EUROPEAN ROMANTICISM

European Romanticism
A Reader

General Editor
STEPHEN PRICKETT

Editor
SIMON HAINES

BLOOMSBURY
LONDON · NEW DELHI · NEW YORK · SYDNEY

Bloomsbury Academic

An imprint of Bloomsbury Publishing Plc

50 Bedford Square	1385 Broadway
London	New York
WC1B 3DP	NY 10018
UK	USA

www.bloomsbury.com

Bloomsbury is a registered trade mark of Bloomsbury Publishing Plc

First published 2010 by Continuum International Publishing Group
Paperback edition first published 2014

British Library Cataloguing-in-Publication Data
A catalogue record for this book is available from the British Library.

ISBN: HB: 978-1-4411-1764-9
PB: 978-1-4725-3544-3

Library of Congress Cataloging-in-Publication Data
A catalog record for this book is available from the Library of Congress.

Typeset by Newgen Knowledge Works (P) Ltd., Chennai, India

Contents

PART II: TEXTS

I. ART AND AESTHETICS

a. British

d. French

e. German

f. Hungarian

CONTENTS

CONTENTS

f. Hungarian

g. Italian

h. Norwegian

i. Polish

l. Russian

m. Spanish

n. Swedish

Acknowledgements

This volume originated in a most unusual international conference that met at Blairquhan Castle, in Ayrshire, Scotland, in 1998. A number of us had become increasingly disillusioned with the standard format of conferences in the humanities where, all too often, graduate students were desperate to show off their wares to bored senior academics, who, in turn, were equally determined to dazzle their peers, while academic superstars, invited to give the much-advertised plenary papers, sometimes failed to show up at all, and if they came, were wont to breeze in and out, without attending other papers, occasionally even giving talks already well known to their fans. It is a world faithfully recorded – and deservedly satirized – by campus novelists such as Malcolm Bradbury and David Lodge. Unlike (maybe?) the scientific conferences, on which these meetings were implicitly modelled, the important thing about such conferences, we felt, was usually not the papers, but the down-time, when one had a chance to meet and talk with other like-minded academics from around the world.

The problem, we all agreed, was that universities normally refuse to pay travel expenses to faculty who do not give a paper. Our answer was to have a conference with *no* papers at all. All that was needed was an attractive venue, a general theme, outstanding participants and open-minded discussions. We therefore made our pitch mostly to senior professors, who were not still struggling to climb the greasy pole of an academic career, and to some hand-picked graduate students, whom we thought might benefit from a weekend in dialogue with leading Romanticists from around the world. Thanks not least to the generosity of the late James Hunter-Blair, who made Blairquhan Castle available to us at a fraction of the normal cost, and to some subsidy from Glasgow University, we were able to assemble a group of 27 academics, representing a variety of languages and cognate disciplines (including history and philosophy), from Australia, Germany, Hungary, Japan, the United Kingdom, and the USA. Later conferences added Romanticists from Denmark, Ireland, Hong Kong, Norway and Sweden. To our delight this proved an astonishingly fertile formula, producing some of the most interesting debates about Romanticism many of us had ever had.

In retrospect, it might have been predictable that our biggest problem was not going to be the traditional academic chestnut of how to define 'Romanticism', but, rather, that none of us knew more than a fraction of what actually constituted 'Romanticism' across Europe. Though there were a number of excellent anthologies of specific national Romanticisms, and some equally excellent comparative studies of, say, Romanticism in two, three or even countries, supported by no less excellent translations from the historical period itself up until the present, there seemed to be no reliable grand overall map of our theme – and certainly nothing that could link *all* the various disparate languages and cultures involved. Our first need, therefore, was simply to try

and draw such an overall chart to guide future discussions. Later conferences hammered out many of the details – the thematic approach, which languages to involve, the decision to have parallel texts with English as the common language and many other minor points.

This has been a huge collective exercise involving probably fifty or more people, some of whose names do not appear in the lists of contributors, like Michael Caesar, of Birmingham University, Lilian Furst of the University of North Carolina, Chapel Hill, Iain McCalman of Sydney University or Thomas Pfau, of Duke University, who gave valuable advice or support to the project while being unable to attend any of the conferences. Others, like Andrew Bowie, of Royal Holloway, Peter Cochran, from Cambridge, Péter Dávidházi, of Eötvös Loránd University, Budapest, James Heffernan of Dartmouth College, New Hampshire and Jim McKusick now of the University of Montana, Missoula, have been closely involved with the project right from the start, attended every conference in the series and contributed greatly to the planning and contents of the project. Still others, like Walter and Miriam Arndt, of Dartmouth, have contributed translations and crossed the Atlantic at some personal difficulty, to be with us on at least one occasion. While their names do not appear as sectional editors, or as authors of particular national introductions in this volume, without their support, criticism and encouragement, it is unlikely that this project would have sustained its momentum or reached its conclusion.

The central props of this whole edifice have been, nevertheless, our sectional editors and writers of their respective introductions, Gudliev Bø, Richard Cardwell, Gérard Gengembre, László Gyapay, Simon Haines, Mihaela Irimia, Carlos Leone, Ayumi Mizukoshi, Mirosława Modrzewska, Håkan Möller, Anne O'Connor, Martin Procházka, Nicholas Saul, Chris Strathman, Marie-Louise Svane, and Dmitry Usenco. Without the hard work put in by them the whole enterprise would have been impossible. As will be obvious, though the General Introduction is under my name, there has been invaluable input from this team as well as from Peter Cochran, whose knowledge of Byron is as encyclopaedic as it is variegated. For any errors and omissions I am, needless to say, solely responsible. Special mention should also be made here of the work of Simon Haines, who not merely attended every one of the preparatory conferences, co-edited and wrote the introduction to the English section, but also worked tirelessly on the thankless task of gaining permissions and raised financial support for the project. But behind these editors lie other translators, assistants, graduate students, and others who have worked long hours searching for obscure translations, editing, photocopying, scanning, and struggling with unexpected changes in typeface and even script. That Russians use Cyrillic or Germans gothic script is well known, but few of us were aware before we began this enterprise that Romanian was written in Cyrillic in the eighteenth century, Roman in the nineteenth, but in between–almost exactly the period we deal with here–a transitional script was often used, with letters taken promiscuously from both Cyrillic and Roman alphabets. We are much indebted to the translations of David Hill and Bernard Adams from Hungarian; to David J. White and Anne Gwin who translated from the French; to Adina Ciugureanu, who laboured hard over complex Romanian texts, and Jamie Crouse, who co-edited the Russian material; and our many researchers and assistants, Patricia Erskine-Hill, Jane Drake-Brockman, Angela Diehl, Sarah Freeland, Jan Lloyd-Jones, Benjamin Morris, Virginia Jarrell, Emily Sgarlata, Dana Telep and Bethany Smith. We are also grateful for the support of András and József Láng, of Argumentum; for that of our editors at Continuum, Colleen Coalter and Anna Fleming; and for the new paperback

edition, David Avital of Bloomsbury; we also wish to thank Norbert Lennartz for taking over the German editorship.

Finally, we should like to express our warm appreciation for the financial support offered at various stages by Baylor University, Texas, the University of Glasgow, the University of Kent at Canterbury, by the Australian National University and, through the Research Centre for Human Values at the Chinese University of Hong Kong, the Philomathia Foundation.

The Volume Editor and contributors would like to acknowledge, thank and extend their gratitude to the following for their translations:

Richard C. Cardwell for all the translations from the Spanish in this volume; Mihaela Irimia and Patricia Erskine-Hill, for Alecsandri's 'By the Fire Side'; Mihaela Irimia, Adina Ciugureanu and Virginia Jarrell for Russo's 'Hymn to Romania' and Rădulescu's 'The Ballad of the Flying Dragon'; Mihaela Irimia for the extract from Rădulescu's *The National Theatre* and all other translations from Romanian.

Anne Gwin for the translation from Nodier's 'On the Literature of the Fantastic'; Hugo's 'Response to an Indictment'; 'The End of Satan'; 'The Djinns' and 'What the Shadow-Mouth Said'; and Anne Gwin and David J. White for the translations from Balzac's *The Alkahest*; and from Michelet's *Introduction to Universal History*.

Carlos Leone and Bethany Smith for translations from the Portuguese.

Charles Wharton Stork for the translation of texts by Bjørnstjerne Bjørnson, J. S. C. Welhaven and A. O. Vinje.

Kjetil Myskja for the translation of 'The Norwegian' by Ivar Aasen.

Marayde O'Brien and Anne O'Connor for translations from Italian; Bernard Adams for his translations of Ferenc Kölcsey, 'National Traditions', 'Historical Enquiry' and 'Fragments on Religion'; Károly Sükei, 'Literary Auditor'; Sándor Petőfi, 'A Letter to János Arany, Pest 4 February 1847'; János Erdélyi, 'Individual and Ideal'; Gábor Döbrenti, 'A Letter to Ferenc Kölcsey, Kolozsvár, 20 November 1813' and Mihály Vörösmarty 'On Mankind', with acknowledgement to Valerie Becker Makkai, Neville Masterman and Adam Makkai.

John Northam for the translation of the text by Henrik Ibsen.

Walter Arndt, and by courtesy Penguin, for his translation of Alexander Pushkin. 'The Gypsies'. *Pushkin Threefold: Narrative, Lyric, Polemic, and Ribald Verse*. Trans. Walter Arndt. New York: E. P. Dutton, 1972. 59–80.

Walter A. Aue for his translation of Joseph von Eichendorff, 'Divining Rod'.

Yelena Borisova and Jamie S. Crouse for their translations of Appollon Grigoriev, 'A secret power has been given to me over you . . .'; Afansy Fet, 'When I am tired with life . . .'; Belinsky, V. G. 'Misfortune from Intelligence' and Alexei Konstantinovich Tolstoy, 'My Little Bluebells.'

Jean Hersholt for the translation of Hans Anderson. 'The Shadow'. *The Complete Andersen*. Heritage, New York, 1949. 1–6.

David Hill for his translations of János Arany, 'The Wandering Jew' and 'Dante'.

Joseph Luzzi for his translation of Alessandro Manzoni 'Letter on Romanticism': Publications of the Modern Language Association, 119 (2004): 315.2.

Dmitri Nabokov, Proprietor, the Estate of Vladimir Nabokov, and by courtesy Penguin, for Vladimir Nabokov's translation of Fyodor Tyuchev, 'Silentium!', *The Portable Nineteenth-Century Russian Reader*. Ed. George Gibian. Trans. Vladimir Nabokov. New York : Penguin, 1993. 278.

Ivan Panin for his translation of Alexander Pushkin's 'The Prophet'.

Dmitry Usenco for his translations of Koltsov, A. V. 'The Forest' and Pyotr Chaadaev, 'Philosophical Letters', from *Letter the First*, 1836.

The Editor and publisher would also like to acknowledge and extend our grateful thanks to the following writers, publishers and literary representatives for extracts from other copyright works. We have made every effort to contact copyright holders. If by oversight, or misinformation or inability to obtain information, we have omitted any name from this list we apologize and will, of course, seek to remedy the situation. The publishers would welcome correspondence from any copyright holders they have been unable to trace.

Angel Books for Heinrich Heine. *Deutschland*. Trans. T. J. Reed, second (bilingual) edition). Angel Books: London, 1997. 37, 39, 41.

Beck for *In Gespräche mit Goethe in den letzten Jahren seines Lebens*, Johann Peter Eckermann, Beck, Munchen, 1988. 286.

Cambridge Scholars Publishing for Juliusz Slowacki. 'Beniowski'. Trans. Peter Cochran and Mirosława Modrzewska; *Poland's Angry Romantic: Two poems and a Play*. Ed and Trans. Peter Cochrane and Bill Johnston, Mirosława Modrzewska and Catherine O'Neill. Cambridge Scholars Publishing: Newcastle upon Tyne, 2009.

Cambridge University Press for *Johann Gottlieb Fichte, Zweite Einleitung in de Wissenschaftslehre*. Ed. and Trans. Peter Heath and John Lachs. Cambridge University Press, 1982.

Cambridge University Press for Friedrich Schleiermacher, 'On the Essence of Religion' speech 2. Ed. and Trans. Richard Coulter, Cambridge University Press, London, 1996. 19–25.

Carcanet for Friedrich Schiller. *On the Naive and Sentimental in Literature*. Trans. Helen Watanabe. Carcanet: Manchester, 1981.

Electric City Press for Antoni Malczewski. *Marya. A Tale of Ukraine*. Trans. Arthur Prudden Coleman and Marion Moore Coleman, Electric City Press Inc. Schenectady: New York, 1935.

Gyldendal norsk forlag of Oslo for G. M. Gathorne-Hardy's translation of Henrik Wergeland's 'The First Embrace'.

Farrar, Strauss and Giroux, L. L. C. for *Adam Mickiewicz. 1798 – 1855*. Ed. Clark Mills. *Selected Poems*. New York: The Noonday Press, New York, 1956: from 'The Books of Polish Pilgrimage'. 112–114, Book 13. Trans. Ludwik Krzyzanowski. 12–13, Book 18. Trans. Jon F. Leich. 13–14. 'Spin Love'. Trans. Kimball Flaccius. 115–116, 'Within their silent, perfect glass'. Trans. Cecil

Hemley. 116–117: from 'The Crimean Sonnets': VI: Bakhchisarai. Trans. Angelica Caro. 81–82, X: Baidar. Trans. George Reavey. 82, XIII; Chatir Dah. Trans. John Saly. 83; 'The Romantic'. Trans. W. H. Auden. 67–69.

Harper & Row for Johann Gottlieb Fichte, *Speeches to the German Nation*. Trans. George Armstrong Kelly. New York,1968. 2–15.

Hippocrene Press for Adam Mickiewicz, *Pan Tadeusz*. Trans. Kenneth Mackenzie. New York: Hippocrene, 1992. 176–182; from Book XI, 'Rok 1812' ('Year 1812'. 484–488; from 'Discussion on art'). 132–140.

lthurielli Spear for Friedrich Hölderlin, 'Bread and Wine'. In *Poems of Friedrich Hölderlin*. Selected and Trans. James Mitchell. Ithurielli Spear: San Francisco, 2007. 7–29.

James Clarke, of Cambridge, for John Jepson Egglishaw and Niels Lyhne Jenson's translation of Grundtvig's 'The Land of the Living', 1984.

Makkai, Adam for his kind permissions for Mihály Vörösmarty. 'Thoughts in the Library', 'On Mankind' and 'Csongor and Tünde' extract from 'The Soliloquy of the Night' and Sándor Petőfi. 'The Tisza'. *In Quest of the 'Miracle Stag': The Poetry of Hungary*. Trans. Peter Zollman, Watson Kirkconnell and Hyman H. Hart. Trans. and Ed. Adam Makkai, Atlantis-Centaur, M. SzivaÅLrvaÅLny and Corvina, Chicago and Budapest,1996. 228–233, 239–240, 315–317, 479, 835.

Methuen for Novalis, *The Disciples at Sais*. Trans. F. V. M. T. and Una Birch. London: Methuen. 1903. 112–119.

Norbertinum for Juliusz Słowacki, *Kordian*, Act III, scene iv. Ed. and Trans. Michael J. Mikoś. Lublin: Norbertinum, 1999.

Norwegian University Press for John Northam's translation of Ibsen's *The Miner*.

Orion Publishing Group for Heinrich von Kleist. 'Über die allmähliche Verfertigung der Gedanken beim Reden (On the Gradual Production of Thoughts Whilst Speaking)', *Henrich Von Kleist: Selected Writings*. Ed. and Trans. David Constantine. J. M Dent, 1997.

Oxford University Press for Theodor Korner. *Lied der Schwarzen Jager*. Trans. G. F. Richardson, 2 vol. London: David Nutt, 295–298.

Pax, Oslo for poems from Ivar Havnevik. Ed. *Den store norske diktboken*. 2005.

Penguin for Ludwig Tieck. 'Über Shakespeares Behandlung des Wunderbaren'. Trans. Louise Adrey, in Jonathan Bate, *The Romantics on Shakespeare*. Shakespeare Library, Penguin, 1992.

Penguin for Odoevsky, V. F. 'The Last Suicide'. *Russian Nights*, Trans. Olga Koshansky-Olienikov and Ralph E. Matlaw. Evanston: Northwestern University Press, 1977. 91–97.

Pennsylvania State University Press for Friedrich Schlegel, 'A Letter on the Novel'. Trans. Ernst Behler and Roman Struc: Pennsylvania State University Press, 1968.

Princeton University Press for Soren Kierkegaard, Howard V. Hong and Edna H. Hong Ed. *Kierkegaard's Writings, Vol 2: The Concept of Irony*. 246–248; and for Wharton Stork's translation of Welhaven's 'My Saint'.

Raduga for Mikhail Lermontov, Mikhail. 'Words are there so baffling . . .' *Russian 19th-Century Verse: Pushkin, Baratynsky, Tyutchev, Koltsov, Lermontov, Tolstoy, Fet, Nekrasov*. Trans. Irina Zheleznova. Ed. Irina Zheleznova, Raduga, USSR, 1983. 136–137.

Random House for Nikolai Gogol. 'The Portrait'. *The Complete Tales of Nikolai Gogol*. Vol. 2. Ed. Leonard J. Kent. Trans. Constance Garnet (*c*.1923), revised by Leonard J. Kent. New York: Random House, 1964. 285–303.

Random House-Modern Library for Nikolai Gogol. *Dead Souls*. Trans. Constance Garnett (1912). New York: Random House-Modern Library, 1923. 76–78, 264–265.

Slavica Publishers for Adam Mickiewicz, 'Ode to Youth', 'Forefathers' Eve'. *Polish Romantic Literature. An Anthology*. Ed. and Trans. Michael J. Mikoś. Bloomington: Slavica Publishers, 1998.

State University of New York Press for Novalis. 'Fragmente: On Goethe and Antiquity; on music; on creativity; Wilhelm Meisters Lehrjahre; Marchen; Romanticism; Translation; Criticism; Death; Poesy as absolute real' and 'Glauben und Liebe', *Novalis: Philosophical Writings*. Trans and Ed. Margaret Mahony Stoljar, State University of New York Press, 1997.

Suhrkamp Insel for Heinrich Heine, 'Jehuda ben Halevy'. *The Complete Poems of Heinrich Heine*. Trans. Hal Draper. Boston: Suhrkamp/Insel, 1982. 655–677.

Suhrkamp Insel for 'Goethe on Polarität und Steigerung Die Natur; Erläuterung'. *Scientific Studies*. Trans. and Ed. Douglas Miller. New York: Suhrkamp, 1988.

Suhrkamp Insel for Johann Wolfgang von Goethe, 'The Sorrows of Young Werther', Johann Wolfgang von Goethe. *Collected Works*. Ed. Victor Lange, Eric A. Blackall and Cyrus Hamlin, 12 vols. New York: Suhrkamp, 1983–1989, XI (1988). 36–37.

Temple Lodge Publishing for Novalis, 'When No Longer Numbers and Figures . . .'

Heinrich von Ofterdingen, Part II From Stein, W. J. *The Ninth Century and the Holy Grail*. Sussex: Temple Lodge Publishing, 2001. 90.

Ungar for Novalis. *Henry von Ofterdingen. A Novel*. Trans. Palmer Hilty. New York: Ungar, 1964. 54–62.

University of California Press for Adam Mickiewicz. 'Song of the Wajdelota'. *Konrad Wallenrod*. Trans. Jewell Parish, Dorothea Prall Radin, George Rapall Noyes and others. Berkeley: University of California Press, 1925.

And for extract from Chateaubriand, *René*. Trans. Irving Putter, 1967.

University of Minnesota Press for Friedrich Schlegel, *Lucinde and the Fragments*. Trans. with an introduction by Peter Firchow. Minneapolis: University of Minnesota Press, 1971. 10–12.

Winter Press for Wilhelm Heinrich Wackenroder. *Sämtliche Werke und Briefe. Historisch-kritische Ausgabe*. Eds Silvio Vietta and Richard Littlejohns, 2 vols, Winter, Heidelberg, 1999, Vol II. 216–223.

List of Contributors

EDITORS

Stephen Prickett is an honorary professor at the University of Kent, Canterbury and Regius Professor Emeritus of English at the University of Glasgow. Until recently he was Margaret Root Brown Professor and Director of the Armstrong Browning Library at Baylor University in Texas. Born in Sierra Leone, educated in Canterbury, he has degrees from both Cambridge and Oxford. He has taught in Nigeria, the University of Sussex, the Australian National University in Canberra, as well as in visiting posts at Smith College, Massachusets, the University of Minnesota, Aarhus University, Denmark, the National University of Singapore and Duke University, NorthCarolina. He is a Fellow of the Australian Academy of the Humanities, former Chairman of the UK Higher Education Foundation and President of the European Society for the Study of Literature and Theology, President of the George MacDonald Society, Fellow of the English Association, and holds an honorary doctorate from the University of Artois, in France. He has published one novel, ten monographs, seven edited volumes and over ninety articles on Romanticism, Victorian Studies and related topics, especially on literature and theology – as well as editing the World's Classics Bible. He was General Editor of the Macmillan 'Romanticism in Perspective' Series, and the Baylor University Press 'The Making of the Christian Imagination' Series. His latest book is *Modernity and the Reinvention of Tradition: Backing into the Future* (2009). He is the general editor of The Edinburgh Companion to the Bible and the Arts (Edinburgh University Press, 2014).

Gudleiv Bø is Professor of Scandinavian Literature at the University of Oslo, Norway. He has degrees in Russian, English and Norwegian from that university. His main works are: *Garborg og Tolstoj* (comparative study of Arne Garborg and the Russian author), Oslo 1973; *Populærlitteratur og kjønnsroller* (on popular fictions, doctoral thesis), Oslo 1991; *Nationale subjekter* (Henrik Ibsen's romantic dramas), Oslo 2000; *Veslemøys verden* (Guide to Garborg's 'The Fairy'/ Haugtussa), Oslo 2002; *Å dikte Norge* (nationalist themes in Norwegian Literature), Bergen 2006.

Anne O'Connor is a lecturer in Italian Studies at National University of Ireland, Galway. A graduate of University College Cork, Johns Hopkins University and the University of Birmingham, she specializes in nineteenth-century Italian literature and history. She has published a variety of articles and a book on the culture of death and memory in nineteenth-century Florence (*Firenze: La città e la memoria nell'Ottocento*, Firenze, Città di Vita, 2008). Her research interests also include travel literature and she has published numerous articles on travellers to Italy in the nineteenth century and the reaction of locals to the visitors. She is currently working on the tensions between Irish and Italian nationalism during the Risorgimento.

Richard A. Cardwell was Professor and Head of the Department of Hispanic and Latin American Studies in the University of Nottingham, Great Britain, from 1983 until 1998: he retired as Emeritus Professor of Modern Hispanic Literatures in 2003. He continues to teach part-time and supervise postgraduate students. His principal interests are in the fields of European Romanticism and Symbolist Decadence, in both of which he has published widely. His works include books, editions and articles on authors and topics including studies of the reception of Lord Byron in Europe, on Keats, Shelley, Espronceda, Rivas and Bécquer and the themes of metaphysical anguish and the dream in the Romantic period. He has also written on French and Spanish poets in the *fin de siècle* including the work of the Nobel poet, Juan Ramon Jimenez. He also teaches a course on the impact of the Islamic invasion of Spain. He has been Visiting Professor in the Universities of Johns Hopkins and Boulder (Colorado), has lectured in Spain, Portugal, France, Holland, Germany, Denmark, Hungary, Georgia, Italy, Argentina, Brazil and the USA and acted as External Examiner internationally. He is currently writing a study of the Symbolist Decadence in Spain.

Gérard Gengembre, professor of French Literature at the University of Caen (Basse-Normandie, France) and at New York University in France, specializes in nineteenth-century studies, and particularly in relation to counter-revolutionary theory, the thought of Mme de Staël and of the Coppet Circle, the romantic movement. His main works are *La Contre-Révolution ou l'Histoire désespérante* (Paris, Imago, 1989), *Balzac, le Napoléon des lettres* (Paris, Gallimard-Découvertes, 1992), *Le Théâtre français au XIXe siècle* (Paris, Armand Colin, 1999), *Le Romantisme* (Paris, Ellipses, 1995), *Napoleon, History and Myth*, London, Hachette Illustrated, 2003), *Le Roman historique*, Paris, Klincksieck, 2006).

László Gyapay is an assistant professor at University of Miskolc. He comes from a family of Budapest teachers, and has a degree in English and Hungarian from Eötvös Loránd University. After a three-year research grant from the Hungarian Academy of Sciences in 1984, he taught in several schools, before, in 1991, joining the editorial team working on the critical edition of the poet-critic Ferenc Kölcsey becoming a researcher in the Institute for Literary Studies of the Hungarian Academy of Sciences. Meantime he was one of the period-editors of the New Hungarian Literary Lexicon published in 1994. He was responsible for the articles on the second half of the nineteenth century. His monograph *'By the Rules of More Refined Taste': The Start of Kölcsey's Career as a Critic* came out in 2001, followed by the first volume of Kölcsey's *Critical and Aesthetic Writings* (1808–1823) in 2003 (second volume due 2014). In 1995 he began teaching Hungarian literature at the University of Miskolc, where he has been Head of the Department of the History of Hungarian Literature, since 2002. His main field of interest is the history of eighteenth and nineteenth-century Hungarian literary criticism. He joined the 'Blair-quhan-Group' in 2004.

Simon Haines is Professor of English at the Chinese University of Hong Kong. Previously he was Reader at the Australian National University and Head of the School of Humanities from 2005–2007. He is a Co-Director of the International Centre for Human Values at ANU and CUHK. After graduate work in Oxford he worked as a banker in the City of London before joining the Australian Department of Foreign Affairs, where he held a number of positions

including (for three years) Chairman of the Budget Committee of the Organization of Economic Co-operation and Development (OECD) in Paris. He subsequently left Foreign Affairs for an intelligence analysis role in Canberra, before eventually returning to academic life at ANU in 1990. Professor Haines' academic research has principally been in Romanticism and the literature of the long nineteenth century; and, on a broader canvas, in the relationships between literature and philosophy, especially in their representations of the self, within the European tradition. His principal publications include *Shelley's Poetry: The Divided Self* (Macmillan, 1997) and *Poetry and Philosophy from Homer to Rousseau: Romantic Souls, Realist Lives* (Palgrave, 2005), as well as numerous articles and papers on Romantic and nineteenth-century poetry, European classical and Renaissance literature, modern literary theory and the contribution made by modern moral philosophy to literary studies. His current research interests include the representation of time in literature and philosophy, concepts of evil in Milton and Shakespeare, and the idea of spontaneity in Wordsworth and Kant. His current book projects are *Wordsworth to Wittgenstein: The Romantic and Modernist Self in Poetry and Philosophy* and *Romanticism and the Making of the Post-Christian Imagination*. His latest book is *Redemption in Poetry and Philosophy: Wordsworth, Kant, and the making of the Post-Christian Imagination*, Baylor University Press, 2013.

Mihaela Anghelescu Irimia is Professor of English Literature and Cultural Theory, and Director of Studies of the Cultural Studies Centre and Director of the Centre of Excellence for the Study of Cultural Identity at the University of Bucharest. Her professional affiliations comprise: the Romanian Philological Association, the Romanian Association for English and American Studies, the British Society for Eighteenth-Century Studies, the Romanian Society for Eighteenth-Century Studies, the International Society for Eighteenth-Century Studies, the Romanian Society for Romantic Studies, the German Society for English Romanticism, the Romanian Comparative Literature Association. She has been Fulbright Professor at Harvard, fellow of St. John's College, Oxford, research fellow at Yale, and is currently alumna of New Europe College. Her publications in the field include: 'The Ineffectual Angel of Political Hijacking: Shelley in Romanian Culture', in Michael Rossington and Susanne Schmid (eds), *The Reception of Shelley in Europe* (2008); *Lures and Ruses of Modernity / Leurres et ruses de la modernité* (2007) (editor); *Travel (of) Writing* (2006) (editor with Adina Ciugureanu); 'The Byron Phenomenon in Romanian Culture', in Richard A. Cardwell (ed.), *The Reception of Byron in Europe* (2004); *Dicționarul universului britanic* (A Dictionary of Britishness) (2002); *The Stimulating Difference: Avatars of a Concept* (1999, 2005); *The Rise of Modern Evaluation* (1999); *Postmodern Revaluations* (1999); *An Anthology of English Literature: The Romantic Age* (1989) (with Ioan-Aurel Preda, Maria Mociornița and Monica Săulescu), *An Anthology of English Literature: The Age of Sentiment and Sensibility* (1987) (with Ioan-Aurel Preda, Maria Mociornița and Monica Săulescu).

Carlos Leone holds a PhD from the New University of Lisbon (2004) and teaches in the Universidade Lusófona, Lisbon, in the History of Ideas, Portuguese Culture and methods of Social Sciences in modern and contemporary periods. He has published extensively in Portuguese and in English in journals from USA, United Kingdom, Romania and France. As a scholar he has visited Brown, Cambridge and Oxford and he taught as visiting professor in the Language

Department of Rutgers-Newark. Currently he is editor of Prelo, a quarterly journal of the Portuguese National Press. His present research mainly concerns Portuguese in exile during the twentieth century, although his intellectual interests are increasingly more directed to problems of constructivism and history of political ideas.

Ayumi Mizukoshi is an associate professor at Teikyo University, Japan, where she teaches English literature as well as English as a foreign language. She was educated at Kobe College (BA in English) and the University of Kyoto (MA in English) in Japan. She continued her research into British Romantic poetry at Oxford, from where she received her doctorate in 1998. Her doctoral thesis evolved into her first book, *Keats, Hunt and the Aesthetics of Pleasure* (Palgrave, 2001). She is currently working on a study of modernity, subjectivity and Romanticism in Japan at the turn of the twentieth century.

Mirosława Modrzewska is an assistant professor at the Institute of English, University of Gdańsk, Poland. Her interests are teaching eighteenth- and nineteenth-century English literature. She is chiefly interested in Romantic studies and the variety of Romantic canons as established in Polish and English, as well as other European literary historical traditions. She has published articles concerning the works of Lord Byron: on the problems of artistic language, literary traditions and genres in Lord Byron's dramas; on the Polish Romantic translations of Byron's poetry and various aspects of it's literary reception in nineteenth- and twentieth-century Poland. She has co-edited translations of the Polish Romantic poet Juliusz Słowacki into English. She is currently working on G. G. Byron and his affinities with seventeenth-century literature and culture, as well as the works of Robert Burns and their reception in Poland. She is a friend of The International Byron Society, a member of Polish Shakespearian Society and German Society for English Romanticism.

Håkan Möller is a theologian and literary historian. He teaches at the University of Uppsala, and also at the University of Helsinki. He holds Doctorates both in Divinity (1998), and Philosophy (2001) from the University of Uppsala. In 2003 he was approved as docent in Literature at University of Uppsala and in 2004 in Scandinavian Literature at the University of Helsinki. His editorial experience includes work for the Royal Swedish Academy. During the academic year 1996/1997 he was Visiting Scholar in the Faculty of Divinity in Cambridge. His early studies were in the interdisciplinary field of Literature and Religion, especially from the seventeenth to the beginning of the nineteenth century. His doctoral dissertation in Divinity was on the hymnography of Johan Olof Wallin (1779–1839) and the groundbreaking new hymn-book of 1819 for the Church of Sweden, (*The Wallin Hymn*, 1997). His literary dissertation, *The Wallin Poem: From the Early Poems to Angel of Death* (2000) concerns mainly the poetry of Wallin from his first poems of the early nineteenth century up to 'The Angel of Death' (1839), his last major poem. He has recently published a study of one of the most distinguished and famous Swedish authors of the twentieth century, the 1951 Nobel prize-winner in Literature, Pär Lagerkvist (1891–1974): *Pär Lagerkvist. From a Writer's Tale to the Nobel Prize* (2009). The study deals with the literary career of Lagerkvist, from his early dream of becoming a famous writer to the success of the novel Barabbas (1950) and the Nobel Prize 1951.

Martin Procházka, CSc., Professor of English, American and Comparative Literature, is Head of the Department of English and American Studies at Charles University, Prague. He is the

author of *Romantismus a osobnost* (Romanticism and Personality, 1996), a critical study of English romantic aesthetics, Coleridge and Byron, *Transversals* (2007), essays on post-structuralist readings of English and American romantics, and a co-author (with Zdeněk Hrbata) of *Romantismus a romantismy* (Romanticism and Romanticisms, 2005), a comparative study on the chief discourses in the West European, American and Czech Romanticism. With Zdeněk Stříbrný he edited *Slovník spisovatelů: Anglie . . .* (An Encyclopaedia of Writers: England . . . 1996, 2003). He has published two textbooks: *Literary Theory* (1995, 1997, 2007) and *Lectures on American Literature* (2002, 2007), the latter jointly with Hana Ulmanová, Justin Quinn and Erik Roraback. Among his other publications there are book chapters and articles on Shakespeare, Romanticism and Post-structuralism, a translation of Byron's *Manfred* (1991) and M. H. Abrams's *The Mirror and the Lamp* into Czech (2001). He is the founding editor of an international academic journal *Litteraria Pragensia* and a member of editorial boards of five international academic journals. He has been Visiting Professor at the universities of Bristol and Bowling Green (Ohio), Visiting Lecturer at the University of Heidelberg (Germany), Distinguished Visiting Scholar at the University of Adelaide and Visiting Scholar at the University of California at Berkeley.

Nicholas Saul is Professor of German at the University of Durham, England. He has held Guest Professorships at the University of Cologne and the University of Vermont. His chief scholarly interests are Romanticism, Realism, Classical Modernism, Romanies and literary Darwinism. He has published essays on Wilhelm Bölsche, Clemens Brentano, Wilkie Collins, Frederick the Great of Prussia, Goethe, Gutzkow, Hackl, Julius Hart, Carl Hauptmann, Hebbel, Hofmannsthal, Jensen, Keller, Novalis, Raabe, Sailer and Schleiermacher, Schnabel, Stifter, Stoker, Werner, also on the problem of suicide, on aesthetic humanism, on subjectivity, on death and on utopias. His most recent publications are *German Philosophy and Literature 1700-1990* (2002), *The Role of the Romanies* (2004), *Romantik und Aufklärung . . . Festschrift zu Ehren Roger Paulins* (2006), *Gypsies and Orientalism in German Literature and Anthropology of the Long Nineteenth Century* (2007), and *The Cambridge Companion to German Romanticism* (2009). He is currently editing a volume of essays on European Darwinism *The Evolution of Literature* (2010) and writing a monograph on German literary Darwinism 1859–2008.

Christopher A. Strathman is a lecturer in English and acting Director of Writing Foundations at Case Western Reserve University in Cleveland, Ohio. His publications include *Romantic Poetry and the Fragmentary Imperative: Schegel, Byron, Joyce* Blanchot (2006), a genealogical study of the fragmentary work of romantic poetry. A graduate of the University of Notre Dame, his scholarly interests include romantic poetry, literary theory, poetry and poetics, and writing across the humanities. He has also authored, or co-authored, essays on hermeneutics, Blake and the Bible, Byron's poetics and Hopkins's idea of nature. He is currently at work on two book-length projects: a reappraisal of Byron's poetics of departure and a study of the relationship between poetry and experimental science in the late eighteenth- and early nineteenth centuries. He has been a National Endowment for the Humanities Fellow and a Visiting Scholar in English at the University of Notre Dame. He has also been a Golda Meir Postdoctoral Fellow in the Humanities at the Hebrew University of Jerusalem.

Marie-Louise Svane is associate professor in comparative literature at Copenhagen University. She has written largely on European art and literature and with a special focus on the romantic period. Among her published books are *Set gennem kroppen* (*Seen through the Body*, about the German women artists Käthe Kollwitz and Paula Modersohn-Becker) 1994, *Romanticism in Theory* 2001 (an anthology edited with Lis Møller), *Formationer I europćisk romantik* (*Formations in European Romanticism*) 2003. She is a co-writer of a forthcoming *Danish Literary History*, and engaged in a new research project on *Islam in European Literary History*.

Dmitry Usenco graduated from the Moldovan State University with a Masters degree in Modern Languages in 1991. He spent further three years at the Institute of World Literature in Moscow, working on his doctoral dissertation (*Browning and Romanticism*), which he finally defended in 1998. Afterwards he pursued an academic occupation, teaching English Literature at the International Independent University of Moldova from 1998 till 2004. During that period he became interested in comparative literary studies and published articles about Anglo-Russian and Anglo-French cultural connections. He wrote the introduction to the first complete Russian translation of *The Sonnets from the Portuguese* by Elizabeth Barrett Browning and was actively involved in its publication. In 2004 he moved to the United Kingdom where he became a translator and independent researcher. He is currently based in Basildon, Essex, where he is an active member of the local literary society.

TRANSLATORS

Bernard Adams is a translator of prose and poetry. He has a degree in Modern and Medieval Languages – Hungarian and Russian – from Pembroke College, Cambridge (BA 1961; MA 1965). After being a fellow in Turkish at the School of Oriental and African Studies, University of London, and teaching French and Russian at Highgate School he became a freelance translator in 1991, translating mostly from Hungarian, occasionally from Russian. In 2006 he moved to Hungary. In 2008 he was awarded an American PEN translation fund grant and was second in the John Dryden Translation Competition, and in 2009 received a Füst Milán translation award. His translations of Ady, Apor Péter, Arany, Bethlen Kata, Bethlen Miklós, Katona József, Kosztolányi, Mikes, Mikszáth, Móricz, Örkény etc. have been published by Hungarian and other European publishers.

Yelena Borisova, a native of Smolensk, Russia, has a Master of Divinity from Southwestern Theological Seminary in Fort Worth, Texas, a Bachelor of Science degree from Smolensk Pedagogical Institute, and is a candidate for a Ph.D. in Historical Theology at Baylor University. She worked as an interpreter for Smolensk Baptist Church and Smolensk Bible Institute as well as the editor of a magazine, *The Source of Life* and as a book reviewer for a local TV station before coming to the USA to continue her education.

Adina Ciugureanu is Professor of English and American Literature at Ovidius University Constanta, Romania. She got her BA in English and French and her Ph.D. in British and American literature at the University of Bucharest. Since 2004 she has been the Dean of the Faculty of Letters. As an academic, Professor Ciugureanu has published and edited extensively. She is the

author of *High Modernist Poetic Discourse* (1997), based on her Ph.D. dissertation. Following a Fulbright research grant in the USA, she wrote and published a study on American popular culture, *The Boomerang Effect* (2002), seen as remodelling European cultural patterns. The study was translated into Romanian and published in 2008. Her main interests are however concerned with English Victorianism and British and American modernism. She published two studies, Victorian Selves (2004), in which she discussed major Victorian texts with a view to evincing the treatment of the self, and Modernism and the Idea of Modernity, published in the same year, in which she focuses on early twentieth-century modernity as expressed in modernist aesthetics. Her latest study, Post-War Anxieties (2006), is an analysis of the English literature of the 1950s and 1960s through existentialist lenses. She has also published a large number of articles and essays on English and American culture in Romania and abroad.

Jamie S. Crouse holds a Ph.D. in English from the University of Kent, specializing in nineteenth-century literature. Her thesis focuses on the rise of Victorian women's religious poetry. She has published articles on Margaret Fuller, Anna Laetitia Barbauld, Emily Bronte and Hannah More. She currently teaches English at the University of Mary Hardin-Baylor. She minored in Russian at Belhaven College and participated in a study abroad programme at the University of Nizhni Novgorod in Nizhni Novgorod, Russia.

Patricia Erskine-Hill has lived, studied and worked in England, France, Ireland, Italy, Scotland, Switzerland, Spain and the USA. Her principal languages are English, Italian, French and Spanish. She has worked as a court interpreter and freelance translator in Rome, London and Glasgow, and translated a book for UNESCO. Her degrees are in Modern Languages (Trinity College, Dublin) and Economic and Social History (Edinburgh). She has taught Italian language, medieval literature and Italian renaissance literature at Baylor University in Texas. She currently lives in Kent, giving occasional talks on Venetian print culture, Dante and related topics.

Anne Gwin earned her Ph.D. in French literature from the University of Texas. She teaches at Thomas Jefferson Independent Day School in Joplin, Missouri.

David Hill is a writer, editor and translator of prose and verse. He is the author of *Consumed* (USA, 2008), the English lyricist for the Hungarian band Kistehen, and a contributor to Europe-UpClose.com and the Financial Times group. His translations of Hungarian poetry have appeared in *The Times Literary Supplement, The Hungarian Quarterly*, and anthologies including *New Order* (United Kingdom, 2010). In 2004 he co-curated the Hungarian-British literary festival Converging Lines, and in 2001 he co-founded *The Bardroom*, Budapest's English-language literary cabaret. His website is www.davidhill.biz

Virginia Jarrell is a Master's candidate in English Literature at Baylor University in Waco, Texas. She received a Bachelor of Arts in Letters from the University of Oklahoma in 2006. During her undergraduate career Virginia spent a year studying English at the University of Aberdeen in Aberdeen, Scotland. She is a member of Phi Beta Kappa. Her research interests include Eighteenth and Nineteenth Century British Literature. After completing her MA, she plans to pursue a Ph.D. in Literature.

Benjamin Morris completed his Ph.D. in Archaeology at the University of Cambridge, where his research focused on the relationship between cultural heritage and the environment and the rebuilding of New Orleans after Hurricane Katrina. A native of Mississippi, he has a BA in English and Philosophy from Duke University and an M.Sc. in English Literature from the University of Edinburgh. His creative work (poetry, prose, and plays) has been published and has won recognition in both the USA and the United Kingdom, and he has co-edited two anthologies of poetry and fiction, *Stolen Stories* (2008) and *The Golden Hour Book: Volume II* (2009), both from Forest Publications in Edinburgh.

Bethany J. Smith's doctoral dissertation at Baylor University centred on *ekphrasis* in the poetry of Irish writers W. B. Yeats and Eavan Boland. She remains interested in the relationship between literature and the visual arts and with the ethical implications of artistic representation. In addition to teaching composition for the Baylor English Department and Honors Colloquia for the Honors College, she has also taught a course on British and European Romanticism at Houghton College, New York State.

David J. White has a BA in Classics from the University of Akron, M.L.I.S. from Kent State University, and MA in Classical Studies from the University of Pennsylvania. He has taught at the University of Pennsylvania, University of the Arts, St. Joseph's University, Lehigh, Rutgers, and the University of Akron. He has worked as a special collections librarian at the University of Pennsylvania, the Cleveland Museum of Art, and the Western Reserve Historical Society. He is an amateur thespian, specializing in Shakespeare and Gilbert and Sullivan, and is a beginning Esperantist. He is currently a lecturer in Classics at Baylor University.

PART 1

Historical Introductions

General Introduction:
Of Fragments, Monsters and Translations

Stephen Prickett

Peter Quince: 'Bless thee, Bottom! bless thee! thou art translated.'
[Midsummer Night's Dream, *III. i. 118*]

It is, perhaps, surprising that no comprehensive anthology of European Romanticism has so far ever been created. There may be a number of reasons for this – and all, in their different ways, tell us something important about Romanticism.

I

The first is simply that any such anthology necessarily involves much translation, and translation (as Bottom found) is always difficult – very difficult. Indeed, theories of translation are in themselves highly contentious; according to the linguistic arguments of many romantics, impossible. Coleridge, for one, argued fiercely that it could not be done, even while publishing his own translations of Schiller (with acknowledgement) and Frederika Brun (without). Certainly good translation from one language into another is among the most difficult of all arts. Vladimir Nabokov in his 1958 translation of Lermontov's *A Hero of Our Time* has argued that 'we must dismiss once and for all the conventional notion that a translation should "read smoothly" and "should not sound like a translation"':

> In point of fact, any translation that does not sound like a translation is bound to be inexact upon inspection; while on the other hand, the only virtue of a good translation is faithfulness and completeness. Whether it reads smoothly or not depends on the model, not the mimic.[1]

This, of course, is part of a long-running debate over translation that has raged ever since Jerome undertook the Vulgate, and re-ignited when vernacular translations of the Vulgate began to appear in the wake of the Reformation in the sixteenth century.[2] Should the images and metaphors of another culture, with a quite different linguistic and historical experience, be

[1] Vladimir Nabokov. Preface to his translation of Mihail Lermontov's *A Hero of our Time*. New York: Doubleday, 1958. xii.
[2] See Stephen Prickett. *Origins of Narrative: The Romantic Appropriation of the Bible*. Cambridge UP, 1996. Esp. Ch. 2.

assimilated into the conventional terms of the host language, or be permitted to intrude with radical and even, perhaps, uncouth novelty?[3]

In fact, of course, great and influential translations can be found at both ends of the spectrum – and in many places between. Among the latter, more literal category, are, of course, Jerome's Vulgate, which was responsible for turning Classical Latin into Church Latin, as well as Luther's and Tyndale's Bibles; on the other hand, the crudity and inappropriateness of really literal translation – such as that produced by computer programmes and some restaurant menus – have rightly become the butt of jokes. At the other end of the scale, certain great translations have so integrated themselves into the aesthetics of the host language as to become classics in themselves – one thinks of Carlyle's English translation of Goethe's *Wilhelm Meister*, Chateaubriand's of Milton's *Paradise Lost*, the translations of Shakespeare into German and Hungarian by August Schlegel and Mihály Vörösmarty, respectively. Even more ambitious in its spread was perhaps Vassily Zhukovsky, who not content with a Russian translation of Gray's *Elegy* from English, produced no less than three translations of Gottfried August Bürger's German poem *Lenore* – in the first the eponymous heroine appears as Lyudmilla, in the second as Svetlana and only in the third does she reappear with her original German name. All three have proved seminal works in different ways within the Russian canon. Contrast John Harrington's 1592 English translation of Ariosto's *Orlando Furioso* with the repeated translations of Dante into English: the former is a foundational work in its own right in the receptor language; contrarywise, though there have been a spate of excellent English Dante translations – especially recently – none yet (and certainly not Carey's eighteenth-century version) has made Dante a part of the English tradition in the way that, say, Shakespeare has become in German. There may be, arguably, internal reasons that make Dante essentially less translatable than Shakespeare, but such theoretical arguments[4] have a way of collapsing in the face of outstanding achievement of the so-called impossible on the occasions when it occurs.

II

A second factor that has historically tended to inhibit the creation of an anthology such as this concerns the way that the new European Romanticism also encouraged a new nationalism – what Mme de Staël was to stress as 'a fuller sense of nationhood'. From Byron in Greece, Herder in Germany, Scott in Scotland, to Foscolo in Italy, the qualities hailed (often retrospectively) as 'Romantic' involved a rejection of Enlightenment 'uniformitarianism'[5] – not to mention the French cultural hegemony that this so often tacitly implied. It is a commonplace of cultural studies that nations are 'imagined communities'. But in practice the collective imaginations of different communities could, and did,

---

[3] See, for instance, Eugene A. Nida. 'Principles of Translation as Exemplified by Bible Translating'. *On Translation*. Ed. Ruben A. Brower. Cambridge, MA: Harvard UP, 1959. 11–31; Louis G. Kelly. *The True Interpreter: A History of Translation Theory and Practice in the West*. Oxford: Blackwell, 1979; also the discussion in Prickett, *Origins of Narrative*. 64–65 and passim.

[4] Including those of Dante, who believed true translation of poetry was impossible: 'Therefore everyone should know that nothing harmonized according to the rules of poetry can be translated from its native tongue into another without destroying all its sweetness and harmony. This is the reason why Homer has not been translated from Greek into Latin as have been other writings we have of theirs'. *Il Convivio*, Book I, chapter 7. (Lansing translation)

[5] The assumption that all people, everywhere and probably at all times, were essentially similar, despite apparent differences of wealth, rank and culture.

take many forms. For countries like Germany and Italy, then without visible or historical political unity, such collective imaginings centred around a sense of national difference, often based on assertions of the uniqueness of a shared language. Indeed, there is a sense in which any study of this period involves a redefinition of the word 'nationality'.

For the English-speaking peoples of what is now the United Kingdom the primary meaning of the word has usually been political, referring to citizens of a particular country – even if, like Scotland and Wales, that country may be part of a larger political unit. For the Irish, on the other hand, as the nineteenth century went on, their own imagined community increasingly did not include the British. For central, eastern, and southern Europe, and in particular the area occupied by the Austrian Empire, the word takes on extra and rather different connotations.[6] In places such as the Balkans, where there are diverse ethnicities, languages, cultures and religions (not merely Catholic and Orthodox, but substantial Muslim minorities) the notion of 'nationality' involves a kind of communal self-description that may involve some *or* all of those factors. Thus the people usually known in 1800 as 'Wallachians', now better-known as 'Romanians', extending from Hungary to and into the Republic of Moldova, are as ethnically mixed as most in that very diverse area, may be Orthodox or Catholic, and may speak any of about five languages besides Romanian, but still feel a cultural attachment to others of their kind.. As a result, romanticists themselves have often tended to be cultural nationalists – at their best, with a strong sense of their cultural qualities, at worst, with a deep suspicion of other cultures as polluting the perceived purity of their own. One only has to look at the claims made by biblical translators for the uniqueness of their particular language to see this process at work – often long before the Romantic period. English, French, Hungarian, Italian and Swedish, for instance, have all been shown (at least to their authors' satisfaction) to be uniquely fit vehicles for the translation of the Hebrew Bible.[7] Similarly, if English romanticists have all too frequently assumed that Romanticism was primarily a British phenomenon, and ignored 'continental' influences, this is a narrowness of vision too often shared by their French or German counterparts. Twentieth-century French deconstructionist critics have sometimes failed to mention the origins of their ideas in those of German Romanticsm.[8]

More delicate is the problem of Nationalism *within* the United Kingdom. For the purposes of this reader, should we have treated England, Ireland, Scotland and Wales as separate cultural entities – with (in two cases at least) material in languages other than English? For someone like myself, with long residence in Scotland, the case is in some ways an attractive one, but in the end we decided that to divide 'English literature' – in the sense of 'the literature of the English language' – would raise more problems than it solved. How, for instance, could one treat Scott or Burns as if they were not part of the same print-culture as Coleridge and Wordsworth (Blake, not Scott, would surely be the odd man out here!). Similarly, Byron was, of course, a Scot, and in some ways remained a man suspended between two very different cultures, but here, in this context, we have to treat him primarily as a European figure. Others (we hope) may wish to follow our broad map-making, with more detailed local charts.

---

[6] See, for instance, both the Hungarian and Romanian Introductions below.

[7] See James L. Kugel. *The Idea of Biblical Poetry: Parallelism and History*. New Haven, CT: Yale University Press, 1981. 301; David Norton. *History of the Bible as Literature*. 2 vols. Cambridge: Cambridge UP, 1993. Vol. 1, 278–279.

[8] A point well brought out by Andrew Bowie's book, *From Romanticism to Critical Theory: The Philosophy of German Literary theory*. London: Routledge, 1997.

III

The third reason is allied to such questions of linguistic nationalism, and concerns the thorny practical question of a host language for any such anthologized translation. Implicit in the rise of cultural nationalism is a strong presupposition that to do justice to any writer, he or she *must* be read in the original language. In a sense this is obviously true, but aside from the question of practicality (only a few in any generation can read every European language with sufficient ease to appreciate the artistic merits of each!) such a conviction destroys not merely the very idea of a reader, but it actually strikes against the equally Romantic belief in the *value* of translation. As we shall see very clearly in the contents of this volume, all European languages and cultures have been immeasurably enriched over the centuries by works translated from other cultures.

Sterne's Yorrick begins his *Sentimental Journey* with the immortal words ' "They do these things better in France," I said.' Whether or not the gentle ironies of that 'I said' could be fully appreciated in every language into which that European best-seller was rapidly translated, the idea (or, rather, multiple *ideas*) of 'sentiment' were to permeate virtually every major literature in the continent by the end of the eighteenth century. Thus in Catherine the Great's Russia, for instance, everybody who was anybody among the tiny literate population ('the chattering classes' of the day) was reading Sterne. When Baroness Dimsdale, wife of Henry Dimsdale, the doctor who inoculated Catherine the Great against smallpox, was introduced to the Empress, her 'gratitude' we are told, 'so far got the better of her good breeding that, when her majesty entered the saloon, instead of half kneeling to kiss the hand held out with so much grace, she flew towards her like a tiger, and almost smothered the poor Empress with hugging and kissing. As soon as the suffering sovereign could disengage herself, and shake her feathers, after so rude and boisterous an embrace, she walked on smiling and told the baron that *madame son épouse* was *très aimable . . .*'[9] Whether or not Catherine's remarkable restraint was, as some have suggested, due to her impression that this was the new English 'sentimental' fashion of greeting,[10] it is certainly true that the Russian notion of sentimentality was never quite the same as the English (or French or German), and the Empress was presumably knowledgeable enough to recognize the fact. Translation is not a neutral idiom – as Bottom knew well, to translate is to change.

Though Catherine, absolute ruler of Russia, was a German by birth, the language of her Court (like most eighteenth-century courts in continental Europe) was, of course, French. As we shall see in the course of this reader, the paradox of French culture in the Romantic period is that it was at once the language of the *ancien régime*, reviled by nationalists, liberals and progressive elements everywhere as the vehicle of the most stultifying convention and formality, *and*, at the same time, the language of new ideas, dangerous revolution, Jacobinism, social equality and free-thought. Even though hindsight might suggest that the Scottish Enlightenment – the world of Francis Hutcheson, David Hume, Thomas Reid, Adam Smith or James Watt[11] – was of greater

---

[9] James Walker. Paramythia (1821) cited in *An English Lady at the Court of Catherine the Great: The Journal of Baroness Elizabeth Dimsdale, 1781.* Ed. A. G. Cross, Cambridge: Crest Publications, 1989. 51.

[10] A view not entirely supported by her alleged remark to her attendents, *Ces choses arrivent quelque fois.*

[11] See James Buchan. *Crowded with Genius.* Harper/Collins, 2003; Arthur Herman. *How the Scots Invented the Modern World: The True Story of How Western Europe's Poorest Nation Created Our World & Every-thing in It.* Edinburgh: Birlinn, 2001. Alexander Broadie. *The Scottish Enlightenment: The Historical Age of the Historical Nation,* 2001. Robert W. Galvin. *America's Founding Secret: What the Scottish Enlightenment Taught Our Founding Fathers.* Lanham: Rowman & Littlefield, 2001.

significance to the world in the long run, France was in almost every sense *seen* as the centre of European culture, thought, and expectations by the rest of a Europe that knew very little about intellectual developments in the far North of Britain. Thus to say that the French Revolution was the most significant event of the period, is not merely to make a statement about European politics, but also about art and literature, manners and customs and even (most controversial of all) about the nature of humanity itself.

'There is nothing in old history that I shall any longer think fabulous'; Fanny Burney wrote to her father in October 1789, 'the destruction of the most wonderful empires on record has nothing more wonderful, nor of more sounding improbability, than the demolition of this great nation, which rises up against itself for its own ruin – perhaps annihilation.'[12] 'The French Revolution', conceded Burke a year later, 'is the most astonishing that has hitherto happened in the world.'[13] Looking back at the end of his life, the radical publisher William Hone, who was born during the Gordon Riots in London in 1780, begins his memoirs with the statement 'In the course of my brief life the most astounding events of modern times have happened . . .'[14] In Revolution or in reaction, France – and its language – was the focal point for much of Europe. Despite the fact that the American Revolution preceded the French, it is remarkable how heavily dependent even the founding fathers of the new nation were on French ideas – down to the rhetoric of garden planning embodied by Jefferson at Montecello.[15] Were this reader being produced 200 years ago there is no doubt which would have been the common language into which all the others would have to be translated.

But today – and not least because of the universality of American influence – Europe has a new *lingua franca*. To make English the common linking language of this reader is scarcely even controversial. It is the common language of Europe, that of business, tourism, medicine – even of air traffic control. As a visit to any Continental European bookshop will demonstrate, more books are translated *from* English than from any other language. Yet the reader of this anthology is likely to be impressed not so much by the quantity of Romantic literature already available in English as by the quantity of original material hitherto un-translated, and which appears here for the first time. In short, this reader seeks to offer a whole new intellectual map which breaks with the limitations of many previous versions of Romanticism. Although the main focus is inevitably European, the fact that we shall include America, the exploration of the Pacific and even the impact of Romantic ideas on Japan, means that Romanticism will be seen ultimately as a global phenomenon, influencing a surprising number of the ways in which the modern world sees itself.

As so often, academic politics also has a part to play. The downside of the increasing world-dominance of English has been the progressive decline of the teaching of other modern languages in the English-speaking world. As any Romantic would have predicted, the result has been an incipient impoverishment of English itself. In recent years 'English studies' has expanded to include a whole series of European and other cultural phenomena which previously were the

---

[12] *Diary and Letters of Madame D'Arblay*, edited by her Niece. 7 vols. London: Henry Colburn. 1842. Vol. V. 66–67.

[13] Edmund Burke. *Reflections on the Revolution in France*. Ed. Conor Cruise O'Brien. Harmondsworth: Penguin Books, 1969. 92.

[14] William Hone. *The Three Trials of William Hone*, 1817.

[15] See, for instance, Malcolm Kelsall. *Jefferson and the Iconography of Romanticism*. London: Macmillan, 1999.

preserve of departments of modern languages – and, as one might expect, much has been lost in translation. To compensate, there has been a growing demand for what they dealt with to be incorporated into a wider conception of literary, philosophical, and cultural studies. Without involving ourselves in any of the theoretical agendas posed by some of these appropriations, we believe that our reader offers one important way to correct the narrow, partisan and ethnocentric biases in the way many of these topics have sometimes been taught. Similarly, traditional areas of study in English literature will also benefit simply from the new perspectives we offer. The idea of valuing cultural diversity for itself has, of course, been a part of Romantic thinking ever since Herder, and this reader aims to live up to that ideal. We have not, therefore, embarked on this project in any spirit of compromise, or in the belief that translation is an inevitable second best to the real thing. If, for those who can read them, there is no substitute for the original work, nevertheless, as we have suggested, the history of translation has repeatedly shown that works re-created in another language and cultural context, if done well – and sometimes even done badly! – can take on a vigour and a life of their own that is wholly unpredictable. Who, for instance, could have predicted that Goethe's description of the miners in *Wilhelm Meister's Travels* would have been transmuted into George MacDonald's fantasies, *The Princess and the Goblin* or *The Golden Key*;[16] or that Dickens' tragicomic portrait of his father, John Dickens, as Mr Micawber, in *David Copperfield*, should have given rise to Dostoevsky's General Ivolgin; that Svidrigailov in *Crime and Punishment* should be based on Lovelace in Richardson's *Clarissa*; or that Mr Pickwick would have laid the foundations of one of the greatest character-studies in the Russian novel, Prince Myshkin, the 'Idiot' of the novel of that title.[17]

Translation has always been the life-blood of cultural vitality. But the history of Romantic translation is more than the history of the appropriation of particular works into other languages. Translation was the midwife to a whole generation of new writers all over Europe. Schleiermacher, the great German critic and theologian, first appeared in print as the translator of English language Sermons by both Blair and Forsyth.[18] Coleridge, like his friend Wordsworth, and later Byron and Shelley had been trained in translation from the classics at school. At the beginning of his poetic career translation helped him to find his own poetic voice.[19] Nor were he and Wordsworth alone. Byron's first publications were translations. Even Scott had translated German ballads before embarking on his work on the 'minstrelsy' of the Scottish borders.[20] Nevertheless, the fact remains that, with a few notable exceptions, such as Volney's *Ruins of Empires* and Goethe's *Sorrows of Young Werther*,[21] unlike the countries of Continental Europe, translation of contemporary literature *into* English was for the most part neither popular nor profitable (see Appendix by Benjamin Morris on George Borrow and John Bowring). In contrast, Byron and Scott constitute a special case in the history of European letters – making a greater and more immediate impact on the culture of Europe than any other British writers of

---

[16] See Stephen Prickett. 'Fictions and Metafictions: *Phantastes, Wilhelm Meister,* and the Idea of the *Bildungsroman*'. *The Golden Key*. Ed. William Raeper. Edinburgh: Edinburgh University Press, 1990.

[17] See Angus Wilson. 'Dickens and Dostoevsky', *Diversity and Depth in Fiction: Selected Critical Writings of Angus Wilson*. Ed. Kerry McSweeney, New York: Viking Press, 1983. 72–78.

[18] See Stephen Prickett. 'Coleridge, Schlegel and Schleiermacher: England, Germany (and Australia) in 1798', *1798*. Ed. Richard Cronin, Basingstoke: Palgrave, 1998. 151–184.

[19] See Stephen Prickett and Peter France. *The Oxford History of Translation*. Vol 4. Oxford: Oxford UP, 2006. Ch. 3.3 'Writers'. 105–106.

[20] Ibid. 106.

[21] See below, 16–17.

any period. Their works were read both in English and in translation with greedy enthusiasm from the Urals to the Atlantic. Their influence was felt in every sphere – poetry, fiction, drama, opera, painting and design – to say nothing of politics. Once war seemed to have ceased, with the abdication of Napoleon early in 1814, accounts of the two new English giants were rapidly spread, via such organs as the *Allgemeine Literatur-Zeitung Intelligenzblatt* of Jena, and the *Bibliothèque britannique* of Geneva.

Of all the British 'romantic' poets Byron owed most to European literature – and contributed most.[22] *Don Juan* is a series of inversions of Homer and Tasso. Voltaire and Stendhal were his idols in prose, and his most sophisticated verse owed its form to the Italian *ottava rima* tradition of Pulci, Berni and the despised and neglected Casti. Though Byron knew no German, *Manfred* was immediately recognized by Goethe as a variation on *Faust* Part I. Its appeal rested not least on the idea that man needed neither demon to tempt him, nor God to damn him: all he needed to destroy himself was his own will. Byron was sufficiently aware of Spanish literature to credit Boscan and Garcilasso with having corrupted the reading of the adolescent Don Juan, and to see Quixote's comic-idealist pilgrimage as a prototype of his own. Russian literature was as closed a book to him as to most people in Western Europe, but he had begun to read it in translation in Cephalonia in 1823 – the year before his death.

This width of reading went hand in hand with a strong liberal analysis of the continent's politics and history. Byron was not alone in England in feeling great disappointment at the triumph of Reaction after Waterloo, and his own later continental career, in Italy and Greece, can be seen as a series of attempts at reversing the verdict on Napoleon. His death at Missolonghi in 1824, made him a mythic figure in the cause of liberty, setting the seal on a life which, as Mickiewicz pointed out, made action the ultimate goal of writing, and the spilling of blood in a nationalist cause the natural extension of that of ink in a 'romantic' one.

Europe indeed became littered with the dead bodies of men who either thought they had, or really had, modelled themselves on Byron. The revolutionary Russian poet Kondraty Rylyeyev, hanged for his part in the Decembrist conspiracy, ascended the scaffold with a single-volume Byron in his pocket; this despite the fact that he had warned Pushkin *against* being influenced by Byron. In France, Byron was admired, without being imitated, by de Vigny, Lamartine, de Staël and Chateaubriand. On the other hand, the irony of Stendhal and the conversational fluency and facetiousness of de Musset, showed how writers who wished could appropriate both his themes and styles.

In Germany, Goethe – that self-proclaimed anti-Romantic – announced Byron to be the only one of his European contemporaries with whom he could stand comparison – including a portrait of him in *Faust* Part II, as Euphorion, the overreaching child of Helen and Faust, who tries to fly heavenwards and disappears in a blaze of light. When the news of Byron's death reached Heine, he lamented that his 'cousin, Lord Byron', had died at Missolonghi. Other poets and playwrights – Lenau, Grillparzer and Grabbe, for example – showed varying degrees of emulation.

Similarly in Spain in the 1830s, José de Espronceda's *El Estudiante de Salamanca* and *El Diablo Mundo*, combined the Byronically erotic, the Byronically misanthropic and the Byronically gothic, in a wonderfully Iberian mixture. Almeida Garrett, the Portuguese playwright and

---

[22] For what follows on Byron I am heavily indebted to Peter Cochran, and the appropriate sectional editors, Richard A. Cardwell (Richard A. Cardwell (ed), *The Reception of Byron in Europe*, Thoemmes Continuum, 2005, 2 vols. The 2 vols cover all of Europe save Iceland.), Mirosława Modrzewska, and others.

self-styled Byronic figure, had read Byron in English and despite Byron's rather dismissive treatment of the Portuguese in *Childe Harold* I, appropriated a Byronic pose in his writing and in his politics to forward Portuguese nationalism and other liberal causes. And while Alexandre Herculano, whose contribution to Portuguese Romanticism was no less significant, was hostile towards Byron, the determination of his opposition also illustrates the force of Byron's influence.

Even in Japan, Kitamura Tôkoku (1868–1894), wrote the *Poem of the Prisoner*, (1889) arguably Japan's longest narrative poem to that date, inspired by Byron's *The Prisoner of Chillon*, and then two years later an (unfinished) poem based on *Manfred*. In true Byronic – or perhaps Wertherean – style, he went on to commit suicide at the age of 25.[23]

Probably Byron's greatest single impact, however, was on Pushkin, who had little Russian poetry of quality on which to model himself. Starting, in poems such as *The Fountain of Bakhchisarai*, and *The Prisoner of the Caucasus*, with imitations of the Turkish Tales, he quickly tired of such orientalist fancy, and in *Evgeny Onegin* outgrew the influence of the early Byron with a creative adaptation of the manner of the later. In *The Little House at Kolomna* he even wrote a *Beppo*-style comedy in *ottava rima*, with the sexual impulse of the heroine as main narrative motiv. Later, Lermontov proclaimed himself not to be Byron, in contexts which showed how eccentrically he thought the reverse. Pechorin, the protagonist of *A Hero of Our Time*, could not be more Byronic; and the Superfluous Man of later Russian literature is a clear descendant of Childe Harold.

Nor was it always necessary to have read Byron to feel his impact. Painters from Turner to Delacroix took what they asserted were Byronic themes and exploited them with great élan, and scant accuracy. In general his reputation varied hugely with local and contextual factors. In Bohemia, for instance, he was viewed with suspicion as a depraved occidental import and therefore as a branch of Austrian imperialism; in Poland – thanks to the championship of Mickiewicz – he was used as an emblem of anti-imperialism, and thus as an invaluable weapon against the Russians. In general, his taboo-breaking works contributed either to the image of a left-wing bogey-man, or to that of a model liberal hero – or, indeed, martyr. In general, his influence was weakest where autocracy was strongest. Thus travellers were warned never to try and get their copy of *Don Juan* through the Russian customs, and anyone who tried to write in a Byronic manner in an Italy dominated by the Papacy, the Bourbons, or the Austrians, risked imprisonment or death. In Italy, Michele Leoni translated *Childe Harold* IV, only to see the whole print run pulped; his compatriot, Silvio Pellico praised the same poem, and was imprisoned. Ironically, such authoritarianism ensured that Byron's literary influence would be least in the continental country where he lived longest.

Indeed, translation actually inspired new art forms. As Anne O'Connor reminds us, though Italy had a number of great Italian Romantic writers, Italy's most lasting contribution to European art was not in literature at all, but in opera – one of the most international art forms ever created. But if it is hard to imagine nineteenth-century Europe without Italian opera, it is harder still to separate that opera from its sources: Rossini without the French of Beaumarchais, Donizetti without Scott, or Verdi without the Bible, Scott and Shakespeare. Nor did Italians miss out on the opportunity to appropriate with ingenuity the politically suspect and omnipresent Byron. Throughout Europe it became easy for a composer to draw attention to his work by giving it a name with a Byronic association: *Il Corsaro, Harold en Italie, Années de Pèlerinage* and so on.

If it is axiomatic that the act of translation from another language always changes the host language, we must remember, finally, that translation into English involves not one, but two host

---

[23] See Ayumi Mizukoshi's Introduction to Japanese Romanticism. 66–67.

languages, divided not merely by rhetoric, traditions and outlook, but even by such mundane matters as spelling. From at least the 1830s onwards, when James Marsh produced his influential translation of Herder's *Spirit of Hebrew Poetry*,[24] an increasing flow of American translations was finding its way into an English-speaking world that was no longer the sole cultural preserve of the United Kingdom.[25] The result was to destabilize a system of spelling that had only slowly achieved any kind of standardization during the previous century. Thus this reader contains translations from American, British and even Australian sources, and it would be both inconsistent and ahistorical of us to amend original spellings in pursuit of any kind of imposed standard. The parallel developments of Webster and the OED tells their own stories of cultural diversity within a linguistic system that has been in itself more and more a multicultural experience.

IV

A fourth possible objection to an reader such as this concerns a natural prejudice against anthologies themselves – and against their inevitable concomitant: excerpts. A work of literature, so this purist argument runs, is whole and indivisible. To break it into fragments, and – worse – to anthologize those unrepresentative fragments is to demean or even destroy the original work. It is, in short, cultural barbarism of the worst kind. Such an argument has indeed strong Romantic roots, and, like the parallel one against translation, is always to be taken seriously. But historically it is, in truth, but one half of yet another Romantic paradox. Just as the Romantics denied the possibility of true translation while embarking on perhaps the greatest wave of translations hitherto attempted in European history, so too they proclaimed the principles of organic unity, while excelling in the production of anthologies, fragments and collections of every kind.

The original meaning of 'anthology' is a collection of flowers – by common metaphorical extension, therefore, a collection of 'flowers of verse'. Shakespeare's fairies, or at least Pease-Blossom and Mustard-Seed in *A Midsummer Night's Dream*, were, therefore, an anthology of sorts, but Bottom with an ass's head is arguably part of an anthology in the more modern sense of an assemblage of disparate elements that suggest a new kind of whole – not always, perhaps, constituting such an ungainly monster, but often enough a new kind of life.

As Shakespeare would probably have known, the most famous literary example of an 'anthology' in the early modern world – and the one that was to give its name to the whole genre – was the *Greek Anthology*, a collection of Greek lyric and epigrammatic poems by many writers, some ancient, and some medieval Christian, assembled in a series of compilations from antiquity onwards.[26] One of the keys to the revival of classical learning in the sixteenth and seventeenth centuries, it served both to popularize Greek literature in a still Latin-dominated Europe, and to

---

[24] See Stephen Prickett. *Modernity and the Reinvention of Tradition: Backing into the Future*. Cambridge: Cambridge UP, 2008. Ch. 7.

[25] Similarly, the standard nineteenth-century translation of Chateaubriand's *Genius of Christianity* (1801) was by James White, and published in Baltimore in 1856.

[26] One form of the anthology had been rediscovered in the fifteenth century and was first published in Florence in 1494 by Janus Lascaris, a well-known Hellenist. This version, known as the Planudean text, had been assembled by a monk named Maximus Planudes at the very end of the thirteenth century. The one most likely to have been known to English readers was a later, larger, and more authoritative text, based on a tenth-century manuscript formerly in the library of the Count Palatine at Heidelberg, which contains a large number of poems not found in the Planudean manuscript. It was brought to England in

popularize and give respectability to anthologies as a genre – also associating them irrevocably with the idea of translation.

It was presumably with this classical example before him in 1798 that one of the fathers of European Romanticism, Friedrich Schlegel – who may even have seen the original of the Palatinate manuscript of *The Greek Anthology* in Heidelberg – latched on to the idea of the fragment as being the perfect form by which to express the new spirit by which antiquity was to be experienced by his contemporary world. To describe that spirit, he coined for it a new/old word: 'Romanticism'. 'Many of the works of the ancients have become fragments,' he wrote. 'Many modern works are fragments as soon as they are written.'[27] Despite appearances, however, this was not in fact intended as an attack on the pigmy status of modern writers (though he was to produce plenty of those elsewhere). For Schlegel, the fragment was to be the chosen art-form for his manifestly uncompleted age.[28] In contrast to the aesthetic completeness and closure assumed by the despised tenets of neo-classicism, Schlegel's Romanticism was of its very essence open-ended. In the words of one of his English admirers, Julius Hare, 'Is not every Gothic minster unfinished? And for the best of reasons, because it is infinite.'[29]

For Rodolphe Gasché, in his Introduction to Schlegel's *Philosophical Fragments*, the Romantic fragment expresses an incompleteness that is universal, essential and whose scope has no comparison to the incompleteness to which the traditional notion of the fragment alludes. Rather it follows from the belief that in order to be an idea, that idea can only exist in the form of an individuality. It cannot be generalized. As befits a practitioner of this principle, Schlegel himself is at once more metaphorical and more concrete than his expositors:

> A dialogue is a chain or garland of fragments. An exchange of letters is a dialogue on a larger scale, and memoirs constitute a system of fragments. But as yet no genre exists that is fragmentary both in form and content, simultaneously completely subjective and individual, and completely objective and like a necessary part in a system of all the sciences.[30]

In defending a similar unity-with-diversity in the Bible, Schlegel turns back to the idea of the *Greek Anthology* again:

> All the classical poems of the ancients are coherent, inseparable; they form an organic whole, they constitute, properly viewed, only a single poem, the only one in which poetry itself appears in perfection. In a similar way, in a perfect literature all books should be only a single book, and in such an eternally developing book, the gospel of humanity and culture will be revealed.[31]

---

manuscript by Erasmus in the early sixteenth century, and, though it forms the basis of modern editions, it was not published until 1616.

[27] Friedrich Schlegel. *Philosophical Fragments*. Trans. Peter Firchow. Foreword by Rodolphe Gasché. Oxford and Minnesota: U of Minnesota P, 1991. 24.

[28] This aesthetic of the unfinished text as an open-ended form is also present in one of the Swedish texts in this anthology: C. J. L. Almqvist's *Om två slags Skrifsätt (About two Ways of Writing)*, 262–266.

[29] Julius and Augustus Hare, *Guesses at Truth* (1827). London: Published for J. Taylor by J. Duncan Vol. 2. 250.

[30] Fragment 77, *Philosophical Fragments*, Op. Cit.

[31] *Ideas, Philosophical Fragments*. 95.

For Schlegel, and his fellow Jena Romantics,[32] the idea of an underlying unity in which all individual works of literature (however complete in themselves) were also but fragments of a wider whole was inseparable from the need for translation. German literature was then only embryonic, clearly dependent on the English, French and Italian works which were widely translated and disseminated to what was, paradoxically, probably the largest and most highly literate reading-public in Europe.[33]

V

A final objection to an anthology such as this concerns the concept of 'Romanticism' itself. There have been a number of notorious debates concerning the problem of definition. One excellent anthology of literature from this period challenges the uncertainties of literary classification by being entitled simply: *British Literature 1780–1830*.[34] Similarly, several of the editors of this volume are so overwhelmed by the variety of possible meanings to the word that they are sceptical as to whether the word has any meaning at all. They have a point. As one distinguished critic has recently noted:

> Some Romantics, self-professed or not, were politically progressive and others reactionary; some were internationalist and cosmopolitan, others fiercely nationalistic; some of them believed in the Enlightenment project of rational perfectibility, while others opposed it. Some Romantics were religious sceptics, while others converted to Catholicism; some vested their hopes in absolute Truth, while others acknowledged the inevitability of relative, subjective truths. Some subscribed to a poetics of subjectivity, others to a literary ideal of non-subjectivity; some wanted literature and the arts to be organic, others highly self-conscious, self-reflexive, auto-referential, and ironic. Some regarded poetry, some the novel, and others the drama as the supreme genre.[35]

For some, indeed, the whole idea of literary classification itself is more than suspect. David Perkins, in a book with the polemical title *Is Literary History Possible?* devotes a chapter specifically to the history of the concept of English Romanticism. He notes that the first person to use the term 'Romantic' to describe the English poets of the period was the French critic Hyppolyte Taine, in his *History of English Literature* (1863), who seems to have constructed English romanticism on the model of the French.[36] Though his *History* appeared in English translation in 1871, the term did not become widespread until the 1890s. Perkins concludes:

> ... it seems that literary classifications have little plausibility. They do not represent realities, and only the naive could believe that they do. For how can groupings of books and authors that are based on the inertia of tradition, on the mere say-so of authors vying with each other

---

[32] Including his brother August, Johann Gottlieb Fichte, Friedrich von Hardenberg (Novalis), Dorothea Mendelssohn, Caroline Michaelis, Friedrich Schelling, Friedrich Schleiermacher, Ludwig Tieck, and, more intermittently, such figures as Brentano, Hölderlin, Hegel and Steffens.

[33] See R. R. Palmer. *The World of the French Revolution.* London: Allen & Unwin, 1971. 233.

[34] *British Literature 1780–1830*. Eds. Anne K. Mellor and Richard E. Matlack, Harcourt, 1996.

[35] Christoph Bode in Nicholas Roe. Ed., *Romanticism, An Oxford Guide*. Oxford: Oxford University Press, 2005. 127.

[36] David Perkins. *Is Literary History Possible?* Baltimore: Johns Hopkins Press, 1992. 96–97.

for notice, on the uncertain perceptions of literary historians, on their need to construct formal symmetries, and on external facts – in other words, not on the objects to be classified but on circumstances adjacent to them – have credibility?[37]

But the fact remains that, as we shall see, this very implausible and indeed artificially constructed category of 'Romanticism', however indefinable, and perhaps even indefensible, had spread like wildfire across Europe, and from Europe to much of the literate world. Moreover, is it *really* naive to believe that the contextual and circumstantial aspects of a work are important? The contexts provided by this reader make it abundantly clear – possibly as never before – how much the English poets had in common with their counterparts in countries right across Europe, and, just as important (as in the case of Byron), how much they were *believed* to have. It is simply not the case that those who make classifications necessarily imagine that their constructs, created for a particular purpose at a particular time (in other words, *also* coming from a specific historical context), represent any kind of absolute 'truth'. Labels such as 'Romantic', 'Gothic' or even 'Sensational' can, for instance, all be applied to a novel like Mary Shelley's *Frankenstein* without suggesting that one excludes any of the others. Classification normally tells us about context and perspective, not about essence. Nor is this an argument for total subjectivity. As E. H. Carr once commented about the study of history, 'the fact that a mountain looks different when seen from different angles does not mean either that it has no shape or an infinity of shapes.'[38]

As the Carr quotation suggests, many of the same arguments have been advanced in the older debate among historians about the possibility of 'intellectual history'. In this context, John Burrow has drawn an analogy between entering the hermeneutical circle of the past and the process of learning another language:

> ... although we can characterize the method in very general and perhaps unnecessarily pretentious terms as hermeneutic, there are no recipes. We may get guidance, tuition, and above all, example, from those who know the language, and we may learn by rote some of the rules of grammar, but ultimately, to come to inhabit a language, we must learn as we say, to play it by ear ...[39]

The analogy may not be perfect – by definition, analogies *can* only be partial – but if we think of 'Romanticism' as a language, it saves us at least from wasting time on definitions. We do not define German. We know it is how people in certain parts of Europe speak. German speakers, whatever their accents, and however different their viewpoints and perspectives, recognize that they speak the same language. It is that act of recognition that is important. Of course any language is a loose and baggy monster, what is important is not how precisely we classify it, but what those who speak it have to say. If we think of reading Romantic literature as an attempt to listen to the conversations of the past, it will at least remind us that learning any language involves submitting to *its* rules, *its* particular ways of describing experience, *its* unique metaphorical structure – and, above all, *its* unique structure of feeling. There is, we might say, a

---

[37] Ibid., 110–111.
[38] E. H. Carr. *What is History?* London: Macmillan, 1961. 21.
[39] John Burrow. 'The Uses of Philology in Victorian England'. *Ideas and Institutions in Victorian Britain.* Ed. Robert Robson. London: Bell, 1967. 19–20ff.

'family resemblance' between widely differing works. We should, perhaps, follow the modest aims of what Karl Popper has called 'methodological nominalism'.

> Instead of finding out what a thing really is, and at defining its true nature, methodological nominalism aims at describing how a thing behaves in various circumstances . . . and it sees in our language, and especially in those of its rules which distinguish properly constructed sentences and inferences from a mere heap of words, the great instrument of scientific description; words it considers rather as subsidiary tools for the task, and not as the name of essences . . .[40]

Perhaps to this end, Christophe Bode, whom we cited earlier on the endless varieties of Romanticism, suggests that we reconceptualize European Romanticism not as a set of beliefs or an aesthetic programme, but 'as a *set of responses*, highly differentiated and at times downright contradictory, to a historically specific *challenge*: the challenge of the ever-accelerating modernization of European society'.[41] Yet the fact remains that, as we shall see, a procession of European writers – Hugo, Manzoni, Stendhal, Sükei and many others cited here – believed that there *was* such a thing, a mood, a response that spoke to them, and to their peers.

It is one of the many paradoxes of Romanticism that, as we have seen, the term itself (not to mention the accompanying theory) actually originated in Germany. Though these first Romantics had loose associations with major creative writers like Goethe, Hölderlin, Novalis and Schiller, the 'idea' of Romanticism (if it may be so called) was primarily the work of a group of critics, philosophers and theologians – including the Schlegel brothers, Schleiermacher and Schelling.[42] Despite the polemical Preface to the contemporary *Lyrical Ballads*, in England, or Shelley's later *Defence of Poetry*, no such collective programmatic thinking animated those whom we now call the English Romantics, such as Blake, Wordsworth and Coleridge, whose work in the late 1790s was far more productive in literary terms. But as we have seen, Goethe, like Schleiermacher and the Schlegels, drew as much from English literature from Shakespeare onwards as they did from German.

In the end, what turned the word 'Romanticism' from the catch-phrase of a small *avant-guarde* coterie in Jena into the banner of a Europe-wide series of intellectual and aesthetic changes was a Frenchwoman of Swiss ancestry, married to a Swede, Mme Germaine de Staël – who employed Friedrich Schlegel's brother, August, as her secretary. A best-selling international novelist and essayist,[43] it was de Staël who first brought Italy to general European consciousness with *Corinne, ou L'Italie* (1807), and then, in effect, hi-jacked and appropriated Romanticism for her own, essentially trans-national, purposes – arguing in *De l'Allemagne* (1810) that what she (at least) meant by the word was an inescapable characteristic of modernity. In the words of John Isbell:

> She found scattered, local and half-formed agendas, from Wordsworth to Chateaubriand, still defined within the ambit of neoclassicism; she brought them a single name, *Romanticism*; a fuller sense of nationhood; a point by point description of the movement's radical

---

[40] Karl Popper. *The Open Society and its Enemies*, 4th edn. London: Routledge, 1962. Vol. 1. 32.

[41] Roe (ed.), *Op. Cit.*, 127.

[42] Goethe, of course, would have been horrified to find himself classified with the 'Romantics', but the author of *Wilhelm Meister* can hardly be considered a 'classical' writer in a sense acceptable to either English or French contemporary critical canons. Similarly, Novalis's extensive critical writings scarcely conform to the narrow definitions of 'Romanticism' advanced by the Schlegels in the *Athenaeum*.

[43] Such as *De la literature* (1800); and *Delphine* (1802).

novelty, extending from religion to the sciences; and terms that allowed it to be adapted for use from Boston to Moscow. This global coherence was not the Germans', it was her own. In brief: Staël took the German term 'Romantic' as a perfect label for her own global agenda, and sold this private agenda to Europe's half-formed anti-Classical reactions. She thereby invented a European Romanticism . . .[44]

Not surprisingly, therefore, in the following pages we shall find the word 'Romantic' deployed in a variety of ways, from a historical term to a critical principal to a deliberate strategic irritant. The vagueness of the concept is well illustrated by the fact that whereas in some countries – Italy, and even Germany, for instance – it was seen as heralding a liberal and even radically democratic agenda, in Spain, as Richard Cardwell points out, A. W. Schlegel's criticism was interpreted as a programme of the far right. Similarly, though Goethe, Foscolo and Leopardi would all have considered themselves neo-classical writers, as we shall see, our editors for the German and Italian sections, Nicholas Saul and Anne O'Connor respectively, here claim them, in some sense at least, as Romantics. Such examples will also serve to remind the reader of the degree to which from de Staël's time onwards the word has always been a controversial and umbrella term. But since the very creation of this volume is polemical, in that it assumes a measure of common ground between the writers reproduced here, we have, for the sake of consistency, chosen (with this caveat) to use a capital for the word 'Romantic' throughout.

At least in de Staël's sense, however, we can say that Romanticism was in its very essence a phenomenon of translation. In the history of European literature, juxtaposition of the familiar and unfamiliar, reshuffling, appropriation and misreading, have always been potent and fertile sources of new ideas and sensibility. Moreover a text shorn of its cultural context can be far more influential than in its original matrix. Bottom translated, we recall, was a far more polyvalent creature than Bottom the would-be actor. Not merely was he the terror of the Athenian forest, but he was also the unlikely lover of the Fairy Queen. Peter Quince was right in thinking that translation is a natural breeding-ground for monsters.

VI

It is, perhaps, appropriate that the first truly translated Romantic character was indeed a monster – whose creation belongs to another woman. Few educations of the romantic period have relied more on translation than the entirely fictional one of Frankenstein's Monster. Not merely was this education preternaturally successful, but it is described to us by Mary Shelley in unusual detail. It begins, as Plato says all education should, with music – played on a guitar by the old blind de Lacey in the cottage next to the shed where the Monster is hiding – but as soon as the Monster has mastered language, and (almost as instantaneously) learned to read, his mind is developed by a strenuous course of books from all over Europe. Starting with Volney's *Ruins of Empires* he continues with *Paradise Lost*, *Plutarch's Lives* and *The Sorrows of Werther*. The cultural range of these few works can scarcely be exaggerated. From the *Ruins*, the Monster tells us, he 'obtained a cursory knowledge of history, and a view of the several empires at present existing in the world', together with 'an insight into the manners, governments, and

[44] John Claiborne Isbell. *The Birth of European Romanticism: Truth and Propaganda in Staël's 'De l'Allemagne' 1810–1813*. Cambridge: Cambridge UP, 1994.

religions of the different nations of the earth'.[45] Goethe's *Werther*, by contrast, appealed inwardly to his emotions, and he wept for the suicide of the hero 'without precisely understanding it'. Plutarch's 'Parallel Lives' gives biographies of 23 Greeks and 23 Romans, arranged in pairs. This, the Monster, tells Frankenstein, gave him not merely a knowledge of ancient history, but also of the ways of men. Finally, Milton's *Paradise Lost*, ostensibly justifying the ways of God to man, was read by the Monster not merely as an expansion of the biblical narrative of the Creation and Fall of man, but as a story of tyranny and injustice in which Satan was a fit 'emblem' of his condition.[46]

In short, the Monster has had a sound education in European Romanticism. From only four books, the mentally agile creature received an insight into the classical and biblical roots of our culture, grasped the meaning of tradition, gained a romantic sense of self amounting to self-invention, a feeling of exile, a yearning for the exotic, and a confessional and autobiographical style of narration. This heady mix of history, religion and sensibility sums up almost every aspect of what we now associate with Romanticism[47] – with one glaring exception. There is here no hint of nationalism. This is scarcely surprising, since the Monster is stateless, rootless, totally without family and non-human. What is significant, however, is that though the Monster lacks cultural, ethnic and social identity, or nationality, he does have a specific language: French. This in itself is revealing, in that a work written wholly in English should imagine as an integral part of its fiction that it was really written partly in English (Walton) but also partly in German (Frankenstein) and partly in French (the Monster). Indeed, we are tacitly asked to take for granted that the conversations between the Monster and his creator are actually a Franco-German dialogue. But though the first book on his unselected reading-list is indeed by a Frenchman – Constantin-François Chassebŝuf de Volney's *Ruins* was presented to the National Assembly in September 1791 – the others are all translations. Milton's *Paradise Lost* had been repeatedly translated into French in the eighteenth century, with four separate versions before the publication of Frankenstein in 1817 (1729, 1754, 1787 and 1805) and was so much admired that it had spawned a whole host of Francophone imitations. For Goethe's *Werther* the Monster also had a wide choice of translation available: between 1774 and 1809 no less than ten different French versions were published. For Plutarch, he would, of course, have read Jacques Amyot's classic French translation of 1559. As his subsequent conversation with de Lacey reveals, the Monster at least knew what many of us too easily forget today, that Romanticism is not the product of any one culture or society, it is of its essence a phenomenon of *translation*.

Each of the Monster's books is metafictional and trans-cultural, depending not merely on translation, but often multiple translations and interpretations of translation. Thus Plutarch's *Lives* was one of the foundational texts of European culture – and North's English translation of 1579 was one of Shakespeare's favourite sources for his plays. North's translation was not,

---

[45] Mary Shelley. *Frankenstein or The Modern Prometheus*. London: Everyman. 1912. 123.
[46] Ibid. 133–136.
[47] This list could be extended indefinitely. Thomas McFarland identifies 'external nature, imagination, egotism, love of the particular, flight into the medieval, flight into the Orient, flight into drugs, a preoccupation with dreams, with melancholy, solitude, suicide, an ubiquitous awareness of process and current, a longing for the infinite and unattainable, an omnipresent involvement with the organic, a profound commitment to symbol, incompleteness, fragmentation, ruin', 'madness' and 'wanderlust' as 'essential determinants of the romantic sensibility'. *Romantic Cruxes*. Oxford: Clarendon, 1987. 13–23.

however, made from the Greek at all, but from Amyot's French version, mentioned above. Volney's *Ruins* is itself a palimpsest of many cross-cultural influences, drawing partly on his own first-hand researches in Greek and Arabic in Syria and the Near East,[48] but no less on the German Higher Criticism of Eichhorn, Lessing and Reimarus, not to mention the researches on Sanskrit in English by Sir William Jones and the Asiatic Society of Calcutta. No less than three separate translations were to appear in English during the 1790s.

For *Werther*, Goethe is drawing on an English tradition of sensibility reaching back through Sterne and Fielding to Shaftsbury, though, of course, the introversion and self-pity of Werther is all his own. First published in German 1774, Goethe's novel was a runaway best-seller. The British Library catalogue lists a French translation in the same year, although the name of the translator is not known. Two more translations followed in 1776, that of Baron S. de Seckendorf (in Erlangen) and G. Deyverdun (in Maastricht). A third, by M. Aubrey, was published in Mannheim in 1777. The fact that all these three French translations were published outside France tells us much about the universality of French at this period. A Danish translation was made in 1776[49] and a Swedish translation followed in 1783.[50] The first Russian translation of Werther was made by F. Galcenkov in 1781.[51] The first English translation, made in 1779 by Daniel Malthus, was made, like that of Plutarch, not from the original, but from a French translation (that of Aubry). Between then and 1815 no less than eight English translations from the German are listed in the British Library catalogue, one of which alone went through ten editions between 1780 and 1799.[52] There is even another translation from Aubrey's French version in 1789 and a translation of a French novel (by a M. Perrin) *The Female Werther* (1792). Mary Shelley's husband, the poet Percy Bysshe Shelley, had himself translated part of another of Goethe's works, *Faust*, into English.

It is easy to forget that Milton was always a European figure, rather than just an English polymath. But it is no accident that he was to prove at least as potent an influence on the development of continental, as on British Romanticism. His learning was notoriously vast and varied, embracing not merely the biblical languages, but the Latin and Italian epic traditions from Virgil to Dante, Ariosto and Tasso. His Satan, however, is uniquely his own creation – for the Romantics, a Byronic hero before his time. Not merely was *Paradise Lost* repeatedly translated into French, by the time Frankenstein's Monster is supposed to have read it, the poem had also been translated in Swedish, Dutch (twice), German (four times), Italian (four times) and Spanish. Moreover the 1796 French translation by Dupré de Saint-Maur and Pierre de Mareuil, made in 1796, at the height of the Revolution, was to be the source of Sándor Bessenyei's Hungarian prose-translations of both *Paradise Lost* and *Paradise Regained*. The Monster was, alas, created too early to have been able to read that ultimate of romantic translations of Milton: that of Chateaubriand himself, which was not published until 1836.

---

[48] In 1781 his examination of Herodotus's chronology had earned him an international reputation as an orientalist, confirmed by his *Voyage en Syrie et en Egypt* (1793) which earned him (among others) a decoration from Catherine the Great of Russia.

[49] Never published, because prohibited by the (Lutheran) Church.

[50] By Erik Wilhelm Weste. It went through three further editions in 1786, 1791 and 1796.

[51] It was printed in St. Petersburg (*Der russische Werther*, red. W. Eggeling and M. Schneider, München, 1988).

[52] Since most of these were anonymous, it is difficult to know without inspecting them all whether they are independent translations or pirated editions of the same translation. I am indebted to Stuart Gillespie for much of this information, and what follows.

Even the story of the creation of the Monster is one of intertextuality and translation. Samuel Taylor Coleridge had given a copy of his as-yet unpublished poem *Christabel* to Walter Scott, and in 1815 this was shown to Byron, who then asked for and obtained his own manuscript copy from Coleridge. The following summer of 1816 Byron met Shelley by arrangement in Geneva. With Shelley were two women: one was Mary Godwin (later to be Mary Shelley) with whom he had just eloped from England, leaving his wife Harriet – who committed suicide. The other was Claire Clairmont, her step-sister, who had had a brief affair with Byron in London earlier in the year, and by whom she was now pregnant. With Byron was a party that included his personal physician and secretary, John William Polidori, an Italian Scot whose sister was later to be mother to the Rossettis – Dante Gabriel, William Michael and Christina. Five years later, at the age of 27, he was also to commit suicide over a gambling debt.

According to the account later published in *The New Monthly Magazine*, 'It appears that one evening Lord Byron, Mr. P. B. Shelley, the two ladies and the gentleman before alluded to, having perused a German work, which was entitled *Phantasmagoriana*, began relating ghost stories; when his lordship, having recited the beginning of *Christabel*, then unpublished, the whole took so strong a hold of Mr Shelley's mind that he suddenly started up and ran out of the room. The physician and Lord Byron followed, and discovered him leaning against a mantlepiece with cold drops of perspiration trickling down his face.'[53] According to another source, he was duly revived with 'a douche of cold water and whiff of ether'. Apparently while he was listening to the famous description of the Lady Geraldine undressing, Shelley had been suddenly overcome by the hallucination of eyes instead of nipples in Mary's breasts.

Whatever this may suggest about the *décolletage* of the 'empire' dresses of the period, the upshot was a competition at writing horror stories. Polidori produced a novella called *The Vampyre*, whose sales he greatly improved by publishing it anonymously and making sure everyone believed it was by Byron. Mary, of course, produced *Frankenstein*. Unfortunately for the legend, other records suggest that the Geneva house-party actually began writing their stories on 17 June 1816, the night before these dramatic events, but Mary's Shelley's account of her difficulties suggest that *Christabel* may, nonetheless, have acted as a trigger to her imagination. What is clear, however, from the foregoing is that whatever her mythical Monster may be supposed to have gleaned from his concentrated reading-course in French, the 19-year-old Mary had benefited at least as much, and more, from those same books in their corresponding English translations – as well as from the English tradition of the Gothic novel, and the extra-biblical stories of the Golem, the Wandering Jew, and of Cain, which animate Coleridge's *Ancient Mariner* and *Christabel*, and Byron's play, *Cain*.

Few would pretend that in *Frankenstein* Mary Shelley had written the best novel of the period,[54] but none can dispute that even in its wildest improbabilities, it offers some of the most dramatic, mysterious and powerful images ever to haunt the European imagination. The unfortunate Monster himself may have been denied descendents, but Mary's novel has spawned as rich and varied a progeny as almost any single literary work – not least, those most eclectic and powerful of monsters, anthologies such as this. That image of the sensitive, self-pitying,

---

[53] See Arthur Nethercott in *The Road to Tyermaine*. New York: Russell & Russell, 1962. 19–20.
[54] Though few would nowadays go as far as George Levine: 'It is so extraordinarily silly a book that it seems either pretentious or absurd to treat it . . . as a text to be edited . . . By most standards of reasonable literary judgment, Frankenstein should have died shortly after its first popular success.' [*The Wordsworth Circle*. VI. 3 (Summer 1975): 208]

self-inventing and yet withal dangerous Byronic hero, as outcast Monster, may also serve us as a metaphor of the dramatic, mysterious and powerful (not to mention fortuitous and accidental) intertextual complexity of European Romanticism itself.

VII

It follows that the organization of our anthology is crucial. To avoid the kind of national compartmentalism mentioned above, and to give some sense of the interaction between various movements the texts themselves are arranged under eight major thematic headings – arranged (in so far as such interconnected themes can be) in a logical progression. [These are: I. Art and Aesthetics, II. The Self, III. History and Politics, IV. Language and Interpretation, V. Myth, Religion and the Supernatural, VI. Nature, VII. The Exotic; VIII. Science.] As indicated, all non-English texts have an accompanying English translation (where possible, contemporary to the period) printed in parallel for ease of reference, the English facing the original language text on the opposite page.

As we are only too well aware, such a set of categories – however much we have debated them – will in the end seem arbitrary and controversial, as indeed they must be. Any competent comparative romanticist could (and no doubt will) construct a different grouping – and we are happy for any to do so. The fact remains that once we had decided to opt for a thematic arrangement, we had to choose a particular set of themes that seemed to bring out best salient features of that phenomenon that we persist in calling 'Romanticism'. Each of our editors has made hard choices to include some texts and, inevitably, to exclude others. Some texts obviously belong under more than one of these headings and this is reflected in the introductory commentaries. One thing to emerge from this arrangement is that – as might be expected – not all countries are represented equally in all the thematic categories – indeed, Czech literature is represented by a single nature poem, *May*. A more surprising omission for some may be the absence of a category of 'the imagination'. But an inspection of the other sections may suggest this to be a theme more missed by English-language readers than by others, since it is a word with notoriously different meanings in different languages (the German word, for instance, is heavily coloured by its Kantian meaning), and not one that has such resonance in all cultures, let alone Romantic movements. But this, too, can, and no doubt will be, challenged by some users of this reader – who may, of course, choose their own selections or topics. As we have said, it is no part of the purpose of this work to impose particular readings of Romanticism, and if one of the results of this compilation is to inspire others to do better, we are all enriched in the long run. On the contrary, by thus taking a series of major themes from the modern period as the headings for the choice of texts, the reader is intended to allow meanings of the term to emerge from the interaction of these themes, rather than attempting an initial definition which would limit the scope of the collection in a predetermined manner. The themes in question play a crucial role in a whole variety of humanities and social science subjects – which may increase the attractiveness of the reader as a resource for these subjects. We observe also that historically Romanticism – even Mme de Staël's version of it – has been a term employed more to designate a *break* with preceding attitudes to major intellectual, political, social and aesthetic questions, than to characterize a specific movement. It is linked to the question of modernity without being identical with it. Of that, and the other thorny questions raised above, we hope that readers of this reader will be in a position, as never before, to judge for themselves.

APPENDIX

CONTEMPORARY TRANSLATORS: GEORGE BORROW AND JOHN BOWRING *Benjamin Morris*

BACKGROUND

The history of literary translation is often as important as the quality, kind and influence of the translations themselves. This is a sketch of two individuals central to the English understanding of other European cultures during what came – with hindsight – to be seen as the Romantic period. Though concerning only two of many such individuals – including not just translators, but printers, publishers and patrons – these notes are intended as a supplement to several of the pieces in the rest of the anthology as well as a springboard for a more sustained programme of works on this phenomenon in its own right.

Born on either side of the publication of *Lyrical Ballads* in 1798 – John Bowring five years before it, George Borrow five years after it – these two translators both grew up with the sensibilities associated with the English Romantic movement. Though both were prolific linguists, writers and translators, neither has gained adequate recognition in the histories of Romantic literature and thought.

George Borrow (1803–1881)

George Borrow was born in Norfolk of a military family in constant relocation. Eventually settling in Norwich, he entered intellectual and political life under the tutelage of William Taylor (himself a prolific translator) before moving to London at the age of 21. Despite literary ambitions, his early efforts began with a year of Grub Street hack work and travels throughout England, usually between Norwich and London via the many Gypsy/Romany communities nearby. Details of these years are vague, scavenged from dubious autobiographical novels written later in life, but in 1829 he returned to London to embark on a collaboration of translations of Scandinavian poetry with John Bowring, whom he had met years before in Norwich. The project fell through, but as Borrow had been accumulating new languages and translating poetry since his youth, the British and Foreign Bible Society sent him abroad (Russia in 1833, Spain in 1835) to distribute copies of the Bible, which included some of his own translations.

Marrying not long after he finished with the Society, he began converting his travels to literary works – finally achieving success with *The Bible in Spain* (1843), a stirring account of his adventures in the Iberian Peninsula which also satisfied evangelical sensibilities of the 1840s.[55] Back in England largely until his death (he continued to travel from time to time), Borrow fictionalized his experiences in novels such as *Lavengro* (1851) and *Romany Rye* (1857). Of his death in 1881 Angus Fraser writes:

His reputation had long been in decline, but revived towards the close of the nineteenth century. Borrow's bibliography is swelled by articles, reviews, compilations, and, above all, his beloved translations: but his enduring legacy was a handful of original works unlike any others, episodic narratives capturing the imagination with strange and at times superbly

---

[55] Angus Fraser. 'Borrow, George Henry (1803–1881)'. *Oxford Dictionary of National Biography*, Oxford: Oxford UP, 2004, online edition. Available at http://www.oxforddnb.com/view/article/2918

presented characters and powerful picaresque sketches. Pervading them all is the opinion-ated but compelling personality of their narrator.[56]

If posterity has been unkind to Borrow's reputation as a translator, it could scarcely be less so than the response of his own day and age. In Borrow's lifetime his translations were hardly known: his earliest substantial translation, F. M. Klinger's *Faustus* (1825), was issued anony-mously. His *Romantic Ballads* of 1826, published by subscription, had only limited circulation. There is no record of any contemporary reaction to his translations from German, Danish and Spanish which appeared in periodicals between 1823–1825,[57] and among a mass of translations he completed in 1828–1830, only those in *The Foreign Quarterly Review* article for June 1830 came to public notice, and their publication was anonymous.[58] Only occasionally did Borrow meet with some success, such as when the Boston *Atheneum* 'gave some prominence to his trans-lations in preference to the many others it might have selected from the English magazines'.[59] Posthumous reception after the publication of the Norwich Edition of his work in 1923, was more favourable, but the fickleness of the reading public for translations, the quality and reputa-tion of his originals and the haphazard manner in which the Norwich Edition and other editions of his work were compiled all weakened his reputation – as did the fact that The 'Songs of Europe' trans-lations, on which Borrow worked all his life, were in some cases published up to 70–80 years after he translated them, with little guidance as to which of the many versions were the preferred ones.[60]

Such delayed publication meant that when George Saintsbury wrote a long obituary for Borrow in *Macmillan's* in 1881, noting that 'Borrow's literary work, even putting aside the "mountains of manuscript" which he speaks of as unpublished, was not inconsiderable'; and that 'his translations . . . though no doubt without value, do not much concern us here',[61] he could have had little knowledge of the full range of Borrow's work.[62] Even when the Norwich Edition was finally compiled, the editors, C. K. Shorter and H. G. Wright, did little to anchor the poems by chronological ordering, annotation or completeness of the text.[63] With poems ripped from their original contexts (except for mentions of the original language), the Norwich Edition offered in effect pieces of poetic driftwood.

John Bowring (1792–1872)
Bowring's life, while considerably more conspicuous – between 1835–1859 he served as MP for Exeter, consul in China and fourth Governor of Hong Kong – still bears remarkable similarities to, and intersections with, Borrow's. Born and educated in Exeter, Bowring learned many of his languages from foreign traders on the Exeter Quayside.[64] Being a decade older he was already established under the wing of Jeremy Bentham by the time Borrow met him in the early 1820s,

---

[56] Ibid.

[57] One of his translations appears in this anthology. See no. 87: Oehlenschläger's 'The Gold Horns'.

[58] Ann Ridler. *George Borrow as Linguist: Images and Contexts*. Privately published doctoral dissertation. Wallingford: A.M. Ridler, 1996. 82–83.

[59] Ibid. 82.

[60] Ibid. 84.

[61] George Saintsbury. 'George Borrow'. *Macmillan's*. (January 1886): 175.

[62] Ridler, 87 n104.

[63] Ibid. 87.

[64] Gerald Stone. 'Bowring, Sir John (1792–1872)'. *Oxford Dictionary of National Biography*, Oxford University Press, September 2004; online edition. http://www.oxforddnb.com/view/article/3087.

and like Borrow his frequent travels provided material for his literary output, primarily translations. These translations came early and often: between 1824–1835, prior to entering public service, Bowring published volumes of Dutch, Spanish, Polish, Serbian, Hungarian (Maygar) and Czech poetry, in his grand design[65] of bringing foreign poetry into England, and he continued to write and publish tracts, pamphlets and other work until his death from prostate disease in 1872. With better political connections than Borrow (such as when he obtained his Consulship in China) he was skilled in exploiting other's efforts and taking the credit for himself.[66] Similarly, he had fewer editorial problems than Borrow. Like many translators he dealt with unfamiliar languages by finding an existing translation into a language like German, which he did know, or a native speaker who could supply a literal rendering into a familiar tongue.[67]

Some of these translations brought temporary fame, but the real problem – the British public's lack of enthusiasm for translations – was never really overcome.[68] (Interestingly, Bowring's son, Edgar Alfred Bowring, apart from serving as an MP like his father, achieved a considerable reputation as a translator as well, having translated Schiller and Goethe's poetry in 1851 and 1853, respectively, and Heine in 1861). If Bowring elder had managed to complete with Borrow the planned anthology of *Songs of Scandinavia* as the latter had hoped, the story might have turned out differently. Their collaboration and later conflict over the anthology is telling: having initially invested considerable time and energy in the project, as time went by Bowring whittled down Borrow's prospectus from four volumes to three, then to two and finally to a single volume. Moreover, as the list of potential subscribers remained stagnant and his political duties took him elsewhere, Bowring eventually lost interest in the book – for which the indigent Borrow was never to forgive him. The ensuing feud between the two was notable for both its duration and intensity; when Borrow published *Romany Rye* in 1851 (one of his more-fiction-than-fact autobiographies), he made a number of professional and personal attacks on Bowring. In addition to having a face 'like that of a convicted pickpocket', Bowring's daughters were labelled as 'too ugly for marriage' and his wife 'looked the very image of shame and malignity'.[69]

Though both were gifted and inquisitive individuals, it does seem clear that Borrow and Bowring's legacies have suffered not just from their personalities, but as well from the third member of the relationship, the nineteenth-century British public that was insufficiently interested to support widespread translation of contemporary European texts beyond the familiar boundaries of France, Germany and Italy. These factors help to explain why their work has not received adequate attention thus far, but there may be another reason as well: Borrow found that 'not poetry, but sentimental moral tales were marketable'.[70] *Plus ça change.*

BRITISH ROMANTICISM *Simon Haines and Christopher A. Strathman*

Where there's a word there's a thing: we tend to reify our abstractions. The words 'Romanticism' and 'Romantic' are egregious examples of this tendency. 'What is Romanticism?'; 'what is

[65] Angus Fraser. 'Two Men of Many Tongues: George Borrow and John Bowring'. *Sir John Bowring 1792–1872: Aspects of His Life and Career.* Ed. Joyce Youings. Exeter: Devonshire Association, 1993. 57.

[66] Ibid., 62.

[67] Ibid., 57–58.

[68] Stone, 15.

[69] Fraser (1993), 66.

[70] British Library. Flysheet from Exhibition Catalogue. 'George Borrow'. Exhibition on display from 8 January–28 June, 1981.

characteristically Romantic/non-Romantic about the poetry of Wordsworth (Blake, Byron)/ novels of Austen (Scott, Peacock)': such questions are sometimes still asked of students, who then feel obliged to say what in their opinion Romanticism 'is', or (worse) what 'romantic' means, before identifying some salient feature or other of the poems or novels under consideration. But A. O. Lovejoy was already complaining 80 years ago that 'the word "romantic" has come to mean so many things that by itself it means nothing'.[1] The era of being admonished to 'discriminate between romanticisms' has now lasted almost as long as the previous undiscriminating era, which itself did not start, at least in Britain, until the 1830s, when it was generally realized that there had been something amounting to a European revolution in literature starting at about the same time as the French Revolution in politics. The literary revolution had no convenient collective English name, although the term *romantisch* had been coined (not to describe his own age) by Friedrich Schlegel in Germany in the late 1790s, promoted by his brother August Wilhelm as the contrary term to *klassisch* in 1801–1804, and then transmitted into the general European literary consciousness by Germaine de Staël in 1814. During the heyday of Wordsworth or Coleridge, Austen or Scott, Byron or Shelley, the term 'romantic' had no meaning beyond its traditional one as 'having the characteristics of romance', of the seventeenth-century Italian, French, Spanish and English romances, in verse and prose, with their medieval subjects, settings and prototypes: fabulous, quixotic, extravagant.

These were 'romances', etymologically speaking, because they were written in the vernacular or Romance languages, which is to say that they were descended from Latin, defined themselves in opposition to Rome; the ancestor of all these *Roman*-tic stories was Virgil's *Aeneid*. But from the 1780s to the 1830s in Britain, during the whole of the era we now think of as 'Romantic', the Lake School of Wordsworth, Southey and Coleridge, the Cockney School of Hazlitt, Keats and Leigh Hunt, the Satanic School of Byron and Shelley, and the novels of Austen, Peacock, Burney and Edgeworth, were never seen as 'romantic' in this old sense, nor as parts of a single literary movement. Many of those writers certainly thought of themselves as living in an age of literary as well as political innovation; in their different ways Wordsworth, Blake, Shelley and Hazlitt all believed that their age had a distinctive and revolutionary 'spirit'. But their conceptions of what was revolutionary about it varied widely.

So according to the Lovejoy view, with its still-current and powerful descendants, 'Romanticism' is a word of such diffuse, varied and even contradictory meanings, especially when the writing canon is broadened from the 'big six' (Blake, Wordsworth, Coleridge, Byron, PB Shelley, Keats) to include all those neglected or contested contemporaries (Austen, Peacock, Mary Shelley, Wollstonecraft, Joanna Baillie, Southey, Crabbe, Felicia Hemans, Leigh Hunt and many more) who may by one definition or another also be termed Romantic, that the only remaining sense we can give the term at least in the British context (Germany is another matter), is a historical one. In this context 'Romantic literature' is normally taken to mean whatever was produced between the 1780s, when Blake and Burns began to publish, and the 1830s, when Coleridge, Scott, Lamb and Hazlitt all died. Even so, we might well want to argue about these dates, since they exclude, say, *Wuthering Heights* and *Jane Eyre*, but include *Pride and Prejudice*. But the deeper problem is that those who consider literature to be bound to history in this way are also liable to argue, with Jerome McGann, that 'poems *are* social and historical products', and that 'the critical study of such products *must* be grounded in a socio-historical

---

[1] Arthur O. Lovejoy. 'On the Discrimination of Romanticisms', *PMLA* 39 (1924), repr. in *Essays in the History of Ideas*, Baltimore: Johns Hopkins Press, 1948. 232.

analytic' (my emphases).[2] If the study of Romantic literature must be 'grounded in' the study of its, and of course our, political and social milieux, then all Romantics turn out to be either 'rebels' or 'reactionari [illegible] der of every literary text must be implicate [illegible] ist observation that far too many scholars [illegible] n of things to attach it to, created here a ki [illegible] rialist approach has been only too willing [illegible]

On the other hand [illegible] apparent heterogeneity, the antithetical [illegible] f an illusion. 'There is, on the contrary, a [illegible] many of them, and we should 'go on spea [illegible] reality to which the word refers is not a hy [illegible] cal ideologies. It is a set of literary represe [illegible] nd coherence', even when it expresses co [illegible] was restating what William Hazlitt had r [illegible] t some other thing, not a vehicle for philo [illegible] social product. This reader, then, is in *Eur* [illegible] *antic Age*. 'Romantic' isn't an historic [illegible] Augustan', a trans-historical disposition [illegible] 'classical', not, say, with 'Enlightenment'. As our reader argues both in its organizational principles and in its title, indeed in its very existence, 'Romanticism' does have both thematic and trans-linguistic coherences, a set of family resemblances.

What is Romanticism?
- defined by history (period from 1780-1830)
- socio-political lense; all romantic authors were rebels or reactionaries
- what do the texts and themes have in common?
Romantic: so many definitions it doesn't mean anything...
In that time - something close to extravagant or fabulous.

What students of literature might prefer to do, then, rather than looking for a definition and then justifying the inclusion of some writer or text under it, is to see for themselves what if anything these contemporary writers, texts and themes have in common *besides* contemporaneity. In this very brief – some might almost say random – selection from the enormous archive of British Romantic writings we begin, for example, under the heading 'Art and Aesthetics', with Wordsworth's famous attack on 'gaudiness and inane phraseology' (linked with his strictures elsewhere against 'sickly and stupid German tragedies'), and his belief in 'beautiful and permanent forms of nature', including human nature. We then find Hazlitt's essay on 'Gusto' (he was a painter before he was a critic) expressing its own belief in 'the truth of passion', in art as a cross-sensory and galvanizing medium of life-perception. Hazlitt's mentor Coleridge, the Plato to his conflicted Aristotle, next advances a related theory of the imagination according to which poetry 'brings the whole soul into activity'. In Shelley's resounding defence poetry 'compels us to feel that which we perceive, and to imagine that which we know'. The art on Keats's Grecian urn aspires to immortality, its frozen images of life preserved in eternal companionship for all the ordinary human lives which are too mortal, too flickeringly ephemeral, to be visible on it, though the implied contrast between them and the visible images gives the poem its poignancy. But Thomas Love Peacock, whose brilliantly ironic, quasi-utilitarian attack on poetry provoked

[2] Jerome J. McGann. *The Romantic Ideology: A Critical Investigation*. Chicago and London: University of Chicago Press, 1983. 3.

[3] Marilyn Butler. *Romantics, Rebels and Reactionaries: English Literature and its Background 1760–1830*. Oxford and London: Oxford University Press, 1981.

[4] René Wellek. 'The Concept of Romanticism in Literary History', *Comparative Literature* 1 (1949), repr. *Concepts of Criticism*. New Haven and London: Yale University Press, 1963. 197.

Shelley's indignant response, calls Wordsworth a 'morbid dreamer', and all the poetic art of their time barbaric, useless and irrational. As Peacock sensed, Romanticism is better understood in terms of its claims for poetry, literature and art than in any other way; its claim is precisely the converse of his charge. Art according to Romanticism is just what *preserves* us from mere utility and rationality, from the 'inane phraseology' of decadent civilization, by recalling for us the 'permanent forms' of human nature. Furthermore, for otherwise this just sounds like classicism, art is the *only* human activity that can do this. In the field of art Romanticism is a belief in the redemptive power of art itself: a belief often explicitly expressed *in* Romantic literature, which represents something of an epoch in cultural history as an art that largely consists in representing the necessity of art.

What this new redemptive art is to redeem is the self, the human awareness of one's own experience *as* one's own. This awareness had by the 1780s been deepened in unprecedented ways by Kant, following the lead of Descartes and other philosophers from the mid-seventeenth century onwards, and especially, very recently, of Rousseau. The new Romantic exploration of the self was conducted mainly as a philosophical enterprise in Germany, but in Britain the thinking was done principally by poets and novelists. To turn back to our selection: Blake's idyllic songs (*eidyllion* means 'a little image', and these poems in their original form *were* little images, the words intertwined with pictures as 'poetical sketches', to use the title of his earlier collection of idylls) enact his sense of the imagining mind's activity as constitutive of life-experience; imagination for him was 'spiritual sensation'. 'I shall not cease from *mental* fight', he declared in the long prophetic book *Milton*; this is the fight that matters when it comes to saving the self. 'Some are born to sweet delight, / Some are born to endless night', he wrote in *Auguries of Innocence*; 'God appears and God is light/ To those poor souls who dwell in Night, / But does a human form display / To those who dwell in realms of day.' Whether we dwell in night or day does not depend on the presence or absence in us of deprivation or suffering. The famous *Tyger* from *Songs of Experience* arguably represents a state of being *inferior* to that represented in its *Songs of Innocence* counterpart *The Lamb*. 'Innocence is a hunter's gown / So clad, we'll abide life's pelting storm', wrote Blake in *Poetical Sketches*. *The Lamb* enacts a unified and integrated self, *The Tyger* a fragmented one: fearful of creation, this fallen and dissociated mind is no longer able to imagine divinity except as artisan, or creation except as mechanical beast. The mind of the speaker of *London* has forged its own manacles. Meanwhile Charlotte Smith's solitary, 'uncursed' with the 'reason' which Blake elsewhere called 'the bound or outward circumference of energy', is saved from a rational knowledge of his own condition by what mere reason would dismiss as madness, though Blake would probably have seen it as 'energy', as 'Imagination & Vision'. Wordsworth's best self or 'calm existence' in the *Prelude* is achieved in the transformation of the 'terrors, pains, and early miseries' of social life, of an experience of the 'mean and vulgar works of man', through an awareness of 'high objects' *via* the 'fearless visitings' in Nature of a 'Spirit of the Universe' perceptible only to the human 'Power' Wordsworth calls 'Imagination'. For Byron the 'I', the ordinary experiencing self, is 'Nothing'; only in the active, creative exercise of the self-conscious mind do we live the 'more intense being' of the true self. P. B. Shelley seeks the same Byronic intensity of being in a heightened Wordsworthian identification with the Spirit of the Universe. Keats's 'fearless visitor' is a solitary nightingale; his own 'sole self', like Byron's, must be expressed either in poetry or in annihilation. In all this poetry we are only ourselves, or are most ourselves, in self-conscious artistic (which is to say, value-adding) re-creation of the natural or human worlds.

[Handwritten note on attached sticky:]

Romanticism
art
- necessity of art
- art redeems self
- In art we are most ourselves
politics
- principles of french revolution; how do they apply to everyone? (Britain)
- redemptive power of politics
- we make the world
language
- we made it & it makes us
- grounded in passion

British political argum[...]ution: the applicability of its principles a[...] and institutions. For Thomas Paine, Mar[...] and Shelley (the husband of their daught[...]rds a 'renovation of the natural order of t[...] attributes affording protection from tyr[...]lution was a *subversion* of the natural o[...] of human nature', in the name of rights, [...]s and breakdown. Byron enlists another [...]-cultural struggle, which Byron was one [...]rdsworth and his friend Southey, who [...] 'pedestrian' poets (though Byron ironic[...] this argument laid claim to a certain mo[...]on permanent conceptual truths at the [...]*idual* self, and thus the aggregate self wh[...]s *between* variegated selves, past as well as present, whi[...]ter) self of civil society. Politically, the Romantic era could be either conservative or radical, relational or conceptual: could appeal either to permanent features of the natural order or distinctive features of the national self. Both sides of the argument (and Hegel was uniting them in Germany, though after him they split again) share a kind of political self-consciousness not seen in earlier Platonic and Aristotelian versions of the two views. Whether we become aware of ourselves as nations, or of ourselves as citizens, what we are doing is becoming aware of ourselves, especially as *self-makers* of and within the political realm: an insight originating with Giambattista Vico in the early eighteenth century (but Vico was unknown to the Romantics). Just as Romanticism in art is a belief in the redemptive power of art, in politics it is a belief in the redemptive power of politics. We must *make* 'the very world, which is the world of all of us': for only in making it can we make ourselves, and only in making ourselves can we redeem ourselves.

Romantic insights into language took a related path. Hugh Blair and Robert Lowth follow Rousseau and, again unknowingly, Vico, in seeing the origins of language as 'poetic': that is, as grounded in passion and metaphor, rather than in correspondences of words and things or words and ideas, as in the ancient Augustinian or recent Lockean traditions. Blake, Wordsworth and P. B. Shelley, though in different terms, think of poetry and art as primal language, figures of speech or stone extruded or impressed by passion. In Anne's conversation with Benwick we see Austen distinguishing, somewhat as Blair does, between the aggravating 'description' or 'imaging' *of* passion in poetry by Scott and Byron, and the rousing and fortifying of the mind *against* it in philosophical or moralizing prose, presumably by a Richard Steele or a Bishop Butler. And in Mary Shelley's even more famous and formative course of literary study, the one self-prescribed by Frankenstein's monstrous creature, that infinitely suffering and unconversible Benwick finds himself first attracted to self-destruction by Goethe's Byronic hero, as many young German men had in fact been: then fortified against it by Plutarch's moralizing *Lives*: and finally (the step Austen does not take) returned to what Blake called the 'Devils' party' by Milton's Satan himself. Whether considering the origins of ordinary language or the formative and moral effects of literary language the British Romantics were interested in what German theorists were calling *bildung*: the dynamic principle of growth in societies and individuals. Language both grew out of feeling, and informed the growth of feeling. We made it, and it makes us.

As for Nature and the transcendent, Watson's response to Gibbon, like Vico's to Descartes, constituted an archetypal Romantic inward turn, towards quality of faith and away from an outward Enlightenment scepticism about claims of fact. The spiritual aridity of Coleridge's Mariner is overcome only by the 'spring of love' gushing from his heart. Paley's counter-argument from wondrous design rebutted standard Enlightenment arguments against deity ('if God has spoken, why is the Universe not convinced?'). Wordsworth's pantheism and Shelley's Neoplatonism alike relied on Nature's 'fearless visitings' to 'see into the life of things' or the 'everlasting universe of things'. In Scott's 'romantic waterfall' and Keats's images of autumn the things of nature derive their life from the observer's own fearless visitings of *them*. We can never know things in themselves, said Kant, but 'we ourselves bring into the appearances [of things] that order and regularity in them that we call nature.'[5] And if we bring order, why not meaning, why not feeling? Why not life?

But surely this order and meaning must then depend on who 'we' are? James Cook's matter-of-fact Easter Islanders and William Beckford's fantastic Gothic-Arabians both catered to that perennial taste (*vide* Herodotus) for the foreign, the alien, the exotic which Romanticism was for the first time domesticating, finding 'their' strangeness reflected within 'us', reviving and recognizing within itself their exotic symphony and song in various forms: the pleasures of Paradise (Abyssinian maids, Juan's Haidee, Ivanhoe's Rebecca); quasi-religious, even drug-induced, epiphanies (De Quincey, Coleridge); primitive sexual drives (Malthus). Indeed if, as Charles Lyell, Paley and Kant himself suggested, God's original act of creation was despite the beauty everywhere manifesting it nevertheless forever hidden from us by thousands of subsequent geological events or 'minute animalcules', then only in the appearances of Nature could God ever again be seen, and 'we ourselves bring' to those appearances whatever order or beauty we find in them. This exploration is therefore as much a matter for a Keats as a Cook, for an Erasmus Darwin as much as a Charles.

Readers not prepared to settle for an entirely historical, or historicized conception of Romanticism, then, may prefer a transcend... ...responsibility of rendering our own exper... ...itself all that gives our lives their value, th... ...the void. This was the Romantic proposal... ...rn out to be impossible (it's still too soon to... ...'European modernity.

CZECH ROMANT...

Emerging rather lat... ...ed with the liberation movement called th... ...d process of cultural and political emanci... ...ng in the 1780s under the influence of the... (1780–1790), interrupted by the Austri... ...g until World War I. The first three phase... y of Czech language, which lost its admir... ...unicative functions after 1627 when the... ...in the aftermath of the unsuccessful up... Habsburg Emperor

[Handwritten note:] Nature & transcendent
- quality of faith over enlightenment skepticism
- If we bring order why not meaning/feeling?
- order & meaning depend on who we are

Self-validation and rendering our own experience is all that gives our lives meaning/value → this delivers us from absurdity and madness ↑ (the romantic proposal)

[5] Immanuel Kant. *Critique of Pure Reason* (1781). Trans. and Ed. Paul Guyer and Allen W. Wood, Cambridge: Cambridge UP, 1998. 241 (A125).

Ferdinand II (1617–1637). Only the last phase, starting in the late 1850s, is marked by the struggle for an adequate political representation of Czechs in the Austrian Empire.

Unlike the first Czech translations heralding the romantic movement, Chateaubriand's *Atala* (1805), Milton's *Paradise Lost* (1811) and major tragedies of Shakespeare (1786–1810), the first works of Czech Romanticism evoke a half-mythological past at the outset of Czech history. A historical novel *Záře nad pohanstvem* (1818, Radiance over the Pagans) by Josef Linda (1789 or 1792–1834), represents the conflict between the pagan and Christian cultures in the tenth century. Neither of the parties, led by St. Wenceslas (the Czech patron-saint) and his brother Boleslav, is victorious. The lyrical narrative with many passages in verse focuses on the archetypal features of Czech character: a mixture of rebellious patriotism and meditative spirituality. Although modelled on François-René Chateaubriand's novel *Les Martyrs* (1809), it does not privilege Christian spirituality but an emotionally expressive pagan idyll believed to represent the 'natural' life of primitive folk-community, later monumentalized in the collections and imitations of traditional oral poetry by František Ladislav Čelakovský (1799–1852) and Karel Jaromír Erben (1811–1870).

Similar purpose characterizes forged fragments of allegedly medieval epic and lyrical poetry, *Rukopis královédvorský* (1817) and *Rukopis zelenohorský* (1818) (The Manuscripts of Dvůr Králové and Zelená Hora; The Manuscripts), influenced by Macpherson's Ossian poems and later used a document to supply missing information about the early national history and creating the awareness of ancient grandeur and mighty sources of Czech culture. While in Ossian poems, Scotland was represented as a centre of the ancient Celtic world, the authors of *The Manuscripts* did not stress the centrality of Czech culture in the world of old Slavs. Rather, they referred to previous, legendary or chronicled, historical narratives which had been incorporated into oral, folk tradition. The attempt to make oral tradition not only literary, but also *literal* (in the form of a historical document), confirms the tendency in the Czech Revival Movement to use literacy as a means of legitimization of Czech nationality and as an instrument that would help to shape a homogenous community of Czech language users.

The invention of Slavic mythology is typical of the Panslavic tendency in Czech Romanticism, represented by Jan Kollár (1793–1852). His monumental sonnet sequence *Slávy dcera* (1824, 1832, The Daughter of Glory; the later edition including 615 sonnets) is an attempt at a universal Slavic epic based on Dante's *Divine Comedy*, Petrarch's sonnets and Byron's *Childe Harold's Pilgrimage*. While the first three parts of the sequence refer to historical events and to the localities in Slavic territories, lamenting the suffering and gradual extermination of Slavic tribes in the lands settled by Germanic nations, the latter two parts concentrate on the timeless space of the Slavic myth, as the ultimate destination of the narrator's pilgrimage. Other representative works of Czech Romanticism include attempts at the frenetic novel in the style of the French *roman noir*, Karel Sabina's (1813–1877), *Hrobník* (1844, The Gravedigger), and ironic, meditative early poetry of Jan Neruda (1834–1891), *Hřbitovní kvítí* (1858, The Graveyard Blossoms).

The works of the most talented representative of Czech Romanticism, Karel Hynek Mácha (1810–1836) were several times rejected by the National Revival movement because of their ideological bias. This happened especially to his masterpiece, a lyrical epic tale called *Máj* (*May*, 1836). Mácha was the first Czech artist to demythologize Czech nationalist ideology by translating it into conflicting romantic discourses. His poetry not only create a powerful metaphor of existential situation of the romantic artist, but also shows the emptiness of the ideological contents of the Revivalist language and the illusory nature of the ideal of a new life. This is evident in the graveyard scenes of Intermezzo I, where the

afterlife of the dead is called 'my newest dream' or in the sequences with catachretic meta-phors in Parts 3 and 4:

The last indignant thoughts of the defeated dead,
Their unremembered names, the clamour of old fights
The worn-out northern lights, after their gleam is fled,
The untuned harp, whose strings distil no more delights,
The deeds of time gone by, quenched starlight overhead,

....

As the smoke of burnt-out fires, as the shatter'd bell's chime,
Are the dead years of the dead, their beautiful childhood time.

Despite their romantic roots (one of the sources is Walter Scott's rendering of a folk saga about the birth of Brian the Hermit in *The Lady of the Lake*, 1810), these lines anticipate modern reflexive poetry and twentieth-century thought about time (Henri Bergson). In *May* poetry no longer seems to serve human ends. Already in Part 2 the world of failed human law, represented by the reflections of the prisoner, opens itself into the boundless universe, symbolized by the endless fall of a star. Mácha's poetry turns itself to *cosmic nature*, creating beauty even in the scenes of death and destruction as those in Part 4 depicting the remains of the executed hero:

Deep in the heart of the lake a secret light is burning;
And the fireflies, shooting stars, about the wheel are showering,
Glittering in their play, touching the pale skull brightly,
Lighting to launch again, and launch again as lightly,
Like fiery falling tears, all his spent tears embowering.

As a result, Mácha's *May* can be said to go beyond the romantic naturalism of Byron or Leopardi and explore the utmost limits of romantic irony.

DANISH ROMANTICISM *Marie-Louise Svane*

In autumn 1802, Henrich Steffens, a Danish mineralogist recently returned from Jena, delivered a series of epoch-making lectures at the University of Copenhagen. While in Jena, Steffens had befriended Schelling and the German Romantic group associated with the *Athenäum*. Now these ideas were eagerly received by Danish intellectuals. His *Introduction to the Philosophical Lectures*, envisions nature as a creative principle pervading the entire universe from the most humble of minerals to the philosophical heights of reflective thinking and artistic genius. For Steffens, the evolution of man and the world were intimately linked because, from creation to the summit of modern civilization, every step could be viewed as dimensions of an everlasting living totality, the emanation of a divine idea. More inspiring than conventional enlightenment beliefs, such was the success of Steffens' lectures that the authorities became alarmed: It was only ten years since the French Revolution, and Frederick VI's absolute monarchy used censorship, police spies and threats of banishment from the country for the outspoken. Steffens was passed over for the appointment as professor of philosophy. Nevertheless, many young people, later prominent as first generation Romantics, came to view Steffens as a prophet of the new era, a 'new Ansgarius from the South' – the messenger from Continental Europe.

Steffens and his younger friend, the poet *Adam Oehlenschläger* (1779–1850), are the two most prominent Danish Romantics. Under Steffens' influence, Oehlenschläger avidly read the poets and philosophers whom Steffens knew: the Schlegels, Tieck, Novalis, Kant, Fichte, Schelling – and, not least, Goethe. Later, travelling in Europe from 1805 to 1809, Oehlenschläger himself also befriended several of these. Unlike Steffens Oehlenschläger was primarily a poet, and, inspired by the new ideas linking nature, history and poetry, he quickly produced many of the finest Danish Romantic poems, such as *The Golden Horns* (1803) and *Journey to Langeland* (1805) among other poems; the comedies, *Midsummer Eve's Play* (1803) and *Aladdin* (1805); and the tragedies *Baldur the Good* (1807) and *Earl Hakon the Rich* (1807). His early works show a novel type of metaphorical diction and a playful form of irony – as in his re-creation of old Nordic Ballads and mythology. Later dramas, influenced by Shakespeare and Schiller, reshape the sagas of nordic kings and heroes in a more pathetic vein.

As a poet, and also professor of aesthetics at Copenhagen University, Oehlenschläger's impact on contemporary literature was formidable, although even he was not immune to criticism. He lectured on European, especially German literature, but he also had a fair knowledge of contemporary English literature (Scott and Byron). Included in this volume is the early poem *The Gold Horns*. It is a piece of programmatic romanticism and has held a central place in the Danish literary canon ever since its publication. Occasioned by the theft in 1802 of two gold horns from the cabinet of curiosities at the Copenhagen collection of antiquities, this loss of irreplaceable national treasures symbolizes the defeat of poetry in a modern world of prose, and in a series of visions the poet imagines a past where man, nature and the godhead coexist in arcane poetic bliss. Oehlenschläger's way of blending myth and the present day in the poem struck contemporaries as new and original, and its taut Norse verse form and dynamic imagery suggested hitherto unexplored poetic potential in the Danish language.

Today, *Niels Frederik Severin Grundtvig* (1783–1872) is primarily known as the founder of the Danish folk high-school movement. This sought to introduce the rural young to a tolerant version of Christianity and to develop a national consciousness that shunned bookishness, replacing it with the spontaneity of oral talks and the treasures of 'the living word'. After the introduction of the bourgeois constitution in 1849, the high school movement played a considerable part in spreading democratic ideas, and from 1808 until his death Grundtvig himself was active both as poet and as a clergyman. His early writings are steeped in romantic thought and moulded on the kind of German Idealism represented by Steffens and Schelling. Like Oehlenschläger, Grundtvig felt a strong attraction to Nordic mythology – though with his own theological and historicist flavour. Oehlenschläger, whom Grundtvig at first admired but from whom he was subsequently estranged, gave Thor, Freya and Baldur universal human characteristics. Grundtvig, on the other hand, used mythology to reinterpret Christianity, depicting the world of the Ases[1] as a prelude to Christianity that, reciprocally, was conceived as fulfilment of the incomplete project of a heathen mythology. This is the central idea behind *Nordic Mythology* (1808), *Scenes from the Fall of the Giants in the North* (1809), *Scenes from the Fights of Nornes and Ases* (1811). Later works include a vast collection of poems and hymns, a poetic paraphrase of *Beowulf*, a reconstruction of Snorre's Icelandic chronicles and of Saxo's *Gesta Danorum* – besides pamphlets dealing with contemporary Christian issues. The hymns, which

---

[1] In Nordic mythology the world is created and sustained by the gods, the Ases (ruled by Odin) who are always fighting the dark and evil powers, personified in the subterranean breed of giants (jotun). The Nornes are deities of fate.

were published in *Song Work for the Danish Church* (1837–1875), are light and unassuming in tone, and achieved an instant popularity which they have never lost. An early hymn, *Land of the Living* (1824), included here, uses characteristic mythological imagery: The key figure is 'bifrost', the rainbow, which in Asa lore is a bridge joining man's Earth to the Heaven of the gods, prefiguring the relationship between a heathen and a Christian world. At the same time, this is also Grundtvig's meta-poetic vision of poetry as a bridge between human life and a higher, divine world.

Hans Christian Andersen (1805–1870), a second generation romanticist, is known worldwide. Besides the popular collections of tales, he also produced less-known poems, plays, novels and travelogues. Like his fellow romantics, Andersen knew German literature and early on in his career he came under the influence of poets like Heine, Tieck and Hoffmann. Later, he also read English literature, being especially attracted to Dickens, whom he visited in London in 1847. Andersen's first published works from around 1830 are experiments in a fantastic-ironic vein, such as his *Journey on Foot from Holmen's Canal to the Eastern Point of Amager* (1829) or in the travel book *Shadow Pictures* (1831). Although written some five or six years before Andersen began the tales, there are early signs of playful metamorphosing images and a use of the ironic narrator, not to mention an animated world where physical objects have thought and speech. Imaginary characters are always embedded in everyday surroundings, reflecting a rural and urban Denmark distinctly Biedermeier[2] in character, and showing an everyday realism scarcely present in his German models, Tieck and Hoffmann. In novels like *The Improvisor* (1835), *OT* (1836) and *The Fiddler* (1837), Andersen finds his personal voice exploring the gap between rich and poor, where individual destinies are ruled by abstract social forces and conflicts; social conflict also figures in several of the tales, where Andersen characteristically transposed it into a world of animals, or paraphrased it into power-struggles between everyday household objects. Social success and recognition are everywhere hard to get. Social inequality is also behind the well-known tale *The Ugly Duckling* – which metamorphoses into a beautiful swan. *Shadow* (1847), included here, is a more complex text. It is the tale of a cultured man whose ambition it is to rule the world on the basis of his lofty ideals, but who himself is ruled in turn by his own shadow. The story is soaked in existential irony.

Of course, this self divided between irony and emptiness is a subject matter far removed from the kind of emotionalized idyll often found in Andersen's tales. In some ways, *Shadow* is perhaps more closely related to Kierkegaard's existentialism than to Andersen's other tales. Our extract from Søren Kierkegaard (1813–1855) comes from his dissertation, *The Concept of Irony, with Continual Reference to Socrates* (1841), and is one of his earliest combined literary and philosophical works. Kierkegaard, too, was greatly influenced by German idealism – especially Hegel – and has been a major influence on the existentialism of Heidegger and Sartre. Though Kierkegaard's ironist is persistently critical of the deadness of habitual thought, the author, characteristically, offers no alternative. Socrates, as ironist, uncovers the illusions barring man from his real self. The ironist is the individual subject who cuts away from traditional social ways and values to achieve self-consciousness and 'the absolute beginning of personal life'.

To Kierkegaard, there is no absolute point of view safeguarding individual existence as in Hegel's philosophy, where the absolute Spirit overcomes the division between soul and body

---

[2] Biedermeier is the labelling of a mental trend in late continental romanticism which cultivates family values and seclusion from the outside world. It is often seen as a counter to 'dark romanticism' with its fascination of existential spleen and demonic sexuality.

and between eternity and temporality. Individual man always lives his life piecemeal. At the same time, his existential morality – that you must take on the life you have been given and work to make it morally meaningful – urges him to unify the individual fragments. Thus Kierkegaard bears witness to a never-ending struggle between division and coherence. In the philosophical novel *Either/Or* (1843), the viewpoint begins with the aesthetes' staging of his life in terms of pleasure-hunting as philosophical reflection, but subsequently shifts to the ethicists' demand that what matters in life is choosing oneself as 'this particular product of this particular society', that is what matters is finding one's place in an orderly world to discover one's individual being.

In Kierkegaard's later works, most notably *Fear and Trembling* (1843), *The Concept of Anxiety* (1844) and *Stages on Life's Way* (1845) the ethicist's commitment to a complete life is replaced by Kierkegaard's famous 'leap of faith'. However, Kierkegaard's Christianity was never dogmatic, but sought to confront the vertiginous absurdity of modern life. Belief, to Kierkegaard, is to hover above a gulf in a state of fearful confidence that meaning, paradoxically, will unveil itself and that faith is 'A rush of enthusiasm against the unknown'.

FRENCH ROMAN[TICISM]

One feels the Ror[...]

[...]ie ou Vocabulaire des [...]nots nouveaux, 1801)

Defining Romantic[...]n it comes to French Romanticism. It is [...] agenda is infinite. It embraces everythin[...] universe, visible and invisible, of course[...] European romantic configurations, its s[...] Art, Aesthetics, Language, Religion, the [...] existential and intellectual array in the [...]inking the destiny of humankind, reshap[...]ign and while at the same time glorifyin[...]

Among many w[...] cultural galaxy, one would stress Georg[...] [...]iences humaines et la pensée occidentale* (1966–1985), he argues convincingly for the intrinsic coherence of Romanticism, as a conception which aims at a complete understanding of the Totality: a synthesis, or a syncretism encompassing all aspects of knowledge, sensation and intellection.

French Romantics inherit several concepts and themes from the Enlightenment, of which they are quite often deeply critical. But their main reference is the French Revolution, which they endeavour to understand, interpret and translate into art and literature, which they dream to pursue, even to transcend, when at the same time they see it as the greatest historical trauma, the greatest divide ever. This political, social and cultural upheaval is construed as the point of origin, the birth certificate of the French version of Romanticism – which actually it is not, since nothing in the intellectual field ever has a single cause. Yet one could not really comprehend the intellectual, spiritual and ideological scope of romantic literary works without viewing them in the light of the Revolution and its consequences. And this cannot be done without some difficulty.

[Handwritten note:]
Goal of the Romanticism
- Infinite agenda
- rethink destiny of mankind
- all encompassing - literally covers like every topic
Is it cohesive/unified?
French Revolution is the birth of French Romanticism?
But nothing in intellectual field has a single cause
Scope of romanticism is huge

When Victor Hugo declares in 1830 that Romanticism can be defined as liberalism in literature – liberalism being the political current claiming its revolutionary agenda – he assigns a mission to the modern writer and artist, exalted as a revolutionary agent, devoting his creative genius to progress, highlighted as an essential part of the dynamics of History. At the same time, in the same energetic gesture, he praises a Promethean Napoleon, with his larger than life stature and his extraordinary destiny. But ten years before, most Romantics, including Hugo himself, had written counter-revolutionary and anti-Napoleonic poetry, in the process of inventing a new literature, and were attempting to revolutionize the theatre, a trend which would culminate in 1829 with the first successful *drame romantique*, Alexandre Dumas' *Henri III et sa cour*.

When Alfred de Musset publishes *La Confession d'un enfant du siècle* in 1836, he voices what is probably the best definition of *mal du siècle*, the depressing feeling of inadequacy in a world void of the epic glory crushed on the plains of Waterloo, a modern melancholy born of an historical situation, set in a social and cultural context explained by the contrast between the memories of more exalting times, the dreams brought forth by two amazing decades, and everyday life after the illusory and disappointing Revolution of July 1830. Yet Chateaubriand, as early as 1802, in *Génie du christianisme*, and in 1805, when he published *René* as a separate work, had first expressed this same feeling of dereliction, this same *état d'âme*, but addressed as the intimate by-product of the Revolution, seen as a theatre of death, a bloodbath, a destruction and the unravelling of the very fabric of society, leaving the wretched individual in an unbearable state of abandonment, like a modern orphan, astray in an historical desert.

When Michelet undertakes his monumental *Histoire de France*, he wants to uncoil the centuries as a chain of events, leading to the Revolution, as the slow but unrelenting shaping of the *Peuple*, asserting itself, becoming more and more conscious of its might. But in her posthumous work, the *Considérations sur la révolution française* (1818), Mme de Staël had made the distinction between a democratic Revolution, conceived as a political translation of the Enlightenment, and a terrorist Revolution, a monstrous caricature, born of heinous passions agitating an alienated People.

These are but a few examples of signifying contradictions. Yet, these writers and thinkers, undoubtedly, are all Romantics, regarded as such, instituted as milestones along the road of literary history. One would tend to conclude that Romanticism doesn't exist *per se*, but changes with every author, and that there are only very different romantic approaches, loosely linked, sharing perhaps one single common idea: the nineteenth century is unlike any other century in history and urgently needs to be understood thanks to spiritual, intellectual and scientific tools which have to be designed for that very purpose. Something decidedly new is afoot. O brave new world!

So, how are we to go about a general presentation of French Romanticism? In the beginning, some trends and concepts of the Enlightenment, opposed to the rationalist systems and to the empire of the classical Reason, can be construed as potential romantic material, liable to be recycled and reinterpreted by the Romantics. Sensibility, a feeling for Nature, melancholy, spleen, nostalgia, generally speaking a world weariness, a number of Rousseauist themes and philosophical ideas, to name a few of these ingredients, compose a complex background upon which romantic writers are free and inspired to imprint their own vision. The lyric sentimentality of the second half of the eighteenth century also paves the way for the expression of the Self.

However, it would be wrong to characterize this literary, aesthetic and philosophical scenery as some sort of Pre-Romanticism, some kind of Ur-Romanticism, just waiting to bloom. The

Revolution is decisive, and sets a new course for the arts and for literature, which undergo a complete metamorphosis thanks to its seminal influence. For instance, Volney's *Ruines,* published in 1791, take from their new context a whole new meaning compared with that of only five years earlier. Likewise, Chateaubriand's *René,* set in the 1720s, depicts the situation of a young man whose loneliness and wretchedness are obviously linked to the trauma of the 1790s.

The most precious gain from the Revolution, perhaps, is a new perspective on the essence of writing and the status of the artist and of the writer. The age of the *Homme de lettres,* assigned to a certain place and function in society, with its institutions like the Salons, the Circles and the Academies, with its aristocratic sponsoring, with its codes and circuits, is past. Now a new breed emerges: the *écrivain* (see Paul Bénichou's *Le Sacre de l'écrivain,* 1973), set in a whole new social and political context, with a mission and an agenda. He must reconsider the meaning of Literature – in all its forms, theatre, poetry, fiction, etc. – of Art, of History, of Religion. One must make a new assessment of the relationship between truth, imagination, reality, literary or artistic licence. One [must] [explore its] [possibili]ties, make use of its entire lexicon. One [must] [make full use] [of] of metaphors, since one must grasp the m[...]

It is time to embra[ce] [...] to the most obscure layers of the personal[...] [...] and its prestigious, seductive exotic land[s] [...] [ev]en the directions of the universe. It beco[mes] [...] sense of it all, and understand the myst[...] [...] Hugo and Michelet. One must endeavour [...] [...] message of Christianity. Such is Lamar[tine] [...]

This accounts for th[e] [...] [Staë]l's *De l'Allemagne,* Hugo's preface to *Cro[mwell]* [...] [prefa]ce to *Mademoiselle de Maupin,* Vigny's pr[...] [revie]ws and newspapers, like Balzac's *Des Artis[tes]* [...] [s]alons. They express the didactics of mode[rn] [...]

This explains also t[he] [...] Poet, with a capital P, in fact a thinker, a p[...] [th]e issues of the generations born from or since the Revolution. French romantic poetry, as exemplified in the works of Lamartine, Hugo or Musset, is an inventory of the moral, intellectual, sensual portrait of the modern individual – *that is* historically situated – and of his desires, sufferings, dreams and despair.

This explains too why some works, like Sainte-Beuve's *Vie, Poésies et Pensées de Joseph Delorme,* invent a new narrative. This also explains in addition why some philosophers, Fabre d'Olivet, Leroux, Fourier, hoped to found new sciences, such as linguistics or sociology. Finally this explains the capital importance of Love. Its significance goes beyond its traditional centrality in the human experience. Love embodies the cosmic energy, blends and coalesces all relationships between the Self and the Other, Microcosm and Macrocosm and naturally Man and Woman. The romantic notion of love should not be reduced to a mere outburst of sentimental effusion or to a poetically exalted attachment. For the Romantics, Love is in essence sublime. Inherent to the human condition, it elevates it to a godlike feeling of omniscience and omnipotence, however illusory. It is another name for knowledge. Love is a universal bond.

French Romanticism is obsessed with an idealistic dream of unity and harmony. To follow the path traced by the Revolution is to pursue the reunification of the individual and society, of the

35

masculine and the feminine values, of Man and the Divine. This would mean the end of History, replaced by a universal bliss. On the other hand, if this utopian design fails, a harmonious unity can be found in a purely imaginary and aesthetic world, a substitute for an unbearable reality. Such is the uneasy dynamic of a fundamental contradiction between a Promethean mythology and a self-centred creative ambition, between an ideological *Weltanschauung* and a retreating motion towards an artistic or poetic hermitage, between an urge to shape the future and a cult of the past, the supernatural or an *Ailleurs*. Whether to change the world or to flee anywhere out of the world: French Romantics oscillate from the one to the other.

This aporetic contradiction probably is the main distinctive trait of a most fascinating phenomenon. Revolutionary *and* counter-revolutionary, utopian *and* regressive, spiritual *and* materialistic, individualistic *and* collectivistic minded. Indeed, Romanticism is a great modernizer of myths – Oedipian, Orphic, Promethean. It is drawn to the mystic or religious aspects of life, spiritually inclined to seek and invoke the afterlife and the fantastic. It glorifies the sublime. But the counterpart of this attraction for the irrational side lies in the romantic passion for the historical destiny of Man and the transformation of reality in order to benefit society. In all cases, attitudes and positions, the Romantics see themselves as historically situated. They can only accept it and assume the responsibility, or reject this yoke. But they cannot escape this determinist factor. Here may very well rest the originality of the French Romantics on the European stage.

This complex setting shouldn't intimidate students of French Romanticism. Some definite general trends and characteristics can be assessed, apart from this stress put upon the historicity of the human condition. We start with the intellectual and aesthetic reaction against classicism. The new literature, born from Chateaubriand's and Madame de Staël's ideas, looking to the northern and gothic skies and times, gained its emancipation from the models of the ancients and promoted Christian and medieval evocations, while stressing the essential role of human passions and poetic inspiration. Rousseau, German philosophy and literature were seminal here. The invention of the melancholic hero, starting in 1802 and again in 1805 with Chateaubriand's René, transformed fiction and poetry. Set in the post-revolutionary political and social context, it was to become a prominent trope during the Restoration period and beyond, from 1815 on.

The inventio[...] thought to be the required signature for t[...] in poetic language began with the politic[...]res, such as the ode or the elegy, were vin[...]ne's *Méditations poétiques* (1820) provide[...]ly was deemed too archaic and was to be r[...]ween their historical situation, duty or r[...]ould be embraced, where modern Fate w[...]nism.

The Romant[...]hich, as Stendhal, Balzac, George Sand ar[...]nalyse society, illustrate in an illuminating[...]social forces or structures – see the *bildun[...]oint of view and the creation of exempla[...]rmits new combinations, such as the alli[...]*de chagrin* (1831). It also encompasses a[...]

Fantastical ta[...]husiasm and despair, fascination for the[...]cation: all these aspects,

[Handwritten note:] do we change the world or flee miserable reality through the imaginary /aesthetic world? Romanticism is full of contradictions... – Romantics view themselves as historically situated. one general endeavor: transform society socially, intellectually, aesthetically, and morally

trends, perspectives, are part of one general endeavour: the writing of the individual, considered as organically linked with the natural and the supernatural world, and capable of transforming society, socially, intellectually, aesthetically, morally. Poetics as poiesis: could this be a valid definition?

GERMAN ROMANTICISM *Nicholas Saul*

Johann Wolfgang von Goethe ruined the reputation of German Romanticism for a century and a half with a throwaway remark in 1829 to his Boswell, Johann Peter Eckermann, that the Romantic was sick and the Classical healthy. Goethe's status – in 1798 Novalis (Friedrich von Hardenberg) had called him the pope of poesy – lent irresistible authority both to the denunciation and the aesthetic or cultural dualism it promulgated. And yet the self-styled Classic Goethe was himself, in European terms, a Romantic. Quite apart from the erroneous pyschopathological content of his judgement in respect of German Romanticism, Goethe's own *Sorrowings of Young Werther* (1774), with their blissfully agonized celebration of the alienated modern individual and emphatically de-Christianized religion of creative nature, of course marked the beginning of the Romantic age. Goethe's later, half-hearted attempts to de-authorize the radical message of *Werther* and mitigate the genuine tensions it disclosed in the history of modern culture by foregrounding his ideal of harmonious personality and idiosyncratic notion of realism in truth merely give him a characteristic place in the wide spectrum of the European (and American) phenomenon which is Romanticism. Only in the 1970s did this more differentiated view develop in Germany, and only after that did the revisionist perspective here taken begin to be adopted in the anglophone world. It is reflected in Goethe's – and his cohort Schiller's – place in this anthology.

The Germany in which there emerged the European Romanticism of Goethe, Schiller, Novalis, the Schlegels, Tieck and the rest was even by eighteenth-century standards a parochial and de-centred place. Politically, Germany still retained a sort of rationalized version of the constitution of the mediaeval Holy Roman Empire. Around 1800 it technically still consisted in a tattered patchwork quilt of 1,800 independent, federated states, some as small as a village, others as large as Saxony. The bigger constituent states, notably Brandenburg, Hanover and Austria, had compelling political interests outside of the Empire and even German-speaking lands, in the shape of their own partner states Prussia, Great Britain and Hungary. The Empire, traditionally a Habsburg fief, was correspondingly weakened by the foreign power bases of its own members. Germany so constituted had little central government and no capital – or, rather, several competing ones.

It nevertheless possessed a unified and rapidly accumulating symbolic – cultural – capital. Still weakened materially even at the start of the eighteenth century by the effects of the Thirty Years War, Germany initially sought cultural improvement beyond its borders. French became the hegemonic language of the cultivated classes. The philosophy of Enlightenment flourished in regional capitals, especially in those of states such as Brandenburg-Prussia, where the religious conformism of the Treaty of Westphalia had been undermined by the multi-confessionality of its subjects and the Voltaire-inspired indifference of its francophone ruler. Later, on the Cartesian foundation of Leibniz's and Wolff's rationalism, German school philosophy developed a highly sophisticated account of the self as a spiritual, intrinsically individual and incomparable – monadic – entity, which followed its own innate path to self-becoming, and yet was also unconnected in any material way with the world around it. Thus, encouraged by Germany's rulers,

[Handwritten annotation on sticky note:]

Germany had no central gov. and essentially no capital (several competing ones)

—did have unified Symbolic capital = cultural capital (national cultural revival)
↳ Some wanted shift to "written" capital (literature = medium for self-actualization)

reunification of humans & nature

a tradition of p[...]r this characteristic baggi-ness of the Ger[...]ell-calculated wars, established Prussia[...]much against Frederick's intentions), did[...]ann Gottfried Herder was the key agent i[...] *Ancient Poetry* to return to national cult[...]er, in his pioneering essay *On the Origin*[...]language vis-à-vis reason, making the for[...]edium in which a cultur-ally relativistic,[...]stablishing a new sense of the native langu[...]ignity. Following Gotthold Ephraim Lessin[...]i-classical model of vigor-ous and movin[...]2) turned the bard into a Youngian origi[...]nglo-Saxon model for the new generation[...]German writers whom we know today as[...]ation, vigour, passion and freedom. Wert[...]national cultural revival. Germans of th[...]fering as it seemed a way forward out of the ruins of feudalism and towards a humane nation-state. But following the widespread German dismay at the course taken by the Revolution, where the Terror seemed to dissipate the original promise of a republican state proportionate to humane norms, Herder in his *Letters on the Furtherance of Humanity* (1793–1797) summarized the German project by reverting to tradition: calling for a *written* capital of German culture, for literature in the widest sense as the medium of the self-realization which Germans lacked.

It was however Friedrich Schiller who found the most influential post-Revolutionary formulations for the German cultural project which became Romanticism. His *On the Naive and Sentimental in Literature* (1795) takes the yearning of the divided Wertherian subject for a Rousseauistic, secularized respite from modern cultural life in an asylum of idealized nature and recognizes in it a lost past and a possible future. That unmediated unity of subject and nature, intellect and sensuality, typified by the ancient Greeks (Homer, Aeschylus), typified ahistorically by privileged modern geniuses such as Goethe and Shakespeare, is the naive. The naive recuperated is, or should be, the destiny of sentimental moderns. As guardians of what is natural in human nature, it is the role of poets and artists in general in the modern age to restore that lost unity through visionary integrations which supplement the recognized deficits of the real. Poets and artists thereby not only become the exceptions, outsiders and borderers, but also the therapists and messiahs in nature's name of a culture diagnosed as sick – a role they still play today. A directly analogous pattern is traced in idealist philosophy. If Kant, in his second preface to the *Critique of Pure Reason*, had valorized the epistemological creativity of the subject at the price of sealing both its division from nature and internal fragmentation, so Fichte, in his *Second Introduction to the Theory of Knowledge*, attempted in response to show that absolute creativity underlay even the subject's self-consciousness, and the *Oldest System Programme of German Idealism* (probably written by a co-operative of Hegel, Hölderlin and Schelling) posited aesthetics as the highest act of reason and reason so understood as mythological therapist of humanity, no less.

Out of Schiller's, not intentionally historical scheme develop both the German Romantic fascination for the aesthetic and its orientation around Goethe and Shakespeare as models of their own aesthetic-cultural ambitions in the time of post-Revolutionary crisis. Novalis admires

Goethe's and Schiller's notion of aesthetic education, shares their estimate of Classical antique and modern culture, shares their aspiration for a modern Classicism, but radicalizes the aesthetic message. Goethe, for him, stops short in his programmatic novel of education *Wilhelm Meister's Years of Apprenticeship* (1795–1796), prosaically sets limits to the potential of creative imagination and aesthetic healing which he does not recognize. In truth, everything – the self, nature, the historical process of cultural development – is the expression of an absolute creative imagination growing in alienation away from its origin but paradoxically also back to mature identity in progressive stages of self-realization, with material nature on its ladder of diverse manifestations as the foundation of spiritual culture. The poet, earthly sovereign of creative imagination, is the privileged possessor of this knowledge. Poesy, finally supplanting the orthodox Christian tradition of the Bible, is the authentic expression of the real absolute. The poet's use of imagination as *natura naturans* makes him into the instrument of transcendental therapy, diviner of connectedness, unifier of the encyclopaedia of the sciences, transformer of dormant or petrified nature into partner in dialogue or singer in chorus, restorer of the naive in fairy tale and folk song, rediscoverer of the lost Golden Age, navigator of humanity across the ocean of history towards its utopian goal.

But Novalis and his chief partner in early German Romanticism, Friedrich Schlegel, intoxicated as they sound, are not naive. For them as moderns, all cultural manifestations, including the self, are recognizable as constructs of the imagination, expressed *as* itself through something – a signifier – which is paradoxically *not* itself. This is the germ of Romantic Irony. Designers of utopia in every domain of human experience as they may be, the German Romantics – in this more radical than Goethe and Schiller – recognized the fundamentally constructed character of their designs for harmony by inscribing in them indicators of self-reflexivity, which simultaneously celebrate and debunk the aesthetic panacea. Thus (for example) images of the author writing his own novel or the novel written by its own chief protagonist have conferred on utopian Romantic texts their characteristically provisional status, the palindromic, self-conscious, self-positing and -retracting constitution typical of Romanticism and of all modernist aesthetic expression since then.

From this emerge all the diverse instantiations of the Romantic in Germany. Schleiermacher's *On Religion*, that unilateral declaration of religion's independence from the Enlightenment tutelage of epistemology and ethics, reduces all 'religion', historical or contemporary, revealed or negative, to imaginative intuition of the universe. Hölderlin's *Bread and Wine*, Hardenberg's *Hymns to Night*, self-consciously remake Greece and Christianity into the modern, constructed religion of myth. In aesthetics proper Tieck relegitimates the marvellous in Shakespeare's *Tempest* or *Hamlet* thanks to its hermetically autonomous evocative power, and Wackenroder self-reflexively (as art in art) celebrates music as an equally sovereign realm of signification. In German folksong and fairytale, Arnim's and the Grimms' restorative collections turn out to be re-collections, apparently naive texts aspiring to return Germans to their roots but in fact in large part remade by the sentimental collectors themselves. On still another level, the literary work (being constitutionally provisional and unclosable) is recognized to be as much written by those who respond to it – critics or other writers – as by the titular, 'original' author. Friedrich Schlegel typically 'completed' Goethe's *Meister*, and some have even argued that 'Novalis' is as much the creation of Hardenberg refracted in the 'other' of Tieck's and Schlegel's imaginations, as it is of his own. Finally, we recall Kleist's – typically Kleistian – radical notions that, thanks to our intricate complicity with the signifier, creative thoughts are as much involuntarily prompted by the words others use as by our own free inner processes of ratiocination; or that beauty, that

irreducible fusion of form and matter, is more successfully instantiated by the automatic, puppet-like movement of the body than our own, excessive self-consciousness.

But German Romanticism is concrete and practical as well as theoretical. If German Romantics thought of existence as quintessentially alien[...] [...]lly provisional and characterized by lack, they also, in thei[...] [...] innovative and far-reaching solutions. The [...] von Humboldt (brother of the naturalist [...] y of gender, which – if not transcending [...] *Héloïse* (1759) – nonetheless attempts to [...] gnizing modern woman's productivity as [...] s superiorities. Schlegel's gender idyll in h[...] into the Platonic ideal of androgynous co[...] an Romanticism did a good deal to cha[...] first woman poet and philosopher of no[...] ite Schlegel's theory to accommodate the [...] a.

In politics and h[...] he with characteristic acuity saw as advoc[...] n, while failing to see that precisely this la[...] it into his historical scheme. His *Faith a[...] g the political problem of the age by not[...] ment, balancing the drawbacks of both m[...] in the shape of an ideally representative poet-m[...] [...]ges two great alternatives. This wholly impracticable design was – i[...] [...]al early Romantic course of things – swiftly retracted in *Christendom, or Europe* (1799). Here the Revolution is seen as the pubertal crisis of a growing organism on the verge of maturity. The earlier synthesis is replaced by an equally utopian idea for a pan-European federation founded *ex negativo* on the ashes of the atheistic and failed Revolution and regulated by the poetic successors of the papacy. But as time passed the historic roots of Romanticism were strengthened and its self-critical faculty weakened. Napoleon's invasion and abolition of the Empire called forth a compensatory outburst of nationalism which retained Novalis's modernist religiosity but swept away his ingrained cosmopolitanism. That produced the undifferentiated, proto-messianic nationalism of Johann Gottlieb Fichte and the self-sacrificial war poet Theodor Körner. Even the scheme of Arnim's friend Clemens Brentano in *The Box with the Peace Doll* for pan-European peace after 1815 is bought at the price of a Jewish scapegoat. The German-Jewish Heinrich Heine made the appropriate comments on nationalism and Theodor Körner in *Germany. A Winter's Tale* (1840).

A similar trajectory is followed by the Romantic view of nature. Goethe's decidedly post-Christian Werther memorably saw nature as mother and monster, both inspiritor and consumer of human fulfilment. The others tend to emphasize both aspects sequentially. Novalis belongs to the former group. As a qualified and practising mining technologist, he was no enemy of natural science, and spent years of his life writing a kind of systematic alternative to the empiricist *Encyclopédie* of the *philosophes*. He shared Goethe's view of nature as fundamentally alive and Goethe's concomitant critique of Newton's *experimentum crucis* and all forms of strictly empirical-analytical, dissectionist natural science as 'killing' its object of knowledge and substituting disassembled parts for the organic whole. Hence he argues that the imaginative poet knows nature better than the strictly rational and experimental scientist, that mathematics and abstract formulae offer only skeletal versions of true Enlightenment, and that they should be

supplemented by imaginative reconstructions of living totality. Eichendorff's notion of the song slumbering in things except for those with ears to hear makes Novalis's ideas concrete, and Novalis's own fairy tale *Hyacinth and Rose-Blossom* (1800) figures this as the hero's eccentric path from abstract knowledge and alienation to dream reunion with a lost beloved, who is also Isis, goddess of nature. Ernst Theodor Amadeus Hoffmann, however, in this a typical late Romantic, deconstructs precisely this motif in his *Mines at Falun*. Hoffmann's Elis too pursues the goddess of nature. But she mortifies him.

However, perha[...] German Romanticism's fascination with recognizing and overcoming alienation is most [...]rs with cultural otherness. As ever, Nov[...]n fundamentalism and apology of Islami[...] Zulima in *Heinrich of Ofterdingen*. This [...]ion of Germanness (it befits a nation whi[...]) and defence of translation (he once de[...] most German Romantics and underlies [...]eign into Germany, not only Shakespeare, [...]oethe's of Hafis, August Wilhelm Schlegel [...] many others. It underlies the self-critiqu[...] Chamisso's account of the natives of Sou[...] as much as it does the fervour of Arnim [...]leist's (*The Betrothal in Santo Domingo*) a[...] this interculturality too decays over time. [...]en Halevy cannot draw the sting of the O[...] apology, and this is the limit of German [...]

[Handwritten marginal note:]
Nature
- criticized enlightenment as killing object of knowledge by substituting disassembled parts for an organic whole
- imaginative poet knows nature better than empirical scientist

- Interculturality
(fascination w/ recognizing & overcoming alienation)

HUNGARIAN ROMANTICISM *László Gyapay*

A key issue for the majority of Hungarian writers of the Romantic period was how to carry on artistic communication within the *whole* of the national community. This is partly why the problem of language and the use of it gained an enormous importance. At that time the population of Hungary consisted of diverse communities of different ethnicities, religions, nationalities and languages, and the country was an inseparable part of the multinational and multilingual Habsburg Empire. According to a rough estimate in 1804 the population of the Hungarian Kingdom and Transylvania amounted to 7.970.000, of which 42 per cent were Hungarians, 18.5 per cent Serbs and Croats, 14 per cent Slovaks, 10 per cent Rumanians, 9.2 per cent Germans, 3.8 per cent Ruthenians, 2.5 per cent other nationalities. Of all these nationalities only the Hungarians and the Croats had societies with the whole spectrum of traditional classes, like nobility, bourgeoisie and peasantry.[1] Though Hungarians made up by far the dominant nationality, they were not in the absolute majority in the country, though divisions of nationalities did not always correspond to those of languages. At the end of the eighteenth century Latin was used in much of state administration, higher jurisdiction and (higher) education. It wasn't until 1848 that Hungarian was officially introduced in the whole country. In line with this development there were animated debates on the standardization of literary language, a sign of which

[1.] See *Magyarország története 1790–1848*, 2 vols. Eds Gyula Mérei and Károly Vörös. Budapest: Akadémiai Kiadó, 1980, Vol. 1. 439.

was the publication of the first spelling rules (1832), a guideline that was authoritative only for texts edited by the Hungarian Academy.

In his pamphlet *Magyarság* [On the Hungarian Language] (1778) György Bessenyei (1747–1811) regarded the Hungarian language as one among the specific signs of the nation, like her legal system, clothing, music and dance.[2] Some decades later, in the Romantic period there was a definite shift in the concept, hence language constituted one of the main factors, if not the very essence, of national identity. The status of Hungarian is well demonstrated by the case of Gusztáv Szontagh (1793–1858), an army officer who became a prominent critic, philosopher and ultimately member of the Hungarian Academy. Born of Hungarian parents in Csetnek, a small town whose immigrant German-speaking population turned Slovakian in the sixteenth century, Szontagh in 1829 confessed: 'Since my early childhood I wrestled with Latin, on leaving school I was to go abroad; ever since I returned to Buda, to our capital, I could hardly practice my national language with the inhabitants of the town. [. . .] if I cease to read and write Hungarian, I shall be degenerate from tip to toe.'[3] All these may explain why the cultivation of the Hungarian language was an issue of great significance. It was above all a patriotic act that bore relation to politics (see l.f.2, l.f.3), to the inner power game of the whole Habsburg Empire, to the career of those being involved, to individual and national self-respect and to art (see IV.f.1). The great poet-critic of the Romantic era, Ferenc Kölcsey (1790–1838) explored the artistic aspects of the Hungarian language in connection with the growing demand for a national literature (see l.f.1). The criteria for national literature were, so his argument goes, that it should be highly artistic and yet comprehensible to all strata of the Hungarian public, not only to the cultural elite. Narrative traditions known to the *whole* of the national community could provide the writers with forms, codes, stories, archetypes and points of view (just like the *Iliad* and the *Odyssey*) by the help of which they could make their message comprehensible to all classes of the Hungarian society. Though there were, in fact, only stray fragments of a naive heroic epic tradition available to the Romantic generations, the collective pursuit of national literature was so strong, and the reaction to the scantiness of reliable sources so creative, that eventually the result turned out to be very productive. All these Romantic aspirations as well as the keen interest in the national past (see l.f.1, III.f.2) and folk poetry contributed to the restructuring of the system of genres in the period. Mihály Vörösmarty (1800–1855) and János Arany (1817–1882) made the most outstanding attempts to create national epics (see l.f.2); Miklós Jósika (1794–1865), József Eötvös (1813–1871), Zsigmond Kemény (1814–1875) and Mór Jókai (1825–1904) published numerous novels many of them historical; several efforts were made to collect popular and folk poetry (songs and ballads) and their poetic reproductions were highly appreciated, especially those by Sándor Petőfi (1823–1849).

Theatre was widely regarded as one of the best institutions for the cultivation and diffusion of the Hungarian language. With the Hungarian king residing in Vienna (since 1541!), there was no permanent royal household in the capital of Hungary (Pest and Buda on both sides of the Danube) to provide support for maintaining a theatre. It was partly the reason why it took decades of unflagging efforts until in 1837 the first permanent Hungarian theatre was opened in Pest, where there had already been a German theatre with 3.200 (!) seats. (It was built in 1812

[2.] György Bessenyei. *Válogatott művei.* Ed. Bíró, Ferenc. Budapest: Szépirodalmi Kiadó, 1987. 589–590.

[3.] 'Gyermekségemtől fogva a' deák nyelvvel bajlódtam; majd az iskolát elhagyván, sorsom külföldre vitt; 's visszatérvén Budára, Fő-Városunkba, ennek polgárai köztt csaknem semmi gyakorlásom sincsen nemzeti beszédünkben. [...] ha magyarúl olvasni és írni megszűnök, tetőmtől talpig elkorcsosulandó vagyok.' (Szontagh, Gusztáv, [Recenzió Kölcsey *Hit, remény, szeretet* című írásáról], Muzarion, 1829. Vol. 4. 89.).

and for the opening ceremony Beethoven composed *King Stephen Overture* in honour of Saint Stephen, the first Hungarian king.) The genesis of modern Hungarian literary institutions mainly coincided with the Romantic period. From the second decade of the nineteenth century the number of Hungarian periodicals began to grow and a slow process of specialization started. The encyclopaedic *Tudományos Gyűjtemény* [Scientific Miscellany] (1817–1841) was the first monthly magazine, whose editor paid honorarium for the articles. By the mid-40s there were a sufficient number of newspapers, fashion journals, magazines, publishing houses and readers, for Petőfi and his family to earn a good living by writing. (Half a century earlier Mihály Csokonai Vitéz (1773–1805), a poet of comparable stature, had to bombard his patrons with desperate letters, yet could hardly keep body and soul together.) Initiated by Count István Széchenyi (1791–1860) in 1825, the Hungarian Academy could rely on financial support mostly from aristocrats. Its principal objective was to encourage the cultivation of the native language. In addition to its representative functions like the annual assembly where even the highest dignitaries were present, it regularly promoted writing for the stage, awarded several prestigious prizes, published dictionaries, financially supported some of its members, and provided jobs for a few employees. Though the post-revolutionary absolutism (1849–1867) introduced drastic measures to paralyse and control social life, the literary institutions of the Romantic period survived this era of oppression and had a decisive influence on the development of the Hungarian literature.

* * *

A NOTE ON THE TEXT

Hungarian orthography was effectively standardized in 1904 – after which there have been no substantial changes. Except for scholarly critical editions the usual procedure in Hungary is to modernize the orthography of texts earlier than 1904. This we did in the present section, always adding the bibliographical data of the first publication. Whenever there was more than one English translation, the first priority was, of course, quality, the second, to choose the more contemporary one. Quite a few of the texts were translated just for this volume: poetry by David Hill; prose by Bernard Adams.

ITALIAN ROMANTICISM *Anne O' Connor*

Italy faced the advent of European Romanticism in a divided and disheartened state. The Congress of Vienna in 1815 had returned the country to its previous fragmented and foreign-dominated status and Italians faced further problems of linguistic disunity, widespread illiteracy, censorship and isolation. Such times influenced the kind of Romanticism which emerged in Italy and resulted in strong trends towards patriotism, cultural nationalism, Catholicism and historicism. These characteristics were able to lie happily with European trends such as the nurturing of the individual and indeed, Romanticism, with all its contradictions, found a fertile arena in Italy.

Ugo Foscolo, for example, is generally considered a neoclassical writer but his novel *Le ultime lettere di Jacopo Ortis* (1798) and monumental poem *Dei Sepolcri* (1807) contain early romantic traits, such as his mixture of patriotic fervour and melancholy, his lyrical subjective prose, and his feelings of rebellion and despair. The actual start of the debate on Romanticism in Italy can be dated to the publication by Madame de Staël in January 1816 in *La biblioteca italiana* of an

article entitled, 'Sulla maniera e la utilità delle traduzioni' (On the manner and usefulness of translations). In this article, she supported the translation of European literature into Italian but then widened her discussion into an exhortation to Italians to abandon their attachment to imitation of the classics. Italians were encouraged to create original works, to take example from German and English literature, and to abandon the pompous, derivative, rhetorical style which she felt prevailed in Italy.

Naturally such an article provoked a response, both for and against de Staël, and her supporters gradually came to be identified as the Romantics. Based mainly in Milan, they expressed their views in the journal *Il Conciliatore* (founded 1818, closed down in 1819). Articles by Ludovico Di Breme, Pietro Borsieri, Giovanni Berchet and Ermes Visconti argued against the unconditional and pedestrian imitation of classical writers, and the use of classical mythology, promoting instead 'truth in poetry'. Di Breme contended that a love for Italy could be expressed through a new form of literature which did not betray the past, while Borsieri claimed that Italians should develop their own creative powers, free from any arbitrary rules created by traditions and scholars. They wished, in the words of Berchet, to create a 'common literary fatherhood', where true poetry must express feelings and emotions common to all people.

Literary wrangles combined with political struggles in Austrian-dominated Lombardy, and Romanticism came to be associated with the Italian nineteenth-century nationalistic effort. Following a crackdown by the Austrian authorities on the leading figures of Italian Romanticism and the closure of *Il Conciliatore*, the liveliest section of the movement seemed to fade from prominence. However, as Alessandro Manzoni, tells us in his Letter on Romanticism (1823): 'In all the wars about Romanticism, the only thing that has perished is the word *Romanticism*. Resurrection of the word is not desirable; this would only renew the wars and perhaps damage the idea, which without a name, lives and grows tranquilly enough.' He continues: 'Romanticism is far from decaying but lives, prospers, and diffuses itself day by day and invades little by little all aesthetic theory, with results that are increasingly reproduced, applied and considered the basis of good judgment in poetic matters.' Manzoni, himself, in his play *Conte di Carmagnola* (1820) moved away from Aristotelian principles of drama which had dominated the artistic form in Italy in previous centuries. More importantly, his novel *I promessi sposi* can be regarded as the first modern Italian novel, showing distinct concern with history and the past, with the wider reading public, and with the importance of language in the national context.

Many writers, although not avowedly Romantic, showed a new approach in their literature which broke with the pre-1816 past. Leopardi, for example, wrote against the Italian Romantic movement in his 1818 publication *Discorso di un italiano intorno alla poesia romantica* (An Italian's discourse on Romantic poetry). However, he is today viewed as the most accomplished Italian Romantic writer. His poetry and much of his prose show sensibility, spontaneity, originality and a uniqueness of form and language. Furthermore, his interest in the destructive power of nature and his expression of the interior reaction show a lyrical expression of the individual. Another contrast emerges in the linguistic field. Although Manzoni attempted in his writing to unify and harmonize the Italian language, Italian Romanticism also saw a linguistic reassertion of the local, exemplified by poets such as Carlo Porta who wrote in his local dialect of Lombardy. Porta's choice of medium is indicative of the trends which favoured an interest in plebian life and the vernacular. There was no black magic or mythology but rather a celebration of the local idiom. Porta summed up the change in Italian literature when he said in his poem *Sestinn per el matrimoni* 'Since I am a Romantic, I am forced to find all that I write within myself.'

As well as the literary field, the world of visual arts was stimulated by these new trends, and some of the most important articulations of Italian Romanticism came in the world of opera. Given limited cultural unity and in particular, limited literacy, opera was a popular cultural form which could reach out to the masses in a manner only imagined by the original theoreticians of Romanticism in Italy. Innovations by Gioachino Rossini, Vincenzo Bellini and Gaetano Donizetti were continued by Giuseppe Verdi, who demonstrated in his operas the poetry of song, the human drama and the spirit of nationalism on the stage. Such developments had a huge impact in Europe and to name just one example, Rousseau found much inspiration for his Romanticism in the music of Italian composers.

Foreigners were not just romantically inspired by developments in Italy; the country itself became a romantic construction in the European imagination. Italy, a country of genius and history, of beauty and tragedy became a popular image for European Romantics. Indeed writers such as Goethe, Byron and Shelly, who would have a fundamental impact on the development and direction of Romanticism in Europe, spent lengthy and influential stays in Italy. Italian Romanticism thus opened many new paths not only to Italian writers but also to artists, musicians and foreign enthusiasts. Many of these paths intertwined as is exemplified in Silvio Pellico's play *Francesca da Rimini*, an historical drama based on the figures of Paolo and Francesca immortalized in Canto V of Dante's *Inferno*. This medieval subject was adapted for modern sensibilities, combining history and a human love story and adding a nationalistic dimension to the story. It was a hugely successful romantic representation of the past which was further popularized through an operatic version of the play and attracted international attention, in particular from Byron. These developments for just one play demonstrate the manner in which Romanticism opened up the Italian cultural scene, defying attempts at definitions and moving beyond the narrow debates between classicists and romantics to a more European intermingling of history, art, public, the self, the nation, melancholy, tragedy and triumph. Though initially accused of introducing anarchy and the wild peculiarities of foreign literature into Italy, the Italian dialogue with Romanticism opened up, in the words of Leopardi, that far horizon and endless spaces beyond.

NORWEGIAN ROMANTICISM *Gudleiv Bø*

Romanticism came late to Norway; we usually speak of a more or less romantic period from around 1820 well into the 1860s. Norwegian romanticism must be seen against the background of the country's political history. Norway had been in a union with Denmark for 400 years, but was in connection with Napoleon's defeat ceded to Sweden. However, Norwegian leaders had made themselves a constitution, and had it accepted by the Swedish leaders. This made Norway a remarkably democratic nation state earlier than many other European countries, and one might add – a very self-conscious one. All this gave the traditions from French enlightenment a very strong position among Norwegian intellectuals. One might argue that enlightenment ideas dominated Norwegian nineteenth-century history when it comes to practical government, whereas romantic ideas influenced the nation building process on an ideological level.

Ideologically it became important that Norway's ruling classes were felt to have a questionable national identity, while only the farming class was considered fully 'Norwegian'. This was because the written language was Danish, the intellectuals had until recently been educated in Denmark and they had close family ties in Denmark. Thus, the culture of Norway's elites could

hardly be distinguished from that of the Danish elites. As a result – in spite of the fact that most of the ideological nation building process took place while Norway was in a union with Sweden, the challenge that really mattered, was to distinguish whatever was Norwegian from everything Danish.

Not only were the farmers 'more Norwegian' than the intellectuals, they were also 'free' in the sense that a majority of them owned the soil they cultivated – as opposed to most peasants of feudal Europe. This was considered an important national asset at a time when Europe was struggling for democracy. Thus, the 'folk' culture of the farming class became an important national symbol – unifying enlightenment ideas of freedom and the fascination for folklore in German 'Heidelberg romanticism' – the heritage of Herder, Brentano, the Grimm brothers etc.

The two most dominant representatives of romantic literature in Norway were Henrik Wergeland and Johan S. C. Welhaven. These two became the living symbols of either side of the particularly Norwegian mix of French enlightenment and Heidelberg romanticism, Wergeland representing the former and Welhaven the latter. Wergeland felt that the fundamental challenge of his generation was to fight for democracy and justice. He published an enormous number of pamphlets and two popular journals to educate ordinary people for active participation in the young democracy. And yet Wergeland also was a genuine romanticist; he was a theologian by education, and he wrote a great myth of world history in verse where Plato and Jesus were leading figures on humankind's striving towards a deistic and just Utopia. (*Creation, Man, and Messiah*, 1829). Wergeland could probably be characterized as a neoplatonic transcendentalist with a leaning towards Jena romanticism in his understanding of nature and of man: The pine tree is a worldly witness of a spiritual world; the loving embrace harmonizes the worldly and the spiritual in man. In his aesthetics Wergeland was an admirer of Shakespeare's exuberance in metaphor, and he revolted against neoclassicist rules of genre and clarity.

This latter point was only one of the reasons why he was furiously attacked by Welhaven, who was a convinced neoclassicist when it came to aesthetic form, but a transcendentalist in general world view. They also opposed each other because Wergeland was a radical democrat and a fervent nation builder resisting the Danish cultural heritage in Norway, while Welhaven took for granted that the educated elite had to rule the country, and that its links through Denmark to continental elites was an advantage for the country. Like Wergeland he did take an interest in the people, but not in order to change them into active participants in democracy – rather as objects of fascination inspired by Heidelberg romanticism. Welhaven wrote a number of romantic 'ballads', none of which are represented here, as they are quite long. He became a central figure in Norwegian national romanticism together with collectors of folklore like Jørgen Moe and Peter Christen Asbjørnsen, famous for their collection of folk tales, and Magnus Brostrup Landstad and Olea Crøger, collectors of ballads.

Both Wergeland and the national romanticists wrote Danish. Both Danish and Norwegian are derived from Old Norse, and are mutually intelligible even today. Written Norwegian had died out partly due to the extinction of Norway's medieval aristocracy by the Black Death, and partly due to the Lutheran reformation that was carried through by Danish authorities during the union with Denmark. In order to demonstrate the new independence in the nineteenth century Wergeland had introduced a small number of words from the Norwegian oral language in his written Danish, but Welhaven and other conservatives resisted that. However, around 1850 Ivar Aasen created a Norwegian written language based on dialects and Old Norse, and he and a few followers started to write in this language. Ivar Aasen was a dedicated follower of

enlightenment ideas, and his basic motivation for his 'New Norwegian' was democratic as well as nationalist. But he shared with romanticism a nostalgia for premodern culture. During the subsequent century the 'New Norwegian' movement triggered a transformation of the Heidelberg heritage into a popular movement of a leftist leaning and considerable strength, particularly towards the end of the nineteenth century and Norway's secession from the union with Sweden in 1905. But 'New Norwegian' remained a minority language. Wergeland's ideas caught on more widely – so that not merely were common Norwegian words accepted in writing, but also (which he did not suggest) words that are common to both Danish and Norwegian are now spelled according to the Norwegian pronunciation.

Aasmund Olafsson Vinje was Norway's first major writer who took up Aasen's New Norwegian. He was in some ways a split personality. He renewed Norwegian journalism and essayistic commentary. As a journalist he was often ironic – sometimes with a tendency towards carnivalism; but as a poet he approaches romantic pantheism.

Bjørnstjerne Bjørnson and Henrik Ibsen were leading authors during the period of realism. But in their youth they had close ties to romanticism, particularly national romanticism. Bjørnson shows in the national anthem that he shares a romantic outlook on history. Henrik Ibsen relates to national romanticism in most of his plays through the 1850s and 60s, including *Pretenders* (1863) and *Peer Gynt* (1867). It was not until *Pillars of Society* (1877) that he turned a realist author.

Even today Norwegian culture is split between French enlightenment and Heidelberg romanticism. Norway's constitution – that is its enlightenment heritage – is celebrated every 17 May. But the Heidelberg heritage is also striking. Not only are a great many of Norwegian classical authors, composers, painters etc. inspired by folk art, but Norwegians also have relatively strong feeling for folk literature, folk music, folk dancing etc. And every 17th May Norwegians wear 'national costumes' with obvious ties back to Heidelberg romanticism.

POLISH ROMANTICISM *Mirosława Modrzewska*

The date traditionally used for marking the historical beginning of Polish Romanticism is1822, the year when the first volume of Adam Mickiewicz's *Ballady i romanse (Ballads and Romances)* was published in Wilno. Its new anti-classicist taste, fantastic Lithuanian and Belorussian folk stories introduced readers to foggy woods and thickets and to mysterious lakes with magic characters, which not only horrified, but also created a new sense of the world as essentially inexplicable and impossible to define in rationalist terms. Such is the theme of the ballad *Romantyczność (The Romantic)*. The situation of the main character, Karusia, who can see her dead lover, but is declared 'out of her senses' by a 'man with a learned air', embodies the epistemological conflict between the narrow rationalism, represented by neoclassicists, and the 'truth of the heart' and 'feelings'. This conflict between the 'heart' and the 'intellect' was to become one of the leading themes of Polish Romanticism.

The way to a new spirituality and understanding of literature was paved by the reading of German and English Romantic poetry and prose, which were also filtered through enthusiastic literary-philosophical essays of Maurycy Mochnacki (1803–1834). In his writings, published between the years 1825–1834, he linked the experience of German Romantic philosophers (A. W. Schlegel, F. Schlegel and F. W. Schelling) with the poetic endeavours of Polish Romantics. Mochnacki represented the generation of Poles born after the complete partitioning of Poland by Prussia, Russia and Austria, and the caesura in his writing, as in that of all Polish writers of

the time, was brought about by the great calamity of the national November Insurrection of 1830–1831[1] and the so-called Great Emigration.[2]

The cleavage between pre- and post-insurrectional Polish Romantic literature was the result not only of the dramatic split of the reading public between émigrés and the oppressed homeland, but also by the November Insurrection. Resulting in massive persecution and exile, this uprising forced Polish writers of the time, who had assumed the role of spiritual and political leadership for their readers, and led them to a military struggle for independence, to rethink and revise all of the previously accepted ideas of their Romantic philosophy, such as inspiration, the necessity of rebellion, and the notion of revolution in history.

In the first phase of Polish Romanticism before 1830, a great variety of lyrical and reflective poetry was published, like Mickiewicz's *Sonety krymskie (Crimean Sonnets, 1826)*, which both established a new artistic language and discovered an unknown, often exotic, poetic world. Byron was a powerful influence during this period, and among numerous narrative tales in verse contributing to the Byronic genre, were *Maria* by Antoni Malczewski (1825) and *Konrad Wallenrod* by Adam Mickiewicz (1828).

A change in poetic taste came after 1831, and the following years marked the height of Romantic *misterium* and a variety of religious lyrical poetry. The great dramas of the later time are *Forefathers' Eve, The Dresden Text*, by Adam Mickiewicz (1832); *Kordian*, by Juliusz Słowacki (1834); and *The Undivine Comedy*, by Zygmunt Krasiński (1835).

The notion of history in the song of the minstrel in *Konrad Wallenrod* (1828) differs considerably from the various historiographies of post-insurrectional drama, for the 'old saga' about the 'men of Litwa' is to be read as political inspiration for action, leading the tragic hero to a treacherous act of vengeance on his masters in the name of liberty. Though its plot includes real historical characters and tragic past events, *Dziady (Forefathers' Eve, 1832)* considers history in its eschatological sense via the *misterium* of sacrifice and murder of the innocent. In Słowacki's *Koridan*, however, history is a matter of the personal decision to act, which the title character is never capable of, and the tragic choice between the immorality of murder, and the hell of inertia in subjection and humiliation, links him with the figure of Shakespeare's Hamlet. The moral obligation to 'act', formulated by *Oda do Młodości (Ode to Youth, 1822)*, was a problem for all of the Polish Romantics and a subject for political disputes till about 1863, the year of the January Insurrection in Poland, as well as the year in which Cyprian Kamil Norwid (1821–1883), an heir and critic of Romanticism, published the only volume of his poetry to appear in his lifetime.

Despite the considerable influence of German and English Romanticism, visible in the choice of poetic style and genres, the literary masterpieces of Polish Romantic writers do have a unique character, which may be explained partly by the demand of the era for originality and 'local character', and partly by the historical coincidence of Romantic ideas with the political and spiritual situation of the Polish people at a time in which writers were endowed with the prerogative of intellectual leadership. This endowment, on the one hand, secured a wide circulation and an immediate response to their works, and, on the other hand, made their literary existence, between individual and collective thought, a very complex matter. Their responsibility was to preserve Polish cultural life, which at that time could only exist and survive in the language.

---

[1] A Polish rebellion that unsuccessfully tried to overthrow Russian rule in the Congress Kingdom of Poland as well as in the Polish provinces of Western Russia.

[2] The emigration of political elites from Poland from 1831–1870.

For a long time the best Romantic works were created in exile. Among such is the digressive poem recognized as the greatest national epic ever written: Adam Mickewicz's *Pan Tadeusz* (1834), an epic based on the poetics of remembrance and nostalgia for a lost idyll.

As we have seen in other European countries, there is no homogeneous image of Polish Romanticism. Just as various authors held often conflicting and changing ideas about human existence in its historical, philosophical or eschatological dimensions, so they also offered a variety of worlds and poetic styles created in a continuous dialogue and commentary. Alongside Mickiewicz's idyllic and pastoral image of Lithuania is the Cossacks' wildness and the bloody past of the Ukrainian part of the Eastern borderlands presented by Antoni Malczewski and Juliusz Słowacki. The melodious poetry of Mickievicz's Eden, saved from oblivion, is dramatically contrasted with the ironic language and imagery of *Beniowski* (1841), in which Słowacki, using Byronic, *donjuanesque* humour and style, reveals the crisis of Polish Romantic expression and looks for a new language and a new kind of literary authenticity.

Any selection from or fragmentation of this part of the Polish literary heritage leaves the editor dissatisfied due to the wealth and variety of the material and the peculiar role Polish Romantic poetry had in the shaping of national culture. Our aim has been primarily literary-historical, and it is to be hoped that, from the few abstracts presented here, the reader will be able to see affinities with other European literatures of the time in terms of themes and style and notice the dynamism of change between the early descriptive lyrical mode of Mickiewicz's *Crimean Sonnets* (1826) and the dramatic force of the *Improvisation* in *Forefathers' Eve* (1832). Likewise, it should be possible to trace the Romantic 'speaking I' in a variety of realizations: the voice of rebellion and emotion in *Ode to Youth* (1820); of biblical prophecy in *The Books of the Polish Nation and Polish Pilgrimage* (1832); or of a mature man, capable of depicting symbolic space of timelessness, *The Lusanne Lyrics* (1839–1840).

FURTHER READING

Bachórz, Józef and Alina Kowalczykowa, eds. *Słownik literatury polskiej XIX wieku*. Wrocław: Ossolineum, 1994.
Janion, Maria. *Gorączka romantyczna*. Warszawa: Państwowy Instytut Wydawniczy, 1975.
Miłosz, Czesław. *The History of Polish Literature*. London: Macmillan, 1969.
Siwicka, Dorota. *Romantyzm. 1822–1863*. Warszawa: Wydawnictwo Naukowe PWN, 1995.
Zgorzelski, Czesław. *O sztuce poetyckiej Mickiewicza*. Warszawa: Państwowy Instytut Wydawniczy, 1976.

PORTUGUESE ROMANTICISM *Carlos Leone and Bethany Wilson*

Even to consider Romanticism in Portugal assumes that categories of intellectual history common in most of Western Europe have universal relevance. The Portuguese case, however, like several others in southern Europe, defies such categorization. Before attempting to define Portuguese Romanticism, we must first consider the nation's unusual Enlightenment.

Although Portugal was one of the leading European nations throughout the XV and XVI centuries, due to the overseas expansion of its naval powers, Portugal's contact with modern Europe declined in the seventeenth century. This breach lead to a cultural decline, evident even in the seventeenth century, and the consensus among modern Portuguese and European scholars is that the Inquisition and the period of joint monarchy with Spain (1580–1640) are the main causes of Portugal's stagnation at the dawn of the modern world. Even Portugal's restored national independence proved inadequate to re-establish the scientific culture of modernity and Portuguese

Enlightenment, which was never as socially influential as other European Enlightenments. Interestingly, it was Lisbon's earthquake of 1755 that again placed Portugal at the centre of a key debate about progress and optimism in European culture. Soon after though, the combination of *ancien regime* brutality and Lockean empiricism protracted by the enlightened despotism of the Marquis of Pombal, alienated sympathy for Portugal's regime, and, as such external commentaries as Diderot's Enclopedie only emphasized, made the Iberian Peninsula[1] as a whole look like nothing more than a gothic anachronism in the period.

The historical period that immediately precedes Romanticism in Portugal is difficult to define. The background out of which Portuguese modernity developed did not change significantly until the Napoleonic invasions in the first decade of the nineteenth century. Marginalized from the major trends of Enlightenment culture, the Portuguese did not participate in the formation of Romanticism's most significant artistic, political and scientific innovations. Only after 1820, with the triumph of a liberal constitution, did Romanticism in Portugal acquire enough cultural significance to justify inclusion in this anthology. The work of two key figures in Portuguese Romanticism, Almeida Garrett and Alexandre Herculano, highlight the connection between Portugal's shift from an absolutist government to a constitutional monarchy and its aesthetic affirmation of a new school in literature and the arts. Both Garrett and Herculano were in exile during the struggle for liberalism and both were politically active in the early days of the constitutional monarchy. Although brothers in arms, they disagreed on many subjects in art and in politics. For instance, in 1851 Herculano opposed a treaty that Garrett was negotiating with France about matters of literary property, concerning the trade in Belgian-printed books. Garrett and Herculano are the only cultural figures worthy of standing alongside other European Romantic figures. Not only do they recognize external influences on Portuguese Romanticism, but they were themselves quickly recognized in Europe as authors who deserved to be translated.

Edgar Prestage's English version of Garrett's play *Frei Luis de Souza* (1844) and several translations of his travel novel *Viagens na Minha Terra* (1846)[2] have made Garrett the best known of pre-twentieth-century Portuguese writers. Since these other works are so well-known, only an excerpt of the Introduction to *Um Auto de Gil Vicente* (1841), a play about the early modern founder of Portuguese drama, is included here. This Introduction aptly illustrates Garrett's political stance and his vision of Portuguese cultural independence. The selections from Herculano's texts on Portuguese history portray him as a modern theorist and empirical researcher as well as a hardy polemicist. Unfortunately the selections printed here leave out his contributions to European polemics of his day, such as his essay on the Pope's infallibility. In choosing the passages for this anthology an attempt has been made to emphasize cultural elements unique to the Portuguese, and therefore issues like the papal one, commented on throughout Europe, are excluded. Herculano's work as a journalist, a librarian, a poet and the greatest Portuguese historical novelist of his time have also been left out.

Precisely to compensate for these shortcomings, two Portuguese literary critics are represented by short excerpts that illustrate how Europeans perceived the greatness of Garrett and Herculano. These passages by Lopes de Mendonça, the first Portuguese literary critic, and

---

[1] 'Iberian Peninsula' often appears in these excerpts as 'Hespanha'.

[2] Garrett's *Frei Luis de Suoza* is translated as *Brother Luis de Souza*, Altrincham, 1900. A recent English translation of *Viagens na Minha Terra* titled *Travels in my Homeland* (2003) is available in the Adamastor Book Series from the UMass Dartmouth Press.

Rebello da Silva, the most praised literary critic of nineteenth-century Portugal, emphasize the centrality of theatre for Portuguese Romanticism and highlight the connections between the Portuguese and other European cultures. They were first published in periodicals and later collected in books, and while their influence among the literate classes was significant, it must be remembered that in the early nineteenth century the Portuguese people were largely illiterate.

In conclusion, this very narrow selection focuses on key themes in well-established Romantic authors, but it also raises a less familiar problem evident in several Romantic traditions (also apparent elsewhere): can there be an historical logic responsible for intellectual development across different cultures? Did Enlightenment turn into Romanticism in each European tradition? What if there were no Enlightenment, at least in the usual sense, to begin with? These small excerpts cannot possibly illustrate this problem fully, but they introduce one of its primary cultural effects: the meshing of Enlightenment with Romantic themes. The problem of defining Romanticism begins with the problem of defining the Enlightenment, or indeed any cultural movement in history.

ROMANIAN ROMANTICISM *Mihaela Anghelescu Irimia*

For Romanian culture, Romanticism in all its forms – from the conceptual to the philosophic, aesthetic, moral, civic, political *and* national – is inseparable from the process of modernization. Historically, this process overlaid two previous cultural traditions: the Wallachian-Moldavian, with its Byzantine-Slavonic background, and the Transylvanian, with its Austro-Hungarian one. Behind both, however, lies an essentially Romance identity concealed in Cyrillic script, so that what sounds Latin to the ear reads Slav to the eye. What Călinescu (1941) was to see as a 'bygone age' of religious literature, courtly chronicles and princely edicts, was irreversibly overtaken by Westernization between the late eighteenth century and the first half of the nineteenth century. Lacking either a Western-style Renaissance, with the exception of Polish influence in Moldavia, or a genuine Enlightenment, with the exception of the Transylvanian School (Şcoala Ardeleană), Romanian Romanticism found itself defending an agenda at once nationalist and pan-European. Hence its strong civic component, the national and nationalistic accents and its militant tone. As a latecomer, this Romanian modernity – 'the age of Biedermeier' (Nemoianu 1984) – combined Enlightenment with Romantic principles, values and institutions.

The period between 1820 and 1850 witnessed the shaping of a 'national idea' that 'burned' long phases of historical evolution and 'combined genres' (Cornea 1972). Synchronization with the Occident became the rule of the day: the elite travelled to the West, adopting the French fashion in dress and hairstyles, and enjoying translations from world literature (Molière, Voltaire, Montesquieu, Goethe, Ossian, Young, Volney, Chateaubriand, Lamartine, Scott, Byron, Hugo, Schiller, Pushkin), and seeing it as their duty to promote civilization and progress, following the *Encyclopédie* and the French Revolution. In strictly literary terms, this is the time when Romanian won the battle to be finally accepted as the national language of the three historic principalities, Wallachia, Moldavia and Transylvania, concluding what had previously been a schizophrenic condition. It also marked the end of 'the transitional script' between Cyrillic and Roman types. From now on, what sounds Latin to the ear reads Latin to the eye. The first literary text to be printed exclusively in Roman script was Byron's *Don Juan*, Cantos I and II, translated from the French (!), which appeared in 1847, just one year before the revolutions of 1848. This is a good example of the Romanian salon taste for Englishness – via a French cultural filter – in both Wallachia and Moldavia. In Transylvanian intellectual circles, German was the

usual literary conduit. Thus the establishment of an institutionalized national culture went hand in hand with cosmopolitanism.

Nationalistic press agitation for increased 'Romanianness' preceded the historic union of Wallachia and Moldavia as the national state in 1859, while full national independence from Ottoman rule was not finally achieved until 1877. Education leaped forward, with universities founded in Iaşi (Jassy) and Bucureşti (Bucharest) focusing mainly on national literature, while the theatre and numerous cultural societies also emphasized Romanian identity. As elsewhere in Europe, this national spirit was part concept and part sentiment, half-discovered and half-invented. The Transylvanian School took up the old chroniclers' slogan 'we come from Rome.' This radical Romanticism involved a bundle of related beliefs, among which were convictions of racial and linguistic purity, and that national frontiers, given to humans by nature and God, were sacrosanct. Eliade Rădulescu's manifesto in support of *The National Theatre* (1830) shows an obsession with the heroic grandeur of national history, echoing almost to the letter Mihail Kogălniceanu's *Introduction* to the *Literary Dacia* (1840), which asserts that 'all Romanians have one language and one literature common to all of them' and urging as corollary the 'moral commandment' of union through culture.

After this, Russo's *Hymn to Romania* in the following decade comes as little surprise, and can be grouped in the company of popular ballads rewritten as literary masterpieces under the pen of the 'national bard' Vasile Alecsandri. The latter had travelled to Paris, Florence and London, as well as to Constantinople, Gibraltar, Morocco and Tangiers, acted as an ardent promoter of original Romanian writings in the periodical *Literary Romania* (founded in 1855), and occupied governmental and diplomatic positions during a flourishing public career. In the early 1850s Alecsandri promoted a literary taste for the 'wild' and 'primitive' works of the 'organic community', populating the 'cultural periphery' of Europe and fostering the purest 'popular culture' (Burke 1978), seeing in the national landscape a repository of national history.

The ethnogenetic vision underlying the *Miorița* (*Mioritza*) ballad, like the myth of the birth of culture couched in *Meşterul Manole* (*Master Manole*), point to the autochthonous element in Romanian Romantic and romanticized literature. Redolent of Bolintineanu's *Muma lui Ştefan cel Mare* (*Stephen the Great's Mother*), Alecsandri's own cult of the Moldavian prince, like his cult of the Roman Emperor Trajan, tunes in with his visionary *Deşteptarea României* (*Romania's Awakening*) a couple of years before 1877, and *Cântecul gintei latine* (*Song to the Latin Race*), for which he was awarded the Prix du Chant Latin immediately after the victorious conclusion of the Independence War. This extraordinary twining of the indigenous with the cosmopolitan element is a filogenetic reiteration of the ontogenetic phenomenon in the Romanian culture of the day. The '*bonjourists*' had opposed the '*anti-bonjourists*' in the atmosphere preceding the revolutions of 1848. Western-educated and open-minded, they were nicknamed 'the young ones', 'the French' or 'the Germans' by the opposed conservative camp of the newly established public sphere. The former upheld innovative middle-class values, the latter still nourished the outmoded Phanariot spirit of 'the old', as they were scornfully labelled by their opponents.

At the same time, Dacia was dug out of the collective unconscious and circulated as at once a cultural-literary space and the actual historical reality from which the national stock could be claimed. The parallel between *Literary Dacia* and *Literary Romania* within the span of one and a half decades is indicative. Both encouraged the union of national forces through letters and underlined the sacred duty of vernacular authors' contributions in mystical nationalistic terms, while proclaiming the virtues of the modern profession of literature in its own right.

The late Romantic Mihai Eminescu, 'the' national poet of the Romanians, is currently regarded as the epitome of the modern spirit – in itself, of course, a Romantic idea. He appears to embody both the messianic and the utopian, the radical and the conservative, the exotic and the national in a literature ambitious of achieving a European identity and presence. Like Eliade Rădulescu in the early century, who had endeavoured to render celebrated texts of world literature in the Romanian vernacular, like Alecsandri in the mid-century, who had mixed Romantic and classic genres in his writings, Eminescu was the outstanding Romanian writer of the late nineteenth century. Drawing on contemporary German and other Western ideas, he theorizes on the nature of poetry and the poet's mission as he explores cosmogonic and cosmological themes in his *Scrisoarea I (First Epistle)*. He looks for outworldly roots to human creativity in his masterpiece, *Luceafărul (Hyperion)*, seeing nature as the first and greatest book of the poet, like Lamartine, Wordsworth or Keats, and identifies in the rippling lake or the sky-blue flower the wide world on a small scale, in a perfect isomorphic relationship with the cosmos, like Blake. Fascinated by the glorious past of the nation, like the generation of '48, he holds a similar vision of future national apotheosis in *Ce-ți doresc eu ție, dulce Românie (What I wish you, sweet Romanian land)*. He is the most Westernized Romanian Romantic, and the greatest exponent of folklore turned into original national culture. Author of *doinas* – typical popular lyrics – and of songs, he draws on folklore for his rather unsuccessful historical drama, while investing it with all the historical significance of a Victor Hugo.

As a member of the Junimea (Young Generation) literary society based in Iaşi, Eminescu stands in a metonymic relation to 'the 1870 movement', echoing 'the 1855 moment' embodied by Alecsandri, which in turn harks back to the 'Romantic moment' (Călinescu 1941) with Eliade as its central cultural activist, creator and citizen. All the way between the 1820s and the 1870s, Romanian Romanticism does justice to Lovejoy's 'discrimination of Romanticisms'. Aware of the historical fault-line separating Western from Central-Eastern Europe, and using methodologies from *Mentalités*, History of Ideas, and Cultural Identity approaches, recent Romanian studies have managed to balance an understanding of the native 'Romantic phenomenon' with foreign, pre-eminently Western 'sources', in constructing a picture of the cultural turmoil of the period.

BIBLIOGRAPHY

Burke, Peter. *Popular Culture in Early Modern Europe*. London: Temple Smith, 1978.
Călinescu, George. *Istoria literaturii române dela origini până în prezent*. Bucureşti: Fundaţia Regală pentru Literatură şi Artă, 1941.
Cornea, Paul. *Originile romantismului românesc – Spiritul public, mişcarea ideilor şi literatura între 1780–1840*. Bucureşti: Editura Minerva, 1972.
Lovejoy, Arthur O. 'On the Discrimination of Romanticisms', *The Romantic Movement*. Ed. Anthony Thorlby. London & Harlow: Longmans, 1969 (© 1966). 14–19.
Nemoianu, Virgil. *The Taming of Romanticism: European Literature and the Age of Biederemeier*. Cambridge, Massachusetts and London: Harvard University Press, 1984.
Porter, Roy and Mikuláš Teich, eds. *Romanticism in National Context*, Cambridge: Cambridge University Press, 1988.

RUSSIAN ROMANTICISM *Dmitry Usenco*

If Russian Romanticism were to be outlined in a single phrase, the most appropriate would be *Apprenticeship struggling for mastery*. Pure imitation and reproduction of Western models

common in the eighteenth century were being overcome and a search for a national identity starting. This search went on through the twentieth century and beyond, and is still, with numerous modifications and reservations, a major topic on the Russian cultural agenda. One can say with a reasonable degree of certainty that most of the 'accursed questions' that have troubled the reflecting part of the Russian society during its tumultuous history sprang into being in the Romantic period – germinating the seeds of what were to later flower as full-scale aesthetic movements. Although there was still a lot of borrowing and rediscovery of things that seemed trivial for the more 'progressive' West, by the middle of the nineteenth century resistance to uncritical assimilation of imported ideas and methods was getting stronger. To identify the sources of later literary campaigns and controversies we need a closer look at the first half of that century.

One of the permanent troubles of modern Russia has been the discrepancy between its relatively advanced cultural development on the one hand, and its economic and political backwardness on the other. The period under consideration is no exception – moreover, the realization of that incongruity by the Russian intelligentsia was more acute than ever. The mediaeval institution of serfdom, abandoned by Europe centuries before, still constituted the basis of the social system. It meant that nearly two-thirds of the country's population were legally deprived of essential human rights, which instead were delegated to and exercised by their landlords. Putting aside the question whether both classes were happy or unhappy with such a bargain, and whether its origin derived from economic conditions peculiar to Russia, or from the 'spirit of slavery' that, according to some later observers, dominated the Russian mentality, by the late eighteenth century the Russian establishment found itself in a rather ambiguous position. With the French revolution underway, ideas of liberty, fashionable among the upper class, were inexorably penetrating the whole society. At the same time, new laws in support of serfdom were tacitly introduced. An average Russian nobleman faced a difficult dilemma: his upbringing (usually by a French resident tutor), his reading (usually Voltaire and the Encyclopaedists) prompted him to embrace modern ideas, while his economic considerations dictated to him the dire necessity to carry on in the role of 'tyrant' and 'oppressor' in order to maintain his household and appropriate lifestyle. Serfdom was not a popular subject in the literature of that period not only because of strict censorship exercised by the state, but also because of the personal concerns of many writers. However, the problem could not but tell on contemporary attitudes, breeding a sense of guilt and contributing much to the Romantic concept of 'dual reality', realized in a way very different from the Western understanding of it.

The most prominent historic event in early nineteenth-century Russia – the defeat of Napoleon's invasion – only contributed to that intellectual dichotomy. France, universally acknowledged the bearer of the Enlightenment, suddenly turned into an aggressor, a threat to Russian independence. The overwhelming majority of the Russian aristocracy spoke French far better than any other language (in fact Russian had to be seriously learnt only by those who wished to go into literature), and many of them regarded the French Emperor as a political paragon. Advanced European ideas had unexpectedly entered Russia by means of military force, and had to be physically (if not intellectually) counteracted. Consequently, final victory could not be unambiguously interpreted as a triumph of good over evil, but was overshadowed by second thoughts suggesting a defeat of civilization by barbarism.

The most outstanding domestic event of the period was undoubtedly the Decembrist uprising of 1825 organized by a group of high-rank army officers in an attempt to liberalize Russia. The programmes and goals of the conspirators were controversial and sometimes even odious.

The most radical of them, for example, planned to exterminate the royal family, deport all Jews to Asia Minor and 'temporarily' impose some sort of military dictatorship. Once again, it is a subject of speculation whether the revolt, if victorious, would have made the nation more democratic, rather than bringing the Great Terror a hundred years forward. Whatever their aims, they achieved the opposite: the new Tsar Nicholas I was appalled by the uprising and adopted much stricter policies than his liberal-minded predecessor Alexander I. Probably the most unfortunate result was the growing alienation between the monarch and his bureaucracy on the one hand, and the intelligentsia on the other. This unhappy breach has persisted throughout all the later periods of Russian history. The intelligentsia persistently declared their indifference towards politics at best, which was often complicated by secret or even open hostility towards the existing regime. A situation when a man of letters could be a tutor of the heir to the throne (like the early Romantic, Zhukovsky) or even a government minister (like his contemporary, the classicist Ivan Dmitriev), quite acceptable under Alexander, became impossible under Nicholas and his successors.

The unique geopolitical situation of Russia made its Romanticism also very specific, even at its 'imitative' stage. Thus the acquaintance with and the borrowings from Western literature were rather sporadic and unsystematic; many of them nowadays look rather surprising from the viewpoint of the established Romantic 'canon'. The initial and principal source of influence was certainly France. French Romanticism, however, was a belated literary phenomenon itself, still in its bud at the turn of the century. So, paradoxically enough, most Russian Romanticism grew out of pre-Romantic French poetry whose representatives are now almost forgotten in their homeland but are still remembered in Russia thanks to their influence on major authors. One of the best-known examples is the work of Evariste de Forges de Parny, which exerted an enormous influence on the early poetry of Pushkin whose own achievements virtually immortalized his modest predecessor. Things did not change much with the advent of a new fashion – German poetry. Both Vasily Zhukovsky and Mikhail Lermontov, for instance, translated Joseph Christian von Zedlitz, an Austrian author now completely forgotten but for these brilliant Russian renderings (*Die nächtliche Heerschau* and *Das Geisterschiff*). German philosophers' influence was more mainstream – as testified by the numerous Russian followers of Hegel, some of whom even had a chance to attend his lectures (though Russian soil grew almost no Kantians). Here, however, the outcome was no less surprising – for Hegel was later adopted to voice the ideas of the Slavophil movement.

English Romanticism started to play an important role in Russia only with the spread of works by Lord Byron (usually in French translations). For a while it brought a radical change in fashion – the posture of pessimism and disillusionment assumed by the British poet proved to be in tune with the mindset of many literary men on the banks of the Neva. Yet, as we shall see shortly, this influence once again bore unique fruit on the Russian soil.

But what was the main 'national feature' with which Russian culture could identify itself in the global context? The first, and easiest, solution would be to adopt Western-made subjects to a specifically Eurasian locale. A good example can be once more found in the poetry of Zhukovsky. His initial popularity was due to the adaptation of *Lenore*, a short narrative poem by the German author Gottfried August Bürger. In the first Russian version the title character is called by a Russian name, Lyudmila; the original text is followed rather closely, however it avoids any Western references and sticks to essentially Slavonic vocabulary. However, Zhukovsky did not stop there. Apparently finding his adaptation not Russian enough, some time later, he came up with another version under a different title – *Svetlana* (thanks to Zhukovsky both names

have been extremely popular among the Russians ever since). This time the poem is obviously set in Russia – it incorporates descriptions of some folk customs practised on the eve of Epiphany. Unlike the original and the preceding version, the poem has a happy ending. The Russian poet did not stop here either – later on he made a closer translation of *Lenore*, reintroducing Western names and loan words. All three undertakings can be considered independent pieces of writing, having their own artistic value.

The new generation of poets, led by Pushkin, felt themselves less restrained by European models, at least in terms of the setting. This was made easier by the variety of Russian scenery, offering numerous places even more exotic than Sir Water Scott's Highlands (extremely popular in Russia) or the Turkish forts of Byron. Finland, the Caucasus, even Siberia became the scene of many an epic and lyric poem, with lots of authentic or not so authentic ethnic details and elements of folklore. In most cases, however, they feature a Byronic hero, alienated from the philistine society and searching for spiritual redemption in communication with nature or in espousing some political movement. In the course of time, the interest in folklore grew more genuine and played a significant part in the earlier works of Gogol (who wrote in Russian using chiefly Ukrainian material) as well as influenced the famous collectors of indigenous vocabulary (Vladimir Dahl) and folk tales (Alexander Afanasiev).

The estranged Romantic hero, so vividly presented in the works of Byron and Shelley, also experienced an intriguing development when transplanted to Russian soil, giving rise to a whole series of what was later to be styled as 'superfluous people'. A typical member of this class would be a young aristocrat in his 20s who has seen some of the world and become completely disenchanted with it. The only thing he faces for the rest of his life is everlasting ennui and desperate search for new sensations. This, however, does not normally involve amorality, although it does lead to some controversial acts (both Pushkin's Onegin and Lermontov's Pechorin kill their friends in a duel). Nevertheless the main accent in depicting this 'gallery' is existential rather than social, and anticipates many brilliant psychological studies later in the century, above all in Dostoyevsky.

Another way of differentiation from Western models was to have recourse to the rich mystical and ritualistic tradition of the Eastern Orthodox Church. This tradition was obviously at odds with the more popular rationalistic philosophy, therefore the proponents of orthodoxy usually had to assign themselves to a separate ideological camp. Most of its representatives sided with the Slavophil movement, claiming that Russia had its own way of progressing different from the West. Although they often received their education at European universities, their attitude to Europe was predominantly critical. Here we can discern the origin of the shift towards the cultural opposition mentioned before. Although the adepts of Slavophilism (Khomyakov, Kireyevsky) did not develop any consistent or comprehensive system and published very little in their lifetime, later on, when their notebooks and letters became known, they exerted a considerable influence on intellectual trends in the second half of the century, giving rise to the doctrine of Panslavism – unification of all the Slavic people under the patronage of the Russian tsar. Its famous proponents are Alexey Tolstoy and Fyodor Tyutchev, even though the latter's manifests itself chiefly in his essays rather than his poetry.

This is the unstable background of nineteenth-century Russian literature. It remains to say that the poetic and narrative technique of the Russian Romantics was, in general, up to a very high standard. It was brought to perfection in the 'golden age' of Russian culture – late nineteenth century, marked by co-existence between the successors of earlier Romantics and the Realists. Predictably, both schools influenced each other, although the outcomes differed from author to

author. Dostoyevsky, for example, although predominantly a Realist, is much more of a Romantic than his other great contemporary Tolstoy. As for the poets, they reveal almost opposite tendencies. Some, such as Nekrasov, adopted realism as their literary creed, so, despite their originality, are inappropriate for this anthology. Others, on the contrary, distanced themselves from realism, escaping to the realms of philosophy and archaic diction (Tyutchev), art for art's sake (Fet) or Bohemian-style fatalism with a touch of fashionable 'decadency' (Grigoriev). All three were, however, top-class artists, deserving a place among the cream of Russian writers.

The apprenticeship completed, what was still by European standards a young literature was quickly acquiring an original and international voice. Though there is little unanimity as to what exactly it had to say, perhaps, in the context of this anthology, its themes will become more generally appreciated and better understood.

SPANISH ROMANTICISM *Richard A. Cardwell*

In 1940 E. Allison Peers, in *A History of the Romantic Movement in Spain* (Cambridge: Cambridge University Press, 1940), argued that Spain's reaction was fundamentally eclectic (combining classical and romantic elements) and purely literary in nature. Yet as Alcalá Galiano's 1834 *Preface* to Rivas' *El moro expósito* (The Orphan Moor), and Eugenio de Ochoa's 1835 essay, 'Romanticismo', in *El Artista* both indicate, the basis of the Spanish response was clearly ideological. In the former Alcalá Galiano distinguishes between what he calls 'historical romanticism', associated with the works of Walter Scott, and 'present-day romanticism' which he associates with Lord Byron. The following year Ochoa implicitly contrasted his own conservative attitude with a more subversive model when he observed that 'the word 'Romantic' for them is the same as a heretic, as a man capable of any crime. That is to say that they are the sons of Beelzebub'. The Romantic movement in Spain is to be understood, then, in the light of these two responses: the one profoundly conservative, allied to throne and altar; the second liberal, progressive and, at the same time, deleterious to established beliefs and conventions. The struggle between these opposing groups was to be played out against the historical background of invasion, war, political struggle, the Congress of Verona and the restoration of thrones, a reign of terror, exile and persecution.

Yet the origins of Romanticism in Spain began with a subtle shift in sensibility rather than ideology. Although the word *romántico* did not appear until June 1818 in the Madrid newspaper *Crónica Científica y Literaria*, the general term for the new spirit was *romancesco* (associated with *novelesco* and meaning 'odd' or 'exaggerated') and generally restricted to literature. The first Romantic work, arguably, was the anacreontic collection, *Ocios de mi juventud* (Pastimes of Youth, 1773) by José Cadalso, also author of the posthumous *Noches lúgubres* (Lugubrious Nights 1792). Both expressed the European cult of sensibility found in writers like Thomson and Saint-Lambert. Here was a radical shift in the presentation of the poetic self, personal experience and nature, differing markedly from previous classical traditions. Emotion is expressed through the pathetic fallacy. Sensual adjectives are psychological rather than descriptive. Nature is sad because the poet is sad – the first expression and presence of that cosmic anguish which was to be termed *Weltschmertz* or *mal de siècle*. By 1794, the verses of Meléndez Valdés gave Spain her own term: *fastidio universal*. In 1839 García Tassara coined the term *fiebre del siglo* (fever of the age). In the intermediate period we find an increasing awareness of spiritual distress in an age of war and political convulsion and the consequent collapse of systems of belief and value. In 1812, the young Martínez de la Rosa was among the first to express that typical

Romantic contrast between past felicity and present loss and despair where youthful visions of flowers become present deserts, a contrast which anticipates the work of Espronceda in the mid-1830s.

But these anguished outpourings were soon contested by the political and ideological interpretation of Romanticism in 1814 after the restoration of Ferdinand VII and the reestablishment of absolutism. In 1814 Johann Nikolas Böhl von Faber, a German scholar resident in Cadiz, began a debate which was to shape and consolidate a specific view of Romanticism. Böhl was a monarchist and arch-conservative and, under the influence of the Vienna lectures of A. W. Schlegel (whose writings were to dominate literary and historiographical thinking in Spain for the next century and a half), identified Romanticism with Christian literature from the medieval period onwards and, especially, with the Golden Age dramas of Calderón. By contrast with the uniformity and rationality of classicism, Spanish literature was popular, heroic, unbound by precept and, above all, monarchist and Catholic. Underneath these discriminations lay Böhl's hatred of the Enlightenment, France and its Revolution and the subversion of morals and religion in the 'new' literature. These medievalizing tenets by Böhl, Durán and other literary and historical critics, popularized by the translation and imitation of Walter Scott, entered the cultural mainstream through an upsurge of historical plays and novels, *leyendas*, articles on national history and heroes, architecture and customs. The regenerationist interpretation of tradition was the hallmark of the new sensibility and determined the patterns of thought for decades despite the reaction of liberal and progressive writers 20 years later. Indeed, its clear political motivation is expressed in the endeavour to make history serve a purpose different from the prevalent influence of the Enlightenment. Amid the general spiritual crisis and the breakdown of beliefs and established values for which the Enlightenment was held responsible, the idea of a new organic community with a close-knit and harmonious set of structures was soon to become an accepted view of the new spirit. The vogue for the past was no Romantic veneer; it marked a political and intellectual programme for the recovery of conservative values and faith. To this end José Zorrilla's *Cantos del trovador* (Songs of the Troubador, 1841), his historical plays and *leyendas* and his celebrated drama, *Don Juan Tenorio* (1844) all express the author's adherence to national and patriotic Catholic values. Zorrilla was the most lionized poet of the age. His overt statement of his adherence to this value system recognized the presence of the liberal and unorthodox resistance to the Schlegelian project which was unleashed after the death of Ferdinand and the return of the exiles in 1834.

The two writers who best express this rebellious, even negative and subversive attitude to accepted beliefs and values are José de Espronceda and Mariano José de Larra. Briefly, a group of dramatists – Rivas, García Gutiérrez and Martínez de la Rosa – writing in the period 1834–1844 also express the 'fever of the age' and a sense of injustice, the failure of human ideals and a sense of emptiness. Espronceda's early poems, written in exile, show a hostility to social conventions and systems of justice. His 'The Hangman' and 'The Condemned Man' express the Romantic motif of 'the prison house of life' which, in *The Student of Salmanca* (1840) is developed as a metaphor for eternal forces of evil and cosmic injustice against which the solitary hero must assert his will, an anticipation by over a century of Camus' *l'homme révolté*. Rivas' *Don Álvaro* (1834) had already expressed the same view where fate and coincidence (cosmic injustice) hound the hero and his lover to their doom. If *The Student* expresses a contest of wills between a malign divinity and a seeker after knowledge, the unfinished epic poem *El diablo mundo* (It's an Absurd World, 1840–1841) carries Espronceda's anguished negative response to belief a stage further. Striving to

outdo Byron's *Don Juan* in wit and technique, Espronceda sets the scene in contemporary Madrid where his innocent hero is remorselessly stripped of all his ideals. With Espronceda's untimely death in 1842 the voice of protest virtually ceases. Larra's contribution, apart from two historical plays and a novel which express similar negative sentiments, is mainly as a satirist and literary critic. He attacks social manners and hypocrisy, contrasted with a deep patriotism and despair over the condition of Spain. Yet in a review of Dumas' *Antony*, for all his desire for new guiding ideals, he discovered a 'truth' which failed to connect with his own longing for 'the expression of human progress'. His confrontation with what Byron called 'the fatal truth', his failure in politics, his break with his wife and his mistress all led to his suicide in 1837.

The immediate aftermath of Larra's suicide saw the reassertion of the conservative view of a patriotic and organic community, Catholic and monarchical, and an attempt to assuage the 'fever of the age'. Pastor Díaz, in the introduction to Zorrilla's poems in 1837 recognized that the dominant theme of contemporary Romantic literature was the collapse of collectively accepted beliefs and echoed the violent hostility which it provoked. Between 1837 and 1842 Salas y Quiroga, Mesonero Romanos, Gil, Ventura de la Vega and Mora, among many, had all accused 'present day romanticism' of fomenting disbelief and immorality. Bermúdez de Castro in his *Ensayos poéticos* of 1840 spoke of 'the sad fact of a disconsoling and chilling scepticism . . . the outcome of the poisoned atmosphere that the present generation has breathed in'. By the mid-1840s orthodox intellectual opinion clamoured for reassurance which was soon forthcoming in the writings of Balmes and Donoso Cortés. The former offered a reassertion of traditional belief and his *El Criterio* (1845) had a strong popular appeal. Donoso's *Ensayo sobre el catolicismo, el liberalismo y el socialismo* (1851) performed a *volte face* from his earlier support of negative Romanticism, advocating the Schlegelian interpretation of history and social organization. Analysis, he now proclaimed, was a form of blasphemy, and praised on practical and utilitarian grounds 'the beauty of Catholic solutions'. Campoamor who, too, had expressed his own spiritual distress soon began to 'tame' the anguished voice with his *doloras* where doubt and scepticism were turned into witty and whimsical epigrams.

Not until the end of the century, between 1895 and 1910, did the two strains of Romanticism come together in the work of the young progressive writers for whom the notion of an organic society and the 'soul' of the nation became the means to respond to a general sense of spiritual distress. The intellectuals' failure to solve the nation's ills was, indirectly, to lead to more practical solutions – and eventually to the generals who attempted to resolve Spain's future in the armed struggle which broke out in July 1936, almost a century after the high tide of Romanticism itself.

SWEDISH ROMANTICISM *Håkan Möller*

When Gustav III was murdered during a masquerade ball in the opera house in Stockholm 1792 an epoch was ended. The period following the golden age of Gustav III's reign, up to the bloodless coup d'état 1809, has been called the iron age of Swedish cultural life. Throughout the eighteenth century intellectuals had suffered severe restrictions and press censorship, which affected also the theatre, and the importing of books. A year after the coup d'état 1809 a new special press law was issued (rewritten 1812). This opened the floodgates for a wave of new publications – including literary calendars, periodicals and newspapers of different kinds. Young romantics in Stockholm and Uppsala were by this time well prepared and they took on their revolutionary task with eagerness and energy.

In fact signs of the new literature they were looking for had already appeared, and the battle they fought was already underway in the eighteenth century. Johan Henric Kellgren (1751–1795), often said to be the first writer in Sweden who made a living entirely by his pen, was already one of the most prominent authors during Gustav III's reign when, at the end of his life, he wrote several poems exposing pre-romantic stylistic ideals, among them *The New Creation, or The World of the Imagination* (1790). The main theme of this rondo-structured piece of poetry is the liberating power of love. The image of the beloved is reflected everywhere, and nature is being re-created in the gaze of the speaker – under the spell of his passion the subject of the poem takes the same position as the God of Genesis, the poet becomes a Creator. Not least, the intense presence of the speaking subject points to a central aspect of romantic poetry.

Politics ensured that after 1792 the capital of Sweden lost ground as an intellectual and cultural centre, and instead it was the university-towns that started to develop as centres of creativity. For the romantics, Uppsala was the most important. It was in the old university-town the poet, critic and literary historian P. D. A. Atterbom (1790–1855) and his fellows started Musis Amici, a society with the agenda for reforming the entire cultural life. By a new poetry a new world should be created. The romantics looked upon the dispute with the Enlightenment as a shift as dramatic as from night to day. Their explicit mission was nothing less than the creation of a new epoch – in Friedrich Schlegel's sense of a history of literature divided into literary epochs – to restore poetry to its former glorious standard, which, they believed, had been thoroughly destroyed by classicism. In a European perspective they were not unique in this respect. In Germany the romantics were criticized, but they never found it necessary to get together and strike back as a group. Typically enough it was in Sweden and France with their powerful Academies that the romantics organized themselves in societies with rules and orders imitating the institutionalized opponents. They adopted their opponent's structures to be more efficient, but their literary mission was to break with the aesthetic ideals represented by the Academies.

Central to the romantic revolution in Sweden was the publishing house of author and critic V. F. Palmblad (1788–1852). He not only produced romantic literature in periodicals, an important medium for the popularization of romanticism, but also translations of foreign romantic authors, including novels by Byron, Tieck and Hugo, and the collected works of Schelling. With high ambitions they started the weekly paper, *Svensk Literatur-Tidning* (1813–1823; Swedish literary journal), in which they reviewed new literature. Witty and spiteful satire was used together with reviews in a drawn-out debate with the 'Old school'. The sense of vocation, of striving for a common goal, and shared aesthetic themes in the struggle between the 'New school' and the 'Old school' is clearly displayed at the end of Atterbom's review of The Annual Report of the Swedish Academy (1813).

The contentious young romantics in Uppsala and Stockholm were perhaps more important as critical revolutionaries – especially in introducing and developing continental ideas – than as successful writers. Instead someone in the other old university-town, Lund, in southern Sweden, Esaias Tegnér (1782–1846) emerged as the most important poet of the age. Tegnér was a classicist whose poetry combined eloquence, extraordinary metrical skilfulness and metaphorical innovation. But the rhetorical armour was bursting under the pressure of the new metaphorical style. What has been described as a 'romantic break-through' occurs in his lyrical poetry of 1812–1813, where his divinization of art, his belief in the power of poetry and his view of inspiration made him a romantic poet in a most general sense – expressed in for instance his poem 'Song to the sun' whose lyrical subjectivism and absence of classical rhetoric breaks decisively with neoclassical formalism.

Early in the 1810s Tegnér joined 'Götiska förbundet' (the Old Norse League), publishing his romantic poetry in their recently started journal, *Iduna* (1811–1824) as well as the first songs of his celebrated romantic verse narrative *Frithiofs saga* (1825), which was soon translated into German and English (1833) and in time well known in Europe. In this, what was eventually to become the national epic of Sweden, Tegnér blended well-known romantic ingredients: Norse mythology, Christian interpretations of parts of the old saga, and a hero sometimes characterized by a desolate Byronic mood.

Founded in Stockholm, The Old Norse League soon attracted the historian Erik Gustaf Geijer (1783–1847) as its most influential member. *Iduna*, with its historical interest in Old Norse literature and mythology, was the natural home for Geijer's poems 'Vikingen', 'Manhem', and 'Odalbonden' (The yeomen farmer) – the latter as important for the Old Norse renaissance in Sweden as Oehlenschläger's 'Guldhornerne' in Denmark. The romantics' historical interests also appeared in their ambition to collect and publish folk songs and folk tales. Following the lead of the German Heidelberg School, Geijer and Arvid August Afzelius (1785–1871) published *Swedish Folk Songs from Ancient Times* (1814–1817).

The romantics also sought contemporary authors to express the new literary ideals. One such was the eccentric poet and dramatist, Erik Johan Stagnelius (1793–1823), a lyrical poet of incomparable skill and originality. The leading critic of the period, Lorenzo Hammarsköld, who early noticed his talent, edited his literary remains after his early death. Thanks to more complete and authoritative modern editions, Stagnelius has come to be seen as the most astonishing of the romantic poets – writing in a more widely spoken language than Swedish he would undoubtedly have been a major European poet of the romantic period.

Stagnelius early used and mastered many classical forms, such as the canzone, the sonnet and *ottava rima*, with a correspondingly rich variety of matters and themes. Stagnelius's elegy 'Friend! In the moment of Devastation' offers the human soul consolation and hope in a moment of utter despair. Is there no hope? The answer is biblical; the same power that once created the world out of chaos and still keeps the world in order can also restore and save the human soul out of its inner state of chaos. The didactic 'The Mystery of Sighs', expresses the tragedy of existence through the breathing in and out of the 'sigh', a rhythm present on all levels of creation. In this most elementary life-expression the Poet finds the two basic rules for the human life, the will to desire and the need to abandon. The poem shows Stagnelius's poetical skills, his unique tone and his very personal blend of speculative, gnostically coloured, ideas, Hegel's dialectics and Schelling's Philosophy of Nature. Stagnelius's originality transformed the Swedish didactic poem. The reader is left uncertain as to who is being addressed – and by whom? Is it an inner part of the self or/and every new reader of the poem?

In time, the Romantic outsiders became the most admired authors. Carl Jonas Love Almqvist (1793–1866), like Stagnelius, was a man of many literary talents. Spanning several decades, his literary output includes short stories, novels, poetry, music, and drama, essays on politics and poetics, and educational books. His most astonishing and, in a European perspective unique, literary project, *The Book of the Briar Rose*, is a fictional framework within which he organized nearly all his literary creations. This gigantic all-encompassing work, published from 1833–1851 in 17 volumes in two different series, set out to answer nothing less than such questions as how does one describe the world in its entirety, and how could one reach truth through language, poetry, science, and religion.

With Stockholm friends Almqvist founded the society 'Manna-Samfund' (Society of Men), a parallel to Atterbom's Uppsala circle, and from this period springs *Parjumouf* (1817), a short

story showing the young author's attempt to write like Lafontaine with his taste for the exotic, inspired by the travel writing characteristic of the period. The narrative is modelled on Romeo and Juliet but is set in Australia.

A brilliant example of Almqvist's continuous theorizing over authorship in *The Book of the Briar Rose* is *On two ways of Writing* (from *Dialogue on How to end Pieces*, 1835). Many modern critics have found here a premodern discussion about the open text and the co-creative reader, but a more historical interpretation notes that Almqvist's display of narrative control and rhetorical tools shows his authorial powers to lead his readers as he wishes.

In 'The Poet's Night', probably written 1825–1826, but not published until 1838, we can follow the Poet's path from despair to strength-giving trust in God. Art and religion are deeply interwoven in much of Almqvist's romantic writing, and the main theme of this cunningly designed prose poem is the Poet's relation to life. When the relationship to God is restored, the distancing and falseness of art vanish and instead become a free play. With words echoing of Goethe's famous lines, 'Ich hab' mein Sach' auf nichts gestellt', the Poet formulates his insight: 'to stand on nothing, and lean against nothing'. But this freedom of creativity has a price, the artist becomes alienated from life itself.

FINNISH ROMANTICISM *Håkan Möller*

Finland formally became a state after the Russian conquest 1808–1809, and therewith the political prerequisite for a national literature arose. At a time when many nations in Europe followed Herder's model in searching for the poetical manifestations of the folk-soul, and bards were found or created, the quest for the folk songs became urgent in Finland as well. The result was the national-epic Kalevala, and the name of the bard was Väinämöinen.

Elias Lönnrot (1802–1884) and Johan Ludvig Runeberg (1804–1877) were the leading figures of the Romantic Movement in Finland, and together with their friends they strove to create a national literature. Runeberg was the poet and Lönnrot, the researcher, publicist and collector of Finnish folklore, was the man behind the Kalevala.

From an enormous body of Finnish folk-poetry he put together the national-epic. The first version (1835–1836) contained 32 songs (12,078 lines). The new and more extensive version of the Kalevala, the so-called New Kalevala (1849), contains 50 songs (22,795 lines). The lyrical elements are reinforced in the later version, and this is clearly shown not at least in the striking use of parallelism in song XLIV, 'Väinämöinen's new *Kantele*'.

AMERICAN ROMANTICISM *Christopher A. Strathman*

Although romanticism arrived late to America's shores – emerging fully formed only with Ralph Waldo Emerson's essay *Nature* (1836) – its impact was neverthless lasting and profound. In the work that announced his entrance onto the international stage, Emerson draws on several European intellectual currents, as well as his own experience, to offer a distinctly American vision of the Self in relation to God and Nature. Having lost none of its original force, *Nature* opens with an impassioned plea:

> The foregoing generations beheld God and nature face to face; we, through their eyes. Why should not we also enjoy an original relation to the universe? Why should not we have a poetry and philosophy of insight and not of tradition, and a religion by revelation to us, and

not a history of theirs? . . . why should we grope among the dry bones of the past, or put the living generation into masquerade out of its faded wardrobe? The sun shines to-day also.[1]

What Emerson calls the desire for an 'original relation to the universe' has shaped the contours of American life in a way that has few parallels. The reasons for this are varied and complex, but one can begin with a simple observation. Unlike England, where Wordsworth, Coleridge and Southey renounced the revolutionary Jacobinism of their youth and – to Hazlitt's everlasting dismay – embraced the Tory spirit of the Regency; or France, where Napoleon's defeat at Waterloo led to the restoration of the Bourbon dynasty, American romanticism developed in tandem with many of the economic, political, and religious forces that drove the nation's expansion. In the USA, that is, romanticism did not so much lead to a counter-revolutionary reaction as recalibrate the commercial and spiritual aspirations at the heart of the budding American dream. This goes some way towards explaining not only the more optimistic mood of much nineteenth-century romantic, or 'transcendentalist', literature, but also the warm reception that European, especially British, romanticism often receives in the American academy.

At the centre of American romanticism, and of the American intellectual tradition, are Emerson and Henry David Thoreau. Emerson, especially, created a new cultural ground out of his experience, much as he remade his life after the death of his first wife, Ellen Tucker Emerson, in 1831. But he did not create this ground in a vacuum. Partly as a result of a trip to England in 1832–1833 and meetings with Wordsworth, Coleridge and Carlyle, Emerson underwent a gradual but decisive transformation that bore fruit not only in the essay *Nature* but in lectures and addresses such as 'The American Scholar' (1837) and the Divinity School Address (1838), two series of *Essays* (1841, 1844), the often (unjustly) overlooked *Representative Men* (1850) and the late work *The Conduct of Life* (1860). Known for his searching essays, among which 'Self-Reliance', 'Circles', 'The Poet', 'Experience' and 'Fate', are perhaps representative, it is hard to overestimate his influence on authors such as Bronson Alcott, Margaret Fuller, Nathaniel Hawthorne, Edgar Allan Poe, Herman Melville, Emily Dickinson and Walt Whitman. In a very real sense, Emerson is responsible for the initial 'grounding' of American literature.[2]

At the same time, Emerson gestures towards something greater. In a well-known fragment Friedrich Schlegel gave his assessment of modern literature as follows: "The whole history of modern poetry is a running commentary on the following brief philosophical text: all art should become science and all science [should become] art; poetry and philosophy should be united."[3] The works of Emerson and Thoreau, especially Emerson's, embody what 'modern poetry' in this sense might look like in an American context, just as the works of Coleridge and Wordsworth do in an English one. Only this time, the apotheosis of romantic poetry's fragmentary imperative – always becoming but never completed – is the essay. As if instructed to carry out Schlegel's new program for poetry, Emerson confesses at the end of 'Experience' (1844): 'Illusion, Temperament, Succession, Surface, Surprise, Reality, Subjectiveness, – these are threads on the loom of time, these are the lords of life. I dare not assume to give their order, but I name them as I find them in

---

[1] Ralph Waldo Emerson. *Selected Essays*. Ed. Larzer Ziff. New York: Penguin, 1982. 35. All quotations are hereafter taken from this edition and cited by page number.

[2] I borrow this idea from Stephen Fredman. *The Grounding of American Poetry: Charles Olson and the Emersonian Tradition*. Cambridge: Cambridge University Press, 1993.

[3] Friedrich Schlegel, *Philosophical Fragments*. Trans. Peter Firchow, 1971; Minneapolis and Oxford: University of Minneapolis Press, 1991. 14.

my way. I know better than to claim any completeness for my picture. I am a fragment, and this is a fragment of me' (309).

In the introduction to *The Visionary Company* (1971), the critic Harold Bloom articulates a counter-narrative of English literary tradition that is designed to displace the syllabus established by the poet and critic T. S. Eliot in a series of books and essays written during the first half of the twentieth century. With uncommon clarity, Bloom writes:

> To understand fully the link between the Revolution and English Romantic literature, it is perhaps most immediately illuminating to consider the case, not of one of its great poets, but of the critic William Hazlitt . . .
>
> Like that of all the English Romantic poets, Hazlitt's religious background was in the tradition of Protestant dissent, the kind of nonconformist vision that descended from the Left Wing of England's Puritan movement. There is no more important point to be made about English Romantic poetry than this one, or indeed about English poetry in general, particularly since it is a displaced Protestantism, or a Protestantism astonishingly transformed by different kinds of humanism or naturalism. The poetry of the English Romantics is a kind of religious poetry, and the religion is in the Protestant line, though Calvin or Luther would have been horrified to contemplate it. Indeed, the entire continuity of English poetry that T. S. Eliot and his followers attacked is a radical Protestant or displaced Protestant tradition.[4]

In this brief text Bloom counters Eliot's version of English literary history by rewriting the story dialectically, answering the older critic by reinserting his conservative Anglo-Catholic tradition into a larger cultural conservation in which the major role is actually played by an endlessly protean, if radical, Protestantism. It is a dazzling image of tradition that captures something essential about literature and, the tendency for overreaching aside, one in which either Emerson or Thoreau could easily be substituted for Hazlitt.

This is so because, for better and for worse, such a reading is profoundly American. Thoreau, the author of *Walden* (1854), would certainly share Bloom's – and Hazlitt's – disdain for religious formalism and, equally, celebrate the inner colloquy that animates authentic spiritual experience. In a late essay called 'Life without Principle' (1858), Thoreau characteristically quips: 'In proportion as our inward life fails, we go more constantly and desperately to the post-office.'[5] A witty moment to be sure, but such was Thoreau's view of the lengths to which human beings will go in order to avoid contact with their interior paramours. In a memorial tribute titled simply 'Thoreau' (1862), written after his friend's death, Emerson writes: 'He was born a protestant' (394). Moreover, '[h]e was a protestant *á outrance* [to the fullest extent], and few lives contain so many renunciations' (395). The idea that Thoreau 'renounced' things lends the essay an aura of spiritual biography, as if Emerson were recounting the life of some monk or hermit who lived life according to the discipline of a religious rule. Moreover, the use of the word 'protestant' to describe Thoreau communicates Emerson's faith in the renewable energy of protest at

---

[4] Harold Bloom. 'Prometheus Rising: The Backgrounds of Romantic Poetry' xiii–xxv in *The Visionary Company: A Reading of English Romantic Poetry*, revised and enlarged edition, 1961; Ithaca and London: Cornell University Press, 1971. xvii–xix.

[5] *Henry David Thoreau: Collected Essays and Poems*. Ed. Elizabeth Hall Witherell. New York: Library of America, 2001. 361.

work within the larger structures of institutionalized Protestantism, an energy needed in order to keep it honest and faithful, free from the temptation of empty ritual. In short, writes Emerson with obvious admiration, overlaying religious with explicitly political significance, '[n]o truer American existed than Thoreau' (398).

Much the same could actually be said of Emerson. In one of his best-known essays, 'Self-Reliance' (1841), Emerson strikes a bold note regarding the self. He writes:

> To believe your own thought, to believe that what is true for you in your private heart is true for all men, – that is genius. Speak your latent conviction, and it shall be the universal sense; for the inmost in due time becomes the outmost, and our first thought is rendered back to us by the trumpets of the Last Judgment. . . . In every work of genius we recognize our own rejected thoughts; they come back to us with a certain alienated majesty. Great works of art have no more affecting lesson for us than this. They teach us to abide by our spontaneous impression with good-humored inflexibility then most when the whole cry of voices is on the other side. Else to-morrow a stranger will say with masterly good sense precisely what we have thought and felt at the time, and we shall be forced to take with shame our own opinion from another. (175–176)

This is an exhortation that perhaps only an American could fully appreciate. Of course, it smacks of a stubborn New England piety that resists outside interference. But, truth be told, the trace of a radical reinterpretation of Kant's categorical imperative – 'to believe that what is true for you in your private heart is true for all men' – is also clearly visible. Emerson, for his part, surely means to advocate something more than self-interest or juvenile egotism. His is a vision of the mature self finally awakened from its slumbers and ready to spend its inheritance, a self at long last willing to trust that God sometimes speaks extraordinary truths through the lips of ordinary women and men.

The mention of Kant is not an idle gesture. In a series of lectures and essays published over the years, the philosopher Stanley Cavell has argued that Emerson and Thoreau can profitably be read as part of a genealogy of indigenous American reflection on the idea of the ordinary, and the accompanying idea of acknowledgement as an alternative to knowing, that hearkens back to Kant, via Coleridge and Wordsworth, and that anticipates the later work of both Heidegger and Wittgenstein. In claiming this, Cavell pays special attention to Emerson's essay 'Experience'. Reconsidering his early preference for Thoreau – articulated in *The Senses of Walden* (1972) – and discerning clear echoes of Kant in the essay, Cavell writes: 'Now I see that I might, even ought to, have seen Emerson ahead of me, since, for example, his essay on "Experience" is about the epistemology, or say the logic, of moods.'[6] He goes on to press the idea of Emerson-as-thinker:

> My claim is that Emerson is out to destroy the ground on which such a problem [whether the successive colors or moods of the universe are subjective or objective] takes itself seriously, I mean interprets itself as a metaphysical fixture. The universe is separate from me, but as intimately a part of me, as one on whose behalf I contest, and who therefore wears my color. We are in a state of 'romance' with the universe (to use a word from the last sentence of the essay); we do not possess it, but our life is to return to it, in ever-widening circles . . .

[6] Stanley Cavell. *The Senses of Walden: An Expanded Edition*, 1972; Chicago and London: University of Chicago Press, 1992. 125–126. Hereafter cited by page number.

The Kantian ring of the idea of the universe as inevitably wearing our color is, notwithstanding, pertinent. Its implication is that the way specifically Kant understands the generation of the universe keeps it solipsistic, still something partial, something of our, of my, making. Emerson's most explicit reversal of Kant lies in his picturing the intellectual hemisphere of knowledge as passive or receptive and the intuitive or instinctive hemisphere as active or spontaneous. (128)

Like Wordsworth, then (on a certain way of reading him), Emerson holds the world with a wise passiveness accountable only to itself, and indicates that if the world answers to our conceptions of it, it nonetheless answers in ways that leave room for withdrawal, mystery, even second-thoughts. It answers to our conceptions of it, in other words, not logically or systematically but, as it were, romantically and gratuitously, as a gift which gives in a way that could never have been anticipated and whose gifts are as surprising as they are unwarranted.

THE IMPACT OF EUROPEAN ROMANTICISM ON JAPAN *Ayumi Mizukoshi*

Does Japanese Romanticism exist at all? The answer is, it certainly did. Take any dictionary of or companion to modern Japanese literature, and you will find the definition of 'Romanticism' (*roman shugi*): a literary movement characterized by an uninhibited celebration of self, by an exaltation of personal, natural feelings and by a yearning for individual freedom from any moral and social constraints. You will also find out that the Japanese Romantic movement lasted for about two decades at the turn of the twentieth century, roughly from 1890 to 1910.[1] This nearly hundred-year time lag between European Romanticism and its Japanese counterpart was due not only to geographical distance but to Japan's specific geopolitical position on the world map in the mid-nineteenth century.

While the European powers were relentlessly expanding their colonial empires over the globe throughout the seventeenth and eighteenth centuries, Japan had chosen to cut off all diplomatic and commercial ties with Western countries (except those with the Dutch) to enjoy relative peace and prosperity in seclusion for more than two hundred years. It should not be, therefore, hard to imagine how rudely shocked and totally disorientated the Japanese felt in 1853, when Matthew Perry of the USA with a squadron of four warships arrived at the entrance to Tokyo Bay (then called Edo Bay), eventually to force them to open up their country. In the eyes of the Japanese, Commodore Perry's 'black ships' (*kurofune*) symbolized the indisputably superior military strength and industrial power of the West. The following decade witnessed the unprecedented social upheaval and political turmoil, fuelled not only by external imperialistic pressures but also by internal power struggles. In 1867, finally, the enfeebled shogunate agreed to return sovereign power to the imperial dynasty which had ruled Japan until the twelfth century. The following year the 'Restoration' of rule to the Emperor was proclaimed and Edo was renamed Tokyo, which marked the beginning of the 'modern' period in Japanese history.

The nature of the Restoration of 1868, say, whether it was a military coup or a nationalist revolution, or whether it was the product of the Western impact or the ultimate outcome of the gradual social and economic changes during the period of seclusion, has been the subject of

[1] We are not concerned here with the 'Japan Romantic School' (*Nihon romanha*), a group of ultra-right nationalist writers who in the late 1930s fiercely criticized Western-imported modernity and advocated the restoration of the Japanese tradition. As you might guess, these writers modelled themselves on the German Romantics.

much debate. Yet no historian would deny the fact that the year 1868 inaugurated Japan's dramatic transformation from a feudal country into a modern nation state. Under the banner of equality with the great powers of the world, Japan plunged into a swift and sweeping modernization programme, replacing feudal institutions with Western-style political, social, economic and educational systems: the British-style navy, the French-style army and the Prussian-style constitution, to name but a few. The hereditary four-status system (warriors, farmers, artisans and merchants) had been abolished by the mid-1870s, which transformed the majority of the samurai, the former feudal elite, into a mere small portion of the entire populace. In the consequent more mobile and meritocratic social order, the whole nation underwent an identity crisis struggling for social, economic, cultural and psychological survival. In the meantime Japan managed to win the Sino-Japanese War (1894–1895) and the Russo-Japanese War (1904–1905) in succession, and by the end of the first decade of the twentieth century it became one of the world's major powers.

The Japanese Romantics, having been born after the 1868 Restoration and grown up with the cataclysmic changes whose impact may well be comparable to that of the French Revolution, belonged to the first generation of modern Japan. What characterized them most was their eager and enthusiastic embrace of Western individualism, that is, to quote Janet A. Walker, 'the idea that the existence, the energy, and the morality of the individual are valuable in their own right and worthy of cultural attention and respect'.[2] And it was chiefly through Western (especially Romantic) literature, along with Christianity, that the Japanese Romantic writers absorbed and appropriated the idea of individualism.[3] The self, or more precisely the inner self, was now seen as the sole agent of artistic activity, and the only purpose of art (or even of life) as self-expression. With this new sense of self, liberated (so they hoped) from the social and moral burden of the feudal past, the young Japanese Romantics launched their literary careers in the brave new modern world. The standard history of Japanese literature classifies its Romantic writers into two groups: the 'early' Romantics whose works mostly appeared in their coterie magazine *Literary World* (*Bungakkai*) in the 1890s, and the 'late' Romantics clustering around the poetry and fine arts magazine *Morning Star* (*Myôjô*) in the 1900s. The major Japanese Romantics to be treated in this essay are two male writers such as Kitamura Tôkoku and Shimazaki Tôson from the former group, and a female poet Yosano Akiko from the latter.[4]

Kitamura Tôkoku (1868–1894), the charismatic leader of the *Literary World* circle, was the eldest son of a former (low-ranking) samurai. Unlike his class of youths who desperately tried to make it in the newly modern and mobile world, however, Tôkoku aspired not to earthly wealth but to spiritual freedom.[5] As an impassioned and impressionable teenager Tôkoku

---

[2] Janet A. Walker. *The Japanese Novel of the Meiji Period and the Ideal of Individualism*. Princeton: Princeton University Press, 1979. vii–viii.

[3] The two-and-a-half-century ban on Christianity was lifted in 1873. See Otis Cary. *A History of Christianity in Japan*. 2 vols. New York: Fleming H. Revell Company, 1909.

[4] Japanese names are given in the Japanese order of last name first. I follow the general rule that the writers who thrived in the early stage of modern Japanese literature are normally referred to by their first names, for example, Tôkoku for Kitamura Tôkoku.

[5] Samuel Smile's *Self-Help* (translated in 1870), which was (mis)read as a treatise on worldly success, turned out to be *the* best-seller among the ambitious youth of samurai origin. See Earl H. Kinmonth. *The Self-Made Man in Meiji Japanese Thought: From Samurai to Salary Man*. Berkeley: University of California Press, 1981.

became involved with the political movement for 'Freedom and People's Rights' (*jiyû minken*), but within a few years euphoria turned into disillusionment.[6] Subsequent events in his life, such as his falling love with Ishizuka Mina, a devout Christian and the daughter of an illustrious leader of the People's Rights movement, his conversion to Christianity under Mina's influence followed by their marriage in church (Tôkoku was barely twenty years old, and Mina was twenty-three), and the financial difficulties which put a great strain on what was once a passionate relationship (their premarital private correspondence was probably the first recorded example of romantic love in Japan), all contributed to precipitating Tôkoku's 'inward' turn. His poetry may duly be called the poetry of the interiorized self. In 1889 when he was 20, Tôkoku privately published *The Poem of the Prisoner* (*Soshû no shi*) which renders the solitary self as an internalized prison. *The Poem of the Prisoner*, evidently inspired by Byron's *The Prisoner of Chillon*, was not only Tôkoku's first work but also arguably the earliest Japanese attempt at a long narrative poem written in the 'new style'. So-called new-style verse (*shintaishi*), as distinguished from such traditional verse forms as 31-syllable *waka* (literally, 'Japanese song') and 17-syllable *haiku*, was a kind of free and much longer verse heavily influenced by the Western notion of 'poetry'. And this newly introduced literary genre, freed from the strict rules of poetic diction and syllabic meter (5-7-5-7-7 for *waka*, and 5-7-5 for *haiku*), was then hailed as an apposite means of expressing the complex thoughts and emotions of the modern individual. Two years later, Tôkoku again privately published *The Sacred Mountain* (*Hôraikyoku*), an unfinished dramatic poem modelled on Byron's *Manfred*. In the preface Tôkoku declares that the poem is not meant to be performed on the stage but to give expression to his inmost emotions. Indeed the author's inner conflict is revealed through the anguished speech the poem's Byronic hero delivers: he is tormented by his own sense of divided self – the flesh and the spirit, the human and the divine, and the finite and the infinite. Tôkoku's desire for the freedom of the spirit, to be released from the confines of the flesh, was so intense that one contemporary critic dubbed him the 'Romantic Idealist' (*romanchikku aideiarisuto*).

Being one of the pioneers in the sphere of modern Japanese poetry, however, Tôkoku's reputation rests on his critical essays rather than on his poetic attempts. During his short literary career from 1889 to 1894, Tôkoku contributed a large number of essays to the *Literary World* and other periodicals, among which those discussing 'the inner life' are the finest expressions of his uniquely (almost un-Japanese) 'Romantic' strain. In his essay 'On the Inner Life' (*Naibu seimei ron*) published a year before his tragic death, Tôkoku insisted that man's 'life' should be seen not as a mere life of 50 years but as the embodiment of the fundamental, 'inner life', without which any religion, any philosophy, any literature and indeed any human experience would be hollow and worthless. Tôkoku undoubtedly derived the idea of the inner life from the Christian (especially Protestant) emphasis on the inner self of the individual, for he praised the missionaries for having planted 'the tree of life' in the Japanese mind. Yet developing the notion of the God-given inner life, Tôkoku took a step forward in the Romantic direction: only the inspired *poet* can fully experience his own inner life being in the state of communion with the spirit of the universe, or with God. Hence, as Tôkoku passionately proclaims, the duty of the poet-philosopher is to convey to the world the 'Various Manifestations' (he writes this phrase in English) of the inner life. For all his belief in this life-giving principle, however, he suffered from increasingly severe depression, and committed suicide. It may be argued that Tôkoku's

---

[6] John Stuart Mill's *On Liberty* (translated in 1871) was the bible for the People's Rights movement which flourished in the late 1870s and early 1880s.

short life was an archetypal, though unsuccessful, struggle to acquire a new mode of subjectivity with its newly created inner depth.

Shimazaki Tôson (1872–1943), the closest friend of and acknowledged successor to Tôkoku, was one of the most renowned 'new-style' poets of the day, and is now widely recognized as the founder of modern Japanese poetry. Born into a distinguished family of the rural gentry, Tôson spent his formative years in a Western-style school founded by American and Scottish Presbyterians. He was baptized at the age of 16 (though he lost his faith a few years later), but his baptism was not so much in Christianity itself as in Western literature. Young Tôson became infatuated with the canonical works of European literature such as Wordsworth, Byron, Shelley, Shakespeare, Milton, Burns, Goethe and Dante (the latter two read in English translation), among whom he was particularly enamoured of the English Romantics. What thrilled the young Romantic-to-be was the discovery that his own innermost feelings – youthful passion, love, angst and wanderlust – were happily expressed in Wordsworth, Byron and Shelley.[7] Following his graduation from the Presbyterian school in 1891, Tôson tentatively embarked on a literary career and began to publish small pieces of translation. (This was against the expectations of his family who wanted him to go into business.) Yet it was through his association with the *Literary World* (founded in 1892) that Tôson gradually acquired his own language of self-expression which was to become a new poetic voice for the first modern generation. Tôson's first collection of new-style verse, *Seedlings* (*Wakanashû*), was published in 1897 when he was 25, and this slim volume took young men and women by Romantic storm. In contrast with Tôkoku's privately published poems which was, though pioneering, virtually unknown at the time, Tôson's *Seedlings* was acclaimed as the first book of new-style verse that gave full voice to the sentiments of the modern individual. Tôson's popular appeal was due to his offering a new structure of feeling, especially that of romantic love, in revolt against the poetic and social ancien régime.[8] In addition, the poet's use of the traditional meter consisting of seven and five syllables and the consequent pleasurable recitability also contributed to the immense popularity of *Seedlings*. This strange mingling of *waka*-derived diction with novel imagery taken from Romantic poetry, the Bible and Christian hymns (the translation of hymn books began as early as 1874) struck contemporary readers as the dawn of modern Japanese poetry. Tôson published another three poetical volumes between 1898 and 1901, after which he left poetry for prose. Throughout the rest of his long career as a novelist, Tôson never ceased to explore the possibilities of representing the self. In the sphere of poetry, however, Tôson's creation of modern subjectivity was succeeded by Yosano Akiko's even more celebratory song of the 'I'.

Yosano Akiko (1878–1942) reigned as queen of the late Japanese Romantics whose organ *Morning Star* (founded in 1900) with its poetic creed of originality and individuality drew a

[7] It must be noted that the Japanese reception of English Romanticism in the late nineteenth century was heavily influenced and curiously refracted by Hippolyte Taine's *Histoire de la litterature anglaise* (1863–1864), the English translation of which *History of English Literature* (1871) was widely read in intellectual circles and frequently used as a textbook in private schools that were then proliferating. Interestingly, Taine was the first person to categorize the English poets of the early nineteenth century as the 'romantic school', under the label of which were included Lamb, Coleridge, Southey, Moore, Scott, Wordsworth, Shelley and Byron (Blake got no mention, and the name of Keats appeared only once). See David Perkins. *Is Literary History Possible?* Baltimore: The Johns Hopkins University Press, 1992. 96–97.

[8] For the introduction of romantic love into modern Japan, see Takayuki Yokota-Murakami, *Don Juan East/West: On the Problematics of Comparative Literature*. Albany: State University of New York Press, 1998. 35–80.

constellation of young poets and artists. The leader of the *Morning Star* society (and later Akiko's husband) was Yosano Tekkan (1873–1935), one of the major reformers of the traditional *waka* genre. However, it was Akiko's *Tangled Hair* (*Midaregami*) published in 1901 that revived and revolutionized the 1,400-year-old Japanese lyric. Classical *waka* burdened with stylistic conventions was now renamed and successfully modernized into *tanka* (literally, 'short song') as a vehicle for the spontaneous overflow of powerful, individual feelings. While abiding by the time-honoured 5-7-5-7-7 syllabic meter, Akiko suffused her 399 *tanka* in *Tangled Hair* with distinctly modern sentiments. Her total affirmation of sensual love and of (her own) female beauty, together with her daring defiance of classical decorum and of Confucian morality, made 22-year-old Akiko an overnight sensation. Akiko's poetic persona – an emancipated young woman – was no doubt derived from her real-life experiences. Akiko was born as the third daughter of a family who ran an established confectionary in a port city near Osaka. Although she was given an unusually high education for a girl from a mercantile background, Akiko left school at the age of 17 as expected of any woman in that early modern period. While helping manage the family business, in her leisure hours she immersed herself not only in the classics (such as *The Tale of Genji*) but also in new literature (including the *Literary World* her brother in Tokyo sent her). Through Tōson and other new-style poets, as Donald Keene puts it, 'she directly absorbed the Japanese Romanticism of the *Bungakkai* [*Literary World*] group, and indirectly the European Romanticism that had inspired them.'[9] As a girl with a poetic turn of mind, Akiko started dabbling in both old-style *waka* and new-style verse. And her encounter with Tekkan's *tanka* (whose colloquial diction deeply impressed her) and later with Tekkan himself finally and completely transformed the demure maiden into a passionate, Romantic poetess. Within a year of their meeting, Akiko fled her home to Tokyo to live with Tekkan who had not yet separated from his (second) wife and their child. Akiko's *Tangled Hair* which came out only two months after this tempestuous love affair scandalized the traditional stratum of society as well as electrified the younger generation. In the eyes of ardent admirers, Akiko was the modern 'I' incarnate – independent, individualist and free from the shackles of (what they saw as) the benighted feudal era.

European Romanticism, as has been argued, served as a catalyst for the invention of the modern Japanese self. You may recall that the Romantic writers discussed above were all young poets: Tōkoku killed himself at the age of 25, Tōson left the realm of poetry before he became 30, and Akiko's popularity had declined by 1908 when the *Morning Star* was discontinued. Short-lived as it was, the Japanese Romantic movement played an integral part of the modernizing process of Japanese literature. According to the standard literary history, the Romantic project of expressing the true voice of feeling laid the foundation for the 'I-novel' (*shi-shōsetsu*), a type of autobiographical novel which is generally accepted as 'the most salient and unique form of modern Japanese literature'.[10] The very ideas of literary history and of national literature originated most probably from European Romanticism, but a full discussion of that topic is beyond the scope of this humble essay.

---

[9] Donald Keene. *A History of Japanese Literature* IV. New York: Columbia University Press, 1999. 22.
[10] Tomi Suzuki, *Narrating the Self: Fictions of Japanese Modernity*. Stanford: Stanford University Press, 1996. 1.

PART 2

Texts

I. Art

The texts chosen here reflect the ways in [...] [...] life [...]
both of Romantic thinking and of Roman[...] [...] [...]
as the main figure in a text. The growth o[...] [...] simple expressions)
by the emergence of serious philosophical r[...] [...] [...]
aspects of human life. The themes of the ima[...] [...] [...]
for a substitute for religion, art and politics, t[...] ence/regular feeling
play a major role in the choice of texts. The special status of 'literature' that emerges with
Romanticism is also explored. This section includes the primary Romantic manifestos, most
of them German or English, but with a few French examples: Wordsworth, Coleridge, Shelley
and the Schlegels. Also important are theories of irony: not just the obvious German ironists,
but also Kierkegaard in Denmark and Peacock in England.

a. BRITISH

I.a.1. WILLIAM WORDSWORTH, from Advertisement to *Lyrical Ballads*

The majority of the following poems are to be considered as experiments. They were written
chiefly with a view to ascertain how far the language of conversation in the middle and lower
classes of society is adapted to the purposes of poetic pleasure. Readers accustomed to the
gaudiness and inane phraseology of many modern writers, if they persist in reading this book
to its conclusion, will perhaps frequently have to struggle with feelings of strangeness and awk-
wardness: they will look round for poetry, and will be induced to inquire by what species of
courtesy these attempts can be permitted to assume that title. It is desirable that such readers,
for their own sakes, should not suffer the solitary word Poetry, a word of very disputed meaning,
to stand in the way of their gratification; but that, while they are perusing this book, they should
ask themselves if it contains a natural delineation of human passions, human characters, and
human incidents; and if the answer be favourable to the author's wishes, that they should consent to be pleased in spite of that most dreadful enemy to our pleasures, our own pre-established
codes of decision.

[1798]

I.a.2. WILLIAM WORDSWORTH, from Preface to *Lyrical Ballads*

The principal object, then, proposed in these Poems was to choose incidents and situations
from common life, and to relate or describe them, throughout, as far as was possible in a selection
of language really used by men, and, at the same time, to throw over them a certain colouring of

imagination, whereby ordinary things should be presented to the mind in an unusual aspect; and, further, and above all, to make these incidents and situations interesting by tracing in them, truly though not ostentatiously, the primary laws of our nature: chiefly, as far as regards the manner in which we associate ideas in a state of excitement. Humble and rustic life was generally chosen, because, in that condition, the essential passions of the heart find a better soil in which they can attain their maturity, are less under restraint, and speak a plainer and more emphatic language; because in that condition of life our elementary feelings coexist in a state of greater simplicity, and, consequently, may be more accurately contemplated, and more forcibly communicated; because the manners of rural life germinate from those elementary feelings, and, from the necessary character of rural occupations, are more easily comprehended, and are more durable; and, lastly, because in that condition the passions of men are incorporated with the beautiful and permanent forms of nature. The language, too, of these men has been adopted (purified indeed from what appear to be its real defects, from all lasting and rational causes of dislike or disgust) because such men hourly communicate with the best objects from which the best part of language is originally derived; and because, from their rank in society and the sameness and narrow circle of their intercourse, being less under the influence of social vanity, they convey their feelings and notions in simple and unelaborated expressions. Accordingly, such a language, arising out of repeated experience and regular feelings, is a more permanent, and a far more philosophical language, than that which is frequently substituted for it by Poets, who think that they are conferring honour upon themselves and their art, in proportion as they separate themselves from the sympathies of men, and indulge in arbitrary and capricious habits of expression, in order to furnish food for fickle tastes, and fickle appetites, of their own creation.

I cannot, however, be insensible to the present outcry against the triviality and meanness, both of thought and language, which some of my contemporaries have occasionally introduced into their metrical compositions; and I acknowledge that this defect, where it exists, is more dishonourable to the Writer's own character than false refinement or arbitrary innovation, though I should contend at the same time, that it is far less pernicious in the sum of its consequences. From such verses the Poems in these volumes will be found distinguished at least by one mark of difference, that each of them has a worthy purpose. Not that I always began to write with a distinct purpose formerly conceived; but habits of meditation have, I trust, so prompted and regulated my feelings, that my descriptions of such objects as strongly excite those feelings, will be found to carry along with them a purpose. If this opinion be erroneous, I can have little right to the name of a Poet. For all good poetry is the spontaneous overflow of powerful feelings: and though this be true, Poems to which any value can be attached were never produced on any variety of subjects but by a man who, being possessed of more than usual organic sensibility, had also thought long and deeply. For our continued influxes of feeling are modified and directed by our thoughts, which are indeed the representatives of all our past feelings; and, as by contemplating the relation of these general representatives to each other, we discover what is really important to men, so, by the repetition and continuance of this act, our feelings will be connected with important subjects, till at length, if we be originally possessed of much sensibility, such habits of mind will be produced, that, by obeying blindly and mechanically the impulses of those habits, we shall describe objects, and utter sentiments, of such a nature, and in such connexion with each other, that the understanding of the Reader must necessarily be in some degree enlightened, and his affections strengthened and purified.

* * *

I have said that poetry is the spontaneous overflow of powerful feelings: it takes its origin from emotion recollected in tranquillity: the emotion is contemplated till, by a species of reaction, the tranquillity gradually disappears, and an emotion, kindred to that which was before the subject of contemplation, is gradually produced, and does itself actually exist in the mind. In this mood successful composition generally begins, and in a mood similar to this it is carried on; but the emotion, of whatever kind, and in whatever degree, from various causes, is qualified by various pleasures, so that in describing any passions whatsoever, which are voluntarily described, the mind will, upon the whole, be in a state of enjoyment. If Nature be thus cautious to preserve in a state of enjoyment a being so employed, the Poet ought to profit by the lesson held forth to him, and ought especially to take care, that, whatever passions he communicates to his Reader, those passions, if his Reader's mind be sound and vigorous, should always be accompanied with an overbalance of pleasure. Now the music of harmonious metrical language, the sense of difficulty overcome, and the blind association of pleasure which has been previously received from works of rhyme or met___ ____ ____ or similar construction, an indistinct perception perpetually renewed of langu_ _____ __ ___ ____ ____ _____ in the circumstance of metre, differing from it so _ ____ _____ _____ _____ _____ ng of delight, which is of the most import_ _____ _____ _____ _____ ermingled with powerful descriptions of t_ _____ _____ _____ _____ _athetic and impassioned poetry; while, i_ _____ _____ _____ _____ _ich the Poet manages his numbers are the_ _____ _____ _____ _____ on of the Reader.

[1800]

[handwritten note:]
- Poems of romantleism are not arbitray/ caprecious and thus have a worthy purpose (not trivial/mean)
- they do not seperate themselves from the sympatrics of men
- worthy purpose sets these poems apart
- poetry should come from spontaneous overflow of powerful feelings and Wires men to think deeply

I.a.3. WILL___ _____ _____ _____ _____ _____ [expanded text]

Taking up the_ _____ _____ _____ _____ _____ s meant by the word Poet? What is a Poe_ _____ _____ _____ _____ _____ _age is to be expected from him? – He is a_ _____ _____ _____ _____ _____ more lively sensibility, more enthusiasm a_ _____ _____ _____ _____ _____ nature, and a more comprehensive soul, _ _____ _____ _____ _____ _ man pleased with his own passions and v_ _____ _____ _____ _____ e spirit of life that is in him; delighting to co_ _____ _____ _____ _____ sted in the goings-on of the Universe, and habitually impelled to cr___ _____ _____ find them. To these qualities he has added a disposition to be affected more than other men by absent things as if they were present; an ability of conjuring up in himself passions, which are indeed far from being the same as those produced by real events, yet (especially in those parts of the general sympathy which are pleasing and delightful) do more nearly resemble the passions produced by real events, than anything which, from the motions of their own minds merely, other men are accustomed to feel in themselves: – whence, and from practice, he has acquired a greater readiness and power in expressing what he thinks and feels, and especially those thoughts and feelings which, by his own choice, or from the structure of his own mind, arise in him without immediate external excitement.

I.a.4. WILLIAM HAZLITT, from 'On Gusto'

Gusto in art is power or passion defining any object. – It is not so difficult to explain this term in what relates to expression (of which it may be said to be the highest degree) as in what relates to things without expression, to the natural appearances of objects, as mere colour or form. In

one sense, however, there is hardly any object entirely devoid of expression, without some character of power belonging to it, some precise association with pleasure or pain: and it is in giving this truth of character from the truth of feeling, whether in the highest or the lowest degree, but always in the highest degree of which the subject is capable, that gusto consists.

There is a gusto in the colouring of Titian. Not only do his heads seem to think – his bodies seem to feel. This is what the Italians mean by the *morbidezza*[1] of his flesh-colour. It seems sensitive and alive all over; not merely to have the look and texture of flesh, but the feeling in itself. For example, the limbs of his female figures have a luxurious softness and delicacy, which appears conscious of the pleasure of the beholder. As the objects themselves in nature would produce an impression on the sense, distinct from every other object, and having something divine in it, which the heart owns and the imagination consecrates, the objects in the picture preserve the same impression, absolute, unimpaired, stamped with all the truth of passion, the pride of the eye, and the charm of beauty. Rubens makes his flesh-colour like flowers; Albano's is like ivory; Titian's is like flesh, and like nothing else. It is as different from that of other painters, as the skin is from a piece of white or red drapery thrown over it. The blood circulates here and there, the blue veins just appear, the rest is distinguished throughout only by that sort of tingling sensation to the eye, which the body feels within itself. This is gusto. – Vandyke's flesh colour, though it has great truth and purity, wants gusto. It has not the internal character, the living principle in it. It is a smooth surface, not a warm, moving mass. It is painted without passion, with indifference. The hand only has been concerned. The impression slides off from the eye, and does not, like the tones of Titian's pencil, leave a sting behind it in the mind of the spectator. The eye does not acquir[e] ⟨...⟩ ⟨...⟩ in painting is where the impression made o[n] ⟨...⟩

[1816]

I.a.5.   SAMUEL TAYLOR C⟨OLERIDGE⟩

[From Chapter XIII]

The IMAGINATION then I c⟨onsider⟩ ⟨...⟩ IMAGINA-
TION I hold to be the living P⟨ower⟩ ⟨...⟩ a repetition
in the finite mind of the etern⟨al⟩ ⟨...⟩ magination
I consider as an echo of the fo⟨rmer⟩ ⟨...⟩ entical with
the primary in the *kind* of its ⟨...⟩ f its operation. It dissolves, diffuses, d⟨...⟩ is rendered
impossible, yet still at all ever ⟨...⟩ *ital*, even as
all objects (*as* objects) are ess⟨...⟩

FANCY, on the contrary, ⟨...⟩ finites. The
fancy is indeed no other than ⟨...⟩ e and space,
and blended with, and modif⟨ied by⟩ ⟨...⟩ e express by
the word CHOICE. But equally with the ordinary memory it must receive all its materials ready made from the law of association . . .

Handwritten note:
> a.5 IMAGINATION
> Primary: agent of all human
> Perception / extension of
> the infinite in the finite mind
> Secondary: echo of first
> works with concious will
> (similar to primary in action
> but different in amount &
> method)
> FANCY: mode of memory
> seperate from time/space
> & influenced by CHOICE (will)

* * *

[1] Softness or delicacy.

[From Chapter XIV] Chapter XIV

During the first year that Mr. Wordsworth and I were neighbours, our conversations turned frequently on the two cardinal points of poetry, the power of exciting the sympathy of the reader by a faithful adherence to the truth of nature, and the power of giving the interest of novelty by the modifying colours of imagination. The sudden charm, which accidents of light and shade, which moonlight or sun-set diffused over a known and familiar landscape, appeared to represent the practicability of combining both. These are the poetry of nature. The thought suggested itself (to which of us I do not recollect) that a series of poems might be composed of two sorts. In the one, the incidents and agents were to be, in part at least, supernatural; and the excellence aimed at was to consist in the interesting of the affections by the dramatic truth of such emotions as would naturally accompany such situations, supposing them real. And real in this sense they have been to every human being who, from whatever source of delusion, has at any time believed himself under supernatural agency. For the second class, subjects were to be chosen from ordinary life; the characters and incidents were to be such, as will be found in every village and its vicinity, where there is a meditative and feeling mind to seek after them, or to notice them, when they present themselves.

In this idea originated the plan of the 'Lyrical Ballads;' in which it was agreed, that my endeavours should be directed to persons and characters supernatural, or at least romantic, yet so as to transfer from our in[ner nature a human interest and a semblance of truth] sufficient to procure for these shadow[s of imagination that willing suspension of disbelief] for the moment, which constitutes poe[tic faith . . . Mr. Wordsworth, on the other hand, was to pro]pose to himself as his object, to give the [charm of novelty to things of every day, and to excite] a feeling analogous to the supernatural, b[y awakening the mind's attention from the lethargy of] custom, and directing it to the loveliness [and the wonders of the world before us; an inexhausti]ble treasure, but for which in consequenc[e of the film of familiarity and selfish solicitude we ha]ve eyes, yet see not, ears that hear not, an[d hearts that neither feel nor understand.]

With this view I w[rote . . . For the second volume, I had prepared the 'Dark Ladie,' and the 'Chr[istabel' . . . But Mr. Wordsworth's industry had proved so much more than I had done in my first [attempt . . . that I was compelled to acknowledge . . . he had reali]zed my ideal, than I had done in my first [attempt . . . that I was compelled to acknowledge . . . he had reali] much more successful, and the number of hi[s poems so much greater, that my compositions, instead] of forming a balance, appeared rather an in[terpolation of heterogeneous matter. Mr. Wordsworth] added two or three poems written in his ow[n character . . . the tale of the female vagrant . . . in dic]tion, which is characteristic of his genius. In[the 'Thorn,' the 'Idiot Boy' . . . his words were . . . w]ere presented by him as an *experiment*, whether [subjects, which from their nature rejected the] ornaments and extracolloquial style of poems in [a language fitted to their respective importanc]e of ordinary life as to produce the pleasurable interest, which it is the po[et's duty to] impart. To the second edition he added a preface of considerable length; in which notwithstanding some passages of apparently a contrary import, he was understood to contend for the extension of this style to poetry of all kinds, and to reject as vicious and indefensible all phrases and forms of style that were not included in what he (unfortunately, I think, adopting an equivocal expression) called the language of *real* life. From this preface, prefixed to poems in which it was impossible to deny the presence of original genius, however mistaken its direction might be deemed, arose the whole long continued controversy. For from the conjunction of perceived power with supposed heresy I explain the inveteracy and in some instances, I grieve to say, the acrimonious passions, with which the controversy has been conducted by the assailants.

POETRY

1. gain sympathy of reader through truth of nature

2. making it new through imagination

2 kinds of poems
- derived from supernatural
- derived from ordinary life

[...]on of forms not [...]ed in language of "real life"

Had Mr. Wordsworth's poems been the silly, the childish things, which they were for a long time described as being; had they been really distinguished from the compositions of other poets merely by meanness of language and inanity of thought; had they indeed contained nothing more than what is found in the parodies and pretended imitations of them; they must have sunk at once, a dead weight, into the slough of oblivion, and have dragged the preface along with them. But year after year increased the number of Mr. Wordsworth's admirers. They were found too not in the lower classes of the reading public, but chiefly among young men of strong ability and meditative minds; and their admiration (inflamed perhaps in some degree by opposition) was distinguished by its intensity, I might almost say, by its *religious* fervour. These facts, and the intellectual energy of the author, which was more or less consciously felt, where it was outwardly and even boisterously denied, meeting with sentiments of aversion to his opinions, and of alarm at their consequences, produced an eddy of criticism, which would of itself have borne up the poems by the violence, with which it whirled them round and round. With many parts of this preface in the sense attributed to them and which the words undoubtedly seem to authorize, I never concurred; but on the contrary objected to them as erroneous in principle, and as contradictory (in appearance at least) both to other parts of the same preface, and to the author's own practice in the greater number of the poems themselves. Mr. Wordsworth in his recent collection has, I find, degraded this prefatory disquisition to the end of his second volume, to be read or not at the reader's choice. But he has not, as far as I can discover, announced any change in his poetic creed. At all events, considering it as the source of a controversy, in which I have been honoured more than I deserve by the frequent conjunction of my name with his I think it expedient to declare once for all, in what points I coincide with his opinions, and in what points I altogether differ. But in order to render myself intelligible I must previously, in as few words as possible, explain my ideas, first, of a POEM; and secondly, of POETRY itself, in *kind*, and in *essence*.

The office of philosophical *disquisition* consists in just *distinction*; while it is the privilege of the philosopher to preserve himself constantly aware, that distinction is not division. In order to obtain adequate notions of any truth, we must intellectually separate its distinguishable parts; and this is the technical process of philosophy. But having so done, we must then restore them in our conceptions to the unity, in which they actually co-exist; and this is the *result* of philosophy. A poem contains the same elements as a prose composition; the difference therefore must consist in a different combination of them, in consequence of a different object proposed. According to the ⟨...⟩ combination. It is possible, that the object ⟨...⟩ facts or observations by artificial arrange⟨...⟩ because it is distinguished from compositio⟨...⟩ intly. In this, the lowest sense, a man mig⟨...⟩ umeration of the days in the several mont⟨...⟩

Thirty days h⟨...⟩
April, June, a⟨...⟩

and others of t⟨...⟩ is found in anticipating
the recurrence o⟨...⟩ this charm superadded,
whatever be thei⟨...⟩

(Handwritten note:)
POEM & POETRY

truth can only be found by breaking down into distinguishable parts

(vertical:) process of philosophy of philosophy

However, **must** be returned to unity

result of philosophy

poems have a kind of charm

So mu[...] contents supplies an additional
ground o[...]nication of truths; either of truth
absolute [...]erienced and recorded, as in history. Plea[...]may *result* from the *attainment* of
the end; b[...]communication of pleasure may
be the im[...]llectual, ought to be the ultimate
end, yet t[...]lass to which the work belongs.
Blessed in[...]ose would be baffled by the perversion of [...]n or imagery could exempt the
Bathyllus [...]t and aversion!

But the [...]bject of a work not metrically
composed [...]ed, as in novels and romances.
Would the [...]yme, entitle *these* to the name
of poems? [...]hich does not contain in itself
the reason [...], all other parts must be made
consonant [...]and distinct attention to each
part, which [...]d are calculated to excite. The
final defini[...] then so deduced, may be thus worded. A poem is that species of composition,
which is opposed to works of science [...]ruth;
and from all other species (having th[...]pos-
ing to itself such delight from the wh[...]each
component *part*.

Controversy is not seldom excited [...]rent
meaning to the same word; and in fe[...]utes
concerning the present subject. If a [...]h is
rhyme, or measure, or both, I must le[...]east
competent to characterize the writer'[...]vise
entertaining or affecting, as a tale, or a[...]s as
another fit ingredient of a poem, and [...]hat
of a legitimate poem, I answer, it mus[...]ain
each other; all in their proportion ha[...]wn
influences of metrical arrangement. Th[...]ate
judgement of all countries, in equally [...]o a
series of striking lines or distichs, each[...]to
itself disjoins it from its context, and n[...]rt;
and on the other hand, to an unsustain[...]he
general result unattracted by the component parts. The reader should be carried forward, not
merely or chiefly by the mechanical impulse of curiosity, or by a restless desire to arrive at the
final solution; but by the pleasurable activity of mind excited by the attractions of the journey
itself. Like the motion of a serpent, which the Egyptians made the emblem of intellectual power;
or like the path of sound through the air; at every step he pauses and half recedes, and from the
retrogressive movement collects the force which again carries him onward. *Precipitandus est
liber* spiritus[2], says Petronius Arbiter most happily. The epithet, *liber*, here balances the preceding
verb; and it is not easy to conceive more meaning condensed in fewer words.

[2] The *free* spirit must be hurried onward.

But if this should be admitted as a satisfactory character of a poem, we have still to seek for a definition of poetry. The writings of PLATO, and Bishop TAYLOR, and the Theoria Sacra of BURNET, furnish undeniable proofs that poetry of the highest kind may exist without metre and even without the contradistinguishing objects of a poem. The first chapter of Isaiah (indeed a very large proportion of the whole book) is poetry in the most emphatic sense, yet it would be not less irrational than strange to assert, that pleasure, and not truth, was the immediate object of the prophet. In short, whatever *specific* import we attach to the word, poetry, there, will be found involved in it, as a necessary consequence, that a poem of any length neither can be, or ought to be, all poetry. Yet if an harmonious whole is to be produced, the remaining parts must be preserved *in keeping* with the poetry; and this can be no otherwise effected than by such a studied selection and artificial arrangement, as will partake of one, though not a *peculiar*, property of poetry. And this again can be no other than the property of exciting a more continuous and equal attention, than the language of prose aims at, whether colloquial or written.

My own conclusions on the nature of poetry, in the strictest use of the word, have been in part anticipated in the preceding disquisition on the fancy and imagination. What is poetry? is so nearly the same question with, what is a poem? that the answer to the one is involved in the solution of the other. For it is a distinction resulting from the poetic genius itself, which sustains and modifies the images, thoughts, and emotions of the poet's own mind. A poet, described in *ideal* perfection, brings the whole soul of man into activity, with the subordination of its faculties to each other, according to their relative worth and dignity. He diffuses a tone, and spirit of unity, that blends, and (as it were) *fuses*, each into each, by that synthetic and magical power, to which we have exclusively appropriated the name of imagination. This power, first put in action by the will and understanding, and retained under their irremissive, though gentle and unnoticed, control (*laxis effertur habenis*[3]) reveals itself in the balance or reconciliation of opposite or discordant qualities: of sameness, with difference; of the general, with the concrete; the idea, with the image; the individual, with the representative; the sense of novelty and freshness, with old and familiar objects; a more than usual state of emotion, with more than usual order; judgement ever awake and steady self-possession, with enthusiasm and feeling profound or vehement; and while it blends and harmonizes the natural and the artificial, still subordinates art to nature; the manner to the matter; and our admiration of the poet to our sympathy with the poetry.

[1817]

I.a.6. JOHN KEATS, 'Ode on a Grecian Urn'

1

Thou still unravish'd bride of quietness,
    Thou foster-child of silence and slow time,
Sylvan historian, who canst thus express
    A flowery tale more sweetly than our rhyme:
What leaf-fring'd legend haunts about thy shape
    Of deities or mortals, or of both,
        In Tempe or the dales of Arcady?
    What men or gods are these? What maidens loth?

---

[3] It is carried onwards with loose reins.

What mad pursuit? What struggle to escape?
  What pipes and timbrels? What wild ecstasy?

2

Heard melodies are sweet, but those unheard
  Are sweeter; therefore, ye soft pipes, play on;
Not to the sensual ear, but, more end
  Pipe to the spirit
Fair youth, beneath t
  Thy song, nor ever
    Bold Lover, neve
  Though winning n
She cannot fade, thoug
    Forever wilt thou

Ah, happy, happy bough
  Your leaves, nor ever
And, happy melodist, un
    Forever piping songs fo
More happy love! more ha
  For ever warm and still
    For ever panting, and
  All breathing human pa   above,
That leaves a heart high-sorrowful and cloy'd,
    A burning forehead, and a parching tongue.

4

Who are these coming to the sacrifice?
  To what green altar, O mysterious priest,
Lead'st thou that heifer lowing at the skies,
  And all her silken flanks with garlands dressed?
What little town by river or sea shore,
  Or mountain-built with peaceful citadel,
    Is emptied of this folk, this pious morn?
  And, little town, thy streets for evermore
Will silent be; and not a soul to tell
    Why thou art desolate, can e'er return.

5

O Attic shape! Fair attitude! with brede
  Of marble men and maidens overwrought,

With forest branches and the trodden weed;
   Thou, silent form, dost tease us out of thought
As doth eternity: Cold Pastoral!
   When old age shall this generation waste,
     Thou shalt remain, in midst of other woe
Than ours, a friend to man, to whom thou say'st,
'Beauty is truth, truth beauty, – that is all
   Ye know on earth, and all ye need to know.'

[1820]

I.a.7.   THOMAS LOVE PEACOCK, from 'The Four Ages of Poetry'

A poet in our times is a semi-barbarian in a civilized community. He lives in the days that are past. His ideas, thoughts, feelings, associations, are all with barbarous manners, obsolete customs, and exploded superstition. The march of his intellect is like that of a crab, backward. The brighter the light diffused around him by the progress of reason, the thicker is the darkness of antiquated barbarism, in which he buries himself like a mole, to throw up the barren hillocks of his Cimmerian labours. The philosophic mental tranquility which looks round with an equal eye on all external things, collects a store of ideas, discriminates their relative value, assigns to all their proper place, and from the materials of useful knowledge thus collected, appreciated, and arranged, forms new combinations that impress the stamp of their power and utility on the real business of life, is diametrically the reverse of that frame of mind which poetry inspires, or from which poetry can emanate. The highest inspirations of poetry are resolvable into three ingredients: the rant of unregulated passion, the whining of exaggerated feeling, and the cant of factitious sentiment: and can therefore serve only to ripen a splendid lunatic like Alexander, a puling driveller like Werter, or a morbid dreamer like Wordsworth. It can never make a philosopher, nor a statesman, nor in any class of life an useful or rational man. It cannot claim the slightest share in any one of the comforts and utilities of life of which we have witnessed so many and so rapid advances.

[1820]

1.a.8.   PERCY BYSSHE SHELLEY, from *A Defence of Poetry*

Poetry is indeed something divine. It is at once the centre and circumference of knowledge; it is that which comprehends all science, and that to which all science must be referred. It is at the same time the root and blossom of all other systems of thought; it is that from which all spring, and that which adorns all; and that which, if blighted, denies the fruit and the seed, and withholds from the barren world the nourishment and the succession of the scions of the tree of life. It is the perfect and consummate surface and bloom of all things; it is as the odor and the color of the rose to the texture of the elements which compose it, as the form and splendor of unfaded beauty to the secrets of anatomy and corruption. What were virtue, love, patriotism, friendship – what were the scenery of this beautiful universe which we inhabit; what were our consolations on this side of the grave – and what were our aspirations beyond it, if poetry did not ascend to bring light and fire from those eternal regions where the owl-winged faculty of calculation dare not ever soar? Poetry is not like reasoning, a power to be exerted according to the determination of the will. A man cannot say, 'I will compose poetry.' The greatest poet even

cannot say it; for the mind in creation is as a fading coal, which some invisible influence, like an inconstant wind, awakens to transitory brightness; this power arises from within, like the colour of a flower which fades and changes as it is developed, and the conscious portions of our natures are unprophetic either of its approach or its departure. Could this influence be durable in its original purity and force, it is impossible to predict the greatness of the results; but when composition begins, inspiration is already on the decline, and the most glorious poetry that has ever been communicated to the world is probably a feeble shadow of the original conceptions of the poet. I appeal to the greatest poets of the present day, whether it is not an error to assert that the finest passages of poetry are produced by labour and study. The toil and the delay recommended by critics can be justly interpreted to mean no more than a careful observation of the inspired moments, and an artificial connection of the spaces between their suggestions by the intertexture of conventional expressions; a necessity only imposed by the limitedness of the poetical faculty itself; for Milton conceived the *Paradise Lost* as a whole before he executed it in portions. We have his own authority also for the Muse having 'dictated' to him the 'unpremeditated song.'

And let this be [an answer to those who would allege the fifty-six vari]ous readings of the first line of the *Orlando* [Furioso. Compositions so produced are to poetry w]hat mosaic is to painting. This instinct an[d intuition of the poetical faculty is still more observ]able in the plastic and pictorial arts; a gr[eat statue or picture grows under the power of the art]ist as a child in a mother's womb; and the [very mind which directs the hands in formation is i]ncapable of accounting to itself for the or[igin, the gradations, or the media of the process.]

Poetry is the [record of the best and happiest moments of the happi]est and best minds. We are aware of evane[scent visitations of thought and feeling sometimes as]sociated with place or person, sometime[s regarding our own mind alone, and always arising] unforeseen and departing unbidden, but [elevating and delightful beyond all expression: so that] even in the desire and the regret they lea[ve, there cannot but be pleasure, participating as it i]s in the nature of its object. It is as it were [the interpenetration of a diviner nature through our ow]n; but its footsteps are like those of a wind [over the sea which the coming calm erases, and who]se traces remain only as on the wrinkled s[and which paves it. These and corresponding condition]s of being are experienced principally by [those of the most delicate sensibility and the most enl]arged imagination; and the state of mind [produced by them is at war with every base desire. The] enthusiasm of virtue, love, patriotism, an[d friendship is essentially linked with such emotion]s; and whilst they last, self appears as wh[at it is, an atom to a universe. Poets are not only subj]ect to these experiences as spirits of the most refined organization, but they can colour all that they combine with the evanescent hues of this ethereal world; a word, a trait in the representation of a scene or a passion will touch the enchanted chord, and reanimate, in those who have ever experienced these emotions, the sleeping, the cold, the buried image of the past. Poetry thus makes immortal all that is best and most beautiful in the world; it arrests the vanishing apparitions which haunt the interlunations of life, and veiling them, or in language or in form, sends them forth among mankind, bearing sweet news of kindred joy to those with whom their sisters abide – abide, because there is no portal of expression from the caverns of the spirit which they inhabit into the universe of things. Poetry redeems from decay the visitations of the divinity in man.

Poetry turns all things to loveliness; it exalts the beauty of that which is most beautiful, and it adds beauty to that which is most deformed; it marries exultation and horror, grief and pleasure, eternity and change; it subdues to union under its light yoke all irreconcilable things. It transmutes all that it touches, and every form moving within the radiance of its presence is changed by wondrous sympathy to an incarnation of the spirit which it breathes: its secret alchemy turns to potable

gold the poisonous waters which flow from death through life; it strips the veil of familiarity from the world, and lays bare the naked and sleeping beauty, which is the spirit of its forms.

All things exist as they are perceived: at least in relation to the percipient. 'The mind is its own place, and of itself can make a heaven of hell, a hell of heaven.' But poetry defeats the curse which binds us to be [...]. And whether it spreads its own figured [...] ene of things, it equally creates for us a b[...] world to which the familiar world is a cha[...] re portions and percipients, and it purges [...] scures from us the wonder of our being. [...] agine that which we know. It creates anew [...] minds by the recurrence of impressions bl[...] ords of Tasso – *Non merita nome di creator*[...]

A poet, as he[...] ure, virtue, and glory, so he ought personally[...] st illustrious of men. As to his glory, let time[...] ther institutor of human life be comparable to[...] nd the best, inasmuch as he is a poet, is equall[...] of the most spotless virtue, of the most consu[...] erior of their lives, the most fortunate of men: [...] essed the poetic faculty in a high yet inferior d[...] ather than destroy the rule. Let us for a moment stoop to the arbitration of popular breath, and usurping and uniting in our own persons the incompatible characters of accuser, witness, judge, and executioner, let us decide without trial, testimony, or form, that certain motives of those who are 'there sitting where we dare not soar,' are reprehensible. Let us assume that Homer was a drunkard, that Vergil was a flatterer, that Horace was a coward, that Tasso was a madman, that Lord Bacon was a peculator, that Raphael was a libertine, that Spenser was a poet laureate. It is inconsistent with this division of our subject to cite living poets, but posterity has done ample justice to the great names now referred to. Their errors have been weighed and found to have been dust in the balance; if their sins 'were as scarlet, they are now white as snow'; they have been washed in the blood of the mediator and redeemer, Time. Observe in what a ludicrous chaos the imputations of real or fictitious crime have been confused in the contemporary calumnies against poetry and poets; consider how little is as it appears – or appears as it is; look to your own motives, and judge not, lest ye be judged.

Poetry, as has been said, differs in this respect from logic, that it is not subject to the control of the active powers of the mind, and that its birth and recurrence have no necessary connection with the consciousness or will. It is presumptuous to determine that these are the necessary conditions of all mental causation, when mental effects are experienced unsusceptible of being referred to them. The frequent recurrence of the poetical power, it is obvious to suppose, may produce in the mind a habit of order and harmony correlative with its own nature and with its effects upon other minds. But in the intervals of inspiration, and they may be frequent without being durable, a poet becomes a man, and is abandoned to the sudden reflux of the influences under which others habitually live. But as he is more delicately organized than other men, and sensible to pain and pleasure, both his own and that of others, in a degree unknown to them, he will avoid the one

> *[Handwritten annotation:]* As also described by Coleridge & Wordsworth; Poetry lifts the veil of familiarity which prevents wonder at our own existence
>
> Poet ≠ logic (it is not subject to active powers of mind / connection to consciousness or will)

---

[4] 'None deserve the name of creator except God and the Poet.'

and pursue the other with an ardor proportioned to this difference. And he renders himself obnoxious to calumny, when he neglects to observe the circumstances under which these objects of universal pursuit and flight have disguised themselves in one another's garments.

But there is nothing necessarily evil in this error, and thus cruelty, envy, revenge, avarice, and the passions purely evil have never formed any portion of the popular imputations on the lives of poets.

I have thought it most favorable to the cause of truth to set down these remarks according to the order in which they were suggested to my mind, by a consideration of the subject itself, instead of observing the formality of... ...which they contain be just, they will be fo... ...etry, so far at least as regards the first divi... ...d have moved the gall of some learned and... ...I confess myself, like them, unwilling to b... ...y. Bavius and Mævius undoubtedly are, as... ...a philosophical critic to distinguish rather...

The first part of th... ...principles; and it has been shown, as well a... ...what is called poetry, in a restricted sense,... ...d of beauty, according to which the mat... ...and which is poetry in an universal sense...

The second part w... ...to the present state of the cultivation of p... ...dern forms of manners and opinions, an... ...and creative faculty. For the literature of E... ...ceded or accompanied a great and free d... ...om a new birth. In spite of the low-thoug... ...porary merit, our own will be a memorable age in intellectual achievements, and we live among such philosophers and poets as surpass beyond comparison any who have appeared since the last national struggle for civil and religious liberty. The most unfailing herald, companion, and follower of the awakening of a great people to work a beneficial change in opinion or institution, is poetry. At such periods there is an accumulation of the power of communicating and receiving intense and impassioned conceptions respecting man and nature. The person in whom this power resides, may often, as far as regards many portions of their nature, have little apparent correspondence with that spirit of good of which they are the ministers. But even whilst they deny and abjure, they are yet compelled to serve, that power which is seated on the throne of their own soul. It is impossible to read the compositions of the most celebrated writers of the present day without being startled with the electric life which burns within their words. They measure the circumference and sound the depths of human nature with a comprehensive and all penetrating spirit, and they are themselves perhaps the most sincerely astonished at its manifestations; for it is less their spirit than the spirit of the age. Poets are the hierophants of an unapprehended inspiration; the mirrors of the gigantic shadows which futurity casts upon the present; the words which express what they understand not; the trumpets which sing to battle, and feel not what they inspire; the influence which is moved not, but moves. Poets are the unacknowledged legislators of the world.

(1821) [1840]

[Handwritten note: Critique of Enlightenment? — will and conciousness are not necessary for all mental action as we experience mental effects without them being called upon. Poetry = companion for beneficial change in opinion or institution]

d. FRANÇAIS

I.d.1. HONORÉ de BALZAC, de «*Des artistes*»

Un homme qui dispose de la pensée est un souverain. Les rois commandent aux nations pendant un temps donné, l'artiste commande à des siècles entiers; il change la face des choses, il jette une révolution en moule; il pèse sur le globe, il le façonne. […] Un artiste tient par un fil plus ou moins délié, par une accession plus ou moins intime au mouvement qui se prépare. Il est une partie nécessaire d'une immense machine, soit qu'il condense une doctrine, soit qu'il fasse faire un progrès de plus à l'ensemble de l'art. Aussi le respect que nous accordons aux grands hommes morts ou aux chefs, doit-il revenir à ces courageux soldats auxquels il n'a manqué peut-être qu'une circonstance pour commander.

D'où vient donc, en un siècle aussi éclairé que le nôtre paraît l'être, le dédain avec lequel on traite les artistes, poètes, peintres, musiciens, sculpteurs, architectes? Les rois leur jettent des croix, des rubans, hochets dont la valeur baisse tous les jours, distinctions qui n'ajoutent rien à l'artiste; il leur donne du prix plutôt qu'il n'en reçoit. Quant à l'argent, jamais les arts n'en ont moins obtenu du gouvernement. […]

Beaucoup de difficultés sociales viennent de l'artiste, car tout ce qui est conformé autrement que le vulgaire, froisse, gêne et contrarie le vulgaire.

Soit que l'artiste ait conquis son pouvoir par l'exercice d'une faculté commune à tous les hommes; soit que la puissance dont il use vienne d'une difformité du cerveau, et que le génie soit une maladie humaine comme la perle est une infirmité de l'huître; soit que sa vie serve de développement à un texte, à une pensée unique gravée en lui par Dieu, il est reconnu qu'il n'est pas lui-même dans le secret de son intelligence. Il opère sous l'empire de certaines circonstances, dont la réunion est un mystère. Il ne s'appartient pas. Il est le jouet d'une force éminemment capricieuse.

Tel jour, et sans qu'il le sache, un air souffle et tout se détend. Pour un empire, pour des millions, il ne toucherait pas à son pinceau, il ne pétrirait pas un fragment de cire à mouler, il n'écrirait pas une ligne; et s'il essaye, ce n'est pas lui qui tient le pinceau, la cire ou la plume, c'est un autre, c'est son double, son Sosie: celui qui monte à cheval, fait des calembours, a envie de boire, de dormir, et n'a d'esprit que pour inventer des extravagances. […]

Tel est l'artiste: humble instrument d'une volonté despotique, il obéit à un maître. Quand on le croit libre, il est esclave; quand on le voit s'agiter, s'abandonner à la fougue de ses folies et de ses plaisirs, il est sans puissance et sans volonté, il est mort. Antithèse perpétuelle, qui se trouve dans la majesté de son pouvoir comme dans le néant de sa vie:il est toujours un dieu ou toujours un cadavre.

[…] L'artiste dont la mission est de saisir les rapports les plus éloignés, de produire des effets prodigieux par le rapprochement de deux choses vulgaires, doit paraître déraisonner fort souvent. Là où un public voit du rouge, il voit du bleu. Il est tellement intime avec les causes secrètes qu'il s'applaudit d'un malheur, qu'il maudit une beauté; il loue un défaut et défend un crime; il a tous les symptômes de la folie, parce que les moyens qu'il emploie paraissent toujours aussi loin d'un but qu'ils en sont près. La France tout entière s'est moquée des coquilles de noix de Napoléon au camp de Boulogne, et quinze ans après nous comprîmes que l'Angleterre n'avait jamais été si près de sa perte. L'Europe entière n'a jamais été dans le secret du plus hardi dessein de ce géant que quand il est tombé. Ainsi l'homme de talent peut ressembler dix fois par jour à un niais. Des hommes qui brillent dans les salons prononcent qu'on ne peut en faire qu'un courtaut de boutique. Son esprit est presbyte; il ne voit pas les petites choses auxquelles le monde donne tant d'importance et qui sont près de lui, tandis qu'il converse avec l'avenir. Alors sa femme le prend pour un sot.

d. FRENCH

I.d.1. HONORÉ de BALZAC, from 'On Artists'

A man who has thought at his disposal is a sovereign. Kings command nations for a given time, the artist commands whole centuries; he changes the face of things, he molds a revolution; he weighs on the globe, he fashions it. [. . .] An artist holds by a tighter or looser thread, by a more or less intimate accession to the movement which is preparing itself. He is a necessary part of an immense machine, whether he condenses a doctrine, or whether he causes the art as a whole to make one more advance. Thus the respect which we grant to great dead men or to chiefs, should return to these courageous soldiers who perhaps lacked only one circumstance to command. Whence, therefore, comes in a century as enlightened as ours appears to be, the disdain with which are treated artists, poets, painters, musicians, sculptors, architects? Kings toss them medals,[1] ribbons, toys whose value goes down daily, distinctions which add nothing to the artist; he gives them more worth than he receives from them. As for money, never have the arts received less from the government. [. . .]

Many social difficulties come from the artist, for everything which is formed differently from the vulgar, ruffles, bothers, and annoys the vulgar.

Whether the artist has conquered his power by the exercise of a faculty common to all men; whether the strength he uses comes from a deformity of the brain, and genius is a human malady as the pearl is a weakness of the oyster; whether his life serves as the development of a text, as a unique thought engraved in him by God, it is recognized that he is not himself in on the secret of his intelligence. He works in the grip of certain circumstances, whose gathering is a mystery. He does not belong to himself. He is the plaything of an eminently capricious force.

On such-and-such a day, without his knowing, a breeze blows and everything relaxes. For an empire, for millions, he would not touch his brush, he would not knead a fragment of molding wax, he would not write a line; and if he tries, it is not he who holds the brush, the wax or the pen, it is another, it is his double, his Doppelgänger: the one who rides on horseback, makes puns, wants to drink and sleep, and has no wit except for inventing extravagances. [. . .]

Such is the artist: humble instrument of a despotic will, he obeys a master. When one thinks him free, he is a slave; when one sees him moving restlessly, giving himself up to the fire of his madness and his pleasures, he is without strength and without will, he is dead. Perpetual antithesis, which occurs in the majesty of his power as in the nothingness of his life: he is always a god or always a corpse.

[. . .] The artist whose mission is grasping the farthest links, producing prodigious effects by the bringing together of two vulgar things, must seem very often to rave. There where an audience sees red, he sees blue. He is so intimate with the secret causes that he congratulates himself on a misfortune, that he curses a beauty; he praises a fault and defends a crime; he has all the symptoms of madness, because the means which he uses always appear as far from a goal as they are near to it. The whole of France made fun of Napoleon's walnut shells in the Boulogne camp, and fifteen years later we understood that England had never been so close to being lost. None of Europe was in on the secret of this giant's most daring plan until he fell. Thus the talented man may look like a simpleton ten times a day. Men who shine in the salons announce that nothing can be made of him but a dumpy little shopman. His mind is farsighted; he does not see the little things which society finds so important and which are close to him, while he converses with the future. So his wife takes him for a fool.

---

[1] Translator's note: 'croix' here means 'croix de la Légion d'honneur'.

La morale de ces observations peut se résoudre par un mot: *Un grand homme doit être malheureux.* Aussi, chez lui, la résignation est-elle une vertu sublime. Sous ce rapport le Christ en est le plus admirable modèle. Cet homme gagnant la mort pour prix de la divine lumière qu'il répand sur la terre et montant sur une croix où l'homme va se changer en Dieu, offre un spectacle immense: il y a là plus qu'une religion: c'est un type éternel de la gloire humaine. Le Dante en exil, Cervantès à l'hôpital, Milton dans une chaumière, le Corrège expirant sous le poids d'une somme en cuivre, le Poussin ignoré, Napoléon à Sainte-Helène, sont des images du grand et divin tableau que présente le Christ sur la croix, mourant pour renaître, laissant sa dépouille mortelle pour régner dans les cieux. Homme et Dieu: homme d'abord, Dieu après; homme, pour le plus grand nombre; Dieu, pour quelques fidèles; peu compris, puis tout à coup adoré; enfin ne devenant Dieu que quand il s'est baptisé de son sang.

En poursuivant l'analyse des causes qui font réprouver l'artiste, nous en trouverons une qui suffirait pour le faire exclure du monde extérieur où il vit. En effet, avant tout, un artiste est l'apôtre de quelque vérité, l'organe du Très-Haut qui se sert de lui, pour donner un développement nouveau à l'œuvre que nous accomplissons tous avec aveuglement. Or, l'histoire de l'esprit humain, est unanime sur la répulsion vive, sur la révolte qu'excitent les nouvelles découvertes, les vérités, et les principes les plus influents sur la destinée de l'Humanité. La masse des sots qui occupent le haut du pavé décrète qu'il y a des vérités nuisibles, comme si la révélation d'une idée neuve, n'était pas l'effet de la volonté divine; et comme si le mal lui-même n'entrait pas dans son plan comme un bien, invisible à nos faibles yeux. Alors toute la colère des passions tombe sur l'artiste, sur le créateur, sur l'instrument. L'homme qui s'est refusé aux vérités chrétiennes et qui les a roulées dans un flot de sang, combat les saines idées d'un philosophe qui développe l'évangile, d'un poète qui coordonne la littérature de son pays aux principes d'une croyance nationale, d'un peintre qui restaure une école, d'un physicien qui redresse une erreur, d'un génie qui détrône la stupidité d'un enseignement immémorial dans sa routine. Aussi, de cet apostolat, de cette conviction intime, il résulte une accusation grave que presque tous les gens irréfléchis portent contre les gens de talent.

Les sauvages et les peuples qui se rapprochent le plus de l'état de nature sont bien plus grands dans leurs rapports avec les hommes supérieurs, que les nations plus civilisées. Chez eux, les êtres à *seconde vue,* les bardes, les improvisateurs sont regardés comme des créatures privilégiées. Leurs artistes ont une place au festin, sont protégés par tous, leurs plaisirs sont respectés, leur sommeil et leur vieillesse également. Ce phénomène est assez rare chez une nation civilisée, et le plus souvent quand une lumière brille, on accourt pour l'éteindre; car on la prend pour un incendie.

[*Publié dans La Silhouette*, 1830]

The moral of these observations may be summed up in a word: *A great man must be unhappy.* Therefore, in him, resignation is a sublime virtue. From this point of view, Christ is the most admirable model. This man earning death as the price of the divine light which he spreads on earth, and mounting a cross where man will change into God, offers an immense spectacle: there is more here than a religion: it is an eternal example of the glory of humanity. Dante in exile, Cervantes in the hospital, Milton in a cottage, Correggio dying under the weight of a sum of copper, Poussin unknown, Napoleon at Saint Helena, are images of the great and divine tableau presented by Christ on the cross, dying to be reborn, leaving his mortal remains to reign in heaven. Man and God: man first, God later; man, for most people; God, for a few faithful; little understood, then all at once adored; finally becoming God only when he baptized himself with his blood.

In pursuing the analysis of the reasons which cause the artist to be condemned, we find one which would be enough to exclude him from the exterior world in which he lives. Indeed, above all, an artist is the apostle of some truth, the mouthpiece of the Most High who uses him, to give a new development to the work, which we all do blindly. The history of the human spirit is unanimous in the keen repugnance, in the revolt excited by the new discoveries, the truth, and the principles which have most influenced Humanity's destiny. The mass of fools who take pride of place decree that there are harmful truths, as if the revelation of a new idea was not the effect of divine will; and as if evil itself did not enter in his plan as a good, invisible to our feeble eyes. Thus all the passions' anger falls on the artist, on the creator, on the instrument. The man who rejected Christian truths and rolled them in a stream of blood fights the healthy ideas of a philosopher who develops the gospel, of a poet who coordinates the literature of his country with the principles of a national belief, of a painter who restores a school, of a physician who rectifies an error, of a genius who dethrones the stupidity of a teaching age-old in its routine. Thus, from this apostolate, from this intimate conviction, there results a grave accusation which nearly all unthinking people make against the talented.

Savages and those peoples who most nearly approach a state of nature are much greater in their relationships with superior men than more civilized nations. In them, people with *second sight,* bards, improvisers are seen as privileged creatures. Their artists have a place at the feast, are protected by all, their pleasures are respected, as are their sleep and their old age. This phenomenon is rather rare in a civilized nation, and most often when a light shines, people run to put it out; for it is taken for a fire.

[*Published in La Silhouette, 1820. Translated by Anne Gwin*]

I.d.2. CHARLES BAUDELAIRE, Salon de 1859, III dans la *Revue française*

Dans ces derniers temps nous avons entendu dire de mille manières différentes: «Copiez la nature; ne copiez que la nature. Il n'y a pas de plus grande jouissance ni de plus beau triomphe qu'une copie excellente de la nature.» Et cette doctrine, ennemie de l'art, prétendait être appliquée non seulement à la peinture, mais à tous les arts, même au roman, même à la poésie. A ces doctrinaires si satisfaits de la nature un homme imaginatif aurait certainement eu le droit de répondre: «Je trouve inutile et fastidieux de représenter ce qui est, parce que rien de ce qui est ne me satisfait. La nature est laide, et je préfère les monstres de ma fantaisie à la trivialité positive.» Cependant il eût été plus philosophique de demander aux doctrinaires en question, d'abord s'ils sont bien certains de l'existence de la nature extérieure, ou, si cette question eût paru trop bien faite pour réjouir leur causticité, s'ils sont bien sûrs de connaître toute la nature, tout ce qui est contenu dans la nature. Un oui eût été la plus fanfaronne et la plus extravagante des réponses. Autant que j'ai pu comprendre ces singulières et avilissantes divagations, la doctrine voulait dire, je lui fais l'honneur de croire qu'elle voulait dire: L'artiste, le vrai artiste, le vrai poète, ne doit peindre que selon qu'il voit et qu'il sent. Il doit être réellement fidèle à sa propre nature. Il doit éviter comme la mort d'emprunter les yeux et les sentiments d'un autre homme, si grand qu'il soit; car alors les productions qu'il nous donnerait seraient, relativement à lui, des mensonges, et non des réalités. Or, si les pédants dont je parle (il y a de la pédanterie même dans la bassesse), et qui ont des représentants partout, cette théorie flattant également l'impuissance et la paresse, ne voulaient pas que la chose fût entendue ainsi, croyons simplement qu'ils voulaient dire: «Nous n'avons pas d'imagination, et nous décrétons que personne n'en aura.»

Mystérieuse faculté que cette reine des facultés! Elle touche à toutes les autres; elle les excite, elle les envoie au combat. Elle leur ressemble quelquefois au point de se confondre avec elles, et cependant elle est toujours bien elle-même, et les hommes qu'elle n'agite pas sont facilement reconnaissables à je ne sais quelle malédiction qui dessèche leurs productions comme le figuier de l'Evangile.

Elle est l'analyse, elle est la synthèse; et cependant des hommes habiles dans l'analyse et suffisamment aptes à faire un résumé peuvent être privés d'imagination. Elle est cela, et elle n'est pas tout à fait cela. Elle est la sensibilité, et pourtant il y a des personnes très sensibles, trop sensibles peut-être, qui en sont privées. C'est l'imagination qui a enseigné à l'homme le sens moral de la couleur, du contour, du son et du parfum. Elle a créé, au commencement du monde, l'analogie et la métaphore. Elle décompose toute la création, et, avec les matériaux amassés et disposés suivant des règles dont on ne peut trouver l'origine que dans le plus profond de l'âme, elle crée un monde nouveau, elle produit la sensation du neuf. Comme elle a créé le monde (on peut bien dire cela, je crois, même dans un sens religieux), il est juste qu'elle le gouverne. Que dit-on d'un guerrier sans imagination? Qu'il peut faire un excellent soldat, mais que, s'il commande des armées, il ne fera pas de conquêtes. Le cas peut se comparer à celui d'un poète ou d'un romancier qui enlèverait à l'imagination le commandement des facultés pour le donner, par exemple, à la connaissance de la langue ou à l'observation des faits. Que dit-on d'un diplomate sans imagination? Qu'il peut très bien connaître l'histoire des traités et des alliances dans le passé, mais qu'il ne devinera pas les traités et les alliances contenus dans l'avenir. D'un savant sans imagination? Qu'il a appris tout ce qui, ayant été enseigné, pouvait être appris, mais qu'il ne trouvera pas les lois non encore devinées. L'imagination est la reine du vrai, et le possible est une des provinces du vrai. Elle est positivement apparentée avec l'infini.

I.d.2. CHARLES BAUDELAIRE, from *Salon of 1859,* III in Art in Paris:1845–1862:
Baudelaire's Reviews of Salons and Other Exhibitions

In recent years we have heard it said in a thousand different ways, 'Copy nature; just copy nature.
There is no greater delight, no finer triumph than an excellent copy of nature.' And this doctrine
(the enemy of art) was alleged to apply not only to painting but to all the arts, even to the novel
and to poetry. To these doctrinaires, who were so completely satisfied by Nature, a man of imagination would certainly have had the right to reply: 'I consider it useless and tedious to represent
what exists, because nothing that exists satisfies me. Nature is ugly, and I prefer the monsters of
my fancy to what is positively trivial.'

And yet it would have been more philosophical to ask the doctrinaires in question first of all
whether they were quite certain of the existence of external nature, or (if this question might
seem too well calculated to pander to their sarcasm) whether they were quite certain of knowing
all nature, that is, all that is contained in nature. A 'yes' would have been the most boastful and
extravagant of answers. So far as I have been able to understand its singular and humiliating
incoherences, the doctrine meant – at least I do it the honour of believing that it meant: The
artist, the true artist, the true poet, should only paint in accordance with what he sees and with
what he feels. He must be really faithful to his own nature. He must avoid like the plague borrowing the eyes and the feelings of another man, however great that man may be; for then his
productions would be lies in relation to himself, and not realities. But if these pedants of whom
I am speaking (for there is a pedantry even among the mean-spirited) and who have representatives everywhere (for their theory flatters impotence no less than laziness) – if these pedants,
I say, did not wish the matter to be understood in this way, let us simply believe that they meant
to say, 'We have no imagination, and we decree that no one else is to have any.'

How mysterious is imagination, that Queen of the Faculties? It touches all the others; it rouses
them and sends them into combat. At times it resembles them to the point of confusion, and yet
it is always itself, and those men who are not quickened thereby are easily recognizable by some
strange curse which withers their productions like the fig tree in the Gospel.

It is both analysis and synthesis; and yet men who are clever at analysis and sufficiently quick
at summing up, can be devoid of imagination. It is that, and it is not entirely that. It is sensitivity,
and yet there are people who are very sensitive, too sensitive perhaps, who have none of it. It is
Imagination that first taught man the moral meaning of colour, of contour, of sound and of
scent. In the beginning of the wand it created analogy and metaphor. It decomposes all creation,
and with the raw materials accumulated and disposed in accordance with rules whose origins
one cannot find save in the furthest depths of the soul, it creates a new world, it produces the
sensation of newness. As it has created the world (so much can be said, I think, even in a religious sense), it is proper that it should govern it. What would be said of a warrior without imagination? that he might make an excellent soldier, but that if he is put in command of an army, he
will make no conquests. The case could be compared to that of a poet or a novelist who took
away the command of his faculties from the imagination to give it, for example, to his knowledge of language or to his observation of facts. What would be said of a diplomat without imagination? that he may have an excellent knowledge of the history of treaties and alliances in the
past, but that he will never guess the treaties and alliances held in store by the future. Of a
scholar without imagination? that he has learnt everything that, having been taught, could be
learnt, but that he will never discover any laws that have not yet been guessed at. Imagination is
the queen of truth, and the possible is one of the provinces of truth. It has a positive relationship

Sans elle, toutes les facultés, si solides ou si aiguisées qu'elles soient, sont comme si elles n'étaient pas, tandis que la faiblesse de quelques facultés secondaires, excitées par une imagination vigoureuse, est un malheur secondaire. Aucune ne peut se passer d'elle, et elle peut suppléer quelques-unes. Souvent ce que celles-ci cherchent et ne trouvent qu'après les essais successifs de plusieurs méthodes non adaptées à la nature des choses, fièrement et simplement elle le devine. Enfin elle joue un rôle puissant même dans la morale; car, permettez-moi d'aller jusque-là, qu'est-ce que la vertu sans imagination? Autant dire la vertu sans la pitié, la vertu sans le ciel; quelque chose de dur, de cruel, de stérilisant, qui, dans certains pays, est devenu la bigoterie, et dans certains autres le protestantisme.

Malgré tous les magnifiques privilèges que j'attribue à l'imagination, je ne ferai pas à vos lecteurs l'injure de leur expliquer que mieux elle est secourue et plus elle est puissante, et, que ce qu'il y a de plus fort dans les batailles avec l'idéal, c'est une belle imagination disposant d'un immense magasin d'observations.

with the infinite. Without imagination, all the faculties, however sound or sharpened they may be, are as though they did not exist, whereas a weakness in some of the secondary faculties, so long as they are excited by a vigorous imagination, is a secondary misfortune. None of them can do without it, but the lack of some of them can be made up by it. Often when our other faculties only find what they are seeking after successive trials of several different methods which are ill-adapted to the nature of things, imagination steps in, and proudly and simply guesses the answer. Finally, it plays a powerful role even in ethical matters; for – allow me to go so far and to ask, What is virtue without imagination? You might as well speak of virtue without pity, virtue without Heaven – it is a hard, cruel, sterilizing thing, which in some countries has become bigotry and in others Protestantism.

In spite of all the magnificent privileges that I attribute to the imagination, I will not pay your readers the insult of explaining to them that the more it is helped in its work, the more powerful it is, and that there is nothing more formidable in our battles with the ideal than a fine imagination disposing of an immense armoury of observed fact. Nevertheless, to return to what I was saying a moment ago concerning the prerogative of making up deficiencies, which the imagination owes to its divine origin, I should like to quote you an example, a tiny example, which I hope you will not scorn. Do you think that the author of *Antony*, of *Count Hermann*, and of *Monte Cristo*, is a scholar? I imagine not. Do you suppose that he has steeped himself in the practice of the arts and has made a patient study of them? Of course not. I should even imagine that to do so would be antipathetic to his nature. Very well then, he is an example to prove that the imagination, although unassisted by practice or by acquaintance with technical terms, is nevertheless incapable of producing heretical nonsense in a matter which is, for the most important part, within its province. Not long ago I was in a train and I was pondering over the article which I am now writing: I was considering above all that singular reversal of values which has permitted (in a century, I grant you, in which, for man's chastening, everything has been permitted hire) a disdain of the most honourable and the most useful of the moral faculties. And then I saw lying on a nearby cushion a forgotten copy of the Independence Belge. Alexandre Dumas had taken over this year's account of the works in the Salon. This circumstance aroused my curiosity. You can guess my delight when I discovered my reflections amply verified by an example thrown in my way by chance.

[*Translated and edited by Jonathan Mayne. Oxford: Phaidon, 1995*]

I.d.3. FRANÇOIS-RENÉ de CHATEAUBRIAND, *Génie du christianisme*, IIIe partie, Livre I, chapitre 8

Chaque chose doit être mise en son lieu, vérité triviale à force d'être répétée, mais sans laquelle, après tout, il ne peut y avoir rien de parfait. Les Grecs n'auraient pas plus aimé un temple égyptien à Athènes que les Egyptiens un temple grec à Memphis. Ces deux monuments changés de place auraient perdu leur principale beauté, c'est-à-dire leurs rapports avec les institutions et les habitudes des peuples. Cette réflexion s'applique pour nous aux anciens monuments du christianisme. Il est même curieux de remarquer que dans ce siècle incrédule les poètes et les romanciers, par un retour naturel vers les mœurs de nos adieux, se plaisent à introduire dans leurs fictions des souterrains, des fantômes, des châteaux, des temples gothiques: tant ont de charmes les souvenirs qui se lient à la religion et à l'histoire de la patrie! Les nations ne jettent pas à l'écart leurs antiques moeurs comme on se dépouille d'un vieil habit. On leur en peut arracher quelques parties, mais il en reste des lambeaux, qui forment avec les nouveaux vêtements une effroyable bigarrure.

On aura beau bâtir des temples grecs bien élégants, bien éclairés, pour rassembler le bon peuple de saint Louis et lui faire adorer un Dieu métaphysique, il regrettera toujours ces Notre-Dame de Reims et de Paris, ces basiliques toutes moussues, toutes remplies des générations des décédés et des âmes de ses pères; il regrettera toujours la tombe de quelques messieurs de Montmorency, sur laquelle il soulait se mettre à genoux durant la messe, sans oublier les sacrées fontaines où il fut porté à sa naissance. C'est que tout cela est essentiellement lié à nos moeurs; c'est qu'un monument n'est vénérable qu'autant qu'une longue histoire du passé est pour ainsi dire empreinte sous ses voûtes toutes noires de siècles. Voilà pourquoi il n'y a rien de merveilleux dans un temple qu'on a vu bâtir et dont les échos et les dômes se sont formés sous nos yeux. Dieu est la loi éternelle; son origine et tout ce qui tient à son culte doit se perdre dans la nuit des temps.

On ne pouvait entrer dans une église gothique sans éprouver une sorte de frissonne ment et un sentiment vague de la Divinité. On se trouvait tout à coup reporté à ces temps où les cénobites, après avoir médité dans les bois de leurs monastères se venaient prosterner à l'autel et chanter les louanges du Seigneur dans le calme et le silence de la nuit. L'ancienne France semblait revivre: on croyait voir ces costumes singuliers, ce peuple si différent de ce qu'il est aujourd'hui; on se rappelait et les révolutions de ce peuple, et ses travaux et ses arts. Plus ces temps étaient éloignés de nous, plus ils nous paraissaient magiques, plus ils nous remplissaient de ces pensées qui finissent toujours par une réflexion sur le néant de l'homme et la rapidité de la vie.

L'ordre gothique, au milieu de ces proportions barbares, a toutefois une beauté qui lui est particulière.[2]

Les forêts ont été les premiers temples de la Divinité, et les hommes ont pris dans les forêts la première idée de l'architecture. Cet art a donc dû varier selon les climats. Les Grecs ont tourné l'élégante colonne corinthienne avec son chapiteau de feuilles sur le modèle du palmier.[3] Les

---

[2] On pense qu'il nous vient des Arabes, ainsi que la sculpture du même style. Son affinité avec les monuments de l'Egypte nous porterait plutôt à croire qu'il nous a été transmis par les premiers chrétiens d'Orient, mais nous aimons mieux encore rapporter son origine à la nature.

[3] Vitruve raconte autrement l'invention du chapiteau, mais cela ne détruit pas ce principe général, que l'architecture est née dans les bois. On peut seulement s'étonner qu'on n'ait pas, d'après la variété des arbres, mis plus de variété dans la colonne. Nous concevons, par exemple, une colonne qu'on pourrait appeler palmiste, et qui serait la représentation naturelle du palmier. Un orbe de feuilles un peu recourbées d'un léger fût de marbre ferait, ce nous semble, un effet charmant dans un portique.

d3, d7, d9

I.d.3.   FRANÇOIS-RENÉ de CHATE[...]
Part III, Book I, Chapter 8: Of[...]

Every thing ought to be put in its pro[...]ut
without its due observance, there can[...]et-
ter pleased with an Egyptian temple [...] at
Memphis. These two monuments, by [...]ty,
that is to say, their relations with the [...] is
equally applicable to the monuments [...]his
infidel age, the poets and novelists, b[...]rs,
and Gothic churches into their fictio[...]ith
religion, and the history of our count[...]

In vain would you build Grecian te[...]e of
assembling the *good people* of St. Loui[...]ys-
ical God; still they would regret those[...]he-
drals, overgrown with moss, full of g[...]ers;
still would they regret the tombs of those heroes the morning mass: to say nothing of the sacred
fonts to which they were carried at their birth. The reason is, that all these things are essentially
interwoven with their manners, that a monument is not venerable, unless a long history of the
past be, as it were, inscribed beneath its vaulted canopy, black with age. For this reason also,
there is nothing marvelous in a temple, whose erection we have witnessed, whose echoes and
whose domes were formed before our faces. God is the eternal law; his origin, and whatever is
attached to him, out to be enveloped in the night of time.

You could not enter a Gothic church without feeling a kind of awe and a vague sentiment of
the divinity. You were all at once carried back to those times when a fraternity of cenobites, after
having mediated in the woods of their monasteries, met to prostrate themselves before the altar,
and to chant the praises of the Lord, amid the tranquility and the silence of night. Ancient
France seemed to revive altogether; you beheld all those singular costumes, all that nation so
different from what it is at present; you were reminded of its revolutions, its productions, and its
arts. The more remote were these times, the more magical they appeared, the more they inspired
ideas which always end with a reflection on the nothingness of man and the rapidity of life.

The Gothic style, notwithstanding its barbarous proportions, possesses a beauty peculiar to
itself.[4]

The forests were the first temples of the divinity, and in them men acquired the first idea of
architecture. This art must, therefore, have varied according to climates. The Greeks turned the
elegant Corinthian column, with its capital of foliage, after the model of the palm tree.[5] The

---

[4] Gothic architecture, as well as the sculpture in the same style is conjectured to have been borrowed by us
of the Arabs. Its affinity to the monuments of Egypt, would rather lead us to imagine, that it was transmitted to us by the first Christians of the East; but it is still more congenial with our sentiments, to refer its
origin to nature.

[5] Vitruvius gives a different account of the invention of the Corinthian capital; but his does not confute the
general principle, that architecture originated in the woods. We are only astonished that there should not
be more variety in the column, after the varieties of trees. We have a conception, for example, of a column
that might be termed Palmist, and be a natural representation of a palm-tree. An orb of foliage An orb of
foliage slightly bowed and sculptured on the top of a light shaft of marble, would, in our opinion, produce
a very pleasing effect in a portico.

énormes piliers du vieux style égyptien représentent le sycomore, le figuier oriental, le bananier et la plupart des arbres gigantesques de l'Afrique et de l'Asie.

Les forêts des Gaules ont passé à leur tour dans les temples de nos pères, et nos bois de chênes ont ainsi maintenu leur origine sacrée. Ces voûtes ciselées en feuillages, ces jambages qui appuient les murs et finissent brusquement comme des troncs brisés, la fraîcheur des voûtes, les ténèbres du sanctuaire, les ailes obscures, les passages secrets, les portes abaissées, tout retrace les labyrinthes des bois dans l'église gothique, tout en fait sentir la religieuse horreur, les mystères et la divinité. Les deux tours hautaines plantées à l'entrée de l'édifice surmontent les ormes et les ifs du cimetière et font un effet pittoresque sur l'azur du ciel. Tantôt le jour naissant illumine leurs têtes jumelles; tantôt elles paraissent couronnées d'un chapiteau de nuages ou grossies dans une atmosphère vaporeuse. Les oiseaux eux-mêmes semblent s'y méprendre et les adopter pour les arbres de leurs forêts: des corneilles voltigent autour de leurs faîtes et se perchent sur leurs galeries.

Mais tout à coup des rumeurs confuses s'échappent de la cime de ces tours et en chassent les oiseaux effrayés. L'architecte chrétien, non content de bâtir des forêts, a voulu, pour ainsi dire, en imiter les murmures, et au moyen de l'orgue et du bronze suspendu il a attaché au temple gothique jusqu'au bruit des vents et des tonnerres, qui roulent dans la profondeur des bois. Les siècles, évoqués par ces sons religieux, font sortir leurs antiques voix du sein des pierres et soupirent dans la vaste basilique: le sanctuaire mugit comme l'antre de l'ancienne Sibylle, et tandis que l'airain se balance avec fracas sur votre tête, les souterrains voûtés de la mort se taisent profondément sous vos pieds.

[1802]

I.d.4. EUGÈNE DELACROIX, 'Réflexions sur le beau'

Le sentiment du beau est-il celui qui nous saisit à la vue d'un tableau de Raphaël ou de Rembrandt indifféremment, d'une scène de Shakespeare ou de Corneille, quand nous disons: «que c'est beau!» ou se borne-t-il à l'admiration de certains types en dehors desquels il ne soit point de beauté? En un mot, l'*Antinoüs*, la *Vénus*, le *Gladiateur*, et en général les purs modèles que nous ont transmis les Anciens, sont-ils la règle invariable, le *canon* dont il ne faut point s'écarter sous peine de tomber dans la monstruosité, ces modèles impliquant nécessairement avec l'idée la grâce, de la vie même, celle de la régularité?

L'antique ne nous a pas exclusivement transmis de semblables types. Le *Silène* est beau, le *Faune* est beau, *Socrate* même est beau: cette tête est pleine d'une certaine beau té, malgré son petit nez épaté, sa bouche lippue et ses petits yeux. Elle ne brille pas, il est vrai, par la symétrie et la belle proportion des traits, mais elle est animée par le reflet de la pensée et d'une élévation intérieure. Encore le *Silène*, le *Faune* et tant d'autres figures de caractère sont-elles de la pierre dans l'antique. On concevra facilement que la pierre, le bronze et le marbre demandent dans l'expression des traits une certaine sobriété qui est e la roideur et de la sécheresse quand on l'imite en peinture. Ce dernier art, qui a la couleur, l'effet, qui se rapproche davantage de l'imitation immédiate, admet des détails plus palpitants, moins conventionnels, et qui s'écarteraient encore davantage de la forme sévère.

Les écoles modernes ont proscrit tout ce qui s'écarte de l'antique régulier; en embellissant même le *Faune* et le *Silène,* en ôtant des rides à la vieillesse, en supprimant les disgrâces inévitables et souvent caractéristiques qu'entraînent dans la représentation de la forme humaine les

enormous pillars of the ancient Egyptian style represent the massive sycamore, the oriental gig, the banana, and most of the gigantic trees of Africa and Asia. The forests of Gaul were, in their turn, introduced into the temples of our ancestors, and those celebrated woods of oaks thus maintained their sacred character. Those ceilings sculptured into foliage of different kinds, those buttresses which prop the walls and terminate abruptly like the broken trunks of trees, the coolness of the vaults, the darkness [...] the dim twilight of the ailes, the chapels resembling grottoes, the secret passa[...] [...]thic church reminds you of the labyrinth[...] [...]e, of mystery, and of divinity.

The steeple, or the two lofty tower[...] [...]s and yew-trees of the church-yard, and p[...] [...]aven. Sometimes their twin heads are il[...] [...]pear crowded with a capital of clouds, [...] [...]selves seem to make a mistake in regard [...] [...]; they hover over their summits, and per[...] [...]denly issue from the top of these towers, [...] [...]nitect, not content with building forests, [...] [...]ans of the organ and of bells, he has atta[...] [...]nders that roll in the recesses to the wood[...] [...]e their venerable voices from the bosom [...] [...]nedral. The sanctuary re-echoes like the ca[...] [...]r your head, which the vaults of death un[...]

[handwritten note: Beauty is different from culture to culture. The Gothic cathedral reminds me of John Keat's "ode to a Grecian urn". Monuments are modeled after forests]

[..., 1856]

I.d.4. EUGÈNE DELACROIX, from 'Reflections on the Beautiful'

Is the sentiment of the beautiful that which comes over us at the sight of a painting of either Raphael or Rembrandt, of a scene of Shakespeare or Corneille, when we say: 'Oh, it's beautiful!' or is it limited to the admiration of certain types outside of which there is no beauty? In a word, are the *Antinoüs,* the *Venus,* the *Gladiator,* and in general the pure models which the ancients have handed down to us, the invariable rule, the *canon* from which one must not stray on pain of falling into monstrosity, these models necessarily implying with the idea of grace, of life itself, that of regularity?

The antique style has not exclusively handed down to us types of that sort. The *Silenus* is beautiful, the *Faun* is beautiful, even *Socrates* is beautiful: this head is full of a certain beauty, in spite of its flat little nose, its thick-lipped mouth, and its small eyes. It does not shine, it is true, by the symmetry and beautiful proportion of its features, but it is animated by the reflection of thought and of an interior elevation. Too, in the antique style, the *Silenus,* the *Faun* and many other character studies are of stone. One will easily understand that stone, bronze, and marble demand a certain sobriety in the expression of features which is stiffness and dryness when one imitates it in painting. This last art, which has color and effect, which more nearly approaches immediate imitation, allows details that are more thrilling and less conventional, and which stray even farther from the severe form.

The modern schools have prohibited everything which moves away from classical regularity; by making even the *Faun* and the *Silenus* more attractive, by removing the wrinkles of old age, by suppressing the inevitable and often characteristic infelicities which natural accidents and

accidents naturels et le travail, elles ont donné naïvement la preuve que le beau pour elles ne consistait que dans une suite de recettes. Elles ont pu enseigner le beau comme on enseigne l'algèbre, et non seulement l'enseigner mais en donner de faciles exemples. Quoi de plus simple, en effet, à ce qu'il semble? Rapprocher tous les caractères d'un modèle unique, atténuer, effacer les différences profondes qui séparent dans la nature les tempéraments et les âges divers de l'homme, éviter les expressions compliquées ou les mouvements violents, capables de déranger l'harmonie des traits ou des membres, tels sont en abrégé les principes à l'aide desquels on tient le beau comme dans sa main! Il est facile alors de le faire pratiquer à des élèves et de le transmettre de génération en génération comme un dépôt.

Mais la vue des beaux ouvrages de tous les temps prouve que le beau ne se rencontre pas à de semblables conditions: il ne se transmet ni ne se concède comme l'héritage d'une ferme; il est le fruit d'une inspiration persévérante qui n'est qu'une suite de labeurs opiniâtres; il sort des entrailles avec des douleurs et des déchirements, comme tout ce qui est destiné à vivre; il fait le charme et la consolation des hommes, et ne peut être le fruit d'une application passagère ou d'une banale tradition. Des palmes vulgaires peuvent couronner de vulgaires efforts; un assentiment passager peut accompagner, pendant la durée de leur succès, des ouvrages enfantés par le caprice du moment; mais la poursuite de la gloire commande d'autres tentatives: il faut une lutte obstinée pour arracher un de ses sourires; ce serait peu encore: il faut, pour l'obtenir, la réunion de mille dons et la faveur du destin. La simple tradition ne saurait produire un ouvrage qu fasse qu'on s'écrie: «Que c'est beau!» Un génie sorti de terre, un homme inconnu et privilégié va renverser cet échafaudage de doctrines à l'usage de tout le monde et qui ne produisent rien. Un Holbein avec son imitation scrupuleuse des rides de ses modèles et qui compte pour ainsi dire leurs cheveux, un Rembrandt avec ses types vulgaires, remplis d'une expression si profonde, ces Allemands et ces Italiens des écoles primitives avec leurs figures maigres et contournées et leur ignorance complète de l'art des anciens, étincellent de beautés et de cet idéal qui les écoles vont chercher la toise à la main. Guidés par une naïve inspiration, puisant, dans la nature qui les entoure et dans un sentiment profond, l'inspiration que l'érudition ne saurait contrefaire, ils passionnent autour d'eux le peuple et les hommes cultivés, ils expriment des sentiments qui étaient dans toutes les âmes: ils ont trouvé naturellement ce joyau sans prix qu'une inutile science demande en vain à l'expérience et à des préceptes.

La nature a donné à chaque talent un talisman palier, que je comparerais à ces métaux inestimables de l'alliage de mille métaux précieux, et qui rendent des sons ou charmants ou terribles, suivant les proportions diverses des éléments dont ils sont formés. Il est des talents délicats qui ne peuvent facilement se satisfaire: attentifs à captiver l'esprit, ils s'adressent à lui par tous les moyens dont l'art dispose; ils refont cent fois un morceau, ils sacrifient la touche, l'exécution savante, qui fait ressortir plus ou moins les détails, à l'unité et à la profondeur de l'impression. Tel est Léonard de Vinci, tel est Titien. Il est d'autres talents, comme Tintoret, mieux encore comme Rubens, et je préfère ce dernier parce qu'il va plus avant dans l'expression, qui sont entraînés par une sorte de verve qui est dans le sang et dans la main. La force de certaines touches, sur lesquelles on ne revient point, donne aux ouvrages de ces maîtres une animation et une vigueur auxquelles ne parvient pas toujours une exécution plus circonspecte.

[*Revue des Deux Mondes*, 15 Juillet, 1854]

work bring to the representation of the human form, they have naïvely proved that for them, the beautiful consisted only of a set of recipes. They were able to teach the beautiful as one teaches algebra, and not only teach it but give easy examples of it. Indeed, what could be simpler, seemingly? Bringing together all the characteristics of a unique model, toning down, erasing the deep differences which, in nature, separate the temperaments and the different ages of man, avoiding complicated expressions or violent movements capable of disturbing the harmony of features or of limbs, these, in a nutshell, are the principles by means of which one can hold the beautiful in one's hand! It is easy then to have students practice it and to hand it down from generation to generation like a trust.

But the sight of the beautiful works of every age proves that the beautiful is not found under such conditions; it is not handed down nor granted like the inheritance of a farm; it is the fruit of a persevering inspiration which is nothing but a series of stubborn labors; it comes from one's womb with pain and tearing, like everything which is destined to live; it is the charm and the consolation of men, and cannot be the fruit of a passing effort or of a banal tradition. Vulgar laurels may crown vulgar efforts; a passing assent may accompany, during their success, works brought forth by the caprice of the moment; but the pursuit of glory commands other attempts: an unyielding fight is necessary to snatch one of its smiles; that would be little enough: to obtain it one must have a thousand gifts and destiny's favor. Simple tradition could not produce a work which caused people to cry out 'Oh, it's beautiful!' A genius come out of earth, an unknown and privileged man will topple this scaffold of doctrines for everyone's use, which produce nothing. A Holbein with his scrupulous imitation of his models' wrinkles, who counts their hairs, so to speak, a Rembrandt with his vulgar types filled with such deep expression, these Germans and these Italians of the primitive schools, with their thin, crooked figures and their complete ignorance of ancient art, sparkle with beauties and with that ideal which the schools chase after, ruler in hand. Guided by a naïve inspiration, drawing the inspiration which erudition cannot counterfeit from the nature which surrounds them and from a deep feeling, they excite around them both the people and cultivated men, they express sentiments which were in every soul: they have naturally found this priceless jewel which a useless science vainly asks of experience and precepts.

Nature has given to each talent a particular talisman, which I would compare to these metals invaluable in the alloying of a thousand precious metals, and which give sounds either charming or terrible, according to the different proportions of the elements which form them. There exist delicate talents which cannot easily be satisfied: seeking to captivate the spirit, they address it with all the means at their disposal; they remake a piece a hundred times, they sacrifice the touch, the trained execution, which brings out the details to a greater or lesser degree, to the unity and depth of the impression. Such a one is Leonardo da Vinci, such a one is Titian. There are other talents, like Tintoretto, or even better like Rubens, and I prefer the latter because he goes farther forward in expression, talents which are swept along by a sort of verve which is in the blood and the hand. The strength of certain touches, which are not considered here, gives to the works of these masters an animation and a vigor which a more circumspect execution does not always reach.

[*From the Revue des Deux Mondes*, 15 July 1854. *Translated by Anne Gwin*]

99

I.d.5. THÉOPHILE GAUTIER, Préface de *Mademoiselle de Maupin*

Il est aussi absurde de dire qu'un homme est un ivrogne parce qu'il décrit une orgie, un débauché parce qu'il raconte une débauche que de prétendre qu'un homme est vertueux parce qu'il a fait un livre de morale; tous les jours on voit le contraire. – C'est le personnage qui parle et non l'auteur; son héros est athée, cela ne veut pas dire qu'il soit athée; il fait agir et parler les brigands en brigands, il n'est pas pour cela un brigand. A ce compte, il faudrait guillotiner Shakespeare, Corneille et tous les tragiques; ils ont plus commis de meurtres que Mandrin et Cartouche; on ne l'a pas fait cependant, et je ne crois même pas qu'on le fasse de longtemps, si vertueuse et si morale que puisse devenir la critique.

C'est une des manies de ces petits grimauds à cervelle étroite que de substituer toujours l'auteur à l'ouvrage et de recourir à la personnalité pour donner quelque pauvre intérêt de scandale à leurs misérables rapsodies, qu'ils savent bien que personne ne lirait si elles ne contenaient que leur opinion individuelle.

Nous ne concevons guère à quoi tendent toutes ces criailleries, à quoi bon toutes ces colères et tous ces abois, – et qui pousse messieurs les Geoffroy au petit pied à se faire les don Quichotte de la morale, et, vrais sergents de ville littéraires, à empoigner et à bâtonner, au nom de la vertu, toute idée qui se promène dans un livre la cornette posée de travers ou la jupe troussée un peu trop haut. – C'est fort singulier. L'époque, quoi qu'ils en disent, est immorale (si ce mot-là signifie quelque chose, ce dont nous doutons fort), et nous n'en voulons pas d'autre preuve que la quantité de livres immoraux qu'elle produit et le succès qu'ils ont. – Les livres suivent les moeurs et les moeurs ne suivent pas les livres. – La Régence a fait Crébillon, ce n'est pas Crébillon qui a fait la Régence. es petites bergères de Boucher étaient fardées et débraillées, parce que les petites marquises étaient fardées et débraillées. – Les tableaux se font d'après les modèles et non es modèles d'après les tableaux. je ne sais qui a dit je ne sais où que la littérature et les rts influaient sur les moeurs. Qui que ce soit, c'est indubitablement un grand sot. – C'est omme si l'on disait: Les petits pois font pousser le printemps; les petits pois poussent u contraire parce que c'est le printemps, et les cerises parce que c'est l'été. Les arbres ortent les fruits, et ce ne sont pas les fruits qui portent les arbres assurément, loi éternelle t invariable dans sa variété; les siècles se succèdent, et chacun porte son fruit qui n'est as celui du siècle précédent; les livres sont les fruits des moeurs.

A côté des journalistes moraux, sous cette pluie d'homélies comme sous une pluie 'été dans quelque parc, il a surgi, entre les planches du tréteau saint-simonien, une théorie de petits champignons d'une nouvelle espèce assez curieuse, dont nous allons faire l'histoire naturelle.

Ce sont les critiques utilitaires. Pauvres gens qui avaient le nez court à ne le pouvoir hausser de lunettes, et cependant n'y voyaient pas aussi loin que leur nez. Quand un uteur jetait sur leur bureau un volume quelconque, roman ou poésie, – ces messieurs se enversaient nonchalamment sur leur fauteuil, le mettaient en équilibre sur ses pieds de errière, et, se balançant d'un air capable, ils se rengorgeaient et disaient:

– A quoi sert ce livre? Comment peut-on l'appliquer à la moralisation et au bien-être e la classe la plus nombreuse et la plus pauvre? Quoi! pas un mot des besoins de la ociété, rien de civilisant et de progressif! Comment, au lieu de faire la grande synthèse e l'humanité, et de suivre, à travers les événements de l'histoire, les phases de l'idée égénératrice et providentielle, peut-on faire des poésies et des romans qui ne mènent à ien, et qui ne font pas avancer la génération dans le chemin de l'avenir? Comment peut-on s'occuper de la forme, du style, de la rime en présence de si graves intérêts? – Que ous font, à nous, et le style et la rime, et la forme? c'est bien de cela qu'il s'agit (pauvres enards, ils sont trop verts)! – La société souffre, elle est en proie à un grand

I.d.5. THÉOPHILE GAUTIER, from Preface to *Mademoiselle de Maupin*

It is as absurd to say that a man is a drunkard because he describes an orgy, or a debauchee because he recounts a debauch, as to pretend that a man is virtuous because he has written a moral book; every day we see the contrary. It is the character who speaks and not the author; the fact that his hero is an atheist does not make him an atheist; his brigands act and speak like brigands, but he is not therefore a brigand himself. At that rate it would be necessary to guillotine Shakespeare, Corneille, and all the tragic writers; they have committed more murders than Mandrin and Cartouche. This has, nevertheless not been done, and I think that it will be long before it is done, however virtuous and moral criticism may come to be. It is one of the manias of these narrow-brained scribblers to substitute always the author for the work and have recourse to personalities, in order to give some poor scandalous interest to their wretched rhapsodies which they are quite aware nobody would read if they contained only their own individual opinions.

We find it hard to understand the purport of all this bawling, the good of all this temper and despair, and who it is that impels the miniature Geoffreys to constitute themselves the Don Quixotes of morality, and like true literary policemen, to seize and cudgel, in the name of virtue, every idea which makes its appearance in a book with its mob-cap awry or its skirt tucked up a little to high. It is very singular.

Say what they will, the age is an immoral one (if this word signifies anything, of which we have strong doubts), and we wish for no other proof than the quantity of immoral books it produces and the success that attends them. Books follow morals, and not moral books. The Regency made Crébillon, and not Crébillon the Regency. Boucher's little shepherdesses had their faces painted and their bosoms bare, because the little marchionesses had the same. Pictures are made according to models, and not models according to pictures. Some one has said somewhere that literature and the arts influence morals. Whoever he was, he was undoubtedly a great fool. It was like saying green peas make the spring grow, whereas green peas grow because it is spring, and cherries because it is summer. Trees bear fruits; it is certainly not the fruits that bear the trees, and this law is eternal and invariable in its variety; the centuries follow one another, and each bears its own fruit, which is not that of the preceding century; books are the fruits of morals.

By the side of the moral journalists, under this rain of homilies as under summer rain in some park, there has sprung up between the planks of the Saint-Simonian stage a theory of little mushrooms, of a novel and somewhat curious species, whose natural history we are about to give. These are the utilitarian critics. Poor fellows! Their noses are too short to admit of their wearing spectacles, and yet they cannot see the length of their noses.

If an author threw a volume of romance or poetry on their desk, these gentlemen would turn round carelessly in their easy-chair, poise it on its hinder legs, and balancing themselves with a capable air, say loftily:–

'What purpose does this book serve? How can it be applied for the moralization and well-being of the poorest and most numerous class? What! not a word of the needs of society, nothing about civilization and progress? How can a man, instead of making the great synthesis of humanity, and pursuing the regenerating and providential idea through the events of history, how can he write novels and poems which lead to nothing, and do not advance our generation on the path of the future? How can he busy himself with form, and style, and rhyme in the presence of such grave interests? What are style, and rhyme, and form to us? They are of no

déchirement ntérieur (traduisez: personne ne veut s'abonner aux journaux utiles). C'est au poète à hercher la cause de ce malaise et à le guérir. Le moyen, il le trouvera en sympathisant de oeur et d'âme avec l'humanité (des poètes philanthropes! ce serait quelque chose de rare et de charmant). Ce poète, nous l'attendons, nous l'appelons de tous nos voeux. Quand l paraîtra, à lui les acclamations de la foule, à lui les palmes, à lui les couronnes, à lui le rytanée – .

A la bonne heure; mais, comme nous souhaitons que notre lecteur se tienne éveillé usqu'à la fin de cette bienheureuse préface, nous ne continuerons pas cette imitation très fidèle du style utilitaire, qui, de sa nature, est passablement soporifique, et pourrait remplacer, avec avantage, le laudanum et les discours d'académie.

Non, imbéciles, non, crétins et goitreux que vous êtes, un livre ne fait pas de la soupe à la gélatine; – un roman n'est pas une paire de bottes sans couture; un sonnet, une seringue à jet continu; un drame n'est pas un chemin de fer, toutes choses essentiellement civilisantes, et faisant marcher l'humanité dans la voie du progrès.

De par les boyaux de tous les papes passés, présents et futurs, non et deux cent mille fois non. On ne se fait pas un bonnet de coton d'une métonymie, on ne chausse pas une comparaison en guise de pantoufle; on ne se peut servir d'une antithèse pour parapluie; malheureusement, on ne saurait se plaquer sur le ventre quelques rimes bariolées en manière de gilet. J'ai la conviction intime qu'une ode est un vêtement trop léger pour l'hiver, et qu'on ne serait pas mieux habillé avec la strophe, l'antistrophe et l'épode que cette femme du cynique qui se contentait de sa seule vertu pour chemise, et allait nue comme la main, à ce que raconte l'histoire.

Cependant le célèbre M. de La Calprenède eut une fois un habit, et, comme on lui demandait quelle étoffe c'était, il répondit: Du Silvandre. – Silvandre était une pièce qu'il venait de faire représenter avec succès.

De pareils raisonnements font hausser les épaules par-dessus la tête, et plus haut que le duc de Glocester.

Des gens qui ont la prétention d'être des économistes, et qui veulent rebâtir la société de fond en comble, avancent sérieusement de semblables billevesées.

Un roman a deux utilités: – l'une matérielle, l'autre spirituelle, si l'on peut se servir d'une pareille expression a l'endroit d'un roman. – L'utilité matérielle, ce sont d'abord les quelques mille francs qui entrent dans la poche de l'auteur, et le lestent de façon que le diable ou le vent ne l'emportent; pour le libraire, c'est un beau cheval de race qui piaffe et saute avec son cabriolet d'ébène et d'acier, comme dit Figaro; pour le marchand de papier, une usine de plus sur un ruisseau quelconque, et souvent le moyen de gâter un beau site; pour les imprimeurs, quelques tonnes de bois de campêche pour se mettre hebdomadairement le gosier en couleur; pour le cabinet de lecture, des tas de gros sous très prolétairement vert-de-grisés, et une quantité de graisse, qui, si elle était convenablement recueillie et utilisée, rendrait superflue la pêche de la baleine. – L'utilité spirituelle est que, pendant qu'on lit des romans, on dort, et on ne lit pas de journaux utiles, vertueux et progressifs, ou telles autres drogues indigestes et abrutissantes.

Qu'on dise après cela que les romans ne contribuent pas à la civilisation. – je ne parlerai pas des débitants de tabac, des épiciers et des marchands de pommes de terre frites, qui ont un intérêt très grand dans cette branche de littérature, le papier qu'elle emploie étant, en général, de qualité supérieure à celui des journaux.

En vérité, il y a de quoi rire d'un pied en carré, en entendant disserter messieurs les utilitaires républicains ou saint-simoniens. – Je voudrais bien savoir d'abord ce que veut dire précisément ce grand flandrin de substantif dont ils truffent quotidiennement le vide de leurs colonnes, et

consequence (poor foxes! they are too sour). Society is suffering, it is a prey to great internal anguish (translate – no one will subscribe to utilitarian journals). It is for the poet to seek the cause of this uneasiness and to cure it. He will find the means of doing so by sympathizing from his heart and soul with humanity – (philanthropic poets, they would be something uncommon and charming). This poet we await, and on him we call with all our vows. When he appears, his will be the acclamations of the crowd, his the palm, his the crown, his the Prytaneum.'

Well and good! But as we wish our reader to remain awake until the end of this blissful preface, we shall continue this very faithful imitation of the utilitarian style, which is, in its nature, tolerably soporific, and might, with advantage, take the place of laudanum and Academic discourses.

No, fools, no, goitrous cretins that you are, a book does not make gelatine soup; a novel is not a pair of seamless boots; a sonnet, a syringe with a continuous jet; or a drama, a railway – all things which are essentially civilizing and adapted to advance humanity on its path of progress.

By the guts of all the popes past, present, and future, no, and two hundred thousand times no! We cannot make a cotton cap out of a metonymy, or put on a comparison like a slipper; we cannot use an antithesis as an umbrella, and we cannot, unfortunately, lay a medley of rhymes on our body after the fashion of a waistcoat. I have an intimate conviction that an ode is too light a garment for winter, and that we should not be better clad in strophe, antistrophe, and epode than was the cynic's wife who contented herself with merely her virtue as chemise, and went about as naked as one's hand, so history relates.

However, the celebrated Monsieur de La Calprenède had once a coat, and when asked of what material it was made, he replied, 'Of Silvandre.' *Silvandre* was the name of a piece which he had just brought out with success. Such arguments make one elevate one's shoulders above the head, and higher than the Duke of Gloucester's.

People who pretend to be economists, and who wish to reconstruct society from top to bottom, seriously advance similar nonsense.

A novel has two uses – one material and the other spiritual – if we may employ such an expression in reference to a novel. Its material use means first of all some thousands of francs which find their way into the author's pocket, and ballast him in such a fashion that neither devil nor wind can carry him off; to the bookseller, it means a fine thoroughbred horse, pawing and prancing with its cabriolet of ebony and steel, as Figaro says; to the papermaker, another mill beside some stream or other, and often the means of spoiling a fine site; to the printers, some tons of logwood for the weekly staining of their throats; to the circulating library, some piles of pence covered with very proletarian verdigris, and a quantity of fat which, if it were properly collected and utilized, would render whale-fishing superfluous. Its spiritual use is that when reading novels we sleep, and do not read useful, virtuous, and progressive journals, or other similarly indigestible and stupefying drugs.

Let any one say after this that novels do not contribute to civilization. I say nothing of tobacco-sellers, grocers, and dealers in fried potatoes, who have a very great interest in this branch of literature, the paper employed in it being commonly of a superior quality to that of newspapers.

In truth, it is enough to make one burst with laughing to hear the dissertations of these Republican or Saint-Simonian utilitarian gentlemen. I should, first of all, very much like to know the precise meaning of this great lanky substantive with which the void in their columns

qui leur sert de schibroleth et de terme sacramentel. – Utilité: quel est ce mot, et à quoi s'applique-t-il?

Il y a deux sortes d'utilité, et le sens de ce vocable n'est jamais que relatif. Ce qui est utile pour l'un ne l'est pas pour l'autre. Vous êtes savetier, je suis poète. – Il est utile pour moi que mon premier vers rime avec mon second. – Un dictionnaire de rimes m'est d'une grande utilité; vous n'en avez que faire pour carreler une vieille paire de bottes, et il est juste de dire qu'un tranchet ne me servirait pas à grand-chose pour faire une ode. – Après cela, vous objecterez qu'un savetier est bien au-dessus d'un poète, et que l'on se passe mieux de l'un que de l'autre. Sans prétendre rabaisser l'illustre profession de savetier, que j'honore à l'égal de la profession de monarque constitutionnel, j'avouerai humblement que j'aimerais mieux avoir mon soulier décousu que mon vers mal rimé, et que je me passerais plus volontiers de bottes que de poèmes. Ne sortant presque jamais et marchant plus habilement par la tête que par les pieds, j'use moins de chaussures qu'un républicain vertueux qui ne fait que courir d'un ministère à l'autre pour se faire jeter quelque place.

Je sais qu'il y en a qui préfèrent les moulins aux églises, et le pain du corps à celui de l'âme. A ceux-là, je n'ai rien à leur dire. Ils méritent d'être économistes dans ce monde, et aussi dans l'autre.

Y a-t-il quelque chose d'absolument utile sur cette terre et dans cette vie où nous sommes? D'abord, il est très peu utile que nous soyons sur terre et que nous vivions. je défie le plus savant de la bande de dire à quoi nous servons, si ce n'est à ne pas nous abonner au Constitutionnel ni à aucune espèce de journal quelconque.

Ensuite, l'utilité de notre existence admise a priori, quelles sont les choses réellement utiles pour la soutenir? De la soupe et un morceau de viande deux fois par jour, c'est tout ce qu'il faut pour se remplir le ventre, dans la stricte acception du mot. L'homme, à qui un cercueil de deux pieds de large sur six de long suffit et au-delà après sa mort, n'a pas besoin dans sa vie de beaucoup plus de place. Un cube creux de sept à huit pieds dans tous les sens, avec un trou pour respirer, une seule alvéole de la ruche, il n'en faut pas plus pour le loger et empêcher qu'il ne lui pleuve sur le dos. Une couverture, roulée convenablement autour du corps, le défendra aussi bien et mieux contre le froid que le frac de Staub le plus élégant et le mieux coupé.

Avec cela, il pourra subsister à la lettre. On dit bien qu'on peut vivre avec 25 sous par jour; mais s'empêcher de mourir, ce n'est pas vivre; et je ne vois pas en quoi une ville organisée utilitairement serait plus agréable à habiter que le Père-la-Chaise.

Rien de ce qui est beau n'est indispensable à la vie. – On supprimerait les fleurs, le monde n'en souffrirait pas matériellement; qui voudrait cependant qu'il n'y eût plus de fleurs? je renoncerais plutôt aux pommes de terre qu'aux roses, et je crois qu'il n'y a qu'un utilitaire au monde capable d'arracher une plate-bande de tulipes pour y planter des choux.

A quoi sert la beauté des femmes? Pourvu qu'une femme soit médicalement bien conformée, en état de faire des enfants, elle sera toujours assez bonne pour des économistes.

A quoi bon la musique? à quoi bon la peinture? Qui aurait la folie de préférer Mozart à M. Carrel, et Michel-Ange à l'inventeur de la moutarde blanche?

Il n'y a de vraiment beau que ce qui ne peut servir à rien; tout ce qui est utile est laid, car c'est l'expression de quelque besoin, et ceux de l'homme sont ignobles et dégoûtants, comme sa pauvre et infirme nature. – L'endroit le plus utile d'une maison, ce sont les latrines. [...]

(1834)

is daily truffled, and which serves them as a shibboleth and sacramental term – utility. What is this word, and to what is it applicable?

There are two sorts of utility, and the meaning of the vocable is always a relative one. What is useful for one is not useful for another. You are a cobbler; I am a poet. It is useful to me to have my first line rhyme with my second. A rhyming dictionary is of great utility to me; you do not want it to cobble an old pair of boots, and it is only right to say that a shoe-knife would not be of great service to me in making an ode. To this you will object that a cobbler is far above a poet, and that people can do without the one better than without the other. Without affecting to disparage the illustrious profession of cobbler, which I honor equally with that of constitutional monarch, I humbly confess that I would rather have my shoes unstitched than my verse badly rhymed, and that I should be more willing to go without boots than without poems. Scarcely ever going out, and walking more skillfully with my head than with my feet, I wear out fewer shoes than a virtuous Republican, who is always hastening from one minister to another in the hope of having some place flung to him.

I know that there are some who prefer mills to churches, and bread for the body to that for the soul. To such I have nothing to say. They deserve to be economists this world and also in the next.

Is there anything absolutely useful on this earth and in this life of ours? To begin with, it is not very useful that we are on the earth and alive. I defy the most learned of the band to tell us of what use we are, unless it be not to subscribe to the 'Constitutionnel,' nor any other species of journal whatsoever.

Next, the utility of our existence being admitted *a priori*, what are the things really useful for supporting it? Some soup and a piece of meat twice a day is all that is necessary to fill the stomach in the strict acceptation of the word. Man who finds a coffin six feet long by two wide more than sufficient after his death does not need much more room during his life. A hollow cube measuring seven or eight feet every way, with a hole to breathe through, a single cell in the hive, nothing more is wanted to lodge him and keep the rain off his back. A blanket properly rolled around his body will protect him as well and better against the cold than the most elegant and best cut dress-coat by Staub. With this he will be able, literally, to subsist. It is truly said that it is possible to live on a shilling a day. But to prevent one's self from dying is not living; and I do not see in what respect a town organized after the utilitarian fashion would be more agreeable to dwell in than the cemetery of Père-la-Chaise.

Nothing that is beautiful is indispensable to life. You might suppress flowers, and the world would not suffer materially; yet who would wish that there were no more flowers? I would rather give up potatoes than roses, and I think that there is none but an utilitarian in the world capable of pulling up a bed of tulips in order to plant cabbages therein.

What is the use of women's beauty? Provided that a woman be medically well formed, and in condition to bear children, she will always be good enough for economists.

What is the good of music? of painting? Who would be foolish enough to prefer Mozart to Monsieur Carrel, and Michael Angelo to the inventor of white mustard? There is nothing truly beautiful but that which can never be of any use whatsoever; everything useful is ugly, for it is the expression of some need, and man's needs are ignoble and disgusting like his own poor and infirm nature. The most useful place in a house is the water-closet.

(1834) [*Translated by Burton Rascoe. New York: Knopf, 1926. 21–27*]

I.d.6. VICTOR HUGO, préface de *Cromwell*

Ainsi, pour résumer rapidement les faits que nous avons observés jusqu'ici, la poésie a trois âges, dont chacun correspond à une époque de la société: l'ode, l'épopée, le drame. Les temps primitifs sont lyriques, les temps antiques sont épiques, les temps modernes sont dramatiques. L'ode chante l'éternité, l'épopée solennise l'histoire, le drame peint la vie. Le caractère de la première poésie est la naïveté, le caractère de la seconde est la simplicité, le caractère de la troisième, la vérité. Les rhapsodes marquent la transition des poëtes lyriques aux poëtes épiques, comme les romanciers des poëtes épiques aux poëtes dramatiques. Les historiens naissent avec la seconde époque; les chroniqueurs et les critiques avec la troisième. Les personnages de l'ode sont des colosses, – Adam, Caïn, Noé; ceux de l'épopée sont des géants, – Achille, Atrée, Oreste; ceux du drame sont des hommes, – Hamlet, Macbeth, Othello. L'ode vit de l'idéal, l'épopée du grandiose, le drame du réel. Enfin, cette triple poésie découle de trois grandes sources, la Bible, Homère, Shakespeare.

Telles sont donc, et nous nous bornons en cela à relever un résulat, les diverses physionomies de la pensée aux différentes ères de l'homme et de la société. Voilà ses trois visages, de jeunesse, de virilité et de vieillesse. Qu'on examine une littérature en particulier, ou toutes les littératures en masse, on arrivera toujours au même fait: les poëtes lyriques avant les poëtes épiques, les poëtes épiques avant les poëtes dramatiques. En France, Malherbe avant Chapelain, Chapelain avant Corneille; dans l'ancienne Grèce, Orphée avant Homère, Homère avant Eschyle; dans le livre primitif, la *Genèse* avant les *Rois*, les *Rois* avant *Job*; ou, pour reprendre cette grande échelle de toutes les poésies que nous parcourions tout à l'heure, la Bible avant l'*Iliade*, l'*Iliade* avant Shakespeare.

La société, en effet, commence par chanter ce qu'elle rêve, puis raconte ce qu'elle fait, et enfin se met à peindre ce qu'elle pense. C'est, disons-le en passant, pour cette dernière raison que le drame, unissant les qualités les plus opposées, peut-être tout à la fois plein de profondeur et plein de relief, philosophique et pittoresque.

Il serait conséquent d'ajouter ici que tout dans la nature et dans la vie passe par ces trois phases, du lyrique, de l'épique et du dramatique, parce que tout naît, agit et meurt. S'il n'était pas ridicule de mêler les fantasques rapprochements de l'imagination aux déductions sévères du raisonnement, un poëte pourrait dire que le lever du soleil, par exemple, est un hymne, son midi une éclatante épopée, son coucher un sombre drame où luttent le jour et la nuit, la vie et la mort. Mais ce serait là de la poésie, de la folie peut-être; et *qu'est-ce que cela prouve*?

Tenons-nous-en aux faits rassemblés plus haut; complétons-les d'ailleurs par une observation importante. C'est que nous n'avons aucunement prétendu assigner aux trois époques de la poésie un domaine exclusif, mais seulement fixer leur caractère dominant. La Bible, ce divin monument lyrique, renferme, comme nous l'indiquions tout à l'heure, une épopée et un drame en germe, les *Rois* et *Job*. On sent dans tous les poèmes homériques un reste de poésie lyrique et un commencement de poésie dramatique. L'ode et le drame se croisent dans l'épopée. Il y a tout dans tout; seulement il existe dans chaque chose un élément générateur auquel se subordonnent tous les autres, et qui impose à l'ensemble son caractère propre.

Le drame est la poésie complète. L'ode et l'épopée ne le contiennent qu'en germe; il les contient l'une et l'autre en développement; il les résume et les enserre toutes deux. Certes, celui qui a dit: *les français n'ont pas la tête épique,* a dit une chose juste et fine; si même il eût dit *les modernes,* le mot spirituel eût été un mot profond, II est incontestable cependant qu'il y a surtout du génie épique dans cette prodigieuse *Athalie,* si haute et si simplement sublime que le siècle royal ne l'a

I.d.6.   VICTOR HUGO, from Preface to *Cromwell*

Thus, to sum up hurriedly the facts that we have noted thus far, poetry has three periods, each of which corresponds to an epoch of civilization: the ode, the epic, and the drama. Primitive times are lyrical, ancient times epical, modern times dramatic. The ode sings of eternity, the epic imparts solemnity to history, the drama depicts life. The characteristic of the first poetry is ingenuousness, of the second, simplicity, of the third, truth. The rhapsodists mark the transition from the lyric to the epic poets, as do the romancists that from the lyric to the dramatic poets. Historians appear in the second period, chroniclers and critics in the third. The characters of the ode are colossi – Adam, Cain, Noah; those of the epic are giants – Achilles, Atreus, Orestes; those of the drama are men – Hamlet, Macbeth, Othello. The ode lives upon the ideal, the epic upon the grandiose, the drama upon the real. Lastly, this threefold poetry flows from three great sources – The Bible, Homer, Shakespeare.

Such then – and we confine ourselves herein to noting a single result – such are the diverse aspects of thought in the different epochs of mankind and of civilization. Such are its three faces, in youth, in manhood, in old age. Whether one examines one literature by itself or all literatures *en masse,* one will always reach the same result: the lyric poets before the epic poets, the epic poets before the dramatic poets. In France, Malherbe before Chapelain, Chapelain before Corneille; in ancient Greece, Orpheus before Homer, Homer before Æschylus; in the first of all books, *Genesis* before *Kings, Kings* before *Job;* or to come back to that monumental scale of all ages of poetry, which we ran over a moment since, The Bible before the *Iliad,* the *Iliad* before Shakespeare.

In a word, civilization begins by singing of its dreams, then narrates its doings, and lastly, sets about describing what it thinks. It is, let us say in passing, because of this last, that the drama, combining the most opposed qualities, may be at the same time full of profundity and full of relief, philosophical and picturesque.

It would be logical to add here that everything in nature and in life passes through these three phases, the lyric, the epic, and the dramatic, because everything is born, acts, and dies. If it were not absurd to confound the fantastic conceits of the imagination with the stern deductions of the reasoning faculty, a poet might say that the rising of the sun, for example, is a hymn, noonday a brilliant epic, and sunset a gloomy drama wherein day and night, life and death, contend for mastery. But that would be poetry – folly, perhaps – and *what does it prove?*

Let us hold to the facts marshaled above; let us supplement them, too, by an important observation, namely that we have in no wise pretended to assign exclusive limits to the three epochs of poetry, but simply to set forth their predominant characteristics. The Bible, that divine lyric monument, contains in germ, as we suggested a moment ago, an epic and a drama – *Kings* and *Job.* In the Homeric poems one is conscious of a clinging reminiscence of lyric poetry and of a beginning of dramatic poetry. Ode and drama meet in the epic. There is a touch of all in each; but in each there exists a generative element to which all the other elements give place, and which imposes its own character upon the whole.

The drama is complete poetry. The ode and the epic contain it only in germ; it contains both of them in a state of high development, and epitomizes both. Surely, he who said: 'The French have not the epic brain,' said a true and clever thing; if he had said, 'The moderns,' the clever remark would have been profound. It is beyond question, however, that there is epic genius in that marvelous *Athalie,* so exalted and so simple in its sublimity that the royal century was unable to comprehend it. It is certain, too, that the series of Shakespeare's chronicle dramas presents a grand

pu comprendre. Il est certain encore que la série des drames-chroniques de Shakespeare présente un grand aspect d'épopée. Mais c'est surtout la poésie lyrique qui sied au drame; elle ne le gêne jamais, se plie à tous ses caprices, se joue sous toutes les formes, tantôt sublime dans Ariel, tantôt grotesque dans Caliban. Notre époque, dramatique avant tout, est par cela même éminemment lyrique. C'est qu'il y a plus d'un rapport entre le commencement et la fin; le coucher du soleil a quelques traits de son lever; le vieillard redevient enfant. Mais cette dernière enfance ne ressemble pas à la première; elle est aussi triste que l'autre est joyeuse. Il en est de même de la poésie lyrique. Éblouissante, rêveuse à l'aurore des peuples, elle reparaît sombre et pensive à leur déclin. La Bible s'ouvre riante avec la *Genèse*, et se ferme sur la menaçante *Apocalypse*. L'ode moderne est toujours inspirée, mais n'est plus ignorante. Elle médite plus qu'elle ne contemple; sa rêverie est mélancolie. On voit, à ses enfantements, que cette muse s'est accouplée au drame.

Pour rendre sensibles par une image les idées que nous venons d'aventurer, nous comparerions la poésie lyrique primitive à un lac paisible qui reflète les nuages et les étoiles du ciel; l'epopée est le fleuve qui en découle et court, en réfléchissant ses rives, forêts, campagnes et cités, se jeter dans l'océan du drame. Enfin, comme le lac, le drame réfléchit le ciel; comme le fleuve, il réfléchit ses rives; mais seul il a des abîmes et des tempêtes.

C'est donc au drame que tout vient aboutir dans la poésie moderne. Le *Paradis perdu* est un drame avant d'être une épopée. C'est, on le sait, sous la première de ces formes qu'il s'était présenté d'abord à l'imagination du poëte, et qu'il reste toujours imprimé dans la mémoire du lecteur, tant l'ancienne charpente dramatique est encore saillante sous l'édifice épique de Milton! Lorsque Dante Alighieri a terminé son redoutable *Enfer*, qu'il en a refermé les portes, et qu'il ne lui reste plus qu'à nommer son oeuvre, l'instinct de son génie lui fait voir que ce poëme multiforme est une émanation du drame, non de l'épopée; et sur le frontispice du gigantesque monument, il écrit de sa plume de bronze: *Divina Commedia*.

On voit donc que les deux seuls poètes des temps modernes qui soient de la taille de Shakespeare se rallient à son unité. Ils concourent avec lui à empreindre de la teinte dramatique toute notre poésie; ils sont comme lui mêlés de grotesque et de sublime; et, loin de tirer à eux dans ce grand ensemble littéraire qui s'appuie sur Shakespeare, Dante et Milton sont en quelque sorte les deux arcs-boutants de l'édifice dont il est le pilier central, les contreforts de la voûte dont il est la clef.

Qu'on nous permette de reprendre ici quelques idées déjà énoncées, mais sur lesquelles il faut insister. Nous y sommes arrivé, maintenant il faut que nous en repartions. Du jour où le christianisme a dit à l'homme: – Tu es double, tu es composé de deux êtres, l'un périssable, l'autre immortel, l'un charnel, l'autre éthéré, l'un enchaîné par les appétits, les besoins et les passions, l'autre emporté sur les ailes de l'enthousiasme et de la rêverie, celui-ci enfin toujours courbé vers la terre, sa mère, celui-là sans cesse élancé vers le ciel, sa patrie; – de ce jour le drame a été créé. Est-ce autre chose en effet que ce contraste de tous les jours, que cette lutte de tous les instants entre deux principes opposés qui sont toujours en présence dans la vie, et qui se disputent l'homme depuis le berceau jusqu'à la tombe?

La poésie née du christianisme, la poésie de notre temps est donc le drame; le caractère du drame est le réel; le réel résulte de la combinaison toute naturelle de deux types, le sublime et le grotesque, qui se croisent dans le drame, comme ils se croisent dans la vie et dans la création. Car la poésie vraie, la poésie complète, est dans l'harmonie des contraires.

(1827)

epic aspect. But it is lyric poetry above all that befits the drama; it never embarrasses it, adapts itself to all its caprices, disports itself in all forms, sometimes sublime as in Ariel, sometimes grotesque as in Caliban. Our era being above all else dramatic, is for that very reason eminently lyric. There is more than one connection between the beginning and the end; the sunset has some features of the sunrise; the old man becomes a child once more. But this second childhood is not like the first; it is as melancholy as the other is joyous. It is the same with lyric poetry.

Dazzling, dreamy, at the dawn of civilization, it reappears, solemn and pensive, at its decline. The Bible opens joyously with *Genesis* and comes to a close with the threatening *Apocalypse*. The modern ode is still inspired, but is no longer ignorant. It meditates more than it scrutinizes; its musing is melancholy. We see, by its painful labour, that the muse has taken the drama for her mate.

To make clear by a metaphor the ideas that we have ventured to put forth, we will compare early lyric poetry to a placid lake which reflects the clouds and stars; the epic is the stream which flows from the lake, and rushes on, reflecting its banks, forests, fields and cities, until it throws itself into the ocean of the drama. Like the lake, the drama reflects the sky; like the stream, it reflects its banks; but it alone has tempests and measureless depths.

The drama, then, is the goal to which everything in modern poetry leads. *Paradise Lost* is a drama before it is an epic. As we know, it first presented itself to the poet's imagination in the first of these forms, and as a drama it always remains in the reader's memory, so prominent is the old dramatic framework still beneath Milton's epic structure! When Dante had finished his terrible *Inferno,* when he had closed its doors and nought remained save to give his work a name, the unerring instinct of his genius showed him that that multiform poem was an emanation of the drama, not of the epic; and on the front of that gigantic monument, he wrote with his pen of bronze: *Divina Commedia.*

Thus we see that the only two poets of modern times who are of Shakespeare's stature follow him in unity of design. They coincide with him in imparting a dramatic tinge to all our poetry; like him, they blend the grotesque with the sublime; and, far from standing by themselves in the great literary *ensemble* that rests upon Shakespeare, Dante and Milton are, in some sort, the two supporting abutments of the edifice of which he is the central pillar, the buttresses of the arch of which he is the keystone.

Permit us, at this point, to recur to certain ideas already suggested, which, however, it is necessary to emphasize. We have arrived, and now we must set out again.

On the day when Christianity said to man: 'Thou art twofold, thou art made up of two beings, one perishable, the other immortal, one carnal, the other ethereal, one enslaved by appetites, cravings and passions, the other borne aloft on the wings of enthusiasm and reverie – in a word, the one always stooping toward the earth, its mother, the other always darting up toward heaven, its fatherland' – on that day the drama was created. Is it, in truth, anything other than that contrast of every day, that struggle of every moment, between two opposing principles which are ever face to face in life, and which dispute possession of man from the cradle to the tomb? The poetry born of Christianity, the poetry of our time, is, therefore, the drama; the real results from the wholly natural combination of two types, the sublime and the grotesque, which meet in the drama, as they meet in life and in creation. For true poetry, complete poetry, consists in the harmony of contraries.

(1827) [*From The Harvard Classics (1909–1914)*]

I.d.7. STENDHAL, *Racine et Shakespeare*

Le *romanticisme* est l'art de présenter aux peuples les œuvres littéraires qui, dans l'état actuel de leurs habitudes et de leurs croyances, sont susceptibles de leur donner le plus de plaisir possible.

Le *classicisme,* au contraire, leur présente la littérature qui donnait le plus grand plaisir à leurs arrière-grands-pères.

Sophocle et Euripide furent éminemment romantiques; ils donnèrent aux Grecs rassemblés au théâtre d'Athènes les tragédies qui, d'après les habitudes morales de ce peuple, sa religion, ses préjugés sur ce qui fait la dignité de l'homme, devaient lui procurer le plus grand plaisir possible.

Imiter aujourd'hui Sophocle et Euripide, et prétendre que ces imitations ne feront pas bâiller le Français du XIXe siècle, c'est du classicisme.

Je n'hésite pas à avancer que Racine a été romantique; il a donné aux marquis de la cour de Louis XIV une peinture des passions, tempérée par *l'extrême dignité* qui alors était de mode, et qui faisait qu'un duc de 1670, même dans 'es épanchements les plus tendres de l'amour paternel, ne manquait jamais d'appeler son fils *Monsieur.*

C'est pour cela que le Pylade *d'Andromaque* dit toujours à Oreste: *Seigneur;* et cependant quelle amitié que celle d' Oreste et de Pylade!

Cette dignité-là n'est nullement dans les Grecs, et c'est cause de cette *dignité,* qui nous glace aujourd'hui, que Racine a été romantique.

Shakespeare fut romantique parce qu'il présenta aux Anglais de l'an 1590, d'abord les catastrophes sanglantes menées par les guerres civiles, et pour reposer de ces tristes spectacles, une foule de peintures fines des mouvements du coeur, et des nuances de passions les plus délicates. Cent ans de guerres civiles et de troubles presque continuels, une foule de trahisons, de supplices, de dévouements généreux, avaient préparé les sujets d'Elisabeth à ce genre de tragédie, qui ne produit presque rien de tout *le factice* de la vie des cours et de la civilisation des peuples tranquilles. Les Anglais de 1590, heureusement fort ignorants, aimèrent à contempler au théâtre l'image des malheurs que le caractère ferme de leur reine venait d'éloigner de la vie telle. Ces mêmes détails naïfs, que nos vers alexandrins repousseraient avec dédain, et que l'on prise tant aujourd'hui dans *Ivanhoé* et dans *Rob-Roy,* eussent paru manquer de dignité aux yeux des fiers marquis de Louis XIV.

Ces détails eussent mortellement effrayé les poupées sentimentales et musquées qui, sous Louis XV, ne pouvaient voir une araignée sans s'évanouir. Voilà, je le sens bien, une phrase peu digne.

Il faut du courage pour être romantique, car il faut *hasarder.*

Le *classique* prudent, au contraire, ne s'avance jamais sans être soutenu, en cachette, par quelque vers d'Homère, ou par une remarque philosophique de Cicéron, dans son traité *De Senectute.*

Il me semble qu'il faut du courage à l'écrivain presque autant qu'au guerrier; l'un ne doit pas plus songer aux journalistes que l'autre à l'hôpital.

(1823)

I.d.7.   STENDHAL, from *Racine and Shakespeare*

Romanticism is the art of presenting to different peoples those literary works which, in the existing state of their habits and beliefs, are capable of giving them the greatest possible pleasure.

Classicism, on the contrary, presents to them that literature which gave the greatest possible pleasure to their great-grandfathers.

Sophocles and Euripides were eminently romantic. To the Greeks assembled in the theatre of Athens, they presented those tragedies which, in accordance with the moral usages of that people, its religion, and its prejudices in the matter of what constitutes the dignity of man, would provide for it the greatest possible pleasure.

To imitate Sophocles and Euripides today, and to maintain that these imitations will not cause a Frenchman of the nineteenth century to yawn with boredom, is classicism.

I do not hesitate to state that Racine was a romantic. He gave the *marquis* of the court of Louis XIV a portrayal of the passions tempered by the *extreme formalism* then in style, which was such that a duke of 1670, even in the most tender effusions of paternal love, never failed to call his son *Monsieur*.

It was for this reason that the Pylades of *Andromaque* always calls Orestes *Seigneur*. And yet how great was the friendship between Orestes and Pylades!

That formalism did not exist at all among the Greeks; and it is because of that formalism, which today we find chilling, that Racine was romantic. Shakespeare was romantic because he presented to the English of 1590, first, the bloody catastrophes brought on by the civil wars and then, by way of relief from those sad spectacles, a wealth of exact portrayals of the emotions and the most delicate nuances of feeling. A hundred years of civil wars and almost continuous troubles, with countless acts of treason, torturings, and generous acts of devotion, had prepared the subjects of Elizabeth for this kind of tragedy, which reproduces almost none of the *artificial* element in the court life and civilization of the tranquil nations. The English of 1590, fortunately very ignorant, loved to contemplate on the stage the image of those misfortunes that had recently been removed from real life thanks to the firm character of their queen. These same fresh details, which our alexandrine lines would repulse with disdain and which are so much appreciated today in *Ivanhoe* and *Rob Roy*, would have seemed to the proud marquis of Louis XIV to be lacking in dignity.

Those details would have mortally frightened the sentimental and perfumed dolls who, under Louis XV, could not see a spider without fainting. (This sentence, I realize, is most undignified.)

It requires courage to be a romant[...]

The prudent *classicist*, on the cont[...] etly, by a line from Homer or by a phi[...] *De Senectute*.

It seems to me that the writer mu[...]mer must give no more thought to the jou[...]

(1823) [Trans[...]-39]

[Handwritten note:] Romanticism: presenting a literary work that will produce the greatest pleasure

It requires courage to be romantic (one must take a chance)

romanticism depends on period

I.d.8. CHARLES NODIER, de *'De la littérature fantastique'*

Le fantastique demande à la vérité une virginité d'imagination et de croyances qui manque aux littératures secondaires, et qui ne se reproduit chez elle qu'à la suite de ces révolutions dont le passage renouvelle tout; mais, alors, et quand les religions elles-mêmes ébranlées jusque dans leurs fondements ne parlent plus à l'imagination, ou ne lui portent que des notions confuses de jour en jour obscurcies par un scepticisme inquiet, il faut bien que cette faculté de produire le merveilleux dont la nature l'a douée s'exerce sur un genre de création plus vulgaire, et mieux approprié aux besoins d'une intelligence matérialisée. L'apparition des fables recommence au moment où finit l'empire de ces vérités réelles ou convenues, qui prêtent un reste d'âme au mécanisme usé de la civilisation. Voilà ce qui a rendu le fantastique si populaire en Europe depuis quelques années, et ce qui en fait la seule littérature essentielle de l'âge de décadence ou de transition où nous sommes parvenus. Nous devons même reconnaître en cela un bienfait spontané de notre organisation, car si l'esprit humain ne se complaisait encore dans de vives et brillantes chimères, quand il a touché à nu toutes les repoussantes réalités du monde vrai, cette époque de désabusement serait en proie au plus violent désespoir, et la société offrirait la révélation effrayante d'un besoin unanime de dissolution et de suicide. Il ne faut donc pas tant crier contre le romantique et contre le fantastique. Ces innovations prétendues sont l'expression inévitable des périodes extrêmes de la vie politique des nations, et sans elles, je sais à peine ce qui nous resterait aujourd'hui de l'instinct moral et intellectuel de l'humanité. [...]

Parmi les hommes d'élection qu'un instinct profond de génie a jeté, dans ces derniers temps, à la tête des littératures, il n'en est point qui n'ait senti l'avertissement de cette muse d'une société qui tombe, et qui n'ait obéi à ses inspirations, comme à la voix imposante d'un mourant dont la fosse est déjà ouverte. L'école romanesque de Lewis, l'école romantique des Lackistes, et, par-dessus tout, ces grands maîtres de la parole, Byron, et Walter Scott, et Lamartine, et Hugo, s'y sont précipités à la recherche de la vie idéale, comme si un organe particulier de divination, que la nature a donné au poète, leur avait fait pressentir que le souffle de la vie positive était près de s'éteindre dans l'organisation caduque des peuples. [...]

Ce que j'ose croire, c'est que si la liberté dont on nous parle n'est pas, comme je l'ai craint quelquefois, une déception de jongleurs, ses deux principaux sanctuaires sont dans la croyance de l'homme religieux et dans l'imagination du poète. Quelle autre compensation promettez-vous à une âme profondément navrée de l'expérience de la vie, quel autre avenir pourra-t-elle se préparer désormais dans l'angoisse de tant d'espérances déchues, que les révolutions emportent avec elles, je le demande à vous, hommes libres qui vendez aux maçons le cloître du cénobite, et qui portez la sape sous l'ermitage du solitaire, où il s'était réfugié à côté du nid de l'aigle? Avez-vous des joies à rendre aux frères que vous repoussez qui puissent les dédommager de la perte d'une seule erreur consolant et vous croyez-vous assez sûrs des vérités que vous fait payer si cher aux nations, pour estimer leur aride amertume au prix de la douce et inoffensive rêverie du malheureux qui se rendort sur un songe heureux? Cependant tout jouit chez vous, il faut le dire, d'une liberté sans limites, si ce n'est la conscience et le génie.

[*Publié dans la Revue de Paris, Novembre 1830*]

I.d.8. CHARLES NODIER, from 'On the Literature of the Fantastic'

The fantastic demands of truth a virginity of imagination and beliefs which is lacking in second-ary literatures, and which recurs in the truth only after those revolutions whose passage renews everything; but then, and when the religions themselves, shaken to their very foundations, no longer speak to the imagination, or bring it only confused notions obscured from day to day by a worried skepticism, it is indeed necessary that this faculty of producing the marvelous with which nature has endowed it, should be exercised on a more vulgar type of creation, better suited to the needs of a materialized intelligence.

The appearance of fables begins anew at the moment where ends the influence of those real or conventional truths which lend a remnant of soul to the well-worn mechanism of civilization. That is what has made the fantastic so popular in Europe for some years now, and what makes it the only essential literature of the age of decadence or transition which we have reached. We ought even to recognize in this a spontaneous benefit of our organization, for if the human spirit did not still delight in lively and brilliant chimeras, when it has touched all the uncovered, repulsive reali-ties of the real world, this period of disillusionment would fall prey to the most violent despair, and society would offer the fearsome revelation of a unanimous need for dissolution and suicide. One should not therefore scold the romantic and fantastic so much. These so-called innovations are the inevitable expression of extreme periods of the political life of nations, and without them, I hardly know what would remain to us today of the moral and intellectual instinct of humanity. [. . .]

Among the chosen men which the deep instinct of genius has of late thrown to the head of literatures, there is not one who has not felt the warning of this muse of a falling society, and who has not obeyed her inspirations, as the imposing voice of a dying man whose grave is already open. The romanesque school of Lewis, the romantic school of the Lackists, and above all, these great masters of the word, Byron, and Walter Scott, and Lamartine, and Hugo, have rushed to search for the ideal life, as if a particular organ of divination, which nature has given to the poet, had made them feel a premonition that the breath of positive life had nearly died out in the lapsed organization of the peoples. [. . .]

I dare to believe that if the liberty we hear about is not, as I have sometimes feared, a juggler's deception, its two principal sanctuaries are in the belief of the religious man and in the imagination of the poet. What other compensation do you promise to a soul profoundly sickened by the expe-rience of life, what other future can it prepare for itself henceforth in the anguish of so many fallen hopes, that the revolutions carry with them, I ask you, free men who sell to masons the cenobite's cloister, and who dig a sapper's tunnel under the hermit's cell, where he had taken refuge beside the eagle's nest? Have you joys to return to the brothers whom you push away which can make up for the loss of a single consoling error and do you believe yourselves sure enough of the truths for which you cause the nations to pay so dearly, to appraise their arid bitterness at the price of the gentle, inoffensive reverie of the unhappy man who goes back to sleep on a happy dream? Yet with you, everything enjoys a limitless freedom, it must be said, except for conscience and genius.

[*Published in the Revue des Deux Mondes, November 1830*]
[*Translated by Anne Gwin*]

I.d.9.   ANNE LOUISE GERMAINE de STAËL, de *De l'Allemagne, Pt. II, Ch. XI.*
De la Poésie Classique et de la Poésie Romantique

Le nom de *romantique* a été introduit nouvellement en Allemagne pour désigner la poésie, dont les chants des troubadours ont été l'origine, celle qui est née de la chvalerie et du christianisme. Si l'on n'admet pas que le paganisme et le christianisme, le Nord et le Midi, l'antiquité et le moyen âge, la chevalerie et les institutions grecques et romaines, se sont partagé l'empire de la littérature, l'on ne parviendra jamais à juger sous un point de vue philosophique le goût antique et le goût moderne.

On prend quelquefois le mot classique comme synonyme de perfection. Je m'en sers ici dans une autre acception, en considérant la poésie classique comme celle des anciens, et la poésie romantique comme celle qui tient de quelque manière aux traditions chevaleresques. Cette division se rapporte également aux deux ères du monde: celle qui a précédé l'établissement du christianisme, et celle qui l'a suivi.

On a comparé ainsi dans divers ouvrages allemands la poésie antique à la sculpture, et la poésie romantique à la peinture; enfin l'on a caractérisé de toutes les manières la marche de l'esprit humain, passant des religions matérialistes aux religions spiritualistes, de la nature à la Divinité.

La nation française, la plus cultivée des nations latines, penche vers la poésie classique, imitée des Grecs et des Romains. La nation anglaise, la plus illustre des nations germaniques, aime la poésie romantique et chevaleresque, et se glorifie des chefs-d'œuvre qu'elle possède en ce genre. Je n'examinerai point ici lequel de ces deux genres de poésie mérite la préference; il suffit de montrer que la diversité des goûts, à cet égard, dérive non seulement de causes accidentelles, mais aussi des sources primitives de l'imagination et de la pensée.

Il y a dans les poëmes épiques et dans les tragédies des anciens un genre de simplicité qui tient à ce que les hommes étaient identifiés à cette époque avec la nature, et croyaient dépendre du destin comme elle de la nécessité. L'homme, réfléchissant peu, portait toujours l'action de son âme au dehors; la conscience elle-même était figurée par des objets extérieurs, et les fambeaux des furies secouaient les remords sur la tête des coupables. L'événement était tout dans l'antiquité; le caractère tient plus de place dans les temps modernes; et cette réflexion inquiète, qui nous dévore comme le vautour de Prométhée, n'eût semblé que de la folie au milieu des rapports clairs et prononcés qui existaient dans l'état civil et social des anciens.

On ne faisait en Grèce, dans le commencement de l'art, que des statues isolées; les groupes ont été composés plus tard. On pourrait dire de même avec vérité que dans tous les arts il n'y avait point de groupes; les objets représentés se succédaient comme dans des bas-reliefs, sans combinaison, sans complication d'aucun genre. L'homme personnifiait la nature: des nymphes habitaient les eaux, des hamadryades les forêts; mais la nature à son tour s'emparait de l'homme, et l'on eût dit qu'il ressemblait au torrent, à la foudre, au volcan, tant il agissait par une impulsion involontaire, et sans que la réflexion pût en rien altérer les motifs ni les suites de ses actions. Les anciens avaient, pour ainsi dire, une âme corporelle dont tous les mouvements étaient forts, directs et conséquents; il n'en est pas de même du coeur humain développé par le christianisme: les modernes ont puisé dans le repentir chrétien l'habitude de se replier continuellement sur eux-mêmes.

Mais, pour manifester cette existence tout intérieur, il faut qu'une grande variété dans les faits présente, sous toutes les formes, les nuances infinies de ce qui se passe dans l'âme. Si de nos jours les beaux-arts étaient astreints à la simplicité des anciens, nous n'atteindrions pas à la force

I.d.9. ANNE LOUISE GERMAINE de STAËL, from *On Germany, Part II,*
Chapter XI *Of Classic and Romantic Poetry*

The word *romantic* has been lately introduced in Germany to designate that kind of poetry which is derived from the songs of the Troubadours; that which owes its birth to the union of chivalry and Christianity. If we do not admit that the empire of literature has been divided between paganism and Christianity, the North and the South, antiquity and the middle ages, chivalry and the institutions of Greece and Rome, we shall never succeed in forming a philosophical judgment of ancient and of modern taste.

We sometimes consider the word classic as synonymous with perfection. I use it at present in a different acceptation, considering classic poetry as that of the ancients, and romantic, as that which is generally connected with the traditions of chivalry. This division is equally suitable to the two eras of the world, – that which preceded, and that which followed the establishment of Christianity.

In various German works, ancient poetry has also been compared to sculpture, and romantic to painting; in short, the progress of the human mind has been characterized in every manner, passing from material religions to those which are spiritual, from nature to the Deity.

The French nation, certainly the most cultivated of all that are derived from Latin origin, inclines towards classic poetry imitated from the Greeks and Romans. The English, the most illustrious of the Germanic nations, is more attached to that which owes its birth to chivalry and romance; and it prides [...] it possesses. I will not, in this place, exam[...] reference; it is sufficient to show, that th[...] ng from accidental causes, but are derived [...] ought.

There is a kind of si[...] ncients; because at that time men were c[...] lves controlled by fate, as absolutely as [...] g but little, always bore the action of his s[...] al objects, and the torch of the Furies sh[...]. In ancient times, men attended to event[...] r importance; and that uneasy reflection, [...] devours us, would have been folly amid [...] they existed in the civil and social state o[...]

When the art of sc[...] rmed; groups were composed at a later p[...] e no groups in any art: objects were repre[...] tion, without complication of any kind. [...] s, hamadryads the forests; but nature, in turn, possessed herself of man, and, it might be said, he resembled the torrent, the thunderbolt, the volcano, so wholly did he act from involuntary impulse, and so insufficient was reflection in any respect, to alter the motives or the consequences of his actions. The ancients, thus to speak, possessed a corporeal soul, and its emotions were all strong, decided, and consistent; it is not the same with the human heart as developed by Christianity: the moderns have derived from Christian repentance a constant habit of self-reflection.

But in order to manifest this kind of internal existence, a great variety of outward facts and circumstances must display, under every form, the innumerable shades and gradations of that which is passing in the soul. If in our days the fine arts were confined to the simplicity of the

primitive qui les distingue, et nous perdrions les émotions intimes et multipliées dont notre âme est susceptible. La simplicité de l'art, chez les modernes, tournerait facilement à la froideur et à l'abstraction, tandis que celle des anciens était pleine de vie. L'honneur et l'amour, la bravoure et la pitié sont les sentiments qui signalent le christianisme chevaleresque; et ces dispositions de l'âme ne peuvent se faire voir que dans les dangers, les exploits, les amours, les malheurs, l'intérêt romantique enfin, qui varie sans cesse les tableaux. Les sources des effets de l'art sont donc différentes à beaucoup d'égards dans la poésie classique et dans la poésie romantique: dans l'une, c'est le sort qui règne; dans l'autre, c'est la Providence; le sort ne compte pour rien les sentiments des hommes, la Providence ne juge les actions que d'après les sentiments. Comment la poésie ne créerait-elle pas un monde d'une tout autre nature, quand il faut peindre l'oeuvre d'un destin aveugle et sourd, toujours en lutte avec les mortels, ou cet ordre intelligent auquel préside un être suprême que notre coeur interroge et qui répond à notre coeur!

La poésie païenne doit être simple et saillante comme les objets extérieurs; la poésie chrétienne a besoin des mille couleurs de l'arc-en-ciel pour ne pas se perdre dans les nuages. La poésie des anciens est plus pure comme art, celle des modernes fait verser plus de larmes; mais la question pour nous n'est pas entre la poésie classique et la poésie romantique; mais entre l'imitation de l'une et l'inspiration de l'autre. La littérature des anciens est chez les modernes une littérature transplantée; la littérature romantique ou chevalesque est chez nous indigène, et c'est notre religion et nos institutions qui l'ont fait éclore. Les écrivains imitateurs des anciens se sont soumis aux règles du goût les plus sévères; car, ne pouvant consulter ni leur propre nature ni leurs propres souvenirs, il a fallu qu'ils se consulter ni leur propre nature ni leurs propres souvenirs, il a fallu qu'ils se conformassent aux loix d'après lesquelles les chefs-d'oeuvre des anciens peuvent être adaptés à notre goût, bien que toutes les circonstances politiques et religieuses qui ont donné le jour à ces chef-d'oeuvre soient changées. Mais ces poésies d'apès l'antique, quelque parfaites qu'elles soient, sont rarement populaires, parce qu'elles ne tiennent, dans le temps actuel, à rien de national.

La poésie française étant la plus classique de toutes les poésies modernes, elle est la seule qui ne soit pas répandue parmi le peuple. Les stances du Tasse sont chantées par les gondoliers de Venise; les Espagnols et les Portugais de toutes les classes savent par coeur les vers de Calderon et de Camoëns. Shakespeare est autant admiré par le peuple en Angleterre que par la classe supérieure. Des poëmes français sont admirés par tout ce qu'il y a d'esprits cultivés chez nous et dans le reste de l'Europe; mais ils sont tout à fait inconnus aux gens du peuple et aux bourgeois même des villes, parce que les arts en France ne sont pas, comme ailleurs, natifs du pays même où leurs beautés se développent.

Quelques critiques français ont prétendu que la littérature des peuples germaniques était encore dans l'enfance de l'art; cette opinion est tout à fait fausse: les hommes les plus instruits dans la connaissance des langues et des ouvrages des anciens n'ignorent certainement pas les inconvénients et les avantages du genre qu'ils adoptent ou de celui qu'ils rejettent; mais leur caractère, leurs habitudes et leurs raisonnements les ont conduits à préférer la littérature fondée sur les souvenirs de la chevalerie, sur le merveilleux du moyen âge, à celle dont la mythologie des Grecs est la base. La littérature romantique est la seule qui soit susceptible encore d'être perfectionnée, parce qu'ayant ses racines dans notre propre sol, elle est la seule qui puisse croître et se vivifier de nouveau; elle exprime notre religion; elle rappelle notre histoire; son origine est ancienne, mais non antique.

La poésie classique doit passer par les souvenirs du paganisme pour arriver jusqu'à nous: la poésie des Germains est l'ère chrétienne des beaux-arts; elle se sert de nos impressions

ancients, we should ne[...] s them, and we should lose those intima[...] eptible. Simplicity in the arts would, am[...] bstraction, while that of the ancients was [...] y, were the sentiments which distinguish[...] sitions of the soul could only be displayed [...] interest, in short, by which pictures are i[...] its effect are then very different in classic [...] eigns, in the other it is Providence. Fate co[...] e judges of actions according to those sent[...] y different nature, when its object is to p[...] f, maintaining an endless contest with r[...] lligent order, over which the Supreme Be[...] rts supplicate, and who mercifully answe[...]

The poetry of the p[...] d as the objects of nature; while that of Christianity requires the various colors of the rainbow to preserve it from being lost in the clouds. The poetry of the ancients is more pure as an art; that of the moderns more readily calls forth our tears. But our present object is not so much to decide between classic and romantic poetry, properly so called, as between the imitation of th[...] e and the inspiration of the other. The li[...] planted literature; that of chivalry and ro[...] ce of our religion and our institutions. W[...] themselves to the rules of strict taste alo[...] ture or their own recollections, it is neces[...] efs-d'oeuvre of the ancients may be adapte[...] cal and religious, which gave birth to thes[...] written in imitation of the ancients, ho[...] n our days, it has no connection whateve[...]

The French being th[...] east calculated to become familiar among[...] are sung by the gondoliers of Venice; th[...] art the verses of Calderon and Camoëns.[...] n England as by those of a higher class. The[...] epeated from the banks of the Rhine to the sh[...] herever there are cultivated minds, either in o[...] e quite unknown to the common people, and e[...] e arts, in France, are not, as elsewhere, natives o[...] country in which their beauties are displayed.

Some French critics have asserted that German literature is still in its infancy. This opinion is entirely false; men who are best skilled in the knowledge of languages and the works of the ancients, are certainly not ignorant of the defects and advantages attached to the species of literature which they either adopt or reject; but their character, their habits, and their modes of reasoning, have led them to prefer that which is founded on the recollection of chivalry, on the wonders of the middle ages, to that which has for its basis the mythology of the Greeks. Romantic literature is alone capable of further improvement, because, being rooted in our own soil, that alone can continue to grow and acquire fresh life: it expresses our religion; it recalls our history; its origin is ancient, although not of classical antiquity. Classic poetry, before it comes

personnelles pour nous émouvoir; le génie qui l'inspire s'adresse immédiatement à notre coeur, et semble évoquer notre vie elle-même comme un fantôme le plus puissant et le plus terrible de tous.

(1810)

e. DEUTSCH

I.e.1. FRIEDRICH SCHILLER, aus *Über naive und sentimentalische Dichtung*

Es gibt Augenblicke in unserm Leben, wo wir der Natur in Pflanzen, Mineralien, Tieren, Landschaften, sowie der menschlichen Natur in Kindern, in den Sitten des Landvolks und der Urwelt, nicht weil sie unsern Sinnen wohltut, auch nicht weil sie unsern Verstand oder Geschmack befriedigt (von beiden kann oft das Gegenteil stattfinden), sondern bloß *weil sie Natur ist*, eine Art von Liebe und von rührender Achtung widmen. Jeder feinere Mensch, dem es nicht ganz und gar an Empfindung fehlt, erfährt dieses, wenn er im Freien wandelt, wenn er auf dem Lande lebt oder sich bei den Denkmälern der alten Zeiten verweilet, kurz, wenn er in künstlichen Verhältnissen und Situationen mit dem Anblick der einfältigen Natur überrascht wird. Dieses nicht selten zum Bedürfnis erhöhte Interesse ist es, was vielen unsrer Liebhabereien für Blumen und Tiere, für einfache Gärten, für Spaziergänge, für das Land und seine Bewohner, für manche Produkte des fernen Altertums u. dgl. zum Grund liegt; vorausgesetzt, daß weder Affektation noch sonst ein zufälliges Interesse dabei im Spiele sei. Diese Art des Interesses an der Natur findet aber nur unter zwei Bedingungen statt. Fürs erste ist es durchaus nötig, daß der Gegenstand, der uns dasselbe einflößt, *Natur* sei oder doch von uns dafür gehalten werde; zweitens, daß er (in weitester Bedeutung des Worts) *naiv* sei; d. h. daß die Natur mit der Kunst im Kontraste stehe und sie beschäme. Sobald das letzte zu dem ersten hinzukommt, und nicht eher, wird die Natur zum Naiven.

Natur in dieser Betrachtungsart ist uns nichts anders als das freiwillige Dasein, das Bestehen der Dinge durch sich selbst, die Existenz nach eignen und unabänderlichen Gesetzen.

Diese Vorstellung ist schlechterdings nötig, wenn wir an dergeichen Erscheinungen Interesse nehmen sollen. Könnte man einer gemachten Blume den Schein der Natur mit der vollkommensten Täuschung geben, könnte man die Nachahmung des Naiven in den Sitten bis zur höchsten Illusion treiben, so würde die Entdeckung, daß es Nachahmung sei, das Gefühl, von dem die Rede ist, gänzlich vernichten. Daraus erhellet, daß diese Art des Wohlgefallens an der Natur kein ästhetisches, sondern ein moralisches ist; denn es wird durch eine Idee vermittelt, nicht unmittelbar durch Betrachtung erzeugt; auch richtet es sich ganz und gar nicht nach der Schönheit der Formen. Was hätte auch eine unscheinbare Blume, eine Quelle, ein bemooster Stein, das Gezwitscher der Vögel, das Summen der Bienen usw. für sich selbst so Gefälliges für uns? Was könnte ihm gar einen Anspruch auf unsere Liebe geben? Es sind nicht diese Gegenstände, es ist eine durch sie dargestellte Idee, was wir in ihnen lieben. Wir lieben in ihnen das stille schaffende Leben, das ruhige Wirken aus sich selbst, das Dasein nach eignen Gesetzen, die innere Notwendigkeit, die ewige Einheit mit sich selbst.

Sie *sind*, was wir *waren*; sie sind, was wir wieder *werden sollen*. Wir waren Natur wie sie, und unsere Kultur soll uns, auf dem Wege der Vernunft und der Freiheit, zur Natur zurückführen. Sie sind also zugleich Darstellung unserer verlorenen Kindheit, die uns ewig das Teuerste bleibt;

home to us, must pass through our recollections of paganism: that of the Germans is the Christian era of the fine arts; it employs our personal impressions to excite strong and vivid emotions; the genius by which it is inspired addresses itself immediately to our hearts, and seems to call forth the spirit of our own lives, of all phantoms at once the most powerful and the most terrible.

(1810) [*Cambridge, MA: Houghton, 1879. 198–204*]

e. GERMAN

I.e.1. FRIEDRICH SCHILLER, from *On the Naive and Sentimental in Literature*

There are moments in our life when we accord to nature in plants, minerals, animals, landscapes, as well as to human nature in children, in the customs of country people and of the primitive world, a sort of love and touching respect, not because it pleases our senses nor because it satisfies our intellect or taste (the opposite of both can often be the case) but merely *because it is nature*. Every sensitive person who is not wholly lacking in feeling experiences this when he wanders in the open air, when he lives in the country or lingers among the monuments of ancient times, in short, when in artificial conditions and situations he is surprised by a sight of simple nature. This interest, elevated quite often to a need, is what lies at the bottom of many of our fancies for flowers and animals, for, simple gardens, for walks, for the country and its inhabitants, for many a product of distant antiquity and such like things; always presupposing that neither affectation nor any other accidental interest plays a part here. This sort of interest in nature, however, only comes to pass under two conditions. Firstly, it is absolutely necessary that the object which inspires it in us should be *natural* or at least should be held by us to be so; secondly, that it should (in the widest sense of the word) be *naive*, i.e., that nature should stand in contrast to art and put it to shame. As soon as the last is joined to the first and not before, the natural becomes the naive.

In this way of looking at things, nature for us is nothing other than voluntary existence, the continuation of things through themselves, existence according to its own unchangeable laws.

This concept is absolutely necessary if we are to take an interest in such phenomena. If one could give an artificial flower the appearance of nature so that it deceived completely, if one could push the imitation of the naive in manners and customs to the highest degree of illusion, then the discovery that it was imitation would completely destroy the feeling under discussion. From this it emerges that this sort of pleasure in nature is not an aesthetic but a moral one; for it is conveyed by means of an idea, not produced directly by observation; nor is it governed at all by the beauty of natural forms. What could a modest flower, a spring, a mossy stone, the twittering of the birds, the humming of the bees, etc. have in themselves that would be so pleasing to us? What could give them a claim on our love, even? It is not these objects, it is an *idea* represented by them which we love in them. In them we love the calm, creative life, the quiet functioning from within themselves, the existence according to their own laws, the inner necessity, the eternal unity with themselves.

They *are* what we *were*; they are what we *should become* again. We were natural like them and our culture should lead us back to nature along the path of reason and freedom. They are, therefore, at the same time a representation of our lost childhood, which remains eternally most

daher sie uns mit einer gewissen Wehmut erfüllen. Zugleich sind sie Darstellungen unserer höchsten Vollendung im Ideale, daher sie uns in eine erhabene Rührung versetzen.

[. . .]

Die Dichter sind überall, schon ihrem Begriffe nach, die *Bewahrer* der Natur. Wo sie dieses nicht ganz mehr sein können und schon in sich selbst den zerstörenden Einfluß willkürlicher und künstlicher Formen erfahren oder doch mit demselben zu kämpfen gehabt haben, da werden sie als die *Zeugen* und als die *Rächer* der Natur auftreten. Sie werden entweder Natur *sein*, oder sie werden die verlorene *suchen*. Daraus entspringen zwei ganz verschiedene Dichtungsweisen, durch welche das ganze Gebiet der Poesie erschöpft und ausgemessen wird. Alle Dichter, die es wirklich sind, werden, je nachdem die Zeit beschaffen ist, in der sie blühen, oder zufällige Umstände auf ihre allgemeine Bildung und auf ihre vorübergehende Gemütsstimmung Einfluß haben, entweder zu den *naiven* oder zu den *sentimentalischen* gehören.

Der Dichter einer naiven und geistreichen Jugendwelt, sowie derjenige, der in den Zeitaltern künstlicher Kultur ihm am nächsten kommt, ist streng und spröde, wie die jungfräuliche Diana in ihren Wäldern, ohne alle Vertraulichkeit entflieht er dem Herzen, das ihn sucht, dem Verlangen, das ihn umfassen will. Die trockne Wahrheit, womit er den Gegenstand behandelt, erscheint nicht selten als Unempfindlichkeit. Das Objekt besitzt ihn gänzlich, sein Herz liegt nicht wie ein schlechtes Metall gleich unter der Oberfläche, sondern will wie das Gold in der Tiefe gesucht sein. Wie die Gottheit hinter dem Weltgebäude, so steht er hinter seinem Werk; er ist das Werk, und das Werk ist er; man muß des erstern schon nicht wert oder nicht mächtig oder schon satt sein, um nach ihm nur zu fragen.

So zeigt sich z.B. Homer unter den Alten und Shakespeare unter den Neuern; zwei höchst verschiedene, durch den unermeßlichen Abstand der Zeitalter getrennte Naturen, aber gerade in diesem Charakterzuge völlig eins. Als ich in einem sehr frühen Alter den letztern Dichter zuerst kennenlernte, empörte mich seine Kälte, seine Unempfindlichkeit, die ihm erlaubte, im höchsten Pathos zu scherzen, die herzzerschneidenden Auftritte im *Hamlet*, im *König Lear*, im *Macbeth* usf. durch einen Narren zu stören, die ihn bald da festhielt, wo meine Empfindung forteilte, bald da kaltherzig fortriß, wo das Herz so gern stillgestanden wäre. Durch die Bekanntschaft mit neuern Poeten verleitet, in dem Werke den Dichter zuerst aufzusuchen, *seinem* Herzen zu begegnen, *mit ihm* gemeinschaftlich über seinen Gegenstand zu reflektieren; kurz, das Objekt in dem Subjekt anzuschauen, war es mir unerträglich, daß der Poet sich hier gar nirgends fassen ließ und mir nirgends Rede stehen wollte. Mehrere Jahre hatte er schon meine ganze Verehrung und war mein Studium, ehe ich sein Individuum liebgewinnen lernte. Ich war noch nicht fähig, die Natur aus der ersten Hand zu verstehen. Nur ihr durch den Verstand reflektiertes und durch die Regel zurechtgelegtes Bild konnte ich ertragen, und dazu waren die sentimentalischen Dichter der Franzosen und auch der Deutschen, von den Jahren 1750 bis etwa 1780, gerade die rechten Subjekte. Übrigens schäme ich mich dieses Kinderurteils nicht, da die bejahrte Kritik ein ähnliches fällte und naiv genug war, es in die Welt hineinzuschreiben.

Dichter von dieser naiven Gattung sind in einem künstlichen Weltalter nicht so recht mehr an ihrer Stelle. Auch sind sie in demselben kaum mehr möglich, wenigstens auf keine andere Weise möglich, als daß sie in ihrem Zeitalter *wild laufen* und durch ein günstiges Geschick vor dem verstümmelnden Einfluß desselben geborgen werden. Aus der Sozietät selbst können sie nie und nimmer hervorgehen; aber außerhalb derselben erscheinen sie noch zuweilen, doch mehr als Fremdlinge, die man anstaunt, und als ungezogene Söhne der Natur, an denen man sich ärgert. So wohltätige Erscheinungen sie für den Künstler sind, der sie studiert, und für den

precious to us and thus they fill us with a certain sadness. At the same time they are representations of our highest perfection in the/ideal, so that they transport us into a state of elevated emotion.

[...]

Poets everywhere are by definition the *preservers* of nature. Where they can no longer be so completely and already experience in themselves the destructive influence of arbitrary and artificial forms or have even, had to fight against them, then they appear as the *witnesses* and the *avengers* of nature. They therefore will either be nature or they will *look for* lost nature. From this stem two quite different types of poetry, by which the whole poetic territory is exhausted and measured. All poets who really are poets, according to the nature of the period in which they flourish or according to what accidental circumstances have an influence on their general education and on their passing mental state, will belong either to the *naive* or the *sentimental* type.

*

The poet of a naive and clever youthful world, like him who in eras of artificial culture approaches him most nearly, is severe and reserved like the virgin Diana in her woods; without any intimacy he flees the heart which seeks him, the desire which wants to embrace him. The dry truth with which he treats his subject often appears insensitive. The subject possesses him utterly, his heart does not lie like base metal just under the surface but needs like gold to be sought for in the depths. As the godhead stands behind the edifice of the world, so does he stand behind his creation, *he* is the creation and the creation is *he*, one has to be unworthy of the creation, not strong enough for it or tired of it even to look for the creator.

This is how, for example, *Homer* among the ancients and *Shakespeare* among the moderns appear, two very different natures, separated by the immeasurable distance of their eras but in this characteristic completely one. When I first became acquainted with Shakespeare at a very early age, I was shocked by his coldness, the lack of feeling which allowed him to joke in the midst of the greatest pathos, to break up the heart-rending scenes in *Hamlet, King Lear, Macbeth* etc., by the introduction of a fool, which at times stopped him where my emotions rushed on, at times bore him cold-heartedly on where the heart would gladly have paused. Misled by my acquaintance with more modern poets to look first of all in the work for the author, to encounter *his* heart, to reflect on his subject-matter together *with him*, in short to look for the subject-matter in the person, it was unbearable to me that here the poet could nowhere be grasped, was nowhere answerable to me. He had already possessed my entire admiration and had been my study for several years before I learned to love his personality. I was not yet capable of understanding nature at first hand. I could only bear her image filtered by the understanding and ordered by rules, and for this the sentimental French and also German writers of the years 1750 to approximately 1780 were just the right subjects. However, I am not ashamed of this childish judgment, since critics well on in years formed a similar one and were naive enough to publish it to the world.

[...]

Poets of this naive type are no longer really in place in an artificial era. Neither are they possible any longer in such an era or at least only possible in so far as they fail to *conform* to their age and are protected by a favourable destiny from its mutilating influence. They can never emerge as part of society but sometimes they appear outside of it, rather as outsiders whom one wonders at and badly-brought up sons of nature at whom one is annoyed though they are refreshing figures for the artist who studies them and for the real connoisseur who knows how to appreciate

echten Kenner, der sie zu würdigen versteht, so wenig Glück machen sie im ganzen und bei ihrem Jahrhundert. Das Siegel des Herrschers ruht auf ihrer Stirne; wir hingegen wollen von den Musen gewiegt und getragen werden. Von den Kritikern, den eigentlichen Zaunhütern des Geschmacks, werden sie als *Grenzstörer* gehaßt, die man lieber unterdrücken möchte; denn selbst Homer dürfte es bloß der Kraft eines mehr als tausendjährigen Zeugnisses zu verdanken haben, daß ihn diese Geschmacksrichter gelten lassen; auch wird es ihnen sauer genug, ihre Regeln gegen sein Beispiel, und sein Ansehen gegen ihre Regeln zu behaupten.

Der Dichter, sagte ich, ist entweder Natur, oder er wird sie *suchen.* Jenes macht den naiven, dieses den sentimentalischen Dichter.

[...]

Solange der Mensch noch reine, es versteht sich, nicht rohe Natur ist, wirkt er als ungeteilte sinnliche Einheit und als ein harmonierendes Ganze. Sinne und Vernunft, empfangendes und selbsttätiges Vermögen, haben sich in ihrem Geschäfte noch nicht getrennt, viel weniger stehen sie im Widerspruch miteinander. Seine Empfindungen sind nicht das formlose Spiel des Zufalls, seine Gedanken nicht das gehaltlose Spiel der Vorstellungskraft; aus dem Gesetz der *Notwendigkeit* gehen jene, aus der *Wirklichkeit* gehen diese hervor. Ist der Mensch in den Stand der Kultur getreten, und hat die Kunst ihre Hand an ihn gelegt, so ist jene *sinnliche* Harmonie in ihm aufgehoben, und er kann nur noch als *moralische* Einheit, d. h. als nach Einheit strebend sich äußern. Die Übereinstimmung zwischen seinem Empfinden und Denken, die in dem ersten Zustande *wirklich* stattfand, existiert jetzt bloß *idealisch*: sie ist nicht mehr in ihm, sondern außer ihm; als ein Gedanke, der erst realisiert werden soll, nicht mehr als Tatsache seines Lebens. Wendet man nun den Begriff der Poesie, der kein andrer ist, *als der Menschheit ihren möglichst vollständigen Ausdruck zu geben*, auf jene beiden Zustände an, so ergibt sich, daß dort in dem Zustande natürlicher Einfalt, wo der Mensch noch, mit allen seinen Kräften zugleich, als harmonische Einheit wirkt, wo mithin das Ganze seiner Natur sich in der Wirklichkeit vollständig ausdrückt, die möglichst vollständige *Nachahmung des Wirklichen* — daß hingegen hier in dem Zustande der Kultur, wo jenes harmonische Zusammenwirken seiner ganzen Natur bloß eine Idee ist, die Erhebung der Wirklichkeit zum Ideal oder, was auf eins hinausläuft, *die Darstellung des Ideals den Dichter machen muß*. Und dies sind auch die zwei einzig möglichen Arten, wie sich überhaupt der poetische Genius äußern kann. Sie sind, wie man sieht, äußerst voneinander verschieden, aber es gibt einen höhern Begriff, der sie beide unter sich faßt, und es darf gar nicht befremden, wenn dieser Begriff mit der Idee der Menschheit in eins zusammentrifft.

Es ist hier der Ort nicht, diesen Gedanken, den nur eine eigene Ausführung in sein volles Licht setzen kann, weiter zu verfolgen. Wer aber nur irgend, dem Geiste nach und nicht bloß nach zufälligen Formen, eine Vergleichung zwischen alten und modernen Dichtern anzustellen vetrsteht, wird sich leicht von der Wahrheit desselben überzeugen können. Jene rühren uns durch Natur, durch sinnliche Wahrheit, durch lebendige Gegenwart; diese rühren uns durch Ideen.

Dieser Weg, den die neueren Dichter gehen, ist übrigens derselbe, den der Mensch überhaupt sowohl im einzelnen als im ganzen einschlagen muß. Die Natur macht ihn mit sich eins, die Kunst trennt und entzweiet ihn, durch das Ideal kehrt er zur Einheit zurück. Weil aber das Ideal ein Unendliches ist, das er niemals erreicht, so kann der kultivierte Mensch in *seiner* Art niemals vollkommen werden, wie doch der natürliche Mensch es in der seinigen zu werden vermag. Er müßte also dem letzteren an Vollkommenheit unendlich nachstehen, wenn bloß auf das Verhältnis, in welchem beide zu ihrer Art und zu ihrem Maximum stehen, geachtet wird. Vergleicht man hingegen die Arten selbst miteinander, so zeigt sich, daß das Ziel, zu welchem der Mensch durch

them, yet they do not get on well on the whole and in their epoch. The seal of a ruler rests on their forehead; we on the other hand want to be cradled and carried by the muses. They are hated by the critics, the actual border guards of taste, as *boundary breakers* who should rather be suppressed. For even Homer has the strength of the witness of more than a thousand years to thank that these guardians of good taste approve of him. They find it a bitter enough task to have to maintain their rules in the face of his prestige and his prestige in the face of their rules. The poet, as I have said, either is nature or he will seek it. The former constitutes the naive, the second the sentimental poet.

[. . .]

As long as man consists of pure, not of course of crude, nature, then he gives the impression of an undivided sensual unit and of a harmonious whole. The senses and the reason, the receptive and the spontaneous capacity, have not yet separated in their function, much less are they in opposition to each other. His emotions are not the formless play of accident, his thoughts are not the meaningless play of the imagination; the former proceed from the law of *necessity*, the latter from *reality*. If man has entered into a state of culture and if art has placed her hand on him, then that *sensual* harmony has been removed from him and he can only express himself as a *moral* unit, i.e., as someone striving for unity. The correspondence between his feeling and his thinking which existed in *reality* in the first state, now only exists *as an ideal*; it is no longer in him but outside of him, as an idea which must first be realized, no longer as a fact of his life. If one now applies the concept of poetry, which means nothing else than *to give humanity its most complete expression possible*, to both of these states, then in the state of natural simplicity, where man still functions together with all his powers as a harmonious unit, where the whole of his nature expresses itself completely in reality, the result is that the most complete possible *imitation of the real* must constitute the poet—that, on the other hand, here in the state of culture where that harmonious cooperation of his whole nature is merely an idea, it is the elevation of reality to the ideal or, what comes to the same thing, *the representation of the ideal which must make the poet*. And these are the two sole possible ways in which the poetic spirit can ever express itself. They are, as one can see, extremely different from each other, but there is a higher concept which subsumes both of them and it should not surprise us when this concept coincides with the idea of humanity.

Here is not the place to pursue this idea which can only be displayed in its full light by a separate discussion. He who knows how to institute a comparison between ancient and modern poets according to some spiritual criterion and not just according to accidental forms will easily be able to convince himself of the truth of it. The older poets touch us through nature, through sensual truth, through the living present; the modern ones touch us through ideas.

This path on which the modern poets are moving is, moreover, the same one on which man individually and mankind as a whole must travel. Nature makes him one with himself, art separates and divides him, through the ideal he returns to that unity. Because, however, the ideal is an infinite one which he never attains, the cultivated man can never become perfect in his *own* way as the natural man is able to do in his. He would, therefore, necessarily be immeasurably inferior to the latter in perfection if one were only to consider the relationship of both to their type and to their maximum potential. If, on the other hand, one compares the types themselves with each other, then it emerges that, the goal for which man *strives* through culture is immeasurably preferable to that which he *reaches* through nature. One, therefore, has his value because of his absolute attainment of a finite greatness, the other because of his approximation to an

Kultur *strebt*, demjenigen, welches er durch Natur *erreicht*, unendlich vorzuziehen ist. Der eine erhält also seinen Wert durch absolute Erreichung einer endlichen, der andre erlangt ihn durch Annäherung zu einer unendlichen Größe. Weil aber nur die letztere *Grade* und einen *Fortschritt* hat, so ist der relative Wert des Menschen, der in der Kultur begriffen ist, im ganzen genommen niemals bestimmbar, obgleich derselbe im einzelnen betrachtet sich in einem notwendigen Nachteil gegen denjenigen befindet, in welchem die Natur in ihrer ganzen Vollkommenheit wirkt. Insofern aber das letzte Ziel der Menschheit nicht anders als durch jene Fortschreitung zu erreichen ist und der letztere nicht anders fortschreiten kann, als indem er sich kultiviert und folglich in den erstern übergeht, so ist keine Frage, welchem von beiden in Rücksicht auf jenes letzte Ziel der Vorzug gebühre.

Dasselbe, was hier von den zwei verschiedenen Formen der Menschheit gesagt wird, läßt sich auch auf jene beiden ihnen entsprechenden Dichterformen anwenden.

Man hätte deswegen alte und moderne — naive und sentimentalische — Dichter entweder gar nicht oder nur unter einem gemeinschaftlichen höhern Begriff (einen solchen gibt es wirklich) miteinander vergleichen sollen. Denn freilich, wenn man den Gattungsbegriff der Poesie zuvor einseitig aus den alten Poeten abstrahiert hat, so ist nichts leichter, aber auch nichts trivialer, als die modernen gegen sie herabzusetzen. Wenn man nur das Poesie nennt, was zu allen Zeiten auf die einfältige Natur gleichförmig wirkte, so kann es nicht anders sein, als daß man den neuern Poeten gerade in ihrer eigensten und erhabensten Schönheit den Namen den Dichter wird streitig machen müssen, weil sie gerade hier nur zu dem Zögling der Kunst sprechen und der einfältigen Natur nichts zu sagen haben. Wessen Gemüt nicht schon zubereitet ist, über die Wirklichkeit hinaus ins Ideenreich zu gehen, für den wird der reichste Gehalt leerer Schein und der höchste Dichterschwung Überspannung sein. Keinem Vernünftigen kann es einfallen, in demjenigen, worin Homer groß ist, irgendeinen Neuern ihm an die Seite stellen zu wollen, und es klingt lächerlich genug, wenn man einen Milton oder Klopstock mit dem Namen eines neuern Homer beehrt sieht. Ebensowenig aber wird irgendein alter Dichter und am wenigsten Homer in demjenigen, was den modernen Dichter charakteristisch auszeichnet, die Vergleichung mit demselben aushalten können. Jener, möchte ich es ausdrücken, ist mächtig durch die Kunst der Begrenzung; dieser ist es durch die Kunst des Unendlichen.

[1795] [*Friedrich Schiller. Sämtliche Werke. Ed. Herbert G. Göpfert and Gerhard Fricke.*
Munich: Hanser, 1959. V, 694–719 (extracts)]

I.e.2.   LUDWIG TIECK, Über Shakespear's Behandlung des Wunderbaren

Man hat oft Shakspeare's Genie bewundert, das in so vielen seiner Kunstwerke die gewöhnliche Bahn verläßt, und neue Pfade sucht; bald Leidenschaften bis in ihre feinsten Schattierungen, bald bis zu ihren entferntesten Grenzen verfolgt; bald den Zuschauer in die Geheimnisse der Nacht einweiht, und ihn in einen Kreis von Hexen und Gespenstern versetzt; ihn dann wieder mit Feen und Geistern umgiebt, die jenen fürchterlichen Erscheinungen völlig unähnlich sind. Man hat zu oft über die Kühnheit, mit der Shakspeare die gewöhnlichen Regeln des Dramas verletzt, die ungleich größere Kunst übersehen, mit der er den Mangel der Regel unbemerkbar macht; denn eben darin besteht der Probierstein des ächten Genie's, daß es für jede verwegene Fiktion, für jede ungewöhnliche Vorstellungsart, schon im voraus die Täuschung des Zuschauers zu gewinnen weiß; daß der Dichter nicht unsre Gutmütigkeit in Anspruch nimmt, sondern die Phantasie, selbst wider unsern Willen, so spannt, daß wir die Regeln der Äesthetik, mit allen Begriffen unsers aufgeklärteren Jahrhunderts vergessen, und uns ganz dem schönen Wahnsinn des Dichters überlassen; daß sich die Seele, nach dem Rausch, willig der Bezauberung von

infinite one. However, because only the latter has *degrees* and a *progression*, then the relative value of him who is caught up in culture is on the whole never determinable, although looked at individually he must always find himself at a disadvantage compared to him in whom nature is functioning in all her perfection. In so far, however, as the ultimate goal of humanity cannot be reached except by means of that progression and the natural man cannot progress except by cultivating himself and as a result merges with the former, then there is no question as to which of the two deserves greater merit with regard to that ultimate goal.

What has been said here of two different forms of humanity can also be applied to the two types of poet who correspond to them.

For this reason we should have compared ancient and modern – naive and sentimental – poets either not at all or under a common but higher category (there really is such a one). For indeed if one has previously derived the definition of poetry one-sidedly from the ancient poets, then nothing is easier, but also more trivial, than to disparage the moderns in comparison with them. If one only calls that poetry which at all times has the same effect on simple natures, then the result must be that one will have to deny to the modern poets the name of poet at exactly the moment of their most individual and most elevated beauty, because it is just here that they only speak to the pupil of art and have nothing to say to simple natures. He whose spirit is not already prepared to go beyond reality into the realm of ideas will find the richest content empty illusion and the highest poetic flight exaggeration, It cannot occur to a sensible person to place a modern on an equal footing with Homer in the areas in which he is great and it sounds ridiculous enough when one sees a Milton or a Klopstock honored with the name of a modern Homer. Just as little, however, can any ancient poet and Homer least of all survive comparison with a modern poet in that area in which he characteristically excels. The ancient, if I may so express it, is powerful through the art of limitation; the modern through the art of the infinite.

[1795] [*Translated by Helen Watanabe. Manchester: Carcanet, 1981. 21–24*]

I.e.2.   LUDWIG TIECK, from 'Shakspeare's Treatment of the Marvellous'

Admiration has often been expressed for Shakspeare's genius, which in so many of his artistic works leaves the common course behind and seeks out new pathways, following the passions now into their most subtle nuances, now to their uttermost bounds, now initiating the spectator into the mysteries of the night, transporting him into the company of witches and ghosts, then again surrounding him with fairies wholly different from those terrible apparitions. Given the boldness with which Shakspeare offends against the customary rules of the drama, we too often overlook the immeasurably greater artistry with which he conceals from our notice such want of regularity: for the touchstone of true genius is to be found in the fact that, for every audacious fiction, every unusual angle of depiction, it is able to predispose the mind of the spectator to the acceptance of illusion; that the poet does not presume on our goodwill but so excites our imagination, even against our wishes, that we forget the rules of aesthetics, together with all the notions of our enlightened century, and abandon ourselves completely to the lovely delusions of the poet; that after intoxication the soul willingly yields to fresh

neuem hingibt, und die spielende Phantasie durch keine plötzliche und widrige Überraschung aus ihren Träumen geweckt wird.

In dieser größten unter den dramatischen Vollkommenheiten, wird Shakspeare vielleicht stets unnachahmlich bleiben; — diese große Alchymie, durch die alles, was er berührte, in Gold verwandelt ward, scheint mit ihm verloren. Denn so sehr seine Meisterstücke auch von seinen Zeitgenossen und späteren Dichtern, von Engländern und Deutschen nachgeahmt sind, so hat sich doch keiner nach ihm in jenen magischen Kreis gewagt, in welchem er so groß und furchtbar erscheint. Die wenigen, die es versucht haben, ihn hierin zu erreichen, stehen gegen ihn wie Beschwörer da, denen, trotz ihren geheimnißvollen Formeln, trotz allen ihren Cirkeln und ihrem Zauber-Apparatus, kein Geist gehorcht; und die am Ende nur Langeweile erregen, weil sie die Kunst nicht besitzen, den richtenden Verstand einzuschläfern.

Shakspeare war in seinem Zeitalter mehr als jeder andere Schriftsteller, der Dichter seiner Nation; er schrieb nicht für den Pöbel, aber für sein Volk; und die dramatischen Meisterstücke der Alten, selbst wenn er sie gekannt hätte, waren daher nicht das Tribunal, vor dem er seine Schauspiele zog, sondern durch ein aufmerksames Studium des Menschen hatte er gelernt, was auf die Gemüter wirkt, und nach seinem eigenen Gefühl, und den Regeln, die er aus der Erfahrung abstrahiert hatte, dichtete er seine Kunstwerke. Eben daher kommt es, daß die meisten seiner Stücke bei der Vorstellung und beim Lesen so allgemein wirken, und nothwendig wirken müssen; denn vielleicht hat kein Dichter in seinen Kunstwerken so sehr den theatralischen Effekt berechnet, als Shakspeare, ohne doch leere Theatercoups zum Besten zu geben, oder durch armselige Überraschungen zu unterhalten. Er hält die Aufmerksamkeit, ohne die Kunstgriffe mancher intriguanten Dichter, und ohne den Beistand der *Neugier* bis zum Schluß in Spannung, und erschüttert durch kühne Schläge seines Genie's innig, und bis zum Erschrecken.

Seine wunderbare Welt besteht daher nicht aus den Römischen oder Griechischen Gottheiten, oder aus unwirksamen allegorischen Wesen, die man vor ihm, und selbst noch zu seiner Zeit, häufig auf dem Theater sah, obgleich die Zuschauer durch diese an die übernatürlichen Wesen gewissermaßen gewöhnt waren; — sondern als Volksdichter ließ er sich zu der Tradition seines Volkes hinab.

Da die Phantasie des gemeinen Volks den Aberglauben erschafft und ausschmückt, so ist es natürlich, daß in den Produkten der erhitzten und geängstigten Einbildungskraft immer eben so viel Kindisches als Schreckliches liegt, eben so viel widrige und abgeschmackte Züge, als schöne und fürchterliche. Hätte Shakspeare ohne Unterschied diese Vorstellungsarten des Volks adoptiert, so hätte er freilich wohl auf den Beifall des Pöbels rechnen können, aber jeder Leser von einigem Geschmack und geläuterter Phantasie hätte dann auch unwillig die Mißgeburten seines Gehirns aus den Händen geworfen. Er zeigte aber hier sein feineres Gefühl; als einem echten Dichter, war es ihm nicht genug, sich zu den Vorstellungsarten des Volkes herabzulassen, sondern er hob diese Vorstellungen zugleich zu seinem eigenen Geiste hinauf; — er begegnete der Phantasie des Volks, aber er forderte von diesem auch eine Veredlung und Verfeinerung des Gefühls. In dieser Vereinigung veredlte er den gemeinen Aberglauben zu den schönsten poetischen Fiktionen, er sonderte das Kindische und Abgeschkmackte davon ab, ohne ihm das Seltsame und Abenteuerliche zu nehmen, ohne welches die Geisterwelt dem gewöhnlichen Leben zu nahe kommen würde.

Shakspeare ist ein ganz verschiedener Künstler als Tragiker, und in seinen sogenannten Lustspielen. Jeder Leser wird beim ersten Anblick auf die Bemerkung geführt sein, daß das

enchantments and the playful imagination is not awoken from its dreams by any sudden, unpleasant surprise.

In this highest achievement of dramatic art Shakspeare will perhaps remain forever inimitable – that great alchemy which transformed everything he touched into gold seems to have died with him. For however much his masterpieces are imitated by his contemporaries and by later poets, by the English and the Germans, not one of them has ventured to follow him into that magic circle in which he appears so great and so terrible. Those few who have tried to rival him in this appear in comparison to him like conjurors whom no spirit will obey, despite their mysterious spells, their mystic circles and all their magical apparatus, and who in the end arouse only boredom because they do not possess the artistry to lull to sleep our powers of reason and judgement.

At the time when he lived, Shakspeare, more than any other writer, was the poet of his people; he did not write for the rabble but for his nation, and so, whether he knew the masterpieces of antiquity or not, they were not the tribunal to which he brought his plays, on the contrary, he had learnt what produces an effect on people's minds by studious observation of mankind, and he created his works of art according to his own instinct and the rules which he had derived from experience. This is the reason why most of his plays are so generally effective in performance and when read, and why they must necessarily be effective, for perhaps there is not a poet who has calculated the theatrical effect of his works as carefully as Shakespeare, though without treating his audience to hollow *coups de théâtre,* or entertaining them with feeble surprises. He holds their attention rapt to the very end without recourse to the artifices dear to many a calculating poet and without any appeal to curiosity, and he moves them intensely, even to the point of terror, with his bold strokes of genius.

It is not Roman or Greek deities who people his marvellous world, nor those colourless allegorical creatures which were often seen in the theatre before and even during his lifetime, although these had to some extent accustomed his audiences to supernatural beings – no, as a poet of his people he descended to the level of his people's tradition.

Since it is the fantasy of the common people which creates and embellishes superstition, it is natural that, in the products of the alarmed and heated imagination, we should find as much that is childish as is dreadful, as many repulsive and tasteless features as we do lovely and terrible ones. Had Shakespeare indiscriminately adopted the same conceptions as the people themselves, he could certainly have counted on the applause of the rabble, but any reader possessed of some taste and imaginative refinement would then have cast away those misshapen fantasies in exasperation. Here he demonstrated his finer feelings, however, as a genuine poet, it did not satisfy him to lower himself to the same conceptions as the people themselves; instead he raised the products of their imagination up to the level of his own mind – he met the people's fantasy halfway, but also demanded from them an ennoblement and refinement of feeling. By this act of unification he refined common superstition to create the loveliest of poetic fictions and removed childish and tasteless elements without taking away what was strange and exotic, without which the spirit world would come too close to everyday life.

Shakspeare is a completely different artist as a writer of tragedies and in his so-called comedies. Every reader will immediately observe that the use of the marvellous in *Macbeth* and *Hamlet* is totally different to the use of the marvellous in *The Tempest* and *A Midsummer Night's Dream.* I shall turn first to these latter plays.

Shakspeare's plays can be divided up into many classes. Only a few bear any resemblance to one another; virtually every one has some stamp of particularity, a sprit of its own which

Wunderbare im Macbeth und Hamlet, dem Wunderbaren im Sturm und Sommernachtstraum, durchaus unähnlich sey. Ich wende mich zuerst zu den letztern Stücken.

[...]

Shakspeare's Schauspiele können in viele Klassen geteilt werden. Nur wenige sehen sich unter einander ähnlich; fast jedes hat irgend ein Gepräge der Eigenthümlichkeit, einen eigenen Geist, der es von den übrigen absondert. Alle sind treue Spiegel der Seele des Dichters; fast jedes ist ein Produkt einer eigenen, den übrigen unähnlichen Empfindung. Dem Sturm kann man kein anderes Schauspiel gegenuber stellen, als den Sommernachtstraum; man findet hier ohngefähr dieselbe Welt, und ähnliche Charaktere wieder; eben die blühende, ewig lebendige Phantasie, und die zarte Empfindung; eben den leisen Fortschrtt einer Begebenheit von kleinem Umfange; eben die Mischung des Ernsthaften und Komischen. Wenn ich auch nicht mit Malone die Dichtung des Sommernachtstraums 17 Jahre vor der des Sturms setzen möchte, so bin ich doch überzeugt, daß das letztere ungleich später als jenes geschrieben ward; denn man kann vielleicht sagen, daß der Sturm eine schönere und mehr vollendete Wiederhohlung des Sommernachtstraums sey.

Das *Wunderbare*, und die Art der Behandlung desselben, ist es vorzüglich, die diese Schauspiele in eine besondre Klasse stellt, und sie den übrigen Dichtungen der Shakspeareschen Muse unähnlich macht. Es scheint mir daher der Mühe werth, etwas genauer zu untersuchen, auf welche Art der Dichter die neue Bahn betritt, und ein Gemälde aufstellt, das wir mit eben so hoher Bewunderung als seine andern Meisterstücke betrachten.

Wenn man so eben von der Lesung des Macbeth oder Othello zurückkommt, so wird man versucht, den Sturm und Sommernachtstraum sehr tief unter diese großen Zeichnungen zu setzen; denn diese sanften und freundlichen Gemälde kontrastiren sehr gegen jene gigantischen Figuren. Man findet hier keine Schule der Leidenschaften, keine Geisterwelt, die uns mit Schrecken und Schauder füllt. Shakspeare läßt seine Donner schweigen, um ungestört die Imagination bei den reizenden Bildern verweilen zu lassen; er weiht in diesen Stücken den Zuschauer in seine Zauberwelt ein, und läßt ihn mit hundert magischen Gestalten in eine vertrauliche Bekanntschaft treten, ohne daß ihn Schrecken und Schauder von der geheimnißvollen Werkstatt in einer grauenhaften Entfernung halten. Man darf daher im Sturm nicht Szenen erwarten, die denen im Macbeth oder Hamlet ähnlich sind. Der Dichter hat uns hier die Geisterwelt näher gerückt, sie nicht in jener furchtbaren Entfernung gelassen, nicht mit jenem undurchdringlichen Schleier umhüllt, der die Blicke der Sterblichen zurückschreckt. Das Reich der Nacht ist hier von einem sanften Mondschein erhellt: wir treten dreist zu den freundlichen und ernsten Gestalten hinzu, die uns eben so wenig schrecklich als schädlich sind.

[...]

Der Sturm und der Sommernachtstraum lassen sich vielleicht mit heitern Träumen vergleichen: in dem letztern Stück hat Shakspeare sogar den Zweck, seine Zuschauer gänzlich in die Empfindung eines Träumenden einzuwiegen; und ich kenne kein anderes Stück, das, seiner ganzen Anlage nach, diesem Endzweck so sehr entspräche. Shakspeare, der so oft in seinen Stücken verrät, wie vertraut er mit den leisesten Regungen der menschlichen Seele sei, beobachtete sich auch wahrscheinlich in seinen Träumen, und wandte die hier gemachten Erfahrungen auf seine Gedichte an. Der Psychologe und der Dichter können ganz ohne Zweifel ihre Erfahrungen sehr erweitern, wenn sie dem Gange der Träume nachforschen: hier läßt sich gewiß oft der Grund entdecken, warum manche Ideenkombinationen so heftig auf die Gemüter wirken; der Dichter kann hier am leichtesten bemerken, wie sich eine Menge von Vorstellungen an einander reihen, um eine wunderbare, unerwartete Wirkung hervorzubringen. Jedermann von lebhafter

distinguishes it from the rest. Every one is a faithful mirror of the poet's soul; almost every one is a product of a distinct sentiment, quite different from the rest. There is no other play with which one can compare *The Tempest* save *A Midsummer Night's Dream*: here one finds again roughly the same world and similar characters, just the same flourishing, inexhaustibly lively imagination and delicacy of feeling, the same gradual development of a small-scale event; just the same mixture of serious and comic elements. Even though, unlike Malone, I am not inclined to set the composition of *A Midsummer Night's Dream* 17 years before that of *The Tempest*, I am nevertheless certain that the latter was written a great deal later than the former, for one might perhaps say that *The Tempest* is a lovelier and more perfect reprise of *A Midsummer Night's Dream*.

It is primarily the marvellous, and Shakespeare's way of treating it, that places these plays in a class of their own and makes them dissimilar to any other product of the Shakspearian muse. Consequently, it seems to me worthwhile to examine somewhat more closely the way in which the poet embarks upon this new course and creates a picture which we contemplate with the same intense admiration as we do his other masterpieces.

Anyone who has just returned from reading *Macbeth* or *Othello* is tempted to set *The Tempest* or *A Midsummer Night's Dream* far beneath these great compositions, for the gentle, amiable views Shakspeare paints in these last-named plays contrast powerfully with the gigantic profiles of the former. Here there is no school of passions, no spirit world to fill us with terror and awe: Shakespeare's thunder is silenced and he allows the imagination to dwell unhindered on the lovely images he creates; in these plays he initiates the spectator into his fairytale world and allows him close acquaintance with a hundred magical figures, without his being kept at a cruel distance from the mysterious workshop by terror and awe. Thus it would be wrong to expect from *The Tempest* scenes similar to those in *Macbeth* or *Hamlet*. The poet has brought the spirit world closer to us, has not kept it at that dreadful distance, has not concealed it beneath that impenetrable veil which discourages mortal gaze. The Kingdom of night is illuminated here by a pale moonlight: We join the friendly, earnest figures with assurance, for they are no more frightening to us than they are harmful. . .

One might perhaps compare *The Tempest* and *A Midsummer Night's Dream* to sweet dreams: in this last-named play Shakespeare's purpose is indeed to lull his audience into perceiving things as if in a dream, and I know no other play which in its every aspect answers this purpose so well. Shakspeare, who in his plays so often reveals his familiarity with the faintest stirrings of the human soul, probably observed himself also while dreaming and applied what he discovered here to his poetry. The psychologist and the poet can undoubtedly broaden their experience considerably by examining the course of dreams: here, surely, is often to be found the reason why certain combinations of ideas have such a powerful effect on the mind; here the poet can most readily observe how a myriad notions are linked together to create a marvellous and unexpected effect. Anyone with a lively imagination will doubtless often have suffered or experienced happiness when a dream has transported him into the realm of ghosts and monsters, or into a lovely fairy-land. In the midst of the dream the soul is itself very often on the point of refusing to believe in such chimeras, of tearing itself away from the illusion and declaring the whole thing to be nothing but the false figures of a dream. At such moments, when the spirit is so to speak at odds with itself, the sleeper is always close to wakefulness, for his fantasies lose some of their illusory reality, the power of judgement reasserts itself and the whole magical experience is on the point of disappearing. If, however, one continues to dream, the maintenance of the illusion arises on each occasion from the infinite number of new magical figures which are brought forth inexhaustibly from

Phantasie wird gewiß schon oft gelitten, oder sich glücklich gefühlt haben, indem ihn ein Traum in das Reich der Gespenster und Ungeheuer, oder in die reizende Feenwelt versetzte. Mitten im Traume ist die Seele sehr oft im Begriff, den Phantomen selbst nicht zu glauben, sich von der Täuschung loszureißen, und alles nur für betrügerische Traumgestalten zu erklären. In solchen Augenblicken, wo der Geist gleichsam mit sich selber zankt, ist der Schlafende immer dem Erwachen nahe; denn die Phantasien verlieren an ihrer täuschenden Wirklichkeit, die Urtheilskraft sondert sich ab, und der erste Zauber ist im Begriff zu verschwinden. Träumt man aber weiter, so entsteht die Nicht-Unterbrechung der Illusion jedesmal von der unendlichen Menge neuer magischen Gestalten, die die Phantasie unerschöpflich hervorbringt. Wir sind nun in einer bezauberten Welt festgehalten: wohin wir uns wenden, tritt uns ein Wunder entgegen; alles, was wir anrühren, ist von einer fremdartigen Natur; jeder Ton, der uns antwortet, erschallt aus einem übernatürlichen Wesen. Wir verlieren in einer unaufhörlichen Verwirrung den Maßstab, nach dem wir sonst die Wahrheit zu messen pflegen; eben, weil nichts Wirkliches unsre Aufmerksamkeit auf sich heftet, verlieren wir in der ununterbrochenen Beschäftigung unsrer Phantasie, die Erinnerung an die Wirklichkeit; der Faden ist hinter uns abgerissen, der uns durch das rätselhafte Labyrinth leitete; und wir geben uns am Ende völlig den Unbegreiflichkeiten preis. Das Wunderbare wird uns itzt gewöhnlich und natürlich: weil wir von der wirklichen Welt gänzlich abgeschnitten sind, so verliert sich unser Mißtrauen gegen die fremdartigen Wesen, und nur erst beim Erwachen werden wir überzeugt, daß sie Täuschung waren.

Die ganze Welt von Wunderbarem ist es, die unsre Phantasie in manchen Träumen so lange beschäftiget, wo wir auf eine Zeit lang ganz die Analogie unsrer Begriffe verlieren, und uns eine neue erschaffen, und wo alles diesen neuerworbenen Begriffen entspricht. — Alles dieses, was die Phantasie im Traume beobachtet, hat Shakspeare im Sturm durchgeführt. Die vorzüglichste Täuschung entsteht dadurch, daß wir uns durch das ganze Stück nicht wieder aus der wundervollen Welt verlieren, in welche wir einmal hinein geführt sind, daß kein Umstand den Bedingungen widerspricht, unter welchen wir uns einmal der Illusion überlassen haben. Shakspeare beobachtet eben dies im Sommernachtstraum, aber nicht auf eine so vorzügliche Art, als im Sturm. *Hier* führt uns nichts in die wirkliche Welt zurück; Begebenheiten und Charaktere sind gleich außerordentlich; die Handlung des Stücks hat nur einen kleinen Umfang, aber sie ist durch so wunderbare Vorfälle, durch eine Menge von Übernatürlichkeiten vorbereitet und durchgeführt, daß wir die Grundbegebenheit des Stücks fast ganz darüber vergessen, und uns nicht so sehr für den Zweck des Dichters interessieren, als für die Mittel, durch die er seinen Zweck erreicht.

[...]

Prospero ist aber noch mehr, als ein edler Mensch; der Dichter läßt ihn zugleich als ein über-menschliches Wesen auftreten, dessen Befehlen die Natur willig gehorcht, der durch das Stu-dium der Magie eine Herrschaft über die Geister erlangt hat, durch die alle Umstände nach seinem Willen lenkt.

[...]

Prospero führt seinen Plan durch Hülfe seiner dienstbaren Geister aus: Ariel ist der oberste seiner Diener. Der Zuschauer wird nun selbst zu den geheimsten Anschlägen zugelassen; er sieht alle Mittel, durch welche Prospero wirkt; kein Umstand bleibt ihm verborgen. Die Macht der Geister selbst ist ihm zwar unbegreiflich; aber es ist ihm genug, daß sie wirken, und Prospero's Gebote erfüllen sieht. Er verlangt keine näheren Aufschlüsse; er glaubt sich in alle Geheimnisse eingeweiht, indem keine Wirkung erfolgt, die er nicht gleichsam selber zubereiten sah, — keine Erscheinung, kein Wunder eintritt, von dem er nicht vorher wußte, daß

the imagination. We are now held fast in an enchanted world: wherever we turn we encounter a miracle; everything we touch is strange to us; every call which answers ours resounds from a supernatural being. In this never-ending confusion we lose the yardstick with which we are normally wont to measure truth; precisely because nothing real commands our attention, we lose, in this incessant appeal to our imagination, all memory of reality; the thread which was guiding us through the mysterious labyrinth is broken off behind us and in the end we abandon ourselves totally to the unfathomable. The marvellous now seems to us ordinary and natural; because we are cut off completely from the real world, our mistrust of the strange beings is dissipated, and it is only upon awakening that we are convinced they were an illusion.

It is the whole world of the marvellous that engages our imagination for so long in many a dream. All these things, observed in the dream state by our imagination, are given concrete form by Shakspeare in the *The Tempest*. The most admirable illusion is created by the fact that, once we have been led into it, we do not stray for a moment in the course of the play from the world of the marvellous, not a single circumstance contravenes the conditions according to which we abandoned ourselves to the illusion in the first place. Nothing here leads us back into the real world, events and characters are equally extraordinary; action is on a small scale, but introduced and executed by means of such marvellous occurrences, so many supernatural events, that they cause us to forget the primary facts of the plot almost completely, so that we are less interested in the poet's purpose than in the means by which he accomplishes that purpose. . .

Prospero is more than just a noble man; the poet presents him at the same time as a superhuman being whose commands Nature willingly obeys, and who by the study of magic has achieved mastery over the spirits, through whom he directs all events according to his will. He carries out his plan with the help of his serviceable spirits; Ariel is the Chief of his servants. The spectator himself is allowed access to the most secret calculations; he is privy to all the means by which Prospero achieves his ends; no circumstance remains hidden from him. He cannot comprehend the power of the spirits, it is true, but it is enough that he sees them perform and fulfil Prospero's commands. He demands no more precise information: he believes that he has been initiated into every secret, for no effect is achieved which he has not himself seen prepared, so to speak-no apparition, no marvel supervenes without his knowing in advance that it would supervene at that very moment. Thus nothing *surprises* or *shocks* him, although everything puts him into a state of amazement and dreamlike intoxication, as a result of which he comes to feel quite at home in the world of the marvellous. –

It is primarily through the characters of Ariel and Caliban that Shakspeare creates this whole marvellous world around us; they are, so to speak, the guardians who never permit our minds to return to the realm of reality; in every serious scene we are reminded by the presence of Ariel of where we are, in every comic scene, by that of Caliban. Prospero's magical contrivances, which occur one after the other without interruption, do not for a single moment permit our eyes to return to the reality which would instantly reduce all the chimeras of the poet to dust and ashes. Even the strange contrast between Ariel and Caliban enhances our faith in the marvellous. The creation of that exotic figure was a most felicitous idea on the part of the poet; in this figure he shows us the strangest mixture of absurdity and abomination; this monster is so remote from humanity and is portrayed with such extreme plausibility and conviction that Caliban's presence alone would persuade us that we had been transported to an utterly strange, as yet unknown world . . .

[1793] [*Translated by Louise Adey. From: The Romantics on Shakespeare. Ed. Jonathan Bate. Harmondsworth: Penguin, 1992. 60–66.*]

es in demselben Augenblick eintreten würde. Er wird daher durch nichts *überrascht* oder *erschreckt*, ob ihn gleich alles in ein neues Erstaunen und in einen traumähnlichen Rausch versetzt, durch welchen er sich am Ende in einer wunderbaren Welt, wie in seiner Heimat befindet. — Durch die Charaktere *Ariels* und *Calibans* erschafft Shakspeare vorzüglich diese ganze wunderbare Welt um uns her; sie sind gleichsam die Wächter, die unsern Geist nie in das Gebiet der Wirklichkeit zurücklassen: Ariels Gegenwart erinnert uns in allen ernsten, Calibans in allen komischen Scenen, wo wir uns befinden. Prospero's magische Veranstaltungen, die ununterbrochen eine nach der andern einfallen, lassen das Auge auf keinen Moment in die Wirklichkeit zurück, die sogleich alle Phantome des Dichters zu Schanden machen würde. Auch der seltsame Kontrast zwischen Ariel und Caliban erhöht unsern Glauben an das Wunderbare. Die Schöpfung dieses abentheuerlichen Wesens war die glücklichste Idee des Dichters; er zeigt uns in dieser Darstellung die seltsamste Mischung von Lächerlichkeit und Abscheulichkeit; dies Ungeheuer steht so weit von der menschlichen Nature entfernt, und ist mit so höchst täuschenden und überzeugenden Zügen geschildert, daß wir uns schon durch die Gegenwart des Caliban in eine ganz fremde, bis ist uns unbekannte Welt, versetzt zu sein glauben würden.

[Ludwig Tieck, Schriften 1789-1794. Ed. Achim Hölter. Frankfurt am Main:
Deutscher Klassiker Verlag 1991. 681–722]

I.e.3. WILHELM HEINRICH WACKENRODER, 'Das eigentümliche innere Wesen der Tonkunst, und die Seelenlehre der heiligen Instrumentalmusik', aus *Phantasien über die Kunst*

Der Schall oder Ton war ursprünglich ein grober Stoff, in welchem die wilden Nationen ihre unförmlichen Affecten auszudrücken strebten, indem sie, wenn ihr Inneres erschüttert war, auch die umgebenden Lüfte mit Geschrey und Trommelschlag erschütterten, gleichsam um die äußere Welt mit ihrer inneren Gemüthsempörung in's Gleichgewicht zu setzen. Nachdem aber die unaufhaltsam-wirkende Natur die ursprünglich in Eins verwachsenen Kräfte der menschlichen Seele, durch viele Säkula hindurch, in ein ausgebreitetes Gewebe von immer feineren Zweigen aus einander getrieben hat; so ist, in den neueren Jahrhunderten, auch aus *Tönen* ein kunstreiches System aufgebaut, und also auch in diesem Stoff, so wie in den Künsten der Formen und Farben, ein sinnliches Abbild und Zeugniß, von der schönen Verfeinerung und harmonisehen Vervollkommung des heutigen menschlichen Geistes, niedergelegt worden. Der einfarbige Lichtstrahl des Schalls ist in ein buntes, funkelndes Kunstfeuer zersplittert, worin alle Farben des Regenbogens flimmern; dies konnte aber nicht anders geschehen, als das zuvor mehrere weise Männer in die Orakelhöhlen der verborgensten Wissenschaft hinunterstiegen, wo die allzeugende Natur selbst ihnen die Urgesetze des Tons enthüllte. Aus diesen geheimnißreichen Grüften brachten sie die neue Lehre, in tiefsinnigen Zahlen geschrieben, an's Tageslicht, und setzten hiernach eine feste, weisheitsvolle Ordnung von vielfachen einzelnen Tönen zusammen, welche die reiche Quelle ist, aus der die Meister die mannigfaltigsten Tonarten schöpfen.

Die *sinnliche* Kraft, welche der Ton von seinem Ursprunge her in sich führt, hat sich durch dieses gelehrte System eine verfeinerte Mannigfaltigkeit erworben.

Das Dunkle und Unbeschreibliche aber, welches in der Wirkung des Tons verborgen liegt, und welches bey keiner andern Kunst zu finden ist, hat durch das System eine wunderbare Bedeutsamkeit gewonnen. Es hat sich zwischen den einzelnen mathematischen Tonverhältnissen und in den einzelnen Fibern des menschlichen Herzens eine unerklärliche Sympathie offenbart, wodurch die Tonkunst ein reichhaltiges und bildsames Maschinenwerk zur Abschilderung menschlicher Empfindungen geworden ist.

I.e.3. WILHELM HEINRICH WACKENRODER, 'The Characteristic Inner Nature of the Musical Art and the Psychology of Today's Instrumental Music', from *Fantasias on Art*

The sound wave or note was originally a crude material in which uncivilized peoples strove to express their undeveloped emotions. When their souls were deeply shaken, they also shook the surrounding air with screaming and the beating of drums, as if to bring the external world into balance with their inner spiritual excitation. However, after incessantly active Nature has, over many centuries, developed the originally stunted powers of the human soul into an extensive web of finer and finer branches, so too, in the more recent centuries, an ingenious system has been built up out of tones, whereby in this material too, just as in the arts of forms and colors, there has been set down a sensual copy of and testimony to the beautiful refinement and harmonious perfection of the human mind of today. The monochrome beam of sound has been broken up into a bright, sparkling fire of art, in which all the colors of the rainbow glitter; this could not have occurred, however, had not many wise men first descended into the oracle caves of the most occult sciences, where Nature, begetter of all things, herself unveiled for them the fundamental laws of sound. Out of these secret vaults they brought to the light of day the new theory, written in profound numbers. In accordance with this, they constructed a fixed, knowledgeable order of multitudinous individual notes, which is the plentiful fountain-head from which the masters draw the most varied tonal combinations.

The sensual power which the tone has carried within itself from its origin has, through this learned system, acquired a refined diversity.

The dark and indescribable element, however, which lies hidden in the effect of the tone and which is to be found in no other art, has gained a wonderful significance through the system. Between the individual, mathematical, tonal relationships and the individual fibers of the human heart an inexplicable sympathy has revealed itself, through which the musical art has become a comprehensive and flexible mechanism for the portrayal of human emotions.

Thus has the characteristic inner nature of today's music developed. In its present perfection it is the youngest of all the arts. No other is capable of fusing these qualities of profundity, of

So hat sich das eigenthümliche Wesen der heutigen Musik, welche, in ihrer jetzigen Vollend-ung, die jüngste unter allen Künsten ist, gebildet. Keine andre vermag diese Eigenschaften der Tiefsinnigkeit, der sinnlichen Kraft, und der dunkeln, phantastischen Bedeutsamkeit, auf eine so räthselhafte Weise zu verschmelzen. Diese merkwürdige, enge Vereinigung so widerstrebend-scheinender Eigenschaften macht den ganzen Stolz ihrer Vorzüglichkeit aus; wiewohl eben die-selbe auch viele seltsame Verwirrungen in der Ausübung und im Genusse dieser Kunst, und viel thörichten Streit unter Gemüthern, welche sich niemals verstehen können, hervorgebracht hat.

Die wissenschaftlichen Tiefsinnigkeiten der Musik haben manche jener speculirenden Geis-ter herangelockt, welche in allem ihren Thun streng und scharf sind, und das Schöne nicht aus offener, reiner Liebe, um sein selbst willen, aufsuchen, sondern es nur des Zufalls halber schätzen, daß besondre, seltene Kräfte daran aufzureiben waren. Anstatt das Schöne auf allen Wegen, wo es sich freundlich uns entgegenbietet, wie einen Freund willkommen zu heißen, betrachten sie ihre Kunst vielmehr als einen schlimmen Feind, suchen ihn im gefährlichsten Hinterhalt zu bekämpfen, und triumphiren dann über ihre eigne Kraft. Durch diese gelehrten Männer ist das innere Maschinenwerk der Musik, gleich einem künstlichen Weberstuhle für gewirkte Zeuge, zu einer erstaunenswürdigen Vollkommenheit gebracht worden; ihre einzelnen Kunststücke aber sind oftmals nicht anders als in der Mahlerey vortreffliche anatomische Stu-dien und schwere academische Stellungen zu betrachten.

Traurig anzusehn ist es, wenn dies fruchtbare Talent sich in ein unbeholfenes und empfindungsarmes Gemüth verirrt hat. In einer fremden Brust schmachtet alsdann das phantastische Gefühl, das unberedt in Tönen ist, nach der Vereinigung, - indeß die Schöpfung, die Alles erschöpfen will, mit solchen schmerzlichen Naturspielen nicht ungern wehmüthige Versuche anzustellen scheint.

Demnach hat keine andre Kunst einen Grundstoff, der schon an sich mit so himmlischen Geiste geschwängert wäre, als die Musik. Ihr klingender Stoff kommt mit seinem geordneten Reichthume von Akkorden den bildenden Händen entgegen, und spricht schon schöne Emp-findungen aus, wenn wir ihn auch nur auf eine leichte, einfache Weise berühren. Daher kommt es, daß manche Tonstücke, deren Töne von ihren Meistern wie Zahlen zu einer Rechnung, oder wie die Stifte zu einem musivischen Gemählde, bloß regelrecht, aber sinnreich und in glückli-cher Stunde, zusammengesetzt wurden, - wenn sie auf Instrumenten ausgeübt werden, eine herrliche, empfindungsvolle Poesie reden, obwohl der Meister wenig daran gedacht haben mag, daß in seiner gelehrten Arbeit, der in dem Reiche der Töne verzauberte Genius, für eingeweihte Sinne, so herrlich seine Flügel schlagen würde.

Dagegen fahren manche, nicht ungelehrte, aber unter unglücklichem Stern gebohrne, und innerlich harte und unbewegliche Geister täppisch in die Töne hinein, zerren sie aus ihren eigenthümlichen Sitzen, so daß man in ihren Werken nur ein schmerzliches Klaggeschrey des gemarterten Genius vernimmt.

Wenn aber die gute Natur die getrennten Kunstseelen in *eine* Hülle vereinigt, wenn das Gefühl des Hörenden noch glühender im Herzen des tiefgelehrten Kunstmeisters brannte, und er die tiefsinnige Wissenschaft in diesen Flammen schmelzt; dann geht ein unnennbar-köstli-ches Werk hervor, worin Gefühl und Wissenschaft so fest und unzertrennlich in einander han-gen, wie in einem Schmelzgemählde Stein und Farben verkörpert sind. –

Von denjenigen, welche die Musik und alle Künste nur als Anstalten betrachten, ihren nüchternen und groben Organen die nothdürftig sinnliche Nahrung zu verschaffen, — da doch die Sinnlichkeit nur als die kräftigste, eindringlichste und menschlichste Sprache anzusehn ist, worin das Erhabene, Edle und Schöne zu uns reden kann, - von diesen unfruchtbaren Seelen ist

sensual power, and of dark, visionary significance in such an enigmatical way. This remarkable, close fusion of such apparently contradictory qualities constitutes the whole pride of its superiority; although precisely this same thing has produced many strange confusions in the exercise and in the enjoyment of this craft and many a foolish argument between mentalities which can never understand each other.

The scientific profundities of music have attracted many of those speculative minds, who are rigorous and sharp-witted in all of their activities and who do not seek the beautiful for its own sake, out of an open, pure love, but treasure it only because of the coincidence that unusual, strange powers can be aroused by it. Rather than welcoming that which is beautiful, like a friend, on all pathways where it presents itself to us in a friendly manner, they regard their art as a dangerous enemy instead, seek to subdue it in the most perilous ambush, and triumph thereupon over their own strength. The inner machinery of music, like an ingenious weaver's loom for woven cloth, has been developed to a level of perfection worthy of astonishment by these learned men; their individual works of art, however, are often to be regarded no differently from excellent anatomical studies and difficult academic postures in the art of painting.

It is sad to behold, when this fruitful talent has gone astray into an ungainly and emotionally impoverished soul. Then, in a breast foreign to it, the inventive feeling, which is lacking eloquence in sounds, yearns for union, – while Creation, which wants to exhaust everything, seems to enjoy initiating pitiful attempts with such painful tricks of Nature.

Furthermore, no other art but music has a raw material which is, in and of itself, already impregnated with such divine spirit. Its vibrating material with its ordered wealth of chords comes to meet the creating hands halfway and expresses beautiful emotions, even if we touch it in an elementary, simple way. Thus it is that many musical pieces, whose notes were arranged by their composers like numbers in an accounting or like the pieces in a mosaic, merely according to the rules, but ingeniously and at a fortunate hour, – speak a magnificent, emotionally rich poetry when they are performed on instruments, although the composer may have little imagined that, in his scholarly work, the enchanted spirit in the realm of music would beat its wings so magnificently for initiated senses.

On the other hand, many internally rigid and immovable minds, who are not unlearned but are born under an unfortunate star, enter clumsily into the realm of tones, pull them out of their proper places, so that one hears in their works only a painful, plaintive outcry of the martyred spirit.

But, whenever benevolent Nature unites these separate souls of art in one mortal frame, when the emotion of the one who hears burns even more ardently in the heart of the highly learned master of art, and he dissolves the profound science in these flames, then an inexpressibly beautiful work emerges, in which emotion and scholarship are as firmly and inseparably commingled as stone and colors in a ceramic painting.

Those individuals who regard music and all the arts only as institutions to provide their dull and coarse organs with the necessitous sensual nourishment, – since, after all, sensuality is to be regarded merely as the most powerful, most penetrating, and most human language in which that which is exalted, noble, and beautiful can speak to us, – these sterile souls are not to be mentioned. If they were capable of it, they ought to worship the deeply founded, immutable holiness which is characteristic of this art above all others, that in its works the fixed, oracular law of the system, the natural magnificence of the triad, cannot be destroyed and defiled even by the most infamous hands, – and that it is not even capable of expressing that which is defiled,

nicht zu reden. Sie sollten, wenn sie es vermöchten, die tiefgegründete, unwandelbare *Heiligkeit*, die dieser Kunst vor allen andern eigen ist, verehren, daß in ihren Werken das feste Orakelgesetz des Systems, der ursprüngliche Glanz des Dreyklangs, auch durch die verworfensten Hände nicht vertilgt und befleckt werden kann, - und daß sie *gar nicht vermag* das Verworfene, Niedrige und Unedle des menschlichen Gemüths auszudrücken, sondern an sich nicht mehr als *rohe* und *grelle* Melodieen geben kann, denen die sich anhängenden irrdischen Gedanken erst das Niedrige leihen müssen.

Wenn nun die Vernünftler fragen: wo denn eigentlich der Mittelpunkt dieser Kunst zu entdecken sey, wo ihr eigentlicher Sinn und ihre Seele verborgen liege, die alle ihre verschiedenartigen Erscheinungen zusammenhalte? — so kann ich es ihnen nicht erklären oder beweisen. Wer das, was sich nur von innen heraus fühlen läßt, mit der Wünschelruthe des untersuchenden Verstandes entdecken will, der wird ewig nur Gedanken über das Gefühl, und nicht das Gefühl selber, entdecken. Eine ewige feindselige Kluft ist zwischen dem fühlenden Herzen und den Untersuchungen des Forschens befestigt, und jenes ist ein selbstständiges verschlossenes göttliches Wesen, das von der Vernunft nicht aufgeschlossen und gelöst werden kann. — Wie jedes einzelne Kunstwerk nur durch dasselbe Gefühl, von dem es hervorgebracht ward, erfaßt und innerlich ergriffen werden kann, so kann auch das Gefühl überhaupt nur vom Gefühl erfaßt und ergriffen werden: - gerade so, wie, nach der Lehre der Mahler, jede einzelne Farbe nur vom gleichgefärbten Lichte beleuchtet ihr wahres Wesen zu erkennen giebt. — Wer die schönsten und göttlichsten Dinge im Reiche des Geistes mit seinem Warum? und dem ewigen Forschen nach Zweck und Ursache untergräbt, der kümmert sich eigentlich nicht um die Schönheit und Göttlichkeit der Dinge selbst, sondern um die Begriffe, als die Gränzen und Hülsen der Dinge, womit er seine Algebra anstellt — Wen aber, — dreist zu reden, — von Kindheit an, der Zug seines Herzens durch das Meer der Gedanken, pfeilgrade wie einen kühnen Schwimmer, auf das Zauberschloß der Kunst allmächtig hinreißt, der schlägt die Gedanken wie störende Wellen muthig von seiner Brust, und dringt hinein in das innerste Heiligthum, und ist sich mächtig bewußt der Geheimnisse, die auf ihn einstürmen. –

Und so erkühn' ich mich denn, aus meinem Innersten den wahren Sinn der Tonkunst auszusprechen, und sage:

Wenn alle die inneren Schwingungen unsrer Herzensfibern, — die zitternden der Freude, die stürmenden des Entzückens, die hochklopfenden Pulse verzehrender Anbetung, — wenn alle die Sprache der Worte, als das *Grab* der innern Herzenswuth, mit *einem* Ausruf zersprengen: — dann gehen sie unter fremdem Himmel, in den Schwingungen holdseliger Harfensaiten, wie in einem jenseitigen Leben in verklärter Schönheit hervor, und feyern als Engelgestalten ihre Auferstehung. —

Hundert und hundert Tonwerke reden Fröhlichkeit und Lust, aber in jedem singt ein andrer Genius, und einer jeden der Melodieen zittern andre Fibern unsres Herzens entgegen. - Was wollen sie, die zaghaften und zweifelnden Vernünftler, die jedes der hundert und hundert Tonstücke in Worten erklärt verlangen, und sich nicht darin finden können, daß nicht jedes eine nennbare Bedeutung hat, wie ein Gemählde? Streben sie die reichere Sprache nach der ärmern abzumessen, und in Worte aufzulösen, was Worte verachtet? Oder haben sie nie ohne Worte empfunden? Haben sie ihr hohles Herz nur mit Beschreibungen von Gefühlen ausgefüllt? Haben sie niemals im Innern wahrgenommen das stumme Singen, den vermummten Tanz der unsichtbaren Geister? oder glauben sie nicht an die Mährchen? —

Ein fließender Strom soll mir zum Bilde dienen. Keine menschliche Kunst vermag das Fließen eines mannigfaltigen Stroms, nach allen den tausend einzelnen, glatten und bergigten,

base, and ignoble in the human spirit but can, in itself, present no more than crude and harsh melodies, to which the quality of baseness must be lent by the earthly thoughts attaching themselves to these melodies.

Now, when the subtle reasoners ask: where, actually, the center of this art is to be found, where its true meaning and its soul lie hidden, where all its varied manifestations are held together? – then I cannot explain or demonstrate it to them. Whoever wants to discover with the divining-rod of the investigating intellect that which can only be felt from within will perpetually discover only thoughts about emotion and not emotion itself. An eternally hostile chasm is entrenched between the feeling heart and the investigations of research, and the former is an independent, tightly sealed, divine entity, which cannot be unlocked and opened up by the reason. – Just as every individual work of art can be comprehended and inwardly grasped by emotion: – just as every individual color, according to the teachings of painters, reveals its true nature when illuminated by light of the same color. – He who undermines the most beautiful and most holy things in the realm of the spirit with his 'Why?' and with relentless searching for Purpose and Cause, is actually not concerned with the beauty and divinity of the things themselves but with the concepts, as the boundaries and husks of the things, with which he sets up his algebra. – However, he – to speak boldly, whose heart's desire carries him almightily through the sea of thoughts from childhood on, straight as an arrow like a daring swimmer, up to the magic castle of art, such a one pushes thoughts courageously from his breast like interfering waves and penetrates into the innermost sanctuary and is intensely aware of the secrets which rush in upon him. –

And, therefore, I venture to express from the depths of my being the true meaning of the musical art and say:

Whenever all the inner vibrations of our heartstrings – the trembling ones of joy, the tempestuous ones of delight, the rapidly beating pulse of all-consuming adoration, – when all these burst apart with one outcry the language of words, as the grave of the inner frenzy of heart: – then they go forth under a strange sky, amidst the vibrations of blessed harp-strings, in transfigured beauty as if in another life beyond this one, and celebrate as angelic figures their resurrection. –

Hundreds and hundreds of musical works express gaiety and pleasure, but in each one a different spirit sings and toward each of the melodies different fibers of our hearts respond with trembling. – What do they want, the faint-hearted and doubting reasoners, who require each of the hundreds and hundreds of musical pieces explained in words, and who cannot understand that not every piece has an expressible meaning like a painting? Are they trying to measure the richer language by the poorer and to resolve into words that which disdains words? Or have they never felt without words? Have they filled up their hollow hearts merely with descriptions of feelings? Have they never perceived within themselves the mute singing, the masked dance of invisible spirits? Or do they not believe in fairy tales? –

A rushing river shall serve as my image. No human art is capable of sketching for the eye with words the flowing of an immense river, following all the thousands of individual smooth and mountainous, plunging and foaming waves. – Language can only inadequately count and name the changes, not visibly portray for us the interdependent transformations of the drops. And so it is also with the secret river in the depths of the human soul. Language counts and names and describes its transformations, in a foreign medium; – the musical art causes it to flow past us ourselves. It reaches spiritedly into the mysterious harp, it strikes certain obscure, marvelous

stürzenden und schäumenden Wellen, mit *Worten* für's *Auge* hinzuzeichnen, - die Sprache kann die Veränderungen nur dürftig *zählen* und *nennen*, nicht die an einanderhängenden Verwandlungen der Tropfen uns sichtbar vorbilden. Und eben so ist es mit dem geheimnißvollen Strome in den Tiefen des menschlichen Gemüthes beschaffen. Die Sprache zählt und nennt und beschreibt seine Verwandlungen, in fremdem Stoff; — die Tonkunst strömt ihn uns selber vor. Sie greift beherzt in die geheimnißvolle Harfe, schlägt in der dunkeln Welt bestimmte, dunkle Wunderzeichen in bestimmter Folge an, - und die Saiten unsres Herzens erklingen, und wir verstehen ihren Klang.

In dem Spiegel der Töne lernt das menschliche Herz sich selber kennen; sie sind es, wodurch wir das *Gefühl fühlen* lernen; sie geben vielen in verborgenen Winkeln des Gemüths träumenden Geistern, lebendes Bewußtseyn, und bereichern mit ganz neuen zauberischen Geistern des Gefühls unser Inneres.

Und alle die tönenden Affekten werden vor dem trocknen wissenschaftlichen Zahlensystem, wie von den seltsamen wunderkräftigen Beschwörungsformeln eines alten furchtbaren Zauberers, regiert und gelenkt. Ja, das System bringt, auf merkwürdige Weise, manche wunderbar neue Wendungen und Verwandlungen der Empfindungen hervor, wobey das Gemüth über sein eignes Wesen erstaunt, — so wie etwa die Sprache der Worte manchmal von den Ausdrücken und Zeichen der Gedanken neue Gedanken zurückstrahlt, und die Tänze der Vernunft in ihren Wendungen lenkt und beherrscht. –

Keine Kunst schildert die Empfindungen auf eine so künstliche, kühne, so *dichterische*, und eben darum für kalte Gemüther so erzwungene Weise. Das *Verdichten* der im wirklichen Leben verloren herumirrenden Gefühle in mannichfaltige feste Massen, ist das Wesen aller Dichtung; sie trennt das Vereinte, vereint fest das Getrennte, und in den engeren, schärferen Gränzen schlagen höhere, empörtere Wellen. Und wo sind die Gränzen und Sprünge schärfer, wo schlagen die Wellen höher als in der Tonkunst?

Aber in diesen Wellen strömt recht eigentlich nur das reine, *formlose* Wesen, der Gang und die Farbe, und auch vornehmlich der tausendfältige *Übergang* der Empfindungen; die idealische, engelreine Kunst weiß in ihrer Unschuld weder den *Ursprung*, noch das *Ziel* ihrer Regungen, kennt nicht den Zusammenhang ihrer Gefühle mit der wirklichen Welt.

Und dennoch empört sie bey aller ihrer Unschuld, durch den mächtigen Zauber ihrer *sinnlichen Kraft*, alle die wunderbaren, wimmelnden Heerschaaren der *Phantasie*, die die Töne mit magischen Bildern bevölkern, und die formlosen Regungen in bestimmte Gestalten menschlicher Affekten verwandeln, welche wie gaukelnde Bilder eines magischen Blendwerks unsern Sinnen vorüberziehn.

Da sehen wir die hüpfende, tanzende, kurzathmende Fröhlichkeit, die jeden kleinen Tropfen ihres Daseyns zu einer geschlossenen Freude ausbildet.

Die sanfte, felsenfeste Zufriedenheit, die ihr ganzes Daseyn aus *einer* harmonischen, beschränkten Ansicht der Welt herausspinnt, auf alle Lagen des Lebens ihre frommen Überzeugungen anwendet, nie die Bewegung ändert, alles Rauhe glättet, und bey allen Übergängen die Farbe vertreibt.

Die männliche, jauchzende Freude, die bald das ganze Labyrinth der Töne in mannichfacher Richtung durchläuft, wie das pulsirende Blut warm und rasch die Adern durchströmt, - bald mit edlem Stolz, mit Schwung und Schnellkraft sich wie im Triumph in die Höhen erhebt.

Das süße, sehnsüchtige Schmachten der Liebe, das ewig wechselnde Anschwillen und Hinschwinden der Sehnsucht, da die Seele aus dem zärtlichen Schleichen durch benachbarte Töne sich auf einmal mit sanfter Kühnheit in die Höhe schwingt und wieder sinkt, — aus einem unbefriedigten

signals in the dark world in a definite succession, and the strings of our hearts resound and we understand their ringing.

The human heart becomes acquainted with itself in the mirror of musical sounds; it is they through which we learn to feel emotion; to many spirits, dreaming in hidden crannies of the mind, they give living consciousness, and they enrich our souls with entirely new, bewitching essences of feeling.

And all the resounding emotions are directed and guided by the dry, scientific system of numbers, as by the strange, miraculous incantations of an old, frightful sorcerer. Indeed, in a curious way, the system brings forth many wondrously new changes and transformations of the emotions, so that the mind is astounded by its own nature, – just as, for instance, the language of words sometimes reflects new thoughts from the expressions and signs of thoughts and directs and governs the dances of reason in their movements. – No art portrays the emotions in such an artistic, bold, such a poetic and, therefore, for cold minds such a forced manner. The essence of all art is the poetization of the emotions, wandering around lost in real life, into manifold, fixed masses; it separates what is united, unites firmly what is separated, and, in the narrower, more sharply defined boundaries, there beat higher, more surging waves. And where are the boundaries and leaps sharper, where do the waves beat higher than in the musical art?

However, in actuality, only the pure, formless essence, the motion and the color, and also primarily the thousandfold nuances of the emotions flow in these waves; ideal, angelically pure art knows in its innocence neither the origin nor the goal of its excitations, does not know the relationship of its emotions to the real world.

And, despite all its innocence, nevertheless, through the overwhelming magic of its sensual force, it arouses all the wonderful, teeming hosts of the fantasy, which populate the musical strains with magical images and transform the formless excitations into distinct shapes of human emotions, which draw past our senses like elusive pictures in a magical deception.

There we see the leaping, dancing, breathless gaiety which perfects every little drop of its existence into a harmonious entity of joy.

The gentle, rock-solid contentedness, which spins its entire existence out of one harmonious, limited view of the world, applies its pious convictions to all situations of life, never alters its movement, smooths all roughnesses, and rubs away the color in all nuances.

The masculine, exulting joy, which sometimes passes through the entire labyrinth of musical tones in many a direction, like pulsating blood flows warmly and quickly through the veins, – sometimes elevates itself to the heights as if in triumph, with noble pride, with verve and elasticity.

The sweet, ardent yearning of love, the ever-alternating swelling and receding of desire, when with gentle boldness the soul suddenly soars out of its tender creeping through nearby musical strains into the heights, and sinks down again, – turns from one unsatisfied striving to another with lascivious displeasure, rests willingly on gently painful chords, strives eternally for resolution and, in the end, only dissolves in tears.

The deep pain, which sometimes drags along as if in chains, sometimes moans interrupted sighs, then gushes forth in long laments, wanders through all types of pain, lovingly perfects its own suffering and, amidst the dark clouds, only infrequently catches sight of faint shimmers of hope.

The mischievous, liberated, gay mood, like a whirlpool that causes all earnest feelings to be shipwrecked and plays with their fragments in the gay vortex, – or like a grotesque demon that mocks all human dignity and all human pain with farcical mimicry and delusively mimics

Streben sich mit wollüstigem Unmuth in ein andres windet, gem auf sanftschmerzlichen Akkorden ausruht, ewig nach Auflösung strebt, und am Ende nur mit Thränen sich auflöst.

Der tiefe Schmerz, der bald sich wie in Ketten daherschleppt, bald abgebrochene Seufzer ächzt, bald sich in langen Klagen ergießt, alle Arten des Schmerzes durchirrt, sein eigenes Leiden liebend ausbildet, und in den trüben Wolken nur selten schwache Schimmer der Hoffnung erblickt.

Die muthwillige, entbundene fröhliche Laune, die wie ein Strudel ist, der alle ernsthaften Empfindungen scheitern macht, und im fröhlichen Wirbel mit ihren Bruchstücken spielt, — oder wie ein grottesker Dämon, der alle menschliche Erhabenheit und allen menschlichen Schmerz durch possenhafte Nachäffung verspottet, und gaukelnd sich selber nachäfft, - oder wie ein unstät schwebender luftiger Geist, der alle Pflanzen aus ihrem festen irrdischen Boden reißt und in die unendlichen Lüfte streut, und den ganzen Erdball verflüchtigen möchte.

Aber wer kann sie alle zählen und nennen, die luftigen Phantasieen, die die Töne wie wechselnde Schatten durch unsre Einbildung jagen?

Und doch kann ich's nicht lassen, noch den letzten höchsten Triumph der Instrumente zu preisen: ich meyne jene göttlichen großen Symphoniestücke, (von inspirirten Geistern hervorgebracht,) worin nicht eine einzelne Empfindung gezeichnet, sondern eine ganze Welt, ein ganzes Drama menschlichen Affekten ausgeströmt ist. Ich will in allgemeinen Worten erzählen, was vor meinen Sinnen schwebt.

Mit leichter, spielender Freude steigt die tönende Seele aus ihrer Orakelhöhle hervor, — gleich der Unschuld der Kindheit, die einen lüsternen Vortanz des Lebens übt, die, ohne es zu wissen, über alle Welt hinwegscherzt, und nur auf ihre eigene innerliche Heiterkeit zurücklächelt. — Aber bald gewinnen die Bilder um sie her festen Bestand, sie versucht ihre Kraft an stärkeres Gefühl, sie wagt sich plötzlich mitten in die schäumenden Fluthen zu stürzen, schmiegt sich durch alle Höhen und Tiefen, und rollt alle Gefühle mit muthigem Entzücken hinauf und hinab. — Doch wehe! sie dringt verwegen in wildere Labyrinthe, sie sucht mit kühn-erzwungener Frechheit die Schrecken des Trübsinns, die bittern Quaalen des Schmerzes auf, um den Durst ihrer Lebenskraft zu sättigen, und mit einem Trompetenstoße brechen alle furchtbaren Schrecken der Welt, alle die Kriegsschaaren des Unglücks von allen Seiten mächtig wie ein Wolkenbruch herein, und wälzen sich in verzerrten Gestalten fürchterlich, schauerlich wie ein lebendig gewordenes Gebirge über einander. Mitten in den Wirbeln der Verzweiflung will die Seele sich muthig erheben, und sich stolze Seligkeit ertrotzen, — und wird immer überwältigt von den fürchterlichen Heeren. — Auf einmal zerbricht die tollkühne Kraft, die Schreckengestalten sind furchtbar verschwunden, — die frühe, ferne Unschuld tritt in schmerzlicher Erinnerung, wie ein verschleyertes Kind, wehmüthig hüpfend hervor, und ruft vergebens zurück, — die Phantasie wälzt mancherley Bilder, zerstückt wie im Fiebertraum, durch einander, — und mit ein paar leisen Seufzern zerspringt die ganze lauttönende lebenvolle Welt, gleich einer glänzenden Lufterscheinung, in's unsichtbare Nichts.

Dann, wenn ich in finsterer Stille noch lange horchend da sitze, dann ist mir, als hätt' ich ein Traumgesicht gehabt von allen mannigfaltigen menschlichen Affekten, wie sie, gestaltlos, zu eigner Lust, einen seitsamen, ja fast wahnsinnigen pantominischen Tanz zusammen feyern, wie sie mit einer furchtbaren *Willkühr*, gleich den unbekannten, räthselhaften Zaubergöttinnen des Schicksals, frech und frevelhaft durch einander tanzen.

Jene wahnsinnige Willkühr, womit in der Seele des Menschen Freude und Schmerz, Natur und Erzwungenheit, Unschuld und Wildheit, Scherz und Schauder sich befreudet und oft plötzlich die Hände bieten: — welche Kunst führt auf ihrer Bühne jene *Seelenmysterien* mit so dunkler, geheimnißreicher, ergreifender Bedeutsamkeit auf? -

itself, – or like a restlessly floating, airy spirit, that tears all plants out of their firm, terrestrial soil and scatters them into the infinite breezes and would like to curse the entire world.

But who can count and name them all, the ephemeral fantasies which chase the musical strains through our imagination like changing shadows?

And yet, I cannot refrain from extolling, in addition, the latest, highest triumph of musical instruments: I mean those divine, magnificent symphonic pieces (brought forth by inspired spirits), in which not one individual emotion is portrayed, but an entire world, an entire drama of human emotions, is poured forth. I wish to relate in general terms what hovers before my senses.

With easy, playful joy the resounding soul rises forth from its oracular cave, – like the innocence of childhood, which is practicing a lustful opening dance of life, which unknowingly jests above and beyond the whole world and smiles back only upon its own inner gaiety. – But soon the images around it acquire firmer contours; it tests its power on stronger emotion; it suddenly dares to plunge itself into the midst of the foaming flood-tides, moves lithely through all heights and depths, and rolls all emotions up and down with spirited delight. – But alas! it penetrates rashly into wilder labyrinths; with boldly forced impudence it seeks out the horrors of dejection, the bitter torments of pain, in order to quench the thirst of its vital energy; and, with one burst of the trumpet, all frightful horrors of the world, all the armies of misfortune break in violently from all sides like a cloudburst and roll in upon each other in distorted shapes, frightfully, gruesomely, like a mountain range come alive. In the midst of the whirlwinds of despair the soul desires to elevate itself courageously and defiantly obtain for itself proud salvation, – and is continuously overpowered by the frightful armies. – All at once the madly bold power is shattered, the figures of horror have dreadfully disappeared, – the early, distant innocence emerges in painful recollection, hopping sadly like a veiled child, and calls back in vain, – the fantasy intermingles a host of images in confusion, dismembered as in a feverish dream, – and with a few gentle sighs the entire, loudly resounding world full of life explodes, like a shining mirage, into the invisible void.

Then, as I sit there listening for a long while in more ominous stillness, then it seems to me as if I had experienced a vision of all the manifold human emotions, how they incorporeally celebrate a strange, indeed, an almost mad pantomimic dance together for their own pleasure, how they dance between each other impudently and wantonly, with a frightful spontaneity, like the unknown, enigmatical sorcerer-goddesses of Fate.

That mad spontaneity, with which joy and pain, nature and artificiality, innocence and wildness, jesting and shuddering, befriend each other in the soul of the human being and often suddenly extend a hand to each other: – what art presents those mysteries of the soul on its stage with such dark, secret, gripping significance? –

Indeed, our hearts fluctuate every moment in response to the very same tones, whether the resounding soul will boldly despise all vanities of the world and strive with noble pride upwards toward heaven, or whether it will despise all heavens and gods and press with shameless striving merely toward one single earthly bliss. And precisely this mischievous innocence, this frightful, oracularly ambiguous obscurity, makes the musical art truly a divinity for human hearts. –

But why do I, foolish one, strive to melt words into tones? It is never as I feel it. Come, Thou musical strains, draw near and rescue me from this painful earthly striving for words, envelop me in Thy shining clouds with Thy thousandfold beams, and raise me up into the old embrace of all-loving heaven.

[1799] [*Translated by Mary Hurst Schubert. University Park and London: Pennsylvania UP, 1971*]

Ja, jeden Augenblick schwankt unser Herz bey *denselben* Tönen, ob die tönende Seele kühn alle Eitelkeiten der Welt verachtet, und mit edlem Stolz zum Himmel hinaufstrebt, - oder ob sie alle Himmel und Götter verachtet, und mit frechem Streben nur einer einzigen irdischen Seligkeit entgegendringt. Und eben diese frevelhafte *Unschuld*, diese furchtbare, orakelmäßig-zweydeutige Dunkelheit, macht die Tonkunst recht eigentlich zu einer Gottheit für *menschliche Herzen*. — —

Aber was streb' ich Thörichter, die Worte zu Tönen zu zerschmelzen? Es ist immer nicht, wie ich's fühle. Kommt thr Töne, ziehet daher und errettet mich aus diesem schmerzlichen irrdischen Streben nach Worten, wickelt mich ein mit Euren tausendfachen Strahlen in Eure glänzende Wolken, und hebt mich hinauf in die alte Umarmung des allliebenden Himmels!

[1799] [*Edited by Silvio Vietta and Richard Littlejohns. Heidelberg:*
Winter 1999. 216–223]

I.e.4. NOVALIS, Fragmente: Goethe und die Antike; Schaffende Einbildungskraft
i *Wilhelm Meisters Lehrjahre*; Märchen; Romantik; Übersetzung;
Kritik; Tod; Poesie

[ÜBER GOETHE]

445. Göthe ist ganz practischer Dichter. Er ist in seinen Wercken – was der Engländer in seinen Waaren ist – höchst einfach, nett, bequem und dauerhaft. Er hat in der deutschen Litteratur das gethan, was Wedgwood in der englischen Kunstwelt gethan hat – Er hat, wie die Engländer, einen natürlich oeconomischen und einen durch Verstand erworbenen edeln Geschmack. Beydes verträgt sich sehr gut und hat eine nahe Verwandtschaft, im *chemischen* Sinn. In seinen physicalischen Studien wird es recht klar, daß es seine Neigung ist eher etwas Unbedeutendes ganz fertig zu machen — ihm die höchste Politur und Bequemlichkeit zu geben, als eine Welt anzufangen und etwas zu thun, wovon man vorauswissen kann, daß man es nicht vollkommen ausführen wird, daß es gewiß ungeschickt bleibt, und daß man es nie darinn zu einer meisterhaften Fertigkeit bringt. Auch in diesem Felde wählt er einen romantischen oder sonst artig verschlungnen Gegenstand. Seine Betrachtungen des Lichts, der Verwandlung der Pflanzen und der Insecten sind Bestätigungen und zugleich die überzeugendsten Beweise, daß auch der vollkommne Lehrvortrag in das Gebiet des Künstlers gehört. Auch dürfte man im gewissen Sinn mit Recht behaupten, daß Göthe der erste Physiker seiner Zeit sey — und in der That Epoke in der Geschichte der Physik mache. Vom Umfang der Kenntnisse kann Hier nicht die Rede seyn, so wenig auch Entdeckungen den Rang des Naturforschers bestimmen dürften. Hier kommt es darauf an, ob man die Natur, wie ein Künstler die Antike, betrachtet — denn ist die Natur etwas anders, als eine lebende Antike. Natur und Natureinsicht entstehn zugleich, wie Antike, und Antikenkenntniß; denn man irrt sehr, wenn man glaubt, daß es Antiken giebt. Erst jezt fängt die Antike an zu entstehen. Sie wird unter den Augen und der Seele des Künstlers. Die Reste des Alterthums sind nur die specifischen Reitze zur Bildung der Antike. Nicht mit Händen wird die Antike gemacht. Der Geist bringt sie durch das Auge hervor — und der gehaune Stein ist nur der Körper, der erst durch sie Bedeutung erhält, und zur Erscheinung derselben wird. Wie der Physiker Göthe sich zu den übrigen Physikern verhält, so der Dichter zu den ubrigen Dichtern. An Umfang, Mannichfaltigkeit und Tiefsinn wird er hie und da übertroffen, aber an Bildungskunst, wer dürfte sich ihm gleich stellen? Bey ihm ist alles That — wie bey andern alles Tendenz

[handwritten note]
e4, e5

nature = living antiquity

antiquity grows under
hands / eyes of artist

Antiquity ≠ made w/ hands

spirit produces it
through eye

I.e.4. NOVALIS, Fragmente: On Goeth
Meisters Lehrjahre; Marchen; Ron
Death; Poesy

[ON GOETHE]

Goethe is a wholly practical poet. He is in his works – what the Englishman is in his goods – extremely simple, neat, comfortable, and durable. He has done for German literature what Wedgwood has for the English art world. Like the Englishman he has a naturally economical and noble taste acquired through the understanding. Both qualities tolerate each other very well and have a close affinity, in the *chemical* sense. In his scientific studies it becomes very clear that his inclination is rather to finish completely something insignificant – to give it the greatest polish and ease of expression, than to begin a whole world and do something in respect of which one can know in advance that it will not be possible to carry it out completely, that it will probably remain clumsy and that a masterly level of skill will never be achieved in it. In this field too he chooses a Romantic or otherwise nicely convoluted subject. His observations on light, on the transformation of plants and insects are at once confirmations and the most convincing proofs that the perfect didactic essay also belongs to the realm of the artist. One would also be justified in maintaining in a certain sense that Goethe is the first physicist of his age – indeed that his work is epoch-making in the history of physics. There can be no question of the scope of his knowledge, however little any discoveries may determine the rank of the scientist. It is a question of whether one contemplates nature as an artist does antiquity – for nature is nothing other than living antiquity. Nature and insight into nature come into being at the same time, like antiquity and the knowledge of antiquities; for one is greatly in error if one believes that antiquities exist. Antiquity is only now coming into being. It grows under the eyes and soul of the artist. The remains of ancient times are only the specific stimuli for the formation of antiquity. Antiquity is not made with hands. The spirit produces it through the eye – and the carved stone is only the body which first receives meaning through antiquity and becomes its appearance. As Goethe the physicist is to other physicists, so Goethe the poet is to other poets. Here and there he is surpassed in range, diversity, and profundity, but in the art of creation, who could aspire to be his equal? With him everything is deed – as with others everything is only tendency. He really makes something, while others only make something possible – or

nur ist. Er macht wircklich etwas, während andre nur etwas möglich — oder nothwendig machen. Nothwendige und mögliche Schöpfer sind wir alle — aber wie wenig Wirckliche. Der Philosoph der Schule würde dies vielleicht activen Empirismus nennen. Wir wollen uns begnügen Göthens Künstlertalent zu betrachten und noch einen Blick auf seinen Verstand werfen. An ihm kann man die Gabe zu abstrahiren in einem neuen Lichte kennen lernen. Er abstrahirt mit einer seltnen Genauigkeit, aber nie ohne das Object zugleich zu construiren, dem die Abstraction entspricht. Dies ist nichts, als angewandte Philosophie — und so fänden wir ihn am Ende zu unserm nicht geringen Erstaunen auch als anwendenden, practischen Philosophen, wie denn jeder ächte Künstler von jeher nichts anders war. Auch der *reine* Philosoph wird practisch seyn, wenn gleich der anwendende Philosoph sich nicht mit reiner Philosophie abzugeben braucht — denn dies ist eine Kunst für sich. /Göthens Meister./ Der Sitz der eigentlichen Kunst ist lediglich im Verstande. Dieser konstruirt nach einem eigenthümlichen Begriff. Fantasie, Witz und Urtheilskraft werden nur von ihm requirirt. So ist Wilhelm Meister ganz ein Kunstproduct — ein Werck des Verstandes. Aus diesem Gesichtspunct sieht man manche sehr mittelmäßige Werke im Kunstsaal — hingegen die meisten vortrefflich geachteten Schriften davon ausgeschlossen. Die Italiaener und Spanier haben bey weitem häufigeres Kunsttalent, als wir. Auch selbst den Franzosen fehlts nicht daran — die Engländer haben schon weit weniger und ähneln hierinn uns, die ebenfalls äußerst selten *Kunsttalent* besitzen — wenn gleich unter allen Nationen am reichhaltigsten und besten mit jenen Fähigkeiten versehn sind — die der Verstand bey seinen Wercken anstellt. Dieser Überfluß an Kunstrequisiten macht freylich die wenigen Künstler unter uns so einzig — so hervorragend, und wir können sichre Rechnung machen, daß unter uns die herrlichsten Kunstwercke entstehn werden, denn in energischer Universalitaet kann keine Nation gegen uns auftreten. Wenn ich die neuesten Freunde der Litteratur des Alterthums recht verstehe, so haben sie mit ihrer Foderung, die klassischen Schriftsteller nachzuahmen nichts anders im Sinn, als uns zu Künstlern zu bilden — Kunsttalent in uns zu erwecken. Keine moderne Nation hat den Kunstverstand in so hohen Grad gehabt, als die Alten. Alles ist bey ihnen Kunstwerck — aber vielleicht dürfte man nicht zu viel sagen, wenn man annähme, daß sie es erst für uns sind, oder werden können. Der classischen Litteratur geht es, wie der Antike; sie ist uns eigentlich nicht gegeben — sie ist nicht vorhanden — sondern sie soll von uns erst hervorgebracht werden. Durch fleißiges und geistvolles Studium der Alten entsteht erst eine klassische Litteratur für uns — die die Alten selbst nicht hatten. Die Alten würden sich eine umgekehrte Aufgabe nehmen müssen — denn der bloße Künstler ist ein einseitiger, beschränckter Mensch. An Strenge steht Göthe wohl den Alten nach — aber er übertrifft sie an Gehalt — welches Verdienst jedoch nicht das Seinige ist. Sein Meister kommt ihnen nah genug — denn wie sehr ist er Roman schlechtweg, ohne Beywort — und wie viel ist das in dieser Zeit!

Göthe wird und muß übertroffen werden — aber nur wie die Alten übertroffen werden können, an Gehalt und Kraft, an Mannichfaltigkeit und Tiefsinn — als Künstler eigentlich nicht — oder doch nur um sehr wenig, denn seine Richtigkeit und Strenge ist vielleicht schon musterhafter, als es scheint.

SCHAFFENDE EINBILDUNGSKRAFT

226. * Wie der Mahler mit ganz andern Augen, als der gemeine Mensch die sichtbaren Gegenstände sieht — so erfährt auch der Dichter die Begebenheiten der äußren und innern Welt nuf eine sehr verschiedne Weise vom gewöhnlichen Menschen. Nirgends aber ist es auffallender, daß es nur der Geist ist, der die Gegenstände, die Veränderungen des Stoffs poëtisirt, und daß

necessary. We are all necessary and possible creators but how few of us are real ones. The scholastic philosopher would perhaps call this active empiricism. We shall content ourselves with contemplating Goethe's artistic talent and casting another glance at his understanding. By this one can come to see the gift of generalization in a new light. He generalizes with a rare exactitude, but never without at the same time representing the object to which the generalization corresponds. This is nothing but applied philosophy – and so in the end we should find him, with more than a little astonishment, to be also a practical philosopher who applies his knowledge, as every true artis[...] will be practical, although the applied p[...] ny – for this is an art in itself. Goethe's M[...]nding. The latter construed according to [...] are required only by this. Thus *Wilhelm* [...]erstanding. From this point of view one [...]n the other hand most works of literatur[...]ans and the Spanish show talent for art [...]much less and are similar in this respect [...]y rarely – even if among all nations we a[...] which the understanding employs in it[...]rtainly makes the few artists among us s[...]he most splendid works of art will be pr[...]rgetic universality. If I understand the m[...]tly, they have with their demand that we [...]cultivate artists for us – to awaken the tal[...] understanding of art in such high degre[...]rt – but perhaps it would not be saying to[...]r can be so. Classical literature is like antiquity; it is not really given to us – it is not present – rather it is to be only now produced by us. Through diligent and inspired study of the ancients, classical literature is only now coming into being for us – a literature that the ancients themselves did not have. The ancients would have had to apply themselves to the contrary task – for he who is only an artist is a one-sided, narrow person. Goethe may well not be the equal of the ancients in rigor – but he surpasses them in content – which merit however is not his own. His *Meister* approaches them closely enough – for how very much is it an absolute novel, without any adjective – and how much that is in our time!

Goethe will and must be surpassed – but only as the ancients can be surpassed, in content and energy, in diversity and profundity—not really as an artist – or only by very little, for his rightness and his rigor are perhaps already more exemplary than they appear.

ON CREATIVITY

*As the painter sees visible objects with quite different eyes from those of the common person – so too the poet experiences the events of the outer and the inner world very differently from the ordinary person. But nowhere is it more striking than in music – that it is only the spirit that poeticizes the objects and the changes of the material, and that the beautiful, the subject of art, is not given to us nor can it be found ready in phenomena. All sounds produced by nature are rough – and empty of spirit – only the musical soul often finds the rustling of the forest – the whistling of the wind, the song of the nightingale, the babbling of the brook

Handwritten note: authentic art rooted in understanding (imagination, wit, judgement required by this) — everyone can be an artist but not many are — no modern nation possesses understanding of art as good as the ancients.

145

das Schöne, der Gegenstand der Kunst uns nicht gegeben wird oder in den Erscheinungen schon fertig liegt — als in der Musik. Alle Töne, die die Natur hervorbringt sind rauh — und geistlos — nur der musikalischen Seele dünkt oft das Rauschen des Waldes — das Pfeifen des Windes, der Gesang der Nachtigall, das Plätschern des Bachs melodisch und bedeutsam. Der Musiker nimmt das Wesen seiner Kunst aus sich — auch nicht der leiseste Verdacht von Nachahmung kann ihn treffen. Dem Mahler scheint die sichtbare Natur überall vorzuarbeiten — durchaus sein unerreichbares Muster zu seyn — Eigentlich ist aber die Kunst des Mahlers so unabhängig, so ganz a priori entstanden, als die Kunst des Musikers. Der Mahler bedient sich nur einer unendlich schwereren *Zeichensprache*, als der Musiker — der Mahler mahlt eigentlich mit dem Auge — Seine Kunst ist die Kunst regelmäßig, und Schön zu sehn. Sehn ist hier ganz activ — durchaus bildende Thätigkeit. Sein Bild ist nur seine Chiffer — sein Ausdruck — Sein Werckzeug der Reproduktion. Man vergleiche mit dieser künstlichen Chiffer — die *Note*. Die mannichfaltige Bewegung der Finger, der Füße und des Mundes dürfte der Musiker noch eher dem Bilde des Mahlers entgegenstellen. Der Musiker hört eigentlich auch active — Er hört heraus. Freylich ist dieser umgekehrte Gebrauch der Sinne den Meisten ein Geheimniß, aber jeder Künstler wird es sich mehr oder minder deutlich bewußt seyn. Fast jeder Mensch ist in geringen Grad schon Künstler — Er sieht in der That heraus und nicht herein — Er fühlt heraus und nicht herein. Der Hauptunterschied ist der; der Künstler hat den Keim des selbstbildenden Lebens in seinen Organen belebt — die Reitzbarkeit derselben *für den Geist* erhöht und ist mithin im Stande Ideen nach Belieben — ohne äußre Sollicitation — durch sie heraus zu strömen — Sie, als Werckzeuge, zu *beliebigen* Modificationen der wircklichen Welt zu gebrauchen — dahingegen sie beym Nichtkünstler nur durch Hinzutritt einer äußren Sollicitation ansprechen und der Geist, wie die trage Materie, unter den Grundgesetzen der Mechanik, daß alle Veränderungen eine äußre Ursache voraussetzen und Wirckung und Gegenwirkung einander jederzeit gleich seyn mussen, zu stehn, oder sich diesem Zwang zu unterwerfen scheint. Tröstlich ist es wenigstens zu wissen, daß dieses mechanische Verhalten dem Geiste unnatürlich und wie alle geistige Unnatur, *zeitlich* sey.

Gänzlich richtet sich indeß auch bey dem gemeinsten Menschen, der Geist nach den Gesetzen der Mechanik nicht — und es ware daher auch bey jedem möglich diese höhere Anlage und Fähigkeit des Organs auszubilden.

Um aber auf die Unterschiede der Mahlerey und Musik zurückzukommen, so ist gleich das auffallend, das bey der Musik Chiffer, Werckzeug und Stoff getrennt, bey der Mahlerey aber Eins sind und eben deshalb bey ihr jedes in abstracto so unvollkommen erscheint. So viel, dünkt mich, werde daraus gewiß, daß die Mahlerey bey weiten *schwieriger,* als die Musik, sey. Daß sie eine Stufe gleichsam dem Heiligthume des Geistes näher, und daher, wenn ich so sagen darf, edler, als die Musik sey ließe sich wohl gerade aus dem gewöhnlichen encomischen Argumente der Lobredner der Musik folgern, daß die Musik viel stärkere und allgemeinere Wirckung thue. Diese physische Größe dürfte nicht der Maaßstab der intellectuellen Höhe der Künste seyn, und eherkontraindiciren. <Musikkennen und haben schon die Thiere — von Mahlerey haben sie aber keine Idee. Die schönste Gegend, das reizendste Bild werden sie eigentlich nicht sehn. Ein gemahlter Gegenstand aus dem Kreise ihrer Bekanntschaft betrügt sie nur —Aber, als Bild, haben sie keine Empfindung daran.>

Ein guter Schauspieler ist in der That ein plastisches und poëtisches Instrument. Eine Oper, ein Ballet sind in der That plastisch poëtische Koncerte — Gemeinschaftliche Kunstwercke mehrerer plastischer Instrumente. /Thatiger Sinn des Gefühls. *Poësie.l*

melodious and meaning[...] [...]hin himself – not
even the slightest suspic[...] [...]ble nature seems
everywhere to be doing [...] model. But really
the painter's art has aris[...] [...]sician's. Only the
painter uses an infinitel[...] the painter really
paints with his eye – his [...]g is quite active –
entirely a formative acti[...] his reproducing
tool. Suppose we compa[...] [...]e musician might
rather counter the pain[...] [...], the feet, and the
mouth. Really the musi[...] For most people
this reversed use of the[...] [...]ore or less clearly
aware of it. Almost eve[...] [...]t he sees actively
and not passively – he f[...] this: the artist has
vivified the germ of self[...] [...]xcitability of these
for the spirit and is the[...] without! external
prompting — to use th[...] *as he will.* On the
other hand for the nor[...] [...]ternal prompting,
and the spirit, like ine[...] [...]e constraint of the
basic laws of mechanics, namely that all changes presuppose an external cause and that effect
and countereffect must equal each other at all times. At least it is some consolation to know that
this mechanical behavior is unnatural to the spirit and is *transient,* like all that is spiritually
unnatural.

[handwritten note overlaying text:] poet experiences outer/inner world different from everyon[e] (most evident in music) (only) a musical soul can find sounds of nature melodious & he can not imitate anything) Painters: seem to have a template in nature but really original like musician

Yet even with the most humble person the spirit does not wholly obey the law of
mechanics – and hence it would be possible for everyone to develop this higher propensity and
skill of the organ.

But to come back to the differences between painting and music, what is immediately striking
is that in music sign, tool, and material are separate, but in painting they are one, and just for
this reason in the latter each element *in abstracto* appears so incomplete. So much can be established with certainty from this, it seems to me, namely that painting is far more *difficult* than
music. That it is as it were one step closer to the holy place of the spirit and therefore nobler than
music, if I may put it that way, may well be inferred from just that usual encomiastic argument
of the admirers of music, that music exercises a much stronger and more general effect. This
physical quantity ought not to be the yardstick of the intellectual stature of the arts, and would
be rather a contraindication of it. Even animals know music and have it themselves – but they
have no idea of painting. They would really not see the most beautiful scene or the most charming picture. A painted object from the circle of their acquaintance only deceives them – but qua
picture they have no sensation of it.

A good actor is indeed a tangible and poetic instrument. Opera and ballet are indeed tangible
poetic concerts – cooperative works of art employing several tangible instruments. The active
sense of feeling. *Poetry.*

26. In the same way as we move our mental organ at will – modify its movement at will –
observe this and its products – and express them in diverse ways – in the same way as we
articulate the movements of our mental organ – as we externalize them in gestures – give them
form in action, as in general we move and behave freely – combine and separate our movements – in just the same way we must also move the inner organs of our bodies, constrain

247. * Auf dieselbe Art, wie wir unser Denkorgan in beliebige Bewegung setzen — seine Bewegung beliebig modificiren — dieselbe und ihre Produkte beobachten — und mannichfaltig ausdrücken — auf dieselbe Art, wie wir die Bewegungen des Denkorgans zur Sprache bringen — wie wir sie in Geberden äußern — in Handlungen ausprägen, wie wir uns überhaupt willkührlich bewegen und aufhalten — unsre Bewegungen vereinigen und vereinzeln — auf eben dieselbe Art müssen wir auch die innern Organe unsers Körpers bewegen, hemmen, vereinigen und vereinzeln, *lernen.* Unser ganzer Körper ist schlechterdings fähig vom Geist in beliebige Bewegung gesezt zu werden. Die Wirckungen der Furcht, des Schreckens — der Traurigkeit, des Zorns — des Neides — der Schaam, der Freude, der Fantasie etc. sind Indikationen genug — Überdem aber hat man genugsam Beyspiele von Menschen — die eine willkührliche Herrschaft über einzelne, gewöhnlich d[er] Willkühr entzogene Theile ihres Körpers erlangt haben. Dann wird jeder sein eigner Arzt seyn — und sich ein vollständiges, sichres und genaues Gefühl seines Körpers erwerben können — dann wird der Mensch erst wahrhaft unabhängig von der Natur, vielleicht im Stande sogar seyn verlorne Glieder zu restauriren, sich blos durch seinen Willen zu tödten, und dadurch erst wahre Aufschlüsse über Korper — Seele — Welt, Leben — Tod und Geisterwelt zu erlangen. Es wird vielleicht nur von ihm dann abhängen einen Stoff zu beseelen — Er wird seine Sinne zwingen ihm die Gestalt *zu produciren,* die er verlangt — und im eigentlichsten Sinn in *Seiner* Welt leben können. Dann wird er vermögend seyn sich von seinem Körper zu trennen — wenn er es fur gut findet — er wird sehn [,] hören — und fühlen — was, wie und in welcher Verbindung er will.

Fichte hat den thätigen Gebrauch des Denkorgans gelehrt — und entdeckt. Hat Fichte etwa die Gesetze des thätigen Gebrauchs der Organe überhaupt entdeckt. Intellectuale Anschauung ist nicht anders.

WILHELM MEISTERS LEHRJAHRE

505. Wilhelm Meisters Lehrjahre sind gewissermaaßen durchaus *prosaïsch* – und modern. Das Romantische geht darinn zu Grunde – auch die Naturpoësie, das Wunderbare – Er handelt blos von gewöhnlichen *menschlichen* Dingen – die Natur und der Mystizism sind ganz vergessen. Es ist eine poëtisirte bürgerliche und häusliche Geschichte. Das Wunderbare darinn wird ausdrücklich, als Poesie und Schwärmerey, behandelt. Künstlerischer Atheïsmus ist der Geist des Buchs. Sehr viel Oeconomie – mit prosaïschen, wohlfeilen Stoff ein poëtischer Effect erreicht.

536. *Gegen* Wilhelm Meisters Lehrjahre. Es ist im Grunde ein fatales und albernes Buch — so pretentios und pretiös — undichterisch im hochsten Grade, was den Geist betrift — so poëtisch auch die Darstellung ist. Es ist eine Satyre auf die Poësie, Religion etc. Aus Stroh und Hobelspänen ein wolschmeckendes Gericht, ein Götterbild zusammengesezt. Hinten wird alles Farçe. Die Oeconomische Natur ist die Wahre — *Übrig bleibende.*

Göthe hat auf alle Fälle einen widerstrebenden Stoff behandelt. *Poëtische Maschinerie.*

Wilhelm Meisters Lehrjahre, oder die Wallfahrt nach dem Adelsdiplom.

W[ilhelm] M[eisters] ist eigentlich ein Candide, gegen die Poësie gerichtet.

MÄRCHEN

195. Es liegt nur an der Schwäche unsrer Organe, und der Selbstberührung, daß wir uns nicht in einer Feenwelt erblicken. Alle Mährchen sind nur Träume von jener heymathlichen Welt, die überall und nirgends ist. Die höhern Mächte in uns, die einst, als Genien, unsern Willen vollbringen werden, sind jezt Musen, die uns auf dieser mühseligen Laufbahn mit süßen Errinnerungen erquicken.

them, combine and separate them, [...] moved by the spirit at will. The effects of f[...] [...]ation etc. are sufficient indications. Besi[...] [...]ieved voluntary mastery over individual [...]ontrol of the will. Then everyone will be [...] com- plete, sure, and exact way. Then fo[...] [...]lent of nature, perhaps even in a positior[...] [...]ll, and thereby to achieve for the first tim[...] [...]th and the world of spirits. Perhaps ther[...] [...]e will compel his senses to *produce* for [...] e in *his* world in the truest sense. Then h[...] – if he finds it good to do so. He will see[...] [...]nation he will.

Fichte taught – and discovered [...]ps dis- covered the laws of the active use of the organs in general. [...] [...]othing else.

handwritten note overlaid:
the artist can get ideas to flow out without external prompting

painting = more difficult than music

(in music, sign, tool, material are all seperate)

even animals have music but no painting

intellectual perception = active use of mental organ

ON WILHELM MEISTER'S APPRENTICESHIP

23. *Wilhelm Meister's Apprenticeship* is to a certain extent thoroughly *prosaic* – and modern. The Romantic quality is destroyed in it – also the nature poetry, the marvelous. He deals with merely ordinary, *human* things – nature and mysticism are quite forgotten. It is a poeticized bourgeois and domestic story. The marvelous element in it is expressly treated as poetic and eccentric. Artistic atheism is the spirit of the book.

Very much economy – a poetic effect achieved with prosaic, cheap material.

28. *Against Wilhelm Meister's Apprenticeship.* It is at bottom a fatal and foolish book – so pre- tentious and precious – unpoetic to the highest degree, as far as the spirit is concerned – how- ever poetic the description. It is a satire on poetry, religion etc. A palatable dish, a divine image put together from straw and shavings. Behind it everything becomes farce. Economic nature is true – and *what remains.*

In any case Goethe has treated a recalcitrant subject matter. *Poetic machinery.* [...]
Wilhelm Meister's Apprenticeship, or the pilgrimage to the title of nobility.
Wilhelm Meister is actually a Candide directed against poetry.

ON FAIRY TALE

3. It is only because of the weakness of our organs and of our contact with ourselves that we do not discover ourselves to be in a fairy world. All fairy tales are only dreams of that familiar world of home which is everywhere and nowhere. The higher powers in us, which one day will carry out our will like genies, are now muses that refresh us with sweet memories along this arduous path.

14. ROMANTICISM et cetera. In a true fairytale everything must be marvelous – mysterious and unconnected – everything must be animated. Each in its different way. The whole of nature must be mixed in a strange way with the whole of the spirit world. Time of general anarchy – lawlessness – freedom – the *natural state* of *nature* – the time before the *world* (state). This time before the world brings with it, as it were the scattered features of the *time after the world* – as the

[234.] ROMANT[IK] ETC. In einem ächten Märchen muß alles wunderbar — geheimnißvoll und unzusammenhängend seyn — alles belebt. Jedes auf eine andre Art. Die ganze Natur muß auf eine wunderliche Art mit der ganzen Geisterwelt vermischt seyn. Die Zeit der allg[emeinen] Anarchie — Gesezlosigkeit — Freyheit — der *Naturstand* der *Natur* — die Zeit vor der *Welt* (Staat.) Diese Zeit vor der Welt liefert gleichsam die zerstreuten Züge der Zeit *nach der Welt* — wie der Naturstand ein *sonderbares Bild* des ewigen Reichs ist. Die Welt des Märchens ist die *durchausentgegengesezte* Welt der Welt der Wahrheit (Geschichte) — und eben darum ihr so *durchaus ähnlich* —wie das *Chaos* der *vollendeten Schöpfung.* (Über *die Idylle.*)

In der *künftigen* Welt ist alles, wie in der *ehmaligen* Welt — und *doch alles ganz Anders.* Die *künftige* Welt ist das *Vernünftige* Chaos — das Chaos, das sich selbst durchdrang — in sich und außer sich ist — *Chaos* 2 oder ∞.

Das *ächte Märchen* muß zugleich *Prophetische Darstellung* — idealische Darstell[ung] — abs[olut] nothwendige Darst[ellung] seyn. Der ächte Märchendichter ist ein Seher der Zukunft.

Bekenntnisse eines wahrhaften, synth[etischen] *Kindes* — eines idealischen Kindes. (Ein Kind ist weit klüger und weiser, als ein Erwachsener — d[as] Kind muß durchaus *ironisches* Kind seyn.) — Die Spiele d[es] K[indes] — *Nachahmung* der Erwachsenen. (Mit der Zeit muß d[ie] Gesch[ichte] Märchen werden — sie wird wieder, wie sie anfieng.)

940. Das Mährchen ist gleichsam der *Canon* der *Poësie* — alles poëtische muß mährchenhaft seyn. Der Dichter betet den Zufall an.

ROMANTIK

105. Die Welt muß romantisirt werden. So findet man den urspr[ünglichen] Sinn wieder. Romantisiren ist nichts, als eine qualit[ative] Potenzirung. Das niedre Selbst wird mit einem bessern Selbst in dieser Operation identificirt. So wie wir selbst eine solche qualit[ative] Potenzenreihe sind. Diese Operation ist noch ganz unbekannt. Indem ich dem Gemeinen einen hohen Sinn, dem Gewöhnlichen ein geheimnißvolles Ansehn, dem Bekannten die Würde des Unbekannten, dem Endlichen einen unendlichen Schein gebe so romantisire ich es — Umgekehrt ist die Operation für das Höhere, Unbekannte, Mystische, Unendliche — dies wird durch diese Verknüpfung logarythmisirt — Es bekommt einen geläufigen Ausdruck. romantische Philosophie. *Lingua romana.* Wechselerhöhung und Erniedrigung.

ÜBERSETZUNG

68. Eine Übersetzung ist entweder grammatisch, oder verändernd, oder mythisch. Mythische Übersetzungen sind Übersetzungen im hochsten Styl. Sie stellen den reinen, vollendeten Karacter des individuellen Kunstwercks dar. Sie geben uns nicht das wirckliche Kunstwerck, sondern das Ideal desselben. Noch existirt, wie ich glaube kein ganzes Muster derselben. Im Geist mancher Kritiken und Beschreibungen von Kunstwercken trift man aber helle Spuren. Es gehört ein Kopf dazu, indem sich poëtischer Geist und philosophischer Geist in ihrer ganzen Fülle durchdrungen haben. Die griechische Mythologie ist zum Theil eine solche Übersetzung einer Nationalreligion. Auch die moderne Madonna ist ein solcher Mythus.

Grammatische Übersetzungen sind die Übersetzungen im gewohnlichen Sinn. Sie erfodern sehr viel Gelehrsamkeit — aber nur discursive Fähigkeiten.

Zu den Verändernden Übersetzungen gehört, wenn sie ächt seyn sollen, der höchste, poëtische Geist. Sie streifen leicht in die Travestie — wie Bürgers Homer in Jamben — Popens Homer —

state of nature is a *strange picture* of the eternal kingdom. The world of the fairy tale is the *absolutely opposite* world to the world of truth (history) – and just for this reason it is so *absolutely similar* to it – as *chaos* is to *accomplished creation*. (On the *idyll*).

In the *future* world everything is as it is in the *former* world – and *yet everything is quite different*. The *future* world is *reasonable* chaos – chaos which penetrated itself – is inside and outside itself – *chaos* squared or infinity.

The *true fairy tale* must be at once a *prophetic representation* – an ideal representation – an absolutely necessary representation. The maker of true fairy tales is a prophet of the future.

Confessions of a truly synthetic *child* – an ideal child. A child is far cleverer and wiser than an adult – the ⬚⬚⬚⬚ ⬚⬚⬚ ⬚⬚⬚ mes – *imitation* of adults. In time history ⬚⬚⬚⬚ ⬚⬚⬚⬚ it was in the beginning.

940. The ⬚ ⬚⬚⬚ oetic must be like a fairy tale. The poet wo⬚⬚

[... dia. Das Allgemeine Brouillon.
roduction by David W. Wood,
ew York Press, Albany, S. 167]

ON ROMAN⬚⬚

66. The worl⬚ ⬚⬚⬚⬚⬚⬚ e original meaning again. To make Roma⬚ ⬚⬚⬚⬚⬚⬚⬚ ⬚r. In this operation the lower self will bec⬚⬚ ⬚⬚⬚⬚⬚⬚ ⬚ch a qualitative exponential series. This ⬚⬚⬚⬚⬚⬚ commonplace with a higher meaning, th⬚ ⬚⬚⬚⬚⬚⬚ dignity of the unknown, the finite with th⬚ ⬚⬚⬚⬚⬚⬚ The operation for the higher, unknown, m⬚⬚⬚⬚⬚⬚⬚ rithmic change through this connection – ⬚⬚⬚⬚⬚⬚ philosophy. *Lingua romana.* Raising and lowering by turns.

ON TRANSLATION

68. A translation is either grammatical, or modifying, or mythical. Mythical translations are translations of the highest kind. They represent the pure, perfected character of the individual work of art. They do not give us the real work of art but the ideal of it. There still does not exist, I believe, a complete example of such a translation. But in the spirit of many a critique and description of works of art clear signs are to be found. A mind is needed where the spirit of poetry and the spirit of philosophy have saturated each other in all their fullness. Greek mythology is in part such a translation of a national religion. The modern Madonna too is such a myth.

Grammatical translations are translations in the usual sense. They require a great deal of learning – but only discursive abilities.

Modifying translations, if they are to be genuine, demand the highest poetic spirit. They easily slip into travesty – like Bürger's Homer in iambics – Pope's Homer – all French translations. The true translator of this kind must indeed be an artist himself and be able to produce the idea of the whole at will in one way or another. He must be the poet of the poet and thus be able to let him speak according to his own and the poet's idea *at the same time*.

The genius of humanity stands in a similar relation to each single person. Not only books but everything can be translated in these three ways.

die Französischen Übersetzungen insgesammt. Der wahre Übersetzer dieser Art muß in der That der Künstler selbst seyn und die Idee des Ganzen beliebig so oder so geben können — Er muß der Dichter des Dichters seyn und ihn also nach seiner und des Dichters eigner Idee *zugleich* reden lassen können.

In einem ähnlichen Verhältnisse steht der Genius der Menschheit mit jedem einzelnen Menschen.

Nicht blos Bücher, alles kann auf diese drey Arten übersezt werden.

KRITIK

125. Der wahre Leser muß der erweiterte Autor seyn. Er ist die höhere Instanz, die die Sache von der niedern Instanz schon vorgearbeitet erhält. Das Gefühl, vermittelst dessen der Autor die Materialien seiner Schrift geschieden hat, scheidet beim Lesen wieder das Rohe und Gebildete des Buchs — und wenn der Leser das Buch nach seiner Idee bearbeiten würde, so würde ein 2ter Leser noch mehr läutern, und so wird dadurch daß die bearbeitete Masse immer wieder in frischthätige Gefäße kömmt die Masse endlich wesentlicher Bestandtheil — Glied des wircksamen Geistes.

TOD

[30.] Der Tod ist das romantisirende Princip unsers Lebens. Der Tod ist – das Leben +. Durch den Tod wird das Leben verstärkt.

POESIE

473. Die Poësie ist das ächt absolut Reelle. Dies ist der Kern meiner Phil[osophie]. Je poëtischer, je wahrer.

> [*Novalis Schriften. Historisch-kritische Ausgabe. Ed. Paul Kluckhohn, Richard Samuel,*
> *Hans-Joachim Mähl and Gerhard Schulz. 7 Vols. Stuttgart, Berlin, Cologne, Mainz:*
> *Kohlhammer, 1960. II, 438–647; III, 280–647 (extracts)]*

1.e.5. FRIEDRICH SCHLEGEL, aus 'Athenaeum Fragmentes'

ROMANTIK

116. Die romantische Poesie ist eine progressive Universalpoesie. Ihre Bestimmung ist nicht bloß, alle getrennte Gattungen der Poesie wieder zu vereinigen, und die Poesie mit der Philosophie und Rhetorik in Berührung zu setzen. Sie will, und soll auch Poesie und Prosa, Genialität und Kritik, Kunstpoesie und Naturpoesie bald mischen, bald verschmelzen, die Poesie lebendig and gesellig, und das Leben und die Gesellschaft poetisch machen, den Witz poetisieren, und die Formen der Kunst mit gediegnem Bildungsstoff jeder Art anfüllen und sättigen, und durch die Schwingungen des Humors beseelen. Sie umfaßt alles, was nur poetisch ist, vom größten wieder mehre Systeme in sich enthaltenden Systeme der Kunst, bis zu dem Seufzer, dem Kuß, den das dichtende Kind aushaucht in kunstlosen Gesang. Sie kann sich so in das Dargestellte verlieren, daß man glauben möchte, poetische Individuen jeder Art zu charakterisieren, sei ihr Eins und Alles; und doch gibt es noch keine Form, die so dazu gemacht wäre, den Geist des Autors vollständig auszudrücken: so daß manche Künstler, die nur auch einen Roman schreiben wollten, von ungefähr sich selbst

ON CRITICISM

125. The true reader must be a ~~case already prepared by the l~~ ~~rated out the materials of his~~ ~~formed aspects of the book - a~~ ~~own idea, a second reader wou~~ ~~been worked through would~~ become an essential compone

[handwritten note:] modifying translations require a poet ⌐ must be able to still communicate the whole idea through his own idea & poets idea at the same time

reader must be extension of the author

ON DEATH

5. Death is the Romanticizing ~~death = romanticizing~~ *[handwritten:]* death = romanticizing Principle of life
ened through death.

ON P

[handwritten:] Poetry = truth absolute real

24. P ~~y philosophy. The more poetic the~~
more

[handwritten:] the more poetic the more true

r. Margaret Mahony Stoljar. Albany: New York P, 1997. 32–117(extracts)]

I.e.5 *[handwritten:]* [e.5] goal of romanticism:

ROM

116. ~~ts aim isn't merely to reunite all the~~
sepa ~~philosophy and rhetoric. It tries to~~
and ~~and criticism, the poetry of art and~~
the p ~~, and life and society poetical; poet-~~
icize ~~very kind of good, solid matter for~~
instru ~~mor. It embraces everything that is~~
purely poetic, from the greatest ~~~~ ~~~~ing within themselves still further
systems, to the sigh, the kiss that the poetizing child breathes forth in artless song. It can so
lose itself in what it describes that one might believe it exists only to characterize poetical
individuals of all sorts; and yet there still is no form so fit for expressing the entire spirit of
an author: so that many artists who started out to write only a novel ended up by providing
us with a portrait of themselves. It alone can become, like the epic, a mirror of the whole

153

dargestellt haben. Nur sie kann gleich dem Epos ein Spiegel der ganzen umgebenden Welt, ein Bild des Zeitalters werden. Und doch kann auch sie am meisten zwischen dem Dargestellten und dem Darstellenden, frei von allem realen und idealen Interesse auf den Flügeln der poetischen Reflexion in der Mitte schweben, diese Reflexion immer wieder potenzieren und wie in einer endlosen Reihe von Spiegeln vervielfachen. Sie ist der höchsten und der allseitigsten Bildung fähig; nicht bloß von innen heraus, sondern auch von außen hinein; indem sie jedem, was ein Ganzes in ihren Produkten sein soll, alle Teile ähnlich organisiert, wodurch ihr die Aussicht auf eine grenzenlos wachsende Klassizität eröffnet wird. Die romantische Poesie ist unter den Künsten was der Witz der Philosophie, und die Gesellschaft, Umgang, Freundschaft und Liebe im Leben ist. Andre Dichtarten sind fertig, und können nun vollständig zergliedert werden. Die romantische Dichtart ist noch im Werden; ja das ist ihr eigentliches Wesen, daß sie ewig nur werden, nie vollendet sein kann. Sie kann durch keine Theorie erschöpft werden, und nur eine divinatorische Kritik dürfte es wagen, ihr Ideal charakterisieren zu wollen. Sie allein ist unendlich, wie sie allein frei ist, und das als ihr erstes Gesetz anerkennt, daß die Wilkür des Dichters kein Gesetz über sich leide. Die romantische Dichtart ist die einzige, die mehr als Art, und gleichsam die Dichtkunst selbst ist: denn in einem gewissen Sinn ist oder soll alle Poesie romantisch sein.

FRANZÖSISCHE REVOLUTION, GOETHE, FICHTE:

216. Die Französische Revolution, Fichtes Wissenschaftslehre, und Goethes Meister sind die größten Tendenzen des Zeitalters. Wer an dieser Zusammenstellung Anstoß nimmt, wem keine Revolution wichtig scheinen kann, die nicht laut und materiell ist, der hat sich noch nicht auf den hohen weiten Standpunkt der Geschichte der Menschheit erhoben. Selbst in unsern dürftigen Kulturgeschichten, die meistens einer mit fortlaufendem Kommentar begleiteten Variantensammlung, wozu der klassische Text verloren ging, gleichen, spielt manches kleine Buch, von dem die lärmende Menge zu seiner Zeit nicht viel Notiz nahm, eine größere Rolle, als alles, was diese trieb.

IRONIE Nr.1:

51. Naiv ist, was bis zur Ironie, oder bis zum steten Wechsel von Selbstschöpfung und Selbstvernichtung natürlich, individuell oder klassisch ist, oder scheint. Ist es bloß Instinkt, so ists kindlich, kindisch, oder albern; ists bloße Absicht, so entsteht Affektation. Das schöne, poetische, idealische Naive muß zugleich Absicht, und Instinkt sein. Das Wesen der Absicht in diesem Sinne ist die Freiheit. Bewußtsein ist noch bei weitem nicht Absicht. Es gibt ein gewisses verliebtes Anschauen eigner Natürlichkeit oder Albernheit, das selbst unsäglich albern ist. Absicht erfordert nicht gerade einen tiefen Calcul oder Plan. Auch das Homerische Naive ist nicht bloß Instinkt: es ist wenigstens so viel Absicht darin, wie in der Anmut lieblicher Kinder, oder unschuldiger Mädchen. Wenn Er auch keine Absichten hatte, so hat doch seine Poesie und die eigentliche Verfasserin derselben, die Natur, Absicht.

IRONIE Nr.2:

42. Die Philosophie ist die eigentliche Heimat der Ironie, welche man logische Schönheit definieren möchte: denn überall wo in mündlichen oder geschriebenen Geaprächen, und nur nicht ganz systematisch philosophiert wird, soll man Ironie leisten und fordern; und sogar die Stoiker hielten die Urbanität für eine Tugend. Freilich gibts auch eine rhetorische Ironie, welche sparsam gebraucht vortreffliche Wirkung tut, besonders im Polemischen; doch ist sie gegen die erhabne Urbanität der sokratischen Muse, was die Pracht der glänzendsten Kunstrede gegen

circumambient world, an image of the
hover at the midpoint between the po
self-interest, on the wings of poetic ref
to a higher power, can multiply it ir
the highest and most variegated refine
without inwards; capable in that it org
effects – the parts along similar lines,
increasing classicism. Romantic poetr
society and sociability, friendship and
are now capable of being fully analyze
becoming; that, in fact, is its real esse
perfected. It can be exhausted by no th
characterize its ideal. It alone is infini
commandment that the will of the po
of poetry is the only one that is more
certain sense all poetry is or should be

[Handwritten note overlaying text: "Novels/poems become a portrait of the author and mirror of an age (focus on author/creator). Romanticism is in the arts what friendship & love are in life. romantic poetry = still in a state of becoming"]

FRENCH REVOLUTION, GOETHE, FICHTE:

216. The French Revolution, Fichte's philosophy, and Goethe's Meister are the greatest tendencies of the age. Whoever is offended by this juxtaposition, whoever cannot take any revolution
seriously that isn't noisy and materialistic, hasn't yet achieved a lofty, broad perspective on the
history of mankind. Even in our shabby histories of civilization, which usually resemble a collection of variants accompanied by a running commentary for which the original classical text
has been lost; even there many a little book, almost unnoticed by the noisy rabble at the time,
plays a greater role than anything they did.

IRONY No.1:

51. Naive is what is or seems to be natural, individual, or classical to the point of irony, or else to
the point of continuously fluctuating between self-creation and self-destruction, if it's simply
instinctive, then it's childlike, childish, or silly; if it's merely intentional, then it gives rise to affectation. The beautiful, poetical, ideal naive must combine intention and instinct. The essence of
intention in this sense is freedom, though intention isn't consciousness by a long shot. There is
a certain kind of self-infatuated contemplation of one's own naturalness or silliness that is itself
unspeakably silly. Intention doesn't exactly require any deep calculation or plan. Even Homeric
naiveté isn't simply instinctive; there is at least as much intention in it as there is in the grace of
lovely children or innocent girls. And even if Homer himself had no intentions, his poetry and
the real author of that poetry, Nature, certainly did.

IRONY No.2:

42. Philosophy is the real homeland of irony, which one would like to define as logical beauty: for
wherever philosophy appears in oral or written dialogues – and is not simply confined into rigid
systems – there irony should be asked for and provided. And even the Stoics considered urbanity a virtue. Of course, there is also a rhetorical species of irony which, sparingly used, has an
excellent effect, especially in polemics; but compared to the sublime urbanity of the Socratic
muse, it is like the pomp of the most splendid oration set over against the noble style of an

eine alte Tragödie in hohem Styl. Die Poesie allein kann sich auch von dieser Seite bis zur Höhe der Philosophie erheben, und ist nicht auf ironische Stellen begründet, wie die Rhetorik. Es gibt alte und moderne Gedichte, die durchgängig im Ganzen und überall den göttlichen Hauch der Ironie atmen. Es lebt in ihnen eine wirklich transzendentale Buffonerie. Im Innern, die Stimmung, welche alles übersieht, und sich über alles Bedingte unendlich erhebt, auch über eigne Kunst, Tugend, oder Genialität: im Äußern, in der Ausführung die mimische Manier eines gewöhnlichen guten italiänischen Buffo.

IRONIE Nr.3:

48. Ironie ist die Form des Paradoxen. Paradox ist alles, was zugleich gut und groß ist.

FRAGMENT:

206. Ein Fragment muß gleich einem kleinen Kunstwerke von der umgebenden Welt ganz abgesondert und in sich selbst vollendet sein wie ein Igel.

> [1798] [*Edited by Ernst Behler, Paderborn, Munich, Vienna, Zürich:*
> *Schöningh, 1958. 182–197*]

I.e.6. FRIEDRICH SCHLEGEL, aus 'Brief über den Roman'

Ich muß, was ich gestern zu Ihrer Verteidigung zu sagen schien, zurücknehmen, liebe Freundin! und Ihnen so gut als völlig unrecht geben. Sie selbst geben es sich am Ende des Streites darin, daß Sie sich so tief eingelassen, weil es gegen die weibliche Würde sei, aus dem angebornen Element von heiterm Scherz und ewiger Poesie zu dem gründlichen oder schwerfälligen Ernst der Männer sich, wie Sie es richtig nannten, herabzustimmen. Ich stimme Ihnen gegen Sie selbst bei, daß Sie unrecht haben. Ja ich behaupte noch außerdem, daß es nicht genug sei, Unrecht anzuerkcnnen; man muß es auch büßen, und die wie mirs scheint, ganz zweckmäßige Buße dafür, daß Sie sich mit der Kritik gemein gemacht haben, soll nun sein, daß Sie sich die Geduld abnötigen, diese kritische Epistel über den Gegenstand des gestrigen Gesprächs zu lesen.

Ich hätte es gleich gestern sagen können, was ich sagen will; oder vielmehr ich konnte es nicht, meiner Stimmung und der Umstände wegen. Mit welchem Gegner hatten Sie zu tun, Amalia? Freilich versteht er das, wovon die Rede war, recht wohl und wie sichs für einen tüchtigen Virtuosen nicht anders gebührt. Er würde also darüber sprechen können so gut wie irgend einer, wenn er nur überhaupt sprechen könnte. Dieses haben ihm die Götter versagt; er ist, wie ich schon sagte, ein Virtuose und damit gut; die Grazien sind leider ausgeblieben. Da er nun so gar nicht ahnden konnte, was Sie im innersten Sinne meinten, und das äußerliche Recht so ganz auf seiner Seite war, so hatte ich nichts Angelegeners, als mit ganzer Stärke für Sie zu streiten, damit nur das gesellige Gleichgewicht nicht völlig zerstört würde. Und überdem ists mir natürlicher, wenn as ja sein muß, schriftliche Belehrungen zu geben als mündliche, die nach meinem Gefühl die Heiligkeit des Gesprächs entweihen.

Das unsrige fing damit an, daß Sie behaupteten, Friedrich Richters Romane seien keine Romane, sondern ein buntes Allerlei von kränklichem Witz. Die wenige Geschichte sei zu schlecht dargestellt um für Geschichte zu gelten, man müsse sie nur erraten. Wenn man aber auch alle zusammennehmen und sie rein erzählen wolle, würde das doch höchstens Bekenntnisse geben. Die Individualität des Menschen sei viel zu sichtbar, und noch dazu eine solche!

Das letzte übergehe ich, weil es doch wieder nur Sache der Individualität ist. Das bunte Allerlei von kränklichem Witz gebe ich zu, aber ich nehme es in Schutz und behaupte dreist, daß

ancient tragedy. Only poetry can also reach the heights of philosophy in this way, and only poetry does not restrict itself to isolated ironical passages, as rhetoric does. There are ancient and modern poems that are pervaded by the divine breath of irony throughout and informed by a truly transcendental buffoonery. Internally: the mood that surveys everything and rises infinitely above all limitations, even above its own art, virtue, or genius externally, in its execution: the mimic style of an averagely gifted Italian buffo.

IRONY No.3:

48. Irony is the form of paradox. Paradox is everything simultaneously good and great.

FRAGMENT:

206. A fragment, like a miniature work of art, has to be entirely isolated from the surrounding world and be complete in itself like a porcupine.

[1798] [Translated by Peter Firchow. Minneapolis: _____nesota P, 1971]

I.e.6.   FRIEDRICH SCH

I must retract, my dear la____ _____ ____ ____ __ ___say that you are almost completely wrong ____ _____ ____ ___ ___ ___gument, having become involved so deep ___ ___ ___ ____ ____ ___ __ ____ __ tone, as you so aptly put it, from the inn___ ___ ____ ____ ___ ___ __ __ough or heavy-handed earnestness of th___ ___ ___ ____ ___ __ ___ __vrong. Indeed, I maintain that it is not en___ ___ ___ ___ __ ___ __ __for it and, as it seems to me, proper am____ ___ ___ ___ ___ ___ __ __would now be that you force yourself t___ ___ ___ ___ __ __ __ ___bout the subject of yesterday's conversatio____

What I want to say I co____ ___ ____ ___ ___ __use of my mood and the circumstances. ____ ___ ____ ___ ___ __a? Certainly he understands quite well w____ ___ ____ ___ ___ ___ver virtuoso. He could have talked about i____ ___ ____ ___ ___is the gods have denied him; he is, as I have already said, a virtuoso and that's it; the Graces, unfortunately, stayed away. Since he was not quite certain what you meant in the deepest sense, and externally the right was so completely on your side, I made it my business to argue for you with all my might, to prevent the convivial balance from being destroyed. And besides, it is more natural for men, if it really has to be done, to give written instructions rather than oral which I feel violate the dignity of conversation.

Our conversation began when you asserted that Friedrich Richter's novels are not novels but a colorful hodgepodge of sickly wit; that the meager story is too badly presented to be considered a story; one simply had to guess it. If, however, one wanted to put it all together and just tell it, it would at best amount to a confession. The individuality of the man is much too visible, and such a personality at that.

I disregard this last point because it is only a question of individuality. I admit the colorful hodgepodge of sickly wit; but I shall defend it and emphatically maintain that such grotesques and confessions are the only romantic productions of our unromantic age.

solche Grotesken und Bekenntnisse noch die einzigen romantischen Erzeugnisse unsers unromantischen Zeitalters sind.

Lassen Sie mich bei dieser Gelegenheit ausschütten, was ich lange auf dem Herzen habe! Mit Erstaunen und mit innerm Grimm habe ich oft den Diener die Haufen zu Ihnen hereintragen sehn. Wie mögen Sie nur mit Ihren Händen die schmutzigen Bände berühren? — Und wie können Sie den verworrnen, ungebildeten Redensarten den Eingang durch Ihr Auge in das Heiligtum der Seele verstatten? — Stundenlang Ihre Fantasie an Menschen hingeben, mit denen von Angesicht zu Angesicht nur wenige Worte zu wechseln Sie sich schämen würden? — Es frommt wahrlich zu nichts, als nur die Zeit zu töten und die Imagination zu verderben! Fast alle schlechten Bücher haben Sie gelesen von Fielding bis zu Lafontaine. Fragen Sie sich selbst was Sie davon gehabt haben. Ihr Gedächtnis selbst verschmäht das unedle Zeug, was eine fatale Jugendgewohnheit Ihnen zum Bedürfnis macht, und was so emsig herbeigeschafft werden muß, wird sogleich rein vergessen.

Dagegen erinnern Sie sich noch vielleicht, daß es eine Zeit gab, wo Sie den Sterne liebten, sich oft ergötzten, seine Manier anzunehmen, halb nachzuahmen, halb zu verspotten. Ich habe noch einige scherzhafte Briefchen der Art von Ihnen, die ich sorgsam bewahren werde. — Sternes Humor hatte Ihnen also doch einen bestimmten Eindruck gegeben; wenngleich eben keine idealisch schöne, so war es doch eine Form, eine geistreiche Form, die Ihre Fantasie dadurch gewann, und ein Eindruck, der uns so bestimmt bleibt, den wir so zu Scherz und Ernst gebrauchen und gestalten können, ist nicht verloren; und was kann einen gründlichern Wert haben als dasjenige, was das Spiel unsrer innern Bildung auf irgend eine Weise reizt oder nährt.

Sie fühlen es selbst, daß Ihr Ergötzen an Sternes Humor rein war, und von ganz andrer Natur, als die Spannung der Neugier, die uns oft ein durchaus schlechtes Buch, in demselben Augenblick, wo wir es so finden, abnötigen kann. Fragen Sie sich nun selbst, ob Ihr Genuß nicht verwandt mit demjenige war, den wir oft bei Betrachtung der witzigen Spielgemälde empfanden, die man Arabesken nennt. — Auf den Fall, daß Sie sich selbst nicht von allem Anteil an Sternes Empfindsamkeit freisprechen können, schicke ich Ihnen hier ein Buch, von dem ich Ihnen aber, damit Sie gegen Fremde vorsichtig sind, voraussagen muß, daß es das Unglück oder das Glück hat, ein wenig verschrien zu sein. Es ist Diderots FATALISTE. Ich denke, es wird Ihnen gefallen, und Sie werden die Fülle des Witzes hier ganz rein finden von sentimentalen Beimischungen. Es ist mit Verstand angelegt, und mit sicher Hand ausgeführt. Ich darf es ohne Übertreibung ein Kunstwerk nennen. Freilich ist es keine hohe Dichtung, sondern nur eine — Arabeske. Aber eben darum hat es in meinen Augen keine geringen Ansprüche; denn ich halte die Arabeske für eine ganz bestimmte und wesentliche Form oder Äußerungsart der Poesie.

Ich denke mir die Sache so. Die Poesie ist so tief in dem Menschen gewurzelt, daß sie auch unter den ungünstigsten Umständen immer noch zu Zeiten wild wächst. Wie wir nun fast bei jedem Volk Lieder, Geschichten im Umlauf, irgendeine Art wenngleich rohe Schauspiele im Gebrauch finden: so haben selbst in unserm unfantastischen Zeitalter, in den eigentlichen Ständen der Prosa, ich meine die sogenannten Gelehrten und gebildeten Leute, einige einzelne eine seltne Originalität der Fantasie in sich gespürt und geäußert, obgleich sie darum von der eigentlichen Kunst noch sehr entfernt waren. Der Humor eines Swift, eines Sterne, meine ich, sei die Naturpoesie der höhern Stände unsers Zeitalters.

Ich bin weit entfernt, sie neben jene Großen zu stellen; aber Sie werden mir zugeben, daß wer für diese, für den Diderot Sinn hat, schon besser auf dem Wege ist, den göttlichen Witz, die Fantasie eines Ariost, Cervantes, Shakespeare verstehn zu lernen, als ein andrer, der auch noch nicht einmal bis dahin sich erhoben hat. Wir dürfen nun einmal die Foderungen in diesem

On this occasion let me get something off my mind that I have been thinking about for a long time.

With astonishment and inner anger, I have often seen your servant carry piles of volumes in to you. How can you touch with your hands those dirty volumes? And how can you allow the confused and crude phrases to enter through your eye to the sanctuary of your soul? To yield your imagination for hours to people with whom, face to face, you would be ashamed to exchange even a few words? It serves no purpose but to kill time and to spoil your imagination. You have read almost all the bad books from Fielding to La Fontaine. Ask yourself what you profited by it. Your memory scorns this vulgar stuff which has become a necessity through an unfortunate habit of your youth; what has to be acquired so laboriously, is entirely forgotten.

But then perhaps you remember that there was a time when you loved Sterne and enjoyed assuming his manner, partially to imitate, partially to ridicule him. I still have a few jocular letters of this kind from you which I will carefully save. Sterne's humor did make a definite impression on you. Even though it was no ideally perfect form, yet it was a form and a witty one which captivated your imagination. And an impression that is so definite that we make use of it and cultivate it in seriousness and jest is not lost. And what can have a more fundamental value than those things which in some way stimulate or nourish the play of our inner makeup.

You feel yourself that your delight in Sterne's humor was pure and of an entirely different nature than the suspense which can be often forced upon us by a thoroughly bad book, at the very time that we find it bad. Now ask yourself if your enjoyment was not related to what we often experience while viewing the witty paintings called arabesques. In case you cannot deny some sympathy with Sterne's sensibility, I am sending you a book, but I have to warn you about it so that you will be careful with regard to strangers, for it has the fortune or misfortune to be somewhat notorious. It is Diderot's The Fatalist. I think you will like it and will find in it an abundance of wit, quite free of sentimental admixtures. It is designed with understanding and executed with a firm hand. Without exaggerating, I can call it a work of art. To be sure, it is not a work of high rank, but only an arabesque. But for that reason it has in my eyes no small merit; for I consider the arabesque a very definite and essential form or mode of expression of poetry.

This is how I think of the matter. Poetry is so deeply rooted in man that at times, even under the most unfavorable circumstances, it grows without cultivation. Just as we find in almost every nation songs and stories in circulation and, even though crude, some kind of plays in use, so in our unfantastic age, in the actual estate of prose, and I mean the so-called educated and cultured people, we will find a few individuals who, sensing in themselves a certain originality of the imagination, express it, even though they are still far removed from true art. The humor of a Swift, a Sterne is, I believe, natural poetry of the higher classes of our age.

I am far from putting them next to the great ones; but you will admit that whoever has a sense for these, for Diderot, has a better start on the way to learning to appreciate the divine wit, the imagination of an Ariosto, Cervantes, Shakespeare, than one who did not even rise to that point. We simply must not make exaggerated demands on the people of our times; what has grown in such a sickly environment naturally cannot be anything else but sickly. I consider this circumstance, however, rather an advantage, as long as the arabesque is not a work of art but a natural product, and therefore place Richter over Sterne because his imagination is far more sickly, therefore far more eccentric and fantastic. Just go ahead and read Sterne again. It has been a long time since you read him and I think you will find him different. Then compare our German with him. He really does have more wit, at least for one who takes him wittily, for he could easily

Stück an die Menschen der jetzigen Zeit nicht zu hoch spannen, und was in so kränklichen Verhältnissen aufgewachsen ist kann selbst natürlicherweise nicht anders als kränklich sein. Dies halte ich aber, so lange die Arabeske kein Kunstwerk sondern nur ein Naturprodukt ist, eher für einen Vorzug, und stelle Richtern also auch darum über Sterne, weil seine Fantasie weit kränklicher, also weit wunderlicher und fantastischer ist. Lesen Sie nur überhaupt den Sterne einmal wieder. Es ist lange her, daß Sie ihn nicht gelesen haben, und ich denke er wird Ihnen etwas anders vorkommen wie damals. Vergleichen Sie dann immer unsern Deutschen mit ihm. Er hat wirklich mehr Witz, wenigstens für den, der ihn witzig nimmt: denn er selbst könnte sich darin leicht Unrecht tun. Und durch diesen Vorzug erhebt sich selbst seine Sentimentalität in der Erscheinung über die Sphäre der engländischen Empfindsamkeit.

Wir haben noch einen äußern Grund diesen Sinn für das Groteske in uns zu bilden, und uns in dieser Stimmung zu erhalten. Es ist unmöglich, in diesem Zeitalter der Bücher nicht auch viele, sehr viele schlechte Bücher durchblättern, ja sogar lesen zu müssen. Einige unter diesen sind, darauf darf man mit einiger Zuversicht rechnen, glücklicherweise immer von der albernen Art, und da kommt es wirklich nur auf uns an, sie unterhaltend zu finden, indem wir sie nämlich als witzige Naturprodukte betrachten. Laputa ist nirgends oder überall, liebe Freundin; es kommt nur auf einen Akt unsrer Willkür und unsrer Fantasie an, so sind wir mitten darin. Wenn die Dummheit eine gewisse Höhe erreicht, zu der wie sie jetzt, wo sich alles schärfer sondert, meistens gelangen sehn, so gleicht sie auch in der äußern Erscheinung der Narrheit. Und die Narrheit, werden Sie mit zugeben, ist das Lieblichste, was der Mensch imaginieren kann, und das eigentliche letzte Prinzip alles Amüsanten. In dieser Stimmung kann ich oft ganz allein für mich über Bücher, die keinesweges dazu bestimmt scheinen, in ein Gelächter verfallen, was kaum wieder aufhören will. Und es ist billig, daß die Natur mir diesen Ersatz gibt, da ich über so manches, was jetzt Witz und Satire heißt, durchaus nicht mitlachen kann. Dagegen werden mir nun gelehrte Zeitungen z. B. zu Farcen, und diejenige welche sich die allgemeine nennt, halte ich mir ganz ausdrücklich, wie die Wiener den Kasperle. Sie ist aus meinem Standpunkte angesehen, nicht nur die mannigfaltigste von allen, sondern auch in jeder Rücksicht die unvergleichlichste: denn nachdem sie aus der Nullität in eine gewisse Plattheit gesunken, und aus dieser ferner in eine Art von Stumpfheit übergegangen war, ist sie zuletzt auf dem Wege der Stumpfheit endlich in jene närrische Dummheit verfallen.

Dieses ist im ganzen für Sie schon ein zu gelehrter Genuß. Wollen Sie aber, was Sie leider nicht mehr lassen können, in einem neuen Sinn tun, so will ich nicht mehr über den Bedienten schelten, wenn er die Haufen aus der Leihbibliothek bringt. Ja ich erbiete mich selbst für dieses Bedürfnis Ihr Geschäftsträger zu sein, und verspreche Ihnen eine Unzahl der schönsten Komödien aus allen Fächern der Literatur zu senden.

Ich nehme den Faden wieder auf: denn ich bin gesonnen Ihnen nichts zu schenken, sondern Ihren Behauptungen Schritt vor Schritt zu folgen.

Sie tadelten Jean Paul auch, mit einer fast wegwerfenden Art, daß er sentimental sei.

Wollten die Götter, er wäre es in dem Sinne wie ich das Wort nehme, und es seinem Ursprunge und seiner Natur nach glaube nehmen zu müssen. Denn nach meiner Ansicht und nach meinem Sprachgebrauch ist eben das romantisch, was uns einen sentimentalen Stoff in einer fantastischen Form darstellt.

Vergessen Sie auf einen Augenblick die gewöhnliche übel berüchtigte Bedeutung des Sentimentalen, wo man fast alles unter dieser Benennung versteht, was auf eine platte Weise rührend und tränenreich ist, und voll von jenen familiären Edelmutsgefühlen, in deren Bewußtsein Menschen ohne Charakter sich so unaussprechlich glücklich und groß fühlen.

put himself in the wrong. And this excellence raises his sentimentality in appearance over the sphere of English sensibility.

There is another external reason why we should cultivate in ourselves this sense for the grotesque and remain in this mood. It is impossible in this age of books not to have to leaf through very many bad books, indeed, read them. Some of them always – one can depend on it – are fortunately of a silly kind, and thus it is really up to us to find them entertaining by looking at them as witty products of nature. Laputa is everywhere or nowhere, my dear friend; only by an act of our freedom and imagination and we are in the midst of it. When stupidity reaches a certain height, which we often see now when everything is more severely differentiated, stupidity equals foolishness even in the external appearance. And foolishness, you will admit, is the loveliest thing that man can imagine, and the actual and ultimate principle of all amusement. In such a mood I can often break out in almost incessant laughter over books which seem in no way meant to provoke it. And it is only fair that nature gave me this substitute, since I cannot laugh at all at many a thing nowadays called anecdote and satire. For me, on the other hand, learned journals, for example, become a farce, and the one called Die Allgemeine Zeitung I subscribe to very obstinately, as the Viennese keep their Jack Pudding. Seen from my point of view, it is not only the most versatile of them all but in every way the most incomparable: having sunk from nullity to a certain triviality and from there to a kind of stupidity, now by way of stupidity it has finally fallen into that foolish silliness.

This in general is too learned a pleasure for you. If, however, you were to carry on what unfortunately you cannot stop doing, then I will no longer scorn your servant when he brings you the stacks of books from the loan library. Indeed, I offer myself as your porter for this purpose and promise to send you any number of the most beautiful comedies from all areas of literature.

I now take up the thread again: for I am determined to spare you nothing but to follow up your statements step by step.

You also criticized Jean Paul, in an almost cavalier manner, for being sentimental.

May the gods grant it was in the sense in which I understand the word and as I feel I must understand it according to its origin and nature. For according to my point of view and my usage, that is romantic which presents a sentimental theme in a fantastic form.

Forget for a moment the usual notorious meaning of the sentimental, by which one understands almost everything which, in a shallow way, is maudlin and lachrymose and full of those familiar noble feelings whose awareness makes people without character feel so unspeakably happy and great.

Think rather of Petrarch or Tasso, whose poetry in comparison to the more fantastic Romanzo of Ariosto can well be called sentimental; I cannot recall offhand an example where the contrast is so clear and the superiority so decisive as here.

Tasso is more musical, and the picturesque in Ariosto is certainly not the worst. Painting is no longer as fantastic, if I can trust my feeling, as it was prior to its best period: in numerous masters of the Venetian school, also in Correggio, and perhaps not only in the arabesque of Raphael. Modern music, on the other hand, as far as the ruling power of man in it is concerned, has remained true on the whole to its character, so that I would dare to call it without reservation a sentimental art.

What then is this sentimental? It is that which appeals to us, where feeling prevails, and to be sure not a sensual but a spiritual feeling. The source and soul of all these emotions is love, and the spirit of love must hover everywhere invisibly visible in romantic poetry. This is what is meant by this definition. As Diderot so comically explains in The Fatalist, the gallant passions

Denken Sie dabei lieber an Petrarca oder an Tasso, dessen Gedicht gegen das mehr fantastische Romanzo des Ariost, wohl das sentimentale heißen könnte; und ich erinnre mich nicht gleich eines Beispiels, wo der Gegensatz so klar und das Übergewicht so entschieden wäre wie hier.

Tasso ist mehr musikalisch und das Pittoreske im Ariost ist gewiß nicht das schlechteste. Die Malerei ist nicht mehr so fantastisch, wie sie es bei vielen Meistern der venezianischen Schule, wenn ich meinem Gefühl trauen darf, auch im Correggio und vielleicht nicht bloß in den Arabesken des Raffael, ehedem in ihrer großen Zeit war. Die moderne Musik hingegen ist, was die in ihr herrschende Kraft des Menschen betrifft, ihrem Charakter im ganzen so treu geblieben, daß ichs ohne Scheu wagen möchte, sie eine sentimentale Kunst zu nennen.

Was ist denn nun dieses Sentimentale? Das was uns anspricht, wo des Gefühl herrscht, und zwar nicht ein sinnliches, sondern das geistige. Die Quelle und Seele aller dieser Regungen ist die Liebe, und der Geist der Liebe muß in der romantischen Poesie überall unsichtbar sichtbar schweben; das soll jene Definiton sagen. Die galanten Passionen, denen man in den Dichtungen der Modernen, wie Diderot im FATALISTEN so lustig klagt, von dem Epigramm bis zur Tragödie nirgends entgehn kann, sind dabei grade das wenigste, oder vielmehr sie sind nicht einmal der äußre Buchstabe jenes Geistes, nach Gelegenheit auch wohl gar nichts oder etwas sehr Unliebliches und Liebloses. Nein, es ist der heilige Hauch, der uns in den Tönen der Musik berührt. Er läßt sich nicht gewaltsam fassen und mechanisch greifen, aber er läßt sich freundlich locken von sterblicher Schönheit und in sie verhüllen, und auch die Zauberworte der Poesie können von seiner Kraft durchdrungen und beseelt werden. Aber in dem Gedicht, wo er nicht überall ist, oder überall sein könnte, ist er gewiß gar nicht. Er ist ein unendliches Wesen und mitnichten haftet und klebt sein Interesse nur an den Personen, den Begebenheiten und Situationen und den individuellen Neigungen: für den wahren Dichter ist alles dieses, so innig es auch seine Seele umschließen mag, nur Hindeutung auf das Höhere, Unendliche, Hieroglyphe der Einen ewigen Liebe und der heiligen Lebensfülle der bildenden Natur.

Nur die Fantasie kann das Rätsel dieser Liebe fassen und als Rätsel darstellen; und dieses Rätselhafte ist die Quelle von dem Fantastischen in der Form aller poetischen Darstellung. Die Fantasie strebt aus allen Kräften sich zu äußern, aber das Göttliche kann sich in der Sphäre der Natur nur indirect mitteilen und äußern. Daher bleibt von dem, was ursprünglich Fantasie war, in der Welt der Erscheinungen nur das zurück was wir Witz nennen.

Noch eines liegt in der Bedeutung des Sentimentalen, was grade das Eigentümliche der Tendenz der romantischen Poesie im Gegensatz der antiken betrifft. Es is darin gar keine Rücksicht genommen auf den Unterschied von Schein und Wahrheit, von Spiel und Ernst. Darin liegt der große Unterschied. Die alte Poesie schließt sich durchgängig an die Mythologie an, und vermeidet sogar den eigentlich historischen Stoff. Die alte Tragödie sogar ist ein Spiel, und der Dichter, der eine wahre Begebenheit, die das ganze Volk ernstlich anging, darstelle, ward bestraft. Die romantische Poesie hingegen ruht ganz auf historischem Grunde, weit mehr als man es weiß und glaubt. Das erste beste Schauspiel, das Sie sehn, irgend eine Erzählung die Sie lesen; wenn eine geistreiche Intrige darin ist, können Sie fast mit Gewißheit darauf rechnen, daß wahre Geschichte zum Grunde liegt, wenngleich vielfach umgebildet. Boccaz ist fast durchaus wahre Geschichte, ebenso andre Quellen, aus denen alle romantische Erfindung hergeleitet ist.

Ich habe ein bestimmtes Merkmal des Gegensatzes zwischen dem Antiken und dem Romantischen aufgestellt. Indessen bitte ich Sie doch, nun nicht sogleich anzunehmen, daß mir das Romantische und das Moderne völlig gleich gelte. Ich denke es ist etwa ebenso verschieden, wie die Gemälde des Raffael und Correggio von den Kupferstichen die jetzt Mode sind. Wollen Sie sich den Unterschied völlig klar machen, so lessen Sie gefälligst etwa die EMILIA GALOTTI die

which one cannot escape in the works of the moderns from the epigram to tragedy are the least essential, or more, they are not even the external letter of that spirit; on occasion they are simply nothing or something very unlovely and loveless. No, it is the sacred breath which, in the tones of music, moves us. It cannot be grasped forcibly and comprehended mechanically, but it can be amiably lured by mortal beauty and veiled in it. The magic words of poetry can be infused with and inspired by its power. But in the poem in which it is not everywhere present nor could be everywhere, it certainly does not exist at all. It is an infinite being and by no means does it cling and attach its interest only to persons, events, situations, and individual inclinations; for the true poet all this – no matter how intensely it embraces his soul – is only a hint at something higher, the infinite, a hieroglyph of the one eternal love and the sacred fullness of life of creative nature.

Only the imagination can grasp the mystery of this love and present it as a mystery; and this mysterious quality is the source of the fantastic in the form of all poetic representation. The imagination strives with all its might to express itself, but the divine can communicate and express itself only indirectly in the sphere of nature. Therefore, of that which originally was imagination there remains in the world of appearances only what we call wit.

One more thing resides in the meaning of the sentimental which concerns precisely the peculiar tendency of romantic poetry in contrast with ancient. No consideration is taken in it of the difference between appearance and truth, play and seriousness. Therein resides the great difference. Ancient poetry adheres throughout to mythology and avoids the specifically historical themes. Even ancient tragedy is play, and the poet who presented a true event of serious concern for the entire nation was punished. Romantic poetry, on the other hand, is based entirely on a historical foundation, far more than we know and believe. Any play you might see, any story you read – if it has a witty plot – you can be almost sure has a true story at its source, even if variously reshaped. Boccaccio is almost entirely true history, just as all the other sources are from which all Romantic ideas originate.

I have set up a definite characteristic of the contrast between the antique and the Romantic. Meanwhile, please do not immediately assume that the Romantic and the Modern are entirely identical for me. I consider them approximately as different as the paintings of Raphael and Correggio are from the etchings which are fashionable now. If you wish to realize the difference clearly, read just Emilia Galotti, which is so extremely modern and yet not in the least Romantic, and then think of Shakespeare, in whom I would like to fix the actual center, the core of the Romantic imagination. This is where I look for and find the Romantic – in the older moderns, in Shakespeare, Cervantes, in Italian poetry, in that age of knights, love, and fairytales in which the thing itself and the word for it originated. This, up to now, is the only thing which can be considered as a worthy contrast to the classical productions of antiquity; only these eternally fresh flowers of the imagination are worthy of adorning the images of the ancient gods. Certainly all that is best in modern poetry tends toward antiquity in spirit and even in kind, as if there were to be a return to it. Just as our literature began with the novel, so the Greek began with the epic and dissolved in it.

The difference is, however, that the Romantic is not so much a literary genre as an element of poetry which may be more or less dominant or recessive, but never entirely absent. It must be clear to you why, according to my views, I postulate that all poetry should be Romantic and why I detest the novel as far as it wants to be a separate genre.

Yesterday when the argument became most heated, you demanded a definition of the novel; you said it as if you already knew that you would not receive a satisfactory answer. I do not

so unaussprechlich modern und doch im geringsten nicht romantisch ist, und erinnern sich dann an Shakespeare, in den ich das eigentliche Zentrum, den Kern der romantischen Fantasie setzen möchte. Da suche und finde ich das Romantische, bei den ältern Modernen, bei Shakespeare, Cervantes, in der italiänischen Poesie, in jenem Zeitalter der Ritter, der Liebe und der Märchen, aus welchem die Sache und das Wort selbst herstammt. Dieses ist bis jetzt das einzige, was einen Gegensatz zu den klassischen Dichtungen des Altertums abgeben kann; nur diese ewig frischen Blüten der Fantasie sind würdig die alten Götterbilder zu umkränzen. Und gewiß ist es, daß alles Vorzüglichste der modernen Poesie dem Geist und selbst der Art nach dahinneigt; es müßte denn eine Rückkehr zum Antiken sein sollen. Wie unsre Dichtkunst mit dem Roman, so fing die der Griechen mit dem Epos an und löste sich wieder darin auf.

Nur mit dem Unterschiede, daß das Romantische nicht sowohl eine Gattung ist als ein Element der Poesie, das mehr oder minder herrschen und zurücktreten, aber nie ganz fehlen darf. Es muß Ihnen nach meiner Ansicht einleuchtend sein, daß und warum ich fordre, alle Poesie solle romantisch sein; den Roman aber, insofern er eine besondre Gattung sein will, verabscheue.

Sie verlangten gestern, da der Streit eben am lebhaftesten wurde, eine Definition, was ein Roman sei; mit einer Art, als wüßten Sie schon, Sie würden keine befriedigende Antwort bekommen. Ich halte dieses Problem eben nicht für unauflöslich. Ein Roman ist ein romantisches Buch. – Sie werden das für eine nichtssagende Tautologie ausgeben. Aber ich will Sie zuerst nur darauf aufmerksam machen, daß man sich bei einem Buche schon ein Werk, ein für sich bestehendes Ganze denkt. Alsdann liegt ein sehr wichtiger Gegensatz gegen das Schauspiel darin, welches bestimmt ist angeschaut zu werden: der Roman hingegen war es von den ältesten Zeiten für die Lektüre, und daraus lassen sich fast alle Verschiedenheiten in der Manier der Darstellung beider Formen herleiten. Das Schauspiel soll auch romantisch sein, wie alle Dichtkunst; aber ein Roman ists nur unter gewissen Einschränkungen, ein angewandter Roman. Der dramatische Zusammenhang der Geschichte macht den Roman im Gegenteil noch keineswes zum Ganzen, zum Werk, wenn er es nicht durch die Beziehung der ganzen Komposition auf eine höhere Einheit, als jene Einheit des Buchstabens, über die er sich oft wegsetzt und wegsetzen darf, durch das Band der Ideen, durch einen geistigen Zentralpunkt wird.

Dies abgerechnet, findet sonst so wenig ein Gegensatz zwischen dem Drama und dem Roman statt, daß vielmehr das Drama so gründlich und historisch wie es Shakespeare z. B. nimmt und behandelt, die wahre Grundlage des Romans ist. Sie behaupteten zwar, der Roman habe am meisten Verwandtschaft mit der erzählenden ja mit der epischen Gattung. Dagegen erinnre ich nun erstlich, daß ein Lied ebenso gut romantisch sein kann als eine Geschichte. Ja ich kann mir einen Roman kaum anders denken, als gemischt aus Erzählung, Gesang und andern Formen. Anders hat Cervantes nie gedichtet, und selbst der sonst so prosaische Boccaccio schmückt seine Sammlung mit einer Einfassung von Liedern. Gibt as einen Roman, in dem dies nicht stattfindet und nicht stattfinden kann, so liegt es nur in der Individualität des Werks, nicht im Charakter der Gattung; sondern es ist schon eine Ausnahme von diesem. Doch das ist nur vorläufig. Mein eigentlicher Einwurf ist folgender. Es ist dem epischen Stil nichts entgegengesetzter als wenn die Einflüsse der eignen Stimmung im geringsten sichtbar werden; geschweige denn, daß er sich seinem Humor so überlassen, so mit ihm spielen dürfte, wie es in den vortrefflichsten Romanen geschieht.

Nachher vergaßen Sie Ihren Satz wieder oder gaben ihn auf und wollten behaupten: alle diese Einteilungen führten zu nichts; es gebe nur Eine Poesie, und es komme nur darauf an, ob etwas schön sei; nach der Rubrik könne nur ein Pedant fragen. — Sie wissen, was ich von den Klassi-

consider this problem insolvable. A novel is a romantic book. You will pass that off as a mean-ingless tautology. But I want to draw your attention to the fact that when one thinks of a book, one thinks of a work, an existing whole. There is then a very important contrast to drama, which is meant to be viewed; the novel, on the other hand, was from the oldest times for reading, and from this fact we can deduce almost all the differences in the manner of presentation of both forms. The drama should also be romantic, like all literature; but a novel is that only under cer-tain limitations, an applied novel. On the contrary, the dramatic context of the story does not make the novel a whole, a work, if the whole composition is not related to a higher unity than that of the letter which it often does and should disregard; but it becomes a work through the bond of ideas, through a spiritual central point.

Having made this allowance, there is otherwise so little contrast between the drama and the novel that it is rather the drama, treated thoroughly and historically, as for instance by Shake-speare, which is the true foundation of the novel. You claimed, to be sure, that the novel is most closely related to the narrative, the epic genre. On the other hand, I want to admonish you that a song can as well be romantic as a story. Indeed, I can scarcely visualize a novel but as a mixture of storytelling, song, and other forms. Cervantes always composed in this manner and even the otherwise so prosaic Boccaccio adorns his collections of stories by framing them with songs. If there is a novel in which this does not or cannot occur, it is only due to the individuality of the work and not the character of the genre; on the contrary, it is already an exception. But this is only by the way. My actual objection is as follows. Nothing is more contrary to the epic style than when the influence of the subjective mood becomes in the least visible; not to speak of one's ability to give himself up to his humor and play with it, as it often happens in the most excellent novels.

Afterwards you forgot your thesis or gave it up, and decided to claim that all those divisions lead to nothing; that there is one poetry, and what counts is whether something is beautiful, and only a pedant would bother with titles and headings. You know what I think of the classifica-tions in current use. And yet I realize that it is quite necessary for each virtuoso to limit himself to a well-defined goal. In my historical research I came upon several fundamental forms which are not further reducible. Thus, in the sphere of Romantic poetry, for instance, novellas and fairy tales seem to me, if I may say so, infinitely contrasted, I only wish that an artist would reju-venate each of these genres by restoring them to their original character.

If such examples became known, then I would have the courage for a theory of the novel which would be a theory in the original sense of the word; a spiritual viewing of the subject with calm and serene feeling, as it is proper to view in solemn joy the meaningful play of divine images. Such a theory of, the novel would have to be itself a novel which would reflect imagi-natively every eternal tone of the imagination and would again confound the chaos of the world of the knights. The things of the past would live in it in new forms; Dante's sacred shadow would arise from the lower world, Laura would hover heavenly before us, Shakespeare would converse intimately with Cervantes, and there Sancho would jest with Don Quixote again.

These would be true arabesques which, together with confessions, as I claimed at the outset of my letter, are the only romantic products of nature in our age.

It will no longer appear strange to you that I include confessions here, when you have admit-ted that true story is the foundation of all romantic poetry; and you will – if you wish to reflect on it – easily remember and be convinced that what is best in the best of novels is nothing but a more or less veiled confession of the author, the profit of his experience, the quintessence of his originality.

fikationen, die so im Umlauf sind, halte. Aber doch sehe ich ein, daß es für jeden Virtuosen durchaus notwendig ist, sich selbst auf einen durchaus bestimmten Zweck zu beschränken; und in der historischen Nachforschung komme ich auf mehre ursprüngliche Formen, die sich nicht mehr ineinander auflösen lassen. So scheinen mir im Umkreise der romantischen Poesie selbst Novellen und Märchen z. B., wenn ich so sagen darf, unendlich entgegengesetzt. Und ich wünsche nichts mehr, als daß ein Künstler jede dieser Arten verjüngen möge, indem er sie auf ihren ursprünglichen Charakter zurückführt.

Wenn solche Beispiele ans Licht träten, dann würde ich Mut bekommen zu einer *Theorie des Romans*, die im ursprünglichen Sinne des Wortes eine Theorie wäre: eine geistige Anschauung des Gegenstandes mit ruhigem, heitern ganzen Gemüt, wie es sich ziemt, das bedeutende Spiel göttlicher Bilder in festlicher Freude zu schauen. Eine solche Theorie des Romans würde selbst ein Roman sein müssen, der jeden ewigen Ton der Fantasie fantastisch wiedergäbe, und das Chaos der Ritterwelt noch einmal verwirrte. Da würden die alten Wesen in neuen Gestalten leben; da würde der heilige Schatten des Dante sich aus seiner Unterwelt erheben, Laura himmlisch vor uns wandeln, und Shakespeare mit Cervantes trauliche Gespräche wechseln; — und da würde Sancho von neuem mit dem Don Quixote scherzen.

Das wären wahre Arabesken und diese nebst Bekenntnissen, seien, behauptete ich im Eingang meines Briefs, die einzigen romantischen Naturprodukte unsers Zeitalters.

Daß ich auch die Bekenntnisse dazu rechnete, wird Ihnen nicht mehr befremdend sein, wenn Sie zugegeben haben, daß wahre Geschichte das Fundament aller romantischen Dichtung sei; und Sie werden sich, wenn Sie darüber reflektieren wollen, leicht erinnern und überzeugen, daß das Beste in den besten Romanen nichts anders ist als ein mehr oder minder verhülltes Selbstbekenntnis des Verfassers, der Ertrag seiner Erfahrung, die Quintessenz seiner Eigentümlichkeit.

Alle sogenannten Romane, auf die meine Idee von romantischer Form freilich gar nicht anwendbar ist, schätze ich dennoch ganz genau nach der Masse von eigner Anschauung und dargestelltem Leben, die sie enthalten; und in dieser Hinsicht mögen denn selbst die Nachfolger des Richardson, so sehr sie auf der falschen Bahn wandeln, willkommen sein. Wir lernen aus einer CECILIA BEVERLEY wenigstens, wie man zu der Zeit, da das eben Mode war, sich in London ennuyierte, auch wie eine britische Dame vor Delikatesse endlich zu Boden stürzt und sich blutrünstig fällt; das Fluchen, die Squires und dergleichen sind im Fielding wie aus dem Leben gestohlen, und der WAKEFIELD gibt uns einen tiefen Blick in die Weltansicht eines Landpredigers; ja dieser Roman wäre vielleicht, wenn Olivia ihre verlorne Unschuld am Ende wieder fände, der beste unter allen engländischen Romanen.

Aber wie sparsam und tropfenweise wird einem in allen diesen Büchern das wenige Reelle zugezählt! Und welche Reisebeschreibung, welche Briefsammlung, welche Selbstgeschichte wäre nicht für den, der sie in einem romantischen Sinne liest, ein besserer Roman als der beste von jenen? —

Besonders die Confessions geraten meistens auf dem Wege des Naiven von selbst in die Arabeske, wozu sich jene Romane höchstens am Schluß erheben, wenn die bankerotten Kaufleute wieder Geld und Kredit, alle armen Schlucker zu essen bekommen, die liebenswürdigen Spitzbuben ehrlich und die gefallnen Mädchen wieder tugendhaft werden.

Die CONFESSIONS von Rousseau sind in meinen Augen ein höchst vortrefflicher Roman; die HELOISE nur ein sehr mittelmäßiger.

Ich schicke Ihnen hier die Selbstgeschichte eines berühmten Mannes, die Sie, so viel ich weiß, noch nicht kennen: die Memoirs von Gibbon. Es ist ein unendlich gebildetes und ein unendlich drolliges Buch. Es wird Ihnen auf halbem Wege entgegenkommen, und wirklich ist der komische

Yet I appreciate all the so-called novels to which my idea of romantic form is altogether inapplicable, according to the amount of self-reflection and represented life they contain. And in this respect even the followers of Richardson, however much they are on the wrong track, are welcome. From a novel like Cecilia Beverley, we at least learn how they lived there in London in boredom, since it was the fashion, and also how a British lady for all her daintiness finally tumbles to the ground and knocks herself bloody. The cursing, the squires, and the like in Fielding are as if stolen from life, and Wakefield grants us a deep insight into the world view of a country preacher; yes, this novel would perhaps – if Olivia regained her lost innocence at the end – be the best among all the English novels.

But how sparingly and only drop by drop even the small amount of the real in all those books is handed out. Which travelogue, which collection of letters, which autobiography would not be a better novel for one who reads them in the romantic sense than the best of these Confessions, especially, mainly by way of the naive, develop of themselves into arabesques. But at best those novels rise to the arabesque only at the end, when the bankrupt merchants regain their money and credit, all the poor devils get to eat, the likeable scoundrels become honest, and the fallen women become virtuous again.

The Confessions of Rousseau is in my opinion a most excellent novel, Héloise only a very mediocre one.

I will send you the autobiography of a famous man which, as far as I know, you are not acquainted with: Gibbon's Memoirs. It is an infinitely civilized and infinitely funny book. It will meet you half way, and really the comic novel contained in it is almost complete. You will see before your eyes, as clearly as you could wish, the Englishman, the gentleman, the virtuoso, the scholar, the bachelor, the well-bred dandy in all his affected absurdity, through the dignity of the historic periods. One can go through many bad books and many insignificant men before finding so much to laugh about gathered in one place.

[. . .]

After Antonio had read this epistle, Camilla began to praise the goodness and forebearance of women: that Amalia did not object to receiving such an amount of instruction and, that in general, women were a model of modesty since they remained patient in the face of men's seriousness and, what is more, remained serious and even expressed a certain belief in the art of men. If by modesty you mean this belief, added Lothario, this premise of an excellence which we do not yet possess, but whose existence and dignity we begin to realize; then it would be the firmest basis of a noble education for excellent women. Camilla asked if pride and self-complacency had this function for men, since every one of them considered himself the more unique the more incapable he was of understanding what the other wanted. Antonio interrupted her by remarking that he hoped for the sake of mankind that that belief was not as necessary as Lothario thought, for it was a rare quality. Women, he said, as far as he could observe, think of art, antiquity, philosophy, and such as of unfathomed traditions, prejudices with which men impress each other in order to pass the time.

Marcus announced some observations about Goethe. 'What, again a characterization of a living poet' asked Antonio. 'You will find the answer to your objection in the essay itself,' replied Marcus, and he began to read:

[1798] [*Translated by Ernst Behler and Roman Struc: Pennyslvania State UP, 1968*]

Roman, der darin liegt, fast ganz fertig. Sie werden den Englander, den Gentleman, den Virtuosen, den Gelehrten, den Hagestolzen, den Elegant vom guten Ton in seiner ganzen zierlichen Lächerlichkeit durch die Würde dieser historischen Perioden so klar vor Augen sehn, wie Sie nur immer wünschen können. Gewiß man kann viel schlechte Bücher und viele unbedeutende Menschen durchsehn, ehe man so viel Lachstoff auf einem Haufen beisammen findet.

Nachdem Antonio diese Epistel vorgelesen hatte, fing Camilla an die Güte und Nachsicht der Frauen zu rühmen: daß Amalia ein solches Maß von Belehrung anzunehmen nicht für zu gering geachtet; und überhaupt wären sie ein Muster von Bescheidenheit, indem sie bei dem Ernst der Männer immer geduldig, und, was noch mehr sagen wolle, ernsthaft blieben, ja sogar einen gewissen Glauben an ihr Kunstwesen hätten. — Wenn Sie unter der Bescheidenheit diesen Glauben verstehn, setzte Lothario hinzu, diese Voraussetzung einer Vortrefflichkeit, die wir noch nicht selbst besitzen, deren Dasein und Würde wir aber zu vermuten anfangen: so dürfte sie wohl die sicherste Grundlage aller edlen Bildung für vorzügliche Frauen sein. — Camilla fragte, ob es für die Männer etwa der Stolz und die Selbstzufriedenheit sei; indem sich jeder meistens um so mehr für einzig hielte, je unfähiger er sei zu verstehen, was der andre wolle. — Antonio unterbrach sie mit der Bemerkung, er hoffe zum Besten der Menschheit, jener Glaube sei nicht so notwendig als Lothario meine; denn er sei wohl sehr selten. Meistens halten die Frauen, sagte er, so viel ich habe bemerken können, die Kunst, das Altertum, die Philosophie und dergleichen für ungegründete Traditionen, für Vorurteile, die sich die Manner untereinander weismachen, um sich die Zeit zu vertreiben.

[1798] [*Edited by Ernst Behler. Paderborn, Munich, Vienna, Zürich: Schöningh, 1958. 329–339*]

I.e.7.   KLEIST, 'Über die allmähliche Verfertigung der Gedanken beim Reden'

Wenn du etwas wissen willst und es durch Meditation nicht finden kannst, so rate ich dir, mein lieber, sinnreicher Freund, mit dem nächsten Bekannten, der dir aufstößt, darüber zu sprechen. Es braucht nicht eben ein scharfdenkender Kopf zu sein, auch meine ich es nicht so, als ob du ihn darum befragen solltest: nein! Vielmehr sollst du es ihm selber allererst erzählen. Ich sehe dich zwar große Augen machen, und mir antworten, man habe dir in frühern Jahren den Rat gegeben, von nichts zu sprechen, als nur von Dingen, die du bereits verstehst. Damals aber sprachst du wahrscheinlich mit dem Vorwitz, *andere*, ich will, daß du aus der verständigen Absicht sprechest, *dich* zu belehren, und so könnten, für verschiedene Fälle verschieden, beide Klugheitsregeln vielleicht gut neben einander bestehen. Der Franzose sagt, l'appétit vient en mangeant, und dieser Erfahrungssatz bleibt wahr, wenn man ihn parodiert, und sagt, l'idée vient en parlant. Oft sitze ich an meinem Geschäftstisch über den Akten, und erforsche, in einer verwickelten Streitsache, den Gesichtspunkt, aus welchem sie wohl zu beurteilen sein möchte. Ich pflege dem gewöhnlich ins Licht zu sehen, als in den hellsten Punkt, bei dem Bestreben, in welchem mein innerstes Wesen begriffen ist, sich aufzuklären. Oder ich suche, wenn mir eine algebraische Aufgabe vorkommt, den ersten Ansatz, die Gleichung, die die gegebenen Verhältnisse ausdrückt, und aus welcher sich die Auflösung nachher durch Rechnung leicht ergibt. Und siehe da, wenn ich mit meiner Schwester davon rede, welche hinter mir sitzt, und arbeitet, so erfahre ich, was ich durch ein vielleicht stundenlanges Brüten nicht herausgebracht haben würde. Nicht, als ob sie es mir, im eigentlichen Sinne *sagte;* denn sie kennt weder das Gesetzbuch, noch hat sie den Euler, oder den Kästner studiert. Auch nicht, als ob sie mich durch geschickte Fragen auf den Punkt hinführte, auf welchen es ankommt, wenn schon dies letzte häufig der Fall sein mag. Aber weil

I.e.7.   KLEIST, 'On the Gradual Production of Thoughts Whilst Speaking'

If there is something you wish to know and by meditation you cannot find it, my advice to you, my ingenious old friend, is: speak about it with the first acquaintance you encounter. He does not need to be especially perspicacious, nor do I mean that you should ask his opinion, not at all. On the contrary, you should yourself tell him at once what it is you wish to know. I see astonishment in your face. I hear you reply that when you were young you were advised only to speak of things you already understood. But in those days, doubtless, you spoke in the presumption of instructing others but my wish is that you speak in the sensible intention of instructing yourself, and so, different rules applying in different circumstances, both may perhaps be allowed to stand. The French say 'l'appétit vient en mangeant' and this maxim is just as true if we parody it and say 'l'idée' vient en parlant'. Often I have sat at my desk over the papers of a difficult case and sought the point of view from which it might be grasped. My habit then, in this striving of my innermost being after enlightenment, is to gaze into the lamplight, as into the brightest point. Or a problem in algebra occurs to me and I need a starting point, I need the equation which expresses the given relationships and from which by simple calculation the solution may be found. And lo and behold! If I speak about it to my sister sitting behind me at her work, I learn more than I should have arrived at by perhaps hours of brooding. Not that she in any real sense *tells* me, for she is not familiar with the penal code nor has she studied Euler or Kästner. Nor is it that by skilful questioning she brings me to the crux of the matter, though that might often be the way to do it, I daresay. But because I do have some dim conception at the outset, one distantly related to what I am looking for, if I boldly make a start with that, my mind, even as my speech proceeds, under the necessity of finding an end for that beginning, will shape my first

ich doch irgend eine dunkle Vorstellung habe, die mit dem, was ich suche, von fern her in einiger Verbindung steht, so prägt, wenn ich nur dreist damit den Anfang mache, das Gemüt, während die Rede fortschreitet, in der Notwendigkeit, dem Anfang nun auch ein Ende zu finden, jene verworrene Vorstellung zur völligen Deutlichkeit aus, dergestalt, daß die Erkenntnis, zu meinem Erstaunen, mit der Periode fertig ist. Ich mische unartikulierte Töne ein, ziehe die Verbindungs- wörter in die Länge, gebrauche auch wohl eine Apposition, wo sie nicht nötig wäre, und bediene mich anderer, die Rede ausdehnender, Kunstgriffe, zur Fabrikation meiner Idee auf der Werkstätte der Vernunft, die gehörige Zeit zu gewinnen. Dabei ist mir nichts heilsamer, als eine Bewegung meiner Schwester, als ob sie mich unterbrechen wollte; denn mein ohnehin schon angestrengtes Gemüt wird durch diesen Versuch von außen, ihm die Rede, in deren Besitz es sich befindet, zu entreißen, nur noch mehr erregt, und in seiner Fähigkeit, wie ein großer General, wenn die Umstände drängen, noch um einen Grad höher gespannt. In diesem Sinne begreife ich, von welchem Nutzen Molière seine Magd sein konnte; denn wenn er derselben, wie er vorgibt, ein Urteil zutraute, das das seinige berichten konnte, so ist dies eine Bescheidenheit, an deren Dasein in seiner Brust ich nicht glaube. Es liegt ein sonderbarer Quell der Begeisterung für denjenigen, der spricht, in einem menschlichen Antlitz, das ihm gegenübersteht; und ein Blick, der uns einen halbausgedrückten Gedanken schon als begriffen ankündigt, schenkt uns oft den Ausdruck für die ganze andere Hälfte desselben. Ich glaube, daß mancher große Redner, in dem Augenblick, da er den Mund aufmachte, noch nicht wußte, was er sagen würde. Aber die Überzeugung, daß er die ihm nötige Gedankenfülle schon aus den Umständen, und der daraus resultierenden Erregung seines Gemüts schöpfen würde, machte ihn dreist genug, den Anfang, auf gutes Glück hin, zu setzen. Mir fällt jener »Donnerkeil« des Mirabeau ein, mit welchem er den Zeremonienmeister abfertigte, der nach Aufhebung der letzten monarchischen Sitzung des Königs am 23. Juni, in welcher dieser den Ständen auseinander zu gehen anbefohlen hatte, in den Sitzungssaal, in welchem die Stände noch verweilten, zurückkehrte, und sie befragte, ob sie den Befehl des Königs vernommen hatten? »Ja«, antwortete Mirabeau, »wir haben des Königs Befehl vernommen« - ich bin gewiß, daß er bei diesem humanen Anfang, noch nicht an die Bajonette dachte; mit welchen er schloß: »ja, mein Herr«, wiederholte er, »wir haben ihn vernommen « - man sieht, daß er noch gar nicht recht weiß, was er will. »Doch was berechtigt Sie«- fuhr er fort, und nun plötzlich geht ihm ein Quell ungeheurer Vorstellungen auf - »uns hier Befehle anzudeuten? Wir sind die Repräsentanten der Nation. « - Das war es was er brauchte! » Die Nation gibt Befehle und empfängt keine. « - um sich gleich auf den Gipfel der Vermessenheit zu schwingen. »Und damit ich mich Ihnen ganz deutlich erkläre « - und erst jetzo findet er, was den ganzen Widerstand, zu welchem seine Seele gerüstet dasteht, ausdrückt: »so sagen Sie Ihrem Konige, daß wir unsre Plätze anders nicht, als auf die Gewalt der Bajonette verlassen werden. « - Worauf er sich, selbstzufrieden, auf einen Stuhl niedersetzte. - Wenn man an den Zeremonien- meister denkt, so kann man sich ihn bei diesem Auftritt nicht anders, als in einem völligen Geistesbankerott vorstellen; nach einem ähnlichen Gesetz, nach welchem in einem Körper, der von dem elektrischen Zustand Null ist, wenn er in eines elektrisierten Körpers Atmosphäre kommt, plötzlich die entgegengesetzte Elektrizität erweckt wird. Und wie in dem elektrisierten dadurch, nach einer Wechselwirkung, der ihm inwohnende Elektrizitätsgrad wieder verstärkt wird, so ging unseres Redners Mut, bei der Vernichtung seines Gegners zur verwegensten Begeisterung über. Vielleicht, daß es auf diese Art zuletzt das Zucken einer Oberlippe war, oder ein zweideutiges Spiel an der Manschette, was in Frankreich den Umsturz der Ordnung der Dinge bewirkte. Man liest, daß Mirabeau, sobald der Zeremonienmeister sich entfernt hatte, aufstand, und vorschlug: 1) sich sogleich als Nationalversammlung, und 2) als unverletzlich, zu

confused idea into complete clarity so that, to my amazement, understanding is arrived at as the sentence ends. I put in a few unarticulated sounds, dwell lengthily on the conjunctions, perhaps make use of apposition where it is not necessary, and have recourse to other tricks which will spin out my speech, all to gain time for the fabrication of my idea in the workshop of the mind. And in this process nothing helps me more than if my sister makes a move suggesting she wishes to interrupt; for such an attempt from outside to wrest speech from its grasp still further excites my already hard-worked mind and, like a general when circumstances press, its powers are raised a further degree. This, in my view, was how Molière used his maid; for to allow her judgement to correct his, as he said he did, would show more modesty than I can believe he had. It is a strangely inspiring thing to have a human face before us as we speak; and often a look announcing that a half-expressed thought is already grasped gives us its other half's expression. I believe many a great speaker to have been ignorant when he opened his mouth of what he was going to say. But the conviction that he would be able to draw all the ideas he needed from the circumstances themselves and from the mental excitement they generated made him bold enough to trust to luck and make a start. I think of the 'thunderbolt' with which Mirabeau dismissed the Master of Ceremonies who, after the meeting of 23 June, the last under the *ancien régime,* when the King had ordered the estates to disperse, returned to the hall in which they were still assembled and asked them had they heard the King's command. 'Yes,' Mirabeau replied, 'we have heard the King's command.' – I am certain that beginning thus humanely he had not yet thought of the bayonets with which he would finish. 'Yes, my dear sir,' he repeated, 'we have heard it.' – As we see, he is not yet exactly sure what he intends. 'But by what right . . .' he continues, and suddenly a source of colossal ideas is opened up to him, 'do you give us orders here? We are the representatives of the nation.' – That was what he needed! – 'The nation does not take orders. It gives them.' – Which launches him there and then to the highest pitch of boldness. – 'And to make myself perfectly plain to you . . .' – And only now does he find words to express how fully his soul has armed itself and stands ready to resist – 'Tell your king we shall not move from here unless forced to by bayonets.' – Whereupon, well content with himself, he sat down. – As to the Master of Ceremonies, we must imagine him bankrupted by this encounter of all ideas. For a law applies rather similar to the law which says that if a body having no electricity of its own enters the zone of a body which has been electrified at once the latter's electricity will be produced in it. And just as in the electrified body, by a reciprocal effect, a strengthening of the innate electricity then occurs, so our speaker's confidence, as he annihilated his opponent, was converted into an inspired and extraordinary boldness. In this way it was perhaps the twitching of an upper lip or an equivocal tugging at the cuffs that brought about the overthrow of the order of things in France. We read that Mirabeau as soon as the Master of Ceremonies had withdrawn stood up and proposed (i) that they constitute themselves a national assembly at once, and (ii) declare themselves inviolable. For having, like a Kleistian jar, discharged himself now he was neutral again. Returning from boldness, speedily he made way for caution and fear of the Châtelet. – We have here a remarkable congruence between the phenomena of the physical world and those of the moral world which, if we were to pursue it, would hold good in the subsidiary circumstances too. But I shall leave my comparison and return to the matter in hand. La Fontaine also, in his fable 'Les animaux malades de la peste', where the fox is obliged to justify himself to the lion and does not know what material to draw on, gives us a remarkable example of the gradual completion of thought out of a beginning made under pressure. The fable is well known. Plague is raging among the animals, the lion summons the grandees of the kingdom and informs them that heaven, if it is to be propitiated, must have a sacrifice. There are many sinners among the people,

konstituieren. Denn dadurch, daß er sich, einer Kleistischen Flasche gleich, entladen hatte, war er nun wieder neutral geworden, und gab, von der Verwegenheit zurückgekehrt, plötzlich der Furcht vor dem Chatelet, und der Vorsicht, Raum. – Dies ist eine merkwürdige Übereinstimmung zwischen den Erscheinungen der physischen und moralischen Welt, welche sich, wenn man sie verfolgen wollte, auch noch in den Nebenumständen bewähren würde. Doch ich verlasse mein Gleichnis, und kehre zur Sache zurück. Auch Lafontaine gibt, in seiner Fabel: Les animaux malades de la peste, wo der Fuchs dem Löwen eine Apologie zu halten gezwungen ist, ohne zu wissen, wo er den Stoff dazu hernehmen soll, ein merkwürdiges Beispiel von einer allmählichen Verfertigung des Gedankens aus einem in der Not hingesetzten Anfang. Man kennt diese Fabel. Die Pest herrscht im Tierreich, der Löwe versammelt die Großen desselben, und eröffnet ihnen, daß dem Himmel, wenn er besänftigt werden solle, ein Opfer fallen müsse. Viele Sünder seien im Volke, der Tod des größesten müsse die übrigen vom Untergang retten. Sie möchten ihm daher ihre Vergehungen aufrichtig bekennen. Er, für sein Teil gestehe, daß er, im Drange des Hungers, manchem Schafe den Garaus gemacht; auch dem Hunde, wenn er ihm zu nahe gekommen; ja, es sei ihm in leckerhaften Augenblicken zugestoßen, daß er den Schäfer gefressen. Wenn niemand sich größerer Schwachheiten schuldig gemacht habe, so sei er bereit zu sterben. »Sire«, sagt der Fuchs, der das Ungewitter von sich ableiten will, »Sie sind zu großmütig. Ihr edler Eifer führt Sie zu weit. Was ist es, ein Schaf erwürgen? Oder einen Hund, diese nichtswürdige Bestie? Und: quant au berger«, fährt er fort, denn dies ist der Hauptpunkt: »on peut dire«, obschon er noch nicht weiß was? »qu'il méritoit tout mal«, auf gut Glück; und somit ist er verwickelt; »étant«, eine schlechte Phrase, die ihm aber Zeit verschafft: »de ces gens là«, und nun erst findet er den Gedanken, der ihn aus der Not reißt: »qui sur les animaux se font un chimérique empire.« - Und jetzt beweist er, daß der Esel, der blutdürstige! (der alle Kräuter auffrißt) das zweckmäßigste Opfer sei, worauf alle über ihn herfallen, und ihn zerreißen. - Ein solches Reden ist ein wahrhaftes lautes Denken. Die Reihen der Vorstellungen und ihrer Bezeichnungen gehen neben einander fort, und die Gemütsakten für eins und das andere, kongruieren. Die Sprache ist alsdann keine Fessel, etwa wie ein Hemmschuh an dem Rade des Geistes, sondern wie ein zweites, mit ihm parallel fortlaufendes, Rad an seiner Achse. Etwas ganz anderes ist es wenn der Geist schon, vor aller Rede, mit dem Gedanken fertig ist. Denn dann muß er bei seiner bloßen Ausdrückung zurückbleiben, und dies Geschäft, weit entfernt ihn zu erregen, hat vielmehr keine andere Wirkung, als ihn von seiner Erregung abzuspannen. Wenn daher eine Vorstellung verworren ausgedrückt wird, so folgt der Schluß noch gar nicht, daß sie auch verworren gedacht worden sei; vielmehr könnte es leicht sein, daß die verworrenst ausgedrückten grade am deutlichsten gedacht werden. Man sieht oft in einer Gesellschaft, wo durch ein lebhaftes Gespräch, eine kontinuierliche Befruchtung der Gemüter mit Ideen im Werk ist, Leute, die sich, weil sie sich der Sprache nicht mächtig fühlen, sonst in der Regel zurückgezogen halten, plötzlich mit einer zuckenden Bewegung, aufflammen, die Sprache an sich reißen und etwas Unverständliches zur Welt bringen. Ja, sie scheinen, wenn sie nun die Aufmerksamkeit aller auf sich gezogen haben, durch ein verlegnes Gebärdenspiel anzudeuten, daß sie selbst nicht mehr recht wissen, was sie haben sagen wollen. Es ist wahrscheinlich, daß diese Leute etwas recht Treffendes, und sehr deutlich, gedacht haben. Aber der plötzliche Geschäftswechsel, der Übergang ihres Geistes vom Denken zum Ausdrücken, schlug die ganze Erregung desselben, die zur Festhaltung des Gedankens notwendig, wie zum Hervorbringen erforderlich war, wieder nieder. In solchen Fällen ist es um so unerläßlicher, daß uns die Sprache mit Leichtigkeit zur Hand sei, um dasjenige, was wir gleichzeitig gedacht haben, und doch nicht gleichzeitig von uns geben können, wenigstens so schnell, als möglich, auf einander folgen zu

the death of the greatest must save the rest from destruction. Accordingly, he bids them make him a candid confession of all their crimes. He, for his part, admits that, driven by hunger, he has cut short the lives of many a sheep; dogs likewise, when they came too near; indeed, in delicious moments he has even been known to eat the shepherd. If no one is guilty of worse weaknesses than these then he, the lion, will gladly be the one to die. 'Sire,' says the fox, wishing to ward the lightning off himself, 'in your zeal and generosity you have gone too far. What if you have done a sheep or two to death? Or a dog, a vile creature? And: 'quant au berger,' he continues, for this is the chief point, 'on peut dire,' though he still does not know what, 'qu'il méritoit tout mal,' trusting to luck, and with that he has embroiled himself, 'étant,' a poor word but which buys him time, 'de ces gens là,' and only now does he hit upon the thought that gets him out of his difficulty, 'qui sur les animaux se font un chimérique empire.' – And he goes on to prove that the donkey, the bloodthirsty donkey, (devourer of grass and plants) is the most fitting sacrifice. And with that they fall on him and tear him to pieces. – Speech of that kind is truly a thinking aloud. The ideas in succession and the signs for them proceed side by side and the mental acts entailed by both converge. Speech then is not at all an impediment; it is not, as one might say, a brake on the mind but rather a second wheel running along parallel on the same axle. It is a quite different matter when the mind, before any utterance of speech, has completed its thought. For then it is left with the mere expression of that thought, and this business, far from exciting the mind, has, on the contrary, only a relaxing effect. Thus if an idea is expressed confusedly we should by no means assume that it was thought confusedly too; on the contrary, it might well be the case that the most confusedly expressed ideas are the clearest thought. In any gathering where by a lively conversation a continuous insemination of minds with ideas is under way you will often see people who, not feeling in control of language, have usually held back, all of a sudden, with a convulsive movement, take fire, seize a chance to speak and bring something incomprehensible into the world. Indeed, having drawn the whole company's attention upon themselves, they seem then by embarrassed gestures to indicate that they themselves no longer quite know what it was they wanted to say. It is probable that such a person has thought something very apt, and very clearly. But the sudden shift of activity, the mind's transition from thinking to expression, caused the lapsing of all its excitement, which it needed both to hold on to the thought and then to utter it. In such cases it is all the more necessary that we have language readily at our disposal so that the things we have thought of all at once but have not all at once been able to utter we may as quickly as possible deliver in sequence. And in general if two men have the same clarity of thought the faster speaker will always have an advantage since he brings, so to speak, more forces to the battle than his opponent. That a certain excitement of the intelligence is necessary even to revivify ideas we have already had is amply demonstrated whenever open-minded and knowledgeable people are being examined and without any preamble are asked such questions as: What is the state? Or: What is property? Things of that kind. If these young people had been in company and for a while the subject of conversation had been the state or property they would by a process of comparison, discrimination and summary perhaps with ease have arrived at the definition. But being wholly deprived of any such preparation they are seen to falter and only an obtuse examiner will conclude from this that they do not *know*. For it is not *we* who know things but pre-eminently a certain *condition* of ours which knows.

Only very commonplace intellects, people who yesterday learned by heart what the state is and today have forgotten it again, will have their answers pat in an examination. Indeed, there may be no worse opportunity in the world for showing oneself to advantage than a public examination. Besides the fact that it offends and wounds our sense of decency and incites us to

lassen. Und überhaupt wird jeder, der, bei gleicher Deutlichkeit, geschwinder als sein Gegner spricht, einen Vorteil über ihn haben, weil er gleichsam mehr Truppen als er ins Feld führt. Wie notwendig eine gewisse Erregung des Gemüts ist, auch selbst nur, um Vorstellungen, die wir schon gehabt haben, wieder zu erzeugen, sieht man oft, wenn offene, und unterrichtete Köpfe examiniert werden, und man ihnen ohne vorhergegangene Einleitung, Fragen vorlegt, wie diese: was ist der Staat? Oder: was ist das Eigentum? Oder dergleichen. Wenn diese jungen Leute sich in einer Gesellschaft befunden hätten, wo man sich vom Staat, oder vom Eigentum, schon eine Zeitlang unterhalten hätte, so würden sie vielleicht mit Leichtigkeit durch Vergleichung, Absonderung, und Zusammenfassung der Begriffe, die Definition gefunden haben. Hier aber, wo diese Vorbereitung des Gemüts gänzlich fehlt, sieht man sie stocken, und nur ein unverständiger Examinator wird daraus schließen daß sie nicht *wissen*. Denn nicht wir wissen, es ist allererst ein gewisser *Zustand* unsrer, welcher weiß. Nur ganz gemeine Geister, Leute, die, was der Staat sei, gestern auswendig gelernt, und morgen schon wieder vergessen haben, werden hier mit der Antwort bei der Hand sein. Vielleicht gibt es überhaupt keine schlechtere Gelegenheit, sich von einer vorteilhaften Seite zu zeigen, als grade ein öffentliches Examen. Abgerechnet, daß es schon widerwärtig und das Zartgefühl verletzend ist, und daß es reizt, sich stetig zu zeigen, wenn solch ein gelehrter Roßkamm uns nach den Kenntnissen sieht, um uns, je nachdem es fünf oder sechs sind, zu kaufen oder wieder abtreten zu lassen: es ist so schwer, auf ein menschliches Gemüt zu spielen und ihm seinen eigentümlichen Laut abzulocken, es verstimmt sich so leicht unter ungeschickten Händen, daß selbst der geübteste Menschenkenner, der in der Hebeammenkunst der Gedanken, wie Kant sie nennt, auf das Meisterhafteste bewandert wäre, hier noch, wegen der Unbekanntschaft mit seinem Sechswöchner, Mißgriffe tun könnte. Was übrigens solchen jungen Leuten, auch selbst den unwissendsten noch, in den meisten Fällen ein gutes Zeugnis verschafft, ist der Umstand, daß die Gemüter der Examinatoren, wenn die Prüfung öffentlich geschieht, selbst zu sehr befangen sind, um ein freies Urteil fällen zu können. Denn nicht nur fühlen sie häufig die Unanständigkeit dieses ganzen Verfahrens: man würde sich schon schämen, von jemandem, daß er seine Geldbörse vor uns ausschütte, zu fordern, viel weniger, seine Seele: sondern ihr eigener Verstand muß hier eine gefährliche Musterung passieren, und sie mögen oft ihrem Gott danken, wenn sie selbst aus dem Examen gehen können, ohne sich Blößen, schmachvoller vielleicht, als der, eben von der Universität kommende, Jüngling gegeben zu haben, den sie examinierten.

[Die Fortsetzung folgt] H.V.K.
[*Heinrich von Kleist. Sämtliche Werke und Briefe. Ed. Helmut Sembdner.*
2 vols. Munich: Hanser, 1993. II, 319–324]

I.e.8.   Johann Peter Eckermann, Gespräche mit Goethe in den letzten Jahren
seines Lebens (Zur Klassik und Romantik)

Von diesen kamen wir auf die neuesten französischen Dichter und auf die Bedeutung von *klassisch* und *romantisch*. »Mir ist ein neuer Ausdruck eingefallen«, sagte Goethe, »der das Verhältnis nicht übel bezeichnet. Das Klassische nenne ich das Gesunde und das Romantische das Kranke. Und da sind die Nibelungen klassisch wie der Homer, denn beide sind gesund und tüchtig. Das meiste Neuere ist nicht romantisch, weil es neu, sondern weil es schwach, kränklich und krank ist, und das Alte ist nicht klassisch, weil es alt, sondern weil es stark, frisch, froh und gesund ist. Wenn wir nach solchen Qualitäten Klassisches und Romantisches unterscheiden, so werden wir bald im reinen sein.

[2 April 1829] [*Gespräche mit Goethe in den letzten Jahren seines Lebens*]

recalcitrance to have some learned horsedealer looking into how many things we know who then, depending on whether they are five or six, either buys us or dismisses us: it is so difficult to play upon a human mind and induce it to give forth its peculiar music, it so easily under clumsy hands goes out of tune, that even the most practised connoisseur of human beings, a real master in what Kant calls the midwifery of thinking, even he, not being acquainted with the one whose labour he is assisting at, may make mistakes. And if such young people, even the most ignorant among them, do most often achieve good marks this is because the minds of the examiners, if the examination is in public, are themselves too embarrassed to deliver a true judgement. For not only do they themselves feel the indecency of the whole procedure: we should be ashamed to ask a person to tip out the contents of his purse before us, let alone his soul: but their own intelligences come under dangerous appraisal and they may count themselves lucky if they manage to leave the examination without having revealed more shameful weaknesses than the young finalist himself has whom they have been examining.

(To be continued.)

Heinrich von Kleist. Selected Writings, ed. David Constantine, London, 2004, pp. 405–409.

I.e.8.   Goethe in Eckermann, on Classicism and Romanticism

Thence we turned to the latest French writing and the meaning of *classic* and *romantic*. 'A new terminology has occurred to me,' said Goethe, 'which defines the relation not at all badly. The Classic I call the Healthy and the Romantic the Sick. In this sense the *Nibelungen* are as classic as Homer, since both are healthy and fit. Most of the new is not romantic because it is new but because it is weak, sickly and sick, and the old is not classic because it is old but because it is strong, fresh, glad and healthy. If we discriminate Classic and Romantic according to these qualities, we shall soon be clear.'

[2 April 1829]

f. MAGYAR

I.f.1. KÖLCSEY FERENC, *Nemzeti hagyományok (Részletek)*

Egész nemzeteknek, szintúgy mint egyes embereknek, meg vagynak az ő különböző koraik. Gyermekkorból virul fel ifjúságok, ifjúból érnek férfivá, s férfikoroknak erejét az öregségnek lankadása váltja fel.

A férfit a lélek érettségének nyugalma bélyegzi; fő pontjára jutott erejével nehéz dolgokat vehet célba s vihet véghez, de okos számvetéssel tudja magát a sorssal s a környülményekkel öszvemérni, s előre nézve midőn kezd, vigyázva lépteiben, fáradatlan a küzdés közt, felemelkedett és magos érzelmeiben bámulattal elegy tiszteletet gerjeszt maga körül; az ő neve: *nagy*.

Az ifjúság kebelében a jövendő férfinak ereje áradozó bővségben habzik, forr és vív önmagával. Az ő karakterében tűz és nyugtalanság önti ki magát: céljai nincsenek, csak reményei: principiumokat nem követ, csak sejdítéseket; gondolatai a képzeletben süllyednek el, s képzeleteinek a kívánság emelvén fáklyát, mértéket, határt és lehetetlenséget nem ismer, s kezd és csinál több lánggal mint erővel, több szenvedelemmel mint ésszel, s így szerencsében és szerencsétlenségben, akaratán és tettein bizonyos *regényes* szín ömlik el.

A nemzetek ifjúsága félig vad állapot. Kevés tapasztalással és ismerettel, sok kitörekedő, munkába folyni akaró tűzzel, felébredező, gyakran homályos és szempillantatnyi kívánságokkal: boldog nemzet, melyet ilyenkor külső és belső akadályok vagy magába záródva eltespedni, vagy haszon és következés nélkül széjjeláradozni nem kényszerítenek; melyet sors vagy történet kedvező, szép pályára vonz! Munka és szélvész közt, jó és balszerencse befolyásaiban kiforrva s megtisztulva, magát megpróbált erővel s időnként szélesedő ismeretekkel fog ő egykor *regénységeinek* csillogása közül kilépve a való nagyság világosságában állani. Az ő regénytettei a dicsőség sugáraiban fognak késő századokra általfényleni, hogy általok a jövendő költőnek lelkesedése táplálatot, s az unokának patriotizmusa fennszárnyallatot találjon.

Az új mindég, kisebb nagyobb mértékben, lelket lep, s ez a meglepés annál érezhetőbb, annál különösebb, mennél újabb maga a meglepett lélek, azaz, mennél kevesebb tapasztalásokkal tudja a feltűnő újat öszvehasonlítani. Ki nem emlékezik vissza a maga kifejlésének kezdő éveire? Minő sejdítések, minő kimagyarázhatatlan homályos érzelmek, minő varázslathoz hasonló állapot: midőn a körülvevő jeleneteket[1] legelőszer figyelembe venni kezdettük! Az ég, mely a láthatár halmain nyugodni látszik, a szivárvány, mely a felhőn ragyog, a sziklájából felbuzgó forrás, a habokon lebegő csolnak s minden egyebek úgy hatnak reánk, mint valamely tündérvilágnak képei. Mindaddig, míg okot és következést messzéről sem sejdítünk, a tüneményeket úgy tekintjük, mintha azok ismeretlen magasságú lénynek rendkívül való munkálódásai lennének. Egy valóságos költői helyhezet![2] A fejleni kezdő fiatalka léleknek éppen úgy sötéttisztában, homályon általsugárzó glória közt tetszik fel a természet, mint a költő előtt; csakhogy a költő a lelkesedés pillantatiban a tapasztalás nyomvasztó világából kikapva él, a fiatal lélek pedig még abba nem lépett.

Midőn egy merész embercsoport legelőszer csatlotta öszve magát, s valamely szomszéd társaságocskát nyugodalmas mezein felvert és kirablott; midőn egy tengerparti lakos kivájt fatörzsökét legelőszer a habokra vonta, s a szomszéd sziget partjáig evezett: természetes, ha ezen tettek mind a tevőben, mind egykorúiban különös érzéseket gerjesztettek, s minden bizonnyal különösebbeket, mint időnkben egy százezerekből álló táborozás, s egy út az egész planéta körül. [...]

[1] jelenségeket, tapasztalati tények
[2] költői helyzet, ihletett állapot

f. HUNGARIAN

I.f.1. FERENC KÖLCSEY,[3] from *National Traditions*

Whole nations, like individual people, have their various ages. Childhood defers to youth, youth to adulthood, while the feebleness of age supplants the vitality of the pride of life.

Adulthood is characterised by the calm of spiritual maturity; matters of weight are proposed and accomplished as strength reaches its peak, but maturity knows how to pit itself against fate and circumstance with shrewd calculation, looks ahead as it begins, proceeds cautiously, is unwearied in the many trials, and in its exalted, lofty sentiments inspires around it admiration and respect; its name is *great*.

The strength of coming adulthood which swells the youthful breast foams, seethes and battles against itself. It is by nature brimming with fire and restlessness; it has no goals, only hopes; it follows no precepts, only conjectures; its thoughts wallow in the mire of imagination, and as desire holds aloft the torch of that imagination it knows neither moderation, limitation nor impossibility, it begins and acts with more fire than strength, more passion than sense, and so in fortune good and bad alike, in its ambitions and its deeds it is tinged with a certain *romance*.

The youth of nations is a half-wild condition. Experience and awareness are slight, ebullient fire is eager to flow into action, burgeoning desires are often unclear and fleeting. Happy the nation that is, at such a time, neither confined by obstacles internal or external to stagnate within itself, nor forced into dispersion without profit or consequence, and which fate or history guide onto a favourable, fine path! It will emerge from its erstwhile *romancings*, purged and purified by toil and tempest, by fair fortune and foul, its strength proven and its awareness broadened with the passage of time, to stand illumined by true greatness. The glories of its marvellous deeds will irradiate centuries to come, food for the inspiration of the future poet and wings for the soaring patriotism of generations yet unborn.

The novel always, to a greater or lesser degree, takes the spirit by surprise, and this surprise is all the more palpable, all the more unexpected, the newer the surprised spirit is, that is, the fewer the experiences with which it can compare the rising novelty. Who does not recall their own salad days? What conjectures, what inexplicable, murky emotions, what a state verging on enchantment, when we first began to notice the scenery around us! The sky, which seems to rest on the hills at the horizon, the rainbow shining in the clouds, the spring bursting from its rock, the boat bobbing on the waves and everything else affects us like pictures of some fairyland. While we have not the remotest conception of cause and effect we regard those phenomena as the extraordinary works of a being of unfathomable superiority. A truly poetic situation! To the youthful spirit on the threshold of development nature appears as in the eyes of a poet, in a glory gleaming in chiaroscuro and through a mist; the poet, however, in moments of inspiration, is exalted above the crushing world of experience, while the youthful spirit has not yet entered there.

When for the first time a venturesome tribe mustered to assault and plunder the peaceful lands of some small neighbouring community; when a dweller by the sea first launched upon the waves a hollowed-out tree-trunk and paddled to the shore of a nearby island; it was natural that these acts should arouse, in the performers and in their contemporaries alike, strange feelings, in all probability stranger than do in our day the raising of armies a hundred thousand strong and journeys around the entire planet. [. . .]

---

[3] Ferenc Kölcsey (1790–1838), poet (author of the national anthem, *Hymnus*), critic and politician who substantially influenced the liberal political opposition in the 30s.

Amely nemzet a hatalom és míveltség magas pontjain áll, nagy dolgokat vihet ugyan véghez, de ezen nagy dolgok a história teljes fényében láttatván, természeteseknek lenni megismertetnek, s a maradékra a való piperétlen színében szállanak keresztül. A széles kiterjedésű míveltség koraiban az individuális nagyság tüneményei ritkábbak s kevésbé ragyogók; a mesterség, fortély és tudomány közönségessé váltában a magányos erők nagyrészént alsóbb rendet foglalnak el; s a már régebben feltűnt találmányok hosszú sora s a geniális lélek ezerféle jelenségei után, az eredetiség színét megnyerni felette nehéz, s a genienek bélyegvonásai ritkábban ismertetnek ki.

Másképpen van a dolog a fejleni csak most kezdő népeknél. Itt lelki és testi erők messzére kitündöklő fénnyel ragyognak. Itt minden jeles, a vitézség tetteiben s a genienek műveiben és találmányaiban, egyes pontokban mutatkozik. Itt minden, amit a gondolkozó ész s a találó elme előhoz, az eredetiség vonásaival jelen meg. Az, ki a vadon talált magot legelébb a földbe vetette, ki a kézmívességnek legszükségesbeit legelőszer ismeretbe hozta; ki fegyvert adott a vitéznek, s a legelső hadi rendet kiszabta; ki a házasság oly egyszerű törvényét javallatba tette, stb.: kétségkívül szokatlan fényben jelent meg, s szokatlan behatással munkált egykorúi közt. S ki nem tudja, hogy éppen a behatás mennyisége teszi a nagy embernek és nagy tetteknek külső mértékét? S a behatásnak mennyisége hol lehet nagyobb, hol szembetűnőbb, mint félvad nemzetnél?

Mikor tehát valamely nemzet a maga félvad állapotában, messze a puhálkodás veszedelmeitől, s hódításban támadólag, vagy szabadságért védelmezőleg küzdve él és forr; mikor benne a genienek és erőnek jelenségei sűrűn, de egyes alakokban feltűnnek; mikor ezen tünemények lelkesedéssel fogadtatnak, s az, ami bennek új és hasznos és szép és nagy, a költői érzelemhez hasonlóval éreztetnek, következőleg szív és képzelet segedelme által megdicsőíttetnek: ekkor szokott a hőskor feltetszeni. S mivel feltetszik bizonyos sötéttisztában, mivel tüneményi a jelenkorban elragadtatással fogadtatnak, s így a jövőnek a hagyomány glóriájában adatnak által; mivel a históriai vizsgálat későn fellobbanó fáklyája ezen sötéttisztán és glórián a közvéleményben többé erőt nem vehet: természetes, ha a hősi kor a maga regényes alakját századról századra nem csak megtartja, de öregbíti, s a nemzeti lelkesedésnek és poézisnek sokáig tartó táplálatot nyújt.

Különbség van aközt, ha a hősi korra nyíló nemzet a míveltség magosbb pontjain álló népek közelében lakik-e, vagy magához hasonlóktól vétetik környül? Midőn a durva embercsoport mívelt lelkű nagy néppel jön öszveérésbe és küzdésbe, vagy hatalommal vagy világossággal fog elboríttatni. A szép virágzatú hőskor a nagyra menendő nemzet pontonként terjedésének s fejlődésének lépcsői közé tartozik; s csak lassanként kell a teljes míveltség korába általolvadnia, hogy a maga poétai varázsalakját maradandólag megtarthassa.

Az ifjú lélek forró ereje s küzdő érzelmei vagy az emberből ki, vagy belől az emberben munkálnak. Kifelé munkáltokban tettek által hősségre törekednek, bennmunkáltok alatt gondolati derengés és sejdítési borongás közt szövik a poézisnek fátyolát. A munkálatnak mindegyik módja a fantázia befolyásával történik; s így a hősségre kitörekedő és a poézis fátyola alatt bennküzdő fiatal lelkek rokonok egymással. Egyforma tünemények közt, egyforma helyhezetben tűnnek fel, s egyformán meg nem vesztegetett friss forrásokból buzognak ki. A költői szellem a maga eredetében éppen oly erős, mint a hősi, puha ellágyulás és ellágyító a érzelékenység nélkül; mindegyik nemzet individuális karaktere és helyhezete szerént egyképpen vígabb vagy búsabb, vadabb vagy szelídebb, több vagy kevesebb svermerséggel[4] elborult. Európának utazó

---

[4] rajongással, ábrándozással

The nation that stands at the acme of power and culture can indeed achieve great things; but when these great things are seen in the full light of history they are recognised as natural, and come down to posterity in the drab of reality. Instances of individual greatness are less frequent and less brilliant in times of widespread culture; when skill, artifice and science have become universal, solitary powers for the most part take a lower place; after a lengthy series of long-forgotten discoveries and manifold revelations of fertile minds it becomes exceedingly hard to achieve even the semblance of originality, and the stamp of genius is less often recognised.

The situation is different in the case of a nation that is only just beginning to develop. Here spiritual and physical powers gleam with a distant light. Here all that is excellent shows itself at isolated points, in deeds of valour and works and discoveries of genius. Here everything that thoughtful mind and inventive wit produce bears the mark of originality. He who first planted in the earth seed found in the wild, that first understood the essence of craftsmanship; who placed weapons in the hands of warriors and shaped the first military formation; who formulated the so simple law of marriage, etc., without doubt appeared in an unusual light and exercised an unaccustomed influence on his contemporaries. And who does not know that it is the amount of their influence that sets the external measure of great men and great deeds? And where can that influence be greater, where more obvious, than in a half-wild nation?

When, then, some nation lives and seethes in its own half-wild state, far from the dangers of laxity, poised to conquer or struggling to preserve liberty; when signs galore of genius and power appear in it, though in individuals; when these appearances are received with enthusiasm, when that which is in them is new and useful and beautiful and great, they are perceived with a sentiment akin to the poetic and are consequently acclaimed by heart and fancy alike, then the heroic age is dawning, and as it dawns in chiaroscuro, as its wonders are received with delight in the present, so they are bequeathed to the future in a glory of tradition; and since the later blazing torch of historical examination can no longer overcome in the common mind this clear darkness and halo, it is natural for the heroic age not only to preserve but to increase its romantic qualities as the centuries pass, and provides long-lasting sustenance for national fervour and poetry.

There is a difference between a nation blossoming into its heroic age and situated in the vicinity of peoples at higher stages of culture, and one surrounded by others like itself. When the uncouth tribe comes into contact and conflict with a large people of cultured spirit it will be enveloped in either power or enlightenment. The flowering of a heroic age is one of the steps in the gradual expansion and development of a people on its way to greatness, and it must mellow only slowly into the age of full culture in order that it may preserve permanently its magic poetic status.

The seething power of the youthful spirit and its struggling emotions will work either outwards from a man or inwardly within him. Through the deeds of the extrovert they strive for heroism, through those of the introvert they weave the veil of poetry amidst contemplative dawning and brooding premonition. Both are brought about by the workings of fantasy; thus it is that the youthful spirits that burst out into heroism and struggle inwardly beneath the veil of poetry are kindred one to another. They arise amid the same phenomena, in the same situation, and spring from sources which are as yet unsullied. The poetic spirit is, in its origin, every bit as strong as the heroic, lacking tender tranquility and enervating sentimentality alike; every nation is, according to its individual character and situation, gayer or sadder, wilder or more gentle, endowed with greater or lesser flights of fancy. The sons of Europe on their travels have heard

fiai az új-zélandi kannibál szájából csatadalokat hallottak, s Tahiti szelíd ege alatt énekeseket találtak, kik módjokkal a Homerídákra emlékeztetnek; ezek éppen oly jelenetek, mint az Argonauták mellett Orpheus, s mint a Morvai hősek közt Ossian.

Mikor a kifejlés útján előre haladó nemzet közeledik azon ponthoz, hol a tettek nagysága az ismeretek nagyságával párosul, hol az ész világa a képzelet csillogásának ellenében feltámad, s a históriának pályája megnyílik, akkor az érzések közönségesen zajlott csapongása szűnni kezd, a tisztán természeti állapot mesterségesebbre megy által, s már maga az a komolyabb, hidegebb tekintet, mellyel az érett ész a körülvevő dolgokat tekinti, nem egyéb, mint ezen mesterségesb állapotnak következése. Mennél inkább elhidegszik a jelenlét, annál hátrább vonulnak a régibb kor tündérképei, s a poézis, mely a forróbb élettel együtt ébredett és járt, lassanként elvonja magát az életkörtől. S íme itt van a pont, hol a hőskor határai észrevétlenül eltűnnek; a poézis pedig a maga legtündöklőbb sugáraiban ragyoghat. Az ilyenkor született költő, szintúgy lángkebellel, mint az előbbi kor gyermeke, de kitisztultabb fejjel s gazdagabb ismeretekkel, midőn az őtet körülvevő élettől elvonul, természetesen egy jobbat, szebbet, belsőjével rokonabbat keresni kényszeríttetik. Boldog ő, ha ezen jobbat, szebbet s rokonabbat saját hazájának régiségeiben felleli! A költő, ki nem lél magának a régiségben kielégítő világot, nyugtalanul csapong cél és határ nélkül magából kifelé; s vagy eltompulás a végtelenségben, vagy megromlott képzelődés a formátlanságban, vagy vészes érzékenység az epedés által, lészen csapongásának következése: midőn a hőskor maradéka bátran veti a múltra tekintetét, annak képeit a távolság miatt megszelídült fényben láthatja, képzelete a bizonyos célra repületben erőt és formát nyer, s ugyanez által érzelmei kitisztulnak és nyugalommal szállonganak, nyugalommal, mely a nemzeti karakterszínhez képest vagy derültebb vagy borultabb, de mindég felemeli a lelket, s művészi virágzatban tenyész.

A poézisnek legkedvezőbb pillantatok tehát akkor nyílnak, midőn a nemzet a zajló ifjúság korából a tisztább és józanabb míveltség csendesebb világába lépni kezd. A nyelv ilyenkor kap hajlékonyságot, s a poétának kívánságai s szükségei szerént ezerféle alakra változhat el; az érzés ilyenkor nyér fellengést, mivel a jelenkoron vagy felül vagy túl emelvén magát, más ragyogóbb tartományba siet vissza; a képzelet ilyenkor talál szabad lebegést, mivel a körülfogó valóság által meg nem szoríttatván, az előtte felnyitott messze tartományt sajátjának tekinti, s annak képeit önkéje szerént[5] öntheti el varázssugáraival: s így nyelv, érzés és képzelet a magok kedvezőbb pontját elérvén, mi kell egyéb, hogy a költő a legtündöklőbb alakban tűnjön fel?

A nemzeti hőskor hagyja maga után a nemzeti hagyományt; s nemzeti hagyomány és nemzeti poézis szoros függésben állanak egymással. Ahol ősi hagyomány vagy éppen nincsen, vagy igen keskeny határokban áll, ott nemzeti poézis sem származhatik; az ott születendő énekes vagy saját (tisztulást és folyamot[6] nem található) lángjában süllyed el, vagy külföldi poézis világánál fog fáklyát gyújtani; s hangjai örökre idegenek lesznek hazájában. Mert a nemzeti poézis a nemzeti történet körében kezdi pályáját, s a lírának később feltámadó s individuális érzelmeket tárgyazó zengése is csak ott lehet hazaivá, hol az a nemzeti történet régibb múzsájától kölcsönöz sajátságot, s személyes érzeményeit a nemzeti hagyomány és nemzeti megnemesített életkör nimbuszán keresztül sugároztatja.

Ha ezen fejtegetéseket a históriára akarjuk alkalmaztatni: hova fordítsuk inkább szemeinket, mint a görögökre? Soha nemzeti poézis ragyogóbb hőskorra vissza nem tekintett, és soha nemzeti hőskor ragyogóbb poézist maga után nem vont, mint őnálok. Ifjúságok felvirulását azon idegeneknek köszönték, kik hozzájok míveltebb népektől jöttenek, s köztök magasabb ismereteikkel

---

[5] önkénye szerint, önkényesen
[6] tartósságot

war-songs from the lips of New Zealand cannibals, and beneath the gentle skies of Tahiti have found singers whose melodies remind us of the Homeric bards; these are just such scenes as Orpheus singing beside the Argonauts, and Ossian among the heroes of Morva.

As the nation advancing along the road of development approaches the point at which greatness of deeds is commensurate with that of knowledge, where the world of the mind rises to counter the glitter of the imagination and the course of History opens before it; then the communal turbulence of emotions begins to cease, the purely natural state changes to one more artificial, and then the more serious, cooler view with which the mature mind looks at its surroundings is nothing more than the natural sequel to that more artificial condition. The more the present cools, the more distant seem the charmed images of the former age, and poetry, which awoke and moved together with life when the pace was hotter, gradually withdraws from the real world until, of a sudden, comes the point at which the boundaries of the heroic age imperceptibly vanish; poetry, however, can shine in its own most brilliant rays. The poet born at such a time, though his bosom is afire like the child of the former age, is naturally obliged, with his clearer head and richer awareness, to seek something better, finer, more attuned to what is within him when he retires from the life around him. Happy is he, if he discovers that better, finer, more attuned thing in the antiquities of his fatherland. The poet that does not find himself a satisfying world in antiquity drifts restlessly, aimlessly, vaguely out of sorts, and the outcome of his wanderings will be either foundering in an infinity of apathy, a ruined, perverted imagination, or a sensitivity rendered morbid by yearning; whereas the scion of the heroic age turns his gaze boldly upon the past and sees its images in a light softened by distance; his imagination gains strength and form as it flies to a certain goal, and indeed his feelings are thereby purified and are wafted serenely, in a serenity which, depending on the national character, may be more or less happy or sad, but in either case will elevate the spirit and bring forth a flowering of art.

The moments most favourable for poetry, therefore, occur when the nation is beginning to step from the time of turbulent youth into the quieter world of purer and more sober culture. At such times the language acquires flexibility and can assume a thousand forms to suit the desires and needs of the poet; feeling is heightened at such times, since it elevates itself above or beyond the present age, hastening back to more illustrious ground; imagination at such times finds itself free to soar, since it is not confined by the reality that surrounds it, regards the region that opens before it as its own and can flood its images with magic rays at will; thus language, feeling and imagination come to a favourable high point, and what more is needed for the poet to appear in the most brilliant aspect?

A nation's heroic age leaves behind it national tradition, and national tradition and national poetry are closely dependent one on another. Where ancient tradition is either quite non-existent, or is very restricted, national poetry cannot develop; the bard born there will either (unable to attain purification or permanence) founder in his own fire, or will light a torch in the world of foreign poetry, and his voice will be for ever alien in his native land. Because national poetry begins its course in the sphere of national history and beams its personal sentiments through the nimbus of national tradition, the sound of the lyre that is later tuned to individual feelings can only be at home where it borrows its complexion from the older Muse of national history.

If we wish to apply these remarks to History, where better to turn our eyes than to the Greeks? Never has a national poetry looked back on a more brilliant heroic age, never has a nation's heroic age given rise to more brilliant poetry than the Greek. They had others, who came among them from more cultured nations and shone with their higher knowledge, to thank for the

fenn ragyogtak ugyan, de nem úgy, mint Banks vagy Forster Tahitinak lakosai közt; mert Triptolemus, Cadmus, Cecrops, Danaus s mások több tapasztalások mellett is lelkek ifjúságára s emberiségök kifejlésére nézve egy lépcsőn vagy legalább hasonlón állottak azokhoz, kiknek tartományában megtelepedtenek; s midőn nekik némely új ismeretet, némely új szokást hoztanak, ugyanakkor nyelvöket s nemzetiségöket elfogadván, mind magokat, mind ismereteiket és szokásaikat a görög földön meghonosították. E környülménynek két következése lőn. Első, hogy a hellén a maga serdületének kezdetében hirtelen teljes kifejlésre nem hívattatván, lépcsőnként haladhatott az érelem[7] nagy pontja felé, s hosszú, szép ifjúságot élhetett. Másik, hogy idegen világosság által a nemzeti körből ki nem kapatott, s az eredetiség színét ott is megtarthatta, hol kölcsönzött vonásokkal ékesült. […]

Midőn a hellén faj nemzetiségéről szólunk, a religiót sem kell elfelednünk. A religiónak alapideái, akár a görög földön magán tűntek fel valaha, akár idegenből szállongottak által, mindenképpen nemcsak a históriának, hanem a hősi kor hagyományainak határain is túl a gyermekemberiség szűkebb körében vettek lételt; s minden bizonnyal ha nem tisztán is, legalább sejdítésben az emberi természeten felül s az emberi életen és történeteken túl fekvő s egy más ismeretlen világból általfolyó erőket vettek tárgyazatba. A görög ezen ideákat nemcsak az emberi életbe hozta le, hanem a maga nemzetiségébe s nemzeti történeteibe olvasztotta. Az istenségi erők a hellén föld gyermekeiben individualizáltattak, s így egy félig religiói sejdítésekből, félig történeti hagyományokból öszvealkotott hazai mitológia készült, mely a maga ezerféleképpen különböző, gyakran csudálatos, de mindég mosolygó alakjában egy vidámon exaltált poézisnek örök tárgya lett, s ezáltal a görög poézist a görög hazaisággal elválaszthatatlanul öszveforrasztotta. Ily boldog öszvejövések közt származhatott Homerus, ki nemcsak a maga költői elérhetetlen nagysága miatt érdemel figyelmet, hanem még sokkal inkább azon példátlan behatás miatt, mellyel ő az egész görög népet, annak százképpen megszaggatott polgári alkotványai közt, egy közönséges[8] nemzeti szellemmel eltöltvén, a maga költői munkálkodása körében egyesítette; s religiót, s játékszíni és lírai poézist, művészséget, filozófiát és életet egyformán lelkesítvén, mindezeket bizonyos varázskörbe foglalta, melyen belöl örök virágzatban, sanyarkodás nélkül, szabad lebengéssel tenyésznek.

A római nemzet, mely a maga kicsinységéből óriási nagyságra századokon keresztül tartott küzdés közt emelkedett, úgy látszik, hogy a legszebb tündöklésű hőskort teremtette elő tetteiből. De a Tiberis mellett nem azon esetek jőnek öszve, melyek a hellén ég alatt oly szerencsés befolyással dolgoztak. Egy sokfelől egybecsoportozott fiatal rabló népet pillantunk meg ott Romulusnak zászlója alatt, s ezen rabló nép megjelenésén felül a Romulus mesés születéséig, s innen Aeneásig és Latinusig s tovább Faunus és Saturnus uralkodásáig, egy alkalmasint setétben fekvő kornak perspektívája nyílik meg tekinteteinknek. Hazaivá lett félhistóriai mítosz az, mely ezen perspektívában rajzoltatik; de a rajzolatnak két fő pontjai (a trójai szökevények és a látiumi régiség homálya) behatásaira nézve messze maradnak azon ragyogó táblának[9] színeitől, mely a régi Hellászt terjeszti elő; s mindazért, mivel különbféleséggel nem bírnak, mindazért mivel a későbbi kor temérdek tettei mellett igen parányi alakban jelennek meg: lehetetlen vala, hogy a nemzettel valamely különösen lelkesítő öszvetételben állhassanak. Adjuk hozzá, hogy a római nép mindjárt kezdetkor erővel teljes ifjúságban lép elő, s korához képest igen is komoly kinézések[10] közt magát

---

[7] kifejlődés, érettség
[8] általános
[9] képnek; vö. táblakép, azaz fára vagy vászonra festett kép
[10] külső, forma

upturn of their youth, but these were not like Banks[11] and Forster[12], among the people of Tahiti; for Triptolemus, Cadmus, Cecrops, Danaus and others were, despite their greater experience, in terms of youthfulness of spirit and development of human qualities on a level with, or at least similar to, those in whose lands they settled; and whereas the newcomers brought new awareness, new practices, they absorbed the Greek language and national characteristics and assimilated themselves, their knowledge and customs, to the land of Greece. This led to two consequences. Firstly, that the Hellene was not summoned to a sudden complete development in early adolescence, but was able to advance in stages to the acme of maturity and to enjoy a long and splendid youth. Secondly, that he was not driven from his national sphere by foreign enlightenment, and was able to preserve the appearance of originality even though adorned with borrowed plumage. [. . .]

In speaking of the Hellene race we must not forget religion. Whether the fundamental notions of religion appeared in the Greek world itself at some time, or were brought in from outside, they came into being somewhere beyond the fringe not only of history but of the heroic age too, in the narrower world of infant humanity; and in all probability, if not quite clearly, were an attempt to account for forces flowing through from another, unknown world which lay, supposedly at least, above human nature and beyond human life and history. The Greek not only brought these notions down into human life, but blended them into his own nationality and national history. The divine powers were personified in the children of the Greek world, and so there grew up a native mythology compounded of religious hypothesis and historical tradition, which, in its thousand-faceted, often miraculous but always smiling form, became the perpetual subject of a cheerfully exalted poetry, and thereby blended indissolubly Greek poetry and Greekness. This so happy union was able to give birth to Homer, who commands attention not only because of his peerless poetic greatness, but also – indeed, much more so – because of the unequalled influence by which he filled the whole Greek world with a common national spirit and united it, with its hundredfold discords, in the sphere of his poetic works; and he inspired religion, dramatic and lyric poetry, art, philosophy and life alike, enclosed them all, as it were, in a magic circle in which to proliferate in an eternal flowering, soaring in freedom unrestrained.

It would appear that the Roman race, which rose through centuries of struggle from a tiny beginning to gigantic size, produced the most glittering heroic age by its deeds. Beside the Tiber, however, the same conjunctions that functioned with such fortunate effect beneath the Hellenic sky did not take place. Under the banner of Romulus we glimpse a randomly gathered band of young robbers, and beyond the appearance of that robber band there opens before us a view of an age for the most part shrouded in obscurity, back to Romulus' fabulous birth, to Aeneas and Latinus and to the rule of Faunus and Saturn; that which is outlined in this view has become a patriotic semi-historical myth; but as concerns the two main points of the outline (the flight from Troy and the obscurity of the antiquity of Latium), in terms of their impact they are far removed from the colours of that glittering page which displays to us ancient Hellas; and both because they display no variety and because in comparison with the illustrious deeds of later ages they seemed trifling, it was impossible for them jointly to offer any particular inspiration to the nation. Let us add that from its very beginning the Roman people marched forward in a youth full of power and, with a

---

[11] Sir Joseph Banks (1743–1820), an English botanist, who took part in Captain James Cook's first voyage around the globe (1768–1771).

[12] This name can refer to both Johann Reinhold Forster (1729–1798) and his son Johann George (1754–1794). They were German naturalists, who both took part in Captain James Cook's second expedition (1772–1775).

a rokon nemzetektől külön választván, fáradatlan hévvel politikai nagyságra törekszik; s innen Romulustól fogva a később százakig még nyilván mesés történetein is históriai szín ömlik el. Mindezek nem valának a nemzeti poézis felderülésének kedvező vezércsillagi; annyival is inkább, mivel a római művészet és tudomány elébb hetrúriai, majd görög befolyás alatt, mint egészen idegen plánta nevekedett fel, s az eredetiség színével, mely nélkül a nemzetiség fenn nem állhat, nem bírhata. A római poézis görög magvakból, görög színekkel virágzott ki; s ha Livius Andronicust s közel követőit nem említjük is, de maga Virgilnek ragyogó pompájú nyelve, s a horatiusi líra mi vala egyéb Hellászban szedett zsákmánynál?

Midőn római nagyság és görög míveltség a történeti játékszínről lassanként tűnni kezdettenek, több fiatal nemzetek állottak elő Európában, melyek egy zajgással és munkával teljes életkörben nyughatatlanul kerengvén, s forrás által tisztulást, nyomás által emelkedést keresvén, egyfelől nyers ifjúságokban a birodalom aggságával, másfelől csapongó vadságokban a keresztyénség szelídségével a legkitetszőbb ellentételt formálták. Fegyvereik hatalmasok valának, de lelkeik a római míveltség elborító világa által leverettek, s régi nyelvüket sokan, honi vallásokat pedig mindnyájan felcserélvén, egy egészen új, isméretlen életbe mentek által, melynek tüneményei szokatlan világításban valának feltünendők.

Vad nép közelített a míveltség hosszú századaiban elpuhult nemzethez, mely már minden poétai szellem s lelkesedés nélkül, még csak a vallásban találhata hevületet, azon vallásban, mely a földiektől elvon, s utat ugyan az ég felé mutat, de egyszersmind az emberi lelket romlottságának s kicsiny voltának hathatós éreztetése által poriglan nyomja le. Hevület ég felé, s megaláztatás ezen hevületben: minő ellentétel ennek kimagyarázhatatlan érzelme, s azon emberi vidám érzelem közt, mely egykor a mitológia tündérképei körül lebegett! A mitológiával együtt elsüllyedt a görög poézisnek világa a maga utolsó visszasugárzásaiban is; tudomány, szív, lélek s az emberi élet egész folyamja a religió szent körében koncentráltattak, s így a keresztyénség kebelében új életszakot kezdő vad népek azt a változást, melyet érzelmeikre, szokásaikra s egész valóságokra nézve szükségesen szenvedniük kellett, csaknem egyedül a religió befolyásai alatt szenvedték. Íme tehát egyfelől míveletlen, nyers ifjúságban, csapongó indulatok közt zajló emberfaj; másfelől vallás, mely az emberi szívet nehéz önáldozat és határtalan emberszeretet által a maga-megtagadásnak és szelídségnek elérhetetlen pontja felé buzdítja. Egyfelől ki nem fejlett, de a természet örök rendénél fogva kifejlésre indulandó nemzetek, melyek a római nagyság és míveltség omladékai közt bolyonganak; másfelől vallás, mely az emberi értelmet, nagyságot és míveltséget megalázza, s földi példáktól elvonván, az isteni véghetetlen s megfoghatatlan tökély követésére hív. Minő öszvejövetelek az ellenkezésben! Hosszú forrás lett ezeknek következése, mely alatt a régi nemzeti formák elváltoztanak, s a vallás közönséges befolyásával a nemzetek különféleségében egy közönséges szellem kezdett lengeni, mely az európai hőskort, s azt követő európai poézist a görög régiségtől különböző alakban hozta fel.

Vallás szentsége küzdött emberi gyarlósággal. Amaz terjesztett nyugalmat szelídség és áhítat által: emez nyugtalanságot a tenni akarásban. Amaz parancsolt a kívánságnak zabolát: ez fáklyát gyújtott a szenvedelmeknek. Amaz az embert testi köréből felkapni, ez a maga örvényébe lemeríteni igyekezett. Így leve, hogy az emberiség nagy masszája az ég és föld között megoszlani kényszeríttetett. Keveseknek jutott az erő, hogy magokat Isten előtt megsemmisítsék, s életeket a religió gyakorlásaiban elsüllyesztvén, az emberi kívánságoknak meghaljanak; a sokaság hódíthatatlan kívánságaival, s a gyarlóság kisértéi[13] között félénken vetette olykor-olykor a vallás kifüggesztett törvényeire pillantatit; s vágy és rettegés, szenvedelem és megtagadás közt fejlett ki a helléni korban ismeretlen szentimentalizmus. [...]

[13] kísértései

bearing very serious for its time, set itself apart from related nations and strove with indefatigable zeal for political greatness; and from the time of Romulus until later centuries a tinge of authenticity covers even its clearly apocryphal history. All these were not guiding stars favourable to the awakening of a national poetry; all the more so as Roman art and science came first under Etruscan, then Greek influence, and grew up as a completely exotic plant quite devoid of the originality without which national qualities cannot be. Roman poetry burgeoned from Greek seed and in Greek colours, and to say nothing of Livius Andronicus and his close followers, what were the magnificent language of Vergil himself and the lyrics of Horace but booty acquired in Greece?

When Roman greatness and Greek culture began gradually to vanish from the scene, there emerged in Europe other young nations which moved restlessly in a milieu full of uproar and toil, seeking purification through turbulence and elevation through pressure. The raw youthfulness of some offered the most complete contrast to the age of the empire, as did the nomadic savagery of others to the mildness of Christianity. Their weapons were powerful, but their spirits were subdued by the world of Roman culture; many changed their languages and all their religions, and they entered upon a completely new, unfamiliar way of life, the phenomena of which were to appear in an unusual light.

A primitive people approached a nation, softened by long centuries of culture, now devoid of poetic spirit and enthusiasm, and which could find passion only in religion, that religion which rejects the things of earth and shows the way heavenward, but at the same time utterly crushes the human spirit by imparting a strong sense of its corrupt and insignificant nature. A passionate desire for heaven and humiliation in that desire – what a contrast between the inexplicable feeling of that and the cheerful human feeling which had once floated about the magical images of mythology! The world of Greek poetry down to its final glimmerings had foundered along with Greek mythology; learning, heart, spirit and the whole of human life had become concentrated in religion, and so the primitive peoples that began a new phase of life in the bosom of Christianity suffered that change which they had of necessity to undergo in respect of their feelings, their customs and their ways as a whole – almost entirely under the influence of religion. See, on the one hand an uncultured tribe in raw youth, adrift in unstable emotions; and on the other a religion which urged the human heart towards an unattainable level of self-denial and meekness by way of grievous self-sacrifice and boundless love of man. On the one hand nations as yet undeveloped, but about to embark on the development that accords with the eternal order of things, roamed the ruins of the culture and greatness of Rome; on the other hand a religion which set no store by human worth, greatness and culture, rejected earthly criteria and bade men seek the infinite and incomprehensible perfection of God. What a meeting of opposites! The outcome was a long period of unrest, during which the ancient nations were transformed and, under the influence of religion a common spirit began to rise among the miscellany of nations and brought into being the European heroic age and the consequent European poetry in a form different from the Greek.

The holiness of religion fought against human vileness. The former dispensed peace by means of meekness and piety; the latter unrest in the desire for action. The former commanded desire to be curbed, the letter lit the way for passion. The former strove to elevate man from the bodily sphere, the latter to plunge him into his own abyss. Thus it was that the great mass of humanity was perforce torn between heaven and earth. Few had the strength to reduce themselves to nothing before God, to immerse their lives in the practice of religion, to die to human desires; the majority, among the temptations of vileness, cast with irrepressible desire occasional timid glances at the laws set out by religion, and among yearning and fear, suffering and self-denial, there grew up Sentimentalism, unknown in the era of Hellenism. [. . .]

A középkor szilaj gyermeke a maga erejének rendetlen érzelmében, klíma és vallási befolyás által elkomolyított fantáziával, tetteiben és műveiben óriási nagyságra, s csudálatosságra törekedett. A hellén s a hellént utánzó római művész még feledve volt, s ne lett légyen bár; de mi módon fogott volna az egyszerű nagyságnak szép, de nem szembeszökőleg szép képe a hatalomérzésben még kemény, még durva hősre munkálni? Az ő érzelmei s ízlése más úton indultak, mint az argonauták unokáiké. Ezeknek képzeletét a grácia vezérlette vissza egy vidámon s magosított emberiséggel ragyogó hőskorba, s onnan vissza a társaságos élet kellemes körébe. Csendes nyugalomban belülről, szállongott a tárgyak szép külsőjén tekintetük; s lélekvonás és szívérzelem, bánat és öröm, remény és esdeklés mosolygó megtestesülésben lebegtek szemeik előtt. A középkori magzat fantáziája, elfordíttatván az ősi sötét és vad mítoszoktól, a vallás testetlen országába ragadtatott, hol meghatározott formákat nem talált. Vedd hozzá, hogy a vallásnak felségesen komoly szelleme az emberi lélek hiuságát, s az emberi képzet[14] és érzelem játékos csapongásait nem táplálhatta, következésképpen egy határtalan szabadsággal lebegő poézisnek gerjesztője nem lehetett. Hol leljen tehát a költői lelkesedés célt és hazát? A pogány régiségben? Azon félig ismeretlen homály, félig a keresztyénségnek átka feküdött. A jelenkor vala hátra, melyben és melyből a költő felemelkedésért törekedhetett. Egzaltált szerelemérzés, és a rittervilági hőskor nyitottak pályát nékie; két tünemény, egyformán alkalmatosak a fantáziát rendetlen hevületbe hozhatni. Hevült is az rendetlenül; s ez által leve, hogy az életet magosítani s az emberiség határait kiterjeszteni akaró költő bizonyos mitológiának nem létében egy csudálatos formákból alkotott tündérvilág felé csapongott; s így tündérezés, ritterség és szerelem vallási buzgósággal és köznépi babonával elvegyülve rendkívül való, bizarr világításban tüntették fel a romantikát, mely az európai poézisre még akkor sem szűnt meg fő behatással munkálni, mikor a görög és római művek új életre hozatván, követés tárgyaivá tétettek.

Most görög formák közt lebegő s görög és római színt és lelket utánzó romantikai szellem befolyása kezdett az európai költés művein megismerszeni; egy félig eredeti állapot, mely a délieknél inkább lágyság és enthusiasmus, az északiaknál inkább magába-vonulás és epedés, a franciáknál inkább elmésség és udvariság kitetsződbb vonásaiban jelengette magát; aszerént amint ezek a nemzeti karakterben is kisebb vagy nagyobb mértékben a kitetsződbb vonások voltanak.

[...] Annyi bizonyos, hogy [nemzeti] karakter és [nemzeti] nyelv a poéta művére egyforma behatással munkálnak. A nyelvbeli különbség Európának régi és új mívelt népei közt, nem keveset tesz arra, hogy a görög és európai új poézis minden hasonlítani akarás mellett is egymástól különbözzenek. Akcentuáltság s onnan következett rím és német prozódiai sajátság, s a régi nyelvekénél kevésbé szabad szintaxis, már magokban nevezetes elhajlásokat csinálnak; mi nem leszen még, ha a nyelvvel a különböző nevelés, erkölcs, szokás, ítélet és tudomány következéseit öszvekapcsoljuk? Maga az újaknál oly közönségesen elterjedett szentimentalizmus a költés minden nemeiben új meg új színeket hoz elegyedésbe; midőn nemcsak a komolyabb indulatokon önti el magát, de magának a jókedvnek csapongásaira is gyakran általfoly. A görög költőnek, mint a görög művész szobrának, busongása is szép és nyugalmas; vidámsága pedig tiszta, mint a felhőtlen ég. Az újkori lelkes költőnek bánatja gyakran a vérzésig gyötör; s vidámsága sok ízben annyi komolysággal vegyül fel, hogy e vegyületben egy egészen újalakú lélekállapot áll elő: *humor* tudniillik, mely a régieknél ismeretlen.

Ha régi és új poézis különbségeiről van szó, azt sem kell elfelednünk, hogy az új Európa költője a maga nemzetével nem áll a göröggel egyforma jóltevő öszvefüggésben. Keresztyén vallás

---

[14] képzelet

The unruly child of the Middle Ages had a capricious sense of his own strength, and strove, with a fantasy rendered serious by climate and religious influence, for tremendous greatness and miraculous achievement in deeds and art. The Hellene and the Roman artist that had imitated him were forgotten – if only they had not been! – but how was the beautiful, if not strikingly beautiful, image of simple greatness going to affect the hero who was still hard, still uncouth in the awareness of power? His sensibilities and tastes took a different direction from that of the descendants of the Argonauts. Grace led their imagination back to a heroic age that gleamed cheerfully and with elevated humanity, and thence back to the pleasant milieu of communal life. In peace and quiet their gaze moved from inside to the beautiful exteriors of things, and intellectual attraction and feelings of the heart, grief and pleasure, hope and entreaty appeared in corporeal form before their eyes. The fantasy of the scion of the Middle Ages, forced away from the dark and uncouth myths of old, clutched at the incorporeal world of religion, where it could find no defined forms. Add to that, that the exaltedly solemn spirit of religion could nourish neither the vanity of the human spirit nor the whimsical meanderings of the human imagination and emotions, and in consequence could not be the inspiration of a poetry that would soar in boundless freedom. Where then was poetic fervour to find a purpose and a native land? In pagan antiquity? Over that lay both a veil of ignorance and the curse of Christianity. There remained the present day, in which and from which the poet could strive to rise. Lofty ideals of love and the heroic age of chivalry opened a way before him, two subjects equally suitable for exciting the fantasy to ungoverned passion. And ungoverned it was, through which it came about that for want of a reliable mythology the poet who wished to elevate life and expand the limits of humanity drifted towards a magic world of marvellous forms; and thus belief in the supernatural, chivalry and love combined in an extraordinary, bizarre light with religious zeal and popular superstition to give rise to the romantic, which had not ceased to exercise the principal influence on European poetry by the time that Greek and Roman works were revived and made objects of imitation.

Now the influence of a romantic spirit, soaring among things Greek and imitative of Greek and Roman colours and spirit, began to make itself felt in the world of European poetry; a semi-original condition, which showed itself in the south in warmth and enthusiasm, in the north in introverted nostalgia and yearning, and among the French rather in wit and refinement, according to the greater or lesser degree with which those qualities manifested themselves in the national character.

[. . .] What is certain is that [national] character and [national] language have equal influence on the work of a poet. The linguistic difference between the old and new cultured peoples of Europe is the main cause of the difference between the Greek and the new European poetry, despite every attempt to find common ground. Rhythmic metre, the rhyme and the special features of German prosody which it entailed and the syntax less free than that of the ancient languages constitute in themselves notable departures; if we add to language the consequences of education, morals, customs, judgement and learning, what more need be said? The very sentimentalism which spread so generally among the new peoples mixed ever newer colours in every type of poetry, since it flooded not only more serious moods but often overflowed into flights of levity too. The reverie of the Greek poet, like that of the Greek sculptor's statuary, is beautiful and calm, its cheerfulness as unsullied as the cloudless sky. The grief of the poet of the new age often torments to the point of drawing blood, while his cheerfulness is on many occasions blended with so much solemnity that in the mixture there emerges a quite new spiritual condition: *humour*, that is to say, which was unknown to the ancients.

In speaking of the differences between the ancient poetry and the new we must not forget that the poet of the new Europe and his nation did not enjoy the same beneficial rapport the Greeks did.

The Christian religion and the scientific culture of Europe strove equally for cosmopolitanism. Thence it comes that that exclusive, self-centred, but at the same time spirit-raising sense of nationality which characterised the Hellene is not to be found in Europe. The various peoples, with all their political and moral inclinations, all their different physical situations, are as distinct from one another by virtue of religion, culture and outlook as were the Greeks of Athens from those of Sparta, those of Ephesus from those of Rhodes. The Greeks, however, for all their manifold diversity, did achieve, in terms of language, drama, tradition and a national poetry founded thereon, a certain cohesive force which is not realised in Europe, either because of the growing distinctiveness of peoples as nationalities merged or because of the merging of nationalities as peoples became distinct. That is why in later times no nation could produce so widely influential a poet as Homer; for is it not evident that both Ariosto and his imitators in their enchanted world and Milton and Klopstock in the sacred territories of religion placed before their peoples images just as much divorced from nationality as those who restored Greek mythology to life? [. . .] Greek tradition came down to later generations in unbroken sequence and was always held in respect, and that did not happen with this European tradition. For that reason national poetry in the true meaning of the term is not to be found in a single European people, because the poet, even when singing of the events of his own time, does not cease from standing at a certain distance from the sons of his native land as he is unable to reach that level of contact at which Greek poetry stood *vis-à-vis* the Greek nation.

The three principal forms of poetry – epic, dramatic and lyric – attracted the Greek world to them with equal charm. The first, since Homer made the ancestral traditions of all the Hellenes shine in an all-encompassing circle; the second, since it was drawn from national traditions and at the same time closely associated with the national religion as a festive item; lyric too, because it likewise served religion and likewise glorified the traditions.

The poet of the new age seems close to the nation only in the theatre. But what a profound difference there is between the Athenian theatre and the new theatre of Europe! The latter is open to a very tiny part of the people as a private entertainment; the former took to its bosom the whole Athenian people as communal celebrants. The latter is outside the boundaries of religion; the former grew and blossomed in a religious milieu. The latter so sets out the traditions and events of times ancient and modern, things domestic and foreign, that the audience cannot find any national spirit in the thousand-fold churning, and cannot sustain a national feeling; the former was created and selected its subjects within the limits of nationality. The Greek saw other Greeks before his eyes, and as he looked at the stage found himself in the world of his own nation; whereas the European is dragged from one end of the earth to the other, and can only understand his poet through knowledge remotely acquired.

Instead of pursuing these matters at a distance, the time has come for us to turn our attention to our own nation and to consider events in our history and the connection of our national qualities and poetry with them.

If we look at antiquity the Huns are the people that appear on the most distant horizon of our traditions. The name of Bendegúz rings in our ears, and we see the fame of Attila[19] gleam; but that gleam vanishes before our eyes like a flash of lightning, and from that time until the Avars[20] the memory of our nation is shrouded in obscurity. Not a single thing from the whole history of

[19] According to sources Kölcsey may have used, Bendegúz was the father of Attila the Hun (*c.* 406–453).
[20] The Avars were a nomadic people of Eurasia. From the second half of the sixth until the beginning of the ninth century they occupied most of the Carpathian basin. Kölcsey believed, as many of his contemporaries did, that the Magyars were related to the Avars.

közfényű csillogásában állana; s így Attilától fogva Álmosig századokon keresztül semmit sem találunk, amivel nemzeti érzésünket öszveolvaszthatnók.

Minő helyhezet! Íme tudósaink a görög hagyományt a káosztól és Kronostól fogva Prometheuson, Heraklesen s az egész közben folyt és követő időn keresztül a história századáig nyomról nyomra követhetik; midőn saját nemzeti hagyományunk oly parányi s egymástól oly messze fekvő töredékeken fundáltatik.[21] A nemzeti hagyomány pedig sok tekintetben megbecsülhetetlen kincs. Nemcsak azért, mivel a históriai tudománynak, ha emlékeket nem is, de legalább nyomokat mutat; hanem sokkal inkább azért, mert az a nemzeti lelkesedésnek s annál fogva a honszeretetnek vezércsillaga. A római statusalkotvány,[22] patriotizmus és abból folyó nagyság mítoszon épült, s mítosszal tápláltatott; s még azok is, kik a Scipiókkal, Aemiliusokkal s több nagyokkal együtt éltenek, tisztelettel hevülő érzések közt pillantottak vissza a tettekkel gazdag jelenkorból a mítosz szentté lett képeire; mert jelenkor és valóság nagyon tiszta, nagyon emberi fényben állanak, midőn a hajdankor mesés ugyan, de hitelt talált tüneményei némiképpen emberfeletti világításban sugároznak.

Mi annak oka, ha valamely nemzetnek hagyományai úgy megcsonkulnak: mint például, a miénk Álmoson felül? A régiséggel dicsekedő nemzetek a világ teremtéséig szoktak felhágni tradícióikban, s történeteiket, habár mesés alakban is, az eredettől fogva emlegetik. Azt fogjuk-e következtetni, hogy a nemzet, mely ezt nem teheti, egészen új ága valamely régibb törzsöknek, melyből tekintetet nem érdemlő kicsinységben szakadt ki, s elvadulván, többé kiszakadásáról semmit sem tudott? Azt-e, hogy a hagyománytalan nemzet gyáván, tettek nélkül vesztegle, s emlékezetét unokáira által nem plántálhatta? De a magyarnak nyelve eredetiséget bizonyít, s rokonsága sok kiholt nyelvekkel régiségét mutatja; az a környülmény pedig, mely szerént Álmos s fia Árpád egy félelmet gerjesztő nagyságban s erővel teljes ifjúságban fénylő nemzettel szállottak elő a Kárpátok megől, hagy-e kételkedni afelett, hogy e nemzetnek már az előtt hosszú küzdések alatt kellett a vérpályára kikészülve[23] lennie.

Nem gondolt talán a nemzet saját tetteivel? De olvassuk, hogy Attilának asztalánál bárdok[24] énekletenek; s Anonymus is említi a köznép énekeit, melyekben régi tettek dicsőíttetének. Ami Attila alatt s az Árpád unokáinak idejében s még Mátyás alatt is megtörtént, miért ne történhetett volna meg a köztük lefolyt korban is? Idő hosszúsága és statusfelforgató szélvészek tehették, hogy a hőskor nyomai elfeledtettek; tehette talán az unokáknak vétkes elhűlése is a régiségnek, nemzetiségnek s hazafiságnak emlékei eránt. Nem merném meghatározni, ha úgy volt-e századok előtt, de már hosszú idő olta vétkeinket ki nem menthetjük. […]

A hagyomány annál poétaibb alakot nyer magának, mennél több egyes történetekre oszlik fel, oly egyes történetekre tudniillik, melyek a regénység színét viselvén, az egésznek elevenítő fényt kölcsönözhetnek. A görög hagyomány tele van ilyenekkel, s az ilyenek abban még több költői felemelkedéssel bírnak azon oknál fogva, mert vagy mítoszokká tétettek, vagy mítoszokkal vegyültenek. A magyar hagyományban semmi mitológiai nyomokat észre nem veszünk; s ezek különben is a keresztyénség után idegenekké fogtak volna lenniek. A hagyomány annál fogva Álmostól kezdve egészen históriai formát visel, s ezen formában is az egyes vonások igen ritkák

---

[21] alapul, nyugszik
[22] államrend, állami berendezkedés
[23] a harcokra felkészültté, alkalmassá válva
[24] énekesek, dalnokok

the Avars has left any mark on tradition, and so in the centuries from Attila to Álmos[25] we can find nothing to which we can link our sense of nationhood.

What a situation! See, our scholars can trace Greek tradition step by step from chaos and Kronos onward to the times of Prometheus, Herakles and the rest and later to the centuries of historiography; whereas our own national tradition is based on such minute and widely scattered fragments. And in many respects national tradition is a treasure beyond price – not only because, even if it cannot provide historical science with records, it can provide it at least with clues but much more because it is the guiding star of national zeal and thence of love of the fatherland. The constitution and patriotism of Rome and their ensuing greatness were built on myths, and were nourished by them; and even those who lived with the Scipios, the Aemiliuses and other great men looked back with sentiments warmly respectful from a present rich in deeds to the sanctified images of mythical times; because the present time and reality are illuminated by a very pure, very human light, whereas the past is indeed fabulous, but those of its events that have gained credibility somehow shine with a light that is superhuman.

What is the reason for the traditions of a nation being so cut off as our pre-Álmos ones? Nations that rejoice in a glorious past often go back to the creation of the world in their Legends, and their history, if only in fanciful form, is recounted from the very beginning. Are we to infer that the nation that cannot do this is a completely new branch of some more ancient tribe, from which it broke away when still so tiny as to be unworthy of attention, and having grown savage no longer knows anything about its separation? Or that the traditionless nation dallied in cowardly fashion, without achievements, and failed to plant the remembrance of it in posterity? Yet the language of the Hungarians is evidence of originality, and its relationship to numerous dead languages demonstrates its antiquity; does the circumstance, however, that Álmos and his son Árpád emerged from beyond the Carpathians with a nation large enough to spread terror and radiant in the full power of youth, leave any room for doubt that that nation must by then have been hardened for running the gauntlet in the course of lengthy previous struggles?

Did the nation, perhaps, not care about its deeds? We read, however, that Bards were employed to perform at Attila's table, and Anonymous[26] too refers to the songs of the common people in which deeds of old were glorified. Why should what happened under Attila, in the days of the Árpád posterity and even in the reign of Mátyás[27] not have taken place in the intervening period too? The passage of time and disruptive political events must have caused what remained of the heroic age to be forgotten; the reprehensible cooling of posterity towards memories of antiquity, nationality and patriotism may also have been responsible. I would not venture to state categorically that this is what occurred centuries ago, but we cannot continue to make excuses for our mistakes, as we have for so long. [. . .]

Tradition gains for itself a more poetic form the more it divides into individual events, such individual events, that is, as can shed a vivifying light on the whole under the guise of antiquity. Greek tradition is full of such events, and they possess even more poetic elevation because they have either been made into myth or are mixed with myth. In Hungarian tradition we can detect no mythological traces, and these would have been particularly alien after the adoption of Christianity. For that reason from the time of Álmos onward tradition has had an entirely

[25] The occupation of the Carpathian Basin by the Magyars under Prince Álmos (819–895) and his son Prince Árpád (*c*. 845–*c*. 907) is traditionally dated at 896.

[26] The unknown author of the earliest extant *Gesta Hungarorum*, probably dating from the reign of Béla III (1172–1196), is traditionally called Anonymous.

[27] Mátyás I/Mátyás Hunyadi/King Matthias Corvinus (1443–1490; reigned from 1458) was the Magyars' great, national, renaissance monarch, who later became the symbol of power, justice and culture.

[…]. Ha nemzetünkben akkor több poézisre gerjesztő lélek lakott, mint később, úgy mindent bírt, ami a nemzetiség hatalmas érzésének, s egy szép nemzeti poézisnek előteremtésére megkívántatott. Erős ifjúság, küzdéssel egybekötött vándorlás, ősi birtok visszanyerésének reménye, vér, önáldozat, tettek és győzelmek s kielégült kívánság általok: nem elég okok-e, melyek a hazafit és költőt ezer történeti különbféleség közt a honi dicsőség és hatalom érzelmében lángra gyújthassák? De meg kell jegyezni, hogy nem minden vitéz nép körében ébred fel a poétai szellem saját erejében. Példát lelünk Romában, mely nagy tetteket önmagából állíta fel, poézist pedig sokkal későbben Hellástól kölcsönzött. […]

Nem hiszem, hogy volna tartomány, melynek földében a költésnek bármely kevés virágai is ne tenyésznének. Mindenütt vagynak a köznépnek dalai, mindenütt megdicsőítetnek a merész tettek, bármely együgyű[28] énekben is. De vagynak népek, kik az együgyű ének hangját időről időre megnemesítik, az énekes magasabb reptet vesz, s honának történeteit nevekedő fényben terjeszti elő. Az ének lépcsőnként hágó ereje lassanként vonja maga után az egykorúakat, s mindég a nemzetiség körében szállongván, állandóul ismerős marad nékiek, míg végre a pórdalból egy selmai ének, vagy éppen egy Ilias tűnik fel. Másutt a pórdal állandóul megtartja eredeti együgyűségét, s a nemzet szebb része felfelé hágván a míveltség lépcsőin, a bölcsőben fekvő nemzeti költést messze hagyja magától. Ily környűlményben a magasabb poézis többé belső szikrából szép lángra nem gerjed; idegen tűznél kell annak meggerjednie, s a nemzet egészének nehezen fog világítani. Velünk, úgy látszik, e történt meg.

Úgy vélem, hogy a való nemzeti poézis eredeti szikráját a köznépi dalokban kell nyomozni; szükség tehát, hogy pórdalainkra ily céllal vessünk tekintetet. Két rendbelieknek leljük azokat; mert vagy történeteket énekelnek, vagy a szempillantat személyes érzéseit zengik el. Nagyon régieket sem egy, sem más nemben nem lelünk, s ez is igazolja jegyzésemet, mely magyarainknak a régiség eránt lett elhűléséről felebb tétetett. Ki merné azt tagadni, hogy a hajdankor tiszteletesb tárgyú dalokkal ne bírt légyen, mint a mostani? A több százados daltöredék, mely a magyar gyermek ajkán mai napiglan zeng: *Lengyel László jó Királyunk, az is nékünk ellenségünk,* bizonyítja, hogy valaha a köznépi költő messzebb kitekintett a haza történeteire, ahelyett, hogy a mostani énekekben csak a felfüggesztett[29] rablónak, s a szerencsétlenül járt lánykának emlékezete forog fenn. Legrégibb dalaink, melyekben még nemzeti történet említetik a kurucvilágból maradtak reánk; [….] s ezekben a poétai lelkesedésnek nyilvánságos[30] nyomai láttatnak, amit az újabb pórtörténeti pórdalban[31] hiába fogsz keresni.

A másod rendbeli dalok közt több poétai szikra csillámlik. Némelyekben, habár soronként is, való érzés, bizonyos gondatlan könnyű szállongás, s tárgyról tárgyra geniális szökdelés lep meg bennünket; de tagadhatatlan az is, hogy legközönségesbb karakterök nem egyéb, mint üres, ízetlen rímjáték, mely miatt a legidegenebb ideák egymással öszvefűzetnek, s a köztök olykor elvegyült egymáshoz illőbbel nevetséges tarkaságot formálnak.

---

[28] egyszerű; itt: művészietlen
[29] felakasztott, kivégzett
[30] nyilvánvaló, könnyen érzékelhető
[31] az alsóbb társadalmi osztályok életéről szóló népdal

historical form, and even in that form individual features are very rare. [. . .] If there lived in our nation at that time a spirit that inspired more poetry than was the case later, then it had everything that was required for the creation of a strong sense of nationhood and a fine national poetry. A powerful youth, wandering from struggle to struggle, the hope of regaining ancestral lands, blood, self-sacrifice, deeds, victories and expectations realised through them: are these not reasons enough to kindle a flame in patriot and poet as they sense the power and glory of their land among a thousand historical diversities? It must, however, be pointed out that the poetic spirit is not awakened in its own strength in the sphere of every valiant people. We see that in Rome, for example, which itself did great deeds, but borrowed poetry much later from Hellas. [. . .]

I do not believe that there is a country in whose soil the flowers of poetry, ever so few though they may be, do not grow. The songs of common folk are everywhere, and daring deeds are extolled even if only in song ever so simple. There are peoples, however, the voice of whose simple song is from time to time ennobled, as the singer aims higher and sets out the history of his native land in a brightening light. The power of song, rising step by step, gradually draws its contemporaries after it and, soaring always within the national sphere, remains permanently familiar to them, until at length there appears out of the rustic ditty a lay of Ossian or even an Iliad. Elsewhere the rustic ditty keeps for ever its original form, while the more refined part of the nation ascends the steps of culture, leaving national poetry far behind in the cradle. In such circumstances the higher poetry no longer bursts into flame from an internal spark; it must be ignited at a foreign fire, and will scarcely give light to the whole of the nation. This, it seems, is what has happened to us.

In my opinion the original spark of true national poetry must be sought in the songs of the common people; we must therefore consider our folk songs with this in mind. We shall find that they are of two orders: either they sing of historical events, or they proclaim the personal feelings of the moment. In neither sort do we find any that are very ancient, and that confirms my remark made above to the effect that our Hungarians have cooled towards antiquity. Who would venture to deny that past ages had songs on more honourable subjects than the present? The snatch of the centuries-old song *Lengyel László jó királyunk, Az is nekünk ellenségünk*[32] which is heard to this day on the lips of Hungarian children proves that at one time the popular poet took a closer look at the history of the fatherland rather than perpetuate only the memory of robbers hanged and maidens forlorn, as prevails in the songs of today. Our most ancient songs in which national history is so much as mentioned are those that come to us from the *kuruc*[33] world [. . .] and in these are seen evident traces of the poetic inspiration that will be sought in vain in more recent folk-historical folk songs.

More poetic sparks gleam among the songs of the second order. In some, if only in odd lines, we are surprised by real feeling, a certain light, carefree soaring, a dexterous jumping from subject to subject; but it cannot be denied that their most general characteristic is nothing other than an inane, tasteless play on rhymes which causes the yoking together of the most heterogeneous ideas, and the occasional mixing in with them of the better constructed leads to a ridiculous hotchpotch.

[32] 'Polish László is our good king, he is also our enemy.' These are lines from a children's song, which contains an allusion to the Hungarian King Ulászló I (1424–1444), who, as Wladislaw III, was king of Poland too.

[33] The term *kuruc* is used for the anti-Habsburg fighters in Royal Hungary in the late seventeenth and early eighteenth centuries. The movement produced some significant poetry. (See *In Quest of the 'Miracle Stag': The Poetry of Hungary*. Ed. Adam Makkai. Chicago and Budapest: Atlantis-Centaur, M. Szivárvány and Corvina, 1996. 99–110.)

Azt kell-e hinnünk, hogy a nemzeti poézis már régen felemelkedvén, azt nem többé a mai pórnépnél, hanem a nemzet magasb míveltségű rendében fogjuk fellelni? Lépjünk vissza egy kevéssé, s keressük az utat, melyen poézisünk az írói nyelvbe által menvén, megnemesedhetett. Az *Emlékezzünk régiekről* tűnik legelőszer szemünkbe, mely valóban minden meztelensége[34] mellett is nem érdemel megvetést, mert lépcsővé tétethetett a magosb emelkedésre vágyónak. A reformáció kora jön sorba, s látunk nép számára készült énekeket, melyek a költés határain kívül feküsznek. A mohácsi vészt közel érő kor számos történeti verseket hagyott reánk, melyeknek az akkori hőstettek nyújtottak alkalmat; nagy nevek ragyognak azokban, de Tinódi s egykorúi nem tevének egyebet, mint az tenne, ki újságleveleket foglalna versekbe. Ki nem kénytelen megvallani, hogy maga a rómaiaktól tanult, legalább mitológiát, és ovidiusi deskripció-viszketeget, és eláradozást tanult Gyöngyösi sem adott a nemzetnek semmit, ami való poétai nevet érdemeljen? Az ő tárgyai többnyire hazaiak, de nem csak hogy a lelketlen előterjesztés miatt hevületbe nem hoznak, hanem azonfelül a sok római tudománynál fogva a nemzetiség köréből kicsaponganak. [...] Melyik magyar találhassa fel magát saját nemzetiségében, ha nemcsak az idegen mitológia képeire, hanem ez vagy amaz római verselőnek ez vagy amaz sorában álló ez vagy amaz névre is emlékeznie kell, ha poétáját érteni akarja? A görög költő csak kitisztult érzést ízléssel párosulva kíván hazája fiától, hogy lelkére hasson dalával: nekünk ellenben antiquáriusi tudományt kell szereznünk, hogy költőnket olvashassuk; s ha megértettük is, minő behatást tehet reánk a mitológiának világa, mely nekünk csak valamely allegóriai tarka festés gyanánt jelen meg? Valljuk meg, hogy nem jó úton kezdettünk a rómaiaktól tanulni. Ahelyett, hogy segédöknél fogva tulajdon körünkben emelkedtünk volna, szolgai követésre hajlottunk; ahelyet hogy az ő szellemüket magunkba szívtuk és saját világunkban sajátunkká tettük volna, az ő világokba költöztünk által; de ott egészen fel nem találhatván magunkat, honunk felé visszapillongunk,[35] s örökre megoszlott képzelettel itt is, ott is idegenek maradunk. Nem nyilván van-e, hogy a való nemzeti költésnek csak a nemzet kebelében lehet, s kell szárnyára kelnie? Az idegen tűznél gyújtott fény a nemzetnek csak homály közül sugárzik.

Azonban úgy akarta a sors, hogy a magyar költés szelleme idegen világból lengjen által hozzánk; s minekutána ez a római néppel is megtörtént, szükség-e pirulnunk? [...]

A poézis minden nemei közt [a játékszíni költés] áll a közönséges életkörrel legegyenesb s legkönnyebben érezhető öszvefüggésben. Az eposz és líra mind ketten életet hagynak szemeink előtt lebegni, de ezen élet a poétával együtt tűnik fel, s bizonyos távolságban, bizonyos emelkedésben áll felettünk: a drámából ki kell a poétának tűnnie,[36] mellettünk és körülöttünk ömledez a megnemesített élet, s csalatásunk a való színét kapván meg, kikelni látszunk önmagunkból, s észrevétlenül a költő világába vegyülünk. Boldog költő, ki bennünket ily kellemes csalódásba rengethet által, s kinek világából hideg érdeklések, kellemetlen öszveütközés, vagy idegenbe tévedezés vissza nem taszítják képzetinket! Az ő műveiben alkotná öszve magát azon való költői tartomány, melyben a magosított nemzetiség tulajdon hazáját fellelné; az ő műveiben ölelkeznék a hősi szép kor a jelenvalóval, emberiség érzelme a hazafisággal; mi pedig emlékezet és részvétel

---

[34] itt: dísztelensége, egyszerűsége
[35] visszapillantunk, visszatekintünk, visszanézünk
[36] A drámában a közvetlen költői jelenlétnek el kell tűnnie, vagy legalább kisebbnek kell lennie, mint az eposz és a líra esetében.

Are we to believe that national poetry has long since been elevated and that we shall no longer find it among the common people but at the more highly cultivated level of the nation? Let us go back a little and look for the way in which our poetry entered literary language and was ennobled. The first thing to come to mind is *Emlékezzünk régiekről*,[37] which, for all its lack of elegance, does not deserve to be scorned because it offered a stairway for those so desiring to ascend. Follows the age of Reformation, and we see songs written for the people which lie outside the bounds of poetry. The period shortly following the disaster of Mohács[38] has left us numerous historical verses for which the heroic deeds of the day provided material; great names shine in them, but Tinódi[39] and his contemporaries did no more than one that versified news-reports. Who is not forced to confess that Gyöngyösi[40]himself, who learnt from the Romans at least mythology, an Ovidian urge to describe and a tendency to exaggeration, gave to the nation nothing worthy of the name of poetry? His subjects are for the most part Hungarian, but they fail to warm the heart not so much because of spiritless presentation as because, in addition, they stray from the national sphere by virtue of preoccupation with things Roman. [. . .] What Hungarian can feel at home in his own nationality if he has to remember not only the images of foreign mythology, but this or that name in this or that line of this or that Roman poetaster when he wishes to understand his poet? The Greek poet requires the son of his fatherland to have nothing more than unimpaired feeling coupled with taste if he is to touch his soul with his song; we, on the other hand, have to acquire the erudition of the antiquary to read our poet; and even if we have understood him, what effect can the world of mythology have on us if it appears as a multicoloured allegorical painting? Let us confess that we have not done well in studying the Romans. Instead of elevating ourselves within our own world with their assistance we have bowed to them in servile imitation; instead of breathing their spirit into ourselves and making them ours in our own world, we have removed into theirs; but feeling ourselves quite out of place there we have glanced back home and are left strangers both here and there with imagination eternally divided. Is it not obvious that true national poetry can and must rise on its wings only in the bosom of the nation? The lamp lit at a foreign flame shines only dimly for the nation.

Fate has, however, willed that the spirit of Hungarian poetry shall flutter hither from an alien world; and as that happened to the Roman people too, must we blush? [. . .]

Of all the varieties of poetry, dramatic verse stands most on a level with the everyday life, and in the most easily perceived connection to it. Both epic and lyric verse make life soar before our eyes, but that life, together with the poet, appears at a certain distance, a certain elevation above us; the poet must vanish from the drama and ennobled life will flood beside and around us, and as our deception takes on the colour of reality we seem to rise out of ourselves and imperceptibly become caught up in the poet's world. Happy the poet, who can shake us into so pleasant a deceit, and from whose world neither cold interest, unpleasant shocks or becoming lost among things alien drag back our imagination! In his works that true poetic land would be created in which exalted nationality would find its real home; in his world the fine heroic age would enfold the present day, the

---

[37] 'Let us remember men of old.' It is the opening line of Demeter Csáti's poem (from around 1526), which tells the story how Árpád conquered the land of Hungary.

[38] Mohács a town about 200kms south of Budapest is where the Turks inflicted a tragic defeat on the Hungarian army in 29 August 1526. This catastrophe later led to the disintegration of the country.

[39] Sebestyén Tinódi 'the Lutenist' (*c.*1505–1556), a poet who is most famous for his versified war chronicles. (See *In Quest of the 'Miracle Stag': The Poetry of Hungary*. Ed. Adam Makkai. Chicago and Budapest: Atlantis-Centaur, M. Szivárvány and Corvina, 1996. 57–64.)

[40] István Gyöngyösi (1629–1704), an epic poet who gained much popularity in Hungary.

által vissza-visszakapatván megőriztetnénk azon veszedelemtől, hogy a szüntelen előre és messzebb távozás alatt eredeti színeinket lassanként elveszessük, s kebelünk többé felmelegedni ne tudhasson.

[…]

[First published: Élet és Literatúra, 1826. 15–59. Modern edition: Kölcsey, Ferenc, Kölcsey Ferenc összes művei, 3 vols. Budapest: Szépirodalmi, 1960, vol. 1. 490–523.]

I.f.2. PETŐFI SÁNDOR, *Levél Arany Jánoshoz, Pest, 1847. február 4.* (Részlet)

Üdvezlem Önt! Ma olvastam a *Toldit*, […] minél hamarabb akarom Önnek tudtára adni azon meglepetést, azon örömet, azon elragadtatást, melyet műve költött bennem. Hiába, a népköltészet az igazi költészet. Legyünk rajta, hogy ezt tegyük uralkodóvá! Ha a nép uralkodni fog a költészetben, közel áll ahhoz, hogy a politikában is uralkodjék, s ez a század föladata, ezt kivívni célja minden nemes kebelnek, ki megsokalta már látni, mint mártírkodnak milliók, hogy egypár ezren henyélhessenek és élvezzenek. Égbe a népet, pokolba az arisztokráciát! […]

[Critical edition: Petőfi, Sándor, Petőfi Sándor összes művei, vol. 7, Petőfi Sándor levelezése. Eds József Kiss and Nyilassy, V. Vilma. Budapest: Akadémiai, 1964. 41–42]

I.f.3. SÜKEI KÁROLY, *Irodalmi ellenőr* (Reszletek)

Előtájékozás

[…] Mi a legújabb jelenkor gyermekei vagyunk, és szeretjük azt bűneiben is. Mert úgy vétkezni, miként a jelenkor gyermekei tudnak, csak a szép hellén világ dicső istenei valának képesek.

Igen! mi nem akarjuk a szenvedélyt, mint valami rakoncátlan ebet, pórázra fűzni – hogy elvégre is teljes szellemi rugalmatlanság gyáva bilincseiben élő halottak legyünk –, sőt inkább szabadon eresztve megszelídítjük a szépnek dicső harmóniája által; s erkölcsi fönségünk érzetében, fölülemelkedve a puszta törvény vakondtúrásán, nem akarunk azon egykori quakerhez hasonlítani, ki a legszebb fügeleveletlen, hitregei festményeket összevásárolván – azokat csupa szűzies érzésből elégette.

Szeretjük pedig a jelenkort rontva teremtő irányú romantikájával; szeretjük szabadszelleműségét, mely megdönti azon általánosságokat, melyek a természetet és életet anticipáló szemlélődés útján lőnek ténylegesítve; szeretjük filozófiáját a humorisztika vagy – ha éppen magatoknak úgy tetszik – az újdonászati modor burleszk öltözetében is.

Hódolunk pedig ezen iránynak egyfelül azért, mert bennünk, a fiatalságban fejlődött az idő kezdetén eszmei öntudatosságra. A fiatalság eszméi pedig örökkévalók.

Irányunk központja a népszellem.

És ha a művészet nap, mely látköre tárgyaiból gyűjti a világosság sugarait, úgy e látkörnek a nyilvános népéletnek kell lenni. Annyival is inkább, mert a világszellem történeti fejlődése rányomta a népélet nyilatkozataira az organikai szükségesség bélyegét, s vonjátok el a művészetet erről a térről, mint Herkules által földanyjától elszakasztott Anteusz óriás, elveszti minden erejét.

feeling of humanity embrace patriotism; we, however, being brought back time and again by memory and participation would be guarded from the danger of gradually losing our original colours through constant to-ing and fro-ing, and of our hearts being no longer capable of feeling warmth.

[. . .]

[Translated by Bernard Adams]

I.f.2. SÁNDOR PETŐFI,[41] from *A Letter to János Arany,*[42] *Pest, 4 February 1847*

Greetings! Today I have been reading *Toldi*[43] [. . .] and I wish to convey to you as quickly as possible the surprise, the pleasure, the delight which your work has aroused in me. Folk poetry is indeed the true poetry. Let us set about making it supreme! If the people rules in poetry the day cannot be far off when it will rule in politics too, and that is the task of the age, the achievement of which is the aim of every noble breast that is sickened to see millions afflicted so that a few thousand may lead lives of ease and pleasure. To heaven with the people, to hell with the aristocracy! [. . .]

[Translated by Bernard Adams]

I.f.3. KÁROLY SÜKEI,[44] from *Literary Auditor*

Introduction

[. . .] We are children of the latest present age and love it, faults and all. Because only the glorious gods of the beautiful Hellenic world have been capable of offending like the children of the present age.

Yes! We do not intend to hold passion on the leash, like some unruly dog – so as finally to become living dead in the cowardly fetters of total spiritual rigidity – indeed, we will rather let it run free and train it by the glorious harmony of the beautiful; and sensible of our moral superiority, rising above the molehill of sterile law, we do not intend to resemble that Quaker of old who purchased the finest figleaf-free mythological paintings and burned them simply out of a sense of propriety.

But we love the present age and the wrecking-creating tendency of its romanticism; we love its free-spiritedness, which shatters those generalities that have become established by anticipating nature and life; we love its philosophy, even in the guise of humour – or, if you prefer – modern-style burlesque.

We follow this tendency, however, because it has developed in us, the youth, to a conceptual self-awareness. And the concepts of the young are eternal.

The focal point of our tendency is the spirit of the people.

And if art is a sun which gathers rays of brightness from objects in its field of vision, so this field of vision must be the evident life of the people. All the more so as the historical development of the spirit of the world has impressed upon the declarations of the life of the people the seal of organic necessity, and if you take art away from this sphere, like Anteus the giant when lifted from Mother Earth by Hercules, it loses all its strength.

---

[41] Sándor Petőfi (1823–1849), poet who was a key figure in the revolution of 1848.
[42] János Arany (1817–1882), poet, critic, editor and translator.
[43] *Toldi*, the first part of the folk epic trilogy by János Arany was written in 1846.
[44] Károly Sükei (1824–1845), critic, poet and translator. For four months (July–October) in 1847 he published *A Literary Auditor*, a critical column in the weekly magazine *Életképek*.

Látjuk a népszellemet cselekvő életre ébredni; látjuk, hogy az akaraté a kezdeményezés, és ez akarat új eget, új földet teremtő erőhatályának szimbolikája nekünk – mitológiánk.

Kezdetben vala az ige, mondja az evangélista; kezdetben vala a szerelem, mondja korunk legnagyobb lángelméje; kezdetben vala az akarat, vagy ha magatoknak jobban tetszik – a tetterő, hirdetjük mi.

Azzal ugyanis, ha őseink hitregéjének idő viharai által szétszaggatott jelkép-cafrangjait búvárkodva keresitek mindenfelé, hogy abból aztán madárperspektíven keresztül betűzzétek ki a szellemet – nem fogjátok soha a költészet központját megalapítani. El kell ismernetek – vagy akarjátok, vagy nem – a népszellem minden oldalú kijelentéseit ténylegesnek, emeljétek ezeket az uralkodó világnézeti egység harmóniájára, teremtsetek a harmóniás egység törvényei szerint; s így, és csak így fog a magyar nemzeti szépirodalom idő folytával kifejlődni.

Hagyjatok föl pedig minden amolyan „világirodalom"-féle üres szavak bálványozásával. Éppen úgy nem lehet ezt jelenkorunkban a való élet szempontjából érteni, miként a világpolgárság eszméjét.

Higgyétek el, hogy míg önmagatokat [az] előadott szempontból nem tudjátok tájékozni, addig minden, általános elméletek nyomán keletkezett, s a míveltség fölött álló teremtés manifesztációira erőszakolt kritika hasztalan, s legföllebb is csak a szó sztereotip értelmében vett tudást segíti elő, mi egyébiránt – önmagában véve – hogy mennyire szükséges, mennyire nem, attól függ: minő szempontból fogjuk föl az emberiség jelenlegi törekvéseinek történetfilozófiáját. [...]

Következetlenség

[...] [A]z esztétikusok, jelesen a német szemlélődő filozófia iskolájához tartozók – igen kevés kivétellel – az esztétikát a filozófia elvont formáiba szorítják, s nem tudván azt, hogy a szépet csupán szép által lehet kimagyarázni, sejtelmetlen és költőietlen iskolás értelmezéseikkel igen barbár módra bántak az esztétikával [...].

Egyébiránt hiábavaló minden esztétizálás, míg a *szépnek* érzése nemzeti életükből határozott világnézet alapján ki nem fejlődik. Itt pedig a *nemzeti jellem* lévén a legelső föltétel, hiábavaló mindig és mindig *ízlésről* beszélni, mert a szépirodalmat nem csupán ízlés, sőt inkább teremtő erő és géniusz éltetik. – E szempontból nagy anomáliát követett el a kritika. Petőfivel s legújabban Jósika Miklóssal; ugyanis ahelyett, hogy a költői szellem új fázisaiba itt és amott igyekezett volna magát bele találni: saját iskolai értelmezései torzító szemüvegén keresztül ugyancsak prózai boncolás volt egész eljárása. [...]

Rendszeresség

A nép szava, isten szava.

Ha szükség volna reá: tudnók e tételt az általános elvszerűség szempontjából is fejtegetni; tudnánk e részben, minden szubjektív ösztönszerűségen fölül álló tekintélyeket idézni, minők pl. Arisztotelész és Goethe; de erre semmi szükség, mert csak a világszellem történeti fejlődésének legújabb fázisát kell megtekintenünk, hogy meggyőződhessünk róla, miszerint a nép szava, isten szava.

Ugyanis a közép- és újkorban tekintély s egyéni szellem túlnyomóságot gyakoroltak a közszellem fölött; de a legújabb jelenkorban tekintély s egyéni nagyságok kezdeményezése megszűnt, és a tömegé az, ami kezdődik.

We see the spirit of the people waking to active life; we see that the initiative belongs to the will, and that this will is to us the symbol of a force that will create a new heaven and a new earth – our mythology.

In the beginning was the Word, says the Evangelist; in the beginning was love, says the greatest genius of our age; what we proclaim is that in the beginning was will, or, if you prefer, energy.

That is to say, you will never establish the central point of poetry if you rummage in the symbol-trappings, scattered by the ravages of time, of our ancestors' mythology and search around to make out there the spirit, as from a bird's-eye view. You will have to admit – whether you will or no – that the manifold revelations of the spirit of the people are genuine, elevate them to the harmony of the ruling ideological concord and create in accordance with the laws of the harmonious whole; thus, and only thus, will Hungarian national literature develop with the passage of time.

Give up the idolatry of such empty words as 'world literature'. From the point of view of real life in our present age this cannot be understood any more than the concept of world citizenship.

Believe that, until you get your bearings from the said point, any critique based on the general ideas and forced on revelations of creation in precedence over culture is profitless, and at the most advances knowledge only in the stereotype sense of the word, which otherwise – taken in itself, however necessary or not – depends on the point of view from which we accept the historical philosophy of the present endeavours of humanity. [. . .]

Inconsistency

[. . .] [T]he aestheticians, in particular those belonging to the German school of contemplative philosophy – with very few exceptions – force aesthetics into the abstract forms of philosophy, do not know that the beautiful can only be explained by means of the beautiful, deal with aesthetics in a most barbarous manner with scholastic interpretations lacking insight and poetic quality [. . .].

Moreover, all aestheticising is futile, as the feeling of the *beautiful* is not derived from the life of the nation on the basis of a precise world-view. Here, however, the *national character* is the first condition, and it is futile to be for ever talking about *taste*, because it is not merely taste that gives life to literature, but rather creative power and genius. From that point of view criticism has been guilty of a great anomaly in the case of Petőfi and, most recently, Miklós Jósika;[45] that is to say, instead of making the effort to find its way into the new phases of the poetic spirit, its whole procedure has been a prosaic dissection through a distorting lens of interpretations of its own school. [. . .]

Regularity

The word of the people is the word of God.

If there were need, we could analyse this thesis from the point of view of general principle; we could, in this respect, quote authorities who are above all subjective instinctivity, such as Aristotle and Goethe; but there is no need of that, because we have only to consider the latest phase of the historical development of the spirit of the world to be convinced that the word of the people is the word of God.

That is to say, in medieval and modern times authority and individual mind dominated the public mind; in the most recent times, however, the supremacy of authority and the individual mind is fading, and that of the masses is coming in.

---

45 Miklós Jósika (1794–1865), a popular and prolific novel writer.

Midőn a tömeg kezdeményez, ott eszme helyett tény uralkodik; ott már a nemen túl vagyunk, és kezdődik az igen; ott az egyéni értelem alkotta rendszerek hatalmán mindig fölül áll a tényező akarat. Hagyjatok föl tehát a szoros rendszeresség ok nélküli bálványozásával. Ugyanis napjainkban kész rendszerrel előállni akarni annyi, mint kilépni az alakuló korszellem sodró folyamából. Mert azon világnézet, mit eddigelé a bevégzett, és jelesen a német hipotetikus rendszerek ténylegesítettek, éppen úgy be van fejezve jelenleg Hegelben, mint volt hajdan Arisztotelészben a hellén világ, s ami ezután következik, az csupán e rendszerek kritikája – `fölbomlás lehet.

Innen egy vagy más irányt, művészetben éppen úgy, mint szellemünk egyéb emanációjában nem az határoz, ha vajon van-e benne rendszeresség vagy nincs, hanem az, ha vajon az uralkodó közszellem igaz valódiságának konkrét alkatrésze-e, vagy pedig nem. Jelenleg nem az a kérdés: ideál vagy reál, empíria vagy spekuláció, hanem az: vajon München és Berlin, vagy Düsseldorf és Párizs?

Innen mi, kik a tény szempontjából indulunk ki, igen helyesnek találjuk, hogy korunkban a politika túlnyomó a művészet fölött. S azzal, hogy ez általános irányban a rendszeresség nem kézzel fogható, azzal nem sokat törődünk, mert hisszük, hogy az elvet meg fogjuk találni majd az eljárás végén, midőn egy új organizáció a nemzeti és népi elem egységében minden egyebet fölolvaszt.

Ez álláspontról minden uralkodó egyoldalúságot meg lehet fejteni. Ugyanis az általános történeti fejlődés e mondottuk stádiumában, a tetté alakulandó eszmék valódi élete bizonyos sajátszerű korlátoltságban jelenik meg mindig és mindenütt; és ilyszerű esetben a világért sem nemlegesítő kritika teendő, hanem az, hogy az irányt, különnemű sajátos szétágazásaiban – szintetikus úton – a szabad állapotok harmóniájára emeljük.

Tudjuk a frank romantikáról, hogy a júliusi forradalom előtt – nem rázhatván le magáról teljesen a középkor lebernyegét – nem volt megtisztulva a különnemű pártelemektől, és így sok tekintetben korlátolt vala; de miután nem csupán az érzés és eszme, hanem egyszersmind a tény szempontjából is igyekezett kategorikus helyet foglalni el; – azóta mint határozott világszemlélet nyilvánítja magát szellemünk konkrét tüneményeiben.

Ha pedig saját körünkben vizsgálódunk, úgy fogjuk találni, hogy korunk fönnebb vázolt iránya nemzetünk egyéni jellemével nagyon megegyezik. A magyar nem szemlélődő nemzet; egyetlen eszme van, mit föltétlenül és határozottan elfogad – s melyen túl reá nézve megszűnt a szemlélődő értelem, és kezdődik a cselekvő akarat –, és ez az eszme a nemzetiség. És e tekintetben teljesen hasonlítunk az angolokhoz, kik egyedül az alkotmányos szabadság eszméjét fogadják el mint föltétlent és állandót, s innen van, hogy az irodalom sem nálunk, sem Angliában nincs főhatalmasságnak elismerve.

E mondottak nyomán nemcsak hogy szabad, sőt inkább kategorice szükséges a nemzeti költőknek politikai tekintetben átellenes viszonyba jutni egymással – különben hatásra egyáltalában nem számíthatnak.

Azt pedig egyáltalában ne higgyétek, hogy ezáltal a tisztán emberi kockáztatva van. Ugyanis, mi a tisztán emberi? A szabadság. S mi a szabadság egyéb, mint az embernek azon saját cselekvősége, melyre támaszkodva teremti önmagát és saját világát? Itt pedig a cselekvő értelem s értelmes cselekvés különböznek egymástól, s ahelyett, hogy értelmünk világába vonulva az ember éppen a cselekvéstől akarjuk szabaddá tenni, úgy állítjuk elő a tisztán emberit, ha az egyénben a cselekvő embert valósítjuk.

[*First published: Életképek, vol. 2. 4 July 1847. 20–21; 18 July. 87; 8 August. 182. Modern edition: Szöveggyűjtemény a forradalom és szabadságharc korának irodalmából, 2 vols, eds Kerényi, Ferenc and Tamás, Anna. Budapest: Tankönyvkiadó, 1980, vol. 1. 391–395*]

When the masses take the initiative fact will rule instead of thought; we are now beyond 'no' and 'yes' is beginning; there positive will always prevail over the power of the systems established by the individual intellect.

So give up the groundless idolatry of close orderliness. That is, in our day to wish to come forward with a ready system is tantamount to stepping out of the swirling stream of the inchoate spirit of the age. For that world-view which hitherto the exhausted, and particularly the German, hypothetical systems practised has now reached its climax in Hegel, just as the Hellenic world in time gone by did in Aristotle, and what follows can only be a critique i.e. the collapse of those systems.

From this point, in art as in other emanations of the mind, the tone will be decided not by whether there is or is not orderliness in it, but by whether or not it is a genuine constituent of the true reality of the dominant public mind. At present the question is not ideal or real, empiricism or speculation, but is it to be Munich and Berlin, or Düsseldorf and Paris?

Hence we, who start out from the point of view of fact, find it perfectly correct that in our age politics predominates over art. And we are not greatly concerned that orderliness is not manifest in that general tendency, because we believe that we shall find principle at the end of the process, when the new organisation will dissolve everything else in the unity of national and popular mind.

From that standpoint all dominant bias can be explained. That is, at the stage of general development described above the real life of ideas becoming deeds appears at all times and in all places in a certain characteristic restrictedness; and in such a case negative criticism is not to be offered at any price, but let us raise the tendency in its own divergent proliferation – by a synthetic way – to the harmony of free conditions.

We know about the French Romantic, that before the July revolution – having been unable to shake completely off the cloak of the Middle Ages – it was not free of a range of factions and so in many respects was restricted; but after it made the effort to take a precise place in terms of not only feeling and ideas but also of fact – since then it has revealed itself as a precise world-view among the clear visions of our minds.

If, however, we look around in our own sphere we shall find that the tendency of our age as outlined above is very much in keeping with the individual character of our nation. The Hungarian is not a contemplative nation; it has a single idea, which it holds unconditionally and decisively – and beyond which, as far as it is concerned, contemplative intellect ends and active will begins – and that idea is nationhood. And in this respect we are completely like the English, who alone hold the concept of constitutional liberty as unconditional and permanent, and hence neither in Hungary nor in England is literature recognised as a supreme power.

In view of the foregoing it is not only permissible, it is indeed rather categorically necessary for the nation's poets, as regards politics, to form an opposition – otherwise they cannot count on exercising any influence at all.

Do not, however, believe at all that by this the purely human will be jeopardised. Actually, what is the 'purely human'? Liberty. And what is liberty but a man's own activity on which he relies to create himself and his world? Here, however, active intelligence and intelligent activity are distinct one from the other, and instead of withdrawing into the world of our intellect and wishing to free man from action, let us so produce the purely human as to realise the man of action in the individual.

[*Translated by Bernard Adams*]

g. ITALIANO

I.g.1. GIOVANNI BERCHET, *Lettera semiseria di Grisostomo al suo figliuolo*

Il Bürger portava opinione che «la sola vera poesia fosse la popolare». Quindi egli studiò di derivare i suoi poemi quasi sempre da fonti conosciute, e di proporzionarli poi sempre con tutti i mezzi dell'arte alla concezione del popolo. Anche delle composizioni che ti mando oggi tradotte, l'argomento della prima è ricavato da una tradizione volgare; quello della seconda è inventato, imitando le tradizioni comuni in Germania; il che vedremo in seguito piú distesamente. Anche in entrambi questi componimenti v'ha una certa semplicità di narrazione che manifesta nel poeta il proponimento di gradire alla moltitudine.

Forse il Bürger, com'è destino talvolta degli uomini d'alto ingegno, trascorreva in quella sua teoria agli estremi. Ma perché i soli uomini d'alto ingegno sanno poi di per sé stessi ritenersene giudiziosamente nella pratica, noi, leggendo i versi del Bürger, confessiamo che neppure il dotto vi scapita, né ha ragione di dolersi del poeta. L'opinione nondimeno che la poesia debba essere popolare non albergò solamente presso del Bürger; ma a lei s'accostarono pur molto anche gli altri poeti sommi d'una parte della Germania. Né io credo d'ingannarmi dicendo ch'ella pende assai nel vero. E se, applicandola alla storia dell'arte e pigliandola per codice nel far giudizio delle opere dei poeti che furono, ella può sembrare troppo avventata – giacché al Petrarca, a modo d'esempio, ed al Parini, benché, rade volte popolari, bisogna, pur fare di cappello – parmi che, considerandola come consiglio a' poeti che sono ed ammettendola con discrezione, ella sia santissima. E dico così, non per riverenza servile a' Tedeschi ed agli Inglesi, ma per libero amore dell'arte e per desiderio che tu, nascente poeta d'Italia, non abbia a dare nelle solite secche che da qualche tempo in qua impediscono il corso agli intelletti e trasmutano la poesia in matrona degli sbadigli.

Questa è la precipua cagione per la quale ho determinato che tu smetta i libri del Blair, del Villa e de' loro consorti, tosto che la barba sul mento darà indizio di senno in te più maturo. Allora avrai da me danaro per comperartene altri, come a dire del *Vico*, del *Burke*, del *Lessing*, del *Bouterwek*, dello *Schiller*, del *Beccaria*, di *Madama de Staël*, dello *Schlegel* e d'altri che fin qui hanno pensate e scritte cose appartenenti alla *Estetica*: né il *Platone in Italia* del Consigliere Cuoco sarà l'ultimo dei doni ch'io ti farò.

[…]

Tutti gli uomini, da Adamo in giù fino al calzolaio che ci fa i begli stivali, hanno nel fondo dell'anima una tendenza alla Poesia. Questa tendenza, che in pochissimi è attiva, negli altri non è che passiva; non è che una corda che risponde con simpatiche oscillazioni al tocco della prima. La natura, versando a piene mani i suoi doni nell'animo di que' rari individui ai quali ella concede la tendenza poetica attiva, pare che si compiaccia di crearli differenti affatto dagli altri uomini in mezzo a cui li fa nascere. Di qui le antiche favole sulla quasi divina origine de' poeti, e gli antichi pregiudizi sui miracoli loro, e l'«*est Deus in nobis*». Di qui il più vero dettato di tutti i filosofi; che i Poeti fanno classe a parte, e non sono cittadini di una sola società ma dell'intero universo. E per verità chi misurasse la sapienza delle nazioni dalla eccellenza de' loro poeti, parmi che non iscandaglierebbe da savio. Né savio terrei chi nelle dispute letterarie introducesse i rancori e le rivalità nazionali. Omero, Shakespeare, il Calderon, il Camoens, il Racine, lo Schiller per me sono italiani di patria tanto quanto Dante, l'Ariosto e l'Alfieri.

La repubblica delle lettere non è che una, e i poeti ne sono concittadini tutti indistintamente. La predilezione con cui ciascheduno di essi guarda quel tratto di terra ove nacque, quella lin-

g. ITALIAN

I.g.1. GIOVANNI BERCHET, from *Semi-serious Letter* from *Grisostomo to His Son*

Bürger was of the opinion that 'the only true poetry was popular poetry'. Therefore he almost always sought to derive his poems from known sources, and to adjust them to the views of the people using all artistic methods. Also in the translated compositions that I give you today, the subject of the first is drawn from a vulgar tradition; that of the second is invented, imitating the common traditions in Germany; the reason for this we will see in more detail later. Also together these components provide a certain simplicity of narration that manifests in the poet the resolution to appeal to the masses.

Maybe Bürger, as is sometimes the destiny of men of high intelligence, brought his theory to its limits. But why do only men of great intelligence know how to consider themselves judicious in practice, reading the verses of Bürger, we confess that not even the learned man is unaffected and neither has the poet a right to lament. Nevertheless the opinion that poetry should be popular is harboured not only by Bürger; but is also supported by the other great poets of a certain part of Germany. Neither do I believe that I am deceiving myself by saying that it [this opinion] leans very much towards the truth. And if, applying it to the history of art and taking it as a system by which to judge the works of poets of the past, – it can seem too rash because if applied to Petrarch, for example, and to Parini, who even if rarely popular, must be acknowledged and saluted – it seems to me that, considering this opinion as advice to actual poets and admitting it with discretion, it is sacred. And I say this, not out of servile reverence towards the Germans and the English, but out of unrestrained love of art and a desire that you, a rising poet of Italy, will not give in to the usual dry shallowness which has for some time impeded the course of the intellectuals and transformed poetry into a matron of yawning.

This is the principle reason for which I determined that you stop reading the books of Blair, of Villa and of their consorts, as soon as the beard on your chin gives a sign of more mature judgment in you. At that point you will have money from me to buy others, like something by *Vico*, by *Burke*, by *Lessing*, by *Bouterwek*, by *Schiller*, by *Beccaria*, by *Madame de Staël*, by *Schlegel* and others who up to now have thought and written material belonging to the school of *Esthetics*: neither will *Platone in Italia* by Consigliere Cuoco be the last of the gifts which I will give you.

[. . .]

All men, from Adam down to the shoemaker who makes us beautiful boots, have in the depths of their soul a tendency towards Poetry. This tendency, which is active in only very few, and in others is only passive; is only a chord that responds with pleasant oscillation to the first touch. It seems that Nature, generously pouring its gifts into the soul of those rare individuals to whom it concedes the active poetic tendency, satisfies herself in creating them completely different to the other men in whose midst they are born. Thus arise the old fairytales about the almost divine origin of poets, and the ancient superstitions about their miracles, and the 'est Deus in nobis'. Thus arises the truest dictate of all the philosophers; that Poets are a class apart, and are not citizens of only one society but of the entire universe. And truly it seems to me that whoever would measure the wisdom of nations by the excellence of their poets would not create scandal amongst the wise. Neither would I consider wise the person who who introduces rancour and national rivalry in literary disputes. Homer, Shakespeare, Calderon, Camoens, Racine, Schiller are for me as much Italians as are Dante, Ariosto and Alfieri.

gua che da fanciullo imparò, non nuoce mai, né alla energia dell'amore che il vero poeta consacra per istinto dell'arte sua a tutta insieme la umana razza, né alla intensa volontà, per la quale egli studia colle opere sue di provvedere al diletto ed alla educazione di tutta insieme l'umana razza. Però questo amore universale, che governa l'intenzione de' poeti, mette universalmente nella coscienza degli uomini l'obbligo della gratitudine e del rispetto; e nessuna occasione politica può sciogliere noi da questo sacro dovere. Fin anche l'ira della guerra rispetta la tomba d'Omero e la casa di Pindaro.

Il poeta, dunque, sbalza fuori dalle mani della natura in ogni tempo, in ogni luogo. Ma per quanto esimio egli sia, non arriverà mai a scuotere fortemente l'animo de' lettori suoi, né mai potrà ritrarne alto e sentito applauso, se questi non sono ricchi anch'essi della tendenza poetica passiva. Ora siffatta disposizione degli animi umani, quantunque universale, non è in tutti gli uomini egualmente squisita.

[…]

Che s'egli [il poeta] considera che la sua nazione non la compongono que' dugento che gli stanno intorno nelle veglie o ne' conviti; se egli ha mente a questo, che mille e mille famiglie pensano, leggono, scrivono, piangono, fremono, e sentono le passioni tutte, senza pure avere un nome ne' teatri, può essere che a lui si schiarisca innanzi un altro orizzonte; può essere che egli venga accostandosi ad altri pensieri ed a più vaste intenzioni.

[…]

La lode che al poeta viene da questa minima parte della sua nazione non può davvero farlo andare superbo; quindi anche il biasimo ch'ella sentenzia, non ha a mettergli grande spavento. La gente ch'egli cerca, i suoi veri lettori stanno a milioni nella terza classe. E questa, cred'io, deve il poeta moderno aver di mira, da questa deve farsi intendere, a questa deve studiar di piacere, s'egli bada al proprio interesse ed all'interesse vero dell'arte. Ed ecco come la sola vera poesia sia la popolare: salve le eccezioni sempre, come ho già detto; e salva sempre la discrezione ragionevole con cui questa regola vuole essere interpretata. Se i poeti moderni d'una parte della Germania menano tanto romore di sé in casa loro, e in tutte le contrade d'Europa, ciò è da ascriversi alla popolarità della poesia loro. E questa salutare direzione ch'eglino diedero all'arte fu suggerita loro dagli studi profondi fatti sul cuore umano, sullo scopo dell'arte, sulla storia di lei e sulle opere ch'ella in ogni secolo produsse: fu suggerita loro dalla divisione in *classica* e *romantica* ch'eglino immaginarono nella poesia.

(1816) [*Edizione di riferimento: I manifesti romantici del 1816 e gli scritti principali del «Conciliatore» sul Romanticismo, a cura di Carlo Calcaterra, Unione tipografico-editrice torinese, Torino, ristampa 1964*]

There is just one republic of the arts and all poets are, without exception, citizens of it. The fondness with which every one of them regards that tract of land where he was born, that language which he learned as a child, never interferes with either the energy of love which the true poet instinctively dedicates in his art to the whole human race, nor the intense will, with which he studies his works to provide for the delight and education of the whole of the human race. But this universal love that governs poets' intentions, universally gives men an obligation of gratitude and respect; and no political situation can release us from this sacred duty. Even the wrath of war respects Homer's tomb and Pindaro's house.

The poet, therefore, leaps out of the hands of nature in every age, in every place. But as much as he is esteemed, he will never succeed in vigorously shaking the souls of his readers, nor will he ever be able to gain lofty and sustained applause, if they are not also rich in the passive poetic tendency. Today such a disposition of the human spirit, however universal, is not equally refined in all men.

[...]

If he [the poet] takes into account that his nation is not just composed of those two hundred people who surround him at vigils and banquets; if he has this in mind, that thousands and thousands of families think, read, write, cry, tremble, and all feel the passions, without even having a reputation in the theatre, it may be that another horizon brightens in front of him; it may be that he is supported by different thoughts and broader intentions.

[...]

The praise that the poet receives from this small part of his nation cannot truly make him arrogant; therefore the disapproval that it also delivers cannot make him afraid. The people whom he seeks, his true readers, are to be found in their millions in the third class. And this [the third class] I believe, is what the modern poet, if he cares for his own interests and for the true interests of art, should have as his aim, to make himself understood by them, to seek to please them. And thus, the one true poetry is popular poetry; always save for the exceptions, as I have already said; and always allowing for the reasonable discretion with which this rule wishes to be interpreted. If the modern poets of a part of Germany create a lot of discussion about themselves at home, and in all quarters of Europe, it is to be attributed to the popularity of their poetry. And this healthy direction in which they lead art was suggested to them by profound studies done on the human heart, on the purpose of art, on its history and its works produced in every century: it was suggested to them by the *classical* and *romantic* divisions which they imagined existed in poetry.

(1816) [*Translated by Marayde O'Brien and Anne O'Connor*]

h. NORSK

I.h.1. JOHAN SEBASTIAN CAMMERMEYER WELHAVEN, 'Digtets Aand'

Hvad ei med Ord kan nævnes
i det rigeste Sprog,
det Uudsigelige
skal Digtet røbe dog.

Af Sprogets strenge Bygning,
af Tankeformers Baand
stiger en frigjort Tanke,
og den er Digtets Aand.

Den boede i Sjelen
før Strophens Liv blev til,
og Sprogets Malm er blevet
flydende ved dens Ild

Den gjennemtrænger Ordet
lig Duft, der stiger op
af Rosentræets Indre
i den aabnede Knop.

Og skjønt den ei kan præges
i Digtets Tankerad,
den er dog der tilstede
som Duft i Rosenblad.

Glem da den gamle Klage,
at ingen Kunst formaaer
at male Tankefunken,
hvoraf et Digt fremstaaer.

Thi hvis den kunde bindes
og sløres af paa Prent,
da var i denne Skranke
dens Liv og Virken endt.

Den vil med Aandens Frihed
svæve paa Ordets Klang;
den har i Digtets Rhythmer
en stakket Gjennemgang,

En Gjennemgang til Livet
i Læserens Bryst;
der vil den vaagne atter
i Sorrig eller Lyst,

Og næres og bevæges
og blive lig den Ild,

h. NORWEGIAN

I.h.1. JOHAN SEBASTIAN CAMMERMEYER WELHAVEN, 'The Soul of Poetry'

What else no speech could utter,
No power of words unseal,
The music of the poet
Availeth to reveal.

Out of the verse-form's texture
So rigorously wrought
A free-born spirit rises,
The poet's primal thought.

It dwelt long, long within him
In formless, vague desire,
And there the ore of language
Was melted by its fire.

It steeps the words like fragrance
That hearts of roses hold,
To breathe out in the springtime
When first their buds unfold.

And though 'tis never fettered
In logic's printed net,
Like perfume in the rose leaves
Its presence lingers yet.

Heed not the ancient adage,
When fools and dullards mourn
That art can never capture
The spark whence thought is born.

For if the printed symbol
Could hold it when 'twas caught,
Its force, its very being
Would quickly come to naught.

It craves the right of spirits
To float as in a trance,
And on the wings of rhythm
To find brief utterance,

To seek the reader's bosom
And there to live again
In re-awakened beauty
A life of joy or pain,

To grow there, to be nourished
Within its new-found nest,

der laae i Digtersjælen,
før Strophens Liv blev til.

Kun da bevarer Digtet
sin rette Tryllemagt,
det Uudsigelige
er da i Ordet lagt.

Betragt den stille Lykke,
der gjør en Digter varm,
mens Aanden i hans Sang
svæver fra Barm til Barm.

Lad kun hans Rygte hæves
mod Sky af Døgnets Vind,
det er dog ei den sande
Kvægelse for hans Sind.

Men naar hans Tankebilled
med eller uden Ry,
finder et lutret Indre,
og fødes der paany –

O, bring ham da et Budskap
om dette Aandens Bliv,
thi dermed er der lovet
hans Verk et evig Liv.

[1845] [*All Norwegian poems in this volume are from Ivar Havnevik. Ed.
Den store norske diktboken. Oslo: Pax, 2005*]

i. POLSKI

I.i.1. ADAM MICKIEWICZ, 'Oda do Młodości'

Bez serc, bez ducha, to szkieletów ludy;
Młodości! dodaj mi skrzydła!
Niech nad martwym wzlecę światem
W rajską dziedzinę ułudy:
Kędy zapał tworzy cudy,
Kędy zapał tworzy cudy,
I obleka w nadziei złote malowidła.

Niechaj, kogo wiek zamroczy,
Chyląc ku ziemi poradlone czoło,
Takie widzi świata koło,
Jakie tępymi zakreśla oczy.

Młodości! ty nad poziomy
Wylatuj, a okiem słońca
Ludzkości całe ogromy
Przeniknij z końca do końca.

And be once more the fire
That filled the poet's breast.

'Tis only there the radiance
of poetry is shed,
what else no speech could utter
may only there be said.

What rapture has the p
How fervent, deep and
While this his spirit pa
From breast to breast i

When transient tongue
And critics praise his a
He finds not there the
He longed for in his he

But when his glowing
Unknown to common
Finds out another bos
And springs once mor

O tell him that his spi
Once more is burning
That is his one assurar
His poem cannot die.

[1845] [*Translated by Charles Wharton Stork. Princeton UP, 1942*]

i. POLISH

I.i.1. ADAM MICKIEWICZ, 'Ode to Youth'

No heart, no soul, they're crowds of skeletons,
O Youth! Bestow upon me wings!
I'll rise over the world that's lifeless
To heaven's realm of rare illusions,
Where rapture creates dream visions,
Stirs up the flower of freshness,
And covers it with hope's golden paintings.

Let him who is dazed by year's sway,
His furrowed brow bending down low,
Of this world's sphere only as much know
As his feeble eyes can survey.

O Youth! Soar above the earth's flatness,
And with the sun's piercing eye,
All mankind's gigantic vastness
From end to end probe as you fly.

Patrz na dół – kędy wieczna mgła zaciemia
Obszar gnuśności zalany odmętem:
　To ziemia!

Patrz, jak nad jej wody trupie
Wzbił się jakiś płaz w skorupie.
Sam sobie sterem, żeglarzem, okrętem;
Goniąc za żywiołkami drobniejszego płazu,
To się wzbija, to w głąb wali:
Nie lgnie do niego fala ani on do fali;
A wtem jak bańka prysnął o szmat głazu.
Nikt nie znał jego życia, nie zna jego zguby:
　To samoluby!

Młodości! tobie nektar żywota
Natenczas słodki, gdy z innymi dzielę:
Serca niebieskie poi wesele,
Kiedy je razem nić powiąże złota.

Razem, młodzi przyjaciele!…
W szczęściu wszystkiego są wszystkich cele;
Jednością silni, rozumni szałem,
Razem, młodzi przyjaciele!…
I ten szczęśliwy, kto padł wśród zawodu,
Jeżeli poległym ciałem
Dał innym szczebel do sławy grodu.
Razem, młodzi przyjaciele!…
Choć droga stroma i śliska,
Gwałt i słabość bronią wchodu:
Gwałt niech się gwałtem odciska,
A ze słabością łamać uczmy się za młodu!

Dzieckiem w kolebce kto łeb urwał Hydrze,
Ten młody zdusi Centaury
Piekłu ofiarę wydrze,
Do nieba pójdzie po laury.
Łam sięgaj, gdzie wzrok nie sięga;
Łam, czego rozum nie złamie:
Młodości! orla twych lotów potęga,
Jako piorun twoje ramię.

Hej! ramię do ramienia! spólnymi łańcuchy
Opaszmy ziemskie kolisko!
Zestrzelmy myśli w jedno ognisko
I w jedno ognisko duchy! …
Dalej, bryło, z posad świata!
Nowymi cię pchniemy tory,
Aż opleśniałej zbywszy się kory,
Zielone przypomnisz lata.

Look down – where eternal mist darkens
The region of sloth in chaos afloat:
   That is the earth!

Look, how above its deathly waters
A shell-clad mollusk upward stirs,
It is its own rudder, sailor, and boat;
Pursuing water creatures of the smaller stock,
It rises now, now sinks in deep caves:
Waves do not cling to it, it does not cling to waves;
Then, like a bubble, bursts on a piece of rock:
None knew its life, none knows that it no more exists:
   Such are all egoists!

O Youth! Life's nectar is sweet whenever
I share it around with my fellow men:
Our hearts are nourished by mirth from heaven,
When a golden thread binds them together.

Together as one, my young friends!
In common happiness each man's goal blends;
Strong in accord, prudent yet with passion,
Together as one, my young friends!
And he is happy who in battle fell,
If only his body, death-stricken,
Gave other a rung to Fame's citadel.
Together as one, my young friends!
Although the road is slippery and steep,
Violence and weakness defend the fortress:
Let violence with violence meet,
And let's learn in youth to struggle with weakness!

A child in the crib that tore off Hydra's head,
In youth will strangle the Centaurs;
He will from hell wrest out the dead,
To heaven will go for laurels.
Reach far beyond the range of your sight,
Conquer what reason can't conquer:
Youth! Strong as an eagle in flight,
As a thunderbolt is your shoulder.

So shoulder to shoulder! As with a common chain
Let us encircle the whole planet!
Let's swiftly aim our thoughts at one target
And spirits into one domain!
Terrestrial globe, away from your base!
We will push you onto a new lane,
Until freed from moldy bark once again,
You will recall your verdant days.

A jako w krajach zamętu i nocy,
Skłóconych żywiołów waśnią,
Jednym «stań się» z bożej mocy
Świat rzeczy stanął na zrębie;
Szumią wichry, cieką głębie,
A gwiazdy błękit rozjaśnią –
W krajach ludzkości jeszcze noc głucha:
Żywioły chęci jeszcze są w wojnie:
Oto miłość ogniem zionie,
Wyjdzie z zamętu świat ducha:
Młodość go pocznie na swoim łonie,
A przyjaźń w wieczne skojarzy spojnie.

Pryskają nieczułe lody
I przesądy światło ćmiące;
Witaj jutrzenko swobody,
Zbawienia za tobą słońce!

(1820) [1827] [*Edited by Czesław Zgorzelski. Warszawa: Czytelnik, 1993*]

I.i.2. ADAM MICKIEWICZ, *Pan Tadeusz,* Księga III (fragment)

«Pani, rzekł Hrabia, racz mej śmiałości darować,
Przychodzę i przepraszać, i razem dziękować.
Przepraszać, że jej kroków śledziłem ukradkiem;
I dziękować, że byłem jej dumania świadkiem;
Tyle ją obraziłem! winienem jej tyle!
Przerwałem chwile dumań: winienem ci chwile
Natchnienia! chwile błogie! potępiaj człowieka,
Ale sztukmistrz twojego przebaczenia czeka!
Na wielem się odważył, na więcej odważę!
Sądź!» – tu ukląkł i podał swoje peizaże.

Telimena sądziła malowania proby
Tonem grzecznej, lecz sztukę znającej osoby;
Skąpa w pochwały, lecz nie szczędziła zachętu:
«Brawo, rzekła, winszuję, niemało talentu.
Tylko Pan nie zaniedbuj; szczególniej potrzeba
Szukać pięknej natury! O szczęśliwe nieba
Krajów włoskich! różowe Cezarów ogrody!
Wy, klasyczne Tyburu spadające wody!
I straszne Pauzylipu skaliste wydroże!
To, Hrabio, kraj malarzów! U nas, żal się Boże!
Dziecko muz, w Soplicowie oddane na mamki,
Umrze pewnie. Moi Hrabio, oprawię to w ramki
Albo w album umieszczę do rysunków zbiorku,
Które zewsząd skupiałam: mam ich dosyć w biorku».

As in the regions of chaos and night
Beset by the strife of elements,
By one 'Let there be' of God's might
The world of living things arose;
The storm blusters, deep water flows,
And stars throw light upon the heavens.
In our lands dead night still lies;
Human desires are still at war;
But love emits its fire beacon;
The spirit's world from chaos will rise:
Youth will conceive it in its bosom
And friendship bond it forevermore.

The numb icecaps suddenly quail,
So does prejudice that dims light's radiance.
O morning star of freedom, hail,
Behind you the sun of deliverance!

(1820) [1827] [*Edited and translated by Michael J. Mikoś. Polish Romantic Literature.
An Anthology.* Bloomington: Slavica Publishers, 1998]

I.i.2. ADAM MICKIEWICZ, from *Pan Tadeusz*, 'Discussion on Art' (fragment)

'Forgive me,' said the Count, 'if I intrude;
I come for pardon and with gratitude:
For pardon for your privacy abusing,
With thanks for being witness of your musing.
My boldness has inflicted great distress,
And I must own my great indebtedness.
I have disturbed a moment's meditation;
But I have gained a lifetime's inspiration.
Oh, happy moments! You may reprobate
The man; the artist shall for pardon wait.
Much have I dared nor shall from daring cease!
Be judge!' He knelt and showed his masterpiece.

Telimena judged the sketch in courteous part
But not as one unconversant with art.
She spared the praise not yet forbore to cheer:
'Well done!' she cried, 'a pretty talent here,
But you must foster it and specially try
To seek out lovely scenes. O happy sky
Of Italy! O Caesar's rosary,
Ye classic waterfalls of Tivoli,
Ye craggy paths of Posilipo's grot!
O land of painters! Pity our sad lot!
The Muses' child, in Soplicowo raised,
Would surely die, I'll have your picture glazed,

Zaczęli więc rozmowę o niebios błękitach,
Morskich szumach i wiatrach wonnych, i skał szczytach,
Mieszając tu i ówdzie, podróżnych zwyczajem,
Śmiech j urąganie się nad ojczystym krajem.

A przecież wokoło nich ciągnęły się lasy
Litewskie! tak poważne i tak pełne krasy! –
Czeremchy oplatane dzikich chmielów wieńcem,
Jarzębiny ze świeżym pasterskim rumieńcem,
Leszczyna jak menada z zielonymi berły,
Ubranymi, jak w grona, w orzechowe perły,
A niżej dziatwa leśna: głóg w objęciu kalin,
Ożyna czarne usta tuląca do malin.
Drzewa i krzewy liśćmi wzięły się za ręce,
Jak do tańca stające panny i młodzieńce
Wkoło pary małżonków. Stoi pośród grona
Para, nad całą leśną gromadą wzniesiona
Wysmukłością kibici i barwy powabem:
Brzoza biała, kochanka, z małżonkiem swym grabem.
A dalej, jak by starce na dzieci i wnuki
Patrzą, siedząc w milczeniu: tu sędziwe buki,
Tam matrony topole i mchami brodaty
Dąb, włożywszy pięć wieków na swój kark garbaty,
Na dębów, przodków swoich, skamieniałych trupach.

Pan Tadeusz kręcił się, nudząc niepomału
Długą rozmową, w której nie mógł brać udziału;
I wyliczać z kolei wszystkich drzew rodzaje:
Pomarańcze, cyprysy, oliwki, migdały,
Kaktusy, aloesy, mahonie, sandały,
Cytryny, bluszcz, orzechy włoskie, nawet figi,
Wysławiając ich kształty, kwiaty i łodygi –
Tadeusz nie przestawał dąsać się i zżymać,
Na koniec nic mógł dłużej od gniewu wytrzymać.

Był on prostak, lecz umiał czuć wdzięk przyrodzenia
I patrząc w las ojczysty, rzeki pełen natchnienia:
«Widziałem w botanicznym wileńskim ogrodzie
Owe sławione drzewa rosnące na wschodzie
I na południu, w owej pięknej włoskiej ziemi;
Któreż równać się może z drzewami naszemi?
Czy aloes z długimi jak konduktor pałki?
Czy cytryna, karlica z złocistymi gałki,
Z liściem lakierowanym, krótka i pękata,
Jako kobieta mała, brzydka, lecz bogata?
Czy zachwalony cyprys, długi, cienki, chudy!
Co zdaje się być drzewem nie smutku, lecz nudy?

Or put it in the great portfolio
Of pictures I collect in my bureau.

And so they started talking of blue sky,
Of murmuring seas, sweet airs and mountains high,
As travellers do, mingling from time to time
Contempt and laughter for their native clime.
Yet all around in solemn splendour stood
The glory of the Lithuanian wood!
The wild hop wreathed upon the currant bush;
The service tree with shepherdess's blush;
The hazel like a maenad clad with shapes
Of thyrsuses and nut-brown pearls like grapes;
The forest children, shorter than the rest,
The hawthorn with the elder on his breast,
And blackberry to the lips of raspberry pressed.
The trees and bushes joined their leafy hands
Like men and girls preparing for a dance
Around a married couple. Midst the host
Of forest tress stood forth the pair that must
Excel in slenderness and lovely hue,
The darling silver birch and her spouse true,
The hornbeam; while afar in silence sate
The matron poplar and the beech sedate,
Watching their children; and with mossy beard
An oak on his humped back five centuries reared
Above the fossils of his ancestors,
As on the broken shafts of sepulchres.

Tadeusz heard this lengthy conversation,
In which he could not share, with much vexation.
But when they praised the trees of foreign climes,
The cypresses and oranges and limes,
The aloes, olives, figs and cactuses,
The sandalwoods and the mahoganies,
The ivy even and the walnut trees,
Lauding the shapes and flowers and barks of these,
he sniffed and frowned and frowned and sniffed again,
His rage no longer able to contain.

Though simple, he by natural charm was moved
And, gazing at the ancestral trees he loved,
Began as one inspired: 'I too have seen
Those vaunted trees in Wilno when I've been
In the botanic garden, and I know
The kinds that in the south and east do grow
And in that land of Italy so fair.
But which of them with our trees can compare?

Mówią, że bardzo smutnie wygląda na grobie:
Jest to jak lokaj Niemiec we dworskiej żałobie,
Nie śmiejący rąk podnieść ani głowy skrzywić,
Aby się etykiecie niczym nic sprzeciwić.

Czyż nie piękniejsza nasza poczciwa brzezina,
Która jako wieśniaczka, kiedy płacze syna,
Lub wdowa męża, ręce załamie, roztoczy
Po ramionach do ziemi strumienic warkoczy!
Niema z żalu, postawą jak wymownie szlocha!
Czemuż Pan Hrabia, jeśli w malarstwie się kocha,
Nie maluje drzew naszych, pośród których siedzi?
Prawdziwie, będą z Pana żartować sąsiedzi,
Że mieszkając na żyznej litewskiej równinie,
Malujesz tylko jakieś skały i pustynie».

«Przyjacielu! rzekł Hrabia, piękne przyrodzenie
Jest formą, iłem, materią, a duszą natchnienie,
Które na wyobraźni unosi się skrzydłach;
Poleruje się gustem, wspiera na prawidłach.
Nie dość jest przyrodzenia, nie dosyć zapału,
Sztukmistrz musi ulecieć w sfery ideału!
Nie wszystko, co jest piękne, wymalować da się!
Dowiesz się o tym wszystkim z książek w swoim czasie.
Co się tycze malarstwa: do obrazu trzeba
Punktów widzenia, grupy, ansamblu i nieba,
Nieba włoskiego! stąd też w kunszcie pejzażów
Włochy były, są, będą, ojczyzną malarzów.
Stąd też oprócz Brejgela, lecz nie Van der Helle,
Ale pejzażysty (bo są dwaj Brejgele),
I oprócz Ruisdala, na całej północy
Gdzież był pejzażysta który pierwszej mocy?
Niebios, niebios potrzeba!» – «Nasz malarz Orłowski,
Przerwała Telimena, miał gust Soplicowski.
(Trzeba wiedzieć, że to jest Supliców choroba,
Że im oprócz Ojczyzny nic się nie podoba).
Orłowski, który życie strawił w Peterburku,
Sławny malarz (mam jego kilka szkiców w biurku),
Mieszkał tuż przy cesarzu, na dworze, jak w raju,
A nie uwierzy Hrabia, jak tęsknił po kraju,
Lubił ciągle wspominać swej młodości czasy.
Wysławiał wszystko w Polszcze; ziemię, niebo, lasy…»

«I miał rozum! zawołał Tadeusz z zapałem:
Te Państwa niebo włoskie, jak o nim słyszałem.
Błękitne, czyste, wszak to jak zamarzła woda;
Czyż nie piękniejsze stokroć wiatr i niepogoda?

The aloe like a lightning-rod so tall?
The dwarfish lemon with its golden ball
And lacquered leaves, in shape so short and stumpy
Like a small woman, ugly, rich and dumpy?
Or that much vaunted cypress, tall and thin,
To boredom rather than to grief akin?
They say that on a grave it looks forlorn –
More like a German flunkey dressed to mourn,
Afraid to lift an arm or head to bend,
Lest somehow he may etiquette offend.'

'Is not our honest birch a fairer one,
That's like a peasant weeping for her son,
Or widow for her husband, as she stands,
Hair streaming to the ground, and wrings her hands,
Her silent form than sobs more eloquent?
If, Count, on painting you are so intent,
Why don't you paint the trees that round you thrive?
The neighbours will make fun of you, that live
Upon the fertile Lithuanian plain
And all but rocks and desert scenes disdain.'

'Fair nature,' said the Count, 'is not the whole
Of art, but only form and theme. The soul
Of art, that gives it life, is inspiration,
Which soars on pinions of imagination,
But also must be polished by good taste
And on the rules of painting firmly based.
Nor nature nor enthusiasm suffice;
The artist into ideal realms must rise.
For art not all things beautiful are fit,
Which you may learn in time from books on it.
And as for painting you must know this too:
A picture needs arrangement, point of view,
Ensemble and grouping – most of all a sky,
Italian sky! And that's the reason why
The land of Italy for landscape art
Was ever dearest to the painter's heart.
Except for Breughel (no, not Van der Helle,
The landscapist's the one of whom I tell)
And Ruysdael, where is found in all the north
A landscape artist of the highest worth?
The sky – 'Here Telimena cut him short:
'Orlowski's' taste was the Soplica sort;
Soplicas, it's well known, have this disease,
No country but their fatherland can please.
That painter lived in Petersburg, you know,

U nas dość głowę podnieść, ileż to widoków!
Ileż scen i obrazów z samej gry obłoków!
Bo każda chmura inna. na przykład jesienna
Pełźnie jak żółw leniwa, ulewą brzemienna,
I z nieba aż do ziemi spuszcza długie smugi
Jak rozwite warkocze, to są deszczu strugi;
Chmura z gradem, jak balon, szybko z wiatrem leci,
Krągła. ciemnobłękitna, w środku żółto świeci,
Szum wielki słychać wkoło; nawet te codzienne,
Patrzcie Państwo, te białe chmurki, jak odmienne!
Zrazu stada dzikich gęsi lub łabędzi,
A z tyłu wiatr jak sokół do kupy je pędzi:
Ściskają się, grubieją, rosną, nowe dziwy!
Dostają krzywych karków, rozpuszczają grzywy,
Wysuwają nóg rzędy i po niebios sklepie
Przelatują jak tabun rumaków po stepie:
Wszystkie białe- jak srebro, zmieszały się nagle
Z ich karków rosną maszty, z grzyw szerokie żagle,
Tabun zmienia się w okręt i wspaniale płynie
Cicho, z wolna, po niebios błękitnej rowninie!»
Hrabia i Telimena poglądali w górę;
Tadeusz jedną ręką pokazał im chmurę,
A drugą ścisnął z lekka rączkę Telimeny;
Kilka już upłynęło minut cichej sceny;
Hrabia rozłożył papier na swym kapeluszu
I wydobył ołówek; wtem przykry dla uszu
Odezwał się dzwon dworski, i zaraz śród lasu
Cichego pełno było krzyku i hałasu.

Hrabia kiwnąwszy głową, rzekł poważnym tonem:
«Tak to na świecie wszystko los zwykł kończyć dzwonem,
Rachunki myśli wielkiej, plany wyobraźni,
Zabawki niewinności, uciechy przyjaźni,
Wylania się serc czułych! gdy spiż z dala ryknie –
Wszystko miesza się, zrywa, mąci się i niknie!»
Tu obróciwszy czuły wzrok ku Telimenie:
«Cóż zostaje?» – a ona mu rzekła: «Wspomnienie».

[1834] [*Edited by Zbigniew Jerzy Nowak. Warszawa: Czytelnik, 1995*]

(I have some works of his in my bureau)
Close to the emperor's court in splendid style,
Yet longed for his own country all the while.
He loved to call to mind his boyhood days,
And Polish earth and sky and woods to praise.'
'And he was right,' Tadeusz grew more bold,
'For your Italian sky, as I've been told,
Is clear like frozen water and serene –
What varied sights one sees here every day!
How many pictures in the clouds at play!
Each cloud is different: when autumn lours,
Some crawl like tortoises and teem with showers,
And let down to the earth a streaming train
Like flowing tresses, rivulets of rain.
The hail cloud rides balloon-like on the storm,
A gleam of gold within its dark-blue form,
A might roar around. E'en ordinary
Small clouds like these, how rapidly they vary!
First, like a flock of geese or swans the wind
Compels them like a falcon from behind;
They huddle close and swell and suddenly lo!
Curved necks and rows of legs begin to grow,
And o'er the heavenly vault with spreading manes
Fly like a herd of horses on the plains,
All silver-white; then suddenly confounded,
Masts spring from necks and sails from manes are rounded,
The herd becomes a ship, and o'er the sea
Of heaven floats in silent majesty.'

The Count and Telimena looked up high;
Tadeusz pointed one hand at the sky,
And with the other gently squeezed her fingers.
This quiet scene for several minutes lingers;
The Count a paper on his hat deploys
And takes his pencil. Then, unwelcome noise,
The house bell rings; immediately all round
The silent woods with shouts and din resound.

The noble shook his head and gravely spoke:
'Thus fate ends all things with a clapper stroke.
The mind's profoundest thoughts and fancy's flights,
The joys of friendship, innocent delights,
The hear's outpourings – at the brazen roar
All's broken and confused and is no more.'
Then glancing at the lady feelingly:
'What then remains?' She answered, 'Memory.'

[1834] [*Translated by Kenneth R. Mackenzie. New York: Hippocrene, 1992*]

j. PORTUGUÊS

I.j.1. JOAO BAPTISTA de SILVA LEITAO de ALMEIDA GARRETT,
excerto «de Introdução a *Um Auto de Gil Vicente*»

Em Portugal nunca chegou a haver teatro; o que se chama teatro nacional, nunca: até nisso se parece a nossa literatura com a latina, que também o não teve. A cena romana viveu sempre de emprésti-mos gregos, nunca houve renda própria; a nossa andou fazendo «operações mistas» com Itália e Castela, até que, fatigada de uma existência difícil, toda de privações e sem glória, arreou a bandeira nacional, que nunca içara com verdadeiro e bom direito, e entregou-se à invasão francesa.

Napoleão mandou à conquista de Portugal um dos seus generais mais brilhantes. Mas a gente que, bons trinta anos antes disso, tinha vindo, em nome das perfeições francesas, apoderar-se do nosso teatro era bicha reles – algum troço de guarda-barreiras de província.

O que se traduziu, o que se traduziu, e como?

E todavia Gil Vicente tinha lançado os fundamentos de uma escola nacional. Mas foi como se a pintura moderna acabasse no Perugino. Os alicerces da escola eram sólidos como os do «erário novo» à Cotovia; mas não houve quem edificasse para cima, e entraram a fazer barracas de madeira no meio, e casinholas de taipa, que iam apodrecendo e caindo, até que vieram os refor-madores, como é moda agora, destruíram tudo, alicerces e tudo, fizeram muitos planos, e não construíram nada, – nem sequer deixaram o terreno limpo.

A causa desta esterilidade dramática, desta como negação para o teatro em um povo de tanto engenho, em que outros ramos de literatura se têm cultivado tanto... não se pode explicar, dizem todos, e eu também o tenho dito. Mas é que nada se acha sem procurar. Ora vamos a ver.

O teatro é um grande meio de civilização, mas não prospera onde a não há. Não têm procura os seus produtos enquanto o gosto não forma os hábitos e com eles a necessidade. Para prin-cipiar, pois, é mister criar um mercado factício. É o que fez Richelieu em Paris, e a corte de Espanha em Madrid; o que já tinham feito os certames e concursos públicos em Atenas, e o que em Lisboa tinham começado a fazer D. Manuel e D. João III. Depois de criado o gosto público, o gosto público sustenta o teatro: é o que sucedeu em França e em Espanha; é o que teria suce-dido em Portugal, se o misticismo belicoso d'el-reí D, Sebastião, que não tratava senão de brigar e rezar, – e logo a dominação estrangeira que nos absorveu, não tivessem cortado à nascença a planta que ainda precisava muito abrigo e muito amparo.

(...)

O marquês de Pombal, sobretudo depois que travou luta de morte com os Jesuítas, com a corte velha – e com toda a sociedade velha- quis servir-se do teatro; mas o estado de guerra social era já muito violento de mais, andava no ar muito foracao de filosofias abstractas que não deixavam medrar o que se plantava, e a terra não se revolvera ainda bastante para lhe dar substância nova.

Neste primeiro começar das transições sociais não se cria.

Como se há-de então criar hoje? Hoje, o estado é outro; já se revolveu a terra, já mudou todo o modo de ser antigo; não está completa a transição, mas já leva um século de começada – que a principiou o marquês de Pombal.

Drogas que se não fazem na terra que remédio há senão mandá-las vir de fora! O marquês de Pombal mandou vir uma ópera italiana para el-rei.

O povo compôs-se a exemplo do rei: traduziam em português as óperas de Metastásio, metiam-lhes graciosos, – chamava-se a isto acomodar ao gosto português, – e meio rezado, meio cantarolado, lá se ia representando.

(...)

j. PORTUGUESE

I.j.1. JOAO BAPTISTA de SILVA LEITAO de ALMEIDA GARRETT, from 'Introduction of His play *A Play of Gil Vicente*'

(. . .)

The Portuguese never developed a national theatre tradition. Like the Roman stage, which borrowed heavily from the Greeks, our stage was defined by combined efforts with Italy and Castile until we surrendered to the French invasion. After a time of great hardship and scarcity, our national flag was brought down where it once had flown free and true. But even thirty years before the French military invasion, when Napoleon sent one of his most brilliant generals, Junot, to conquer Portugal, a small-minded, provincial French contingency had already usurped the Portuguese stage in the name of 'French perfection.' What characteristics of the Portuguese theatre are a mere translation of French fashion?

In the early sixteenth-century, however, Gil Vicente had established the foundation for a Portuguese national theatre. The foundations were as solid as those of the 'erário novo' at Cotovia,[1] but no one built upon them; it was as if artists had failed to develop modern painting after Perugino. Instead, lesser playwrights set up their shacks around Vicente's foundation, all of which rotted or blew away. A wave of reformists inspired hope, but as usual with reformists, they destroyed the foundation along with everything else, drew plenty of sketches, and left without even clearing the land. The cause of this dramatic sterility in a nation which has nurtured ingenuity in other forms of literature is difficult to determine, but let us examine history more closely for the answer.

The birth of a theatrical tradition depends upon the development of a culture with clearly-defined tastes. D. Manuel and D. João III began this process in Lisbon by creating an artificial market like the fairs and competitions in ancient Athens, as Richelieu had done in Paris and the Court of Spain in Madrid. A taste for theatre would have developed in Portugal, as it had in France and Spain, had it not been for the mystical bellicosity of King D. Sebastião. His obsession with religion and war allowed foreign cultural influences to strangle the fragile bud of national drama.

(. . .) [*Garrett comments on the Portuguese Ancient Regime of the 17 and 18th centuries, referring to the marquis of Pombal, Portuguese Prime Minister from 1750 to 1778 who tried to steer Portugal into the Enlightenment.*]

The marquis of Pombal tried to revive the theatre in the eighteenth century after taking power from the Jesuits and the old Court, but the social situation was still in turmoil. Typhoons of abstract philosophies kept the seeds of theatre from blossoming, and the land was still not sufficiently cultivated to provide nourishment. In this first stage of social transition, nothing was created.

But shouldn't we be able to create today? Now the soil is tilled and the social changes the marquis of Pombal started a century ago is nearly complete. Goods unavailable here must be imported! To compensate for his nation's lack of a theatrical tradition, the marquis of Pombal commissioned an Italian opera for the king; the popular interest in Italian opera which followed prompted Portuguese translations of Metastasio's operas. The Portuguese inserted *graciosos* into the opera – which they called 'adapting the operas to Portuguese taste.'[2]

[*Garrett refers to two traditional eighteenth-century Portuguese playwrights.*]

---

[1] A reference to Lisbon's urbanzation in the eighteenth and nineteenth centuries.

[2] Inherited from the servus of Latin comedy, the *gracioso* is a type of clown or jester associated with all kinds of trouble and deceit in Spanish and Portuguese comedy. Northrop Frye identifies him as a type of tricky slave.

221

és európai tudományos kultúra egyenlően kozmopolitizmusra törekednek. Innen van, hogy az a kirekesztő, saját centruma körül forgó, de egyszersmind lelket emelő nemzetiség, mely a hellénnek tulajdona volt, Európában nem találtatik. Ezen sokféle népek minden politikai és morális elhajlásaik, s minden különböző fizikai fekvésük mellett is, vallás s míveltség és kinézéseknél fogva csak úgy választatnak meg egymástól, mint az athénai görög a spártaitól, mint az ephesusitól a rhodusi. Azonban a görög a maga sokfelé ágaztában is nyelv, játék,[15] hagyomány és azon épült nemzeti poézis által bizonyos[16] öszvehúzó középpontot nyere, mely középpont Európában sem a nemzetek egybefolyásában a népek különválása, sem a népek különválásában a nemzetek egybefolyása miatt nem lél helyet. Ez az oka, miért az újabb időkben egy nemzetnek is oly nagy behatású költője, mint Homer nem születhetett; mert nem nyilván van-e, hogy mind Ariosto és hasonlói a magok tündérvilágában, mind Milton és Klopstock a religió szent tartományiban éppen úgy a nemzetiségtől különválasztott képeket állítottak fel népeik előtt: mint azok, kik a görög mitológiát hozák új életre? [...] A görög hagyomány szakadatlan idősorban, s mindég tiszteletben tartva szállott a késő unokákra, s ez az európai hagyománnyal nem történt. Ezért nemzeti poézis való értelemben egy európai népnél sem találkozik,[17] mert a poéta, még midőn saját korának történeteit énekli is, nem szűnik meg hazája fiaitól bizonyos távolságban állani, nem jöhetvén az öszveérésnek azon pontjaihoz, melyekben a görög poézis állott a görög nemzettel.

A költés három fő nemei, eposz, dráma és líra egyforma varázslattal vonták a görög nép egyetemét magokhoz. Az első, mivel Homer, a mindenhellének ősi hagyományait egy közönségesen általölelő körben hagyá ragyoglani; a másik, mivel a nemzeti hagyományokból meríttetett, s egyszersmind a nemzeti religióval, mint innepi tárgy, szorosan öszvefüggött; s így a líra is, mely hasonlóul a religiónak szolgált, s hasonlóul a hagyományokat dicsőítette meg.

Az újkori költő csak a játékszínen látszik a nemzethez közel állani. De mely különbség az athénai és az európai új játékszín között! Ez a nép egyik igen kicsiny részének nyílik fel mint magányos mulatság;[18] amaz az athénai nép egészét, mint közönséges öröminnep, fogadta keblébe. Ez a religió határain kívül áll; az a religiónak körében kapott fakadást és virágzatot. Ez a régi és új kor hagyományait és történeteit, a kül- és belföldi dolgokat úgy terjeszti elő, hogy a néző az ezerféle vegyítésben nemzeti szellemet fel nem találhat, s nemzeti érzést nem táplálhat; az a nemzetiség határain belől alkotta öszve magát, s választotta tárgyait. A görög testvéri formákat látott maga előtt lebegni, s a szcéna előtt is saját nemzetének világában lelte magát; midőn az európai a világ egyik sarkától a másikig ragadtatik, s poétáját csak messzünnen szerzett tudomány által értheti meg.

Ahelyett, hogy ezeket messzebb nyomoznók, ideje leszen saját nemzetünkre fordítani figyelmünket, s történeteinkre, s nemzetiségünknek s poézisünknek azokkal való egybefüggésére vetni egy tekintetet.

Ha nézzük a régiséget, a hunnusok azok, kik hagyományaink legtávolabb határszélén előttünk feltűnnek. Bendegúznak neve hangzik fülünkbe, s Attilának dicsőségét látjuk ragyogni; de ezen ragyogás, mint egy villám elenyész szemünk elől, s ez időtől fogva az Avarokig sötétség borul el népünk emlékezetén. Az avarok egész történetsorából egy pont sincs kiemelve, mely a hagyomány

---

[15] színházi játék, dráma; vö. játékszín, vagyis színház
[16] határozott
[17] van, létezik
[18] privát szórakozás, nem közösségi időtöltés

No reinado seguinte era pecado subirem mulheres à cena. Façam lá *Zairas* ou *Ifigénias* para representarem barbatolas!

Demais a mais, a invasão literária francesa, de que falei, veio por este tempo. Completa ela, já não era possível haver teatro: a literatura dramática é, de todas, a mais ciosa da independência nacional.

Essas poucas e deslavadas tragédias que se fizeram, – clássicas puritanas da gema, – eram francesas na mesma alma, não tinham de português senão as palavras... algumas – uma ou duas, apenas o título e os nomes das pessoas.

E a Academia das Ciências a oferecer prémios aos dramas originais! E escritores de bom talento a traduzir Racine, Voltaire e Crébillon e Arnaud! Nada; não renascia; ou, propriamente, não nascia o teatro nacional.

Nem ele tinha onde nascer, o pobre: que só a humildade da Eterna Grandeza escolheu para nascer um presepe. Havia aí duas arribanas, uma no Salitre, outra na rua dos Condes, onde alternada e lentamente agonizava um velho decrépito que alguns tafuis de botequim alcunhavam de teatro português; e iam lá de vez cm quando ouvir o terrível estertor do moribundo: – que atroz divertimento!

O povo não; esse não ia lá. Conhecia o estrangeiro, não lhe tinha amor nem ódio, mas deixava-o morrer e berrar com dores e com fome. Não ia lá.

O povo tinha razão.

E mais razão teria se fosse pôr dali fora o velho e os tafuis, e queimasse as arribanas, que eram um insulto e uma desonra para ele, povo, que não tinha culpa. Tinha; mas em sofrer.

Fizeram-se revoluções; as primeiras sem o povo saber: eram desavenças entre frades, fidalgos, desembargadores e soldados, sobre quais haviam de governar. E o povo a ver. Caíram uns, levantaram-se outros; disputaram muito dos direitos do homem, depois do trono e do altar; cada um puxava para a sua banda pela velha máquina social, até que ela desabou toda, e quebrou a cabeça à maior parte dos disputantes.

O povo começou a levantar a sua.

(...)

Fizeram-se escolas e academias, decretou-se o Panteão...

Foi – poesia; mas não da glosa sediça dos tais poetas de outeiro que nos trepanam a cabeça há tantos anos. – Mofaram dele os sensaborões: pois deviam-se envergonhar, que era um pensamento nobre, nacional, útil, exequível, necessário, que podia salvar tanto monumento para a História, ressuscitar tantas memórias que se apagam, levantar tanto ânimo baixo que decai, fazer renascer talvez o antigo entusiasmo português pela glória, que morreu afogado nas teorias utilitárias. – Cá nesta pobre terra nem sequer de teorias passaram!

Decretou-se também o Teatro Nacional e o Conservatório Dramático. – «Foi o irmão gémeo do Panteão», disse ainda o outro dia um dos tais. – Seria, foi; e fizeram-lhe a mesma chacota a mesma gente, – os poetas do outeiro perpétuo, que nunca fizeram, nem podem, nem sabem, nem hão-de fazer nada – mas não querem que ninguém o faça. Eles aí estão outra vez a glosar o seu mote, a fazer promessas e proclamações. Vejam as estradas que macadamizam, os canais por que navegam – e os Camões que os cantam!

Ora eu, que sou um pobre homem, gostei do Panteão e do Teatro Nacional e do Conservatório; mas não cria muito neles – não por eles em si que são muito possíveis e fazíveis – mas porque sei onde vivo e com quem.

Among other changes during Pombal's reign, it became a sin to have women on stage: imagine *Zaira* and *Iphigenia* played by bearded men!

The French invasion, which I have already mentioned, completed the defeat of an emerging national theatre during Pombal's reign. Once the French invasion was complete, theatre could no longer thrive: dramatic literature is, of all literary genres, the most mindful of national independence. A few pitiful tragedies were created in Portuguese, but they evoked a pure French sensibility. Some of them were Portuguese in language only, and in one or two, only the title and names of the characters were Portuguese. The Academy offered prizes for original dramas, but talented writers persisted in translating Racine, Voltaire, Crébillon and Arnaud! Nothing seemed able to bring the theatre back to life; or perhaps more appropriately, the national theatre wouldn't be born.

So where could the poor theatre be born? Some people perceived Portuguese drama as a crippled old man, and occasionally took a perverse pleasure in patronizing his productions in the desolate Salitre and Rua dos Condes Theatres. What atrocious entertainment to listen to the terrifying screams of a dying old man! The birth of a national theatre on these barren stages was unlikely, for only the Son of God chose to be born in a stable. But most of the people stayed away. They knew the strange dying man, neither loved nor hated him, but let him die in agony.

The people were right to let him die.

It would have been even better if they had chased him out with his audience and burned the offensive stages, all of which were an affront to the people who had no reason to suffer such terrible productions.

The people were to blame, but only for enduring the old man for so long. Meanwhile, political revolutions emerged, and the people watched as priests, noblemen, judges, and soldiers quarrelled over human rights, the throne, and the church. Each tried to pull the old social machine to their side until it finally collapsed and crushed the heads of those who fought over it.

And the people finally had a chance to raise their own heads.

(. . .) [*Garrett refers to early nineteenth-century liberalism, after the Napoleonic invasions.*]

Schools and Academies were created and a Pantheon of national poets was finally established.

The imitative poets whose songs filled our heads for so long mocked the new poetry but were really ashamed that they did not hold such high ideals. The new poets believed in reviving the fragments of Portuguese history and cultural memory, to recover its fallen spirit and enthusiasm for glory that drowned among the utilitarian theories of recent centuries. But in such a harsh environment, their noble ideals of creating a national poetry never surpassed the theory stage. The National Theatre and Arts School suffered a similar fate. It was called the 'twin brother of the Pantheon,' and the same people who mocked the Pantheon mocked it: the same imitative artists who had never accomplished anything but couldn't stand for others to achieve glory either!

(. . .)

I was at the immediate disadvantage of liking the Pantheon and the National Theatre and Arts School. I never put much faith in them, however, not because I didn't think their ideals could be realized, but because I know where and with whom I live. The Pantheon was delayed out of fear of ridicule. They shouldn't have feared; we must have the spirit to go face to face with ridicule. He is the worst of enemies, but we must face him straight in the eye without fear if we want to do something useful and good, particularly where there are so many small-minded people.

And so I supported the Arts School and the Theatre, and continued to work and achieve success disregarding the opposition.

Acanharam-se, recuaram com o Panteão; fizeram mal. E preciso ter ânimo para afrontar até com o ridículo; é o pior inimigo que há, mas é necessário encarar com ele de olhos direitos, e não lhe ter medo, quem quer fazer qualquer coisa útil e boa, em terras pequenas sobretudo, e onde há tanta gente pequena.

É o que eu fiz com o Conservatório e o teatro. Fui por diante, não fíz caso dos sensaborões, e levava-os de vencida.

Mas têm maus fígados, a tal gentinha. Quebrou-se-lhes a arma do ridículo, tomaram sem escrúpulo a da calúnia. Veio a religião, veio a economia, chamou-se tudo para anatematizar um pobre instituto inocente cuja despesa é insignificante, cujo proveito é tamanho.

– Que proveito?

– O de criar um teatro nacional que não temos.

[1841] [*Edited by Manuel dos Santos Rodrigues. Editora Replicação, Lisboa, 1996*]

But our accusers had few scruples and did not stop when ridicule failed to be effective; They pulled out the card of slander, first using religion, then finances to overthrow a poor institution whose insignificant expenditure represents such a great profit for society. How do we profit society? By creating the national theatre society has always lacked. How does it accomplish this? By its manner of directing theatrical censorship; by supporting young playwrights; by developing actors – the most difficult part of all –; and by building a house worthy of the investments of a cultured nation. If there are any faults in the institution, they should be corrected, but destroying the whole institution for a few faults would be barbaric.

I was entrusted with this great national endeavour, and when Her Majesty the Queen sent for me, I told her the following: 'One of the most beautiful jewels Portugal lost under Spanish rule[3] was our promising national theatre tradition. Just as the power of the Portuguese empire weakened after the reign of His Majesty the King D. Manuel, so too was the fledgling national theatre weakened after the death of Gil Vicente. Other nations usurped our trade routes, and other muses occupied the theatre we abandoned.

It seems always to be Portugal's fate to see others finish the great ideas its own people started. We fall asleep under the dim light of a torch we lit, but we awaken to darkness! The Portuguese theatre never recovered when the nation regained independence. Other modern societies followed the road we paved toward dramatic greatness, but we went back on our road and never found our way forward again.

Some attempts have been made to revive the national theatre, but they have all failed because the three necessary elements never came together: a national subject, the playwrights, and good actors. Gil Vicente's plays and the operas of the unfortunate António José[4] were our only truly national theatrical productions, but both artists' works, for different reasons, are now obsolete.

But now Portugal has the opportunity to revive its theatrical talent once again. Your Majesty has only to call the elements from the chaos in which they struggle, and a beautiful form will respond to your voice. Your Majesty will take personal pleasure in it and also gain world-wide fame under the illustrious title, Patron of the Fine Arts.'

(. . .) [*Garrett ends his Introduction explaining how his play relates to Portugal's Art and History.*]

[1841] [*Translated by Carlos Leone and Bethany Smith*]

---

[3] Portugal remained officially under Spanish rule from 1580–1640.

[4] Antonio Jose da Silva (1705–1739), also known as 'The Jew', a popular Portuguese playwright of the eighteenth century, whose comedies, puppet shows, and comic operas were performed frequently in the 1730s. The Inquisition arrested and tortured him in 1737 for refusing to renounce Judaism and finally burnt him at the stake in a spectacular *auto da fe* in 1739.

k. ROMÂNĂ

I.k.1. CEZAR BOLLIAC, din 'Poezia'[1]

VI

[...] O! Poetul s-a ocupat prea mult cu cerul şi a ajuns să-şi piarză cu totul proprietatea pe pământ! [...] pământul s-a scăpat acum de cer, şi poetul trebuie să se considere numai ca un conducător al omului pe pământ, şi pentru ca aceasta să ajungă odată simţită de obşte, trebuie să se deştepte mai întâi într-însul. [...] poetul este geniul şi artiştii sunt talentul. Ideea ce va deştepta el, aceea a să zboare peste vulg, aceea a să invite şi a să dirige acel flux şi reflux al patimilor şi al dorinţelor populilor. [...]

VII

Unde stă cea d-întâi inegalitate socială? – În sclavia fămeiei. [...] Să emancipeze dar poezia pe fămeie, să dea libertate amorului; să desfiinţeze toate iluziile pe care se mai reazimă viaţa cea religioasă şi politică a omului [...]; să facă ca populii, prin cultivare, să se organizeze şi să se cârmuiască de sine, să-şi administreze justiţia de sine în viaţa publică şi în dregătoria publică; [...] să facă ca nici o parte a societăţii să nu stea în inactivitate la republică; să facă ca proletarul cel necultivat, cel lipsit astăzi de cultură spirituală şi de îndestularea materială să se aridice prin educaţia generală la cetăţeanul actual, la demnitatea de om; să facă ca totalitatea acestor cetăţeni, în adevăr liberi, să se împărtăşească de cele mai înalte interesuri ale statului lor, – de legislaţie, judicătorie şi administraţie [...]; [...] şi în sfârşit să facă vorbirea şi scrisul, – care sunt expresia cugetării, expresia omului născut a fi liber, – să zboare fără stavili; şi totodată să nu uite a pregăti fiece popul la ideea frăţiei generale, la ideea de cosmopolitism, ca ultimul ferice al locuitorilor globului. Aceste principuri sunt misia poeziei moderne, căci pe aceste principuri se va clădi edificiul societăţii celei noi.

(1846)

I.k.2. MIHAI EMINESCU, din 'Epigonii'

Când privesc zilele de-aur a scripturelor române,
Mă cufund ca într-o mare de visări dulci şi senine
Şi în jur parcă-mi colindă dulci şi mândre primăveri,
Sau văd nopţi ce-ntind deasupră-mi oceanele de stele,
Zile cu trei sori în frunte, verzi dumbrăvi cu filomele,
Cu izvoare-ale gândirii şi cu râuri de cântări.

....

Iară noi? noi, epigonii?... Simţiri reci, harfe zdrobite,
Mici de zile, mari de patimi, inimi bătrâne, urâte,
Măşti râzânde, puse bine pe-un caracter inimic;
Dumnezeul nostru: umbră, patria noastră: o frază;

---

[1] Sometimes described as Voltairian in its rejection of religion, and defending a ëreligion of reason' as its only progressive replacement, this manifesto comes closer to socialist views of Joseph Fourier and Saint-Simon. Bolliac's *engagé* tone echoes his critical positions in other debates like the slavery of Gypsies, women's subaltern place in society, or the humiliation of the poor, and puts one in mind of Shelley's radicalism, especially when it comes to poetry being defined as the original law-giver of righteousness.

k. ROMANIAN

I.k.1. CEZAR BOLLIAC, from 'Poesy'

VI

[. . .] O, the poet has been too long preoccupied with the heavens and lost his place on earth! [. . .] earth is now free of heaven, so that the poet can now consider himself the guide of man on earth, but for this to be felt by his fellows, it must first awaken him. [. . .] the poet is the genius, the artists are the talent. It is his ideas that will dominate the people, that will summon and control the ebb and tide of the peoples' passions and desires. [. . .]

VII

[. . .] Where lies the original social inequality? – In woman's slavery. [. . .] Let poesy therefore emancipate woman, and render love free; tear down the illusions which vainly prop up man's religious and political life [. . .]; let the people, through education, organize and govern themselves, and administer their own justice in public life and public functions; [. . .] let no component of society try to opt out of the republic; let the least educated proletarian, with least culture or possession rise via state education to the full dignity of citizenship; let all these truly free citizens participate to the full in the workings of their society – its legislation, justice and administration [. . .]; [. . .] and let speech and writing – which are the true expression of thought, the expression of man born free – soar unhindered; let everybody be prepared for general fraternity, cosmopolitanism, and the ultimate happiness of humanity throughout the globe. These are the true principles and mission of modern poesy, for upon these foundations will the new society be built. [. . .]

(1846) [*Translated by Mihaela Anghelescu Irimia*]

I.k.2. MIHAI EMINESCU, from 'The Epigones'

When I see the golden era of Romanian writ, it seems
That I plunge into an ocean of delicious cloudless dreams;
That on all sides I am girdled by sweet-scented vernal flowers;
I see nights that stretch above me endless starry citadels,
Days with three suns in their foreheads, verdant groves with philomels,
Wells of subtle meditation and of songs no end of showers.

. . . .

And we, epigones, their offspring? Chilly feelings, broken harps,
Too big-headed, too small-minded, impotent and worn out hearts,
Each a grinning mask adjusted aptly on a scurvy mind,
All Our Holy is a phantom and our homeland merely bluster,

În noi totul e spoială, totu-i lustru fără bază;
Voi credeați în scrisul vostru, *noi nu credem în nimic!*
....

Noi? Privirea scrutătoare ce nimica nu visează,
Ce tablourile minte, ce simțirea simulează,
Privim reci la lumea asta – vă numim vizionari.
O convenție e totul; ce-i azi drept mâine-i minciună;
Ați luptat luptă deșartă, ați vânat țintă nebună,
Ați visat zile de aur pe-astă lume de amar.
"Moartea succede vieții, viața succede la moarte",
Alt sens n-are lumea asta, n-are alt scop, altă soarte;
Oamenii din toate cele fac icoană și simbol;
Numesc sânt, frumos și bine ce nimic nu însemnează,
Împărțesc a lor gândire pe sisteme numeroase
Și pun haine de imagini pe cadavrul trist și gol.
Ce e cugetarea sacră? Combinare măiestrită
Unor lucruri nexistente; carte tristă și-ncâlcită,
Ce mai mult o încifrează cel ce vrea a descifra.
Ce e poezia? Înger palid cu priviri curate,
Voluptos joc cu icoane și cu glasuri tremurate.
Strai de purpură și aur peste țărâna cea grea.
Rămâneți dară cu bine, sânte firi vizionare,
Ce făceați valul să cânte, ce puneați steaua să zboare,
Ce creați o altă lume pe-astă lume de noroi;
Noi reducem tot la pravul azi în noi, mâini în ruină,
Proști și genii, mic și mare, sunet, sufletul, lumină, –
Toate-s praf... *Lumea-i cum este...* și ca dânsa suntem noi.

[1870]

With us everything is varnish, everything but surface lustre.
You believed in your own writings, *we to all belief are blind.*
....

We? Cold dreamless eyes, inspectors of concrete things and connexions,
Misinterpreting all pictures, simulating all affections,
At this world we look with coldness and we call you visionaries,
Everything is mere convention; what's good now, tomorrow's bad.
You have striven for chimeras, fought for aims considered mad
And awakened golden fancies in a world of woes and worries.
Death and life succeed each other as the night succeeds the day – ,
Things can have no other meaning, purpose, destiny or way,
Human beings make an icon and a symbol out of all,
They call sacred, good and gracious what is simply worthless lumber,
Range and classify their thinking into systems without number,
And upon the bare dead body put a many-coloured pall.
What is sacred meditation? A majestic honey-comb
Rife with non-existing matter; an entangled wretched tome,
Made still darker by researchers who will guide those gone astray.
What is verse? A pallid angel with looks chaste, never dissembling,
A voluptuous play with icons and with voices weak and trembling,
A large robe of gold and purple on the heavy-weighing clay.
Farewell, visionary natures, saints that yearned after the sky,
Setting ocean-waves to music, making luminaries fly,
And creating a new planet from this world of mud and grime;
We reduce *all* to the ashes now within ourselves, tomorrow
In the rubble; dolts or adepts, old, young, sound, soul, light, or sorrow,
All is dust . . . *The world is brainless* and it is the world we mime.

[1870] [*Translated by Leon Levițchi*]

I.k.3.   MIHAI EMINESCU, *'Luceafărul'*

A fost odată ca-n povești,
A fost ca niciodată.
Din rude mari împărătești,
O prea frumoasă fată.

Și era una la părinți
Și mândră-n toate cele,
Cum e Fecioara între sfinți
Și luna între stele.

Din umbra falnicelor bolți
Ea pasul și-l îndreaptă
Lângă fereastră, unde-n colț
Luceafărul așteaptă.

Privea în zare cum pe mări
Răsare și străluce,
Pe mișcătoarele cărări
Corăbii negre duce.

Îl vede azi, îl vede mâini,
Astfel dorința-i gata;
El iar, privind de săptămâni,
Îi cade draga fată.

Cum ea pe coate-și răzima
Visând ale ei tâmple,
De dorul lui și inima
Și sufletu-i se împle.

Și cât de viu s-aprinde el
În orișicare sară,
Spre umbra negrului castel
Când ea o să-i apară.

                    *

Și pas cu pas pe urma ei
Alunecă-n odaie,
Țesând cu recile-i scântei
O mreajă de văpaie.

I.k.3. MIHAI EMINESCU, *'Hyperion'*[2]

Upon a time, as people said,
In fairy-tales of old,
There lived a high-born, royal maid
Of grace and charms untold.

She was her parents' only child,
In all beyond compare,
As is 'mid saints the Virgin mild,
The Moon 'mid stars, so fair.

She leaves the stately colonnade;
Her steps will gain anon
The window where, beyond the shade,
Awaits Hyperion.

She looked and saw how on the seas
He rose and shone e'ermore,
How the black-painted argosies
On restless paths he bore.

She sees him nightly, now, anew,
Straight forward the desire;
He, gazing for some fortnights, too,
Grows brighter with new fire.

And as she, dreamful, rests her head
Upon her snow-white hands,
To love for him her soul is wed,
Her heart with love expands.

And with what brightness does he speak
And glitter every night,
When in the castle's shadows dark
She comes into his sight.

***

And step by step pursuing her,
He glides into her room
And weaves a glistening gossamer
Upon her frozen loom.

---

[2] The original Romanian title is *Luceafărul*, literally *The Morning Star*. It also suggests the fallen angel, Lucifer, 'the carrier of God's light'. The name Hyperion points to the immortal condition of the male protagonist, who fatally falls in love with the young princess. Their incompatible relationship is underlined by the earthly intervention of the courtly page Cătălin, who takes the upper hand. Leaving the suffering demon 'deathless and dead cold' in his superhuman world, the tragic denouement allots each of the three lovers their own sphere with frontiers impossible to trespass. Like fundamental texts of Western Romantic poetry, Eminescu's masterpiece opens up a cosmological avenue, as it operates with religious syncretism and combines these grand themes with social and moral criticism.

Şi când în pat se-ntinde drept
Copila să se culce,
I-atinge mâinile pe piept,
I-nchide geana dulce;

Şi din oglindă luminiş
Pe trupu-i se revarsă,
Pe ochii mari, bătând închişi
Pe faţa ei întoarsă.

Ea îl privea cu un surâs,
El tremura-n oglindă,
Căci o urma adânc în vis
De suflet să se prindă.

Iar ea vorbind cu el în somn,
Oftând din greu suspină:
– O, dulce-al nopţii mele domn,
De ce nu vii tu? Vină!

Cobori în jos, luceafăr blând,
Alunecând pe-o rază,
Pătrunde-n casă şi în gând
Şi viaţa-mi luminează!

El asculta tremurător,
Se aprindea mai tare
Şi s-arunca fulgerător,
Se cufunda în mare;

Şi apa unde-au fost căzut
În cercuri se roteşte,
Şi din adânc necunoscut
Un mândru tânăr creşte.

Uşor el trece ca pe prag
Pe marginea ferestei
Şi ţine-n mână un toiag
Încununat cu trestii.

Părea un tânăr voievod
Cu păr de aur moale,
Un vânăt giulgi se-ncheie nod
Pe umerele goale.

Iar umbra feţei străvezii
E albă ca de ceară –
Un mort frumos cu ochii vii
Ce scânteie-n afară.

And when, to seek her nightly rest,
Supine in bed she lies,
He strokes her hands crossed on her breast
And closes her sweet eyes.

Upon her body mirrors cast
A flood of golden light,
Upon her eyes that beat so fast
Beneath her lids closed tight.

She smiled at him with sweet assent,
He in the glass did thrill
And in her dreams pursued her, bent
On winning of her will.

While sleeping deeply in her room,
She heaves a heavy sigh:
'O gentle sov'reign of my gloom,
Will you not come? Draw nigh!

Descend, O mild Hyperion,
Glide down upon a ray,
Into my home and thoughts anon
And brighten up my way!'

The more he thrilled at such discourse,
The brighter kindled he;
He hurled himself with all his force
And sank into the sea;

The water where he fell whirled round,
In ripples and, forsooth,
From the mysterious profound
Up sprang a princely youth.

A threshold is not easier spanned
Than is the window's edge;
He has a truncheon in his hand
And it is crowned with sedge.

A very voievode[3], he was young,
Had soft and golden hair,
A knotted purple mantle hung
Upon his shoulders bare.

The shade of his translucid face
Was white, as white as snow –
A handsome corpse with living eyes
That cast abroad their glow.

[3] Medieval Slavic term for *prince*.

– Din sfera mea venii cu greu
Ca să-ţi urmez chemarea,
Iar cerul este tatăl meu
Şi mumă-mea e marea.

Ca în cămara ta să vin,
Să te privesc de-aproape,
Am coborât cu-al meu senin
Şi m-am născut din ape.

O, vin'! odorul meu nespus,
Şi lumea ta o lasă;
Eu sunt luceafărul de sus,
Iar tu să-mi fii mireasă.

Colo-n palate de mărgean
Te-oi duce veacuri multe,
Şi toată lumea-n ocean
De tine o s-asculte.

– O, eşti frumos, cum numa-n vis
Un înger se arată,
Dară pe calea ce-ai deschis
N-oi merge niciodată;

Străin la vorbă şi la port,
Luceşti fără de viaţă,
Căci eu sunt vie, tu eşti mort,
Şi ochiul tău mă-ngheaţă.

***

Trecu o zi, trecură trei
Şi iarăşi, noaptea, vine
Luceafărul deasupra ei
Cu razele-i senine.

Ea trebui de el în somn
Aminte să-şi aducă
Şi dor de-al valurilor domn
De inim-o apucă:

– Cobori în jos, luceafăr blând,
Alunecând pe-o rază,
Pătrunde-n casă şi în gând
Şi viaţa-mi luminează!

Cum el din cer o auzi,
Se stinse cu durere,
Iar ceru-ncepe a roti
În locul unde piere;

'However hard, I left my skin
To gratify your plea,
My father is the heaven high,
My mother is the sea.

To slip into your room and, dumb,
To gaze at you from near,
Down with my azure am I come,
Born from the waters' sphere.

O come, my treasure! Leave afar
The world where you abide;
My love, I am the evening star
And you shall be my bride.

We shall the coral castles gain,
There will you dwell for aye,
And all the people of the main
Shall unto you obey.'

'You are so very handsome, yea,
Like angels in a dream –
But I shall never go the way
You show me with your beam.

You're alien-spoken, alien-bred,
And lifeless is your glow,
I am alive and you are dead,
Your eyes they freeze me so.'

    ***

There passed a day, then three, then four,
The night clooed in again,
And over her the star once more
His beams serene did rain.

By images of his o'erawed
So often in her sleep,
She felt a yearning for the lord
Of the unquiet deep.

'Descend, o sweet Hyperion,
Glide down upon a ray
Into my home and thoughts anon
And brighten up my way.'

When, from above, he heard the girl,
The evening-star shone dead,
The skies began to reel and whirl
Where used to be his stead;

235

În aer rumene văpăi
Se-ntind pe lumea-ntreagă,
Și din a chaosului văi
Un mândru chip se-ncheagă;

Pe negre vițele-i de păr
Coroana-i arde pare,
Venea plutind în adevăr
Scăldat în foc de soare.

Din negru giulgi se desfășor
Marmoreele brațe,
El vine trist și gânditor
Și palid e la față;

Dar ochii mari și minunați
Lucesc adânc himeric,
Ca două patimi fără saț
Și pline de-ntuneric.

– Din sfera mea venii cu greu
Ca să te-ascult ș-acuma,
Și soarele e tatăl meu,
Iar noaptea-mi este muma;

O, vin', odorul meu nespus,
Și lumea ta o lasă;
Eu sunt luceafărul de sus,
Iar tu să-mi fii mireasă.

O, vin', în părul tău bălai
S-anin cununi de stele,
Pe-a mele ceruri să răsai
Mai mândră decât ele.

– O, ești frumos cum numa-n vis
Un demon se arată,
Dară pe calea ce-ai deschis
N-oi merge niciodată!

Mă dor de crudul tău amor
A pieptului meu coarde,
Și ochii mari și grei mă dor,
Privirea ta mă arde.

– Dar cum ai vrea să mă cobor?
Au nu-nțelegi tu oare,
Cum că eu sunt nemuritor,
Și tu ești muritoare?

With crimson torches in the air,
The world's far ends are rife,
And from the valleys of nowhere
A proud shape comes to life;

And on the locks of his black hair
The crown seems all ablaze;
He came and floated, one would swear,
As bathed in the sun's rays.

The marble arms form the black shroud
Reach out as for embrace,
He comes so pensive, sad and proud,
And wax-pale is his face;

But his large eyes, of eerie spell,
Chimerically spark,
Two passions bottomless and fell
And overfull of dark.

"Twas hard to leave my sphere and come
And lend to you my ear,
The night she is my mother glum,
The sun, my father dear.

O, come, my treasure! Leave afar
The world where you abide;
My love, I am the evening star
And you shall be my bride.

O, come, and on your fair-haired head
A wreath of stars I'll lay,
That from my heavens you may shed
More glorious light than they.'

'You are as handsome as in sleep
Can but a daemon be;
Yet never shall I take and keep
The path you show to me.

My heartstrings ache when every eve
You vent your cruel desire,
Your eyes, so gloomy, make me grieve,
And scorching is their fire.'

'How could I possibly descend?
You ought to realize
That my life here will have no end,
Whilst yours just gleams and dies.'

– Nu caut vorbe pe ales,
Nici ştiu cum aş începe –
Deşi vorbeşti pe înţeles,
Eu nu te pot pricepe;

Dar dacă vrei cu crezământ
Să te-ndrăgesc pe tine,
Tu te coboară pe pământ,
Fii muritor ca mine.

– Tu-mi cei chiar nemurirea mea
În schimb pe-o sărutare,
Dar voi să ştii asemenea
Cât te iubesc de tare;

Da, mă voi naşte din păcat,
Primind o altă lege;
Cu vecinicia sunt legat,
Ci voi să mă dezlege.

Şi se tot duce... S-a tot dus.
De dragu-unei copile,
S-a rupt din locul lui de sus,
Pierind mai multe zile.

***

În vremea asta Cătălin,
Viclean copil de casă,
Ce umple cupele cu vin
Mesenilor la masă,

Un paj ce poartă pas cu pas
A-mpărătesii rochii,
Băiat din flori şi de pripas,
Dar îndrăzneţ cu ochii,

Cu obrăjei ca doi bujori
De rumeni, bată-i vina,
Se furişează pânditor
Privind la Cătălina.

Dar ce frumoasă se făcu
Şi mândră, arz-o focul;
Ei, Cătălin, acu-i acu
Ca să-ţi încerci norocul.

Şi-n treacăt o cuprinse lin
Într-un ungher degrabă.
– Da' ce vrei, mări Cătălin?
Ia du-t' de-ţi vezi de treabă.

'I do not make of words a choice,
I know not how to start,
Though you speak clearly, with men's voice,
I fail to read your heart;

But if you really want that I
Should your beloved be,
Descend on earth from there on high,
Be mortal just like me.'

'My immortality you take
As ransom for a kiss;
Yet you must know how sore I ache,
How sore your love I miss;

I shall be born, whate'er betide,
In sin, take a new law;
Though to eternity I'm tied,
I shall be tied no more.'

And off he goes . . . For a girl's love
E'er faster does he wend,
Estranged from his abode above,
And lost for days on end.

***

At this time, cunning Cătălin,
A boy brought up so fine,
That at each sumptuous banquet scene
He fills the cups of wine,

A page who step by step does hold
The robe-trains of the queen,
A tramp born out of wedlock, bold,
With eyes unduly keen,

With cheeks like rosy flowers in bloom,
On tiptoe, oh the sinner!
He steals into the dim-lit room
To look at Cătălina.

My goodness! She is near her prime . . .
How lovely is the duck!
Well, Cătălin, now is the time
For you to try your luck.

So when she slid into a nook,
He clasped her unawares.
'What is it, Cătălin? Now look –
Go, mind your own affairs!'

– Ce voi? Aş vrea să nu mai stai
Pe gânduri totdeauna,
Să râzi mai bine şi să-mi dai
O gură, numai una.

– Dar nici nu ştiu măcar ce-mi ceri,
Dă-mi pace, fugi departe –
O, de luceafărul din cer
M-a prins un dor de moarte.

– Dacă nu ştii, ţi-aş arăta
Din bob în bob amorul,
Ci numai nu te mânia,
Ci stai cu binişorul.

Cum vânătoru-ntinde-n crâng
La păsărele laţul,
Când ţi-oi întinde braţul stâng
Să mă cuprinzi cu braţul;

Şi ochii tăi nemişcători
Sub ochii mei rămâie...
De te înalţ de subsuori
Te-nalţă din călcâie;

Când faţa mea se pleacă-n jos,
În sus rămâi cu faţa,
Să ne privim nesăţios
Şi dulce toată viaţa;

Şi ca să-ţi fie pe deplin
Iubirea cunoscută,
Când sărutându-te mă-nclin,
Tu iarăşi mă sărută.

Ea-l asculta pe copilaş
Uimită şi distrasă,
Şi ruşinos şi drăgălaş,
Mai nu vrea, mai se lasă,

Şi-i zice-ncet: – Încă de mic
Te cunoşteam pe tine,
Şi guraliv şi de nimic,
Te-ai potrivi cu mine...

Dar un luceafăr, răsărit
Din liniştea uitării,
Dă orizon nemărginit
Singurătăţii mării;

'What is it?! Thinking stifles you,
And you call that great fun!
You'd better smile and give me, do,
A hearty kiss, just one.'

'I don't know what you ask, or why –
Leave me in peace, be gone!
I'm deadly love-sick, and on high
Is he – Hyperion.'

'You don't' know! Well, I can – I bet –
Show you, and piecemeal, too,
What is love – only do not fret,
And hold your peace, mind you.

As in the grove the fowler lays
His snare upon the tree,
When I reach out my arm sideways,
With both your arms clasp me;

Then, as I gaze into your eyes,
Don't move them to and fro,
And when I lift you up, just rise
On tiptoe and stand so;

And, also, when my face bends down,
Do hold your face supine,
A lifetime in your looks I'll drown
And you will melt in mine.

So that your love may fully know
And all its magic learn,
When, kissing you, I bend full low,
Do kiss me in your turn.'

She listened listless to the boy,
Though struck by his strange tone,
She was now passionate, now coy,
Now hostile, now half-prone.

She quoth, 'I knew you from a child,'
In a low voice she quoth,
'A mouthy ne'er-do-well, and wild,
We'd get on smoothly both.

A star, however, born to freeze
In bleak oblivion's quiet,
Lends scope unbounded to the sea's
Vast solitude and riot;

Şi tainic genele le plec,
Căci mi le umple plânsul
Când ale apei valuri trec
Călătorind spre dânsul;

Luceşte c-un amor nespus,
Durerea să-mi alunge,
Dar se înalţă tot mai sus,
Ca să nu-l pot ajunge.

Pătrunde trist cu raze reci
Din lumea ce-l desparte...
În veci îl voi iubi şi-n veci
Va rămânea departe...

De-aceea zilele îmi sunt
Pustii ca nişte stepe,
Dar nopţile-s de-un farmec sfânt
Ce nu-l mai pot pricepe.

– Tu eşti copilă, asta e...
Hai ş-om fugi în lume,
Doar ni s-or pierde urmele
Şi nu ne-or şti de nume,

Căci amândoi vom fi cuminţi,
Vom fi voioşi şi teferi,
Vei pierde dorul de părinţi
Şi visul de luceferi.

***

Porni luceafărul. Creşteau
În cer a lui aripe,
Şi căi de mii de ani treceau
În tot atâtea clipe.

Un cer de stele dedesubt,
Deasupra-i cer de stele –
Părea un fulger ne'ntrerupt
Rătăcitor prin ele.

Şi din a chaosului văi,
Jur împrejur de sine,
Vedea, ca-n ziua cea dentâi,
Cum izvorau lumine;

Cum izvorând îl înconjor
Ca nişte mări, de-a-notul...
El zboară, gând purtat de dor,
Pân' piere totul, totul;

My lashes secretly I bend
For I can't choose but cry
When the sea's foamy billows tend
Towards his seat on high.

To soothe my grief he shines so bright,
With love that can't be told,
But he attains e'er greater height,
E'er farther for my hold.

He sadly comes with his cold ray
From his own world, earth-proof,
For aye I'll love him and for aye
He will remain aloof.

And that is why my days are dry
As is a desert land,
So hallowed, yet, the nights that I
Their charm can't understand.'

'You're just a girl, that's what you are . . .
Let's travel far and wide,
They'll lose our traces near and far
And think that we have died.

We shall be wise and gay, we'll roam
Sound both in mind and limb,
You will forget your parents' home,
And all star-prompted whim.'

***

Off went the star. And as he went,
His wings grew more and more
And myriads of years were spent
For every hour that wore.

There was a sky of stars beneath,
A sky of stars o'erhead –
Like to a bolt with ne'er a death
Among the worlds he sped.

And from the valleys of the pit
He upwards spun his way;
He saw how lights sprang up and lit
As on the earliest day,

How like a sea they girdled him,
And swam and heaved about . . .
And flew and flew, an ache-borne whim
Till everything died out;

Căci unde-ajunge nu-i hotar,
Nici ochi spre a cunoaşte,
Şi vremea-ncearcă în zadar
Din goluri a se naşte.

Nu e nimic şi totuşi e
O sete care-l soarbe,
E un adânc asemene
Uitării celei oarbe.

– De greul negrei vecinicii,
Părinte, mă dezleagă
Şi lăudat pe veci să fii
Pe-a lumii scară-ntreagă;

O, cere-mi, Doamne, orice preţ
Dar dă-mi o altă soarte,
Căci tu izvor eşti de vieţi
Şi dătător de moarte;

Reia-mi al nemuririi nimb
Şi focul din privire,
Şi pentru toate dă-mi în schimb
O oră de iubire...

Din chaos, Doamne,-am apărut
Şi m-aş întoarce-n chaos...
Şi din repaos m-am născut,
Mi-e sete de repaos.

– Hyperion, ce din genuni
Răsai c-o-ntreagă lume,
Nu cere semne şi minuni
Care n-au chip şi nume;

Tu vrei un om să te socoţi
Cu ei să te asameni?
Dar piară oamenii cu toţi,
S-ar naşte iarăşi oameni.

Ei numai doar durează-n vânt
Deşerte idealuri –
Când valuri află un mormânt,
Răsar în urmă valuri;

Ei doar au stele cu noroc
Şi prigoniri de soarte,
Noi nu avem nici timp, nici loc
Şi nu cunoaştem moarte.

For where he reached there was no bourn,
To see there was no eye,
And from the chaos to be born
Time vainly made a try.

And there was nothing. There was, though,
A thirst that did oppress,
A gaping gulf above, below,
Like blind forgetfulness.

'From heavy, dark eternity
Deliver me, of Lord,
For ever hallowed may'st Thou be
And praised throughout the world!

O, ask me, Father, anything
But change my fortune now;
O'er Fount of Life Thou art the king,
The death-dispenser Thou;

My aura of eternity,
My fiery looks retrieve,
And, in exchange, for love grant me
A single hour's leave.

From chaos come, I would return
To chaos, oh, most Blessed,
For out of rest eternal born,
I yearn again for rest.'

'Wan star, which from the world's confines
Dost with the cosmos rise,
Ask not for miracles and signs
That have no name nor guise!

What, wouldst thou deem thyself to be
A fellow of those men?
If all of them drowned in the sea,
Men would be born again.

For, it is men alone who, blind,
Build castles in the air;
When waves have found their grave, behind,
Waves simmer everywhere;

Or lucky stars or Fate's disgrace
Are only humans' lot,
While we have neither time nor place
And death can strike us not.

Din sânul vecinicului ieri
Trăieşte azi ce moare,
Un soare de s-ar stinge-n cer
S-aprinde iarăşi soare;

Părând pe veci a răsări,
Din urmă moartea-l paşte,
Căci toţi se nasc spre a muri
Şi mor spre a se naşte.

Iar tu, Hyperion, rămâi
Oriunde ai apune...
Cere-mi cuvântul meu dentâi –
Să-ţi dau înţelepciune?

Vrei să dau glas acelei guri,
Ca dup-a ei cântare
Să se ia munţii cu păduri
Şi insulele-n mare?

Vrei poate-n faptă să arăţi
Dreptate şi tărie?
Ţi-aş da pământul în bucăţi
Să-l faci împărăţie.

Îţi dau catarg lângă catarg,
Oştiri spre a străbate
Pământu-n lung şi marea-n larg,
Dar moartea nu se poate...

Şi pentru cine vrei să mori?
Întoarce-te, te-ndreaptă
Spre-acel pământ rătăcitor
Şi vezi ce te aşteaptă.

***

În locul lui menit din cer
Hyperion se-ntoarse
Şi, ca şi-n ziua cea de ieri,
Lumina şi-o revarsă.

Căci este sara-n asfinţit
Şi noaptea o să-nceapă;
Răsare luna liniştit
Şi tremurând din apă

Şi umple cu-ale ei scântei
Cărările din crânguri.
Sub şirul lung de mândri tei
Şedeau doi tineri singuri:

From yesterday's eternal womb
Lives now whatever dies,
And if a sun should meet its doom,
New suns would mount the skies.

Although they seem e'er to ascend,
Death pricks them with his thorn,
All that are born die in the end
To live on a new morn.

Hyperion thou must remain
Wherever thou dost rise . . .
Wouldst thou hear my first word again
And so become more wise?

Wilt thou that I my mouth should ope
To sing the song that wiles
The mountains with their wooded slope,
The sea's uncounted isles?

Or wilt thou prove by deed thy worth,
That right and might canst helm?
I would in clods give thee the earth
To make it a great realm!

Or give the vessels, masts on masts,
And hosts that land and sea
Will cross, the power to ride and blast,
But death – that cannot be . . .

And when, think'st thou, thy death is worth?
Turn back, turn down once more
And see what on the straying earth
There is for three in store.'

***

Hyperion finds back his way
To his predestined stead
And, once again, as yesterday,
His radiant light does shed.

The sun does with the dusk compete,
The night will gather soon,
Out of the waters, trembling, sweet,
Uprises the full moon.

To gild with sparkles the soft breeze,
The paths in grass unmown.
Under a clump of linden-trees
A young pair sat alone.

– O, lasă-mi capul meu pe sân,
Iubito, să se culce
Sub raza ochiului senin
Şi negrăit de dulce;

Cu farmecul luminii reci
Gândirile străbate-mi,
Revarsă linişte de veci
Pe noaptea mea de patimi.

Şi de asupra mea rămâi
Durerea mea de-o curmă,
Căci eşti iubirea mea dentâi
Şi visul meu din urmă.

Hyperion vedea de sus
Uimirea-n a lor faţă:
Abia un braţ pe gât i-a pus
Şi ea l-a prins în braţe...

Miroase florile-argintii
Şi cad, o dulce ploaie,
Pe creştetele-a doi copii
Cu plete lungi, bălaie.

Ea, îmbătată de amor,
Ridică ochii. Vede
Luceafărul. Şi-ncetişor
Dorinţele-i încrede:

– Cobori în jos, luceafăr blând,
Alunecând pe-o rază,
Pătrunde-n codru şi în gând,
Norocu-mi luminează!

El tremură ca alte dăţi
În codri şi pe dealuri,
Călăuzind singurătăţi
De mişcătoare valuri;

Dar nu mai cade ca-n trecut
În mări din tot înaltul:
– Ce-ţi pasă ţie, chip de lut,
Dac-oi fi eu sau altul?

Trăind în cercul vostru strâmt
Norocul vă petrece,
Ci eu în lumea mea mă simt
Nemuritor şi rece.

[1883]

248

'O, rest my head upon your breast!
There, sweetheart, let it lie,
Under the heaven's eye, more blest,
More sweet with every sigh;

Imbue my thoughts for evermore
With your light's frozen balm,
Upon my light of passion pour
Your everlasting calm.

Abide o'er me and from above
Assuage with your pale beam
My grief, for you are my first love
And, also, my last dream.'

Hyperion, in heavens, read
Amaze upon their face;
No sooner had he clasped her head
That she did him embrace . . .

Two children with long flaxen hair
Are lying 'mid the flowers,
Upon the blooms fall from the air
In scented, silver showers.

Love-struck, she raises up her eyes
And sees the star. Afire
She trusts him in a gentle wise
With her unquenched desire:

'Descend, o mild Hyperion,
Glide down upon a ray
Into the woods and thoughts anon,
Light up my fortune's way!'

He trembles as he often would
In forests, hills and leas,
And guides the awesome solitude
Of ever restless seas.

Yet he no more, as yesterday,
Falls down into the sea;
'What dost thou care, o, shape of clay,
If it is I or he?

You live accompanied by weal
In your all-narrow fold,
Whilst in my boundless world I feel
Both deathless and dead cold.'

[1883] [*Translated by Leon Leviţchi*]

249

I.k.4. ION ELIADE RĂDULESCU, din *Teatrul naţional*

[...] Oraşul nostru liniştit d-odată simţi trebuinţa teatrului şi de o pornire tot mişcat, într-o inimă a hotărât să înlesnească de bunăvoie şi să dea fieştecare o mică sumă după starea sa şi ca să se zidească un teatru după chipul celor europeneşti. [...] Râvna acestora încredinţează pe oricine că în scurtă vreme se va alcătui şi o companie rumânească şi vom dobândi un teatru naţional, şcoala cea dintâi a gustului, a moralului şi a formării obiceiurilor, petrecerea cea mai nobilă şi mai nevinovată, cinstea şi îmfrumuseţarea politicii, locul unde, cu vreme, vom auzi şi vom vedea încorunaţi pe poeţii şi autorii noştri, loc în care limba se îmfrumuseţează şi se înalţă în treapta ce i se cuvine şi în care este făcută şi hotărâtă ca să o ţie odată, puindu-se d-alăturea ca o tânără logodnică cu surorile ei şi luând moştenirea ce legiuit i-a lăsat-o maica sa, latina. [...] Istoria noastră este plină de întâmplări şi fapte mari şi eroice, şi este izvorul de unde să se adape duhurile şi cu tragedii originale. Daţi dară ajutor tinerilor simţitori, începeţi a alcătui şi a tâlmăci ca să înzestraţi biblioteca teatrului cu faptele voastre!

[1830]

l. РУССКИЙ

I.l.1. АЛЕКСАНДР ПУШКИН, «ПРОРОК»

Духовной жаждою томим,
В пустыне мрачной я влачился, –
И шестикрылый серафим
На перепутье мне явился.
Перстами легкими как сон
Моих зениц коснулся он.
Отверзлись вещие зеницы,
Как у испуганной орлицы.
Моих ушей коснулся он, –
И их наполнил шум и звон:
И внял я неба содроганье,
И горний ангелов полет,
И гад морских подводный ход,
И дольней лозы прозябанье.
И он к устам моим приник,
И вырвал грешный мой язык,
И празднословный и лукавый,
И жало мудрыя змеи

I.k.4.   ION ELIADE RĂDULESCU, from *The National Theatre*[4]

[. . .] Our quiet city suddenly felt a need for the theatre. Driven by this need, they have decided with one heart and one mind that each inhabitant should donate a small sum, according to their income, towards the building of a theatre in the European style. [. . .] Their industry and work ethic are a guarantee that soon there will be a Romanian theatre company and we will boast a national theatre. The theatre will embody taste and morality, and will educate the people in our customs and mores. The theatre – the noblest and purest of pastimes, the honour and grace of the government – will, over time, see our poets and playwrights crowned with fame. It is a place where language dwells, growing in beauty and honour, as a young fiancé, by the side of its sisters, inheriting the legacy of its mother, Latin. [. . .] Our history boasts great and heroic deeds and exploits, it is a spring from which those spirits looking for original tragedies can drink. Support our sensitive youth, I urge you, start writing and translating so as to endow the theatre library with your doings!

[1830] [*Translated by Mihaela Anghelescu Irimia and Virginia Jarrell*]

l.   RUSSIAN

I.l.1.   ALEXANDER PUSHKIN, 'The Prophet'

With soul athirst I wandered lost
Through darkling of a desert land
And at the place where pathways crossed
Beheld the six-wing'd Seraph stand.
His fingers light as sleep he turned
To touch mine eyes and lo they burned,
And like a startled eaglet's eyes
They opened wild on prophecies,
And at his touch my mortal ears
Filled with the sounding of the spheres:
I fathomed shudderings of the sky
The sweep of angel hosts on high,
The creep of creatures in the seas,
The seeping sap of valley trees.
Then leaning to my lips he wrung
Thereout my sinful earthen tongue
And all its guile and perfidy;
And his right hand where blood was wet

---

[4] A believer in the social mission of culture, Eliade Rădulescu employed a persuasive strategy in the name of national values. He spoke as a public figure of firm convictions, aware that his voice would play no little role in shaping such an important institution as a national theatre in Bucharest, at a time of servile imitation of Western models, if not of still Greek ones. But, more than anything else, he conceived of the new institution as the right dwelling of the Romanian language, a proud inheritor of its mother, Latin. Eliade's linguistic purist mania was to push him into ridiculous positions, as when, out of an utterly disproportionate love for Italian, he devised an Italianite Romanian which nobody ever used even in the elite intellectual circles in which he moved. While this is a joke now, it shows the ardour of the national debate about the Latinity of the Romanians in the years preceding the 1859 Union.

В уста замершие мои
Вложил десницею кровавой.
И он мне грудь рассек мечом,
И сердце трепетное вынул,
И угль, пылающий огнем,
Во грудь отверстую водвинул.
Как труп в пустыне я лежал,
И Бога глас ко мне воззвал:
«Восстань, пророк, и виждь, и внемли,
Исполнись волею моей,
И, обходя моря и земли,
Глаголом жги сердца людей».

(1826)

I.1.2. ВИССАРИОН БЕЛИНСКИЙ, из статьи «*Горе от ума*»

Поэзия есть истина в форме созерцания; ее создания – воплотившиеся идеи, видимые, *созерцаемые* идеи. Следовательно, поэзия есть та же философия, то же мышление, потому что имеет то же содержание – абсолютную истину, но только не в форме диалектического развития идеи из самой себя, а в форме непосредственного явления идеи в образе. Поэт мыслит образами; он не *доказывает* истины, а *показывает* ее. Но поэзия не имеет цели вне себя – она сама себе цель; следовательно, поэтический образ не есть что-нибудь внешнее для поэта, или второстепенное, не есть средство, но есть цель: в противном случае он не был бы образом, а был бы символом. Поэту представляются образы, а не идея, которой он из-за образов не видит и которая, когда сочинение готово, доступнее мыслителю, нежели самому творцу. Посему поэт никогда не предполагает себе развить ту или другую идею, никогда не задает себе задачи: без ведома и без воли его возникают в фантазии его образы, и, очарованный их прелестию, он стремится из области идеалов и возможности перенести их в действительность, то есть видимое одному ему сделать видимым для всех. Высочайшая действительность есть истина; а как содержание поэзии – истина, то и произведения поэзии суть высочайшая действительность. Поэт не украшает действительности, не изображает людей, какими они должны быть, но каковы они суть. Есть люди, – это все они же, все романтические же классики, – которые от всей души убеждены, что поэзия есть мечта, а не действительность, и что в наш век, как *положительный* и *индюстриальный*, поэзия невозможна. Образцовое невежество! нелепость первой величины! Что такое мечта? Призрак, форма без содержания, порождение расстроенного воображения, праздной головы, колобродствующего сердца! И *такая* мечтательность нашла своих поэтов в Ламартинах и свои поэтические произведения в идеально чувствительных романах, вроде «Аббаддонны»[1]; но разве Ламартин поэт, а не мечта, – и разве «Аббаддонна» поэтическое произведение, а не мечта?.. И что за жалкая, что за устарелая мысль о *положительности* и *индюстриальности* нашего века, будто бы враждебных искусству? Разве не в нашем веке явились Байрон, Вальтер Скотт, Купер, Томас Мур, Уордсворт, Пушкин, Гоголь, Мицкевич, Гейне, Беранже, Эленшлегер, Тегнер и другие? Разве не в нашем веке действовали Шиллер и Гете? Разве не наш век оценил и

---

[1] Известный немецкий роман какого-то господина идеальштюкмахера. (*Прим. В. Г. Белинского.*)

Parted my palsied lips and set
A Serpent's subtle sting in me.
He raised a blade and cleft my chest
Reft out my quaking heart entire
And, in my breast asunder, pressed
A coal alight with living fire.
I lay in desert land as dead
Until the Voice from Heaven said:
"Arise O Prophet! Work my will,
Thou that hast now perceived and heard.
On land and sea thy charge fulfill
And burn Man's heart with this My Word."

(1826) [*Translated by Ivan Panin*]

I.1.2.   VISSARION BELINSKY, from *Misfortune from Intelligence*[2]

Poetry is truth in a form of contemplation – incarnate ideas, visible, *contemplative*[3] ideas. Therefore, poetry is the same as philosophy, the same as thinking, because it has the same contents, namely, the absolute truth, only not in a form of a dialectical development of an idea out of itself, but in the form of a direct appearance of the idea as an image. A poet thinks in images; he does not prove the truth but rather *demonstrates* it. But poetry has no goal beyond itself – it is its own goal; therefore, a poetic image is not anything exterior, or secondary; for a poet, it is not the means, but it is the goal: otherwise, it would not be an image, but rather it would be a symbol. It is images that appear to a poet, and not an idea, which he does not see behind the images, and which, when a composition is completed, is more accessible for a thinker, than for its creator. This is why a poet never intends to develop one idea or another; he never gives himself a task: without his knowing and without his willing his images emerge in his imagination, and, allured by their seductiveness, he strives to transport them from the realm of ideals and possibility into reality, that is, to make that which is visible for him alone visible for all. The most sublime reality is truth; and since the content of poetry is truth, the works of poetry are the most sublime reality. A poet does not embellish reality, he does not depict people as they ought to be, but as they are. There are people, – they are these same people, these same romantic classics, – who are convinced with all their heart that poetry is a dream, and not a reality, and that in our age, since it is *positive* and *industrial*, poetry is impossible.

What an exemplary ignorance! What complete nonsense! What is a dream? A phantom, a form without contents, the deformed offspring of a sick imagination, of an idle head, of a wayward heart! And this kind of dreaminess is found in the followers of Lamartine and the ideally sentimental novels, a sort of *Abbaddonna*;[4] but is Lamartine a poet, and not a dream? – and is *Abbaddonna* a piece of poetry, and not a dream? And what a pitiful, outmoded thought is the belief that our age, being *positive* and *industrial*, would be hostile towards art? Wasn't it in our

---

[2]   *Misfortune from Intelligence* is a neo-classical comedy by Alexander Griboedov (a piece of dramatic art that has always enjoyed unflagging popularity in Russia). Belinsky preludes his review of this play with an extensive exposition of his own aesthetic programme, revealing a strong influence of Hegelian philosophy (to be overcome at the later stages of the critic's career).

[3]   Lit. 'that which can be contemplated', 'contemplatable' – if there were such a word.

[4]   A famous German novel by some Mister Idealstückmacher. (A comment of V. G. Belinsky.)

понял создания классического искусства и Шекспира? Неужели это еще не факты? Индустриальность есть только одна сторона многостороннего XIX века, и она не помешала ни дойти поэзии до своего высочайшего развития в лице поименованных нами поэтов, ни музыке в лице ее Шекспира – Бетховена, ни философии в лице Фихте, Шеллинга и Гегеля. Правда, наш век – враг мечты и мечтательности, но потому-то он и великий век! Мечтательность в XIX веке так же смешна, пошла и приторна, как и сентиментальность. *Действительность* – вот пароль и лозунг нашего века, действительность во всем – и в верованиях, и в науке, и в искусстве, и в жизни. Могучий, мужественный век, он не терпит ничего ложного, поддельного, слабого, расплывающегося, но любит одно мощное, крепкое, существенное. Он смело и бестрепетно выслушал безотрадные песни Байрона и, вместе с их мрачным певцом, лучше решился отречься от всякой радости и всякой надежды, нежели удовольствоваться нищенскими радостями и надеждами прошлого века. Он выдержал рассудочный критицизм Канта, рассудочное положение Фихте; он перестрадал с Шиллером все болезни внутреннего, субъективного духа, порывающегося к действительности путем отрицания. И зато в Шеллинге он увидел зарю бесконечной действительности, которая в учении Гегеля осияла мир роскошным и великолепным днем и которая, еще прежде обоих великих мыслителей, непонятая, явилась непосредственно в созданиях Гете… Только в наш век искусство получило полное

свое значение, как примирение христианского содержания с пластицизмом классической формы, как новый момент уравновешения идеи с формою. Наш век есть век примирения, и он так же чужд романтического искусства, как и классического. Средние века были моментом нецельным, неслитным, но отвлеченным; мы видим в нем только романтические элементы, которыми человечество запасалось на будущую жизнь и которые только теперь явились в своей слитной действительности и проникли нашу частную, домашнюю и даже практическую сторону жизни, так что одна сторона не отрицает другой, но обе являются в неразрывном единстве, взаимно проникнув одна другую. Этого-то слитного единства и не было в действительности средних веков, которых романтические элементы обозначались в какой-то отвлеченной особенности. И вот почему рыцарь иногда при одном подозрении в неверности жены или безжалостно умерщвлял ее собственною рукою, или сожигал живую, – ее, которая некогда была царицею дум и мечтаний души его, перед которою робко преклонял он колени, едва осмеливаясь возвести взоры на свое божество, и которой бескорыстно посвящал он и свое кипящее мужество, и силу железной руки, и беспокойную, бродячую волю свою… Да и вообще, находя жену, он терял идеальное, бесплотное, ангелоподобное существо. В новейшем периоде человечества напротив: Юлия Шекспира обладает всеми романтическими элементами; любовь была религиею и мистикою ее девственного сердца; встреча с родною ей душою была великим и торжественным актом ее души, вдруг сознавшей себя и возросшей до действительности; а между тем, это существо не облачное, не туманное, все *земное*, – да, земное, но насквозь проникнутое небесным. Романтическое искусство переносило землю на небо, его стремление было вечно туда, по ту сторону действительности и жизни: наше новейшее искусство переносит небо на землю и земное просветляет небесным. В наше время только слабые и болезненные души видят в действительности юдоль страдания и бедствий и в туманную сторону идеалов переносятся своей фантазиею, на жизнь и радость в мечте: души нормальные и крепкие находят свое блаженство в живом сознании живой действительности, и для них прекрасен божий мир, и само страдание есть только форма блаженства, а блаженство – жизнь в бесконечном. Мечтательность была высшею

age when Byron, Walter Scott, Cooper, Thomas Moore, Wordsworth, Pushkin, Gogol, Mickie-wicz, Heine, Beranger, Elenschleger[5], Tegnér, and others, appeared? Wasn't it in our age, when Schiller and Goethe worked? Wasn't it our age that appreciated and understood the works of classical art and of Shakespeare? Are these facts still not enough? Industrialization is only one side of the multisided 19th century, and it has not prevented poetry from achieving its highest development in the poets named by us, nor has it prevented music to achieve its highest devel-opment in the person of its 'Shakespeare,' Beethoven, nor has it prevented philosophy to achieve its highest development in the persons of Fichte, Shelling, and Hegel. It is true that our age is an enemy of dream and of dreaminess, but for this very reason it is also a great age! Dreaminess in the 19th century is as ridiculous, banal, and cloying, as sentimentality. *Reality* – this is the pass-word and the motto of our age, reality in everything – in beliefs, in science, in art, and in life. This mighty, manly age does not tolerate anything false, counterfeit, weak, and ambiguous, but it loves only that which is mighty, strong, and substantial. Courageously and intrepidly it lis-tened to the cheerless songs of Byron, and, together with their somber singer, it decided that it is better to deny all joy and all hope, than to find satisfaction in the miserable joys and hopes of the preceding age. It withstood the rational criticism of Kant, the rational thesis of Fichte; together with Schiller it suffered all the maladies of the interior subjective spirit, aspiring to reality by way of negation. In Schelling, however, it perceived the dawn of the infinite reality, which in the teaching of Hegel illuminated the world with a splendid and magnificent day, and which, even before these two great thinkers, had appeared, though misunderstood by others, directly in works of Goethe. . .

Only in our age art has received its full meaning, as the reconciliation of Christian content with the plasticity of classical form, as a new time of equilibrium of idea and form. Our age is the age of reconciliation, and it is as alienated from romantic art as it is from classical art. The Middle Ages were an incomplete, disjointed, and rather abstract time period; in it we only see romantic elements, which humankind was stocking up for a life to come, and which have only now appeared in their integral reality and penetrated our private, domestic, and even practical side of life, so that one side does not deny the other, but both appear in indissoluble unity, hav-ing interpenetrated one another. It is this very indissoluble unity that was absent from the reality of the Middle Ages, the romantic elements of which were appearing in a certain abstract isolation. And this is why a knight, from just a suspicion of infidelity of his wife, would some times either ruthlessly murder her with his own hand, or burn her alive, – she, who had once been a queen of the thoughts and dreams of his soul, before whom he bashfully bent his knees, hardly daring to lift his eyes to his deity, and to whom he had selflessly devoted his boiling courage, and the force of his iron hand, and his restless vagrant will . . . And in general, having found a wife, he would loose an ideal, incorporeal, angel-like being. In the modern age of humanity it is the opposite: Shakespeare's Julia possesses all romantic elements; love was a reli-gion and mystique of her virgin heart; the encounter with her soul mate was a magnificent and solemn action of her own soul, which had suddenly realized itself as having grown up to real-ity; and, in the meanwhile, this being is not nebulous, not ethereal, but entirely *earthly*, – yes, earthly, but permeated by the heavenly through and through. Romantic art transported the earth into heaven, its aspiration was eternally directed beyond, outside reality and life; our modern art transports heaven to earth, and illumines the earthly by the heavenly. In our time only weak and ailing souls perceive in reality the vale of sufferings and of disasters, and, by

---

[5] Adam Gottlob Oehlenschläger. It appears that it is sometimes spelled Elenschleger.

действительностию только в периоде юношества человеческого рода; тогда и формы поэзии улетучивались в фимиам молитвы, во вздох блаженствующей любви или тоскующей разлуки. Поэзия же мужественного возраста человечества, наша, новейшая поэзия осязаемо изящную форму просветляет эфиром мысли и наяву действительности, а не во сне мечтаний, отворяет таинственные врата священного храма духа. Короче: как романтическая поэзия была поэзиею мечты и безотчетным порывом в область идеалов, так новейшая поэзия есть *поэзия действительности*, поэзия жизни.

Разделение поэзии на три рода – лирическую, эпическую и драматическую – выходит из ее значения как *сознания истины* и, следовательно, из взаимных отношений сознающего духа – *субъекта*, к предмету сознания – *объекту. Лирическая* поэзия выражает субъективную сторону человека, открывает нашему взору *внутреннего* человека, и потому вся она – ощущение, чувство, музыка. *Эпическая* поэзия есть объективное изображение совершившегося во времени события, картина, которую показывает вам художник, выбирая для вас лучшие точки зрения, указывая на все ее стороны. *Драматическая* поэзия есть примирение этих двух сторон, субъективной, или лирической, и объективной, или эпической. Перед вами не *совершившееся*, но *совершающееся* событие; не поэт вам сообщает его, но каждое действующее лицо выходит к вам само, говорит вам за самого себя. В одно и то же время видите вы его с двух точек зрения: оно увлекается общим водоворотом драмы и действует волею и неволею сообразно с своими отношениями к прочим лицам и идее целого создания – вот его объективная сторона; оно раскрывает перед вами свой внутренний мир, обнажает все изгибы сердца своего; вы подслушиваете его немую беседу с самим собою – вот его субъективная сторона. Поэтому-то в драме всегда видите вы два элемента: эпическую объективность действия в целом и лирические выходки и излияния в монологах, до того лирические, что они непременно должны быть писаны стихами и, переданные в переводе прозою, теряют свой поэтический букет и переходят в надутую прозу, чему доказательством могут служить лучшие места Шекспировых драм, переведенных прозою. В лирической поэзии поэт является нам субъектом, и потому-то в ней так часто и такую важную роль играет его личность, его *я*, а ощущения и чувства, о которых он говорит, как о своих собственных, будто бы одному ему принадлежащих, мы приписываем себе, узнаем в них моменты собственного духа. Эпический поэт, скрываясь за событиями, которые заставляет нас созерцать, только подразумевается как лицо, без которого мы не знали бы о совершившемся событии; он даже и не всегда бывает незримо присутствующим лицом: он может позволять себе обращения и к самому себе, говорить о себе или, по крайней мере, подавать свой голос об изображаемых им событиях. В драме, напротив, личность поэта исчезает совсем и как бы даже не предполагается существующею, потому что в драме и событие говорит само за себя, современно представляясь совершающимся, и каждое из действующих лиц говорит само за себя, современно развиваясь и с внутренней и с внешней стороны своей.

Драматическую поэзию обыкновенно разделяют на два вида: *трагедию* и *комедию*. Разовьем необходимость этого разделения из сущности идеи поэзии, а не из внешних форм и признаков. Для этого мы должны разделить на две стороны самую поэзию, какая бы она ни была – лирическая, эпическая или драматическая: на *поэзию положения, или действительности*, и *поэзию отрицания, или призрачности*[6].

---

[6] Мы уверены, что это слово никому не покажется странным, хоть оно и ново. Всякий, понимающий слово «призрак», верно, поймет и «призрачность», означающую совокупность свойств призрака, точно так же, как «разум» и «разумность», и проч. (*Прим. В. Г. Белинского.*)

means of their imagination they transport themselves into a hazy country of ideals, for a life and joy found in a dream; normal and robust souls find their bliss in a living recognition of a living reality, and for them God's world is beautiful, and suffering itself is only a form of bliss, and bliss is the life in the infinite. Dreaminess was the ultimate reality only in the adolescence of humanity; then forms of poetry also vanished into the incense of prayer, into a sigh of a blissful love or a longing separation[7]. But the poetry of a mature state of humanity, our, modern poetry enlightens a palpably-fine form with the ether of thought, and in alertness of reality, and not in the slumber of dreaming, it opens the mysterious gates of the holy temple of spirit. In short: just as romantic poetry was poetry of dream and an unconscious impulse towards the realm of ideals, so modern poetry is the poetry of reality, the poetry of life.

Division of poetry into three types – lyric, epic, and dramatic – comes out of its meaning as the *apprehension of truth*, and, consequently, out of mutual relations of the apprehending spirit, which is the subject, to that which is apprehended, its object. *Lyric* poetry expresses the subjective side of man, reveals the *inner* man to our sight, and for this reason all of it is sensation, feeling, music. *Epic* poetry is the objective depiction of an event which occurred in time, a picture which the artist is showing to you, choosing for you the best visual vantage points, pointing at all its sides. *Dramatic* poetry is a reconciliation of these two sides, the subjective, or lyric, and the objective, or epic. That which is in front of you, is not an event that *has happened*, but an event that *is happening*; it is not the poet who relates it to you, but rather each character himself comes out to you and speaks with you for himself. At the same time you observe him from two viewpoints: he is carried along with the total vortex of the drama, and acts, willingly and unwillingly, in accordance with his relations to other characters, and to the idea of the entire work – this is his objective side; he opens his inner world before you, exposing every bend of his heart; you overhear his silent conversation with himself – this is his subjective side. It is for this reason that in drama you always see two elements: epic objectivity of an action in totality, and lyric escapades and outpours in monologues, lyrical to such an extent that they should have necessarily been written in verse, and, communicated by means of prose in translation, they lose their poetic bouquet and turn into turgid prose, as a proof of which the best passages of Shakespeare's dramas translated in prose may serve. In lyric poetry the poet appears to us as the subject, and this is why his personality, his 'I', plays a role in it so often, and such an important role, and the sentiments and feelings, of which he speaks as though they were his own, as if they belonged to him only, but we ascribe them to ourselves; in them we recognize instances of our own spirit. An epic poet, hiding behind the events which he makes us contemplate, is only implied as a character without whom we would not have known about the event that has occurred; and he does not even always exist as an invisibly present figure: he can afford to address himself, speak about himself, or, at least, speak about the events he depicts. On the contrary, in a drama the person of the poet completely disappears, as if it were not even assumed that he exists because in a drama an event speaks for itself, at the same time appearing as occurring, and every character also speaks for himself, at the same time developing inwardly and outwardly.

Dramatic poetry is usually divided into two types: *tragedy* and *comedy*. Let us deduce the necessity of this division on the basis of the essence of the idea of poetry, rather than on the basis of exterior forms and features. In order to do this we have to divide poetry itself, of whichever

---

[7] 1 I.e., a separation which makes one grieve.

Предмет поэзии есть *действительность*, или *истина в явлении*. Те, которые думают, что ее предмет – мечты и вымыслы никогда и нигде небывалого, кроме воображения поэта, сбиваются словами «идеал» и «идеализирование действительности». Конечно, создания поэта не суть списки или копии с действительности, но они сами суть действительность, как *возможность*, получившая свое *осуществление*, и получившая это осуществление по непреложным законам самой строгой необходимости: идея, рождающаяся в душе поэта, есть тайна, как младенец, зачинающийся во чреве матери: кто может угадать заранее индивидуальную форму той или другого? и та и другая не есть ли *возможность*, стремящаяся получить свое *осуществление*, *не* есть ли совершенно никогда и нигде небывалое, но долженствующее быть сущим? Идеал не есть собрание рассеянных по природе черт одной идеи и сосредоточенных на одном лице, потому что собирание не может не быть механическим, – а это противоречит динамическому процессу творчества. Еще менее идеал может быть воображением того, чего и нет и быть не может, то есть мечтою, или украшенною природою и усовершенствованными людьми – людьми не как они суть, а какими будто бы они должны быть. *Идеал* есть общая (абсолютная) идея, отрицающая свою общность, чтобы стать частным явлением, а ставши им, снова возвратиться к своей общности. Объясним это примером. Какая идея Шекспирова «Отелло»? Идея ревности, как следствия обманутой любви и оскорбленной веры в любовь и достоинство женщины. Эта идея не была сознательно взята поэтом в основание его творения, но, без ведома его, как незримо падшее в душу зерно, развилась в образы Отелло и Дездемоны, то есть совлеклась своей безусловной и отвлеченной общности, чтобы стать частными явлениями, личностями Отелло и Дездемоны. Но как лица Отелло и Дездемоны не суть лица какого-нибудь известного Отелло и какой-нибудь известной Дездемоны, а лица типические, благодаря общей идее, воплотившейся в них, то следует второе отрицание идеи, или возвращение общей идеи к самой себе. Следовательно, идеализировать действительность значит совсем не украшать, но являть ее как божественную идею, в собственных недрах своих носящую творческую силу своего осуществления из небытия в живое явление. Другими словами, «идеализировать действительность» значит в частном и конечном явлении выражать общее и бесконечное, не списывая с действительности какие-нибудь случайные явления, но создавая *типические* образы, обязанные своим типизмом общей идее, в них выражающейся. Портрет, чей бы он ни был, не может быть художественным произведением, ибо он есть выражение частной, а не общей идеи, которая одна способна явиться типически; но лицо, в котором бы, например, всякий узнал *скупого*, есть идеал, как типическое выражение общей родовой идеи скупости, которая заключает в себе возможность всех своих случайных явлений; поэтому, как скоро она стала образом, то в этом образе всякий видит портрет не *какого-нибудь* скупца, но портрет всякого *какого-нибудь* скупца, хотя бы этот *какой-нибудь* и имел совершенно другие черты лица.

Под словом «действительность» разумеется все, что есть, – мир видимый и мир духовный, мир фактов и мир идей. Разум в сознании и разум в явлении – словом, открывающийся самому себе дух есть *действительность*; тогда как все частное, все случайное, все неразумное есть *призрачность*, как противоположность действительности, как ее отрицание, как *кажущееся*, но не *сущее*. Человек пьет, ест, одевается – это мир *призраков*, потому что в этом нисколько не участвует дух его; человек чувствует, мыслит, сознает себя органом, сосудом духа, конечною частностию общего и бесконечного – это мир *действительности*. Человек служит царю и отечеству вследствие возвышенного

sort it may be – lyrical, epic, or dramatic – into two categories: poetry of affirmation, or of reality, and poetry of negation, or of ghostliness.[8]

Reality, or truth as a phenomenon, is the subject of poetry. Those who think that its subject is dreams and fantasies of that which has never existed anywhere, except in imagination of a poet, are bewildered by the words 'ideal', or 'idealization of reality'. Obviously, the works of a poet are not reproductions or copies of reality, rather, they are themselves reality, as a potentiality that has achieved its realization, and it has achieved this realization according to the inviolable laws of the strictest necessity: an idea, born in poet's soul, is a mystery, like an infant being conceived in the mother's womb: who can guess ahead of time the individual form of the one[9]or of the other?[10] Aren't both of them a potentiality, striving to achieve its actualization; are they not that which had never existed anywhere, but must come into existence[11]? An ideal is not an assembly of features of one idea dispersed in the nature and focused in one individual because an assembly cannot help but be mechanical, – but this contradicts the dynamic creative process. Even more so, an ideal cannot be the imagining of that which does not, and cannot, exist, that is, a dream, or embellished nature, or perfected humans – not humans as they are, but humans as they ought to be. An *ideal* is a universal, an absolute, idea, negating its universality in order to become a particular phenomenon, but, having become a particular phenomenon, it returns to its universality. Let us explain this by an example. What is the idea of Shakespeare's *Othello*? It is an idea of jealousy, as a consequence of cheated love and insulted belief in love and in woman's dignity. This idea was not consciously taken by the poet as a foundation of his creation, but, without his awareness, as a seed that invisibly fell into the soul, it developed into the characters of Othello and Desdemona, that is, the idea stripped off its non-contingent and abstract universality in order to become a particular phenomenon, namely, the persons of Othello and Desdemona. However, since the characters, Othello and Desdemona, are not the characters of some actual Othello or Desdemona, but character-types, due to the universal idea embodied in them, then the second transformation follows, that is, the return of the universal idea to itself. It follows that to idealize reality does not mean at all to embellish it, but rather to reveal it as a divine idea, which carries in its own depths a creative force of its actualization out of non-being into a live phenomenon. In other words, 'to idealize reality' means to express, in a particular and finite phenomenon, the universal and the infinite, not by copying some accidental phenomena from reality, but rather creating *typical* images, which owe their typology to the universal idea which is being expressed in them. A portrait, no matter whose, cannot be a work of art, because it is an expression of a particular rather than a universal idea, which alone can appear as a type; but a face in whom, for instance, everybody would recognize a miser, is an ideal, as a typical expression of a universal generic idea of miserliness, which comprises in itself a potentiality of all its particular occurrences; therefore, as soon as it became an image, in this image everyone sees, not a portrait of a *certain* miser, but rather a portrait of every *certain* miser, even though this certain one might have completely different facial features.

Everything that exists is implied by the word 'reality' – both the visible world and the spiritual world, the world of facts and the world of ideas. Reason in consciousness, and reason in

---

[8] *We are certain that no one will find this word strange, even though it is new. Everyone who understands the word 'ghost', will, no doubt, also understand 'ghostliness' which means a totality of qualities of a ghost, just like 'intellect' and 'intelligence', etc (Belinsky.)*

[9] That is, of the idea.

[10] That is, of the infant.

[11] Lit., 'become existing'.

понятия о своих обязанностях к ним, вследствие желания быть орудием истины и блага, вследствие сознания себя как части общества, своего кровного и духовного родства с ним – это мир действительности. «Овому талант, овому два», – и потому, как бы ни была ограничена сфера деятельности человека, как бы ни незначительно было место, занимаемое им не только в человечестве, но и в обществе, но если он, кроме своей конечной личности, кроме своей ограниченной индивидуальности, видит в жизни нечто общее и в сознании этого общего, по степени своего разумения, находит источник своего счастия, – он живет в действительности и есть действительный человек, а не призрак, – истинный, *сущий*, а не *кажущийся* только человек. Если человеку недоступны объективные интересы, каковы жизнь и развитие отечества, ему могут быть доступны интересы своего сословия, своего городка, своей деревни, так что он находит какое-то, часто странное и непонятное для самого себя, наслаждение для их выгод лишаться собственных личных выгод – и тогда он живет в действительности. Если же он не возвышается и до таких интересов, – пусть будет он супругом, отцом, семьянином, любовником, но только не в животном, а в человеческом значении, источник которого есть любовь, как бы ни была она ограничена, лишь бы только была отрицанием его личности, – он опять живет в действительности. На какой бы степени ни проявился дух, он – действительность, потому что он любовь или бессознательная разумность, а потом разум или любовь, сознавшая себя.

(1835)

m.   ESPAÑOL

I.m.1.   JOSÉ ZORRILLA Y MORAL, 'Granada. Fantasía'

¿Qué es un poeta? Un ave en la sombría
selva del mundo por su Dios lanzada
para llenar sus manos de armonía;
mas no para gorjear desatinada
día y noche, la selva ensordeciendo,
malgastando la voz que le fue dada
para elevarla audaz sobre el estruendo
mundanal y con fe consoladora
la gloria de Dios enalteciendo.
No al poeta se dio la voz sonora
como engañosa voz a la sirena
ni como al cocodrilo voz traidora;
la del poeta el ánimo serena
del hombre por la tierra peregrino,
dulce y divina voz que le enajena,
la patria celestial de donde vino

phenomena, in a word, the spirit revealing itself to itself is *reality*; while everything particular, everything incidental, everything unreasonable is *ghostliness*, as the opposite of reality, as its negation, as something appearing yet not existing. A man drinks, eats, gets dressed – this is the world of ghosts, because his spirit does not participate in this at all; a man feels, thinks, recognizes himself as an organ, a vessel of spirit, as a finite particularity of the universal and the infinite – this is the world of *reality*. The man serves the king and the fatherland in consequence of a lofty understanding of his obligations with respect to them, in consequence of the desire to be an instrument of truth and of the good, in consequence of recognizing himself as part of society, of his relation to it by blood and by spirit – this is the world of reality. 'To one he gave one talent, to another two,'[12] – and for this reason, no matter how limited a sphere of human activity may be, no matter how insignificant may be the place which he occupies not only in humanity, but also in society; but if, besides his finite personality, and besides his limited individuality, he sees something universal in life, and, in realization of this universality, to the degree of his understanding, he finds the source of his happiness, – he lives in reality, and he is a real human being rather than a ghost, – the true, the existing, rather than only appearing, man. If objective interests, such as the life and the development of the fatherland, are not accessible for a man, interests of his class, his town, his village may be accessible for him, so that he finds some satisfaction, often strange and incomprehensible for himself, to give up his own personal advantages for their sake, – in this case he also lives in reality. If, however, he does not even ascend to the interests of this kind, – let him be a husband, a father, a family man, a lover, but only not in an animal, but in a human sense, the source of which is love, no matter how limited it may be, if only it could be a denial of himself,– again, he lives in reality. No matter on which stage the spirit may become apparent, it is reality, because it is love and the unconscious rationality, and, because of this, it is reason and love which has become aware of itself.

[Translated by Yelena Borisova. Edited by Jamie S. Crouse]

m. SPANISH

I.m.1. JOSÉ ZORRILLA Y MORAL, 'Granada. A Fantasy'

What is a poet? A bird in the shadowy wood of the world cast by God to fill his hands with harmony, but not to warble madly night and day, deafening the wood, squandering the voice given him to raise it audaciously above the bustle of the world but, with consoling faith, raising the glory of God on high. The poet was not given his sonorous voice as the enchanting tones of the siren nor like the treacherous voice of the crocodile; that of the poet, the spirit of man serene, a pilgrim through the land, a sweet and divine voice which makes him an outcast, the heavenly motherland from which he hails is always recalled and gives relief in the mortal fatigue of his journey. Alas the poet who, singing without faith, only raised a murmur like the sighing of water and the wind. Alas the poet who does not sing his faith and the glory of the nation in which he was born, vainly letting his throat grow hoarse, a butterfly and not a bee! This has been the reason which has sustained me tenaciously in this my very work and in my assiduous desire. My poetry changes with my reason and in the light of my faith I proclaim once more that I have been a butterfly this day. In the thirty years I have dwelt in this land I have been a senseless bird chirping in the forest with useless warbling and I now must use my divine inspiration which

---

[12] Refers to the Parable of the Talents (Mt. 25.14–30).

recordándole siempre y aliviando
la fatiga poeta mortal de su camino.
¡Ay del poeta que, sin fe cantando,
sólo murmullo efímero levanta
como el agua y el viento susurrando!
¡Ay del poeta que su fe no canta
y la gloria del pueblo en que ha nacido,
enroqueciendo en vano su garganta,
mariposa y no abeja! Tal ha sido
la causa que tenaz de esta obra mía
en el asiduo afán me ha sostenido.
Cambia con mi razón mi poesía
y a la luz de la fe recapacito
que he sido mariposa hasta este día.
Ha siete lustros que la tierra habito,
ave insensata que en la selva trina
con inútil gorjear y necesito
utilizar la inspiración divina
que al poeta da Dios, el sacrosanto
sino cumpliendo a que mi ser destina.
Y he aquí porque, cuando hoy mi voz levanto,
Cristiano y español, con fe y sin miedo
Canto mi religión, mi patria canto.

(1847) [1852]

n. SVENSKA

I.n.1. C. J. L. ALMQVIST, *Om två slags Skrifsätt*, ur *Dialog om Sättet att sluta Stycken*

Det har ett särdeles behag för Läsaren, när äfven han får uppfinna något, får vara verksam.

Man kan skrifva så, att man ordentligt och riktigt ger besked i allt, hvad ämnet tillhörer, så att för läsaren ingenting återstår att göra, mer än blott – hvad för honom väl ock tycks vara det lämpligaste – läsa.

Men man kan äfven skrifva på ett annat sätt. Man kan låta bli att yttra allt; kanske ej en gång i orden lägga det hufvudsakligaste. Hvad man yttrar kan dock vara af sådan beskaffenhet, att det sätter läsaren i ett perspektiv, i en stämning, i en önskan och förmåga att gå fram i ämnets riktning – och han uppfinner på egen hand allt det öfriga osagda; ja kanske mycket mer, än som ens hade kunnat sägas af författaren.

Läsaren får då vara, ej blott läsare, utan äfven menniska: han får vara produktiv. Han bekommer tråden af författaren, men får gå med den på sitt sätt. Tråden måste likväl vara sådan, att läsaren dermed ej löper annorstädes, än författaren ville, ehuru det kan ske i variationer efter olika läsares lynnen.

Besynnerligt nog väckes i en läsares själ och sinne ofta helt annat genom uttrycken i en skrift, än hvad orden sjelfva, tagna efter orden, innehålla. Men den verld, som författaren hos sin läsare[1] manar fram till lif och egen verksamhet, – den verlden är egentligen hans verk, och orden i hans skrift (det synliga verket) ingenting annat än ett *moyen*.

[1] NB. en, som icke missförstår honom.

God, the sacrosanct, gives poetry, only fulfilling what is destined for my being. And here, I state my reason, when today I raise my voice, *Christian and Spanish, with faith and feeling,*

I sing my religion, I sing my motherland.

(1847) [1852]

Zorrilla, like Campoamor, was one of the most popular poets of the age and he caught the public mood exactly. Famed, principally, for his revision of the Don Juan theme in his play of 1844 (still put on every year), in his youth he reacted strongly against an archconservative father. His early verses express something of the anguish of the age. At the funeral of the suicide, Larra, on 15 February 1837, he read an elegy which propelled him to instant fame as the spokesman for the conservative wing of Spanish Romanticism. He soon, through his poems based on an historicist reading of history and legend, as well as a series of dramas, became the 'national' poet, expressing conservative ideals in a medievalizing dress. He also, as expressed here, elaborated a special divinely inspired role for poets as the voice of national ideals and of the Catholic faith. Also, like Arolas (see below), he cultivated the Oriental, especially in his long, unfinished, poem Granada, *based on the fall of the city in 1492. His meditations, in his last collections, on poetic inspiration and the creative act paved the way for Spanish Symbolism.*

n.   SWEDISH

I.n.1.   C. J. L. ALMQVIST, 'On Two Ways of Writing', from *Dialogue on How to End Pieces*

It is particularly enjoyable for the Reader when he also invents or creates something.

A text may be written so as to provide complete, exhaustive information on everything pertaining to the subject, so that nothing remains for the *reader* other than – and this he may well find appropriate – to *read*.

But one can also write in a different manner. One can stop short of saying everything; perhaps not even put the gist of arguments into words. What one does articulate can, however, be written in such a way as to give the reader a perspective, a mood, a desire and ability to follow along the tracks laid by the subject. Thus he invents what is left unsaid, indeed perhaps much more than the writer could have said.

The reader can thus be not only reader, but also a human being: he becomes productive. He receives the thread from the author, but can unwind it after his own fashion. The thread must nevertheless be spun so as to prevent the reader from running in a direction not intended by the author, although variations may arise with different readers.

Oddly enough, the soul and mind of a reader are stirred by the expressive spirit of a piece rather than by what is literally expressed through the words. But the world that the author calls to life and sets in motion in the empathetic reader– that world is his true creation and the actual words in his work (the tangible achievement) nothing less than an instrument.

Många gamla saker har jag sett, som till uttrycken äro föga poetiska; bistra, torra. Men de stämma läsaren hemlighetsfullt till poesi, musik, piktur i hans egen verld, i hans inbildning. Läsaren dröjer här så mycket hellre, som han anser den verlden för sin egen; och hon är äfvenså till hälften. Han dröjer der så mycket längre, som han känner det hos sig oförmodadt uppkomna än vidare kunna fortgå i uppfinningar, utan gräns. Han dröjer der med så mycket sannare tillfredsställelse, som han på detta sätt egentligen bildas – *han blir sjelf Verket* – i stället att för ögonen hafva ett redan bildadt verk att betrakta. Han icke blott läser poesi – han blir poesi; och, såsom väckt till verksamhet i sin egen inbildnings verld, är han der äfven poet (ποιητής, görare, frambringare). Efter detta skrifsätt äro författaren och hans läsare två samverkande faktorer till det arbete, som utföres. Och verket sjelf – som på papperet, der det ligger för ögonen, icke kan anses färdigt mer än till det, i bokstäfverna befintliga, artistiska anslaget – blir oupphörligt mer och mer färdigt genom läsarne. Och emedan desse under tidernas lopp blifva fler och fler, så kan man säga, att författarens arbete sålunda ständigt allt vidare fortfar att förfärdigas, så länge verlden står. Innebär det ej en outtömlighet, en viss evighet, som icke saknar interesse?

Det första skrifsättet, det direkta, det sjelfuttömda, har andra fördelar. Det bildar verk, som redan äro färdiga för läsarens ögon och således existera oberoende af honom. Men de hafva emot sig, hvad allt färdigt och fulländadt har, nemligen att vara slut. Och, liksom de äro oberoende af läsaren, så händer ock, att han kommer i en stämning af oberoende mot dem – som vill säga, han röres stundom ej så mycket af dem. Författaren och läsaren äro icke nu två faktorer, samarbetande till ett enda, oupphörligt blifvande och uppkommande verk; utan de äro begge ett slags egoister, utom hvarann, stundom kalla nog för hvarann.

Det är en stor konst att skrifva så, att man riktigt fulländar sitt ämne, matieren må vara vettenskaplig eller artistisk. Men att, utan synlig fulländning i arbetets för ögonen stående linier, likväl göra det så, att hos läsaren eller betraktaren just de toner anslås, just den verld väckes, som skall. väckes; och på det sätt, att han på egen hand går vidare fram i Verkets bana; det är ock en konst.

Men härtill behöfvas visserligen läsare och betraktare, som äro väckbara. Frågas dock, om ej äfven ett arbete af det sjelftillräckliga slaget, af en synliga fulländningen, af det sjelf-uttömda skrifsättet, fordrar läsare med intresse, såvida verket af dem skall genomgås till ändan? – Fordran på receptivitet må icke förblandas med författare-egoism. Receptivitet kan icke undvaras af någon, emedan behofvet deraf grundas på en helig naturlag, som gjort alla varelser till fraktionärer. Individerna äro skapade till hemisferer (ingenting hade annars ansigte, face); ingen skall då fulländas, utan genom andra; och det hela genom alla.

Det fullkomliga och sjelfständiga, hos menniskor som annat, har visst förekommit mig älskvärdt: men aldrig utan med vilkor, att tillika vara fraktionärt, på ett ädelt sätt brutet och behöfvande, hemisferiskt. Hvem förlåter icke gerna sina vänner all fullkomlighet och storhet, blott de tillika äro ofullkomliga?

Ingenting är ett ärligt och rätt fulländadt Helt, mer än blott sjelfva det Hela (Universum). Således tyckes hvart individuelt väsende, sin egen lilla helhet oaktadt, vara i stor mening ett bråk, som blott genom ett annat kan förvandlas till helt tal. Är icke lifvet så?

Ett skrifsätt och dess betraktare, ett verk och dess läsare, böra de ej vara två halfheter, som ömsevis upptaga och fullända hvarann? När derföre ett individuelt framställer sig – menniska eller skrift – med anspråk och form af ett slutet och fullbordadt för sig, utan någon annans medarbete; så går liksom en falsk ande deromkring, det har en bismak. Emedan all varelse af lif, jemte sin individuella helhet, tillika nödvändigt är ett fragment; så ångar en besynnerlig

I have seen many things that are not expressed poetically; texts that are grim, arid. But they secretly call the reader to poetry, music, prose in his own world, in *his own* imagination. The reader would perhaps rather stop here, regarding that world as his own; and so it is, in part. He may even feel that this sudden sense of inventing and creating will be indefinitely prolonged. He experiences a satisfaction more profound as he is altered himself by this action – *he becomes the Text* – instead of having set before him a text already created. He not only reads poetry – he *becomes* poetry; and, as he is stirred into activity in the world of his own imagination, he is also a poet (ποιητής, a doer and conjuror). In this creative process the author and his reader work side by side as the work takes shape. And the piece itself – which on paper, before our eyes, is incomplete, a mere set of characters arranged artistically – the piece becomes increasingly complete through its readers. And because they increase in number with time, one can say that the author's work continues to come into being as long as the world exists. Does this not suggest an inexhaustibility, an 'infiniteness', itself of great interest?

There are advantages to the first, direct, self-limited method of writing. It produces work that lies ready before the eyes of the reader and exists independently of him. But it has the disadvantage of all things ready and complete, namely that it is *finished*. And as it is independent of the reader he comes to feel equally independent of it – that is to say, he is not so moved by it. The author and the reader are now not side by side, cooperating towards one continuously emerging work; instead they have become two selves, separate, even distanced from one another.

Enormous artistic skill is required to write perfectly about any subject, whether scholarly or artistic. But even where the actual lines of the text are far from perfect, there are times when they strike precisely those chords needed to awaken the very world that must be awakened. When this enables the observer to follow independently the trajectory of the Work; that is also Art.

But receptive readers and observers are needed for this process. One may ask, also, if works of that other, self-sufficient, visibly perfect, self-limited type , may not also require readers who wish to engage with and develop the argument. The demand for a receptive readership must not be confused with authorial selfishness. Such a readership is needed for both kinds of writing, a need based on the innate propensity of all creatures to dissent, to take sides. By definition any individual must thus favour a single hemisphere (otherwise nothing would have countenance, *face*). It follows therefore that no individual is perfect; perfection can be reached only through others, and the whole through all.

I have always had the highest regard for the beings thus perfected and self-sufficient: but this is never achieved unconditionally. To dissent, to take sides, can be a noble state, though imperfect: who will not willingly forgive his friends all perfection and greatness, as long as they also are incomplete?

Nothing is a true and rightly perfected Whole, other than the Whole itself (the Universe). Thus, every individual being, in spite of its own little wholeness, seems to be a fraction of something else, which can only be made whole through another. Is this not a reflection of the way life itself works?

A written work and its reader, are they not two halves that both absorb and perfect each other? When an individual entity – man or text – appears or claims to be complete, without outside contribution, it is as if a deceptive spectre roams around it, it somehow looks wrong. Since all living creatures are both individually whole and of necessity also fragmentary, a

köld och afdödhet ifrån hvarje ting, som framstår med *blott och bar* fullständighet, helhet, sjelfhet.

Men om allt lefvande är ett *amabile fractum*, så följer deraf för ingen del, att det skall eller får vara en trasa, en slurfvig sammansättning, ett rafs. Ett rätt fragment, sådant som lifvet, är mera artistiskt brutet, än om det vore helt.

[1835]

I.n.2. P. D. A. ATTERBOM, från recensionen av *Svenska Akademiens Handlingar (1813)* i *Svensk Literatur-Tidning,* 4 November 1815.

[...]

Den Fransyska tonen i vettenskap och konst har tillräckligt uppdagat sina frukter. Den moquanta sensualismen, den bellettristiska jargonen, den mot religion, philosophi och poesi lika protesterande materialistiska fanatismen hafva äntligen bragt sitt hemland till det mål, hvarifrån Rousseaus och Hemsterhuis' i öknen ropande röster ej förmådde aflägsna det. Äfven dess tillgifnaste anhängare inse nu det rysliga tillstånd af fullkomlig upplösning, det moraliska och politiska brådjup, i hvilket detta fordom, så rättvist beundrade, ännu i så många enskilda fall älskvärdt ridderliga folk sunkit under och förtärs. Och likväl prisa de till vår efterföljd dessa kärnlösa mönster, der man förgäfves söker lifvets ord, dessa författare utan hjerta, utan tro, utan allvar, som med sina pestaktiga utdunstningar förgiftat Europa och andligen mördat sin nation! Genom hvad annat underkufvade Napoelon, som i sin person representerar all den storhet, hvartill jordens ande skild ifrån ljusets kan hinna, nästan hela den bildade verlden, om ej genom den egoism och den slappa lättsinnighet, som från Voltaires fosterjord bemäktigat sig nästan allheten af Europas förnäma, ståndspersoner och embetsmän? Och hvarigenom blef han krossad, om genom reaktionen af ett yngre slägte, uppfostradt i andra grundsatser, och af de män, som under den förflutna jerntiden med outtröttligt nit förberedt sanningens välde? Den som ännu är blind för den litterära verldens omedelbara sammanhang med den politiska, han betrakte det ljus af kraft och seger, som ändtligen fulländat den Germaniska stammens ära. Preussen har slagit tidens Babel genom elektriseringen af sina tänkares ideer och sina konstnärers tjuskraft. För att bevisa detta, hvilket ligger för allas ögon som umgåtts med personer af Tysklands bildade stånd, behöfs ej engång erinras, att dessa tänkare och dessa konstnärer sjelfve fäktat i led med de landsmän de uppeldat, att Körners unga blod för frihetens sak strömmade öfver hans lyra, att Fichte dog af militäriska mödor, eller att Steffens bär jernkorsets hjelteorden och var en af korstågets hufvudmän. Det är i *principerna* af den vettenskapliga och ästhetiska bildningen hos våra ädla stamförvanter, som bevisen böra sökas för det phenomen, att äfven den mechaniska taktiken brutits af de krafter, hvilka i förväg bröto den mechaniska verldsåsigten och den mechaniska konstläran. Det är sant, jemväl i Tyskland finnas nattfåglar, som grina mot ljuset; men till tidens och mensklighetens heder låter det af inga pappersbalar hämma sig. Det är äfven sant, att strålarne af detta ljus, som upplöser alla motsatser, abstraktioner och ensidigheter till harmonisk grundval för en gemensam verldscultur, förbländat och förvirrat många svagt organiserade sinnen, och att det tillstånd af chaotisk fermentation, som måste föregå stora skapelser, ofta frambringar förunderliga missfoster i alla den högre bildningens elementer. Många bland dem, som hoptals tränga sig fram omkring genialiska författares fanor, synas blott vilja gifva sig sjelfva en liten märkvärdighet med att räknas till deras lärjungar, och behandla saken med samma lättsinnighet, som berodde den endast på öfvergången från ett gammalt mode till ett nytt.

peculiar coldness and dead quality emanate from any which pretend *simply and solely* to be totally complete and contained within themselves.

But if life itself is an *amabile fractum,* a lovable fragment of a whole, we cannot then dismiss it as worthless scrap, mere flotsam. A true fragment, such as human life, is more artistic when broken than when whole.

[1835] [*Translated by Mattias Bolkéus Blom and Patricia Erskine-Hill*]

1.n.2. P. D. A. ATTERBOM, from Review of 'Svenska Akademiens Handlingar' ['The Proceedings of the Swedish Academy'] (1813) in *Svensk Literatur-Tidning,* November the 4th 1815

[. . .]

French scholarship and art have been seen for what they are. The mocking sensuality and belle-lettrist jargon, the materialist fanaticism against religion, philosophy and poetry have finally brought France to the end from which Rousseau and Hemsterhuis, calling out in the desert, could not save it. Even its most ardent supporters now realize the horrid dissolution, the moral and political abyss, into which this once much admired people, still in so many individual cases amiably chivalrous, has sunk and been consumed. And still they urge us to follow these pointless shadows, to which you look in vain for the word of life, these writers without heart, faith or sincerity, who have poisoned Europe and murdered their nation spiritually with their pestilent vapours! How else did Napoleon, who in his person represents all the greatness that can come from an earthly spirit deprived of light, conquer almost all the educated world, if not through the selfishness and lax frivolity of the native soil of Voltaire, enveloping almost all of Europe's persons of quality and its public officials? And how else was he crushed, if not by this younger breed, raised with other principles, and by the men who during the past iron age with indefatigable ardour have prepared the reign of truth? He who is still blind to the close link between the literary world and the political sees the light of strength and victory that has finally made the glory of the Germanic tribe complete. Prussia has struck the Babel of our time with the electrification of its thinkers and the charm of its artists. This is crystal-clear to anyone acquainted with Germany's educated classes; there is no need for a reminder that these thinkers and these artists have fought alongside the countrymen whom they have inflamed. Körner's young blood ran down his lyre for the sake of freedom, Fichte died from military pains and Steffens carried the heroic order of the Iron Cross and was at the head of the crusade. We must look for proof that this has occurred in the principles of the scholarly and aesthetic education of our 'noble kinsmen' : even the mechanical tactics have been broken by the forces that previously broke the mechanical world view and the mechanical school of art. There may well still be night-birds in Germany who fret in the light; but to the credit of the times and of mankind, light will not be dimmed by reams of paper. It is also true that this light, which dissolves all contradiction, abstraction and bias and creates the harmony needed for a common world culture, has blinded and confused many weak minds. The chaotic fermentation that precedes a great new order often creates strange monstrosities throughout higher education. Many who gather around the banners of great writers seem only to aspire to being numbered among their disciples and are as frivolous as if simply taking up a new fancy.

Att sådan icke är Redaktionens sinnesart, förmodar hon att billiga kännare skola medgifva. Vårt sätt att resonnera i vettenskapliga ämnen är ej ett slafviskt efterpladdrande af missförstådda begrepp och missbrukade termer, och de ledamöter, som sysselsätta sig med Poesi, äga åtminstone den förtjensten att den är deras egen. Föröfrigt ämnade vi aldrig att öfverflytta den Tyska litteraturen, såsom sådan, på Svensk grund; utan blott det, som för hela Norden bör vara gemensamt af denna litteratur: friheten, allvaret, natursinnet och andakten. Tyskland är i andligt afseende Europas hjerta: må Skandinavien inse, att naturen i samma afseende bestämt vår halvö till dess hufvud! Att utbilda detta ursprungliga förhållande mellan hufvud och hjerta, till en gudomlig och varaktig sammanklang – det är Svenska Akademiens, det är alla svenska vettenskapsidkares och konstvänners bestämmelse. Det är ej nu fråga om att *härma*, utan att *göra sjelf*; det är ej nu fråga om att uppsätta en liten täck hedendom på altaret i Culturens tempel, utan att återställa den gamla goda christendomen i sina rättigheter, och med henne sammansmälta lifvet, forskningen och sången. En ny organisation är i detta hänseende börjad med Sveriges national-bildning; den skall segra genom det ungdomliga i sin princip; tiden är visserligen stormig, men den fordrar också kraftiga ideer och modiga charakterer. En ny paradisisk verld uppstiger långsamt ur alstrande böljor, och vill man bosätta sig der, så måste man ännu ej sky mödan att simma eller brottas med vågorna. De makter, som ställa sig emot henne, blotta redan derigenom sitt öde, att de *skryta öfver sin föräldring*; de skola försvinna såsom agnar från jorden, och efter-verlden, om deras namn hinna dit, skall dömma dem utan förskoning.

[1815]

It is presumed that those in authority, however base, acknowledge that this is not the approach of the Editors. Our way of reasoning in scholarly matters is not a slavish parroting of misunderstood conceptions and misused terms. The members who are concerned with Poetry may at least claim that it is their own. We never intended to transfer the German literary canon to Swedish ground: we wish instead for that which ought to be common to all Nordic literature; freedom, sincerity, a sense of nature, and devotion. Germany is the spiritual heart of Europe; may the Scandinavian countries realize that nature has destined our peninsula to be its head! To elevate this connection between head and heart to a divine and lasting harmony – that is the aim of the Swedish Academy and of all Swedish scholars and friends of the arts. It is now not a question of *imitating*, but of *doing it ourselves*; not a question of placing a small pretty pagan idol on the altar of the Temple of Culture, but of restoring the ancient, good Christianity to its rightful place, infused with life, study and song. To achieve this a new educational body has been created for Sweden. It will conquer through the youthfulness of its principles; times may be stormy and they require powerful ideas and a brave heart. A new paradisiacal world slowly rises from the waves; if you want to dwell there you must be prepared to swim and wrestle with the waves. The powers that stand in her way show their true nature as they *boast of their refinement*; they will disappear like chaff from wheat, and posterity, if indeed it hears their names at all, will judge them without mercy.

[1815] [*Translated by Mattias Bolkéus Blom and Patricia Erskine-Hill*]

II. The Self

Romanticism is a major source of modernity's concern with the nature of selfhood, and of the relationship between subjective experience and the objectivity discovered in nature by the sciences. The self is experienced both in terms of an ever-growing 'inner space' as well as the location of what was seen as a new and liberated human capacity for cognitive, moral and aesthetic exploration. At the same time, these Enlightenment tropes could be experienced in very un-Enlightenment terms, as something essentially mysterious and not transparent to itself. Heroic and divided selves are explored through both literary and philosophical texts. The new role of human feeling and its place in the objective world is, paradoxically, inseparable from the rise of the idea of the 'unconscious'. In addition to such psychodramas as Anderson's The Shadow, this section includes examples of the confessional genre from Rousseau to De Quincy, but its central concern will be with the creation of 'self' in the writing of the period – including the emphasis on that new creative power, the 'imagination'.

The fact that this new sense of self occurred at a time of political turmoil and conservative reaction, when such writers as Paine, Cobbett, Chateaubriand and Foscolo were driven into exile as a direct consequence of revolutionary activity, while such figures as Shelley and Byron chose exile as the result of sexual and social transgression, was partly (but only partly) contingent. The effect, in both cases was to reinforce the notion of the artist's condition as one of spiritual or physical isolation and exile – often symbolized by the myths of the wanderings of Cain, or the Wandering Jew.

a. BRITISH

II.a.1. WILLIAM BLAKE, Introduction to *Songs of Innocence*

Piping down the valleys wild,
Piping songs of pleasant glee,
On a cloud I saw a child,
And he laughing said to me:

'Pipe a song about a Lamb!'
So I piped with merry cheer.
'Piper, pipe that song again.'
So I piped: he wept to hear.

'Drop thy pipe, thy happy pipe;
Sing thy songs of happy cheer!'
So I sung the same again,
While he wept with joy to hear.

'Piper, sit thee down and write
In a book, that all may read.'
So he vanished from my sight;
And I plucked a hollow reed,

And I made a rural pen,
And I stained the water clear,
And I wrote my happy songs
Every child may joy to hear.

[1789, 1794]

II.a.2.   WILLIAM BLAKE, 'The Lamb'

Little lamb, who made thee?
Dost thou know who made thee,
Gave thee life, and bid thee feed
By the stream and o'er the mead;
Gave thee clothing of delight,
Softest clothing, woolly, bright;
Gave thee such a tender voice,
Making all the vales rejoice?
Little lamb, who made thee?
Dost thou know who made thee?

Little lamb, I'll tell thee;
Little lamb, I'll tell thee:
He is callèd by thy name,
For He calls Himself a Lamb.
He is meek, and He is mild,
He became a little child.
I a child, and thou a lamb,
We are callèd by His name.
Little lamb, God bless thee!
Little lamb, God bless thee!

[1789, 1794]

II.a.3.   WILLIAM BLAKE, Introduction to *Songs of Experience*

Hear the voice of the Bard,
Who present, past, and future, sees;
Whose ears have heard
The Holy Word
That walked among the ancient trees;

Calling the lapsed soul,
And weeping in the evening dew;
That might control
The starry pole,
And fallen, fallen light renew!

'O Earth, O Earth, return!
Arise from out the dewy grass!
Night is worn,
And the morn
Rises from the slumbrous mass.

'Turn away no more;
Why wilt thou turn away?
The starry floor,
The watery shore,
Is given thee till the break of day.'

[1789, 1794]

II.a.4. WILLIAM BLAKE, 'The Tyger'

Tyger! Tyger! burning bright
In the forests of the night
What immortal hand or eye
Could frame thy fearful symmetry?

In what distant deeps or skies
Burnt the fire of thine eyes?
On what wings dare he aspire?
What the hand dare sieze thy fire?

And what shoulder, & what art,
Could twist the sinews of thy heart?
And why thy heart began to beat,
What dread hand? & what dread feet?

What the hammer? what the chain?
In what furnace was thy brain?
What the anvil? what dread grasp
Dare its deadly terrors clasp?

When the stars threw down their spears
And water'd heaven with their tears,
Did he smile his work to see?
Did he who made the Lamb make thee?

Tyger! Tyger! burning bright
In the forests of the night,
What immortal hand or eye
Dare frame thy fearful symmetry?

[1789, 1794]

II.a.5.   WILLIAM BLAKE, 'London'

I wandered through each chartered street,
Near where the chartered Thames does flow,
And mark in every face I meet,
Marks of weakness, marks of woe.

In every cry of every man,
In every infant's cry of fear,
In every voice, in every ban,
The mind-forged manacles I hear:

How the chimney-sweeper's cry
Every blackening church appals,
And the hapless soldier's sigh
Runs in blood down palace-walls.

But most, through midnight streets I hear
How the youthful harlot's curse
Blasts the new-born infant's tear,
And blights with plagues the marriage-hearse.

[1789, 1794]

II.a.6.   CHARLOTTE SMITH, 'On Being Cautioned against Walking on an Headland Overlooking the Sea, because It was Frequented by a Lunatic'

Is there a solitary wretch who hies
    To the tall cliff, with starting pace or slow,
And, measuring, views with wild and hollow eyes
    Its distance from the waves that chide below;
Who, as the sea-born gale with frequent sighs
    Chills his cold bed upon the mountain turf,
With hoarse, half-utter'd lamentation, lies
    Murmuring responses to the dashing surf?
In moody sadness, on the giddy brink,
    I see him more with envy than with fear;
He has no *nice felicities* that shrink
    From giant horrors; wildly wandering here,
He seems (uncursed with reason) not to know
The depth or the duration of his woe.

(1797–1800)

II.a.7.   WILLIAM WORDSWORTH, from *The Prelude*

[*From Book I*]

Fair seed-time had my soul, and I grew up
Fostered alike by beauty and by fear:

Much favoured in my birth-place, and no less
In that beloved Vale to which erelong
We were transplanted; – there were we let loose
For sports of wider range. Ere I had told
Ten birth-days, when among the mountain slopes
Frost, and the breath of frosty wind, had snapped
The last autumnal crocus, 'twas my joy
With store of springes o'er my shoulder hung
To range the open heights where woodcocks run
Along the smooth green turf. Through half the night,
Scudding away from snare to snare, I plied
That anxious visitation; – moon and stars
Were shining o'er my head. I was alone,
And seemed to be a trouble to the peace
That dwelt among them. Sometimes it befell
In these night wanderings, that a strong desire
O'erpowered my better reason, and the bird
Which was the captive of another's toil
Became my prey; and when the deed was done
I heard among the solitary hills
Low breathings coming after me, and sounds
Of undistinguishable motion, steps
Almost as silent as the turf they trod.
   Nor less, when spring had warmed the cultured Vale,
Moved we as plunderers where the mother-bird
Had in high places built her lodge; though mean
Our object and inglorious, yet the end
Was not ignoble. Oh! when I have hung
Above the raven's nest, by knots of grass
And half-inch fissures in the slippery rock
But ill sustained, and almost (so it seemed)
Suspended by the blast that blew amain,
Shouldering the naked crag, oh, at that time
While on the perilous ridge I hung alone,
With what strange utterance did the loud dry wind
Blow through my ear! the sky seemed not a sky
Of earth – and with what motion moved the clouds!
   Dust as we are, the immortal spirit grows
Like harmony in music; there is a dark
Inscrutable workmanship that reconciles
Discordant elements, makes them cling together
In one society. How strange, that all
The terrors, pains, and early miseries,
Regrets, vexations, lassitudes interfused
Within my mind, should e'er have borne a part,
And that a needful part, in making up

The calm existence that is mine when I
Am worthy of myself! Praise to the end!
Thanks to the means which Nature deigned to employ;
Whether her fearless visitings, or those
That came with soft alarm, like hurtless light
Opening the peaceful clouds; or she would use
Severer interventions, ministry
More palpable, as best might suit her aim.
   One summer evening (led by her) I found
A little boat tied to a willow tree
Within a rocky cave, its usual home.
Straight I unloosed her chain, and stepping in
Pushed from the shore. It was an act of stealth
And troubled pleasure, nor without the voice
Of mountain-echoes did my boat move on;
Leaving behind her still, on either side,
Small circles glittering idly in the moon,
Until they melted all into one track
Of sparkling light. But now, like one who rows,
Proud of his skill, to reach a chosen point
With an unswerving line, I fixed my view
Upon the summit of a craggy ridge,
The horizon's utmost boundary; far above
Was nothing but the stars and the grey sky.
She was an elfin pinnace; lustily
I dipped my oars into the silent lake,
And, as I rose upon the stroke, my boat
Went heaving through the water like a swan;
When, from behind that craggy steep till then
The horizon's bound, a huge peak, black and huge,
As if with voluntary power instinct,
Upreared its head. I struck and struck again,
And growing still in stature the grim shape
Towered up between me and the stars, and still,
For so it seemed, with purpose of its own
And measured motion like a living thing,
Strode after me. With trembling oars I turned,
And through the silent water stole my way
Back to the covert of the willow tree;
There in her mooring-place I left my bark, –
And through the meadows homeward went, in grave
And serious mood; but after I had seen
That spectacle, for many days, my brain
Worked with a dim and undetermined sense
Of unknown modes of being; o'er my thoughts
There hung a darkness, call it solitude

Or blank desertion. No familiar shapes
Remained, no pleasant images of trees,
Of sea or sky, no colours of green fields;
But huge and mighty forms, that do not live
Like living men, moved slowly through the mind
By day, and were a trouble to my dreams.
    Wisdom and Spirit of the universe!
Thou Soul that art the eternity of thought
That givest to forms and images a breath
And everlasting motion, not in vain
By day or star-light thus from my first dawn
Of childhood didst thou intertwine for me
The passions that build up our human soul;
Not with the mean and vulgar works of man,
But with high objects, with enduring things –
With life and nature – purifying thus
The elements of feeling and of thought,
And sanctifying, by such discipline,
Both pain and fear, until we recognise
A grandeur in the beatings of the heart.
Nor was this fellowship vouchsafed to me
With stinted kindness. In November days,
When vapours rolling down the valley made
A lonely scene more lonesome, among woods,
At noon and 'mid the calm of summer nights,
When, by the margin of the trembling lake,
Beneath the gloomy hills homeward I went
In solitude, such intercourse was mine;
Mine was it in the fields both day and night,
And by the waters, all the summer long. (ll. 301–424)

[*From Book VI*]
               That very day,
From a bare ridge we also first beheld
Unveiled the summit of Mont Blanc, and grieved
To have a soulless image on the eye
That had usurped upon a living thought
That never more could be. The wondrous Vale
Of Chamouny stretched far below, and soon
With its dumb cataracts and streams of ice,
A motionless array of mighty waves,
Five rivers broad and vast, made rich amends,
And reconciled us to realities;
There small birds warble from the leafy trees,
The eagle soars high in the element,
There doth the reaper bind the yellow sheaf,

The maiden spread the haycock in the sun,
While Winter like a well-tamed lion walks,
Descending from the mountain to make sport
Among the cottages by beds of flowers.
    Whate'er in this wide circuit we beheld,
Or heard, was fitted to our unripe state
Of intellect and heart. With such a book
Before our eyes, we could not choose but read
Lessons of genuine brotherhood, the plain
And universal reason of mankind,
The truths of young and old. Nor, side by side
Pacing, two social pilgrims, or alone
Each with his humour, could we fail to abound
In dreams and fictions, pensively composed:
Dejection taken up for pleasure's sake,
And gilded sympathies, the willow wreath,
And sober posies of funereal flowers,
Gathered among those solitudes sublime
From formal gardens of the lady Sorrow,
Did sweeten many a meditative hour.
    Yet still in me with those soft luxuries
Mixed something of stern mood, an underthirst
Of vigour seldom utterly allayed:
And from that source how different a sadness
Would issue, let one incident make known.
When from the Vallais we had turned, and clomb
Along the Simplon's steep and rugged road,
Following a band of muleteers, we reached
A halting-place, where all together took
Their noon-tide meal. Hastily rose our guide,
Leaving us at the board; awhile we lingered,
Then paced the beaten downward way that led
Right to a rough stream's edge, and there broke off;
The only track now visible was one
That from the torrent's further brink held forth
Conspicuous invitation to ascend
A lofty mountain. After brief delay
Crossing the unbridged stream, that road we took,
And clomb with eagerness, till anxious fears
Intruded, for we failed to overtake
Our comrades gone before. By fortunate chance,
While every moment added doubt to doubt,
A peasant met us, from whose mouth we learned
That to the spot which had perplexed us first
We must descend, and there should find the road,
Which in the stony channel of the stream

Lay a few steps, and then along its banks;
And, that our future course, all plain to sight,
Was downwards, with the current of that stream.
Loth to believe what we so grieved to hear,
For still we had hopes that pointed to the clouds,
We questioned him again, and yet again;
But every word that from the peasant's lips
Came in reply, translated by our feelings,
Ended in this, – *that we had crossed the Alps.*

    Imagination – here the Power so called
Through sad incompetence of human speech,
That awful Power rose from the mind's abyss
Like an unfathered vapour that enwraps,
At once, some lonely traveller. I was lost;
Halted without an effort to break through;
But to my conscious soul I now can say –
'I recognise thy glory:' in such strength
Of usurpation, when the light of sense
Goes out, but with a flash that has revealed
The invisible world, doth greatness make abode,
There harbours; whether we be young or old,
Our destiny, our being's heart and home,
Is with infinitude, and only there;
With hope it is, hope that can never die,
Effort, and expectation, and desire,
And something evermore about to be.
Under such banners militant, the soul
Seeks for no trophies, struggles for no spoils
That may attest her prowess, blest in thoughts
That are their own perfection and reward,
Strong in herself and in beatitude
That hides her, like the mighty flood of Nile
Poured from his fount of Abyssinian clouds
To fertilise the whole Egyptian plain.

    The melancholy slackening that ensued
Upon those tidings by the peasant given
Was soon dislodged. Downwards we hurried fast,
And, with the half-shaped road which we had missed,
Entered a narrow chasm. The brook and road
Were fellow-travellers in this gloomy strait,
And with them did we journey several hours
At a slow pace. The immeasurable height
Of woods decaying, never to be decayed,
The stationary blasts of waterfalls,
And in the narrow rent at every turn
Winds thwarting winds, bewildered and forlorn,

The torrents shooting from the clear blue sky,
The rocks that muttered close upon our ears,
Black drizzling crags that spake by the way-side
As if a voice were in them, the sick sight
And giddy prospect of the raving stream,
The unfettered clouds and region of the Heavens,
Tumult and peace, the darkness and the light –
Were all like workings of one mind, the features
Of the same face, blossoms upon one tree;
Characters of the great Apocalypse,
The types and symbols of Eternity,
Of first, and last, and midst, and without end. (ll. 523–640)

[1850]

II.a.8. GEORGE GORDON, LORD BYRON, from *Childe Harold's Pilgrimage*

III

In my youth's summer I did sing of One,
The wandering outlaw of his own dark mind;
Again I seize the theme, then but begun,
And bear it with me, as the rushing wind
Bears the cloud onwards: in that tale I find
The furrows of long thought, and dried-up tears,
Which, ebbing, leave a sterile track behind,
O'er which all heavily the journeying years
Plod the last sands of life – where not a flower appears.

IV

Since my young days of passion – joy, or pain,
Perchance my heart and harp have lost a string,
And both may jar: it may be, that in vain
I would essay as I have sung to sing.
Yet, though a dreary strain, to this I cling,
So that it wean me from the weary dream
Of selfish grief or gladness – so it fling
Forgetfulness around me – it shall seem
To me, though to none else, a not ungrateful theme.

V

He who, grown aged in this world of woe,
In deeds, not years, piercing the depths of life,
So that no wonder waits him; nor below

Can love or sorrow, fame, ambition, strife,
Cut to his heart again with the keen knife
Of silent, sharp endurance: he can tell
Why thought seeks refuge in lone caves, yet rife
With airy images, and shapes which dwell
Still unimpaired, though old, in the soul's haunted cell.

VI

'Tis to create, and in creating live
A being more intense, that we endow
With form our fancy, gaining as we give
The life we image, even as I do now.
What am I? Nothing: but not so art thou,
Soul of my thought! with whom I traverse earth,
Invisible but gazing, as I glow
Mixed with thy spirit, blended with thy birth,
And feeling still with thee in my crushed feelings' dearth. (III, ll. 19–54)

[1816]

II.a.9. GEORGE GORDON, LORD BYRON, from *Manfred*

MANFRED

It is not noon – the sunbow's rays still arch
The torrent with the many hues of heaven,
And roll the sheeted silver's waving column
O'er the crag's headlong perpendicular,
And fling its lines of foaming light along,
And to and fro, like the pale courser's tail,
The Giant steed, to be bestrode by Death,
As told in the Apocalypse. No eyes
But mine now drink this sight of loveliness;
I should be sole in this sweet solitude,
And with the Spirit of the place divide
The homage of these waters. – I will call her.

[MANFRED takes some of the water into the palm of his hand, and flings it in the air, muttering the adjuration. After a pause, the WITCH OF THE ALPS rises beneath the arch of the sunbow of the torrent]

MANFRED

Beautiful Spirit! with thy hair of light,
And dazzling eyes of glory, in whose form
The charms of Earth's least-mortal daughters grow
To an unearthly stature, in an essence
Of purer elements; while the hues of youth, –

Carnation'd like a sleeping infant's cheek,
Rock'd by the beating of her mother's heart,
Or the rose tints, which summer's twilight leaves
Upon the lofty glacier's virgin snow,
The blush of earth embracing with her heaven, –
Tinge thy celestial aspect, and make tame
The beauties of the sunbow which bends o'er thee.
Beautiful Spirit! in thy calm clear brow,
Wherein is glass'd serenity of soul,
Which of itself shows immortality,
I read that thou wilt pardon to a Son
Of Earth, whom the abstruser powers permit
At times to commune with them – if that he
Avail him of his spells – to call thee thus,
And gaze on thee a moment.

WITCH

    Son of Earth!
I know thee, and the powers which give thee power;
I know thee for a man of many thoughts,
And deeds of good and ill, extreme in both,
Fatal and fated in thy sufferings.
I have expected this – what wouldst thou with me?

MANFRED

To look upon thy beauty – nothing further.
The face of the Earth hath madden'd me, and I
Take refuge in her mysteries, and pierce
To the abodes of those who govern her –
But they can nothing aid me. I have sought
From them what they could not bestow, and now
I search no further.

WITCH

    What could be the quest
Which is not in the power of the most powerful,
The rulers of the invisible?

MANFRED

    A boon;
But why should I repeat it? 'twere in vain.

WITCH

I know not that; let thy lips utter it.

MANFRED

Well, though it torture me, tis but the same;
My pang shall find a voice. From my youth upwards
My spirit walk'd not with the souls of men,
Nor look'd upon the earth with human eyes;
The thirst of their ambition was not mine,
The aim of their existence was not mine;
My joys, my griefs, my passions, and my powers,
Made me a stranger; though I wore the form,
I had no sympathy with breathing flesh,
Nor midst the creatures of clay that girded me
Was there but one who but of her anon.
I said, with men, and with the thoughts of men,
I held but slight communion; but instead,
My joy was in the Wilderness, to breathe
The difficult air of the iced mountain's top,
Where the birds dare not build, nor insect's wing
Flit o'er the herbless granite; or to plunge
Into the torrent, and to roll along
On the swift whirl of the new breaking wave
Of river-stream, or ocean, in their flow.
In these my early strength exulted; or
To follow through the night the moving moon,
The stars and their development; or catch
The dazzling lightnings till my eyes grew dim;
Or to look, list'ning, on the scattered leaves,
While Autumn winds were at their evening song.
These were my pastimes, and to be alone;
For if the beings, of whom I was one, –
Hating to be so, – cross'd me in my path,
I felt myself degraded back to them,
And was all clay again. And then I dived,
In my lone wanderings, to the caves of death,
Searching its cause in its effect; and drew
From wither'd bones, and skulls, and heap'd up dust,
Conclusions most forbidden. Then I pass'd
The nights of years in sciences untaught,
Save in the old-time; and with time and toil,
And terrible ordeal, and such penance
As in itself hath power upon the air,
And spirits that do compass air and earth,
Space, and the peopled infinite, I made
Mine eyes familiar with Eternity,
Such as, before me, did the Magi, and
He who from out their fountain dwellings raised

Eros and Anteros, at Gadara,
As I do thee; – and with my knowledge grew
The thirst of knowledge, and the power and joy
Of this most bright intelligence, until –

WITCH

Proceed.

MANFRED

      Oh! I but thus prolonged my words,
Boasting these idle attributes, because
As I approach the core of my heart's grief –
But to my task. I have not named to thee
Father or mother, mistress, friend, or being,
With whom I wore the chain of human ties;
If I had such, they seem'd not such to me –
Yet there was one

WITCH

      Spare not thyself – proceed.

MANFRED

She was like me in lineaments – her eyes,
Her hair, her features, all, to the very tone
Even of her voice, they said were like to mine;
But soften'd all, and temper'd into beauty;
She had the same lone thoughts and wanderings,
The quest of hidden knowledge, and a mind
To comprehend the universe: nor these
Alone, but with them gentler powers than mine,
Pity, and smiles, and tears – which I had not;
And tenderness – but that I had for her;
Humility – and that I never had.
Her faults were mine – her virtues were her own –
I loved her, and destroy'd her! (II, ii, 1–117)

[1817]

II.a.10.   PERCY BYSSHE SHELLEY, 'Ode to the West Wind'

I

O wild West Wind, thou breath of Autumn's being,
Thou, from whose unseen presence the leaves dead
Are driven, like ghosts from an enchanter fleeing,

Yellow, and black, and pale, and hectic red,
Pestilence-stricken multitudes: O thou,
Who chariotest to their dark wintry bed

The winged seeds, where they lie cold and low,
Each like a corpse within its grave, until
Thine azure sister of the Spring shall blow

Her clarion o'er the dreaming earth, and fill
(Driving sweet buds like flocks to feed in air)
With living hues and odors plain and hill:

Wild Spirit, which art moving everywhere;
Destroyer and preserver; hear, oh, hear!

II

Thou on whose stream, 'mid the steep sky's commotion,
Loose clouds like earth's decaying leaves are shed,
Shook from the tangled boughs of Heaven and Ocean,

Angels of rain and lightning: there are spread
On the blue surface of thine aery surge,
Like the bright hair uplifted from the head

Of some fierce Maenad, even from the dim verge
Of the horizon to the zenith's height,
The locks of the approaching storm. Thou dirge

Of the dying year, to which this closing night
Will be the dome of a vast sepulchre,
Vaulted with all thy congregated might

Of vapors, from whose solid atmosphere
Black rain, and fire, and hail will burst: oh, hear!

III

Thou who didst waken from his summer dreams
The blue Mediterranean, where he lay,
Lulled by the coil of his crystalline streams,

Beside a pumice isle in Baiae's bay,
And saw in sleep old palaces and towers
Quivering within the wave's intenser day,

All overgrown with azure moss and flowers
So sweet, the sense faints picturing them! Thou
For whose path the Atlantic's level powers

285

Cleave themselves into chasms, while far below
The sea-blooms and the oozy woods which wear
The sapless foliage of the ocean, know

Thy voice, and suddenly grow gray with fear,
And tremble and despoil themselves: oh, hear!

IV

If I were a dead leaf thou mightest bear;
If I were a swift cloud to fly with thee;
A wave to pant beneath thy power, and share

The impulse of thy strength, only less free
Than thou, O uncontrollable! If even
I were as in my boyhood, and could be

The comrade of thy wanderings over Heaven,
As then, when to outstrip thy skiey speed
Scarce seemed a vision; I would ne'er have striven

As thus with thee in prayer in my sore need.
Oh, lift me as a wave, a leaf, a cloud!
I fall upon the thorns of life! I bleed!

A heavy weight of hours has chained and bowed
One too like thee: tameless, and swift, and proud.

V

Make me thy lyre, even as the forest is:
What if my leaves are falling like its own!
The tumult of thy mighty harmonies

Will take from both a deep, autumnal tone,
Sweet though in sadness. Be thou, Spirit fierce,
My spirit! Be thou me, impetuous one!

Drive my dead thoughts over the universe
Like withered leaves to quicken a new birth!
And, by the incantation of this verse,

Scatter, as from an unextinguished hearth
Ashes and sparks, my words among mankind!
Be through my lips to unawakened earth

The trumpet of a prophecy! O Wind,
If Winter comes, can Spring be far behind?

[1820]

II.a.11. JOHN KEATS, 'Ode to a Nightingale'

I

My heart aches, and a drowsy numbness pains
   My sense, as though of hemlock I had drunk,
Or emptied some dull opiate to the drains
   One minute past, and Lethe-wards had sunk:
'Tis not through envy of thy happy lot,
   But being too happy in thine happiness,
      That thou, light-winged Dryad of the trees,
        In some melodious plot
Of beechen green, and shadows numberless,
   Singest of summer in full-throated ease.

II

O, for a draught of vintage! that hath been
   Cool'd a long age in the deep-delved earth,
Tasting of Flora and the country green,
   Dance, and Provencal song, and sunburnt mirth!
O for a beaker full of the warm South,
   Full of the true, the blushful Hippocrene,
      With beaded bubbles winking at the brim,
        And purple-stained mouth;
That I might drink, and leave the world unseen,
   And with thee fade away into the forest dim:

III

Fade fare away, dissolve, and quite forget
   What thou among the leaves hast never known,
The weariness, the fever, and the fret
   Here, where men sit and hear each other groan;
Where palsy shakes a few, sad, last gray hairs,
   Where youth grows pale, and spectre-thin, and dies;
      Where but to think is to be full of sorrow
        And leaden-eyed despairs,
Where Beauty cannot keep her lustrous eyes,
   Or new Love pine at them beyond to-morrow.

IV

Away! away! for I will fly to thee,
   Not charioted by Bacchus and his pards,
But on the viewless wings of Poesy,
   Though the dull brain perplexes and retards:

Already with thee! tender is the night,
  And haply the Queen-Moon is on her throne,
    Cluster'd around by all her starry Fays;
      But here there is no light,
  Save what from heaven is with the breezes blown
    Through verdurous glooms and winding mossy ways.

V

I cannot see what flowers are at my feet,
  Nor what soft incense hangs upon the boughs,
But, in embalmed darkness, guess each sweet
  Wherewith the seasonable month endows
The grass, the thicket, and the fruit-tree wild;
  White hawthorn, and the pastoral eglantine;
    Fast fading violets cover'd up in leaves;
      And mid-May's eldest child,
  The coming musk-rose, full of dewy wine,
    The murmurous haunt of flies on summer eves.

VI

Darkling, I listen; and, for many a time
  I have been half in love with easeful Death,
Call'd him soft names in many a mused rhyme,
  To take into the air my quiet breath;
Now more than ever seems it rich to die,
  To cease upon the midnight with no pain,
    While thou art pouring forth thy soul abroad
      In such an ecstasy!
  Still wouldst thou sing, and I have ears in vain –
    To thy high requiem become a sod.

VII

Thou wast no born for death, immortal Bird!
  No hungry generations tread thee down;
The voice I hear this passing night was heard
  In ancient days by emperor and clown:
Perhaps the self-same song that found a path
  Through the sad heart of Ruth, when, sick for home,
    She stood in tears amid the alien corn;
      The same that oft-time hath
Charm'd magic casements, opening on the foam
  Of perilous seas, in faery lands forlorn.

VIII

Forlorn! the very word is like a bell
  To toll me back from thee to my sole self!
Adieu! the fancy cannot cheat so well
  As she is fam'd to do, deceiving elf.
Adieu! adieu! they plaintive anthem fades
    Past the near meadows, over the still stream,
      Up the hill-side; and now 'tis buried deep
        In the next valley glades:
  Was it a vision, or a waking dream?
    Fled is that music: – Do I wake or sleep?

[1820]

c. DANSK

II.c.1. SØREN KIERKEGAARD, fra *Om Begrebet Ironi*, 'Orienterende Betragtninger'

Der var en Tid og ikke ret længe tilbage, da man ogsaa her kunde gjøre sin Lykke med en *Smule Ironi*, der gjorde Fyldest for alle Mangler i andre Henseender og hjalp En hæderligen gjennem Verden, gav En Anseelse af at være dannet, at have Blik paa Livet, Forstand paa Verden, betegnede En for de Indviede som Medlem af et vidtudstrakt aandeligt Frimureri. Man træffer endnu stundom en eller anden Repræsentant for denne svundne Tid, der har conserveret dette fine, betydningsfulde, tvetydigt saa Meget forraadende Smiil, denne aandelige Hofmandstone, hvormed han gjorde fortune i sin Ungdom, og som han havde bygget hele sin Fremtid paa, i det Haab, at han havde overvundet Verden. Ak, men det var en Skuffelse! Forgjeves søger hans speidende Øie en ligestemt Sjæl, og hvis hans Glands-Periode ikke var endnu for En og Anden i frisk Minde, saa vilde hans Ansigts Muskelspil blive en gaadefuld Hieroglyph for den Samtid, i hvilken han lever som en Fremmed og Udlænding. Thi vor Tid, den fordrer mere, den fordrer, om ikke høi, saa dog *høirøstet Pathos,* om ikke Speculation, saa dog Resultat, om ikke Sandhed, saa dog Overbeviisning, om ikke Ærlighed, saa dog Forsikkringer derom, om ikke Følelse, saa dog Vidtløftigheder den betræffende. Den udpræger derfor ogsaa en ganske anden Art af privilegerede Ansigter. Den tillader ikke, at Munden trodsigt lukker sig, eller at Overlæben bæver i Kaadhed, den fordrer, at Munden skal staae aaben; thi hvorledes kunde man vel tænke sig en sand og ægte Fædrelandsven uden talende, hvorledes en dybsindig Tænkers dogmatiske Ansigt uden med en Mund, der var istand til at sluge hele Verden, hvorledes kunde man forestille sig en Virtuos paa det levende Ords Overflødighedshorn, uden med opspilet Mund? Den tillader ikke, at man staaer stille og fordyber sig, at gaae langsomt er allerede mistænkeligt, og hvorledes skulde man ogsaa kunne finde sig i Sligt i det bevægede Øieblik, i hvilket vi leve, i den skjæbnesvangre Tid, hvorom Alle ere blevne enige, at den gaaer frugtsommelig med det Overordentlige? Den hader Isolation, og hvorledes skulde den ogsaa kunne taale, at et Menneske fik den fortvivlede Idee, at gaae ene gjennem Livet, den Tid, der selv, Haand i Haand og Arm i Arm (ligesom reisende Haandværkssvende og Landsoldater), lever for Menighedens Idee?[1]

Men om det nu end er langtfra, at Ironi er Særkjendet for vor Tid, saa følger deraf dog *ingenlunde,* at *Ironien ganske* skulde være *forsvunden.* Vor Tid er saaledes heller ingen tvivlende Tid, men desuagtet er der dog bleven mange Yttringer af Tvivl tilbage, i hvilke man ligesom kan studere Tvivlen, om der end bliver en qvalitativ Forskjel mellem en speculativ Tvivl og en vulgær Tvivl om dette eller hint. I det oratoriske Foredrag forekommer saaledes hyppigt en Figur, som bærer Navn af Ironi, hvis Charakteristiske er dette, at sige det Modsatte af hvad man mener. Her have vi allerede en Bestemmelse, der gaaer gjennem al Ironi, den nemlig, at *Phænomenet ikke er Væsenet, men det Modsatte* af Væsenet. Idet jeg taler, er Tanken, Meningen Væsenet, Ordet Phænomenet. Disse to Momenter ere absolut nødvendige, og det er i denne Forstand, at Plato har bemærket, at al Tænken er en Talen. Sandheden fordrer nu Identiteten; thi dersom jeg havde Tanken uden Ordet, da havde jeg ikke Tanken, og dersom jeg havde Ordet uden Tanken, da havde jeg heller ikke Ordet, som man jo heller ikke kan sige om Børn og Afsindige, at de tale. Seer jeg dernæst hen til det talende Subject, saa har jeg atter en Bestemmelse, der gaaer igjennem al Ironi, *Subjectet* er nemlig *negativ frit.* Naar jeg, idet jeg taler, er mig bevidst, at det, jeg siger, er min Mening, og at det Udsagte er et adæqvat Udtryk for min Mening, og jeg forudsætter,

---

[1] Hermed skal ingenlunde Tidens alvorlige Stræben være miskjendt eller forkleinet, men det var visselig at ønske, at den i sin Alvor var mere alvorlig.

c. DANISH

II.c.1. SØREN KIERKEGAARD, from *The Concept of Irony*, 'Observations'

There was a time, and not so long ago, when one could score a success also here with a bit of irony, which compensated for all other deficiencies and helped one get through the world rather respectably, gave one the appearance of being cultured, of having a perspective on life, an understanding of the world, and to the initiated marked one as a member of an extensive intellectual freemasonry. Occasionally we still meet a representative of that vanished age who has preserved that subtle, sententious, equivocally divulging smile, that air of an intellectual courtier with which he had made his fortune in his youth and upon which he had built his whole future in the hope that he had overcome the world.

Ah, but it was an illusion! His watchful eye looks in vain for a kindred soul, and if his days of glory were not still a fresh memory for a few, his facial expression would be a riddle to the contemporary age, in which he lives as a stranger and a foreigner. Our age demands more; it demands, if not lofty pathos then at least loud pathos, if not speculation then at least conclusions, if not truth then at least persuasion, if not integrity then at least protestations of integrity, if not feeling then at least verbosity about feelings. Therefore, it also coins a totally different kind of privileged faces. It will not allow the mouth to be defiantly compressed or the upper lip to quiver mischievously; it demands that the mouth be open, for how, indeed, could one imagine a true and genuine patriot who is not delivering speeches; how could one visualize a profound thinker's dogmatic face without a mouth able to swallow the whole world; how could one picture a virtuoso on the cornucopia of the living word without a gaping mouth? It does not permit one to stand still and to concentrate; to walk slowly is already suspicious; and how could one even put up with anything like that in the stirring period in which we live, in this momentous age, which all agree is pregnant with the extraordinary? It hates isolation; indeed, how could it tolerate a person's having the daft idea of going through life alone – this age that hand in hand and arm in arm (just like itinerant journeymen and soldiers) lives for the idea of community?[2]

But even if irony is far from being the distinctive feature of our age, it by no means follows that irony has totally disappeared. Our age is not an age of doubt, either, but nevertheless many manifestations of doubt still survive, in which one can, as it were, study doubt, even though there is a qualitative difference between speculative doubt and common doubt about this or about that. In oratory, for example, there frequently appears a figure of speech with the name of irony and the characteristic of saying the opposite of what is meant. Already here we have a quality that permeates all irony – namely, that the phenomenon is not the essence but the opposite of the essence. When I am speaking, the thought, the meaning, is the essence, and the word is the phenomenon. These two elements are absolutely necessary, and it is in this sense that Plato has said that all thinking is a discourse. Now, truth demands identity, for if I had the thought without the word, then I would not have the thought; and if I had the word without the thought, then I would not have the word, either – just as one cannot say of children and deranged people that they speak. If I next consider the speaking subject, I once again have a qualification that permeates all irony – namely, the subject is negatively free. When I am aware as I speak that what I am saying is what I mean and that what I have said adequately expresses my meaning, and I assume that the person to whom I am talking grasps my meaning completely, then I am bound in what has been

---

[2] This is not meant to depreciate or deprecate the earnest efforts of the age, but it is certainly to be wished that the age were more earnest in its earnestness.

at den, til hvem jeg taler, i det Udsagte har min Mening heel og holden, saa er jeg bunden i det Udsagte, det er, jeg er positiv fri deri. Her gjelder det gamle Vers: semel emissum volat irrevocabile verbum. Ogsaa med Hensyn til mig selv er jeg bunden, og kan ikke frigjøre mig derfra, hvad Øieblik jeg vil. Dersom derimod det Udsagte ikke er min Mening, eller er det Modsatte af min Mening, saa er jeg fri i Forhold til Andre og til mig selv.

Den *ironiske Talefigur hæver* imidlertid *sig selv,* idet Taleren forudsætter, at Tilhørerne forstaae ham, og saaledes bliver dog, gjennem en Negation af det umiddelbare Phænomen, Væsenet i Identitet med Phænomenet. Naar det stundom hændes, at en saadan ironisk Tale bliver misforstaaet, saa er dette ikke Talerens Skyld, uden forsaavidt han har givet sig i Kast med en saadan rænkefuld Patron, som Ironien er, der ligesaa gjerne spiller sine Venner som sine Fjender et Puds. Man siger ogsaa om en saadan ironisk Vending i Talen: det er ikke Alvor med den Alvor. Yttringen er saa alvorlig, saa det er en Gru, men den vidende Tilhører er indviet i Hemmeligheden, der stikker bag derved. Men netop derved er Ironien igjen hævet. Det er den almindeligste Form af Ironi, at man siger Noget alvorligt, som dog ikke er meent alvorligt. Den anden Form, at man siger Noget for Spøg spøgende, som er meent alvorligt, forekommer sjeldnere.[3]

Men som sagt, den ironiske Talefigur hæver sig selv, den er som en Gaade, paa hvilken man i samme Øieblik har Opløsningen. Imidlertid har den ironiske Talefigur en Egenskab, som ogsaa er eiendommelig for al Ironi, *en vis Fornemhed,* som hidrører fra, at den, om den end vil forstaaes, dog ikke vil ligefrem forstaaes; som gjør, at denne Figur ligesom seer ned paa den slet og rette Tale, hvilken Enhver øieblikkelig kan forstaae; den reiser ligesom i et fornemt Incognito, og seer fra dette høie Stade medlidende ned paa den almindelige pedestre Tale. I den daglige Omgang forekommer den ironiske Talefigur især i de høiere Kredse som et Prærogativ, der hører under samme Kategori som den bonton, der fordrer at smile over Uskyldighed, og at ansee Dyd for en Bornerthed, skjøndt man dog til en vis Grad troer derpaa.

Forsaavidt som nu de høiere Kredse, (dette maa naturligviis forstaaes efter en aandelig Rangforordning), ligesom Konger og Fyrster tale fransk, saaledes tale ironisk, for at Lægfolk ikke skal forstaae dem, forsaavidt er Ironien i Færd med at *isolere sig,* den ønsker ikke i Almindelighed at blive forstaaet. *Her hæver* altsaa *Ironien ikke sig selv.* Det er ogsaa kun en underordnet Form af den ironiske Forfængelighed, der ønsker Vidner, for at forvisse og forsikkre sig om sig selv, ligesom det ogsaa kun er en Inconseqvents, Ironien har tilfælleds med ethvert negativt Standpunkt, at den, der efter sit Begreb er Isolation, søger at constituere et Samfund, vil, da den ikke kan hæve sig til Menighedens Idee, realisere sig i Conventikler. Men der er derfor ogsaa ligesaalidet Samfunds-Eenhed i et Cotteri af Ironikere, som der i Sandhed er Ærlighed i en Røverstat. Men see vi nu bort fra den Side, igjennem hvilken Ironien aabner sig for de Medsammensvorne, og betragte den i Forhold til de Uindviede, i Forhold til dem, imod hvilke dens Polemik retter sig, i Forhold til den Tilværelse, den opfatter ironisk, da pleier den at yttre sig paa *tvende Maader.* Enten *identificerer* nemlig Ironikeren sig med det Uvæsen, han vil bekjæmpe, eller han stiller sig i et *Modsætnings- forhold* dertil, men naturligviis bestandig saaledes, at han er sig bevidst, at hans Tilsyneladelse er Modsætningen til det, han selv holder fast ved, og at han nyder Glæden over dette Misforhold.

I Forhold til en taabelig opblæst Viden, der veed Beskeed om Alt, er det ironisk rigtigt, *at gaae med,* at være henrykt over al denne Viisdom, at anspore den ved sit jublende Bifald til bestandig at stige høiere og høiere i bestandig høiere og høiere Galenskab, skjøndt Ironikeren derunder er

---

[3] Hvor den hyppigst forekommer, er gjerne i Forbindelse med en vis Fortvivlelse, og den findes derfor ofte hos Humorister, saaledes naar f. Ex. **Heine** i den meest spøgefulde Tone overveier, hvad der er værst, Tandpine eller en ond Samvittighed, og erklærer sig for den første.

said – that is, I am positively free therein. Here the old verse is appropriate: *semel emissum volat irrevocabile verbum* [the word once let slip flies beyond recall]. I am also bound with respect to myself and cannot free myself any time I wish. If, however, what I said is not my meaning or the opposite of my meaning, then I am free in relation to others and to myself.

The ironic figure of speech cancels itself, however, inasmuch as the one who is speaking assumes that his hearers understand him, and thus, through a negation of the immediate phenomenon, the essence becomes identical with the phenomenon. If it sometimes happens that an ironic figure of speech such as this is misunderstood, this is not the fault of the one who is speaking, except insofar as he has come to grips with such a crafty fellow as irony, who likes to play tricks just as much on friends as on foes. In fact, we say of such an ironic turn of speech: Its earnestness is not in earnest. The remark is so earnest that it is shocking, but the hearer in the know shares the secret lying behind it. But precisely thereby the irony is once again canceled. It is the most common form of irony to say something earnestly that is not meant in earnest. The second form of irony, to say as a jest, jestingly, something that is meant in earnest, is more rare.[4] But, as was mentioned, the ironic figure of speech cancels itself; it is like a riddle to which one at the same time has the solution.

The ironic figure of speech has still another property that characterizes all irony, a certain superiority deriving from its not wanting to be understood immediately, even though it wants to be understood, with the result that this figure looks down, as it were, on plain and simple talk that everyone can promptly understand; it travels around, so to speak, in an exclusive incognito and looks down pitying from this high position on ordinary, prosaic talk. In everyday affairs, the ironic figure of speech appears especially in the higher circles as a prerogative belonging to the same category as the *bon ton* [good form] that requires smiling at innocence and looking upon virtue as narrow-mindedness, although one still believes in it up to a point.

Just as kings and princes speak French, the higher circles (this, of course, must be understood according to an intellectual ordering of rank) speak ironically so that lay people will not be able to understand them, and to that extent irony is in the process of isolating itself; it does not wish to be generally understood. Consequently, irony does not cancel itself here. Moreover, it is only a secondary form of the ironic vanity that desires witnesses in order to assure and reassure itself of itself, just as it also is only an inconsistency irony has in common with every negative position that irony, which is isolation according to its concept, seeks to form a society and, when it cannot elevate itself to the idea of community, tries to actualize itself in conventicles. This is why there is just as little social unity in a coterie of ironists as there is real honesty in a band of thieves.

Leaving this aspect of irony through which it opens itself to the inner circle and looking at irony in relation to the uninitiated, in relation to those against whom the polemic is directed, in relation to the existence it ironically interprets, we see that ordinarily it has two modes of expression. Either the ironist identifies himself with the odious practice he wants to attack, or he takes a hostile stance to it, but always, of course, in such a way that he himself is aware that his appearance is in contrast to what he himself embraces and that he thoroughly enjoys this discrepancy.

When it comes to a silly, inflated, know-it-all knowledge, it is ironically proper to go along, to be enraptured by all this wisdom, to spur it on with jubilating applause to ever greater lunacy, although the ironist is aware that the whole thing underneath is empty and void of substance.

---

[4] This most frequently happens in connection with a certain despair and thus is often found in humorists, for example, when Heine waggishly ponders which is worse, a toothache or a bad conscience, and declares himself for the first.

sig bevidst, at det Hele er tomt og indholdsløst. Ligeoverfor en fad og inept Begeistring er det ironisk rigtigt *at overbyde* denne i stedse mere og mere himmelraabende Jubel og Lovsang, skjøndt Ironikeren er sig bevidst, at denne Begeistring er den største Taabelighed af Verden. Og jo mere det lykkes Ironikeren at skuffe, jo bedre hans Falskneri faaer Fremgang, desto større er hans Glæde. Men denne Glæde nyder han ganske ene, og det er ham netop om at gjøre, at Ingen mærker hans Bedrageri. – Dette er en Form af Ironi, som kun sjeldnere forekommer, skjøndt den er ligesaa dyb og lettere at gjennemføre end den Ironi, der optræder under en Modsætnings Form. I det Mindre seer man den vel stundom anvendt mod et Menneske, der er paa Veien til at lide af en eller anden fix Idee; mod et Menneske der bilder sig ind, at han er smuk, eller især har smukke Bakkenbarter; eller bilder sig ind, at han er vittig eller dog engang har sagt en Vittighed, der ikke ofte nok kan høres; eller mod et Menneske, hvis Liv ligesom er gaaet op i en eneste Begivenhed, som han bestandig kommer tilbage paa, og som man i ethvert Øieblik kan bringe ham til at fortælle, naar man blot veed at trykke paa den rigtige Fjeder o. s. v. I alle disse Tilfælde er det Ironikerens Glæde selv *at synes besnæret* i den samme Hildethed, som den Anden er fangen i. Det er en af Ironikerens store Glæder overalt at opdage saadanne svage Sider; og jo mere udmærket det Menneske er, hos hvem de findes, desto mere glæder det ham at kunne dupere ham, at have ham i sin Magt, skjøndt han ikke selv veed deraf, saa at endog et udmærket Individ bliver i enkelte Øieblikke for Ironikeren som en Dukke, han har en Snor i, en Gliedermann, han kan faae til at gjøre de Bevægelser, som han vil, at han skal gjøre, eftersom han trækker i Snoren; og, det er besynderligt nok, Menneskets svage Sider nærme sig meget mere til at være Klangfigurer, der bestandig komme tilsyne, naar man stryger rigtigt, end Menneskets gode, de synes ligesom at have en Naturnødvendighed i sig, medens man saa ofte maa sørge over, at de gode Sider ligge under for Inconseqventser.

Men paa den anden Side er det Ironien ligesaa eiendommeligt at træde op under et Modsætningsforhold. Ligeoverfor en Viisdommens Overflødighed at være saa uvidende, saa dum, en saa *complet* **Arv** som muligt, men dog bestandig tillige saa lærvillig og saa godmodig, at Viisdommens Forpagtere ret have Glæde af at lade En slippe med ind paa deres frugtbare Græsgange; ligeoverfor en sentimental, smægtende Begeistring at være *for indskrænket,* til at fatte det Sublime, der begeistrer Andre, men dog altid at forraade den gode Villie, der saa gjerne vilde fatte og forstaae, hvad der hidtil var En en Gaade – ere fuldkommen normale Yttringer af Ironi. Og jo mere troskyldig Ironikerens Dumhed viser sig, jo mere uforfalsket hans ærlige og oprigtige Stræben synes, desto større er hans Glæde. Man seer deraf, at det kan være ligesaa meget ironisk at lade vidende, skjøndt man veed, at man er uvidende, som at lade uvidende, skjøndt man veed, man er vidende. – Ogsaa paa en mere indirecte Maade kan Ironien vise sig gjennem et Modsætningsforhold, naar Ironien udvæl|ger de eenfoldigste og meest indskrænkede Mennesker, ikke for at spotte dem, men for at spotte Viismændene.

I alle disse Tilfælde viser Ironien sig nærmest som den, der opfatter Verden, der søger at mystificere den omgivende Verden, ikke saa meget for selv at være skjult, som for at *faae Andre* til at *aabenbare sig*. Men Ironien kan ogsaa vise sig, idet Ironikeren søger at bringe *Omverdenen paa Vildspor* sig selv betræffende. I vor Tid, hvor de borgerlige og selskabelige Forhold næsten gjøre enhver *hemmelig Kjærlighedshistorie* umulig, hvor Byen eller Omegnen som oftest allerede mange Gange har lyst fra Prædikestolen for det lykkelige Par, førend Præsten har gjort det første Gang; i vor Tid, hvor det selskabelige Liv vilde see sig en af sine kjæreste Forrettigheder berøvet, hvis det ikke havde Magtfuldkommenhed til at knytte Kjærlighedsbaand, og tillige at have paa egen (ikke paa Præstens) Opfordring meget derimod at sige, saa at den offentlige Omtale først giver en Kjærlighedsforstaaelse sin Gyldighed, og en Forbindelse indgaaet uden Byens Vidende

Over against an insipid and inept enthusiasm, it is ironically proper to outdo this with scandalous praise and plaudits, although the ironist is himself aware that this enthusiasm is the most ludicrous thing in the world. Indeed, the more successful the ironist is in beguiling, the further his fakery proceeds, the more joy he has in it. But he relishes this joy in private, and the source of his joy is that no one realizes his deception. – This is a form of irony that appears only rarely, although it is just as profound as the irony that appears under the form of opposition and is easier to carry through. On a small scale, it is sometimes seen used against a person about to be afflicted with one or another fixed idea, or against someone who imagines himself to be a handsome fellow or has especially beautiful sideburns or fancies himself to be witty or at least has said something so witty it cannot be repeated enough, or against someone whose life is wrapped up in a single event, to which he comes back again and again, and which he can be prompted to tell at any time merely by pressing the right button etc.

In all these cases, it is the ironist's joy to seem to be caught in the same noose in which the other person is trapped. It is one of the ironist's chief joys to find weak sides such as this everywhere, and the more distinguished the person in whom it is found, the more joy he has in being able to take him in, to have him in his power, although that person himself is unaware of it. Thus at times even a distinguished person is like a puppet on a string for the ironist, a jumping-jack he can get to make the motions he wants it to make by pulling the string. Strangely enough, it is the weaker sides of the human being more than the good sides that come close to being Chladni figures that continually become visible when made to vibrate properly; they seem to have an intrinsic, natural necessity, whereas the good sides, to our dismay, so often suffer from inconsistencies.

But, on the other hand, it is just as characteristic of irony to emerge in an antithetical situation. Faced with a superfluity of wisdom and then to be so ignorant, so stupid, such a complete Simple Simon as is possible, and yet always so good-natured and teachable that the tenant farmers of wisdom are really happy to let someone slip into their luxuriant pastures; faced with a sentimental, soulful enthusiasm, and then to be too dull to grasp the sublime that inspires others, yet always manifesting an eager willingness to grasp and understand what up until now was a riddle – these are altogether normal expressions of irony. And the more naïve the ironist's stupidity appears to be, the more genuine his honest and upright striving seems, the greater his joy. Thus we perceive that it can be just as ironic to pretend to know when one knows that one does not know as to pretend not to know when one knows that one knows. – Indeed, irony can manifest itself in a more indirect way through an antithetical situation if the irony chooses the simplest and dullest of persons, not in order to mock them but in order to mock the wise.

In all these cases, irony manifests itself rather as the irony that comprehends the world, seeks to mystify the surrounding world, seeking not so much to remain in hiding itself as to get others to disclose themselves. But irony can also be in evidence when the ironist tries to mislead the outside world concerning himself. In our day, when the civic and social situation practically makes every secret love affair impossible, when the city or neighborhood usually has already read the banns for the happy pair many times from the pulpit before the pastor has done it once; in our day, when society would consider itself robbed of one of its most precious prerogatives if it did not have the absolute power to tie the love knot and also at its own request (not at the pastor's) to speak out against it, with the result that a love affair is first validated by public discussion, and a relationship entered into without the town's knowing about it is almost considered invalid or at least a shameful invasion of its rights, just as undertakers regard suicide as an inadmissible sneaking out of the world – in our day, I say, it may certainly at times seem necessary for someone to cheat if he does not want the town to assign itself the honorable

næsten ansees for ugyldig eller idetmindste for et skammeligt Indgreb i dens Rettigheder, lige-som Bedemænd ansee Selvmord for en utilladelig Listen sig ud af Verden – i vor Tid, siger jeg, kan det vel stundom forekomme En og Anden nødvendigt at spille falsk, naar han ikke ønsker, at Byen skal paatage sig det hæderlige Hverv at frie for ham, saa han selv blot behøver at vise sig med det sædvanlige Frieransigt ad modum Peder Erik Madsen, med hvide Handsker paa og en skizzeret Haandtegning over sine Livs-Udsigter i Haanden, tilligemed andre bedaarende Tryl-lemidler (et ærbødigst Promemoria ikke at forglemme), der bruges ved det sidste Angreb. Er det nu mere udvortes Omstændigheder, der gjøre en vis Hemmelighedsfuldhed nødvendig, saa bliver den Mystification, der anvendes, mere slet og ret *Forstillelse*. Men jo mere Individet opfat-ter disse Mystificationer som Episoder i sin egen Kjærlighedshistorie, jo mere overgiven han er i sin Glæde over at henlede Folks Opmærksomhed paa et ganske andet Punkt, desto mere fremtræder *Ironien*. Ironikeren nyder hele Kjærlighedens Uendelighed, og den Udvidelse, Andre søge ved at have Fortrolige, den forskaffer han sig ved at have høit Betroede, der dog Intet veed. Lignende Mystificationer ere stundom ogsaa nødvendige i *Literaturen,* hvor man overalt omspændes af en Mængde aarvaagne Literatusser, der opdage Forfattere, ligesom Kirsten Giftekniv stifter Partier. Jo mindre det nu er en udvortes Grund (Familiehensyn, Hensyn til Befordring, Frygtagtighed o. s. v.), der bestemmer En til at lege Skjul; jo mere det er en vis *indre Uendelighed,* der ønsker at frigjøre sit Værk fra ethvert endeligt Forhold til sig selv, ønsker at see sig fritaget for al Condolation af Ulykkeskammerater, og al Gratulation af Forfatternes ømme Broderskab – desto mere er Ironien fremtrædende. Gaaer det nu saavidt, at man kan faae en eller anden kaglende Hane, der saa uendelig gjerne vilde lægge et Æg, til, halv undvigende, halv bestyrkende Folk i deres Vildfarelse, at lade sig paadutte Paterniteten, saa har Ironikeren vundet Spil. Ønsker man undertiden, hvad vel let i vor Tid En og Anden kan fristes til, at afføre sig den Habit, Enhver i Forhold til sin *Stilling i Samfundet* efter Rangforordningen allerunderdanigst maa anlægge og bære; ønsker En engang imellem idetmindste at vide, at han har det Fortrin for dømte Personer, at han tør vise sig iført andre end Husets Klæder: saa bliver ogsaa her en vis Mystification nødvendig. Jo mere nu det, der bestemmer En til en slig Mystification er et ende-ligt Hensyn, som naar en Kjøbmand reiser incognito for at fremskynde en Speculations heldige Udfald, en Konge for at overraske Kassebetjente, en Politiembedsmand for til Afvexling selv at komme som en Tyv – om Natten, en Mand i en underordnet Stilling i Staten af Frygt for høie Foresatte o. s. v., desto mere nærmer det sig til en slet og ret Forstillelse. Jo mere det derimod er en Trang til engang imellem at være Menneske og ikke evig og altid Cancelliraad, jo mere *poetisk Uendelighed,* der er deri, med jo mere Kunst Mystificationen gjennemføres, desto mere er Ironien fremtrædende. Ja lykkes det endog reent at lede Folk paa Afveie, maaskee at blive anholdt som en mistænkelig Person, eller indblandet i interessante Familieforhold, saa har Iron-ikeren opnaaet, hvad han ønsker.

Men det, som i alle disse og lignende Tilfælde er det Fremtrædende i Ironien, er den *subjective Frihed,* der i ethvert Øieblik har *Muligheden af en Begyndelse* i sin Magt og ikke er generet af tidligere Forhold. Der er noget forførerisk ved al Begyndelse, fordi Subjectet endnu er frit, og det er *denne Nydelse,* Ironikeren attraaer. Virkeligheden taber i saadanne Øieblikke sin Gyldighed for ham, han er fri over den. Dette er Noget, den romersk-catholske Kirke paa enkelte Punkter er bleven sig bevidst, og i Middelalderen pleiede den derfor til visse Tider at hæve sig selv over sin absolute Realitet og opfatte sig selv ironisk, f. Ex. ved Æselsfesten, Narrefesten, Paaskelatter o. s. v. En lignende Følelse laae til Grund for den Tilladelse, de romerske Soldater havde til at synge Spotteviser over Triumphator. Her blev man sig paa eengang Livets Glands og Hæders Realitet bevidst, og i samme Øieblik var man ironisk ude derover. Saaledes skjulte der sig ogsaa,

task of proposing marriage for him so that all he needs to do is present himself with the conventional demeanor of someone who is proposing (*ad modum* [in the manner of] Peder Erik Madsen), wearing white gloves and carrying an outlined sketch of his life prospects, together with other charms and amulets (not to forget a most deferential reminder) to be used in the final assault. Now, if there are circumstances of a primarily more external nature that make a certain secrecy necessary, the mystification to be used becomes more and more outright dissimulation. But the more the individual sees these mystifications as episodes in his own love affair, the more exuberant he is in his joy over drawing people's attention to a totally different point, the more pronounced is the irony. The ironist relishes the whole infinity of love, and the amplification others seek by having confidants he obtains by having highly trusted associates who still know nothing.

Similar mystifications are sometimes also necessary in literature, where one is surrounded on all sides by a crowd of alert literati who discover authors the way Mrs. Matchmaker arranges matches. The less it is an external reason (family reasons, timidity, regard for promotion, etc.) that makes someone decide to play the game of secrecy, the more it is a kind of inner infinity that desires to emancipate its creation from every finite relation to itself, wants to see itself freed from all the condolences of fellow sufferers and from all the congratulations of the tender, loving brotherhood of authors – the more pronounced is the irony. If it goes so far that one can get some cackling rooster who would so very much like to lay an egg to support imputed paternity, half evading, half encouraging people in their error, then the ironist has won the game. If one sometimes wishes to take off the garments something some one or other can easily be tempted to do in our day everyone obsequiously must put on and wear according to his station in society; if one now and then at least wants to know that one has the advantage over convicts of daring to appear dressed in something other than the uniform of the penitentiary – then a certain mystification becomes necessary here also. Now, the more it is a finite reason that makes someone decide upon a mystification such as this, as when a merchant travels incognito to promote the closing of a business venture, a king in order to take his pursers by surprise, a police officer for a change to come as a thief in the night, a subordinate public official afraid of his superiors, etc. – the more it approaches outright dissimulation. However, the more it is an urge to be a human being once in a while and not always and forever the chancellor, the more poetic infinity there is in it, and the more skillfully the mystification is carried out, the more pronounced is the irony. And if one is totally successful in hoaxing people, perhaps even to the point of being arrested as a suspicious character or becoming entangled in an interesting family situation, the ironist has achieved what he desires.

But in all these and similar incidents, the salient feature of the irony is the subjective freedom that at all times has in its power the possibility of a beginning and is not handicapped by earlier situations. There is something seductive about all beginnings, because the subject is still free, and this is the enjoyment the ironist craves. In such moments, actuality loses its validity for him; he is free and above it. This is something the Roman Catholic Church has realized at certain points, and therefore in the Middle Ages it tended to rise above its absolute reality at certain times and to view itself ironically – for example, at the Feast of the Ass, the Feast of Fools, the Easter Comedy, etc. A similar feeling was the basis for allowing the Roman soldiers to sing satirical songs about the victor. There was simultaneously an awareness of the prestige of life and the reality of glory, and at the very same time there was an ironical detachment beyond it. Likewise, without needing the mockery of a Lucian, there was much irony in the lives of the Greek deities; not even the heavenly actuality of the gods was spared the sharp blasts of irony. Just as

uden at man behøver en Lucians Spotterier, megen Ironi i det græske Gudeliv, hvor Gudernes himmelske Virkelighed heller ei var forskaanet for Ironiens skarpe Vindpust. Saavist som det nu er, at der er megen Tilværelse, der ikke er Virkelighed, og at der er Noget i Personligheden, der idetmindste momentviis er incommensurabelt for Virkeligheden, saavist er det ogsaa, at der ligger en Sandhed i Ironien. Hertil kommer, at, saaledes som vi hidtil have opfattet Ironien, er den mere bleven seet som en momentan Yttring, saa at vi i alle disse Tilfælde endnu ikke kunne tale om den rene Ironi, eller om Ironi som Standpunkt. Jo mere derimod den Betragtning af Forholdet mellem Virkelighed og Subject, som her leilighedsviis blev gjort gjeldende, griber om sig, desto mere nærme vi os til det Punkt, hvor Ironien viser sig i sin usurperede Totalitet.

En *Diplomats Opfattelse* af Verden er i mange Maader ironisk, og den bekjendte Yttring af Talleyrand, at Mennesket havde faaet Talen ikke for at aabenbare, men for at skjule sine Tanker, indeholder en dyb Ironi over Verden, og er fra Statsklogskabens Side aldeles svarende til en anden ægte diplomatisk Sætning, mundus vult decipi, decipiatur ergo. Imidlertid følger dog deraf endnu ingenlunde, at den diplomatiske Verden betragter Tilværelsen ironisk, den har tvertimod Meget, den for Alvor vil gjøre gjeldende. – Forskjellen mellem alle de her antydede *Yttringer* af *Ironi* er derfor en blot qvantitativ, et Mere eller Mindre, hvorimod *Ironien sensu eminentiori* qvalitativt adskiller sig fra den her beskrevne Ironi, ligesom den speculative Tvivl qvalitativt adskiller sig fra den vulgære og empiriske. Ironien *sensu eminentiori* retter sig ikke mod dette eller hint enkelte Tilværende, den retter sig mod hele den til en vis Tid og under visse Forhold givne Virkelighed. Den har derfor en Aprioritet i sig, og det er ikke ved successivt at tilintetgjøre et Stykke af Virkeligheden efter det andet, at den kommer til sin Total-Anskuelse, men det er i Kraft af denne, at den destruerer i det Enkelte. Det er ikke dette eller hint Phænomen, men det er Tilværelsens Totale, den betragter sub specie ironiæ. Forsaavidt seer man Rigtigheden af den hegelske Betegnelse af Ironien som den *uendelig absolute Negativitet.*

Forinden vi imidlertid gaae over til den nærmere Udvikling heraf, synes det rigtigst at orientere os i den Begrebs-Omgivelse, hvor Ironien har hjemme. Man maa til den Ende adskille, hvad man kunde kalde en *executiv Ironi*[5] fra en *contemplativ Ironi.*

---

[5] Til den executive eller, som den og kunde kaldes, den dramatiske Ironi hører ogsaa *Naturens Ironi,* forsaavidt nemlig Ironien ikke er bevidst i Naturen, men kun for den, der har Øiet for den, for hvem det da er, som drev Naturen, som en Person, sit Spøg med ham, eller som den betroede ham sin Sorg og sin Smerte. I Naturen ligger ikke dette Misforhold, dertil er den for naturlig og altfor naiv, men for den, der er ironisk udviklet, viser det sig i Naturen. **Schubert** (i hans Symbolik des Traumes, Bamberg 1821) har til behageligt Udvalg en Mangfoldighed af saadanne ironiske Træk i Naturen. Han bemærker, at Naturen med dyb Spot Klage mit Lust, Fröhlichkeit mit Trauer wunderlich paart, gleich jener Naturstimme, der Luftmusik auf Ceylon, welche im Tone einer tiefklagenden, herzzerschneidenden Stimme, furchtbar lustige Menuetten singt (Pag. 38). Han gjør opmærksom paa *Naturens ironiske Sammenstilling* af de fjerneste Extremer, smlgn. Pag. 41: Unmittelbar auf den vernünftigen gemäßigten Menschen, folgt in der Ideenassociation der Natur der tolle Affe, auf den weisen, keuschen Elephanten das unreine Schwein, auf das Pferd der Esel, auf das häßliche Cameel die schlanken Reharten, auf die mit dem gewöhnlichen Loos der Säugthiere unzufriedne, dem Vogel nachäffende Fledermaus, folgt in verschiedener Hinsicht die Maus, die sich kaum aus der Tiefe herauswagt. Men alt Sligt er ikke i Naturen, men *det ironiske Subject* seer det deri. Saaledes kan man ogsaa opfatte alle Sandsebedrag som en Ironi af Naturen. Men for at blive sig det bevidst, fordres der en Bevidsthed, der selv er ironisk. Jo mere polemisk et Individ er udviklet, desto mere Ironi vil han ogsaa finde i Naturen. En saadan Betragtning af Naturen tilhører derfor *mere* den *romantiske* Udvikling *end* den *classiske.* Den græske Harmoni fandt vanskelig slige Spydigheder i Naturen. Jeg vil oplyse dette ved et Exempel. I det lykkelige Grækenland blev Naturen sjelden Vidne til

298

much of life now is not actuality and just as there is something in personality that at least momentarily is incommensurate with actuality, so also there is a truth in irony. Add to this the fact that heretofore we have more or less viewed irony as a momentary manifestation and thus in all these instances are still unable to speak of pure irony or of irony as a position. But the further we extend consideration of the relation between actuality and subject, which has been asserted here only occasionally, the closer we shall approach the point where the irony manifests itself in its usurped totality.

A diplomat's view of the world is ironic in many ways, and Talleyrand's famous statement that man did not acquire speech in order to reveal his thoughts but in order to conceal them contains a profound irony about the world and from the angle of political prudence corresponds entirely to another genuinely diplomatic principle: *mundus vult decipi, decipiatur ergo* [the world wants to be deceived; therefore let it be deceived]. Still this does not necessarily mean that the diplomatic world views existence ironically; on the contrary, there is much it earnestly wants to affirm.

The difference, therefore, between all the manifestations of irony suggested here is merely a quantitative difference, a more or less, whereas irony *sensu eminentiori* [in the eminent sense] qualitatively differs from the irony described here in the same way that speculative doubt differs qualitatively from common, empirical doubt. Irony *sensu eminentiori* is directed not against this or that particular existing entity but against the entire given actuality at a certain time and under certain conditions. Thus it has an intrinsic apriority, and it is not by successively destroying one portion of actuality after another that it arrives at its total view, but it is by virtue of this that it destroys in the particular instance. It is not this or that phenomenon but the totality of existence that it contemplates *sub specie ironiae* [under the aspect of irony]. To this extent we see the correctness of Hegel's view of irony as infinite absolute negativity.

However, before we go on to discuss this in more detail, it seems best to orient ourselves in the conceptual milieu to which irony belongs. To that end we must distinguish between what could be called executive irony[6] and contemplative irony. We shall first consider what we ventured to

---

[6] Also belonging to executive or, as it could be called, dramatic irony, is nature's irony – that is, provided the irony is not conscious in nature but is conscious only to the one who has an eye for it, to whom it seems as if nature, like a person, were playing its joke on him or confiding its grief and pain to him. This discrepancy is not intrinsic to nature – it is too natural and far too naïve for that, but it appears in nature to the person who is ironically advanced. In his *Symbolik des Traumes* (Bamberg: 1821), Schubert has an engaging selection of many such ironic figures in nature. He notes (38) that nature, with profound mockery, 'Klage mit Lust, Fröhlichkeit mit Trauer wunderlich paart, gleich jener Naturstimme, der Luftmusik auf Ceylon, welche im Tone einer tiefklagenden, herzzerschneidenden Stimme, furchtbar lustige Menuetten singt [curiously joins lament with merriment, joy with sorrow, like that voice of nature on Ceylon, the air music, which sings a frightfully merry minuet in the tones of a profoundly plaintive, heartrending voice].' He points out nature's ironic juxtaposition of outrageous extremes (41): 'Unmittelbar auf den vernünftigen gemäszigten Menschen, folgt in der Ideenassociation der Natur der tolle Affe, auf den weisen, keuschen Elephanten das ureine Schwein, auf das Pferd der Esel, auf das häszliche Cameel die schlanken Reharten, auf die mit dem gewöhnlichen Loos der Säugthiere unzufriedne, dem Vogel nachäffende Fledermaus, folgt in verschiedener Hinsicht die Maus, die sich kaum aus der Tiefe herauswagt [In nature's association of ideas, the rational and moderate human being is immediately succeeded by the ridiculous ape, after the wise and pure elephant comes the unclean swine, after the horse the ass, after the hideous camel the slender deer, and after the bat, dissatisfied with the ordinary lot of the mammal and imitating the bird, comes the mouse, which, dissatisfied in a different sense, scarcely ventures

Vi betragte først, hvad vi vovede at kalde den *executive* Ironi. Forsaavidt som Ironien gjør Modsætningsforholdet gjeldende i alle dets forskjellige Nuancer, forsaavidt kunde det synes, at Ironi blev identisk med *Forstillelse.*[7]

I Almindelighed pleier man for Kortheds Skyld at oversætte Ironi ved Forstillelse. Men Forstillelse betegner mere den *objective* Act, der fuldbyrder Misforholdet mellem Væsen og Phænomen; Ironi betegner tillige den subjective Nydelse, idet Subjectet ved Ironien frigjør sig fra den Bundethed, i hvilken Livsforholdenes Continuitet holder ham, som man jo derfor ogsaa kan sige om Ironikeren, at han slaaer sig løs. Hertil kommer, at Forstillelse, forsaavidt man vil bringe den i Forhold til Subjectet, har en Hensigt, men denne Hensigt er en udvortes Hensigt, en Forstillelsen selv fremmed; derimod har Ironien ingen Hensigt, dens Hensigt er immanent i den selv, det er en metaphysisk Hensigt. Hensigten er ikke noget Andet end Ironien selv. Naar Ironikeren saaledes viser sig som en anden, end han virkelig er, saa kunde det vistnok synes, at hans Hensigt var den, at faae Andre til at troe dette; men hans egentlige Hensigt er dog den, at føle sig fri, men dette er han netop ved Ironien, og saaledes har Ironien altsaa ikke nogen anden Hensigt, men er Selvhensigt. Man seer derfor let, at Ironi er forskjellig fra den Jesuitisme, hvori Subjectet vel er frit i Valget af Midler til at udføre sin Hensigt, men ingenlunde frit i den Forstand som i Ironien, hvor Subjectet ingen Hensigt har.

Forsaavidt som det er Ironien væsentligt at have et Udvortes, der er det Indvortes modsat, kunde det synes, at den blev identisk med *Hykleri.* Paa Dansk har man vel ogsaa stundom oversat Ironi ved Skalkagtighed, og en Hykler pleier man jo at kalde en Øienskalk. Men Hykleri hører egentlig hjemme paa det *moralske* Gebet. Hykleren stræber bestandig at synes god, skjøndt han er ond. Ironien derimod ligger paa et metaphysisk Gebet, og det er Ironikeren bestandig blot om at gjøre at synes en anden, end han virkelig er, saa at, ligesom Ironikeren skjuler sin Spøg i Alvor, sit Alvor i Spøg (omtrent som Naturlydene paa Ceylon), saaledes kan det ogsaa falde ham ind at lade ond, skjøndt han er god. Kun maa man erindre, at de moralske Bestemmelser egentlig ere for concrete for Ironien.

Men Ironien har ogsaa en theoretisk eller *contemplativ* Side. Betragte vi Ironien som et underordnet Moment, saa er Ironien jo det sikkre Blik for det Skjæve, det Forkeerte, det Forfængelige i Tilværelsen. Idet den nu opfatter dette, kunde det synes, at Ironi blev identisk med *Spot, Satire, Persiflage* o. s. v. En Lighed har den naturligviis hermed, forsaavidt som den ogsaa seer det Forfængelige; men idet den vil fremstille sin Observation, afviger den, idet den ikke tilintetgjør det Forfængelige, ikke er, hvad den straffende Retfærdighed er i Forhold til Lasten, ikke har det Forsonende ved sig, som det Comiske har, men den *bestyrker* snarere det Forfængelige i dets Forfængelighed, den gjør det Gale endnu galere. Dette er hvad man kunde kalde Ironiens Forsøg paa at mediere de discrete Momenter, ikke i en høiere Enhed, men i en høiere Galskab.

Andet end en ligelig stemt Sjæls blide og milde Harmonier, thi selv den græske Sorg var skjøn, derfor var Echo en venlig *Nymphe.* I den nordiske Mythologi derimod, hvor Naturen gjenlød af vilde Klageskrig, hvor Natten ikke var lys og klar, men mørk og taaget, angstfuld og rædsom, hvor Sorgen ikke formildedes ved en stille Erindring, men ved et dybt Suk og evig Glemsel, der var Echo en *Trold.* I den nordiske Folketro hedder Echo derfor Dvergmål eller Bergmål, smlgn. **Grimm:** Irische Elfenmärchen Pag. LXXVIII Færøiske Qvæder. Randers 1822 Pag. 464. Denne Ironi i Naturen har her fundet Plads i en Note, fordi det dog egentlig først er for det humoristiske Individ, at den gaaer op; thi det er egentlig først igjennem Betragtningen af *Synden* i Verden, at den ironiske Opfattelse af Naturen ret træder frem.

[7] Saaledes er Ironi opfattet af **Theophrast,** cfr. Theophrasti Characteres ed. Astius pag. 4 Cap. I: περὶ εἰρωνείας. Her defineres Ironi saaledes: προσποίησις ἐπὶ χεῖρον πράξεων καὶ λόγων (simulatio dissimulatioque fallax et fraudulenta).

call executive irony. Insofar as irony asserts contradistinction in all its various nuances, it might seem that irony would be identical with dissimulation.[8] For the sake of conciseness, the word 'irony' is customarily translated as 'dissimulation.' But dissimulation denotes more the objective act that carries out the discrepancy between essence and phenomenon; irony also denotes the subjective pleasure as the subject frees himself by means of irony from the restraint in which the continuity of life's conditions holds him – thus the ironist can literally be said to kick over the traces. Add to this the fact that dissimulation, insofar as it is brought into relation to the subject, has a purpose, but this purpose is an external objective foreign to the dissimulation itself. Irony, however, has no purpose; its purpose is immanent in itself and is a metaphysical purpose. The purpose is nothing other than the irony itself. If, for example, the ironist appears as someone other than he actually is, his purpose might indeed seem to be to get others to believe this; but his actual purpose still is to feel free, but this he is precisely by means of irony – consequently irony has no other purpose but is self-motivated. We readily perceive, therefore, that irony differs from Jesuitism, in which the subject is, to be sure, free to choose the means to fulfill his purpose but is not at all free in the same sense as in irony, in which the subject has no purpose.

Insofar as it is essential for irony to have an external side that is opposite to the internal, it might seem that it would be identical with hypocrisy. Indeed, irony is sometimes translated in Danish as *Skalkagtighed* [roguishness], and a hypocrite is usually called an *Řienskalk* [eye-rogue]. But hypocrisy actually belongs to the sphere of morality. The hypocrite is always trying to appear good, although he is evil. Irony, on the other hand, lies in the metaphysical sphere, and the ironist is always only making himself seem to be other than he actually is; thus, just as the ironist hides his jest in earnestness, his earnestness in jest (somewhat like the sounds of nature on Ceylon), so it may also occur to him to pretend to be evil, although he is good. Only remember that the moral categories are actually too concrete for irony.

But irony also has a theoretical or contemplative side. If we regard irony as a minor element, then irony, of course, is the unerring eye for what is crooked, wrong and vain in existence. Regarded in this way, irony might seem to be identical with mockery, satire, persiflage, etc. There is, of course, a resemblance insofar as irony sees the vanity, but it diverges in making its observation, because it does not destroy the vanity; it is not what punitive justice is in relation to vice, does not have the redeeming feature of the comic but instead reinforces vanity in its

forth from the depths].' Now all such things are not in nature, but the ironic subject sees them in nature. Similarly, we can also interpret all sensory illusions as irony on the part of nature. But it takes a consciousness that is itself ironic to become aware of this. The more polemically developed an individual is, the more irony he will also find in nature. Therefore, such a view of nature belongs more to the romantic than to the classical trend. It was difficult for Greek harmoniousness to find such sarcasm in nature. I shall illustrate with this example. In happy Greece, nature seldom witnessed anything but the soft and gentle harmonies of an even-tempered psyche, for even Greek sorrow was beautiful, and therefore Echo was a friendly nymph. But in Norse mythology, where nature resounded with wild lament, where the night was not light and clear but dark and foggy, full of anxiety and terror, where grief was assuaged not by a quiet recollection but by a deep sigh and everlasting oblivion, there Echo was a troll. Thus in Norse mythology, Echo is called *Dvergmall* or *Bergmaal* (see Grimm, *Irische Elfenmärchen* p. LXXVIII; *Færøiske Qvæder* [Randers: 1822], p. 464). This irony in nature has been placed in a footnote because only the humorous individual actually perceives it, since it is actually only through the contemplation of *sin* in the world that the ironic interpretation of nature really emerges.

[8] Irony is interpreted in this way by Theophrastus. See *Theophrasti Characteres*, edited by Ast, chs 1, 4; (*simulatio dissimulatioque fallax et fraudulenta*) [false and fraudulent dissimulation and concealment].

Betragte vi Ironien, idet den vender sig *mod hele Tilværelsen,* saa fastholder den atter her Modsætningen mellem Væsen og Phænomen, mellem det Indvortes og det Udvortes. Det kunde nu synes, at den blev, som den absolute Negativitet, identisk med *Tvivlen.* Men deels maa man erindre, at Tvivl er en Begrebsbestemmelse, Ironi en *Subjectivitetens* Forsigværen; deels at Ironien væsentlig er *practisk,* og at den kun er theoretisk for atter at være practisk, med andre Ord, at det ikke er Ironien om Sagen, men om den selv at gjøre. Naar derfor Ironien kommer under Veir med, at der bag Phænomenet maa stikke noget Andet end det, der ligger i Phænomenet, saa er det, der bestandig er Ironien magtpaaliggende, det, at Subjectet føler sig frit, saa at Phænomenet bestandig ikke faaer Realitet for Subjectet. Bevægelsen er derfor og aldeles modsat. I Tvivlen vil Subjectet bestandig ind i Gjenstanden, og hans Ulykke er den, at Gjenstanden bestandig flyer for ham. I Ironien vil Subjectet bestandig ud af Gjenstanden, hvilket han opnaaer derved, at han i ethvert Øieblik bliver sig bevidst, at Gjenstanden ingen Realitet har. I Tvivlen er Subjectet Vidne til en Erobringskrig, i hvilken ethvert Phænomen tilintetgjøres, fordi Væsenet bestandig maa ligge bag derved. I Ironien retirerer Subjectet bestandig, afdisputerer ethvert Phænomen Realitet, for at frelse sig selv, det vil sige, for at bevare sig selv i den negative Uafhængighed af Alt.

Forsaavidt endelig Ironien, idet den bliver sig bevidst, at Tilværelsen ingen Realitet har, udtaler den samme Sætning, som det fromme Gemyt, kunde det synes, at Ironien blev en Slags *Andagt.* I Andagten taber ogsaa, om jeg saa maa sige, den lavere Virkelighed, det vil sige Verdensforholdene, sin Gyldighed, men dette skeer dog kun forsaavidt, som *Gudsforholdene* i samme Øieblik gjøre deres absolute Realitet gjeldende. Det andagtsfulde Sind udsiger ogsaa, at Alt er Forfængelighed; men det er dog kun forsaavidt, som ved denne Negation alt Forstyrrende skaffes tilside, og det evigt Bestaaende kommer tilsyne. Hertil kommer, at naar det andagtsfulde Sind finder Alt forfængeligt, saa gjør det ingen Undtagelse med sin egen Person, gjør ingen Ophævelser med den, tvertimod, den maa ogsaa tilside, for at det Guddommelige ikke skal stødes tilbage ved dens Modstand, men udgyde sig i det ved Andagten sig aabnende Sind. Ja i de dybere gaaende Opbyggelsesskrifter see vi, at det fromme Sind netop agter sin egen endelige Personlighed at være det Usleste af Alt. I Ironien derimod bliver, idet Alt forfængeliggjøres, Subjectiviteten fri. Jo mere Alt bliver forfængeligt, desto lettere, desto indholdsløsere, desto flygtigere bliver Subjectiviteten. Og medens Alt bliver Forfængelighed, bliver det ironiske Subject *ikke sig selv* forfængeligt, men frelser sin egen Forfængelighed. For Ironien bliver Alt Intet; men Intet kan tages paa flere Maader. Det speculative Intet er det i ethvert Øieblik for Concretionen Forsvindende, da det selv er det Concretes Trang, dets nisus formativus; det mystiske Intet er et Intet for Forestillingen, et Intet, der dog er ligesaa indholdsrigt, som Nattens Taushed er høirøstet for den, der har Øren at høre med; det ironiske Intet endelig er den Dødsstilhed, i hvilken Ironien gaaer igjen og spøger (dette sidste Ord taget aldeles tvetydigt).

vanity and makes what is lunatic even more lunatic. This is what could be called irony's attempt to mediate the discrete elements – not into a higher unity but into a higher lunacy.

If we consider irony as it turns against all existence, here again it maintains the contradiction between essence and phenomenon, between the internal and the external. It might seem now that as the absolute negativity it would be identical with doubt. But one must bear two things in mind – first that doubt is a conceptual qualification, and irony is subjectivity's being-for-itself; second, that irony is essentially practical, that it is theoretical only in order to become practical again – in other words, it has to do with the irony of itself and not with the irony of the situation. Therefore, if irony gets an inkling that there is something more behind the phenomenon than meets the eye, then precisely what irony has always insisted upon is this, that the subject feel free, so that the phenomenon never acquires any reality [*Realitet*] for the subject. Therefore, the movement is continually in the opposite direction. In doubt, the subject continually wants to enter into the object, and his unhappiness is that the object continually eludes him. In irony, the subject continually wants to get outside the object, and he achieves this by realizing at every moment that the object has no reality. In doubt, the subject is an eyewitness to a war of conquest in which every phenomenon is destroyed, because the essence must continually lie behind it. In irony, the subject is continually retreating, talking every phenomenon out of its reality in order to save itself – that is, in order to preserve itself in negative independence of everything.

Finally, insofar as irony, when it realizes that existence has no reality [*Realitet*], pronounces the same thesis as the pious mentality, irony might seem to be a kind of religious devotion. If I may put it this way, in religious devotion the lower actuality [*Virkelighed*], that is, the relationships with the world, loses its validity, but this occurs only insofar as the relationships with God simultaneously affirm their absolute reality. The devout mind also declares that all is vanity, but this is only insofar as through this negation all disturbing factors are set aside and the eternally existing order comes into view. Add to this the fact that if the devout mind finds everything to be vanity, it makes no exception of its own person, makes no commotion about it; on the contrary, it also must be set aside so that the divine will not be thrust back by its opposition but will pour itself into the mind opened by devotion. Indeed, in the deeper devotional literature, we see that the pious mind regards its own finite personality as the most wretched of all.

In irony, however, since everything is shown to be vanity, the subject becomes free. The more vain everything becomes, all the lighter, emptier, and volatilized the subject becomes. And while everything is in the process of becoming vanity, the ironic subject does not become vain in his own eyes but rescues his own vanity. For irony, everything becomes nothing, but nothing can be taken in several ways. The speculative nothing is the vanishing at every moment with regard to the concretion, since it is itself the craving of the concrete, its *nisus formativus* [formative impulse]; the mystic nothing is a nothing with regard to the representation, a nothing that nevertheless is just as full of content as the silence of the night is full of sounds for someone who has ears to hear. Finally, the ironic nothing is the dead silence in which irony walks again and haunts (the latter word taken altogether ambiguously).

[1841] [*Translated by V. Howard and Edna H. Hong. Princeton, NJ: Princeton UP, 1989*]

II.c.2. HANS CHRISTIAN ANDERSEN, *Skyggen*

I de hede Lande, der kan rigtignok Solen brænde! Folk blive ganske mahognibrune; ja i de aller-
hedeste Lande brændes de til Negre, men det var nu kun til de hede Lande, en lærd Mand var
kommen fra de kolde; der troede han nu at han kunde løbe om, ligesom der hjemme, jo det blev
han snart vant fra. Han og alle fornuftige Folk maatte blive inde, Vindues-Skodder og Døre
bleve lukkede den hele Dag; det saae ud som hele Huset sov eller der var ingen hjemme. Den
smalle Gade med de høie Huse, hvor han boede, var nu ogsaa bygget saaledes at Solskinnet fra
Morgen til Aften maatte ligge der, det var virkeligt ikke til at holde ud! - Den lærde Mand fra de
kolde Lande, det var en ung Mand, en klog Mand, han syntes, han sad i en gloende Ovn; det tog
paa ham, han blev ganske mager, selv hans Skygge krøb ind, den blev meget mindre end hjemme,
Solen tog ogsaa paa den. - De levede først op om Aftenen, naar Solen var nede.

Det var ordentlig en Fornøielse at see paa; saasnart Lyset blev bragt ind i Stuen, strakte Skyggen
sig heelt op ad Væggen, ja saa gar hen ad Loftet, saa lang gjorde den sig, den maatte strække sig
for at komme til Kræfter. Den Lærde gik ud paa Altanen, for at strække sig der, og altsom
Stjernerne kom frem i den deilige klare Luft, var det for ham, som kom han tillive igjen. Paa alle
Altaner i Gaden, og i de varme Lande har hvert Vindue en Altan, kom Folk frem, for Luft maa
man have, selvom man er vant til at være mahogni! Der blev saa levende oppe og nede. Skomag-
ere og Skræddere, alle Folk fløttede ud paa Gaden, der kom Bord og Stol, og Lyset brændte, ja
over tusind Lys brændte, og den ene talte og den anden sang, og Folk spadserede, Vognene kjørte,
Æslerne gik: klingelingeling! de har Klokker paa; der blev Liig begravede med Psalmesang, Gad-
edrengene skjød med Troldkjællinger, og Kirkeklokkerne ringede, jo der var rigtig nok levende
nede i Gaden. Kun i det ene Huus, som laa ligeoverfor hvor den fremmede lærde Mand boede,
var der ganske stille; og dog boede der Nogen, for der stod paa Altanen Blomster, de groede saa
deiligt i den Solhede, og det kunde de ikke, uden at de bleve vandede, og Nogen maatte jo vande
dem; Folk maatte der være. Døren derovre kom ogsaa halv op ud paa Aftenen, men der var mørkt
derinde, i det mindste i det forreste Værelse, dybere inde fra lød Musik. Den fremmede lærde
Mand syntes, den var ganske mageløs, men det kunde nu ogsaa gjerne være at han kun bildte sig
det ind, for han fandt Alting mageløst derude i de varme Lande, naar der kun ingen Sol havde
været. Den Fremmedes Vert sagde at han ikke vidste, hvem der havde leiet Gjenboens Huus, man
saae jo ingen Folk og hvad Musiken angik, syntes han, at den var gruelig kjedelig. »Det er ligesom
om En sad og øvede sig paa et Stykke, han ikke kan komme ud af, altid det samme Stykke. »»Jeg
faaer det dog ud!«« siger han nok, men han faaer det dog ikke ud hvor længe han spiller.«

En Nat vaagnede den Fremmede, han sov for aaben Altandør, Gardinet foran den løftede sig
i Vinden, og han syntes at der kom en forunderlig Glands fra Gjenboens Altan, alle Blomsterne
skinnede som Flammer, i de deiligste Farver, og midt imellem Blomsterne stod en slank, yndig
Jomfru, det var som om ogsaa hun lyste; det skar ham virkeligt i Øinene, han lukkede dem nu
ogsaa saa forfærdelig meget op og kom lige af Søvnen; i et Spring var han paa Gulvet, ganske
sagte kom han bag Gardinet, men Jomfruen var borte, Glandsen var borte; Blomsterne skinnede
slet ikke, men stode meget godt, som altid; Døren var paa klem, og dybt inde klang Musiken
saa blød og deilig, man kunde ordentlig falde hen i søde Tanker derved. Det var dog ligesom
en Trolddom og hvem boede der? Hvor endvar den egentlige Indgang? Hele Stue-Etagen var
Boutik ved Boutik, og der kunde Folk jo dog ikke altid løbe igjennem.

En Aften sad den Fremmede ude paa sin Altan, inde i Stuen bag ved ham brændte Lyset, og
saa var det jo ganske naturligt at Skyggen af ham gik over paa Gjenboens Væg; ja der sad den lige
over for mellem Blomsterne paa Altanen; og naar den Fremmede rørte sig, saa rørte Skyggen sig
ogsaa, for det gjør den. -

II.c.2. HANS CHRISTIAN ANDERSEN, *The Shadow*

It is in the hot countries that the sun burns down in earnest, turning the people there a deep mahogany-brown. In the hottest countries of all they are seared into negroes, but it was not quite that hot in this country to which a man of learning had come from the colder north. He expected to go about there just as he had at home, but he soon discovered that this was a mistake. He and other sensible souls had to stay inside. The shutters were drawn and the doors were closed all day long. It looked just as if everyone were asleep or away from home. The narrow street of high houses where he lived was so situated that from morning till night the sun beat down on it – unbearably! To this young and clever scholar from the colder north, it felt as if he were sitting in a blazing hot oven. It exhausted him so that he became very thin, and even his shadow shrank much smaller than it had been at home. Only in the evenings, after sundown, did the man and his shadow begin to recover.

This was really a joy to see. As soon as a candle was brought into the room, the shadow had to stretch itself to get its strength back. It stretched up to the wall, yes, even along the ceiling, so tall did it grow. To stretch himself, the scholar went out on the balcony. As soon as the stars came out in the beautifully clear sky, he felt as if he had come back to life.

In warm countries each window has a balcony, and in all the balconies up and down the street people came out to breathe the fresh air that one needs, even if one is already a fine mahogany-brown. Both up above and down below, things became lively. Tailors, shoemakers – everybody – moved out in the street. Chairs and tables were brought out, and candles were lighted, yes, candles by the thousand. One man talked, another sang, people strolled about, carriages drove by, and donkeys trotted along, *ting-a-ling-a-ling*, for their harness had bells on it. There were church bells ringing, hymn singing, and funeral processions. There were boys in the street firing off Roman candles. Oh yes, it was lively as lively can be down in that street.

Only one house was quiet – the one directly across from where the scholarly stranger lived. Yet someone lived there, for flowers on the balcony grew and thrived under that hot sun, which they could not have done unless they were watered. So someone must be watering them, and there must be people in the house. Along in the evening, as a matter of fact, the door across the street was opened. But it was dark inside, at least in the front room. From somewhere in the house, farther back, came the sound of music. The scholarly stranger thought the music was marvelous, but it is quite possible that he only imagined this, for out there in the warm countries he thought everything was marvelous – except the sun. The stranger's landlord said that he didn't know who had rented the house across the street. No one was ever to be seen over there, and as for the music, he found it extremely tiresome. He said: 'It's just as if somebody sits there practicing a piece that's beyond him – always the selfsame piece. "I'll play it right yet," he probably says, but he doesn't, no matter how long he tries.'

One night the stranger woke up. He slept with the windows to his balcony open, and as the breeze blew his curtain aside he fancied that a marvelous radiance came from the balcony across the street. The colors of all the flowers were as brilliant as flames. In their midst stood a maiden, slender and lovely. It seemed as if a radiance came from her too. It actually hurt his eyes, but that was because he had opened them too wide in his sudden awakening. One leap, and he was out of bed. Without a sound, he looked out through his curtains, but the maiden was gone. The flowers were no longer radiant, though they bloomed as fresh and fair as usual. The door was ajar and through it came music so lovely and soft that one could really feel very romantic about it. It was like magic. But who lived there? What entrance did they use? Facing the street, the lower floor of the house was a row of shops, and people couldn't run through them all the time.

»Jeg troer min Skygge er det eneste Levende, man seer derovre!« sagde den lærde Mand. »See hvor net den sidder mellem Blomsterne, Døren staaer * paa klem, nu skulde Skyggen være saa snild og gaae indenfor, see sig om, og saa komme og fortælle mig hvad den havde seet! ja Du skulde gjøre Gavn!« sagde han i Spøg! »Vær saa god at træde indenfor! naa! gaaer Dut« og saa nikkede han til Skyggen og Skyggen nikkede igjen. »Ja saa gaa, men bliv ikke borte!« og den Fremmede reiste sig og hans Skygge ovre paa Gjenboens Altan reiste sig ogsaa; og den Fremmede dreiede sig og Skyggen dreiede sig ogsaa; ja dersom Nogen ordentligt havde lagt Mærke dertil, da havde de tydeligt kunnet see, at Skyggen gik ind af den halvaabne Altandør hos Gjenboen, lige i det den Fremmede gik ind i sin Stue og lod det lange Gardin falde ned efter sig.

Næste Morgen gik den lærde Mand ud for at drikke Kaffe og læse Aviser. »Hvad er det?« sagde han, da han kom ud i Solskinnet, »jeg har jo ingen Skygge! saa er den virkelig gaaet i Aftes og ikke kommet igjen; det er noget kjedeligt Noget!«

Og det ærgrede ham, men ikke saa meget fordi at Skyggen var borte, men fordi han vidste, at der var en Historie til om en Mand uden Skygge, den kjendte jo alle Folk hjemme i de kolde Lande, og kom nu den lærde Mand der og fortalte sin, saa vilde de sige, at han gik og lignede efter, og det behøvede han ikke. Han vilde derfor slet ikke tale derom, og det var fornuftigt tænkt.

Om Aftenen gik han ud paa sin Altan igjen, Lyset havde han meget rigtig sat bag ved sig, for han vidste at Skyggen vil altid have sin Herre til Skjærm, men han kunde ikke lokke den; han gjorde sig lille, han gjorde sig stor, men der var ingen Skygge, der kom ingen! Han sagde: hm! hm! men det hjalp ikke.

Ærgerligt var det, men i de varme Lande der voxer nu Alting saa gesvindt, og efter otte Dages Forløb mærkede han, til sin store Fornøielse, at der voxede ham en ny Skygge ud fra Benene, naar han kom i Solskin, Roden maatte været blevet siddende. Efter tre Uger havde han en ganske taalelig Skygge, der, da han begav sig hjem til de nordlige Lande, voxte paa Reisen meer og meer, saa at den tilsidst var saa lang og saa stor at det Halve var nok.

Saa kom den lærde Mand hjem og han skrev Bøger om hvad der var Sandt i Verden, og om hvad der var Godt og hvad der var Smukt, og der gik Dage og der gik Aar; der gik mange Aar.

Da sidder han en Aften i sin Stue og saa banker det ganske sagte paa Døren.

»Kom ind!« siger han, men der kom Ingen; saa lukker han op og der stod for ham saadan et overordentligt magert Menneske, saa han blev ganske underlig. Forresten var Mennesket særdeles fiint klædt paa, det maatte være en fornem Mand.

»Hvem har jeg den Ære at tale med?« spurgte den Lærde.

»Ja det tænkte jeg nok!« sagde den fine Mand, »at De ikke kjendte mig! jeg er blevet saa meget Legeme, jeg har ordentlig faaet Kjød og Klæder. De har nok aldrig tænkt at see mig i saadan en Velmagt. Kjender De ikke deres gamle Skygge? Ja De har vist ikke troet at jeg mere kom igjen. Mig er det gaaet særdeles vel siden jeg sidst var hos dem, jeg er i alle Henseender bleven meget formuende! skal jeg kjøbe mig fri fra Tjenesten, saa kan jeg!« og saa raslede han med et heelt Bundt kostbare Signeter, som hang ved Uhret, og han stak sin Haand ind i den tykke Guldkjæde, han bar om Halsen; nei hvor alle Fingrene glimrede med Diamants Ringe! og det var Altsammen virkeligt.

»Nei, jeg kan ikke komme til mig selv!« sagde den lærde Mand, »hvad er dog alt det!«

»Ja noget Almindeligt er det ikke!« sagde Skyggen, »men De selv hører jo heller ikke til det Almindelige, og jeg, det veed De nok, har fra Barnsbeen traadt i deres Fodspoer. Saasnart De fandt, jeg var moden til at gaae alene ud i Verden, gik jeg min egen Vei; jeg er i de allerbrillanteste Omstændigheder, men der kom en Slags Længsel over mig efter engang at see Dem før de døer, De skal jo døe! jeg vilde ogsaa gjerne gjensee disse Lande, for man holder dog altid af

On another evening, the stranger sat out on his balcony. The candle burned in the room behind him, so naturally his shadow was cast on the wall across the street. Yes, there it sat among the flowers, and when the stranger moved, it moved with him. 'I believe my shadow is the only living thing to be seen over there,' the scholar thought to himself. 'See how he makes himself at home among the flowers. The door stands ajar, and if my shadow were clever he'd step in, have a look around, and come back to tell me what he had seen.' 'Yes,' he said as a joke, 'you ought to make yourself useful. Kindly step inside. Well, aren't you going?' He nodded to the shadow, and the shadow nodded back. 'Run along now, but be sure to come back.' The stranger rose, and his shadow across the street rose with him. The stranger turned around, and his shadow turned too. If anyone had been watching closely, he would have seen the shadow enter the half-open balcony door in the house across the way at the same instant that the stranger returned to his room and the curtain fell behind him.

Next morning, when the scholar went out to take his coffee and read the newspapers, he said, 'What's this?' as he came out in the sunshine. 'I haven't any shadow! So it really did go away last night, and it stayed away. Isn't that annoying?'

What annoyed him most was not so much the loss of his shadow, but the knowledge that there was already a story about a man without a shadow. All the people at home knew that story. If he went back and told them his story they would say he was just imitating the old one. He did not care to be called unoriginal, so he decided to say nothing about it, which was the most sensible thing to do.

That evening he again went out on the balcony. He had placed the candle directly behind him, because he knew that a shadow always likes to use its master as a screen, but he could not coax it forth. He made himself short and he made himself tall, but there was no shadow. It didn't come forth. He hemmed and he hawed, but it was no use.

This was very vexing, but in the hot countries everything grows most rapidly, and in a week or so he noticed with great satisfaction that when he went out in the sunshine a new shadow was growing at his feet. The root must have been left with him. In three weeks' time he had a very presentable shadow, and as he started north again it grew longer and longer, until it got so long and large that half of it would have been quite sufficient. The learned man went home and wrote books about those things in the world that are true, that are good, and that are beautiful. The days went by and the years went past, many, many years in fact.

Then one evening when he was sitting in his room he heard a soft tapping at his door. 'Come in,' said he, but no one came in. He opened the door and was confronted by a man so extremely thin that it gave him a strange feeling. However, the man was faultlessly dressed, and looked like a person of distinction.

'With whom do I have the honor of speaking?' the scholar asked.

'Ah,' said the distinguished visitor, 'I thought you wouldn't recognize me, now that I've put real flesh on my body and wear clothes. I don't suppose you ever expected to see me in such fine condition. Don't you know your old shadow? You must have thought I'd never come back. Things have gone remarkably well with me since I was last with you. I've thrived in every way, and if I have to buy my freedom, I can.' He rattled a bunch of valuable charms that hung from his watch, and fingered the massive gold chain he wore around his neck. Ho! how his fingers flashed with diamond rings – and all this jewelry was real.

'No, I can't get over it!' said the scholar. 'What *does* it all mean?'

'Nothing ordinary, you may be sure,' said the shadow. 'But you are no ordinary person and I, as you know, have followed in your footsteps from childhood. As soon as you thought me sufficiently experienced to strike out in the world for myself, I went my way. I have been immeasurably

Fædrelandet! - Jeg veed De har faaet en anden Skygge igjen, har jeg noget at betale til den eller dem? De vil bare være saa god at sige det.«

»Nei, er det virkelig Dig!« sagde den lærde Mand, »det er dog høist mærkværdig! aldrig havde jeg troet at Ens gamle Skygge kunde komme igjen som Menneske!«

»Siig mig hvad jeg har at betale!« sagde *Skyggen*, »for jeg vil nødig staae i nogen Slags Gjæld!«

»Hvor kan Du tale saaledes!« sagde den lærde Mand. »Hvad Gjæld er her at snakke om! vær saa fri, som Nogen! jeg glæder mig overordentlig ved din Lykke! sid ned, gamle Ven og fortæl mig bare lidt om hvorledes det er gaaet til, og hvad Du saae ovre hos Gjenboens, der i de varme Lande!« -

»Ja, det skal jeg fortælle Dem,« sagde *Skyggen* og satte sig ned, »men saa maa De ogsaa love mig, at De aldrig til Nogen her i Byen, hvor De endogsaa træffer mig, siger at jeg har været deres Skygge! jeg har isinde at forlove mig; jeg kan føde mere end een Familie!« -

»Vær ganske rolig!« sagde den lærde Mand, »jeg skal ikke sige Nogen hvem Du egenlig er! her er min Haand! jeg lover det og en Mand et Ord!«

»Et Ord en Skygge!« sagde Skyggen, og saaledes maatte den jo tale.

Det var ellers virkelig ganske mærkværdigt hvormeget Menneske den var; ganske sortklædt var den og i det allerfineste sorte Klæde, lakerede Støvler, og Hat der kunde smække sammen, saa at den blev bar Pul og Skygge, ikke at tale om hvad vi allerede veed her var, Signeter, Guldhalskjæde og Diamantringe; jo, Skyggen var overordentlig godt klædt paa, og det var just det, som gjorde at den var ganske et Menneske.

»Nu skal jeg fortælle!« sagde *Skyggen*, og saa satte den sine Been med de lakerede Støvler saa haardt, den kunde, ned paa Ærmet af den lærde Mands nye Skygge, der laa som en Puddelhund ved hans Fødder, og det var nu enten af Hovmod eller maaskee for at faae den til at hænge ved; og den liggende Skygge, holdt sig saa stille og rolig, for ret at høre efter; den vilde nok vide hvorledes man saaledes kunde komme løs og tjene sig op til sin egen Herre.

»Veed De, hvem der boede i Gjenboens Huus?« sagde Skyggen, »det var den deiligste af Alle, det var *Poesien*! Jeg var der i tre Uger og det er ligesaa virkende, som om man levede i tre tusind Aar og læste Alt hvad der var digtet og skrevet, for det siger jeg og det er rigtigt. Jeg har seet Alt og jeg veed Alt!«

»Poesien!« raabte den lærde Mand! »ja, ja - hun er tidt Eremit i de store Byer! Poesien! ja jeg har seet hende et eneste kort Øieblik, men Søvnen sad mig i Øinene! hun stod paa Altanen og skinnede som Nordlyset skinner! Fortæl, fortæl! Du var paa Altanen, Du gik ind ad Døren og saa - -!«

»Saa var jeg i Forgemakket!« sagde Skyggen. »De har altid siddet og seet over til Forgemakket. Der var slet intet Lys, der var en Slags Tusmørke, men den ene Dør stod aaben ligefor den anden i en lang Række Stuer og Sale; og der var lyst op, jeg var reent blevet slaaet ihjel af Lys, var jeg kommet heelt ind til Jomfruen; men jeg var besindig, jeg gav mig Tid og det skal man gjøre!«

»Og hvad saae Du saa?« spurgte den lærde Mand.

»Jeg saae Alting, og jeg skal fortælle Dem det, men, - det er slet ingen Stolthed af mig, men - som Fri og med de Kundskaber jeg har, ikke at tale om min gode Stilling, mine fortræffelige Omstændigheder, - saa ønskede jeg gjerne at de vilde sige De til mig!«

»Om Forladelse!« sagde den lærde Mand, »det er gammel Vane, som sidder fast! - De har fuldkommen Ret! og jeg skal huske det! men nu fortæller De mig Alt hvad De saae!«

»Alting!« sagde *Skyggen*, »for jeg saae Alt og jeg veed Alt!«

successful. But I felt a sort of longing to see you again before you die, as I suppose you must, and I wanted to see this country again. You know how one loves his native land. I know that you have got hold of another shadow. Do I owe anything to either of you? Be kind enough to let me know.'

'Well! Is it really you?' said the scholar. 'Why, this is most extraordinary! I would never have imagined that one's own shadow could come back in human form.'

'Just tell me what I owe,' said the shadow, 'because I don't like to be in debt to anyone.'

'How can you talk that way?' said the student. 'What debt could there be? Feel perfectly free. I am tremendously pleased to hear of your good luck! Sit down, my old friend, and tell me a bit about how it all happened, and about what you saw in that house across the street from us in the warm country.'

'Yes, I'll tell you all about it,' the shadow said, as he sat down. 'But you must promise that if you meet me anywhere you won't tell a soul in town about my having been your shadow. I intend to become engaged, for I can easily support a family.'

'Don't you worry,' said the scholar. 'I won't tell anyone who you really are. I give you my hand on it. I promise, and a man is as good as his word.'

'And a word is as good as its – shadow,' the shadow said, for he couldn't put it any other way. It was really remarkable how much of a man he had become, dressed all in black, with the finest cloth, patent-leather shoes, and an opera hat that could be pressed perfectly flat till it was only brim and top, not to mention those things we already know about – those seals, that gold chain, and the diamond rings. The shadow was well dressed indeed, and it was just this that made him appear human.

'Now I'll tell you,' said the shadow, grinding his patent-leather shoes on the arm of the scholar's new shadow, which lay at his feet like a poodle dog. This was arrogance, perhaps, or possibly he was trying to make the new shadow stick to his own feet. The shadow on the floor lay quiet and still, and listened its best, so that it might learn how to get free and work its way up to be its own master.

'Do you know who lived in the house across the street from us?' the old shadow asked. 'She was the most lovely of all creatures – she was Poetry herself. I lived there for three weeks, and it was as if I had lived there three thousand years, reading all that has ever been written. That's what I said, and it's the truth! I have seen it all, and I know everything.'

'Poetry!' the scholar cried. 'Yes, to be sure she often lives as a hermit in the large cities. Poetry! Yes, I saw her myself, for one brief moment, but my eyes were heavy with sleep. She stood on the balcony, as radiant as the northern lights. Tell me! Tell me! You were on the balcony. You went through the doorway, and then – '

'Then I was in the anteroom,' said the shadow. 'It was the room you were always staring at from across the way. There were no candles there, and the room was in twilight. But the door upon door stood open in a whole series of brilliantly lit halls and reception rooms. That blaze of lights would have struck me dead had I gone as far as the room where the maiden was, but I was careful – I took my time, as one should.'

'And then what did you see, my old friend?' the scholar asked.

'I saw everything, and I shall tell everything to you, but – it's not that I'm proud – but as I am a free man and well educated, not to mention my high standing and my considerable fortune, I do wish you wouldn't call me your old friend.'

'I beg your pardon!' said the scholar. 'It's an old habit, and hard to change. You are perfectly right, my dear sir, and I'll remember it. But now, my dear sir, tell me of all that you saw.'

'All?' said the shadow, 'for I saw it all, and I know everything.'

»Hvorledes saae der ud i de inderste Sale?« spurgte den lærde Mand. »Var der som i den friske Skov? Var der som i en hellig Kirke? Vare Salene som den stjerneklare Himmel, naar man staaer paa de høie Bjerge?«

»Alting var der!« sagde *Skyggen*. »Jeg gik jo ikke ganske heelt ind, jeg blev i det forreste Værelse i Tusmørket, men der stod jeg særdeles godt, jeg saae Alting og jeg veed Alting! Jeg har været ved Poesiens Hof, i Forgemakket.«

»Men hvad saae De? Gik gjennem de store Sale alle Oldtidens Guder? Kjæmpede der de gamle Helte? Legede søde Børn og fortalte deres Drømme?«

»Jeg siger Dem, jeg var der og De begriber, jeg saae Alting, hvad der var at see! havde De kommet derover, var De ikke blevet Menneske, men det blev jeg! og tillige lærte jeg at kjende min inderste Natur, mit Medfødte, det Familieskab, jeg havde med Poesien. Ja den Gang jeg var hos Dem, tænkte jeg ikke over det, men altid, De veed det, naar Sol gik op og Sol gik ned, blev jeg saa underlig stor; i Maaneskin var jeg næsten ved at være tydeligere end De selv; jeg forstod ikke den Gang min Natur, i Forgemakket gik det op for mig! jeg blev Menneske! - Moden kom jeg ud, men De var ikke længere i de varme Lande; jeg skammede mig som Menneske ved at gaae som jeg gik, jeg trængte til Støvler, til Klæder, til hele denne Menneske-Fernis, som gjør et Menneske kjendeligt. - Jeg tog Vei, ja, Dem siger jeg det, De sætter det jo ikke i nogen Bog, jeg tog Vei til Kagekonens Skjørt, under det skjulte jeg mig; Konen tænkte ikke paa hvor meget hun gjemte; først om Aftenen gik jeg ud; jeg løb om i Maaneskinnet paa Gaden; jeg gjorde mig lang op ad Muren, det killer saa deiligt i Ryggen! jeg løb op og jeg løb ned, kiggede ind af de høieste Vinduer, ind i Salen og paa Taget, jeg kiggede hvor Ingen kunde kigge og jeg saae hvad ingen Andre saae, hvad Ingen skulde see! Det er i Grunden en nedrig Verden! jeg vilde ikke være Menneske, dersom det nu ikke engang var antaget at det var noget at være det! Jeg saae det Allerutænkeligste hos Konerne, hos Mændene, hos * Forældrene og hos de søde mageløse Børn; - jeg saae«, sagde *Skyggen*, »hvad ingen Mennesker maatte vide, men hvad de Allesammen saa gjerne vilde vide, Ondt hos Naboen. - Havde jeg skrevet en Avis, den var bleven læst! men jeg skrev lige til Personen selv, og der blev en Forfærdelse i alle Byer hvor jeg kom. De bleve saa bange for mig! og de holdt saa overordentlig af mig. Professorerne gjorde mig til Professor, Skræderne gav mig ny Klæder, jeg er godt forsynet; Myntmesteren slog Mynt for mig, og Konerne sagde, jeg var saa kjøn! - og saa blev jeg den Mand jeg er! og nu siger jeg Farvel; her er mit Kort, jeg boer paa Solsiden og er altid hjemme i Regnvejr!« og saa gik *Skyggen*.

»Det var dog mærkeligt!« sagde den lærde Mand.

Aar og Dag gik, saa kom *Skyggen* igjen.

»Hvorledes gaaer det?« spurgte den.

»Ak!« sagde den lærde Mand, »jeg skriver om det Sande og det Gode og det Skjønne, men Ingen bryder sig om at høre Sligt, jeg er ganske fortvivlet, for jeg tager mig det saa nær!«

»Men det gjør jeg ikke!« sagde *Skyggen*, »jeg bliver feed, og det er det man skal see at blive! ja De forstaaer dem ikke paaVerden. De bliver daarlig ved det. De maa reise! jeg gjør en Reise til Sommer; vil De med? Jeg gad nok have en Reisekammerat! vil De reise med, som Skygge? Det skal være mig en stor Fornøielse at have Dem med, jeg betaler Reisen!«

»Det gaaer vel vidt!« sagde den lærde Mand.

»Det er ligesom man tager det!« sagde *Skyggen*. »De vil have grumme godt af at reise! vil De være min Skygge saa skal De faae Alting frit paa Reisen!«

»Det er for galt!« sagde den lærde Mand.

»Men saadan er nu Verden!« sagde *Skyggen*, »og saaledes bliver den!« og saa gik *Skyggen*.

'How did the innermost rooms look?' the scholar asked. 'Was it like a green forest? Was it like a holy temple? Were the rooms like the starry skies seen from some high mountain?'

'Everything was there,' said the shadow. 'I didn't quite go inside. I stayed in the dark anteroom, but my place there was perfect. I saw everything, and I know everything. I have been in the antechamber at the court of Poetry.'

'But what did you see? Did the gods of old march through the halls? Did the old heroes fight there? Did fair children play there and tell their dreams?'

'I was there, I tell you, so you must understand that I saw all that there was to be seen. Had you come over, it would not have made a man of you, as it did of me. Also, I learned to understand my inner self, what is born in me, and the relationship between me and Poetry. Yes, when I was with you I did not think of such things, but you must remember how wonderfully I always expanded at sunrise and sunset. And in the moonlight I almost seemed more real than you. Then I did not understand myself, but in that anteroom I came to know my true nature. I was a man! – I came out completely changed. But you were no longer in the warm country. Being a man, I was ashamed to be seen as I was. I lacked shoes, clothes, and all the surface veneer which makes a man. – I went into hiding – this is confidential, and you must not write it in any of your books. I went into hiding under the skirts of the cake-woman. Little she knew what she concealed. Not until evening did I venture out. I ran through the streets in the moonlight and stretched myself tall against the walls. It's such a pleasant way of scratching one's back. Up I ran and down I ran, peeping into the highest windows, into drawing rooms, and into garrets. I peered in where no one else could peer. I saw what no one else could see, or should see. Taken all in all, it's a wicked world. I would not care to be a man if it were not considered the fashionable thing to be. I saw the most incredible behavior among men and women, fathers and mothers, and among those "perfectly darling" children. I saw what nobody knows but everybody would like to know, and that is what wickedness goes on next door. If I had written it in a newspaper, oh, how widely it would have been read! But instead I wrote to the people directly concerned, and there was the most terrible consternation in every town to which I came. They were so afraid of me, and yet so remarkably fond of me. The professors appointed me a professor, and the tailor made me new clothes – my wardrobe is most complete. The master of the mint coined new money for me, the women called me such a handsome man; and so I became the man I am. Now I must bid you good bye. Here's my card. I live on the sunny side of the street, and I am always at home on rainy days.' The shadow took his leave.

'How extraordinary,' said the scholar.

The days passed. The years went by. And the shadow called again. 'How goes it?' he asked.

'Alack,' said the scholar, 'I still write about the true, the good, and the beautiful, but nobody cares to read about such things. I feel quite despondent, for I take it deeply to heart.'

'I don't,' said the shadow. 'I am getting fat, as one should. You don't know the ways of the world, and that's why your health suffers. You ought to travel. I'm taking a trip this summer. Will you come with me? I'd like to have a traveling companion. Will you come along as my shadow? It would be a great pleasure to have you along, and I'll pay all the expenses.'

'No, that's a bit too much,' said the scholar.

'It depends on how you look at it,' said the shadow. 'It will do you a lot of good to travel. Will you be my shadow? The trip won't cost you a thing.'

'This has gone much too far!' said the scholar.

'Well, that's the way the world goes,' the shadow told him, 'and that's the way it will keep on going.' And away he went.

Den lærde Mand havde det slet ikke godt, Sorg og Plage fulgte ham, og hvad han talte om det Sande og det Gode og det Skjønne, det var for de Fleste ligesom Roser for en Ko! - han var ganske syg tilsidst.

»De seer virkelig ud ligesom en Skygge!« sagde Folk til ham, og det gjøs i den lærde Mand, for han tænkte ved det.

»De skal tage til Bad!« sagde *Skyggen*, som kom og besøgte ham, »der er ikke andet for! jeg vil tage Dem med for gammelt Bekjendtskabs Skyld, jeg betaler Reisen og De gjør Beskrivelsen og er saadan lidt morsom for mig paa Veien! jeg vil til et Bad, mit Skjæg groer ikke ud som det skulde, det er ogsaa en Sygdom, og Skjæg maa man have! Vær De nu fornuftig og tag imod Tilbudet, vi reise jo som Kammerater!«

Og saa reiste de; *Skyggen* var da Herre og Herren var da Skygge; de kjørte med hinanden, de rede og gik sammen, Side ved Side, forud og bag efter, saaledes som Solen stod; Skyggen vidste altid at holde sig paa Herrepladsen; og det tænkte den lærde Mand nu ikke saadanne over; han var et meget godt Hjerte, og særdeles mild og venlig, og da sagde han en Dag til Skyggen: »da vi nu saaledes ere blevne Reisekammerater, som vi er det og vi tillige ere voxne op fra Barndommen sammen, skulle vi saa ikke drikke Duus, det er dog mere fortroligt!«

»De siger noget!« sagde Skyggen, som jo nu var den egentlige Herre. »Det er meget ligefremt og velmeent sagt, jeg vil være ligesaa velmenende og ligefrem. De, som en lærd Mand, veed vistnok hvor underlig Naturen er. Somme Mennesker kunne ikke taale at røre ved graat Papir, saa faae de ondt; Andre gaaer det gjennem alle Lemmer, naar man lader et Søm gnide mod en Glasrude; jeg har ligesaadan en Følelse ved at høre Dem sige Du til mig, jeg føler mig ligesom trykket til Jorden i min første Stilling hos Dem. De seer at det er en Følelse, det er ikke Stolthed; jeg kan ikke lade Dem sige Du til mig, men jeg skal gjerne sige Du til Dem, saa er det halve gjort!«

Og saa sagde *Skyggen* Du til sin forrige Herre.

»Det er dog vel galt,« tænkte han, »at jeg maa sige *De* og han siger *Du*,« men nu maatte han holde ud.

Saa kom de til et Bad, hvor der vare mange Fremmede og imellem disse en deilig Kongedatter, som havde den Sygdom at hun saae altfor godt og det var nu saa ængsteligt.

Ligestrax mærkede hun at han, der var kommet, var en ganske anden Person end alle de Andre; »han er her for at faae sit Skjæg til at voxe, siger man, men jeg seer den rette Aarsag, han kan ikke kaste Skygge.«

Nysgjærrig var hun blevet; og saa gav hun sig strax paa Spadsereturen i Tale med den fremmede Herre. Som en Kongedatter behøvede hun ikke at gjøre mange Omstændigheder, og saa sagde hun, »Deres Sygdom er at De ikke kan kaste Skygge.«

»Deres kongelige Høihed maa være betydelig i Bedring!« sagde *Skyggen*, »jeg veed, Deres Onde er at De seer alt for godt, men det har tabt sig, De er helbredet, jeg har just en ganske usædvanlig Skygge! Seer de ikke den Person, som altid gaaer med mig! Andre Mennesker have en almindelig Skygge, men jeg holder ikke af det Almindelige. Man giver tidt sin Tjener finere Klæde i Liberiet end man selv bruger, og saaledes har jeg ladet min Skygge pudse op til Menneske; ja, De seer, at jeg endogsaa har givet *ham* en Skygge. Det er meget kostbart, men jeg holder af have noget for mig selv!« -

»Hvad?« tænkte Prindsessen, »skulde jeg virkelig være kommet mig! Dette Bad er det første der er til! Vandet har i vor Tid ganske forunderlige Kræfter. Men jeg tager ikke bort, for nu bliver her morsomt; den Fremmede synes jeg overordenligt om. Bare hans Skjæg ikke voxer, for saa reiser han!«

Om Aftenen i den store Balsal dandsede Kongedatteren og Skyggen. Hun var let, men han var endnu lettere, saadan en Dandser havde hun aldrig havt. Hun sagde ham fra hvad Land hun var,

The learned man was not at all well. Sorrow and trouble pursued him, and what he had to say about the good, the true, and the beautiful, appealed to most people about as much as roses appeal to a cow. Finally he grew quite ill.

'You really look like a shadow,' people told him, and he trembled at the thought.

'You must visit a watering place,' said the shadow, who came to see him again.

'There's no question about it. I'll take you with me, for old friendship's sake. I'll pay for the trip, and you can write about it, as well as doing your best to amuse me along the way. I need to go to a watering place too, because my beard isn't growing as it should. That's a sort of disease too, and one can't get along without a beard. Now do be reasonable and accept my proposal. We shall travel just like friends!'

So off they started. The shadow was master now, and the master was the shadow. They drove together, rode together, and walked together, side by side, before or behind each other, according to the way the sun fell. The shadow was careful to take the place of the master, and the scholar didn't much care, for he had an innocent heart, besides being most affable and friendly. One day he said to the shadow, 'As we are now fellow-travelers and have grown up together, shall we not call each other by our first names, the way good companions should? It is much more intimate.'

'That's a splendid idea!' said the shadow, who was now the real master. 'What you say is most open-hearted and friendly. I shall be just as friendly and open-hearted with you. As a scholar, you are perfectly well aware how strange is man's nature. Some men cannot bear the touch of gray paper. It sickens them. Others quail if they hear a nail scratched across a pane of glass. For my part, I am affected in just that way when I hear you call me by my first name. I feel myself ground down to the earth, as I was in my first position with you. You understand. It's a matter of sensitivity, not pride. I cannot let you call me by my first name, but I shall be glad to call you by yours, as a compromise.' So thereafter the shadow called his one-time master by his first name.

'It has gone too far,' the scholar thought, 'when I must call him by his last name while he calls me by my first!' But he had to put up with it.

At last they came to the watering place. Among the many people was a lovely Princess. Her malady was that she saw things too clearly, which can be most upsetting. For instance, she immediately saw that the newcomer was a very different sort of person from all the others. 'He has come here to make his beard grow, they say. But I see the real reason. He can't cast a shadow.'

Her curiosity was aroused, and on the promenade she addressed this stranger directly. Being a king's daughter, she did not have to stand upon ceremony, so she said to him straight: 'Your trouble is that you can't cast a shadow.'

'Your Royal Highness must have improved considerably,' the shadow replied. 'I know your malady is that you see too clearly, but you are improving. As it happens, I do have a most unusual shadow. Don't you see that figure who always accompanies me? Other people have a common shadow, but I do not care for what is common to all. Just as we often allow our servants better fabrics for their liveries than we wear ourselves, so I have had my shadow decked out as a man. Why, you see I have even outfitted him with a shadow of his own. It is expensive, I grant you, but I like to have something uncommon.'

'My!' the Princess thought. 'Can I really be cured? This is the foremost watering place in the world, and in these days water has come to have wonderful medicinal powers. But I shan't leave just as the place is becoming amusing. I have taken a liking to this stranger. I only hope his beard won't grow, for then he would leave us.'

That evening, the Princess and the shadow danced together in the great ballroom. She was light, but he was lighter still. Never had she danced with such a partner. She told him what

og han kjendte Landet, han havde været der, men da var hun ikke hjemme, han havde kiget ind af Vinduerne foroven og forneden, han havde seet baade det Ene og det Andet, og saa kunde han svare Kongedatteren og gjøre Antydninger, saa hun blev ganske forundret; han maatte være den viseste Mand paa hele Jorden! hun fik saadan en Agtelse for hvad han vidste, og da de saa dandsede igjen, saa blev hun forliebt, og det kunde *Skyggen* godt mærke, for hun var færdig at see lige igjennem ham. Saa dandsede de nok engang og saa var hun lige ved at sige det, men hun var besindig, hun tænkte paa sit Land og Rige og paa de mange Mennesker, hun skulde regjere over. »En viis Mand er han,« sagde hun til sig selv, »det er godt! og deiligt dandser han, det er ogsaa godt, men mon han har grundige Kundskaber, det er ligesaa vigtigt! han maa exami-neres.« Og saa begyndte hun saa smaat at spørge ham om noget af det Allervanskeligste, hun kunde ikke selv have svart paa det; og Skyggen gjorde et ganske underligt Ansigt.

»Det kan de ikke svare paa!« sagde Kongedatteren.

»Det hører til min Børne-Lærdom,« sagde *Skyggen,* »jeg troer saagar min Skygge der henne ved Døren kan svare derpaa!«

»Deres Skygge!« sagde Kongedatteren, »det vilde være høist mærkeligt!«

»Ja, jeg siger ikke bestemt at han kan!« sagde Skyggen, »men jeg skulde troe det, han har nu i saa mange Aar fulgt mig, og hørt efter, - jeg skulde troe det! men deres Kongelige Høihed tillader, at jeg gjør Dem opmærksom paa, at han har saa megen Stolthed af at gaae for et Menneske, at naar han skal være i rigtig Humeur, og det maa han være for at svare godt, saa maa han behan-dles ganske som et Menneske.«

»Det kan jeg godt lide!« sagde Kongedatteren.

Og saa gik hun hen til den lærde Mand ved Døren, og hun talte med ham om Sol og Maane, og om Menneskene baade uden paa og inden i og han svarede saa klogt og godt.

»Hvad det maa være for en Mand, der har saa viis en Skygge!« tænkte hun, »det vil være en reen Velsignelse for mit Folk og Rige om jeg valgte ham til min Gemal; - jeg gjør det!«

Og de vare snart enige, baade Kongedatteren og Skyggen, men Ingen skulde vide derom før hun kom hjem i sit eget Rige.

»Ingen, ikke engang min Skygge!« sagde *Skyggen,* og det havde han nu saadan sine egne Tanker ved! -

»Hvad det maa være for en Mand, der har saa viis en Skygge!« tænkte hun, »det vil være en reen Velsignelse for mit Folk og Rige om jeg valgte ham til min Gemal; - jeg gjør det!«

Og de vare snart enige, baade Kongedatteren og Skyggen, men Ingen skulde vide derom før hun kom hjem i sit eget Rige.

»Ingen, ikke engang min Skygge!« sagde *Skyggen,* og det havde han nu saadan sine egne Tanker ved! -Saa vare de i Landet hvor Kongedatteren regjerede naar hun var hjemme.

»Hør min gode Ven!« sagde *Skyggen* til den lærde Mand, »nu er jeg blevet saa lykkelig og mægtig, som Nogen kan blive, nu vil jeg ogsaa gjøre noget særdeles for Dig! du skal altid boe hos mig paa Slottet, kjøre med mig i min kongelige Vogn og have hundrede tusinde Rigsdaler om Aaret; men saa maa Du lade dig kalde Skygge af Alle og Enhver; Du maa ikke sige at du har nogensinde været Menneske og engang om Aaret, naar jeg sidder paa Altanen i Solskin og lader mig see, maa Du ligge ved mine Fødder, som en Skygge skal! jeg skal sige dig, jeg gifter Konge-datteren, i Aften skal Brylluppet holdes.«

»Nei det er dog altfor galt!« sagde den lærde Mand, »det vil jeg ikke, det gjør jeg ikke! det er at bedrage hele Landet og Kongedatteren med! Jeg siger Alting! at jeg er Mennesket, og at du er Skyggen, du er bare klædt paa!«

»Det er der Ingen som troer!« sagde *Skyggen,* »vær fornuftig, eller jeg kalder paa Vagten!« -

country she came from, and he knew it well. He had been there, but it was during her absence. He had looked through every window, high or low. He had seen this and he had seen that. So he could answer the Princess and suggest things that astounded her. She was convinced that he must be the wisest man in all the world. His knowledge impressed her so deeply, that while they were dancing she fell in love with him. The shadow could tell, for her eyes transfixed him, through and through. They danced again, and she came very near telling him she loved him, but it wouldn't do to be rash. She had to think of her country, and her throne, and the many people over whom she would reign. 'He is a clever man,' she said to herself, 'and that is a good thing. He dances charmingly, and that is good too. But is his knowledge more than superficial? That's just as important, so I must examine him.'

Tactfully, she began asking him the most difficult questions, which she herself could not have answered. The shadow made a wry face.

'You can't answer me?' said the Princess.

'I knew all that in my childhood,' said the shadow. 'Why, I believe that my shadow over there by the door can answer you.'

'Your shadow!' said the Princess. 'That would be remarkable indeed!'

'I can't say for certain,' said the shadow, 'but I'm inclined to think so, because he has followed me about and listened to me for so many years. Yes, I am inclined to believe so. But your Royal Highness must permit me to tell you that he is quite proud of being able to pass for a man, so if he is to be in the right frame of mind to answer your questions he must be treated just as if he were human.'

'I like that!' said the Princess.

So she went to the scholar in the doorway, and spoke with him about the sun and the moon, and about people, what they are inside, and what they seem to be on the surface. He answered her wisely and well.

'What a man that must be, to have such a wise shadow!' she thought. 'It will be a godsend to my people, and to my country if I choose him for my consort. That's just what I'll do!'

The Princess and the shadow came to an understanding, but no one was to know about it until she returned to her own kingdom.

'No one. Not even my shadow!' said the shadow. And he had his own private reason for this.

Finally they came to the country that the Princess ruled when she was at home.

'Listen, my good friend,' the shadow said to the scholar, 'I am now as happy and strong as one can be, so I'll do something very special for you. You shall live with me in my palace, drive with me in my royal carriage, and have a hundred thousand dollars a year. However, you must let yourself be called a shadow by everybody. You must not ever say that you have been a man, and once a year, while I sit on the balcony in the sunshine, you must lie at my feet as shadows do. For I tell you I am going to marry the Princess, and the wedding is to take place this very evening.'

'No! That's going too far,' said the scholar. 'I will not. I won't do it. That would be betraying the whole country and the Princess too. I'll tell them everything – that I am the man, and you are the shadow merely dressed as a man.'

'No one would believe it,' said the shadow. 'Be reasonable, or I'll call the sentry.'

'I'll go straight to the Princess,' said the scholar.

'But I will go first,' said the shadow, 'and you shall go to prison.' And to prison he went, for the sentries obeyed the one who, they knew, was to marry the Princess.

'Why, you're trembling,' the Princess said, as the shadow entered her room. 'What has happened? You mustn't fall ill this evening, just as we are about to be married.'

»Jeg gaaer lige til Kongedatteren!« sagde den lærde Mand. »Men jeg gaaer først!« sagde *Skyggen*, »og du gaaer i Arrest!« - og det maatte han, for Skildvagterne de lystrede ham, som de vidste Kongedatteren vilde have.

»Du ryster!« sagde Kongedatteren, da Skyggen kom ind til hende, »er der skeet Noget? Du maa ikke blive syg til iaften, nu vi skal have Bryllup.«

»Jeg har oplevet det Grueligste, der kan opleves!« sagde Skyggen, »tænk Dig - ja, saadan en stakkels Skyggehjerne kan ikke holde meget ud! - Tænk Dig, min Skygge er blevet gal, han troer at han er Mennesket og at jeg - tænk dig bare, - at jeg er hans Skygge!«

»Det er frygteligt!« sagde Prindsessen, »han er dog spærret inde?«

»Det er han! Jeg er bange han kommer sig aldrig.«

»Stakkels Skygge!« sagde Prindsessen, »han er meget ulykkelig; det er en sand Velgjerning at frie ham fra den Smule Liv han har, og naar jeg rigtig tænker over det, saa troer jeg det bliver nødvendigt at det bliver gjort af med ham i al Stilhed!«

»Det er rigtignok haardt!« sagde Skyggen, »for det var en tro Tjener!« og saa gav han ligesom et Suk. »De er en ædel Characteer!« sagde Kongedatteren.

Om Aftenen var hele Byen illumineret, og Kanonerne gik af: bum! og Soldaterne præsenterede Gevær. Det var et Bryllup! Kongedatteren og *Skyggen* gik ud paa Altanen for at lade sig see og faae nok en Gang Hurra!

Den lærde Mand hørte ikke noget til Alt det, for ham havde de taget Livet af. –

[1847] [*Edited by Erik Dahl. Copenhagen: DSL/Hans Reitzel, 1960–1990*]

d. FRANÇAIS

II.d.1. FRANÇOIS RENÉ DE CHATEAUBRIAND, *René*

«Je me trouvai bientôt plus isolé dans ma patrie, que je ne l'avois été sur une terre étrangère. Je voulus me jeter pendant quelque temps dans un monde qui ne me disoit rien et qui ne m'entendoit pas. Mon ame, qu'aucune passion n'avoit encore usée, cherchoit un objet qui pût l'attacher; mais je m'aperçus que je donnois plus que je ne recevois. Ce n'étoit ni un langage élevé, ni un sentiment profond qu'on demandoit de moi. Je n'étois occupé qu'à rapetisser ma vie, pour la mettre au niveau de la société. Traité partout d'esprit romanesque, honteux du rôle que je jouois, dégoûté de plus en plus des choses et des hommes, je pris le parti de me retirer dans un faubourg pour y vivre totalement ignoré.

«Je trouvai d'abord assez de plaisir dans cette vie obscure et indépendante. Inconnu, je me mêlois à la foule: vaste désert d'hommes!

«Souvent assis dans une église peu fréquentée, je passois des heures entières en méditation. Je voyois de pauvres femmes venir se prosterner devant le Très-Haut, ou des pécheurs s'agenouiller au tribunal de la pénitence. Nul ne sortoit de ces lieux sans un visage plus serein, et les sourdes clameurs qu'on entendoit au dehors sembloient être les flots des passions et les orages du monde qui venoient expirer au pied du temple du Seigneur. Grand Dieu, qui vis en secret couler mes larmes dans ces retraites sacrées, tu sais combien de fois je me jetai à tes pieds, pour te supplier de me décharger du poids de l'existence, ou de changer en moi le vieil homme! Ah! qui n'a senti quelquefois le besoin de se régénérer, de se rajeunir aux eaux du torrent, de retremper son âme a la fontaine de vie? Qui ne se trouve quelquefois accablé du fardeau de sa propre corruption, et incapable de rien faire de grand, de noble, de juste?

'I have been through the most dreadful experience that could happen to anyone,' said the shadow. 'Just imagine! Of course a poor shadow's head can't stand very much. But imagine! My shadow has gone mad. He takes himself for a man, and – imagine it! He takes me for his shadow.'

'How terrible!' said the Princess. 'He's locked up, I hope!'

'Oh, of course. I'm afraid he will never recover.'

'Poor shadow,' said the Princess. 'He is very unhappy. It would really be a charitable act to relieve him of the little bit of life he has left. And, after thinking it over carefully, my opinion is that it will be necessary to put him out of the way.'

'That's certainly hard, for he was a faithful servant,' said the shadow. He managed to sigh.

'You have a noble soul,' the Princess told him.

The whole city was brilliantly lit that evening. The cannons boomed, and the soldiers presented arms. That was the sort of wedding it was! The Princess and the shadow stepped out on the balcony to show themselves and be cheered, again and again. The scholar heard nothing of all this, for they had already done away with him.

[1847] [*Translated by Hans Hersholt*]

d.   FRENCH

II.d.1.   FRANÇOIS RENÉ DE CHATEAUBRIAND, from *René*

Soon I found myself lonelier in my native land than I had been on foreign soil. I was tempted to plunge for a time into a totally new environment which I could not understand and which did not understand me. My heart was not yet wasted by any kind of passion, and I sought to find someone to whom I could become attached. But I soon discovered that I was giving more of myself than I was receiving of others. It was neither lofty language nor deep feeling which the world asked of me. I was simply reducing my being to the level of society. Everywhere I was taken for an impractical dreamer. Ashamed of the role I was playing and increasingly repulsed by men and things, I finally decided to return to some smaller community [*sic*] where I could live completely by myself.

At first I was happy enough in this secluded, independent life. Unknown by everyone, I could mingle with the crowd – that vast desert of men! Often I would sit in some lonely church, where I could spend hour after hour in meditation. I saw poor women prostrating themselves before the Almighty or sinners kneeling at the seat of penitence. None emerged from this retreat without a more serene expression, and the muffled noises drifting in from outside seemed like waves of passion or storms of the world subsiding at the foot of the Lord's temple. Mighty God, who from Thy solitude couldst see my tears falling in that holy shelter, Thou knowest how many times I threw myself at Thy feet, imploring Thee to relieve me of the weight of my existence or make over the old man within me! Ah, who has never felt a need of regeneration, of growing young in the waters of the spring and refreshing his soul in the fountain of life? Who does not sometimes feel himself crushed by the burden of his own corruption and incapable of anything great or noble or just!

«Quand le soir étoit venu, reprenant le chemin de ma retraite, je m'arrêtois sur les ponts, pour voir se coucher le soleil. L'astre, enflammant les vapeurs de la cité, sembloit osciller lentement dans un fluide d'or, comme le pendule de l'horloge des siècles. Je me retirois ensuite avec la nuit, à travers un labyrinthe de rues solitaires. En regardant les lumières qui brilloient dans les demeures des hommes, je me transportois par la pensée, au milieu des scènes de douleur et de joie qu'elles éclairoient; et je songeois que sous tant de toits habités, je n'avois pas un ami. Au milieu de mes réflexions, l'heure venoit frapper à coups mesurés dans la tour de la cathédrale gothique; elle alloit se répétant sur tous les tons et à toutes les distances d'église en église. Hélas! chaque heure dans la société ouvre un tombeau, et fait couler des larmes.

«Cette vie, qui m'avoit d'abord enchanté, ne tarda pas à me devenir insupportable. Je me fatiguai de la répétition des mêmes scènes et des mêmes idées. Je me mis à sonder mon coeur, à me demander ce que je desirois. Je ne le savois pas; mais je crus tout-à-coup que les bois me seroient délicieux. Me voilà soudain résolu d'achever, dans un exil champêtre, une carrière à peine commencée, et dans laquelle j'avois déjà dévoré des siècles.

«J'embrassai ce projet avec l'ardeur que je mets à tous mes desseins; je partis précipitamment pour m'ensevelir dans une chaumière, comme j'étois parti autrefois pour faire le tour du monde.

«On m'accuse d'avoir des goûts inconstans, de ne pouvoir jouir longtemps de la même chimère, d'être la proie d'une imagination qui se hâte d'arriver au fond de mes plaisirs, comme si elle étoit accablée de leur durée; on m'accuse de passer toujours le but que je puis atteindre: hélas! je cherche seulement un bien inconnu, dont l'instinct me poursuit. Est-ce ma faute, si je trouve partout les bornes, si ce qui est fini n'a pour moi aucune valeur? Cependant je sens que j'aime la monotonie des sentimens de la vie, et si j'avois encore la folie de croire au bonheur, je le chercherois dans l'habitude.

«La solitude absolue, le spectacle de la nature, me plongèrent bientôt dans un état presqu'impossible à décrire. Sans parens, sans amis, pour ainsi dire seul sur la terre, n'ayant point encore aimé, j'étois accablé d'une surabondance de vie. Quelquefois je rougissois subitement, et je sentois couler dans mon coeur, comme des ruisseaux d'une lave ardente; quelquefois je poussois desi cris involontaires, et la nuit étoit également troublée de mes songes et de mes veilles. Il me manquoit quelque chose pour remplir l'abyme de mon existence: je descendois dans la vallée, je m'élevois sur la montagne, appelant de toute la force de mes désirs l'idéal objet d'une flamme future; je l'embrassois dans les vents; je croyois l'entendre dans les gémissemens du fleuve: tout étoit ce fantôme imaginaire, et les astres dans les cieux, et le principe même de vie dans l'univers.

«Toutefois cet état de calme et de trouble, d'indigence et de richesse, n'étoit pas sans quelques charmes. Un jour je m'étois amusé à effeuiller une branche de saule sur un ruisseau, et à attacher une idée à chaque feuille que le courant entraînoit. Un roi qui craint de perdre sa couronne par une révolution subite, ne ressent pas des angoisses plus vives que les miennes, à chaque accident qui menaçoit les débris de mon rameau. O foiblesse des mortels! O enfance du coeur humain qui ne vieillit jamais! Voilà donc à quel degré de puérilité notre superbe raison peut descendre! Et encore est-il vrai que bien des hommes attachent leur destinée à des choses d'aussi peu de valeur que mes feuilles de saule.

«Mais comment exprimer cette foule de sensations fugitives, que j'éprouvois dans mes promenades? Les sons que rendent les passions dans le vuide d'un coeur solitaire, ressemblent au murmure que les vents et les eaux font entendre dans le silence d'un désert: on en jouit, mais on ne peut les peindre.

«L'automne me surprit au milieu de ces incertitudes: j'entrai avec ravissement dans les mois des tempêtes. Tantôt j'aurois voulu être un de ces guerriers errant au milieu des vents, des nuages et des fantômes; tantôt j'enviois jusqu'au sort du pâtre que je voyois réchauffer ses mains à l'humble

When night had closed in I would start back to my retreat, pausing on the bridges to watch the sunset. As the great star kindled the mists of the city, it seemed to swing slowly in a golden fluid like the pendulum of some clock of the ages. Then I retired with the night through a labyrinth of solitary streets. As I passed lights shining in the dwellings of men, I imagined myself among the scenes of sorrow and joy which they revealed, and I reflected that under all those roofs sheltering so many people, I had not a single friend. In the midst of these thoughts, the hour began tolling in measured cadence from the tower of the Gothic cathedral, and its message was taken up from church to church in a wide range of tones and distances. Alas! Every hour in society lays open a grave and draws fresh tears.

But this life, which at first was so delightful, soon became intolerable. I grew weary of constantly repeating the same scenes and the same thoughts, and I began to search my soul to discover what I really sought. I did not know; but suddenly it occurred to me that I might be happy in the woods. Immediately I resolved to adopt a country exile where I could spend the rest of my days, for, though scarcely begun, my life had already consumed centuries.

I adopted this plan with the ardor typical of all my projects and left at once to retire into seclusion in some rustic cabin, just as previously I had left to travel around the world.

People accuse me of being unpredictable in my tastes, of being unable for long to cherish any single illusion. They consider me the victim of an imagination which plunges toward the end of all pleasure as though it suffered from their duration. They accuse me of forever overreaching the goal I can achieve. Alas! I am only in search of some unknown good, whose intuition pursues me relentlessly. Am I to blame if everywhere I find limitations, if all that is finite I consider worthless? And yet, I feel that I love the monotony in the feelings of life, and, if I were still foolish enough to believe in happiness, I would seek it in an orderly existence.

Total solitude and the spectacle of nature soon brought me to a state almost impossible to describe. Practically bereft of relatives and friends on earth, and ever having been in love, I was furiously driven by an excess of life. Sometimes I blushed suddenly and felt torrents of burning lava surging through my heart. Sometimes I would cry out involuntarily, and the night was disturbed both by my dreams and by sleepless cares. I felt I needed something to fill the vast emptiness of my existence. I went down into the valley and up on the mountain, calling with all the strength of my desire, for the ideal creature of some future passion I embraced her in the winds and thought I heard her in the river's moaning. Everything became this version of my imagination – the stars in the skies and the very principle of life in the universe.

Nevertheless, this state of calm and anxiety, of poverty and wealth was not wholly without charm. One day I amused myself by stripping the leaves from a willow branch, one by one, and throwing them into the stream, attaching a thought to each leaf as the current carried it off. A king in fear of losing his crown in a sudden revolution does not feel sharper pangs of anguish than did I, as I watched each peril threatening the remains of my bough. O frailty of mortal man! O childishness of the human heart, which never grows old! How infantile our haughty reason can become! And yet how many men attach their existence to such petty things as my willow leaves!

How can I describe the host of fleeting sensations I felt in my rambles? The echoes of passion in the emptiness of a lonely heart are like the murmurings of wind and water in the silence of the wilderness – they offer their joy, but cannot be portrayed.

Autumn came upon me in the midst of this uncertainty, and I welcomed the stormy months with exhilaration. Sometimes I wished I were one of those warriors who wander amongst winds, clouds, and phantoms, while at other times I was envious even of the shepherd's lot, as I watched him warming his hands by the humble brushwood fire he had built in a corner of the woods.

feu de broussailles qu'il avoit allumé au coin d'un bois. J'écoutois ses chants mélancoliques, qui me rappeloient que dans tout pays, le chant naturel de l'homme est triste, lois même qu'il exprime le bonheur. Notre coeur est un instrument incomplet, une lyre où il manque des cordes, et où nous sommes forcés rendre les accens de la joie, sur le ton consacré aux soupirs.

«Le jour je m'égarois sur de grandes bruyères terminées par des forêts. Qu'il falloit peu de chose à ma rêverie: une feuille séchée que le vent chassoit devant moi une cabane dont la fumée s'élevoit dans la cime dépouillée des arbres, la mousse qui trembloit au souffle du nord sur le tronc d'un chêne, une roche écartée, un étang désert où le jonc flétri murmuroit! Le clocher du hameau, s'élevant au loin dans la vallée, a souvent attiré mes regards; souvent j'ai suivi des yeux les oiseaux de passage qui voloient au-dessus de ma tête. Je me figurais les bords ignorés, les climats lointains où ils se rendent; j'aurois voulu être sur leurs ailes. Un secret instinct me tourmentoit; je sentois que je n'étois moi-même qu'un voyageur; mais une voix du ciel sembloit me dire:

«Homme, la saison de ta migration n'est pas encore venue; attends que le vent de la mort se lève, alors tu déploieras ton vol vers ces régions inconnues que ton coeur demande».

«Levez-vous vîte, orages desirés, qui devez emporter René dans les espaces d'une autre vie! Ainsi disant, je marchois à grands pas, le visage enflammé, le vent sifflant dans ma chevelure, ne sentant ni pluie ni frimas, enchanté, tourmené, et comme possédé par le démon de mon coeur.

«La nuit, lorsque l'aquilon ébranloit ma chaumière, que les pluies tomboient en torrent sur mon toit, qu'à travers ma fenêtre, je voyais la lune sillonner les nuage amoncelés, comme un pâle vaisseau qui laboure les vagues, il me sembloit que la vie redoubloit au fond de mon coeur, que j'aurois eu la puissance de créer des mondes. Ah! si j'avois pu faire partager à une autre les transports que j'éprouvois! O Dieu! si tu m'avois donné une femme selon mes désirs; si, comme à notre premier père, tu m'eusses amené par la main une Ève tirée de moimême. ... Beauté céleste, je me serois prosterné devant toi; puis, te prenant dans mes bras, j'aurois prié l'Éternel de te donner le reste de ma vie.

«Hélas! j'étois seul, seul sur la terre! Une langueur secrète s'emparoit de mon corps. Ce dégoût de la vie que j'avois ressenti dès roon enfance, revenoit avec une force nouvelle. Bientôt mon coeur ne fournit plus d'aliment à ma pensée, et je ne m'apercevois de mon existence que par un profond sentiment d'ennui.

«Je luttai quelque temps centre mon mal, mais avec indifférence et sans avoir la ferme résolution de le vaincre. Enfin, ne pouvant trouver de remède a cette étrange blessure de mon coeur, qui n'étoit nulle part et qui étoit partout, je résolus de quitter la vie.

«Prêtre du Très-Haut, qui m'entendez, pardonnez à un malheureux que le ciel avoit presque privé de la raison. J'étois plein de religion, et je raisonnois en impie; mon cœur aimoit Dieu, et mon esprit le méconnoissoit; ma conduite, mes discours, mes sentimens, mes pensées, n'étoient que contradiction, ténèbres, mensonges. Mais l'homme sait-il bien toujours ce qu'il veut, est-il toujoirs sûr de ce qu'il pense?

«Tout m'échappoit à la fois, l'amitié, le monde, la retraite. J'avois essayé de tout, et tout m'avoit été fatal. Repoussé par la sociéété, abandonné d'Amélie, quand la solitude vint à me manquer, que me restoit-il? C'étoit la dernière planche sur laquelle j'avois espéré me sauver, et je la sentois encore s'enfoncer dans l'abyme!

«Décidé que j'étois a me débarrasser du poids de la vie, je résolus de mettre toute ma raison dans cet acte insensé. Rien ne me pressoit: je ne fixai point le moment du départ, afin de savourer a longs traits les derniers momens de l'existence, et de recueillir toutes mes forces, à l'exemple d'un ancien, pour sentir mon âme s'échapper.

[Edited by Armand Weil. Paris: Libraire E. Droz, 1935]

I listened to his melancholy airs and remembered that in every land the natural song of man is sad, even when it renders happiness. Our heart is a defective instrument, a lyre with several chords missing, which forces us to express our joyful moods in notes meant for lamentation.

During the day I roamed the great heath with its forests in the distance. How little I needed to wander off in reverie – a dry leaf blown before me by the wind, a cabin with smoke drifting up through the bare tree tops, the moss trembling in the north wind on the trunk of an oak, an isolated rock, or a lonely pond where the withered reed whispered . . . The solitary steeple far off in the valley often drew my attention. Many times, too, my eyes followed birds of passage as they flew overhead. I imagined the unknown shores and distant climes for which they were bound – and how I would have loved to be on their wings! A deep intuition tormented me; I felt that I was no more than a traveler myself, but a voice from heaven seemed to be telling me, 'Man, the season for thy migration is not yet come; wait for the wind of death to spring up, then wilt thou spread thy wings and fly toward those unexplored realms for which thy heart longs.'

Rise swiftly, coveted storms, coming to bear me off to the spaces of another life! This was my plea, as I plunged ahead with great strides, my face all aflame and the wind whistling through my hair, feeling neither rain nor frost, bewitched, tormented, and virtually possessed by the demon of my heart.

At night, when the fierce wind shook my hut and the rain fell in torrents on my roof, as I looked out through my window and saw the moon furrowing the thick clouds like a pallid vessel ploughing through the waves, it seemed to me that life grew so strong in the depths of my heart that I had the power to create worlds. Ah, if only I could have shared with someone else the delight I felt! O Lord, if only Thou hadst given me a woman after my heart's desire, if Thou hadst drawn from my side an Eve, as Thou didst once for our first father, and brought her to me by the hand . . . Heavenly beauty! I would have knelt down before you, and then, clasping you in my arms, I would have begged the Eternal Being to grant you the rest of my life!

Alas! I was alone, alone in the world! A mysterious apathy gradually took hold of my body. My aversion for life, which I had felt as a child, was returning with renewed intensity. Soon my heart supplied no more nourishment for my thought, and I was aware of my existence only in a deep sense of weariness.

For some time I struggled against my malady, but only halfheartedly, with no firm will to conquer it. Finally, unable to find any cure for this strange wound of my heart, which was nowhere and everywhere, I resolved to give up my life.

Priest of the Almighty, now listening to my story, forgive this poor creature whom Heaven had almost stripped of his reason. I was imbued with faith, and I reasoned like a sinner; my heart loved God, and my mind knew Him not. My actions, my words, my feelings, my thoughts were nothing but contradictions, enigmas, and lies. But does man always know what he wished, and is he always sure of what he thinks?

Affection, society, and seclusion, everything was slipping away from me at once. I had tried everything, and everything had proved disastrous. Rejected by the world and abandoned by Amelia, what had I left now that solitude had failed me? It was the last support which I had hoped could save me, and now I felt it too giving way and dropping into the abyss!

Having decided to rid myself of life's burden, I now resolved to use the full consciousness of my mind in committing this desperate act. Nothing made it necessary to take action quickly. I did not set a definite time for my death, so that I might savor the final moments of my existence in long, full draughts and gather all my strength, like the men of antiquity, to feel my soul escaping.

[*Translated by Irving Putter. Berkeley, CA: U of California P, 1967*]

II.d.2. FRANÇOIS RENÉ DE CHATEAUBRIAND, *Le Génie du christianisme*,
Partie II, Livre 3, chapitre 9: « Du vague des passions »

Il reste à parler d'un état de l'âme qui, ce nous semble, n'a pas encore été bien observé: c'est celui qui précède le développement des passions, lorsque nos facultés, jeunes, actives, entières, mais renfermées, ne se sont exercées que sur elles-mêmes, sans but et sans objet. Plus les peuples avancent en civilisation, plus cet état du vague des passions augmente; car il arrive alors une chose fort triste: le grand nombre d'exemples qu'on a sous les yeux, la multitude de livres qui traitent de l'homme et de ses sentiments rendent habile sans expérience. On est détrompé sans avoir joui; il reste encore des désirs, et l'on n'a plus d'illusions. L'imagination est riche, abondante et merveilleuse; l'existence pauvre, sèche et désenchantée. On habite avec un coeur plein un monde vide, et sans avoir usé de rien on est désabusé de tout.

L'amertume que cet état de l'âme répand sur la vie est incroyable; le coeur se retourne et se replie en cent manières, pour employer des forces qu'il sent lui être inutiles. Les anciens ont peu connu cette inquiétude secrète, cette aigreur des passions étouffées qui fermentent toutes ensemble: une grande existence politique, les jeux du gymnase et du Champ-de-Mars, les affaires du Forum et de la place publique, remplissaient leurs moments et ne laissaient aucune place aux ennuis du coeur.

D'une autre part, ils n'étaient pas enclins aux exagérations, aux espérances, aux craintes sans objets, à la mobilité des idées et des sentiments, à la perpétuelle inconstance, qui n'est qu'un dégoût constant; dispositions que nous acquérons dans la société des femmes. Les femmes, indépendamment de la passion directe qu'elles font naître chez les peuples modernes, influent encore sur les autres sentiments. Elles ont dans leur existence un certain abandon qu'elles font passer dans le nôtre; elles rendent notre caractère d'homme moins décidé, et nos passions, amollies par le mélange des leurs, prennent à la fois quelque chose d'incertain et de tendre.

Enfin, les Grecs et les Romains, n'étendant guère leurs regards au delà de la vie et ne soupçonnant point des plaisirs plus parfaits que ceux de ce monde, n'étaient point portés comme nous aux méditations et aux désirs par le caractère de leur culte. Formée pour nos misères et pour nos besoins, la religion chrétienne nous offre sans cesse le double tableau des chagrins de la terre et des joies célestes, et par ce moyen elle fait dans le cúur une source de maux présents et d'espérances lointaines, d'où découlent d'inépuisables rêveries. Le chrétien se regarde toujours comme un voyageur qui passe ici-bas dans une vallée de larmes et qui ne se repose qu'au tombeau. Le monde n'est point l'objet de ses voeux, car il sait que l'homme vit peu de jours, et que cet objet lui échapperait vite.

Les persécutions qu'éprouvèrent les premiers fidèles augmentèrent en eux ce dégoût des choses de la vie. L'invasion des barbares y mit le comble, et l'esprit humain en reçut une impression de tristesse et peut-être même une teinte de misanthropie qui ne s'est jamais bien effacée. De toutes parts s'élevèrent des couvents, où se retirèrent des malheureux trompés par le monde et des âmes qui aimaient mieux ignorer certains sentiments de la vie que de s'exposer à les voir cruellement trahis. Mais de nos jours, quand les monastères ou la vertu qui y conduit ont manqué à ces âmes ardentes, elles se sont trouvées étrangères au milieu des hommes. Dégoûtées par leur siècle, effrayées par leur religion, elles sont restées dans le monde sans se livrer au monde: alors elles sont devenues la proie de mille chimères; alors on a vu naître cette coupable mélancolie qui s'engendre au milieu des passions, lorsque ces passions, sans objet, se consument d'elles-mêmes dans un coeur solitaire.

[1802]

II.d.2. FRANÇOIS RENÉ DE CHATEAUBRIAND, from *The Genius of Christianity*,
Part II, Book 3, Chapter 9: Of the Unsettled State of the Passions

We have yet to treat of a state of the soul, which, as we think, has not been accurately describe; we mean that which precedes the development of the strong passions, when all the faculties, fresh, active, and entire, but confined in the breast, act only upon themselves, without object, and without end. The farther nations advance in civilization, the more this unsettled state of the passions predominates: for then our imagination is rich, abundant, and full of wonders; but our existence is poor, insipid, and destitute of charms. With a full heart, we dwell in an empty world; and scarcely have we advanced a few steps when we have nothing more to learn.

It is inconceivable what a shade this state of the soul throws over life; the heart turns a hundred different ways to employ the energies which it feels to be useless to it. The ancients knew but little of this secret inquietude, this acerbity of the stifled passions fermenting all together: political affairs, the sports of the Gymnasium and of the Campus Martius, the business of the forum and of the popular assemblies, engaged all their time, and left no room of this tedium of the heart.

On the other hand, they were not disposed to exaggerations, to hopes and fears without object, to versatility in ideas and sentiments, and to perpetual inconstancy, which is but a continual disgust; dispositions which we acquire in the familiar society of the fair sex. Women, independently of the direct passion which they excite among all the modern nations, also possess an influence over all other sentiments. They have in their nature a certain ease which they communicate to ours; they render the marks of the masculine character less distinct; and out passions, softened by the mixture of theirs, assume, at one and the same time, something ambiguous and tender.

Finally, the Greeks and Romans, looking scarcely any farther than the present life, and having no conception of pleasures more perfect than those which this world affords, were not disposed, like us by the character of their religion, to reveries and desires. In the spirit of christianity, we must seek the reason of this unsettled state of the feelings, so common among the people of modern times. Framed for our afflictions and for our wants, the Christian religion incessantly exhibits to our view the two-fold picture of terrestrial griefs and heavenly joys, and thus creates in the heart a source of present evils and distant hopes, whence spring inexhaustible abstractions and meditations. The Christian always looks upon himself as no more than a pilgrim traveling here below through a vale of tears, and finding no repose till he reaches the tomb. The world is not the object of his wishes, for he knows that the days of man are few, and that this object would speedily escape from his grasp.

The persecutions which the first believers underwent had the effect of strengthening in them this disgust of the things of this life. The invasion of barbarians raised this feeling to the highest pitch, and the human mind received from it an impression of melancholy, and, perhaps even a slight tincture of misanthropy, which has never been thoroughly removed. On all sides arose convents; disappointments of the world, or souls who chose rather to remain strangers to certain sentiments of life, than to run the risk of finding themselves cruelly deceived. A determined pensiveness was the result of this monastic life; and this sentiment, somewhat confused in its nature, mingling with all the others, stamped upon them its own indecisive character. But at the same time, by a truly remarkable effect, the unsettled state into which melancholy plunges the sentiments gives birth to it again; for it springs up in the midst of the passions, when these passions, without object, subside of themselves in a solitary heart.

[1802] [*Translated by Charles White. Baltimore: John Murphy & Co, 1856*]

II.d.3. ETIENNE PIVERT DE SENANCOUR, *Oberman*, Lettre 18

Même ici, je n'aime que le soir. L'aurore me plait un moment: je crois que je sentirais sa beauté, mais le jour qui va la suivre doit être si long! ... Rien ne m'opprime ici, rien ne me satisfait. Je crois même que l'ennui augmente: c'est que je ne souffre pas assez. Je suis donc plus heureux? Point du tout: souffrir ou être malheureux, ce n'est pas la même chose; jouir ou être heureux, ce n'est pas non plus une même chose.

Ma situation est douce, et je mène une triste vie. Je suis ici on ne peut mieux; libre, tranquille, bien portant, sans affaires, indifférent sur l'avenir dont je n'attends rien, et perdant sans peine le passé dont je n'ai pas joui. Mais il est en moi une inquiétude qui ne me quittera pas; c'est un besoin que je ne connais pas, qui me commande, qui m'absorbe, qui m'emporte au delà des être périssables.

Vous vous trompez, et je m'y étais trompé moi-même; ce n'est pas le besoin d'aimer. Il y a une distance bien grande du vide de mon coeur à l'amour qu'il a tant désiré; mais il y a l'infini entre ce que je suis et ce que j'ai besoin d'être. L'amour est immense, il n'est pas infini. Je ne veux point jouir; je veux espérer, je voudrais savoir! Il me faut des illusions sans bornes, qui s'éloignent pour me tromper toujours. Que m'importe ce qui peut finir? L'heure qui arrivera dans soixante années est là près de moi. Je n'aime point ce qui se prépare, s'approche, arrive, et n'est plus. Je veux un bien, un rêve, une espérance enfin qui soit toujours devant moi, au delà de moi, plus grande que mon attente elle-même, plus grande que ce qui passe. Je voudrais être tout intelligence, et que l'ordre éternel du monde... Et, il y a trente ans, l'ordre était, et je n'étais point!

(1865?)

II.d.4. ALFRED DE MUSSET, *Les Nuits*

LA NUIT D'OCTOBRE

LE POETE.

> Le mal dont j'ai souffert s'est enfui comme un rêve.
> Je n'en puis comparer le lointain souvenir
> Qu'à ces brouillards légers que l'aurore soulève,
> Et, qu'avec la rosée on voit s'évanouir.

LA MUSE.

> Qu'aviez-vous done, ô mon poëte!
> Et quelle est la peine secrète
> Qui de moi vous a séparé?
> Hélas! je m'en ressens encore.
> Quel est done ce mal que j'ignore
> Et dont j'ai si longtemps pleuré?

LE POETE.

> C'était un mal vulgaire et bien connu des hommes;
> Mais, lorsque nous avons quelque ennui dans le coeur,
> Nous nous imaginons, pauvres fous que nous sommes,
> Que personne avant nous n'a senti la douleur.

II.d.3.   ETIENNE PIVERT DE SENANCOUR, from *Obermann*, Letter 18

Even here I love only the evening. The dawn delights me for a moment; it seems as though I should feel its beauty, but the day which is to follow in its train must be so long!

Here, nothing crushes me, nothing satisfies me. I even believe that my weariness is on the increase; it is because I do not suffer enough. Am I, then, happier? Ah, no; suffering and unhappiness are not the same; neither are enjoyment and happiness. My lot is easy, but my life is sad. I am in the best of surroundings: free, tranquil, well, without cares, indifferent towards the future, from which I expect nothing, and drifting away without regret from the past, which has brought me no joy. But I am filled with an unrest that will never leave me; it is a craving I do not comprehend, which overrules me, absorbs me, lifts me above the things that perish.

You are mistaken, and I too was once mistaken; it is not the desire for love. A great distance lies between the void that fills my heart and the love that I have so deeply desired; but the infinite stretches between what I am and what I crave to be. Love is vast, but it is not the infinite. I do not desire enjoyment; I long for hope, I crave knowledge! I need endless illusions, which shall ever lure me onwards, and ever deceive me. What do I care for things that will cease to be? The hour that will come in sixty years is near me now. I have no liking for what is prearranged, for what approaches, arrives, and is then no more. I desire a good, a dream, a hope, that shall be ever before me, beyond me, greater even than my expectation, greater than what passes away. I should like to be pure intelligence, and I wish that the eternal order of the world. . . . And thirty years ago the order was, and I was not!

[Translated by Jessie Frothingham. Cambridge: Riverside P, 1901]

II.d.4.   ALFRED DE MUSSET, from *The Nights*

THE NIGHT OF OCTOBER

THE POET

> My griefs have vanished like a midnight dream;
> All I remember of them I compare
> To those light mists that rise at morning's gleam.
> And, with the dewdrops, melt into the air.

THE MUSE

> What grief was it, O Poet, tell,
> That seared your heart up like a spell,
> And parted our fond souls in twain?
> Tho' deeply in your heart conceal'd,
> Each accent and each glance reveal'd
> The woes I've long time mourned in vain.

THE POET

> It was a vulgar evil, and well known;
> But oftentimes when we are sick at soul,
> We think that we, of all the world alone,
> Are crushed with misery beyond control.

LA MUSE.

> Il n'est de vulgaire chagrin
> Que celui d'une âme vulgaire.
> Ami, que ce triste mystère
> S'échappe aujourd'hui de ton sein.
> Crois-moi, parle avec confiance;
> Le sévère dieu du silence
> Est un des frères de la Mort;
> En se plaignant on se console,
> Et quelquefois une parole
> Nous a délivrés d'un remord.

LE POETE.

> S'il fallait maintenant parler de ma souffrance,
> Je ne sais trop quel nom elle devrait porter,
> Si c'est amour, folie, orgueil, expérience,
> Ni si personne au monde en pourrait profiler.
> Je veux bien toutefois t'en raconter l'histoire,
> Puisque nous voilà seuls, assis près du foyer.
> Prends cette lyre, approche, et laisse ma mémoire
> Au son de tes accords doucement s'éveiller.

LA MUSE.

> Avant de me dire ta peine,
> O poëte! en es-tu guéri?
> Songe qu'il t'en faut aujourd'hui
> Parler sans amour et sans haine.
> S'il to souvient que j'ai reçu
> Le doux nom de consolatrice,
> Ne fais pas de moi la complice
> Des passions qui t'ont perdu.

LE POETE.

> Je suis si bien guéri de cette maladie,
> Que j'en doute parfois lorsque j'y veux songer;
> Et quand je pense aux lieux où j'ai risqué ma vie,
> J'y crois voir à ma place un visage étranger.
> Muse, sois donc sans crainte; au souffle qui t'inspire
> Nous pouvons sans péril tous deux nous confier.
> Il est doux de pleurer, il est doux de sourire
> Au souvenir des maux qu'on pourrait oublier.

LA MUSE.

> Comme une mère vigilante
> Au berceau d'un fils bien-aimé,
> Ainsi je me penche tremblante

THE MUSE

> It cannot be a vulgar grief
> That comes not from a vulgar mind;
> But tell me all that lurks behind,
> And give your aching heart relief.
> Oh, trust me, and confess with truth
> That Silence' God, in very sooth,
> Is brother to the God of Death.
> Telling our woes we ofttimes heal
> The very ills that we reveal,
> And mourn and cure them in a breath.

THE POET

> If I must tell thee of my suffering,
> I scarcely know what name it ought to bear,
> Whether it rose from love, or was a thing
> Of pride and folly and my own despair.
> But now I will unfold my burning pain,
> Since we are here, alone beside the fire,
> If thou, dear Muse, wilt lull my racking brain,
> As in my happier days, with thy loved lyre.

THE MUSE

> Before you tell me your harsh fate
> Drive cruel rancor far away;
> For, Poet, you must speak to-day
> Without a trace of love or hate.
> If you remember long ago
> You held me soother of your heart –
> Then would you have me take a part
> In passions which have wrought your woe?

THE POET

> So well I conquered all this hideous strife,
> That sometimes when I dream me of my ill,
> In those same spots I risked my boyhood's life
> A stranger takes the place I wont to fill.
> Be fearless then, O Muse, and mark, that while
> I tell my woes, there is no fond regret;
> Sweet it is to weep, but sweeter still to smile
> At the thoughts of woes we are able to forget.

THE MUSE

> Like a watchful mother bending
> O'er the cradle of her son,
> So I rest, while you are blending

Sur ce coeur qui m'était fermé.
Parle, ami, – ma lyre attentive
D'une note faible et plaintive
Suit déjà l'accent de ta voix,
Et dans un rayon de lumière,
Comme une vision légère,
Passent les ombres d'autrefois.

LE POETE.

Jours de travail! seuls jours où j'ai vécu!
O trois fois chère solitude!
Dieu soit loué, j'y suis donc revenu,
A ce vieux cabinet d'étude!
Pauvre réduit, murs tant de fois déserts,
Fauteuils poudreux, lampe fidèle,
O mon palais, mon petit univers,
Et toi, Muse, ô jeune immortelle,
Dieu soit loué, nous allons donc chanter!

II.d.5. ALPHONSE DE LAMARTINE, « L'isolement » *Méditations poétiques*

Souvent sur la montagne, à l'ombre du vieux chêne,
Au coucher du soleil, tristement je m'assieds;
Je promène au hasard mes regards sur la plaine,
Dont le tableau changeant se déroule à mes pieds.
Ici gronde le fleuve aux vagues écumantes;
Il serpente, et s'enfonce en un lointain obscur;
Là, le lac immobile étend ses eaux dormantes
Où l'étoile du soir se lève dans l'azur.
Au sommet de ces monts couronnés de bois sombres,
Le crépuscule encor jette un dernier rayon;
Et le char vaporeux de la reine des ombres
Monte, et blanchit déjà les bords de l'horizon.
Cependant, s'élançant de la flèche gothique,
Un son religieux se répand dans les airs;
Le voyageur s'arrête, et la cloche rustique
Aux derniers bruits du jour mêle de saints concerts.
Mais à ces doux tableaux mon âme indifférente
N'éprouve devant eux ni charme ni transports;
Je contemple la terre ainsi qu'une ombre errante
Le soleil des vivants n'échauffe plus les morts.
De colline en colline en vain portant ma vue,
Du sud à l'aquilon, de l'aurore au couchant,
Je parcours tous les points de l'immense étendue,

Future hopes with deeds misdone.
Speak, O Poet, and my lyre
Shall every trembling accent fire,
And lull you with its wonted lays,
Till, in a flood of silver light,
Like some vision gay and bright,
Fades all the gloom of bygone days.

THE POET

Loved nights of toil, of darling solitude,
O nights of toil when life sped fast –
To my old study, in my wonted mood,
Thank God! I have come back at last.
Tho' oft deserted, how I love each wall –
Each book upon the dusty shelves!
Remember, Muse, how it was all in all,
A universe for our two selves!
When to the careless scoffing world I told
The burning songs I heard from you.

[*Translated by George Santayana et al. New York: Brainard, 1908*]

II.d.5.   ALPHONSE DE LAMARTINE, from *Meditations Poetiques*, 'Isolation'

On the mountain, in the old oak's domain,
Often at dusk I sadly take my seat,
And glance haphazardly across the plain
Whose varied scene unfolds beneath my feet.
Here growls the river with its frothy surge:
It winds far off, and vanishes from view;
There the calm lake extends its sleeping verge
Where evening's star arises in the blue.
On these dark woods crowning the mountains' height
Twilight is sending out its final ray,
While the blurred chariot of the queen of night
Rises, and pales the skyline far away.
Meanwhile the ringing of a Gothic bell
Casts a religious sound across the breeze;
The traveller pauses, and the rustic knell
With day's last noise blends sacred harmonies.
Yet my soul, unmoved by this pleasant view,
Feels neither charmed with it nor comforted;
I see the earth as wandering spirits do:
The sun of the living never warms the dead.
Vainly from hill to hill, look where I may,
From south to north, from dawn to dusk, I stare;
I scan the whole of the vast realm, and say:

Et je dis: «Nulle part le bonheur ne m'attend.»
Que me font ces vallons, ces palais, ces chaumières,
Vains objets dont pour moi le charme est envolé?
Fleuves, rochers, forêts, solitudes si chères,
Un seul être vous manque, et tout est dépeuplé!
Que le tour du soleil ou commence ou s'achève,
D'un œil indifférent je le suis dans son cours;
En un ciel sombre ou pur qu'il se couche ou se lève,
Qu'importe le soleil? je n'attends rien des jours.
Quand je pourrais le suivre en sa vaste carrière,
Mes yeux verraient partout le vide et les déserts:
Je ne désire rien de tout ce qu'il éclaire,
Je ne demande rien à l'immense univers.
Mais peut-être au delà des bornes de sa sphère,
Lieux où le vrai soleil éclaire d'autres cieux,
Si je pouvais laisser ma dépouille à la terre,
Ce que j'ai tant rêvé paraîtrait à mes yeux!
Là, je m'enivrerais à la source où j'aspire;
Là, je retrouverais et l'espoir et l'amour,
Et ce bien idéal que toute âme désire,
Et qui n'a pas de nom au terrestre séjour!
Que ne puis-je, porté sur le char de l'Aurore,
Vague objet de mes vœux, m'élancer jusqu'à toi!
Sur la terre d'exil pourquoi resté-je encore?
Il n'est rien de commun entre la terre et moi.
Quand la feuille des bois tombe dans la prairie,
Le vent du soir s'élève et l'arrache aux vallons;
Et moi, je suis semblable à la feuille flétrie:
Emportez-moi comme elle; orageux aquilons!

[*Edited by Jean des Cognets. Paris: Garnier, 1956*]

e. DEUTSCH

II.e.1. IMMANUEL KANT, *Kritik der reinen Vernunft*, aus Vorrede zur 2.
Auflage (1787)

Ob die Bearbeitung der Erkenntnisse, die zum Vernunftgeschäfte gehören, den sicheren Gang einer Wissenschaft gehe oder nicht, das läßt sich bald aus dem Erfolg beurteilen. Wenn sie nach viel gemachten Anstalten und Zurüstungen, so bald es zum Zweck kommt, in Stocken gerät, oder, um diesen zu erreichen, öfters wieder zurückgehen und einen andern Weg einschlagen muß; imgleichen wenn es nicht möglich ist, die verschiedenen Mitarbeiter in der Art, wie die gemeinschaftliche Absicht erfolgt werden soll, einhellig zu machen: so kann man immer überzeugt sein, daß ein solches Studium bei weitem noch nicht den sicheren Gang einer Wissenschaft eingeschlagen, sondern ein bloßes Herumtappen sei, und es ist schon ein Verdienst um die Vernunft, diesen Weg wo möglich ausfindig zu machen, sollte auch manches als vergeblich

'There is no happiness for me anywhere.'
What are these vales, towers, cottages to me?
Vain things, whose charm for me has long abated;
Streams, rocks, woods – places loved and solitary –
One creature goes . . . all is depopulated.
Whether the passing sun may set or rise,
With an indifferent eye I watch its way;
It comes or goes, through clear or cloudy skies –
No matter! I have no hope any day.
If I could follow it throughout its flights,
Everywhere I should see voids, wastes, and worse;
I care for none of all the things it lights,
I ask for nothing of the universe.
Yet perhaps past the boundaries of its sphere,
Where the true Sun enlightens other skies,
If I could leave my trappings on earth here,
What I have dreamed might stand before my eyes.
Filled at the fountain to which I aspire,
There I might find both hope and love once more –
The ideal goodness that all souls desire,
Which never can be named on this world's shore!
O that, within Dawn's chariot, I were sent
To the dim object of my longings there!
Why linger in the land of banishment?
The earth and I have nothing that we share.
When forest leaves fall in the open waste,
The night wind, rising, blows them from the vales;
And I am such a leaf, dry and debased:
Sweep me away like them, you stormy gales!

[*Edited by E. H. Blackmore and A. M. Blackmore. New York: Oxford UP, 2000*]

e. **GERMAN**

II.e.1. IMMANUEL KANT, *Critique of Pure Reason*, from Preface to the
2nd Edition (1787)

Whether the treatment of that portion of our knowledge which lies within the province of pure reason advances with that undeviating certainty which characterizes the progress of science, we shall be at no loss to determine. If we find those who are engaged in metaphysical pursuits, unable to come to an understanding as to the method which they ought to follow; if we find them, after the most elaborate preparations, invariably brought to a stand before the goal is reached, and compelled to retrace their steps and strike into fresh paths, we may then feel quite sure that they are far from having attained to the certainty of scientific progress and may rather be said to be merely groping about in the dark. In these circumstances we shall render an important service to reason if we succeed in simply indicating the path along which it must

aufgegeben werden müssen, was in dem ohne Überlegung vorher genommenen Zwecke enthalten war.

[...]

Die *Mathematik* ist von den frühesten Zeiten her, wohin die Geschichte der menschlichen Vernunft reicht, in dem bewundernswürdigen Volke der Griechen den sichern Weg einer Wissenschaft gegangen. Allein man darf nicht denken, daß es ihr so leicht geworden, wie der Logik, wo die Vernunft es nur mit sich selbst zu tun hat, jenen königlichen Weg zu treffen, oder vielmehr sich selbst zu bahnen; vielmehr glaube ich, daß es lange mit ihr (vornehmlich noch unter den Ägyptern) beim Herumtappen geblieben ist, und diese Umänderung einer *Revolution* zuzuschreiben sei, die der glückliche Einfall eines einzigen Mannes in einem Versuche zu Stande brachte, von welchem an die Bahn, die man nehmen mußte, nicht mehr zu verfehlen war, und der sichere Gang einer Wissenschaft für alle Zeiten und in unendliche Weiten eingeschlagen und vorgezeichnet war. Die Geschichte dieser Revolution der Denkart, welche viel wichtiger war als die Entdeckung des Weges um das berühmte Vorgebirge, und des Glücklichen, der sie zu Stande brachte, ist uns nicht aufbehalten. Doch beweiset die Sage, welche *Diogenes der Laertier* uns überliefert, der von den kleinesten, und, nach dem gemeinen Urteil, gar nicht einmal eines Beweises benötigten, Elementen der geometrischen Demonstrationen den angeblichen Erfinder nennt, daß das Andenken der Veränderung, die durch die erste Spur der Entdeckung dieses neuen Weges bewirkt wurde, den Mathematikern äußerst wichtig geschienen haben müsse, und dadurch unvergeßlich geworden sei. Dem ersten, der den *gleichseitigen Triangel* demonstrierte (er mag nun *Thales* oder wie man will geheißen haben), dem ging ein Licht auf; denn er fand, daß er nicht dem, was er in der Figur sahe, oder auch dem bloßen Begriffe derselben nachspüren und gleichsam davon ihre Eigenschaften ablernen, sondern durch das, was er nach Begriffen selbst a priori hineindachte und darstellete (durch Konstruktion), hervorbringen müsse, und daß er, um sicher etwas a priori zu wissen, er der Sache nichts beilegen müsse, als was aus dem notwendig folgte, was er seinem Begriffe gemäß selbst in sie gelegt hat.

Mit der Naturwissenschaft ging es weit langsamer zu, bis sie den Heeresweg der Wissenschaft traf; denn es sind nur etwa anderthalb Jahrhunderte, daß der Vorschlag des sinnreichen *Baco* von Verulam diese Entdeckung teils veranlaßte, teils, da man bereits auf der Spur derselben war, mehr belebte, welche eben sowohl nur durch eine schnell vorgegangene Revolution der Denkart erklärt werden kann. Ich will hier nur die Naturwissenschaft, so fern sie auf *empirische* Prinzipien gegründet ist, in Erwägung ziehen.

Als *Galilei* seine Kugeln die schiefe Fläche mit einer von ihm selbst gewählten Schwere herabrollen, oder *Torricelli* die Luft ein Gewicht, was er sich zum voraus dem einer ihm bekannten Wassersäule gleich gedacht hatte, tragen ließ, oder in noch späterer Zeit *Stahl* Metalle in Kalk und diesen wiederum in Metall verwandelte, indem er ihnen etwas entzog und wiedergab: so ging allen Naturforschern ein Licht auf. Sie begriffen, daß die Vernunft nur das einsieht, was sie selbst nach ihrem Entwurfe hervorbringt, daß sie mit Prinzipien ihrer Urteile nach beständigen Gesetzen vorangehen und die Natur nötigen müsse, auf ihre Fragen zu antworten, nicht aber sich von ihr allein gleichsam am Leitbande gängeln lassen müsse; denn sonst hängen zufällige, nach keinem vorher entworfenen Plane gemachte Beobachtungen gar nicht in einem notwendigen Gesetze zusammen, welches doch die Vernunft sucht und bedarf. Die Vernunft muß mit ihren Prinzipien, nach denen allein übereinkommende Erscheinungen für Gesetze gelten können, in einer Hand, und mit dem Experiment, das sie nach jenen ausdachte, in der anderen, an die Natur gehen, zwar um von ihr belehrt zu werden, aber nicht in der Qualität eines Schülers,

travel, in order to arrive at any results – even if it should be found necessary to abandon many of those aims which, without reflection, have been proposed for its attainment.

[. . .]

In the earliest times of which history affords us any record, mathematics had already entered on the sure course of science, among that wonderful nation, the Greeks. Still it is not to be supposed that it was as easy for this science to strike into, or rather to construct for itself, that royal road, as it was for logic, in which reason has only to deal with itself. On the contrary, I believe that it must have remained long – chiefly among the Egyptians – in the stage of blind groping after its true aims and destination, and that it was revolutionized by the happy idea of one man, who struck out and determined for all time the path which this science must follow, and which admits of an indefinite advancement. The history of this intellectual revolution – much more important in its results than the discovery of the passage round the celebrated Cape of Good Hope – and of its author, has not been preserved. But Diogenes Laertius, in naming the supposed discoverer of some of the simplest elements of geometrical demonstration – elements which, according to the ordinary opinion, do not even require to be proved – makes it apparent that the change introduced by the first indication of this new path, must have seemed of the utmost importance to the mathematicians of that age, and it has thus been secured against the chance of oblivion. A new light must have flashed on the mind of the first man (Thales, or whatever may have been his name) who demonstrated the properties of the isosceles triangle. For he found that it was not sufficient to meditate on the figure, as it lay before his eyes, or the conception of it, as it existed in his mind, and thus endeavour to get at the knowledge of its properties, but that it was necessary to produce these properties, as it were, by a positive a priori construction; and that, in order to arrive with certainty at a priori cognition, he must not attribute to the object any other properties than those which necessarily followed from that which he had himself, in accordance with his conception, placed in the object.

A much longer period elapsed before physics entered on the highway of science. For it is only about a century and a half since the wise Bacon gave a new direction to physical studies, or rather – as others were already on the right track – imparted fresh vigour to the pursuit of this new direction. Here, too, as in the case of mathematics, we find evidence of a rapid intellectual revolution. In the remarks which follow I shall confine myself to the empirical side of natural science.

When Galilei experimented with balls of a definite weight on the inclined plane, when Torricelli caused the air to sustain a weight which he had calculated beforehand to be equal to that of a definite column of water, or when Stahl, at a later period, converted metals into lime, and reconverted lime into metal, by the addition and subtraction of certain elements; a light broke upon all natural philosophers. They learned that reason only perceives that which it produces after its own design; that it must not be content to follow, as it were, in the leading-strings of nature, but must proceed in advance with principles of judgement according to unvarying laws, and compel nature to reply its questions. For accidental observations, made according to no preconceived plan, cannot be united under a necessary law. But it is this that reason seeks for and requires. It is only the principles of reason which can give to concordant phenomena the validity of laws, and it is only when experiment is directed by these rational principles that it can have any real utility. Reason must approach nature with the view, indeed, of receiving information from it, not, however, in the character of a pupil, who listens to all that his master chooses to tell him, but in that of a judge, who compels the witnesses to reply to those questions which

der sich alles vorsagen läßt, was der Lehrer will, sondern eines bestallten Richters, der die Zeugen nötigt, auf die Fragen zu antworten, die er ihnen vorlegt. Und so hat sogar Physik die so vorteilhafte Revolution ihrer Denkart lediglich dem Einfalle zu verdanken, demjenigen, was die Vernunft selbst in die Natur hineinlegt, gemäß, dasjenige in ihr zu suchen (nicht ihr anzudichten), was sie von dieser lernen muß, und wovon sie für sich selbst nichts wissen würde. Hiedurch ist die Naturwissenschaft allererst in den sicheren Gang einer Wissenschaft gebracht worden, da sie so viel Jahrhunderte durch nichts weiter als ein bloßes Herumtappen gewesen war.

Der *Metaphysik*, einer ganz isolierten spekulativen Vernunfterkenntnis, die sich gänzlich über Erfahrungsbelehrung erhebt, und zwar durch bloße Begriffe (nicht wie Mathematik durch Anwendung derselben auf Anschauung), wo also Vernunft selbst ihr eigener Schüler sein soll, ist das Schicksal bisher noch so günstig nicht gewesen, daß sie den sichern Gang einer Wissenschaft einzuschlagen vermocht hätte; ob sie gleich älter ist, als alle übrigen, und bleiben würde, wenn gleich die übrigen insgesamt in dem Schlunde einer alles vertilgenden Barbarei gänzlich verschlungen werden sollten. Denn in ihr gerät die Vernunft kontinuierlich in Stecken, selbst wenn sie diejenigen Gesetze, welche die gemeinste Erfahrung bestätigt (wie sie sich anmaßt), a priori einsehen will. In ihr muß man unzählige mal den Weg zurück tun, weil man findet, daß er dahin nicht führt, wo man hin will, und was die Einhelligkeit ihrer Anhänger in Behauptungen betrifft, so ist sie noch so weit davon entfernt, daß sie vielmehr ein Kampfplatz ist, der ganz eigentlich dazu bestimmt zu sein scheint, seine Kräfte im Spielgefechte zu üben, auf dem noch niemals irgend ein Fechter sich auch den kleinsten Platz hat erkämpfen und auf seinen Sieg einen dauerhaften Besitz gründen können. Es ist also kein Zweifel, daß ihr Verfahren bisher ein bloßes Herumtappen, und, was das Schlimmste ist, unter bloßen Begriffen, gewesen sei.

Woran liegt es nun, daß hier noch kein sicherer Weg der Wissenschaft hat gefunden werden können? Ist er etwa unmöglich? Woher hat denn die Natur unsere Vernunft mit der rastlosen Bestrebung heimgesucht, ihm als einer ihrer wichtigsten Angelegenheiten nachzuspüren? Noch mehr, wie wenig haben wir Ursache, Vertrauen in unsere Vernunft zu setzen, wenn sie uns in einem der wichtigsten Stücke unserer Wißbegierde nicht bloß verläßt, sondern durch Vorspiegelungen hinhält, und am Ende betrügt! Oder ist er bisher nur verfehlt: welche Anzeige können wir benutzen, um bei erneuertem Nachsuchen zu hoffen, daß wir glücklicher sein werden, als andere vor uns gewesen sind?

Ich sollte meinen, die Beispiele der Mathematik und Naturwissenschaft, die durch eine auf einmal zu Stande gebrachte Revolution das geworden sind, was sie jetzt sind, wäre merkwürdig genug, um dem wesentlichen Stücke der Umänderung der Denkart, die ihnen so vorteilhaft geworden ist, nachzusinnen, und ihnen, so viel ihre Analogie, als Vernunfterkenntnisse, mit der Metaphysik verstattet, hierin wenigstens zum Versuche nachzuahmen. Bisher nahm man an, alle unsere Erkenntnis müsse sich nach den Gegenständen richten; aber alle Versuche, über sie a priori etwas durch Begriffe auszumachen, wodurch unsere Erkenntnis erweitert würde, gingen unter dieser Voraussetzung zu nichte. Man versuche es daher einmal, ob wir nicht in den Aufgaben der Metaphysik damit besser fortkommen, daß wir annehmen, die Gegenstände müssen sich nach unserer Erkenntnis richten, welches so schon besser mit der verlangten Möglichkeit einer Erkenntnis derselben a priori zusammenstimmt, die über Gegenstände, ehe sie uns gegeben werden, etwas festsetzen soll. Es ist hiemit eben so, als mit den ersten Gedanken des *Kopernikus* bewandt, der, nachdem es mit der Erklärung der Himmelsbewegungen nicht gut fort wollte, wenn er annahm, das ganze Sternheer drehe sich um den Zuschauer, versuchte, ob es nicht besser gelingen möchte, wenn er den Zuschauer sich drehen, und dagegen die Sterne in Ruhe ließ. In der Metaphysik kann man nun, was die *Anschauung* der Gegenstände betrifft, es auf ähnliche Weise versuchen. Wenn

he himself thinks fit to propose. To this single idea must the revolution be ascribed, by which, after groping in the dark for so many centuries, natural science was at length conducted into the path of certain progress.

We come now to metaphysics, a purely speculative science, which occupies a completely isolated position and is entirely independent of the teachings of experience. It deals with mere conceptions – not, like mathematics, with conceptions applied to intuition – and in it, reason is the pupil of itself alone. It is the oldest of the sciences, and would still survive, even if all the rest were swallowed up in the abyss of an all-destroying barbarism. But it has not yet had the good fortune to attain to the sure scientific method. This will be apparent; if we apply the tests which we proposed at the outset. We find that reason perpetually comes to a stand, when it attempts to gain a priori the perception even of those laws which the most common experience confirms. We find it compelled to retrace its steps in innumerable instances, and to abandon the path on which it had entered, because this does not lead to the desired result. We find, too, that those who are engaged in metaphysical pursuits are far from being able to agree among themselves, but that, on the contrary, this science appears to furnish an arena specially adapted for the display of skill or the exercise of strength in mock-contests – a field in which no combatant ever yet succeeded in gaining an inch of ground, in which, at least, no victory was ever yet crowned with permanent possession.

This leads us to inquire why it is that, in metaphysics, the sure path of science has not hitherto been found. Shall we suppose that it is impossible to discover it? Why then should nature have visited our reason with restless aspirations after it, as if it were one of our weightiest concerns? Nay, more, how little cause should we have to place confidence in our reason, if it abandons us in a matter about which, most of all, we desire to know the truth – and not only so, but even allures us to the pursuit of vain phantoms, only to betray us in the end? Or, if the path has only hitherto been missed, what indications do we possess to guide us in a renewed investigation, and to enable us to hope for greater success than has fallen to the lot of our predecessors?

It appears to me that the examples of mathematics and natural philosophy, which, as we have seen, were brought into their present condition by a sudden revolution, are sufficiently remarkable to fix our attention on the essential circumstances of the change which has proved so advantageous to them, and to induce us to make the experiment of imitating them, so far as the analogy which, as rational sciences, they bear to metaphysics may permit. It has hitherto been assumed that our cognition must conform to the objects; but all attempts to ascertain anything about these objects a priori, by means of conceptions, and thus to extend the range of our knowledge, have been rendered abortive by this assumption. Let us then make the experiment whether we may not be more successful in metaphysics, if we assume that the objects must conform to our cognition. This appears, at all events, to accord better with the possibility of our gaining the end we have in view, that is to say, of arriving at the cognition of objects a priori, of determining something with respect to these objects, before they are given to us. We here propose to do just what Copernicus did in attempting to explain the celestial movements. When he found that he could make no progress by assuming that all the heavenly bodies revolved round the spectator, he reversed the process, and tried the experiment of assuming that the spectator revolved, while the stars remained at rest. We may make the same experiment with regard to the intuition of objects. If the intuition must conform to the nature of the objects, I do not see how we can know anything of them a priori. If, on the other hand, the object conforms to the nature of our faculty of intuition, I can then easily conceive the possibility of such an a priori knowledge. Now as I cannot rest in the mere intuitions, but – if they are to become cognitions – must refer

die Anschauung sich nach der Beschaffenheit der Gegenstände richten müßte, so sehe ich nicht ein, wie man a priori von ihr etwas wissen könne; richtet sich aber der Gegenstand (als Objekt der Sinne) nach der Beschaffenheit unseres Anschauungsvermögens, so kann ich mir diese Möglichkeit ganz wohl vorstellen. Weil ich aber bei diesen Anschauungen, wenn sie Erkenntnisse werden sollen, nicht stehen bleiben kann, sondern sie als Vorstellungen auf irgend etwas als Gegenstand beziehen und diesen durch jene bestimmen muß, so kann ich entweder annehmen, die *Begriffe*, wodurch ich diese Bestimmung zu Stande bringe, richten sich auch nach dem Gegenstande, und denn bin ich wiederum in derselben Verlegenheit, wegen der Art, wie ich a priori hiervon etwas wissen könne; oder ich nehme an, die Gegenstände, oder, welches einerlei ist, die *Erfahrung*, in welcher sie allein (als gegebene Gegenstände) erkannt werden, richte sich nach diesen Begriffen, so sehe ich sofort eine leichtere Auskunft, weil Erfahrung selbst eine Erkenntnisart ist, die Verstand erfordert, dessen Regel ich in mir, noch ehe mir Gegenstände gegeben werden, mithin a priori voraussetzen muß, welche in Begriffen a priori ausgedrückt wird, nach denen sich also alle Gegenstände der Erfahrung notwendig richten und mit ihnen übereinstimmen müssen. Was Gegenstände betrifft, so fern sie bloß durch Vernunft und zwar notwendig gedacht, die aber (so wenigstens, wie die Vernunft sie denkt) gar nicht in der Erfahrung gegeben werden können, so werden die Versuche, sie zu denken (denn denken müssen sie sich doch lassen), hernach einen herrlichen Probierstein desjenigen abgeben, was wir als die veränderte Methode der Denkungsart annehmen, daß wir nämlich von den Dingen nur das a priori erkennen, was wir selbst in sie legen.

Dieser Versuch gelingt nach Wunsch, und verspricht der Metaphysik in ihrem ersten Teile, da sie sich nämlich mit Begriffen a priori beschäftigt, davon die korrespondierenden Gegenstände in der Erfahrung jenen angemessen gegeben werden können, den sicheren Gang einer Wissenschaft. Denn man kann nach dieser Veränderung der Denkart die Möglichkeit einer Erkenntnis a priori ganz wohl erklären, und, was noch mehr ist, die Gesetze, welche a priori der Natur, als dem Inbegriffe der Gegenstände der Erfahrung, zum Grunde liegen, mit ihren genugtuenden Beweisen versehen, welches beides nach der bisherigen Verfahrungsart unmöglich war. Aber es ergibt sich aus dieser Deduktion unseres Vermögens a priori zu erkennen im ersten Teile der Metaphysik ein befremdliches und dem ganzen Zwecke derselben, der den zweiten Teil beschäftigt, dem Anscheine nach sehr nachteiliges Resultat, nämlich daß wir mit ihm nie über die Grenze möglicher Erfahrung hinauskommen können, welches doch gerade die wesentlichste Angelegenheit dieser Wissenschaft ist. Aber hierin liegt eben das Experiment einer Gegenprobe der Wahrheit des Resultats jener ersten Würdigung unserer Vernunfterkenntnis a priori, daß sie nämlich nur auf Erscheinungen gehe, die Sache an sich selbst dagegen zwar als für sich wirklich, aber von uns unerkannt, liegen lasse. Denn das, was uns notwendig über die Grenze der Erfahrung und aller Erscheinungen hinaus zugehen treibt, ist das *Unbedingte*, welches die Vernunft in den Dingen an sich selbst notwendig und mit allem Recht zu allem Bedingten, und dadurch die Reihe der Bedingungen als vollendet verlangt. Findet sich nun, wenn man annimmt, unsere Erfahrungserkenntnis richte sich nach den Gegenständen als Dingen an sich selbst, daß das Unbedingte *ohne Widerspruch gar nicht gedacht* werden könne; dagegen, wenn man annimmt, unsere Vorstellung der Dinge, wie sie uns gegeben werden, richte sich nicht nach diesen, als Dingen an sich selbst, sondern diese Gegenstände vielmehr, als Erscheinungen, richten sich nach unserer Vorstellungsart, *der Widerspruch wegfalle*; und daß folglich das Unbedingte nicht an Dingen, so fern wir sie kennen (sie uns gegeben werden), wohl aber an ihnen, so fern wir sie nicht kennen, als Sachen an sich selbst, angetroffen werden müsse: so zeiget sich, daß, was wir anfangs nur zum Versuche annahmen, gegründet sei.

[1787] [*Immanuel Kant: Werke, 12 vols. Edited by Wilhelm Weischedel. Frankfurt am Main: Suhrkamp, 1977. III, 20–28*]

them, as representations, to something, as object, and must determine the latter by means of the former, here again there are two courses open to me. Either, first, I may assume that the conceptions, by which I effect this determination, conform to the object – and in this case I am reduced to the same perplexity as before; or secondly, I may assume that the objects, or, which is the same thing, that experience, in which alone as given objects they are cognized, conform to my conceptions – and then I am at no loss how to proceed. For experience itself is a mode of cognition which requires understanding. Before objects, are given to me, that is, a priori, I must presuppose in myself laws of the understanding which are expressed in conceptions a priori. To these conceptions, then, all the objects of experience must necessarily conform. Now there are objects which reason thinks, and that necessarily, but which cannot be given in experience, or, at least, cannot be given so as reason thinks them. The attempt to think these objects will hereafter furnish an excellent test of the new method of thought which we have adopted, and which is based on the principle that we only cognize in things a priori that which we ourselves place in them.

This attempt succeeds as well as we could desire, and promises to metaphysics, in its first part – that is, where it is occupied with conceptions a priori, of which the corresponding objects may be given in experience – the certain course of science. For by this new method we are enabled perfectly to explain the possibility of a priori cognition, and, what is more, to demonstrate satisfactorily the laws which lie a priori at the foundation of nature, as the sum of the objects of experience – neither of which was possible according to the procedure hitherto followed. But from this deduction of the faculty of a priori cognition in the first part of metaphysics, we derive a surprising result, and one which, to all appearance, militates against the great end of metaphysics, as treated in the second part. For we come to the conclusion that our faculty of cognition is unable to transcend the limits of possible experience; and yet this is precisely the most essential object of this science. The estimate of our rational cognition a priori at which we arrive is that it has only to do with phenomena, and that things in themselves, while possessing a real existence, lie beyond its sphere. Here we are enabled to put the justice of this estimate to the test. For that which of necessity impels us to transcend the limits of experience and of all phenomena is the unconditioned, which reason absolutely requires in things as they are in themselves, in order to complete the series of conditions. Now, if it appears that when, on the one hand, we assume that our cognition conforms to its objects as things in themselves, the unconditioned cannot be thought without contradiction, and that when, on the other hand, we assume that our representation of things as they are given to us, does not conform to these things as they are in themselves, but that these objects, as phenomena, conform to our mode of representation, the contradiction disappears: we shall then be convinced of the truth of that which we began by assuming for the sake of experiment; we may look upon it as established that the unconditioned does not lie in things as we know them, or as they are given to us, but in things as they are in themselves, beyond the range of our cognition.

[*Translated by J. M. D. Meiklejohn, 1855. 11–15*]

II.e.2. FICHTE, 'Zweite Einleitung in die Wissenschaftslehre'

1.

Ganz besonders ist diese vorläufige Untersuchung über die Methode bei der Wissenschaftslehre nöthig, deren ganzer Bau und Bedeutung von dem Bau und der Bedeutung der philosophischen Systeme, die bisher gäng und gäbe waren, völlig verschieden ist. Die Verfertiger der Systeme, welche ich im Sinne habe, gehen von irgend einem Begriffe aus; ganz unbesorgt, woher sie diesen selbst genommen, und woraus sie ihn zusammengesetzt haben, analysiren sie ihn, combiniren ihn mit anderen, über deren Ursprung sie ebenso unbekümmert sind; und dieses ihr Raisonnement ist selbst ihre Philosophie. Ihre Philosophie besteht sonach in ihrem eigenen Denken. Ganz anders verhält es sich mit der Wissenschaftslehre. Dasjenige, was sie zum Gegenstande ihres Denkens macht, ist nicht ein todter Begriff, der sich gegen ihre Untersuchung nur leidend verhalte, und aus welchem sie erst durch ihr Denken etwas mache, sondern es ist ein Lebendiges und Thätiges, das aus sich selbst und durch sich selbst Erkenntnisse erzeugt, und welchem der Philosoph bloss zusieht. Sein Geschäft in der Sache ist nichts weiter, als dass er jenes Lebendige in zweckmässige Thätigkeit versetze, dieser Thätigkeit desselben zusehe, sie auffasse, und als Eins begreife. Er stellt ein Experiment an. Das zu untersuchende in die Lage zu versetzen, in der bestimmt diejenige Beobachtung gemacht werden kann, welche beabsichtigt wird, ist seine Sache; es ist seine Sache, auf die Erscheinungen aufzumerken, sie richtig zu verfolgen und zu verknüpfen; aber wie das Object sich äussere, ist nicht seine Sache, sondern die des Objects selbst, und er würde seinem eigenen Zwecke gerade entgegenarbeiten, wenn er dasselbe nicht sich selbst überliesse, sondern in die Entwickelung der Erscheinung Eingriffe thäte. Der Philosoph von der ersten Gattung hingegen verfertigt ein Kunstproduct. Er rechnet im Objecte seiner Bearbeitung nur auf die Materie, nicht auf eine innere, selbstthätige Kraft desselben. Ehe er an die Arbeit geht, muss diese innere Kraft schon getödtet seyn, ausserdem würde sie seiner Bearbeitung widerstehen. Aus dieser todten Masse verfertigt er etwas lediglich durch seine eigene Kraft, und bloss nach seinem eigenen, schon vorher entworfenen Begriffe. In der Wissenschaftslehre giebt es zwei sehr verschiedene Reihen des geistigen Handelns: die des Ich, welches der Philosoph beobachtet, und die der Beobachtungen des Philosophen. In den entgegengesetzten Philosophien, auf welche ich mich soeben bezog, giebt es nur *eine* Reihe des Denkens, die der Gedanken des Philosophen; da sein Stoff selbst nicht als denkend eingeführt wird. [...]

2.

Nach dieser vorläufigen Erinnerung, deren weitere Anwendung in unserer gegenwärtigen Abhandlung enthalten seyn wird, — wie wird die Wissenschaftslehre zu Werke gehen, um ihre Aufgabe zu lösen?

Die Frage, welche sie zu beantworten hat, ist, wie bekannt, folgende: woher das System der vom Gefühle der Nothwendigkeit begleiteten Vorstellungen? oder: wie kommen wir dazu, dem, was doch nur subjectiv ist, objective Gültigkeit beizumessen? Oder, da objective Gültigkeit durch Seyn bezeichnet wird: wie kommen wir dazu, ein Seyn anzunehmen? Da diese Frage von der Einkehr in sich selbst, von der Bemerkung, dass das unmittelbare Object des Bewusstseyns doch lediglich das Bewusstseyn selbst sey, ausgeht, so kann sie von keinem anderen Seyn, als von einem Seyn für uns reden; und es wäre völlig widersinnig, sie mit der Frage nach einem Seyn ohne Beziehung auf ein Bewusstseyn für einerlei zu halten. Jedoch gerade das widersinnigste pflegt in unserem philosophischen Zeitalter von den Philosophen am gewöhnlichsten zu geschehen.

II.e.2. FICHTE, 'Second Introduction to the Science of Knowledge. *For readers who already have a philosophical system*' (1797)

1

This preliminary inquiry into method is most particularly necessary in regard to the Science of Knowledge, whose entire structure and significance are utterly different from those of the philosophical systems that have been customary hitherto. The system-makers I have in mind proceed from some concept or other; without caring in the least where they got it from, or whence they have concocted it, they analyze it, combine it with others to whose origin they are equally indifferent, and in reasonings such as these their philosophy itself is comprised. It consists, in consequence, of their own thoughts. The Science of Knowledge is a very different matter. Its chosen topic of consideration is not a lifeless concept, passively exposed to its inquiry merely, of which it makes something only by its own thought, but a living and active thing which engenders insights from and through itself, and which the philosopher merely contemplates. His role in the affair goes no further than to translate this living force into purposeful activity, to observe the activity in question, to apprehend it and grasp it as a unity. He undertakes an experiment. His affair it is, to put the object of inquiry in a position where precisely those observations that were intended can be made; his affair also, to take note of the phenomena, to follow them correctly, and to connect them together; but how the object manifests is not his affair, but that of the object itself, and he would be operating directly counter to his own aim if he did not leave it to itself, and sought to intervene in the development of the phenomenon. The philosopher of the first type, by contrast, is fashioning an artefact. In the object of his labours he reckons only upon the matter, not upon an inner, self-active force thereof. Before he goes to work, this inner force must already have been killed, or it would offer resistance to his efforts. From this dead mass he fashions something, purely through his own powers, and in accordance only with his own concept, already devised beforehand. In the Science of Knowledge there are two very different sequences of mental acts: that of the self, which the philosopher observes, and that of the philosopher's observations. In the opposite philosophies just referred to, there is only *one* sequence of thought that of the philosopher's meditations; for the content thereof is not itself introduced as thinking. [...]

2

After these preliminary remarks, whose further application will be found in discussion now in hand – how is the Science of Knowledge to go about the solution of its problem?

The question it has to answer is, as we know, the following: Whence arises the system of presentations accompanied by the feeling of necessity? or: How do we come to attribute objective validity to what in fact is only subjective? or, since objective validity is described as existence: How do we come to believe in an existent? Since this question arises from a reversion into oneself, from observing that the immediate object of consciousness is in fact only consciousness itself, it can refer to no other existence than an existence for us; and it would be perfectly absurd to assimilate it to the question as to an existence unrelated to consciousness. Yet it is precisely the greatest absurdities that seem most commonly to be put forth by the philosophers of our day.

The question proposed, namely: How is an existent possible for us? itself abstracts from all existence: which is to say, not that it supposes a nonexistence, whereby this concept would be

Die aufgestellte Frage: wie ist ein Seyn für uns möglich? abstrahirt selbst von allem Seyn: d. h. nicht etwa, sie denkt ein Nicht-Seyn, wodurch dieser Begriff nur negirt, nicht aber von ihm abstrahirt wurde, sondern sie denkt sich den Begriff des Seyns überhaupt gar nicht, weder positiv, noch negativ. Sie fragt nach dem Grunde des Prädicats vom Seyn überhaupt, werde es nun beigelegt oder abgesprochen; aber der Grund liegt allemal ausserhalb des begründeten, d. i. er ist demselben entgegengesetzt, Die Antwort muss, wenn sie eine Antwort auf *diese* Frage seyn soll, und auf dieselbe wirklich eingehen will, gleichfalls von allem Seyn abstrahiren. [...]

3.

Wer ist es nun, der die geforderte Abstraction von allem Seyn vornimmt: in welcher von den beiden Reihen liegt sie? Offenbar in der Reihe des philosophischen Raisonnements; eine andere Reihe ist bis jetzt noch nicht vorhanden.

Das, woran allein er sich hält, und woraus er das zu erklärende zu erklären verspricht, ist das Bewusstseyende, das Subject, welches er sonach rein von aller Vorstellung des Seyns auffassen müsste, um in ihm erst den Grund alles Seyns— für dasselbe, wie sich vorsteht — aufzuweisen. Aber dem Subjecte kömmt, wenn von allem Seyn desselben und fur das selbe abstrahirt ist, nichts zu, denn ein Handeln; es ist insbesondere in Beziehung auf das Seyn das handelnde. In seinem Handeln sonach müsste er es auffassen, und von diesem Puncte aus würde jene doppelte Reihe erst anheben.

Die Grundbehauptung des Philosophen, als eines solchen, ist diese: So wie das Ich nur für sich selbst sey, entstehe ihm zugleich nothwendig ein Seyn ausser ihm; der Grund des letzteren liege im ersteren, das letztere sey durch das erstere bedingt: Selbstbewusstseyn und Bewusstseyn eines Etwas, das nicht wir selbst — seyn solle, sey nothwendig verbunden; das erstere aber sey anzusehen als das bedingende, und das letztere als das bedingte. Um diese Behauptung zu erweisen, nicht etwa durch Raisonnement, als gültig für ein System der Existenz an sich, sondern durch Beobachtung des ursprünglichen Verfahrens der Vernunft, als gültig für die Vernunft, müsste er zeigen, zuvörderst: wie das Ich für sich sey und werde; dann, dass dieses Seyn seiner selbst für sich selbst nicht möglich sey, ohne dass ihm auch zugleich ein Seyn ausser ihm entstehe.

Die erste Frage sonach wäre die: wie ist das Ich für sich selbst? das erste Postulat: denke dich, construire den Begriff deiner selbst, und bemerke, wie du dies machst.

Jeder, der dies nur thue, behauptet der Philosoph, werde finden, dass im Denken jenes Begriffs seine Thätigkeit, als Intelligenz, in sich selbst zurückgehe, sich selbst zu ihrem Gegenstande mache.

Ist dies nun richtig, und wird es zugestanden, so ist die Weise der Construction des Ich, der Art seines Seyns für sich (und von einem anderen Seyn ist nirgends die Rede), bekannt, und der Philosoph könnte nun fortschreiten zum Erweise, dass diese Handlung nicht möglich sey ohne eine andere, wodurch dem Ich ein Seyn ausser ihm entstehe.

So, wie wir es jetzt beschrieben, knüpft die Wissenschaftslehre ihre Untersuchungen an. Jetzt unsere Betrachtungen darüber, mit welchem Rechte sie so verfahre.

4.

Zuvörderst, was gehört in dem beschriebenen Acte dem Philosophen an, als Philosophen; — was dem durch ihn zu beobachtenden Ich? Dem Ich nichts weiteres, als das Zurückkehren in sich; alles übrige gehört zur Relation des Philosophen, für den als blosses Factum das System der gesammten Erfahrung schon da ist, welches vom Ich unter seinen Augen zu Stande gebracht werden soll, damit er die Entstehungsart desselben kennen lerne.

340

neither negated, nor yet abstracted from, but that it does not entertain the concept of existence in general at all, either positively or negatively. It inquires as to the ground of the predicate of existence in general, imputed or withheld, as the case may be; but the ground is always external to the grounded, that is, it is opposed to the latter. The answer, if it is to be an answer to *this* question, and genuinely seeks to be addressed thereto, must similarly abstract from all existence. [...]

3

Who is it now, who performs the required abstraction from all existence: in which of the two series does it lie? Obviously, in that of philosophical ratiocination; no other series has so far made its appearance.

The only thing the philosopher adheres to, and from which he proposes to account for what is to be explained, is the conscious being, or subject, which he will therefore have to conceive as stripped of any presentation of existence, in order first to point therein to the ground of all existence – existence for itself, naturally. But when all existence of or for the subject is taken away, it has nothing left but an act; more especially in relation to existence, it is that which acts. So he will therefore have to view it in its acting, and from this point on the double series will first commence.

The basic contention of the philosopher, as such, is as follows: Though the self may exist only for itself, there necessarily arises for it at once an existence external to it; the ground of the latter lies in the former, and is conditioned thereby: self-consciousness and consciousness of something that is to be – not ourselves – are necessarily connected; but the first is to be regarded as the conditioning factor, and the second as the conditioned. To establish this claim, not by argument, indeed – as valid for a system of existence-in-itself – but, by observation of the original procedure of reason, as valid for reason, he will have to show, firstly, how the self is and may be for itself; then, that this existence of itself for itself would be impossible, unless there also at once arose for it an existence outside itself.

Thus the first question would be: How does the self exist for itself? The first postulate: Think of yourself, frame the concept of yourself; and notice how you do it.

Everyone who does no more than this, so the philosopher claims, will find that in the thinking of this concept his activity as an intelligence reverts into itself and makes itself its own object.

Now if this be correct, and once it is admitted, we know the mode of construction of the self, the manner in which it exists for itself (and no other existence is in question here); the philosopher can thereupon proceed to his demonstration that this act would be impossible without another, whereby there arises for the self an existence outside itself.

Thus, as we have now described it, does the Science of Knowledge knit its investigations together. We next have to consider its right to proceed in this fashion.

4

First of all, what elements in the act described are to be assigned to the philosopher as such, – and what to the self that is to be observed by him? The self has nothing beyond the reversion into itself; everything else pertains to the relation thereto of the philosopher, for whom the entire system of experience is already given as a mere fact, which is to be brought into being before his eyes by the self, so that he may come to know the manner of its genesis.

Das Ich geht zurück *in sich selbst*, — wird behauptet. Ist es denn also nicht schon vor diesem Zurückgehen, und unabhängig von demselben da für sich; muss es nicht für sich schon da seyn, um sich zum Ziele eines Handelns machen zu können; und, wenn es so ist, setzt denn nicht eure Philosophie schon voraus, was sie erklären sollte?

Ich antworte: keineswegs. Erst durch diesen Act, und lediglich durch ihn, durch ein Handeln auf ein Handeln selbst, welchem bestimmten Handeln kein Handeln überhaupt vorhergeht, wird das Ich *ursprünglich* für sich selbst. Nur *für den Philosophen* ist es vorher da als Factum, weil dieser die ganze Erfahrung schon gemacht hat. Er muss sich so ausdrücken, wie er sich ausdrückt, um nur verstanden zu werden; und er kann sich so ausdrücken, weil er alle die dazu erforderlichen Begriffe schon längst aufgefasst hat.

Was ist nun, um zuvörderst auf das beobachtete Ich zu sehen, dieses sein Zurückgehen in sich selbst; unter welche Klasse der Modificationen des Bewusstseyns soll es gesetzt werden? Es ist kein *Begreifen:* dies wird es erst durch den Gegensatz eines Nicht-Ich, und durch die Bestimmung des Ich in diesem Gegensatze. Mithin ist es eine blosse *Anschauung.* — Es ist sonach auch kein Bewusstseyn, nicht einmal ein Selbstbewusstseyn; und lediglich darum, weil durch diesen blossen Act kein Bewusstseyn zu Stande kommt, wird ja fortgeschlossen auf einen anderen Act, wodurch ein Nicht-Ich für uns entsteht; lediglich dadurch wird ein Fortschritt des philosophischen Raisonnements und die verlangte Ableitung des Systems der Erfahrung möglich. Das Ich wird durch den beschriebenen Act bloss in die Möglichkeit des Selbstbewusstseyns, und mit ihm alles übrigen Bewusstseyns versetzt; aber es entsteht noch kein wirkliches Bewusstseyn. Der angegebene Act ist bloss ein Theil, und ein nur durch den Philosophen abzusondernder, nicht aber etwa ursprünglich abgesonderter Theil der ganzen Handlung der Intelligenz, wodurch sie ihr Bewusstseyn zu Stande bringt.

Wie verhält es sich dagegen mit dem Philosophen, als solchem? Jenes sich selbst construirende Ich ist kein anderes, als sein eigenes. Er kann den angegebenen Act des Ich nur in sich selbst anschauen, und um ihn anschauen zu können, muss er ihn vollziehen. Er bringt ihn willkürlich und mit Freibeit in sich hervor.

Aber — kann man dabei fragen, und hat man dabei gefragt, — wenn diese ganze Philosophie auf etwas durch einen Act der blossen Willkür zu Stande gebrachtes aufgebaut wird, wird sie nicht dadurch ein Hirngespinnst, eine blosse Erdichtung? Wie will denn der Philosoph dieser nur subjectiven Handlung ihre Objectivität, wie will er denn dem, das doch offenbar nur empirisch ist, und in eine Zeit fällt — in die Zeit, da sich der Philosoph zum Philosophiren anschickt, — seine Ursprünglichkeit zusichern? Wie will er denn erweisen, dass sein gegenwärtiges freies Denken mitten in der Reihe seiner Vorstellungen, dem nothwendigen Denken, wodurch er überhaupt für sich geworden, und wodurch die ganze Reihe dieser Vorstellungen, angeknüpft worden, entspreche? Ich antworte: diese Handlung ist ihrer Natur nach objectiv. Ich bin für mich; dies ist Factum. Nun kann ich mir nur durch ein Handeln zu Stande gekommen seyn, denn ich bin frei; und nur durch dieses bestimmte Handeln: denn durch dieses komme ich mir in jedem Augenblicke zu Stande, und durch jedes andere kommt mir etwas ganz anderes zu Stande. Jenes Handeln ist eben der Begriff des Ich, und der Begriff des Ich ist der Begriff jenes Handelns, beides ist ganz dasselbe; und es wird unter jenem Begriffe nichts anderes gedacht, und kann nichts anderes gedacht werden, als das angezeigte. *Es ist so,*—weil ich es *so mache.* Der Philosoph macht sich nur klar, was er eigentlich denkt und von jeher gedacht hat, wenn er *sich* denkt; dass er aber sich denke, ist ihm unmittelbares Factum des Bewusstseyns. — Jene Frage nach der Objectivität gründet sich auf die sonderbare Voraussetzung, dass das Ich noch etwas anderes sey, als sein eigener Gedanke von sich, und dass diesem Gedanken noch irgend etwas ausser dem Gedanken — Gott mag sie verstehen, was! — zu Grunde liege, über dessen eigentliche Beschaffenheit sie in Sorgen sind. Wenn sie nach einer solchen objectiven

The self, we say, reverts *into itself*. So is it not therefore already present for itself before the occurrence of this reversion, and independently thereof? Must it not already be there for itself, in order that it may make itself the object of an act? And if so, doesn't your philosophy in that case already presuppose what it was meant to explain?

I answer: Not at all. It is only through this act, and first by means of it, by an act upon an act itself, which specific act is preceded by no other whatever, that the self *originally* comes to exist for itself. Only *for the philosopher* is it there beforehand, as a fact, since he himself has already run through the whole course of experience. He is obliged to express himself as he does, if only to be understood; and is able so to express himself, because he has already long since acquired all the concepts that are needed for the purpose.

Now what – to look first at the self under observation – is this reversion it makes into itself; to what class of modifications of consciousness is it to be assigned? It is not a *conceiving*; this it only becomes by contrast with a not-self, and through determination of the self within this opposition. Hence it is a mere intuition. – It is also, accordingly, no consciousness, not even a consciousness of self; and simply because no consciousness comes about through this mere act, we may indeed infer further to another act, whereby a not-self arises for us; only so can we make progress in our philosophical argument, and derive as required the system of experience. By the act described, the self is merely endowed with the possibility of self-consciousness, and therewith of all other consciousness; but no true consciousness comes into being as yet. The act in question is merely a part, and a part not originally separated, but only to be distinguished by the philosopher, of that entire enterprise of the intellect, whereby it brings its consciousness into being.

How does it fare, on the other hand, with the philosopher as such?

This self-constructing self is none other than his own. He can intuit the aforementioned act of the self in himself only, and in order that he may intuit it, he has to carry it out. Freely, and by his own choice, he brings it about in himself.

But – it may be asked, and asked it has been – if this whole philosophy is erected on something brought about by an act of mere arbitrary choice, does it not thereby become a fancy of the brain, a mere fabrication? How then is the philosopher to ensure the objectivity of this purely subjective act? How is he to accord this primordial character to what is obviously empirical merely, and occurs at a time – the time when he sets about philosophizing. How is he to prove that this current free thought of his, in the middle of his series of presentations, corresponds to the necessary thought whereby he came to exist for himself at all, and which ties the whole sequence of these presentations together? I answer: This act is by its nature objective. That I exist for myself, is a fact. Now I can only have come about for myself through acting, for I am free; and through this particular act only; for by this I come about for myself at every instant, and by every other, something wholly different comes about for me. The act in question is simply the concept of the self, and the concept of the self is the concept of this act; both are exactly the same; and by means of this concept nothing else is thought, nor can be thought, save what we have referred to. It *is* so, because I *make* it so. The philosopher merely makes clear to himself what he actually thinks, and always has thought, when he thinks of *himself*; that he thinks of himself is, however, an immediate fact of consciousness for him. – The query about objectivity is based on the strange assumption that the self is something over and above its own thought of itself, and that this thought is underlaid by something else – Heaven knows what! – apart from the thought itself, and whose true nature is a matter of concern. If people wish to make inquiry

Gültigkeit des Gedankens, nach dem Bande zwischen diesem Objecte und dem Subjecte fragen, so gestehe ich, dass die Wissenschaftslehre hierüber keine Auskunft geben kann. Sie mögen selbst auf die Entdeckung dieses Bandes in diesem, oder in irgend einem Falle ausgehen; bis sie sich etwa besinnen, dass jenes unbekannte, was sie suchen, abermals ihr Gedanke, und das, was sie diesem Gedanken etwa wieder unterlegen werden, auch nur ihr Gedanke ist, und so ins unendliche; und dass sie überhaupt nach nichts fragen und von nichts reden können, ohne es eben zu denken.

In diesem Acte nun, der für den Philosophen, als solcher, willkürlich ist und in der Zeit, fur das Ich aber, das er sich, seinem soeben erwiesenen Rechte nach, dadurch für seine folgenden Beobachtungen und Schlüsse construirt, nothwendig und ursprünglich: — in diesem Acte, sage ich, sieht der Philosoph sich selbst zu, er schaut sein Handeln unmittelbar an, er weiss, was er thut, weil *er — es thut*.

Entsteht ihm denn nun hierin ein Bewusstseyn? Ohne Zweifel: denn er schaut nicht nur an, sondern er *begreift* auch. Er begreift seinen Act, als ein *Handeln überhaupt*, von welchem er zufolge seiner bisherigen Erfahrung schon einen Begriff hat; und als dieses *bestimmte, in sich zurückgehende Handeln*, wie er es in sich anschaut: er greift es durch diesen charakteristischen Unterschied aus der Sphäre des Handelns überhaupt heraus. — *Was* Handeln sey, lässt sich nur anschauen, nicht aus Begriffen entwickeln und durch Begriffe mittheilen; aber das in dieser Anschauung liegende wird begriffen durch den Gegensatz des blossen *Seyns*. Handeln ist kein Seyn, und Seyn ist kein Handeln; eine andere Bestimmung giebt es durch den blossen Begriff nicht; für das wahre Wesen muss man sich an die Anschauung wenden. [...]

5.

Dieses dem Philosophen angemuthete Anschauen seiner selbst im Vollziehen des Actes, wodurch ihm das Ich entsteht, nenne ich *intellectuelle Anschauung*. Sie ist das unmittelbare Bewusstseyn, dass ich handle, und was ich handle: sie ist das, wodurch ich etwas weiss, weil ich es thue. Dass es ein solches Vermögen der intellectuellen Anschauung gebe, lässt sich nicht durch Begriffe demonstriren, noch, was es sey, aus Begriffen entwickeln. Jeder muss es unmittelbar in sich selbst finden, oder er wird es nie kennen lernen. Die Forderung, man solle es ihm durch Raisonnement nachweisen, ist noch um vieles wunderbarer, als die Forderung eines Blindgeborenen seyn würde, dass man ihm, ohne dass er zu sehen brauche, erklären müsse, was die Farben seyen.

Wohl aber lässt sich jedem in seiner von ihm selbst zugestandenen Erfahrung nachweisen, dass diese intellectuelle Anschauung in jedem Momente seines Bewusstseyns vorkomme. Ich kann keinen Schritt thun, weder Hand noch Fuss bewegen, ohne die intellectuelle Anschauung meines Selbstbewusstseyns in diesen Handlungen; nur durch diese Anschauung weiss ich, dass ich es thue, nur durch diese unterscheide ich mein Handeln und in demselben mich, von dem vorgefundenen Objecte des Handelns. Jeder, der sich eine Thätigkeit zuschreibt, beruft sich auf diese Anschauung. In ihr ist die Quelle des Lebens, und ohne sie ist der Tod.

Nun aber kömmt diese Anschauung nie allein, als ein vollständiger Act des Bewusstseyns, vor; wie denn auch die sinnliche Anschauung nicht allein vorkommt, noch das Bewusstseyn vollendet, sondern beide müssen *begriffen* werden. Nicht aber allein dies, sondern die intellectuelle Anschauung ist auch stets mit einer *sinnlichen* verknüpft. Ich kann mich nicht handelnd finden, ohne ein Object zu finden, auf welches ich handle, in einer sinnlichen Anschauung, welche begriffen wird; ohne ein Bild von dem, was ich hervorbringen will, zu entwerfen, welches gleichfalls begriffen wird. Wie weiss ich denn nun, was ich hervorbringen will, und wie könnte

concerning such an objective validity of thought, or the bond between this object and the subject, I confess that the Science of Knowledge can give no information on the point. Let them set out on their own to discover such a bond, in this or any other case; until they bethink themselves, perhaps, that this unknown they are in search of is still their own thought, and that what they may again wish to lay beneath it is also merely a thought of theirs, and so on forever; and that they are wholly unable to inquire or to speak about anything, without in fact thinking of it.

In this act, then, which for the philosopher as such is arbitrary and temporal, but for the self is that which be necessarily and primarily constructs for himself, as by right now established, for the observations and inferences that are to follow – in this act, I say, the philosopher contemplates himself, scans his act directly, knows what he does, because *he – does* it.

Does, then, a consciousness arise for him therein? Undoubtedly; for he not only intuits, but also *conceives*. He conceives his act as an *acting in general*, of which he already has a concept in consequence of his previous experience; and as this *specific, self-reverting act*, as he intuits it in himself; by this characteristic difference he singles it out from the sphere of action in general. – What acting is, can only be intuited, not evolved from concepts or communicated thereby; but the import of this intuition is grasped by contrast with mere *being*. Acting is not being, and being is not acting; the mere concept furnishes no other determination; for the true nature of things, one must have recourse to intuition. [...]

5

This intuiting of himself that is required of the philosopher, in performing the act whereby the self arises for him. I refer to it as *intellectual intuition*. It is the immediate consciousness that I act, and what I enact; it is that whereby I know something because I do it. We cannot prove from concepts that this power of intellectual intuition exists, nor evolve from them what it may be. Everyone must discover it immediately in himself, or he will never make its acquaintance. The demand to have it proved for one by reasoning is vastly more extraordinary than would be the demand of a person born blind to have it explained to him what colors are, without his needing to see.

Everyone, to be sure, can be shown, in his own admitted experience, that this intellectual intuition occurs at every moment of his consciousness. I cannot take a step, move hand or foot, without an intellectual intuition of my self-consciousness in these acts; only so do I know that *I* do it, only so do I distinguish my action, and myself therein, from the object of action before me. Whosoever ascribes an activity to himself, appeals to this intuition. The source of life is contained therein, and without it there is death.

This intuition, however, never occurs in isolation, as a complete act of consciousness; any more than sensory intuition occurs singly or renders consciousness complete; for both must be *brought under concepts*. Nor is this all, indeed, for intellectual intuition is also constantly conjoined with an intuition of *sense*. I cannot find myself in action without discovering an object on which I act, in the form of a conceptualized sensory intuition; without projecting a picture, no less conceptual, of what I wish to bring about. For how do I know what I seek to accomplish, and how could I know this, without having an immediate regard to myself, in projecting the target-concept as an act? – Only this whole set of circumstances, in uniting the given manifold, completes the sphere of consciousness. It is

ich dies wissen, ausser dass ich mir im Entwerfen des Zweckbegriffes, als einem Handeln, unmittelbar zusehe? — Nur dieser ganze Zustand in Vereinigung des angegebenen Mannigfaltigen vollendet das Bewusstseyn. Nur der Begriffe, des vom Objecte, und des vom Zwecke, werde ich mir bewusst; nicht aber der beiden ihnen zum Grunde liegenden Anschauungen. [...]

Eine hiervon ganz unterschiedene Aufgabe ist es, diese intellektuelle Anschauung, die hier als Factum vorausgesetzt wird, ihrer *Möglichkeit* nach zu erklären, und sie durch diese Erklärung aus dem Systeme der gesammten Vernunft, gegen den Verdacht der Trüglichkeit und Täuschung zu vertheidigen, den sie durch ihren Widerstreit gegen die ebenfalls in der Vernunft gegründete dogmatische Denkart auf sich zieht; den *Glauben* an ihre Realität, von welchem der transcendentale *Idealismus* nach unserem eigenen ausdrüklichen Geständnisse allerdings ausgeht, durch etwas noch höheres zu bewähren, und das Interesse selbst, auf welches er sich gründet, in der Vernunft nachzuweisen. Dies geschieht nur lediglich durch Aufweisung des Sittengesetzes in uns, in welchem das Ich als etwas über alle ursprüngliche Modification durch dasselbe, Erhabenes vorgestellt, in welchem ihm ein absolutes, nur in ihm und schlechthin in nichts anderem begründetes Handeln angemuthet, und es sonach als ein absolut Thätiges charakterisirt wird. In dem Bewusstseyn dieses Gesetzes, welches doch wohl ohne Zweifel nicht ein aus etwas anderem gezogenes, sondern ein unmittelbares Bewusstseyn ist, ist die Anschauung der Selbstthätigkeit und Freiheit begründet; ich werde mir durch mich selbst als etwas, das auf eine gewisse Weise thätig seyn soll, gegeben, ich werde mir sonach durch mich selbst als thätig überhaupt gegeben; ich habe das Leben in mir selbst, und nehme es aus mir selbst. Nur durch dieses Medium des Sittengesetzes erblicke ich *mich;* und erblicke ich mich dadurch, so erblicke ich mich nothwendig als selbstthätig; und dadurch entsteht mir das ganz fremdartige Ingrediens der reellen Wirksamkeit meines Selbst in einem Bewusstseyn, das ausserdem nur das Bewusstseyn einer Folge meiner Vorstellungen seyn würde.

Diese intellektuelle Anschauung ist der einzige feste Standpunct für alle Philosophie. Von ihm aus lässt sich alles, was im Bewusstseyn vorkommt, erklären; aber auch nur von ihm aus. Ohne Selbstbewusstseyn ist überhaupt kein Bewusstseyn; das Selbstbewusstseyn ist aber nur möglich auf die angezeigte Weise: ich bin nur thätig. Von ihm aus kann ich nicht weiter getrieben werden; meine Philosophie wird hier ganz unabhängig von aller Willkür, und ein Product der eisernen Nothwendigkeit, inwiefern Nothwendigkeit für die freie Vernunft stattfindet; d. h. Product der *praktischen* Nothwendigkeit.

[1797] [*Philosophisches Journal, V (1797). S. 319–378*]

only the concepts of object and goal that I come to be aware of, however, not the two intuitions that underlie them.

It is a wholly different task to explain this intellectual intuition – here presupposed as fact – in terms of its *possibility*, and, by this deduction from the system of reason as a whole, to defend it against the suspicion of fallacy and delusion which it incurs by conflicting with the dogmatic mode of thought that is no less grounded in reason; to confirm on yet higher grounds the *belief* in its reality, from which, by our own express admission, transcendental idealism assuredly sets out, and to vindicate in reason even the interest on which it is based. This comes about solely by exhibition of the moral law in us, wherein the self is presented as a thing sublime beyond all original modifications effected by that law; is credited with an absolute activity founded only in itself and in nothing else whatever; and is thus characterized as an absolute agency. The consciousness of this law, which itself is doubtless an immediate consciousness derived from no other, forms the basis for the intuition of self-activity and freedom; I am given to myself, by myself, as something that is to be active in a certain fashion, and am thereby given to myself as active in general: I have life within me, and draw it from myself. Only through this medium of the moral law do I behold *myself*; and in thus seeing myself. I necessarily see myself as self-active; and thereby arises for me the wholly alien factor of my self's real efficacy, in a consciousness that would otherwise be merely that of a succession among my presentations.

Intellectual intuition is the only firm standpoint for all philosophy. From thence we can explain everything that occurs in consciousness; and moreover, only from thence. Without self-consciousness there is no consciousness whatever; but self-consciousness is possible only in the manner indicated: I am simply active. Beyond that I can be driven no further; here my philosophy becomes wholly independent of anything arbitrary, and a product of iron necessity, insofar as the free reason is subject to the latter; a product, that is, of *practical* necessity.

[*From J. G. Fichte. Science of Knowledge, with the First and Second Introductions. Edited and translated by Peter Heath and John Lachs. Cambridge: Cambridge UP, 1982. 29–41 (extracts)*]

II.e.3.   FRIEDRICH SCHLEGEL, aus *Lucinde*, 'Dithyrambische Phantasie über
die schönste Situation'

Eine große Träne fällt auf das heilige Blatt, welches ich hier statt Deiner fand. Wie treu und wie einfach hast Du ihn aufgezeichnet, den kühnen alten Gedanken zu meinem liebsten und geheimsten Vorhaben. In Dir ist er groß geworden, und in diesem Spiegel scheue ich mich nicht, mich selbst zu bewundern und zu lieben. Nur hier sehe ich mich ganz und harmonisch, oder vielmehr die volle ganze Menschheit in mir und in Dir. Denn auch Dein Geist steht bestimmt und vollendet vor mir; es sind nicht mehr Züge, die erscheinen und zerfließen: sondern wie eine von den Gestalten, die ewig dauern, blickt er mich aus hohen Augen freudig an und öffnet die Arme, den meinigen zu umschließen. Die flüchtigsten und heiligsten von jenen zarten Zügen und Äußerungen der Seele, die dem, welcher das Höchste nicht kennt, allein schon Seligkeit scheinen, sind nur die gemeinschaftliche Atmosphäre unsers geistigen Atmens und Lebens.

Die Worte sind matt und trübe; auch würde ich in diesem Gedränge von Erscheinungen nur immer das eine unerschöpfliche Gefühl unsrer ursprünglichen Harmonie von neuem wiederholen müssen. Eine große Zukunft winkt mich eilends weiter ins Unermeßliche hinaus, jede Idee öffnet ihren Schoß und entfaltet sich in unzählige neue Geburten. Die äußersten Enden der zügellosen Lust und der stillen Ahndung leben zugleich in mir. Ich erinnere mich an alles, auch an die Schmerzen, und alle meine ehemaligen und künftigen Gedanken regen sich und stehen wider mich auf. In den geschwollnen Adern tobt das wilde Blut, der Mund durstet nach Vereinigung, und unter den vielen Gestalten der Freude wählt und wechselt die Fantasie und findet keine, in der die Begierde sich endlich erfüllen und endlich Ruhe finden könnte. Und dann gedenke ich wieder plötzlich und rührend der dunkeln Zeit, da ich immer wartete, ohne zu hoffen, und heftig liebte, ohne daß ich es wußte; da mein innerstes Wesen sich ganz in unbestimmte Sehnsucht ergoß und sie nur selten in halb unterdrückten Seufzern aushauchte.

Ja! Ich würde es für ein Märchen gehalten haben, daß es solche Freude gebe und solche Liebe, wie ich nun fühle, und eine solche Frau, die mir zugleich die zärtlichste Geliebte und die beste Gesellschaft wäre und auch eine vollkommene Freundin. Denn in der Freundschaft besonders suchte ich alles, was ich entbehrte und was ich in keinem weiblichen Wesen zu finden hoffte. In Dir habe ich es alles gefunden und mehr, als ich zu wünschen vermochte: aber Du bist auch nicht wie die andern. Was Gewohnheit oder Eigensinn weiblich nennen, davon weißt Du nichts. Außer den kleinen Eigenheiten besteht die Weiblichkeit Deiner Seele bloß darin, daß Leben und Lieben für sie gleichviel bedeutet; Du fühlst alles ganz und unendlich, Du weißt von keinen Absonderungen, Dein Wesen ist eins und unteilbar. Darum bist Du so ernst und so freudig; darum nimmst Du alles so groß und so nachlässig, und darum liebst Du mich auch ganz und überläßt keinen Teil von mir etwa dem Staate, der Nachwelt oder den männlichen Freunden. Es gehört Dir alles, und wir sind uns überall die nächsten und verstehn uns am besten. Durch alle Stufen der Menschheit gehst Du mit mir, von der ausgelassensten Sinnlichkeit bis zur geistigsten Geistigkeit, und nur in Dir sah ich wahren Stolz und wahre weibliche Demut.

Das äußerste Leiden, wenn es uns nur umgäbe, ohne uns zu trennen, würde mir nichts scheinen als ein reizender Gegensatz für den hohen Leichtsinn unsrer Ehe. Warum sollten wir nicht die herbeste Laune des Zufalls für schönen Witz und ausgelassene Willkür nehmen, da wir unsterblich sind wie die Liebe? Ich kann nicht mehr sagen, meine Liebe oder Deine Liebe; beide sind sich gleich und vollkommen eins, soviel Liebe als Gegenliebe. Es ist Ehe, ewige Einheit und Verbindung unsrer Geister, nicht bloß für das, was wir diese oder jene Welt

II.e.3. FRIEDRICH SCHLEGEL, from *Lucinde,* 'A Dithyrambic Fantasy on the Loveliest Situation in the World'

A large tear falls on this sacred page that I've found here in place of you. How honestly and simply you've expressed the old, daring thought of my most cherished and secret intention. In you it's come to fruition and I'm not afraid to admire and love myself in such a mirror. Only here do I see myself complete and harmonious, or rather, see all of humanity in me and in you. For your spirit, too, stands well defined and perfected before me; no longer does it consist of features that appear and melt away. No: like one of those beings that live forever, your spirit looks at me joyfully through noble eyes and opens its arms to embrace me. The slightest and holiest of those fragile features and expressions of the soul that seem like bliss to those who don't know the greatest joy are merely the everyday atmosphere of our spiritual breath and life.

These words are dull and turbid. Still, amid this throng of impressions I can do no more than repeat and repeat forevermore the single inexhaustible feeling of our pristine harmony. A great future beckons me to rush deeper into infinity: every idea opens its womb and brings forth innumerable new births. The farthest reaches of unbridled lust and silent intimation exist simultaneously in me. I remember everything, even my sufferings, and all my former and future thoughts bestir themselves and arise against my will. Wild blood rages in my swollen arteries, my mouth thirsts for union, and my imagination, alternately choosing and, rejecting among the many forms of joy, finds none in which desire can finally fulfill itself and be at peace at last. And then I think suddenly and movingly again of that dark time when I was always waiting without hope, when I loved intensely without knowing it, when my inmost being was completely filled with an indeterminate yearning that was only seldom expressed in half-suppressed sighs.

Yes: I would have thought it a fairy tale that there could be such happiness and such love as I feel now – and such a woman, at once the most delicate lover, the most wonderful companion, and the most perfect friend. For in friendship particularly I sought for all that I lacked and didn't expect to find in any woman. In you I've found everything and even more than I could have hoped for; but, then, you're not like the others. You're untouched by the faults that custom and caprice call female. Aside from your little idiosyncrasies, the femininity of your soul consists simply in your making life and love synonymous. You feel completely and infinitely; you know of no separations; your being is one and indivisible. That is why you are so serious and so joyful. That is why you take every thing so solemnly and so negligently, and also why you love me completely and don't relinquish any part of me to the state, to posterity, or to my friends. Everything belongs to you, and we are in every respect closest to each other and understand each other best. You're at my side at every stage of human experience, from the most passionate sensuality to the most spiritual spirituality; and only in you have I seen true pride and true womanly modesty.

The most extreme sorrows, if they merely enveloped us and didn't separate us, would seem to me nothing more than a refreshing contrast to the sublime frivolity of our marriage. Why shouldn't we interpret the bitterest whim of chance as a lovely witticism and an exuberant caprice, since we, like love, are immortal? I can no longer say *my* love or *your* love: both are identical and perfectly united, as much love on one side as on the other. This is marriage, the timeless union and conjunction of our spirits, not simply for what we call this world or the world beyond death, but for the one, true, indivisible, nameless, unending world, for our whole eternal life and being. Therefore, if I thought the time had come, I'd drink a cup of poison with you just as gladly and easily as the last glass of champagne we drank together when I said: 'This

nennen, sondern für die eine, wahre, unteilbare, namenlose, unendliche Welt, für unser ganzes ewiges Sein und Leben. Darum würde ich auch, wenn es mir Zeit schiene, ebenso froh und ebenso leicht eine Tasse Kirschlorbeerwasser mit Dir ausleeren, wie das letzte Glas Champagner, was wir zusammen tranken, mit den Worten von mir: "So laß uns den Rest unsers Lebens austrinken." — So sprach und trank ich eilig, ehe der edelste Geist des Weins verschäumte; und so, das sage ich noch einmal, so laß uns leben und lieben. Ich weiß, auch Du würdest mich nicht überleben wollen, Du würdest dem voreiligen Gemahle auch im Sarge folgen und aus Lust und Liebe in den flammenden Abgrund steigen, in den ein rasendes Gesetz die indischen Frauen zwingt und die zartesten Heiligtümer der Willkür durch grobe Absicht und Befehl entweiht und zerstört.

Dort wird dann vielleicht die Sehnsucht voller befriedigt. Ich bin oft darüber erstaunt: jeder Gedanke und was sonst gebildet in uns ist, scheint in sich selbst vollendet, einzeln und unteilbar wie eine Person; eines verdrängt das andre, und was eben ganz nah und gegenwärtig war, sinkt bald in Dunkel zurück. Und dann gibt es doch wieder Augenblicke plötzlicher, allgemeiner Klarheit, wo mehrere solche Geister der innern Welt durch wunderbare Vermählung völlig in eins verschmelzen und manches schon vergessene Stück unsers Ich in neuem Lichte strahlt und auch die Nacht der Zukunft mit einem hellen Scheine öffnet. Wie im Kleinen, so, glaube ich, ist es auch im Großen. Was wir ein Leben nennen, ist für den ganzen ewigen innern Menschen nur ein einziger Gedanke, ein unteilbares Gefühl. Auch für ihn gibt's solche Augenblicke des tiefsten und vollsten Bewußtseins, wo ihm alle die Leben einfallen, sich anders mischen und trennen. Wir beide werden noch einst in Einem Geiste anschauen, daß wir Blüten Einer Pflanze oder Blätter Einer Blume sind, und mit Lächeln werden wir dann wissen, daß, was wir jetzt nur Hoffnung nennen, eigentlich Erinnerung war.

Weißt Du noch, wie der erste Keim dieses Gedankens vor Dir in meiner Seele aufsproßte und auch gleich in der Deinigen Wurzel faßte? — So schlingt die Religion der Liebe unsre Liebe immer inniger und stärker zusammen, wie das Kind die Lust der zärtlichen Eltern dem Echo gleich verdoppelt.

Nichts kann uns trennen, und gewiß würde jede Entfernung mich nur gewaltsamer an Dich reißen. Ich denke mir, wie ich bei der letzten Umarmung im Gedränge der heftigen Widersprüche zugleich in Tränen und in Lachen ausbreche. Dann würde ich still werden und in einer Art von Betäubung durchaus nicht glauben, daß ich von Dir entfernt sei, bis die neuen Gegenstände um mich her mich wider Willen überzeugten. Aber dann würde auch meine Sehnsucht unaufhaltsam wachsen, bis ich auf ihren Flügeln in Deine Arme sänke. Laß auch die Worte oder die Menschen ein Mißverständnis zwischen uns erregen! Der tiefe Schmerz würde flüchtig sein und sich bald in vollkommenere Harmonie auflösen. Ich würde ihn so wenig achten, wie die liebende Geliebte im Enthusiasmus der Wollust die kleine Verletzung achtet.

Wie könnte uns die Entfernung entfernen, da uns die Gegenwart selbst gleichsam zu gegenwärtig ist. Wir müssen ihre verzehrende Glut in Scherzen lindern und kühlen, und so ist uns die witzigste unter den Gestalten und Situationen der Freude auch die schönste. Eine unter allen ist die witzigste und die schönste: wenn wir die Rollen vertauschen und mit kindischer Lust wetteifern, wer den andern täuschender nachäffen kann, ob Dir die schonende Heftigkeit des Mannes besser gelingt oder mir die anziehende Hingebung des Weibes. Aber weißt Du wohl, daß dieses süße Spiel für mich noch ganz andre Reize hat als seine eignen? Es ist auch nicht bloß die Wollust der Ermattung oder das Vorgefühl der Rache. Ich sehe hier eine wunderbare, sinnreich bedeutende Allegorie auf die Vollendung des Männlichen und Weiblichen zur vollen, ganzen Menschheit. Es liegt viel darin, und was darin liegt, steht gewiß nicht so schnell auf wie ich, wenn ich Dir unterliege.

is how we should drain the rest of our life to the dregs.' Having uttered these words, I drank hurriedly before the noblest spirit of the wine could vanish; and so – I repeat once again – so let us live and love. I know that you wouldn't want to outlive me either. You too would follow your rash husband into the grave, and willingly and lovingly descend into the flaming abyss into which an insane law forces Indian women and, by its rude intention and command, desecrates and destroys freedom's most delicate shrines.

Perhaps yearning will be satisfied more fully there. I often marvel at that: every idea and whatever else is formed within us seems perfect in itself, as unique and indivisible as a person. One idea supplants the other and what just now seemed near and immediate soon vanishes again into obscurity. And yet then again, there are moments of sudden, universal clarity, when, through some miraculous marriage, several such spirits of the inner world fuse completely into one, when many a forgotten fragment of our Ego shines with a new light, illuminating with its bright radiance even the night of the future. The same is true, I think, on both small and large scales. What we call a life is for the complete, timeless, inner human being only a single idea, an indivisible feeling. For him too there are such moments of the deepest and most complete consciousness when all lives occur to him, combine in various ways, and then separate again. There will come a time when the two of us will perceive in a single spirit that we are blossoms of a single plant or petals of a single flower, and then we will know with a smile that what we now call merely hope is really remembrance.

Do you still remember how the first seed of this idea grew in my soul, and how it immediately took root in yours as well? So is it that the religion of love weaves our love ever more closely and tightly together, just as the child, echolike, redoubles the happiness of its tender parents.

Nothing can separate us and certainly every absence would only draw me more powerfully to you. I imagine how, in our final embrace, torn violently by conflicting emotions, I would break out simultaneously in tears and laughter. Then I would grow quiet and, in a kind of stupor, absolutely refuse to believe that I was away from you until my new surroundings would convince me against my will. But then irresistibly my yearning would also grow until, brought to you on its wings, I would sink into your arms. Let men or words try to bring misunderstanding between us! That deep pain would quickly ebb and soon resolve itself into a more perfect harmony. I'd pay as little attention to it as a woman in love does to the slight hurt she suffers in the heat of pleasure.

How could distance make us more distant, since for us the present is, as it were, too present? We have to lessen and cool the consuming fire with playful good humor, and therefore the wittiest of all the shapes and situations of happiness is for us also the loveliest. One above all is wittiest and most beautiful: when we exchange roles and in childish high spirits compete to see who can mimic the other more convincingly, whether you are better at imitating the protective intensity of the man, or I the appealing devotion of the woman. But are you aware that this sweet game still has quite other attractions for me than its own – and not simply the voluptuousness of exhaustion or the anticipation of revenge? I see here a wonderful, deeply meaningful allegory of the development of man and woman to full and complete humanity. There is much in it – and what is in it certainly doesn't rise up as quickly as I do when I am overcome by you.

That was my dithyrambic fantasy on the loveliest situation in the most beautiful world! I remember well how you received it at the time and what you thought of it. But I think I know just as well what your opinion of it will be when you run across it here in this little book in which you expected to find more faithful history, plain truth, calm reason, and, yes, even morality, the charming morality of love. 'How can you want to write what you should hardly talk about, what

Das war die dithyrambische Fantasie über die schönste Situation in der schönsten Welt! Ich weiß noch recht gut, wie Du sie damals gefunden und genommen hast. Aber ich glaube auch eben so gut zu wissen, wie Du sie hier finden und nehmen wirst, hier in diesem Büchelchen, von dem Du mehr treue Geschichte, schlichte Wahrheit und ruhigen Verstand, ja sogar Moral, die liebenswürdige Moral der Liebe erwartest. "Wie kann man schreiben wollen, was kaum zu sagen erlaubt ist, was man nur fühlen sollte?" — Ich antworte: Fühlt man es, so muß man es sagen wollen, und was man sagen will, darf man auch schreiben können.

Ich wollte Dir erst beweisen und begründen, es liege ursprünglich und wesentlich in der Natur des Mannes ein gewisser tölpelhafter Enthusiasmus, der gern mit allem Zarten und Heiligen herausplatzt, nicht selten über seinen eignen treuherzigen Eifer ungeschickterweise hinstürzt und mit einem Worte leicht bis zur Grobheit göttlich ist.

Durch diese Apologie wäre ich zwar gerettet, aber vielleicht nur auf Unkosten der Männlichkeit selbst: denn soviel ihr auch im einzelnen von dieser haltet, so habt ihr doch immer viel und vieles wider das Ganze der Gattung.

[1799] [*Edited by Ernst Behler. Paderborn, Munich, Vienna, Zürich: Schöningh, 1958. 10–13*]

f. MAGYAR

II.f.1. VÖRÖSMARTY MIHÁLY, *Az emberek*

I

Hallgassatok, ne szóljon a dal,
Most a világ beszél,
S megfagynak forró szárnyaikkal
A zápor és a szél,
Könyzápor, melyet bánat hajt,
Szél, melyet emberszív sóhajt.
Hiába minden: szellem, bűn, erény;
Nincsen remény!

II

Hallátok a mesét: a népnek
Atyái voltanak,
S amint atyáik vétkezének,
Ők úgy hullottanak:
A megmaradt nép fölsüvölt:
Törvényt! s a törvény újra ölt.
Bukott a jó, tombolt a gaz merény:
Nincsen remény!

you only should feel?' My answer: if you feel something, then you should want to tell it too, and what you want to tell, you should also be allowed to write.

First I wanted to demonstrate and prove to you that there is essentially and congenitally in the nature of the male a certain doltish enthusiasm that readily blurts out all sorts of delicate and holy things. It often stumbles over its own guileless zeal, and in a word, is godlike almost to grossness.

To be sure, I should be safe because of this apology, but perhaps only at the expense of my reputation for masculinity, for as highly as you women think of men in individual cases, you still hold a great many grudges against the species as a whole.

[1799] [*Translated by Peter Firchow. Minneapolis:*
U of Minnesota P, 1971. 46–50]

f. HUNGARIAN

II.f.1.   MIHÁLY VÖRÖSMARTY,[1] *On Mankind*

I

You wind, that sigh from doleful heart,
Your fiery wings be ice.
You flowing waters too, freeze hard,
You tears from grieving eyes.
Let now your sound no more be heard,
Of virtue, crime or wit no word;
Silent be all while Earth tells out its pain:
All hope is vain!

II

The tale's well known: Humanity
From Adam sprang full brave,
But as he sinned posterity
Went, like him, to the grave.
Those that came next, now wiser, willed:
'Let there be Law' – but Law too killed.
The virtuous fell while evil raged amain:
All hope is vain.

[1] Mihály Vörösmarty (1800–1855) poet, dramatist, editor and translator.

III

És jöttek a dicsők, hatalmas
Lábok törvény felett.
Volt munka: pusztított a vas!
S az ember kérkedett.
S midőn dicsői vesztenek,
Bújában egymást marta meg.
S a hír? villám az inség éjjelén:
Nincsen remény!

IV

És hosszu béke van s az ember
Rémítő szapora,
Talán hogy a dögvésznek egyszer
Dicsőbb legyen tora:
Sovár szemmel néz ég felé,
Mert hajh a föld! az nem övé,
Neki a föld még sírnak is kemény:
Nincsen remény!

V

Mi dús a föld, s emberkezek még
Dúsabbá teszik azt,
És mégis szerte dúl az inség
S rút szolgaság nyomaszt.
Így kell-e lenni? vagy ha nem,
Mért oly idős e gyötrelem?
Mi a kevés? erő vagy az erény?
Nincsen remény!

VI

Istentelen frígy van közötted,
Ész és rosz akarat!
A butaság dühét növeszted,
Hogy lázítson hadat.
S állat vagy ördög, düh vagy ész,
Bármelyik győz, az ember vész:
Ez őrült sár, ez istenarcu lény!
Nincsen remény!

VII

Az ember fáj a földnek; oly sok
Harc- s békeév után

III

Then came the men of might, who trod
The Law beneath their feet.
Man conquered iron, turned the sod;
Boundless was his conceit.
And when the mighty were no more
Man, in his anguish, turned to war.
In misery the word shone forth again:
All hope is vain.

IV

Then a long age of peace ensued;
Man mightily increased,
Although his numbers only grew
To spread 'fore plague a feast.
Man looks on Heaven with longing eyes,
For Earth his ownership denies;
E'en for a grave too hard is its terrain:
All hope is vain.

V

How bountiful, how rich the Earth,
Made richer by Man's flair!
Yet everywhere there still is dearth,
Oppression everywhere.
Must it be always thus? If no,
Why all this time has it been so?
Virtue and strength – can Man not these retain?
All hope is vain.

VI

An impious covenant has been made
'Twixt reason and despite!
Men rage and folly cultivate
To urge their armies fight.
Beast or devil, heart or head,
No matter which wins, men lie dead.
Made in the form of God? Clay gone insane!
All hope is vain!

VII

Man pains the Earth. After the train
Of years of peace and war

A testvérgyülölési átok
Virágzik homlokán;
S midőn azt hinnők, hogy tanúl,
Nagyobb bűnt forral álnokúl.
Az emberfaj sárkányfog-vetemény:
Nincsen remény! nincsen remény!

[*First published: Honderü, vol. 1, no. 18, May 1846. 342–343. Critical edition:*
Vörösmarty, Mihály, Vörösmarty Mihály összes művei, vol. 3,
Kisebb költemények 3, (1840–1855). Edited by Tóth, Dezső.
Budapest: Akadémiai, 1962. 145–147]

II.f.2. ERDÉLYI JÁNOS, *Egyéni és eszményi* (Részlet)

Mikor a művészetről úgy gondolkozunk, hogy az teremt, mint a természet, nem hiszünk egyebet által, mint analogonát a természet működésének. E tekintetben a természettudósok fognának bennünket eligazítani s tudományuk tekintélyével megnyugtatni, ha előadnák, miképp igyekszik a teremtő erő minden kis teremtményeiben új meg új tulajdonnal, sajátsággal különböztetni meg egyiket a másiktól. Látjuk ezt a lények úgynevezett országaiban, hol a nemek csak fajokban nyilatkoznak, sőt a fajoknak is tömérdek változata vagyon, például a zöld vagy vörös szín árnyéklatai. Ha megismerjük, hogy a művészeti formák őstípusai: a költői ritmus, a zene időmértéke, a festészet elevensége, a szobrok mintája a természetben nyilatkoznak először, s csak azután lesznek ismeretté, mely a természet példaadásával magunkból fejlett ki: miért ne mernénk azon módok vizsgálatába is ereszkedni, melyekkel a természet minden benne látható tüneménynek lételt ad. Itt az organizmus törvényét fedezzük föl, s azt mondjuk: minden életnek saját eleme és célja vagyon, még akkor is, ha nem találunk bennök egyebet, mint az ugyanazon alkotó elemeknek külön adagú vegyítését.

Hogy feladatunknál, mely a művészet, maradjunk, az emberi élet s különösen az ennek alapját tevő négy vérmérsék ugyanannyiféle vegyítékben nyilatkozik, amennyi az ember, s így a legkülönfélébb változatosságot állítja elő; és mivel az embert mint erkölcsi lényt magasabb tulajdonságok jegyzik, mint az állatot és növényt, mikor előáll az *egyed:* ő a fajtában nem pusztán fajt tenyész, hanem még a fajt is személyességig viszi, mikor előáll az *egyén.*

Ezen különváltságban és önállásban fogni fel és visszatükrözni költőnek az embert feladata, szerintünk, a művészetnek, legyen ez szóló vagy képző. Mások evvel csaknem átellenesen gondolkozván, nem engedik emez utolsó, feloszthatlan élő egységig menni a művészetet, hanem megállapodnak a fajnál vagy a nemnél, mikor így fejezik ki magokat, hogy a művészetnek egyénben a *nemet* kell előállítani, és ezt nevezik aztán idealizálásnak vagy *eszményítésnek.*

Az elmondott elvek után már az esztétikusok mindkét oldalon rendszert alkottak, és szorosan megvonták a határt a két rendszer között, úgyhogy egyik a másikba nem csaphat át végveszedelme nélkül, mert mint mondani szokták, csak egy kőnek kell kimozdulni az épületből, hogy utána romoljon az egész. Ezen rendszerek ugyan senkit nem tesznek költővé, de azt, ki már annak született, szabályozzák; így azoktól többet várni balság volna, mire nézve a két rendszer egyikének sincs elsősége a másik felett. Nem arról van tehát szó, miképp teremtsünk elő költőket; hanem arról, mi utat kell választani költőinknek, hogy költészetünk életrevaló legyen. A rendszer ekképp úgy tekintetik, mint a gondolkozó ész törvényeinek kényszerűsége,

Now too the ancient curse of Cain
Springs on its brow once more.
And when we think that Man will learn
To greater crime he'll basely turn,
Sow Cadmus' fateful dragon's teeth again.
All hope is vain! All hope is vain!

[*Translated by Bernard Adams with acknowledgement to Valerie Becker Makkai, Neville Master-man and Adam Makkai. See, In Quest of the 'Miracle Stag': The Poetry of Hungary. Edited by Adam Makkai. Chicago and Budapest, Atlantis-Centaur, M. Szivárvány and Corvina, 1996. 239–240, with the kind permission of Adam Makkai.*]

II.f.2.   JÁNOS ERDÉLYI,[2] from *Individual and Ideal*

When we think of Art as creating as does Nature, we mean by that nothing more than an analogy with the working of Nature. In that regard, the naturalist would seek to correct and disarm us with the authority of his science by expounding force endeavours in all its little creations to distinguish one from another by ever more properties and characteristics. This we can see in the so-called natural world, in which genera consist of species and species have large numbers of varieties, for example shades of green or red. If we recognise that the archetypes of artistic forms – poetic rhyme, musical rhythm, realism in painting and modelling in statuary – are first displayed in Nature and only subsequently become knowledge which Nature has brought out in us by its exam-ple: why should we not venture to engage in the examination of those means by which Nature gives rise to all the phenomena that may be observed in it? In so doing we discover the law of the organ-ism and say: every life-form has its own quintessence and purpose, even when we find nothing in it other than a mixture of the very same constituent elements in different proportions.

To keep to our subject, which is Art: human life, and in particular its four fundamental humours, appears in the same number of mixtures as there are men and thus produces the greatest number of varieties; and since Man, as a moral being, is characterised by higher proper-ties than animals and plants, when the *specific* is singled out it does not simply give rise to a species within a species but carries the species to the personal level, at which point the *individ-ual* comes into play.

To conceive of and reflect man in this separateness and independence is the task of the poet and, in our view, of art whether verbal or representational. Others see this in an almost entirely different light and do not permit Art to go as far as the ultimate, indivisible living unit, but stop at the species or genus, express the view that Art must represent the *genus* in an individual, and then call that *idealisation*.

On these principles aestheticians have devised systems on both sides and have clearly delineated the boundary between the two, so that the one may not trespass upon the other without extreme danger because, as the saying goes, only one stone need be removed from a building for the whole to collapse. Although these systems make no one a poet, they do regulate him that is born one; it would be a mistake to expect more of them, and so neither system is superior to the other. The issue is not, therefore, how we are to create poets; but what direction we are to choose for our poets, that our poetry may be viable. A system is thus seen as a necessary consequence of an enquiring mind,

---

[2] János Erdélyi (1814–1868), poet, critic and philosopher.

miért, ha egyszer kifejtők mindkettőt, csak úgy lehet megnyugodni egyik vagy másikban, amint tételeik az elv egyszerűségétől kezdve minden részleteken át szigorúan, kimozdíthatatlanul egybefüggenek, de szigorú egybefüggésök is akkor lesz minden becsre méltó, ha gyakorlatban kivihető leszen, vagy ha szerencsére minél nagyobb költőkben látjuk azt megtestesítve.

Két elv és rendszer van eszerint szóban: *egyéniség* és *eszményiség*. Az egyéniség védelme az ismereten alapszik, vagyis a képzelődő erőhöz még egy más erőt társítunk, az ismerőt, mely szükséges föltételül szabja, hogy tárgyával a költő legszorosabban tartozik megbarátkozni, azaz megtudni annak állandó és múló, tehát szükséges és esetleges jegyeit. Ezen lépés megszerzi költőnek a felfogás helyességét, azaz segíti felfogni tárgyát annak természete, belsője szerint úgy, amint más tárgy fel nem fogható, csak éppen az. Mihelyt ezen független különbségben áll előttünk vásznon vagy szoborban vagy költeményben valami, akkor elmondhatjuk s elmondjuk, hogy az egyénileg van felfogva, egyszersmind jellemzetesnek, valódinak, életrevalónak hisszük azt, mert az élet más forma alatt nem jelenhetik meg, mint egyénileg. Mi tehát magából a belső természetéből szeretjük kifejteni a művészeti tárgyat, s a költő ismeretét nem kitűzött elv szigora után óhajtjuk tökéletesíttetni, melyet ha egyszer elismertünk, kivétel nélkül kell alkalmaznunk minden alfogalomra: hanem minden új tárgyhoz, úgyszólván, külön új tanulmányt kívánunk, mert csak így lehet az egyféle eszmét vagy tárgyat is a külön egyéniségben előtüntetni mikép Shakespeare a cselszövő gazembert III. Richard, Edmund és Jago képében anélkül, hogy egyik gazember a másikat is eszünkbe juttatná. Tehát különbséget kell tenni a dolgokban létező tulajdonok és a mi fejünk fogalmainak tulajdonságai között, mert a fogalom, például a gazember fogalma, rendesen úgy van szerkesztve, hogy az minden olyanra ráillik; de az megint az élet és az egyéniség kényszerűségében áll, hogy külön-külön minden gazembernek van valami éltető jele, mely által egymástól különböznek, holott a fogalomnál fogva mindnyájan egyenlők s ugyanazok, mert egy a mérték. Hibáznak azért, kik az egyéniség fogalmát igen anyaginak hiszik, mert mi nem kívánunk egyebet, mint eszméhez éppen a neki és nem egyszersmind másnak is való öltözetet, mennyi alatt életében megjelenhetik az, s állításunk egyre megy a természettudósok azon tételével: minden test olyan nagy, minő a teriméje[3] (volumen); szerintünk pedig minden költői eszme annyit ér, mennyi testet elbír. Tehát gondolataink folyvást a szellem és anyag összhangzása körül forognak, s egyiket a másik fölött éppen úgy nem akarják túlnyomóvá tenni, mint a fizikai test nem terjedhet túl teriméje határain, de viszont kisebb sem lehet annál. Az anyagiság vádja egyedül csak akkor volt érvényes, mikor a régi iskola szerint a *természet utánzása* mondatott főelvül, mivel az utánzás csak külsőre terjedhet, az pedig az anyag; mi ellenben az *eszményiségre* a szellemiség túlnyomásának vádját hisszük jogosan illőnek, melynél fogva gondolkozás útján készített fogalom szerint állíttatik elő az ember; s éppen e két szélsőség túlságait kerülőleg fogadnók el az egyéniség elvét, hol, mint láttuk, nem a kettő (szellemi és anyagi) közül egyiknek vagy másiknak felülkerekedése, hanem éppen a kettőnek lelkes test alakjában együvé engesztelése minden törekvésünk, mi a forma és tartalom korreszpondenciája.

Meg kell annálfogva mondanunk, hogy nem hisszük életrevalónak, vagyis egyénben megjelenhetőnek az elvontat, s nem hisszük szerencsés eljárásnak költészetben a mintául felállított elvemberek típusát, s pedig azért nem, mivel az előbb-utóbb modort idéz elő a változatosság legkisebb játéka nélkül, mikor aztán költészeti ember úgy készül, mint a lábbeli – kapta után.

---

[3] térfogata

for which reason, once both have been elaborated, it is possible to submit to one or the other, as their theses, from simplicity of principle through all details, are strictly, unshakeably, closely related, but even their strict, close relationship will only be of value if it can be put into effect or if we have the good fortune to see it embodied in the greatest possible poets.

Accordingly, there are two principles and two systems, termed *individuality* and *idealisation*. The defence of individuality is based on awareness, that is, we associate with the power of imagination another power, that of learning, which makes it a necessary condition that the poet be intimately acquainted with his subject, that is, he must discover its permanent and impermanent, and therefore necessary and fortuitous manifestations. That step will gain for the poet soundness of perception, that is, will help him to conceive of his subject by virtue of its nature and essence in a way that no other subject can be conceived of, but only it. As soon as something stands before us in this independent dissimilarity, be it on canvas, in a statue or in a poem, then we can and do say that it has been individually conceived, and we believe it to be at the same time characteristic, authentic and viable because life cannot appear in any form other than the individual. We therefore like to set out the object of Art by its innermost nature, and do not wish to improve the awareness of the poet by the rigour of a set principle which, once we have recognised it, we shall have to apply to every fundamental idea sub-principle without exception: but we desire, so to speak, a separate new approach to every new subject, because only in this way is it possible for concepts or objects of the same kind to be portrayed in distinct individuality, as Shakespeare portrays the scheming villain in the guise of Richard III, Edmund and Iago, without any of the three bringing to mind the others. A distinction has therefore to be made between the properties actually inherent in things and those attributed to them in our mentally held concepts, because a concept – for example, that of the villain – is commonly so contrived as to fit all such; but again, life and individuality make it necessary for each and every separate villain to have some vital mark by which he is distinguished from all others, whereas according to the concept they are all equal and identical, for there is a single pattern. They are in error, therefore, that hold that the concept of individuality is simply material, because we ask for nothing but that a concept be clothed in a manner that fits only it and not another at the same time, as it appears in real life, and our statement agrees with the naturalist's thesis: every body is as large as its measurements (volumen); we believe, however, that every poetic concept is worth as much as the amount of body that it can bear. Our thoughts, therefore, revolve constantly around the consonance of mind and matter, and have no desire to make the one prevail over the other, as the physical body cannot extend beyond the limits of its measurements, but likewise neither can it be smaller than them. The accusation of materialism was only valid when what the old school termed *imitation of Nature* was stated as a main principle, as imitation can only have an outward extension, and that a material one; we, on the contrary, hold that the accusation of overweening intellectuality is justly levelled at *abstraction*, by virtue of which Man is the product of a concept formulated by mental process; and we would adopt, as avoiding the excesses of these two extremes, the principle of individuality, in which, as we have seen, our sole interest lies not in the achievement of superiority by either of the two (the intellectual or the material), but in the reconciliation of the two in the shape of a body that has a soul, the concord of form and content.

Therefore we must say that we do not consider the abstract viable, that is, capable of appearing in an individual, nor do we consider the type of principle-men set up as patterns in poetry to be a happy development, because sooner or later this would give rise to a fashion without the least pretence at variation, when later men in poetry were made like pairs of boots – on a last.

Ezt lehet észrevenni költők- s művészeken egyformán, ha ezen útra térnek, s műveiken örökleg megtetszik a mérték, a mindenkire illő s ugyanazért senkit különösen nem jelölő általány, mi egyhangúságot szül, s unalomba ejt. – De hogy elleneink gondolatát az anyagiság vádjára nézve megtéríthessük, csak azt kérdezzük: anyagiság-e az, mikor mi, úgyszólván, minden tárgynak a lényegét keressük, s éppen külsőleg is akarjuk láttatni ezt? A kőhöz például általánosan a keménység képzetét párosítjuk, azért minden kövön, mely ecset alól kijő, látni óhajtjuk a neki való keménységet. Így vagyunk az arcképekkel; s mint kinek-kinek vonásain látjuk a belsőt, úgy óhajtjuk szintén akkor is, ha leföstetik az; így akarunk lelket, magát a belső embert hallani a költői szóban, hogy az magát mondja s tárja fel előttünk szíve legtitkosabb redőiig; és az egyéniség fogalmát nem csak szóra, hanem az abból fejlő cselekvényre is átvisszük pedig, s akarjuk, hogy ami drámában cselekvényi jelenetként előfordul, soha ne történhessék meg más körülmények között és föltételek alatt, mint éppen ott, hol azt a kellet[4] kényszerűsége parancsolja, s a jelen lélekállapot előhozza; sőt elérni véljük általa még ama dicsőségét is az előadásnak, melyért Schiller úgy felmagasztalá Shakespeare-t,

„Was er weise verschweigt, zeigt mir den Meister des Styls"[5]

mert a ki nem mondottat a költő elhallgatása mellett egyedül úgy érthetni meg, ha olyan egyéni körülmények közé van téve a hallgató lelke, melyek között csak az mondathatik, ami el van mondva, mikor az is értve lesz, ami elhallgattatik. Ez nem anyagiság, mint a természet utánzásából eredni szokott, nem is túlnyomólag szellemi, miképp az eszményiség útján megtörténhető. Itt a testen lélek, a lelken test vagyon, egyik a másikat magyarázza, s minden dolog, minden tárgy úgy szól hozzánk művészetből, mintha természetben, az életben volna; tehát nem a puszta természet meglelése, hanem az életnek test és lélek összeforrtában fölfedezett állapota, mely úgy ment a szélsőségek kicsapongásaitól, mint az előttünk megjelenő ember, ki sem test, sem lélek külön, hanem a kettő együtt.

[*János Erdélyi and Imre Henszlmann anonymously published a series of articles titled Egyéni és eszményi (Individual and Ideal) of which the second written by Erdélyi has been republished in this volume. First published: Magyar Szépirodalmi Szemle, vol. 2, no. 7, 15 August. 97–100. Annotated edition: Erdélyi, János, Filozófiai és esztétikai írások. Edited by Erdélyi, T. Ilona. Budapest: Akadémiai, 1981. 580–582.*]

II.f.3.   ARANY JÁNOS, Az örök zsidó

Pihenni már. – Nem, nem lehet:
Vész és vihar hajt engemet,
Alattam a föld nem szilárd,
Fejem fölött kétélü bárd ...
  Tovább! tovább!

Az út, hová talpam nyomul,
Sűlyed, ropog, átvékonyul;
Ónsúllyal a kolosszi lég
Elzúzna, ha megállanék ...
  Tovább! tovább!

---

[4] szükségszerűség
[5] Amit bölcsen elhallgat, az mutatja nekem a stílus mesterét. (Schiller, Der Meister [A mester])

That can be observed in poets and artists alike if they take that road, and the standard is always to be found in their works, a generalisation suitable for all and for that reason not signifying anyone in particular, which gives rise to monotony and leads to boredom. – In order, however, to be able to counter our opponents' thoughts of the charge of materialism, we need only ask: is it materialism when we, so to speak, seek the essence of every object and precisely wish to make it outwardly visible? For example, we generally associate with stone the idea of hardness, and so in every stone that comes from the painter's brush we desire to see the hardness appropriate to it. We are the same with portraits; as we see the inner man in the features of each, so we desire to see him when he is painted; thus we wish to hear in the words of a poet a soul, the inner man, speaking and revealing himself to us in the most secret recesses of his heart; and we carry over the concept of individuality not only to speech but also to the action that derives from it, and we wish that it should never be possible for what transpires in the scenes of action in a drama to happen under circumstances and conditions other than where the force of necessity commands it and the present frame of mind proposes; indeed, we believe that thereby even that glory of exposition for which Schiller extolled Shakespeare would be attained:

Was er weise verschweigt, zeigt mir den Meister des Styls[6]

because it is possible to understand what remains unsaid in a poet's silence if the soul of the hearer is made privy to individual circumstances under which only that may be said which has been said, and when that also will be understood which remains unsaid. That is not materialism such as derives from the imitation of Nature, nor is it excessively intellectual, as is that which may occur through idealisation. Here there is soul in body and body in soul, the one accounts for the other, and every act, every object, speaks to us through Art as if it were natural, alive; it is not, therefore, the discovery of Nature alone, but the condition revealed in life's knitting together body and soul which saves us from the excesses of extremity, like the man that we see before us, who is neither body nor soul separately, but both together.

[Translated by Bernard Adams]

II.f.3. JÁNOS ARANY, *The Wandering Jew*[7]

I need to rest. But no time yet.
Propelled by conflict and regret,
On unfirm ground I lay my tracks,
Above my head a two-edged axe . . .
    Move on! Move on!

The road on which my feet press down
Begins to crack, so thin it's grown.
The air would crush me with lead weight
If ever I should hesitate . . .
    Move on! Move on!

---

[6] What he cleverly leaves unsaid reveals to me the master of style. (Schiller, *Der Meiter* [The Master])
[7] There are many variants of the legend of the Wandering Jew, who insulted Jesus during his suffering. Later he was cursed to wander around the earth until the last judgement.

Rettent a perc, a létező,
S teher minden következő;
Új léptem új kigyón tapod:
Gyülőlöm a mát s holnapot ...
    Tovább! tovább!

Éhes vagyok: ennem iszony;
Láng az ital, midőn iszom;
Álmam szilaj fölrettenés,
Kárpit megől szivembe kés ...
    Tovább! tovább!

S melyet hazud a sivatag,
Mint délibáb: tó és patak;
Gyümölcs unszol, friss balzsamu:
Kivűl arany, belűl hamu ...
    Tovább! tovább!

Rohannom kell – s a földi boly
Mellettem gyorsan visszafoly:
Ködfátyol-kép az emberek:
Én egy arcot sem ismerek ...
    Tovább! tovább!

Oh, mily tömeg! s én egyedűl,
Útam habár közé vegyül:
Érzem, mint csónak a habot,
Hogy átmenet mind rám csapott ...
    Tovább! tovább!

Az üstökös meg' visszatér,
Kiröppent nyíl oda is ér,
Az eldobott kő megpihen:
Én céltalan, én szüntelen
    Tovább! tovább!

Pusztán folyam mért nem vagyok,
Hogy inna fel aszú homok!
Mért nem futó, veszett vihar,
Mely ormokon egyszer kihal ...
    Tovább! tovább!

Irígylem az ágról szakadt
Levélkét: hisz majd fennakad;
Irígylem az ördögszekért:

The present moment scares me so.
The future's load will bend me low.
On snakes I'm stepping all the way.
I hate tomorrow and today . . .
    Move on! Move on!

I'm hungry, but it hurts to eat.
A cool drink burns me with its heat.
I sleep, but wake up with a start
On dreaming knife-blades pierce my heart . . .
    Move on! Move on!

The desert throws up visions fake:
A babbling stream, a sparkling lake,
And golden fruit with outside fresh,
But full of ash instead of flesh . . .
    Move on! Move on!

I'm forced to run – the other folks
All run the other way in flocks.
They gather like a foggy cloud.
I know not one face in the crowd . . .
    Move on! Move on!

What is this mob that's all around,
Through whom on lonely path I'm bound?
I'm like a boat by all waves tossed.
From each change, I'm the one who's lost . . .
    Move on! Move on!

A comet comes at intervals.
An arrow to its target falls.
A thrown rock won't forever roll.
My journey's constant, with no goal . . .
    Move on! Move on!

Why couldn't I just be a stream,
To wet parched sands along my seam?
Why not a thunderstorm, which raves,
But soon dies out in mountain caves?
    Move on! Move on!

How lucky are the leaves that drop:
There's always someplace where they stop.
How lucky is the tumbleweed –

Árokba hull: céljához ért ...
Tovább! tovább!

Szegény zsidó ... Szegény szivem:
Elébb-utóbb majd megpihen.
Az irgalom nagy és örök,
Megszán s átkom nem mennydörög:
Tovább! tovább!

[*First published: Szépirodalmi Figyelő, vol. 1, no. 4, 28 November 1860.*
Critical edition: Arany, János, Arany János összes művei, vol. 1,
Kisebb költemények. Edited by Voinovich, Géza. Budapest:
Akadémiai, 1951. 296–297]

g. ITALIANO

II.g.1.   GIACOMO LEOPARDI, 'A Se Stesso'

Or poserai per sempre,
Stanco mio cor. Perì l'inganno estremo,
Ch'eterno io mi credei. Perì. Ben sento,
In noi di cari inganni,
Non che la speme, il desiderio è spento.
Posa per sempre. Assai
Palpitasti. Non val cosa nessuna
I moti tuoi, nè di sospiri è degna
La terra. Amaro e noia
La vita, altro mai nulla; e fango è il mondo.
T'acqueta omai. Dispera
L'ultima volta. Al gener nostro il fato
Non donò che il morire. Omai disprezza
Te, la natura, il brutto
Poter che, ascoso, a comun danno impera,
E l'infinita vanità del tutto.

(c. 1835) [*In Giacomo Leopardi, Canti, a cura di Giuseppe e Domenico*
De Robertis. Milano: Oscar Studio Mondadori, 1978]

It finds a ditch in which to seed . . .
    Move on! Move on!

Poor wand'ring Jew: within my breast
Resides a heart which yearns for rest.
Some mercy one day might be found,
And nevermore my curse will sound:
    Move on! Move on!

[Translated by David Hill]

g.   ITALIAN

II.g.1.   GIACOMO LEOPARDI, 'To himself'

Now you will rest forever
My weary heart. The extreme deceit perished
That I thought myself eternal. Perished. I truly feel
Not the hope, but the desire in us
For dear deceits, is dead.
Left forever. Much
You throbbed. Worthless your impulses,
Undeserving of sighs
Is the earth. Bitter and burdensome
Is life, never anything else and the world is mud.
Now be calm. Despair
A final time. To our people fate
Gave only death. Now despise
Yourself, nature, the ugly
Power which, hidden, stands over common damage
And the infinite futility of all.

(c. 1835) *[Translated by Anne O'Connor]*

II.g.2.   GIACOMO LEOPARDI, 'L'infinito'

Sempre caro mi fu quest'ermo colle,
E questa siepe, che da tanta parte
Dell'ultimo orizzonte il guardo esclude.
Ma sedendo e mirando, interminati
Spazi di là da quella, e sovrumani
Silenzi, e profondissima quiete
Io nel pensier mi fingo; ove per poco
Il cor non si spaura. E come il vento
Odo stormir tra queste piante, io quello
Infinito silenzio a questa voce
Vo comparando: e mi sovvien l'eterno,
E le morte stagioni, e la presente
E viva, e il suon di lei. Così tra questa
Immensità s'annega il pensier mio:
E il naufragar m'è dolce in questo mare.

(1819) [*In Giacomo Leopardi, Canti, a cura di Giuseppe e Domenico
De Robertis. Milano: Oscar Studio Mondadori, 1978*]

h.   NORSK

II.h.1.   HENRIK WERGELAND, 'Den første Omfavnelse'

Kommer nu Sorger! knuger mit Bryst
at det ei sprænges af jublende Lyst!
Himmel! med Uheld, Helved! med Qvaler
tæmmer dets Bølger! Thi der har hun hvilt!
    Fiendenag
aabne dets Aarer! Din Piilodd kun svaler.
    Thi ved dets Slag
har hun jo zittret og smilt.

Sorgen har tabt sin Tyngde og Magt,
hvor hendes yndige Aasyn har lagt.
Sank hun den ned i sit svømmende Øje?
Drak hun dens Gift med sin Mund? Thi jeg saae
    Vemodets Smiil
bævende Skygger om Læben at bøje;
    dunklere blaa
sværmede Øjnenes Ild.

Du har forsont, uskyldige Brud,
Sjelen med Verden, Blodet med Gud;
Den gang din hellige Pande du sænkte,

II.g.2. GIACOMO LEOPARDI, 'The infinite'

This lonely hill was always dear to me
And this hedge which hides
So much of this far horizon from my view.
But sitting and gazing, endless
Spaces beyond, and unearthly
Silences and deepest peace
I imagine in my mind, and my heart
Is close to fear. And as I hear the wind
Rustling among these plants, I compare
That infinite silence to this voice
And I am reminded of the eternal,
And the dead seasons and the present one
Alive, the sound of it. Thus in this
Immensity my thought is drowned:
And sinking in this sea is dear to me.

[1819] [*Translated by Anne O'Connor*]

h. NORWEGIAN

II.h.1. HENRIK WERGELAND, 'The First Embrace'

Come to me, grief, on my bosom press,
Lest it should burst with joy's excess:
Heaven, with disaster, hell, with your pains,
Calm its commotion. For here awhile
   She has lain. Strike, foes!
Your shafts but soothe, when they pierce the veins
   Of a breast that glows
With the bliss of her thrill and her smile.

Sorrow and trouble have died away
Here, where her face in its loveliness lay.
Drowned she these in the deep of her eye?
Or sucked she their venom? I seemed to mark,
   On her smiling lips,
How a tremulous shadow of pain passed by:
   And the blue grew dark,
As her eyes' light found eclipse.

Innocent bride, thou hast joined afresh
Soul with earth, and with God the flesh.
When on my breast, as pure and bright

straalreen som Naadens skinnende Lin,
    over mit Bryst,
borttog du Synden, den taarebestænkte.
    Nu er mit Sind
reent som et Tempel og lyst.

Rødmende Uskyld speilte Du ind,
Brud, i mit Bryst med jomfruelig Kind.
Hviftet af himmelske Due fornemmed
jeg i den Lok, som omsvævede mig.
    Hil mig, min Geist,
forhen dæmonisk, for Himmelen fremmed,
    er nu ved Dig,
Elskede, hellig gjenreist!

Der, hvor din Læbe rørte mit Bryst,
indenfor blev det glorielyst.
Kjærlighedshymner derinde fremsprunge
under dit sandsløse, drømmende Kys.
    Sødmen deri
drak Fantasien med glødende Tunge.
    Styrke og Lys
Skjænkte det Ømheds Geni.

Den gang du laa ved mit Hjerte, min Brud,
var det som Blomster sprang derifra ud:
Blomster, som levte, drømte og tænkte.
Mandel og Abild ei vajer saa fuld.
    Solen sit Blod
ikke saa rig over Roserne sprængte.
    Sjelen sit Muld
drømmende saligt forlod.

Fjern dig, min Sjel, du mørkblaa Seraf!
Eller en Stund i mit Blod dig begrav!
Herskende lad det rulle saa længe!
Nerven lad aabne sin zittrende Mund!
    Samling berøvt
høre du opfyldt med tonende Strenge
    Brystet, hvor Hun
hvilede elskovsbedøvt.

*[This poem was addressed to his young wife, and was
first printed in Poesier, 1838]*

As a saint's white robe, thy perfect brow
   Gently was lain,
Guilt with its tear-steins vanished quite,
   And my mind is now
Like a cleansed and lighted fane.

My heart reflected an inward grace
From the sinless blush of thy maiden face:
To the waft of celestial wings was changed
The tress that wavered over me;
   And, O joy, my soul,
Demoniac once, from heaven estranged,
   Is, thanks to thee,
Darling, restored and whole.

I feel, where thy loving lips have pressed
A glory shining within my breast,
And O, the paeans of love that burst,
At the touch of thy passionless, drowsy kiss.
   I was fired and manned, –
While my fancy drank with a burning thirst
   All the sweet of this
By a tender angel's hand.

Love, while you lay by my beating heart,
What burgeoning blossoms seemed to start!
Blossoms that lived, and dreamed, and thought.
Almond or apple was never so gay;
   So rich a stream
Of the sun's blood never the roses caught.
   My soul its clay
Left in a blissful dram.

Cold, dark spirit, hold thee apart,
Or blend with the blood that stirs my heart;
Let it flow supreme in its pulses still,
Let nerves aquiver their passion prove,
   And in ecstasy
Hark to the breast's tense chords athrill,
   Where, tranced in love,
She late at rest did lie.

     [1838] [*Translated by G. M. Gathorne-Hardy. Oslo: Gyldendal norsk forlag, 1960*]

II.h.2.   JOHAN S. C. WELHAVEN, 'Den Salige'

O, vær hilset atter og velsignet
blide Aand, fra Salighedens Hjem!
Ingen Glæde paa min Vei har lignet
den, du kaldte af min Vaardrøm frem;
ingen Kval kan falde paa mit Hjerte
tungt som den, du klaged i min Favn.
O, du Salige, i Fryd og Smerte
har min Sjel en Gjenlyd af dit Navn.

Alt er følt, fuldkommet og erindret,
Alt fornyes evig i mit Sind;
mildt og ømt har Sorgen, der er lindret,
spredet Mindets Fred om mine Trin.
Sorgen vaaged hvor din Aske blunder,
og den vandred gjennem Ørkner hen,
og tilsidst ved Kjerlighedens Under,
fik jeg dig du Salige igjen.

Og da kom du fra de stille Lande,
og den lange Sørgenat blev klar,
klar ved Skinnet om din rene Pande
og ved Straalen, som dit Øie har;
og paany din Salighed er over
mine Drømme som et Lysets Bad,
og jeg hører atter hva du lover,
at vi aldrig mer skal skilles ad.

*[1848, this poem was dedicated to the memory of the
poet's fiancée, who died in 1840]*

i.   POLSKI

II.i.1.   ADAM MICKIEWICZ, from *Dziady*, Scene ii

IMPROWIZACJA

Konrad
(po długim milczeniu)

Samotność – cóż po ludziach, czym śpiewak dla ludzi?
Gdzie człowiek, co z mej pieśni całą myśl wysłucha,
Obejmie okiem wszystkie promienie jej ducha?
Nieszczęsny, kto dla ludzi głos i język trudzi:
Język kłamie głosowi, a głos myślom kłamie;
A słowa myśl pochłoną i tak drżą nad myślą,
Myśl z duszy leci bystro, nim się w słowach złamie,
Jak ziemia nad połkniętą, niewidzialną rzeką:

II.h.2. JOHAN S. C. WELHAVEN, 'My Saint'

Welcome, spirit borne on wings of rapture
From thy sacred dwelling-place above!
Never on life's road could I recapture
Joys like those we shared in youthful love.
Never knew my heart a pang as bitter
As the agony of thy distress,
O my saint, and never music sweeter
Than thy name in grief or happiness.

Thou art with me in thy hallowed semblance,
Bringing to my thoughts a glad release;
And my mourning, softened by remembrance,
Is a pathway to the realms of peace.
Sorrow slept not, but in desolation
Wandered through the wilderness of pain,
Till at last by love's transfiguration
Lo! I have thee, dearest, once again.

From the silent lands thou'rt wafted now, love,
And a glory shines in sorrow's night
From the radiance of thy perfect brow, love,
And thine eyes, that stream with purest light.
And I feel thy holy influence welling
Round my dreams as once in days of yore,
And again I hear thy promise, telling
That we never shall be parted more.

[1848] [*Translated by C. Wharton Stork. Princeton: Princeton UP, 1942*]

i.   POLISH

II.i.1.   ADAM MICKIEWICZ, from *Forefathers Eve*, Scene ii

THE IMPROVISATION

Konrad
(After a long silence)

Alone – what's the use of people, what's a bard to them?
Where is he who will hear out the full sense of my song,
Who will see all the rays that from its spirit stem?
How wretched he whose voice and tongue strain for a throng:
The tongue belies the voice, while the voice belies the thought;
Thoughts fly from the soul swiftly, till in words they are caught,
And the words engulf thoughts and tremble over them,
As does the earth over a swallowed, unseen river.

Z drżenia ziemi czyż ludzie głąb nurtu docieką,
Gdzie pędzi, czy się domyślą? –

Uczucie krąży w duszy, rozpala się, żarzy,
Jak krew po swych głębokich, niewidomych cieśniach;
Ile krwi tylko ludzie widzą w mojej twarzy,
Tyle tylko z mych uczuć dostrzegą w mych pieśniach.

Pieśni ma, tyś jest gwiazdą za granicą świata!
I wzrok ziemski, do ciebie wysłany za gońca,
Choć szklanne weźmie skrzydła, ciebie nie dolata,
Tylko o twoję mleczną drogę się uderzy;
Domyśla się, że to słońca,
Lecz ich nie zliczy, nie zmierzy.

Wam, pieśni, ludzkie oczy, uszy niepotrzebne;
Płyńcie w duszy mej wnętrznościach,
Świećcie na jej wysokościach,
Jak strumienie podziemne, jak gwiazdy nadniebne.
Ty Boże, ty naturo! dajcie posłuchanie. –
Godna to was muzyka i godne śpiewanie. –
Ja mistrz!
Ja mistrz wyciągam dłonie!
Wyciągam aż w niebiosa i kładę me dłonie
Na gwiazdach jak na szklannych harmoniki kręgach.
To nagłym, to wolnym ruchem
Kręcę gwiazdy moim duchem;
Milijon tonów płynie; w tonów milijonie
Każdy ton ja dobyłem, wiem o każdym tonie;
Zgadzam je, dzielę i łączę,
I w tęcze, i w akordy, i we strofy plączę,
Rozlewam je we dźwiękach i w błyskawic wstęgach. –

Odjąłem ręce, wzniosłem nad świata krawędzie,
I kręgi harmoniki wstrzymały się w pędzie.
Sam śpiewam, słyszę me śpiewy –
Długie, przeciągłe jak wichru powiewy,
Przewiewają ludzkiego rodu całe tonie,
Jęczą żalem, ryczą burzą,
I wieki im głucho wtórzą;
A każdy dźwięk ten razem gra i płonie,
Mam go w uchu, mam go w oku,
Jak wiatr, gdy fale kołysze,
Po świstach lot jego słyszę,
Widzę go w szacie obłoku.
Boga, natury godne takie pienie!
Pieśń to wielka, pieśń-tworzenie;
Taka pieśń jest siła, dzielność,

From that trembling will people trace depth of currents then,
Where it rushes will they infer?

This feeling goes round in my soul, it burns, it glows,
Like blood in its deep, unseen straits moving along;
People will see just as much blood as my face shows,
And as much of my feelings they will glimpse in my song.

My song, you are a star far beyond the world's bounds!
And human eye, pursuing you like a messenger,
Though it take wings of glass, will not reach your grounds,
But only strike against your milky way;
       That these are the suns it will gather,
       But will not count them nor survey.

You, songs, have no use at all for human eyes and ears; –
       Flow in my soul's deepest recess,
       Shine in its soaring loftiness,
Like subterranean streams, like stars above the spheres.
You, Almighty, and you, nature! Give heed to.
This music and this singing are worthy of you.
           I am master!
      I, master, stretch my hands out!
   High up to the skies and upon the stars throughout
As on a harmonica's glass spheres I put my hands.
       Now with a fast, now a slow twirl,
       My spirit will make the stars whirl.
   A million tones flow on; in the million that's flown
I produced every tone, I know of every tone;
   I harmonize, split, and bind them,
   I weave them in rainbows, in chords, in a poem,
I spill them over in sounds and in lightning bands.

I pulled back, raised my hands over the rims of the world,
The spheres of the harmonica had stopped where they swirled.
       I sing alone, I hear my song,
       Drawn out like the gusts of the wind and long,
       It blows throughout the depths of the whole human race,
       It roars with storm, it moans with woe,
       And the centuries faintly echo;
    Each sound chimes and at the same time is ablaze,
       I have it in my ear, in my sight,
       Like the wind, when it rocks the water,
       From its whistles I can glean its flight,
       I see it in the cloud vesture.
   Of God and nature worthy this incantation!
My song is grand, my singing is creation.
This song is grand, my singing is creation.

Taka pieśń jest nieśmiertelność!
Ja czuję nieśmiertelność, nieśmiertelność tworzę,
Cóż Ty większego mogłeś zrobić – Boże?
Patrz, jak te myśli dobywam sam z siebie,
Wcielam w słowa, one lecą,
Rozsypują się po niebie,
Toczą się, grają i świecą;
Już dalekie, czuję jeszcze,
Ich wdziękami się lubuję,
Ich okrągłość dłonią czuję,
Ich ruch myślą odgaduję:
Kocham was, me dzieci wieszcze!
Myśli moje! gwiazdy moje!
Czucia moje! wichry moje!
W pośrodku was jak ojciec wśród rodziny stoję,
Wy wszystkie moje!

Depcę was, wszyscy poeci,
Wszyscy mędrce i proroki,
Których wielbił świat szeroki.
Gdyby chodzili dotąd śród swych dusznych dzieci,
Gdyby wszystkie pochwały i wszystkie oklaski
Słyszeli, czuli i za słuszne znali,
I wszystkie sławy każdodziennej blaski
Promieniami na wieńcach swoich zapalali,
Z całą pochwał muzyką i wieńców ozdobą,
Zebraną z wieków tyla i z pokoleń tyla;
Nie czuliby własnego szczęścia, własnej mocy,
Jak ja dziś czuję w tej samotnej nocy:
Kiedy sam śpiewam w sobie,
Śpiewam samemu sobie.
Tak! – czuły jestem, silny jestem i rozumny. –
Nigdym nie czuł, jak w tej chwili –
Dziś mój zenit, moc moja dzisiaj się przesili,
Dziś poznam, czym najwyższy, czylim tylko dumny;
Dziś jest chwila przeznaczona,
Dziś najsilniej wytężę duszy mej ramiona –
To jest chwila Samsona,
Kiedy więzień i ślepy dumał u kolumny.
Zrzucę ciało i tylko jak duch wezmę pióra –
Potrzeba mi lotu,
Wylecę z planet i gwiazd kołowrotu,
Tam dojdę, gdzie graniczą Stwórca i natura.
I mam je, mam je, mam – tych skrzydeł dwoje;
Wystarczą – ad zachodu na wschód je rozszerzę,
Lewym o przeszłość, prawym o przyszłość uderzę,
I dojdę po promieniach uczucia – do Ciebie!

This song is might, great vitality,
I feel immortality, immortality I create,
What greater deed, o God, could You originate?
Look, how I draw these ideas from my inmost center,
Embody them in words, they take flight,
All over the skies they scatter,
They roll, they sound, they give forth light;
Though they are far, I still feel them,
I delight in their comeliness,
I feel with my hand their roundness,
I divine in my mind their progress:
I love you, my poetic children!
O my thoughts! Stars of mine!
O my feelings! Tempests of mine!
I stand among you like a father with his family,
You all belong to me!

All poets, I trample upon you,
All prophets as well as wise men,
Whom the wide world admired then.
Had they walked among their soul children hitherto,
Had they heard all the praise and all acclaim
And felt it all and known it to be right,
Had they had the glamour of daily fame
Kindled on their laurel wreaths with the rays of light;
With all this music of praise and wreaths of adornment,
Gathered from so many centuries and generations,
They would not feel their own happiness, their own might,
As I feel today in this lonely night:
When I sing within myself,
When I sing unto myself.
Yes, I am loving, I am strong and judicious,
Never have I felt as at this hour –
Today's my zenith, today's my height of power,
Today I will know if I'm highest or just vainglorious,
Today is the fated moment,
Today I'll strain my soul's arms to reach their full extent –
This is Samson's moment,
When he brooded by the pillar, enslaved and eyeless.
I'll cast off the flesh and like a ghost will feather –
It is flight that I need,
From planets and revolving stars freed,
I will reach where Creator borders with nature.
I have them now, I have them – these two wings; they'll do:
I will spread them from the west to the east in flight,
I'll strike the past with the left, the future with the right,
And I will rise up on beams of feeling – to You!

I zajrzę w uczucia Twoje,
O Ty! o którym mówią, że czujesz na niebie.
Jam tu, jam przybył, widzisz, jaka ma potęga,
Aż tu moje skrzydło sięga;
Lecz jestem człowiek, i tam, na ziemi me ciało;
Kochałem tam, w ojczyźnie sérce me zostało. –

Ale ta miłość moja na świecie,
Ta miłość nie na jednym spoczęła człowieku
Jak owad na róży kwiecie,
Nie na jednej rodzinie, nie na jednym wieku.
Ja kocham cały naród! – objąłem w ramiona
Wszystkie przeszłe i przyszłe jego pokolenia,
Przycisnąłem tu do łona,
Jak przyjaciel, kochanek, małżonek, jak ojciec;
Chcę go dźwignąć, uszczęśliwić,
Chcę nim cały świat zadziwić –
Nie mam sposobu i tu przyszedłem go dociec.
Przyszedłem zbrojny całą myśli władzą,
Tej myśli, co niebiosom Twe gromy wydarła,
Śledziła chód Twych planet, głąb morza rozwarła –
Mam więcej, tę Moc, której ludzie nie nadadzą,
Mam to uczucie, co się samo w sobie chowa
Jak wulkan, tylko dymi niekiedy przez słowa.

I Mocy tej nie wziąłem z drzewa edeńskiego,
Z owocu wiadomości złego i dobrego;
Nie z ksiąg ani z opowiadań,
Ani z rozwiązania zadań,
Ani z czarodziejskich badań;
Jam się twórcą urodził:
Stamtąd przyszły siły moje,
Skąd do Ciebie przyszły Twoje,
Boś i Ty po nie nie chodził:
Masz, nie boisz się stracić – i ja się nie boję.
Czyś Ty mi dał, czy wziąłem, skąd i Ty masz – oko
Bystre, potężne: w chwilach mej siły – wysoko
Kiedy na chmur spójrzę szlaki
I wędrowne słyszę ptaki,
Żeglujące na ledwie dostrzeżonym skrzydle;
Zechcę, i wnet je okiem zatrzymam jak w sidle –
Stado pieśń żałosną dzwoni,
Lecz póki ich nie puszczę, Twój wiatr ich nie zgoni.
Kiedy spójrzę w kometę z całą mocą duszy,
Dopóki na nią patrzę, z miejsca się nie ruszy.
Tylko ludzie skazitelni,
Marni, ale nieśmiertelni,

And I'll look into your feelings,
   Of You, of whom they say You feel in the heavens!
I am here, I have come, You can see my great power!
   My pinions reach even hither.
But I am a man, over there, on earth my body was laid;
There I loved, there in the native land my heart stayed.

   This love of mine on the earth, however,
   This love has not rested on a single person
   Like an insect on a rose flower;
   Neither on one family, nor on one season.
   I love the whole nation! I've clasped in my embrace
   All of its past and its future generations,
   Close to my bosom is their place,
   As friend, as lover, as husband, and as father;
   I want to lift it up, make it content,
   An object of the world's wonderment.
I lack the means and seeking it I came hither.
   I came armed with the full power of thought,
   of thought that tore Your lightning bolts from the heavens,
Observed the planets move, opened the deep seas expanse –
   I have more, this Might which people will not allot,
   I have this feeling, which within itself hidden,
   Like a volcano, emitting words now and then.

And I have not taken this might of Eden's tree,
Of the fruit of the knowledge of good and evil for me;
Not from books and tales it teems,
Not from solving complex themes,
Not from sorcerous schemes.
I was born a creator:
My powers come from the same source
Whence You, Almighty God, draw Yours,
As You did not seek them ever:
You have them, fear not to lose them; I fear neither.
Whether from You or taken from where You got them –
My keen, potent eye, in the hour of empowerment,
When I look at the cloudy trail
And hear the birds of passage sail,
On their barely visible wings high above there,
I but will it and my eye stops them as in a snare –
The flock clangs a mournful song,
Yet till I let them go, Your wind won't catch them on.
When I gaze at a comet with my soul's full power,
As long as I look, it won't move from its center.
     Only unchaste people,
     Feeble but immortal,

Nie służą mi, nie znają – nie znają nas obu,
Mnie i Ciebie;
Ja na nich szukam sposobu
Tu w niebie.
Tę władzę, którą mam nad przyrodzeniem,
Chcę wywrzeć na ludzkie dusze,
Jak ptaki i jak gwiazdy rządzę mym skinieniem,
Tak bliźnich rozrządzać muszę.
Nie bronią – broń broń odbije,
Nie pieśniami – długo rosną,
Nie nauką – prędko gnije,
Nie cudami – to zbyt głośno.
Chcę czuciem rządzić, które jest we mnie;
Rządzić jak Ty wszystkimi zawsze i tajemnie:
Co ja zechcę, niech wnet zgadną,
Spełnią, tym się uszczęśliwią,
A jeżeli się sprzeciwią,
Niechaj cierpią i przepadną.
Niech ludzie będą dla mnie jak myśli i słowa,
Z których, gdy zechcę, pieśni wiąże się budowa; –
Mówią, że Ty tak władasz!
Wiesz, żem myśli nie popsuł, mowy nie umorzył;
Jeśli mnie nad duszami równą władzę nadasz,
Ja bym mój naród jak pieśń żywą stworzył,
I większe niźli Ty zrobiłbym dziwo,
Zanuciłbym pieśń szczęśliwą!
Daj mi rząd dusz! – Tak gardzę tą martwą budową,
Którą gmin światem zowie i przywykł ją chwalić,
Żem nie probował dotąd, czyli moje słowo
Nie mogłoby jej wnet zwalić.
Lecz czuję w sobie, że gdybym mą wolę
Ścisnął, natężył i razem wyświecił,
Może bym sto gwiazd zgasił, a drugie sto wzniecił –
Bo jestem nieśmiertelny! i w stworzenia kole
Są inni nieśmiertelni – wyższych nie spotkałem. –
Najwyższy na niebiosach! – Ciebie tu szukałem,
Ja najwyższy z czujących na ziemnym padole.
Nie spotkałem Cię dotąd – żeś Ty jest, zgaduję;
Niech Cię spotkam i niechaj Twą wyższość uczuję –
Ja chcę władzy, daj mi ją lub wskaż do niej drogę;
O prorokach, dusz władcach, że byli, słyszałem,
I wierzę; lecz co oni mogli, to ja mogę,
Ja chcę mieć władzę, jaką Ty posiadasz,
Ja chcę duszami władać, jak Ty nimi władasz.

Do not serve me, do not know me – they know neither
          You nor me.
    How to deal with them I seek to discover
          Here, in heavenly city.
This power I hold over nature
          I want to exert on human souls,
Just as I rule birds and stars with my one gesture,
          I must rule over my neighbors.
          Not with arms – arms fend off arms,
          Not with songs – too long to flourish,
          Not with learning – it swiftly mars,
          Not with miracles – that's too garish
I want to rule by the feeling that is in me;
Rule all men like You forever and secretly:
          What I desire, let them at once guess,
          Fulfill it, and find happiness,
          But if they go against my wish,
          Let them all suffer and perish.
Let people become for me just like thoughts and words,
From which, if I wish, I build the frame of my verse;
          They say that You rule this way!
You know I didn't spoil thought nor did speech any wrong;
If over souls You provide me with equal sway,
I would create my nation like a living song,
And a greater wonder than Yours I would perform,
          I would intone a happy song!
Give me the rule over souls! I so much disdain
What common men call the world and praise it withal,
That I have never tried whether my word might fain
Bring this dead structure to a fall.
But if I tightened my will, that's my feeling,
Then strained it and at once shot the rays of light,
A hundred stars I might put out, a hundred ignite,
For I am immortal! And in creation's ring
Are other such men; – yet I have met none higher –
All Highest in the Heavens! I have sought you hither,
I, the highest on this earth who can feel something.
I have not met You yet – but that You are I guess;
Let me encounter You and perceive Your greatness –
I want power, give it to me or show the way!
I heard of prophets, masters of souls, they lived earlier,
I believe; but what they could do, I can do today,
I want to have power such as You possess,
I want to rule souls, just as You rule them, no less.

(Długie milczenie)
(z ironią)

Milczysz, milczysz! wiem teraz, jam Cię teraz zbadał,
Zrozumiałem, coś Ty jest i jakeś Ty władał. –
Kłamca, kto Ciebie nazywał miłością,
Ty jesteś tylko mądrością.
Ludzie myślą, nie sercem, Twych dróg się dowiedzą;
Myślą, nie sercem, składy broni Twej wyśledzą –
Ten tylko, kto się wrył w księgi,
W metal, w liczbę w trupie ciało,
Temu się tylko udało
Przywłaszczyć część Twej potęgi.
Znajdzie truciznę, proch, parę,
Znajdzie blaski, dymy, huki,
Znajdzie prawność i złą wiarę
Na mędrki i na nieuki.
Myślom oddałeś świata użycie,
Serca zostawiasz na wiecznej pokucie,
Dałeś mnie najkrótsze życie
I najmocniejsze uczucie. –

(Milczenie)

Czym jest me czucie?
Ach, iskrą tylko!
Czym jest me życie?
Ach, jedną chwilką!
Lecz te, co jutro rykną, czym są dzisiaj gromy?
Iskrą tylko.
Czym jest wieków ciąg cały, mnie z dziejów wiadomy?
Jedną chwilką.
Z czego wychodzi cały człowiek, mały światek?
Z iskry tylko.
Czym jest śmierć, co rozproszy myśli mych dostatek?
Jedną chwilką.
Czym był On, póki światy trzymał w swoim łonie?
Iskrą tylko.
Czym będzie wieczność świata, gdy On go pochłonie?
Jedną chwilką.

Głos z lewej strony

   Wsiąść muszę
     Na duszę
   Jak na koń.
    Goń! Goń
  W cwał, w cwał!

Głos z prawej

   Co za szał!
Brońmy go, brońmy,
Skrzydłem osłońmy
   Skroń.

(Long silence)
(with irony)

Silent, still silent! I know now, I comprehend You,
I understand who You are and how You rule, too.
He was a liar who Your name 'Love' did call,
You are mere wisdom, that is all.
People learn of Your ways not with heart, but with thoughts;
With thought, not with heart, Your arsenals they can spot –
    For only he who delved in books at length,
    Examined metals, corpses, numbers,
    Only he chanced upon right measures
    To appropriate a part of Your strength.
    He will find poison, powder, steam,
    He will blaze, rumble, and smoke,
    He will find rightful law and faithless scheme
    For know-all men and witless folk.
    You've given over the world's use to thought,
    While You left hearts to eternal penance,
    My life drew from You the shortest lot
    And the feeling which is most intense.

(Silence)

What is my feeling?
    Ah, only a spark!
What's my life herein?
    Ah, just a brief mark!
Thunders that will roar tomorrow's, what are they today?
    Ah, only a spark.
What's the whole span of centuries that records convey?
    Just a brief mark.
From where does the whole man, the little world, come out?
    Only from a spark.
What is death that will scatter my teeming thoughts about?
    Just a brief mark.
What was He when He nourished the wide world in His breast?
    Only a spark.
What's the world's eternity when He engulfs it next?
    Just a brief mark.

Voice from the left side
    I must climb
On his soul meantime
    As on a horse
Run, run the course,
    Gallop, gallop!

Voice from the right
    What a madness!
Let's shield him now,
Let's protect his brow
    With our wings.

Chwila i iskra, gdy się przedłuża, rozpala –
Stwarza i zwala.
Śmiało, śmiało! tę chwilę rozdłużmy, rozdalmy,
Śmiało, śmiało! tę iskrę rozniećmy,: rozpalmy –
Teraz – dobrze – tak. Jeszcze raz Ciebie wyzywam,
Jeszcze po przyjacielsku duszę Ci odkrywam.
Milczysz – wszakżeś z Szatanem walczył osobiście?
Wyzywam Cię uroczyście.
Nie gardź mną, ja nie jeden, choć sam tu wzniesiony.
Jestem na ziemi sercem z wielkim ludem zbratan,
Mam ja za sobą wojska, i mocy, i trony;
Jeśli ja będę bluźnierca,
Ja wydam Tobie krwawszą bitwę niźli Szatan:
On walczył na rozumy, ja wyzwę na serca.
Jam cierpiał, kochał, w mękach i miłości wzrosłem;
Kiedyś mnie wydarł osobiste szczęście,
Na własnej piersi ja skrwawiłem pięście,
Przeciw Niebu ich nie wzniosłem.

Głos

Rumaka
Przedzierzgnę w ptaka
Orlimi pióry
Do góry!
W lot!

Głos

Gwiazdo spadająca!
Jaki szał
W otchłań cię strąca!

Teraz duszą jam w moję ojczyznę wcielony;
Ciałem połknąłem jej duszę,
Ja i ojczyzna to jedno.
Nazywam się Milijon – bo za milijony
Kocham i cierpię katusze.
Patrzę na ojczyznę biedną,
Jak syn na ojca wplecionego w koło;
Czuję całego cierpienia narodu,
Jak matka czuje w łonie bole swego płodu.
Cierpię, szaleję – a Ty mądrze i wesoło
Zawsze rządzisz,
Zawsze sądzisz,
I mówią, że Ty nie błądzisz!
Słuchaj, jeśli to prawda, com z wiarą synowską
Słyszał, na ten świat przychodząc,
Że Ty kochasz; – jeżeliś Ty kochał świat rodząc,
Jeśli ku zrodzonemu masz miłość ojcowską; –
Jeżeli serce czułe było w liczbie żwierząt,
Któreś Ty w arce zamknął i wyrwał z powodzi; –
Jeśli to serce nie jest potwór, co się rodzi

The brief mark and the spark, when they stretch, set ablaze –
    They create and raze.
Come on, come on! Let's prolong and stretch this brief mark,
Come on, come on! Let's kindle and set ablaze this spark –
Now – that's right – yes. I challenge You once more,
I bare my soul to You like a friend as before.
Still silent? And yet You fought Satan in person?
    I challenge You hereon.
Don't scorn me, I'm not by myself, thought raised alone here.
My heart on earth to a great nation a brother,
Behind me armies, and Powers, and Thrones, stand near;
    If I am to curse You,
I'll give You a bloodier battle than Lucifer;
He fought with his mind, on heart my challenge I'll issue.
I suffered, loved, I have grown in torment and love;
And when You tore all happiness out of my breast,
I bloodied my fists upon my chest,
    I didn't raise them against Heaven above

Voice

The horse I'll convert
  Into a bird.
Its eagle feathers
Upward will traverse!
  Fly up!

Voice

Falling star!
What madness
Throws you into the abyss

Now with my whole soul I am in my native region;
    My body has swallowed its soul,
    I and my country are one whole.
    My name is 'Million' – since for many a million
    I love and suffer great torment.
    I look upon my poor homeland,
    As a son at his father broken on the wheel;
    The suffering of the whole nation I feel,
    As a mother feels in the womb her embryo's plight.
    I suffer, rave – while You, wisely and with delight
      Always order,
      Always measure
      And they say that You never err!
   Listen to me, if that be true what I once heard,
   With filial faith when I first drew breath,
   That You love; – if You loved when creating this earth,
   If for Your offspring fatherly love You assert;
If the loving heart was with the animals' number,
Which You put in the ark and saved from the flood once,
If this heart is not a monster that's born by chance

Przypadkiem, ale nigdy lat swych nie dochodzi; –
Jeśli pod rządem Twoim czułość nie jest bezrząd,
Jeśli w milijon ludzi krzyczących «ratunku!»
Nie patrzysz jak w zawiłe zrównanie rachunku; –
Jeśli miłość jest na co w świecie Twym potrzebną
I nie jest tylko Twoją omyłką liczebną...

Głos

Orła w hydrę!
Oczy mu wydrę.
Do szturmu dalej!
Dymi! pali!
Ryk, grzmot!

Głos

Z jasnego słońca
Kometo błędu!
Gdzie koniec twego pędu?
Bez końca, bez końca!

Milczysz! – Jam Ci do głębi serce me otworzył,
Zaklinam, daj mi władzę – jedna część jej licha,
Część tego, co na ziemi osiągnęła pycha,
Za jedną cząstką ileż ja bym szczęścia stworzył!
Milczysz! – nie dasz dla serca, dajże dla rozumu. –
Widzisz, żem pierwszy z ludzi i z aniołów tłumu,
Że Cię znam lepiej niźli Twoje archanioły,
Wart, żebyś ze mną władzą dzielił się na poły –
Jeślim nie zgadł, odpowiedz – milczysz! ja nie kłamię,
Milczysz i ufasz, że masz silne ramię –
Wiedz, że uczucie spali, czego myśl nie złamie –
Widzisz to moje ognisko – uczucie,
Zbieram je, ściskam, by mocniej pałało,
Wbijam w żelazne woli mej okucie,
Jak nabój w burzące działo.

Głos

Ognia! pal!

Głos

Litość! żal!

Odezwij się – bo strzelę przeciw Twej naturze;
Jeśli jej w gruzy nie zburzę,
To wstrząsnę całym państw Twoich obszarem;
Bo wystrzelę głos w całe obręby stworzenia,
Ten głos, który z pokoleń pójdzie w pokolenia:
Krzyknę, żeś Ty nie ojcem świata, ale...

Głos diabła

Carem!

(Konrad staje chwilę, słania się i pada)

Duchy z lewej strony
Pierwszy

Depc, chwytaj!

And never lives long enough in age to advance;
If under Your rule affection is not disorder,
If at a million people crying 'Save us all!,'
You don't look as if at a tangled count to equal;
If love in Your world is of use for anything,
And is not merely Your error in accounting . . .

Voice

The eagle will be a hydra!
  I'll pluck out his eyes,
    Onward we rise!
  In smoke and swelter
    Roar! Thunder!

Voice

From the brightest sun
  The stray comet!
Where's the end of your run?
  No end, no end yet!

Still silent! I have opened to you my whole heart,
I beseech You, give me power: its smallest part,
A fraction of that which pride has attained on earth,
From that one fraction I would create such great mirth!
Still silent! If not for the heart, give for the mind.
You see I am foremost of angels and mankind
Much better than Your archangels I have known You,
I'm worthy of receiving half of Your power, too –
If I haven't been right, respond – silent! I do not lie.
You keep silent and trust in Your strong arm's reply –
But know that feeling can burn what mind can't break hereby –
You see this raging fire of mine: feeling,
I gather it, compress it so it burns strong,
I drive it into my will's iron fitting,
Like a charge into a heavy cannon.

Voice

Aim! Fire!

Voice

Mercy! Pity!

Say something – or I will fire against Your nature;
If I don't wreck it altogether,
I will shake the whole range of Your lands near and far;
For I will shout throughout the whole creation:
The voice that from generation to generation
Will cry You are not the world's father, but . . .

Voice of the devil

The tsar!

(*Konrad stands for a moment, totters, and falls*)

Spirits from the left side

First Spirit

Trample, catch him!

Drugi

Jeszcze dysze.

Pierwszy

Omdlał, omdlał, a nim
Przebudzi się, dodusim.

Duch z prawej strony

Precz – modlą się za nim.

Duch z lewej

Widzisz, odpędzają nas.

Pierwszy z lewej

Ty bestyjo głupia!
Nie pomogłeś mu słowo ostatnie wyrzygnąć,
Jeszcze o jeden stopień w dumę go podźwignąć!
Chwila dumy – ta czaszka już byłaby trupia.
Być tak blisko tej czaszki! i nie można deptać!
Widzieć krew w jego ustach, i nie można chłeptać!
Najgłupszy z diabłów, tyś go wypuścił w pół drogi.

Drugi

Wróci się, wróci –

Pierwszy

Precz stąd, bo wezmę na rogi
I będę cię lat tysiąc niosł, i w paszczę samą Szatana wbiję.

Drugi

Cha! cha! straszysz, ciociu! mamo!
Ja dziecko będę płakać –

(płacze)

Masz –

(uderza rogiem)

A co, nie chybił?
Leć i nie wyłaź z piekła – aha, do dna przybił –
Rogi me, brawo, rogi –

Pierwszy

Sacrédieu!

Drugi

(uderza)

Masz.

Second Spirit

He's still breathing.

First Spirit

He swooned, swooned hereon,
Before he wakes, we'll smother him.

Spirit from the right side

Some pray for him – begone.

Spirit from the left side

Now just see, they chase us away.

First Spirit from the left

You stupid beast!
You did not help him to throw up the last word,
And raise him up one more degree in his proud world!
A moment of pride – his skull would be deceased.
So close to this skull! And not to trample him up!
To see blood in his mouth and not to lap it up!
Most foolish devil, you let him get off halfway.

Second Spirit

He will come back, he will come back –

First Spirit

Just get away –
Or I'll ram you, carry for a thousand years, and spear
Into Satan's jaws.

Second Spirit

Ha, ha, mama, auntie, I fear!
I'll cry like a child –

(he cries)

Take that!

(Strikes him with his horn)

Now did I aim well?
Be off and don't leave hell – now nailed to bottom level –
My horns, bravo –

First Spirit

Sacrédieu!

Second Spirit

(Strikes him)

Take that!

Pierwszy

W nogi.

(Słychać stukanie i klucz we drzwiach)

Drugi duch

Pop, klecha, przyczajmy się i schowajmy rogi.

(1832) [*Edited by Zofia Stefanowska. Warszawa: Czytelnik, 1995*]

k. ROMÂNĂ

II.k.1. VASILE ALECSANDRI, 'La gura sobei'

Aşezat la gura sobei noaptea pe când viscoleşte
Privesc focul, scump tovarăş, care vesel pâlpâieşte,
Şi prin flacăra albastră vrescurilor de aluni
Văd trecând în zbor fantastic a poveştilor minuni.

Iat-o pasere măiastră prinsă-n luptă c-un balaur;
Iată cerbi cu stele-n frunte carii trec pe punţi de aur;
Iată cai ce fug ca gândul; iată zmei înaripaţi
Care-ascund în mari palaturi mândre fete de-mpăraţi.

Iată pajuri năzdrăvane care vin din neagra lume,
Aducând pe lumea albă feţi-frumoşi cu falnic nume;
Iată-n lacul cel de lapte toate zânele din rai...
Nu departe stă Pepelea, tupilat în flori de mai.

Dar pe mine ce m-atrage, dar pe mine ce mă-ncântă
E Ileana Cosânzeana!... în cosiţă floarea-i cântă.
Până-n ziuă stau pe gânduri şi la ea privesc uimit,
Că-mi aduce viu aminte de-o minune ce-am iubit!

First Spirit

Let's run away!

(*Knocking at the door and the sound of a key in the lock*)

Second Spirit

A priest, cassock, let's skulk and draw in our horns today.

(1832) [*Mickiewicz, Adam from Forefathers' Eve. Part III. Translated and edited by Michael J. Mikoś, Polish Romantic Literature. An Anthology. Bloomington: Slavica Publishers, 2002. 48–58, Act I, scene 2*]

k.   ROMANIAN

II.k.1.   VASILE ALECSANDRI, 'By the Fire Side'

By the fireside seated, while the snowstorm blows wildly,
I stare deep into the fire which shows me dear company;
Through the flames of hazel boughs which burn so blue,
My fantastic brain conjures up realms of wonders rare and new.

Here a wondrous bird struggles with a dread ogre;
Here are deer with starry foreheads on golden bridges;
Here horses fly like thought and winged dragons over swift waters
Hiding in majestic castles beauteous imperial daughters.

Here brave and mighty falcons from the black world descend,
To the white world, blending the princely and royal;
Here on the milk-white lake fly fairies from high heavens . . .
And swift Puck[1] in May flowers hidden, lies asleep nearby.

Yet what so attracts me hither and so thoroughly enchants
Is my Fairy Sweet Ileana![2] . . . In her tresses she plants flowers.
I keep gazing till the dawn breaks and, rapt in pensive mood,
Fondly I recall these memories which have so soon escaped.

[*Translated by Mihaela Anghelescu Irimia and Patsy Erskine-Hill*]

---

[1] We have chosen the closest possible equivalent in English folklore for the Romanian Pepelea figure, the typical trickster in fairy tales revived from anonymous sources by most Romantics, Eminescu included.

[2] In Romanian legends and fairy tales Ileana Cosânzeana is the mythical bride saved by Prince Charming, who defeats the Ogre, himself in love with her. In Romantic literature she is associated with the fairy, as her own name indicates: *Sânziana* is an echo of the Roman goddess of the hunt, now conflated with the Christian tradition into 'Saint Diana'.

II.k.2. MIHAI EMINESCU, din 'Scrisoarea I'

Când cu gene ostenite sara suflu-n lumânare,
Doar ceasornicul urmează lung-a timpului cărare,
Căci perdelele-ntr-o parte când le dai, și în odaie
Luna varsă peste toate voluptoasa ei văpaie,
Ea din noaptea amintirii o vecie-ntreagă scoate
De dureri, pe care însă le simțim ca-n vis pe toate.

Lună tu, stăpân-a mării, pe a lumii boltă luneci
Și gândirilor dând viață, suferințele întuneci;
Mii pustiuri scânteiază sub lumina ta fecioară,
Și câți codri-ascund în umbră strălucire de izvoară!
Peste câte mii de valuri stăpânirea ta străbate,
Când plutești pe mișcătoarea mărilor singurătate!

Câte țărmuri înflorite, ce palate și cetăți,
Străbătute de-al tău farmec ție singură-ți arăți!
Și în câte mii de case lin pătruns-ai prin ferești,
Câte frunți pline de gânduri, gânditoare le privești!
Vezi pe-un rege ce-mpânzește globu-n planuri pe un veac,
Când la ziua cea de mâine abia cuget-un sărac...
Deși trepte osebite le-au ieșit din urna sorții,
Deopotrivă-i stăpânește raza ta și geniul morții;
....
Pe când luna strălucește peste-a tomurilor bracuri,
Într-o clipă-l poartă gândul îndărăt cu mii de veacuri,
La-nceput, pe când ființă nu era, nici neființă,
Pe când totul era lipsă de viață și voință,
Când nu s-ascundea nimica, deși tot era ascuns...
Când pătruns de sine însuși odihnea cel nepătruns.
Fu prăpastie? genune? Fu noian întins de apă?
N-a fost lume pricepută și nici minte s-o priceapă,
Căci era un întuneric ca o mare făr-o rază,
Dar nici de văzut nu fuse și nici ochi care s-o vază.
Umbra celor nefăcute nu-ncepuse-a se desface,
Și în sine împăcată stăpânea eterna pace!...
Dar deodat-un punct se mișcă... cel întâi și singur. Iată-l
Cum din chaos face mumă, iară el devine Tatăl!...
Punctu-acela de mișcare, mult mai slab ca boaba spumii,

II.k.2. MIHAI EMINESCU, from 'First Epistle'[3]

When, at night, with drooping eyelids, I blow out the candle's flare,
Time's unending path is followed only by the old clock there;
For just draw aside the curtain and the moon will flood the room
With a fire of passion summoned by the ardours of her gloom;
From the night of recollection she will resurrect an eon
Of distress – which we, however, sense as in a dream-like paean.

Moon, arch-mistress of the ocean, you glide o'er the planet's sphere,
You give light in thoughts unthought-of and eclipse sorrow and fear;
Oh, how many deserts glimmer under your soft virgin light
And how many woods o'ershadow brooks and rivers burning bright!
There are many waves which you dispose of as you please,
When you sail upon the ever restless solitude of seas;

Of resplendent climes, or gardens, palaces and castles old,
Which you impregnate with magic and to your own view unfold;
Of the dwellings that you enter tiptoe by the window-pane
To gaze thoughtfully at foreheads that so many thoughts enchain!
A king's plans enmesh the planet for a century or more,
While the pauper hardly thinks of what his morrow has in store.
Though Fate has allotted them different rungs and ways,
Both submit alike to Death's beckoning rays.

....

While the moon shines over mouldy books penned by sages,
His thoughts take him back through the bygone ages
To the very first, when being and non-being were nought still,
When there was utter absence of both life-impulse and will,
When nothing was unopened, although everything was hidden,
When, by His own self pervaded, resting lay the All-forbidden.
Was it an abyss? a chasm? wat'ry plains without an end?
There was no estate of wisdom, nor a mind to comprehend.
For the darkness was steel-solid just like the shadows' ocean,
And there were no eyes at all to form of it a notion.
Of the unmade things the shadows had not yet begun to gleam
And, with its own self contented, peace eternal reigned supreme.
Suddenly, a dot starts moving – the primeval, lonely Other...
It becomes the Father potent, while the void becomes the mother.
Weaker than a drop of water, this small dot that moves and bounds
Is the unrestricted ruler of the world's unbounded bounds.

[3] In 1881 Eminescu composed a set of five epistles, also referred to (by the poet himself) as satires. The overall theme of the epistles is the plight of the erudite scholar in the midst of a superficial, corrupt, frivolous and ignorant society, in tones reminding one of Shakespeare's Sonnet 66. While the savant in epistle I grasps the essence of cosmogonic processes, the moon, which is his constant visitor and inspirer, invites the inner eye to take over from the outer eye and keeps vigil over the Romanian poet's 'bliss of solitude', so similar to the Wordsworthian experience.

E stăpânul fără margini peste marginile lumii...
De-atunci negura eternă se desface în fâșii,
De atunci răsare lumea, lună, soare și stihii...
De atunci și până astăzi colonii de lumi pierdute
Vin din sure văi de chaos pe cărări necunoscute
Și în roiuri luminoase izvorând din infinit,
Sunt atrase în viață de un dor nemărginit.
Iar în lumea asta mare, noi copii ai lumii mici,
Facem pe pământul nostru mușunoaie de furnici;
Microscopice popoare, regi, oșteni și învățați
Ne succedem generații și ne credem minunați;
Muști de-o zi pe-o lume mică de se măsură cu cotul,
În acea nemărginire ne-nvârtim uitând cu totul
Cum că lumea asta-ntreagă e o clipă suspendată,
Că-ndărătu-i și-nainte-i întuneric se arată.
Precum pulberea se joacă în imperiul unei raze,
Mii de fire viorie ce cu raza încetează,
Astfel, într-a veciniciei noapte pururea adâncă,
Avem clipa, avem raza, care tot mai ține încă...
Cum s-o stinge, totul piere, ca o umbră-n întuneric,
Căci e vis al neființei universul cel himeric...

....

Între ziduri, printre arbori ce se scutură de floare,
Cum revarsă luna plină liniștita ei splendoare!
Și din noaptea amintirii mii de doruri ea ne scoate;
Amorțită li-i durerea, le simțim ca-n vis pe toate,
Căci în propria-ne lume ea deschide poarta-ntrării
Și ridică mii de umbre după stinsul lumânării...
Mii pustiuri scânteiază sub lumina ta fecioară,
Și câți codri-ascund în umbră strălucire de izvoară!
Peste câte mii de valuri stăpânirea ta străbate,
Când pluteşti pe mişcătoarea mărilor singurătate,
Și pe toți ce-n astă lume sunt supuși puterii sorții
Deopotrivă-i stăpâneşte raza ta și geniul morții!

[1881]

Ever since the vasty dimness has been splitting slice by slice,
Ever since come into being earth, sun, moon, light, heat and ice.
Ever since up to the present galaxies of planets lost
Follow up mysterious courses, chaos-bred and chaos-tossed,
And in endlessness begotten, endless swarms of light and thronging
Towards life, forever driven by an infinity of longing;
And in this great world, we, children of a world grotesquely small,
Raise upon our tiny planet anthills to o'ertop the All.
Lilliputian kings and peoples, soldiers, both unread and erudite,
We engender generations, reckoning ourselves full bright!
One-day moths upon a mudball measurable with the chip,
We rotate in the great vastness and forget 'twixt cup and lip
That this world is really nothing but a moment caught in light,
That behind, or else before it, all that one can see is night.
Just like whirls of dust and powder thousands of live granules play
In the glorious beam's brilliance and then vanish with the ray.
Thus against the never-failing night of time without a bound,
The spontaneous ray, the moment, still fails not to go the round;
When it dies, all dies – like shadows melting in the murky distance
For the universe chimeric is a dream of non-existence.

....

Among walls, and trees, and blossoms that are falling white and tender,
How the full moon spreads her own calm and radiant splendour!
From the night of recollection myriads of longings beam
And their pain is mitigated, we feel them as in a dream.
She opens wide the entrance to our inner world of doubt,
Conjuring a host of shadows when the candlelight is out.
Oh, how many deserts glimmer under your soft virgin light,
And how many woods o'ershadow brooks and rivers bright!
How many waves you dispose of as you please,
When you sail over the ever restless solitude of seas;
And all those who in their lifetime are subjected to Fate's ways
Both submit alike to Death's beckoning rays!

[1881] [*Adapted from translation by Leon Leviţchi*]

I. РУССКИЙ

II.I.1. МИХАИЛ ЛЕРМОНТОВ, из романа «Герой нашего времени»

Что ж? умереть так умереть! потеря для мира небольшая; да и мне самому порядочно уж скучно. Я – как человек, зевающий на бале, который не едет спать только потому, что еще нет его кареты. Но карета готова... прощайте!

Пробегаю в памяти все мое прошедшее и спрашиваю себя невольно: зачем я жил? для какой цели я родился?.. А, верно, она существовала, и, верно, было мне назначение высокое, потому что я чувствую в душе моей силы необъятные... Но я не угадал этого назначения, я увлекся приманками страстей пустых и неблагодарных; из горнила их я вышел тверд и холоден, как железо, но утратил навеки пыл благородных стремлений – лучший свет жизни. И с той поры сколько раз уже я играл роль топора в руках судьбы! Как орудие казни, я упадал на голову обреченных жертв, часто без злобы, всегда без сожаления... Моя любовь никому не принесла счастья, потому что я ничем не жертвовал для тех, кого любил: я любил для себя, для собственного удовольствия: я только удовлетворял странную потребность сердца, с жадностью поглощая их чувства, их радости и страданья – и никогда не мог насытиться. Так, томимый голодом в изнеможении засыпает и видит перед собой роскошные кушанья и шипучие вина; он пожирает с восторгом воздушные дары воображения, и ему кажется легче; но только проснулся – мечта исчезает... остается удвоенный голод и отчаяние!

И, может быть, я завтра умру!.. и не останется на земле ни одного существа, которое бы поняло меня совершенно. Одни почитают меня хуже, другие лучше, чем я в самом деле... Одни скажут: он был добрый малый, другие – мерзавец. И то и другое будет ложно. После этого стоит ли труда жить? а все живешь – из любопытства: ожидаешь чего-то нового... Смешно и досадно!

(1839, 1841)

II.I.2. АПОЛЛОН ГРИГОРЬЕВ, «Над тобою мне тайная сила дана...»

Над тобою мне тайная сила дана,
Это – сила звезды роковой.
Есть преданье – сама ты преданий полна –
Так послушай: бывает порой,
В небесах загорится, средь сонма светил,
Небывалое вдруг иногда,
И гореть ему ярко господь присудил –
Но падучая это звезда...
И сама ли нечистым огнем сожжена,
Или, звездному кругу чужда,
Серафимами свержена с неба она, –
Рассыпается прахом звезда;
И дано, говорят, той печальной звезде

1. RUSSIAN

II.1.1. MIKHAIL LERMONTOV, from *A Hero of Our Time*

Well, what of it? If I am to die, I'll die! The loss to the world will not be large and, anyway, I myself am sufficiently bored. I am like a man who yawns at a ball and does not drive home to sleep, only because his carriage is not yet there. But now the carriage is ready . . . good-bye!

I scan my whole past in memory and involuntarily wonder: why did I live, for what purpose was I born? . . . And yet that purpose must have existed, and my destination must have been a lofty one, for I feel, in my soul, boundless strength. But I did not divine that destination; I became enticed by the lure of hollow and thankless passions. From their crucible, I emerged as hard and cold as iron, but lost forever the ardor of noble yearnings – the best blossom of life. And since then, how many times I have played the part of an axe in the hands of fate! As an executioner's tool, I would fall upon the head of doomed victims, often without malice, always with regret. My love brought happiness to none, because I never gave up anything for the sake of those whom I loved. I loved for myself, for my pleasure; I merely satisfied a bizarre need of my heart, avidly consuming their sentiments, their tenderness, their joys and sufferings – and never could I have my fill. Thus a man, tormented by hunger and fatigue, goes to sleep and sees before him rich viands and sparkling wines; he devours with delight the airy gifts of fancy, and he seems to feel relief; but as soon as he awakes – the vision vanishes. He is left with redoubled hunger and despair!

And, perhaps tomorrow, I shall die! . . . And there will not remain, on earth, a single creature that would have understood me completely. Some deem me worse, others better that I actually am. Some will say he was a good fellow; others will say he was a scoundrel. Both this and that will be false. After this, is it worth the trouble to live? And yet one lives – out of curiosity. One keeps expecting something new . . . Absurd and vexatious!

(1839, 1841) [*Translated by Vladimir Nabokov with Dmitri Nabokov*]

II.1.2. APOLLON GRIGORIEV, 'A Secret Power over You Has Been Given to Me . . .'

A secret power has been given to me over you,
The power of a fatal star.
There is a legend – you yourself are full of legends –
So listen: it happens sometimes,
That an unknown star will suddenly light up the skies,
In the midst of the assembly of luminaries,
And the Lord appointed it to shine brightly,
But this is a falling star[1] . . .
And, whether it burnt itself out by an impure fire,
Or, being alien to the stellar circle,
Was thrown down from heaven by seraphs, –
It is disintegrating to dust;
And, they say, it has been ordained that this somber star

[1] Grigoriev uses the image of a meteor. The allusion is to Isaiah 14.12–15 which is often interpreted as the fall of Lucifer (Satan) from Heaven.

Искушенье посеять одно,
Да лукавые сны, да страданье везде,
Где рассыпаться ей суждено.

Над тобою мне тайная сила дана,
Эту силу я знаю давно:
Так уносит в безбрежное море волна
За собой из залива судно,
Так, от дерева лист оторвавши, гроза
В вихре пыли его закружит,
И, с участьем следя, не увидят глаза,
Где кружится, куда он летит...
Над тобою мне тайная сила дана,
И тебя мне увлечь суждено,
И пускай ты горда, и пускай ты скрытна, –
Эту силу я понял давно.

(1843)

m. ESPAÑOL

II.m.1. FRANCISCO MARTÍNEZ DE LA ROSA, 'La soledad'

Yo vi en la aurora de mi edad florida
sus encantos brindarse a mis deseos;
gloria, riquezas, cuantos falsos bienes
anhela el hombre en su delirio ciego.

***

En presto vuelo pasaron cinco lustros de mi vida,
y el cuadro encantador huyó con ellos;
huyó, volví la vista, lancé un grito...
y en vez de flores encontré un desierto.

(Excerpt, c. 1802) [1833]

II.m.2. FRANCISCO MARTÍNEZ DE LA ROSA, 'Mis penas'

Pasa fugaz la alegre primavera,
rosas sembrando y coronando amores,
y el seco estío, deshojando flores,
haces apiña la tostada era.
Mas la estación de Baco lisonjera
torna a dar vida a campos y pastores
y ya el invierno anuncia sus rigores,
al tibio sol menguando la carrera.
Yo una vez y otra vez vi en mayo rosas

will plant a certain temptation,
and evil dreams, and suffering,
wherever those fatal pieces fall.

A secret power has been given to me over you,
A power I have known for a long time:
Like a wave carries a vessel away from a harbor
Into a boundless sea,
So a thunderstorm, tears a leaf away from a tree,
And spins it in a whirlwind of dust,
And the eyes, following it with compassion, will not see
Where it is spinning around, where it is flying . . .
A secret power has been given to me over you,
And it is destined that I will carry you away
And even though you are proud and secretive,
I have known this power from long ago.

(1843) [*Translated by Yelena Borisova. Edited by Jamie S. Crouse*]

m.   SPANISH

II.m.1.   FRANCISCO MARTÍNEZ DE LA ROSA, 'Solitude'

In the dawn of my flowering youth I saw its enchantments offer themselves to my desires; glory, riches, as many false gifts that man seeks after in his blind delirium. . . . In swift flight twenty five years of my life passed by, and the enchanting picture fled with them; it flew, I turned my gaze, I let out a cry . . . and instead of flowers I saw a desert.

(1802) [1833]

II.m.2.   FRANCISCO MARTÍNEZ DE LA ROSA, 'My Suffering'

The happy spring passes swiftly, scattering roses and crowning love, and the dry summer, scattering petals, gathers together sheaves on the burnt threshing floor. Yet the season flattering Bacchus returns to give life to meadows and shepherds, and winter is about to announce its rigours, slowing down the course of the warm sun. I, once and again and again, was witness to roses in May and seeing the corn wave in summer; I saw the abundant fruit of autumn and the sterile ice of impious winter, the hasty seasons fly by . . . And only my pain lasts eternally!

(c. 1805) [1833]

[*Like many of the writers of his time, Martínez de la Rosa was forced into exile for his liberal views. On his return in 1831 he entered politics and became minister in various governments. His play,*

y la mies ondear en el estío;
vi de otoño las frutas abundosas
y el hielo estéril del invierno impío.
Vuelan las estaciones presurosas...
¡Y sólo dura eterno el dolor mío!

(c. 1805) [1833]

II.m.3.   JOSÉ DE ESPRONCEDA, 'A Jarifa en una orgía'

Trae, Jarifa, trae tu mano,
ven y pósala en mi frente,
que en un mar de lava hirviente
mi cabeza siento arder.
Ven y junta con mis labios
esos labios que me irritan,
donde aún los besos palpitan
de tus amantes de ayer.
¡Qué la virtud, la pureza!
¡Qué la verdad y el cariño!
Mentida ilusión de niño
que halagó mi juventud.
Dadme vino: en él se ahoguen
mis recuerdos; aturdida,
sin sentir, huya la vida
paz me atraiga el ataúd.
El sudor mi rostro quema,
y en ardiente sangre rojos
brillan inciertos mis ojos,
se me salta el corazón.
Huye, mujer; te detesto,
siento tu mano en la mía,
y tu mano siento fría,
y tus besos hielos son.
¡Siempre igual! Necias mujeres,
inventad otras caricias, otras delicias,
¡o maldito sea el placer!
Vuestros besos son mentira,
mentira vuestra ternura,
es fealdad vuestra hermosura,
vuestro gozo es padecer.
Yo quiero amor, quiero gloria,
quiero un deleite divino,
como en mi mente imagino,
como en el mundo no hay;
y es la luz de aquel lucero

La conjuración de Venecia *(1834), contributed to the short-lived triumph of the negative strain in literature, along with Larra, Rivas and Espronceda. His early verses anticipate the mordant scepticism of the late 1830s and the personal questioning of traditional values, belief and values centred on personal experiences. Here he employs nature with its eternal return and its fruitful regeneration as a foil and contrast to his own concerns.*]

II.m.3.   JOSÉ DE ESPRONCEDA, 'To Jarifa in an Orgy'

Come, Jarifa, bring your hand, come and place it on my brow for I feel my head burn in a sea of burning lava. Come and place on my lips those lips which inflame me, where still there hover the kisses of your former lovers. What of virtue, purity! What of truth and love! The deceptive illusion of a child which flattered my youth. Give me wine: may my memories drown in it; bewildered, without feeling, let life go by and the coffin bring me peace. Sweat burns my face and my eyes shine uncertainly, red with flaming blood, my heart leaps. Be off, woman; I hate you, I feel your hand in mine and I feel it cold, and your kisses are like ice. Always the same! Stupid women, invent other caresses, another world, other delights, or cursed be pleasure! Your kisses are deceitful, a lie your tenderness, your beauty ugliness, your enjoyment suffering. I desire love, I desire glory, one not of this world; and it is the light of that star which deceived my imagination, a false flame, a false guide which carried me off, errant and blind. Why did my soul die to pleasure and yet lives for impious pain? Why, if I lie in indolent calm, instead of peace I feel arid loathing? Why this disquieting and burning desire? Why this strange and vague feeling that I myself realise is a delirium and yet I seek its seductive allure? Why do I still imagine loves and pleasures which I feel certain will be falsehood? Why, perhaps, does my foolish heart long after fantastic women if, afterwards, in place of meadows and flowers, it finds arid deserts and thorns, and in stupid and lubricious love affairs will only find disgust and vexation? I threw myself, like a fleeting comet, on the wings of my burning imagination; wherever my impetuous and unquiet mind flew I thought I would find happiness and triumph. I threw myself in a daring flight beyond the world in the ethereal regions and I found doubt, and the radiant heavens I saw converted into an airy illusion. Later, on earth, I sought virtue, glory with anxiety and a delirious passion, and I found nauseous dust and insubstantial dross. I saw women of virginal purity among pure white clouds of celestial light; I touched them and saw their purity change into smoke and mire and corruption. And I found my illusions dissolved and eternal and insatiable my desire, I touched reality and hated life; I only believe in the peace of the grave. Yet I seek and greedily seek and my soul still imagines and desires delights; I question, and a fearful accent 'Alas!', replies, 'despair and die. Die unhappy man: life is a torment, pleasure a deceit; there is no peace on earth for thee, nor happiness, nor contentment, only eternal ambition and eternal struggle. For thus God punishes the daring soul who madly aspires in his insane delirium to discover the unfathomable secret mysteries of truth kept hidden from mortals.' Oh!, cease; no, I wish to see no more, nor know nothing; my soul satiated and prostrate longs only to rest. Feeling has died in me, for my happiness is already dead; neither pleasure nor sadness return to trouble my breast. Pass by, pass by in an illusory distorting glass and deceive other young spirits; pearly images of glory, crowned with gold and laurel, pass by. Pass by, pass by in confusion, voluptuous women, with dance and clamour; pass by like vaporous visions without moving or

que engañó mi fantasía,
fuego fatuo, falso guía
que errante y ciego me tray.
¿Por qué murió para el placer mi alma,
y vive aún para el dolor impío?
¿Por qué si yazgo en indolente calma,
siento en lugar de paz, árido hastío?
¿Por qué este inquieto abrasador deseo?
¿Por qué este sentimiento extraño y vago,
que yo mismo conozco un devaneo,
y busco aún su seductor halago?
¿Por qué aún fingirme amores y placeres
que cierto estoy de que serán mentira?
¿Por qué en pos de fantásticas mujeres
necio tal vez mi corazón delira,
si luego en vez de prados y de flores
halla desiertos áridos y abrojos,
y en sus sandios y lúbricos amores
fastidio sólo encontrará y enojos?
Yo me arrojé, cual rápido cometa,
en alas de mi ardiente fantasía;
doquier mi arrebatada mente inquieta
dichas y triunfos encontrar creía.
Yo me lancé con atrevido vuelo
fuera del mundo en la región etérea,
y hallé la duda, y el radiante cielo
vi convertirse en ilusión aérea.
Luego en la tierrra la virtud, la gloria,
busqué con ansia y delirante amor,
y hediondo polvo y deleznable escoria
mi fatigado espíritu encontró.
Mujeres vi de virginal limpieza
entre albas nubes de celeste lumbre;
yo las toqué, y en humo su pureza
trocarse vi, y en lodo y podredumbre.
Y encontré mi ilusión desvanecida
y eterno e insaciable mi deseo,
palpé la realidad y odié la vida;
sólo en la paz de los sepulcros creo.
Y busco aún y busco codicioso,
y aun deleites el alma finge y quiere;
pregunto, y un acento pavoroso
"¡Ay!", me responde, "desespera y muere.
Muere, infeliz: la vida es un tormento,
un engaño el placer; no hay en la tierra
paz para ti, ni dicha, ni contento,

wounding my heart. And let the toasts and the din of the feast befuddle my confused imagination, and let night fly by and let day surprise me in a stupid and endless lethargy. Come, Jarifa, you, like me, have suffered; you never weep. Yet, o sadness!, you know how bitter is my affliction. We are one in our pain; in vain you hold back your weeping . . . You, too, like me, bear a heart that is rent in pieces.

(c. 1837?) [1840]

sino eterna ambición y eterna guerra.
Que así castiga Dios el alma osada
que aspira loca en su delirio insano,
de la verdad para el mortal velada,
a descubrir el insondable arcano".
¡Oh cesa!; no, yo no quiero
ver más, ni saber ya nada;
harta mi alma y postrada,
sólo anhela descansar.
En mí muera el sentimiento,
pues ya murió mi ventura;
ni el placer ni la tristura
vuelvan mi pecho a turbar.
Pasad, pasad en óptica ilusoria,
y otras jóvenes almas engañad;
nacaradas imágenes de gloria,
coronas de oro y de laurel, pasad.
Pasad, pasad, mujeres voluptuosas,
con danza y algaraza en confusión;
pasad como visiones vaporosas
sin conmover ni herir mi corazón.
Y aturdan mi revuelta fantasía
los brindis y el estruendo del festín,
y huya la noche y me sorprenda el día
en un letargo estúpido y sin fin.
Ven Jarifa; tu has sufrido
como yo; tú nunca lloras.
Mas, ¡ay triste! que no ignoras
cúan amarga es mi aflicción.
Una misma en nuestra pena,
en vano el llanto contienes...
Tú también, como yo, tienes
desgarrado el corazón.

(1837?) [1840]

II.m.4. JOSÉ DE ESPRONCEDA, extracto de *El diablo mundo*, Canto II,
'A Teresa. Descansa en paz'

¿Por qué volvéis a la memoria mía,
tristes recuerdos del placer perdido,
a aumentar la ansiedad y la agonía
de este desierto corazón herido?
¡Ay!, que de aquellas horas de alegría
le quedó al corazón sólo un gemido
y el llanto que el dolor los ojos niegan
lágrimas son de hiel que el alma anegan.
¿Dónde volaron, ¡ay!, aquellas horas
de juventud, de amor y de ventura,
regaladas de músicas sonoras,
adornadas de luz y de hermosura?
Imágenes de oro bullidoras,
sus alas de carmín y nieve pura
al sol de mi esperanza desplegando,
pasaban, ¡ay!, a mi alredor cantando.
Gorjeaban los dulces ruiseñores,
el sol iluminaba mi alegría,
el aura susurraba entre las flores,
el bosque mansamente respondía,
las fuentes murmuraban sus amores...
¡Ilusiones que llora el alma mía!
¡Oh! ¡Cuán suave resonó en mi oído
el bullicio del mundo y su ruido!
Mi vida entonces, cual guerrera nave
que el puerto deja por la vez primera
y al soplo de los céfiros suave
orgullosa desplega su bandera
y, al mar, dejando que a sus pies alabe
su triunfo en roncos cantos, va velera,
una ola tras otra bramadora
hollando y dividiendo vencedora,
¡ay!, en el mar del mundo en ansia ardiente
de amor volaba. El sol de la mañana
llevaba yo sobre mi tersa frente
y el alba pura de su dicha ufana.
Dentro de ella el amor, cual rica fuente
que entre frescura y arboledas mana,
brotaba entonces abundante río
de ilusiones y dulce desvarío.
Yo amaba todo: un noble sentimiento
exaltaba mi ánimo y sentía
en mi pecho un secreto movimiento

II.m.4. JOSÉ DE ESPRONCEDA, from *It's an Absurd World,* Canto II,
'To Teresa. Rest in Peace'

Why do sad memories of lost pleasure return to my memory, to increase the anxiety and agony of this deserted and wounded heart? Alas! Of all those hours of happiness to the heart there only remains a groan and the lamentation of which the eyes deny the pain, the tears of bitterness which overwhelm the soul. Whence did they fly, alas, those hours of youth, of love and happiness, showered with sonorous music, adorned with light and beauty? Images of rippling gold, their wings of carmine and pure snow unfurling at the sun of my hopes passed by, alas, singing about me. The sweet nightingales warbled, the sun illumined my happiness, an aura sighed between the flowers, the wood gently replied, fountains murmured their loves . . . Illusions which my soul laments! Oh! How sweetly the bustle and noise of the world resounded in my ear! My life, then, like a ship-of-war that leaves port for the first time and which, at the breath of the soft zephyrs, proudly unfurls its pennant and, letting the seas at its keel praise its triumph in hoarse songs, goes, sails aloft, humbling and dividing as conqueror, wave after roaring wave; alas!, I flew on the sea of the world with a burning anxiety for love. I bore the morning sun on my unlined brow and my pure soul was exultant with my happiness. In my mind, love, like a rich fountain which trickles between greenness and groves, bubbled up then into an abundant river of illusions and sweet delirium. I loved everything: a noble sentiment exalted my spirit and I felt in my breast a sacred movement, a generous guide to great deeds. Liberty with its immortal breath, holy goddess, lit up my soul, constantly imagining in my pure faith, dreams of worldly glory and of good fortune. [. . .] I, exiled on a stranger's shore, with ecstatic eyes I followed the audacious bark which on a silvery ray of light flew from the harbour of my homeland. When the sun swooned in the West, alone and lost amid the darkening masts, I thought I heard the harmonious accent of a woman across the sigh of the wind. A woman! She grows in colour in the warm beams of the magical moon; she slowly fades away, far off between the clouds at the languid swoon of the setting sun; she shimmers for a second at the break of day on the hilltops which May garlands with flowers; she walks through the dark glade and plays in the waters of the serene river. [. . .] A woman which love fashions to her illusions, a woman who says nothing to the senses, a dream of the sweetest tenderness, an echo which brings pleasure to our ears, the generous and pure flame of love, the sweet delights of fulfilled pleasure which garlands a rich fantasy, pleasures for which the heart avariciously longs. Alas! That woman, only she can hope to gain so much delirious delight and yet that woman so pure and beautiful is the deceitful illusion of my hopes. [. . .] Who would have thought that a day would come when, celestial enchantment lost and the blindfold fallen from the eyes, all that had given delight would give vexation? [. . .] For thus the rapid hours passed by and, at the same pace, our happiness passed away, and never did we count our anxieties; you intoxicated in my love, I in your beauty. The hours, alas!, fleeting by, observed us. [. . .] And the hour finally came. Oh! Who, impiously, alas!, seared the flower of your purity? You were once a crystalline river, a spring of limpid purity; afterwards a torrent of dark colours breaking out between gorges and wild plants; in the end a bog of corrupted waters held back by foetid mud. How did you fall down, thrown from on high to the earth, star of the luminous morning?

(1839–1840) [1840]

[Espronceda is, without doubt, the clearest spokesman of the negative vision in Spanish Romanticism and the most concerned with his inner feelings: his heights of delight and pleasure and the

de grandes hechos generoso guía.
La libertad con su inmortal aliento,
santa diosa, mi espíritu encendía,
contino imaginando en mi fe pura
sueños de gloria al mundo y de ventura.

....

Yo desterrado en extranjera playa
con los ojos extático seguía
la nave audaz que en argentada raya
volaba al puerto de la patria mía.
Yo, cuando en Occidente el sol desmaya,
solo y perdido en la arboleda umbría,
oír pensaba el armonioso acento
de una mujer al suspirar el viento.
¡Una mujer! En el templado rayo
de la mágica luna se colora;
del sol poniente al lánguido desmayo
lejos entre las nubes se evapora;
sobre las cumbres que florece el mayo
brilla fugaz al despuntar la aurora;
cruza tal vez por entre el bosque umbrío,
juega en las aguas de sereno río.

....

Mujer que amor en su ilusión figura,
mujer que nada dice a los sentidos,
ensueño de suavísima ternura,
eco que regaló nuestros oídos,
de amor la llama generosa y pura,
los goces dulces del placer cumplidos
que engalana la rica fantasía,
goces que avaro el corazón ansía.
¡Ay!, aquella mujer, tan sólo aquélla
tanto delirio a realizar alcanza
y esa mujer tan cándida y tan bella
es mentida ilusión de la esperanza.

....

¿Quién pensara jamás llegara un día
en que, perdido el celestial encanto
y caída la venda de los ojos,
cuanto diera placer causara enojos?

....

Que así las horas rápidas pasaban
Y pasaba a la par nuestra ventura,
Y nunca nuestras ansias las contaban,

depths of his despair. His exalted contrasts (following Martínez de la Rosa) between illusion and reality, past and present, imagination and truth (echoing Byron's 'the sad truth'); his charting of the collision of youthful ideals and mature insight, of faith and scepticism, mark him out as the pre-eminent poet of metaphysical despair, of the fastidio universal *of the age. In* 'To Jarifa' *he charts the path from youthful illusion to mature disillusion and, through the mysterious groan, implies the existence of a cruel and unjust God who punishes man for seeking after knowledge, a radical and blasphemous idea which challenged the Christian teaching of a God of Love and a Divine Providence, a tenet central to the Catholic teaching of his day. The* Canto a Teresa *is partly autobiographical and relates the painful and disillusioning love affair between the poet and Teresa Mancha. They met in Lisbon as they went into exile in 1827 and an affair began on shipboard, continuing in London. She married Gregorio Bayo in March 1829 but the affair continued; the couple eloped to Paris in August 1832 leaving Teresa's children behind. In 1833, under the amnesty, they returned to Madrid and she bore the poet a daughter in 1834. After a series of violent quarrels they parted and Teresa died, destitute, in September 1839. This canto, totally unrelated to the rest of the unfinished* El Diablo mundo *(1840), expresses Espronceda's pain at the last of his sustaining ideals: love. With love gone, his epic poem expresses the absurdity of life.*]

tú embriagada en mi amor, yo en tu hermosura,
las horas, ¡ay!, huyendo nos miraban.

....

Y llegaron en fin. ¡Oh! ¿Quién, impío,
¡ay!, agostó la flor de tu pureza?
Tú fuiste un tiempo un cristalino río,
manantial de purísima limpieza;
después torrente de color sombrío,
rompiendo entre peñascos y maleza,
y estanque en fin de aguas corrompidas
entre fétido fango detenidas.
¿Cómo caíste despeñado al suelo,
astro de la mañana luminoso?

(1839–1840) [1840]

II.m.5.   GABRIEL GARCÍA TASSARA, 'En el campo'

Hórrida simpatía
el alma adivinaba
entre la estéril sequedad del suelo
y la aridez del corazón. No hallaba
de amor o de amistad un sentimiento
ni en los otros ni en mí; y en torno
yermado y triste y sin vigor el campo
con un placer estúpido miraba
de su vivaz fecundidad vacío
cual volcán bajo piélagos de lava.
Aquel placer sombrío
gustaba yo del propio sufrimiento
en el ajeno padecer. . . Mi alma
esas horas amargas discurría
que anhelamos tal vez que todo sienta
porque padezca con nosotros todo;
y la pálida flor y al árbol seco
daba yo un alma en mi dolor profundo,
para tener en mi dolor un eco
y consolarme en el dolor del mundo.

(c. 1840) [1872]

II.m.5.   GABRIEL GARCÍA TASSARA, 'In the Countryside'

A ghastly sympathy did my soul divine between the sterile drought of the earth and the aridity of the heat. It found no feeling of love nor amity, neither in others nor myself, and all about, barren and sad, the countryside, without energy, watched me with a stupid satisfaction from her empty and lively fecundity, like a volcano under a sea of lava. I savoured that gloomy pleasure of my suffering in that of others . . . My soul whiled away those bitter hours which, perhaps, we desire that all may feel, for everything suffers with us; and to the pale flowers and the shrivelled tree I gave my soul in deepest pain, to have for my anguish an echo, to console myself in the grief of the world.

(c. 1840) [1872]

[*In part an author of civic poetry who railed against the political compromises of his time and Spain's weakness, at heart García Tassara was a sceptical Romantic in the same sense as was Espronceda, a man troubled by a want of faith nor trust in any guiding absolute value. His early poetry was not collected until 1872. In this poem he employs the Romantic pathetic fallacy first attempted by Cadalso in 1773 as a means to express his personal despair and loss of abiding ideals.*]

II.m.6. GERTRUDIS GÓMEZ DE AVELLANEDA, 'Mi mal'

En vano ansiosa tu amistad procura
adivinar el mal que me atormenta;
en vano, amigo, conmovida intenta
revelarlo mi voz a tu ternura,
puede explicarse el ansia, la locura
con que el amor sus fuegos alimenta;
puede el dolor, la pena más violenta
exhalar por el labio su amargura.
Mas de decir mi malestar profundo
no halla mi voz, mi pensamiento, medio
y al indagar su origen me confundo;
pero es un mal terrible, sin remedio,
que hace odiosa la vida, odioso el mundo,
que seca el corazón... ¡En fin, es tedio!

(1841) [1850]

II.m.7. RAMÓN DE CAMPOAMOR, 'La vida humana'

Velas de amor en golfos de ternura
suelta mi pobre corazón al viento
y encuentra en lo que alcanza su tormento
y espera en lo que no halla su ventura.
Viviendo en esta humana sepultura,
engañar el pesar es mi contento
y este cilicio atroz del pensamiento
no halla un linde entre el genio y la locura.
¡Ay! En la vida ruin que al loco embarga
y que al cuerdo infeliz de horror consterna,
dulce en el nombre, en realidad amarga,
sólo el dolor con el dolor alterna
y, si al contarla a días es muy larga,
midiéndola por horas es eterna.

[1842]

II.m.8. RAMÓN DE CAMPOAMOR, 'Mi vida'

En mi vida infeliz paso las horas
mientras llega la muerte,
convirtiendo en doloras
las tristes ironías de la suerte.

[1845]

II.m.6. GERTRUDIS GÓMEZ DE AVELLANEDA, 'My Sickness'

In vain anxiety your friendship strives to guess the pain which torments me; in vain, my friend, my troubled voice strives to reveal the reason at your tenderness. My anxiety can be explained; the madness with which love feeds its flames, suffering most violent pain, can breathe its bitterness through the lips. Yet to speak of my profound malaise I cannot find my voice, my thoughts; I meditate and in seeking its origins I am left confused; but it is a dreadful pain, without remedy, which makes life hateful, hateful the world, it dries up the heart . . . In short, it is depression!

(1841) [1850]

[*Gómez de Avellaneda is one of the outstanding women writers of the age. Born in Cuba in 1814, she came to Spain at the height of the negative Romantic response in 1836 (shortly after Rivas' deeply pessimistic* Don Álvaro *and the appearance of many of Espronceda's most sceptical poems) and mixed with the leading writers of the day. She suffered a series of nervous crises, especially after an affair with García Tassara by whom she had a child which he refused to recognize. Her novel* Sab *(1841) formed part of the anti-slavery movement (see below under History) and had much the same effect as Stowe's* Uncle Tom's Cabin *in 1852. In this poem she attempts to explain the essence of Romantic* mal *and the pervasive* tedio universal *or* Weltschmertz, *echoing her admired Espronceda.*]

II.m.7. RAMÓN DE CAMPOAMOR, 'Human Life'

My poor heart frees to the wind sails of love in gulfs of tenderness and discovers in what it achieves its torment and longs for its happiness in what it does not discover. Living in this human sepulchre my content is to deceive my weariness and this atrocious cilice of my thought finds no place between genius and madness. Alas! In the contemptible life which overpowers the madman and which alarms the man of reason with horror, sweet in its name, bitter in its reality, only pain alternates with pain and, if relating it daily is tiresome, measuring it by hours is an eternity.

[1842]

II.m.8. RAMÓN DE CAMPOAMOR, 'My Life'

In my unhappy life, which death approaches, I spend my hours changing in song the grim ironies of fate.

[1845]

[*Campoamor expressed the contradictions of the 1840s when the profound scepticism of Larra, Espronceda, Rivas and others was under siege from the conservative revival. His early work expresses the* fiebre del siglo, *a term coined by García Tassara, tinged with a world-weary irony which he offered as a means to assimilate the prevailing mood of doubt into the bourgeois consciousness. See under Language for his later work.*]

II.m.9.   CAROLINA CORONADO, '¡Oh cuál te adoro!'

¡Oh cuál te adoro! Con la luz del día
tu nombre invoco apasionada y triste
y, cuando el cielo en sombras se reviste
aún te llama el alma mía.
Tú eres el tiempo que mis horas guía,
tú eres la idea que mi mente asiste
porque en ti se concentra cuanto existe,
mi pasión, mi esperanza, mi poesía.
No hay ni canto que igualar pueda tu canto
cuando tu amor me cuentas y deliras
revelando la fe de tu contento.
Tiemblo a tu voz y tiemblo si me miras
y quisiera exhalar mi último aliento
abrasada en el aire que respiras.

(1849?)

II.m.10.   GUSTAVO ADOLFO BÉCQUER, 'Rima'

Volverán las oscuras golondrinas
en tu balcón sus nidos a colgar
y otra vez con el ala a sus cristales
jugando llamarán;
pero aquellas que el vuelo refrenaban
tu hermosura y mi dicha a contemplar,
aquellas que aprendieron nuestros nombres,
ésas... ¡no volverán!
Volverán las tupidas madreselvas
de tu jardín las tapias a escalar
y otra vez a la tarde, aún más hermosas,
sus flores abrirán;
pero aquellas cuajadas de rocío
cuyas gotas mirábamos temblar
y caer como lágrimas del día...
ésas... ¡no volverán!
Volverán del amor en tus oídos
las palabras ardientes a sonar;
tu corazón de su profundo sueño
tal vez despertará;
pero, mudo y absorto y de rodillas
como se adora a un Dios ante su altar,
como yo te he querido... desengáñate;
así... ¡no te querrán!

[1868]

II.m.9. CAROLINA CORONADO, 'Oh How I Adore You!'

O how I adore you! At the light of day I invoke your name with passion and sadness and, when the heavens gown themselves with shadows, still my exalted soul calls out your name. You are the mark of time which guides my hours, you are the idea which aids my mind, for in you everything that exists is concentrated, my passion, my hopes, my poetry. There is no song which can equal your song when you tell me of your love and you delight in revealing the faith of your contentment. I tremble at your voice and tremble if you look at me and I would desire to exhale my last breath burned in the air you breathe.

(1849?)

[*From 1848, when she first came to Madrid, Coronado led a celebrated literary circle and was a confidente of Queen Isabel II. She was principally concerned with the condition of women but her earliest poems, including this poem, belong to the period 1843–1852. She is famed for the intensity of her love poetry and here, part of a series addressed to Alberto (whether a real or imagined lover remains unclear), this poem marks the high point of the expression of ecstatic feeling and love.*]

II.m.10. GUSTAVO ADOLFO BÉCQUER, 'Rhyme'

The dark swallows will return to your balcony to hang their nests and, once again, will playfully tap with their wings your window panes; but those who paused in their flight to contemplate your beauty and my happiness, they . . . will not return! The dense honeysuckles in your garden will return to climb the walls and, once again, in the afternoon, even more beautiful, they will open their flowers; but those coated with dew whose droplets we watched as they trembled and fell like the tears of the day . . . they . . . will not return! The ardent words of love will return to sound in your ear; your heart will perhaps awaken from its profound dream; but, dumb and absorbed and on my knees as if worshipping a God before the altar, as I have loved you . . . be not deceived: in that way . . . they will not love you!

[1868]

[*A belated Romantic, Bécquer echoes the profound pessimism of Espronceda and Tassara in his existential questioning and his meditations on death. In this often-quoted* rima, *through the contrast of past and present, he laments the passing of time, the loss of love and the fading of illusions, his only comfort that no other could love as he has, a statement which expresses once more the exalted nature of Romantic love and the pain of non-requital.*]

n. SVENSKA

II.n.1.   JOHAN HENRIC KELLGREN, 'Den nya Skapelsen, eller Inbildningens Verld'

Du, som af Skönheten och Behagen
En ren och himmelsk urbild ger!
Jag såg dig – och från denna dagen
Jag endast dig i verlden ser.

Död låg Naturen för mit öga,
Djupt låg hon för min känsla död –
Kom så en flägt ifrån det höga,
Och ljus och lif i verlden böd.

Och ljuset kom, och lifvet tändes,
En själ i stela massan flöt;
Alt tog et anletsdrag som kändes,
En röst som til mit hjerta bröt.

Kring rymden nya Himlar sträcktes,
Och Jorden nya skrudar drog,
Och Bildningen och Snillet väcktes,
Och Skönheten stod up och log.

Då fann min själ sig Himlaburen,
Sig sprungen af en Gudastam,
Och såg de under i Naturen,
Som aldrig Visheten förnam.

Ej endast storhet och förmåga
Och glans och rymd och rörelse;
Ej blott i dalens djup det låga,
Och endast höjd i klipporne;

Men liflig til mit öra fördes
De höga Spherers harmoni;
På berget Änglars harpor hördes
Ur djupet mörka andars skri.

På fältet logo fridens löjen,
Skräck omsmög i den skumma dal,
Och lunden hviskade om nöjen
Och skogen suckade om qval:

Och vrede var i hafvets vågor,
Och ömhet uti källans sus,
Och majestät i solens lågor,
Och blygsamhet i månans ljus.

n. SWEDISH

II.n.1. JOHAN HENRIC KELLGREN, 'The New Creation, or the World of Imagination'

You are the model and template,
Pure beauty and heavenly delight.
I saw you – and from this day on
I can only see you in the world.

Nature lay dead to my eye
Deep dead she was to all feeling –
Then came a breeze from above,
Comanding light and love into the world.

And light came, and life ignited,
A soul flowed in the stiff mass;
Every feeling thing now had a face,
A voice that took to my heart.

Through space new Heavens stretched
And Earth was dressed anew
And Education and Reason woke up,
And Beauty arose smiling.

My soul felt as if born from Heaven,
Sprung from a lineage of Gods,
Beholding the wonders of Nature,
That Wisdom had never perceived.

Not only greatness and vigour
And splendour and space and movement;
Not just the low-lying valley,
Nor simply the height of the cliffs.

But my ears caught the lively music,
The harmony of the high Spheres;
On the mountain rang out Angels' harps,
From the deep the dark spirits' scream.

The joys of peace smiled on the meadows,
While Fear roamed the sombre valley,
And the grove whispered of pleasures
And the forest sighed of torments.

And there was anger in the waves of the ocean
And tenderness murmurs from the spring,
And majesty in the flames of the sun,
And modesty in the light of the moon.

Hämd gick at blixtens pilar hvässa,
Mod skakade orcanens arm,
Och cedern lyftade en hjessa,
Och blomman öpnade en barm. –

O lefvande förstånd af tingen!
O snillets, känslans hemlighet!
Hvem fattade dig, Skönhet? – ingen
Förutan den som älska vet.

För mig när du naturen målar
Til Himlar utaf ljus och väl,
Hvad är du? – återbrutna strålar
Af *Hilmas* bild uti min jsäl.

Hon är det i min själ, hvars stämpel
Til Skapelsen förkjusning bär;
Och Jorden upstod til et Tempel
Der hon Gudomligheten är.

Du, som af Skönhet och Behagen
En ren och himmelsk urbild ger!
Jag såg dig – och från denna dagen
Jag endast dig i verlden ser.

I alt din lånta teckning kännes,
O evigt samma, evigt ny!
Din växt blef liljans växt, och hennes
Den friska glansen af din hy.

Din blick i dagens blickar blandas,
Din röst fick näktergalens sång,
Jag dig i rosens vällukt andas
Och vestanflägten har din gång.

Ej nog – du sjelfva fasan gläder,
Du fyller afgrundar med ljus;
Du öknarne i blomster kläder,
Och kjusar i ruiners grus.

Och när min tanka hänryckt vimlar
Och flyr, och söker trängtande,
Och söker genom jord och himlar
Det sälla stoftets Skapare;

Och frågar, i hvad skepnad fattas,
At öm, och god och glad och mild

Revenge sharpened the arrows of lightning,
Bravery shook the arm of the hurricane,
And the cedar lifted its head upwards,
And the flower opened its heart. –

Oh, living understanding of things!
Oh! secret of emotion and reason!
Who grasped you, Beauty? – none did –
But only the one who can love.

To me when you picture nature
As Heavens of light and good,
What are you? – refracted rays
Of Hilma's image in my soul.

In my soul, it is only her imprint that
Brings enchantment to Creation;
And Earth is now a hallowed shrine
Where she is the Divinity.

You are the model and template,
Pure beauty and heavenly delight.
I saw you – and from this day on
I can see only you in the world.

In everything your essence returns,
So unchanging, yet ever so new!
Your growth was that of the lily,
and hers the fresh gleam of your skin.

Your gaze becomes one with the daylight,
Your voice is the nightingale's song,
I breathe in you the fragrance of roses
And you sway in the western wind.

And yet more – you make joy out of dread,
Abysses you fill up with light;
You dress the deserts in blossom,
Enchanting each stone of our ruins.

Thus exalted, my thoughts swarm;
Fleeing, eagerly searching,
Searching through earth and heavens
For the Creator of the blessed dust;

Asking in what guise to grasp
The tender and good and joyful and mild one,

Vår högsta dyrkan värdig skattas? –
Då visas Han mig i din bild.

I Kungars Slott, i Hof och Städer,
Jag ser bland tusende blott dig;
Och, när min fot i hyddan träder,
Är du der redan före mig.

Jag gick at Visdoms djupet spörja;
Din tanka ref mig ur des famn.
Jag gick at Hjeltars qväden börja;
Men cithran lärde blott dit namn.

Jag ville Ärans höjder hinna,
Men bortvek i det fjät du gick.
Jag ville Lyckans skatter finna,
Och fann dem alla i din blick.

Du, som af skönhet och behagen
En ren och himmelsk urbild ger!
Jag såg dig – och från denna dagen
Jag endast dig i verlden ser.

Förgäfves ur din åsyn tagen,
Mig blott din tanka unnas mer:
I dina spår af minnet dragen,
Jag endast dig i verlden ser.

(1790)

II.n.2.   C. J. L. ALMQVIST, 'Skaldens Natt'

Natten den 19 November.

Jag låg en natt i min säng i mycken oro, och sömnens dufva hvilade icke öfver mig.

Min själ var i ångest, mitt sinne i sorg. Gränslösa frågor stodo upp och tvifvel omhvärfde mig. Lifvet, verlden, evigheten, tiden – allt satt i qval och vanmakt vid sidan af min bädd. Ingenstädes sammanhang. Och glädje? Ingen.

Konstens skapelser hugsvalade icke mitt hjerta. Dess form att vara är ju icke rät? i ständiga slingringar går dess sätt, falskhet är dess andedrägt, och gift dess botten. Konsten skjuter icke åt samma håll som den måttar. Ack jag ville ärligt se mitt mål, och jag ville ärligt träffa mitt mål. Skall jag nödvändigt bedragas? och bedraga?

Jag tänkte på fordna nätter, på farna stunder då jag varit säll – och varit from. Då hade jag känt min ande i himmelrikets grannskap – o vore jag der jag fordom var.

Så låg jag, och det gick öfver midnatt. Klockan slog ett, hon slog tu. Jag forskade ut åt universum, och jag besåg allt som jag kände i verlden. Renhet fann jag icke: icke hos mig, och icke hos någon.

Då hörde jag i nattens mörker en röst hviska till min själ och säga: "Välj –

What is worthy of our utmost reverence? –
I now see him in the Image of you.

In Halls of Kings, at Courts, in Towns,
Among thousands I see only you;
And when I enter a humble cabin,
You are there already inside.

I had set out to understand Wisdom;
The thought of you tore me away.
I set out to compose songs of Heroes;
But the zither just taught your name.

I wished to reach the heights of Repute,
But I found myself in your footsteps.
I wished to seek treasure and Fortune,
And found them all in your gaze.

You are the model and template,
Pure beauty and heavenly delight.
I saw you – and from this day on
I can see only you in the world.

Desperate, as you are hidden from sight,
The thought of you is my sole reward:
I have just the memory of your imprint,
I can see only you in the world.

(1790) [*Translated by John Swedenmark and Patricia Erskine-Hill*]

II.n.2. C. J. L. ALMQVIST, 'The Poet's Night'

The night of November 19th
I lay in great distress one night in my bed, and the dove of sleep did not rest by my side.

In my soul was agony, sorrow in my mind. Unbounded questions arose and doubt surrounded me. Life, world, eternity, time – they all sat in anguish by my bed. Nowhere coherence. And joy? None.

The creations of art did not comfort my heart. Their shape of being is not straight? in constant coils they find their ways, deception is their breath, and poison their underpinning. Art does not discharge in the same direction as it aims. Alas I wanted truly to see my goal, and I wanted truly to strike my target. Would I unavoidably have to be deceived? And deceive?

I thought of nights of old, on moments that had passed when I had been exultant – and been righteous. Then I had felt my spirit in the quarters of heaven – oh if I were whence I once was.

So I lay, and it passed over midnight. The clock struck one, she struck twain. I explored towards the universe, and I saw all that I knew in the world. Purity I found not: not with myself, and not with anyone.

Then in the darkness of the night I heard a voice whisper to my soul, saying 'Choose – '

"Vill du vara stark, så skall du få den starkes lott, hvilken är kamp och ingen ro. Med allt skall du hafva att strida: ingenting utom dig på jorden skall du finna i lag, utan ständigt skall du vilja fäkta deremot. Och ingenting utom dig på jorden skall heller finna dig i lag, utan ständigt uppresa sig och kämpa emot dig. Så äfven inom dig i ditt tänkande och begrundande hem skall du vara irrande och ditt väsende flygtigt.

"Men vill du vara ett lamm, så kom till mig. Då skall du hafva frid, oskuld och ro hos mig i mitt rum. Jag skall omsluta dig och du skall icke dragas af söndringen, ej slitas af eländets verk. Vill du vara ett lamm, så skall du låta allt göra med dig som det vill; men det skall icke röra dig, ty du är i beskärm. Fast utan hus skall du icke frysa, hos mig skall du hafva värme och ljufhet utan skräck. Dig skall intet nå och ingen ålder hinna, ty jag vill komma och vara ung i dig."

Herre! svarade min själ och sjönk tillsammans – kunde jag få vara ett lamm som du säger . . .

Då flögo som en blixt alla bojor sönder, och en stilla sky, såsom en himmelsk sömn – hvilken dock är vaken i Guds beskådning – omhvärfde mig, och jag kände mig tagen i hägn emot allt.

Då öfvergaf jag i mitt sinne allt, och jag sade: Allt må vara och göra huru det vill.

Med mig må de göra såsom det brukas, de må slagta mig.

Men Herren tog mitt arma hjerta i sitt väsende, och sedan blef allt i verlden för mig en lek.

Oskuld och ro satte sig ned vid min säng, frid upplyfte min sängs omhänge.

Jag låg ända långt framåt morgonen: det har jag sedan alltid gjort. En sång hörde jag vid mitt läger, och en mild nåd upptände ljus omkring min hufvudgärd, dem ingen såg mer än jag.

Jag frågade: skall jag numera lyssna på någonting i verlden? skall jag nånsin läsa, tala eller skrifva mer? Det svarades: "lyssna, tala och skrif!

"Ihågkom blott att stå på intet, och att stödja dig vid intet.

"Då skall intet röra dig, och du sjelf skall ega intet; men du skall få makt med allt.

"Du skall ej få makt till att ega det, ty du skall intet besitta och på intet stå. Men du skall få den bästa af all makt, som är att leka."

Vid dessa svar sjönk mitt hufvud in i en ljusgul sky, och jag förlorade universum.

Men när jag vaknade och steg upp, var jag glad. Konsten vaknade då ny inom mig, och i hvit fägring såg jag den täcka.

Dödt hade nu döden, och endast lifvet lefde för mig.

Jag hörde åskan stiga på molnen, och det förskräckta himlahvalfvet bredde sina vingar darrande öfver jorden. Men jag log och sade: Ljungelden är vacker.

Regnet forsade i störtskurar öfver landet, allt föll, smälte och fördränktes. Jag blef icke våt.

Stormar ilade genom skog och äng, djuren flydde, och menniskorna fröso i märg och ben. Min hand var varm, och jag målade.

Blommor såg jag knoppas, blommor såg jag vissna. Jag målade.

Barn såg jag uppväxa till flickor och gossar. Flickorna såg jag blomstra upp till qvinnor, sköna som lifvets rosor: jag såg dem sedan åldras, jag såg dem vissna och förgå. Gossarne såg jag blifva män, jag hörde dem tala klokt och skarpt, jag såg dem sedan åldras, såg dem blekna och gråna. Men jag fortfor att vara den jag är och varit: intet.

Jag målar blott.

. . . .

Gud – min Gud – detta är min sista bön till dig: låt också mig få vissna och dö som andra.

(1825–1826) [1838]

'If you want to be strong, yours shall be the fate of the strong one, which is struggle and no peace. You shall fight with all: you shall find nothing on earth in place, but you will incessantly want to fence it. And nothing or no one on earth shall find you in place, but will incessantly rise against you and fight you. So too will you within your thoughts and contemplation be wayward and your being not fixed.

'But if you want to be a lamb, then come to me. You shall have peace, innocence and quiet with me in my room. I shall embrace you and you shall not be tugged by disruption, not torn by misery's work. If you want to be a lamb, you shall subject yourself to everything and its command; and it shall not move you, for you are shielded. Although without a house, you shall not be cold, by my side you shall find warmth and delight without terror. Nothing will reach you and no age catch you, for I want to come and be youth within you.'

Lord! My soul answered and bowed down – would I be a lamb as you say . . .

Then all shackles flew off as a bolt of lightning, and a quiet sky, like heavenly sleep – one that still is awaken to God's view – came over me, and I felt sheltered against all.

Then I deserted all in my mind, and I said: Everything may be as it will.

By me, they may do as they might, they may butcher me.

But the Lord took my pitiful heart to his being, and then the world became a child's game to me.

Innocence sat down by my bed, peace lifted the draperies of my bed.

I remained until late morning, and I have always done so ever since. I heard a song by my resting place, and a gentle mercy lit my bed's head, unseen to all but me.

I asked: shall I now listen to anything in the world? Shall I ever read, speak or write again? It answered: 'listen, speak and write.'

'But remember to stand on nothing, and lean against nothing.

'Then nothing shall move you, and you shall own nothing for yourself; but you shall have power with all.

'You shall not have power to own it, for you shall possess nothing and stand on nothing. But you shall have the best of powers, which is to play.'

By these answers my head fell into a pale yellow sky, and I lost the universe.

But when I awoke and got up, I was happy. Art then awoke within me, and in white beauty I saw the pretty.

Death now had died, and only life was alive to me.

I heard the thunder rise above the clouds, and the terrified heavens spread its wings tremblingly across the earth. But I smiled and said 'the flashes of lightning are beautiful.'

The rain came down in torrents upon the land, everything fell, melted and drowned. I did not become wet.

Storms ran through wood and meadow, the animals fled, and men became cold to the marrow. My hand was warm, and I painted.

I saw flowers bud, I saw flowers wither. I painted.

I saw children grow up to be girls and young men. I saw the girls blossom into women, beautiful as the roses of life: then I saw them grow old. I saw the young men become men, I heard them speak wisely and sharply, I then saw them grow old, saw them fade and turn grey. But I continued to be who I am and have been: nothing.

I just paint.

. . . .

God – my God – this is my last prayer to you: let me too wither and die like others.

[Translated by Mattias Bolkéus Blom, 2006]

II.n.3.   ERIK JOHAN STAGNELIUS, 'Vän! I förödelsens stund'

Vän! i förödelsens stund, när ditt inre af mörker betäckes,
    När i ett afgrundsdjup minne och aning förgå,
Tanken famlar försagd bland skuggestalter och irrbloss,
    Hjertat ej sucka kan, ögat ej gråta förmår;
När från din nattomtöcknade själ eldvingarne falla,
    Och du till Intet, med skräck, känner dig sjunka på nytt,
Säg, hvem räddar dig då? – Hvem är den vänliga ängel,
    Som åt ditt inre ger ordning och skönhet igen,
Bygger på nytt din störtade verld, uppreser det fallna
    Altaret, tändande der flamman med presterlig hand? –
Endast det mägtiga Väsen, som först ur den eviga natten
    Kysste Seraphen till lif, solarna väckte till dans.
Endast det heliga Ord, som ropte åt verldarna: "Blifven!" –
    Och i hvars lefvande kraft verldarne röras ännu.
Derföre gläds, o vän! och sjung i bedröfvelsens mörker:
    Natten är dagens mor, Chaos är granne med Gud.

(undated, 1810–)

II.n.3. ERIK JOHAN STAGNELIUS, 'Friend! in the Moment of Devastation'

Friend! in the moment of devastation, your inner self covered with darkness,
    When in an abyss memory and premonition pass away,
Your diffident thought gropes among shadowy figures and glow-worms,
    Your heart cannot sigh, your eye fails to weep,
When from your night-dizzy soul the fire-wings fall
    And you fear yourself anew sinking down into Nothingness,
Tell me, who saves you then? – Who is the friendly angel
    That to your inner self restores order and beauty,
Builds your ruined world anew, raises the fallen
    Altar, lighting its candle with priestly hand? –
Alone the powerful Being, who once out of eternal night
    Kissed the Seraph alive, woke the suns up to dance.
Alone the holy word that made call to the worlds: 'Become!' –
    And in whose living force the worlds still ever move.
Therefore, rejoice, friend! and sing in the darkness of despair:
    Night is the mother of day, chaos is neighbour with God.

            (undated, 1810–) [*Translated by John Swedenmark*]

III.   History and Politics

The rise of Romanticism is clearly linked to the French Revolution and to the appearance of a specifically modern historiography which begins to break with both the older providential, and subsequent Enlightenment historical metanarratives represented by Hume and Gibbon. The texts chosen reflect the ways in which history becomes a problematic concept, and in which ideological and national battles were fought over the notion of history. Many sections discuss the question of what is the state and its relation to the individual. Differing kinds of historiography reflect the Romantic awareness of cultural difference and the attempts to respond to it. We also illustrate the rise of the 'philosophy of history'. Thus in the 1830s John Stuart Mill insisted on the connection between historicism and modernity: The 'spirit of the age' is in some measure a novel expression. 'I do not believe it to be met with in any work exceeding fifty years in antiquity.' The writings chosen here are intended to invite readers to explore how Romantic writers invented the traditions within which they placed themselves – embracing the invention of racial, of national and of literary traditions, extending from topics such as the ballad revival, the recovery of national literary traditions (Dante, Shakespeare, the Niebelungenlied), the claim for the organic identity of the Volk, and the attempt by occupied or fragmented nations such as Germany, Hungary, Italy or Romania to redefine and assert their own national identities.

If this section responds to the French Revolution and the dominating figure of Napoleon, it is equally concerned with the emergence of the notion that the term 'revolution' signals an abrupt and dramatic rupture with the past. Not confining itself to political revolution, it traces the notion in other areas; literary, social (as in the 'revolution in female manners'), scientific and industrial: embracing the Burke/Paine French Revolution debate, the Rights of Man/ Woman; the idea of War and opposition to it; and Waterloo as a metaphor and icon.

a.   BRITISH

III.a.1.   EDMUND BURKE, from *Reflections on the Revolution in France*

Society is indeed a contract. Subordinate contracts for objects of mere occasional interest may be dissolved at pleasure – but the state ought not to be considered as nothing better than a partnership agreement in a trade of pepper and coffee, calico, or tobacco, or some other such low concern, to be taken up for a little temporary interest, and to be dissolved by the fancy of the parties. It is to be looked on with other reverence, because it is not a partnership in things subservient only to the gross animal existence of a temporary and perishable nature. It is a partnership in all science; a partnership in all art; a partnership in every virtue and in all perfection. As the ends of such a partnership cannot be obtained in many generations, it becomes a partnership not only between those who are living, but between those who are living, those who are

dead, and those who are to be born. Each contract of each particular state is but a clause in the great primeval contract of eternal society, linking the lower with the higher natures, connecting the visible and invisible world, according to a fixed compact sanctioned by the inviolable oath which holds all physical and all moral natures, each in their appointed place. This law is not subject to the will of those who by an obligation above them, and infinitely superior, are bound to submit their will to that law. The municipal corporations of that universal kingdom are not morally at liberty at their pleasure, and on their speculations of a contingent improvement, wholly to separate and tear asunder the bands of their subordinate community and to dissolve it into an unsocial, uncivil, unconnected chaos of elementary principles. It is the first and supreme necessity only, a necessity that is not chosen but chooses, a necessity alone can justify a resort to anarchy. This necessity is no exception to the rule, because this necessity itself is a part, too, of that moral and physical disposition of things to which man must be obedient by consent or force; but if that which is only submission to necessity should be made the object of choice, the law is broken, nature is disobeyed, and the rebellious are outlawed, cast forth, and exiled from this world of reason, and order, and peace, and virtue, and fruitful penitence, into the antagonist world of madness, discord, vice, confusion, and unavailing sorrow.

These, my dear Sir, are, were, and, I think, long will be the sentiments of not the least learned and reflecting part of this kingdom. They who are included in this description form their opinions on such grounds as such persons ought to form them. The less inquiring receive them from an authority which those whom Providence dooms to live on trust need not be ashamed to rely on. These two sorts of men move in the same direction, though in a different place. They both move with the order of the universe.

[1790]

III.a.2.   THOMAS PAINE, from *The Rights of Man*, Part I

When we survey the wretched condition of man, under the monarchical and hereditary systems of Government, dragged from his home by one power, or driven by another, and impoverished by taxes more than by enemies, it becomes evident that those systems are bad, and that a general revolution in the principle and construction of Governments is necessary.

What is government more than the management of the affairs of a Nation? It is not, and from its nature cannot be, the property of any particular man or family, but of the whole community, at whose expense it is supported; and though by force and contrivance it has been usurped into an inheritance, the usurpation cannot alter the right of things.

Sovereignty, as a matter of right, appertains to the Nation only, and not to any individual; and a Nation has at all times an inherent indefeasible right to abolish any form of Government it finds inconvenient, and to establish such as accords with its interest, disposition and happiness. The romantic and barbarous distinction of men into Kings and subjects, though it may suit the condition of courtiers, cannot that of citizens; and is exploded by the principle upon which Governments are now founded. Every citizen is a member of the Sovereignty, and, as such, can acknowledge no personal subjection; and his obedience can be only to the laws.

When men think of what Government is, they must necessarily suppose it to possess a knowledge of all the objects and matters upon which its authority is to be exercised. In his view of Government, the republican system, as established by America and France, operates to embrace the whole of a Nation; and the knowledge necessary to the interest of all the parts, is to be found in the center, which the parts by representation form: But the old Governments are on a

construction that excludes knowledge as well as happiness; government by Monks, who knew nothing of the world beyond the walls of a Convent, is as consistent as government by Kings.

What were formerly called Revolutions, were little more than a change of persons, or an alteration of local circumstances. They rose and fell like things of course, and had nothing in their existence or their fate that could influence beyond the spot that produced them. But what we now see in the world, from the Revolutions of America and France, are a renovation of the natural order of things, a system of principles as universal as truth and the existence of man, and combining moral with political happiness and national prosperity.

I. Men are born, and always continue, free and equal in respect of their rights. Civil distinctions, therefore, can be founded only on public utility.

II. The end of all political associations is the preservation of the natural and imprescriptible rights of man; and these rights are liberty, property, security, and resistance of oppression.

III. The nation is essentially the source of all sovereignty; nor can any Individual, or any body of men, be entitled to any authority which is not expressly derived from it.

In these principles, there is nothing to throw a Nation into confusion by inflaming ambition. They are calculated to call forth wisdom and abilities, and to exercise them for the public good, and not for the emolument or aggrandisement of particular descriptions of men or families. Monarchical sovereignty, the enemy of mankind, and the source of misery, is abolished; and the sovereignty itself is restored to its natural and original place, the Nation. Were this the case throughout Europe, the cause of wars would be taken away.

[1791]

III.a.3. MARY WOLLSTONECRAFT, from *A Vindication of the Rights of Woman*

To account for, and excuse the tyranny of man, many ingenious arguments have been brought forward to prove, that the two sexes, in the acquirement of virtue, ought to aim at attaining a very different character; or, to speak explicitly, women are not allowed to have sufficient strength of mind to acquire what really deserves the name of virtue. Yet it should seem, allowing them to have souls, that there is but one way appointed by Providence to lead mankind to either virtue or happiness.

If then women are not a swarm of ephemeron triflers, why should they be kept in ignorance under the specious name of innocence? Men complain, and with reason, of the follies and caprices of our sex, when they do not keenly satirise our headstrong passions and grovelling vices. Behold, I should answer, the natural effect of ignorance! The mind will ever be unstable that has only prejudices to rest on, and the current will run with destructive fury when there are no barriers to break its force. Women are told from their infancy, and taught by the example of their mothers, that a little knowledge of human weakness, justly termed cunning, softness of temper, outward obedience, and a scrupulous attention to a puerile kind of propriety, will obtain for them the protection of man; and should they be beautiful, everything else is needless, for at least twenty years of their lives. Thus Milton describes our first frail mother; though when he tells us that women are formed for softness and sweet attractive grace, I cannot comprehend his meaning, unless, in the true Mahometan strain, he meant to deprive us of souls, and insinuate that we were beings only designed by sweet attractive grace, and docile blind obedience, to gratify the senses of man when he can no longer soar on the wing of contemplation.

How grossly do they insult us who thus advise us only to render ourselves gentle, domestic brutes! For instance, the winning softness so warmly and frequently recommended, that governs by obeying. What childish expressions, and how insignificant is the being – can it be an immortal

one? – who will condescend to govern by such sinister methods? 'Certainly,' says Lord Bacon, 'man is of kin to the beasts by his body; and if he be not of kin to God by his spirit, he is a base and ignoble creature!' Men, indeed, appear to me to act in a very unphilosophical manner, when they try to secure the good conduct of women by attempting to keep them always in a state of childhood. Rousseau was more consistent when he wished to stop the progress of reason in both sexes, for if men eat of the tree of knowledge, women will come in for a taste; but, from the imperfect cultivation which their understandings now receive, they only attain a knowledge of evil. Children, I grant, should be innocent; but when the epithet is applied to men, or women, it is but a civil term for weakness.

[1792]

III.a.4. WILLIAM WORDSWORTH, from *The Prelude*

[From Book IX]

> In both her clamorous Halls,
> The National Synod and the Jacobins,
> I saw the Revolutionary Power
> Toss like a ship at anchor, rocked by storms;
> The Arcades I traversed, in the Palace huge
> Of Orleans; coasted round and round the line
> Of Tavern, Brothel, Gaming-house, and Shop,
> Great rendezvous of worst and best, the walk
> Of all who had a purpose, or had not;
> I stared and listened, with a stranger's ears,
> To Hawkers and Haranguers, hubbub wild!
> And hissing Factionists with ardent eyes,
> In knots, or pairs, or single. Not a look
> Hope takes, or Doubt or Fear is forced to wear,
> But seemed there present; and I scanned them all,
> Watched every gesture uncontrollable,
> Of anger, and vexation, and despite,
> All side by side, and struggling face to face,
> With gaiety and dissolute idleness. (ll. 48–66)

> * * *

> 'Twas in truth an hour
> Of universal ferment; mildest men
> Were agitated, and commotions, strife
> Of passion and opinion, filled the walls
> Of peaceful houses with unquiet sounds.
> The soil of common life was, at that time,
> Too hot to tread upon. Oft said I then,
> And not then only, 'What a mockery this
> Of history, the past and that to come!
> Now do I feel how all men are deceived,
> Reading of nations and their works, in faith,
> Faith given to vanity and emptiness;

Oh! laughter for the page that would reflect
To future times the face of what now is!'
The land all swarmed with passion, like a plain
Devoured by locusts, – Carra, Gorsas, – add
A hundred other names, forgotten now,
Nor to be heard of more; yet, they were powers,
Like earthquakes, shocks repeated day by day,
And felt through every nook of town and field. (ll. 161–180)

[From Book X]

    Domestic carnage now filled the whole year
With feast-days; old men from the chimney-nook,
The maiden from the bosom of her love,
The mother from the cradle of her babe,
The warrior from the field – all perished, all –
Friends, enemies, of all parties, ages, ranks,
Head after head, and never heads enough
For those that bade them fall. They found their joy,
They made it proudly, eager as a child,
(If like desires of innocent little ones
May with such heinous appetites be compared),
Pleased in some open field to exercise
A toy that mimics with revolving wings
The motion of a wind-mill; though the air
Do of itself blow fresh, and make the vanes
Spin in his eyesight, 'that' contents him not,
But with the plaything at arm's length, he sets
His front against the blast, and runs amain,
That it may whirl the faster. (ll. 356–374)

              * * *

Most melancholy at that time, O Friend!
Were my day-thoughts, – my nights were miserable;
Through months, through years, long after the last beat
Of those atrocities, the hour of sleep
To me came rarely charged with natural gifts,
Such ghastly visions had I of despair
And tyranny, and implements of death;
And innocent victims sinking under fear,
And momentary hope, and worn-out prayer,
Each in his separate cell, or penned in crowds
For sacrifice, and struggling with fond mirth
And levity in dungeons, where the dust
Was laid with tears. Then suddenly the scene
Changed, and the unbroken dream entangled me
In long orations, which I strove to plead

Before unjust tribunals, – with a voice
Labouring, a brain confounded, and a sense,
Death-like, of treacherous desertion, felt
In the last place of refuge – my own soul. (ll. 397–415)

[From Book XI]

    O pleasant exercise of hope and joy!
For mighty were the auxiliars which then stood
Upon our side, us who were strong in love!
Bliss was it in that dawn to be alive,
But to be young was very Heaven! O times,
In which the meagre, stale, forbidding ways
Of custom, law, and statute, took at once
The attraction of a country in romance!
When Reason seemed the most to assert her rights
When most intent on making of herself
A prime enchantress – to assist the work,
Which then was going forward in her name!
Not favoured spots alone, but the whole Earth,
The beauty wore of promise – that which sets
(As at some moments might not be unfelt
Among the bowers of Paradise itself)
The budding rose above the rose full blown.
What temper at the prospect did not wake
To happiness unthought of? The inert
Were roused, and lively natures rapt away!
They who had fed their childhood upon dreams,
The play-fellows of fancy, who had made
All powers of swiftness, subtilty, and strength
Their ministers, – who in lordly wise had stirred
Among the grandest objects of the sense,
And dealt with whatsoever they found there
As if they had within some lurking right
To wield it; – they, too, who of gentle mood
Had watched all gentle motions, and to these
Had fitted their own thoughts, schemers more mild,
And in the region of their peaceful selves; –
Now was it that 'both' found, the meek and lofty
Did both find, helpers to their hearts' desire,
And stuff at hand, plastic as they could wish, –
Were called upon to exercise their skill,
Not in Utopia, – subterranean fields, –
Or some secreted island, Heaven knows where!
But in the very world, which is the world
Of all of us, – the place where, in the end,
We find our happiness, or not at all! (ll. 105–144)

      * * *

> Share with me, Friend! the wish
> That some dramatic tale, endued with shapes
> Livelier, and flinging out less guarded words
> Than suit the work we fashion, might set forth
> What then I learned, or think I learned, of truth,
> And the errors into which I fell, betrayed
> By present objects, and by reasonings false
> From their beginnings, inasmuch as drawn
> Out of a heart that had been turned aside
> From Nature's way by outward accidents,
> And which was thus confounded, more and more
> Misguided, and misguiding. So I fared,
> Dragging all precepts, judgments, maxims, creeds,
> Like culprits to the bar; calling the mind,
> Suspiciously, to establish in plain day
> Her titles and her honours; now believing,
> Now disbelieving; endlessly perplexed
> With impulse, motive, right and wrong, the ground
> Of obligation, what the rule and whence
> The sanction; till, demanding formal 'proof',
> And seeking it in every thing, I lost
> All feeling of conviction, and, in fine,
> Sick, wearied out with contrarieties,
> Yielded up moral questions in despair. (ll. 282–305)

[1850]

III.a.5.   GEORGE GORDON, LORD BYRON, *Don Juan*, 'Dedication'

Difficile est proprie communia dicere
–Horace, *Epistola ad Pisones*

I

Bob Southey! You're a poet – Poet-laureate,
    And representative of all the race;
Although 'tis true that you turn'd out a Tory at
    Last – yours has lately been a common case;
And now, my Epic Renegade! what are ye at?
    With all the Lakers, in and out of place?
A nest of tuneful persons, to my eye
Like 'four and twenty Blackbirds in a pye;

II

'Which pye being open'd they began to sing'
    (This old song and new simile holds good),
'A dainty dish to set before the King,'
    Or Regent, who admires such kind of food;

And Coleridge, too, has lately taken wing,
    But like a hawk encumber'd with his hood,
Explaining Metaphysics to the nation –
I wish he would explain his Explanation.

III

You, Bob! are rather insolent, you know,
    At being disappointed in your wish
To supersede all warblers here below,
    And be the only Blackbird in the dish;
And then you overstrain yourself, or so,
    And tumble downward like the flying fish
Gasping on deck, because you soar too high, Bob,
And fall, for lack of moisture quite a-dry, Bob!

IV

And Wordsworth, in a rather long 'Excursion'
    (I think the quarto holds five hundred pages),
Has given a sample from the vasty version
    Of his new system to perplex the sages;
'Tis poetry – at least by his assertion,
    And may appear so when the dog-star rages –
And he who understands it would be able
To add a story to the Tower of Babel.

V

You – Gentlemen! by dint of long seclusion
    From better company, have kept your own
At Keswick, and, through still continu'd fusion
    Of one another's minds, at last have grown
To deem as a most logical conclusion,
    That Poesy has wreaths for you alone:
There is a narrowness in such a notion,
Which makes me wish you'd change your lakes for Ocean.

VI

I would not imitate the petty thought,
    Nor coin my self-love to so base a vice,
For all the glory your conversion brought,
    Since gold alone should not have been its price.
You have your salary; was't for that you wrought?
    And Wordsworth has his place in the Excise.

You're shabby fellows – true – but poets still,
And duly seated on the Immortal Hill.

VII

Your bays may hide the baldness of your brows –
    Perhaps some virtuous blushes – let them go –
To you I envy neither fruit nor boughs –
    And for the fame you would engross below,
The field is universal, and allows
    Scope to all such as feel the inherent glow:
Scott, Rogers, Campbell, Moore and Crabbe, will try
'Gainst you the question with posterity.

VIII

For me, who, wandering with pedestrian Muses,
    Contend not with you on the winged steed,
I wish your fate may yield ye, when she chooses,
    The fame you envy, and the skill you need;
And, recollect, a poet nothing loses
    In giving to his brethren their full meed
Of merit, and complaint of present days
Is not the certain path to future praise.

IX

He that reserves his laurels for posterity
    (Who does not often claim the bright reversion)
Has generally no great crop to spare it, he
    Being only injur'd by his own assertion;
And although here and there some glorious rarity
    Arise like Titan from the sea's immersion,
The major part of such appellants go
To – God knows where – for no one else can know.

X

If, fallen in evil days on evil tongues,
    Milton appeal'd to the Avenger, Time,
If Time, the Avenger, execrates his wrongs,
    And makes the word 'Miltonic' mean 'sublime,'
He deign'd not to belie his soul in songs,
    Nor turn his very talent to a crime;
He did not loathe the Sire to laud the Son,
But clos'd the tyrant-hater he begun.

XI

Think'st thou, could he – the blind Old Man – arise
    Like Samuel from the grave, to freeze once more
The blood of monarchs with his prophecies
    Or be alive again – again all hoar
With time and trials, and those helpless eyes,
    And heartless daughters – worn – and pale – and poor;
Would he adore a sultan? he obey
The intellectual eunuch Castlereagh?

XII

Cold-blooded, smooth-fac'd, placid miscreant!
    Dabbling its sleek young hands in Erin's gore,
And thus for wider carnage taught to pant,
    Transferr'd to gorge upon a sister shore,
The vulgarest tool that Tyranny could want,
    With just enough of talent, and no more,
To lengthen fetters by another fix'd,
And offer poison long already mix'd.

XIII

An orator of such set trash of phrase
    Ineffably – legitimately vile,
That even its grossest flatterers dare not praise,
    Nor foes – all nations – condescend to smile,
Not even a sprightly blunder's spark can blaze
    From that Ixion grindstone's ceaseless toil,
That turns and turns to give the world a notion
Of endless torments and perpetual motion.

XIV

A bungler even in its disgusting trade,
    And botching, patching, leaving still behind
Something of which its masters are afraid,
    States to be curb'd, and thoughts to be confin'd,
Conspiracy or Congress to be made –
    Cobbling at manacles for all mankind –
A tinkering slave-maker, who mends old chains,
With God and Man's abhorrence for its gains.

XV

If we may judge of matter by the mind,
    Emasculated to the marrow It

Hath but two objects, how to serve, and bind,
　　Deeming the chain it wears even men may fit,
Eutropius of its many masters, blind
　　To worth as freedom, wisdom as to Wit,
Fearless – because no feeling dwells in ice,
Its very courage stagnates to a vice.

XVI

Where shall I turn me not to view its bonds,
　　For I will never feel them? – Italy!
Thy late reviving Roman soul desponds
　　Beneath the lie this State-thing breath'd o'er thee –
Thy clanking chain, and Erin's yet green wounds,
　　Have voices – tongues to cry aloud for me.
Europe has slaves – allies – kings – armies still,
And Southey lives to sing them very ill.

XVII

Meantime – Sir Laureate – I proceed to dedicate,
　　In honest simple verse, this song to you,
And, if in flattering strains I do not predicate,
　　'Tis that I still retain my 'buff and blue';
My politics as yet are all to educate:
　　Apostasy's so fashionable, too,
To keep one creed's a task grown quite Herculean;
Is it not so, my Tory, ultra-Julian?

(1818) [1832]

III.a.6.　PERCY BYSSHE SHELLEY, 'England in 1819'

An old, mad, blind, despised, and dying king, –
Princes, the dregs of their dull race, who flow
Through public scorn, – mud from a muddy spring, –
Rulers who neither see, nor feel, nor know,
But leech-like to their fainting country cling,
Till they drop, blind in blood, without a blow, –
A people starved and stabbed in the untilled field. –
An army, which liberticide and prey
Makes as a two-edged sword to all who wield, –
Golden and sanguine laws which tempt and slay;
Religion Christless, Godless – a book sealed;
A Senate, – Time's worst statute unrepealed, –
Are graves, from which a glorious Phantom may
Burst, to illumine our tempestuous day.

(1819) [1839]

c. DANSK

III.c.1. ADAM OEHLENSCHLÄGER, 'Guldhornene'

De higer og söger
i gamle Böger,
i oplukte Höie
med speidende Öie,
paa Sværd og Skiolde
i muldne Volde
paa Runestene
blandt smuldnede Bene.

Oldtids Bedrifter
anede trylle;
men i Mulm de sig hylle,
de gamle Skrifter.
Blikket stirrer,
sig Tanken forvirrer.
i Taage de famle.
»I gamle gamle
hensvundne Dage!
da det straalte i Norden,
da Himlen var paa Jorden,
giv et Glimt tilbage!«

Skyen suser,
Natten bruser,
Gravhöien sukker,
Rosen sig lukker.
De övre Regioner
toner!
De sig möde, de sig möde,
de forklarede Höie,
kampfarvede, röde,
med Stierneglands i Öie.

»I som raver i blinde,
skal finde
et ældgammelt Minde,
der skal komme og svinde!
Dets gyldne Sider
skal Præget bære
af de ældste Tider.

Af det kan I lære.
Med andagtsfuld ære
I vor Gave belönne.

c. DANISH

III.c.1. ADAM OEHLENSCHLÄGER, 'The Golden Horns'

UPON the pages
Of far gone ages
In hills where are lying
The dead they are prying;
On armour rusty,
In ruins musty,
On Rune-stones jumbled,
With bones long crumbled.

Deeds of old, in guesses
Beheld, are enticing,
But a mist possesses
The ancient writing.
With eye-balls fixed,
With thoughts perplexed,
In darkness they grope
Vainly they hope
'You days far gone,
A glimpse anon!
Of Heaven united with Earth
Of a shimmering light in the North!'

Cloud is bustling,
Night is rustling
Grave-hills sighing
Rose petals dying
The reaches above rebound
With voices of godlike sound
The mighty and daring
Their spirits there muster
War stains bearing
In eye star lustre.

'You who are blind,
Straying, praying,
A relic shall find
It glitters and speaks, then leaves you behind
Its red sides of gold
A stamp displaying
Of times most old.

Of this you shall learn
Devotion to earn.
Our gift is your duty!

Det skiönneste Skiönne,
en Möe
skal Helligdommen finde!«
Saa synge de og svinde.
Lufttonerne döe!

Hrymfaxe den sorte
puster og dukker
og i Havet sig begraver.
Morgenens Porte
Delling oplukker,
og Skinfaxe traver
i straalende Lue
paa Himlens Bue.

Og Fuglene synge.
Dugperler bade
Blomsterblade,
som Vindene gynge.
Og med svævende Fied
en Möe hendandser
til Marken afsted.
Violer hende krandser.
Hendes Rosenkind brænder,
hun har Lilliehænder.
Let som en Hind
med muntert Sind,
hun svæver og smiler;
og som hun iler
og paa Elskov grubler –
Hun snubler!
og stirrer og skuer
gyldne Luer,
og rödmer og bæver
og zittrende hæver
med undrende Aand,
af sorten Muld,
med sneehvide Haand,
det röde Guld.

En sagte Torden
dundrer!
Hele Norden
undrer!
Og hen de stimle
i store Vrimle,
og grave og söge

A maid,
Of beauty most rare
The shrine shall dare.'
This said,
Their songs die away in the air.

Hrymfax, the black,
Snorting, ducking
The ocean rolls over his back.
Delling, emerging
Morn's gates unlocking:
Skinfax, advancing,
On sky bow prancing,
With lustre glancing.

Little birds quaver,
Night-pearls weeping,
Flowers steeping
In winds which waver.
A fleet-footed maiden, dancing so gay
Crowned with a garland,
Then gliding away,
Cheeks are burning,
Lily-hands turning;
Light as a hind
Playful in mind
Smiling, frisking
Onwards she's whisking,
Thinks on her lover,
Trips something over!
Eyes declining,
Aware of a shining,
She reddens and shakes,
And trembling she takes,
This wondering sprite
From dingy mould,
With hands snow-white,
The ruddy gold.

A gentle thunder
Peals!
The whole North wonder
Feels!
Forth rush with gabble
A countless rabble
Earth upturning
For treasure burning.

skatten at foröge.
Men intet Guld!
Deres Haab har bedraget.
De see kun det Muld,
hvoraf de er taget.

Et Sekel svinder!!

Over Klippetinder
det atter bruser.
Stormenes Sluser
bryde med Vælde.
Over Norges Fielde
til Danmarks Dale
i Skyernes Sale,
de forklarede Gamle
sig atter samle.

»For de sieldne Faae
som vor Gave forstaae,
som ei Jordlænker binde,
men hvis Siele sig hæve
til det Eviges Tinde,
som ane det Höie
i Naturens Öie,
som tilbedende bæve
for Guddommens Straaler,
i Sole, i Violer,
i det Mindste, i det Störste,
som brændende törste
efter Livets Liv,
som – o store Aand
for de svundne Tider!
see dit Guddomsblik
paa Helligdommens Sider,
for dem lyder atter vort Bliv!
Naturens Sön,
ukiendt i Lön,
men som sine Fædre
kraftig og stor,
dyrkene sin Jord,
ham vil vi hædre,
han skal atter finde!«
Saa synge de og svinde.

Hrymfaxe den sorte
Puster og dukker,
Og i Havet sig begraver.

But there is no gold!
Their hope is mistaken:
They see but the mould,
From where it was taken.

Time passes

Again it blusters
Rain-soaked mountains,
Shattering fountains
Burst in fury.
Spirits of glory
From Norway's highlands
To Denmark's islands,
In clouded halls meet
They join and they greet.

'For the few there below
Who our offering know
Who Earth's fetters spurn
And whose souls are soaring
To the everlasting turn;
Who in the eye of Nature
Behold the Creator;
And tremble adoring,
In rays of His power
In sun and in flower,
The least and the first,
Are burning with thirst
For a life from the spring:
But see, you mighty sprite
Of days passed away on the tide
Behold thy own eye so bright
Reflected in gold on the side
For them our 'Stay!' shall ring.
'Nature's son, of name
Unknown to fame
Digging, planting
Strong-armed and tall,
Like his forefathers all,
His honour we're chanting
He shall reclaim it, all unaided'
They sang and so faded.

Hrymfax, the black,
Snorting, ducking
The ocean rolls over his back.

Morgenens Porte
Delling oplukker,
og Skinfaxe traver
i straalende Lue,
paa Himlens Bue.
Ved lune Skov
Řxnene trække
den tunge Plov,
over sorten Dække.

Da standser Ploven,
og en Gysen farer
igiennem Skoven.
Fugleskarer
pludselig tier.
Hellig Taushed
alt indvier.

Da klinger i Muld
det gamle Guld.

Tvende Glimt fra Oldtidsdage
funkler i de nye Tider.
Selsomt vendte de tilbage,
gaadefyldt paa röde Sider.

Mystisk Helligdom omsvæver
deres gamle Tegn og Mærker.
Guddomsglorien ombæver
Evighedens Underværker.

Hædrer dem, thi Skiebnen skalter!
snart maaskee de er forsvunden.
Jesu Blod paa Herrens Alter
fylde dem, som Blod i Lunden.

Men I see kun deres Lue,
ikke det ærværdigt Höie,
Sætte dem som Pragt tilskue
For et mat nysgierrigt Öie.

Himlen sortner, Storme brage!
Visse Time du er kommen.
Hvad de gav de tog tilbage.
Evig bortsvandt Helligdommen.

[1803]

Delling, emerging
Morn's gates unlocking:
Skinfax, advancing,
On sky bow prancing,
With lustre glancing.

By the sheltering shaws
The oxen striding
A heavy plough draws
The black soil dividing.

The plough stops short, and a drove
Of shudders rushes
All through the grove;
The bird-quire hushes
Sudden its strains;
Holy silence
Everywhere reigns.

Then rings in mould
The ancient gold.

A double glimpse from periods old
In the days we inhabit, sparkling,
Strangely returned those visions of gold,
Their sides with puzzles darkling.

A strange craft hovers
O'er their signs, a sense to ponder
Glory the Godhead covers
These eternal works, such wonder.

Honour them, for nought is stable;
They may vanish, past all seeking.
Let Christ's blood on Christ's own table
Fill them, once with red blood reeking.

But their sheen is all you know
Not their honour high
And their lustre's put on show
For a dull unwitting eye

Storm-winds bellow, blacken heaven!
Comes the fateful hour near;
Back is taken what was given, –
Vanished is the token here.

[1803] [Translated by Claus Bratt Østergaard in an adaptation of
George Borrow's 1854 translation of 'Guldhornene']

d. FRANÇAIS

III.d.1. JULES MICHELET, *Introduction à l'histoire universelle*

C'est aux points de contact des races, dans la collision de leurs fatalités opposées, dans la soudaine explosion de l' intelligence et de la liberté, que jaillit de l' humanité cet éclair céleste qu' on appelle le verbe, la parole, la révélation. Ainsi, quand la Judée eut entrevu l'Egypte, la Chaldée et la Phénicie, au point du plus parfait mélange des races orientales, l'éclair brilla sur le Sinaï, et il en resta la pure et sainte unité. Quand l'unité juive se fut fécondée du génie de la Perse et de l'Egypte grecque, l'unité s'épanouit, et elle embrassa le monde dans l'égalité de la charité divine. La Grèce mythotokos, mère du mythe et de la parole, expliqua la bonne nouvelle; il ne fallut pas moins que la merveilleuse puissance analytique de la langue d'Aristote pour dire aux nations le verbe du muet orient. Au point du plus parfait mélange des races européennes, sous la forme de l'égalité dans la liberté, éclate le verbe social. Sa révélation est successive; sa beauté n'est ni dans un temps ni dans un lieu. Il n'a pu présenter la ravissante harmonie par laquelle le verbe moral éclata en naissant: le rapport de Dieu à l' individu était simple; le rapport de l' humanité à elle-même dans une société divine, cette translation du ciel sur la terre, est un problème complexe, dont la longue solution doit remplir la vie du monde; sa beauté est dans sa progression, sa progression infinie. C'est à la France qu'il appartient et de faire éclater cette révélation nouvelle et de l'expliquer.

Toute solution sociale ou intellectuelle reste inféconde pour l'Europe, jusqu' à ce que la France l'ait interprétée, traduite, popularisée. La réforme du saxon Luther, qui replaçait le nord dans son opposition naturelle contre Rome, fut démocratisée par le génie de Calvin. La réaction catholique du siècle de Louis XIV fut proclamée devant le monde par le dogmatisme superbe de Bossuet. Le sensualisme de Locke ne devint européen qu'en passant par Voltaire, par Montesquieu qui assujettit le développement de la société à l'influence des climats. La liberté morale réclama au nom du sentiment par Rousseau, au nom de l'idée par Kant; mais l'influence du français fut seule européenne.

Ainsi chaque pensée solitaire des nations est révélée par la France. Elle dit le verbe de l'Europe, comme la Grèce a dit celui de l'Asie. Qui lui mérite cette mission? C'est qu'en elle, plus vite qu' en aucun peuple, se développe, et pour la théorie et pour la pratique, le sentiment de la généralité sociale. A mesure que ce sentiment vient à poindre chez les autres peuples, ils sympathisent avec le génie français, ils deviennent France; ils luidécernent, au moins par leur muette imitation, le pontificat de la civilisation nouvelle. Ce qu' il y a de plus jeune et de plus fécond dans le monde, ce n'est point l'Amérique, enfant sérieux qui imitera longtemps; c'est la vieille France, renouvelée par l'esprit. Tandis que la civilisation enferme le monde barbare dans les serres invincibles de l'Angleterre et de la Russie, la France brassera l'Europe dans toute sa profondeur. Son intime union sera, n'en doutons point, avec les peuples de langues latines, avec l'Italie et l'Espagne, ces deux îles qui ne peuvent s'entendre avec le monde moderne que par l'intermédiaire de la France. Alors nos provinces méridionales reprendront l'importance qu'elles ont perdue.

L'Espagne résistera longtemps. La profonde démagogie monacale qui la gouverne, la ferme à la démocratie modérée de la France. Ses moines sortent de la populace et la nourrissent. Si pourtant ce peuple, rassuré du côté de la France, reprend son génie d'aventure, c'est par lui que la civilisation occidentale atteindra l'Afrique, déjà si bien nivelée par le mahométisme.

L'Italie, celtique de race dans les provinces du nord, l'Italie préparée à la démocratie par le génie anti-féodal de l'église et du parti guelfe, appartient de coeur à la France, qui ne lui demande pas plus aujourd'hui. Ces deux contrées sont soeurs; même génie pratique: Salerne

d. FRENCH

III.d.1. JULES MICHELET, from *Introduction to Universal History*

It is at the points of contact of the races, in the collision of their opposed fatalities, in the sudden explosion of intelligence and liberty, that there burst forth from humanity this celestial flash that is called the word, speech, revelation. So, when Judea had glimpsed Egypt, Chaldea, and Phoenicia, at the point of the most perfect mingling of the Oriental races, the flash shone over Sinai, and there remained of it the pure and holy unity. When the Jewish unity was made fruitful by the genius of Persia and of Greek Egypt, the unity opened up and embraced the world in the equality of divine charity. Greece mythotokos, mother of myth and of speech, explained the good news: it lacked nothing less than the marvelous analytical power of the language of Aristotle to tell the nations the word of the mute Orient. At the point of the most perfect mingling of the European races, in the form of equality in liberty, the social word bursts forth. Its revelation is successive; its beauty is neither in a time nor in a place. It was not possible to show the ravishing harmony through which the moral word burst forth in being born: the relation of God to the individual was simple; the relation of humanity to itself in a divine society, this translation of heaven to earth, is a complex problem, whose long solution should fill the life of the world; its beauty is in its progression, its infinite progression.

It is the duty of France both to make this new revolution burst forth and to explain it. Every social or intellectual solution remains unfruitful for Europe, until France has interpreted it, translated it, and popularized it. The reform of the Saxon Luther, which restored the North to its natural opposition to Rome, was democratized by the genius of Calvin. The Catholic reaction of the century of Louis XIV was proclaimed before the world by the lofty dogmatism of Bossuet. The sensualism of Locke did not become European except by passing through Voltaire, through Montesquieu who subjected the development of society to the influence of climates. Moral liberty clamored in the name of sentiment through Rousseau, in the name of idea through Kant; but the influence of French was alone European.

Thus every solitary thought of the nations is revealed by France. She speaks the word of Europe, just as Greece spoke that of Asia. How does she deserve this mission? It is because in France, more quickly than in any other nation, there develops, both in theory and in practice, the sentiment of social generality. To the extent that this sentiment comes to appear among other peoples, they sympathize with the French genius, they become France; they discern in her, at least by their mute imitation, the pontificate of the new civilization. That which is younger and more fruitful in the world is not at all America, an earnest child who will imitate for a long time; it is old France, renewed by the spirit. While civilization encloses the barbarian world within the invincible claws of England and Russia, France will brew up Europe in all its depth. Its intimate union will be – let us doubt it not at all – with the peoples of the Latin tongues, with Italy and Spain, these two islands which cannot get along with the modern world except by the intermediary of France. Then our southern provinces will recover their lost importance (this is merely a personal preference, not a linguistic correction).

Spain will resist for a long time. The profound monkish demagogy which governs it closes it to the moderate democracy of France. Its monks emerge from the populace and nourish it. If, however, this nation, reassured by France, recovers its genius for adventure, it is through them that Western civilization will attain Africa, already so well leveled by Mahometanism. Italy, Celtic by race in the northern provinces, Italy, prepared for democracy by the anti-feudal genius of the Church and of the Guelph party, belongs in its heart to France, which demands nothing

et Montpellier, Bourges et Bologne, n'avaient-elles pas un esprit commun? L'économie politique, née en France, a retenti en Italie. Il y a un double écho dans les Alpes. La fraternité des deux contrées fortifiera le sens social de l'Italie, et suppléera à ce qu'elle laissera toujours à désirer pour l'unité matérielle et politique. Chef de cette grande famille, la France rendra au génie latin quelque chose de la prépondérance matérielle qu'il eut dans l'antiquité, de la suprématie spirituelle qu'il obtint au moyen-âge. Dans les derniers temps, le traité de famille qui unissait la France, l'Italie et l'Espagne, dans une alliance fraternelle, était une vaine image de cette future union qui doit les rapprocher dans une communauté de volontés et de pensées. Mais la vraie figure de cette union future de l'Italie et de la France, c'est Bonaparte. Ainsi Charlemagne figura matériellement l'unité spirituelle du monde féodal et pontifical qui se préparait. Les grandes révolutions ont d'avance leurs symboles prophétiques. Quiconque veut connaître les destinées du genre humain doit approfondir le génie de l'Italie et de la France. Rome a été le noeud du drame immense dont la France dirige la péripétie. C'est en nous plaçant au sommet du capitole que nous embrasserons, du double regard de Janus, et le monde ancien qui s'y termine, et le monde moderne, que notre patrie conduit désormais dans la route mystérieuse de l'avenir.

[1831]

III.d.2.   VICTOR HUGO, *William Shakespeare*

Le dix-neuvième siècle ne relève que de lui-même; il ne reçoit l'impulsion d'aucun aïeul; il est le fils d'une idée. Sans doute, Isaïe, Homère, Aristote, Dante, Shakespeare, ont été ou peuvent être de grands points de départ pour d'importantes formations philosophiques ou poétiques; mais le dix-neuvième siècle a une mère auguste, la Révolution française. Il a ce sang énorme dans les veines. Il honore les génies, et, au besoin, méconnus, il les salue, ignorés, il les constate, persécutés, il les venge, insultés, il les couronne, détrônés, il les replace sur leur piédestal; il les vénère, mais il ne vient pas d'eux. Le dix-neuvième siècle a pour famille lui-même et lui seul. Il est de sa nature révolutionnaire de se passer d'ancêtres.

Étant génie, il fraternise avec les génies. Quant à sa source, elle est où est la lueur; hors de homme. Les mystérieuses gestations du progrès se succèdent selon une loi providentielle. Le dix-neuvième siècle est en enfantement de civilisation. Il a un continent à mettre au monde. La France a porté ce siècle, et ce siècle porte l'Europe.

Le groupe grec a été la civilisation, étroite et circonscrite d'abord à la feuille de mûrier, à la Morée; puis la civilisation, gagnant de proche en proche, s'est élargie, et a été le groupe romain; elle est aujourd'hui le groupe français, c'est-à-dire toute l'Europe; avec des commencements en Amérique, en Afrique et en Asie.

Le plus grand de ces commencements est une démocratic, les États-Unis, éclosion aidée par la France dès le siècle dernier. La France, sublime essayeuse du progrès, a fondé une république en Amérique avant d'en faire une en Europe. *Et vidit quod esset bonum.* Après avoir prêté à Washington cet auxiliaire, Lafayette, la France, rentrant chez elle, a donné à Voltaire éperdu dans son tombeau ce continuateur redoutable, Danton. En présence du passé monstrueux, lançant toutes les foudres, exhalant tous les miasmes, soufflant toutes les ténèbres, allongeant toutes les grifles, horrible et terrible, le progrès, contraint aux mêmes armes, a eu brusquement cent bras, cent têtes, cent langues de flamme, cent rugissements. Le bien s'est fait hydre. C'est ce qu'on nomme la Révolution.

more of it today. These two countries are sisters; the same practical genius: Salerno and Montpellier, Bourges and Bologna, did they not have a common spirit? Political economy, born in France, has resounded in Italy. There is a double echo in the Alps. The fraternity of the two countries will fortify the social sense of Italy, and will make up for that which it will always lack in material and political unity. Head of this great family, France will return to the Latin genius something of the material preponderance which it had in antiquity, something of the spiritual supremacy which it obtained in the Middle Ages. In latter days (personal preference), the family treaty which united France, Italy and Spain, in a fraternal alliance, was a vain image of that future union which should bring them together in a community of wills and thoughts. But the true face of this future union of Italy and France is Bonaparte. Thus Charlemagne materially represented the spiritual unity of the feudal and pontifical world which was being prepared.

The grand revolutions have their prophetic symbols in advance. Whoever wishes to know the destinies of the human race should examine thoroughly the genius of Italy and of France. Rome was the heart of the immense drama whose course is directed by France. It is in placing us at the summit of the Capitol that we will embrace, with Janus' double gaze, both the ancient world, which ends there, and the modern world, which our country leads henceforth into the future's mysterious road.

[1831] [*Translated by David J. White. Edited by Anne Gwin*]

III.d.2.   VICTOR HUGO, from *William Shakespeare*

The nineteenth century holds tenure of itself only; it receives its impulse from no ancestor; it is the offspring of an idea. Doubtless Isaiah, Homer, Aristotle, Dante, Shakespeare, have been or could be great starting-points for important philosophical or poetical growths; but the nineteenth century has for its august mother the French Revolution. This redoubtable blood flows in its veins. It honors men of genius, and if need be salutes them when despised, proclaims them when ignored, avenges them when persecuted, reenthrones them when dethroned: it venerates them, but it does not proceed from them. The nineteenth century has for family itself, and itself alone. It is the characteristic of its revolutionary nature to dispense with ancestors.

Itself a genius, it fraternizes with men of genius. As for its source, it is where theirs is, – beyond man. The mysterious gestations of progress succeed each other according to a providential law. The nineteenth century is a birth of civilization. It has a continent to bring into the world. France has borne this century, and this century bears Europe. When civilization was cöexistent with Greece, it was a first circumscribed by the narrow limits of the Morea, of Mulberry Leaf; then, widening by degrees, it spread over the Roman group of nations. To-day it distinguishes the French group; that is to say, all Europe, with beginnings in America, in Africa, and in Asia.

The greatest of these beginnings is a democracy, the United States, whose first tender growth was fostered by France in the last century. France, sublime essayist in progress, founded a republic in America before making one in Europe. *Et vidit quod esset bonum.* After having lent to Washington an auxiliary, Lafayette, France, returning home, gave to Voltaire, dismayed within his tomb, that formidable successor, Danton. When the Past, that grisly monster, being brought to bay, was hurling all its thunderbolts, exhaling all its miasmas, belching black vapors, protruding horrible talons, Progress, forced to use the same weapons, suddenly put forth a hundred arms, a hundred heads, a hundred fiery tongues, a hundred bellowings. The good took the form of the hydra. And this is what is called the Revolution.

Rien de plus auguste.

La Révolution a clos un siècle et a commencé l'autre.

Un ébranlement dans les intelligences prépare un bouleversement dans les faits; c'est le dix-huitième siècle.

Après quoi la révolution politique faite cherche son expression, et la révolution littéraire et sociale s'accomplit. C'est le dix-neuvième. Romantisme et socialisme, c'est, on l'a dit avec hostilité, mais avec justesse, le même fait. Souvent la haine, en voulant injurier, constate, et, autant qu'il est en elle, consolide.

Une parenthèse. Ce mot, *romantisme*, a, comme tous les mots de combat, l'avantage de résumer vivement un groupe d'idées; il va vite, ce qui plaît dans la mêlée; mais il a, selon nous, par sa signification militante, l'inconvénient de paraître borner le mouvement qu'il représente à un fait de guerre; or ce mouvement est un fait d'intelligence, un fait de civilisation, un fait d'âme; et c'est pourquoi celui qui écrit ces lignes n'a jamais employé les mots *romantisme* ou *romantique*. On ne les trouvera acceptés dans aucune des pages de critique qu'il a pu avoir occasion d'écrire. S'il déroge aujourd'hui à cette prudence de polémique, c'est pour plus de rapidité et sous réserves. La même observation peut être faite au sujet du mot *socialisme*, lequel prête à tant d'interprétations différentes.

Le triple mouvement littéraire, philosophique et social du dix-neuvième siècle, qui est un seul mouvement, n'est autre chose que le courant de la révolution dans les idées. Ce courant, après avoir entraîné les faits, se continue immense dans les esprits.

Ce mot, 93 *littéraire*, si souvent répété en 1830 contre la littérature contemporaine, n'était pas une insulte autant qu'il voulait l'être. Il était, certes, aussi injuste de l'employer pour caractériser tout le mouvement littéraire qu'il est inique de l'employer pour qualifier toute la révolution politique; il y a dans ces deux phénomènes autre chose que 93. Mais ce mot, 93 *littéraire*, avait cela de relativement exact qu'il indiquait, confusément mais réellement, l'origine du mouvement littéraire propre à notre époque, tout en essayant de le déshonorer. Ici encore la clairvoyance de la haine était aveugle. Ses barbouillages de boue au front de la vérité sont dorure, lumière et gloire.

La Révolution, tournant climatérique de l'humanité, se compose de plusieurs années. Chacune de ces années exprime une période, représente un aspect ou réalise un organe du phénomène. 93, tragique, est une de ces années colossales. Il faut quelquefois aux bonnes nouvelles une bouche de bronze. 93 est cette bouche.

Écoutez-en sortir l'annonce énorme. Inclinez-vous, et restez effaré, et soyez attendri.

Dieu la première fois a dit lui-même *fiat lux*, la seconde fois il l'a fait dire.

Par qui?

Par 93.

Donc, nous hommes du dix-neuvième siècle, tenons à honneur cette injure: – *Vous êtes* 93.

Mais qu'on ne s'arrête pas là. Nous sommes 89 aussi bien que 93. La Révolution, toute la Révolution, voilà la source de la littérature du dix-neuvième siècle.

Sur ce, faites-lui son procès, à cette littérature, ou son triomphe, haïssez-la ou aimez-la, selon la quantité d'avenir que vous avez en vous, outragez-la ou saluez-la; peu lui importent les animosités et les fureurs! elle est la déduction logique du grand fait chaotique et génésiaque que nos pères ont vu et qui a donné un nouveau point de départ au monde.

Qui est contre ce fait, est contre elle; qui est pour ce fait, est pour elle. Ce que ce fait vaut, elle le vaut. Les écrivains des réactions ne s'y trompent pas; là où il y a de la révolution, patente ou latente, le flair catholique et royaliste est infaillible; ces lettrés du passé décernent à la littérature contemporaine une honorable quantité de diatribe; leur aversion est de la convulsion; un de leurs journalistes, qui est, je crois, évêque, prononce le mot « poëte » avec le même accent que le

Nothing can be more august.

The Revolution ended one century and began another.

An agitation in the world of mind preparatory to an upheaval in the world of fact: such is the eighteenth century. The political revolution, once accomplished, seeks its expression, and the literary and social revolution takes place: such is the nineteenth century. It has been said with truth, although with hostile intent, that romanticism and socialism are the same fact. Hatred, wishing to injure, often affirms, and, so far as in it lies, consolidates.

A parenthesis. This word 'romanticism' has, like all war-cries, the advantage of sharply epitomizing a group of ideas; it is brief, which pleases in the contest: but it has, to our mind, through its militant signification, the inconvenience of appearing to limit to a warlike action the movement that it represents. Now this movement is intelligence, an act of civilization, an act of soul; and this is why the writer of these lines has never used the words 'romanticism' and 'romantic.' They will be found in none of the pages of criticism that he has had occasion to write. If to-day he departs from his usual prudence in polemics, it is for the sake of greater rapidity, and with every reservation. The same observation may be made on the subject of the word 'socialism,' which admits of so many different interpretations.

The triple movement – literary, philosophical, and social – of the nineteenth century, which is one single movement, is nothing but the current of the revolution in ideas. This current, after having swept away so many facts, flows on, broad and deep, through the minds of men.

The term 'literary '93,' so often repeated in 1830 against the contemporaneous literature, was not so much an insult as it was meant to be. It was certainly as unjust to employ it to characterize the whole literary movement as it is wrong to employ it to describe the whole political revolution; there is in these two phenomena something besides '93. But this term, 'literary '93,' was so far relatively exact that it indicated, confusedly but truthfully, the origin of the literary movement of our epoch, while endeavoring to dishonor that movement. Here again the clairvoyance of hatred was blind. Its daubings of mud upon the face of Truth are gilding, light, and glory.

The Revolution, that grand climacteric of humanity, is made up of several years. Each of these years expresses a period, represents an aspect, or realizes a phase of the phenomenon. Tragic '93 is one of these colossal years. Good news must sometimes be spoken through a brazen mouth; such a mouth is '93. Listen to the tremendous proclamation issuing from it. Bow down, remain awestruck, and be touched. In the beginning God himself said, 'Fiat lux;' the second time, He had it said.

By whom?

By '93.

Hence it is that we men of the nineteenth century glory in the reproach, 'You are of '93.'

But we must not stop here. We are of '89 as well as of '93. The Revolution, the whole Revolution, – this is the source of the literature of the nineteenth century.

Then put this literature on trial, or seek its triumph; hate it or love it; according to the amount of your faith in the future, insult it or salute it: little does it care for your animosity and fury. It is logical deduction from the great chaotic and primordial fact which our fathers witnessed, and which has given the world a new point of departure. He who is against that fact is on its side. What fact is worth the literature is worth. Reactionary writers are not at fault. Wherever there is revolution, patent or latent, the Catholic and Royalist scent is unerring. These ancient men of letters award to contemporary literature an honorable portion of diatribe; their aversion is convulsive. One of their journalists, who is, I believe, a bishop, pronounces the word 'poet' with the same accent as 'Septembrist;' another, less episcopal but equally angry, writes: 'I feel in all this

mot « septembriseur »; un autre, moins évêque, mais tout aussi en colère, écrit: *Je sens dans toute cette littérature-là Marat et Robespierre.* Ce dernier écrivain se méprend un peu, il y a dans « cette littérature-là » plutôt Danton que Marat.

Mais le fait est vrai. La démocratie est dans cette littérature.

La révolution a forgé le clairon; le dix-neuvième siècle le sonne.

Ah! cette affirmation nous convient, et, en vérité, nous ne reculons pas devant elle; avouons notre gloire, nous sommes des révolutionnaires. Les penseurs de ce temps, les poëtes, les écrivains, les historiens, les orateurs, les philosophes, tous, tous, tous, dérivent de la révolution française. Ils viennent d'elle, et d'elle seule. 89 a démoli la Bastille; 93 a découronné le Louvre. De 89 est sortie la Délivrance, et de 93 la Victoire. 89 et 93; les hommes du dix-neuvième siècle sortent de là. C'est là leur père et leur mère. Ne leur cherchez pas d'autre filiation, d'autre inspiration, d'autre origine. Ils sont les démocrates de l'idée, successeurs des démocrates de l'action. Ils sont les émancipateurs. L'idée Liberté s'est penchée sur leurs berceaux. Ils ont tous sucé cette grande mamelle; ils ont tous de ce lait dans les entrailles, de cette moelle dans les os, cette sève dans la volonté, de cette révolte dans la raison, de cette flamme dans l'intelligence.

Ceux-là mêmes d'entre eux, il y en a, qui sont nés aristocrates, qui sont arrivés au monde dépaysés en quelque sorte dans des familles du passé, qui ont fatalement reçu une de ces éducations premières dont l'effort stupide est de contredire le progrès, et qui ont commencé la parole qu'ils avaient à dire au siècle par on ne sait quel bégaiement royaliste, ceux-là, dès lors, dès leur enfance, ils ne me démentiront pas, sentaient le monstre sublime en eux. Ils avaient le bouillonnement intérieur du fait immense. Ils avaient au fond de leur conscience un soulèvement d'idées mystérieuses; l'ébranlement intime des fausses certitudes leur troublait l'âme; ils sentaient trembler, tressaillir, et peu à peu se lézarder leur sombre surface de monarchisme, de catholicisme et d'aristocratie. Un jour, tout à coup, brusquement, le gonflement du vrai a abouti, l'éclosion a eu lieu, l'éruption s'est faite, la lumière les a ouverts, les a fait éclater, n'est pas tombée sur eux, mais, plus beau prodige, a jailli d'eux stupéfaits, et les a éclairés en les embrasant. Ils étaient cratères à leur insu.

Ce phénomène leur a été reproché comme une trahison. Ils passaient en effet du droit divin au droit humain. Ils tournaient le dos à la fausse histoire, à la fausse société, à la fausse tradition, au faux dogme, à la fausse philosophie, au faux jour, à la fausse vérité. Le libre esprit qui s'envole, oiseau appelé par l'aurore, est désagréable aux intelligences saturées d'ignorance et aux foetus conservés dans l'esprit-de-vin. Qui voit offense les aveugles; qui entend indigne les sourds; qui marche insulte abominablement les culs-de-jatte. Aux yeux des nains, des avortons, des aztèques, des myrmidons et des pygmées, à jamais noués dans le rachitisme, la croissance est apostasie.

Les écrivains et les poëtes du dix-neuvième siècle ont cette admirable fortune de sortir d'une genèse, d'arriver après une fin de monde, d'accompagner une réapparition de lumière, d'être les organes d'un recommencement. Ceci leur impose des devoirs inconnus à leurs devanciers, des devoirs de réformateurs intentionnels et de civilisateurs directs. Ils ne continuent rien; ils refont tout. A temps nouveaux, devoirs nouveaux. La fonction des penseurs aujourd'hui est complexe; penser ne suffit plus, il faut aimer. Penser et aimer ne suffit plus, il faut agir; penser, aimer et agir ne suffit plus, il faut souffrir. Posez la plume, et allez où vous entendrez la mitraille. Voici une barricade; soyez-en. Voici l'exil; acceptez. Voici l'échafaud; soit. Qu'au besoin dans Montesquieu il y ait John Brown. Le Lucrèce qu'il faut à ce siècle en travail doit contenir Caton. Eschyle, qui écrivait *l'Orestie*, avait pour frère Cynégire, qui mordait les navires ennemis; cela suffisait à la Grèce au temps de Salamine; cela ne suffit plus à la France après la révolution; qu'Eschyle et Cynégire soient les deux frères, c'est peu; il faut qu'ils soient le même homme. Tels sont les

literature Marat and Robespierre.' This latter writer is slightly in error; Danton, rather than Marat, is to be felt in this literature.

But the fact is true; this literature is full of democracy.

The Revolution forged the bugle; the nineteenth century sounds it.

Ah! this avowal suits us, and in truth we do not shrink from it; let us admit our glory, historians, orators, philosophers – trace their lineage, every one, to the French Revolution. From it they descend, and from it alone. '89 demolished the Bastile; '93 discrowned the Louvre. Deliverance sprang from '89; victory from '93. '89 and '93, – from that source issue the men of the nineteenth century. This is their father and mother. Seek for them no other lineage, no other inspiration, no other breath of life, no other origin. They are the democrats of thought, successors to the democrats of action. They are liberators. Freedom was the nurse that bent over their cradles; that ample breast suckled them all; they all have her milk in their bodies, her marrow in their bones, her granite in their will, her rebellion in their reason, her fire in their intelligence.

Even those among them (and there are some) who were by birth aristocrats, who came into the world strangers in old-time families, who received that fatal early training whose stupid endeavor it is to counteract progress, and who began their message to the century by some unmeaning stammering of royalism, – even these (they will not contradict me) felt within them, even from their infancy, the sublime monster. They felt the inward ferment of the vast reality. In the deeps of consciousness they felt an uprising of mysterious thoughts; their souls were shaken by the profound perturbation of false certitudes; little by little they perceived the somber surface of their monarchism, Catholicism, and aristocracy, trembling, quaking, gaping open. One day the swelling of truth within them abruptly culminated, and suddenly the crust was rent, the eruption took place, and behold them opened, shivered by light which fell not upon them from without, but – nobler miracle! – issued from these astonished men, and illuminated them while it set them aflame. All unawares, they had become volcanic craters.

They have been reproached with this phenomenon, as with treason. In fact, they passed over from right divine to human rights. They turned the back upon false history, false tradition, false dogmas, false philosophy, false daylight, false truth. That dawn-summoned bird, the free-soaring spirit, is offensive to minds saturated with ignorance and to embryos preserved in alcohol. He who sees, offends the blind; he who walks, insults the cripple in his wooden bowl. In the eyes of dwarfs, abortions, Aztecs, myrmidons, and pigmies forever stunted with the rickets, growth is apostasy.

The writers and poets of the nineteenth century have the admirable good fortune of proceeding from a genesis, of arriving after an end of the world, of accompanying a reappearance of light, of being the organs of a new beginning. This imposes on them duties unknown to their predecessors, – the duties of intentional reformers and direct civilizers. They continue nothing; they form everything anew. The new time brings new duties. The function of thinkers in our days is complex: it no longer suffices to think, – one must love; it no longer suffices to think and to love, – one must act. To think, to love, and to act, no longer suffice, – one must suffer. Lay down the pen, and go where you hear the grapeshot. Here is a barricade; take your place there. Here is exile; accept it. Here is the scaffold, – be it so. Let the Montesquieu be able, in case of need, to act the part of John Brown. The Lucretius of this travailing century should contain a Cato. Æschylus, who wrote, 'The Oresteia,' had a brother, Cynegirus, who grappled the enemy's ships; that was sufficient for Greece at the time of Salamis, but it no longer suffices for France after the Revolution. That Æschylus and Cynegirus are brothers, is but little; they must needs be the same man. Such are the present requirements of progress. Those who devote themselves to

besoins actuels du progrès. Les serviteurs des grandes choses urgentes ne seront jamais assez grands. Rouler des idées, amonceler des évidences, étager des principes, voilà le remuement formidable. Mettre Pélion sur Ossa, labeur d'enfants à côté de cette besogne de géants: mettre le droit sur la vérité. Escalader cela ensuite, et détrôner les usurpations au milieu des tonnerres; voilà l'oeuvre.

L'avenir presse. Demain ne peut pas attendre. L'humanité n'a pas une minute à perdre. Vite, vite, dépêchons, les misérables ont les pieds sur le fer rouge. On a faim, on a soif, on souffre. Ah! maigreur terrible du pauvre corps humain! le parasitisme rit, le lierre verdit et pousse, le gui est florissant, le ver solitaire est heureux. Quelle épouvante, la prospérité du ténia! Détruire ce qui dévore, là, est le salut. Votre vie a au dedans d'elle la mort, qui se porte bien. Il y a trop d'indigence, trop de dénûment, trop d'impudeur, trop de nudité, trop de lupanars, trop de bagnes, trop de haillons, trop de défaillances, trop de crimes, trop d'obscurité, pas assez d'écoles, trop de petits innocents en croissance pour le mal! Le grabat des pauvres filles se couvre tout à coup de soie et de dentelles, et c'est là la pire misère; à côté du malheur il y a le vice, l'un poussant l'autre. Une telle société veut être promptement secourue. Cherchons le mieux. Allez tous à la découverte. Où sont les terres promises? La civilisation veut marcher; essayons les théories, les systèmes, les améliorations, les inventions, les progrès, jusqu'à ce que chaussure à ce pied soit trouvée. L'essai ne coûte rien, ou coûte peu. Essayer n'est pas adopter. Mais avant tout et surtout, prodiguons la lumière. Tout assainissement commence par une large ouverture de fenêtres, Ouvrons les intelligences toutes grandes. Aérons les âmes.

Vite, vite, ô penseurs. Faites respirer le genre humain. Versez l'espérance, versez l'idéal, faites le bien. Un pas après l'autre, les horizons après les horizons, une conquête après une conquête; parce que vous avez donné ce que vous avez annoncé, ne vous croyez pas quittes. Tenir, c'est promettre. L'aurore aujourd'hui oblige le soleil pour demain.

Que rien ne soit perdu. Que pas une force ne s'isole. Tous à la manoeuvre! la vaste urgence est là. Plus d'art fainéant. La poésie ouvrière de civilisation, quoi de plus admirable? Le rêveur doit être un pionnier; la strophe doit vouloir. Le beau doit se mettre au service de l'honnête. Je suis le valet de ma conscience; elle me sonne, j'arrive. Va! Je vais. Que voulez-vous de moi, ô vérité, seule majesté de ce monde? Que chacun sente en soi la hâte de bien faire. Un livre est quelquefois un secours attendu. Une idée est un baume, une parole est un pansement; la poésie est un médecin. Que personne ne s'attarde.

La souffrance perd ses forces pendant vos lenteurs. Qu'on sorte de cette paresse du songe. Laissez le kief aux turcs. Qu'on prenne de la peine pour le salut de tous, et qu'on s'y précipite, et qu'on s'y essouffle. N'allez-vous pas plaindre vos enjambées? Rien d'inutile. Nulle inertie. Qu'appelez-vous nature morte? Tout vit. Le devoir de tout est de vivre. Marcher, courir, voler, planer, c'est la loi universelle. Qu'attendez-vous? qui vous arrête? Ah! il y a des heures où il semble qu'on voudrait entendre les pierres murmurer contre la lenteur de l'homme.

Quelquefois on s'en va dans les bois. A qui cela n'arrive-t-il pas d'être parfois accablé? On voit tant de choses tristes. L'étape ne se fournit point, les conséquences sont longues à venir, une génération est en retard, la besogne du siècle languit. Comment! tant de souffrances encore! On dirait qu'on a reculé. Il y a partout des augmentations de superstition, de lâcheté, de surdité, de cécité, d'imbécillité. La pénalité pèse sur l'abrutissement. Ce vilain problème a été posé: faire avancer le bien-être par le recul du droit; sacrifier le côté supérieur de l'homme au côté inférieur; donner le principe pour l'appétit; César se charge du ventre, je lui concède le cerveau; c'est la vieille vente du droit d'aînesse pour le plat de lentilles. Encore un peu, et ce contre-sens fatal ferait faire fausse route à la civilisation. Le porc à l'engrais, ce ne serait plus le roi, mais le peuple.

great and urgent causes can never be too great. To set ideas in motion, to heap up evidence, to scaffold up principles, – such is the formidable endeavor. To heap Pelion on Ossa is the labor of infants beside that work of giants, the establishing of right upon truth. Afterward to scale that height, and to dethrone usurpations in the midst of thunders, – such is the task.

The future presses. To-morrow cannot wait. Humanity has not a minute to lose. Quick! Quick! let us hasten. The wretched have their feet on red-hot iron; they hunger, they thirst, they suffer. Alas! terrible emaciation of the poor human body. Parasitism laughs, the ivy grows green and thrives, the mistletoe flourishes, the solitary slug is happy. How frightful is the prosperity of the tapeworm! To destroy that which devours, in that is safety. Within your life death itself lives and thrives robustly. There is too much poverty, too much privation, too much immodesty, too much nakedness, too many houses of shame, too many convict prisons, too many tatters, too many defalcations, too many crimes, too much darkness; not enough schools; too many little innocents growing up for evil! The pallet of the poor girl is suddenly covered with silk and lace, – and in that is the worst misery; by the side of misfortune there is vice, the one urging on the other. Such a society requires prompt succor. Let us seek out the best. Go, all of you, in this search! Where are the promised lands? Civilization must march forward; let us test theories, systems, ameliorations, inventions, reforms, until the shoe for that foot shall be found. The experiment costs nothing, or costs but little. To try is not to adopt. But before all, above all, let us be lavish of the light. All sanitary purification begins by opening the windows wide. Let us open wide all intellects; let us supply souls with air.

Quick, quick, O thinkers! Let the human race breathe. Shed abroad hope, sow the ideal, do good. One step after another, horizon after horizon, conquest after conquest; because you have given what you promised, do not hold yourself quit of obligation. To perform is to promise. Today's dawn pledges the sun for to-morrow.

Let nothing be lost. Let not one force be isolated. Every one to work! The urgency is supreme. No more idle art. Poetry the worker of civilization, – what could be more admirable? The dreamer should be a pioneer; the strophe should mean something. The beautiful should be at the service of honesty. I am the valet of my conscience; it rings for me: I come. 'Go.' I go. What do you require of me, O Truth! sole monarch of this world? Let each one have within him an eagerness for well-doing. A book is sometimes looked forward to for succor. An idea is a balm; a word may be a dressing for wounds; poetry is a physician. Let no one delay. While you tarry, suffering man grows weaker. Let men throw off this dreamy laziness. Leave hashish to the Turks. Let men labor for the welfare of all; let them rush forward, and put themselves out of breath. Do not be sparing of your strides. Let nothing remain useless. No inertia. What do you call dead nature? Everything lives. The duty of all is to live. To walk, to run, to fly, to soar, – such is the universal law. What are you waiting for? Who stops you? Ah! there are times when one might wish to hear the stones cry out against the sluggishness of man.

Sometimes one wanders away into the woods. To whom does it not sometimes happen to be dejected? – one sees so many sad things. The goal does not appear, the results are long in coming, a generation is behindhand, the work of the age languishes. What! So many sufferings yet? One would say there had been retrogression. There is everywhere increase of superstition, of cowardice, of deafness, of blindness, of imbecility. Brutishness is weighted down by penal laws. The wretched problem has been set, – to augment comfort by neglecting right; to sacrifice the superior side of man to the inferior side; to yield up principle to appetite. César takes charge of the belly, I make over to him the brains: it is the old sale of the birthright for the mess of lentils. A little more, and this fatal counter-movement would set civilization upon the wrong road. The

Hélas! ce laid expédient ne réussit même pas. Nulle diminution de malaise. Depuis dix ans, depuis vingt ans, l'étiage prostitution, l'étiage mendicité, l'étiage crime, marquent toujours le même chiffre; le mal n'a pas baissé d'un degré. D'éducation vraie, d'éducation gratuite, point. L'enfant a pourtant besoin de savoir qu'il est homme, et le père qu'il est citoyen. Où sont les promesses? Où est l'espérance? Oh! la pauvre misérable humanité! On est tenté de crier au secours dans la forêt; on est tenté de demander appui, concours et main-forte à cette grande nature sombre. Ce mystérieux ensemble de forces est-il donc indifférent au progrès? On supplie, on appelle, on lève les mains vers l'ombre. On écoute si les bruits ne vont pas devenir des voix. Le devoir des sources et des ruisseaux serait de bégayer: En avant! on voudrait entendre les rossignols chanter des marseillaises.

Après tout, pourtant, ces temps d'arrêt n'ont rien que de normal. Le découragement serait puéril. Il y a des haltes, des repos, des reprises d'haleine dans la marche des peuples, comme il y a des hivers dans la marche des saisons. Le pas gigantesque, 89, n'en est pas moins fait. Désespérer serait absurde; mais stimuler est nécessaire.

Stimuler, presser, gronder, réveiller, suggérer, inspirer, c'est cette fonction, remplie de toutes parts par les écrivains, qui imprime à la littérature de ce siècle un si haut caractère de puissance et d'originalité. Rester fidèle à toutes les lois de l'art en les combinant avec la loi du progrès, tel est le problème, victorieusement résolu par tant de nobles et fiers esprits.

De là cette parole: *Délivrance*, qui apparaît au-dessus de tout dans la lumière, comme si elle était écrite au front même de l'idéal.

La Révolution, c'est la France sublimée. Il s'est trouvé un jour, que la France a été dans la fournaise; les fournaises à de certaines martyres guerrières font pousser des ailes, et de ces flammes cette géante est sortie archange. Aujourd'hui pour toute la terre la France s'appelle Révolution; et désormais ce mot, Révolution, sera le nom de la civilisation jusqu'à ce qu'il soit remplacé par le mot Harmonie. Je le répète, ne cherchez pas ailleurs le point d'origine et le lieu de naissance de la littérature du dix-neuvième siècle. Oui, tous tant que nous sommes, grands et petits, puissants et méconnus, illustres et obscurs, dans toutes nos oeuvres, bonnes ou mauvaises, quelles qu'elles soient, poëmes, drames, romans, histoire, philosophie, à la tribune des assemblées comme devant les foules du théâtre, comme dans le recueillement des solitudes, oui, partout, oui, toujours, oui, pour combattre les violences et les impostures, oui, pour réhabiliter les lapidés et les accablés, oui, pour conclure logiquement et marcher droit, oui, pour consoler, pour secourir, pour relever, pour encourager, pour enseigner, oui, pour panser en attendant qu'on guérisse, oui, pour transformer la charité en fraternité, l'aumône en assistance, la fainéantise en travail, l'oisiveté en utilité, la centralisation en famille, l'iniquité en justice, le bourgeois en citoyen, la populace en peuple, la canaille en nation, les nations en humanité, la guerre en amour, le préjugé en examen, les frontières en soudures, les limites en ouvertures, les ornières en rails, les sacristies en temples, l'instinct du mal en volonté du bien, la vie en droit, les rois en hommes, oui, pour ôter des religions l'enfer et des sociétés le bagne, oui, pour être frères du misérable, du serf, du fellah, du prolétaire, du déshérité, de l'exploité, du trahi, du vaincu, du vendu, de l'enchaîné, du sacrifié, de la prostituée, du forçat, de l'ignorant, du sauvage, de l'esclave, du nègre, du condamné et du damné, oui, nous sommes tes fils, Révolution!

Oui, génies, oui, poëtes, philosophes, historiens, oui, géants de ce grand art des siècles antérieurs qui est toute la lumière du passé, ô hommes éternels, les esprits de ce temps vous saluent, mais ne vous suivent pas; ils ont vis-à-vis de vous cette loi: tout admirer, ne rien imiter. Leur fonction n'est plus la vôtre. Ils ont affaire à la virilité du genre humain. L'heure du changement d'âge est venue. Nous assistons, sous la pleine clarté de l'idéal, à la majestueuse jonction du beau

swine fattening for the knife would no longer be the king, but the people. . . . Alas! this ugly expedient does not even succeed; there is no diminution of wretchedness. For the last ten years – for the last twenty years – the low-water mark of prostitution, of mendacity, of crime, has been constantly visible; evil has not fallen a single degree. Of true education, of free education, there is none. Nevertheless, the child needs to be told that he is a man, and the father that he is a citizen. Where is the promise? Where is the hope? Oh! poor, wretched humanity, one is tempted to claim support and material assistance from vast and somber Nature. Can this mysterious union of forces be indifferent to progress? We supplicate, we call, we lift our hands toward the shadow. We listen, wondering if the rustlings will become voices. The duty of the springs and streams should be to babble forth the word 'Forward!' and one could wish to hear the nightingales sing new Marseillaises.

But, after all, theses seasons of halting have in them nothing but what is normal. Discouragement would be weakness. There are halts, rests, breathing-times in the march of nations, as there are winters in the progress of the seasons. The gigantic step, '89, is none the less a fact. To despair would be absurd, but to stimulate is necessary.

To stimulate, to press, to chide, to awaken, to suggest, to inspire, – these are the functions which, fulfilled everywhere by writers, impress on the literature of this century so marked a stamp of power and originality. To remain faithful to all the laws of art, while combining them with the law of progress, – such is the problem triumphantly solved by so many noble and lofty minds.

Thence the word 'Deliverance,' shining aloft in the light as if it were written on the very brow of the Ideal.

The Revolution of France is sublimated.

There came a day when France entered the furnace, – the furnace breeds wings upon such warrior martyrs, – and from these flames the giantess came forth an archangel. Throughout the earth to-day the name of France is revolution; and henceforth this word 'revolution' will be the name of civilization, until it can be replaced by the word 'harmony.' Seek nowhere else, I repeat, the starting-point and the birthplace of the literature of the nineteenth century. Ay! every one of us, great and small, powerful and despised, illustrious and obscure, in all our works, good or bad, whatever they may be, poems, dramas, romances, history, philosophy, at the tribune of assemblies as before the crowds of the theatre or in solitary meditation; ay! everywhere and always; ay! to combat violence and imposture; ay! to restore those who are stoned and run down; ay! to draw logical conclusions and to march straight onward; ay! to console, to succor, to relieve, to encourage, to teach; ay! to dress wounds, in hope of curing them; ay! to transform charity into fraternity, alms into helpfulness, sloth into industry, idleness into usefulness, to make centralized power give place to the family, to convert iniquity to justice, the bourgeois into the citizen, the populace into the people, the rabble into the nation, nations into humanity, war into love, prejudice into free inquiry, frontiers into welded joints, barriers into thoroughfares, ruts into rails, vestry-rooms into temples, the instinct of evil into the desire of good, life into right, kings into men; ay! to deprive religions of hell, and societies of the prison-den; ay! to be brothers to the wretched, the serf, the fellah, the poor laborer, the disinherited, the victim, the betrayed, the conquered, the sold, the shackled, the sacrificed, the harlot, the convict, the ignorant, the savage, the slave, the negro, the condemned, the damned, – ay! for all these things we are thy sons, O Revolution!

Ay! men of genius; ay! poets, philosophers, historians; ay! giants of that great art of the early ages which is all the light of the past, – O men eternal, the minds of this day salute you, but do not follow you. Concerning you they hold this law: Admire everything, imitate nothing. Their function is no longer yours. They have to do with the manhood of the human race. The hour of

avec l'utile. Aucun génie actuel ou possible ne vous dépassera, vieux génies, vous égaler est toute l'ambition permise; mais, pour vous égaler, il faut pourvoir aux besoins de son temps comme vous avez pourvu aux nécessités du vôtre. Les écrivains fils de la Révolution ont une tâche sainte. O Homère, il faut que leur épopée pleure, ô Hérodote, il faut que leur histoire proteste, ô Juvénal, il faut que leur satire détrône, ô Shakespeare, il faut que leur *tu seras toi* soit dit au peuple, ô Eschyle, il faut que leur Prométhée foudroie Jupiter, ô Job, il faut que leur fumier féconde, ô Dante, il faut que leur enfer s'éteigne, ô Isaïe, ta Babylone s'écroule, il faut que a leur s'éclaire! Ils font ce que vous avez fait; ils contemplent directement la création, ils observent directement l'humanité; ils n'acceptent pour clarté dirigeante aucun rayon réfracté, pas même le vôtre. Ainsi que vous, ils ont pour seul point de départ, en dehors d'eux, l'être universel, en eux, leur âme; ils ont pour source de leur oeuvre la source unique, celle d'où coule la nature et celle d'où coule l'art, l'infini. Comme le déclarait il y a quarante ans, tout à l'heure* celui qui écrit ces lignes: *les poëtes el les écrivains du dix-neuvième siècle n'ont ni maîtres ni modèles.* Non, dans tout cet art vaste et sublime de tous les peuples, dans toutes ces créations grandioses de toutes les époques, non, pas même toi, Eschyle, pas même toi, Dante, pas même toi, Shakespeare, non, ils n'ont ni modèles ni maîtres. Et pourquoi n'ont-ils ni maîtres ni modèles? C'est parce qu'ils ont un modèle, l'Homme, et parce qu'ils ont un maître, Dieu.

[1864]

III.d.3. ANNE LOUISE GERMAINE DE STAËL,
Considérations sur la Révolution française

Il est temps que vingt-cinq années, dont quinze appartiennent au despotisme militaire, ne se placent plus comme un fantôme entre l'histoire et nous, et ne nous privent plus de toutes les leçons et de tous les exemples qu'elle nous offre. N'y aurait-il plus d'Aristide, de Phocion, d'Epaminondas en Grèce; de Régulus, de Caton, de Brutus à Rome; de Tell en Suisse; d'Egmont, de Nassau en Hollande; de Sidney, de Russel en Angleterre, parce qu'un pays, gouverné longtemps par le pouvoir arbitraire, s'est vu livré pendant une révolution aux hommes que l'arbitraire même avoit pervertis? Qu'y a-t-il de si extraor dinaire dans un tel événement, qu'il doive changer le cours des astres, c'est-à-dire, faire reculer la vérité qui s'avançait avec l'histoire pour éclairer le genre humain? Et par quel sentiment public serions-nous désormais émus, si nous repoussions l'amour de la liberté? Les vieux préjugés n'agissent plus sur les hommes que par calcul; ils ne sont soutenus quepar ceux qui ont un intérêt personnel à les défendre. Qui veut en France le pouvoir absolu par amour pur, c'est-à-dire pour lui-même? Informez-vous de la situation personnelle de chacun de ses défenseurs, et vous connaîtrez bien vite les motifs de leur doctrine. Sur quoi donc se fonderait la fraternité des associations humaines, si quelque enthousiasme ne se développait pas dans les coeurs? Qui serait fier d'être Français, si l'on avait vu la liberté détruite par la tyrannie, la tyrannie brisée par les étrangers, et que les lauriers de la guerre ne fussent pas au moins honorés par la conquête de la liberté? Il ne s'agirait plus que de voir lutter l'un contre l'autre l'égoïsme des privilégiés par la naissance et l'égoïsme des privilégiés par les événements. Mais la France où serait-elle? Qui pourrait se vanter de l'avoir servie, puisque rien ne resterait dans les coeurs, ni des temps passés ni de la réforme nouvelle?

man's majority has struck. We assist, under the full light of the ideal, at the majestic union of the Beautiful with the Useful. No present or possible genius can surpass you, ye ancient men of genius; to equal you we must provide for the needs of our time, as ye supplied the wants of yours! Writers who are sons of the Revolution have a holy task. Their epic must sob, O Homer! their history must protest, O Herodotus! their satire must dethrone, O Juvenal! their 'thou shalt be king' must be said to the people, O Shakespeare! their Prometheus must smite down Jupiter, O Aeschylus! their dunghill must be fruitful, O Job! their hell must be quenched, O Dante! thy Babylon crumbles, O Isaiah! theirs must be radiant with light! They do what you have done, – they contemplate creation directly, they observe humanity directly; they accept as lodestar no refracted ray, not even yours. Like you, they have for their sole starting-point, outside them-selves the Universal Being, within themselves the soul; as the source of their work they have the one source whence flows Nature and whence flows Art, the Infinite. As the writer of these lines declared nearly forty years ago:[1] 'The poets and the writers of the nineteenth century have nei-ther masters nor models.' No, in all that vast and sublime art of all nations, among all those grand creations of all epochs, they find neither masters nor models, – not even thee, O Aeschy-lus! not even thee, O Dante! not even thee, O Shakespeare! And why have they neither masters nor models? It is because they have one model, Man, and because they have one master, God.

[1864] [*Translated by Melville B. Anderson. Chicago: McClurg, 1925*]

III.d.3.   ANNE LOUISE GERMAINE DE STAËL,
Considerations on the French Revolution

It is time that five-and-twenty years, of which fifteen belong to military despotism, should no longer place themselves as a phantom betwixt history and us, and should no longer deprive us of all the lessons and of all the examples which it exhibits. Is Aristides to be forgotten, and Phocion, and Epaminondas, in Greece; Regulus, Cato, and Brutus, at Rome; Tell in Switzerland; Egmont and Nassau in Holland; Sidney and Russel in England; because a country that had long been governed by arbitrary power was delivered, during a revolution, to men whom arbitrary power had corrupted? What is there so extraordinary in such an event, as to change the course of the stars, that is, to give a retrograde motion to truth, which was before advancing with his-tory to enlighten the human race? By what public sentiment shall we be moved henceforth, if we are to reject the love of liberty? The prejudices of other days have now no influence upon men except from calculation; they are defended only by those who have a personal interest in defend-ing them. What man in France desires absolute power from a disinterested feeling, or for its own sake. Inform yourself of the personal situation of its partisans, and you will soon know the motives of their doctrine. On what then would the fraternal tie of human associations be founded, if no enthusiasm were to be developed in the heart? Who could be elated with being a Frenchman, after having seen liberty destroyed by tyranny, and tyranny broken to pieces by for-eign force, unless the laurels of war were at least rendered honourable by the conquest of liberty? We should have to contemplate a mere struggle between the selfishness of those who were priv-ileged by birth, and the selfishness of those who are privileged by events. But where would then be France? Who could take a pride in having served her, since nothing would remain in the heart, either of past times or of the new reform?

[1] Preface to 'Cromwell'.

La liberté! répétons son nom avec d'autant plus de force, que les hommes qui devraient au moins le prononcer comme excuse, l'éloignent par flatterie; répétons-le sans crainte de blesser aucune puissance respectable: car tout ce que nous aimons, tout ce que nous honorons y est compris. Rien que la liberté ne peut remuer l'âme dans les rapports de l'ordre social. Les réunions d'hommes ne seraient que des associations de commerce ou d'agriculture, si la vie du patriotisme n'excitait pas les individus à se sacrifier à leurs semblables. La chevalerie était une confrérie guerrière qui satisfaisait au besoin de dévouement qu'éprouvent tous les coeurs généreux. Les nobles étaient des compagnons d'armes qu'un honneur et un devoir réunissaient; mais depuis que les progrès de l'esprit humain ont créé les nations, c'est-a-dire, depuis que tous les nommes participent de quelque manière aux mêmes avantages, que ferait-on de l'espèce humaine sans le sentiment de la liberté?

Pourquoi le patriotisme français commencerait-il à telle frontière et s'arrêterait-il à telle autre, s'il n'y avait pas cette enceinte des espérances, des jouissances, une émulation, une sécurité, qui font aimer son pays natal par l'âme autant que par l'habitude? Pourquoi le nom de France causerait-il une invincible émotion, s'il n'y avait d'autres liens entre les habitants de cette belle contrée que les privilèges des uns et l'asservissement des autres? Partout où vous rencontrez du respect pour la nature humaine, de l'affection pour ses semblables, et cette énergie d'indépendance qui sait résister à tout sur la terre, et ne se prosterner que devant Dieu, là vous voyez l'homme image de son Créateur, là vous sentez au fond de l'âme un attendrissement si intime qu'il ne peut vous tromper sur la vérité. Et vous, nobles François, pour qui l'honneur étoit la liberté; vous qui, par une longue transmission d'exploits et de grandeur, deviez vous considérer comme l'élite de l'espèce humaine, souffrez que la nation s'élève jusqu'à vous; elle a aussi maintenant les droits de conquête, et tout François aujourd'hui peut se dire gentilhomme, si tout gentilhomme ne veut pas se dire citoyen.

[1818]

III.d.4.   ALFRED DE VIGNY, préface de *Cinq-Mars*

De même que l'on descend dans sa conscience pour juger des actions qui sont douteuses pour l'esprit, ne pourrions-nous pas aussi chercher en nous-mêmes le sentiment primitif qui donne naissance aux formes de la pensée, toujours indécises et flottantes? Nous trouverions dans notre coeur plein de trouble, où rien n'est d'accord, deux besoins qui semblent opposés, mais qui se confondent, à mon sens, dans une source commune: l'un est l'amour du VRAI, l'autre l'amour du FABULEUX. Le jour où l'homme a raconté sa vie à l'homme, l'Histoire est née. Mais à quoi bon la mémoire des faits véritables, si ce n'est a servir d'exemple de bien ou de mal? Or les exemples que présente la succession lente des événements sont épars et incomplets; il leur manque toujours un enchaînement palpable et visible, qui puisse amener sans divergence a une conclusion morale; les actes de la famille humaine sur le théâtre du monde ont sans doute un ensemble, mais le sens de cette vaste tragédie qu'elle y joue ne sera visible qu'à l'oeil de Dieu, jusqu'au dénoûment qui le révélera peut-être au dernier homme. Toutes les philosophies se sont en vain épuisées à l'expliquer, roulant sans cesse leur rocher, qui n'arrive jamais et retombe sur elles, chacune élevant son frêle édifice sur la ruine des autres et le voyant crouler à son tour. Il me semble donc que l'homme, après avoir satisfait à cette première curiosité des faits, désira quelque chose de plus complet, quelque groupe, quelque réduction à sa portée et à son usage des anneaux de cette vaste chaîne d'événements que sa vue ne pouvait embrasser; car il voulait aussi

Liberty! Let us repeat her name with so much the more energy, that the men who ought to pronounce it, at least as an apology, keep it at a distance through flattery: let us repeat it without fear of wounding any power that deserves respect; for all that we love, all that we honour, is included in it. Nothing but liberty can arouse the soul to the interests of social order. Assemblages of men would be nothing but associations for commerce or agriculture, if the life of patriotism did not excite individuals to sacrifice themselves for their fellows. Chivalry was a warlike brother-hood, which satisfied that thirst for self-devotion which is felt by every generous heart. The nobles were companions in arms, bound together by duty and honour; but since the progress of the human mind has created nations, – in other words, since all men participate in some degree in the same advantages, what would become of the human species were it not for the sentiment of liberty? Why should the patriotism of a Frenchman begin at this frontier, and cease at that, if there were not within this compass hopes, enjoyments, an emulation, a security, which make him love his native land as much through the genuine feelings of the soul as through habit? Why should the name of France awaken so invincible an emotion, if there were no other ties among the inhabitants of this fine country, than the privileges of some and the subjection of the rest?

Wherever you meet with respect for human nature, affection for fellow-creatures, and that energy of independence which can resist every thing upon earth, and prostrate itself only before God; there you behold man the image of his Creator, there you feel at the bottom of the soul an emotion which so penetrates its very substance, that it cannot deceive you with respect to truth. And you, nobles of France, for whom honour was freedom, you who by a long series of exploits and greatness were entitled to consider yourselves as a chosen portion of the human race, permit the nation to raise itself to a level with you: she too has rights of conquest; every Frenchman may now call himself a gentleman, if every gentleman is not willing to be called a citizen.

[1818] [*Editors: Duke de Broglie and Baron de Staël. London: Baldwin, Cradock, and Joy, 1821*]

III.d.4. ALFRED DE VIGNY, from Preface to *Cinq-Mars*

Just as we descend into our consciences to judge of actions which our minds can not weigh, can we not also search in ourselves for the feeling which gives birth to forms of thought, always vague and cloudy? We shall find in our troubled hearts, where discord reigns, two needs which seem at variance, but which merge, as I think, in a common source – the love of the true, and the love of the fabulous.

On the day when man told the story of his life to man, history was born. Of what use is the memory of facts, if not to serve as an example of good or of evil? But the examples which the slow train of events presents to us are scattered and incomplete. They lack always a tangible and visible coherence leading straight on to a moral conclusion. The acts of the human race on the world's stage have doubtless a coherent unity, but the meaning of the vast tragedy enacted will be visible only to the eye of God, until the end, which will reveal it perhaps to the last man. All systems of philosophy have sought in vain to explain it, ceaselessly rolling up their rock, which, never reaching the top, falls back upon them – each raising its frail structure on the ruins of the others, only to see it fall in its turn.

I think, then, that man, after having satisfied his first longing for facts, wanted something fuller – some grouping, some adaptation to his capacity and experience, of the links of this vast chain of events which his sight could not take in. Thus he hoped to find in the historic recital

trouver, dans les récits, des exemples qui pussent servir aux vérités morales dont il avait la con-science; peu de destinées particulières suffisaient à ce désir, n'étant que les parties incomplètes du TOUT insaisissable de l'histoire du monde; l'une était pour ainsi dire un quart, l'autre une moitié de preuve; l'imagination fit le reste et les compléta. De là, sans doute, sortit la fable. – L'homme la créa vraie, parce qu'il ne lui est pas donné de voir autre chose que lui-même et la nature qui l'entoure; mais il la créa VRAIE d'une VÉRITÉ toute particulière.

Cette VÉRITÉ toute belle, tout intellectuelle, que je sens, que je vois et voudrais définir, dont j'ose ici distinguer le nom de celui du VRAI, pour me mieux faire entendre, est comme l'âme de tous les arts. C'est un choix du signe caractéristique dans toutes les beautés et toutes les grandeurs du VRAI visible; mais ce n'est pas lui-même, c'est mieux que lui; c'est un ensemble idéal de ses principales formes, une teinte lumineuse qui comprend ses plus vives couleurs, un baume enivrant de ses par-fums les plus purs, un élixir délicieux de ses sucs les meilleurs, une harmonie parfaite de ses sons les plus mélodieux; enfin c'est une somme complète de toutes ses valeurs. A cette seule VÉRITÉ doivent prétendre les oeuvres de l'Art qui sont une représentation morale de la vie, les oeuvres dramatiques. Pour l'atteindre, il faut sans doute commencer par connaître tout le VRAI de chaque siècle, être imbu profondément de son ensemble et de ses détails; ce n'est là qu'un pauvre mérite d'attention, de patience et de mémoire; mais ensuite il faut choisir et grouper autour d'un centre inventé; c'est là l'oeuvre de l'imagination et de ce grand BON SENS qui est le génie lui-même.

A quoi bon les Arts, s'ils n'étaient que le redoublement et la contre-épreuve de l'existence? Eh! bon Dieu, nous ne voyons que trop autour de nous la triste et désenchanteresse réalité: la tiédeur insupportable des demi-caractères, des ébauches de vertus et de vices, des amours irrésolues, des haines mitigées, des amitiés tremblotantes, des doctrines variables, des fidélités qui ont leur hausse et leur baisse, des opinions qui s'évaporent; laissez-nous rêver que parfois ont paru des hommes plus forts et plus grands, qui furent des bons ou des méchants plus résolus; cela fait du bien. Si la pâleur de votre VRAI nous poursuit dans l'Art, nous fermerons ensemble le théâtre et le livre pour ne pas le rencontrer deux fois. Ce que l'on veut des oeuvres qui font mouvoir des fantômes d'hommes, c'est, je le répète, le spectacle philosophique de l'homme profondément travaillé par les passions de son caractère et de son temps; c'est donc la VÉRITÉ de cet HOMME et de ce TEMPS, mais tous deux élevés à une puissance supérieure et idéale qui en concentre toutes les forces. On la reconnaît, cette VÉRITÉ, dans les oeuvres de la pensée, comme l'on se récrie sur la ressemblance d'un portrait dont on n'a jamais vu l'original; car un beau talent peint la vie plus encore que le vivant.

[1826]

e. DEUTSCH

III.e.1. NOVALIS, aus *Glauben und Liebe oder der König und die Königin*

22. Es wird eine Zeit kommen und das bald, wo man allgemein überzeugt seyn wird, daß kein König ohne Republik, und keine Republik ohne König bestehn könne, daß beide so untheilbar sind, wie Körper und Seele, und daß ein König ohne Republik, und eine Republik ohne König, nur Worte ohne Bedeutung sind. Daher entstand mit einer ächten Republik immer ein König zugleich, und mit einem ächten König eine Republik zugleich. Der ächte König wird Republik, die ächte Republik König seyn.

39. Ein wahrhafter Fürst ist der Künstler der Künstler; das ist, der Director der Künstler. Jeder Mensch sollte Künstler seyn. Alles kann zur schönen Kunst werden. Der Stoff des Fürsten sind die Künstler; sein Wille ist sein Meißel: er erzieht, stellt und weist die Künstler an, weil nur er

examples which might support the moral truths of which he was conscious. Few single careers could satisfy this longing, being only incomplete parts of the elusive whole of history of the world; one was a quarter, as it were, the other a half of the proof; imagination did the rest and completed them. From this, without doubt, sprang the fable. Man created it thus, because it was not given him to see more than himself and nature, which surrounds him; but he created it true with a truth all its own.

This Truth, so beautiful, so intellectual, which I feel, I see, and long to define, the name of which I here venture to distinguish from that of the True, that of all the arts. It is the selections of the characteristic token in all the beauties and the grandeurs of the visible True; but it is not the thing itself, it is something better: it is an ideal combination of its principal forms, a luminous tint made up of its brightest colors, an intoxicating balm of its purest perfumes, a delicious elixir of its best juices, a perfect harmony of its sweetest sounds – in short, it is a concentration of all its good qualities. For this Truth, and nothing else, should strive those works of art which are a moral representation of life – dramatic works. To attain it, the first step is undoubtedly to learn all that is true in fact of every period, to become deeply imbued with its general character and with its details; this involves only a cheap tribute of attention, of patience, and of memory. But then one must fix upon some chosen centre, and group everything around it; this is the work of imagination, and of that sublime common-sense which is genius itself.

Of what use were the arts if they were only the reproduction and the imitation of life? Good heavens! We see only too clearly about us the sad and disenchanting reality – the insupportable lukewarmness of feeble characters, of shallow virtues and vices, of irresolute love, of tempered hates, of wavering friendships, of unsettled beliefs, of constancy which has its height and its depth, of opinions which evaporate. Let us dream that once upon a time have lived men stronger and greater, who were more determined for good or for evil; that does us good. If the paleness of your True is to follow us into art, we shall close at once the theatre and the book, to avoid meeting it a second time. What is wanted of works which revive the ghosts of human beings is, I repeat, the philosophical spectacle of man deeply wrought upon by the passions of his character and of his epoch, but both raised to a higher and ideal power, which concentrates all their forces. You recognize this Truth in works of the imagination just as you cry out at the resemblance of a portrait of which you have never seen the original; for true talent paints life rather than the living.

[1826] [*Translated by Robert Arnot. New York: Current Literature Pub. Co., 1910*]

e. GERMAN

III.e.1. NOVALIS, from *Faith and Love or The King and the Queen*

22. A time will come, and soon, when there will be a general conviction that no king could exist without a republic and no republic without a king, that the two are as indivisible as body and soul, and that a king without a republic and a republic without a king are only words without meaning. Hence a king always appeared at the same time as a true republic, and a republic appeared at the same time as a true king. The true king will be a republic, the true republic a king.

39. A true prince is the artist of artists; that is, he is the director of artists. Every person should be an artist. Everything can become a fine art. Artists are the prince's material; his will is his chisel: he teaches, engages, and instructs the artists, because only he can oversee the

461

das Bild im Ganzen aus dem rechten Standpunkte übersieht, weil ihm nur die große Idee, die durch vereinigte Kräfte und Ideen dargestellt, exekutirt werden soll, vollkommen gegenwärtig ist. Der Regent führt ein unendlich mannichfaches Schauspiel auf, wo Bühne und Parterre, Schauspieler und Zuschauer Eins sind, und er selbst Poet, Director und Held des Stücks zugleich ist. Wie entzückend, wenn wie bey dem König, die Directrice zugleich die Geliebte des Helden, die Heldin des Stücks ist, wenn man selbst die Muse in ihr erblickt, die den Poeten mit heiliger Glut erfüllt, und zu sanften, himmlischen Weisen sein Saitenspiel stimmt.

68. Jetzt scheint die vollkommene Demokratie und die Monarchie in einer unauflöslichen Antinomie begriffen zu sein — der Vortheil der Einen durch einen entgegengesetzten Vortheil der Andern aufgewogen zu werden. Das junge Volk steht auf der Seite der erstern, gesetztere Hausväter auf der Seite der zweiten. Absolute Verschiedenheit der Neigungen scheint diese Trennung zu veranlassen. Einer liebt Veränderungen — der Andre nicht. Vielleicht lieben wir alle in gewissen Jahren Revolutionen, freie Concurrenz, Wettkämpfe und dergleichen demokratische Erscheinungen. Aber diese Jahre gehn bei den Meisten vorüber — und wir fühlen uns von einer friedlicheren Welt angezogen, wo eine Centralsonne den Reigen führt, und man lieber Planet wird, als einen zerstörenden Kampf um den Vortanz mitkämpft. Man sei also nur wenigstens politisch, wie religiös, tolerant — man nehme nur die Möglichkeit an, daß auch ein vernünftiges Wesen anders incliniren könne als wir. Diese Toleranz führt, wie mich dünkt, allmälig zur erhabenen Ueberzeugung von der Relativität jeder positiven Form — und der wahrhaften Unabhängigkeit eines reifen Geistes von jeder individuellen Form, die ihm nichts als nothwendiges Werkzeug ist. Die Zeit muß kommen, wo politischer Entheism und Pantheism als nothwendige Wechselglieder aufs innigste verbunden sein werden.

[(1798) *Novalis Schriften. Edited by Paul Kluckhohn, Richard Samuel, et al., 7 vols. Stuttgart, 1960– . II, 490, 497–498, 506*]

III.e.2. JOHANN GOTTLIEB FICHTE, aus *Reden an die Deutsche Nation, Nr 1*

Ich rede für Deutsche schlechtweg, von Deutschen schlechtweg, nicht anerkennend, sondern durchaus bei Seite setzend und wegwerfend alle die trennenden Unterscheidungen, welche unselige Ereignisse seit Jahrhunderten in der einen Nation gemacht haben. Sie, E. V., sind zwar meinem leiblichen Auge die ersten und unmittelbaren Stellvertreter, welche die geliebten Nationalzüge mir vergegenwärtigen, und der sichtbare Brennpunkt, in welchem die Flamme meiner Rede sich entzündet; aber mein Geist versammelt den gebildeten Teil der ganzen deutschen Nation, aus allen den Ländern, über welche er verbreitet ist, um sich her, bedenkt und beachtet unser aller gemeinsame Lage und Verhältnisse, und wünschet, daß ein Teil der lebendigen Kraft, mit welcher diese Reden vielleicht Sie ergreifen, auch in dem stummen Abdrucke, welcher allein unter die Augen der Abwesenden kommen wird, verbleibe, und aus ihm atme, und an allen Orten deutsche Gemüter zu Entschluß und Tat entzünde. Bloß von Deutschen und für Deutsche schlechtweg sagte ich. Wir werden zu seiner Zeit zeigen, daß jedwede andere Einheitsbezeichnung oder Nationalband entweder niemals Wahrheit und Bedeutung hatte, oder, falls es sie gehabt hätte, daß diese Vereinigungspunkte durch unsre dermalige Lage vernichtet, und uns entrissen sind, und niemals wiederkehren können; und daß es lediglich der gemeinsame Grundzug der Deutschheit ist, wodurch wir den Untergang unsrer Nation im Zusammenfließen derselben mit dem Auslande, abwehren, und worin wir ein auf ihm selber ruhendes, und aller Abhängigkeit durchaus unfähiges Selbst, wiederum gewinnen können. Es wird, so wie wir dieses letztere einsehen werden, zugleich der scheinbare Widerspruch dieser

picture as a whole from the right standpoint, because only to him the great idea which is to be represented and executed through combined forces and ideas, is perfectly present. The regent presents an infinitely diverse spectacle, where stage and parterre, actor and spectator are one, and he himself is poet, director, and hero of the play. How delightful if, as is so with the king, the *directrice* is at once the hero's beloved, the heroine of the play, if one sees in her even the muse who fills the poet with sacred fire, and tunes his instrument to play soft, heavenly melodies.

68. Now perfect democracy and the monarchy seem to be in a state of insoluble contradiction – the advantage of the one to be balanced by the opposite advantage of the other. Young people are on the side of the first, more sedate heads of households on the side of the second. This division seems to be caused by total divergence of inclination. One likes change – the other does not. Perhaps in certain years we all like revolutions, free competition, contests, and similar democratic phenomena. But for most people these years pass – and we feel attracted by a more peaceful world where a central sun leads the round dance, and one prefers to be a planet rather than join in a destructive struggle for the prelude to the dance. Thus let us at least be politically tolerant as we are in religious matters – let us at least accept the possibility that even a rational being could have different inclinations from ours. This tolerance, it seems to me, will gradually lead to the sublime conviction of the relativity of every positive form – and the true independence of a mature mind from every individual form, which is nothing to him but a necessary tool. The time must come when political entheism and panthcism will be most closely bound together as necessarily interchangeable parts.

[*(1798) Novalis. Philosophical Writings. Translated by Margaret Mahoney Stoljar. Albany: SUNY, 1997. 89, 95–96, 100*]

III.e.2.   JOHANN GOTTLIEB FICHTE, from *Speeches to the German Nation, No. 1*

I speak for Germans simply, of Germans simply, not recognizing, but setting aside completely and rejecting, all the dissociating distinctions which for centuries unhappy events have caused in this single nation. You, gentlemen, are indeed to my outward eye the first and immediate representatives who bring before my mind the beloved national characteristics, and are the visible spark at which the flame of my address is kindled. But my spirit gathers around it the educated part of the whole German nation, from all the lands in which they are scattered. It thinks of and considers our common position and relations; it hopes that part of the living force, with which these addresses may chance to grip you, may also remain in and breathe from the dumb printed page which alone will come to the eyes of the absent, and may in all places kindle German hearts to decision and action. Only of Germans and simply for Germans, I said. In due course we shall show that any other mark of unity or any other national bond either never had truth and meaning or, if it had, that owing to our present position these bonds of union have been destroyed and torn from us and can never recur; it is only by means of the common characteristic of being German that we can avert the downfall of our nation which is threatened by its fusion with foreign peoples and win back again an individuality that is self-supporting and quite incapable of any dependence upon others. With our perception of the truth of this statement its apparent conflict (feared now, perhaps by many) with other duties and with matters that are considered sacred will completely vanish. [...]

Behauptung mit anderweitigen Pflichten, und für heilig gehaltenen Angelegenheiten, den vielleicht dermalen mancher fürchtet, vollkommen verschwinden.

[...]

So wie das an Reinlichkeit und Ordnung gewöhnte äußere Auge durch einen Flecken, der ja unmittelbar dem Leibe keinen Schmerz zufügt, oder durch den Anblick verworren durch einander liegender Gegenstände dennoch gepeinigt, und geängstet wird, wie vom unmittelbaren Schmerze, indes der des Schmutzes und der Unordnung Gewohnte sich in denselben recht wohl befindet; eben also kann auch das innere geistige Auge des Menschen so gewöhnt und gebildet werden, daß der bloße Anblick eines verworrenen und unordentlichen, eines unwürdigen und ehrelosen Daseins seiner selbst und seines verbrüderten Stammes, ohne Rücksicht auf das, was davon für sein sinnliches Wohlsein zu fürchten oder zu hoffen sei, ihm innig wehe tue, und daß dieser Schmerz dem Besitzer eines solchen Auges, abermals ganz unabhängig von sinnlicher Furcht oder Hoffnung, keine Ruhe lasse, bis er, so viel an ihm ist, den ihm mißfälligen Zustand aufgehoben, und den, der ihm allein gefallen kann, an seine Stelle gesetzt habe. Im Besitzer eines solchen Auges ist die Angelegenheit des ihn umgebenden Ganzen, durch das treibende Gefühl der Billigung oder Mißbilligung, an die Angelegenheit seines eignen erweiterten Selbst, das nur als Teil des Ganzen sich fühlt, und nur im gefälligen Ganzen sich ertragen kann, unabtrennbar angeknüpft; die Sichbildung zu einem solchen Auge wäre somit ein sicheres und das einzige Mittel, das einer Nation, die ihre Selbständigkeit, und mit ihr allen Einfluß auf die öffentliche Furcht und Hoffnung verloren hat, übrig bliebe, um aus der erduldeten Vernichtung sich wieder ins Dasein zu erheben, und dem entstandenen neuen und höheren Gefühle ihre National Angelegenheiten, die seit ihrem Untergange kein Mensch und kein Gott weiter bedenkt, sicher anzuvertrauen. So ergibt sich denn also, daß das Rettungsmittel, dessen Anzeige ich versprochen, bestehe in der Bildung zu einem durchaus neuen, und bisher vielleicht als Ausnahme bei Einzelnen, niemals aber als allgemeines und nationales Selbst, dagewesenem Selbst, und in der Erziehung der Nation, deren bisheriges Leben erloschen, und Zugabe eines fremden Lebens geworden, zu einem ganz neuen Leben, das entweder ihr ausschließendes Besitztum bleibt, oder, falls es auch von ihr aus an andere kommen sollte, ganz und unverringert bleibt bei unendlicher Teilung; mit Einem Worte, eine gänzliche Veränderung des bisherigen Erziehungswesens ist es, was ich, als das einzige Mittel die deutsche Nation im Dasein zu erhalten, in Vorschlag bringe.

Daß man den Kindern eine gute Erziehung geben müsse, ist auch in unserm Zeitalter oft genug gesagt, und bis zum Überdrusse wiederholt worden, und es wäre ein geringes, wenn auch wir unseres Ortes dies gleichfalls einmal sagen wollten. Vielmehr wird uns, so wir ein anderes zu vermögen glauben, obliegen, genau und bestimmt zu untersuchen, was eigentlich der bisherigen Erziehung gefehlt habe, und anzugeben, welches durchaus neue Glied die veränderte Erziehung der bisherigen Menschenbildung hinzufügen müsse.

Man muß, nach einer solchen Untersuchung, der bisherigen Erziehung zugestehen, daß sie nicht ermangelt, irgend ein Bild von religiöser, sittlicher, gesetzlicher Denkart, und von allerhand Ordnung und guter Sitte vor das Auge ihrer Zöglinge zu bringen, auch daß sie hier und da dieselben getreulich ermahnt habe, jenen Bildern in ihrem Leben einen Abdruck zu geben; aber mit höchst seltnen Ausnahmen, die somit nicht durch diese Erziehung begründet waren, indem sie sodann an allen durch diese Bildung hindurch gegangenen, und als die Regel hätten eintreten müssen, sondern die durch andere Ursachen herbeigeführt worden, — mit diesen höchstseltenen Ausnahmen, sage ich, haben die Zöglinge dieser Erziehung insgesamt nicht jenen sittlichen Vorstellungen und Ermahnungen, sondern sie haben den Antrieben ihrer, ihnen natürlich, und ohne

The physical eye, when accustomed to cleanliness and order, is troubled and distressed, as though actually hurt, by a spot which indeed causes the body no actual injury, or by the sight of objects lying in chaotic confusion; while the eye accustomed to dirt and disorder is quite comfortable under such circumstances. So, too, the inner mental eye of man can be so accustomed and trained that the very sight of a muddled and disorderly, unworthy and dishonorable existence of its own or of a kindred race causes it intense pain, apart from anything there may be to fear or to hope from this for its own material welfare. This pain, again apart from material fear or hope, permits the possessor of such an eye no rest until he has removed, insofar as he can, this condition which displeases him, and has set in its place that which alone can please him. For the possessor of such an eye, because of this stimulating feeling of approval or disapproval, the welfare of his whole environment is bound up inextricably with the welfare of his own wider self, which is conscious of itself only as part of the whole and can endure itself only when the whole is pleasing. To educate itself to possess such an eye will therefore be a sure means, and indeed the only means left to a nation which has lost its independence and with it all influence over public fear and hope, of rising again into life from the destruction it has suffered, and of entrusting its national welfare, which since its downfall neither God nor man has heeded, with confidence to this new and higher feeling that has arisen. It follows, then, that the means of salvation that I promised to indicate consists in the fashioning of an entirely new self, which may have existed before perhaps in individuals as an exception, but never as a universal and national self, and in the education of the nation, whose former life has died out and become the supplement of an alien life, to a completely new life, which shall either remain its exclusive possession or, if it must go forth from it to others, shall at least continue whole and undiminished in spite of infinite division. In a word, it is a total change of the existing system of education that I propose as the sole means of preserving the existence of the German nation.

That children must be given a good education has been said often enough, and has been repeated too often even in our age; and it would be a paltry thing if we, too, for our part wished to do nothing but say it once again. Rather will it be our duty, insofar as we think we can accomplish something new, to investigate carefully and definitely what education hitherto has really lacked, and to suggest what completely new element a reformed system must add to the training that has hitherto existed. After such an investigation we must admit that the existing education does not fail to bring before the eyes of the pupils some sort of picture of a religious moral, and law-abiding disposition and of order in all things and good habits, and also that here and there it has faithfully exhorted them to copy such images in their lives. With very rare exceptions however – and these were, moreover, not the outcome of this education (because otherwise they must have appeared and that too as the rule, among all who received such instruction), but were occasioned by other causes – with these very rare exceptions I say, the pupils of this education have in general followed, not those moral ideas and exhortations, but the impulses of self-seeking which developed in them spontaneously and without any assistance from education. This proves beyond dispute that the system may, indeed, have been able to fill the memory with some words and phrases and the cold and indifferent imagination with some faint and feeble pictures; but that it has never succeeded in making its picture of a moral world-order so vivid that the pupil was filled with passionate love and yearning for that order, and with such glowing emotion as to stimulate him to realize it in his life – emotion before which self-seeking falls to the ground like withered leaves. It also proves this education to have been far from reaching right down to the roots of real

alle Beihülfe der Erziehungskunst, erwachsenden Selbstsucht, gefolgt; zum unwidersprechlichen Beweise, daß diese Erziehungskunst zwar wohl das Gedächtnis mit einigen Worten, und Redensarten, und die kalte und teilnehmungslose Phantasie mit einigen matten und blassen Bildern anzufüllen vermocht, daß es ihr aber niemals gelungen, ihr Gemälde einer sittlichen Weltordnung bis zu der Lebhaftigkeit zu steigern, daß ihr Zögling von der heißen Liebe und Sehnsucht dafür, und von dem glühenden Affekte, der zur Darstellung im Leben treibt, und vor welchem die Selbstsucht abfällt, wie welkes Laub, ergriffen worden; daß somit diese Erziehung weit davon entfernt sei, bis zur Wurzel der wirklichen Lebensregung und Bewegung durchzugreifen, und diese zu bilden, indem diese vielmehr, unbeachtet von der blinden und ohnmächtigen, allenthalben wild aufgewachsen sei, wie sie gekonnt habe, zu guter Frucht bei wenigen durch Gott begeisterten, zu schlechter bei der großen Mehrzahl. Auch ist es dermalen vollkommen hinlänglich, diese Erziehung durch diesen ihren Erfolg zu zeichnen, und kann man für unsern Behuf sich des mühsamen Geschäfts überheben, die innern Säfte und Adern eines Baumes zu zergliedern, dessen Frucht dermalen vollständig reif ist, und abgefallen, und vor aller Welt Augen liegt, und höchst deutlich und verständlich ausspricht die innere Natur ihres Erzeugers. Der Strenge nach wäre, dieser Ansicht zu Folge, die bisherige Erziehung auf keine Weise die Kunst der Bildung zum Menschen gewesen, wie sie sich denn dessen auch eben nicht gerühmt, sondern gar oft ihre Ohnmacht, durch die Forderung, ihr ein natürliches Talent, oder Genie, als Bedingung ihres Erfolgs voraus zu geben, freimütig gestanden; sondern es wäre eine solche Kunst erst zu erfinden, und die Erfindung derselben wäre die eigentliche Aufgabe der neuen Erziehung. Das ermangelnde Durchgreifen bis in die Wurzel der Lebens Regung und Bewegung hätte diese neue Erziehung der bisherigen hinzu zu fügen, und wie die bisherige höchstens etwas am Menschen, so hätte diese den Menschen selbst zu bilden, und ihre Bildung keinesweges, wie bisher, zu einem Besitztume, sondern vielmehr zu einem persönlichen Bestandteile des Zöglings zu machen.

Ferner wurde bisher diese also beschränkte Bildung nur an die sehr geringe Minderzahl der eben daher gebildet genannten Stände gebracht, die große Mehrzahl aber, auf welcher das gemeine Wesen recht eigentlich ruht, das Volk, wurde von der Erziehungskunst fast ganz vernachlässigt, und dem blinden Ohngefähr übergeben. Wir wollen durch die neue Erziehung die Deutschen zu einer Gesamtheit bilden, die in allen ihren einzelnen Gliedern getrieben und belebt sei durch dieselbe Eine Angelegenheit; so wir aber etwa hierbei abermals einen gebildeten Stand, der etwa durch den neu entwickelten Antrieb der sittlichen Billigung belebt würde, absondern wollten von einem ungebildeten, so würde dieser letzte, da Hoffnung und Furcht, durch welche allein noch auf ihn gewirkt werden könnte, nicht mehr für uns sondern gegen uns dienen, von uns abfallen, und uns verloren gehen. Es bleibt sonach uns nichts übrig, als schlechthin an alles ohne Ausnahme, was deutsch ist, die neue Bildung zu bringen, so daß dieselbe nicht Bildung eines besondern Standes, sondern daß sie Bildung der Nation schlechthin als solcher, und ohne alle Ausnahme einzelner Glieder derselben, werde, in welcher, in der Bildung zum innigen Wohlgefallen am Rechten nämlich, aller Unterschied der Stände, der in andern Zweigen der Entwicklung auch fernerhin statt finden mag, völlig aufgehoben sei, und verschwinde; und daß auf diese Weise unter uns, keinesweges Volks-Erziehung, sondern eigentümliche deutsche National-Erziehung entstehe.

Ich werde Ihnen dartun, daß eine solche Erziehungskunst, wie wir sie begehren, wirklich schon erfunden ist, und ausgeübt wird, so daß wir nichts mehr zu tun haben, als das sich uns darbietende anzunehmen, welches, so wie ich dies oben von dem vorzuschlagenden Rettungsmittel versprach, ohne Zweifel kein größeres Maß von Kraft erfordert, als man bei unserm Zeitalter billig voraussetzen kann. Ich fügte diesem Versprechen noch ein anderes bei, daß nämlich, was die Gefahr anbelange,

impulse and action in life, and from training them; for these roots, neglected by this blind and impotent system, have everywhere developed wild, as best they could, yielding good fruit in a few who were inspired by God, but evil fruit in the majority. For the present, then, it is quite sufficient to describe this education by these results, and for our purpose we can spare ourselves the wearisome task of analyzing the inner sap and fiber of a tree whose fruit is now fully ripe and lies fallen before the eyes of all, proclaiming most clearly and distinctly the inner nature of its creator. Strictly speaking, according to this view, the present system has been by no means the art of educating men. This, indeed, it has not boasted of doing, but has very often frankly acknowledged its importance by demanding to be given natural talent or genius as the condition of its success. Rather does such an art remain to be discovered, and this discovery should be the real task of the new education. What was lacking in the old system – namely, an influence penetrating to the roots of vital impulse and action – the new education must supply. Accordingly, as the old system was able at best to train some part of man, so the new must train man himself, and must make the training given, not, as hitherto, the pupil's possession, but an integral part of himself.

Moreover, education, restricted in this way, has been brought to bear hitherto only on the very small minority of classes which are for this reason called educated, whereas, the great majority on whom in very truth the commonwealth rests, the people, have been almost entirely neglected by this system and abandoned to blind chance. By means of the new education we want to mold the Germans into a corporate body, which shall be stimulated and animated in all its individual members by a common interest. If by this means we wanted, indeed, to mark off an educated class, which might perhaps be animated by the newly developed motive of moral approval, from an educated one, then the latter would desert us and be lost to us; because the motives of hope and fear, by which alone influence might be exercised over it, would no longer work with us but against us. So there is nothing left for us but just to apply the new system to every German without exception, so that it is not the education of a single class, but the education of the nation, simply as such and without excepting any of its individual members. In this, that is to say in the training of man to take real pleasure in what is right, all distinction of classes which may in the future find a place in other branches of development will be completely removed and vanish. In this way there will grow up among us, not popular education, but real German national education.

I shall prove to you that a system of education such as we desire has actually been discovered and is already being practiced so that we have nothing to do but to accept what is offered us. As I promised you concerning the means of salvation that I should propose, this demands undoubtedly no greater amount of energy than can reasonably be expected of our generation. To that promise I added another, namely, that so far as danger is concerned there is none at all in our proposal because the self-interest of the power that rule over us demands that the carrying-out of such a proposal should be assisted rather than hindered. I consider it appropriate to speak my mind clearly on this point at once in this first address.

It is true that in ancient as in modern times the arts of corrupting and of morally degrading the conquered have very frequently been used with success as a means of ruling. By lying fictions, and by skillful confusion of ideas and of language, princes have been libeled to the people and peoples to princes in order that the two parties because of their dissension, might the more surely be controlled. All the impulses of vanity and of self-interest have been cunningly aroused and fostered, so as to make the conquered contemptible, and thus to crush them with something like a good conscience. But it would be a fatal error to propose this method with us Germans.

bei unserm Vorschlage durchaus keine sei, indem es der eigene Vorteil der über uns gebietenden Gewalt erfordere, die Ausführung jenes Vorschlags eher zu befördern, als zu hindern. Ich finde zweckmäßig, sogleich in dieser ersten Rede über diesen Punkt mich deutlich auszusprechen.

Zwar sind so in alter wie in neuer Zeit gar häufig die Künste der Verführung und der sittlichen Herabwürdigung der Unterworfenen, als ein Mittel der Herrschaft mit Erfolg gebraucht worden; man hat durch lügenhafte Erdichtungen, und durch künstliche Verwirrung der Begriffe und der Sprache, die Fürsten vor den Völkern, und diese vor jenen verleumdet, um die entzweiten sicherer zu beherrschen, man hat alle Antriebe der Eitelkeit und des Eigennutzes listig aufgereizt und entwickelt, um die Unterworfenen verächtlich zu machen, und so mit einer Art von gutem Gewissen sie zu zertreten: aber man würde einen sicher zum Verderben führenden Irrtum begehen, wenn man mit uns Deutschen diesen Weg einschlagen wollte. Das Band der Furcht und der Hoffnung abgerechnet beruht der Zusammenhang desjenigen Teils des Auslandes, mit dem wir dermalen in Berührung gekommen, auf den Antrieben der Ehre und des Nationalruhms; aber die deutsche Klarheit hat vorlängst bis zur unerschütterlichen Überzeugung eingesehen, daß dieses leere Trugbilder sind, und daß keine Wunde, und keine Verstümmelung des Einzelnen durch den Ruhm der ganzen Nation geheilt wird; und wir dürften wohl, so nicht eine höhere Ansicht des Lebens an uns gebracht wird, gefährliche Prediger dieser sehr begreiflichen und manchen Reiz bei sich führenden Lehre werden. Ohne darum noch neues Verderben an uns zu nehmen, sind wir schon in unsrer natürlichen Beschaffenheit eine unheilbringende Beute; nur durch die Ausführung des gemachten Vorschlages können wir eine heilbringende werden: und so wird denn, so gewiß das Ausland seinen Vorteil versteht, dasselbe durch diesen selbst bewegt, uns lieber auf die letzte Weise haben wollen, denn auf die erste.

Insbesondere nun wendet mit diesem Vorschlage meine Rede sich an die gebildeten Stande Deutschlands, indem sie diesen noch am ersten verständlich zu werden hofft, und trägt zu allernächst ihnen an, sich zu den Urhebern dieser neuen Schöpfung zu machen, und dadurch teils mit ihrer bisherigen Wirksamkeit die Welt auszusöhnen, teils ihre Fortdauer in der Zukunft zu verdienen. Wir werden im Fortgange dieser Reden ersehen, daß bis hieher alle Fortentwicklung der Menschheit in der deutschen Nation vom Volke ausgegangen, und daß an dieses immer zuerst die großen Nationalangelegenheiten gebracht, und von ihnen besorgt, und weiter befördert worden; daß es somit jetzo zum erstenmale geschieht, daß den gebildeten Ständen die ursprüngliche Fortbildung der Nation angetragen wird, und daß, wenn sie diesen Antrag wirklich ergriffen, auch dies das erstemal geschehen würde. Wir werden ersehen, daß diese Stände nicht berechnen können, auf wie lange Zeit es noch in ihrer Gewalt stehen werde, sich an die Spitze dieser Angelegenheit zu stellen, indem dieselbe bis zum Vortrage an das Volk schon beinahe vorbereitet und reif sei, und an Gliedern aus dem Volke geübt werde, und dieses nach kurzer Zeit ohne alle unsere Beihülfe sich selbst werde helfen können, woraus für uns bloß das erfolgen werde, daß die jetzigen Gebildeten und ihre Nachkommen zum Volke werden, aus dem bisherigen Volke aber ein anderer höher gebildeter Stand emporkomme.

Nach allem ist es der allgemeine Zweck dieser Reden, Mut und Hoffnung zu bringen in die Zerschlagenen, Freude zu verkündigen in die tiefe Trauer, über die Stunde der größten Bedrängnis leicht und sanft hinüber zu leiten. Die Zeit erscheint mir wie ein Schatten, der über seinem Leichname, aus dem so eben ein Heer von Krankheiten ihn heraus getrieben, steht, und jammert, und seinen Blick nicht loszureißen vermag von der ehedem so geliebten Hülle, und verzweifelnd alle Mittel versucht, um wieder hinein zu kommen in die Behausung der Seuchen. Zwar haben schon die belebenden Lüfte der andern Welt, in die die abgeschiedene eingetreten, sie aufgenommen in

Apart from the tie of fear and hope, the coherence of that part of the outside world with which we have now come into contact is founded on the motives of honor and of national glory. The clear vision of the German, however, has long since come to the unshakable conviction that these are empty illusions, and that no injury or mutilation of the individual is healed by the glory of the whole nation, and we shall indeed, if a wider view of life is not brought before us, probably become dangerous preachers of this very natural and attractive doctrine. Therefore, without taking to ourselves any new corruption, we are already in our natural condition a harmful prey; only by carrying out the proposal that has been made can we become a wholesome one. Then the outside world, as certainly as it knows its own interests, will be guided by them, and prefer to have us in the latter state rather than in the former.

Now in making this proposal, my address is directed especially toward the educated classes in Germany, for I hope that it will be intelligible to them first. My proposal is first and foremost that they become the authors of this new creation, thereby, on the one hand, reconciling the world to their former influence, and on the other, deserving its continuance in the future. We shall see in the course of these addresses that up to the present all human progress in the German nation has sprung from the people, and that to it, in the first instance, great national affairs have always been brought, and by it have been cared for and furthered. Now, for the first time, therefore, it happens that the fundamental reconstruction of the nation is offered as a task to the educated classes, and if they were really to accept this offer, that, too, would happen for the first time. We shall find that these classes cannot calculate how long it will still remain in their power to place themselves at the head of this movement, since it is now almost ready and ripe for proposal to the people, and is being practiced on individuals from among the people; and the people will soon be able to help themselves without any assistance from us. The result of this for us will simply be that the present educated classes and their descendants will become the people; while from among the present people another more highly educated class will arise.

Finally, it is the general aim of these addresses to bring courage and hope to the suffering, to proclaim joy in the midst of deep sorrow, to lead us gently and softly through the hour of deep affliction. This age is to me like a shade that stands weeping over its own corpse, from which it has been driven forth by a host of diseases, unable to tear its gaze from the form so beloved of old, and trying in despair every means to enter again the home of pestilence. Already, it is true, the quickening breezes of that other world, which the departed soul has entered, have taken it unto themselves and are surrounding it with the warm breath of love; the whispering voices of its sisters greet it with joy and bid it welcome; and already in its depths it stirs and grows in all directions toward the more glorious form into which it shall develop. But as yet the soul has no feeling for these breezes, no ear for these voices – or if it had them, they have disappeared in sorrow for the loss of mortal form; for with its form the soul thinks it has lost itself too. What is to be done with it? The dawn of the new world is already past its breaking; already it gilds the mountaintops, and heralds the coming day. I wish, so far as in me lies, to catch the rays of this dawn and weave them into a mirror, in which our grief-stricken age may see itself; so that it may believe in its own existence, may perceive its real self, and, as in prophetic vision, may see its own development, its coming forms pass by. In the contemplation of this, the picture of its former life will doubtless sink and vanish; and the dead body may be borne to its resting place without undue lamenting.

[1806] [*Translated by George Armstrong Kelly. New York: Harper & Row, 1968. 2–15*]

sich, und umgeben sie mit warmem Liebeshauche, zwar begrüßen sie schon freudig heimliche Stimmen der Schwestern, und heißen sie willkommen, zwar regt es sich schon und dehnt sich in ihrem Innern nach allen Richtungen hin, um die herrlichere Gestalt, zu der sie erwachsen soll, zu entwickeln; aber noch hat sie kein Gefühl für diese Lüfte, oder Gehör für diese Stimmen, oder wenn sie es hätte, so ist sie aufgegangen in Schmerz über ihren Verlust, mit welchem sie zugleich sich selbst verloren zu haben glaubt. Was ist mit ihr zu tun? Auch die Morgenröte der neuen Welt ist schon angebrochen, und vergoldet schon die Spitzen der Berge, und bildet vor den Tag, der da kommen soll. Ich will, so ich es kann, die Strahlen dieser Morgenröte fassen, und sie verdichten zu einem Spiegel, in welchem die trostlose Zeit sich erblicke, damit sie glaube, daß sie noch da ist, und in ihm ihr wahrer Kern sich ihr darstelle, und die Entfaltungen und Gestaltungen desselben in einem weissagenden Gesichte vor ihr vorüber gehen. In diese Anschauung hinein wird ihr denn ohne Zweifel auch das Bild ihres bisherigen Lebens versinken, und verschwinden, und der Tote wird ohne übermäßiges Wehklagen zu seiner Ruhestätte gebracht werden können.

[1806] [*Edited by G. Jacobs and Peter Lothar Oesterreich. Frankfurt/ M: Deutscher Klassiker Verlag, 1997. 548–562*]

III.e.3. THEODOR KÖRNER, *Lützows wilde Jagd*

Was glänzt dort vom Walde im Sonnenschein?
   Hör's näher und näher brausen.
Es zieht sich herunter in düsteren Reih'n,
Und gellende Hörner schallen darein
   Und erfüllen die Seele mit Grausen.
Und wenn ihr die schwarzen Gesellen fragt:
Das ist Lützows wilde, verwegene Jagd.

Was zieht dort rasch durch den finstern Wald
   Und streift von Bergen zu Bergen?
Es legt sich in nächtlichen Hinterhalt;
Das Hurra jauchzt und die Büchse knallt;
   Es fallen die fränkischen Schergen.
Und wenn ihr die schwarzen Jäger fragt:
Das ist Lützows wilde, verwegene Jagd.

Wo die Reben dort glühen, dort braust der Rhein,
   Der Wütrich geborgen sich meinte;
Da naht es schnell mit Gewitterschein
Und wirft sich mit rüst'gen Armen hinein
   Und springt ans Ufer der Feinde.
Und wenn ihr die schwarzen Schwimmer fragt:
Das ist Lützows wilde, verwegene Jagd.

Was braust dort im Tale die laute Schlacht,
   Was schlagen die Schwerter zusammen?
Wildherzige Reiter schlagen die Schlacht,
Und der Funke der Freiheit ist glühend erwacht

III.e.3. THEODOR KÖRNER, *Lützow's Wild Chase*

What is it that beams in the bright sunshine,
    And echoes yet nearer and nearer
And see, it spreads out in a long dark line,
And hark how yon horns in the distance combine
    To impress with affright the hearer.
And ask ye what means the daring chase;
This is this is Lützow's wild and desperate chase!

See, they leave the dark wood in silence all,
    And from hill to hill are seen flying;
In ambush they 'll lie 'till the deep nightfall,
Then ye'll hear the hurrah! and the rifle ball!
    And the French will be falling and dying!
And ask ye what means their daring race?
This is – Lützow's wild and desperate chase

Where the vine-boughs twine, the Rhine waves roar,
    And the foe thinks its waters shall hide him;
But see, they, fearless approach the shore;
And they leap in the stream, and swim proudly o'er,
    And stand on the bank beside him!
And ask ye what means the daring race ?
This is – Lützow's wild and desperate chase!

Why roars in the valley the raging fight,
    Where swords clash red and gory?
O fierce is the strife of that deadly fight,
For the spark of young Freedom is newly alight,

Und lodert in blutigen Flammen.
Und wenn ihr die schwarzen Reiter fragt:
Das ist Lützows wilde, verwegene Jagd.

Wer scheidet dort röchelnd vom Sonnenlicht,
   Unter winselnde Feinde gebettet?
Es zuckt der Tod auf dem Angesicht;
Doch die wackern Herzen erzittern nicht.
   Das Vaterland ist ja gerettet.
Und wenn ihr die schwarzen Gefall'nen fragt:
Das war Lützows wilde, verwegene Jagd.

Die wilde Jagd und die deutsche Jagd
   Auf Henkersblut und Tyrannen!
Drum, die ihr uns liebt, nicht geweint und geklagt!
Das Land ist ja frei, und der Morgen tagt,
   Wenn wir's auch nur sterbend gewannen.
Und von Enkeln zu Enkeln sei's nachgesagt:
Das war Lützows wilde, verwegene Jagd.

[1813]

III.e.4.   HEINRICH HEINE, aus *Deutschland, Ein Wintermährchen*

CAPUT III

Zu Aachen, im alten Dome, liegt
Carolus Magnus begraben.
(Man muß ihn nicht verwechseln mit Carl
Mayer, der lebt in Schwaben.)

Ich möchte nicht todt und begraben seyn
Als Kaiser zu Aachen im Dome;
Weit lieber lebt' ich als kleinster Poet
Zu Stukkert am Neckarstrome.

Zu Aachen langweilen sich auf der Straß'
Die Hunde, sie flehn unterthänig:
Gieb uns einen Fußtritt, o Fremdling, das wird
Vielleicht uns zerstreuen ein wenig.

Ich bin in diesem langweilgen Nest
Ein Stündchen herumgeschlendert.
Sah wieder preußisches Militär,
Hat sich nicht sehr verändert.

Es sind die grauen Mäntel noch,
Mit dem hohen, rothen Kragen -
(Das Roth bedeutet Franzosenblut,
Sang Körner in früheren Tagen.)

And it breaks into flames of glory!
And ask ye what means the daring race?
This is – Lützow's wild and desperate chase!

See yon warrior who lies on a gory spot,
    From life compell'd to sever;
Yet he never is heard to lament his lot,
And his soul at its parting shall tremble not,
    Since his country is saved for ever!
And if ye will ask at the end of his race,
Still 'tis – Lützow's wild and desperate chase!

The wild chase, and the German chase
    Against tyranny and oppression!
Therefore weep not, lov'd friends, at this last embrace
For Freedom has dawn'd on our loved birth-place,
    And our deaths shall ensure its possession !
And 't will ever be said from race to race,
This was – Lützow's wild and desperate chase!

[1813] [*Translated by G. F. Richardson, London: Nutt, 1845*]

III.e.4. HEINRICH HEINE, from *Germany: A Winter's Tale*

III.

The bones of Carolus Magnus lie
in Aachen cathedral (maybe a
bit confusing, I don't mean wee
Karl Mayer, he lives in Swabia.)

I wouldn't much like to be buried, for all
that splendid imperial shrining.
I'd rather be living, even down there
in Stuttgart, mis'rably rhyming.

The Aachen dogs are so bored, their tails
implore you with servile wagging.
'Give us a kick, o stranger, perhaps
it'll stop our interest flagging.'

I walked about in that boring hole
for an hour or more together.
I saw the Prussian soldiers again.
They're still the same as ever.

Still the same grey coats, and still
the high and blood-red collar
('The red is for the Frenchies' blood,'
as Körner used to holler).

Noch immer das hölzern pedantische Volk,
Noch immer ein rechter Winkel
In jeder Bewegung, und im Gesicht
Der eingefrorene Dünkel.

Sie stelzen noch immer so steif herum,
So kerzengrade geschniegelt,
Als hätten sie verschluckt den Stock
Womit man sie einst geprügelt.

Ja, ganz verschwand die Fuchtel nie,
Sie tragen sie jetzt im Innern;
Das trauliche Du wird immer noch
An das alte Er erinnern.

Der lange Schnurrbart ist eigentlich nur
Des Zopfthums neuere Phase:
Der Zopf, der ehmals hinten hing,
Der hängt jetzt unter der Nase.

Nicht übel gefiel mir das neue Costum
Der Reuter, das muß ich loben,
Besonders die Pikkelhaube, den Helm,
Mit der stählernen Spitze nach oben.

Das ist so ritterthümlich und mahnt
An der Vorzeit holde Romantik,
An die Burgfrau Johanna von Montfaucon,
An den Freyherrn Fouqué, Uhland, Tieck.

Das mahnt an das Mittelalter so schön,
An Edelknechte und Knappen,
Die in dem Herzen getragen die Treu
Und auf dem Hintern ein Wappen.

Das mahnt an Kreuzzug und Turney,
An Minne und frommes Dienen,
An die ungedruckte Glaubenszeit,
Wo noch keine Zeitung erschienen.

Ja, ja, der Helm gefällt mir, er zeugt
Vom allerhöchsten Witze!
Ein königlicher Einfall wars!
Es fehlt nicht die Pointe, die Spitze!

Nur fürcht' ich, wenn ein Gewitter entsteht,
Zieht leicht so eine Spitze
Herab auf Euer romantisches Haupt
Des Himmels modernste Blitze! – –

They're still a wooden pedantic lot,
their movements still have the graces
of a right-angled triangle.
Arrogance freezes their faces.

And still they strut about as stiff,
as straight and thin as a candle,
as if they'd swallowed the corporal's stick
Old Fritz knew how to handle.

The stick has never quite been lost,
although its use has been banned.
Inside the glove of newer ways
there's still the old iron hand.

The long moustache is the pigtail of old,
transferred to a different place.
The pigtail one hung down behind,
now it droops from the face.

The cavalry's new get-up I quite
approved – one must speak fairly –
especially that spike of steel
which crowns it all so squarely,

so redolent of derring-do,
of knights in times Romantic,
of Lady Jane of Falconmount
and m'lords Fouque, Uhland, Tieck;

Of the good olde Middle Ages so fine,
of pages and noble peers,
who bore in their hearts a trust right true,
and coats of arms on their rears.

Crusade and tourney it conjures up,
and serving a lady for guerdon,
an age of faith without blessing of print,
when newspapers hadn't been heard on.

Oh yes, I like the helmet, it proves
the wit of the Lord's Anointed!
A royal jest it was indeed,
most delicately pointed.

It's really only the thought of storms
that I find a little fright'ning –
that spike on your Romantic heads
might attract some modern lightning.

Zu Aachen, auf dem Posthausschild,
Sah ich den Vogel wieder,
Der mir so tief verhaßt! Voll Gift
Schaute er auf mich nieder.

Du häßlicher Vogel, wirst du einst
Mir in die Hände fallen,
So rupfe ich dir die Federn aus
Und hacke dir ab die Krallen.

Du sollst mir dann, in luftger Höh,
Auf einer Stange sitzen,
Und ich rufe zum lustigen Schießen herbey
Die Rheinischen Vogelschützen.

Wer mir den Vogel herunterschießt,
Mit Zepter und Krone belehn' ich
Den wackern Mann! Wir blasen Tusch
Und rufen: es lebe der König!

[1844] [*Edited by Manfred Windfuhr. Hamburg:*
Hoffman & Campe, 1995. 94–97]

f. MAGYAR

III.f.1. VÖRÖSMARTY MIHÁLY, *Csongor és Tünde*
(Részlet az Éj monológjából)

Sötét és semmi voltak: én valék,
Kietlen, csendes, lény nem lakta Éj,
És a világot szültem gyermekűl.
Mindenható sugárral a világ
Fölkelt ölemből; megrázkódtatá
A semmiségnek pusztaságait,
S ezer fejekkel a nagy szörnyeteg,
A Mind, előállt. Hold és csillagok,
A menny csodái lőnek bujdosók
Kimérhetetlen léghatárokon.
Megszünt a régi alvó nyúgalom:
A test megindúlt, tett az új erő,
S tettekkel és mozgással gazdagon
Megnépesűlt a puszta tér s idő,
Föld és a tenger küzdve osztozának
Az eltolt légnek ősi birtokán;
Megszünteté a tenger habjait,
S melyet haraggal ostromolt imént,
Most felmosolyga mélyiből az ég;

At Aachen I saw that bird I hate
displayed on the staging sign;
back at me he looked with an eye
most poisonously malign.

You ugly devil, just you wait,
if ever I manage to catch you
I'll pluck out your feathers and hack off your claws
and then as follows dispatch you:

I'll set you up on top of a pole
high in the air as a target,
and all the Rhineland marksmen shall come
for a jolly shooting party.

The man who brings you down, I shall
in person scepter-and-crown-him –
the worthy fellow! A fanfare shall blow,
and vivats shall ring all around him.

(1844) [*Translated by T. J. Reed. London: Angel, 1986. 33–35*]

f. HUNGARIAN

III.f.1. MIHÁLY VÖRÖSMARTY, from 'Csongor and Tünde'
(Extract from the Soliloquy of the Night)

Darkness and Void was all: myself alone
seclusive, silent, all-forsaken Night,
then light was born to me, my only child.
As blazing light erupted from my womb
the boundless power of the radiation
perturbed the empty space, and from the Void
an all-pervading thousand-headed monster,
the Universe appeared. The moon, the stars,
great wonders of the firmament, became
lone pilgrims of immense trajectories.
The former passive peace has passed away
as matter moved and action came to power.
Then barren space and time were populated,
alive with action, movement everywhere.
Ocean and earth fought desperately, claiming
their heritance where Void had reigned before,
until the oceans calmed their angry waves
and as the fight let up, the waters brightened
with sunny smiles reflected from the sky.

S mint egy menyasszony, szépen és vidáman
Virágruhába öltözött a föld.
A por mozogni kezdett, és az állat,
S királyi fejjel a lelkes porond,
Az ember lőn, és folytatá faját,
A jámbort, csalfát, gyilkost és dicsőt. –
Sötét és semmi vannak: én vagyok,
A fény elől bujdokló gyászos Éj. –
A féreg, a pillantat búboréka,
Elvész; idő sincs mérve lételének.
Madárt a szárny, a körmök állatot
Nem váltanak meg, kérges büszke fát
Letesznek századoknak súlyai.
Az ember feljő, lelke fényfolyam,
A nagy mindenség benne tűkrözik.
Megmondhatatlan kéjjel föltekint,
Merőn megbámúl földet és eget;
De ifjusága gyorsan elmulik,
Erőtlen aggott egy-két nyár után,
S már nincs, mint nem volt, mint a légy fia.
Kiirthatatlan vággyal, amig él,
Túr és tünődik, tudni, tenni tör;
Halandó kézzel halhatatlanúl
Vél munkálkodni, és mikor kidőlt is,
Még a hiúság műve van porán,
Még kőhegyek ragyognak sírjain,
Ezer jelekkel tarkán s fényesen
Az ész az erőnek rakván oszlopot.
De hol lesz a kő, jel, s az oszlopok,
Ha nem lesz föld, s a tenger eltünik.
Fáradtan ösvényikből a napok
Egymásba hullva, összeomlanak;
A Mind enyész, és végső romjain
A szép világ borongva hamvad el;
És ahol kezdve volt, ott vége lesz:
Sötét és semmi lesznek: én leszek,
Kietlen, csendes, lény nem lakta Éj.

[*First published: Vörösmarty, Mihály, Csongor és Tünde. Székesfehérvár: Számmer, 1831,
Act V. Critical edition: Vörösmarty, Mihály, Vörösmarty Mihály összes művei,
vol. 9, Drámák 4. Edited by Fehér, Géza, Staud, Géza and Taxner-Tóth,
Ernő. Budapest: Akadémiai, 1989. 151–152*]

Now, like a bride, in grace and gaiety
young Earth put on her finery of flowers.
The dust began to move, then came the beasts
and lastly man, the animated clay,
in kingly stile, to multiply his kind,
the true, the false, the sinner and the saint.
Darkness and Void remain: I'm here alone,
a fugitive from daylight, gloomy Night. –
An insect is the bubble of a moment,
that's all the time allowed for its existence.
Its wings won't save a bird, nor claws a beast,
and noble, sturdy trees must all decay
under the weight of passing centuries.
As man arrives, his spirit radiates,
the Universe is mirrored in his person.
He looks around with infinite delight,
reviewing raptly earth and firmament,
but youth will soon desert him to decline
to drowsy dotage, till his term is up,
and then he's gone, mere fly-speck, whence he came.
Unquenchable desires drive him on
to delve, to dream, discern and deeds to do,
he hopes to launch immortal enterprises
with mortal hands, and even in the grave
memorials of vainness guard his dust,
resplendent marble mountains mark the place
with countless lurid, ostentatious signs,
where intellect has paid homage to power.
But what are homage, signs, memorials,
when earth and oceans vanish into air?
The tired suns desert their stable orbits
collapsing into one vast cataclysm,
the Universe decays and its ruins
the melancholy twilight fades away.
And it will end, as once it all began:
Darkness and Void will be: myself alone,
seclusive, silent, all-forsaken Night.

[*Translated by Peter Zollman and reprinted from In Quest of the 'Miracle Stag':
The Poetry of Hungary. Edited by Adam Makkai. Chicago and Budapest,
Atlantis-Centaur, M. Szivárvány and Corvina, 1996. 228–230,
with the kind permission of Adam Makkai*]

III.f.2. KÖLCSEY FERENC, *Történetnyomozás* (Részletek)

1.

Az emberi nemzet történetsora, a kezdet egypár emberétől fogva korunknak ezer milliomáig, nem egyéb, mint egymásból szakadatlanul folyt okoknak és következéseknek szövedéke; – egy hosszú lánc, melynek összefüggő szemein véges tekintet keresztül nem hathat. Ki mérheti meg az időnek hosszúságát, mely alatt az ember beszéd nélkül élt? A beszédfeltalálást megelőzött kor az emberi tudománynak elveszett. A beszéd tette lehetségessé a tradíciókat, melyekben az írás előtti embernyomok bizonytalan történetének maradványai a késő unokákra általszállongottanak; s általszállongottanak ugyan, de oly alakban, hogy többé azokat megismerni, s a való história tárgyaivá tenni nem lehetett. Az emberi nem históriája tehát az írástalálmány után kezdődik.

Ha a régiségnek emlékeit s írásait az idő megkímélé vala, kétségkívül a történt dolgokról véghetetlenül többet tudnánk, mint most tudunk, de bizonyost nehezen. Tekintvén a hajdankor maradványait, mond Schiller, nem látjuk-e a történetek nagyobb részét szenvedelem, értetlenség, s az író sajátságai által alakjaiból kiforgatva, isméretlenné tétetni? Gyanúnk felébred a históriának legrégibb emlékei mellett, s tulajdon korunknak évkönyveinél sem enyészik el. Tanukat hallgatunk ki oly esetekről, mely csak ma, azon emberek között, kikkel élünk, s azon városban, melyet lakunk, történt vala; s ellenkező bizonyításaikból alig tudjuk a valót kifejleszteni: minő bizodalommal viseltethetünk hát azon korhoz, azon nemzetekhez, melyeket erkölcsi különjeik[1] még távolabb tartanak tőlünk, mint a közöttünk lefolyt ezredek?

Szedd öszve azon töredékeket, melyek a régiség emlékeiből hozzánk jutottanak, s az emberiség akkori történetei úgy fognak előtted állani, mint némely öszvetört világnak széjjelszórt maradványai. Látsz magányos vonásokat, melyekből egész képet formálni hiában igyekszel. Öszvenézed azokat, s keresvén hasonlatosságot, következéseket akarsz kivonni; s íme itt két s három vagy egyforma, vagy egymáshoz illő vonás világot látszik gyújtani; de a negyedikre vetsz tekintetet, s újabb sötétség veszen körül.

Azok, kik a természet titkait s törvényeit akarták felvilágosítani, saját fejeikből alkottanak hipotéziseket, s azokat a természetre alkalmaztatván, később bizonyos princípiumokká igyekeztek formálni. Hasznos-e a valónak ezen módját a históriára is alkalmaztatni? Talán nemcsak nem hasznos, sőt felette veszedelmes. A hipotézis alkotója lassanként hozzászokik azt, amit először csak gyanúnak tartott, bizonyosságnak hinni; s nem többé a valót, hanem magának a hipotézisnek megállapítását[2] keresni. Összeköttetéseket, hasonlatosságokat, világosságot nem az emléktöredékektől a hipotézisnek, hanem a hipotézistől kölcsönöz az emléktöredékeknek; s magamagát észrevétlen s akaratlanul megcsalván, mindent hamis fényben kezd tekinteni; s vizsgálódás helyett vak hitre téved el. Nem éppen úgy bánt-e Newton a kronológiával, mint a fizikával? S íme az a nagy ember, ki a természettudománynak annyi fényt kölcsönözött, a históriára fordítván fáklyáját, annak álvilágánál eltévedett.

Voltak, kik hipotéziseiket a régiség töredékei közt csillámló neveken, s névmagyarázatokon fundálták, s a történeti homályt ezek által kívánták eloszlatni. Ezeknek írásaikban bámuljuk az olvasás kiterjedtségét, s azon vasszorgalmat, mely az ezerféle tudósítások összeszedésében mutatkozik. De a morális világ ott, hol az emlékek bennünket elhagynak, éppen oly hozzáférhetetlen,

---

[1] egyedi jellemzőik
[2] fenntartását, igazolását

III.f.2. FERENC KÖLCSEY, from *Historical Enquiry*

1

The history of the human race, from the first couple to the billions of our age, has been nothing but a web of causes and their incessant consequent effects – a long chain, the conjoined links of which a limited vision cannot pierce.

Who can measure the length of time that Man was without language? The period preceding the invention of language is lost to science. Language rendered possible the traditions by which the remnants of the uncertain history of traces of preliterate humanity were handed down to later generations; and handed down they were, but in such a form that it was no longer possible to recognise them and make them into subjects of real historical study. The study of the history of the human species begins, therefore, after the invention of writing.

If time had spared the monuments and writings of antiquity there is no doubt that we would know infinitely more than we do of the affairs of history, but we would hardly know any certainty. With regard to the remnants of former years, says Schiller,[3] do we not see the greater part of histories rendered unknown, twisted out of shape by suffering, incomprehension and the personal inclinations of the writer? Our suspicion is aroused at the most ancient monuments of history, nor is it any the less in the case of the chronicles of our own age. We listen to witnesses concerning events which have taken place only today among the people with whom we live, in the town where we live, and from their conflicting evidence can scarcely make out the truth. With what confidence can we then approach ages and nations whose different ways make them even more remote than do the millennia that have elapsed between us?

Gather together those fragments that have come to us from the monuments of antiquity, and the accounts of humanity of the time will appear before you like the wind-scattered remains of so many broken worlds. You will see isolated features, of which you will try in vain to form a complete picture. You will look them over, seek points of comparison and try to draw conclusions; and see, here two or three features, either identical or similar to one another, seem to shed light, but when you look at a fourth again darkness surrounds.

Those who have wished to illuminate the secrets and laws of Nature have formed hypotheses in their heads, applied them to Nature, and then tried to formulate certain principles. Is it profitable to apply this sort of truth to the study of history? Not only unprofitable, perhaps, but indeed highly dangerous. He that forms a hypothesis slowly comes to believe that what at first he merely suspected is certainty, and no longer seeks the truth but proof of the hypothesis itself. He borrows connections, similarities and illumination not from the fragments of monuments for the hypothesis, but from the hypothesis for the fragments of monuments; imperceptibly and unintentionally he deceives himself and begins to see everything in a false light; instead of examination he strays into blind faith. Did Newton not deal with chronology in the same way as he did with physics? And see, that great man, who shed so much light on natural science, when he shone his torch on history went astray by its delusive light.

There have been some who based their hypotheses on shining names among the fragments of antiquity, and on the explanation of names, and sought to dissipate the obscurity of history by this means. In their writings we admire their erudition and the indefatigability which they show in drawing together myriad strands of knowledge. The moral world, however, is there where the

---

[3] See Friedrich Schiller, *Was heißt und zum welchem Ende studiert man Universalgeschichte?* [What is the Meaning of Universal History and for what Reason do we Study it?] (1789)

481

mint a metafizikának tárgyai. Indukciók és analógiák lehetségekre vihetnek, bizonyosságokra nem. S ott, hol nemcsak egy a lehetséges, mi fogja a választást csalhatatlanul vezetni? Mennél inkább szerelmes valaki a maga hipotézisébe, annál messzebb téveszti el magát, s annál inkább nem veszi észre tévelygését: a mocsárban fellobbanó lángot vezércsillagnak nézi; saját gondolatait a valósággal összetéveszti; széles olvasásától félrevezettetvén, fontosságot a sokaságban keres; s mivel következtetései közt rendet s összefüggést talál, nem is gyanítja, hogy hibáz, nem is gyanítja, hogy sokszor a következtetések közt rend és összefüggés lehet, ha szinte maga a főállítvány azok közé tartozik is, miket a logikusok *petitio principii*[4] névvel neveznek. [...]

2.

A történeti jegyzékeket öszvekeresni, s egymás mellett felállítani; való és valótlan tudósításokat egymástól megkülönböztetni; időszámlálást megjavítani; eredetet, születést és halált nyomozni; ezek s az ilyenek a kompilátornak és kritikusnak tisztében állanak. Az ő írásaikban látjuk a nemzeteket s a magányos embereket feltűnni és munkálni; de csak úgy, mint valamely bábszínen az ugráló bábokat: a kéz, mely a szem előtti mozgásokat rejtekéből igazgatja, láthatatlan marad; s így gyakran szemlélünk következést ok, tettet rúgó s történeteket egybefüggés nélkül. Ily szemlélés által gyűlt ismeretünk emlékezőtehetségünkhöz szól, s lelket nem táplál. A filozófusi történetvizsgáló felvilágosítja az emberi szívnek titkait, s azokban keresi fel a történt dolgoknak kútfejeiket; embert emberrel, nemzetet nemzettel, századot századdal hasonlít öszve; következésből nyomozza az okot, s okból a következést; a külhomályt a belső emberből igyekszik felderíteni; tekintetével a múlttól a jelenkorig, a jelenkortól a múltig hat; a nemzeteket a kifejleni kezdés pontjaitól fogva a teljes virágzás s majd a hervadás koráig nyomról nyomra követi; kilesi a segédnek s akadálynak környűlményeit, a fontosb történeteket, melyek a nevezetesb behatásokat okozták, azon nagybefolyású halandókat, kiknek szenvedelmeik, kinézéseik s gondolkozások az egésznek alkotványára munkáltak: s szakadatlan ügyelemmel fonja előttünk az ariadnéi fonalat, mely a temérdek szövevényben biztos vezetőnk lehessen. Az ily vizsgáló, nyelvművészi sajátságokkal kikészítve, teszi azt, kit nagy történetírónak hívunk; s az ily történetírónak tolla alatt leszen a história a valónak fáklyája, s az emberi életnek tanítómestere.

Akarod-e tudni, hogy ezen nemzetek, melyek most Európának kebelében fény s csillogás közt élnek és mozognak, mik voltanak valaha? Vedd kezedbe az utazóknak írásaikat; s tedd által magadat lélekben a Tűzföldnek, Új-Déli-Walesnak, Új-Zélandnak, Tahitinak partjaira. Olvasd egy történetíró szavaival, minő képet rajzolnak előnkbe az utazók az úgynevezett vad népekről: – – Sokakat ismeretlenségben találtak a legszükségesb mesterségekkel: vas, eke s némelyeket éppen tűz nélkül; sokan még a vadállatokkal küzdöttek eledelök s lakjaik miatt; s némelyeknél a beszéd alig kezdett az állati hangokból értelmes jegyekké kifejleni. Itt még a házasságnak oly egyszerű köteléke sem volt szokásban; ott a tulajdon sem ismertetett. Sok helyt a figyelmetlen lélek a naponként visszaforduló tapasztalást sem tudta megkapni: a vad gondatlanul adá el ágyát, melyen ma feküdött, nem jutván eszébe, hogy holnap ismét aludnia kell. De harc találtatott mindenhol, s a győzedelembér nem ritkán a levert ellenségnek teste volt. Másoknál, kik az életnek több javaival ismerkedvén meg, már a kultúrának magasb polcán állottak, szolgaság és despotizmus rettenetes alakban tűntek fel. Ott egy afrikai despot alattvalóit egy korty égettborért vetette áruba: itt sírhal-

---

[4] bizonyítás olyan tétellel, mely maga is bizonyításra szorul

monuments desert us, just as inaccessible as the things of metaphysics. Induction and analogy can lead us to possibilities but not to certainties. And where more than one thing is possible what will guide one's choice infallibly? The more enamoured one is of one's own hypothesis, the farther one leads oneself astray, and the more one fails to notice one's mistakes; one regards the flame that flickers above the swamp as a guiding star, confuses one's own thoughts with reality; one is distracted by extensive reading and seeks importance in quantity; and as one finds order and coherence among one's conclusions one does not so much as suspect that one is wrong, and that there may often be order and coherence among the conclusions simple because the predicate is one of those things which the logicians call *petitio principii*.[5] [. . .]

2

Collection and collation of historical notes, discrimination between true and untrue information, correcting dates, tracing origins, births and deaths – these and the like are in the province of compiler and critic. In their writings we see nations and individual men appearing and working, but only as puppets in a puppet theatre; the hand that directs the movements that we see remains invisible, and so we often observe consequences without causes, deeds without driving forces and events without interdependence. Knowledge that we gain from such observation addresses our capacity for memory, and does not nourish the spirit. The philosophical investigator of history illuminates the secrets of the human heart, and there seeks out the well springs of what has happened; he compares man to man, nation to nation, century to century; traces cause from effect, effect from cause; tries to clear external mist by the inner man; his gaze scans from past to present, from present to past; follows nations step by step from the point of incipient development to full blossoming and then fading; espies the circumstances that favour and hinder, the more important events which make the greatest impact, those men of great influence whose passions, views and thoughts worked to bring the whole together; and with unceasing care spins before us the thread of Ariadne so that we may have a sure guide in the countless labyrinths. Such an investigator, skilled in the art of language, makes the man whom we call a great historian; and under the pen of such an historian history becomes the torch of truth, the schoolmaster of human life.

Do you wish to know what these nations which now live and move among light and brilliance in the bosom of Europe were previously? Take in your hand the writings of travellers; transfer yourself in spirit to the shores of Tierra del Fuego, New South Wales, New Zealand, Tahiti. Read in the words of a historian the picture that travellers paint for us of the so-called savage peoples: – – Many of them were found to be unfamiliar with the most essential crafts: lacking iron, the plough and in some cases even fire; many were still contesting their food and lodging with wild animals; in some cases language had scarcely begun to develop from animal sounds into meaningful signs. Here even the simple bond of marriage was not practised; there property was unknown. In many places the carefree spirit had not even realized that certain things occurred day after day: the savage would leave the bed in which he had lain that night without a thought, without it crossing his mind that he would have to sleep again next day too. Fighting, however, was found everywhere, and the prize of victory was frequently the body of the enemy. With others, who had become familiar with more good things in life and were now on a higher level of culture, dreadful forms of servitude and despotism were in evidence. There an African despot put his subjects on sale for a

---

[5] A fallacious argument in which the premises are contained in the conclusion.

mánál koncoltattak fel azok, hogy az alvilágban szolgálatjára lehessenek. Ott az együgyűség nevetséges fétisek, itt valamely borzasztó szörny előtt borul le (az ember isteneiben nyomja ki saját karakterét). Amennyire elnyomják őtet ott szolgaság, butaság és babona: annyira nyomorúlttá teszi itt a féketlen szabadság másik extremuma. Mindég támadásra vagy oltalomra készülve, minden zörgéstől felrettenve kémlődik pusztájában a vad; ellenség neki minden, ami új, s jaj a vándornak, kit a szélvész az ő partjaira vetett ki! Vendégi tűzhely nem fog számára füstölni, s egy ajtó sem nyílik meg előtte barátságosan. De még ott is, hol az ember ellenséges magányból társaságos életre, szükségről bővségre s félelemről örömre emelkedik – mi különösnek, mi iszonyúnak látszik mielőttünk! Darabos ízlése vidámságot az elkábulásban, szépséget a fintorgatásban s dicsőséget a mérték-felettiségben keres; rénye[6] is irtózásra hoz; s az, amit ő boldogságnak nevez, bennünk csak szánakozást és csömört gerjeszthet.

Mely különbség az új-zélandi kannibál között és miközöttünk! Polgári alkotványunk oltalmában; földmívelés, mesterségek, művészet, és tudomány által segélve s megszelídülve; gondolattal, ismerettel és kívánsággal földet és eget általölelve; kikapva a jelenlétnek s mindennapinak szűk köréből; a szükségestől a kedvesig, a hasznostól a szépig emelkedve: minő címek, hogy korunk férfiúságának a még gyermekidejű emberfajok ellentételében örvendjünk! A kimívelt európai nem elégedett meg azzal, hogy azt, amit saját földén és saját földének kebelében talált, haszonra fordította, hanem felkutatta a földnek minden részeit; idegen plántákat s állatokat hazájában meghonosított, a távol zónáknak klímáját önnen kertjébe varázsolta; szobája falait, asztalát és testét temérdek távolságban szedett zsákmányokkal borította el. Mi által lettek mindezek lehetségesekké? Kétségkívül a tudomány által. Felvonatott a múlt időnek kárpitja, Hellásnak és Rómának omladékai közül szedettek fel a bölcsességnek magvai, melyek plántálgatás, mívelés és ápolás által oly szép virágokká s oly szép gyümölcsökké lettenek. Tudomány nyitott utat a tengereken keresztül ismeretlen földekig, s a mérföldek ezreivel elválasztott népeket szomszédokká tette; tudomány alkotta öszve státusokat; embernek ember, nemzetnek nemzet ellen oltalmat készített; s lelkeinket az állati ösztönnek felibe emelvén, ismeretszomj és az emberiség felébresztett érzelmei által képesekké tett bennünket, nemcsak egy szűk körű háznépnek tagjává, hanem egy egész nagy kiterjedésű hazának, sőt az egész világnak polgárává lehetnünk.

Kell-e kívánni, hogy az emberi természet maga magát megtagadja, s föld feletti tökélyre hágjon fel? Rossz és jó szükséges viszonyban vannak egymással; s fizikai és morális gonoszok egyformán munkálódtak azon javaknak nagy részét előtüntetni, melyek elébb szükségtől s félelemtől mentettek meg bennünket, később pedig gyönyörűségünknek s felemelődésünknek eszközeivé lettenek. Bátran állíthatjátok, hogy mindazon erkölcsi rosszak, melyek az új világ vad népeinél saját meztelenségökben mutatkoznak, kisebb vagy nagyobb mértékben, többé vagy kevesebbé hasonlító alakban, s többé vagy kevesebbé elleplezve, a legmíveltebb nemzetben is feltaláltatnak: de feltaláltatnak oly javak is, melyeknek magvai a vad nép kebelében még észrevétlen szenderegnek. S az ily magvak miként jöttek ez vagy amaz nemzetnél virágzatba? Mint történt az, hogy ez itt a míveltségnek oly magas polcára hághatott, míg amaz ott a középszerűség lépcsőin, vagy éppen a ki nem fejés alsó pontján marada? Hogyan vándorlott a pallérozottság országokról országokra, keletről nyugotra, délről észak felé? Mi módon lett lehetségessé, hogy bizonyos helyeken a régi nagyság emlékei felett félig vad népek fészkelnek? Ezek, s az ilyen kérdések, természetesen tolakodnak minden gondolkozó fejnek elébe; s feleletet reájok csak a históriának egésze, az egyetemi történetírás ád.

[6] erénye

mouthful of brandy; here they were slaughtered at the grave so that he might have servants in the next world. There simplicity bows before simple, risible fetishes, here to some terrible monster (Man expresses his own character in his gods). As there servitude, superstition and stupidity oppress, here the opposing *extremum* of unfettered liberty renders man wretched. The savage, always ready to attack or defend, keeps a wary eye in his wilderness, alarmed at every sound; everything that is new is hostile to him, and woe betide the traveller that shipwreck has cast up on his shores! No welcoming hearth will smoke for his benefit, not a door will open to him in friendly fashion. Yet even where Man has been elevated from hostile loneliness to social life, from need to plenty and from fear to pleasure – what appears before us that is strange, what terrible! His coarse taste seeks happiness in drunkenness, beauty in distortion and glory in excess; his virtues too horrify us; and what he calls happiness can arouse in us only pity and disgust.

What a difference there is between the New Zealand cannibals and us! In the security of our civil constitution; helped and civilised by agriculture, crafts, art and science; embracing earth and sky with thought, knowledge and desire; elevated from the paltry round of the present and the mundane; raised from the necessary to the pleasing, from the useful to the beautiful: how we are entitled to rejoice in the maturity of our age compared to the races of men that are still in their childhood! The cultivated European is not satisfied with having found and put to use what there is on his own land and in its bosom, but has explored every part of the earth; he has introduced exotic plants and animals to his homeland and charmed into his garden the climate of distant parts; he has covered the walls of his rooms, his table and his body with many things plundered from far away. By what means has all this been possible? Beyond doubt, through science. The curtain of times past has been raised, the seeds of wisdom gathered from the ruins of Hellas and Rome and, planted, cultivated and tended, have yielded such lovely flowers and fine fruit. Science has opened the way over the seas to lands unknown, has made neighbours of peoples separated by thousands of miles, created states; has prepared defence for man against man, nation against nation; and has raised our spirits above animal instincts, and through the feelings which it has aroused of thirst for knowledge and of humanity has rendered us capable not only of becoming members of a narrow domestic circle but citizens of a whole great extensive homeland, indeed, of the whole world.

Do we have to wish that human nature deny itself and strive upward for more than earthly perfection? Bad and good are in a necessary relationship with each other; and evils physical and moral have worked alike to cause the greater part of those good things to come forth which previously saved us from need and fear, but have later become means of our delight and uplifting. You may safely declare that the same moral defects that are nakedly revealed in the savage peoples of the new world are also to be found, in greater or lesser measure, in more or less similar form, more or less overtly, in the most cultured nations: but so are good things, the seed of which still slumbers unnoticed in the bosom of the savage people. And how did such seed bring forth flowers in this people or that? How did it happen that this here had managed to ascend to so high a level of culture while that there has remained at a middle stage, or even at the lowest point of undevelopment? How did refinement drift from country to country, from east to west, from south to north? In what way did it become possible for half-savage peoples to settle in certain places on the remains of past greatness? These and other such questions are naturally to the fore in every thinking head; and the answers to them can only come from the study of history as a whole, universal history.

Az emberi természet köre mind a fizikai, mind a morális világra nézve felette szűk. A memphisi pap hajdan vaknak mondotta a hellént, mivel tekintetének a régiség történetei nyitva nem állottak. S nem tartozhatik-e, bizonyos mértékben, ezen megjegyzés mireánk is? Az, amit história egyetemének nevezünk, csak töredékekből álló szövedék; s ezen töredéken is a földkerekségnek csak egy része tűnik fel. Históriai tudományunk csak néhány népek történetein alapul, de ezen néhányak között sincsen egy is, melyet a maga eredetétől fogva a késő időkig nyomról nyomra követhetnénk. És mégis – mi szép, mi tanúságos[7] végignézni azon kevesen is, ami szemeink előtt elterjed! Hogyan lőn itt egy nemzet kicsinyből naggyá, egy más ott nagyból semmivé? Mi módon lőn néhol kevés számkivetett famíliákból város, a városból birodalom, az összetört birodalom omladékaiból hatalmas országok? Miként ébred itt a világosság a vad nép között, s annak jóltevő fényénél mint alkotja az magát össze kisebb vagy nagyobb társaságokká, mint lépdel találmányról találmányra, ismeretről ismeretre, hatalomról hatalomra mindaddig, míg ragyogó pályájának legmagasb pontján áll? Miképpen borul ott homály a fény és csillogás közt századokat töltött nagy népre; s mint süllyed el saját nagyságának terhe alatt lassanként? [...] Nem való-e, hogy ily dolgokra fordítani szemeinket, szívet emelő tekintet.

3.

Midőn a filozóf az emberiséget körülölelő nagy természetre függeszti figyelmét, lehetetlen, hogy mindabban, amit égen és földön magának kivűle lát, rendnek és öszvefüggésnek csalhatatlanul szembetűnő jeleit ne lássa, ne érezze: az ember az egyedül, ki e tagadhatatlan, ez örök rendnek közepében örök rendetlenségben látszik élni és mozogni. És mégis, ha a magányos embert egész nemzettel, s az egész nemzeteket egymással öszvehasonlítjuk; ha az óceán távol partjain élő gyermeknépek rajzolatját a régiség történeteire alkalmaztatjuk; ha az emberi majd magából kitörekedő, majd magába bevonuló, nyughatatlanul rest és restül nyughatatlan léleknek egyes vonásait a históriának egészében nyomozzuk: tapasztalni fogjuk, hogy az emberek különösen, és az emberi nemzetek közönségesen, minden elhajlások és különzéseik mellett is, mindig és mindenütt ugyanazon körben s ugyanazon mozgások közt forganak. A kertész bevetett egy ágyat tulipánmagokkal; s feltenyészik a virágnép ezerféle színveggyel. Ez a napnak jóltevő sugáraiban áll, amazt hideg árnyék borítja; ez most nyílik, amaz már elvirult, s felette egy újabb emeli magát: de mindegyik ugyanazon alkotmánnyal bír; egyformán tápláltatik, él és enyész; s gyökereiken újabb tavasszal újabb sarjazat virul fel.

Ha a történeteket magányosan tekintjük, gyakran oly vonások tűnnek szemeinkbe, melyek rendkívülieknek, képteleneknek tetszenek; az egésznek öszvefüggésében ezek rendesekké, természetesekké, hihetőkké változnak el. Némely vonások különválva csekélyek s tekintetet alig érdemlők: ezek a maguk rendében az egészre temérdek behatással bírhatnak; s az okok és következések nagy láncában a fő szemet tehetik. Mely fényben jelenik meg minden a filozóf keresztülható s öszvehasonlító lelke előtt! Ő százféle nemzetek sokaságában, ezerféle történetek vegyületében fáradatlan tekintettel követi az emberi lélek mozgásait. A jelenkor tüneményeiről, szakadatlan lépcsőkön, felhág a régiség homályába; s nem többé az emberi történetek külsőjét, nem többé a nemzeteknek egy meghatározott körben egymással és egymás mellett küzdésöket nézvén: magának az emberiségnek belsőjére figyelmez. Felülemeli a nemzeti különségeken pillantatát; s a népeket úgy nézi, mint egy nagy kiterjedésű, de ugyanazon egy famíliának tagjait. Ezen nagy famíliának tagjai ezerféleképpen ágaztak el. Lakjaik, szokásaik, véleményeik, nyelveik

---

[7] tanulságos, tanulsággal járó

As regards both physical and moral worlds the sphere of human nature is extremely restricted. In ancient times the priest of Memphis called the Hellene blind because the events of antiquity were not open to his sight. Does not that description apply to us too, to some extent? What we call the whole of history is merely a weaving together of fragments, and even those fragments have to do with only one part of the world. Our knowledge of the past is based on the histories of only a few peoples, and of those few there is not a single one which we can follow step by step from its origin to later times. And yet, what a fine, instructive thing it is to examine what even those few spread out before us! How did this people become great, that was tiny, and another that was great become nothing? How did in some places a town develop from a number of ostracized families, an empire from the town, and mighty countries from the ruins of that empire when it broke up? How does enlightenment dawn somewhere among a savage people, and how does that people form itself, in that beneficial light, into larger or smaller communities, how go from invention to invention, knowledge to knowledge, power to power, until it stands at the highest pinnacle of its brilliant career? How does obscurity envelop a great people that has lived for centuries in light and brightness, and how does it slowly subside beneath the weight of its own greatness? [. . .] Is not it true that the contemplation of such things lifts up our hearts?

3

When the philosopher turns his attention to the great world of Nature that surrounds humanity it is impossible for him not to perceive in all that he sees about him in the sky and on the earth unmistakably clear signs of order and cohesion; Man is the only being that seems to live and move in eternal disorder amidst this undeniable eternal order. And yet, if we compare the individual man with the whole nation, and whole nations with one another; if we fit descriptions of infant nations dwelling on the remote shores of Ocean to accounts of antiquity; if we trace throughout history the singular features of the human spirit as it now strives to break out of itself, now draws back in, restlessly indolent and indolently restless: it will be our experience that men as individuals, and the nations of men in general, for all their divergence and peculiarities, at all times and in all places move in the same circle and in the same ways. A gardener plants a bed with tulip bulbs; and the flowers open with a thousand mixed colours. One stands in the beneficial rays of the sun, another in cool shade; the latter is open now, the former has already faded and another taken its place; but each is similarly constituted, is similarly nourished, lives and withers, and from its roots new life will emerge next spring.

If we look at histories separately, features which seem extraordinary and absurd often come to light; in conjunction with the whole these become orderly, natural and credible. Some features, seen in isolation, are trifling and scarcely worthy of attention but cumulatively can make a great impact on the whole, and can forge the principal link in the great chain of causes and effects. In what a light they all appear then to the discerning and comparing eye of the philosopher! He follows with tireless eye the movements of the human spirit in a hundred nations and the complexities of a thousand events. He climbs back down a continuous stairway from the phenomena of the present age to the obscurity of antiquity and looks no longer at the externals of human history, the conflicts and alliances of nations in a defined sphere: he watches the inner workings of humanity. He raises his eyes beyond national dissimilarities and looks at peoples as members of a family – extended, but one and the same. The members of this great family have branched out in a thousand directions. They have grown apart by virtue of dwelling-places,

s száz meg száz különözéseik által egymástól eltávoztanak; de mindezen eltávozások között is az a közönséges szellem, mely magát az egész famílián keresztül lehellette, soha sem vész el a bölcs elől. Igyekszik ő ezen szellemet a maga számtalan széjjelfolyásaiban követni és felfogni; a milliomok sokaságában, s státusalkotványok temérdekében az egyes embert felkeresi és megtalálja; megvizsgálja őt azon öszvefüggésben, melyben az egész természettel s a maga földi lakával áll; kilesni azon bel és kül erőket, melyek a fizikai és morális világban vagy őtet munkálkodtatják, vagy őreá munkálnak; a történetek különféleségeiben nyomozza azt a rendet, melyhez az emberi kifejlés és munkálkodás kötve van; s azt kérdi magától, ha mindezen erő, rend és munkálkodás nem valamely bizonyos célra siet-e? Ily nyomozások vezetnek bennünket arra, amit a história filozófiájának nevezhetünk.

[*First published: Muzárion, 1833. 278–291. Modern edition: Kölcsey, Ferenc, Kölcsey Ferenc összes művei, 3 vols. Budapest: Szépirodalmi, 1960. Vol. 1, 1264–1274*]

g. ITALIANO

III.g.1. SILVIO PELLICO, da *Francesca da Rimini* (1818)

ATTO I. SCENA I.

Esce Lanciotto dalle sue stanze per andare al'incontro di Guido, il quale giunge. – Si abbracciano affettuosamente.

GUIDO	Vedermi dunque egli chiedea? Ravenna Tosto lasciai; men della figlia caro Sariami il trono della terra.
LANCIOTTO	Oh Guido! Come diverso tu rivedi questo Palagio mio dal dì che sposo io fui! Di Rimini le vie più non son liete Di canti e danze; più non odi alcuno Che di me dica: Non v'ha rege al mondo Felice al pari di Lanciotto. Invidia Avean di me tutti d'Italia i prenci; Or degno son di lor pietà. Francesca Soavemente commoveva a un tempo Colla bellezza i cuori, e con quel tenue Vel di malinconia che più celeste

customs, opinions, languages and hundreds upon hundreds of marks of difference; but despite all the distances between them, the philosopher never loses sight of that common spirit which infuses the whole family. He endeavours to pursue and capture that spirit in its countless ramifications; he seeks and finds the individual among the millions, in the multiplicity of differently constituted states; he examines him in that relationship in which he stands with the whole of Nature and his own earthly abode; he spies out those internal and external forces which either make him work or work upon him in the physical and moral worlds; he tracks down in the divergence of histories that order to which Man's emergence and functioning are bound, and he asks himself whether all this power, order and workings are not hastening to a definite goal? Such enquiries lead us to what we may call the philosophy of history.

[Translated by Bernard Adams]

g. ITALIAN

III.g.1. SILVIO PELLICO, from *Francesca da Rimini* (1818)

ACT I, SCENE I

Lanciotto comes out of his rooms to meet Guido, who is coming towards him. – They embrace affectionately.

GUIDO	So she asked to see me?
	I left Ravenna at once: the world's throne
	is less dear to me than my daughter.
LANCIOTTO	Oh Guido!
	How altered you will see my palace since I married!
	The streets of Rimini are no longer merry with song and dance;
	You will no longer hear anyone say of me: There is no King in
	all the world as happy as Lanciotto. The princes of all Italy
	envied me then; now I deserve their pity. Then, with her beauty,
	and with that faint veil of melancholy that made her appearance
	more heavenly, Francesca gently perturbed hearts.
	Everyone attributed this to her leaving her father's castles and to
	the reserve of holy maidenhood, which made her shy of
	marriage, of the throne and of applause. Time seemed to be
	dissipating that grief at last. Less melancholy were Francesca's

Fea il suo sembiante. L'apponeva ognuno
All'abbandono delle patrie case
E al pudor di santissima fanciulla,
Che ad imene, ed al trono, ed agli applausi
Ritrosa ha l'alma. – Il tempo ir diradando
Parve alfin quel dolor. Meno dimessi
Gli occhi Francesca al suo sposo volgea;
Più non cercava ognor d'esser solinga;
Pietosa cura in lei nascea d'udire
Degl'infelici le querele, e spesso
Me le recava, e mi diceva . . . Io t'amo
Perchè sei giusto, e con clemenza regni.

GUIDO   Mi sforzi al pianto. – Pargoletta, ell'era
Tutta sorriso, tutta gioja; ai fiori
Parea in mezzo volar nel più felice
Sentiero della vita; il suo vivace
Sguardo in chi la mirava infondea tutto
Il gajo spirto de'suoi giovani anni.
Chi presagir potealo? Ecco ad un tratto
Di tanta gioja esinto il raggio, estinto
Al primo assalto del dolor! La guerra,
Ahimè, un fratel teneramente amato.
Rapiale! . . . Oh infausta rimembranza! . . . Il cielo
Con preghiere continue ella stancava
Pel guerreggiante suo caro fratello . . .

LANCIOTTO   Inconsolabil del fratel perduto
Vive e n'abborre l'uccisor; quell'alma
Sì pia, sì dolce, mortalmente abborre!
Invan le dico: I nostri padri guerra
Moveansi; Paolo, il fratel mio, t'uccise
Un fratello, ma in guerra; assai dorragli
L'averlo ucciso; egli ha leggiadri, umani,
Di generoso cavaliero i sensi.
Di Paolo il nome la conturba. Io gemo
Però che sento del fratel lontano
Tenero amore. Avviso ebbi ch'ei riede
In patria; il core men balzò di gioja;
Alla mia sposa supplicando il dissi,
Onde benigna l'accogliesse. Un grido
A tal annunzio mise. Egli ritorna!
Sclamò tremando e semiviva cadde.
Dirtelo deggio? Ahi, l'ho creduta estinta,
E furente giurai che la sua morte
Io vendicato avrei . . . nel fratel mio!

GUIDO   Lasso! e potevi! . . .

eyes that met her husband's gaze; she no longer sought to be
always on her own; compassionate concern welled up in her on
hearing of unhappy cases, and often she would tell me of them
and say to me . . . I love you because you are just, and you reign
with humanity.

GUIDO

You bring me to tears. – As a child, she was full of smiles, Full
of joy; she seemed to fly among the flowers along the happiest
path of life, whoever gazed at her vivacious face was instilled
with the joyous spirit of her young years. Who could foretell it?
The ray of such joy quenched at a stroke, quenched by the first
onslaught of pain! The war, alas, robbed her of a dearly loved
brother! . . . Oh what an unhappy memory! . . . She used to
weary Heaven with continuous prayer for her dear brother at war.

LANCIOTTO

She is inconsolable for her lost brother and loathes his killer;
That soul so kind, so mild, hates him to death! In vain I say to
her: Our fathers were at war; Paolo, my brother, killed your
brother, but it was in war; it grieves him deeply to have killed
him; he has the sentiments of a noble, humane, generous knight.
Paolo's name upsets her. I mourn because I love my absent
brother dearly. I received notice that he would return to his
fatherland; my heart leapt with joy; imploring my wife I asked
that she would welcome him warmly. At that announcement she
let out a cry. He is coming back! She exclaimed trembling and
falling unconscious. And should I tell you? Oh, I believed her to
be dead, and furious, I swore I would avenge her death . . . on
my brother!

GUIDO

Alas! And could you! . . .

LANCIOTTO   Il ciel disperda l'empio
             Giuramento! L'udì ripeter ella,
             Ed orror n'ebbe, e a me le man stendendo:
             Giura, sclamò, giura d'amarlo; ei solo,
             Quand'io più non sarò, pietoso amico
             Ti rimarrà . . . Ch'io l'ami impone, e l'odia
             La disumana! E andar chiede a Ravenna
             Nel suo natìo palagio, onde gli sguardi
             Non sostener dell'uccisor del suo
             Germano.

GUIDO   Appena ebbi il tuo scritto, inferma
             Temei foss'ella. Ah, quanto io l'ami, il sai!
             Che troppo io viva . . . tu m'indendi . . . io sempre
             Tremo.

LANCIOTTO   Oh, non dirlo! . . . Io pur quando sopita
             La guardo . . . e chiuse le palpebre, e il bianco
             Volto segno non dan quasi di vita,
             Con orrenda ansietà pongo il mio labbro
             Sovra il suo labbro per sentir se spiri;
             E del tremor tuo tremo. – In feste e giochi
             Tenerla volli e sen tediò: di gemme
             Doviziosa e d'oro e di possanza
             Farla, e fu grata, ma non lieta. Al cielo
             Devota è assai; novelle are costrussi.
             Cento vergini e cento alzano ognora
             Preci per lei, che le protegge ed ama.
             Ella s'avvede ch'ogni studio adopro
             Onde piacerle, e me lo dice, e piange. –
             Talor mi sorge un reo pensier . . . Avessi
             Qualche rivale? . . . Oh ciel! ma se da tutta
             La sua persona le traluce il core
             Candidissimo e puro! . . . Eccola.

[. . .]

SCENA V.

(Paolo e Lanciotto si corrono incontro e restano lungamente abbracciati).

LANCIOTTO   Ah, tu sei desso,
             Fratel!

PAOLO   Lanciotto! mio fratello! – Oh sfogo
             Di dolcissime lagrime!

LANCIOTTO   L'amico,
             L'unico amico de' miei teneri anni!
             Da te diviso, oh, come a lungo io stetti!

LANCIOTTO   May Heaven dissolve that wicked oath! She heard me say it
             and filled with horror, and her hands outstretched she turned to
             me: swear, she cried, swear to love him; when I shall be no
             more, he alone will remain your friend . . . She made me love
             him and hate him, that cruel lady! And she asks to go to
             Ravenna to her father's palace, from where she will not have to
             bear the gaze of her brother Germano's murderer.

GUIDO   As soon as I received your summons, I feared she might be ill.
             Ah you know how dearly I love her! I fear always . . . you
             understand my meaning . . . that I live too long.

LANCIOTTO   Oh, do not say that! . . . I also feel like this when I look at her
             sleeping . . . and with her eyes closed and her pale face giving
             no sign of life, with a heavy heart I place my lips over hers to
             see if she still breathes; and as you fear, I fear. – I wished to
             entertain her with feasts and games and she found it tedious;
             I gave her many gems and gold and power, and she was grateful
             but not happy. She is greatly devoted to Heaven; I built new
             shrines. One hundred virgins and one hundred more pray for
             her, that she may protect and love them. She is aware that I
             make every effort to please her, and she tells me so, and weeps. –
             Sometimes a guilty thought occurs to me . . . Might I have a
             rival? . . . Oh Heavens! But her most spotless and pure heart
             shines forth from her whole being! . . . Here she is.

[. . .]

SCENE V

Paolo and Lanciotto
(They run towards each other and embrace for a long time)

LANCIOTTO   Oh, it is you, brother!

PAOLO   Lanciotto! my brother! – I overflow with sweet tears.

LANCIOTTO   My friend, the only friend of my young tender years!
             Oh, how long I have been separated from you!

PAOLO	Qui t'abbracciai l'ultima volta . . . Teco Un altr'uomo io abbracciava; ei pur piangea . . . Più rivederlo io non doveva!
LANCIOTTO	Oh padre!
PAOLO	Tu gli chiudesti i moribondi lumi. Nulla ti disse del suo Paolo?
LANCIOTTO	Il suo figliuol lontano egli moria chiamando.
PAOLO	Mi benedisse? – Egli dal ciel ci guarda, Ci vede uniti e ne gioisce. Uniti Sempre saremo d'or innanzi. Stanco Son d'ogni vana ombra di gloria. Ho sparso Di Bisanzio pel trono il sangue mio, Debellando città ch'io non odiava, E fama ebbi di grande, e d'onor colmo Fui dal clemente Imperador: dispetto In me facean gli universali applausi. Per chi di stragi si macchiò il mio brando? Per lo straniero. E non ho patria forse, Cui sacro sia de'cittadini il sangue? Per te, per te, che cittadini hai prodi, Italia mia, combatterò se oltraggio Ti moverà la invidia. E il più gentile Terren non sei di quanti scalda il sole? D'ogni bell'arte non sei madre, o Italia? Polve d'eroi non è la polve tua? Agli avi miei tu valor desti e seggio, E tutto quanto ho di più caro alberghi!
LANCIOTTO	Vederti, udirti e non amarti . . . umana Cosa non è. – Sien grazie al cielo! Odiarti Ella, no, non potrà.
PAOLO	Chi?
LANCIOTTO	Tu non sai Manca alla mia felicità qui un altro Tenero pegno.
PAOLO	Ami tu forse?
LANCIOTTO	Oh se amo! La più angelica donna amo . . . e la donna Più sventurata.
PAOLO	Io pur amo; a vicenda Le nostre pene confidiamci.
LANCIOTTO	Il padre Pria di morire un imeneo m'impose,

PAOLO Here I embraced you the last time . . . I embraced
Another man with you then; he was weeping too . . .
I was never to see him again!

LANCIOTTO Oh father!

PAOLO You closed his dying eyes. Did he say anything of his Paolo?

LANCIOTTO He died calling his absent son.

PAOLO Would he have blessed me? – he looks down on us from
heaven, he sees us united and he rejoices. From this day forward
we will be forever united. I am tired of every worthless hint of
glory. For Byzantium's throne I have spilled my blood,
defeating cities I did not hate, and I had great fame, and was
given the highest honour by the merciful Emperor; the universal
plaudits disgusted me. For whom did I stain my sword with
slaughter? For a stranger. And have I not a fatherland
where the blood of its citizens is sacred? For you, for you I will
fight, my Italy, and your brave citizens, if envious foes should
stir up trouble. Of all the lands that the sun warms are you not
the most noble? Oh Italy are you not mother of every noble art?
Is your soil not the soil of heroes?
You roused valour in my ancestors and you shelter all that
I hold most dear.

LANCIOTTO To see you, hear you and not love you . . . that is not
humanly possible. – Thanks be to God! Hate you, no,
she cannot hate you.

PAOLO Who?

LANCIOTTO You do not know. All that is lacking from my happiness is
another tender pledge.

PAOLO Are you perhaps in love?

LANCIOTTO Oh am I in love! I am in love with the most angelic lady . . . and
the most unfortunate.

PAOLO I am also in love; let us confide our pain to each other.

LANCIOTTO Our father imposed a marriage on me before he died so that a
lasting peace might come to us. I obeyed his order.

Onde stabile a noi pace venisse.
Il commando esegnii.

PAOLO
Sposa t'è dunque
La donna tua? nè lieto sei? Chi è dessa?
Non t'ama?

LANCIOTTO
Ingiusto accusator, non posso
Dir che non m'ami. Ella così te amasse!
Ma tu un fratello le uccidesti in guerra;
Orror le fai, vederti niega.

PAOLO
Parla.
Chi è dessa? Chi?

LANCIOTTO
Tu la vedesti allora
Che alla Corte di Guido . . .

PAOLO
(Reprimendo la sua orribile agitazione).
Essa . . .

LANCIOTTO
La figlia di Guido.

PAOLO
E t'ama? Ed è tua sposa? – È vero;
Un fratello . . . le uccisi . . .

LANCIOTTO
Ed incessante
Duolo ne serba. Poichè udì che in patria
Tu ritornavi, desolata abborre
Questo tetto.

PAOLO
(Reprimendosi sempre).
Vedermi, anco vedermi
Niega? – Felice io mi credeva accanto
Al mio fratel.– Ripartirò . . . in eterno
Vivrò lontano dal mio patrio tetto.

LANCIOTTO
Fausto ad ambi egualmente il patrio tetto
Sarà. Non fia che tu mi lasci.

PAOLO
In pace
Vivi; a una sposa l'uom tutto pospone.
Amala . . . – Ah, prendi questo brando, il tuo
Mi dona! in rimembranza abbilo eterna
Del tuo Paolo
(Eseguisce con dolce violenza questo cambio).

LANCIOTTO
Fratel . . .

PAOLO
Se un giorno mai
Ci rivedrem, s'io pur vivrò . . . più freddo
Batterà allora il nostro cuor . . . il tempo
Che tutto estingue, estinto avrà . . . in Francesca
L'odio . . . e fratel mi chiamerà.

PAOLO	She is your wife then. Your lady? You are not happy? Who is she? She does not love you?
LANCIOTTO	Unjust accuser; I cannot say she does not love me. She would have loved you too! But you killed her brother in the war; you fill her with horror, she refuses to see you.
PAOLO	Speak. Who is she? Who?
LANCIOTTO	You saw her yourself at Guido's court . . .
PAOLO	*(stifling his dreadful agitation)* Her . . .
LANCIOTTO	Guido's daughter.
PAOLO	And you love her? and she is your wife? – It is true; I have killed . . . her brother . . .
LANCIOTTO	The pain she bears is incessant. Since she heard that you were returning home, she is greatly distressed and hates this house.
PAOLO	*(still restraining himself)* She refuses to even see me? – I believed I was happy at my brother's side. – I will leave again . . . I will live for all eternity far from my father's house.
LANCIOTTO	Our father's house will be equally fortunate for both of us. Do not leave me.
PAOLO	Live in peace; a man should put his wife before everything. Love her . . . – Oh, take this sword, give me yours! Let it be a perpetual reminder of your Paolo. *(he executes this exchange with tender violence).*
LANCIOTTO	Brother . . .
PAOLO	If we ever meet again one day, if I still live . . . our hearts will then beat colder . . . time that extinguishes everything, will have extinguished . . . the hatred in Francesca . . . she will call me brother.

LANCIOTTO	Tu piangi.
PAOLO	Io pure amai! Fanciulla unica al mondo Era quella al mio sguardo . . . ah, non m'odiava, No, non m'odiava.
LANCIOTTO	E la perdesti?
PAOLO	Il cielo me l'ha rapita!
LANCIOTTO	D'un fratel l'amore Ti sia conforto. Alla tua vista, a'modi Tuoi generosi placherassi il core Di Francesca medesma. Or vieni . . .
PAOLO	Dove? A lei dinanzi . . . non fia ch'io venga.

[*Edizione di riferimento: Francesca da Rimini, Firenze, Adriano Salani Editore, 1899*]

III.g.2. ERMES VISCONTI, da *Idee elementari sulla Poesia romantica*

Alla poesia romantica appartengono tutti i soggetti ricavati dalla storia moderna o dal medio evo: le immagini, riflessioni e racconti desunti dal cristianesimo, dalle superstizioni delle plebi cristiane o de' monaci o dall'ignoranza, dalle favole delle fate e geni degli Asiatici, introdotte nei romanzi e naturalizzate in Europa; l'ideale cavalleresco; e generalmente tutte quelle opinioni, e tutti quei gradi e tinte di passioni che non si svilupparono negli animi de' Greci e Romani. Non tutto ciò che è romantico può essere convenientemente ricantato al presente; il poeta stia a livello de' suoi coetanei. Washington e i membri delle Coortes sono gli eroi che fanno al caso nostro, non più Sacripante o Amadigi: la religione può prestarci occasioni di sfoggiare nel maraviglioso; ma essa sola, non il mago Atlante o l'incantatore Merlino.

[. . .]

Le opinioni degli estetici tedeschi, e più ancora quelle enunciate da alcuni fra gli studiosi nostri concittadini, coincidono per moltissimi lati colle idee esposte ne' precedenti articoli. Il romantismo adunque non consiste nel favoleggiare continuamente di streghe o folletti e miracoli degni del *Prato fiorito*, o nel gemere e raccapricciarsi ne' cimiteri. A questo modo, si potrebbe dire con parità di ragione che tutta la poesia degli antichi è ristretta alle metamorfosi d'Ovidio; d'altronde si è già accennato che le fole plebee vanno tralasciate. Un poema, una canzone, ed un dramma possono essere romantici senza il menomo intervento di maraviglioso cristiano. Non lo sono forse persino Brunet e Palomba autore di opere buffe in dialetto di Napoli? Il romantismo non consiste nel lugubre e nel malinconico. Shakespear espose sulle scene la morte di Desdemona, ma verseggiò anche i felici amori di Miranda: similmente Omero cantò l'inestinguibile riso degli Dei e le sciagure di Priamo, i giuochi dello stadio e lo strazio di Ettore. Il genere romantico non tende ad esaltare ciecamente i tempi feudali, né ad invidiarli con desiderio insensato. Altro è encomiare le virtù caratteristiche de' crociati, ed altra cosa è lodarne i vizj, far desiderare l'anarchia ed il fanatismo. Si loda pure il patriottismo di Leonida senza che venga in capo di bramare la schiavitù degl'Iloti; si legge *l'Odissea* in tutte le quattro parti del mondo, e niuna principessa si è mai invogliata di fare la lavandaia. Che se qualche autore ha confuso il bene col male, ed ha tessuto senza accorgersene un panegirico alla barbarie, condannate lui solo: ma anche Orazio celebrò le ingiuste guerre de' Romani,

LANCIOTTO	You are weeping.
PAOLO	I was also in love. To my eyes she was a girl unmatched in all the world . . . oh, she did not hate me, no, she did not hate me.

LANCIOTTO	And you lost her?
PAOLO	Heaven stole her from me!
LANCIOTTO	Let a brother's love comfort you. The sight of you and your gentle manners would melt the heart even of Francesca. Come now . . .

PAOLO	Where? Into her presence . . . I don't dare.

[*Translated by Marayde O'Brien and Anne O'Connor*]

III.g.2.   ERMES VISCONTI, from *Elementary Ideas on Romantic Poetry*

All the subjects drawn from modern and medieval history belong to Romantic poetry: the images, reflections and stories taken from Christianity, from the superstitions of the Christian peasants or from monks, or from ignorance, from Asian tales of fairies and genies first encountered in novels and naturalised in Europe, the knightly ideal, and generally from all those levels and shades of passions which the Greek and Roman minds did not develop. Not all that which we call Romantic can be easily reworked in the present: the poet works to the standard of his contemporaries. Sacriphantes or Amadigi are no longer the heroes to whom we attach importance, but rather Washington and the members of the Cohortes: religion can provide us with opportunities to wonder at the marvellous; but only religion, not the magician Atlas or the wizard Merlin.

[. . .]

   The opinion of the German aesthetes, and even more so those opinions formulated by some of our studious fellow citizens, concur on many points with the ideas expressed in previous articles. Romanticism is not merely an endless stream of tales of witches or elves and miracles worthy of *Prato fiorito*, or of moaning and shuddering with fear in cemeteries. With the same kind of reasoning one could rightly say that all the poetry of the Ancients is restricted to Ovid's *Metamorphoses*: on the other hand it has already been mentioned that the fairytales of the common people are ignored. A poem, a song, and a drama can be classed as Romantic without the inclusion of any Christian marvels. Is this not the case with Brunet and Palomba, writer of *opera buffa* in Neapolitan dialect? Romanticism does not comprise only of the gloomy and depressing, Shakespeare showed the death of Desdemona on the stage, but he also wrote about Miranda's happy love affairs. Similarly Homer spoke of the never-ending laughter of the Gods and also of the misfortunes of Priam, the games in the stadium and the torture of Hector. The genre of Romanticism tends not to blindly glorify feudal times, nor to envy them with foolish longing. It is one thing to pay tribute to the virtues characteristic of the Crusaders and another thing to praise their vices, leading to a desire for anarchy and fanaticism. Leonida's patriotism is praised, but the slavery of the Helots is never desired, the *Odyssey* is read in all four corners of the world and not one princess is ever tempted to be a washerwoman. If some authors have confused good and evil and unwittingly praised barbarity, then condemn only them: but even Horace

e forse per questo l'essenza della poesia latina sta nell'approvare la prepotenza di quelle conquiste?

[. . .]

Si cessi dal calunniare gli esimi stranieri, chiamandoli disprezzatori e invidiosi de' classici greci e romani: essi li ammirano anzi con un sentimento più profondo e più vero, che non gli stessi retori, perché vi scoprono bellezze sublimi a cui non arriva lo sguardo de' retori. Il classicismo in Omero ed in Sofocle corrisponde al romanticismo in Schiller ed in Milton; l'uno e l'altro sono effetti di un'identica causa, cioè dell'entusiasmo spontaneo voluto ed alimentato dal complesso della civilizzazione rispettiva. È il solo classicismo de' moderni che merita biasmo, perché è un'imitazione inopportuna non della natura, ma di preesistenti opere d'arte; è un poetare spurio tanto lungi dal vero buon gusto, quanto le inezie claustrali degli scolastici erano lungi dalla vera filosofia.

> [1818] [*Edizione di riferimento: I manifesti romantici del 1816 e gli scritti principali del Conciliatore sul Romanticismo, a cura di Carlo Calcaterra. Torino: Unione tipografico-editrice torinese, ristampa 1964*]

h. NORSK

III.h.1. HENRIK WERGELAND, 'Sandhedens Armée'

Ord? Som Verden saa foragter?
   Ord i Digt?
Endnu meer foragteligt!
Ak, hvor usle disse Magter
   til at fegte
for den Sandhed I fornegte!

Lyn bør slaa og Tordner rulle
   foran *den.*
Sendt tilhjælp fra Himmelen,
legion af Engle skulde
   sine Fløje
sprede viden om den Høje.

Ak, hvi kommer, himmelbaaren,
   Den ei selv?
synlig, med en Stjernes Hvælv
til en Hjelm om Panden skaaren?
   Bedre, bedre
fløi dens Flugt med Sværd til Fjedre.

Ak, hvi har den sine Telte
   ikke spændt
skinnende paa hver en Skrænt?
Ak, hvi har den sine Helte
   ikke givet
Herredømmet over Livet!

commemorated the unfair wars of the Romans, and maybe this is why the essence of Latin poetry lies in that approval of the arrogance of those conquests.

[...]

One should cease to malign the distinguished foreigners calling them scornful and envious of the Greek and Roman classics: in fact, they admire them with a deeper and truer sentiment than those same rhetoricians, because they find sublime beauty in them which the rhetoricians are not capable of seeing. The Classicism in Homer and Sophocles corresponds to the Romanticism of Schiller and Milton: both brought about in the same way, by the spontaneous enthusiasm, desired and completely nurtured by their respective civilisations. It is only modern Classicism which merits disapproval, because it is an inappropriate imitation not of nature, but of pre-existing works of art; it is a spurious poetry-writing, as far removed from good taste as the cloistered triviality written by the Scholastics was from true philosophy.

[1818] [*Translated by Marayde O'Brien and Anne O'Connor*]

h. NORWEGIAN

III.h.1. HENRIK WERGELAND, 'The Army of Truth'

Words, the world so light esteemeth?
　　Lower yet,
words in poet's stanza set!
O how frail your power seemeth,
　　to be fighting
for the truth mankind is slighting.

Truth should come with thunder pealing,
　　flashing Levin:
To her succour sent from Heaven,
angel hosts their cohorts wheeling,
　　wide extended,
should escort her advent splendid.

Ah! Why comes she not, th'exalted,
　　hither now?
With a helm about her brow,
fashioned of the sky star-vaulted,
　　fiercer looming,
swords her radiant pinions pluming?

Why are not her white tents planted,
　　far and wide,
gleaming on the mountain side?
why are not her warriors granted,
　　in their striving,
mastery over life and living?

Mørkets Vold er steil at storme.
   Overtro
hviler fast paa Søilers Ro.
Talløs som Ægyptens Orme
   Er den sorte
Fordomshær ved Templets Porte.

Fremad dog, I usle Rader!
   Hær af Ord!
Eder Seiren dog paa Jord
lovet er af Lysets Fader,
   naar I tjene
Sandheden, hans Barn, alene.

Fremad, Ord, I Sandheds Helte!
   En avant!
Adamshjerterne engang
blive eders Sejerstelte.
   Straaler spile
vil dem ud til eders Hvile.

Fremad, med Viziret lettet,
   Sandhedsord!
Thi den største Magt paa Jord
Eder er af Gud forgjettet:
   At I kunne
Ikke dø, I Sandhedsmunde!

Derfor modige, I Dverge!
   Sandheds Sag
seirer kun i Nederlag.
Stormer Løgnens Ørkenbjerge!
   Hen I veire
dem og Fordoms Taageleire!

Bastioned night is steep for storming;
    bigotry
rests secure on columns high;
like Egyptian serpents swarming,
    round her temple,
error's black-robed guards assemble.

Onward yet, brave words, undaunted,
    howso few!
Earthly triumph has to you
by the God of light been granted,
    who are serving
truth, his child, with faith unswerving.

Forward, words, the truth's selected
    Hero band!
Soon in human hearts shall stand
your victorious tents erected;
    glory sweeping
sunlit folds above your sleeping.

Forward, then, with fearless faces,
    truth's firm line!
Yours shall be, by pledge divine,
power no earthly might displaces;
    death can never
still thee, voice of truth, for ever.

Cease then, puny host, your quailing,
    truth her cause
through defeat to triumph draws:
Falsehood's desert heights assailing,
    see, your powers
dissipate those phantom towers!

[*Translated by G. M. Gathorne-Hardy, 1960*]

[*Wergeland was a fervent patriot, but a liberal one. He opposed the ban on Jews in the Constitution of Norway of 1814. He published two books of poems, Jøden – The Jew, 1842, and Jødinden – The Jewess, 1844, arguing in favour of the recognition of Jews. He never lived to see the amendment of the Constitution on this point, which was passed in 1855. Our text is the introductory poem of Jøden.*]

III.h.2. IVAR AASEN, 'Nordmannen'

Millom bakkar og berg ut med havet
heve nordmannen fenget sin heim,
der han sjølv heve tufterna gravet
og sett sjølv sine hus uppå deim.

Han såg ut på dei steinutte strender;
der var ingen, som der hadde bygt.
"Lat oss rydja og byggja oss grender,
og so eiga me rudningen trygt."

Han såg ut på det bårutte havet;
der var ruskutt å leggja ut på;
men det leikade fisk ned i kavet,
og den leiken den vilde han sjå.

Fram på vetteren stundom han tenkte:
Giv eg var i eit varmare land!
Men når vårsol i bakkarne blenkte,
fekk han hug til si heimlege strand.

Og når liderna grønka som hagar,
når det lavar av blomar på strå,
og når næter er ljosa som dagar,
kan han ingenstad vænare sjå.

[1863]

[This poem was published in different versions in 1863, 1868 and 1875. It is the 1875 version published here.]

III.h.3. BJØRNSTJERNE BJØRNSON, 'Ja, vi elsker dette landet'

Ja, vi elsker dette landet,
som det stiger frem,
furet, værbitt over vannet,
med de tusen hjem, –
elsker, elsker det og tenker
på vår far og mor
og den saganatt som senker
drømmer på vår jord.

Dette landet Harald berget
med sin kjemperad,
dette landet Håkon verget,
medens Øyvind kvad;
Olav på det land har malet
korset med sitt blod,

III.h.2. IVAR AASEN, 'The Norwegian'

Between cliffs and the billowing breakers
The Norwegian of old found his home
A foundation he laid in these acres
His own hands raised his house from the loam.

He looked out on the boulder-strewn beaches,
Not a settlement was there in sight.
'Let's build farms and clear fields in these reaches,
Thus we win them to be ours by right.'

He saw seas that the storm tore asunder
The rough waves made them risky to row
Yet the fish had their passage thereunder,
And their ways he was eager to know.

In the winter he might fall to pining:
'That I were in a sunnier part!'
But when sun in the springtime was shining
Then his homeland grew dear to his heart.

And when fields are like gardens in May-time,
When each hillside is leafy and green,
And when midnight grows light like in daytime
Nowhere else has such beauty he seen.

[*Translated by Kjetil Myskja, 2002*]

III.h.3. BJØRNSTJERNE BJØRNSON, 'National Song'

This our land – indeed we love it
With its homes, our land,
Rising through the pines above it
On the wave-lashed strand.
Ever with that thought is blending
Those who gave us birth,
And the saga-night descending
Softly on our earth.

Harald's warriors fought to gain it,
Loud their weapons rang.
Haakon struggled to maintain it,
There too Öivind sang.
Olaf set the cross upon it
In his blood outpoured,

fra dets høye Sverre talet
Roma midt imod.

Bønder sine økser brynte
hvor en hær dro frem;
Tordenskjold langs kysten lynte,
så den lystes hjem.
Kvinner selv sto opp og strede
som de vare menn;
andre kunne bare grede,
men det kom igjen!

Visstnok var vi ikke mange;
men vi strakk dog til,
da vi prøvdes noen gange,
og det sto på spill;
ti vi heller landet brente
end det kom til fall;
husker bare hva som hendte
ned på Fredrikshald!

Hårde tider har vi døyet,
ble til sist forstøtt;
men i verste nød blåøyet
frihet ble oss født.
Det ga faderkraft å bære
hungersnød og krig,
det ga døden selv sin ære –
og det ga forlig.

Fienden sitt våpen kastet,
opp visiret fór,
vi med undren mot ham hastet;
ti han var vår bror.
Drevne frem på stand av skammen
gikk vi søderpå;
nå vi står *tre brødre* sammen,
og skal sådan stå!

Norske menn i hus og hytte,
takk din store Gud!
Landet ville han beskytte,
skjønt det mørkt så ut.
Alt hva fedrene har kjempet,
mødrene har grett,

After his bold faith had won it
To receive Our Lord.

When the peasant's axe was flashing,
Foes turned back in dread,
Tordenskjold sent bolts a-crashing
Till the invader fled.
Women even took their places
In the ranks of war;
Others prayed, with weeping faces,
When the guns would roar.

Few we were and sorely tested,
But we never failed.
Oft the battle-tide we breasted,
And our might prevailed.
Better turn our soil to embers
Than one inch to yield.
Grimly Fredrikshall remembers
How we kept the field.

Hard the night of our probation,
Yet it led to morn;
Then was in our desperation
Blue-eyed Freedom born.
So our sires of ancient story
Learned to fight and fast.
Death itself was crowned with glory –
Then came peace at last.

Weapon sheathed and helm unfastened,
Stood our former foe.
Wondering much, to him we hastened;
'Twas our brother, lo!
We were smit alike with shame now,
Gone our cruel pride;
We three brothers are the same now
And shall so abide.

Son of Norway, give thou ever
Thanks to God on high!
He will guard, forsaking never,
When the storm is nigh.
For when women all were weeping,
Men were in the fight,

har den Herre stille lempet,
så vi vant vår rett.

Ja, vi elsker dette landet,
som det stiger frem,
furet, værbitt over vannet,
med de tusen hjem.
Og som fedres kamp har hevet
det av nød til seir,
også vi, når det blir krevet,
for dets fred slå leir.

[*This text was first published in a slightly different version in 1859. In 1864 it was established as the national anthem of Norway. The definitive version, which is rendered here, is from 1869.*]

i. POLSKI

III.i.1.   ADAM MICKIEWICZ, *Konrad Wallenrod* (fragment)

'Pieśń Wajdeloty'

Kiedy zaraza Litwę ma uderzyć,
Jej przyjście wieszcza odgadnie źrenica;
Bo jeśli słuszna wajdelotom wierzyć,
Nieraz na pustych smętarzach i błoniach
Staje widomie morowa dziewica,
W bieliźnie, z wiankiem ognistym na skroniach,
Czołem przenosi białowieskie drzewa,
A w ręku chustką skrwawioną powiewa.
Strażnicy zamków oczy pod hełm kryją,
A psy wieśniaków, zarywszy pysk w ziemi,
Kopią, śmierć wietrzą i okropnie wyją.
Dziewica stąpa kroki złowieszczemi
Na sioła, zamki i bogate miasta;
A ile razy krwawą chustką skinie,
Tyle pałaców zmienia się w pustynie,
Gdzie nogą stąpi, świeży grób wyrasta.

Zgubne zjawisko! – Ale więcej zguby
Wróżył Litwinom od niemieckiej strony
Szyszak błyszczący ze strusimi czuby
I płaszcz szeroki, krzyżem naczerniony.

Gdzie przeszły stopy takiego widziadła,
Niczym jest klęska wiosek albo grodów:
Cała kraina w mogiłę zapadła.
Ach! kto litewską duszę mógł ochronić,

Still our land was in His keeping,
And we won our right.

This our land, indeed we love it
With its homes, our land,
Rising through the pines above it
On the wave-lashed strand.
As our sires in bygone ages
Went to victory;
When once more the conflict rages,
So again will we.

[1859, 1864, 1869] [*Translated by C. Wharton Stork, 1942*]

i. POLISH

III.i.1.   ADAM MICKIEWICZ, from *Konrad Wallenrod*

'Song of the Wajdelota'

Whene'er the plague toward Lithuania turns,
The wajdelota's eye her doom foresees;
For, if the bard relate his tale aright,
Oft o'er the empty graveyards and broad leas
The Maid of Pestilence walks, robed in white:
About her brow a fiery garland burns;
Taller than Bialowieza's trees she stands,
And waves a blood-stained kerchief in her hands.
On castle walls the sentries on their round
Behind their visors fain would hide their eyes;
In village lanes the dogs, with dismal cries,
Dig, scenting death, their muzzles to the ground.
The maiden paces on with steps of doom
Through many a village, castle, and rich town;
But where she casts her bloody kerchief down,
The palaces are sunk in desert gloom;
Where treads her foot, there rises a fresh tomb.
Ah; devastating phantom! – but a loss
Far deadlier shadows forth the casque that shines,
The plume that waves beyond the German lines,
And the broad mantle, blackened with the cross!
Where such an apparition has stalked by,
None says, 'Here was a castle, there a town;'
The whole land in one grave is sunken down.
If there be any who can yet defy

Pójdź do mnie, siądziem na grobie narodów,
Będziemy dumać, śpiewać i łzy ronić.

O wieści gminna! ty arko przymierza
Między dawnymi i młodszymi laty:
W tobie lud składa broń swego rycerza,
Swych myśli przędzę i swych uczuć kwiaty.
Arko! tyś żadnym nie złamana ciosem,
Póki cię własny twój lud nie znieważy;
O pieśni gminna, ty stoisz na straży
Narodowego pamiątek kościoła,
Z archanielskimi skrzydłami i głosem –
Ty czasem dzierżysz i miecz archanioła.

Płomień rozgryzie malowane dzieje,
Skarby mieczowi spustoszą złodzieje,
Pieśń ujdzie cało, tłum ludzi obiega;
A jeśli podłe dusze nie umieją
Karmić ją żalem i poić nadzieją,
Ucieka w góry, do gruzów przylega
I stamtąd dawne opowiada czasy.
Tak słowik z ogniem zajętego gmachu
Wyleci, chwilę przysiądzie na dachu:
Gdy dachy runą, on ucieka w lasy
I brzmiącą piersią nad zgliszcza i groby
Nuci podróżnym piosenkę żałoby.
Słuchałem piosnek – nieraz kmieć stoletni,
Trącając kości żelazem oraczem,
Stanął i zagrał na wierzbowej fletni
Pacierz umarłych; lub rymownym płaczem
Was głosił, wielcy ojcowie – bezdzietni.
Echa mu wtórzą, ja słuchałem z dala,
Tym mocniej widok i piosnka rozżala,
Żem był jedynym widzem i słuchaczem.

Jako w dzień sądny z grobowca wywoła
Umarłą przeszłość trąba archanioła,
Tak na dźwięk pieśni kości spod mej stopy
W olbrzymie kształty zbiegły się i zrosły.
Z gruzów powstają kolumny i stropy,
Jeziora puste brzmią licznymi wiosły
I widać zamków otwarte podwoje,
Korony książąt, wojowników zbroje,
Śpiewają wieszcze, tańczy dziewic grono –
Marzyłem cudnie, srodze mię zbudzono!

Zniknęły lasy i ojczyste góry.
Myśl znużonymi ulatując pióry

That specter – if there still be one to keep
A Lithuanian soul – come to me now!
Above the grave of nations let us bow;
There we will ponder, there will sing and weep.
    Saga! thou ark of that most holy plight
Between the years of yore and younger years,
In thee the folk lays armor of its knight,
Fabric of thoughts, blossoms of joy and tears.
    Ark! thou canst not be broken, while thine own
Take heed of thee! O folk song? thou dost stand
On guard before the nation's inmost shrine
Of memory, and wings and voice are thine
Of an archangel – but not these alone,
For an archangel's sword is in thy hand.
    The flames will gnaw away a painted tale;
The fruits of conquest, vandals will despoil:
The song unscathed springs from the murk and moil,
And, if the sordid souls who hear it, fail
To give it food of grief and drink of hope,
It cleaves to ruins, seeks the rugged slope,
And thence mourns ever for the ancient days.
Thus flies the nightingale forth from the blaze
And on the burning gables fain would rest;
When the roofs fall, she flees to wooded hills,
And over graves, with her sonorous breast,
The pilgrim's lonely path with mourning fills.
    I have heard songs: a peasant, bent and gray,
When his iron plowshare struck forgotten bones,
Has paused, upon his willow flute to play
A requiem; or, with impassioned tones,
To raise a chant for you, Ô ancient sires,
Who have no sons to tend your altar fires!
The echoes made responses far and clear:
I grieved the more, that I alone could hear.
As the archangel on the day of doom
Calls forth the dead past from its sunken tomb,
So, at the song, the bones beneath my feet
Fused into giant forms; from heaps of stone
Columns and ceilings rose again complete,
A thousand oars stirred the deserted lake,
Wide open were the doors of castles thrown:
There did the minstrels sing, the maidens dance,
The light from princely crowns and armor glance –
Bravely I dreamt, and cruelly did awake.
Gone are the forests, gone the ancestral peaks;
Thought, flying back, her wonted refuge seeks,

Spada, w domową tuli się zaciszę;
Lutnia umilkła w otrętwiałym ręku,
Śród żałosnego spółrodaków jęku
Często przeszłości głosu nie dosłyszę!
Lecz dotąd iskry młodego zapału
Tlą w głębi piersi, nieraz ogień wzniecą,
Duszę ożywią i pamięć oświecą.
Pamięć naówczas, jak lampa z kryształu
Ubrana pędzlem w malowne obrazy,
Chociaż ją zaćmi pył i liczne skazy,
Jeżeli świecznik postawisz w jej serce,
Jeszcze świeżością barwy znęci oczy,
Jeszcze na ścianach pałacu roztoczy
Kraśne, acz nieco przyćmione kobierce.

Gdybym był zdolny własne ognie przelać
W piersi słuchaczów i wskrzesić postaci
Zmarłej przeszłości; gdybym umiał strzelać
Brzmiącymi słowy do serca spółbraci:
Może by jeszcze w tej jedynej chwili,
Kiedy ich piosnka ojczysta poruszy,
Uczuli w sobie dawne serca bicie,
Uczuli w sobie dawną wielkość duszy
I chwilę jednę tak górnie przeżyli,
Jak ich przodkowie niegdyś całe życie.
Lecz po co zbiegłe wywoływać wieki?
I swoich czasów śpiewak nie obwini,
Bo jest mąż wielki, żywy, niedaleki,
O nim zaśpiewam, uczcie się, Litwini!

Umilknął starzec i dokoła słucha,
Czy Niemcy dalej pozwolą mu śpiewać;
W sali dokoła była cichość głucha,
Ta zwykła wieszczów na nowo zagrzewać.
Zaczął więc piosnkę, ale innej treści,
Bo głos na spadki wolniejsze rozmierzał,
Po strunach słabiej i rzadziej uderzał
I z hymnu zstąpił do prostej powieści.

[1828] [*Warszawa: Czytelnik, 1994*]

As homes the wearied dove upon spent wings.
In listless hands the lute no longer rings;
Seldom the voice of old can I divine
Through Lithuanian lips, that but repine.
But still the sparks of youthful ardor glow
Deep in my breast, and often kindle there
The flames that warm my soul and brighter show
The scenes of old. For memory, like a rare
Crystalline globe of intricate design,
Though filmed with dust and scratches, if one set
A candle in its heart, again will shine
With limpid color; once again will throw
On palace walls a fair and delicate net,
Though somewhat blurred and darkened, radiant yet.
If only I could pour out mine own fire
Into my hearers' breasts; could I inspire
A second life in phantoms of old time;
Could I but pierce with ringing shafts of rhyme
My brothers' hearts – in that one moment when
Their fathers' song aroused them, they might know
The ancient stirring of the heart, the old
Elation of the soul; one moment then
Might they be lifted up, as free and bold
As lived and died their fathers, long ago.
But why for ages that are vanished yearn?
The bard will not belittle his own day;
A hero liveth yet, not far away:
Of him I sing – ye men of Litwa, learn!

The old man hushed his lute, and paused to see
Whether the Germans would forbid that song;
The thrall of silence held the knightly throng,
Silence, more eloquent than praise can be.
So he began anew; the story ran
In slower cadences, of other things;
With faint, infrequent chords he smote the strings;
Ended the hymn, a simple tale began.

[1828] [*Translated by Jewell Parish, Dorothea Prall Radin,*
George Rapall Noyes and Others. Berkeley:
U of California P, 1925]

III.i.2. ADAM MICKIEWICZ, *Pan Tadeusz*, Book XI

'Rok 1812'

O roku ów! kto ciebie widział w naszym kraju!
Ciebie lud zowie dotąd rokiem urodzaju,
A żołnierz rokiem wojny; dotąd lubią starzy
O tobie bajać, dotąd pieśń o tobie marzy.
Z dawna byłeś niebieskim oznajmiony cudem
I poprzedzony głuchą wieścią między ludem;
Ogarnęło Litwinów serca z wiosny słońcem
Jakieś dziwne przeczucie, jak przed świata końcem,
Jakieś oczekiwanie tęskne i radośne.

Kiedy pierwszy raz bydło wygnano na wiosnę,
Uważano, że chociaż zgłodniałe i chude,
Nie biegło na ruń, co już umaiła grudę,
Lecz kładło się na rolę i schyliwszy głowy,
Ryczało albo żuło swój pokarm zimowy.

I wieśniacy ciągnący na jarzynę pługi
Nie cieszą się, jak zwykle, z końca zimy długiej,
Nie śpiewają piosenek, pracują leniwo,
Jakby nie pamiętali na zasiew i żniwo.
Co krok wstrzymują woły i podjezdki w bronie
I poglądają z trwogą ku zachodniej stronie,
Jakby z tej strony miał się objawić cud jaki,
I uważają z trwogą wracające ptaki.
Bo już bocian przyleciał do rodzinnej sosny
I rozpiął skrzydła białe, wczesny sztandar wiosny;
A za nim, krzykliwymi nadciągnąwszy pułki,
Gromadziły się ponad wodami jaskółki
I z ziemi zmarzłej brały błoto na swe domki.
W wieczor słychać w zaroślach szept ciągnącej słomki,
I stada dzikich gęsi szumią ponad lasem,
I znużone na popas spadają z hałasem,
A w głębi ciemnej nieba wciąż jęczą żurawie.
Słysząc to nocni stróże pytają w obawie,
Skąd w królestwie skrzydlatym tyle zamieszania,
Jaka burza te ptaki tak wcześnie wygania.

Aż oto nowe stada, jakby gilów, siewek
I szpaków, stada jasnych kit i chorągiewek
Zajaśniały na wzgórkach, spadają na błonie.
Konnica! dziwne stroje, nie widziane bronie,
Pułk za pułkiem, a środkiem, jak stopione śniegi,
Płyną drogami kute żelazem szeregi;

III.i.2.   ADAM MICKIEWICZ, from *Pan Tadeusz,* Book XI

'Year 1812'

O year of years! And to have seen thee there!
The people call thee still the harvest year,
The soldiers year of war; the old men long
To tell of thee, and poets dream in song.
By heavenly signs thou wast long heralded,
And rumour vague among the people spread;
The hearts of Lithuanians in that Lent
Were filled with strange presentiment,
As though the ending of the world were nigh,
With joy and yearning and expectancy.

When first the cows were driven from the shed,
Men noticed that, thought hungry and ill-fed,
They did not run out to the winter corn,
That with its greenness did the fields adorn,
But lay with drooping heads upon the mead,
And lowed or listless chewed the winter feed.

Nor did the peasants, as they drove the plough,
Rejoice to see the winter ending now,
And working lazily they sang no rhyme,
As though forgetting seed and harvest time.
The harrower checked his horse at every pace,
And anxious looked towards the western space,
As if he hoped some portent to discern,
And anxiously they watched the birds return.
The stork had flown already to his pine,
Spreading white wings – of spring the early sign.
And then the noisy regiments of swallow,
That gathered o'er the waters, soon did follow,
Collecting for their houses frozen mud.
At eve the woodcocks whispered in the wood,
And flocks of wild geese o'er the forest whirred,
And settling noisily to rest were heard.
The cranes were clamouring in the dark o'erhead,
Whereat the watchman asked in tones of dread,
Whence came such chaos to the winged domain,
What storm had brought the birds so soon again.

And now like flocks of starling, finch and plover
New flocks of pennons and bright plumes came over,
Shone on the hills and to the plains dropped down.
Horsemen! strange uniforms and arms unknown,
Regiment on regiment by every road,

Z lasów czernią się czapki, rzęd bagnetów błyska,
Roją się nieźliczone piechoty mrowiska.

Wszyscy na północ: rzekłbyś, iż wonczas zwyraju
Za ptastwem i lud ruszył do naszego kraju,
Pędzony niepojętą, instynktową mocą.
Konie, ludzie, armaty, orły dniem i nocą
Płyną; na niebie gorą tu i ówdzie łuny,
Ziemia drży, słychać, biją stronami pioruny. –

Wojna! wojna! Nie było w Litwie kąta ziemi,
Gdzie by jej huk nie doszedł; pomiędzy ciemnemi
Puszczami chłop, którego dziady i rodzice
Pomarli, nie wyjrzawszy za lasu granice,
Który innych na niebie nie rozumiał krzyków
Prócz wichrów, a na ziemi prócz bestyi ryków,
Gości innych nie widział oprócz spółleśników –
Teraz widzi: na niebie dziwna łuna pała,
W puszczy łoskot, to kula od jakiegoś działa,
Zbłądziwszy z pola bitwy, dróg w lesie szukała,
Rwąc pnie, siekąc gałęzie. Żubr, brodacz sędziwy,
Zadrżał we mchu, najeżył długie włosie grzywy,
Wstaje na wpół, na przednich nogach się opiera
I potrząsając brodą, zdziwiony spoziera
Na błyskające nagle między łomem zgliszcze:
Był to zbłąkany granat, kręci się, wre, świszcze,
Pękł z hukiem jakby piorun; żubr pierwszy raz w życiu
Zląkł się i uciekł w głębszym schować się ukryciu.

Bitwa! gdzie? w której stronie? pytają młodzieńce,
Chwytają broń; kobiety wznoszą w niebo ręce;
Wszyscy pewni zwycięstwa, wołają ze łzami:
«Bóg jest z Napoleonem, Napoleon z nami!»
O wiosno! kto cię widział wtenczas w naszym kraju,
Pamiętna wiosno wojny, wiosno urodzaju!
O wiosno, kto cię widział, jak byłaś kwitnąca
Zbożami i trawami, a ludźmi błyszcząca,
Obfita we zdarzenia, nadzieją brzemienna!
Ja ciebie dotąd widzę, piękna maro senna!
Urodzony w niewoli, okuty w powiciu,
Ja tylko jedną taką wiosnę miałem w życiu.

[1834] [*Edited by Zbigniew Jerzy Nowak. Warszawa: Czytelnik, 1995*]

Like melted snow the iron-shod column flowed,
Caps darkened from the woods and bayonets gleamed,
And infantry like ants unnumbered streamed.

And all were going north; they seemed to come
Behind the birds from some far sunny home,
As if by instinct driven in their flight.

Men, horses, arms and eagles day and night
Flowed on; the sky glowed with a fiery glare,
Earth shook, and there was thunder everywhere.

War! War! On every side the roar of war
Through all the land of Lithuania!
The clamour reached the innermost recess:
The peasant in the darkest wilderness,
Whose ancestors and kin had lived and died
And never seen beyond the forest side,
Who knew no other voices in the skies
Than of the winds, on earth than wild beasts' cries,
To whom no guests save forest dwellers came,
Now saw the sky with fearful fire aflame –
And then a crash – a cannon ball had strayed
And tearing up the trees a path had made.
The bearded bison in his mossy lair
Trembled, and bristled up his shaggy hair.
Half standing and upon his hind legs raised,
He shook his hoary beard, and saw amazed
The glittering sparks that in the brushwood fell –
It was a twirling, whirling, hissing shell,
That went off with a roar; the first time then
He was afraid, and sought a deeper den.

A battle! Where? The young men asked, which way?
And seized their arms, while women turned to pray;
And everyone was sure of victory,
With tears of joy shouting continually:
'Napoleon shall be victorious,
God with Napoleon, and he with us!'

O spring of springs! Who could forget that spring,
That spring of war, that spring of harvesting.
Who could forget how thou dist blossom then
With corn and grass and glittering of men,
Abounding in events and with hope teeming!
I see thee still, fair phantom of my dreaming!
In slavery born and bound in swaddling chain,
I never saw a spring like that again.

[1834] [*Translated by Kenneth Mackenzie. New York: Hioppocrene, 1992*]

517

III.i.3. JULIUSZ SŁOWACKI, *Kordian,* Act III. Scene iv

Podchorąży

W przeszłość patrzę ciemną
I widzę cień kobiety w żałobie – kto ona?
Patrzę w przyszłość – i widzę tysiąc gwiazd przede mną,
A cień przeszłości ku nim wyciąga ramiona;
Te gwiazdy to sztylety... Kraj nasz dawny widzę.
Mądrość rządców na starém zaszczepiła drzewie
Kraj młody, oba kwitły na jednéj łodydze,
Jako dwie róże barwą różne w jednym krzewie.
Jak dwaj równi rycerze w jednakowéj zbroi
Chodzili pierś przy piersi z wrogiem staczać bitwy...
Jako dwie w łonie Boga tonące modlitwy
Jedną natchnięte myślą – jak dwa pszczelnych roi,
Które pasiecznik zlewa w jednych ulów ściany...
Onego czasu! wielkie południa Tytany
Powstali przeciw Bogu – królom – i niewoli.
Bóg uśmiechnął się tylko na tronie szafirów,
Lecz króle padły na kształt zrąbanéj topoli;
Gilotyna okryta łachmanami kirów,
Niezmordowana, ręką wahała stalową,
A ilekroć skinęła, tłum umniejszał głową.
I widzieli ją króle, bo ta gilotyna
Była tragedią ludu, a króle widzami.
Więc zemsta! Nierządnica i car Katarzyna,
Zabijające oko trzymała nad nami;
Osądziła nas wartych męczeńskiego wieńca,
Wymyśliła męczeństwo... Wziąwszy czaszkę spadłą
Z Burbońskiego tułowu – krwawą i pobladłą,
Wsadziła ją na tułów swego oblubieńca
I dała nam za króla, króla z trupią głową.
Potém spod niego kradła dziedzinę grobową,
A on ręką nie ruszył... I nie stało kiru
Na szatę matki naszéj, więc w troje pocięto.
A dziś – zapytaj mewy lecącéj z Sybiru,
Ilu w kopalniach jęczy? a ilu wyrżnięto?
A ilu przedzierżgniono w zdrajców i skalano?
A wszystkich nas łańcuchem z trupem powiązano,
Bo ta ziemia jest trupem. Brat się wściekł carowi,
Więc go rzucił na Polskę, niech pianą zaraża!
Zębem wściekłym rozrywa. Mściciclc! spiskowi!
Gdy car wkładał koronę u stopni ołtarza,
Trzeba go było jasnym państwa mieczem zgładzić,
I pogrzebać w kościele i kościół wykadzić
Jak od dżumy tureckiéj i drzwi zamurować,

III.i.3.   JULIUSZ SŁOWACKI, from *Kordian,* Act III. Scene iv

Officer Cadet

I look into the dark days gone by
And see a shade of a woman in black – who is she?
I look into the future – one thousand stars I see,
The shade of the past stretches its arms to them high;
Those stars are stilettos . . . I see our ancient land.
The wise rulers had implanted on the old tree
A new land, both blossomed on one stem and they stand
Like two roses on one bush, their colors vary.
Like two equal knights wearing similar armor
Who march side by side to battle the enemy . . .
Like two prayers that sink in the bosom of the Savior,
Inspired by one thought – like two hives in one colony,
Which a beekeeper mingles inside the same walls . . .
Some time ago grand Titans of the south arose
Against the Lord – against kings – against slavery.
The Lord merely gave a smile on his sapphire throne.
But the kings fell down like a cut down poplar tree;
The guillotine, with the tatters of shrouds spread on,
Indefatigable, swung with its arm of steel,
And every time it waved, one head in the crowd would reel.
And the kings would see it, because that guillotine
Was tragedy for people, and the kings – spectators.
Then revenge! That harlot and empress Catherine
Kept her murderous eye upon our citizens;
She judged that we were worthy of the martyr's crown,
She devised a torture . . . She took a head that rolled down
From a Bourbon's body – pallid, covered with gore,
And put it on the body of her paramour,
Giving us for the king, the king with the dead man's pate.
Then she stole from under him the burial estate,
And he didn't move a finger . . . Not enough crape around
For our mother's robe, so it was cut up three ways.
And just now – ask a seagull from Siberia outbound,
How many millions in mines? How many killed these days?
And how many were turned into traitors and stained?
As all of us to a dead body have been chained,
For this land is a corpse. Tsar's brother in madness roars,
So he is sent to Poland, let his froth poison!
He bites with his rabid teeth. Avengers! Conspirators!
When tsar put on the crown at the altar steps thereon,
You should have slaved him with the bright sword of the state,
Bury him in the church, and the church fumigate
As if after Turkish pestilence, then brick the door,

I rzec: o Boże, racz się nad grzesznym zmiłować!...
To wszystko – i nic więcéj... Teraz car za stołem,
Satrapy nasze korni pokładli się czołem,
Win tryskają brylanty z kielichów tysiąca,
I palą się pochodnie, a muzyka grzmiąca
Gipsy ze ścian oprósza. Kobiety dokoła
Rozkwitłe, świeże, wonne jak Saronu róże,
Na rossyjskich ramionach opierają czoła.
silnie
Idźmy tam... i wypalmy ogniami na murze
Wyrok zemsty, zniszczenia, wyrok Baltazara.
Carowi nie dopita z rąk wypadnie czara,
Błękitnym blaskiem mieczów napisane słowa,
Wytłómaczy śmierć mędrsza niż głos Danijela.
A potém kraj nasz wolny! potém jasność dniowa!
Polska się granicami ku morzom rozstrzela,
I po burzliwéj nocy oddycha i żyje.
Żyje! czy temu słowu zajrzeliście w duszę?
Nie wiem... w tém jedném słowie jakieś serce bije,
Rozbieram je na dźwięki, na litery kruszę,
I w każdym dźwięku słyszę głos cały ogromny!
Dzień naszej zemsty będzie wielki – wiekopomny!
A dzień pierwszy wolności, gdy radość roznieci,
Ludzie wesela krzykiem o niebo uderzą,
A potém długą ciemność niewoli przemierzą,
Siądą... i z wielkiém łkaniem zapłaczą jak dzieci,
I słychać będzie płacz ogromny zmartwychwstan.

[1834] [*Edited by Michael J. Mikoś. Lublin: Norbertinum, 1999*]

j. PORTUGUÊS

III.j.1.   ALEXANDRE HERCULANO, *História de Portugal*, «Introdução»

[...]

Pelo meado do século XVI, a idea, contraria aos factos, de que existia certa espécie de unidade nacional entre a nação portuguesa e uma ou mais tribus dos celtas hespanhoes conhecidos pelo nome de lusitanos estava fortemente radicada entre os escríptores, que ahaviam recebido sem exame, lisonjeados com o lustre que criam vinha á sua pátria deste parentesco, tão nobre pelo remoto como pelas façanhas daquelles guerreiros selvagens que tomavam por avós. Para bem conhecer que foi o gosto da erudição clássica que fez remontar a nossa historia a eras e a povos que nella naturalmente não cabiam, e *que, porventura, a supposta convenięncia de substituir um nome conhecido entre os escriptores da idade áurea ao nome latino-barbaro dos portucalenses tem legado aos que tractam da historia portuguesa o improbo e inútil trabalho de encher grossos volumes com os successos reaes ou imaginários de uma successào de séculos anteriores á existęncia da nação; para bem conhecer,* dizemos, quanto a violenta associação de que falamos foi devida

520

And say: 'O Lord! Mercy for the sinner we implore! . . .'
       That's all – and nothing more . . . Now the tsar at the table,
Our satraps bow down before him, most humble,
Wines sparkle with diamonds from thousands of goblets
The torches are aglow, and loud music that spreads
Shakes off plaster from the walls. The women all along
In blossom, fresh, fragrant like roses of Sharon,
Rest their heads on Russian shoulders in this merriment.
             strongly
Let's go there . . . and let's burn out with fires on the wall
The judgment of revenge, ruin, Balthazar's judgment.
The unfinished goblet in the tsar's hand will fall,
The words written with swords in a bluish light ray
Will be explained by death, wiser than Daniel's decrees.
And then our land will be free! Then the light of day!
Poland's frontiers will spread out far towards the seas
And after a stormy night it breathes and has life.
It has life! Did you look into this word's essence?
I don't know . . . in this one word a heart beats in strife,
   I take its sounds apart, break letters into fragments,
And in each sound I hear a voice that's stupendous!
The day of our revenge will be grand – momentous!
When the first day of freedom will kindle merriment,
Joyous cries of people will resound to heaven,
And all will think over their long night of enslavement,
They will sit . . . and will burst into tears like children,
The loud cry of resurrection will be heard then.

    [1834] [*Edited and translated by Michael J. Mikoś. Lublin: Norbertinum, 1999*]

j. PORTUGUESE

III.j.1. ALEXANDRE HERCULANO, Introduction to *The History of Portugal*

[. . .]

By the mid-XVI century, Portuguese historians tended to believe, against all evidence to the contrary, that Portugal and the Celtic Spanish tribes known as *lusitanos* shared a common history. The Portuguese were flattered by the prestige of such a noble kinship, accepting the tribes' long history as their own and the tribes' savage warriors as their ancestors. Because of these historians' groundless pride, contemporary historians are left with lengthy but worthless historical volumes inspired by the imagination but lacking in true scholarship. [. . .][1]

    This false conflation of national identities has its roots in the Renaissance when renewed interest in classical studies – as well as the invention of the printing press – caused a burgeoning

---

[1] The corresponding passage marked in italics in the Portuguese has not been included in the English translation.

á influencia exaggerada do renascimento é digno de notar-se, não só o silencio de todo o género de monumentos históricos da nossa idade média acerca desses chamados tempos primitivos, mas também que a denominação latina de *lusitani* só começa a ser-nos applicada no ultimo quartel do século XV, isto é, quando o ardor dos estudos clássicos e a invenção da imprensa tinham feito commum no occidente da Europa a leitura dos historiadores e geographos gregos e romanos. De feito, o mais antigo uso dessa denomínação parece poder collocar-se entre 1460 e 1490. Mestre Mattheus de Pisano, um dos homens mais instruídos daquelle tempo e que fora chamado a Lisboa pela sua erudição latina para escrever nesta lingua a historia da guerra de Ceuta, compôs o seu livro pelos annos de 1460. Ahi, tendo quasi a cada pagina de mencionar os portugueses, constantemente usa da palavra portucalenses, o que mostra quão longe se estava ainda nessa epocha de se julgarem equivalentes as de lusitano e de portuguẹs, não se podendo attribuir este uso constante a ignorância; porque falando do Douro e de Faro, diz ser aquelle um rio celebre e esta uma cidade, ambos da Lusitânia, o que, segundo as divisões da Hespanha romana, as quaes provavelmente Màttheus de Pisano conhecia melhor que as modernas, é de perfeita exacçáo. O primeiro escriptor, conhecido por nós, que usou da palavra *lusitani* paradesignar os portugueses foi o desgraçado bispo d'Evora D. Garcia de Meneses, victima desse mesmo amor exaggerado das cousas romanas que fez triumphar o poder absoluto de D. João II da organisaçáo politica da idade média, e que, em litteratura, levava aquelle prelado a dar aos seus compatrícios o nome colecttivo de uma porção de tribus celtícas da antiga Hespanha. Nas composições, porém, de Henrique Cayado e de Cataldo Siculo, escriptas nos fins do século XV, e nas subsequentes, de Ayres Barbosa,, Pedro Margalho, Góes, Osório, etc,,as palavras *lusitani* e *Lusitânia* tornam-se constantes para representar os portugueses e o seu território. Na língua vulgar o uso destes vocábulos só vem maistarde; todavia, nos fins do século XVI estava de todo generalisado. A idéa do parentescoentre portugueses e lusitanos passava por incontrastavel, e o livro de Resende é, como dissemos, a completa expressão dessa idéa. Todavia ainda isto não bastava: devia vir Fr. Bernardo de Brito para a exaggerar ate o absurdo. Foi o que elle fez nos dous primeiros volumes do grande corpo histórico chamado a *Monarchia Lusitana*. Aproveitando todas as noticias verdadeiras ou fabulosas achadas em escriptores genuínos ou suppostos, e ajunctando a isto alguns que os melhores críticos suppõem da sua lavra, escudado com elles passeou livremente, não só pelas epochas do dominio carthaginẹs e romano na Península, mas ainda pẹlos tempos que reputamos ante-historicos. Tão imbuído estava o bom do monge da intima relação destes differentes tempos e differentes raças, que são expressões suas trívíalissimas as de *Portugal* e *portugueses*, applicadas aos habitantes do occidente da Hespanha, não só no tempo dos celtas e do domínio carthaginês e romano, mas também nas eras fabulosas, que Brito enfeitou com todas as patranhas que lera ou que inventara. Assim a supersticiosa influencia da litteratura clássica veio resumir-se afinal num livro, permitta-se-nos dizẹ-lo, altamente ridiculo.

Mas apesar deste resultado, a idéa que se incarnara na historia era tão uniformemente reproduzida, estava tão inconcussa em todos os espiritos cultivados, casava-se tanto com as nossas pretensoes fidalgas a uma remota antiguidade, achaque trivial em todas as naçõẹs, que essa opinião triumphou até o presente. Quasí nos nossos dias trẹs homens eminentes, cujos serviços ás letras do seu paiz são indisputávcis, sacrificaram a este preconceito de vão orgulho nacional. Pereira de Figueiredo trabalhou largamente em illustrar as suppostas origens portuguesas e, tractando com o devido desprezo os sonhos de Brito, nem por isso deixou de levar as suas indagações até 1400 annos antes de Christo. António Caetano do Amaral, nas suas importantes Memórias sobre a historia das instituições portuguesas não julgou poder esquivar-se a começar

familiarity with Greek and Roman historians and geographers in Western Europe. Historical documents from the Middle Ages are silent about connections between the Portuguese and the *lusitani*; the Latin name *lusitani* was first used for the Portuguese some time between 1460 and 1490. As late as 1460, Master Matteus of Pisano's history of the war in Ceuta demonstrates how far writers were from conflating the *lusitani* with the Portuguese. Master Matteus, a learned Latin scholar, invariably employed the term *portugalenses* rather than *lusitani* when referring to the Portuguese. We must attribute this choice to careful scholarship rather than ignorance, for his understanding of the political and geographical divisions of Lusitania, according to the divisions defined by ancient Roman *Hespanha*, is impeccable. The first writer known to use the term *lusitani* for the Portuguese is the unfortunate bishop of Évora, D. Garcia de Meneses, whose excessive love of Roman culture caused him to christen his countrymen with the collective name of the Celtic tribes of ancient *Hespanha*. This same enthusiasm for Roman culture led to the defeat of medieval political structures and the triumph of D. João II's absolute power in Renaissance Portugal.

By the late fifteenth century, Henrique Cayado and Cataldo Siculo consistently employed *lusitani* and *Lusitania* to refer to the Portuguese and their territory. Ayres Barbosa, Pedro Margalho, Goes, Osorio and other writers continued this tradition into the sixteenth century, and by the end of the century, the terms were part of common parlance. Finally, in the seventeenth century, Friar Bernardo de Brito exaggerated the kinship between the Portuguese and *lusitanos* to the point of absurdity in the first three volumes of his historical tome, *Monarchia Lusitania*. He gleaned information for his history from both authentic and more questionable sources, and many critics believe that much of the history is completely fabricated. The good friar was so sure of the intimate relation between the two cultures that he included ancient tales and fictitious stories to explain the connection from what he called 'pre-historical' times to the age of the Celts and the ages of Carthaginian and Roman rule on the Iberian Peninsula. In each of these pre-historical and historical ages, he uses the terms *Portugal* and *portugalenses* to name the western region of *Hespanha* and its inhabitants.

Despite the ridiculous result of a trend that began with Meneses' love of classical literature, the common history of the Portuguese and the *lusitani* was so ingrained in scholarship, and the idea so well matched with our desire for a long and noble history, that it has prevailed until just recently. Three eminent contemporary scholars have even helped to perpetuate this unfounded national pride. Pereira de Figueiredo tried to rectify some of Brito's mistakes, but his research of history before 1400 BC is still dubious; Antonio Caetano do Amaral's important *Memoires* give an historical account of Portuguese institutions beginning with the laws and culture of the ancient *lusitanos*; and Mello Freire, joining those historians who weave Portuguese genealogy from Noah's son Tubal, begins his otherwise excellent history of Portuguese jurisprudence by

por expor-nos as leis, usos e costumes dos lusitanos desde que as guerras dos carthagineses e dos romanos os tornaram mais conhecidos. Mello Freire, posto que motejasse os historiadores que tinham remontado a Tubal, o filho de Noé, para tecerem a genealogia da nação portuguesa, lá foi na sua historia da nossa jurisprudęncia indagar o, direito publico e privado da Lusitânia antes e depois da conquista romana para d'ahi começar o seu aliás excellente livro. Finalmente a opinião, de que somos os successores e representantes dos lusitanos não só se firmou e perpetuou entre os eruditos, mas também se tornou por fim uma crença nacional e quasi popular que difficultosamente se poderá desarreigar do commum dos espiritos.

Rejeitando do nosso trabalho, como estranha a elle, a historia de todas as raças ousociedades de qualquer parte da Hespanha anteriores á existencia da nação portuguesa como individuo político, cumpria que nos fizéssemos cargo do systema até aqui recebido e que expuséssemos preliminarmente as considerações que nos obrigam a limitar-nos ao que é rigorosamente historia de Portugal, que mais progressos houvera porventura feito, se não se tivessem malbaratado tantos estudos e tantos talentos históricos verdadeiros em averiguações, não diremos absolutamente ociosas, mas, pelo menos, inúteis para illustra as recordações daquelles que devemos em realidade considerar como nossos maiores.

A palavra nação representa uma idéa complexa. Aggregações de homens ligados porertas condições, todas as sociedades humanas se distinguem entre si por caracteres que determinam a existęncia individual desses corpos moraes. Muitos e diversos são estes caracteres, que podem variar de uns para outros povos; mas ha tręs pęlos quaes commummente se aprecia a unidade ou identidade nacional de diversas gerações successivas. São elles – a raça – a língua – o território. Onde falta a filiação das grandes famílias humanas suppõe-se ficar servindo de laço entre os homens de epochas diversas a semelhança de língua e o haverem nascido debaixo do mesmo céu, cultivado os mesmos campos, vertido o sangue na defesa da pátria commum. E na verdade, fora destas tręs condições, a nação moderna sente-se tão perfeitamente estranha á nação antiga como á que nas mais longínquas regiões vive afastada della.

Todavia estes caracteres não têem um valor real senão á luz histórica. A distíncçáo entre as sociedades humanas funda-se, como todos sabem, em circunstâncias muitas vezes diversas destas. É, porém, historicamente que nós consideramos a filiação portuguesa, e é por isso que nos importa indagar se entre ella e um dos povos ou uma das tribus que habitaram outrora na Hespanha existe um ou mais desses pontos de contacto, que nos obriguem a ir entroncar a nossa, historia em successos que nos parecem inteiramente alheios a ella. Na especialidade que nos interessa, o povo desde o qual os historiadores tęem tecido a genealogia portuguesa está achado – é o dos lusitanos. Na opinião desses escriptores, através de todas as phases politicas e sociaes da Hespanha, durante mais de tręs mil annos, aquella raça de celtas soube sempre, como Anteu, erguer-se viva e forte, reproduzir-se immortal na sua essęncia, e nós os portugueses do século XIX temos a honra de ser os seus legítimos herdeiros e representantes. Pede a boa ordem que principiemos qual era esta gloriosa raça de antepassados nossos e os territórios que habitava, para depois vermos se, no caso de não existir entre ella e nós ao menos a comunidade de território, subsistem as relações mais características de família e de língua.

[. . .]

[1846]

questioning Lusitania's Public and Private Law before and after Roman conquest. The notion that the Portuguese are descendants of the *lusitanos* was not only perpetuated among scholars, but has evolved into a folk tradition that will be difficult for the general public to renounce.

Contemporary Portuguese historians must reject the history of races and societies of any part of *Hespanha* previous to the emergence of the Portuguese nation as a separate political entity; however, we must also acknowledge our fabricated historical tradition and begin the present historical project by rigorously circumscribing what constitutes the history of the Portuguese nation. This project would have progressed further already had not so much good historical talent been wasted on research that is worthless for remembering the truly great leaders in Portuguese history.

We must begin then by defining the complex idea behind the word 'nation.' While societies are differentiated by different elements throughout history, three characteristics by which the identity of a unified nation is defined across the ages are race, language, and territory. Even when race fails to be a defining national characteristic, peoples are often unified by common language and a common sense of homeland. Other than these three aspects, the modern idea of nation has very little in common with more ancient ideas of nationhood, and even these aspects are only valuable as modern tools for simplifying the impossibly complex conditions under which societies and nations develop. Nonetheless, since we must consider the Portuguese nation historically, it is relevant to question whether the Portuguese had any of these three aspects in common with other peoples or tribes of ancient *Hespanha*. Previous historians have shown that the Portuguese are legitimate heirs and representatives of the ancient tribes of *lusitanos*; according to these historians, the spirit of the *lusitanos* remained firm and strong like Antheus[2] throughout the various social and political phases of *Hespanha* and over the course of over three thousand years. This study will commence, then, with a comparison between the race, language, and territory of the ancient *lusitanos* and of historical Portugal to determine to what extent the traditional connection between the two cultures is legitimate.

> [1846] [*Edited by David Lopes, Livrarias Aillaud & Bertrand (Paris, Lisboa) and Livraria Francisco Alves (Rio de Janeiro, S. Paulo, Belo Horizonte), no date*]

---

[2] Mythical giant, ferocious and defeated only by Hercules.

III.j.2. ALEXANDRE HERCULANO, *História de Portugal*,
«Prefácio à 3ª edição»

Quando há dezesete annos publiquei a primeira edição deste volume destinava o encetado trabalho para estudo de um príncipe, então na puerícia, que em futuro remoto, quanto a incerteza das cousas humanas permittia ajuizá-lo, devia reinar em Portugal. Persuadido de que o conhecimento da vida anterior de uma nação é o principal auxilio para se poder e saber usar, sem offensa dos bons principios, do influxo que um rei de homens livres tem forçosamente nos destinos do seu paiz, temperando as generosas, mas nem sempre esclarecidas e prudentes aspirações do progresso pela experiencia e sabedoria de um passado que também já foi progresso, pagava assim ao filho uma divida que contrahira com o pae. Fora a este que eu devera uma situação exempta de pesados encargos, a qual me tornara possível dedicar a maior e melhor parte do tempo ao duro e longo lavor que hoje exige a composição da historia. Entendi e ainda entendo que, trabalhando desse modo para o bem do herdeiro da coroa e, virtualmente, para o bem da terra em que nascera, ava um documento, ao mesmo tempo de gratidão e de patriotismo, mais efficaz do que odos os protestos estéreis com que muitos costumam saldar dividas de uma e de outra ordem. No vigor da idade, povoado o espirito dos sonhos dourados da ambição litteraria, único dos vãos ídolos do mundo a que fiz sacrifícios, habituado ao trabalho preserverante que conquista o pão, e dispensado, emfim, de pensar e adquirir este, podia applicar tempo e hábitos a pagar uma divida e, conjunctamente, a satisfazer uma ambição que hoje me faz sorrir. Excedendo pouco a idade de trinta annos quando delineei os primeiros raços de uma empreza ousada, dotado de organização robusta, medindo os horizontes da existencia não tanto pelo compasso dos annos, como pela intensidade dos esforços de que me sentia capaz, se duvidei de que chegasse a completar o edifício cujos alicerces lançava, tinha firme fé em que ela subiria a uma altura na qual fosse comparativamente fácil a outrem pôr-lhe o remate. Tal foi a origem deste livro. A sua sorte, porém, devia ser diversa da que eu previra.

A publicação da Historia de Portugal tinha chegado ao quarto volume, e as matérias para o quinto, que completava o quadro da primeira epocha da monarchia estavam em parte colligidas. Aobra fizera ruído e suscitara animadversão daqueles que querem accommodar a historia ás crendices do vulgo, ás preocupações nacionais, aos interesses que nellas se estribam, e não corrigir e alluminar o presente pelas licções da história. As repetidas e variadas agressões contra o livro e ainda mais contra auctor denunciavam, em geral, a existencia e os intuitos de uma parcialidade irritada, cujos membros procediam de accordo e cujos interesses a nova publicação viera accidentalmente ferir. Provocado injustamente, repelli essas agressões, porventura com demasiada dureza, e descubrindo nellas um pensamento anti-liberal, fui mais longe. Ao livro sem intenção política fiz seguir um que a tinha. Vendo no partido que engrossara a occultas e que, antigo, se recompusera com elementos novos, um perigo para a sociedade, trouxe á luz uma das mais negras páginas da sua genealogia, pagina que, se não é o seu eterno remorso, há-de ser a sua eterna condemnação perante Deus e os homens. Os tres volumes da *Historia do Estabelecimento da Inquisição* provaram, sem réplica possível, uma verdade importante para a solução da lucta que agita a Europa; provaram que o fanatismo ardente e ainda a simples exaggeração do sentimento religioso são mais raros do que se cuida e que o vulgar é a hypocrisia, de todos os fructos da perversão humana o que mais severamente foi condemnado pelo divino

III.j.2.   ALEXANDRE HERCULANO, Foreword to the 3rd Edition of
The History of Portugal

Foreword

[*The excerpt from the 3rd edition, as reproduced in the fourth, and the 4th edition's foreword allow us to grasp Herculano's own relation to his magnum opus, its immediate reception, and the connection between his work and that of other Romantic historians across Europe.*]

When I published the first edition of this volume seventeen years ago, I intended it to be studied by a Prince who was then still very young, but would someday be the ruler of Portugal. Persuaded that an understanding of a nation's history is, without disregard for good principles, a king's primary tool for knowing how to guide his nation's destiny by moderating progressive aspirations with the experience and wisdom of the past, I thought of my work as paying to the son a debt I had with his father. It was the father who granted me a situation that permitted me to dedicate the longest and finest portion of my time to the long, hard work of composing a history of Portugal. I thought then, as I still do, that by working for the good of the king's heir, I was also working for the good of my homeland while providing a document of more gratitude and patriotism than the formal ways in which debts are usually paid to the king.

In the vigour of youth, with my spirit filled with dreams of literary accomplishment (the sole of the world's vain idols to which I paid tribute) but a body used to working for its sustenance, the king freed me from my hard labour to realize a literary ambition that today makes me smile. I was just over thirty years of age when I first drafted the outline of this bold enterprise. Endowed with an enthusiasm that measured the horizons of existence not by the succession of years but by the intensity of the efforts I felt myself capable of, if ever I doubted my ability to finish the building whose foundations I was laying, I had faith that I would at least raise it to a dimension that would make it easy for others to complete. The project's fortune, however, would be other than I anticipated.

The *History of Portugal* had reached its fourth volume, with the fifth (which would complete the first period of monarchy) well under way, when I detected the need to continue my book with an overt political purpose. The published volumes had aroused vigorous opposition from those who wished to accommodate history to popular beliefs or national interests instead of allowing current issues to be corrected or clarified by lessons from history. The repeated hostility toward the book and its author revealed the existence of an irritated party whose interests were accidentally offended by the new publication. Motivated by what I perceived as anti-liberalism, I continued my book with a new political purpose. From my long study of history, I recognized in this emerging opposition the remnants of an older party who had long ceased to be a danger to society, but whose re-emergence seemed imminent. Hence, I dedicated three volumes to one of the bleakest pages of Portuguese history: the History of the Creation of the Inquisition, which, if it does not prove Portugal's eternal sorrow, will remain Portugal's eternal conviction before God and men.

These three volumes proved that extreme fanaticism and even exaggerated religious feeling are more rare than is usually thought, and that hypocrisy – of all fruits of human sin the most severely condemned by Jesus Christ – is the more typical religious perversion. In my introduction to those volumes I indicated the existence, the nature, the goals, and the behaviour of the reactionaries, and without either exaggerating or hiding anything, I described the risks our free-

fundador do christianismo. Nalgumas linhas que precediam aquelles volumes eu apontava a existęncia, a indole, as miras, o modo de proceder da reacção e, sem os exaggerar, mas também sem os disfarçar, assignalava os riscos que a liberdade corria. Os hábeis, os homens practicos, os estadistas eminentes riram-se. Eu não passava de um visionário. Cinco annos depois a reacção apresentava-se com a face descuberta no campo de batalha, e todos os amigos sinceros da liberdade estavam visionários comigo.

[1853?]

III.j.3. ALEXANDRE HERCULANO, *História de Portugal,*
«Advertência à 4ª edição»

Publicando esta quarta edição do primeiro volume da Historia de Portugal desejaria o auctor proceder previamente a um exame minucioso de centenares de citações de livros impressos, de manuscriptos e de documentos em que a narrativa se estriba, e rectificar quaesquer equivocações ou erros de copia na indicação dos logares onde existem taes manuscriptos e documentos ou onde, nos impressos, se lêem as passagens citadas; erros e equivocações esses que, de futuro, podem tornar enfadonha a comparação dos textos. Para o fazer, porém, ser-lhe-hia necessário frequentar assíduamemente archivos e bíbliothecas urante alguns meses, ao que invencivelmente obsta o teor do seu viver actual. Épor isso que as correcções da presente edição se limitam a pequenas mudanças na forma e estylo da narrativa, e na substituição, addição ou suppressâo de varias passagens que pareceram obscuras, inexactas ou incompletas.

Vindo pela primeira vez á luz publica, o presente volume suscitou vivas polémicas obre a critica das, fontes históricas aproveitadas como legitimas ou rejeitadas como impuras o processo da narração. No meio, porém, dessas discussões ardentes e não raro apaixonadas, nunca se pôs em duvida, a existęncia dos variados monumentos indicados como abonadores das doutrinas do livro. Por este lado nem então, nem agora, o auctor receava ou receia a mínima aggressão fundada, porque tinha e tem a conscięncia da lisura e lealdade com que escreveu. Do que não tem a certeza é de ter sempre interpretado bem os textos obscuros dos monumentos e sabido deduzir delles as verdadeiras illações. Se a vaidade o illudisse nesta parte, os estudos de historia romana de Mommsen depois dos de Niebuhr bastariam para o desiludir. É por isso que desejaria facilitar o exame dos textos pelo rigor da exacção nos algarismos das citações.

A nossa historia, mais ainda do que a de outras nações da Europa, para surgir da sombra das lendas a luz clara da realidade, carece de indagações profundas, e de apreciações sinceras e desinteressadas. Será trabalho mais útil, embora mais difficil, do que certas generalisações e philosophias da historia, hoje de moda, em que se generalisa o erróneo ou o incerto, e se tiram conclusões absolutas de factos que se reputam conformes entre si, e que, provavelmente, mais de uma vez os estudos sérios virão mostrar serem diversos, quando não contrarios. A poesia onde não cabe; a poesia na sciencia é absurda. A imaginativa tem mais próprios objectos da sua fecundidade.

[1875]

dom was again facing because of them.[3] Gifted men, practical men, and statesmen alike laughed and called me but a visionary. Five years later, however, when the reactionaries came forth unmasked and ready to battle liberalism, all the sincere friends of freedom were found to be visionaries like me.[4] [. . .]

[1853?] [*Translated by Carlos Leone and Bethany Smith*]

III.j.3. ALEXANDRE HERCULANO, Foreword to the 4th Edition of
The History of Portugal

For this fourth edition of the first volume of the *History of Portugal*, the author wished o prepare a detailed examination of hundreds of quotations from printed books, manuscripts, and other documents that appear in the *History* to clarify any ambiguities or printing errors regarding where references can be found. To do so, however, I would need to return to archives and libraries for several months, which task my present situation in life prevents. Therefore, corrections in this edition are limited to slight changes in form and style, the elimination or replacement of passages that now seem obscure or inaccurate, and additions to passages that seemed incomplete.

When it first appeared in print, this volume instigated lively polemics about the nature and value of certain historical sources for legitimate scholarship. Amidst these hearty and often passionate discussions, however, there was never a doubt about the existence of documentary evidence for the basic historical principles on which the book is based. I had no fear, as I still do not, that my critics could have any serious basis for rejecting my argument because I had, as I still do, a clear conscience of the straightforwardness and of the fidelity with which I wrote. I am not sure that I have always correctly interpreted historical texts and deduced from them the proper conclusions, but if vanity ever interfered, Mommsen's studies of Roman history, after those of Niebuhr, would be enough to set me straight. I hope that my careful documentation and rigorously cited algorisms will also facilitate the future examination of historical texts.

Our historical tradition, even more than other European nations, needs to be questioned thoroughly in order to separate historical reality from traditional legend. Although a sincere and disinterested study will be more difficult than the more fashionable practice of drawing hasty generalizations and conclusions from poorly examined facts, the results will be more useful and scientific. Poetry where it does not belong is absurd; the imagination has more suited objects than the writing of history.

[1875] [*Translated by Carlos Leone and Bethany Smith*]

---

[3] The 'reactionaries' are those who oppose revolutionary human rights brought about by liberals like Herculano.

[4] [Herculano's note] Today [1875] the reaction already disturbs gravely Europe and threatens Central America.

k. ROMÂNĂ

III.k.1. MIHAI EMINESCU, 'Ce-ţi doresc eu ţie, dulce Românie'

Ce-ţi doresc eu ţie, dulce Românie,
Ţara mea de glorii, ţara mea de dor?
Braţele nervoase, arma de tărie,
La trecutu-ţi mare, mare viitor!
Fiarbă vinu-n cupe, spumege pocalul,
Dacă fiii-ţi mândri aste le nutresc;
Căci rămâne stânca, deşi moare valul,
Dulce Românie, asta ţi-o doresc.

Vis de răzbunare negru ca mormântul
Spada ta de sânge duşman fumegând,
Şi deasupra idrei fluture cu vântul
Visul tău de glorii falnic triumfând,
Spună lumii large steaguri tricoloare,
Spună ce-i poporul mare, românesc,
Când s-aprinde sacru candida-i vâlvoare,
Dulce Românie, asta ţi-o doresc.

Îngerul iubirii, îngerul de pace,
Pe altarul Vestei tainic surâzând,
Ce pe Marte-n glorii să orbească-l face,
Când cu lampa-i zboară lumea luminând,
El pe sânu-ţi vergin încă să coboare,
Guste fericirea raiului ceresc,
Tu îl strânge-n braţe, tu îi fă altare,
Dulce Românie, asta ţi-o doresc.

k. ROMANIAN

III.k.1. MIHAI EMINESCU, 'What I Wish You, Sweet Romanian Land'[1]

What I wish you, homeland, sweet Romanian land,
Land of peerless glory and bold aspiration:
As your mightiest weapon strong and active hands,
For your past, a future worthy of our nation!
Let the wine flow freely, let the goblet sparkle
If such boons are cherished by your children true;
For the cliff shines ever though the wave may darkle,
Sweet Romanian homeland, this I wish to you.

A great dream of vengeance, black as is the grave,
And your broadsword reeking with the blood of foes;
May, above the hydra, in the breezes wave
Your great dream of glory and triumphant blows,
May tricoloured banners,[2] far and wide unfurled,
Tell of what may happen when our mighty nation
Burns with sacred fire, tell to the whole world –
This, o sweet Romania, is my dedication.

May, therefore, Love's angel, Peace's go-between,
Smiling – never proudly – on mild Vesta's shrine,
Dazzle Mars the warlike by his glorious sheen
When his lamp is flying, lightning land and brine,
On your virgin bosom may he still alight,
May he taste the blessings of the heavenly dew,
May you close embrace him, make him altars bright,
Sweet Romanian homeland, this I wish to you.

---

[1] The poem was written one year after the accession to the throne of the German Prince Karl Eitel Friedrich Zephyrinus Ludwig von Hohenzollern-Sigmaringen as Royal Prince of the United Romanian Principalities. Known in Romanian history as Carol I, he became King in 1881. As early as 1866, Carol supported the first Romanian Constitution and played a crucial role in the war against the Ottoman Empire, ending with the 1877 proclamation of independence of the Principalities. During his reign Romanian institutions underwent extensive modernization. What he did on the throne, the militant intellectuals of the '48 and their followers did in writing. Eminescu, a man otherwise of conservative convictions, was obviously delighted by the newly acquired political and civic status of his native land. In wishing it a glowing future to match its glorious past, the poet makes use of the typically Romantic syncretism of religious visions and images (with distinct insistence on Roman mythology), apocalyptic projections and nationalistic rhetoric.

[2] The blue-yellow-red banner, the Romanian national colours, occurs in Romantic paintings illustrating female allegories of the newly founded nation. Such are *Romania Breaking Her Fetters on Liberty Field* and *Revolutionary Romania*, works by the most prominent painter of the 1848 generation, the Jewish artist Rosenthal. Bringing together revolutionary exaltation and female delicacy, they represent personified principles of which, with the tools of poetic imagery, Eminescu himself offers a rich display in his oeuvre.

Ce-ţi doresc eu ţie, dulce Românie,
Tânără mireasă, mamă cu amor!
Fiii tăi trăiască numai în frăţie
Ca a nopţii stele, ca a zilei zori,
Viaţa în vecie, glorii, bucurie,
Arme cu tărie, suflet românesc,
Vis de vitejie, fală şi mândrie,
Dulce Românie, asta ţi-o doresc!

[1867]

III.k.2.   DIMITRIE BOLINTINEANU, 'Muma lui Ştefan Cel Mare'

I

Pe o stâncă neagră, într-un vechi castel,
Unde cură-n poale un râu mititel,
Plânge şi suspină tânăra domniţă,
Dulce şi suavă ca o garofiţă;
Căci în bătălie soţul ei dorit
A plecat cu oastea şi n-a mai venit.
Ochii săi albaştri ard în lacrimele
Cum lucesc în rouă două viorele;
Buclele-i de aur cad pe albu-i sân,
Rozele şi crinii pe faţă-i se-ngân.
Însă doamna soacră lângă ea veghează
Şi cu dulci cuvinte o îmbărbătează.

II

Un orologiu sună noaptea jumătate,
În castel în poartă oare cine bate?
'Eu sunt, bună maică, fiul tău dorit;
Eu, şi de la oaste mă întorc rănit.
Soarta noastră fuse crudă astă dată:
Mica mea oştire fuge sfărâmată.
Dar deschideţi poarta... Turcii mă-nconjor...
Vântul suflă rece... Rănile mă dor!'

III

Tânăra domniţă la fereastră sare.
'Ce faci tu, copilă?' zice doamna mare.

What I wish you deeply, my Romanian land,
Girt with a bride's halo, with a mother's love:
May your sons live ever with ill-feelings banned,
Like the gorgeous daybreak, like the stars above;
Infinite existence, glory, exultation,
The most trustful weapons, a Romanian heart,
Deeds of greatest bravery, honour and elation –
This is what I, dearest, wish you on my part!

[1867] [*Adapted from a translation by Leon Levițchi*]

III.k.2. DIMITRIE BOLINTINEANU, 'Stephen the Great's Mother'[3]

I

On a rugged black rock, in a castle old,
Where a tiny river through the valley rolled,
Was a sobbing princess, whose sad tears did sink
As rain among petals of a sweet soft pink.
Off to a great battle, her husband had gone,
Leading his brave army and left her forlorn.
Her blue eyes they fill now with droplets anew,
As sweet violets' petals are covered with dew.
Golden locks fall over her bosom so white,
Roses and sweet lilies on her brow unite.

II

Suddenly at midnight fearful strikes the clock,
At the castle gate now who doth loudly knock?
'It is I, dear mother, your belovèd son,
I return from battle, but return all done.
Cruel this our fortune for once it hath been:
My outnumbered army is scattered unseen.
Open the gate wide, though, the Turks me surround,
Sore the wounds I suffer, the wind's cold around.'

III

Heading for the window the young princess flies,
'Careful, young lady!', the old queen then cries.

[3] Stephen the Great (1457–1504), prince of the Romanian-speaking historical province of Moldavia, is a central figure in the nineteenth-century construction of national identity. The 'athlete of God', as the Pope in Rome called him at the time, he was a valiant defender of land and faith and stood as a dreaded barrier against the 'fierce Turk'. The Romanian communist regime hijacked him for its own nationalistic purposes. Ironically, in post-communist years he has undergone a process of sanctification and goes by the name of Stephen the Great and the Saint.

Apoi ea la poartă atunci a ieşit.
Şi-n tăcerea nopţii astfel a vorbit:
'Ce spui tu, străine? Ştefan e departe,
Braţul său prin taberi mii de morţi împarte,
Eu sunt a sa mumă; el e fiul meu;
De eşti tu acela, nu-ţi sunt mamă eu!
Însă dacă cerul, vrând să-ngreuieze
Anii vieţii mele şi să mă-ntristeze,
Nobilul său suflet astfel l-a schimbat,
Dacă tu eşti Ştefan cu adevărat,
Apoi tu aice fără biruinţă
Nu poţi ca să intri cu a mea voinţă.
Du-te la oştire! Pentru ţară mori!
Şi-ţi va fi mormântul coronat cu flori!'

IV

Ştefan se întoarce şi din cornu-i sună,
Oastea lui zdrobită de prin văi se-adună.
Lupta iar începe... Duşmanii zdrobiţi
Cad ca nişte spice, de securi loviţi.

[1847]

I. РУССКИЙ

III.l.1. ПЕТР ЧААДАЕВ, «Философические письма», из Письма первого

Народы – в такой же мере существа нравственные, как и отдельные личности. Их воспитывают века, как отдельных людей воспитывают годы. Но мы, можно сказать, некоторым образом – народ исключительный. Мы принадлежим к числу тех наций, которые как бы не входят в состав человечества, а существуют лишь для того, чтобы дать миру какой-нибудь важный урок. Наставление, которое мы призваны преподать, конечно, не будет потеряно; но кто может сказать, когда мы обретем себя среди человечества и сколько бед суждено нам испытать, прежде чем исполнится наше предназначение?

Все народы Европы имеют общую физиономию, некоторое семейное сходство. Вопреки огульному разделению их на латинскую и тевтонскую расы, на южан и северян – все же есть общая связь, соединяющая их всех в одно целое и хорошо видимая всякому, кто поглубже вник в их общую историю. Вы знаете, что еще сравнительно недавно вся Европа называлась христианским миром, и это выражение употреблялось в публичном праве. Кроме общего характера, у каждого из этих народов есть еще свой частный характер, но и тот, и другой всецело сотканы из истории и традиции. Они составляют преемственное идейное наследие этих народов. Каждый отдельный человек пользуется там своею долей этого наследства, без труда и чрезмерных усилий он набирает себе в жизни запас этих знаний и навыков и извлекает из них свою пользу. Сравните сами и скажите, много ли мы находим у себя в повседневном обиходе элементарных идей, которыми могли бы с грехом пополам руководствоваться в жизни? И заметьте, здесь

In the dark of night to the gate she makes way;
To her son in sorrow this speech does she say:
'Mark my words, thou stranger, my Stephen's away,
His brave arm in battle thousands doth it slay.
I to him am mother, he son is to me;
If you be that person, you had better flee.
Should God in his heaven now take me to him,
My years crown with sorrow, my old eyes grow dim,
Should thy soul, so noble, have gone all astray,
Should you be my Stephen, to thee thus I say:
Come you not as victor, come here not at all,
Your will, if it cross mine, shall ne'er stand, but fall!
Go! Go, lead your army, and die for your nation;
Flowers round your tombstone will be your oblation.'

IV

Back into dire battle Stephen blows his horn,
His army re-forms now, that once was forlorn.
Resuming the struggle, their foe is struck down,
As a scythe through wheat-stalks, the hillside is mown.

[1847] [Adapted from a translation by Mihaela Anghelescu Irimia]

1. RUSSIAN

III.1.1. PYOTR CHAADAEV, 'Philosophical Letters', from *Letter the First*

Nations are moral entities, just as individual people are. Nations develop over centuries, while individuals develop over years. But one can say that we are, in some ways, an exceptional nation. Our race appears not to be part of the general run of humankind but exists only to teach some important lesson to the world. The message we exist to convey will not, of course, be lost; but who can say when we shall become part of 'humanity' and how many troubles we shall have to suffer before our destiny is fulfilled?

All the peoples of Europe have a common face, a family likeness. In spite of their alleged separation into the Latin and the Teutonic, into southerners and northerners – there is still a common link that unites them into a single whole, some clue clearly visible to anyone who has searched more deeply into their common history. You know that until quite recently Europe was 'the Christian World', a term used in public law. Within this common fabric each of those nations has its own private strand, all woven together out of history and tradition. These make up the inherited ideological legacy of those nations. Each individual enjoys his share in that legacy; he effortlessly acquires a store of knowledge and life skills. Look at the evidence yourself and tell me where we find in our daily round the many basic ideas which guide us through life. And note that this is not about acquiring knowledge or reading, nor about anything to do with literature or science – it is simply about mental communication, about those ideas which take possession of a child from the cradle, surround him as he plays his childish games and enter him with his

идет речь не о приобретении знаний и не о чтении, не о чем-либо касающемся литературы или науки, а просто о взаимном общении умов, о тех идеях, которые овладевают ребенком в колыбели, окружают его среди детских игр и передаются ему с ласкою матери, которые в виде различных чувств проникают до мозга его костей вместе с воздухом, которым дышит, и создают его нравственное существо еще раньше, чем он вступает в свет и общество. Хотите ли знать, что это за идеи? Это – идеи долга, справедливости, права, порядка. Они родились из самых событий, образовавших там общество, они входят необходимым элементом в социальный уклад этих стран.

Это и составляет атмосферу Запада; это – больше, нежели история, больше чем психология; это – физиология европейского человека. Чем вы замените это у нас? Не знаю, можно ли из сказанного сейчас вывести что-нибудь вполне безусловное и извлечь отсюда какой-либо непреложный принцип; но нельзя не видеть, что такое странное положение народа, мысль которого не примыкает ни к какому ряду идей, постепенно развивавшихся в обществе и медленно выраставших одна из другой, и участие которого в общем поступательном движении человеческого разума ограничивалось лишь слепым, поверхностным и часто неискусным подражанием другим нациям, должно могущественно влиять на дух каждого отдельного человека в этом народе.

Вследствие этого вы найдете, что всем нам недостает известной уверенности, умственной методичности, логики. Западный силлогизм нам незнаком. Наши лучшие умы страдают чем-то большим, нежели простая неосновательность. Лучшие идеи, за отсутствием связи или последовательности, замирают в нашем мозгу и превращаются в бесплодные призраки. Человеку свойственно теряться, когда он не находит способа привести себя в связь с тем, что ему предшествует, и с тем, что за ним следует. Он лишается тогда всякой твердости, всякой уверенности. Не руководимый чувством непрерывности, он видит себя заблудившимся в мире. Такие растерянные люди встречаются во всех странах; у нас же это общая черта. Это вовсе не то легкомыслие, в котором когда-то упрекали французов и которое в сущности представляло собою не что иное, как способность легко усваивать вещи, не исключавшую ни глубины, ни широты ума и вносившую в обращение необыкновенную прелесть и изящество; это – беспечность жизни, лишенной опыта и предвидения, не принимающей в расчет ничего, кроме мимолетного существования особи, оторванной от рода, жизни, не дорожащей ни честью, ни успехами какой-либо системы идей и интересов, ни даже тем родовым наследием и теми бесчисленными предписаниями и перспективами, которые в условиях быта, основанного на памяти прошлого и предусмотрении будущего, составляют и общественную, и частную жизнь. В наших головах нет решительно ничего общего; все в них индивидуально и все шатко и неполно. Мне кажется даже, что в нашем взгляде есть какая-то странная неопределенность, что-то холодное и неуверенное, напоминающее отчасти физиономию тех народов, которые стоят на низших ступенях социальной лестницы. В чужих странах, особенно на юге, где физиономии так выразительны и так оживленны, не раз, сравнивая лица моих соотечественников с лицами туземцев, я поражался этой немотой наших лиц.

Иностранцы ставят нам в достоинство своего рода бесшабашную отвагу, встречаемую особенно в низших слоях народа; но, имея возможность наблюдать лишь отдельные проявления национального характера, они не в состоянии судить о целом. Они не видят, что то же самое начало, благодаря которому мы иногда бываем так отважны, делает нас всегда неспособными к углублению и настойчивости; они не видят, что этому равнодушию

mother's caresses; which penetrate the marrow of his bones together with the air he breathes, creating his moral being even before he enters the world and society. Do you want to know what those ideas are? They are the ideas of duty, justice, law, order. They were formed by the events that shaped each community, they are an integral part of the social pattern.

This is what constitutes the atmosphere of the West; this is more than just history, more than psychology; this is the physiology of the European man. What shall you replace it with in our country? I do not know whether we can derive anything absolute or draw any fundamental principle from what I have said; yet one cannot but see that for a nation whose intellectual capital does not belong to a belief system evolved organically, one idea leading to the next, and whose participation in the general progress of the human mind has been limited to blind, superficial and often clumsy imitation of other nations, this strange situation must have a powerful influence on the spirit of each individual in that nation.

As a consequence, you will find that we all lack a certain confidence, a certain mental rigour or ease with logic. The western syllogism is unfamiliar. Our best intellects suffer from more than mere groundlessness. Our best ideas, for lack of connection or consistency, fade away in our brains and turn to fleshless ghosts. It is common for a human being to get lost when he cannot find a way to connect himself with what comes before or after him. He is deprived then of all firmness, all assurance. Unguided by a sense of continuity, he sees that he is adrift, rudderless. Such confused people can be found everywhere, but in our country they are common. This confusion is not the levity for which the French were once reproached, which was simply the ability to assimilate things easily. Such levity excluded neither depth nor breadth and brought a singular charm and elegance to their discourse. It is instead the void of lives with neither experience nor foresight, lives which take nothing into account save the fleeting existence of an individual torn away from his stock, lives that value neither honour nor success nor even that ancestral inheritance and those numberless prescriptions and perspectives which, when they exist within a culture based on memory of the past and anticipation of the future, constitute both public and private life. The human mind is not general; it is all individual, unsteady, incomplete. It seems to me that even our faces reflect some strange uncertainty, something cold and unconfident, not unlike those of the poor and dispossessed. In other countries, especially in the south, where faces are so expressive and so vivid, not once, comparing the faces of my compatriots with those of the natives, have I been struck by how very numb ours seem.

Foreigners admire our particular kind of reckless bravery, a bravery especially common among our nation's lower classes. Being able, however, to observe only fragmentary manifestations of our national character, they are incapable of judging the whole. They cannot see that the same element that produces this transitory bravery makes us perennially incapable of depth and persistence; they cannot see that this indifference to the vicissitudes of life is matched in us with

к житейским опасностям соответствует в нас такое же полное равнодушие к добру и злу, к истине и ко лжи и что именно это лишает нас всех могущественных стимулов, которые толкают людей по пути совершенствования; они не видят, что именно благодаря этой беспечной отваге даже высшие классы у нас, к прискорбию, не свободны от тех пороков, которые в других странах свойственны лишь самым низшим слоям общества; они не видят, наконец, что, если нам присущи кое-какие добродетели молодых и малоразвитых народов, мы уже не обладаем зато ни одним из достоинств, отличающих народы зрелые и высококультурные.

Я не хочу сказать, конечно, что у нас одни пороки, а у европейских народов одни добродетели; избави Бог! Но я говорю, что для правильного суждения о народах следует изучать общий дух, составляющий их жизненное начало, ибо только он, а не та или иная черта их характера, может вывести их на путь нравственного совершенства и бесконечного развития.

(1836, первоначальный текст по-французски)

III.l.2.   НИКОЛАЙ ГОГОЛЬ, из романа «Мертвые души»

Заключительные абзацы части 1

И в самом деле, Селифан давно уже ехал зажмуря глаза, изредка только потряхивая впросонках вожжами по бокам дремавших тоже лошадей; а с Петрушки уже давно невесть в каком месте слетел картуз, и он сам, опрокинувшись назад, уткнул свою голову в колено Чичикову, так что тот должен был дать ей щелчка. Селифан приободрился и, отшлепавши несколько раз по спине чубарого; после чего тот пустился рысцой, да помахнувши сверху кнутом на всех, примолвил тонким певучим голоском: «Не бойся!» Лошадки расшевелились и понесли, как пух, легонькую бричку. Селифан только помахивал да покрикивал: «Эх! эх! эх!» – плавно подскакивая на козлах, по мере того как тройка то взлетала на пригорок, то неслась духом с пригорка, которыми была усеяна вся столбовая дорога, стремившаяся чуть заметным накатом вниз. Чичиков только улыбался, слегка подлетая на своей кожаной подушке, ибо любил быструю езду. И какой же русский не любит быстрой езды? Его ли душе, стремящейся закружиться, загуляться, сказать иногда: «черт побери все!» – его ли душе не любить ее? Ее ли не любить, когда в ней слышится что-то востороженно-чудное? Кажись, неведомая сила подхватила тебя на крыло к себе, и сам летишь, и все летит: летят версты, летят навстречу купцы на облучках своих кибиток, летит с обеих сторон лес с темными строями елей и сосен, с топорным стуком и вороньим криком, летит вся дорога невесть куда в пропадающую даль, и что-то страшное заключено в сем быстром мельканье, где не успевает означиться пропадающий предмет, – только небо над головою, да легкие тучи, да продирающийся месяц одни кажутся недвижны. Эх, тройка! Птица тройка, кто тебя выдумал? знать, у бойкого народа ты могла только родиться, в той земле, что не любит шутить, а ровнем-гладнем разметнулась на полсвета, да и ступай считать версты, пока не зарябит тебе в очи. И не хитрый, кажись, дорожный снаряд, не железным схвачен винтом, а наскоро живьем с одним топором да долотом снарядил и собрал тебя ярославский расторопный мужик. Не в немецких ботфортах ямщик: борода да рукавицы, и сидит черт знает на чем; а привстал, да замахнулся, да затянул песню – кони вихрем, спицы в колесах смешались в

an equal indifference to good and evil, truth and falsehood. It is precisely this that deprives us of those powerful spurs to improvement; they cannot see that just because of that reckless bravery even our higher classes still, regretfully, cling to those vices which in other countries are only common among the lowest segments of society; finally, they cannot see that, while we share some of the virtues of young and underdeveloped nations, we have none of the advantages that distinguish mature and cultivated ones.

Of course, I do not mean to say that we have only vices and that western nations have only virtues; God forbid! But I do say that to make a right judgment about nations one should study the spirit which animates their way of life, for this alone and no combination of character traits can lead them to moral perfection and infinite development.

(1836, originally written in French) [Translated by Dmitry Usenco]

III.1.2.   NIKOLAI GOGOL, from *Dead Souls*

From the end of Part I

And, indeed, Selifan had for a long time been driving with closed eyes, only occasionally shaking the reins about the sides of the horses who were also dozing; and Petrushka's cap had fallen off long ago, and he had sunk back with his head poking Tchitchikov's legs so that the latter was obliged to give him a nudge. Selifan pulled himself together, and giving the dappled grey a few switches on the back, after which the latter, fell into a trot, and flourishing the whip over them all, cried in a thin sing-song voice: 'Never fear.' The horses bestirred themselves and carried the chaise along as though it were as light as a feather.

Selifan brandished the whip and kept shouting, 'Ech! ech! ech!' smoothly rising up and down on the box, as the three horses darted up or flew like the wind down the little hills which dotted the high road that sloped scarcely perceptibly down hill. Tchitchikov merely smiled as he lightly swayed on his leather cushion, for he loved rapid driving. And what Russian does not love rapid driving? How should his soul that craves to be lost in a whirl, to carouse without stint, to say at times, 'Damnation take it all!' – how should his soul not love it? How not love it when there is a feeling in it of something ecstatic and marvellous? One fancies an unseen force has caught one up on its wing and one flies oneself, and everything flies too: milestones fly by, merchants on the front seats of their tilt-carts fly to meet one, the forest flies on both sides with dark rows of firs and pines, with the ring of the axe and caw of the crows; the whole road flies into the unknown retreating distance; and there is something terrible in this rapid flitting by, in which there is no time to distinguish the vanishing object and only the sky over one's head and the light clouds and the moon that struggles through them seem motionless. Ah! troika, bird of a troika! Who was it first thought of thee? Sure, thou couldst only have been born among a spirited people, – in that land that does not care to do things by halves, but has spread, a vast plain, over half the world, and one may count its milestones till one's eyes are dizzy! And there is nothing elaborate, one would thing, about thy construction; it is not held together by iron screws – no, a deft Yaroslav peasant filled thee up and put thee together, hastily, roughly, with nothing but axe and drill. The driver wears no German top boots: he has a beard and gauntlets, and sits upon goodness knows

один гладкий круг, только дрогнула дорога, да вскрикнул в испуге остановившийся пешеход – и вон она понеслась, понеслась, понеслась!.. И вон уже видно вдали, как что-то пылит и сверлит воздух.

Не так ли и ты, Русь, что бойкая необгонимая тройка несешься? Дымом дымится под тобою дорога, гремят мосты, все отстает и остается позади. Остановился пораженный Божьим чудом созерцатель: не молния ли это, сброшенная с неба? Что значит это наводящее ужас движение? и что за неведомая сила заключена в сих неведомых светом конях? Эх, кони, кони, что за кони! Вихри ли сидят в ваших гривах? Чуткое ли ухо горит во всякой вашей жилке? Заслышали с вышины знакомую песню, дружно и разом напрягли медные груди и, почти не тронув копытами земли, превратились в одни вытянутые линии, летящие по воздуху, и мчится вся вдохновенная Богом!.. Русь, куда ж несешься ты? дай ответ. Не дает ответа. Чудным звоном заливается колокольчик; гремит и становится ветром разорванный в куски воздух; летит мимо все, что ни есть на земле, и, косясь, постораниваются и дают ей дорогу другие народы и государства.

(1842)

Последний абзац части II, большая часть которой была уничтожена
автором и сохранилась только во фрагментах

– Теперь тот самый, у которого в руках участь многих и которого никакие просьбы не в силах были умолить, тот самый бросается теперь к ногам вашим, вас всех просит. Все будет позабыто, изглажено, прощено; я буду сам ходатаем за всех, если исполните мою просьбу. Вот моя просьба. Знаю, что никакими средствами, никакими страхами, никакими наказаньями нельзя искоренить неправды: она слишком уже глубоко вкоренилась. Бесчестное дело брать взятки сделалось необходимостью и потребностью даже и для таких людей, которые и не рождены быть бесчестными. Знаю, что уже почти невозможно многим идти противу всеобщего теченья. Но я теперь должен, как в решительную и священную минуту, когда приходится спасать свое отечество, когда всякий гражданин несет все и жертвует всем,- я должен сделать клич хотя к тем, у которых еще есть в груди русское сердце и понятно сколько- нибудь слово 'благородство'. Что тут говорить о том, кто более из нас виноват. Я, может быть, больше всех виноват; я, может быть, слишком сурово вас принял вначале, может быть, излишней подозрительностью я оттолкнул из вас тех, которые искренно хотели мне быть полезными, хотя и я с своей стороны мог бы также сделать-<им упрек>. Если они уже действительно любили справедливость и добро своей земли, не следовало бы им оскорбиться на надменность моего обращения, следовало бы им подавить в себе собственное честолюбие и пожертвовать своею личностью. Не может быть, чтобы я не заметил их самоотверженья и высокой любви к добру и не принял бы наконец от них полезных и умных советов. Все-таки скорей подчиненному следует применяться к нраву начальника, чем начальнику к нраву подчиненного. Это законней по крайней мере и легче, потому что у подчиненных один начальник, а у начальника сотни подчиненных. Но оставим теперь в стороне, кто кого больше виноват. Дело в том, что пришло нам спасать нашу землю; что гибнет уже земля наша не от нашествия двадцати иноплеменных языков, а от нас самих; что уже мимо законного управленья образовалось другое правленье, гораздо сильнейшее всякого законного. Установились свои условия, все

what; but when he stands up and swings his whip and sets up a song – the horses fly like a whirl-wind, the spokes of the wheels are blended into one revolving disc, the road quivers, and the pedestrian cries out, halting in alarm – and the troika dashes away and away! . . . And already all that can be seen in the distance is something flinging up the dust and whirling through the air.

And, Russia, art not thou too flying onwards like a spirited troika that nothing can overtake? The road is smoking under thee, the bridges rumble, everything falls back and is left behind! The spec-tator stands still, struck dumb by the divine miracle: is it not a flash of lightning from heaven? What is the meaning of this terrifying onrush? What mysterious force is hidden in this troika, never seen before? Ah, horses, horses – what horses! Is the whirlwind hidden under your manes? Is there some delicate sense tingling in every vein? They hear the familiar song over their heads – at once in uni-son they strain their iron chests and scarcely touching the earth with their hoofs are transformed almost into straight lines flying through the air – and the troika rushes on, full of divine inspiration. . . . Russia, whither flyest thou? Answer! She gives no answer. The ringing of the bells melts into music; the air, torn to shreds, whirs and rushes like the wind, everything there is on earth is flying by, and the other states and nations, with looks askance, make way for her and draw aside.

(1842)

From the end of Part II (mostly destroyed by the author and preserved in fragments only)

'Now the very man in whose hand the fate of many lines and whom no supplications could have softened, that very man flings himself now at your feet and entreats you all. All will be forgotten, effaced and forgiven, I will myself be the advocate for all if you grant my request. Here it is. I know that by no means, by no terrors, by no punishments can dishonesty be eradicated. It is too deeply rooted. The dishonest practice of taking bribes has become necessary and inevitable, even for such who are not born to be dishonest. I know that it is almost impossible for many to run counter to the general tendency. But I must now, as at the decisive and sacred moment when it is our task to save our country, when every citizen bears every burden and makes every sacri-fice – I must appeal to those at least who still have a Russian heart and who have still some understanding of the word 'honour.' What is the use of discussing which is the more guilty among us! I am perhaps the most guilty of all; I perhaps received you too sternly at first; perhaps by excessive suspicion I repelled those among you who sincerely wished to be of use to me. If they really cared for justice and the good of their country, they ought not to have been offended by the haughtiness of my manner, they ought to overcome their own vanity and sacrifice their personal dignity. It is not possible that I should not have noticed their selfdenial and lofty love of justice and should not at last have accepted useful and sensible advice from them. It is anyway more suitable for a subordinate to adapt himself to the character of his chief than for a chief to adapt himself to the character of a subordinate. It is more lawful anyway and easier, because the subordinates have only one chief, while the chief has hundreds of subordinates. But let us lay aside the question of who is most to blame. The point is that it is our task to save our country, that our country is in danger now, not from invasion of twenty foreign races, but from ourselves; that, besides our lawful government, another rule has been set up, far stronger than any lawful one. Its conditions are established, everything has its price, and the prices are a matter of com-mon knowledge. And no ruler, though he were wiser than all the legislators and governors, can cure the evil however he may curtail the activity of bad officials, by putting them under the

оценено, и цены даже приведены во всеобщую известность. И никакой правитель, хотя бы он был мудрее всех законодателей и правителей, не в силах поправить зла, как <ни> ограничивай он в действиях дурных чиновников приставленьем в надзиратели других чиновников. Все будет безуспешно, покуда не почувствовал из нас всяк, что он так же, как в эпоху восстанья народов, вооружался против < врагов? >, так должен восстать против неправды. Как русский, как связанный с вами единокровным родством, одной и тою же кровью, я теперь обращаюсь <к> вам. Я обращаюсь к тем из вас, кто имеет понятье какое-нибудь о том, что такое благородство мыслей. Я приглашаю вспомнить долг, который на всяком месте предстоит человеку. Я приглашаю рассмотреть ближе свой долг и обязанность земной своей должности, потому что это уже нам всем темно представляется, и мы едва...

[На этом рукопись обрывается...]

III.l.3.   АЛЕКСЕЙ КОНСТАНТИНОВИЧ ТОЛСТОЙ, «Колокольчики мои... »

Колокольчики мои,
  Цветики степные!
Что глядите на меня,
  Тёмно-голубые?
И о чём звените вы
  В день весёлый мая,
Средь некошеной травы
  Головой качая?

Конь несёт меня стрелой
  На поле открытом;
Он вас топчет под собой,
  Бьёт своим копытом.
Колокольчики мои,
  Цветики степные!
Не кляните вы меня,
  Тёмно-голубые!

Я бы рад вас не топтать,
  Рад промчаться мимо,
Но уздой не удержать
  Бег неукротимый!
Я лечу, лечу стрелой,
  Только пыль взметаю;
Конь несёт меня лихой,-
  А куда? не знаю!

Он учёным ездоком
  Не воспитан в холе,
Он с буранами знаком,
  Вырос в чистом поле;

supervision of other officials. All will be fruitless until every one of us feels that just as at the epoch of the rising up of all the peoples he was armed against the enemy, he must now take his stand against dishonesty. As a Russian, as one bound to you by ties of birth and blood, I must now appeal to you. I appeal to those among you who have some conception of what is meant by an honourable way of thinking. I invite you to remember the duty which stands before a man in every position. I invite you to look more closely into your duty and the obligations of your earthly service for we all have as yet but a dim understanding of it, and we scarcely . . .
(*here the manuscript breaks off*)

[*Translated by Constance Garnett, 1912*]

III.1.3.   ALEXEI KONSTANTINOVICH TOLSTOY, 'My Little Bluebells'

My little bluebells,
    Flowers of the steppe!
Why do you look at me,
    You, azure ones?
And what tinkle you about
    On a happy day of May,
Nodding your heads,
    Amidst unmown grass?

The steed carries me like an arrow
    Over the open field;
He tramples you down underneath,
    Hits you with his hoof.
My little bluebells,
    Flowers of the steppe!
Pray curse me not,
    You, azure ones!

I would be happy not to trample you down,
    Happy to rush along, passing you by,
But one cannot restrain with a bridle
    This indomitable race!
I fly, fly like an arrow,
    Only raising the dust;
The dashing horse carries me, –
    But where? I know not!

Untrained and ungroomed
    By a master rider,
And hardened by blizzards,
    Thou hast grown in an open country;

И не блещет как огонь
   Твой чепрак узорный,
Конь мой, конь, славянский конь,
   Дикий, непокорный!

Есть нам, конь, с тобой простор!
   Мир забывши тесный,
Мы летим во весь опор
   К цели неизвестной.
Чем окончится наш бег?
   Радостью ль? кручиной?
Знать не может человек –
   Знает Бог единый!

Упаду ль на солончак
   Умирать от зною?
Или злой киргиз-кайсак,
   С бритой головою,
Молча свой натянет лук,
   Лежа под травою,
И меня догонит вдруг
   Медною стрелою?

Иль влетим мы в светлый град
   Со кремлем престольным?
Чудно улицы гудят
   Гулом колокольным,
И на площади народ,
   В шумном ожиданье
Видит: с запада идет
   Светлое посланье.

В кунтушах и в чекменях,
   С чубами, с усами,
Гости едут на конях,
   Машут булавами,
Подбочась, за строем строй
   Чинно выступает,
Рукава их за спиной
   Ветер раздувает.

Thou hast no luxurious saddle-cloth
    That sparkles like fire,
My horse, my Slavic horse,
    Wild and unruly!

Steed, we have our freedom!
    Having left the cramped world behind,
We fly in full career
    Towards an unknown goal.
How will our ride end?
    In bliss? or in sorrow?
It is not for man to know –
    Only God knows!

Shall I fall down on the salty marsh
    To die of heat?
Or shall an evil Kirghiz-Kaisak
    With shaved head,
Hiding in the grass,
    Silently, bend his bow
And suddenly overtake me
    With his brazen arrow?

Or shall we dash into the radiant city
    With its regal kremlin?[1]
The streets sound marvelously
    With the chime of bells,
And the people in the square,
    In noiseful expectation behold
A serene embassy
    Coming from the west.

Wearing caftans and doublets,
    With forelocks and mustaches,
The guests ride their steeds,
    Waving their maces;
With a proud port, line after line
    Marches majestically;
The wind blows apart their sleeves
    Behind their backs.

[1] Any walled city, not necessarily the Kremlin of Moscow. The poem is deliberately unclear as to the setting of the final scene – Moscow or Kiev – although the proximity of the steppes, rather than woods, makes the latter a likelier option.

И хозяин на крыльцо
    Вышел величавый;
Его светлое лицо
    Блещет новой славой;
Всех его исполнил вид
    И любви и страха,
На челе его горит
    Шапка Мономаха.

«Хлеб да соль! И в добрый час!-
    Говорит державный.-
Долго, дети, ждал я вас
    В город православный!»
И они ему в ответ:
    «Наша кровь едина,
И в тебе мы с давних лет
    Чаем господина!»

Громче звон колоколов,
    Гусли раздаются,
Гости сели вкруг столов,
    Мед и брага льются,
Шум летит на дальний юг
    К турке и к венгерцу –
И ковшей славянских звук
    Немцам не по сердцу!

Гой вы, цветики мои,
    Цветики степные!
Что глядите на меня,
    Темно-голубые?
И о чем грустите вы
    В день веселый мая,
Средь некошеной травы
    Головой качая?

(1840-е годы)

And the stately host
    Comes out on the porch,
His radiant face
    Shines with a new glory;
His look inspires
    Both love and fear in all,
The Monomach's Cap[2]
    Glistens on his forehead.

'Bread and salt![3] And well met! –
    Says the sovereign. –
Long have I awaited you, children,
    To come to the holy city!'[4]
And they reply to him:
    'We are one blood,
And we have looked to thee as our lord
    Since the days of yore!'

The bells chime louder,
    The gusli[5] ring out,
The guests are seated around the tables,
    Mead and beer flow freely,
The uproar spreads far south
    To the Turk and the Hungarian –
And the Slavic sound of clinking bowls
    Is not to the Germans' liking.

Hail ye, my little bluebells,
    Flowers of the steppe!
Why do you look at me,
    You, azure ones?
And what grieve ye about,
    On a happy May day,
Nodding your heads,
    Amidst unmown grass?

(1840s)

[Translated by Yelena Borisova. Edited by Jamie S. Crouse and Dmitry Usenco]

[2] The crown of all Muscovite grand princes and tsars up to Peter the Great, allegedly a gift from the Byzantine Emperor Constantine IX Monomachus.

[3] An expression of hospitality. To present an offering of bread and salt is a way to express that the guest is welcome.

[4] Literally, orthodox, that is, the city where the faithful are gathered.

[5] An ancient Slavic string musical instrument, a kind of harp.

m. **ESPAÑOL**

III.m.1. ÁNGEL DE SAAVEDRA RAMÍREZ DE BAQUEDANO, DUQUE DE RIVAS, 'Romance'

Con once heridas mortales
hecha pedazos la espada,
el caballo sin aliento
y perdida la batalla,
manchado de sangre y polvo,
en noche oscura y nublada,
en Ontígola vencido
y deshecha mi esperanza,
casi en brazos de la muerte
el laso potro aguijaba
sobre cadáveres yertos
y armaduras destrozadas.
Por una senda oculta
que el cielo me deparara,
entre sustos y congojas
llegar logré a Villacañas.
La hermosísima Filena,
de mi desastre apiadada,
me ofreció su hogar, su lecho
y consuelo a mis desgracias.
Registóme las heridas
y con manos delicadas
me limpió el polvo y la sangre
que en negro raudal manaban.
Curábame las heridas
y mayores me las daba;
curábame las del cuerpo,
me las causaba en el alma.
Yo, no pudiendo sufrir
el fuego que me abrasaba,
díjele: 'Hermosa Filena,
basta de curarme, basta.
Más crueles son tus ojos
que las polonesas lanzas.
Ellas hirieron mi cuerpo
y ellos el alma me abrasan.
Tuve contra Marte aliento
en las sangrientas batallas
y contra el rapaz Cupido
el aliento hora me falta.
Deja esa cura, Filena,
déjala, que más me agravas;

m.   SPANISH

III.m.1.   ÁNGEL DE SAAVEDRA RAMÍREZ DE BAQUEDANO, DUQUE DE RIVAS, 'Romance/ Ballad'

With eleven mortal wounds, sword shattered in pieces, horse without breath and the battle lost, stained with blood and dust on a dark and cloudy night, overwhelmed in Ontígola and my hopes dashed, almost in the arms of death, I spurred on my weary colt over rigid bodies and shattered armour. And by a hidden pathway which the heavens offered me, between frights and distress I managed to reach Villacañas. The most comely Filena, pitying my poor condition, offered me her dwelling, her bed and consolation for my misfortunes. She examined my wounds and with delicate hands, she washed away the dust and blood which streamed from me in a black flood. My wounds healed and I gained greater ones; those of my body were cured, yet my soul brought new ones. I, unable to suffer the fire which consumed me, said to her, 'Beautiful Filena, it is enough to cure me, enough; your eyes are more cruel than Polish lances. They wounded my body and yours burn my soul. I gained a breathing space against Mars in bloody battles and against the boy Cupid my breath now fails me. Leave off this cure, Filena, leave it, for you do me more harm, leave the cure of my body and strive to cure my soul.

[1814] (In the hospital of Baza, 1809)

[*Rivas, later Duque de Rivas on the death of his elder brother, spent twelve years in exile (1823–1834) in England, Malta and France. His major fame rests on his long historical ballads, especially* El moro expósito *(1834), influenced by Byron and Scott. His* Romances históricos *(1841) written in 1829 belong to the conservative medievalizing strain of Romanticism, while his drama,* Don Álvaro *(1835), expresses the same sense of cosmic injustice found in Espronceda. Rivas was wounded in the Battle of Ontígola (1809) against the French, under Marshall Soult, and saved by a fellow soldier, not by the imagined pastoral Filena.*]

deja la cura del cuerpo,
atiende a curarme el alma.'
(En el hospital de Baza, 1809)

[From *Poesías* 1814]

III.m.2.   JOSEFA ESTÉVEZ, 'La esposa'

Cual tortolilla del nido
de su amor abandonada,
sola está la tierna esposa
en pie tras de su ventana,
esperando tristemente
al amado de su alma,
lleno de amargura el pecho,
los ojos llenos de lágrimas.
Nada de la noche augusta
turba el silencio y la calma.
En el reloj de la villa
las doce ha tiempo sonaron,
hora pavorosa y triste
de espectros y de fantasmas,
en que los muertos tal vez
dejan su tumba olvidada
para visitar amantes
a los que en el mundo amaron.
También de sus muertes dichas
los tristes espectros vagan
por la mente de la esposa
que los contempla angustiada.
El uno lleva en su mano
un ramo de rosas blancas:
Es el mismo que la dio
el amado de su alma
cuando por vez primera
las juró amor y constancia.
Otro de flores de azahar
lleva la hermosa guirnalda
que el día de su himeneo
su pura frente adornara.
Mas sus flores ya no tienen
ni frescura ni fragancia
y, cual de la esposa el rostro,
están marchitas y pálidas.
Del bello ramo de rosas
tan sólo espinas quedaron;

III.m.2. JOSEFA ESTÉVEZ, 'The Wife'

Like a tiny dove in its nest, abandoned by its love, the tender wife stands alone awaiting her soul's beloved, her breast filled with bitterness, her eyes filled with tears. Nothing in the August night disturbs the silence and calm. The town clock has struck twelve some time before, a fearful and sad hour of spectres and phantoms, in which the dead, perhaps, leave their forgotten tombs to visit their lovers, those whom in life they loved. And the sad spectres also wander from their happy deaths through the mind of the wife who, anguished, watches them. One bears in his hand a bunch of white roses, the same as the beloved of her soul gave her when first he swore love and constancy. Another bears the beautiful garland of orange blossom which, the day of their nuptials, would adorn her pure brow. Yet their flowers no longer have freshness and fragrance and, like the face of the wife, are faded and pale. Only thorns remain of the beautiful bouquet of roses; the wind has borne away the blossoms just as words have been carried away, the oaths of love of the beloved of her soul. Another, cruelly, repeats to her in a loving and languid voice these words: 'For tender husbands and wives who love one another in delirium, the moments and hours pass as briefly as the dawn; yet, if fickle, the husband, alas o God!, leaves the wife to seek other pleasures like a frivolous butterfly who now disdains the flower which it once anxiously sucked; the hours are slow centuries of torture for the soul.' – 'Flee, cruel memories', cries the wife in anguish, 'flee, fateful spectres of my dead hopes' – But they persecute her the more she rejects them. Of a sudden, oh pleasure!, o happiness!, the noise of steps resounds. 'It is my dearest love!', the wife exclaims in a tremulous voice, 'sad and copious tears flee from my eyes; let a smile shine on my lips and on my face a sweet calm, for it is unjust to receive in lamentation he who is best beloved. Let pleasure glow on my countenance, my heart drink up your tears.'

[1877]

[*Married to the Governor of the Philipines, Estévez, nevertheless, maintained a celebrated literary circle in Madrid each year. At the death of her husband and children she entered a convent. Her first collection, La esposa, evokes the experiences of a wife, here a widow. In spite of the rather clichéd spectral elements she expresses a sense of deep loss and love and, more daringly, introduces the theme of inconstancy and adultery. Her poems mark the emergence of the female voice in the Spanish lyric. With Gómez de Avellaneda, Coronado, Rosalía de Castro, Maturana, Massanés, Armiño, Sinués and many other women poets, Estévez's work illustrates the spirit of freedom for women that certain aspects of Spanish Romanticism heralded. While some of these women had to struggle to be heard, others of more liberal and wealthy families became the central focus of progressive literary salons.*]

las flores las llevó el viento
cual se llevó las palabras
los juramentos de amor
del amado a su alma.
Otro, cruel, repite
con voz amorosa y lánguida:
'Para dos tiernos esposos
que con delirio se aman
los instantes y las horas
pasan breves como el aura;
mas, si voluble el esposo
de la esposa, ¡ay, Dios!, se aparta
por buscar otros placeres
cual mariposa liviana
que ahora desdeña la flor
que antes ansiosa libara,
son lentos siglos las horas
de tortura para el alma'.
– Huid, crueles recuerdos,
dice la esposa angustiada,
Huid, espectros fatídicos
de mis muertes esperanzas – .
Pero ellos más la persiguen
cuando ella más los rechaza.
De repente, ¡oh gozo!, ¡oh dicha!,
el rumor de unas pisadas
resuena. – ¡Es mi bien amado!,
con trémula voz exclama
la esposa: huid de mis ojos
tristes y copiosas lágrimas;
brille la risa en mis labios
y en mi rostro dulce calma,
que no es justo recibir
con llanto al que bien se ama.
brille el gozo en mi semblante,
¡corazón, bebe tus lágrimas! – .

[1877]

III.m.3. JUAN NICASIO GALLEGO, 'A mi vuelta a Zamora en 1807'

Cargado de mortal melancolía,
de angustia el pecho y de memorias lleno,
otra vez torno a vuestro dulce seno,
campos alegres de la patria mía.
¡Cuán otros, ¡ay!, os vio mi fantasía
cuando de pena y de temor ajeno
en mí fijaba su mirar sereno
la infiel hermosa que me amaba un día!
Tú que, en tiempo mejor fuiste testigo
de mi ventura al rayo de la aurora,
selo de mi dolor, césped amigo;
pues si en mi corazón que sangre llora
esperanzas y amor llevé conmigo,
desengaños y amor te traigo ahora.

(1807) [*Published in Versos de Juan Nicasio Gallego, 1829*]

III.m.4. MANUEL JOSÉ QUINTANA, 'A España después de la Revolución de Marzo'

¿Qué era, decidme, la nación que un día
reina del mundo proclamó el destino
la que a todas las zonas extendía
su cetro de oro y su blasón divino?
Volábase a Occidente
y el vasto mar Atlántico sembrado
se hallaba de su gloria y su fortuna.
Do quiera España: en el preciado seno
de América, en el Asia, en los confines
del África, allí España.
...
Qué de plagas, oh Dios! Su aliento impuro
la pestilente fiebre respirando
infestó el aire, emponzoñó la vida;
el hambre enflaquecida
tendió sus brazos lívidos, ahogando
cuanto el contagio perdonó.
...
¿Qué viste ya sino funesto luto,
honda tristeza, sin igual miseria,
de tu vil servidumbre acerbo fruto?
...
Llega el momento en fin; tiende su mano
el tirano del mundo al Occidente
y fiero exclama: 'El Occidente es mío'.
Bárbaro gozo en su ceñuda frente

III.m.3.   JUAN NICASIO GALLEGO, 'On My Return to Zamora in 1807'

Burdened with mortal melancholy, my breast filled with anguish and memories, I return again to your soft bosom, happy meadows of my homeland. How many others, alas, did my fantasy see when, distant from pain and fear, did the unhappy beauty who once loved me, fix on me her serene regard. You who, in happier times, were the witness to my happiness at the first beams of dawn, be the happy sward of my suffering; for if my blood weeps in my heart I bore hopes and love with me, disillusions and love I bear you now.

(1807) [1829]

[*The collapse of the monarchy and the Napoleonic invasion in the new century inspired a host of patriotic poems, including celebrations (in literature and painting) of the Dos de Mayo when the Madrid mob attacked the French troops as the Royal Family were being taken into exile under a French guard. In this sonnet Gallego adapts the bucolic tradition of a lover's return to the context of war and the inevitable disillusion of a Spain devastated by the struggle with France.*]

III.m.4.   MANUEL JOSÉ QUINTANA, 'Spain after the March Revolution'

Tell me, what was the nation which destiny once proclaimed the queen of the world, she who extended her golden sceptre and her divine escutcheon over all parts of the globe? She flew to the West and the vast Atlantic Ocean was seeded with glory and fortune. Wherever Spain found herself: in the valued bosom of America, in Asia, in the vast extremities of Africa, there was Spain. . . . What plagues, o Lord! Pestilent fever, its impure breath cast over us, infests the air, poisons life; shrivelling hunger stretched out its livid arms, smothering everything that contagion permitted. . . . What did you see (*after a series of military and naval defeats*) but baleful mourning, deep sadness, misery without equal, the bitter fruit of your vile servitude? . . . But, at last the moment came; the tyrant of the world [*Napoleon*] extended his hand to the West and fiercely exclaimed: 'The West is mine'. Barbarous pleasure on his grim brow flashed for a moment like a fleeting ray of lightning in summer in the dark bosom of a thunder cloud, adding horror with its sombre glow. . . . Spain stirred at the contemptible commotion which she heard approaching and at the great impulse of her just rage she broke open the volcano which boiled within her. Her ancient despots hid away pallid and in consternation; the echo of revenge sounded all around and the banks of the Tagus responded 'Revenge'. Where are they, o sacred river, the colossi of ignominy and shame who smothered our worth in their insolence? You once represented glory, our splendour now commences and you, proud and fierce, seeing that there still remain Castile and Castilians, hasten your silver waves to the sea crying 'An end to tyrants'. O triumph! O glory! O heavenly moment! . . . Spaniards, to war, to war! In the Guadalquivir see the venerable shade of Ferdinand III arise in anger; see Gonzalo of imperial Granada show his divine face, see the Cid wield his flashing sword. . . . With stern scowl and disdainful of pain, see how they stream through the vain airs and, exhaling the valour which has been enclosed in the hollow of their cold tombs, they cry, with a fierce and hoarse voice, 'War!' . . . Awake, o race of heroes, that moment has now come to throw yourselves into victory; that your name will eclipse our name, that your glory will give shame to our glory. The altar of the motherland raised in vain by your strong hand on this great day has not been in vain. Swear, she demands it of you:

resplandeció como en el seno oscuro
de nube tormentosa en el estío
relámpago fugaz brilla un momento
que añade horror con su fulgor sombrío.
…

Estremecióse España
del indigno rumor que cerca oía
y al grande impulso de su justa saña
rompió el volcán que en su interior hervía.
Sus déspotas antiguos
consternados y pálidos se esconden;
resuena el eco de venganza en torno
y del Tajo las márgenes responden
'Venganza'. ¿Dónde están, sagrado río
los colosos de oprobio y de vergüenza
que nuestro bien en su insolencia ahogaban?
Su gloria fue, nuestro esplendor comienza,
y tú, orgulloso y fiero,
viendo que aún hay Castilla y castellanos,
precipitas al mar tus rubias ondas
diciendo: 'Ya acabaron los tiranos'.
¡Oh triunfo! ¡Oh gloria! ¡Oh celestial momento!
…

¡Guerra, guerra, españoles! En el Betis
ved del tercer Fernando alzarse airada
la augusta sombra; su divina frente
mostrar Gonzalo en la imperial Granada;
blandir el Cid su centelleante espada;
…

En torvo ceño y desdeñosa pena
ved cómo cruzan por los aires vanos
y, el valor exhalando que se encierra
dentro del hueco de sus tumbas frías,
en fiera y ronca voz pronuncian: '¡Guerra!'.
…

Despertad, raza de héroes, el momento
llegó ya de arrojarse a la victoria;
que vuestro nombre eclipse nuestro nombre,
que vuestra gloria humille nuestra gloria.
No ha sido en el gran día
el altar de la patria alzado en vano
por vuestra mano fuerte.
Juradlo, ella os lo manda: '¡antes la muerte
que consentir jamás ningún tirano!'.
Sí, yo lo juro, venerables sombras,
yo lo juro también, y en este instante

'death before we ever consent to any tyrant!' Yes, I swear it, venerable shades, I, too, swear it, and in this moment, I feel I have come of age. Give me a lance, crown me with the fierce and gleaming helmet, let us fly to combat, to vengeance, and he who denies his breast to hope let his cowardly brow sink in the dust. Perhaps the great torrent of devastation will take me off. What does it matter? Will I not die to meet our illustrious forebears? I salute you, fathers of my homeland, I say 'good health'. Heroic Spain, amid universal destruction and horrors raises her bloodied head and, conqueror of her evil destiny, returns to give her frightened land its golden sceptre and her divine escutcheon.

(April 1808) [1808]

[*Quintana was the national poet of inspiring ideals – liberty, homeland, religion – and one of the most celebrated writers of his time. He was among the first to develop the vision of a renewed role for Spain based on traditional values, one of restored grandeur, independence and liberty. He called his countrymen to resist the Napoleonic threat, especially in this long poem, following the mutiny at the Royal Palace at Aranjuez on 17 March 1808 which led to the fall of the King's favourite, Godoy, the abdication of the King and the Napoleonic invasion itself. Ferdinand III (1217–1253) captured Cordoba and Seville from the Moors; Gonzalo Fernández de Córdoba (1453–1515) led the expedition against the Moorish revolt in the Alpujarras after the surrender of Granada in 1492 and the Cid was Spain's greatest medieval warrior who took Valencia from the Moors.*]

ya me siento mayor. Dadme una lanza,
ceñidme el casco fiero y refulgente,
volemos al combate, a la venganza,
y el que niegue su pecho a la esperanza
hunda en el polvo la cobarde frente,
tal vez el gran torrente
de la devastación en su carrera
me llevará. ¿Qué importa? ¿Por ventura
no se muere una vez? ¿No iré expirando
a encontrar nuestros ínclitos mayores?
¡Salud, oh padres de la patria mía,
yo les diré, salud! La heroica España
de entre el estrago universal y horrores
levanta la cabeza ensangrentada
y, vencedora de su mal destino,
vuelve a dar a la tierra amedrentada
su cetro de oro y su blasón divino.

(Abril de 1808) [1808]

III.m.5.   FERNANDO CORRADI, 'El cántico del esclavo'

Cautivo mísero
gimo humillado.
Ni aun tristes súplicas
puedo exhalar.
¡Maldición sobre el fiero homicida
que el primero humilló a sus iguales!
¡Maldición sobre aquellos mortales
que cual dioses pretenden mandar!
¿Quién al hombre le ha dado derecho
de vender y comprar a los hombres
y, entregando al oprobio sus nombres,
con la infamia su frente sellar?
Amo injusto, mi espalda desnuda
tú con vara de hierro golpeas
y en mi amarga aflicción te recreas,
desoyendo mi trémula voz.
¿Corre acaso otra sangre en mis venas?
¿Soy de especie distinta y natura?
¡Es la imagen de Dios, es su hechura
la que ultrajas!, ¡oh dueño feroz!
¡Ay que suerte tan triste la mía!
Por doquier de vergüenza me escondo;
si me llaman, temblando respondo,
la voz siento en mi labio expirar.

III.m.5. FERNANDO CORRADI, 'The Song of the Slave'

A miserable captive, I groan in humiliation. I cannot even breathe out sad supplications. My stern master makes my blood and tears flow for whatever reason. A curse on the wild murderer who first humiliated his equals! A curse on those mortals who believe they can control like gods! Who has given man the right to buy and sell men? Who, delivering their names to opprobrium, do not brand their foreheads with infamy? My unjust master, you beat my naked back with an iron bar and in my bitter affliction you take pleasure, deaf to my tremulous voice. Does other blood run in my veins? Am I of a different species and nature? It is the image of God, it is his creation you insult, o stern master! Alas, what a sad fate is mine! I hide my shame where I can; if they call I respond in trembling, I hear my voice expire on my lips. If they look at me, I drop my eyes and fix them, humiliated, on the ground, like the condemned man stands terrified by his crime before the judge who is about to sentence him. Nor are the sweet caresses of love given me to enjoy. O sadness! For the proud beauty could never love an unfortunate slave. Beauty does not stint her favours for the noble, the valiant, nor for the king of the stars do the flowers their essence and their tints. See the man who calls himself free, how he lifts his brow to the heavens; how his dignified sense of well-being is reflected in his manly face. Seeing him burning with anger and struggling between envy and vexation, it seems as if my downcast and servile state aggrieves his eyes. At once I hear a voice which cries: 'You are a man, you are free, you are strong, and to he whom death brings no fears, never, never will he groan in chains. There is no one who should oppress us though he occupy the canopy of kings. There is no law that makes us slaves, God created men free!' A volcanic flame burns in my breast; I am no longer timid, I am a lion. Tyrannical master give me liberty or I shall break, O treacherous man, your heart.

[1838]

Si me miran, inclino los ojos
y los clavo humillado en la tierra,
como el reo que en un crimen aterra
ante el juez que le va a sentenciar.
Ni el amor las preciosas caricias
no me es dado gozar. ¡Oh tristeza!
Que jamás la orgullosa belleza
pudo amar al esclavo infeliz.
La beldad sólo al noble, al valiente
no escasea sus dulces favores,
como al rey de los astros las flores
no escasean su esencia y matiz.
Ved al hombre que libre se llama
cómo eleva a los cielos la frente;
cómo el digno entusiasmo que siente
se refleja en su faz varonil.
Oigo al punto una voz que me grita:
'Eres hombre, eres libre, eres fuerte,
y a quien nunca temor dio la muerte
nunca, nunca en cadenas gimió.
No hay ninguno que deba oprimirnos
aunque ocupa el dosel de los reyes.
para hacernos esclavos no hay leyes;
libres Dios a los hombres creó'.
Fuego volcánico
mi pecho inflama;
ya no soy tímido,
soy un león.
Dueño tiránico,
libertad dame
o rompo, ¡oh pérfido!,
tu corazón.

[*Published in El Seminario Pintoresco Español, III, 1838*]

n. SVENSKA/SUOMI

III.n.1. ERIK GUSTAF GEIJER, 'Odalbonden'

Å bergig ås, där står mitt hus,
Högt öfver skog och sjö.
Där såg jag första dagens ljus,
Och där vill jag ock dö.

Må hvem som vill gå kring verldens rund:
Vare herre och dräng den det kan!

[*This poem is only one of many anti-slavery works of the period in tune with the liberal ideals of one aspect of Romanticism in Spain. Gómez de Avellaneda's novel* Sab *(1841) and* El cancionero del esclavo *published by the Sociedad Abolicionista Española in 1866 are, arguably, the best examples of the campaign for the emancipation of the slaves. Women writers like Carolina Coronado and Concepción Arenal were also prominent contributors. The earliest anti-slavery poem dates from 1778.*]

n.   SWEDISH/FINNISH

III.n.1.   ERIK GUSTAF GEIJER, 'The Yeoman Farmer'

On a rocky ridge my house stands,
High above forests and lakes.
There I saw the first light of day,
And there it is I wish to die.

May each tour the world at his will:
Be master or servant whoever can!

Men jag står helst på min egen grund,
Och är helst min egen man.

Mig låckar icke ärans namn.
Hon bor dock i mitt bröst.
Min skörd ej gror i rycktets famn.
Jag skär den lugn hvar höst.

Den jorden beherrskar har tusende ben
Och väl tusende armar dertill.
Men svårt är dem röra – *min* arm är ej sen
Att föra ut hvad *jag* vill.

Jag tror ej böljans falska lopp,
Som far förutan ro.
Den fasta jord, hon är mitt hopp,
Hon visar evig tro.

Hon närer sin son ur sin hulda barm
Den tid honom ödet gaf.
Hon fattar den säkert, hon håller den varm,
Då han dör, uti djupan graf.

Ej buller älskar jag och bång.
Hvad stort sker, det sker tyst.
Snart märks ej spår af stormens gång,
Af blixten, se'n den lyst.

Men tyst lägger tiden stund till stund;
Och du täljer dock icke dess dar.
Och tyst flyter böljan i hafvets grund;
Fast regn-bäcken skrålande far.

Så går ock jag en stilla stig:
Man spör om mig ej stort.
Och mina bröder likna mig,
Hvar en uppå sin ort.

Vi reda för landet den närande saft.
Vi föda det – brödet är vårt.
Af oss har det hälsa, af oss har det kraft,
Och blöder det – blodet är vårt.

Hvar plåga har sitt skri för sig,
Men hälsan tiger still;
Derför man talar ej om mig,
Som vore jag ej till.

De väldige Herrar, med skri och med dån,
Slå byar och riken omkull;

But I prefer to stay on my own land,
And I prefer to be my own man.

Fame does nothing for me at all,
Yet her whisper lives on in my breast.
My harvest does not depend on renown.
Calmly I gather it each autumn.

He who rules the earth has a thousand legs
And a thousand arms as well.
But they're hard to move – my arm is never slow
To do whatever I will.

I don't trust the false course of the waves
Going on and on without peace.
The solid earth she is my hope,
Showing eternal trust.

She feeds her son from her gracious breast
During the time he is spared.
She clasps him and holds him warm,
When he dies, in the deep grave.

I do not like brawling or din.
Big tidings always come in silence.
Soon there'll be no trace of the storm,
Or of the flashes of lightning.

Silently time keeps adding on moments;
And yet we never count its days.
Silently the wave returns to the ocean,
While the small brook bawls and brays.

Likewise I too tread a quiet path:
I am never much asked for.
And my brothers look like me,
Each one in his place.

We make nourishing fare for the country.
We feed it – the bread is from us.
We give it its health and its strength,
And if it bleeds – the blood flows from us.

Each torment has its very own cry,
But health always keeps silent;
Therefore no-one notices me,
And I might as well cease to exist.

Mighty Lords, with noise and destruction,
Tear down villages and realms;

Tyst bygga dem Bonden och hans son,
Som så uti blodbestänkt mull.

Mig mycken lärdom ej är tung;
Jag vet blott, vad är *mitt*.
Hvad rätt är ger jag Gud och Kung,
Och njuter resten fritt.

De lärde, de rike de bråka sitt vett
Att utröna hvars rätt som är god.
Mig ren är den rätt, som man värft med sin svett,
Och som man försvart med sitt blod.

Jag går ej stadigt stugan kring;
Ty blir mig hogen varm.
Jag vandrar upp till Svea Ting,
Med skölden på min arm.

Med mång' ord talar vår Lagman ej
För Kungen i allmän sak.
Men kraftigt är Allmogens Ja eller Nej
Under Vapnens skallande brak.

Och om till krig Han uppbåd ger,
Så gå vi man ur gård.
Där Kungen ställer sitt baner,
Där drabbar striden hård.

För älskade panten i moders famn,
För fäder, för hem vill slåss
Och känner ej ryktet vårt dunkla namn,
Svea Konungar känna oss.

* * *

Så sjunger gladt vid sprakande spis,
I den kalla vinter-qväll,
Den gamle man uppå bonde-vis,
Med söner sin i sitt tjäll.

Han sitter och täljer sin ålders staf.
Må hans ätt ej i Sverige se slut!
Bondens minne det sänks uti graf,
Men hans verk varar tiden ut.

(1811)

Silently the Peasant and his son build them up,
Sowing in earth sprinkled with blood.

I am not weighed down by much learning;
The one thing I know is what's mine;
What is right I give to God and the King,
And the rest I enjoy.

The learned, the rich, they tease their brains
To find out whose right is worth most.
To me the right won with sweat is pure,
Defended with one's own blood.

I do not always trample round my hut;
For if my mind gets heated,
I wander up to the Svea moot,
With my shield upon my arm.

Our governor tells us little
Of politics or of the King.
What counts is the mass of the peasantry
And their roar when they rally to arms.

When summoned to fight for the king,
Each must walk away from his farm.
Wherever the king establishes his banner,
There battle will rage at its fiercest.

As we swore in our mothers' arms,
For ancestors and home we will fight
If our names are unknown to the annals of fame
At least the Kings of Sweden do know us.

* * *

Happily he sings by the crackling stove,
On a cold winter night,
The old man in peasant style,
Together with his sons in his homestead.

He counts his years on the calendar wand.
May his kin in Sweden never end!
The memory of the peasant goes into the grave,
But his works and deeds outlast time.

(1811) [*Translated by John Swedenmark*]

III.n.2.   KALEVALA

XLIV Neljäsviidettä runo

Vaka vanha Väinämöinen
arvelevi aivossansa:
"Nytpä soitanto sopisi,
ilon teentä kelpoaisi
näillä uusilla oloilla,
kaunihilla kartanoilla!
Vaan on kantele kaonnut,
iloni iäti mennyt
kalaisehen kartanohon,
lohisehen louhikkohon,   10
meren hauan haltijoille,
Vellamon ikiväelle.
Eikä tuota tuonekana,
Ahto antane takaisin.

"Oi on seppo Ilmarinen!
Taoit ennen, taoit eilen,
taopa tänäki päänä!
Tao rautainen harava,
haravahan piit tiheät,
piit tiheät, varsi pitkä,   20
jolla lainehet haroan,
laposille aallot lasken,
meren ruoikot ru'olle,
rannat kaikki karhikoille,
soitto jälle saa'akseni,
kantelo tavatakseni
kalaisesta kaartehesta,
lohisesta louhikosta!"
Se on seppo Ilmarinen,
takoja iän-ikuinen,   30
takoi rautaisen haravan
varren vaskisen keralla.
Piit takoi satoa syltä,
varren viittä valmisteli.

Siitä vanha Väinämöinen
otti rautaisen haravan.
Astui tietä pikkaraisen,
kulki matkoa palasen

III.n.2. KALEVALA

XLIV Väinämöinen's new Kantele

Väinämöinen goes to seek for his kantele which was lost in the lake, but cannot find it (1–76). He makes himself a new kantele of birchwood, on which he plays, and delights every creature in the neighbourhood (77–334).

Väinämöinen, old and steadfast,
In his mind was thus reflecting;
'Now the time has come for music,
Time to give ourselves to pleasure,
In our dwelling newly chosen,
In our homestead now so charming;
But the kantele is sunken,
And my joy has gone for ever
To the dwelling-place of fishes,
To the rock-caves of the salmon,   10
Where it may enchant the sea-pike,
Likewise Vellamo's attendants;
But they never will return it,
Ahto will no more return it.

O thou smith, O Ilmarinen!
Yestreen and before thou workedst,
Work to-day with equal vigour.
Forge me now a rake of iron,
Let the teeth be close together,
Close the teeth, and long the handle   20
That I rake among the billows,
And my rake the waves together,
And my rake among the sea-weeds,
With the rake rake all the margins,
And my instrument recover,
And the kantele recover,
From the devious paths of fishes,
From the rocky caves of salmon!'
Thereupon smith Ilmarinen,
He the great primeval craftsman,   30
Forged for him a rake of iron,
Furnished with a copper handle,
Teeth in length a hundred fathoms,
And the handle full five hundred.

Then the aged Väinämöinen
Took the mighty rake of iron,
And a little way he wandered,
Made a very little journey,

teloille teräksisille,
vaskisille valkamoille.   40

Tuoss' oli purtta, kaksi purtta,
kaksi valmista venettä
teloilla teräksisillä,
vaskisilla valkamoilla:
yksi pursi uusi pursi,
toinen pursi vanha pursi.

Sanoi vanha Väinämöinen,
virkki uuelle venolle:
"Lähepä, veno, vesille,
pursi, aalloillen ajaite   50
käsivarren kääntämättä,
peukalon pitelemättä!"

Läksipä veno vesille,
pursi aalloillen ajoihe.
Vaka vanha Väinämöinen
itse istuihe perähän;
läksi merta luutimahan,
lainetta lakaisemahan.
Luopi lumpehet kokohon,
haravoipi rannan raiskat,   60
ruoposteli ruo'on ruutut,
ruo'on ruutut, kaislan kaitut,
joka hauanki harasi,
karit kaikki karhieli:
eipä saanut, ei tavannut
hauinluista soittoansa,
ikimennyttä iloa,
kaonnutta kanteloa.

Vaka vanha Väinämöinen
astuvi kohen kotia   70
alla päin, pahoilla mielin,
kaiken kallella kypärin.
Itse tuon sanoiksi kertoi:
"Ei tuota enämpi olle
hauin hampahan iloa,
kalanluista luikutusta!"

Astuessansa ahoa,
saloviertä vierressänsä
kuuli koivun itkeväksi,
puun visan vetistäväksi.   80

Till he reached the quay, steel-fitted,
And the landing-stage of copper.   40

There he found a boat, found two boats,
Both the boats were waiting ready
On the quay, with steel all fitted,
On the landing-stage of copper,
And the first boat was a new one,
And the second was an old one.

Said the aged Väinämöinen,
To the new boat firstly speaking:
'Go, thou boat, into the water,
To the waves, O vessel, rush thou,   50
Even though no arm should turn thee,
Even though no thumbs should touch thee!'

Sped the boat into the water,
Rushed amid the waves the vessel.
Old and steadfast Väinämöinen,
In the stern made haste to seat him,
And he went to sweep the water,
And to sweep among the billows.
Scattered leaves of water-lilies,
Raked he up among the shore-drift,   60
All the rubbish raked together,
All the rubbish, bits of rushes,
Every scrap he raked together,
All the shoals with care raked over,
But he found not, nor discovered,
Where his pike-bone harp was hidden,
And this joy was gone for ever,
With the kantele was sunken.

Väinämöinen, old and steadfast,
Then returned unto his dwelling,   70
Head bowed down, and sadly grieving,
And his cap askew and drooping,
And he said the words which follow:
'Unto me is lost for ever
Pleasure from the harp of pike-teeth,
From the harp I made of fish-bone!'

As he wandered through the meadows,
On the borders of the woodlands,
Then he heard a birch-tree weeping,
And a speckled tree lamenting,   80

Jopa luoksi luontelihe,
lähemmäksi laittelihe.

Kysytteli, lausutteli:
"Mit' itket, ihana koivu,
puu vihanta, vierettelet,
vyöhyt valkea, valitat?
Ei sua sotahan vieä,
ei tahota tappelohon."

Koivu taiten vastaeli,
itse virkki puu vihanta: 90
"Niinpä muutamat sanovi,
moniahat arvelevi
elävän minun ilossa,
riemussa remuelevan:
minä hoikka huolissani,
ikävissäni iloitsen,
panen pakkopäivissäni,
murehissa murmattelen.

"Typeryyttä, tyhjä, itken,
vajauttani valitan,   100
kun olen osatoin, raukka,
tuiki, vaivainen, varatoin
näillä paikoilla pahoilla,
lake'illa laitumilla.
"Osalliset, onnelliset
tuota toivovat alati
kesän kaunihin tulevan,
suven suuren lämpiävän.
Toisinpa minä typerä,
minä vaivainen varoan   110
- kuoreni kolottavaksi,
lehtivarvat vietäväksi!

"Useinpa minun utuisen,
use'in, utuisen raukan,
lapset kerkeän keväimen
luokseni lähenteleikse,
veitsin viisin viiltelevät
halki mahlaisen mahani.
Paimenet pahat kesällä
vievät vyöni valkeaisen,   120
ken lipiksi, ken tupeksi,
kenpä marjatuohiseksi.

And in that direction hastened,
Walking till he reached the birch-tree.

Thereupon he spoke and asked it:
'Wherefore weep'st thou, beauteous birch-tree,
Shedding tears, O green-leaved birch-tree,
By thy belt of white conspicuous?
To the war thou art not taken,
Longest not for battle-struggle.'

Answer made the leaning birch-tree,
And the green-leaved tree responded: 90
'There is much that I could speak of,
Many things I might reflect on,
How I best might live in pleasure,
And I might rejoice for pleasure.
I am wretched in my sorrow,
And can but rejoice in trouble,
Living with my life o'erclouded,
And lamenting in my sorrow.

And I weep my utter weakness,
And my worthlessness lament for,   100
I am poor, and all unaided,
Wholly wretched, void of succour,
Here in such an evil station,
On a plain among the willows.

Perfect happiness and pleasure
Others always are expecting,
When arrives the beauteous summer.
In the warm days of the summer.
But my fate is different, wretched,
Nought but wretchedness awaits me;   110
And my bark is peeling from me,
Down are hewed my leafy branches.

Often unto me defenceless
Oft to me, unhappy creature,
In the short spring come the children,
Quickly to the spot they hurry,
And with sharpened knives they score me,
Draw my sap from out my body,
And in summer wicked herdsmen,
Strip from me my white bark-girdle,   120
Cups and sheaths therefrom constructing,
Baskets too, for holding berries.

"Use'in minun utuisen,
use'in, utuisen raukan,
tytöt allani asuvat,
vierelläni viehkuroivat,
lehvät päältä leikkelevät,
varvat vastoiksi sitovat.

"Use'in minä utuinen,
use'in, utuinen raukka,   130
kaaetahan kaskipuiksi,
pinopuiksi pilkotahan.
Kolmasti tänäi kesänä,
tänä suurena suvena
miehet allani asuivat,
kirvestänsä kitkuttivat
mun poloisen pään menoksi,
heikon henkeni lähöksi.

"Se oli ilo kesästä,
riemu suuresta suvesta.   140
Ei ole talvi sen parempi,
lumen aika armahampi.
"Jopa aina aikaisehen
mure muo'on muuttelevi,
pääni painuvi pahaksi,
kasvot käypi kalveaksi
muistellessa mustat päivät,
pahat ajat arvellessa.

"Siitä tuuli tuskat tuopi,
halla huolet haike'immat: 150
tuuli vie vihannan turkin,
halla kaunihin hamehen.
Niin minä vähävarainen,
minä, koito koivu raukka,
jään aivan alastomaksi,
varsin vaattehettomaksi
vilussa värisemähän,
pakkasessa parkumahan."

Sanoi vanha Väinämöinen:
"Elä itke, puu vihanta,   160
vesa lehti, vierettele,
vyöhyt valkea, valita!
Saat sinä olevan onnen,
elon uuen armahamman;

Often unto me defenceless,
Oft to me, unhappy creature,
Come the girls beneath my branches,
Come beneath, and dance around me.
From my crown they cut the branches,
And they bind them into bath-whisks.

Often too, am I, defenceless,
Oft am I, unhappy creature,   130
Hewed away to make a clearing,
Cut to pieces, into faggots.
Thrice already in this summer,
In the warm days of the summer,
Unto me have come the woodmen,
And have hewed me with their axes,
Hewed the crown from me unhappy,
And my weak life has departed.

This has been my joy in summer,
In the warm days of the summer,   140
But no better was the winter,
Nor the time of snow more pleasant.
And in former times already,
Has my face been changed by trouble,
And my head has dropped with sadness
And my cheeks have paled with sorrow,
Thinking o'er the days of evil,
Pondering o'er the times of evil.

And the wind brought ills upon me,
And the frost brought bitter sorrows;   150
Tore the wind my green cloak from me,
Frost my pretty dress from off me.
Thus am I of all the poorest,
And a most unhappy birch-tree,
Standing stripped of all my clothing,
As a naked trunk I stand here,
And in cold I shake and tremble,
And in frost I stand lamenting.'

Said the aged Väinämöinen:
'Weep no more, O verdant birch-tree!   160
Leafy sapling, weep no longer,
Thou, equipped with whitest girdle!
For a pleasant future waits thee,
New and charming joys await thee.

573

kohta itkenet ilosta,
riemusta remahutellet."

Siitä vanha Väinämöinen
koivun soitoksi kuvasi.
Veisteli kesäisen päivän,
kalkutteli kanteletta   170
nenässä utuisen niemen,
päässä saaren terhenisen.
Veisti kopan kanteletta,
emäpuun iloa uutta,
kopan koivusta lujasta,
emäpuun visaperästä.

Sanoi vanha Väinämöinen,
itse lausui, noin nimesi:
"Tuoss' on koppa kanteletta,
emäpuu iki-iloa.   180
Mistä naulat saatanehe,
vääntimet perittänehe?"

Kasvoi tammi tanhualla,
puu pitkä pihan perällä,
tammessa tasaiset oksat,
joka oksalla omena,
omenalla kultapyörä,
kultapyörällä käkönen.

Kun käki kukahtelevi,
sanoin viisin virkkelevi,   190
kulta suusta kumpuavi,
hopea valahtelevi
kultaiselle kunnahalle,
hope'iselle mäelle:
siitä naulat kantelehen,
vääntimet visaperähän!

Sanoi vanha Väinämöinen,
itse virkki, noin nimesi:
"Sain ma naulat kantelehen,
vääntimet visaperähän.   200
Vielä uupuvi vähäisen,
viittä kieltä kanteloinen.
Mistä tuohon kielet saisin,
äänöset asetteleisin?"

Soon shalt thou with joy be weeping,
Shortly shalt thou sing for pleasure!'

Then the aged Väinämöinen
Carved into a harp the birch-tree,
On a summer day he carved it,
To a kantele he shaped it,   170
At the end of cloudy headland,
And upon the hazy island,
And the harp-frame he constructed,
From the trunk he formed new pleasure,
And the frame toughest birchwood;
From the mottled trunk he formed it.

Said the aged Väinämöinen
In the very words which follow:
'Now the frame I have constructed,
From the trunk for lasting pleasure.   180
Whence shall now the screws be fashioned,
Whence shall come the pegs to suit me?'

In the yard there grew an oak-tree,
By the farmyard it was standing,
'Twas an oak with equal branches,
And on every branch an acorn,
In the acorns golden kernels,
On each kernel sat a cuckoo.

When the cuckoos all were calling,
In the call five tones were sounding,   190
Gold from out their mouths was flowing,
Silver too they scattered round them,
On a hill the gold was flowing,
On the ground there flowed the silver,
And from this he made the harp-screws,
And the pegs from that provided!

Said the aged Väinämöinen
In the very words which follow:
'Now the harp-screws are constructed,
And the harp-pegs are provided.   200
Something even now is wanting,
And five strings as yet are needed.
How shall I provide the harp-strings,
Which shall yield the notes in playing?'

Läksi kieltä etsimähän.
Astuvi ahoa myöten:
istui immikkö aholla,
nuori neitonen norolla.
Ei se impi itkenynnä,
ei varsin ilonnutkana;   210
ilman lauloi itseksensä:
lauloi iltansa kuluksi,
sulhon toivossa tulevan,
armahansa aikehessa.

Vaka vanha Väinämöinen
tuonne kengättä kepitti,
ilman hampsi hattaratta.
Sitte sinne tultuansa
alkoi hapsia anella.
Itse tuon sanoiksi virkki: 220
"Anna, impi, hapsiasi,
hieprukka, hivuksiasi
kanteloisen kielosiksi,
ääniksi ilon ikuisen!"

Antoi impi hapsiansa,
hienoja hivuksiansa;
antoi hasta viisi, kuusi
sekä seitsemän hivusta:
siit' on kielet kantelessa,
ääntimet iki-ilossa.   230

Saip' on soitto valmihiksi.
Siitä vanha Väinämöinen
istuiksen alakivelle,
paatiselle portahalle.

Otti kantelon käsille,
ilon itsensä lähemmä.
Kären käänti taivahalle,
ponnen polville tukesi:
ääniä asettelevi,
säveliä sääntelevi.   240

Sai äänet asetetuksi,
soittonsa sovitetuksi,
niin käänti alakäsille,
poikkipuolin polvillensa.
Laski kynttä kymmenkunnan,

Then he went to seek for harp-strings,
And along the heath he wandered.
On the heath there sat a maiden,
Sat a damsel in the valley,
And the maiden was not weeping,
Neither was she really joyful.   210
To herself she sang full softly,
Sang, that soon might come the evening,
Hoping for her lover's coming,
For the dear one she had chosen.

Väinämöinen, old and steadfast,
Crept without his shoes towards her,
Sprang to her without his stockings,
And as soon as he approached her,
He besought her hair to give him,
And he spoke the words which follow: 220
'Give thy hair to me, O maiden,
Give me of thy hair, O fair one,
Give me hair to form my harp-strings,
For the tones of lasting pleasure!'

Then her hair the maiden gave him,
From her soft locks hair she gave him,
And she gave him five and six hairs,
Seven the hairs she gave unto him,
That he thus might form his harp-strings,
For the tones of lasting pleasure.   230

Now the harp at last was finished,
And the aged Väinämöinen
On a rock his seat selected,
Near the steps, upon a stone bench.

In his hands the harp then taking,
Very near he felt his pleasure,
And the frame he turned to heaven,
On his knees the knob then propping,
All the strings he put in order,
Fit to make melodious music.   240

When he had the strings adjusted,
Then the instrument was ready;
Underneath his hands he placed it,
And across his knees he laid it,
With his ten nails did he play it,

viisi sormea viritti
kielille kapahumahan,
sävelille hyppimähän.

Siinä vanha Väinämöinen
kun on soitti kanteletta   250
käsin pienin, hoikin sormin,
peukaloin ulos kiverin,
jopa virkki puu visainen,
vesa lehti vieretteli,
kukahti käkösen kulta,
hivus impyen ilosi.

Sormin soitti Väinämöinen,
kielin kantelo kajasi:
vuoret loukkui, paaet paukkui,
kaikki kalliot tärähti,   260
kivet laikkui lainehilla,
somerot vesillä souti,
petäjät piti iloa,
kannot hyppi kankahilla.

Kälykset Kalevan naiset,
kesken kirjan neulomisen
ne tuohon jokena juoksi,
kaikki virtana vilisi,
nuoret naiset naurusuulla,
emännät ilolla mielin   270
soitteloa kuulemahan,
iloa imehtimähän.

Mi oli miehiä lähellä,
ne kaikki lakit käessä;
mi oli akkoja lähellä,
ne kaikki käsi posella.
Tyttäret vesissä silmin,
pojat maassa polvillansa
kanteloista kuuntelivat,
iloa imehtelivät.   280
Sanoivat samalla suulla,
yhen kielen kerkesivät:
"Ei ole tuota ennen kuultu
noin suloista soitantoa,
sinä ilmoisna ikänä,
kuuna kullan valkeana!"

And he let five active fingers
Draw the tunes from out the harp-strings,
Making most delightful music.

When the aged Väinämöinen
Thus upon his harp was playing,   250
Fine his hands, his fingers tender,
And his thumbs were gently curving.
Soon rang out the wood so speckled,
Sang the sapling green full loudly,
Loudly called the golden cuckoo,
And rejoiced the hair of maiden.

Thus played Väinämöinen's fingers,
And the harp-strings loud resounded,
Mountains shook and plains resounded,
All the rocky hills resounded,   260
In the waves the stones were rocking,
In the water moved the gravel,
And the pine-trees were rejoicing,
On the heath the stumps were skipping.

All of Kaleva's fair women,
All their fair ones flocked together,
And in streams they rushed together,
Like a river in its flowing.
Merry laughed the younger women,
And the mistresses were joyful,   270
As they heard the music playing,
And they wondered at their pleasure.

Likewise many men were present,
In their hands their caps all holding,
All the old dames in the party
To their cheeks their hands were holding,
And the maidens' eyes shed tear-drops,
On the ground the boys were kneeling,
To the kantele all listening,
And they wondered at their pleasure.   280
With one voice they all were singing,
With one tongue they all repeated:
'Never have we heard aforetime,
Heard before such charming music,
In the course of all our lifetime,
Through the golden years that have passed.'

Kuuluvi sorea soitto,
kuului kuutehen kylähän.
Eik' ollut sitä otusta,
ku ei tullut kuulemahan   290
tuota soittoa suloista,
kajahusta kanteloisen.

Mi oli metsän eläintä,
kyykistyivät kynsillehen
kanteloista kuulemahan,
iloa imehtimähän.
Ilman linnut lentäväiset
varvuille varustelihe,
veen kalaset kaikenlaiset
rantahan rakentelihe.   300
Matosetki maanalaiset
päälle mullan muuttelihe
- käänteleivät, kuuntelevat
tuota soittoa suloista,
kantelen iki-iloa,
Väinämöisen väännätystä.

Siinä vanha Väinämöinen
kyllä soitteli somasti,
kajahutti kaunihisti.
Soitti päivän, soitti toisen   310
yhtehen rupeamahan,
yhen aamun atriahan,
yhen vyönsä vyötäntähän,
yhen paitansa panohon.

Kun hän soitteli kotona,
huonehessa honkaisessa,
niin katot kajahtelivat,
permannot pemahtelivat;
laet lauloi, ukset ulvoi,
kaikki ikkunat iloitsi,   320
kiukoa kivinen liikkui,
patsas patvinen pajahti.

Kun hän kulki kuusikossa,
vaelti petäjikössä,
kuusoset kumartelihe,
männyt mäellä kääntelihe,
käpöset keolle vieri,
havut juurelle hajosi.

Far was heard the charming music,
In six villages they heard it,
There was not a single creature
But it hurried forth to listen,   290
And to hear the charming music
From the kantele resounding.

All the wild beasts of the forest,
Upright on their claws were resting
To the kantele to listen,
And they wondered at their pleasure.
All the birds in air then flying,
Perched upon the nearest branches,
All the fish that swam the waters,
To the margin hastened quickly,   300
And the worms in earth then creeping,
Up above the ground then hastened,
And they turned themselves and listened,
Listened to the charming music,
In the kantele rejoicing,
And in Väinämöinen's singing.

Then the aged Väinämöinen
Played in his most charming manner,
Most melodiously resounding;
And he played one day, a second,   310
Playing on, without cessation,
Every morning all through breakfast,
Girded with the selfsame girdle,
And the same shirt always wearing.

When he in his house was playing,
In his house of fir constructed,
All the roofs resounded loudly,
And the boards resounded likewise,
Ceilings sang, the doors were creaking,
All the windows were rejoicing,   320
And the hearthstones all were moving,
Birchwood columns sang in answer.

When he walked among the firwoods,
And he wandered through the pinewoods,
All the firs bowed down before him,
To the very ground the pine-trees;
On the grass the cones rolled round him,
On the roots the needles scattered.

Kun hän liikahti lehossa
tahi astahti aholla,   330
lehot leikkiä pitivät,
ahot ainoista iloa,
kukat kulkivat kutuhun,
vesat nuoret notkahteli.

[1849]

When he hurried through the greenwood,
Or across the heath was hastening,   330
All the leaves called gaily to him,
And the heath was all rejoicing,
And the flowers breathed fragrance round him,
And the young shoots bowed before him.

[1849]

[*Translated by W. F. Kirby. London, Dover, New Hampshire: Athlone P, 1907*]

IV. Language and Interpretation

Beginning with Rousseau, Hamann and Herder, Romanticism is the source of major ideas about the nature of language which represent one of the key innovations of modern thought. We have here excerpts from some of the classic essays on the origin of languages, together with some of the methodological texts which evince the new awareness of the question of interpretation that is central to Romantic thinking. Texts which reflect the new sense of the importance of poetic language are included, along with texts which reflect the new national awareness of the importance of language to the constitution of national culture and identity.

a. BRITISH

IV.a.1. HUGH BLAIR, from *Lectures on Rhetoric and Belles Lettres*

But suppose Language to have a Divine original, we cannot, however, suppose, that a perfect system of it was all at once given to man. It is much more natural to think, that God taught our first parents only such Language as suited their present occasions; leaving them, as he did in other things, to enlarge and improve it as their future necessities should require. Consequently, those first rudiments of Speech must have been poor and narrow; and we are at full liberty to enquire in what manner, and by what steps, Language advanced to the state in which we now find it. The history which I am to give of this progress, will suggest several things, both curious in themselves, and useful in our future disquisitions.

If we should we suppose a period before any words were invented or known, it is clear, that men could have no other method of communicating to others what they felt, than by the cries of passion, accompanied by such motions and gestures as were farther expressive of passion. For these are the only signs which nature teaches all men, and which are understood by all. One who saw another going into some place where he himself had been frightened, or exposed to danger, and who sought to warn his neighbour of the danger, could contrive no other way of doing so, than by uttering those cries, and making those gestures, which are the signs of fear: just as two men, at this day, would endeavour to make themselves understood by each other, who should be thrown together on a desolate island, ignorant of each other's Language. Those exclamations, therefore, which by Grammarians are called Interjections, uttered in a strong and passionate manner, were, beyond doubt, the first elements or beginnings of Speech.

When more enlarged communication became necessary, and names began to be assigned to objects, in what manner can we suppose men to have proceeded in this assignation of names, or invention of words? Undoubtedly, by imitating, as much as they could, the nature of the object which they named, by the sound of the name which they gave to it. As a Painter, who would represent grass, must employ a green colour; so, in the beginnings of Language, one giving a

name to any thing harsh or boisterous, would of course employ a harsh or boisterous sound. He could not do otherwise, if he meant to excite in the hearer the idea of that thing which he sought to name. To suppose words invented, or names given, to things in a manner purely arbitrary, without any ground or reason, is to suppose an effect without a cause. There must have always been some motive which led to the assignation of one name rather than another; and we can conceive no motive which would more generally operate upon men in their first efforts towards Language, than a desire to paint by Speech the objects which they named in a manner more or less complete, according as the vocal organs had it in their power to effect this imitation.

Wherever objects were to be named, in which sound, noise, or motion were concerned, the imitation by words was abundantly obvious. Nothing was more natural, than to imitate, by the sound of the voice, the quality of the sound of noise which any external object made; and to form its name accordingly. Thus in all Languages, we find a multitude of words that are evidently constructed upon this principle. A certain bird is termed the cuckoo, from the sound which it emits. When one sort of wind is said to *whistle*, and another to *roar*; when a serpent is said to *hiss*; a fly to *buzz*, and a falling timber to *crash*; when a stream is said to *flow*, and hail to *rattle*; the analogy between the word and the thing signified is plainly discernible.

In the names of objects which address the sight only, where neither noise, nor motion are concerned, and still more in the terms appropriated to moral ideas, this analogy appears to fail. Many learned men, however, have been of opinion, that though in such cases it becomes more obscure, yet it is not altogether lost; but that through the radical words of all Languages there may be traced some degree of correspondence with the object signified. With regard to moral and intellectual ideas, they remark, that, in every Language, the terms significant of them, are derived from the names of sensible objects to which they are conceived to be analogous; and with regard to sensible objects pertaining merely to sight, they remark, that their most distinguishing qualities have certain radical sounds appropriated to the expression of them, in a great variety of Languages. Stability, for instance, fluidity, hollowness, smoothness, gentleness, violence, &c. they imagine to be painted by the sound of certain letters or syllables, which have some relation to those different states of visible objects, on account of an obscure resemblance which the organs of voice are capable of assuming to such external qualities. By this natural mechanism, they imagine all Languages to have been at first constructed, and the roots of their capital words formed.

(1783; rev. 1785)

IV.a.2.   WILLIAM BLAKE, from *The Marriage of Heaven and Hell*

The Voice of the Devil.

All Bibles or sacred codes have been the causes of the following Errors:

1. That Man has two real existing principles Viz: a Body & a Soul.
2. That Energy, call'd Evil, is alone from the Body, & that Reason, call'd Good, is alone from the Soul.
3. That God will torment Man in Eternity for following his Energies.

But the following Contraries to these are True:

1. Man has no Body distinct from his Soul for that call'd Body is a portion of Soul discern'd by the five Senses, the chief inlets of Soul in this age

2. Energy is the only life and is from the Body and Reason is the bound or outward circumference of Energy.

3. Energy is Eternal Delight

Those who restrain desire, do so because theirs is weak enough to be restrained; and the restrainer or reason usurps its place & governs the unwilling.

And being restraind it by degrees becomes passive till it is only the shadow of desire.

The history of this is written in Paradise Lost. & the Governor or Reason is call'd Messiah.

And the original Archangel or possessor of the command of the heavenly host, is call'd the Devil or Satan and his children are call'd Sin & Death

But in the Book of Job Miltons Messiah is call'd Satan.

For this history has been adopted by both parties.

It indeed appear'd to Reason as if Desire was cast out. but the Devils account is, that the Messiah fell. & formed a heaven of what he stole from the Abyss.

This is shewn in the Gospel, where he prays to the Father to send the comforter or Desire that Reason may have Ideas to build on, the Jehovah of the Bible being no other than he, who dwells in flaming fire.

Know that after Christs death, he became Jehovah.

But in Milton; the Father is Destiny, the Son, a Ratio of the five senses. & the Holyghost, Vacuum!

Note. The reason Milton wrote in fetters when he wrote of Angels & God, and at liberty when of Devils & Hell, is because he was a true Poet and of the Devils party without knowing it. [From Plates 4–6]

[1793]

IV.a.3. WILLIAM WORDSWORTH, from Preface to *Lyrical Ballads*

Having dwelt thus long on the subjects and aim of these Poems, I shall request the Reader's permission to apprise him of a few circumstances relating to their style, in order, among other reasons, that he may not censure me for not having performed what I never attempted. The Reader will find that personifications of abstract ideas rarely occur in these volumes; and are utterly rejected, as an ordinary device to elevate the style, and raise it above prose. My purpose was to imitate, and, as far as possible, to adopt the very language of men; and assuredly such personifications do not make any natural or regular part of that language. They are, indeed, a figure of speech occasionally prompted by passion, and I have made use of them as such; but have endeavoured utterly to reject them as a mechanical device of style, or as a family language which Writers in metre seem to lay claim to by prescription. I have wished to keep the Reader in the company of flesh and blood, persuaded that by so doing I shall interest him. Others who pursue a different track will interest him likewise; I do not interfere with their claim, but wish to prefer a claim of my own. There will also be found in these volumes little of what is usually called poetic diction; as much pains has been taken to avoid it as is ordinarily taken to produce it; this has been done for the reason already alleged, to bring my language near to the language of men; and further, because the pleasure which I have proposed to myself to impart, is of a kind very different from that which is supposed by many persons to be the proper object of poetry. Without being culpably particular, I do not know how to give my Reader a more exact notion of the style in which it was my wish and intention to write, than by informing him that I have at all

times endeavoured to look steadily at my subject; consequently, there is I hope in these Poems little falsehood of description, and my ideas are expressed in language fitted to their respective importance. Something must have been gained by this practice, as it is friendly to one property of all good poetry, namely, good sense: but it has necessarily cut me off from a large portion of phrases and figures of speech which from father to son have long been regarded as the common inheritance of Poets. I have also thought it expedient to restrict myself still further, having abstained from the use of many expressions, in themselves proper and beautiful, but which have been foolishly repeated by bad Poets, till such feelings of disgust are connected with them as it is scarcely possible by any art of association to overpower.

If in a Poem there should be found a series of lines, or even a single line, in which the language, though naturally arranged and according to the strict laws of metre, does not differ from that of prose, there is a numerous class of critics, who, when they stumble upon these prosaisms as they call them, imagine that they have made a notable discovery, and exult over the Poet as over a man ignorant of his own profession. Now these men would establish a canon of criticism which the Reader will conclude he must utterly reject, if he wishes to be pleased with these volumes. And it would be a most easy task to prove to him, that not only the language of a large portion of every good poem, even of the most elevated character, must necessarily, except with reference to the metre, in no respect differ from that of good prose, but likewise that some of the most interesting parts of the best poems will be found to be strictly the language of prose, when prose is well written . . . the language of Prose may yet be well adapted to Poetry; and I have previously asserted that a large portion of the language of every good poem can in no respect differ from that of good Prose. I will go further. I do not doubt that it may be safely affirmed, that there neither is, nor can be, any essential difference between the language of prose and metrical composition.

[1800]

IV.a.4. WILLIAM WORDSWORTH, from *The Prelude*

[*From Book XII*]

> There are in our existence spots of time,
> That with distinct pre-eminence retain
> A renovating virtue, whence – depressed
> By false opinion and contentious thought,
> Or aught of heavier or more deadly weight,
> In trivial occupations, and the round
> Of ordinary intercourse – our minds
> Are nourished and invisibly repaired;
> A virtue, by which pleasure is enhanced,
> That penetrates, enables us to mount,
> When high, more high, and lifts us up when fallen.
> This efficacious spirit chiefly lurks
> Among those passages of life that give
> Profoundest knowledge to what point, and how,
> The mind is lord and master – outward sense
> The obedient servant of her will. Such moments

Are scattered everywhere, taking their date
From our first childhood. I remember well,
That once, while yet my inexperienced hand
Could scarcely hold a bridle, with proud hopes
I mounted, and we journeyed towards the hills:
An ancient servant of my father's house
Was with me, my encourager and guide:
We had not travelled long, ere some mischance
Disjoined me from my comrade; and, through fear
Dismounting, down the rough and stony moor
I led my horse, and, stumbling on, at length
Came to a bottom, where in former times
A murderer had been hung in iron chains.
The gibbet-mast had mouldered down, the bones
And iron case were gone; but on the turf,
Hard by, soon after that fell deed was wrought,
Some unknown hand had carved the murderer's name.
The monumental letters were inscribed
In times long past; but still, from year to year
By superstition of the neighbourhood,
The grass is cleared away, and to this hour
The characters are fresh and visible:
A casual glance had shown them, and I fled,
Faltering and faint, and ignorant of the road:
Then, reascending the bare common, saw
A naked pool that lay beneath the hills,
The beacon on the summit, and, more near,
A girl, who bore a pitcher on her head,
And seemed with difficult steps to force her way
Against the blowing wind. It was, in truth,
An ordinary sight; but I should need
Colours and words that are unknown to man,
To paint the visionary dreariness
Which, while I looked all round for my lost guide,
Invested moorland waste and naked pool,
The beacon crowning the lone eminence,
The female and her garments vexed and tossed
By the strong wind. When, in the blessed hours
Of early love, the loved one at my side,
I roamed, in daily presence of this scene,
Upon the naked pool and dreary crags,
And on the melancholy beacon, fell
A spirit of pleasure and youth's golden gleam;
And think ye not with radiance more sublime
For these remembrances, and for the power
They had left behind? So feeling comes in aid

Of feeling, and diversity of strength
Attends us, if but once we have been strong.
Oh! mystery of man, from what a depth
Proceed thy honours. I am lost, but see
In simple childhood something of the base
On which thy greatness stands; but this I feel,
That from thyself it comes, that thou must give,
Else never canst receive. The days gone by
Return upon me almost from the dawn
Of life: the hiding-places of man's power
Open; I would approach them, but they close.
I see by glimpses now; when age comes on,
May scarcely see at all; and I would give,
While yet we may, as far as words can give,
Substance and life to what I feel, enshrining,
Such is my hope, the spirit of the Past
For future restoration. . . . (ll. 208–286)

[1850]

IV.a.5.   JANE AUSTEN, from *Persuasion*

While Captains Wentworth and Harville led the talk on one side of the room, and by recurring to former days, supplied anecdotes in abundance to occupy and entertain the others, it fell to Anne's lot to be placed rather apart with Captain Benwick; and a very good impulse of her nature obliged her to begin an acquaintance with him. He was shy, and disposed to abstraction; but the engaging mildness of her countenance, and gentleness of her manners, soon had their effect; and Anne was well repaid the first trouble of exertion.

He was evidently a young man of considerable taste in reading, though principally in poetry; and besides the persuasion of having given him at least an evening's indulgence in the discussion of subjects, which his usual companions had probably no concern in, she had the hope of being of real use to him in some suggestions as to the duty and benefit of struggling against affliction, which had naturally grown out of their conversation. For, though shy, he did not seem reserved; it had rather the appearance of feelings glad to burst their usual restraints; and having talked of poetry, the richness of the present age, and gone through a brief comparison of opinion as to the first-rate poets, trying to ascertain whether Marmion or The Lady of the Lake were to be preferred, and how ranked the Giaour and The Bride of Abydos; and moreover, how the Giaour was to be pronounced, he showed himself so intimately acquainted with all the tenderest songs of the one poet, and all the impassioned descriptions of hopeless agony of the other; he repeated, with such tremulous feeling, the various lines which imaged a broken heart, or a mind destroyed by wretchedness, and looked so entirely as if he meant to be understood, that she ventured to hope he did not always read only poetry, and to say, that she thought it was the misfortune of poetry to be seldom safely enjoyed by those who enjoyed it completely; and that the strong feelings which alone could estimate it truly were the very feelings which ought to taste it but sparingly.

His looks shewing him not pained, but pleased with this allusion to his situation, she was emboldened to go on; and feeling in herself the right of seniority of mind, she ventured to recommend

a larger allowance of prose in his daily study; and on being requested to particularize, mentioned such works of our best moralists, such collections of the finest letters, such memoirs of characters of worth and suffering, as occurred to her at the moment as calculated to rouse and fortify the mind by the highest precepts, and the strongest examples of moral and religious endurances.

Captain Benwick listened attentively, and seemed grateful for the interest implied; and though with a shake of the head, and sighs which declared his little faith in the efficacy of any books on grief like his, noted down the names of those she recommended, and promised to procure and read them.

[1817]

IV.a.6.   MARY WOLLSTONECRAFT SHELLEY, from *Frankenstein*

'One night during my accustomed visit to the neighbouring wood where I collected my own food and brought home firing for my protectors, I found on the ground a leathern portmanteau containing several articles of dress and some books. I eagerly seized the prize and returned with it to my hovel. Fortunately the books were written in the language, the elements of which I had acquired at the cottage; they consisted of *Paradise Lost*, a volume of Plutarch's *Lives*, and the Sorrows of *Werter*. The possession of these treasures gave me extreme delight; I now continually studied and exercised my mind upon these histories, whilst my friends were employed in their ordinary occupations. I can hardly describe to you the effect of these books. They produced in me an infinity of new images and feelings, that sometimes raised me to ecstasy, but more frequently sunk me into the lowest dejection. In the *Sorrows of Werter*, besides the interest of its simple and affecting story, so many opinions are canvassed and so many lights thrown upon what had hitherto been to me obscure subjects that I found in it a never-ending source of speculation and astonishment. The gentle and domestic manners it described, combined with lofty sentiments and feelings, which had for their object something out of self, accorded well with my experience among my protectors and with the wants which were forever alive in my own bosom. But I thought Werter himself a more divine being than I had ever beheld or imagined; his character contained no pretension, but it sank deep. The disquisitions upon death and suicide were calculated to fill me with wonder. I did not pretend to enter into the merits of the case, yet I inclined towards the opinions of the hero, whose extinction I wept, without precisely understanding it.

'As I read, however, I applied much personally to my own feelings and condition. I found myself similar yet at the same time strangely unlike to the beings concerning whom I read and to whose conversation I was a listener. I sympathized with and partly understood them, but I was unformed in mind; I was dependent on none and related to none. 'The path of my departure was free,' and there was none to lament my annihilation. My person was hideous and my stature gigantic. What did this mean? Who was I? What was I? Whence did I come? What was my destination? These questions continually recurred, but I was unable to solve them.

'The volume of Plutarch's *Lives* which I possessed contained the histories of the first founders of the ancient republics. This book had a far different effect upon me from the *Sorrows of Werter*. I learned from Werter's imaginations despondency and gloom, but Plutarch taught me high thoughts; he elevated me above the wretched sphere of my own reflections, to admire and love the heroes of past ages. Many things I read surpassed my understanding and experience. I had a very confused knowledge of kingdoms, wide extents of country, mighty rivers, and boundless seas. But I was perfectly unacquainted with towns and large assemblages of men. The cottage of

my protectors had been the only school in which I had studied human nature, but this book developed new and mightier scenes of action. I read of men concerned in public affairs, governing or massacring their species. I felt the greatest ardour for virtue rise within me, and abhorrence for vice, as far as I understood the signification of those terms, relative as they were, as I applied them, to pleasure and pain alone. Induced by these feelings, I was of course led to admire peaceable lawgivers, Numa, Solon, and Lycurgus, in preference to Romulus and Theseus. The patriarchal lives of my protectors caused these impressions to take a firm hold on my mind; perhaps, if my first introduction to humanity had been made by a young soldier, burning for glory and slaughter, I should have been imbued with different sensations.

'But *Paradise Lost* excited different and far deeper emotions. I read it, as I had read the other volumes which had fallen into my hands, as a true history. It moved every feeling of wonder and awe that the picture of an omnipotent God warring with his creatures was capable of exciting. I often referred the several situations, as their similarity struck me, to my own. Like Adam, I was apparently united by no link to any other being in existence; but his state was far different from mine in every other respect. He had come forth from the hands of God a perfect creature, happy and prosperous, guarded by the especial care of his Creator; he was allowed to converse with and acquire knowledge from beings of a superior nature, but I was wretched, helpless, and alone. Many times I considered Satan as the fitter emblem of my condition, for often, like him, when I viewed the bliss of my protectors, the bitter gall of envy rose within me.

'Another circumstance strengthened and confirmed these feelings. Soon after my arrival in the hovel I discovered some papers in the pocket of the dress which I had taken from your laboratory. At first I had neglected them, but now that I was able to decipher the characters in which they were written, I began to study them with diligence. It was your journal of the four months that preceded my creation. You minutely described in these papers every step you took in the progress of your work; this history was mingled with accounts of domestic occurrences. You doubtless recollect these papers. Here they are.

'Everything is related in them which bears reference to my accursed origin; the whole detail of that series of disgusting circumstances which produced it is set in view; the minutest description of my odious and loathsome person is given, in language which painted your own horrors and rendered mine indelible. I sickened as I read. 'Hateful day when I received life!' I exclaimed in agony. 'Accursed creator! Why did you form a monster so hideous that even YOU turned from me in disgust? God, in pity, made man beautiful and alluring, after his own image; but my form is a filthy type of yours, more horrid even from the very resemblance. Satan had his companions, fellow devils, to admire and encourage him, but I am solitary and abhorred.'

'These were the reflections of my hours of despondency and solitude; but when I contemplated the virtues of the cottagers, their amiable and benevolent dispositions, I persuaded myself that when they should become acquainted with my admiration of their virtues they would compassionate me and overlook my personal deformity. Could they turn from their door one, however monstrous, who solicited their compassion and friendship? I resolved, at least, not to despair, but in every way to fit myself for an interview with them which would decide my fate. I postponed this attempt for some months longer, or the importance attached to its success inspired me with a dread lest I should fail. Besides, I found that my understanding improved so much with every day's experience that I was unwilling to commence this undertaking until a few more months should have added to my sagacity.[']

[1818]

IV.a.7. PERCY BYSSHE SHELLEY, 'Ozymandias'

I met a traveller from an antique land
Who said, 'Two vast and trunkless legs of stone
Stand in the desert. . . . Near them, on the sand,
Half sunk, a shattered visage lies, whose frown,
And wrinkled lip, and sneer of cold command,
Tell that its sculptor well those passions read
Which yet survive, stamped on these lifeless things,
The hand that mocked them and the heart that fed.
And on the pedestal these words appear:
"My name is Ozymandias, king of kings:
Look on my works, ye Mighty, and despair!"
Nothing beside remains. Round the decay
Of that colossal wreck, boundless and bare
The lone and level sands stretch far away.'

d. FRANÇAIS

IV.d.1. ANTOINE FABRE D'OLIVET, *Les Vers dorés de Pythagore*

Si vous daignez, MESSIEURS, suivre le développement de mes idées avec autant d'attention que d'indulgence, vous savez déjà que ce que j'appelle l'essence ou l'esprit de la Poésie, et que sur les pas du fondateur de l'Académie, et du régénérateur des sciences en Europe, je distingue de sa forme, n'est autre chose que le génie allégorique, production immédiate de l'inspiration; vous comprenez aussi que j'entends par inspiration, l'infusion dans l'âme de ce même génie, qui, n'étant encore qu'en puissance dans la nature intellectuelle, se manifeste en acte en passant dans la nature élémentaire, au moyen du travail intérieur du poète qui la revêt d'une forme sensible, selon son talent; vous sentez enfin de quelle manière j'explique, d'après cette simple théorie, les paroles de Platon, et comment je conçois que le poète inspiré transmet aux hommes les idées des Dieux. Je n'ai pas besoin, je pense, de vous dire que je mets une énorme différence entre cette inspiration divine, qui exalte l'âme et la remplit d'un enthousiasme vrai, et cette espèce de mouvement intérieur ou de désordre, que le vulgaire appelle aussi inspiration, laquelle, dans sa plus grande perfection, n'est que la passion excitée par l'amour de la gloire, unie à l'habitude des vers qui constitue le talent, et dans son imperfection, que la passion désordonnée, appelée par Boileau une ardeur de rimer. Ces deux espèces d'inspiration ne se ressemblent en rien; leurs effets sont aussi différents que leurs causes, leurs productions aussi différentes que leurs sources. L'une, sortant de la nature intellectuelle, est immuable comme elle: elle est la même dans tous les temps, chez tous les peuples, au sein de tous les hommes qui la reçoivent; elle seule produit le génie: sa manifestation première est très rare, mais sa manifestation seconde l'est moins, ainsi que je le ferai voir plus loin, en exposant ma pensée à ce sujet. L'autre inspiration, inhérente à la nature sensible, enfantée par la passion, se varie au gré des hommes et des choses, prend la teinte des mœurs et des temps; elle peut faire naître le talent ou du moins le modifier, et, quand elle est secondée par une grande facilité, peut aller jusqu'à feindre le génie, mais jamais plus loin: son véritable domaine est l'esprit. Sa possession n'est pas très rare, même dans sa perfection. On peut quelquefois la trouver unie à l'inspiration vraie, première, comme dans Homère, ou seconde, comme dans Virgile; et alors la forme qu'elle travaille sans cesse, joignant ses beautés sensibles aux beautés intellectuelles du génie, crée les monuments de la science.

[1813]

IV.d.2. VICTOR HUGO, « Réponse a un acte d'accusation », *Les Contemplations*

Donc, c'est moi qui suis l'ogre et le bouc émissaire.
Dans ce chaos du siècle où votre coeur se serre,
J'ai foulé le bon goût et l'ancien vers françois
Sous mes pieds, et, hideux, j'ai dit à l'ombre: – Sois! –
Et l'ombre fut. – Voilà votre réquisitoire.
Langue, tragédie, art, dogmes, conservatoire,
Toute cette clarté s'est éteinte, et je suis
Le responsable, et j'ai vidé l'urne des nuits.

d. FRENCH

IV.d.1. ANTOINE FABRE D'OLIVET, from *The Golden Verses of Pythagoras*

If you deign, *Messieurs,* to follow the development of my ideas with as much attention as indulgence, you already know that what I call the essence or spirit of poetry, and which, following upon the steps of the founder of the Academy and of the regenerator of the sciences of Europe, I distinguish from its form, is no other thing than the allegorical genius, immediate production of the inspiration; you also understand that I mean by inspiration, the infusion of this same genius into the soul which, having power only in the intellectual nature, is manifested in action by passing into the elementary nature by means of the inner labour of the poet who invests it with a sentient form according to his talent; you perceive finally, how, following this simple theory, I explain the words of Plato, and how I conceive that the inspired poet transmits to men the ideas of the gods. I have no need I think of telling you that I make an enormous difference between this divine inspiration which exalts the soul and fills it with a real enthusiasm, and that sort of inner movement or disorder which the vulgar also call inspiration, which in its greatest perfection is only passion excited by the love of glory, united with a habit of verse making, which constitutes the talent, and in its imperfection is only a disordered passion called by Boileau, an ardour for rhyming. These two kinds of inspiration in no wise resemble each other; their effects are as different as their causes, their productions as different as their sources. The one, issuing from the intellectual nature, has its immutability: it alone produces genius: its first manifestation is very rare, but its second manifestation is less so, as I will show later on. The other inspiration, inherent in sentient nature, born of passion, varies with the whim of men and things, and takes on the hue of the customs and the times; it can bring forth talent or at least modify it, and when it is seconded by a great facility, can go to the extent of feigning genius but never farther: its real domain is the mind. Its possession is not very rare even in its perfection. One can sometimes find it united with the true inspiration, first as in Homer, or second as in Vergil; and then the form which it unceasingly works over, joining its sentient beauties to the intellectual beauties of genius, creates the monuments of science.

[1813] [*Translated by Nayán Louise Redfield. New York: Putnam, 1917*]

IV.d.2. VICTOR HUGO, 'Response to an Indictment', from *Contemplations*

So, it is I who am the ogre and the scapegoat.
In this century's chaos where your heart sinks,
I have trampled good taste and old-fashioned French verse
Under my feet, and, hideous, I have said to the shadow, 'Be!'
And there was shadow. – That is your charge.
Language, tragedy, art, dogmas, conservatory,
All that clarity is extinguished, and I am
The one to blame, and I emptied the urn of nights.

De la chute de tout je suis la pioche inepte;
C'est votre point de vue. Eh bien, soit, je l'accepte;
C'est moi que votre prose en colère a choisi;
Vous me criez: Racca; moi je vous dis: Merci!
Cette marche du temps, qui ne sort d'une église
Que pour entrer dans l'autre, et qui se civilise;
Ces grandes questions d'art et de liberté,
Voyons-les, j'y consens, par le moindre côté,
Et par le petit bout de la lorgnette. En somme,
J'en conviens, oui, je suis cet abominable homme;
Et, quoique, en vérité, je pense avoir commis,
D'autres crimes encor que vous avez omis.
Avoir un peu touché les questions obscures,
Avoir sondé les maux, avoir cherché les cures,
De la vieille ânerie insulté les vieux bâts,
Secoué le passé du haut jusques en bas,
Et saccagé le fond tout autant que la forme.
Je me borne à ceci: je suis ce monstre énorme,
Je suis le démagogue horrible et débordé,
Et le dévastateur du vieil A B C D;
Causons.
Quand je sortis du collège, du thème,
Des vers latins, farouche, espèce d'enfant blême
Et grave, au front penchant, aux membres appauvris;
Quand, tâchant de comprendre et de juger, j'ouvris
Les yeux sur la nature et sur l'art, l'idiome,
Peuple et noblesse, était l'image du royaume;
La poésie était la monarchie; un mot
Était un duc et pair, ou n'était qu'un grimaud;
Les syllabes, pas plus que Paris et que Londre,
Ne se mêlaient; ainsi marchent sans se confondre
Piétons et cavaliers traversant le pont Neuf;
La langue était l'état avant quatre-vingt-neuf;
Les mots, bien ou mal nés, vivaient parqués en castes:
Les uns, nobles, hantant les Phèdres, les Jocastes,
Les Méropes, ayant le décorum pour loi,
Et montant à Versaille aux carrosses du roi;
Les autres, tas de gueux, drôles patibulaires,
Habitant les patois; quelques-uns aux galères
Dans l'argot; dévoués à tous les genres bas,
Déchirés en haillons dans les halles; sans bas,
Sans perruque; créés pour la prose et la farce;
Populace du style au fond de l'ombre éparse;
Vilains, rustres, croquants, que Vaugelas leur chef
Dans le bagne Lexique avait marqué d'une F;

I am the inept mattock who brought it all down;
That's your point of view. All right, fine, I accept it;
It is I whom your angry prose has chosen;
You shout at me: Racca; I say to you, Thanks!
This march of time, which leaves one church
Only to go into another, and which becomes civilized;
These great questions of art and liberty,
Let us see them, I agree, from the least side,
And through the wrong end of the telescope. In short,
I admit it, yes, I am that abominable man;
And, although, in truth, I think that I have committed
Other crimes in addition which you have omitted,
I've touched a little on the obscure questions,
I've probed the hurts, I've searched for cures,
Insulted the old baggage of old mulishness,
Shaken the past from top to bottom,
And sacked the meaning just as much as the form,
I limit myself to this: I am this enormous monster
I am the horrible, overblowing demagogue
And the destroyer of the old ABCD.
Let's talk.
When I left school, and Latin translations,
And Latin verses, shy, a rather wan
And serious child, with bent head, with weak limbs;
When, trying to understand and judge, I opened
My eyes to nature and art, the language,
People and nobility, was the image of the kingdom;
Poetry was the monarchy; a word
Was a duke and a peer, or was nothing but a scoundrel;
Syllables, no more than Paris and London,
Did not mix; as they go without mingling
Walkers and riders crossing the Pon'Neuf;
The language was the State before '89;
Words, well- or low-born, lived penned in castes;
These, noble, haunting Phaedras and Jocastas,
Meropes, having decorum as their law,
And going to Versailles to the king's carriages;
The others, a pile of beggars, sinister rogues,
Living in dialects; some in the chain gangs
Of slang; devoted to every low genre,
Torn into rags in the markets; without stockings,
Without wig; created for prose and farce;
Populace of the style in the depths of the scattered shadow;
Villeins, oafs, yokels, which Vaugelas their chief
Had marked with an F[1] in the work-camp of Lexicon;

[1] 'F' = familiar, colloquial. (Translator's note.)

N'exprimant que la vie abjecte et familière,
Vils, dégradés, flétris, bourgeois, bons pour Molière.
Racine regardait ces marauds de travers;
Si Corneille en trouvait un blotti dans son vers,
Il le gardait, trop grand pour dire: Qu'il s'en aille;
Et Voltaire criait: Corneille s'encanaille!
Le bonhomme Corneille, humble, se tenait coi.
Alors, brigand, je vins; je m'écriai: Pourquoi
Ceux-ci toujours devant, ceux-là toujours derrière?
Et sur l'Académie, aïeule et douairière,
Cachant sous ses jupons les tropes effarés,
Et sur les bataillons d'alexandrins carrés,
Je fis souffler un vent révolutionnaire.
Je mis un bonnet rouge au vieux dictionnaire.
Plus de mot sénateur! plus de mot roturier!
Je fis une tempête au fond de l'encrier,
Et je mêlai, parmi les ombres débordées,
Au peuple noir des mots l'essaim blanc des idées;
Et je dis: Pas de mot où l'idée au vol pur
Ne puisse se poser, tout humide d'azur!
Discours affreux! – Syllepse, hypallage, litote,
Frémirent; je montai sur la borne Aristote,
Et déclarai les mots égaux, libres, majeurs.
Tous les envahisseurs et tous les ravageurs,
Tous ces tigres, les Huns les Scythes et les Daces,
N'étaient que des toutous auprès de mes audaces;
Je bondis hors du cercle et brisai le compas.
Je nommai le cochon par son nom; pourquoi pas?
Guichardin a nommé le Borgia! Tacite
Le Vitellius! Fauve, implacable, explicite,
J'ôtai du cou du chien stupéfait son collier
D'épithètes; dans l'herbe, à l'ombre du hallier,
Je fis fraterniser la vache et la génisse,
L'une étant Margoton et l'autre Bérénice.
Alors, l'ode, embrassant Rabelais, s'enivra;
Sur le sommet du Pinde on dansait Ça ira;
Les neuf muses, seins nus, chantaient la Carmagnole;
L'emphase frissonna dans sa fraise espagnole;
Jean, l'ânier, épousa la bergère Myrtil.
On entendit un roi dire: – Quelle heure est-il? –
Je massacrais l'albâtre, et la neige, et l'ivoire,
Je retirai le jais de la prunelle noire,
Et j'osai dire au bras: Sois blanc, tout simplement.
Je violai du vers le cadavre fumant;
J'y fis entrer le chiffre; ô terreur! Mithridate
Du siége de Cyzique eût pu citer la date.

Expressing only abject, familiar life,
Vile, degraded, withered, bourgeois, good for Molière.
Racine looked askance at these rascals;
If Corneille found one nestling in his verse,
He kept it, too great to say: Let it be gone.
And Voltaire cried: Corneille is slumming
That humble fellow Corneille kept quiet.
So, brigand, I came; I cried: Why
These always ahead, those always behind?
And on the Academy, ancestor and dowager,
Hiding under her skirts the frightened tropes,
And on the square battalions of alexandrines,
I caused a revolutionary wind to blow.
I put a Liberty cap on the old dictionary.
Now no word is a senator! no word is a commoner!
I made a tempest in the depths of the inkwell,
And I mixed, among the overflowing shadows,
With the black people of words the white swarm of ideas;
And I said: No word where the pure-flighted idea
Cannot land, all damp with blue!
Awful speech! – Syllepsis, hypallage, litotes,
Trembled; I climbed onto Aristotle's milestone,
And declared words equal, free, adult.
All the invaders and all the destroyers,
All these tigers, the Huns, the Scythians, the Dacians,
Were mere lapdogs next to my daring;
I bounded out of the circle and broke the compass.
I called the pig by its name; why not?
Guicchiardini named Borgia! Tacitus
Named Vitellius! Implacable, explicit beast,
I removed the collar of epithet from the neck of the stupefied dog;
In the grass, in the shade of the covert
I made the cow and the heifer fraternize,
One being Margoton and the other Berenice.
Then the ode, kissing Rabelais, became drunk;
On the summit of Pindus they were dancing 'Ça ira;'
The nine muses, bare-breasted, were singing the Carmagnole;
Emphasis shivered in her Spanish ruff;
Jean the donkey-herder married the shepherdess Myrtle.
A king was heard to say, 'What time is it?'
I massacred alabaster, and snow, and ivory,
I removed the jet from the sloe-eye
And I dared to say to the arm: Be plain white.
I desecrated the steaming corpse of poetry
I caused numbers to enter it; O terror! Mithridates
Could have cited the date of the siege of Cyzicus.

Jours d'effroi! les Laïs devinrent des catins.
Force mots, par Restaut peignés tous les matins,
Et de Louis-Quatorze ayant gardé l'allure,
Portaient encor perruque; à cette chevelure
La Révolution, du haut de son beffroi,
Cria: – Transforme-toi! c'est l'heure. Remplis-toi
– De l'âme de ces mots que tu tiens prisonnière! –
Et la perruque alors rugit, et fut crinière.
Liberté! c'est ainsi qu'en nos rébellions,
Avec des épagneuls nous fîmes des lions,
Et que, sous l'ouragan maudit que nous soufflâmes,
Toutes sortes de mots se couvrirent de flammes.
J'affichai sur Lhomond des proclamations.
On y lisait: – Il faut que nous en finissions!
– Au panier les Bouhours, les Batteux, les Brossettes
– A la pensée humaine ils ont mis les poucettes.
– Aux armes, prose et vers! formez vos bataillons!
– Voyez où l'on en est: la strophe a des bâillons!
– L'ode a des fers aux pieds, le drame est en cellule.
– Sur le Racine mort le Campistron pullule!-
Boileau grinça des dents; je lui dis: Ci-devant,
Silence! et je criai dans la foudre et le vent:
Guerre à la rhétorique et paix à la syntaxe!
Et tout quatre-vingt-treize éclata. Sur leur axe,
On vit trembler l'athos, l'ithos et le pathos.
Les matassins, lâchant Pourceaugnac et Cathos,
Poursuivant Dumarsais dans leur hideux bastringue,
Des ondes du Permesse emplirent leur seringue.
La syllabe, enjambant la loi qui la tria,
Le substantif manant, le verbe paria,
Accoururent. On but l'horreur jusqu'à la lie.
On les vit déterrer le songe d'Athalie;
Ils jetèrent au vent les cendres du récit
De Théramène; et l'astre Institut s'obscurcit.
Oui, de l'ancien régime ils ont fait tables rases,
Et j'ai battu des mains, buveur du sang des phrases,
Quand j'ai vu par la strophe écumante et disant
Les choses dans un style énorme et rugissant,
L'Art poétique pris au collet dans la rue,
Et quand j'ai vu, parmi la foule qui se rue,
Pendre, par tous les mots que le bon goût proscrit,
La lettre aristocrate à la lanterne esprit.
Oui, je suis ce Danton! je suis ce Robespierre!
J'ai, contre le mot noble à la longue rapière,
Insurgé le vocable ignoble, son valet,
Et j'ai, sur Dangeau mort, égorgé Richelet.

600

Days of dread! the Lad's became trollops.
Many words, groomed by Restaut every morning,
And keeping an air of Louis XIV about them,
Still wore wigs; the Revolution
Shouted at this hairstyle, from the top of her belfry,
'Transform! it's time. Fill yourself
With the soul of those words which you hold prisoner!'
And then the wig roared, and was a mane.
Liberty! It is thus that in our rebellions,
Out of spaniels we made lions,
And that, under the accursed hurricane which we blew,
All kinds of words were covered in flames.
I put up proclamations on Lhomond.
They read, 'We must finish with this!
To the basket with the Bouhours, the Batteux, the Brossettes!
They put shackles on human thought.
To arms, prose and verse! Form your battalions!
See where we are: the strophe has been gagged!
The ode is in irons, drama is in a cell.
On the dead Racine swarms the Campistron.'
Boileau ground his teeth; I said to him: From now on,
Silence! and I shouted in the lightning and the wind:
War on rhetoric and peace to syntax!
And '93 exploded. On their axis
We saw the athos, the ithos and the pathos tremble.
The matacchinos dropping Pourceaugnac and Cathos,
Pursuing Dumarsais in their hideous dance,
Filled their reeds with the waves of the Permessus.
The syllable, climbing over the law which sorted it,
The peasantish substantive, the pariah verb,
Came running. Horror was drunk to the dregs.
They were seen to disinter Atalie's dream;
They scattered to the winds the ashes of
Theramen's story; and the star Institute dimmed.
Yes, they made a clean sweep of the Ancien Régime,
And I clapped my hands, drinker of sentences' blood,
When I saw by the foaming stanza, and saying
Things in an enormous, roaring style,
Poesy collared in the street,
And when I saw, among the rushing crowd,
Hanging, by all the words which good tastes proscribes,
The aristocratic letter on the mind's lantern.
Yes, I am this Danton! I am this Robespierre!
I have, against the noble word with the long rapier,
Roused the ignoble term, its valet,
And I have, on dead Dangeau, cut Richelet's throat.

Oui, c'est vrai, ce sont là quelques-uns de mes crimes.
J'ai pris et démoli la bastille des rimes.
J'ai fait plus: j'ai brisé tous les carcans de fer
Qui liaient le mot peuple, et tiré de l'enfer
Tous les vieux mots damnés, légions sépulcrales;
J'ai de la périphrase écrasé les spirales,
Et mêlé, confondu, nivelé sous le ciel
L'alphabet, sombre tour qui naquit de Babel;
Et je n'ignorais pas que la main courroucée
Qui délivre le mot, délivre la pensée.
L'unité, des efforts de l'homme est l'attribut.
Tout est la même flèche et frappe au même but.
Donc, j'en conviens, voilà, déduits en style honnête,
Plusieurs de mes forfaits, et j'apporte ma tête.
Vous devez être vieux, par conséquent, papa,
Pour la dixième fois j'en fais meâ culpâ.
Oui, si Beauzée est dieu, c'est vrai, je suis athée.
La langue était en ordre, auguste, époussetée,
Fleur-de-lys d'or, Tristan et Boileau, plafond bleu,
Les quarante fauteuils et le trône au milieu;
Je l'ai troublée, et j'ai, dans ce salon illustre,
Même un peu cassé tout; le mot propre, ce rustre,
N'était que caporal: je l'ai fait colonel;
J'ai fait un jacobin du pronom personnel;
Dur participe, esclave à la tête blanchie,
Une hyène, et du verbe une hydre d'anarchie.
Vous tenez le *reum confitentem*. Tonnez!
J'ai dit à la narine: Eh mais! tu n'es qu'un nez!
J'ai dit au long fruit d'or: Mais tu n'es qu'une poire!
J'ai dit à Vaugelas: Tu n'es qu'une mâchoire!
J'ai dit aux mots: Soyez république! soyez
La fourmilière immense, et travaillez! Croyez,
Aimez, vivez! – J'ai mis tout en branle, et, morose,
J'ai jeté le vers noble aux chiens noirs de la prose.
Et, ce que je faisais, d'autres l'ont fait aussi;
Mieux que moi. Calliope, Euterpe au ton transi,
Polymnie, ont perdu leur gravité postiche.
Nous faisons basculer la balance hémistiche.
C'est vrai, maudissez-nous. Le vers, qui, sur son front
Jadis portait toujours douze plumes en rond,
Et sans cesse sautait sur la double raquette
Qu'on nomme prosodie et qu'on nomme étiquette,
Rompt désormais la règle et trompe le ciseau,
Et s'échappe, volant qui se change en oiseau,
De la cage césure, et fuit vers la ravine,
Et vole dans les cieux, alouette divine.

Yes, it's true, these are some of my crimes.
I took and demolished the Bastille of rhymes.
I did more: I broke all the iron collars
Which bound the word 'people,' and pulled from hell
All the old damned words, sepulchral legions;
I crushed the spirals of periphrasis,
And mingled, mixed, and leveled under Heaven
The alphabet, somber tower born of Babel,
And I was not unaware that the wrathful hand
Which delivers the word, delivers thought.
Unity is the attribute of man's efforts.
All is the same arrow, all strikes the same target.
Thus, I admit it, there, laid out in an honest style,
Several of my crimes, and I present my head.
You must be old, then, papa,
For the tenth time, I say my mea culpa.
Yes, if Beauzée is god, it's true, I'm an atheist.
Language was in order, august, dusted,
Golden fleurs-de-lis, Tristan and Boileau, blue ceiling,
The forty chairs and the throne in the center;
I disturbed it, and I, in this illustrious room,
Well, I broke everything; the proper word, that lout,
Was only a corporal; I made it a colonel;
I made a Jacobin of the personal pronoun,
Of the participle, that white-haired slave,
A hyena, and of the verb a hydra of anarchy.
You hold the *reum confitentem*. Roar!
I said to the nostril: But you're just a nose!
I said to the long golden fruit: But you're just a pear!
I said to Vaugelas: You're just a jawbone!
I said to the words: Be a republic! be
The immense anthill, and work! Believe,
Love, live! – I shook up everything, and, morose,
I threw the noble verse to the black dogs of prose.
And, that which I did, others did also;
Better than I. Calliope, Euterpe with the transfixed tone,
Polyhymnia, lost their spurious gravity.
We topple the balance of the hemistich.
It is true, curse us. The verse, which, on its forehead
Formerly wore a circlet of twelve plumes,
And ceaselessly jumped on the double racket
Called prosody and etiquette,
Now breaks the ruler and fools the chisel,
And escapes, a shuttlecock which becomes a bird,
From the cesura's cage, and flees toward the ravine,
And flies in the heavens, a divine lark.

Tous les mots à présent planent dans la clarté.
Les écrivains ont mis la langue en liberté.
Et, grâce à ces bandits, grâce à ces terroristes,
Le vrai, chassant l'essaim des pédagogues tristes,
L'imagination, tapageuse aux cent voix,
Qui casse des carreaux dans l'esprit des bourgeois;
La poésie au front triple, qui rit, soupire
Et chante, raille et croit; que Plaute et Shakspeare
Semaient, l'un sur la plebs, et l'autre sur le mob;
Qui verse aux nations la sagesse de Job
Et la raison d'Horace à travers sa démence;
Qu'enivre de l'azur la frénésie immense,
Et qui, folle sacrée aux regards éclatants,
Monte à l'éternité par les degrés du temps,
La muse reparaît, nous reprend, nous ramène,
Se remet à pleurer sur la misère humaine,
Frappe et console, va du zénith au nadir,
Et fait sur tous les fronts reluire et resplendir
Son vol, tourbillon, lyre, ouragan d'étincelles,
Et ses millions d'yeux sur ses millions d'ailes.
Le mouvement complète ainsi son action.
Grâce à toi, progrès saint, la Révolution
Vibre aujourd'hui dans l'air, dans la voix, dans le livre;
Dans le mot palpitant le lecteur la sent vivre;
Elle crie, elle chante, elle enseigne, elle rit,
Sa langue est déliée ainsi que son esprit.
Elle est dans le roman, parlant tout bas aux femmes.
Elle ouvre maintenant deux yeux où sont deux flammes,
L'un sur le citoyen, l'autre sur le penseur.
Elle prend par la main la Liberté, sa soeur,
Et la fait dans tout homme entrer par tous les pores.
Les préjugés, formés, comme les madrépores,
Du sombre entassement des abus sous les temps,
Se dissolvent au choc de tous les mots flottants,
Pleins de sa volonté, de son but, de son âme.
Elle est la prose, elle est le vers, elle est le drame;
Elle est l'expression, elle est le sentiment,
Lanterne dans la rue, étoile au firmament.
Elle entre aux profondeurs du langage insondable;
Elle souffle dans l'art, porte-voix formidable;
Et, c'est Dieu qui le veut, après avoir rempli
De ses fiertés le peuple, effacé le vieux pli
Des fronts, et relevé la foule dégradée,
Et s'être faite droit, elle se fait idée!

(Paris, janvier 1834)
[1856]

All words now soar in brightness.
Writers have set the language free.
And, thanks to these bandits, thanks to these terrorists,
The true, driving out the swarm of sad pedagogues,
The imagination, rowdy with one hundred voices,
Which breaks the windowpanes in the minds of the bourgeois;
Three-faced poetry, which laughs, sighs,
And sings; mocks and believes; which Plautus and Shakespeare
Scattered, one on the plebs, the other on the mob;
Which pours out on the nations with wisdom of Job
And the reason of Horace through its madness;
Which the immense frenzy of blue intoxicates,
And which, sacred madwoman with dazzling glances,
Climbs to eternity on the steps of time,
The muse reappears, takes us back, leads us back,
Begins anew to weep over human misery,
Strikes and consoles, goes from the zenith to the nadir,
And makes on every forehead shine and gleam
Her flight, whirlwind, lyre, hurricane of sparks,
And her millions of eyes on her millions of wings.
The movement thus completes its action.
Thanks to you, holy progress, the Revolution
Vibrates today in the air, in the voice, in the book,
In the palpitating word the reader feels her live;
She shouts, she sings, she teaches, she laughs.
Her tongue is loosed as is her mind.
She is in the novel, whispering to women.
She opens now two eyes that hold two flames,
One on the citizen, the other on the thinker.
She takes her sister Liberty by the hand,
And makes her enter through the pores of every man.
The prejudices, formed, like the madrepore,
From the dark crowding of abuses over time,
Dissolve at the shock of all the floating words,
Full of her will, of her goal, of her soul.
She is prose, she is verse, she is drama;
She is expression, she is sentiment,
Lantern in the street, star in the firmament.
She enters into the depths of the unfathomable language.
She breathes into art, formidable megaphone,
And, as God wills, after having filled
The people with her pride, erased the old crease
From their foreheads, and raised up the degraded crowd,
And having made herself the law, she makes herself the Idea!

(Paris, January 1834)

[1856] [*Translated by Anne Gwin*]

IV.d.3.   PIERRE LEROUX, 'Du style symbolique', paru dans *Le Globe,* 8 avril 1829

Il faut qu'on nous accorde que toute poésie vit de métaphore, et que le poète est un artiste qui saisit des rapports de tout genre par toutes les puissances de son âme, et qui leur substitue des rapports identiques sous forme d'images, de même que le géomètre substitue au contraire des termes purement abstraits, des lettres qui ne représentent rien de déterminé, aux nombres, aux lignes, aux surfaces, aux solides, à tous les corps de la nature, et à tous les phénomènes[2]. En comprenant la métaphore proprement dite, la comparaison, l'emblème, le symbole, l'allégorie, sous le nom général de métaphore, on pourrait dire hardiment que la poésie n'a pas d'autre élément que la métaphore, que poésie et métaphore sont une même chose, et qu'entre nations différentes de même qu'entre différents âges d'un même peuple, l'ampleur de la métaphore est la mesure du génie poétique.

Or, cela étant, supposez qu'il s'introduise tout à coup dans une langue une figure qui permette de substituer continuellement à des termes abstraits des images, à l'expression propre une expression vague et indéterminée; et voyez-en l'effet. L'abstraction disparaîtra de la poésie de ce peuple, et le mystère y naîtra. C'est précisément ce qui est arrivé par l'introduction dans notre langue d'une forme de style que nous appellerions volontiers *comparaison symbolique,* ou, pour être plus bref, *symbole.*

L'artifice de cette forme de langage consiste à ne pas développer l'idée que l'on veut comparer à une autre, mais à développer uniquement cette seconde idée, c'est-à-dire l'image. C'est donc une forme intermédiaire entre la comparaison et l'allégorie proprement dites, plus rapide que la comparaison et moins obscure que l'allégorie. C'est un véritable emblème. De même qu'on remplace le mot propre par une métaphore, ici l'idée est remplacée par son emblème: on a pour ainsi dire la métaphore d'une idée. [. . .]

[2] Dans la science des nombres, on peut multiplier les deux termes d'un rapport sans que le rapport change; on a ainsi deux rapports égaux et une proportion; et si on répète la même opération plusieurs fois, on obtient une suite de rapports, tous identiques, quoique sous des formes différentes, c'est-à-dire une progression, qui peut s'étendre à l'infini. On peut ensuite faire correspondre une série progressive à une autre, et cette correspondance a conduit aux logarithmes, de telle manière qu'on a substitué au calcul des nombres le calcul plus simple de leurs logarithmes.

L'application de l'algèbre à la géométrie est fondée sur le même procédé. Aux lignes, aux surfaces, aux solides, le géomètre substitue des nombres, parce qu'il ne considère que des rapports.

Nous pourrions continuer, et montrer que tout se passe de même dans toute la science mathématique comme dans ses applications.

Mais ce n'est pas seulement dans les sciences qu'il en est ainsi. Le procédé de l'esprit humain est un; et le poète, dans ses inventions, suit la même loi que Napier inventant les logarithmes ou Descartes l'analyse géométrique.

Que fait le poète en effet, que fait tout artiste, et que font en général tous les hommes, sinon substituer continuellement le sensible aux conceptions pures, ou en d'autres termes saisir des rapports et leur substituer des rapports identiques pris dans un autre ordre d'idées, de même que le géomètre substitue à volonté des nombres aux surfaces, des surfaces aux nombres? Newton se comparant dans ses *Mémoires* à un enfant qui ramasse des coquillages au bord du grand océan de la vérité n'est pas différent de Newton écrivant dans une formule algébrique les mouvements des corps célestes ou les lois de la lumière. Dans l'un et l'autre cas, il ne fait qu'abstraire et comparer, c'est-à-dire substituer le rapport de deux termes au rapport identique de deux autres termes.

L'identité est le principe de toutes ces substitutions. En géométrie, comme en poésie, comme en tout, la comparaison est la grande route de l'esprit humain. Le poète rend l'abstrait par le sensible, le géomètre le sensible par l'abstrait; mais tous deux ne font que substituer des rapports à d'autres rapports, ou plutôt reproduire sous des termes différents des rapports identiques. Seulement ils ne travaillent pas sur les mêmes matériaux.

IV.d.3.   PIERRE LEROUX, 'On Symbolic Style', from *Le Globe,* 9 April 1829

One must grant us that all poetry lives by metaphor, and that the poet is an artist who grasps all sorts of relations with all the strength of his soul, and who substitutes for them identical relations in the form of images, just as the geometer substitutes, on the other hand, purely abstract terms, letters which represent nothing determined, for numbers, lines, surfaces, solids, all the bodies of nature, and all the phenomena.[3] By including metaphor in the strict sense, comparison, emblem, symbol, allegory, under the general term of metaphor, one could boldly say that poetry has no other element but metaphor, that poetry and metaphor are the same thing, and that among different nations, just as among different ages of the same people, the breadth of metaphor is the measure of poetic genius.

This being so, suppose that all of a sudden into a language is introduced a figure which allows the continuous substitution of images for abstract terms, a vague and indeterminate phrase for the correct expression; and see the effect. Abstraction will disappear from the poetry of this people, and mystery will be born.

This is precisely what happened on the introduction into our language of a form of style which we would gladly call *symbolic comparison,* or to be brief, *symbol.* The trick of this form of language consists of not developing the idea which one wants to compare to another, but of developing the second idea alone, that is, the image. It is thus an intermediary form between comparison and allegory in the strict sense, more rapid than comparison and less obscure than allegory. It is a true emblem. Just as one replaces the right word by a metaphor, here the idea is replaced by its emblem: one has, as it were, the metaphor of an idea. [. . .]

---

[3] In the science of numbers, one may multiply the two terms of a ratio without the relation changing; one thus has two equal ratios and a proportion; and if one repeats the same operation several times, one obtains a series of ratios, all identical, although in different forms, that is, a progression, which may extend to infinity. One may then correlate one progressive series to another, and this correlation led to logarithms, in such a way that one has substituted for the calculation of numbers the simpler calculation of their logarithms.

The application of algebra to geometry is founded on the same principle. The geometer substitutes numbers for lines, surfaces, solids, because he considers only ratios.

We could continue, and show that everything occurs in the same way in the whole of mathematical science, as in its applications.

But it is not only in the sciences that it is so. The process of the human mind is one; and the poet, in his inventions, follows the same law as Napier inventing logarithms or Descartes analytical geometry.

What does the poet do, in fact, what does any artist, and what do all men do in general, if not continuously substitute the concrete for pure conceptions, or in other words grasp relationships and substitute for them identical relationships taken from another category of ideas, just as the geometer substitutes at will numbers for surfaces, surfaces for numbers? Newton comparing himself in his *Memoirs* to a child gathering shells on the edge of the great ocean of truth is not different from Newton writing in an algebraic formula the movements of heavenly bodies or the laws of light. In both cases, he is simply abstracting and comparing, that is, substituting the relation of two terms to the identical relation of two other terms.

Identity is the principle of all these substitutions. In geometry, as in poetry, as in all things, comparison is the broad road of the human mind. The poet renders the abstract by the concrete, the geometer the concrete by the abstract; but both are only substituting relations for other relations, or rather reproducing in different terms identical relations. Only they do not work with the same materials.

Si nous nous sommes bien fait entendre, on doit distinguer nettement le trope qui, suivant nous, est devenu l'élément d'un style commun aujourd'hui, lequel ne développe jamais l'idée morale en termes abstraits, mais qui prend toujours un emblème de cette idée, qui pour elle donne un symbole, et procède par allégorie, dans le sens restreint que nous avons donné à ce mot.

Parler par symboles, allégoriser, voilà, à ce qu'il nous semble, la grande innovation, en fait de style, depuis cinquante ans. Nous serions presque tenté de ramener la question du romantisme, quant au style poétique, à l'introduction dans la langue d'un trope, non pas nouveau, mais presque inusité pendant deux siècles. [...]

S'il fallait assigner une origine à cette innovation, aussi poétique que la première l'était peu, nous dirions que les ouvrages de J.-J. Rousseau l'ont provoquée, quoique par son style Jean-Jacques n'appartienne aucunement à la famille d'écrivains dont il fut le précurseur. Mais ses cris contre la société, son dédain pour les solutions de la philosophie, la révélation de sa vie solitaire et de ses jouissances contemplatives, portèrent dans beaucoup d'âmes, avec le dégoût du monde, un véritable enthousiasme pour les scènes de la nature. [...] Ainsi ce grand changement dans le style, et par suite dans la langue, n'est pas dû à une puérile imitation, mais à des besoins bien sentis. Il ne s'est pas opéré par l'accession de quelques idiotismes étrangers [...], mais par une force intérieure de développement, et par une sorte de croissance naturelle. Le besoin de poésie, de rénovation des idées morales et religieuses, et l'étude de la nature et de ses mystérieuses harmonies, voilà ce qui l'a engendré. Après cela, mille causes accessoires y ont concouru: on a pris goût au style poétique de la Bible, qui était pour Voltaire un sujet d'ineffables risées, on a pris goût aux littératures étrangères; on a étudié l'Orient; on a eu besoin d'émotions nouvelles; le sentiment de la liberté et de l'individualisme s'est montré partout, s'est appliqué à tout; enfin on retrouve ici, comme dans mille autres questions, l'influence de tout ce qui compose ce qu'on appelle l'esprit du siècle. Et, comme s'il y avait synchronisme pour la propagation des procédés de l'art dans le monde européen, ainsi que pour tout le reste, on voit à la fois ce style naître et se développer en France, en Angleterre, en Allemagne, et toujours sous la plume d'écrivains amoureux de la nature et profondément méditatifs.

[1829]

e. DEUTSCH

IV.e.1. NOVALIS, 'Monolog'

Es ist eigentlich um das Sprechen und Schreiben eine närrische Sache; das rechte Gespräch ist ein bloßes Wortspiel. Der lächerliche Irrtum ist nur zu bewundern, daß die Leute meinen — sie sprächen um der Dinge willen. Gerade das Eigentümliche der Sprache, daß sie sich blos um sich selbst bekümmert, weiß keiner. Darum ist sie ein so wunderbares und fruchtbares Geheimnis, — daß wenn einer blos spricht, um zu sprechen, er gerade die herrlichsten, originellsten Wahrheiten ausspricht. Will er aber von etwas Bestimmtem sprechen, so läßt ihn die launige Sprache das lächerlichste und verkehrteste Zeug sagen. Daraus entsteht auch der Haß, den so manche ernsthafte Leute gegen die Sprache haben. Sie merken ihren Muthwillen, merken aber nicht, daß das verächtliche Schwatzen die unendlich ernsthafte Seite der Sprache ist. Wenn man den Leuten nur begreiflich machen könnte, daß es mit der Sprache wie mit den mathematischen Formeln sei — Sie machen eine Welt für sich aus — Sie spielen nur mit sich selbst, drücken nichts als ihre wunderbare Natur aus, und eben darum sind sie so ausdrucksvoll — eben darum spiegelt sich in ihnen das seltsame Verhältnisspiel der Dinge. Nur durch ihre Freiheit sind sie Glieder der Natur, und nur in ihren freien Bewegungen äußert sich die Weltseele und macht sie zu einem zarten Maßstab und Grundriß der Dinge. So ist es auch mit der Sprache — wer ein feines Gefühl ihrer

If we have made ourselves understood, one should clearly distinguish the trope which, according to us, has become the element of a common style of the day, which never develops the moral idea in abstract terms, but which always takes an emblem of this idea, which gives a symbol for it, and proceeds by allegory, in the restricted sense which we have given to this word.

Speaking in symbols, allegorizing – this, it seems to us, is the greatest innovation, as regards style, in fifty years. We would almost be tempted to bring the question of Romanticism, as regards poetic style, back to the introduction into the language of a trope, not new, but almost unused for two centuries. [. . .]

If it were necessary to assign an origin to this innovation, as poetic as the first was not, we would say that the works of J.-J. Rousseau provoked it, although by his style Jean-Jacques does not in the least belong to the family of writers of which he was the precursor. But his cries against society, his disdain for the solutions of philosophy, the revelation of his solitary life and his contemplative delights, brought into many souls, along with disgust for the world, a veritable enthusiasm for the scenes of nature. [. . .] Thus this great change in style, and consequently in language, is not due to a puerile imitation, but to strongly-felt needs. It did not come about by the rise of a few foreign idioms [. . .], but by an interior force of development, and by a sort of natural growth. The need for poetry and for renewal of moral and religious ideas, and the study of nature and its mysterious harmonies, this is what caused it. After that, a thousand secondary causes converged: one acquired a taste for the poetic style of the Bible, which was for Voltaire a subject of ineffable mockery, one acquired a taste for foreign literatures; one studied the Orient; one needed new emotions; the feeling of liberty and individualism appeared everywhere, was applied to everything; finally one finds here, as in a thousand other questions, the influence of everything which composes what is called the spirit of the age. And, as if there were synchronicity for the propagation of artistic processes in the European world, as there is for all the rest, one sees this style be born and develop in France, in England, in Germany, and always from the pen of profoundly meditative writers in love with nature.

[1829] [*Translated by Anne Gwin*]

e. GERMAN

1V.e.1. NOVALIS, 'Monologue'

There is really something very foolish about speaking and writing; proper conversation is merely a word game. One can only marvel at the ridiculous mistake that people make when they think – that they speak for the sake of things. The particular quality of language, the fact that it is concerned only with itself, is known to no one. Language is such a marvelous and fruitful secret – because when someone speaks merely for the sake of speaking, he utters the most splendid, most original truths. But if he wants to speak about something definite, capricious language makes him say the most ridiculous and confused stuff. This is also the cause of the hatred that so many serious people feel toward language. They notice its mischief, but not the fact that the chattering they scorn is the infinitely serious aspect of language. If one could only make people understand that it is the same with language as with mathematical formulae. These constitute a world of their own. They play only with themselves, express nothing but their own marvelous nature, and just for this reason they are so expressive – just for this reason the strange play of relations between things is mirrored in them. Only through their freedom are they elements of nature and only in their free movements does the world soul manifest itself in them and make them a sensitive measure and ground plan of things. So it is too with language – on the one

Applicatur, ihres Takts, ihres musikalischen Geistes hat, wer in sich das zarte Wirken ihrer innern Natur vernimmt, und danach seine Zunge oder seine Hand bewegt, der wird ein Prophet sein, dagegen wer es wohl weiß, aber nicht Ohr und Sinn genug für sie hat, Wahrheiten wie diese schreiben, aber von der Sprache selbst zum besten gehalten und von den Menschen, wie Kassandra von den Trojanern, verspottet werden wird. Wenn ich damit das Wesen und Amt der Poesie auf das deutlichste angegeben zu haben glaube, so weiß ich doch, daß es kein Mensch verstehn kann, und ich ganz was albernes gesagt habe, weil ich es habe sagen wollen, und so keine Poesie zustande kommt. Wie, wenn ich aber reden müßte? und dieser Sprachtrieb zu sprechen das Kennzeichen der Eingebung der Sprache, der Wirksamkeit der Sprache in mir wäre? und mein Wille nur auch alles wollte, was ich müßte, so könnte dies ja am Ende ohne mein Wissen und Glauben Poesie sein und ein Geheimnis der Sprache verständlich machen? und so wär ich ein berufener Schriftsteller, denn ein Schriftsteller ist wohl nur ein Sprachbegeisterter? —

(1798)

[*Novalis. Schriften, Historisch-kritische Ausgabe by Paul Kluckhohn,*
Richard Samuel, Hans-Joachim Mähl, Gerhard Schulz, 7 vols. Stuttgart,
Berlin, Cologne, Mainz: Kohlhammer, 1960–, II. 438–439]

f. MAGYAR

IV.f.1. DÖBRENTEI GÁBOR, *Levél Kölcsey Ferenchez, Kolozsvár,*
1813. november 20. (Részlet)

A hiperbolákkal, s általában, figurákkal[1] s trópusokkal[2] teljes írás épen nyelve a költőnek; és nyelvének kell lenni, még minekelőtte a retorikát tanulta volna. Állíts nekem valakit elé, aki annak tanulása után hozhatja írásába a soknemű, különös, meglepő, érzékényítő, elragadó, kifejezéseket, ha azok önmagából nem jönnek. És épen mivel a költőben praxisban van, teória nélkül, ezen írásmódja, azért ragadtatik el általak. Minden csendes megfontolás absztraktumokkal való foglalatoskodás kedvetlen előtte, az ő ifjúi fantáziájának istenekkel-társalkodó világában; matériája önmagából ömlik; ír a társaságban is; – nyelvével pedig nem igen gondol (*aus Mangel an Stoff denkt man leicht zu sehr an die Sprache*;[3] mond a szökdöső fantáziájú Jean Paul); de, lassanként hűlvén tüzéből, melyben elébb egeket ostromolni is kész lett volna, megáll repülésében, nyugszik, gondolkozik; ez által s a kritika által ítélete erősödik; ekkor leül versei mellé; melyeket elébb neki csupán a természet lángolása gyújtott, nézegeti, gondolkodik; úgy van mint a képíró,[4] ki elkészített zseniális munkája mellett, melyet felhevüléssel dolgozott, csendesen ül, nézegeti, ítélgeti magában a vonásokat, itt világosság kell még, itt több kinyomás,[5] itt karaktervonás; így a költő verseivel; megbizonyosodott érzése sugdos neki: ez csak szópompa, ez itt nem eléggé tiszta vagy világos kifejezés, ez nem a tárgy tulajdonságát festő szó, itt nincs euritmia,[6] itt nincs erő, itt alatt mászó, nincs egység a munkában, nincs logikai rend; azonban reszketve olvassa a már sokak ítéletén keresztülment s mindentől felségesnek talált munkát, látja ott a bevégzett írás mi

[1] retorikai és költői szóképekkel
[2] szóképekkel
[3] Anyag hiányában túl könnyen gondol az ember a nyelvre.
[4] festő
[5] kifejezőerő
[6] a szöveg helyes, kellemes tagolása, harmóniája.

hand, anyone who is sensitive to its fingering, its rhythm, its musical spirit, who perceives within himself the delicate workings of its inner nature, and moves his tongue or his hand accordingly, will be a prophet; on the other hand, anyone who knows how to write truths like these but does not have ear and sense enough for it will be outwitted by language itself and mocked by people as Cassandra was by the Trojans. Even if in saying this I believe I have described the essence and function of poetry in the clearest possible way, at the same time I know that no one can understand it, and I have said something quite foolish because I wanted to say it, and in this way no poetry comes about. What would it be like though if I had to speak? and this instinct of language to speak were the hallmark of what inspires language, of the efficacy of language within me? and were my will to want only everything that I was obliged to do, in the end could this be poetry without my knowledge or belief and could it make a secret of language understandable? and thus I would be a born writer, for a writer is surely only a language enthusiast?

(1798) [*Translated by Margaret Stoljar. Novalis: Philosophical Writings. New York: SUNY, 1997. 83–84*]

f. HUNGARIAN

IV.f.1. GÁBOR DÖBRENTEI,[7] from A Letter to Ferenc Kölcsey, Kolozsvár, 20 November 1813

Writing full of hyperbole, figures of speech and tropes in general is precisely the language of the poet; and it has to be his language even before he studies rhetoric. Show me anyone that can bring to his writing after such study all the various sorts of expressions – distinctive, surprising, touching, captivating – if they do not come from within himself. And it is precisely because there is at work in the poet such a style of writing, uninfluenced by theory, that he is captivated by them. All silent contemplation, all embroilment with abstraction, is displeasing to him in the world of his youthful fantasy where he communes with the gods; his material pours from him; he writes even when in company – but takes no great thought for his language (*aus Mangel an Stoff denkt man leicht zu sehr an die Sprache*,[8] as says Jean Paul[9] of lively fantasy); slowly, however, the ardour cools in which he would have been prepared to lay siege to the heavens, he pauses in mid-flight, calms himself and ponders; by this means and through criticism his judgement is strengthened; now he sits down to scrutinise his verses, which formerly the blazing fire of nature alone illumined for him; as the painter who sits quietly with the work of genius that he has executed, on which he has worked intensely, and looks at it, criticises it to himself in detail – here more light is wanted, there more expressiveness, there character should be brought out – so is the poet with his verses; his enhanced awareness whispers to him that this is mere verbiage, that expression is not clear or plain enough, this word does not bring out the flavour of the subject, here eurhythmy is lacking, there is weakness, this here is inferior, there is no unity in the work, no logical structure; he shudders, however, as he reads work that has passed the scrutiny of many and been found by all to be mag-

---

[7] Gábor Döbrentei (1785–1851), writer, poet and translator who between 1814 and 1818 edited the ten volumes of Erdélyi Muzéum, one of the first Hungarian literary and critical periodicals.

[8] With the lack of material language is too easily thought of.

[9] Jean Paul, born Johann Paul Friedrich Richter (1763–1825), German writer and critic, whose *Vorschule der Aesthetik* [Preliminary School of Aesthetics] [1804] with his theory of humour was quite influential in Hungary.

legyen? S minthogy a tökéletességnek bizonyos elrejtett sejdítésével kell bírnia, méregeti a magáét, s mindent, amit igaz szépnek nem lel, irgalom nélkül kitörli; végtére feláll csendes bizodalommal, s a magával vívó ifjú felett lebegett múzsa isteni csókját adja neki, s ezt mondja: így légy fiam, és én halhatatlanságot adok neked; eszerint, mint a kollégiomi deák, aki elsőbb esetekben, midőn a csínos-világ tónusát még nem ismeri, pedánt, otromba, fás, nevetséges a maga viseletében, de utóbb igyekezetei, észrevételei s az illendőnek érzése által egészen mássá változik, leszen a költőnek lelke is, megtisztítva mindentől, ami fantáziájának aranyos rongyai voltak ugyan, de, egybeállítva, hogy gyönyörűséget szerezzenek, nem; kitisztult érzése megmarad, csendesebb de méltóságosabb gyulladás teszi azokat szavakká s olyanokká, melyek a jobb szíveken győződelmet vesznek; fantáziájának merész repülése most is szabadon teremt, egybealkot, de csak a megpróbáltat, a valóságos nagyot, a tisztát veszi be ítélgető érezése: most menjen bátran; költése örökre fenn marad. [. . .]

[*Critical edition: Kölcsey, Ferenc, Kölcsey Ferenc minden munkái, Levelezés 1, (1808–1818). Edited by Szabó, G. Zoltán. Budapest: Universitas, 2005. 268–269*]

g. ITALIANO

IV.g.1. CARLO PORTA, da 'Il Romanticismo'

[. . .]

Donca, madamm, che la se rasserenna,
che la comoda in rid quell bell bocchoeu,
ché i Romantegh infin no hin l'ienna,
hin minga el lôff che va a mangià i fioeu,
ma hin fior de Paladin tutt cortesia,
e massim coj donn bej come usciuria.   36

E l'è appunt dal linguagg che i Paladin
parlaven in del temp de Carlo Magn
che i Todisch han creduu, madamm Bibin,
de tirà a voltra on nomm squasi compagn
per battezà sti Paladin novej,
protettor del bon sens e di donn bej.   42

Ora mò, quant al nomm, che no la vaga
a cercà pù de quell che gh'hoo ditt mì,
o brutt o bell el nomm coss'el suffraga?
Ai Todisch ghè piasuu de digh inscì,
e inscì anch nun ghe diremm a marsc dispett
de sti ruga in la cacca col legnett.   48

Tornand mò adess a nun, l'ha da savè
che el gran busilles de la poesia
el consist in de l'arte de piasè,
e st'arte la sta tutta in la magia

nificent, and there sees what the perfected work should be. And as he must possess a certain sixth sense that seeks perfection he weighs his own work and ruthlessly crosses out everything that he does not find true or beautiful; finally he stands up, quietly confident, and the Muse that has fluttered above the youth as he struggled with himself gives him her divine kiss and says 'Be like that, dear boy, and I will confer upon you immortality.' In that way the spirit of the poet too will be like the schoolboy, who, at first, when he does not yet know the ways of the world, is a pedant, clumsy, wooden and risible in his conduct, but later his endeavours, perceptions and sense of what is right change into something quite different. The poet likewise purges his spirit of everything that used to be the gilded shreds of his erstwhile fantasy but which, when assembled to acquire splendour, no longer are; his purified awareness remains, a quieter but more dignified flame makes these shreds into words, and such words as triumph in the better hearts; now too the daring flight of his fantasy is free to create, to compose, but his shrewd awareness will admit only the tried and genuine great and pure. Now let him proceed boldly; his poetry will last for ever. [. . .]

[*Translated by Bernard Adams*]

g. ITALIAN

IV.g.1. CARLO PORTA, from 'Romanticism'

[. . .]

Therefore, Madame, calm yourself
put a smile on your sweet mouth,
because the Romantics are not after all hyenas
they are not wolves off to eat children
they are the flower of paladins, full of courtesy,
especially with beautiful women like you.   36

It is precisely from the language spoken
by the paladins at the time of Charlemagne
my dear Madam Bibin, that the Germans believed
they could coin a similar name
to baptise these new paladins,
protectors of good sense and beautiful women.   42

Now as far as the name is concerned, do not seek
any more or less that what I have told you,
if it is ugly or beautiful, what does it matter?
the Germans were happy to call it thus
and we will use the same to spite those
search-the-dirt-with-a-stick people.   48

To return to us, you must know
that the big snag in poetry
consists of the art of pleasing
and this art lies in the magic

de moeuv, de messedà, come se voeur,
tutt i passion che gh'emm sconduu in del coeur.   54

E siccome i passion coll'andà innanz
varien, baratten fina a l'infinitt,
segond i temp, i loeugh, i circostanz
tal e qual i sò mod di cappellitt,
così i poetta gh'han de tend adree
come coj cappellitt la fa anca lee.   60

E siccome anca lee ai sò tosanett
per moeuvegh la passion de studià
no la ghe esibiss minga on coreghett,
né i scuffion cont i al de cent ann fa,
né i peland a fioramm con sù i paes
che se ved suj crespin, suj cari chines;   66

inscì anch con nun, se voeuren sti poetta
ciappottann i passion, moeuven el coeur,
han de toccann i tast che ne diletta,
ciappann, come se dis, dove ne doeur,
senza andà suj baltresch a tirà a man
i còregh e i scuffion gregh e roman.   72
[. . .]
Sicché i Romantegh fina chì la ved
che n'hin minga sti eretegh, sti settari,
sti gent pericolos che ghe fan cred
i Torquemada del partii contrari,
che tran in aria el cuu e s'innoreggissen
a bon cunt su tutt quell che no capissen.   126

Né l'ha nanca de cred ai strambarij
che ghe dan a d'intend per spaventalla,
che i Romantegh no parlen che de strij,
de pagur, de carr matt, de mort che balla,
ohjbò: coss che ghe creden press'a pocch
come la cred lee al pappa di tarocch.   132

I Romantegh fan anzi profession
de avegh, con soa licenza, in quell servizzi
tutt quell che tacca lid con la reson,
che somena e che cova i pregiudizzi,
vegnend giò da Saturno a quell folett
che ha stremii l'ann passaa tucc i sabett.   138
[. . .]

of moving, of mixing, as one desires
all the passions which we have hidden in our hearts.   54

And because passions vary
with the passing of time, they change infinitely
according to the times, the places, the circumstances
just like your fashions for hats,
thus poets have to follow these trends,
as you do with headwear.   60

And similarly with your daughters
to induce a passion for study
you certainly do not offer them a crinoline
or a bonnet with the brims of one hundred years ago
nor a dress coat with a flowery pattern and with those landscapes
which one sees on fans and Chinese wall hangings.   66

It is the same with us poets
who wishing to stimulate passions, to move hearts
must touch the notes which entertain us
take us, as one says to where it hurts,
without going into the attics to pull out
the crinolines and bonnets of the Greeks and Romans.   72
[. . .]
Up to this, therefore, do you see that the Romantics
are not those heretics, those sectarians
that dangerous people that the Torquemada inquisitor
from the opposition party would have you believe
people who kick and straighten your ears
when faced with that which is not understood.   126

Neither should you believe those eccentricities
which they present with the intentions of frightening you:
that the Romantics only speak of witches,
ghosts, sabbats, of the dead who dance,
tut tut: they believe in these things as much as
you believe in the Queen of Spades.   132

The Romantics rather make a profession
of keeping, with your permission, in its place
all that picks a fight with reason
that germinates and hatches prejudices
from ancient Saturn to that elf
who last year terrified all the old women.   138
[. . .]

Beata lee, madamm, che l'è levada
a boccon coj prezzett di classicista,
che in quij trè or che la stà là incantada
no la perd mai i dò unitaa de vista
e la sa fin che pont lassass andà
coll'illusion, denanz de tornà a cà.   156

Chè quij goff de Todisch, quij ciaj d'Ingles
se lassen mennà attorna di poetta,
e stan via con lor di dì, di mes,
senza accorges che passen la stacchetta,
e riden, piangen come tant poppò
anch che Orazzi e Aristotel voeubbien nò.   162

[. . .]

Ma via là – che la vaga, che l'è vora,
a sentì la Virginia – On olter dì
ghe vuj legg el Macbeth, se la me onora,
franch e sicur che infin la m'ha da dì:
Grazie, Bosin, capissi, noccoralter
i smargiassad no me capponen d'alter.   216

[1819] [*Edizione di riferimento: Carlo Porta, Poesie, a cura di Dante Isella,*
Mondadori, I Meridiani, Milano, 1975]

h. NORSK

IV.h.1.   IVAR AASEN, fra 'Om vort Skriftsprog'

1.

Efterat vort Fædreneland atter er blevet hvad det engang var, nemlig frit og selvstændigt, maa det være os magtpaaliggende at bruge et selvstændigt og nationalt Sprog, eftersom dette er en Nations fornemste Kjendemærke. Saalænge Norge ansaaes som en dansk Provinds, og Landets Embeder for en stor Deel besattes af Danske, ja endog alle Norske, som nød videnskabelig Opdragelse, oplærtes i Danmark og paa Dansk, og følgelig Dansk eller kjøbenhavnsk Tale og Skrift omsider blev herskende hos os, var det naturlig, at vort Sprogs Nationalitet maatte gaae under. Hiin Umyndighedstid er svunden, og vi burde vise Verden, at vi ogsaa i denne, visstnok ikke uvigtige Sag – attraaede at være selvstændige.

(...)

   Vi trænge aldrig til at gaae udenom Grændserne efter et Sprog; vi skulde lede i vore Gjemmer, og see efter, hvad vi selv eiede, førend vi gik hen at laane af Andre. Ligesaa lidet, som det skulde hædre en fri Mand at aftrygle af Andre, hva han selv havde Forraad af, ligesaalidet hædrer det os, at vi heller samle udenlandske ord, end benytte dem, der almindelig kjendes og bruges i vore Bygder.

Lucky you, Madame, who has been brought up
with the precepts of the Classicists
and who in those three hours [in theatre], are enchanted
without ever losing sight of the two unities
knowing well the point to which your illusions can go
before returning home.   156

On the other hand, those clumsy Germans and foolish English
are led by their poets
and with them can spend days and months
without realising that they have passed the limit
and they laugh and cry like many children
even though Horace and Aristotle would disapprove.   162
[. . .]
But away now, go, – it is time
To go and hear *Virginia* – another day
If you do me the honour, I want to read Macbeth to you
And I am sure and certain that at the end you will say to me
Thank you poet, I understand, nothing else is needed
Bragging will entangle me no longer.   216

[1819] [*Translated by Anne O'Connor*]

h.   NORWEGIAN

IV.h.1.   IVAR AASEN, from 'On Our Written Language'

1.

After our fatherland once more has become what it once used to be, a free and independent nation, it ought to be of utmost importance to us to use an independent and national language, as this is the most distinguished symbol of a nation. As long as Norway was looked upon as a province of Denmark, and the leading professions of the country to a great deal were occupied by Danes, and, furthermore, all Norwegians with a scholarly education had been taught in Denmark and in the Danish language, and as a consequence the Danish language – or rather – the dialect of Copenhagen – became the governing language among us, it was only natural that the nationality of our language died. The days of oppression are over, and we ought to show the world that we longed to be independent in this important matter also.

[. . .]

We need not cross the boarders for a language; we should search in our hideouts, and examine what we owned ourselves before we borrowed from others. In the same way that it would be unbecoming to a free man to ask others for goods that he already possessed himself, it would be dishonorable to us to collect foreign words rather than using those that are generally known and used in our valleys.

2.

Da nu Enhver synes bedst om det, han fra Barns Been er tilvant, og da alle Skrivende I vor Generation, ere paa en Maade bundne til det Kjøbenhavnske, og maaskee fordetmeste vante fra Ungdom op, til at foragte vort Folkesprog, saa er det ventelig, at en saadan Reform ansees af de Fleste med mindre Gunst. Imidlertid gives der dog, – det har man seet i vore offentlige Blade og andre Skrifter, – de, der alvorlig ønske at faa vort Sprog, saaledes formet, at man med mer Føie kunde kalde det Norsk. Den mindre dannede Deel af Folket, saa slavisk den endog undergiver sig det Herskende, maa visst længe stiltiende have imødeseet en saadan Forandring. Visstnok skulde mange Misforstaaelser og ubillige Puristerier for en stor Deel forebygges. Det har altid smertet mig bittert, naar jeg hørte vort Almuesprog krænkes og belees, enten af velklædt Uvidenhed, eller af en rigtignok velmeent Renselses-Iver. Skal vi da, tænkte jeg, give Slip paa denne kostelige Skat fra Fortiden, som vore Forfædre gjennem alle sine Trængsler have troligen bevaret og overladt til os som en hellig Arv? Skal dens Besiddelse, saa retfærdig, som den er, endnu gjøres os stridig, nu, da Folkefriheden atter befinder sig mellem vore Klipper?

3.

(...)

Dersom Norge gjennem disse Sekler havde hævdet sin politiske Selvstændighed, da skulde vort Hovedsprog ogsaa været Almuens, det skulde været Sammenligningen af Landets Dialekter, Middelpunktet, hvorom de dreidede sig. Men vi lode os, med en vidunderlig Taalmodighed, i saa lang Tid uretfærdigen beherske af Andre; derfor tabte vi vort Held og Hæder, derfor tabte vi vort Fædrenesprog. At gjenvinde dette er os endnu ikke umulig; vor Nationalære fordrer det, og vort Lands lykkelig forandrede Stilling berettiger os dertil. Bonden har den Ære at være Sprogets Redningsmand; til hans Tale skulde man altsaa lytte.

4.

(...)

At vi, ved den her tilsigtede Reform eller Tillæmpning, skulde faa et altfor plat og pøbelagtigt Hovedsprog, er en Indvending, der kun grunder sig paa Fordom og Vane. Vi ønske os just et Folkesprog, et som enhver Landsmand uden Møie kan tage Deel i; vor Statsforfatning berettiger os til dette Ønske. Og hvorfor skulde vi være saa ængstelige for disse saakaldte Platheder? De ere det ikke; de ere Norskheder. Lad os sætte Fordommene tilside, og ikke undsee os for at bruge vort Lands eget Tungemaal.

5.

Forslag. Det er ikke min Hensigt hermed at fremhæve nogen enkelt af vore Dialekter; nei, ingen saadan bør være Hovedsprog, men dette skulde være en Sammenligning af, et Grundlag for dem Alle. Til et saadant at fuldføre, skulde der gjøres Ordsamlinger for enhver af Landets større Provindser, med grammatikalske Oplysninger og bestemte Ordforklaringer. Til at forfatte disse, skulde Mænd, som ei blot troede at kunne, men og virkelig kunde Almuesproget, opmuntres. Disse Ordsamlinger skulde innsendes til et Selskab, oprettet af sprogkyndige Mænd, som skulde anstille Sammenligninger og gjøre Udvalg, og efterat saaledes Hovedsproget var bestemt, skulde

2.

As everybody prefers what he has been accustomed to since childhood, and as all literate men of our generation are in some way tied to the language of Copenhagen, and perhaps accustomed to ever since their youth to scorn our people's language, one might expect that such a reform would be considered undesirable by most people. However, there are those – so we have seen in public journals and other writings – who sincerely wish to have our language shaped in such a way that one more appropriately might call it Norwegian. The less educated part of our population, however humbly it subordinates itself to the ruling customs, has no doubt silently longed for such a change for a long time. Obviously many misunderstandings and senseless 'corrections' would be avoided. It has always hurt me bitterly to hear our common language violated and ridiculed, either due to well dressed ignorance or anxiousness to purify. Should we, then, I thought, give up this precious treasure from our past, which our ancestors have kept faithfully throughout their strenuous lives, and left to us like a sacred heritage? Should our possession of it, as just as it is, be questioned, even now, when the freedom of our people once more rules among our cliffs?

3.

[...]

If Norway through these centuries had maintained its political independence, our main language would have been that of ordinary people, it would have been the common denominator of all the dialects of our country, the centre around which they all revolved. But we let ourselves with a strange patience for so long unjustly oppress by others; therefore we lost our fortune and our honor, therefore we lost the language of our fathers. To regain it is still possible; our national honor requires it, and the favorably changed situation of our country entitles us to it. The farmer has the honor of being the savior of the language; thus, it is his speech one should listen to.

4.

[...]

That we by the reform or adjustment indicated here should acquire an all too simple and vulgar official language, is an objection, that is based solely on prejudice and custom. We wish for ourselves precisely a people's language, one that every compatriot can participate in with ease; our Constitution entitles us to this desire. And why should we fear these so called platitudes? That is not what they are; they are Norwegian expressions. Let us put prejudice aside, and not be ashamed to use the language of our own country.

5.

Proposal. It is not my intention by this to promote any one of our dialects; no, none of them should be the official language, but this should be a common denominator, a base, for them all. To such an end one should make collections of words from every one of the larger provinces of our land, with grammatical and lexical explanations. To accomplish this one should engage men who not only believed that they knew, but who really knew the language of ordinary people. These collections of words should be sent to a society, established by scholars of language, who could make comparisons and selections, and after the main language thus had been established,

dette Selskab udarbeide en fuldstændig norsk Ordbog, med tilsvarende Grammatikk. Denne nye Sprogform skulde dog aldeles ikke paabydes eller paanødes; man skulde opmuntre til dens Brug, men ellers lade Enhver bruge det Nye eller Gamle efter eget Godtbefindende.

(1836)

i. POLSKI

IV.i.1. JULIUSZ SŁOWACKI, *Beniowski. Poema* (fragmenty)

PIEŚŃ I

25.

O Melancholio! nimfo! skąd ty rodem?
Czyś ty chorobą jest epidemiczną?
Skąd przyszłaś do nas? Co ci jest powodem,
Że teraz nawet szlachtę okoliczną
Zarażasz? – Nimfo! za twoim przewodem
Ja sam wędrówkę już odbyłem śliczną!
I jestem dzisiaj – niech cię porwie trzysta!
– Nie Polak – ale istny bajronista...

26.

Trochę w tym wina jest mojej młodości,
Trochę – tych grobów, co się w Polszcze mnożą,
Trochę – tej ciągłej w życiu samotności,
Trochę – tych duchów ognistych, co trwożą,
Palcami grobów pokazując kości,
Które się na dzień sądny znów ułożą
I będą chodzić skrzypiąc, płacząc, jęcząc,
Aż wreszcie Pana Boga skruszą – dręcząc.

27.

Prześliczna strofa! mógłbym zacząć od niej
Nowy poemat, jak Sąd ostateczny;
I przy eumenid pokazać pochodni,
Jak jest grzech każdy dziwnie niebezpieczny;
Jak w jasnym niebie daleko jest chłodniéj
Niż w piekle, kędy płonie ogień wieczny;
Lecz wolę dzieło to rzucić na późniéj,
Bo do porządku mnie wołają woźni...

this society should develop a complete Norwegian dictionary, with a corresponding grammar. This new language should still not be forced or pushed on anybody; one should encourage people to use it, but other than that let any one use the new or the old at one's own wish.

[1836] [*Translated by G. Bø, 2009*]

[*A peasant's son, Ivar Aasen wrote this – in Danish – in 1836 at the age of 23. Throughout the subsequent 20 years he himself went ahead and created 'New Norwegian' according to the method indicated here. Rendered here from Hanssen, Eskil (ed.), Fra norsk sprakhistorie. En antologi. Oslo: Universitetsforlaget, 1972.*]

i. POLISH

IV.i.1.   JULIUSZ SŁOWACKI, from *Beniowski*

From Canto I

25.

O melancholy! Nymph! Whence comest thou?
Art thou a creeping plague, an epidemic?
From where didst thou originate, and how?
Both aristos and poets academic
Are touched by thee! – Ah, Nymph! I must avow
That I too caught the malady systemic,
And am by now (the devil! – I'm no ironist)
No longer Polish – but a Byronist . . .

26.

'Tis partly guilt at my hot adolescence,
In part the fault of our massed Polish dead,
In part my life of pain (no convalescence),
In part the fiery ghosts which walk in dread,
Exhibiting their dirty deliquescence,
Which will at Judgement Day all spring new-spread,
And walk, with creaks and tears, a horrid horde,
Till their poor Polish dust torments the Lord.

27.

What pretty lines! With them I shall begin
A great new work yclept 'The Final Day',
And as the Furies' fires and whips for sin,
(For every newborn sin is fresh as May,
Though gentle May's much kinder on your skin
Than is hot Hell, that fearful, frazzling fray . . .
But I shall start this work some later date,
Because my mentors can no longer wait).

PIEŚŃ II

12.

O Boże! ileż bym stworzył romansów,
Gdybym chciał wszystkich d.....w być zabawą,
Wyspą dla grubych naszych Sanczo Pansów,
Na której by się uczyli ze sławą
Sylabizować. Lecz z prozą aliansów
Nie chcę – do wiersza mam, jak sądzę, prawo.
Sam się rym do mnie miłośnie nagina,
Oktawa pieści, kocha mię sestyna.

13.

Ktoś to powiedział, że gdyby się słowa
Mogły stać nagle indywiduami,
Gdyby ojczyzną był język i mowa,
Posąg by mój stał, stworzony głoskami,
Z napisem: „Patri patriae." – Jest to nowa
Krytyka. – Stój! – ten posąg błyska skrami,
Spogląda z góry na wszystkie języki,
Lśni jak mozaika, śpiewa jak słowiki;

14.

Otocz go lasem cyprysów, modrzewi,
On się rozjęczy jak harfa Eola,
W róże się same jak dryjada wdrzewi,
Głosem wyleci za lasy na pola
I rozłabędzi wszystko, roześpiewi...
Jak smukła, pełna słowików topola,
Co kiedy w nocy zacznie pieśń skrzydlatą,
Myślisz... że w niebo ulatujesz z chatą,

From Canto II

12.

Oh God! What romances I should create,
If I would be the sport of bookish fools –
Our fat Sanchos, who play and recreate,
And practice hard with all their critics' tools,
And read by syllables. To procreate
With prose is base, and, lulled by poetry's rules,
I fall among the flowers and herbs of rhyme,
Caressed by octaves, and the sestet's chime.

13.

If words, some wit would have us understand,
Could change to individuals through dark art,[1]
And if our language were the fatherland,
Then, formed from words, my bust would stand apart,
With this inscribed: 'Patri patriae.' – Such grand
New criticism! – Halt! – from my bust sparks dart,
As it smiles down, well pleased at such gay Babel,
Like nightingales, or mosaics in the fable;

14.

Surround it with green cypresses and larches,
And like Aeolus' harp 'twill hum, and hymn,
Tree[2] dryad-like into red roses' arches,
Voice to the fields via the forest dim,
And make all earth swing round in swan-like marches –
Like nightingale-infested poplars slim,
Which, when they start their wingéd song at night,
You'll think that with your cottage you're in flight,

---

[1] 'If words could suddenly become individuals' – Słowacki paraphrases Zygmunt Krasiński, who, in his letter to Roman Załuski (1840) says: 'If the words of the Polish language could become individuals, they should gather and contribute for a statue for Juliusz with an inscription *Patri Patriae*, because language then would be the whole motherland.' Krasiński developed his view further in an article sent to *Tygodnik literacki* [Literary Weekly] just after the publication of the lampoon about the *Improvisers*. It was published in the summer 1841. In the years of Słowacki's fight with critics, Zygmunt Krasiński was his only ally. The reference to 'aeolian harp', in the next stanza, comes from Krasiński's letter, 23 February 1840, in which he wrote: 'Julu' [friendly diminutive of Juliusz], 'I beg you, do not care about those hubbubs, which will come back to you. Keep your soul in the shape of Aeolian harp, above all the hands of people, amongst the wafts of heaven.'

[2] *wdrzewi* – 'tree in' word invented by Słowacki, 'the activity of transubstantiating into a tree'.

15.

Że porwał cię głos, jasność księżycowa,
Serce rozkwitłe, rozlatane pieniem.
O! gdyby mogły się na posąg słowa
Złożyć i stanąć pod cyprysów cieniem
Jak marmur, który duszę w sobie chowa
I z wolna złotym wylewa strumieniem,
A tak powoli leje i łagodnie,
Że po tysiącach lat, jak słońce wschodnie

16.

Stoi w nim cała, ogromna... O! gdyby!...
Zachcenia moje są jak Klefta żądze,
Który chciał w trumnie mieć dla słońca szyby
I dla jaskółek... Na co?... Znowu błądzę
Jak Telimena, gdy wyszła na grzyby,
A zbiera mrówki (mrówkami są żądze –
Na wiatr to mówię tylko, lecz w nadziei,
Żem dostrzegł jako poznańczyk – idei).

17.

Czy w poemacie tym równie szczęśliwa
Krytyka równe porobi odkrycia?
Nie wiem. – Czasami myśl w eterze pływa,
Przez piękne bardzo przelatując śnicia,
Lecz późniéj pismo, druk tęcze obrywa
Z kształtów. – A teraz odbłysk mego życia
Na ten poemat pada niezbyt pięknie.
Patrzcie, jak serce wesołe – gdy pęknie!

18.

Szczęściem, że pieśni tej bohater młody,
Świeży, miłosny i ma ciemne oko,

15.

Transported by the voice, or the bright moon,
The full-blown heart, deep-pounding without fade;
Oh! If words to a statue could so soon
Combine, and stand below the cypress' shade,
As marble hard conceals soul in its tune,
And slowly sings soul like a golden blade,
And pours out sad and slow its gentle runs,
That in a thousand years, like eastern suns

16.

It stands a whole, enormous . . . If, alas! . . .
My wants are like the cravings of that Klepht[3]
Whose windowed hearse would let the sunlight pass,
And for the swallows . . . what? I twitch, bereft,
Like Telimen,[4] the mushroom-lusting lass,
Who swatted ants instead (an image deft) –
I'm not just speaking in the wind, but hope,
Like him from Poznań,[5] I'm a sage – no dope.

17.

Will critics, wallowing happily as ever,
Make new discoveries in this sweet confection?
I don't know. – At first it seems a safe endeavour,
Fast-drifting through my dizzy dreams' perfection,
But later, printing it, my rainbows sever
From their first shapes. – So now my life's reflection
Falls in these verses, none too finely spoken;
How merrily the heart beats – when it's broken!

18.

It's lucky the young hero of this canto
Is fresh, in love, and has a darkling eye,

---

[3] Kleft Dimo, the character of *Chants populaires de la Grèce moderne,* recueillis et publiés par C. Fauriel, Paris 1824; the name Kleft, (old Greek: χλέπτης, literally: a thief) was given to the Greek highlanders, who refused to yield to the Turkish yoke and defended their freedom in the mountains; the Klefts gained adequate poetic quality.

[4] In Mickiewicz's *Pan Tadeusz*; see V, 314–340.

[5] An allusion to J. N. Sadowski, a critic from Poznań (under Prussian occupation), who wrote in *Tygodnik literacki* about *Anhelli* by Słowacki and the character of Orcio from the *Non-divine Comedy* by Krasinski, trying to enhance the symbolism of ideas present there in an exaggerated way. Słowacki ironizes Sadowski's analysis in a satirical dialogue: *Krytyka krytyki i literatury* (*Criticism of criticism and literature*)

Złote połyskiem zielonawéj wody,
Lecz niezbyt na świat patrzące głęboko.
Owszem, ma nadto serdecznéj pogody,
Nadto mu prawie na świecie szeroko.
Ach! nieraz szczerze westchniecie z litości,
Widząc, jaki w nim brak artystyczności!

19.

Poezja go otacza. – Czytelniku!
Na jego miéjscu, o! ileż byś razy
Uczuł, że dusza twa na wykrzykniku
Hipogryfując, leci, tnie wyrazy,
Klnie, że wokoło zimnych serc bez liku!
Same szkielety pod nią, same płazy! –
Beniowski, jakby go Bóg o tym ostrzegł,
A priori to czuł – lecz nie spostrzegł.

20.

Co lepsza, nigdy nie mówił, nie pisał –
Biedaczek! brakło mu formy gotowéj!
Nigdy się w myślów dzwon nie rozkołysał,
Idei żadnéj w nim nie było nowej;
Najnowsze z ustek różanych wysysał;
I teraz, patrzcie! w pasiece lipowéj
Klęczy pokornie przy kochanki nodze –
Oboje na zbyt niebezpiecznéj drodze.

(1841) [*Warszawa: Państwowy Instytut Wydawniczy, 1971*]

Gold with the sheen of greenish sea's portmanteau,
But not a very quick, or worldly spy:
He's far too calm and dim to be the man to
See the indifferent planet pass him by.
Ah! Many times you'll sigh all pessimistic,
To see how much his mind is inartistic!

19.

Though poetry engulfs him – Sweet-faced reader!
If you were in his place, how many times
You'd change into an exclamations-breeder,
Which, like a hyppogriff,[6] cuts through the rhymes,
And swears, how cold the heart's about its leader!
Skeletons, white amphibians in their slimes![7] –
Beniowski, as if God had warned him clear,
A priori felt 'em – but didn't see 'em near.

20.

He neither wrote nor even spoke a thing –
Poor little thing! He lacked a ready form!
The bell of his pure thoughts would never swing,
There were no new thoughts in his brain to swarm;
But only such as out of rose-lips spring;
And look! amidst the lime-tree beehives warm,
He kneels by her, as if a dog would pray –
Though both are bound upon on a fearful way.

(1841) [*Translated by Peter Cochran and Mirosława Modrzewska. Newcastle upon Tyne: Cambridge Scholars Publishing, 2009*]

---

[6] To hippogriffin: a verb made from the word Hippogriffon, or horse-gryffon, created by the Italian poet Boiardo, later identified with Pegasus. Słowacki uses it to ironize about early Polish Romantic literature and its love of exclamation marks.

[7] An allusion to Mickiewicz's *Ode to Youth*, which Słowacki parodies in *Krytyka krytyki i literatury* (*Criticism of criticism and literature*) quoting the alleged *Świat zapału* (World of Enthusiasm).

j. PORTUGUÊS

IV.j.1. ANTÓNIO PEDRO LOPES de MENDONCA, «excertos de *Memórias de Literatura Contemporânea*»

I

Porque é que o drama, depois de haver nascido quasi n'este canto da Peninsula, foi abandonado de todo até ao nosso século?

Esta questão é uma questão de philosophia litteraria, que convém examinar com solicitude, porque lança uma grande luz sobre a nossa historia politica, tão mal avaliada, tão mal entendia de quasi toda a velha geração.

Victor Hugo apresentando o drama como a forma cucial da epoca actual, disse uma grande verdade, mas não a desenvolveu pela analyse cuidadosa das transformações sociais.

O drama é a acção, o drama é a expressão do movimento individual, das suas paixões, dos seus seus sentimentos, da combinação da sua vida íntima, com a sociedade aonde nasceu; a sua indole reside toda no antagonismo, na lucta dos indivíduos, das idéas, dos acontecimentos domésticos ou sociaes.

Poderia aquella forma existir nos tempos adormecidos do absolutismo? Aquela existęncia oficial, de alvará, moldada na corte pela etiqueta, arregimentada em corporações, em bandos distinctos nas outras classes, poderia inspirar a poesia a idéa do movimento, que é a alma do drama moderno?

(...)

Em Portugal, além das causas geraes, que accusam a sua esterilidade litteraria, a degeneração progressiva do seu engenho, o genero-drama não podia assimilar-se à litteratura sem a acção da vida social, sem as peripécias dá vida individual, também adormecida como as glorias ao passado.

Podemos afoutamente dizer que alem de Gil Vicente, e das informes tentativas de Camões, nada produzimos no drama; (...)

(...) Digamos a verdade, o drama creou-se no nosso século, e no nosso tempo; e o maior brasão do sr. Garrett, é haver sido o seu poderoso creador. O *Gil Vicente*, o *Alfageme*, o Frei Luiz de Sousa são as glorias, e os fundamentos do nosso theatro moderno.

«Novas Reflexões, I»

A origem do theatro na Península, como em muitos outros paizes da Europa, foi inteiramente clerical. Esta circumstancia explica, como a litteratura dramática poude nascer e desenvolver-se, no meio da atroz perseguição exercida contra as liberdades do espírito.

(...)

Mas como seriam diversos os destinos da Península, se o despotismo político, abraça do com o fanatismo religioso, não houvessem esmagado os germens da renascença intellectual!

(...)

O protestantismo teve um débil echo na Península. A realeza, de mãos dadas com o clero, instaurou essa monarchia teocrática, que consubstancia a reacção no século XVI. O povo hespanhol fugiu espavorido diante da liberdade inquieta e audaciosa, que propunha o dogma

j. PORTUGUESE

IV.j.1. ANTÓNIO PEDRO LOPES de MENDONCA, from
Memories of Contemporary Literature

[*From the chapter «The Theatre since 1834», extracts indicated by reference to the section of the chapter about the History of Portuguese drama.*]

I

Why is it that drama, after its inception in this corner of the Peninsula, was totally abandoned until our century?

The answer to this important question of literary philosophy will shed light on our political history, which has been so misjudged and misunderstood by the last generation. Victor Hugo recognized drama as the characteristic literary genre of the current age, but failed to develop this idea based on careful analysis of social history.

Drama is the action or expression of individual movement, with all of its passion and intimacy, within the society in which it is born; the spirit of drama exists in the antagonism it represents between individuals, ideas, and domestic or national society. Could such a form exist in the culturally negligent days of absolute rule? The official drama of the court, in conformity with the decrees and desires of the powerful, could not inspire the poetry of individual movement that is the soul of modern drama.

[... *References to the social situation and dramatic activity in England, France and Spain*]

In addition to the general causes of Portugal's literary sterility and the degenerating ingenuity of its writers, Portuguese drama could not join literary history without the ability to represent the accidents of individual life in society – a society still asleep with its past glories.

We can boldly say that with the exception of Gil Vicente and some unfinished attempts by Camões,[1] [*A short digression on Portuguese dramatic non-history*] the Portuguese produced nothing in drama until our own time. And the illustrious Mr. Garrett, with his *Gil Vicente, Alfagame*, and *Brother Fr. Luis de Souza*, is credited with having created the glories and foundations of our modern theatre.

New Reflections, I

[*From the chapter «Novas Reflexões», excerpts following the same mode of reference, about the theatre and Iberian culture («I»)*]

Dramatic literature managed to survive on the Peninsula despite the atrocious persecution of intellectual liberty because its origin was entirely clerical, as it was in many other European countries. [...]

How different might the Peninsula's destiny have been, had not political despotism, hand in hand with religious fanaticism, crushed the seeds of intellectual renaissance!

[...]

---

[1] Luis Vaz de Camões (1524–1580) Portuguese lyric poet and dramatist.

do livre exame em face dos prestígios da auctoridade. A sua religião estava por assim dizer vinculada às suas tradições, e aos prodígios do seu esforço. A cruz era a um tempo o symbolo da crença, e o estandarte da victoria. Em 1570 todos os vestígios do protestantismo estavam aniquilados na Península.

O teatro foi por isso essencialmente subordinado não só aos preceitos mas aos preconceitos religiosos. As novellas e os romances populares demonstram eficazmente o espírito de intolerância e o ódio contra todas as seitas anti-católicas. (...)

(...)

A originalidade do theatro hespanhol reside sobretudo nesta situação moral. Historicamente, filia-se às grandes tradições da luta entre a cruz e o crescente: socialmente exprime o antagonismo violento, entre uma devoção sombria e intolerante, e o rancor das paixões desordenadas e soltas. A corrupção de costumes como se desculpava nas asperezas da penitencia, e na largueza e generosidade das fundações pias.

(...)

Portugal nem mesmo poude quinhoar com a Hespanha os seus esplendores litterarios. Os sessenta annos do domínio hespanhol, abafaram quasi todo o esforço da nossa imaginação: e quando, em 1640, reconquistámos a nossa nacionalidade, reinava o seiscentismo, que importado de Itália do cavalleiro Marini, tivera em D. Luiz de Gongora um talentoso interprete, e na língua hespanhola, um instrumento fácil, melodioso, e apto para aqueles turtuosos *concetti*.

A decadęncia do theatro foi instantânea e rápida. As idéas que o aviventaram, esmoreciam de dia para dia, e a devoção era mais exigente, á proporção que se sentia menos forte e influente no espírito publico. As pompas do culto catholico, engrandecidas e multiplicadas de propósito, chamavam a si a attenção popular. Em Portugal, nos princípios do século XVIII, o theatro quase que expira no supplicio do judeu António José, queimado pela inquisição. A Igreja triumpha mesmo nos domínios das letras. Os bacamartes theologicos, e as dissertações seraphicas inundavam as livrarias, e faziam gemer os prelos.

[1855] [*Microfilm of Biblioteca Nacional de Lisboa; excerpts from pages 176–181; 197–205; 206–213*]

Only a small echo of the Reformation could be heard on the Peninsula. Royalty and Catholic clergy worked together to form a theocratic monarchy in response to the potential threats it posed to their authority. For the people of *Hespanha* the religious freedom and individual interpretation of scripture proposed by the Reformation were a threat not only to religious authority but also to their national traditions. The cross was both the symbol of belief and the flag of national victory for the people of *Hespanha*. By 1570, all traces of Reformation were erased from the Peninsula.

Theatre was thus subordinated to both political decree and religious prejudice. Sixteenth-century short stories and popular novels illustrate the spirit of intolerance and hatred against all anti-catholic sects. [. . .]

Spanish theatre is characterized by the expression of several traditions shared to a limited extent by the Portuguese: the historical antagonism between the cross and the crescent and the social antagonism between a spirit of intolerant devotion and a spirit of free and untamed passions. Corrupt behavior was excused by strict penitence and an abundance of pious works.

[. . .] The Portuguese literary tradition was not compatible with the Spanish, and sixty years of Spanish rule smothered almost every effort of our imagination. When we regained our independence in 1640, the Seiscentismo reigned, imported from chevalier Marini's Italy, and with it the poet D. Luis de Gongora, who found in the Spanish language an easy, melodic instrument, appropriate for the tortuous conceits of the Italian fashion.[2]

From there, the decay of the theatre was swift. The ideas that gave it life weakened more every day, and the devotion required of the dramatist to his art grew in proportion to the lack of public support. The people were more interested in the extravagant grandeur of Catholic spectacle, than the subtleties of the theatre, and by the early eighteenth century, the theatre died with the Jew António José at the hands of the Inquisition.[3] The Church triumphed even in the domain of literature, occupying printers and flooding bookshops with theological compendiums and seraphic dissertations.

[1855]

---

[2] The Seiscentismo corresponds to the Italian Baroque period in the arts, roughly during the eighteenth century. Giambattista Marino (or Marini 1569–1625): Neapolitan poet whose style of elaborate metaphors, complicated word play and heavy hyperbole was imitated by many baroque poets. Luis de Gongora y Argote (1561–1627): Spanish poet, playwright, priest whose complicated baroque style became known as 'gongorismo'.

[3] Antonio Jose da Silva (1705–1739), also known as 'The Jew,' a popular Portuguese playwright of the eighteenth century, whose comedies, puppet shows, and comic operas were performed frequently in the 1730s. The Inquisition arrested and tortured him in 1737 for refusing to renounce Judaism and finally burnt him at the stake in a spectacular *auto da fe* in 1739.

IV.j.2. LUÍS REBELLO DA SILVA, excertos de *Apreciações Literárias* (Garrett)

Desta escola, no sentido mais elevado da sua aspiração, é fundador o Sr. Garrett em Portugal. O primeiro que entendeu a beleza ingénua da poesia popular e a requestou com a mais casta devoção foi o autor de *D. Branca*. E a singella Muza tanto tempo desprezada entre o povo não se mostrou esquiva nem ingrata. Até hoje nenhum poeta foi mais favorecido. Familiar com ele, patenteou-lhe todas as graças, e revelou-lhe o raro segredo de prende a inconstância, e de cortar, apesar dos anos, cada vez mais frescas as rosas da sua coroa.

O Sr. Garrett não é só um poeta, é uma literatura inteira. Para o apreciar não basta estudar as obras que tem produzido; torna-se indispensável antes saber donde descende, e como se formou. A genealogia dos escriptores e a sua filiação literária são essenciais à critica para não faltar ao retrato com a verdadeira phisionomia.

Como Chateubriand e Byron (os primeiros inovadores romanticos), o Sr. Garrett colheu no estudo dos modelos gregos e romanos a flor da erudição antiga. (...)

Excerto Sobre Alexandre Herculano

O segredo, bem raro, e entre nós talvez único de Herculano nestas inspiradas reconstruções do passado é a árdua mas perfeita fusão do ideal nos moldes respeitados das sociedades extintas.

É a consciência do historiador e a reflexão do filósofo dando a mão e regrando os devaneios e arrojos da fantasia.

Passando pela sua palheta, os fenómenos naturais, os acidentes físicos e os afecto humanos harmonizam-se e compõem uma perspectiva, ainda que sombria, verdadeira e expressiva do século que traduzem e das localidades que representam.

Quando nos descreve as fúrias do mar e as tormentas do animo, o fragor das armas e a tristeza das cidades assoladas, o pincel é tão firme, os objectos ressaem da tela com tal viveza que os olhos cuidam que os vęem e o espírito hesita entre a fábula e arealidade!

São gandaras e montes como Cooper as sabia figurar, e não florestas e campinas imaginárias, como as de Delille; são castelos e paços torreados, como Walter Scott os desenhava, e não corredores, alçapões e falsos misteriosos como os de Anna Radcliffe, e por isso is sítios de gravam como nossos conhecidos, nas galas do seu estilo nervoso, nas opulęncias do seu engenho descritivo e nos tesouros das suas remeniscęncias idealizadas.

Excerto Sobre Garrett E Herculano

A razão porque ambos merecem a palma que os honra é a mesma porque Scott e Byron, Schiller e Goethe, Chateaubriand e Hugo hão-de sobreviver à plebe dos imitadores que o seu exemplo arrastou.

Não se morre na posteridade quando a memoria de um povo e de grandes épocas vive nas páginas de livros que sobem logo à altura de monumentos.

[1855] [*Empreza de História de Portugal, Lisbon, 1909*]

IV.j.2. LUÍS REBELLO DA SILVA, from *Literary Appraisals*

On Romanticism in Portugal (Garrett)

Almeida Garrett is the founder of Romanticism in Portugal. He was the first to understand the simple beauty of popular poetry, and the Romantic Muse, so long held in contempt among the people, was neither elusive nor ungrateful for his efforts. In fact, she favoured no poet more than Mr. Garrett. She made all her graces familiar to him and revealed to him the secret of defying mutability and plucking fresher and fresher roses from her crown.

Mr. Garrett is not just a poet, but the creator and embodiment of an entire literary tradition. To appreciate his contribution, a study of his works must be supplemented by knowledge of his literary ascendance and formation. By studying the genealogy of his literary affiliations we can understand the formation of his literary physiognomy.

Like Chateaubriand and Byron, the first Romantic innovators, Mr. Garrett plucked the flowers of ancient erudition from his study of Greek and Roman literature. In the ease of his style, in his sentences' fluent gracefulness, and in his exquisite phrasing one immediately feels that the poet is a close friend of the happy Horatio, of Homer and of the sober Aeschylus.

On Alexandre Herculano

The unique contribution of Herculano's inspired reconstructions of Portuguese history is the arduous but perfect fusion of the spiritual ideal in the respected moulds of extinguished societies.

The historian's conscience joined hands with the philosopher's reflections to discipline the temptations of daydreams and fantasy.

Under Herculano's pen, natural phenomena and human affectations are harmonized; they complete each other for a picture of history that is bleak but true and expressive of the spirit of our century.

When he describes the fury of the sea, the torments of the soul, the clash of battle, and the sadness of our besieged cities, his brush is so firm that the objects on the canvas seem alive, and the viewer hesitates between representation and reality.

In Herculano's work we find paths and hills as Cooper portrayed them, not imaginary forests and fields like Delille's. We encounter castles and towered palaces as Walter Scott drew them, not the corridors, hidden trapdoors, and fabricated mysteries of Anne Radcliffe.[4] Herculano's animated style, rich descriptions, and sense of nostalgia fix places in our minds as though we had really known them.

On Garrett and Herculano

Both writers deserve the laurels that honor them for the same reason that Scott and Byron, Schiller and Goethe, Chateaubriand and Hugo will survive their imitators. Writers never die to posterity when the memory of a people live on in the pages of their books; rather their books ascend to monumental stature.

[1855] [*Translated by Carlos Leone and Bethany Smith*]

---

[4] James Fenimore Cooper (1789–1851) American novelist; Jacques Delille (1738–1813) French catholic poet; Sir Walter Scott (1771–1832) Scottish novelist and poet; Anne Radcliffe (1764–1823) English gothic novelist.

k. ROMÂNĂ

IV.k.1. GRIGORE ALEXANDRESCU, din *Câteva cuvinte în loc de prefață*

[...] În zădar strigă unii că critica e primejdioasă, că omoară talentele [...]. [C]ritica [...] care arată greșelele scrierii [...] poate să îndrepteze pe mulți, poate să formeze gustul. Geniul e ca toate puterile lumești, care adorm într-o oarbă încredințare, când nimeni nu le arată adevărul. [...] E destul să aibă cinevași un duh firesc ceva cultivat și niște organe simțitoare, ca să prețuiască talentul. Meritul unui poet stă în plăcuta întipărire ce ne lasă citirea poeziilor sale, și cititorul, chiar de nu va ști regulile, tot poate spune de a simțit mulțumire sau neplăcere, dacă versurile sunt melodioase sau aspre, deslușite sau încurcate, felurite sau monotone. Autorul a împlinit toate condițiile, de va izbuti să-mi mulțămească duhul, inima și urechea, potrivit cu felul la care se apleacă.

[1847]

k. ROMANIAN

IV.k.1. GRIGORE ALEXANDRESCU, from *A Few Words by Way of Preface*[1]

[...] In vain will some proclaim that criticism is dangerous, that it kills talent [...]. [C]riticism [...] which unravels the errors of writing [...] can improve many and shape taste. Genius is like all worldly powers, which sleep in the blind confidence of ignorance. [...] All that is needed to discover and praise talent is to be natural, cultured and sensitive. A poet's merit lies in the imprint of pleasure left on us by the reading of his poems, and his reader, however little he knows of the rules, will still be able to say if he has felt pleasure or displeasure, or if the verse he has read is melodious or rough, clear or dim, various or monotonous. That author who, according to the needs of the art form, can satisfy my spirit, my heart and my ear, successfully meets all these conditions.

[1847] [*Translated by Mihaela Anghelescu Irimia*]

---

[1] The *Preface* to the 1847 edition of his works reveals Alexandrescu's most classical side as it focuses on questions of morality in literature. A progressive spirit trained in the Classics, he is a modern Aesop, the author of fables as popular in Romanian as are La Fontaine's in French literature. He was also an occasional translator of Byron and Lamaratine, whose influence is felt in poems like *Anul 1840* (*The Year 1840*), based on a false prophecy according to which the fate of humanity was to change then, for which reason the text was published anonymously. *Umbra lui Mircea la Cozia* (*Mircea's Shadow at Cozia*) is a militant encomium of the Wallachian prince Mircea the Old (1386–1418), very much like Bolintineanu's praise of Stephen the Great.

IV.k.2. MIHAIL KOGĂLNICEANU, din *Introducţie la Dacia Literară*

[...] O foaie, dar, care, părăsind politica, s-ar îndeletnici numai cu literatura naţională, o foaie carea făcând abnegaţie de loc, ar fi numai o foaie românească, şi prin urmare s-ar îndeletnici cu producţiile româneşti, fie din orice parte a Daciei, numai să fie bune, această foaie, zic, ar împlini o mare lipsă în literatura noastră. O asemenea foaie ne vom sili ca să fie *Dacia literară* [...]. Aşadar foaia noastră va fi un repertoriu general a literaturii româneşti, în carele, ca într-o oglindă, se vor vede scriitorii moldoveni, munteni, ardeleni, bănăţeni, bucovineni, fieştecarele cu ideile sale, cu limba sa, cu chipul său. [...] Critica noastră va fi nepărtinitoare; vom critica cartea, iar nu persoana. Vrăjmaşi ai arbitrarului, nu vom fi arbitrari în judecăţile noastre literare. Iubitori ai păcei, nu vom primi nici în foaia noastră discuţii ce ar pute să se schimbe în vrajbe. Literatura are trebuinţă de unire, iar nu de dezbinare [...]. În sfârşit, ţălul nostru este realizaţia dorinţii ca românii să aibă o limbă şi o literatură comună pentru toţi.

Dorul imitaţiei s-a făcut la noi o manie primejdioasă, pentru că omoară în noi duhul naţional. Această manie este mai ales covârşitoare în literatură. [...] Traducţiile însă nu fac o literatură. Noi vom prigoni cât vom pute această manie ucigătoare a gustului original, însuşirea cea mai preţioasă a unii literaturi. Istoria noastră are destule fapte eroice, frumoasele noastre ţări sunt destul de mari, obiceiurile noastre sunt destul de pitoreşti şi poetice, pentru ca să putem găsi şi la noi sujeturi de scris, fără să avem pentru această trebuinţă să ne împrumutăm de la alte naţii. Foaia noastră va primi cât se poate mai rar traduceri din alte limbi; compuneri originale îi vor umple mai toate coloanele. [...]

[1840]

IV.k.2. MIHAIL KOGĂLNICEANU, from *Introduction to Literary Dacia*[2]

[. . .] A paper that, abandoning politics, would deal only with national literature; a paper that, taking advantage of the place where it is published, would be solely a Romanian paper and, therefore, would deal only with Romanian productions from any part of Dacia, provided they were of good quality, such a paper, I say, would fill a great gap in our literature. We will do everything in our power to make *Literary Dacia* such a publication [. . .]. It will, therefore, offer a general repertoire of Romanian literature,in which, as in a mirror, Moldavian, Wallachian, Transylvanian, and Bucovinan writers will be reflected; each with his own ideas, language, and type. [. . .] Our criticism shall be impartial; we will criticize the book, not the person. As enemies of the arbitrary, we will not be arbitrary in our literary judgments. As lovers of peace, we will not foster discussions in our writings that could turn into fights. Our literature needs unity, not disunity [. . .]. Finally, our aim is the fulfillment of the desire that all Romanians have for one language and one literature common to all.

The penchant for imitation has turned into a dangerous mania with us, for it kills the national spirit. This mania is all the more overwhelming in literature. [. . .] But translations do not constitute a national literature. We will make every effort to suppress this mania, this killer of originality, that most precious feature of any literature. Our history boasts many a heroic deed, our beautiful countries are large enough, our customs are picturesque and poetic enough to enable us to find subjects for our writings here; we need not borrow them from other nations. Our journal will publish translations from other languages as seldom as possible; original compositions, on the contrary, shall fill almost all its columns. [...]

[1840] [*Adapted from a translation by Mihaela Anghelescu Irimia*]

---

[2] Following the 1829 foundation of the *Curierul românesc* (*The Romanian Courier*) in Bucharest, and of the *Albina românesca* (*The Romanian Bee*) in Iaşi (Jassy), the *Curierul de ambe sexe* (*The Courier for Both Sexes*) was issued in Braşov in 1837. Thus the historical Romanian provinces were equipped with the modern institution of the cultural press in their full Romantic age. The most distinguished periodical of the times, however, is *Dacia literară* (*Literary Dacia*), published in Jassy by Mihail Kogălniceanu, the supporter of a unitary literary creed. In the famous *Introduction* to the newly printed periodical, Kogălniceanu expounds upon the principles of what has since been called the national popular current. His argument was typical of the time's debates: indiscriminate translations had bred a disease that would be the duty of the national creators to cure; for this there was a solid repository of values including a glorious history, scenic geography, and respectable mores.

I. РУССКИЙ

IV.I.1.   МИХАИЛ ЛЕРМОНТОВ, «Есть речи – значенье . . .»

Есть речи – значенье
Темно иль ничтожно,
Но им без волненья
Внимать невозможно.

Как полны их звуки
Безумством желанья!
В них слезы разлуки,
В них трепет свиданья.

Не встретит ответа
Средь шума мирского
Из пламя и света
Рожденное слово;

Но в храме, средь боя
И где я ни буду,
Услышав его, я
Узнаю повсюду.

Не кончив молитвы,
На звук тот отвечу,
И брошусь из битвы
Ему я навстречу.

IV.I.2.   ФЕДОР ТЮТЧЕВ, «Silentium!»

Молчи, скрывайся и таи
И чувства и мечты свои –
Пускай в душевной глубине
Встают и заходят оне
Безмолвно, как звезды в ночи, –
Любуйся ими – и молчи.

Как сердцу высказать себя?
Другому как понять тебя?
Поймет ли он, чем ты живешь?
Мысль изреченная есть ложь –
Взрывая, возмутишь ключи,

l. RUSSIAN

IV.l.1. MIKHAIL LERMONTOV, 'Words There are So Baffling'

Words there are so baffling
They seem bare of meaning,
Yet cast a strange spell on
One's whole heart and being.

There is in them passion,
Love's hot, flaming madness,
The joy of reunion,
Of parting the sadness.

A word born of lightning
Drowned by the world's noises,
Will never be answered
And stays oddly voiceless.

And yet fail it cannot
To capture my spirit:
At prayer or in battle,
I know I will hear it.

From church I will hasten,
Afire with its promise,
And out of the fray rush
To answer its summons.

(1840)

IV.l.2. FYODOR TYUCHEV, 'Silentium!'

Speak not, lie hidden, and conceal,
the way you dream, the things you feel.
Deep in your spirit let them rise
akin to stars in crystal skies
that set before the night is blurred:
delight in them and speak no word.

How can a heart expression find?
How should another know your mind?
Will he discern what quickens you?
A thought once uttered is untrue.
Dimmed is the fountainhead when stirred:

Питайся ими – и молчи.
Лишь жить в себе самом умей –
Есть целый мир в душе твоей
Таинственно-волшебных дум –
Их оглушит наружный шум,
Дневные разгонят лучи –
Внимай их пенью – и молчи! ...

(1830)

m.   ESPAÑOL

IV.m.1.   RAMÓN DE CAMPOAMOR, 'Humoradas'

a
Todo en amor es triste;
mas, triste y todo, es lo mejor que existe.

b
La conciencia al final de nuestra vida
sólo es un laberinto sin salida.

c
Es mi fe tan cumplida
que adoro a Dios, aunque me dio vida.

d
Las hijas de las madres que amé tanto
me besan ya como se besa a un santo.

e
Te vendí y me vendiste, está bien hecho:
La venganza, en España, es un derecho.

f
Busqué la ciencia y me enseñó el vacío.
Logré el amor y conquisté el hastío.

g
Viniendo del *no ser*, no estoy seguro
si voy a parte alguna.
¡Misterios del sepulcro y de la cuna,
fantasmas del pasado y del futuro!

[From Humoradas, 1856]

drink at the source and speak no word.
Live in your inner self alone
within your soul a world has grown,
the magic of veiled thoughts that might
be blinded by the outer light,
drowned in the noise of day, unheard . . .
take in their song and speak no word.

[1830] [*Translated by Vladimir Nabokov*]

m.   SPANISH

IV.m.1.   RAMÓN DE CAMPOAMOR, 'Caprices'

A). All in love is sadness; yet, sad, and in all, it is the best we have. B). Conscience at the end of our life is a maze without exit. C).It is my stated faith that I adore God even though he gave me life. D). The daughters of the mothers whom I loved so much kiss me now as they would a saint. E). I betrayed you as you betrayed me, it is well done. Vengeance, in Spain, is a right. F). I sought knowledge and it showed me nothingness, I acquired love and conquered weariness. G). Coming from *not being*, I am unsure whether I am going anywhere. The mysteries of the grave and the cradle, phantoms of the past and the future!

[1856]

[*Campoamor's early poetry expresses the world weariness and inner turmoil typical of the negative strain of the Spanish Romantic lyric. By the early 1840s, when this aspect of the Movement was under attack from the conservative and Catholic establishment, there emerged a less strident voice of dissent, a bourgeois expression of affected world-weariness which served to create a psychological and aesthetic barrier between direct personal experience and the reader. The humoristic, vaguely ironic, even droll expression of Romantic* mal del siglo *became fashionable among the rising middle classes, especially among female readers. Campoamor became the supreme and popular voice of this new reaction to the Romantic loss of ideals.*]

IV.m.2.   GUSTAVO ADOLFO BÉCQUER, 'Rima'

Yo sé un himno gigante y extraño
que anuncia en la noche del alma una aurora
y estas páginas son de ese himno
cadencias que el alma dilata en las sombras.
Yo quisiera escribirle, del hombre
domando el rebelde mezquino idioma,
con palabras que fuesen a un tiempo
suspiros y risas, colores y notas.
Pero en vano es luchar, que no hay cifra
capaz de encerrarle y apenas, ¡oh hermosa!,
si, teniendo en mis manos las tuyas,
podría al oído cantártelo a solas.

[*From Libro de los gorriones, 1868*]

IV.m.2. GUSTAVO ADOLFO BÉCQUER, 'Rhyme'

I know of a gigantic and strange hymn which heralds a dawn in the dark night of the soul and these pages are about that hymn, cadences which dilate the soul in the shadows. I would write of it, dominating the rebellious and inadequate language of men, with words which were at the same time sighs and laughter, colours and musical notes. But it is in vain I struggle, for there is no cypher capable of enshrining it and, yet, o comely one!, if, holding your hands in mine, I could sing it in your ear while we are alone.

[1868]

[*Bécquer's essays and poems on the nature of inspiration, the poetic process and the struggle to express feelings and moods that lie beyond words (use of conditionals, synaesthesia, metaphor, absences and nuance) mark him out as the precursor of Spanish Symbolism and a new poetic language of allusion and suggestion rather than the post-Romantic flamboyant rhetoric that expressed national ideals. His investigation of the inner workings of the mind, the process of poetic inspiration and the recall of memory and dream ensured that, when bourgeois civic ideals began to lose their potency at the end of the 1800s, the young poets of the new century turned to Bécquer as their inspiration.*]

V. Myth, Religion and the Supernatural

The theology that was to emerge from the political, social and intellectual crises of the late eighteenth century represented a radical shift away from the emphasis on reason and 'evidences' that characterized so much enlightenment and deistic religion. At the same time Lessing in Germany and Volney in France were reading Christianity in essentially 'evolutionary' and anthropological terms, while, in the next generation, Feuerbach was to incorporate many of these ideas into his projectionist view of religion (later, and outside the scope of this anthology, to be adopted by Marx and Freud). Extracts from Blake, Coleridge and Schleiermacher stress in their own distinctive ways the inwardness and subjectivity of religious experience. Chateaubriand added to this a passionate defence of what he (though not everyone else!) saw in traditional Christianity as the bedrock not merely of European social values but also of contemporary aesthetics. Schleiermacher built on enlightenment criticism of the Bible in a slightly different way to suggest that all texts from the past needed to be understood within the context of the society and tradition that had engendered them. In England, the Tractarians, like Keble and Newman (again outside our scope here) were to combine romantic subjectivity with the invention of tradition to produce a distinctively new kind of poetry and poetic theory.

a. BRITISH

V.a.1. ROBERT LOWTH, from *Lectures on the Sacred Poetry of the Hebrews*

The sententious style, therefore, I define to be the primary characteristic of the Hebrew poetry, as being the most conspicuous and comprehensive of all. For although that style seems naturally adapted only to the didactic, yet it is found to pervade the whole of the poetry of the Hebrews. There are indeed many passages in the sacred writings highly figurative and infinitely sublime, but all of them manifestly assume a sententious form. There are some, too, and those not inelegant, which possess little more of the characteristics of poetry than the versification, and that terseness or adaptation of the sentences which constitutes so important a part even of the harmony of verse. This is manifest in most of the didactic psalms, as well as in some others, the matter, order, diction, and thoughts of which are clearly historical, but the conformation of the sentences wholly poetical. There is indeed so strict an analogy between the structure of the sentences and the versification, that when the former chances to be confused or obscured, it is scarcely possible to form a conjecture concerning the division of the lines or verses, which is almost the only part of the Hebrew versification that remains. It was therefore necessary, before I could explain the mechanism of the Hebrew verse, to remark many particulars which properly belong to the present topic.

The reason of this (not to detain you with what is obvious in almost every page of the sacred poetry) is as follows. The Hebrew poets frequently express a sentiment with the utmost brevity

and simplicity, illustrated by no circumstances, adorned with no epithets, (which in truth they seldom use;) they afterwards call in the aid of ornament; they repeat, they vary, they amplify the same sentiment; and adding one or more sentences which run parallel to each other, they express the same or a similar, and often a contrary sentiment, in nearly the same form of words. Of these three modes of ornament, at least, they make the most frequent use, namely the amplification of the same ideas, the accumulation of others, and the opposition or antithesis of such as are contrary to each other: they dispose the corresponding sentences in regular distichs adapted to each other, and of an equal length, in which, for the most part, things answer to things, and words to works, as the Son of Sirach says of the works of God, *two and two, one against the other*. These forms again are diversified by notes of admiration, comparison, negation, and more particularly interrogation; whence a singular degree of force and elevation is frequently added to the composition.

(1753, translated from Latin into English by Richard Gregory in 1787)

V.a.2.   THOMAS PAINE, from *The Age of Reason*, Part I

Having now extended the subject to a greater length than I first intended, I shall bring it to a close by abstracting a summary from the whole.

First, That the idea or belief of a word of God existing in print, or in writing, or in speech, is inconsistent in itself for the reasons already assigned. These reasons, among many others, are the want of an universal language; the mutability of language; the errors to which translations are subject, the possibility of totally suppressing such a word; the probability of altering it, or of fabricating the whole, and imposing it upon the world.

Secondly, That the Creation we behold is the real and ever existing word of God, in which we cannot be deceived. It proclaimeth his power, it demonstrates his wisdom, it manifests his goodness and beneficence.

Thirdly, That the moral duty of man consists in imitating the moral goodness and beneficence of God manifested in the creation towards all his creatures. That seeing as we daily do the goodness of God to all men, it is an example calling upon all men to practise the same towards each other; and, consequently, that every thing of persecution and revenge between man and man, and every thing of cruelty to animals, is a violation of moral duty.

I trouble not myself about the manner of future existence. I content myself with believing, even to positive conviction, that the power that gave me existence is able to continue it, in any form and manner he pleases, either.with or without this body; and it appears more probable to me that I shall continue to exist hereafter than.that I should have had existence, as I now have, before that existence began.

It is certain that, in one point, all nations of the earth and all religions agree. All believe in a God, The things in which they disgrace are the redundancies annexed to that belief; and therefore, if ever an universal religion should prevail, it will not be believing any thing new, but in getting rid of redundancies, and believing as man believed at first. Adam, if ever there was such a man, was created a Deist; but in the mean time, let every man follow, as he has a right to do, the religion and worship he prefers.

[1795]

V.a.3. BISHOP RICHARD WATSON, from *An Apology for the Bible: In a Series of Letters, Addressed to Thomas Paine* [From Letter I]

It appears incredible to many, that God Almighty should have had colloquial intercourse with our first parents. That he should have contracted a kind of friendship for the patriarchs and entered into covenants with them. That he should have suspended the laws of nature in Egypt, should have been so apparently partial as to become the God and governor of one particular nation and should have so far demeaned himself as to give to that people a burdensome ritual of worship, statutes and ordinances, many of which seem to be beneath the dignity of attention, unimportant and impolitic. I have conversed with many deists and have always found that the strangeness of these things was the only reason for their disbelief of them. Nothing similar has happened in their time. They will not, therefore, admit that these events have really taken place at any time. As well might a child, when arrived at a state of manhood, contend that he had never either stood in need or experienced the fostering care of a mother's kindness, the wearisome attention of his nurse, or the instruction and discipline of his schoolmaster. The Supreme Being selected one family from an idolatrous world, nursed it up by various acts of his Providence, into a great nation; communicated to that nation a knowledge of his holiness, justice, mercy, power, and wisdom. Disseminated them at various times, through every part of the earth, that they might be a 'leaven to leaven the whole lump,'[1] that they might assure all other nations of the existence of one Supreme God, the creator and preserver of the world, the only proper object of adoration. With what reason can we expect that what was done to one nation, not out of any partiality to them, but for the general good, should be done to all? That the mode of instruction, which was suited to the infancy of the world, should be extended to the maturity of its manhood or to imbecility of its old age? I own to you that when I consider how nearly man, in a savage state, approaches to the brute creation, as to intellectual excellence and when I contemplate his miserable attainments as to the knowledge of God, in a civilized state, when he has had no divine instruction on the subject or when that instruction has been forgotten, for all men have known something of God from tradition. I cannot but admire the wisdom and goodness of the Supreme Being, in having let himself down to our apprehensions; in having given to mankind, in the earliest ages, sensible and extraordinary proofs of his existence and attributes, in having made the Jewish and Christian dispensations mediums to convey to all men, through all ages that knowledge concerning himself, which he had vouchsafed to give immediately to the first. I own it is strange, very strange, that he should have made an immediate manifestation of himself in the first ages of the world. But what is there that is not strange? It is strange that you and I are here; that there is water, and earth, and air, and fire; that there is a sun, and moon, and stars; that there is a generation, corruption, reproduction. I can account ultimately for none of these things without recurring to him who made everything. I also am his workmanship and look up to him with hope of preservation through all eternity. I adore him for his word as well as for his work. His work I cannot comprehend, but his word hath assured me of all that I am concerned to know. That he hath prepared everlasting happiness for those who love and obey him. This you will call preachment. I will have done with it, but the subject is so vast and the plan of Providence, in my opinion, so obviously wise and good, that I can never think of it without having my mind filled with piety, admiration, and gratitude.

[1796]

---

[1] See Galatians 5.9: 'A little leaven leaveneth the whole lump' (KJV).

V.a.4. SAMUEL TAYLOR COLERIDGE, *The Rime of the Ancient Mariner*

Facile credo, plures esse Naturas invisibiles quam visibiles in rerum universitate. Sed horum omnium familiam quis nobis enarrabit? et gradus et cognationes et discrimina et singulorum munera? Quid agunt? quae loca habitant? Harum rerum notitiam semper ambivit ingenium humanum, nunquam attigit. Juvat, interea, non diffiteor, quandoque in animo, tanquam in tabulâ, majoris et melioris mundi imaginem contemplari: ne mens assuefacta hodiernae vitae minutiis se contrahat nimis, et tota subsidat in pusillas cogitationes. Sed veritati interea invigilandum est, modusque servandus, ut certa ab incertis, diem a nocte, distinguamus.

Thomas Burnet, *Archaeologiae Philosphiocae* p. 68[1]

PART I

<table>
<tr><td>

An ancient Mariner meeteth
three gallants bidden to
a wedding feast, and
detaineth one.

</td><td>

IT is an ancient Mariner,
And he stoppeth one of three.
'By thy long beard and glittering eye,
Now wherefore stopp'st thou me?

The Bridegroom's doors are opened wide,
And I am next of kin;
The guests are met, the feast is set:
May'st hear the merry din.'

He holds him with his skinny hand,
'There was a ship,' quoth he.
'Hold off! unhand me, grey-beard loon!'
Eftsoons his hand dropt he.

</td></tr>
<tr><td>

The Wedding-Guest is
spell-bound by the eye of the
old seafaring man, and
constrained to hear his tale.

</td><td>

He holds him with his glittering eye –
The Wedding-Guest stood still,
And listens like a three years' child:
The Mariner hath his will.

</td></tr>
</table>

---

[1] From Thomas Burnet's *Archaeologiae Philosophicae* (1692), translated by Mead and Foxton (1736): 'I can easily believe, that there are more invisible than visible Beings in the universe. But who will declare to us the families of all these, and acquaint us with the agreements, differences, and peculiar talents which are to be found among them? It is true, human wit has always desired a knowledge of these things, though it has never attained it. I will own that it is very profitable, sometimes to contemplate in the mind, as in a draught [picture – Ed.], the image of the greater and better world, lest the soul being accustomed to the trifles of this present life, should contract itself too much, and altogether rest in mean cogitations, but, in the meantime, we must take care to keep to the truth, and observe moderation, that we may distinguish certain from uncertain things, and day from night.' Coleridge has edited the text.

The Wedding-Guest sat on a stone:
He cannot choose but hear;
And thus spake on that ancient man,
The bright-eyed Mariner.

The ship was cheered, the harbour cleared,
Merrily did we drop
Below the kirk, below the hill,
Below the lighthouse top.

The Mariner tells how the ship
sailed southward with a good
wind and fair weather, till it
reached the Line.

The Sun came up upon the left,
Out of the sea came he!
And he shone bright, and on the right
Went down into the sea.

Higher and higher every day,
Till over the mast at noon –
The Wedding-Guest here beat his breast,
For he heard the loud bassoon.

The Wedding-Guest heareth
the bridal music; but the
Mariner continueth his tale.

The bride hath paced into the hall,
Red as a rose is she;
Nodding their heads before her goes
The merry minstrelsy.

The Wedding-Guest he beat his breast,
Yet he cannot choose but hear;
And thus spake on that ancient man,
The bright-eyed Mariner.

The ship drawn by a
storm toward the South Pole.

And now the Storm-blast came, and he
Was tyrannous and strong:
He struck with his o'ertaking wings,
And chased us south along.

With sloping masts and dipping prow,
As who pursued with yell and blow
Still treads the shadow of his foe,
And forward bends his head,
The ship drove fast, loud roar'd the blast,
The southward aye we fled.

And now there came both mist and snow,
And it grew wondrous cold:
And ice, mast-high, came floating by,
As green as emerald.

The land of ice, and of fearful
sounds, where no living thing
was to be seen.

And through the drifts the snowy clifts
Did send a dismal sheen:
Nor shapes of men nor beasts we ken –
The ice was all between.

The ice was here, the ice was there,
The ice was all around:
It cracked and growled, and roared and howled,
Like noises in a swound![2]

Till a great sea-bird, called the
Albatross, came through the
snow-fog, and was received
with great joy and hospitality.

At length did cross an Albatross,
Thorough the fog it came;
As if it had been a Christian soul,
We hail'd it in God's name.

It ate the food it ne'er had eat,
And round and round it flew.
The ice did split with a thunder-fit;
The helmsman steered us through!

And lo! the Albatross proveth
a bird of good omen, and
followeth the ship as it returned
northward through fog and
floating ice.

And a good south wind sprung up behind;
The Albatross did follow,
And every day, for food or play,
Came to the mariner's hollo!

In mist or cloud, on mast or shroud,
It perched for vespers nine;
Whiles all the night, through fog-smoke white,
Glimmered the white moon-shine.'

The ancient Mariner
inhospitably killeth the
pious bird of good omen.

'God save thee, ancient Mariner!
From the fiends, that plague thee thus! –
Why look'st thou so?' – With my crossbow
I shot the Albatross.

PART II

The Sun now rose upon the right:
Out of the sea came he,
Still hid in mist, and on the left
Went down into the sea.

And the good south wind still blew behind,
But no sweet bird did follow,
Nor any day for food or play
Came to the mariners' hollo!

[2] Swoon or a fainting fit.

His shipmates cry out against the ancient Mariner for killing the bird of good luck.

And I had done an hellish thing,
And it would work 'em woe:
For all averred, I had killed the bird
That made the breeze to blow.
Ah wretch! said they, the bird to slay,
That made the breeze to blow!

But when the fog cleared off, they justify the same, and thus make themselves accomplices in he crime.

Nor dim nor red, like God's own head,
The glorious Sun uprist:
Then all averred, I had killed the bird
That brought the fog and mist.
'Twas right, said they, such birds to slay,
That bring the fog and mist.

The fair breeze continues; the ship enters the Pacific Ocean, and sails northward, even till it reaches the Line.

The fair breeze blew, the white foam flew,
The furrow followed free;
We were the first that ever burst
Into that silent sea.

The ship hath been suddenly becalmed.

Down dropt the breeze, the sails dropt down,
'Twas sad as sad could be;
And we did speak only to break
The silence of the sea!

All in a hot and copper sky,
The bloody Sun, at noon,
Right up above the mast did stand,
No bigger than the Moon.

Day after day, day after day,
We stuck, nor breath nor motion;
As idle as a painted ship
Upon a painted ocean.

And the Albatross begins to be avenged.

Water, water, everywhere,
And all the boards did shrink;
Water, water, everywhere,
Nor any drop to drink.

The very deep did rot: O Christ!
That ever this should be!
Yea, slimy things did crawl with legs
Upon the slimy sea.

About, about, in reel and rout
The death-fires danced at night;
The water, like a witch's oils,
Burnt green, and blue, and white.

*A Spirit had followed them;
one of the invisible inhabitants
of this planet, neither departed
souls nor angels; concerning
whom the learned Jew,
Josephus, and the Platonic
Constantinopolitan, Michael
Psellus, may be consulted.
They are very numerous, and
there is no climate or element
without one or more.*

*The shipmates in their sore
distress, would fain throw the
whole guilt on the ancient
Mariner: in sign whereof they
hang the dead sea-bird round
his neck.*

And some in dreams assuréd were
Of the Spirit that plagued us so;
Nine fathom deep he had followed us
From the land of mist and snow.

And every tongue, through utter drought,
Was withered at the root;
We could not speak, no more than if
We had been choked with soot.

Ah! well a-day! What evil looks
Had I from old and young!
Instead of the cross, the Albatross
About my neck was hung.

PART III

There passed a weary time. Each throat
Was parched, and glazed each eye.
A weary time! a weary time!
How glazed each weary eye!
When looking westward, I beheld
A something in the sky.

*The ancient Mariner
beholdeth a sign in the
element afar off.*

At first it seemed a little speck,
And then it seemed a mist;
It moved and moved, and took at last
A certain shape, I wist.

A speck, a mist, a shape, I wist!
And still it neared and neared:
As if it dodged a water-sprite,
It plunged, and tacked, and veered.

*At its nearer approach, it
seemeth him to be a ship;
and at a dear ransom he
freeth his speech from the
bonds of thirst.*

With throats unslaked, with black lips baked,
We could nor laugh nor wail;
Through utter drought all dumb we stood!
I bit my arm, I sucked the blood,
And cried, A sail! a sail!

With throats unslaked, with black lips baked,
Agape they heard me call:
Gramercy![3] they for joy did grin,
And all at once their breath drew in,
As they were drinking all.

A flash of joy;

[3] Grant mercy on us!

*And horror follows. For can
it be a ship that comes onward
without wind or tide?*

See! see! (I cried) she tacks no more!
Hither to work us weal–
Without a breeze, without a tide,
She steadies with upright keel!

The western wave was all a-flame,
The day was well nigh done!
Almost upon the western wave
Rested the broad bright Sun;
When that strange shape drove suddenly
Betwixt us and the Sun.

*It seemeth him but the skeleton
of a ship.*

And straight the Sun was flecked with bars,
(Heaven's Mother send us grace!),
As if through a dungeon-grate he peered
With broad and burning face.

Alas! (thought I, and my heart beat loud)
How fast she nears and nears!
Are those her sails that glance in the Sun,
Like restless gossameres?

*And its ribs are seen as bars
on the face of the setting Sun.
The Spectre-Woman and her
Death-mate, and no other on
board the skeleton ship. Like
vessel, like crew!*

Are those her ribs through which the Sun
Did peer, as through a grate?
And is that Woman all her crew?
Is that a Death? and are there two?
Is Death that Woman's mate?

Her lips were red, her looks were free,
Her locks were yellow as gold:
Her skin was as white as leprosy,
The Nightmare Life-in-Death was she,
Who thicks man's blood with cold.

*Death and Life-in-Death have
diced for the ship's crew, and
she (the latter) winneth the
ancient Mariner.*

The naked hulk alongside came,
And the twain were casting dice;
'The game is done! I've won! I've won!'
Quoth she, and whistles thrice.

*No twilight within the courts
of the Sun.*

The Sun's rim dips; the stars rush out:
At one stride comes the dark;
With far-heard whisper, o'er the sea,
Off shot the spectre-bark.

We listened and looked sideways up!
Fear at my heart, as at a cup,
My life-blood seemed to sip!
The stars were dim, and thick the night,

The steersman's face by his lamp gleamed white;
From the sails the dew did drip –

At the rising of the Moon,

Till clomb above the eastern bar
The hornéd Moon, with one bright star
Within the nether tip.

One after another,

One after one, by the star-dogged Moon,
Too quick for groan or sigh,
Each turned his face with a ghastly pang,
And cursed me with his eye.

His shipmates drop down
dead.

Four times fifty living men
(And I heard nor sigh nor groan),
With heavy thump, a lifeless lump,
They dropped down one by one.

But Life-in-Death begins
her work on the ancient
Mariner.

The souls did from their bodies fly, –
They fled to bliss or woe!
And every soul, it passed me by
Like the whizz of my cross-bow!'

PART IV

The Wedding-Guest feareth
that a spirit is talking to him;

'I fear thee, ancient Mariner!
I fear thy skinny hand!
And thou art long, and lank, and brown,
As is the ribbed sea-sand.

I fear thee and thy glittering eye,
And thy skinny hand so brown.' –

But the ancient Mariner
assureth him of his bodily
life, and proceedeth to relate
his horrible penance.

Fear not, fear not, thou Wedding-Guest!
This body dropt not down.

Alone, alone, all, all alone,
Alone on a wide, wide sea!
And never a saint took pity on
My soul in agony.

He despiseth the creatures
of the calm.

The many men, so beautiful!
And they all dead did lie:
And a thousand thousand slimy things
Lived on; and so did I.

And envieth that they should
live, and so many lie dead.

I looked upon the rotting sea,
And drew my eyes away;
I looked upon the rotting deck,
And there the dead men lay.

I looked to heaven, and tried to pray;
But or ever a prayer had gusht,
A wicked whisper came, and made
My heart as dry as dust.

I closed my lids, and kept them close,
And the balls like pulses beat;
For the sky and the sea, and the sea and the sky
Lay like a load on my weary eye,
And the dead were at my feet.

But the curse liveth for him in
the eye of the dead men.

The cold sweat melted from their limbs,
Nor rot nor reek did they:
The look with which they looked on me
Had never passed away.

An orphan's curse would drag to hell
A spirit from on high;
But oh! more horrible than that
Is the curse in a dead man's eye!
Seven days, seven nights, I saw that curse,
And yet I could not die.

In his loneliness and fixedness
he yearneth towards the
journeying Moon, and the stars
that still sojourn, yet still move
onward; and everywhere the
blue sky belongs to them, and
is their appointed rest and their
native country and their own
natural homes, which they enter
unannounced, as lords that are
certainly expected, and yet there
is a silent joy at their arrival.

The moving Moon went up the sky,
And nowhere did abide:
Softly she was going up,
And a star or two beside –

Her beams bemocked the sultry main,
Like April hoar-frost spread;
But where the ship's huge shadow lay,
The charméd water burnt alway
A still and awful red.

By the light of the Moon he
beholdeth God's creatures
of the great calm.

Beyond the shadow of the ship,
I watched the water-snakes:
They moved in tracks of shining white,
And when they reared, the elfish light
Fell off in hoary flakes.

Within the shadow of the ship
I watched their rich attire:
Blue, glossy green, and velvet black,
They coiled and swam; and every track
Was a flash of golden fire.

Their beauty and their *happiness.*	O happy living things! no tongue Their beauty might declare: A spring of love gush'd from my heart,
He blesseth them in his heart.	And I blessed them unaware: Sure my kind saint took pity on me, And I blessed them unaware.
The spell begins to break.	The selfsame moment I could pray; And from my neck so free The Albatross fell off, and sank Like lead into the sea.

PART V

O sleep! it is a gentle thing,
Beloved from pole to pole!
To Mary Queen the praise be given!
She sent the gentle sleep from Heaven,
That slid into my soul.

By grace of the holy Mother,
the ancient Mariner is
refreshed with rain.

The silly buckets on the deck,
That had so long remained,
I dreamt that they were filled with dew;
And when I awoke, it rained.

My lips were wet, my throat was cold,
My garments all were dank;
Sure I had drunken in my dreams,
And still my body drank.

I moved, and could not feel my limbs:
I was so light – almost
I thought that I had died in sleep,
And was a blesséd ghost.

He heareth sounds and seeth
strange sights and commotions
in the sky and the element.

And soon I heard a roaring wind:
It did not come anear;
But with its sound it shook the sails,
That were so thin and sere.

The upper air burst into life!
And a hundred fire-flags sheen,
To and fro they were hurried about!
And to and fro, and in and out,
The wan stars danced between.

And the coming wind did roar more loud,
And the sails did sigh like sedge;
And the rain pour'd down from one black cloud;
The Moon was at its edge.

The thick black cloud was cleft, and still
The Moon was at its side:
Like waters shot from some high crag,
The lightning fell with never a jag,
A river steep and wide.

The bodies of the ship's crew
are inspired, and the ship
moves on;

The loud wind never reached the ship,
Yet now the ship moved on!
Beneath the lightning and the Moon
The dead men gave a groan.

They groaned, they stirred, they all uprose,
Nor spake, nor moved their eyes;
It had been strange, even in a dream,
To have seen those dead men rise.

The helmsman steered, the ship moved on;
Yet never a breeze up blew;
The mariners all 'gan work the ropes,
Where they were wont to do;
They raised their limbs like lifeless tools –
We were a ghastly crew.

The body of my brother's son
Stood by me, knee to knee:
The body and I pulled at one rope,
But he said naught to me.

But not by the souls of the
men, nor by demons of earth
or middle air, but by a blessed
troop of angelic spirits, sent
down by the invocation of the
guardian saint.

'I fear thee, ancient Mariner!'
Be calm, thou Wedding-Guest!
'Twas not those souls that fled in pain,
Which to their corses came again,
But a troop of spirits blest:

For when it dawned – they dropped their arms,
And clustered round the mast;
Sweet sounds rose slowly through their mouths,
And from their bodies passed.

Around, around, flew each sweet sound,
Then darted to the Sun;
Slowly the sounds came back again,
Now mixed, now one by one.

Sometimes a-dropping from the sky
I heard the skylark sing;
Sometimes all little birds that are,
How they seemed to fill the sea and air
With their sweet jargoning!

And now 'twas like all instruments,
Now like a lonely flute;
And now it is an angel's song,
That makes the Heavens be mute.

It ceased; yet still the sails made on
A pleasant noise till noon,
A noise like of a hidden brook
In the leafy month of June,
That to the sleeping woods all night
Singeth a quiet tune.

Till noon we quietly sailed on,
Yet never a breeze did breathe:
Slowly and smoothly went the ship,
Moved onward from beneath.

*The lonesome Spirit from the
South Pole carries on the ship
as far as the Line, in obedience
to the angelic troop, but still
requireth vengeance.*

Under the keel nine fathom deep,
From the land of mist and snow,
The Spirit slid: and it was he
That made the ship to go.
The sails at noon left off their tune,
And the ship stood still also.

The Sun, right up above the mast,
Had fixed her to the ocean:
But in a minute she 'gan stir,
With a short uneasy motion –
Backwards and forwards half her length
With a short uneasy motion.

Then like a pawing horse let go,
She made a sudden bound:
It flung the blood into my head,
And I fell down in a swound.

*The Polar Spirit's fellow-demons,
the invisible inhabitants of the
element, take part in his wrong;
and two of them relate, one to
the other, that penance long
and heavy for the ancient
Mariner hath been accorded
to the Polar Spirit, who
returneth southward.*

How long in that same fit I lay,
I have not to declare;
But ere my living life returned,
I heard, and in my soul discerned
Two voices in the air.

'Is it he?' quoth one, 'is this the man?
By Him who died on cross,
With his cruel bow he laid full low
The harmless Albatross.

'The Spirit who bideth by himself
In the land of mist and snow,
He loved the bird that loved the man
Who shot him with his bow.'

The other was a softer voice,
As soft as honey-dew:
Quoth he, 'The man hath penance done,
And penance more will do.'

PART VI

First Voice:
But tell me, tell me! speak again,
Thy soft response renewing –
What makes that ship drive on so fast?
What is the Ocean doing?

Second Voice:
Still as a slave before his lord,
The Ocean hath no blast;
His great bright eye most silently
Up to the Moon is cast –

If he may know which way to go;
For she guides him smooth or grim.
See, brother, see! how graciously
She looketh down on him.

*The Mariner hath been cast
into a trance; for the angelic
power causeth the vessel to
drive northward faster than
human life could endure.*

First Voice:
But why drives on that ship so fast,
Without or wave or wind?

Second Voice:
The air is cut away before,
And closes from behind.

Fly, brother, fly! more high, more high!
Or we shall be belated:
For slow and slow that ship will go,
When the Mariner's trance is abated.

*The supernatural motion is
retarded; the Mariner awakes,
and his penance begins anew.*

I woke, and we were sailing on
As in a gentle weather:
'Twas night, calm night, the Moon was high;
The dead men stood together.

All stood together on the deck,
For a charnel-dungeon fitter:
All fixed on me their stony eyes,
That in the Moon did glitter.

The pang, the curse, with which they died,
Had never passed away:
I could not draw my eyes from theirs,
Nor turn them up to pray.

The curse is finally expiated.

And now this spell was snapt: once more
I viewed the ocean green,
And looked far forth, yet little saw
Of what had else been seen –

Like one that on a lonesome road
Doth walk in fear and dread,
And having once turned round, walks on,
And turns no more his head;
Because he knows a frightful fiend
Doth close behind him tread.

But soon there breathed a wind on me,
Nor sound nor motion made:
Its path was not upon the sea,
In ripple or in shade.

It raised my hair, it fanned my cheek
Like a meadow-gale of spring –
It mingled strangely with my fears,
Yet it felt like a welcoming.

Swiftly, swiftly flew the ship,
Yet she sailed softly too:
Sweetly, sweetly blew the breeze –
On me alone it blew.

And the ancient Mariner
beholdeth his native country.

O dream of joy! is this indeed
The lighthouse top I see?
Is this the hill? is this the kirk?
Is this mine own countree?

We drifted o'er the harbour-bar,
And I with sobs did pray –
O let me be awake, my God!
Or let me sleep alway.

The harbour-bay was clear as glass,
So smoothly it was strewn!
And on the bay the moonlight lay,
And the shadow of the Moon.

The rock shone bright, the kirk no less,
That stands above the rock:
The moonlight steeped in silentness
The steady weathercock.

The angelic spirits leave the
dead bodies,

And the bay was white with silent light,
Till rising from the same,
Full many shapes, that shadows were,
In crimson colours came.

And appear in their own
forms of light.

A little distance from the prow
Those crimson shadows were:
I turn'd my eyes upon the deck –
O Christ! what saw I there!

Each corse lay flat, lifeless and flat,
And, by the holy rood!
A man all light, a seraph-man,
On every corse there stood.

This seraph-band, each waved his hand:
It was a heavenly sight!
They stood as signals to the land,
Each one a lovely light;

This seraph-band, each waved his hand,
No voice did they impart –
No voice; but oh! The silence sank
Like music on my heart.

But soon I heard the dash of oars,
I heard the Pilot's cheer;
My head was turned perforce away,
And I saw a boat appear.

The Pilot and the Pilot's boy,
I heard them coming fast:
Dear Lord in Heaven! it was a joy
The dead men could not blast.

I saw a third – I heard his voice:
It is the Hermit good!

He singeth loud his godly hymns
That he makes in the wood.
He'll shrieve my soul, he'll wash away
The Albatross's blood.

PART VII

The Hermit of the Wood.

This Hermit good lives in that wood
Which slopes down to the sea.
How loudly his sweet voice he rears!
He loves to talk with marineres
That come from a far countree.

He kneels at morn, and noon, and eve –
He hath a cushion plump:
It is the moss that wholly hides
The rotted old oak-stump.

The skiff-boat neared: I heard them talk,
'Why, this is strange, I trow!
Where are those lights so many and fair,
That signal made but now?'

*Approacheth the ship
with wonder.*

'Strange, by my faith!' the Hermit said –
'And they answered not our cheer!
The planks looked warped! and see those sails,
How thin they are and sere!
I never saw aught like to them,
Unless perchance it were

'Brown skeletons of leaves that lag
My forest-brook along;
When the ivy-tod is heavy with snow,
And the owlet whoops to the wolf below,
That eats the she-wolf's young.'

'Dear Lord! it hath a fiendish look –
(The Pilot made reply)
I am a-feared' – 'Push on, push on!'
Said the Hermit cheerily.

The boat came closer to the ship,
But I nor spake nor stire'd;
The boat came close beneath the ship,
And straight a sound was heard.

The ship suddenly sinketh.

Under the water it rumbled on,
Still louder and more dread:

It reached the ship, it split the bay;
The ship went down like lead.

The ancient Mariner is saved in
the Pilot's boat.

Stunned by that loud and dreadful sound,
Which sky and ocean smote,
Like one that hath been seven days drowned
My body lay afloat;
But swift as dreams, myself I found
Within the Pilot's boat.

Upon the whirl, where sank the ship,
The boat spun round and round;
And all was still, save that the hill
Was telling of the sound.

I moved my lips – the Pilot shrieked
And fell down in a fit;
The holy Hermit raised his eyes,
And prayed where he did sit.

I took the oars: the Pilot's boy,
Who now doth crazy go,
Laughed loud and long, and all the while
His eyes went to and fro.
'Ha! ha!' quoth he, 'full plain I see
The Devil knows how to row.'

And now, all in my own countree,
I stood on the firm land!
The Hermit stepped forth from the boat,
And scarcely he could stand.

The ancient Mariner earnestly
entreateth the Hermit to shrieve
him; and the penance of life falls
on him.

'O shrieve me, shrieve me, holy man!'
The Hermit crossed his brow.
'Say quick,' quoth he, 'I bid thee say –
What manner of man art thou?'

Forthwith this frame of mine was wrenched
With a woful agony,
Which forced me to begin my tale;
And then it left me free.

And ever and anon throughout
his future life an agony con-
straineth him to travel from land
to land;

Since then, at an uncertain hour,
That agony returns:
And till my ghastly tale is told,
This heart within me burns.

I pass, like night, from land to land;
I have strange power of speech;
That moment that his face I see,
I know the man that must hear me:
To him my tale I teach.

What loud uproar bursts from that door!
The wedding-guests are there:
But in the garden-bower the bride
And bride-maids singing are:
And hark the little vesper bell,
Which biddeth me to prayer!

O Wedding-Guest! this soul hath been
Alone on a wide, wide sea:
So lonely 'twas, that God Himself
Scarce seeméd there to be.

O sweeter than the marriage-feast,
'Tis sweeter far to me,
To walk together to the kirk
With a goodly company! –

To walk together to the kirk,
And all together pray,
While each to his great Father bends,
Old men, and babes, and loving friends,
And youths and maidens gay!

And to teach, by his own example, love and reverence to all things that God made and loveth.

Farewell, farewell! but this I tell
To thee, thou Wedding-Guest!
He prayeth well, who loveth well
Both man and bird and beast.

He prayeth best, who loveth best
All things both great and small;
For the dear God who loveth us,
He made and loveth all.

The Mariner, whose eye is bright,
Whose beard with age is hoar,
Is gone: and now the Wedding-Guest
Turn'd from the bridegroom's door.

He went like one that hath been stunned,
And is of sense forlorn:
A sadder and a wiser man,
He rose the morrow morn.

(1798; rev. 1817)

V.a.5. WILLIAM PALEY, from *Natural Theology*

IN crossing a heath, suppose I pitched my foot against a *stone*, and were asked how the stone came to be there, I might possibly answer, that, for any thing I knew to the contrary, it had lain there for ever: nor would it, perhaps, be very easy to show the absurdity of this answer. But suppose I had found a *watch* upon the ground, and it should be enquired how the watch happened to be in that place, I should hardly think of the answer which I had before given, that, for any thing I knew, the watch might have always been there. Yet why should not this answer serve for the watch, as well as for the stone? Why is it not as admissible in the second case, as in the first? For this reason, and for no other, viz., that, when we come to inspect the watch, we perceive (what we could not discover in the stone) that its several parts are framed and put together for a purpose, e.g. that they are so formed and adjusted as to produce motion, and that motion so regulated as to point out the hour of the day; that, if the different parts had been differently shaped from what they are, of a different size from what they are, or placed after any other manner, or in any other order, than that in which they are placed, either no motion at all would have been carried on in the machine, or none which would have answered the use that is now served by it. To reckon up a few of the plainest of the parts, and of their offices, all tending to one result: – We see a cylindrical box containing a coiled, elastic spring, which, by its endeavor to relax itself, turns round the box. We next observe a flexible chain (artificially wrought for the sake of flexure) communicating the action of the spring from the box to the fusee. We then find a series of wheels, the teeth of which catch in, and apply to, each other, conducting the motion from the fusee to the balance, and from the balance to the pointer; and at the same time, by the size and shape of those wheels, so regulating that motion, as to terminate in causing an index, by an equable and measured progression, to pass over a given space in a given time. We take notice that the wheels are made of brass, in order to keep them from rust; the springs of steel, no other metal being so elastic; that over the face of the watch there is placed a glass, a material employed in no other part of the work, but, in the room of which, if there had been any other than a transparent substance, the hour could not be seen without opening the case. This mechanism being observed, (it requires indeed an examination of the instrument, and perhaps some previous knowledge of the subject, to perceive and understand it; but being once, as we have said, observed and understood), the inference, we think, is inevitable; that the watch must have had a maker; that there must have existed, at some time and at some place or other, an artificer or artificers who formed it for the purpose which we find it actually to answer; who comprehended its construction, and designed its use.

(1802)

c. DANSK

V.c.1. NIKOLAJ FREDERIK SEVERIN GRUNDTVIG, 'De Levendes Land'

O deilige Land,
Hvor Haaret ei graaner og Tid har ei Tand,
Hvor Solen ei brænder og Bølgen ei slaaer,
Hvor Høsten omfavner den blomstrende Vaar,
Hvor Aften og Morgen gaae altid i Dands
Med Middagens Glands!

Livsalige Land
Hvor Glasset ei rinder med Graad eller Gran,
Hvor Intet man savner, som Ønske er værd,
Hvor det ikkun fattes, som smertede her,
Hvert Menneske søger med Længsel i Bryst
Din smilende Kyst!

Forjættede Land!
Du hilses i Morgenens speilklare Strand,
Naar Barnet mon skue din Lignelse skiøn
Og drømmer, du findes, hvor Skoven er grøn,
Hvor Barnet kan dele med Blomster og Siv
Sit Smil og sit Liv!

O, flygtige Drøm
Om Evigheds-Øen i Tidernes Strøm,
Om Templet for Glæden i Taarernes Dal
Om Halvgude-Livet i Dødninge-Sal,
Med dig fra de Fleste henfarer paa Stand
De Levendes Land!

O, skuffende Drøm!
Du skinnende Boble paa Tidernes Strøm!
Forgiæves dig Skjalden, med Mund og med Pen
Af glimrende Skygger vil skabe igien,
Naar Skyggen er ligest, da hulke de Smaa
Som stirre derpaa!

Fortryllende Drøm
Om Evigheds-Perlen i Tidernes Strøm,
Du giækker de Arme, der søge omsonst,

c. DANISH

V.c.1. NIKOLAJ FREDERIK SEVERIN GRUNDTVIG, 'The Land of the Living'

O, wonderful land,
Where hair turns not grey, falls so softly Time's hand;
Where sun does not burn, nor the seas' white waves fling,
Where autumn embraces the flowering Spring,
Where sunset and dawn always glow with the bright
Noon-radiant light.

O, heavenly land,
Where tears do not run like the hour-glasses sand,
Where wish that is worthy is wished not in vain,
Where lacks only that which here causes us pain.
Of all that we seek for, we long for the most
Thy halcyon coast.

O, fair promised land,
We hail in the dawn's smiling crystalline strand!
The child takes as real thy bright image there seen,
And dreams thou art found where the forest grows green,
Where children can share with the flowers of May
Their innocent day.

O, transient dream
Of Eden's green isle in Time's fast-flowing stream,
Of temples of Joy in the Valley of Tears,
Of demigod life in Mortality's spheres.
To most so will vanish to-day as of yore
The life-giving shore.

Delusory dream!
Thou luminous bubble in Time's flowing stream!
In vain does the bard with his song and his pen
From brilliant shades thee create once again;
When likeness comes nearest, then little ones weep
The vision to keep.

Enchanting bright dream:
Eternity's pearl in Time's glittering stream!
Thou mock the stretched arms which seek vainly to hold

Hvad Hjertet begiærer, i Billed og Konst,
Saa varigst de kalde hvad sikkert forgaaer
Som Timer og Aar!

O, Kiærligheds Aand!
Lad barnlig mig kysse din straalende Haand,
Som rækker fra Himlen til Jorderigs Muld,
Og rører vort Øie med Fingre som Guld,
Saa blaalig sig hæver bag buldrende Strand
Det deilige Land!

O, himmelske Navn!
Som aabner for vores din hellige Favn,
Saa Aanden, usmittet, kan røre ved Støv,
Og levendegiøre det visnede Løv,
O, lad mig nedknæle saa dybt i mit Leer,
At Gud mig kun seer!

O, Vidunder-Tro,
Som slaaer over Dybet den hvælvede Bro,
Der Iis-Gangen trodser i buldrende Strand,
Fra Dødninge-Hjem til de Levendes Land,
Sid lavere hos mig, du høibaarne Giæst!
Det huger dig bedst!

Letvingede Haab!
Gud-Broder! gienfødt i den hellige Daab!
For Reiserne mange til Landet bag Hav,
For Tidender gode, for Trøsten du gav,
Lad saa mig dig takke, at Glæde jeg seer,
Naar Haab er ei meer!

O, Kiærlighed selv!
Du rolige Kilde for Kræfternes Elv!
Han kalder Dig Fader, som løser vort Baand,
Al Livs-Kraft i Sjælen er Gnist af din Aand;
Dit Rige er dér, hvor Man Død byder Trods,
Det komme til os!

Vor Fader saa huld!
Du giærne vil throne i Templet af Muld,
Som Aanden opbygger i Midlerens Navn,

The heart's dearest wish, so in picture and mould
Men strive to enfold for all time what they know
Is destined to go.

O, Spirit of Love!
I kiss like a child Thy bright hand which above
From Heaven comes reaching to Earth's heavy mould
And touches our eyelids with fingers of gold,
That heavenlike rises above rumbling strand
The wonderful land.

O, Name of all Grace,
Who open to us Thy celestial embrace!
Unblighted the Spirit can touch human clay,
Reviving the leaf that had withered away.
Bowed low to the ground on my knees let me be,
But God can me see.

O, Faith, Thou most rare!
Whose swaying bridge over the deep can us bear,
Defying the ice-river's loud-roaring strand,
From Death's spectral home to the life-giving land.
Come lower beside me and stay, high-born guest,
As you like it best.

O, Hope on light wing!
Reborn by the fond, my Godbrother, Thou swing
On many swift flights to the land beyond this,
For alle the good tidings Thou brought and this bliss:
When hope is no longer, then joy I shall see;
My thanks be to Thee!

O, Love, Thou calm spring,
That feeds the strength flowing within ev'rything!
He calls Thee His Father who will set us free,
All life of the spirit is kindled by Thee;
Thy Kingdom is found where we death overcome,
The Kingdom to come!

Our Father and Lord!
In temples of flesh Thou will best be adored,
As built by the Ghost in the Saviour's Name,

Med rygende Alter i Menneske-Favn,
Med Himmellys-Bolig af Gnisten i Løn
Til Dig og din Søn!

O, Christelighed!
Du skiænker vort Hjerte hvad Verden ei veed;
Hvad svagt vi kun skimte, mens Øiet er blaat,
Det lever dog i os, det føle vi godt,
Mit Land, siger Livet, er Himmel og Jord,
Hvor Kiærlighed boer!

d. FRANÇAIS

V.d.1. FÉLICITÉ de LAMENNAIS, *Paroles d'un croyant*

Quand vous avez prié, ne sentez-vous pas votre coeur plus léger et votre âme plus contente?

La prière rend l'affliction moins douloureuse et la joie plus pure: elle mêle à l'une je ne sais quoi de fortifiant et de doux, et à l'autre un parfum céleste.

Que faites-vous sur la terre, et n'avez-vous rien à demander à celui qui vous y a mis?

Vous êtes un voyageur qui cherche la patrie. Ne marchez point la tête baissée: il faut lever les yeux pour reconnaître sa route.

Votre patrie, c'est le ciel; et quand vous regardez le ciel, est-ce qu'en vous il ne se remue rien? est-ce que nul désir ne vous presse? ou ce désir est-il muet?

Il en est qui disent: A quoi bon prier? Dieu est trop au-dessus de nous pour écouter de si chétives créatures.

Et qui donc a fait ces créatures chétives, qui leur a donné le sentiment, et la pensée, et la parole, si ce n'est Dieu?

Et s'il a été si bon envers elles, était-ce pour les délaisser ensuite et les repousser loin de lui?

En vérité, je vous le dis, quiconque dit dans son coeur que Dieu méprise ses œuvres, blasphème Dieu.

With smouldering altars within human frame.
Such heaven-bright dwellings Thy spark here has won
For Thee and Thy Son.

O, Christian lot!
That gives to the heart what the World has not got.
We understand vaguely, we see now in part,
It lives still within us, we feel in our heart.
For *my* Land, says Life, is on Earth and above,
My Kingdom of Love!

[*from the Grundvig Anthology: Selections from the writings of N. S. Grundtvig (1783-1872)*
Translated by Edward Broadbridge and Niels Lyhne Jensen; Edited, annotated and
introduced by Niels Lyhne Jensen, William Michelsen, Gustav Albeck,
Hellmut Toftdahl, Chr. Thodberg. General Editor: Niels Lyhne Jensen,
James Clarke & Co, Cambridge (Centrum: Denmark, 1984)]

d. FRENCH

V.d.1. FÉLICITÉ de LAMENNAIS, from *Words of a Believer*

XVIII.

When you have prayed, do you not feel your heart lighter, and your spirit more contented?

Prayer makes affliction less sad, and joy more pure; with the one she mingles something strengthening and sweet, and with the other a celestial odour.

What do you upon the earth, and have you nothing to ask of Him who has placed you here?

You are a traveller seeking a country. Walk not with downcast look; it is fit you should lift your eyes to reconnoitre your way.

Your country is heaven; and when you look upon heaven, is there nothing within you which stirs? does no desire urge you? Or, that desire, is it dumb?

There are those who say: Of what benefit is it to pray? God is too high above us, to hearken to such contemptible creatures.

Who then made these contemptible creatures, who hath given them feeling, and thought, and language, if it be not God?

And if he hath been so good toward them, was it that he might afterward abandon them and cast them far from him?

In truth, I say unto you, whosoever sayeth in his heart, that God despiseth his works, blasphemeth God.

Il en est d'autres qui disent: A quoi bon prier? Dieu ne sait-il pas mieux que nous ce dont nous avons besoin?

Dieu sait mieux que vous ce dont vous avez besoin c'est pour cela qu'il veut que vous le lui dernandiez, car Dieu est lui-même votre premier besoin, et prier Dieu c'est commencer à posséder Dieu.

Le père connaît les besoins de son fils: faut-il à cause de cela que le fils n'ait jamais une parole de demande et d'actions de grâces pour son père?

Quand les animaux souffrent, quand ils craignent ou quand ils ont faim, ils poussent des cris plaintifs. Ces cris sont la prière qu'ils adressent à Dieu, et Dieu l'écoute L'homme serait-il donc dans la création le seul être dont la voix ne dût jamais monter à l'oreille du Créateur?

Il passe quelquefois sur les campagnes un vent qui dessèche les plantes, et alors on voit les tiges flétries pencher vers la terre; mais, humectées par la rosée, elles reprennent leur fraîcheur et relèvent leur tête languissante.

Il y a toujours des vents brûlants, qui passent sur l'âme de l'homme et la dessèchent. La prière est la rosée qui la rafraîchit.

[1834]

V.d.2. VICTOR HUGO, «Ce que dit la bouche d'ombre» *in Les Contemplations*

... Les fleurs souffrent sous le ciseau,
Et se ferment ainsi que des paupières closes;
Toutes les femmes sont teintes du sang des roses;
La vierge au bal, qui danse, ange aux fraîches couleurs,
Et qui porte en sa main une touffe de fleurs,
Respire en souriant un bouquet d'agonies.
Pleurez sur les laideurs et les ignominies,
Pleurez sur l'araignée immonde, sur le ver,
Sur la limace au dos mouillé comme l'hiver,
Sur le vil puceron qu'on voit aux feuilles pendre,
Sur le crabe hideux, sur l'affreux scolopendre,
Sur l'effrayant crapaud, pauvre monstre aux doux yeux,
Qui regarde toujours le ciel mystérieux!
Plaignez l'oiseau de crime et la bête de proie.
Ce que Domitien, César, fit avec joie,
Tigre, il le continue avec horreur. Verrès,
Qui fut loup sous la pourpre, est loup dans les forêts;
Il descend, réveillé, l'autre côté du rêve:
Son rire, au fond des bois, en hurlement s'achève;
Pleurez sur ce qui hurle et pleurez sur Verrès.
Sur ces tombeaux vivants, marqués d'obscurs arrêts,
Penchez-vous attendri! versez votre prière!

Again, there are others who say: Of what benefit is it to pray? Doth not God know better than we what things we have need of?

God doth indeed know better than you, that of which you have need: and it is for that reason he wills that you should ask of him, for God is himself your chief need, and to pray unto God is to begin to posses God.

The father knoweth the wants of his child, but is that a cause why the child should never have a word of petition or of thanks for his father?

When the animals suffer, when they fear, or when they hunger, they send up their plaintive cries. These cries are the prayer which they address to God, and God heareth them.

Should it be, then, that in all creation man is the only being from whom no voice should ever rise to the ear of the Creator?

Sometimes there passeth over the country a wind which withers the plants, and then one may see their drooping stems bend toward the earth; but moistened by the dew they regain their freshness, and lift up their languishing heads.

There are always scorching winds which pass over the soul of man and wither it.
Prayer is the dew which revives it.

[1834] [*New York: Henry Ludwig, 1834*]

V.d.2. VICTOR HUGO, from 'What the Shadow-Mouth Said', in *Les Contemplations*

. . . Flowers suffer under the scissor,
And shut like closed eyelids;
All the women are dyed with the blood of roses;
The virgin at the ball, who dances, angel with fresh colors,
And who carries in her hand a cluster of flowers,
Smilingly breathes in a bouquet of death throes.
Weep over the uglinesses and ignominies,
Weep over the unclean spider, over the worm,
Over the slug with the back that is damp like winter,
Over the vile aphid which one sees hanging from the leaf,
Over the hideous crab, over the horrible centipede,
Over the frightening toad, poor gentle-eyed monster,
Who always looks at the mysterious sky!
Pity the bird of crime and the beast of prey.
That which Domitian, Caesar, did with joy,
Tiger, he continues it with horror. Verres,
Who was a wolf under his purple, is a wolf in the forests;
He descends, awakened, the other side of the dream:
His laugh, in the depths of the forest, ends in a scream;
Weep over that which screams and weep over Verres.
Over these living tombs, marked with obscure decrees,
Lean tenderly! pour out your prayer!

La pitié fait sortir des rayons de la pierre.
Plaignez le louveteau, plaignez le lionceau.
La matière, affreux bloc, n'est que le lourd monceau
Des effets monstrueux, sortis des sombres causes.
Ayez pitié! voyez des âmes dans les choses.
Hélas! le cabanon subit aussi l'écrou;
Plaignez le prisonnier, mais plaignez le verrou;
Plaignez la chaîne au fond des bagnes insalubres;
La hache et le billot sont deux êtres lugubres;
La hache souffre autant que le corps, le billot
Souffre autant que la tête; ô mystères d'en haut!
Ils se livrent une âpre et hideuse bataille;
Il ébrèche la hache et la hache l'entaille;
Ils se disent tout bas l'un à l'autre: Assassin!
Et la hache maudit les hommes, sombre essaim,
Quand, le soir, sur le dos du bourreau, son ministre,
Elle revient dans l'ombre, et luit, miroir sinistre,
Ruisselante de sang et reflétant les cieux;
Et, la nuit, dans l'étal morne et silencieux,
Le cadavre au cou rouge, effrayant, glacé, blême,
Seul, sait ce que lui dit le billot, tronc lui-même.
Oh! que la terre est froide et que les rocs sont durs!
Quelle muette horreur dans les halliers obscurs!
Les pleurs noirs de la nuit sur la colombe blanche
Tombent; le vent met nue et torture la branche;
Quel monologue affreux dans l'arbre aux rameaux verts!
Quel frisson dans l'herbe! Oh! quels yeux fixes ouverts
Dans les cailloux profonds, oubliettes des âmes!
C'est une âme que l'eau scie en ses froides lames;
C'est une âme que fait ruisseler le pressoir.
Ténèbres! l'univers est hagard. Chaque soir,
Le noir horizon monte et la nuit noire tombe;
Tous deux, à l'occident, d'un mouvement de tombe,
Ils vont se rapprochant, et, dans le firmament,
O terreur! sur le jour, écrasé lentement,
La tenaille de l'ombre effroyable se ferme.
Oh! les berceaux font peur. Un bagne est dans un germe.
Ayez pitié, vous tous et qui que vous soyez!
Les hideux châtiments, l'un sur l'autre broyés,
Roulent, submergeant tout, excepté les mémoires.
Parfois on voit passer dans ces profondeurs noires,
Comme un rayon lointain de l'éternel amour;
Alors l'hyène Atrée et le chacal Timour,
Et l'épine Caïphe et le roseau Pilate,
Le volcan Alaric à la gueule écarlate,
L'ours Henri huit, pour qui Morus en vain pria,

Pity makes rays of light come out of the stone.
Pity the wolf cub, pity the lion cub.
Matter, horrible block, is nothing but the heavy heap
Of monstrous effects, come out of dark causes.
Have pity! see souls in things.
Alas! the padded cell also has a lock.
Pity the prisoner, but pity the bolt;
Pity the chain in the depths of unhealthy penal colonies;
The axe and the block are two lugubrious beings;
The axe suffers as much as the body, the block
Suffers as much as the head; O mysteries of on high!
They fight a bitter and hideous battle;
It nicks the axe and the axe notches it;
They whisper to each other: Assassin!
And the axe curses men, shadowed swarm,
When, in the evenings, on the back of the executioner, its minister,
It returns in the darkness, and glints, sinister mirror,
Dripping with blood and reflecting the heavens;
And, at night, in the dismal and silent stall,
The red-necked corpse, frightening, icy, pallid,
Alone, knows what the block said to him, itself a trunk.
Oh! how cold the earth is and how hard the rocks are!
What mute horror in the dim thickets!
The night's black tears on the white dove
Fall; the wind strips and tortures the branch;
What a horrible monologue in the green-branched tree!
What a shudder in the grass! Oh! what wide-open, fixed eyes
In the deep pebbles, souls' oubliettes!
It is a soul which the water saws in its cold blades;
It is a soul which makes the wine-press drip.
Darkness! the universe is haggard. Every evening,
The black horizon climbs and the black night falls;
Both, in the west, in a tomb's movement,
They go, approaching each other, and in the firmament,
O terror! on the day, slowly crushed,
The appalling shadow's pliers close.
Oh! cradles are frightening. A penal colony is in a seed.
Have pity, all of you and whoever you are!
Hideous punishments, one ground on top of the other,
Roll, submerging everything, except memories.
Sometimes one sees passing in these black depths,
Something like a far-off ray of the eternal love;
Then Atreus the hyena and Timur the jackal,
And Caiaphas the thorn and Pilate the reed,
Alaric the volcano with the scarlet muzzle,
Henry VIII the bear, to whom More prayed in vain,

Le sanglier Selim et le porc Borgia,
Poussent des cris vers l'Être adorable; et les bêtes
Qui portèrent jadis des mitres sur leurs têtes,
Les grains de sable rois, les brins d'herbe empereurs,
Tous les hideux orgueils et toutes les fureurs,
Se brisent; la douceur saisit le plus farouche;
Le chat lèche l'oiseau, l'oiseau baise la mouche;
Le vautour dit dans l'ombre au passereau: Pardon!
Une caresse sort du houx et du chardon;
Tous les rugissements se fondent en prières;
On entend s'accuser de leurs forfaits les pierres;
Tous ces sombres cachots qu'on appelle les fleurs
Tressaillent; le rocher se met à fondre en pleurs;
Des bras se lèvent hors de la tombe dormante;
Le vent gémit, la nuit se plaint, l'eau se lamente,
Et, sous l'oeil attendri qui regarde d'en haut,
Tout l'abîme n'est plus qu'un immense sanglot.
[...]
Espérez! espérez! espérez, misérables!
Pas de deuil infini, pas de maux incurables,
Pas d'enfer éternel!
Les douleurs vont à Dieu, comme la flèche aux cibles;
Les bonnes actions sont les gonds invisibles
De la porte du ciel.
Le deuil est la vertu, le remords est le pôle
Des monstres garrottés dont le gouffre est la geôle;
Quand, devant Jéhovah,
Un vivant reste pur dans les ombres charnelles,
La mort, ange attendri, rapporte ses deux ailes
A l'homme qui s'en va.
Les enfers se refont édens; c'est là leur tâche.
Tout globe est un oiseau que le mal tient et lâche.
Vivants, je vous le dis,
Les vertus, parmi vous, font ce labeur auguste
D'augmenter sur vos fronts le ciel; quiconque est juste
Travaille au paradis.
L'heure approche. Espérez. Rallumez l'âme éteinte!
Aimez-vous! aimez-vous! car c'est la chaleur sainte,
C'est le feu du vrai jour.
Le sombre univers, froid, glacé, pesant, réclame
La sublimation de l'être par la flamme,
De l'homme par l'amour!
Déjà, dans l'océan d'ombre que Dieu domine,
L'archipel ténébreux des bagnes s'illumine;
Dieu, c'est le grand aimant;
Et les globes, ouvrant leur sinistre prunelle,

Selim the boar and Borgia the pig,
Cry out to the adorable Being; and the beasts
Which in olden days wore miters on their heads,
The grain-of-sand kings, the blade-of-grass emperors,
All the hideous prides and all the furors,
Break; gentleness seizes the wildest;
The cat grooms the bird, the bird kisses the fly;
The vulture says in shadow to the sparrow: Pardon!
A caress comes out of the holly and the thistle;
All the roars melt into prayers;
The stones are heard to accuse themselves of their crimes;
All these dark cells which are called flowers
Quiver; the rock begins to dissolve into tears;
Arms are raised out of the sleeping tomb;
The wind groans, the night complains, the water laments,
And, under the softened eye which looks on from above,
The whole abyss is nothing now but an immense sob.
[. . .]
Hope! hope! hope, wretches!
No infinite mourning, no incurable ills,
No eternal hell!
Pains to go God, like the arrow to the target;
Good deeds are the invisible hinges
Of the gate of heaven.
Mourning is virtue, remorse is the pole
Of the garroted monsters whose cavern is the jail;
When, before Jehovah,
A living person remains pure in the fleshly shadows,
Death, softened angel, brings its two wings
To the man who is leaving.
Hells remake themselves as Edens; that is their task.
Every globe is a bird which evil holds and releases.
Living people, I say to you,
Virtues, among you, do the august labor
Of increasing heaven on your brows; whoever is just
Works in heaven.
The hour approaches. Hope. Relight the extinguished soul!
Love each other! love each other! for it is the holy warmth,
It is the fire of the true day.
The dark universe, cold, frozen, heavy, reclaims
The sublimation of the being by the flame,
Of men by love!
Already, in the ocean of shadow which God looks over,
The shadowed archipelago of the penal colony is illuminated;
God is the great magnet;
And the globes, opening their sinister eyes,

Vers les immensités de l'aurore éternelle
Se tournent lentement.
Oh! comme vont chanter toutes les harmonies,
Comme rayonneront dans les sphères bénies
Les faces de clarté,
Comme les firmaments se fondront en délires,
Comme tressailleront toutes les grandes lyres
De la sérénité,
Quand, du monstre matière ouvrant toutes les serres,
Faisant évanouir en splendeurs les misères,
Changeant l'absinthe en miel,
Inondant de beauté la nuit diminuée,
Ainsi que le soleil tire à lui la nuée
Et l'emplit d'arcs-en-ciel,
Dieu, de son regard fixe attirant les ténèbres,
Voyant vers lui, du fond des cloaques funèbres
Où le mal le pria,
Monter l'énormité bégayant des louanges,
Fera rentrer, parmi les univers archanges,
L'univers paria!
On verra palpiter les fanges éclairées,
Et briller les laideurs les plus désespérées
Au faîte le plus haut,
L'araignée éclatante au seuil des bleus pilastres
Luire, et se redresser, portant des épis d'astres,
La paille du cachot!
La clarté montera dans tout comme une sève;
On verra rayonner au front du boeuf qui rêve
Le céleste croissant;
Le charnier chantera dans l'horreur qui l'encombre,
Et sur tous les fumiers apparaîtra dans l'ombre
Un Job resplendissant!
O disparition de l'antique anathème!
La profondeur disant à la hauteur: Je t'aime!
O retour du banni!
Quel éblouissement au fond des cieux sublimes!
Quel surcroît de clarté que l'ombre des abîmes
S'écriant: Sois béni!
On verra le troupeau des hydres formidables
Sortir, monter du fond des brumes insondables
Et se transfigurer;
Des étoiles éclore aux trous noirs de leurs crânes,
Dieu juste! et par degrés devenant diaphanes,
Les monstres s'azurer!
Ils viendront, sans pouvoir ni parler ni répondre,
Éperdus! on verra des auréoles fondre

Toward the immensities of the eternal dawn
Turn slowly.
Oh! how all the harmonies will sing,
How, in the blessed spheres, will shine
The faces of brightness,
How the firmaments will melt in delirium,
How they will shiver, all the great lyres
Of serenity,
When, of the monster Matter opening all the greenhouses,
Making all the miseries vanish into splendors,
Changing absinthe into honey,
Flooding with beauty the diminished night,
Just as the sun pulls mist to itself
And fills it with rainbows,
God, with his fixed gaze attracting the shadows,
Seeing toward him, from the depths of funereal cloacae
Where evil begged him,
Climb the stammering enormity of praises,
Will cause to return, among the archangel universes,
The pariah universe!
One will see the illuminated mires throb,
And the most desperate uglinesses shine
On the highest summit,
The dazzling spider at the threshold of the blue pilasters
Will glow, and, bearing ears of stars,
The straw of the dungeon will straighten!
Brightness will rise in everything like sap;
One will see shining on the brow of the dreaming bull
The celestial crescent;
The charnel house will sing in the horror which encumbers it,
And on all the dunghills will appear in the shadow
A resplendent Job!
O disappearance of the antique anathema!
The depth saying to the height: I love you!
O return of the banished!
What dazzling wonder in the depth of the sublime heavens!
What a surfeit of brightness is the shadow of the abyss
Crying out: Be blessed!
One will see the herd of formidable hydras
Come out, rise from the depths of unsoundable mists
And be transfigured;
Stars budding in the black holes of their skulls,
Just God! and by degrees becoming diaphanous,
Monsters becoming azure!
They will come, without being able either to speak or too answer,
Distraught! one will see aureoles melt

Les cornes de leur front;
Ils tiendront dans leur griffe, au milieu des cieux calmes,
Des rayons frissonnants semblables à des palmes;
Les gueules baiseront!
Ils viendront! ils viendront, tremblants, brisés d'extase,
Chacun d'eux débordant de sanglots comme un vase,
Mais pourtant sans effroi;
On leur tendra les bras de la haute demeure,
Et Jésus, se penchant sur Bélial qui pleure,
Lui dira: C'est donc toi!
Et vers Dieu par la main il conduira ce frère!
Et, quand ils seront près des degrés de lumière
Par nous seuls aperçus,
Tous deux seront si beaux, que Dieu dont l'oeil flamboie
Ne pourra distinguer, père ébloui de joie,
Bélial de Jésus!
Tout sera dit. Le mal expirera; les larmes
Tariront; plus de fers, plus de deuils, plus d'alarmes;
L'affreux gouffre inclément
Cessera d'être sourd, et bégaiera: Qu'entends-je?
Les douleurs finiront dans toute l'ombre; un ange
Criera: Commencement!

[1856]

V.d.3.　VICTOR HUGO, 'Fin de Satan'

XV

Oh! l'essence de Dieu, c'est d'aimer. L'homme croit
Que Dieu n'est, comme lui, qu'une âme, et qu'il s'isole
De l'univers, poussière immense qui s'envole;
Mais moi, l'ennemi triste et l'éternel moqueur,
Je le sais, Dieu n'est pas une âme, c'est un coeur.
Dieu, centre aimant du monde, à ses fibres divines
Rattache tous les fils de toutes les racines,
Et sa tendresse égale un ver au séraphin;
Et c'est l'étonnement des espaces sans fin
Que ce coeur effrayant, blasphémé par les prêtres,
Ait autant de rayons que l'univers a d'êtres.
Pour lui créer, penser, méditer, animer,
Semer, détruire, faire, être, voir, c'est aimer.
Splendide, il aime, et c'est par reflux qu'on l'adore;
Tout en lui roule; il tient à la nuit par l'aurore,
Aux esprits par l'idée, aux fleurs par le parfum;
Et ce coeur dans son gouffre a l'infini, moins un.

The horns of their brows;
They will hold in their claws, in the middle of the calm heavens,
Trembling rays like palm fronds;
Muzzles will kiss!
They will come! they will come, trembling, broken with ecstasy,
Each of them overflowing with sobs like a vase,
But nevertheless without dread;
Arms will be held out to them from the high dwelling,
And Jesus, bending over the weeping Belial,
Will say to him: So, it's you!
And to God he will lead by the hand this brother!
And, when they are near the steps of light,
Perceived by us alone,
Both will be so beautiful, that God whose eye flames,
Will not be able to distinguish, this father dazzled with joy,
Belial from Jesus!
All will have been said. Evil will die; tears
Will dry up; no more irons, no more mourning, no more alarms;
The horrible unmerciful cavern
Will cease to be deaf, and will stammer: What do I hear?
Pains will end in all the shadow; an angel
Will shout: Beginning!

[1856] [*Translated by Anne Gwin*]

V.d.3.   VICTOR HUGO, from 'The End of Satan'

XV

Oh! the essence of God is to love. Man believes
That God is, like him, only a soul, and that he isolates himself
From the universe, immense dust which takes wing;
But I, the sad enemy and the eternal mocker,
I know it, God is not a soul, he is a heart.
God, loving center of the world, to his divine fibers
Reattaches all the threads of all the roots,
And his tenderness equates a worm with a seraph;
And it is to the astonishment of the endless spaces
That this frightening heart, blasphemed by preachers,
Has as many rays as the universe has creatures.
For him to create, think, meditate, animate,
Sow, destroy, make, be, see, is to love.
Splendid, he loves, and it is on the ebb that he is adored;
Everything rolls in him; he holds to the night by the dawn,
To minds by the idea, to flowers by the scent;
And this heart in its abyss holds infinity, minus one.

Moins Satan, à jamais rejeté, damné, morne.
Dieu m'excepte. Il finit à moi. Je suis sa borne.
Dieu serait infini si je n'existais pas.
Je lui dis: Tu fis bien, Dieu, quand tu me frappas!
Je ne l'accuse point, non; mais je désespère!
O sombre éternité, je suis le fils sans père.
Du côté de Satan il est, mais n'est plus Dieu.

XVI

Cent fois, cent fois, cent fois, j'en répète l'aveu,
J'aime! Et Dieu me torture, et voici mon blasphème,
Voici ma frénésie et mon hurlement: j'aime!
J'aime à faire trembler les cieux! – Quoi; tout est vain;
Oh! c'est là l'inouï, l'horrible, le divin,
De se dresser, d'ouvrir des ailes insensées,
De s'attacher, sanglant, à toutes les pensées
Qu'on peut saisir, avec des cris, avec des pleurs,
De sonder les terreurs, de sonder les douleurs,
Toutes, celles qu'on souffre et celles qu'on invente,
De parcourir le cercle entier de l'épouvante,
Pour retomber toujours au même désespoir;
Dieu veut que l'homme las s'endorme, il fait le soir;
Il creuse pour la taupe une chambre sous terre;
Il donne au singe, à l'ours, au lynx, à la panthère,
L'âpre hospitalité des antres et des monts;
Aux baleines les mers, aux crapauds les limons,
Les roseaux aux serpents secouant leurs sonnettes;
Il fait tourner autour des soleils les planètes
Et dans la blanche main des vierges les fuseaux;
Il entre dans les nids, touche aux petits oiseaux,
Et dit: La bise vient, j'épaissirai leurs plumes;
Il laisse l'étincelle échapper aux enclumes,
Et lui permet de fuir, joyeuse, les marteaux;
Il montre son grand ciel aux lions de l'Athos;
Il étale dans l'aube, ainsi que des corbeilles,
Sous des flots de rayons, les printemps pleins d'abeilles
Sa grandeur pour le monde en bonté se résout.
Une vaste lueur ardente embrase tout,
De l'archange à la brute et de l'astre à la pierre,
Croise en forêt de feu ses rameaux de lumièrc,
Va, vient, monte, descend, féconde, enflamme, emplit,
Combat l'hiver liant les fleuves dans leur lit,
Et lui fait lâcher prise, et rit dans toute chose,
Luit mollement derrière une feuille de rose,
Chauffe l'énormité sidérale des cieux,

Minus Satan, rejected forever, damned, dismal.
God excepts me. He ends at me. I am his boundary-stone.
God would be infinite if I did not exist.
I say to him: You did well, God, when you struck me!
I do not accuse him, no; but I despair!
O dark eternity, I am the son without a father.
By Satan he is, but is no longer God.

XVI

A hundred times, a hundred times, a hundred times, I repeat the confession,
I love! And God tortures me, and here is my blasphemy,
Here is my frenzy and my howl: I love!
I love so much the skies tremble! – What, all is vain;
Oh! this is the unheard-of, the horrible, the divine,
To stand up, to open extravagant wings,
To tie oneself, bloody, to all the thoughts
That one can seize, with cries, with tears,
To plumb the terrors, to plumb the pains,
All, those one suffers and those one invents,
To travel the whole circle of dread,
To fall back always into the same despair;
God wants the weary man to sleep, he makes night;
He digs an underground room for the mole;
He gives the monkey, the bear, the lynx, the panther,
The bitter hospitality of lairs and hills;
To whales the seas, to toads the silt;
The reeds to the snakes shaking their rattles;
He makes planets turn around suns
And in virgins' white hands the spindles;
He enters the nests, touches the little birds,
And says: The breeze comes, I will thicken their feathers;
He lets the spark escape from the anvils,
And permits it, joyous, to flee the hammers;
He shows his great sky to the lions of Mount Athos;
He spreads out in the dawn, as though they were baskets,
Under streams of rays, the springtimes full of bees;
His greatness for the world is resolved in kindness.
A vast burning light sets all ablaze,
From the archangel to the brute and from the star to the stone,
Crosses in a forest of fire its branches of light,
Goes, comes, climbs, descends, makes fruitful, inflames, fills,
Fights the winter tying the rivers to their bed,
And makes it let go, and laughs in everything,
Shines softly behind a rose leaf,
Warms the sidereal enormity of the skies,

Brille, et de mon côté, prodige monstrueux,
Ce flamboiement se dresse en muraille de glace;
Oui, la création heureuse s'entrelace
Tout entière, clartés et brume, esprits et corps,
Dans le Dieu bon, avec d'ineffables accords;
L'être le plus déchu retrouve l'innocence
Dans sa toute tendresse et sa toute puissance;
Moi seul, moi le maudit, l'incurable apostat,
Je m'approche de Dieu sans autre résultat
Que de faire gronder vaguement le tonnerre!
Dieu veut que cet essaim d'atomes le vénère,
Il leur demande à tous leur coeur, leur chant, leur bruit,
Leur parfum, leur prière; à moi rien, de la nuit.
O misère sans fond; Ecoutez ceci, sphères,
Etoiles, firmaments, ô vieux soleils, mes frères,
Vers qui monte en pleurant mon douloureux souhait,
Cieux, azurs, profondeurs, splendeurs, – l'amour me hait!

e. DEUTSCH

V.e.1. FRIEDRICH HÖLDERLIN, 'Brot und Wein'

An Heinze

1.

Rings um ruhet die Stadt; still wird die erleuchtete Gasse,
Und, mit Fackeln geschmückt, rauschen die Wagen hinweg.
Satt gehn heim von Freuden des Tags zu ruhen die Menschen,
Und Gewinn und Verlust wäget ein sinniges Haupt
Wohlzufrieden zu Haus; leer steht von Trauben und Blumen,
Und von Werken der Hand ruht der geschäftige Markt.
Aber das Saitenspiel tönt fern aus Gärten; vielleicht, daß
Dort ein Liebendes spielt oder ein einsamer Mann
Ferner Freunde gedenkt und der Jugendzeit; und die Brunnen
Immerquillend und frisch rauschen an duftendem Beet.
Still in dämmriger Luft ertönen geläutete Glocken,
Und der Stunden gedenk rufet ein Wächter die Zahl.
Jetzt auch kommet ein Wehn und regt die Gipfel des Hains auf,
Sieh! und das Schattenbild unserer Erde, der Mond,
Kommet geheim nun auch; die Schwärmerische, die Nacht kommt,
Voll mit Sternen und wohl wenig bekümmert um uns,
Glänzt die Erstaunende dort, die Fremdlingin unter den Menschen,
Über Gebirgeshöhn traurig und prächtig herauf.

Shines, and by me, monstrous prodigy,
This flaming rises as a wall of ice;
Yes, happy creation is interlaced
Completely, lights and mist, minds and bodies,
In the God of good, with ineffable accords;
The most fallen being regains innocence
In his omnibenevolence and omnipotence;
I alone, I the cursed, the incurable apostate,
I approach God with no other result
Than to make thunder growl vaguely!
God wants this swarm of atoms to venerate him,
He asks of all of them their heart, their song, their noise,
Their perfume, their prayer; of me nothing, all night.
O bottomless misery; listen to this, spheres,
Stars, firmaments, O old suns, my brothers,
Toward whom rises, crying, my painful wish,
Skies, azures, depths, splendors, – love hates me!

[Translated by Anne Gwin]

e. GERMAN

V.e.1. FRIEDRICH HÖLDERLIN, 'Bread and Wine'

To Heinze

1.

Round about the city rests. The illuminated streets grow
Quiet, and coaches rush along, adorned with torches.
Men go home to rest, filled with the day's pleasures;
Busy minds weigh up profit and loss contentedly
At home. The busy marketplace comes to rest,
Vacant now of flowers and grapes and crafts.
But the music of strings sounds in distant gardens:
Perhaps lovers play there, or a lonely man thinks
About distant friends, and about his own youth.
Rushing fountains flow by fragrant flower beds,
Bells ring softly in the twilight air, and a watchman
Calls out the hour, mindful of the time.
Now a breeze rises and touches the crest of the grove –
Look how the moon, like the shadow of our earth,
Also rises stealthily! Phantastical night comes,
Full of stars, unconcerned probably about us –
Astonishing night shines, a stranger among humans,
Sadly over the mountain tops, in splendor.

2.

Wunderbar ist die Gunst der Hocherhabnen und niemand
Weiß, von wannen und was einem geschiehet von ihr.
So bewegt sie die Welt und die hoffende Seele der Menschen,
Selbst kein Weiser versteht, was sie bereitet, denn so
Will es der oberste Gott, der sehr dich liebet, und darum
Ist noch lieber, wie sie, dir der besonnene Tag.
Aber zuweilen liebt auch klares Auge den Schatten
Und versuchet zu Lust, eh es die Not ist, den Schlaf,
Oder es blickt auch gern ein treuer Mann in die Nacht hin,
Ja, es ziemet sich, ihr Kränze zu weihn und Gesang,
Weil den Irrenden sie geheiliget ist und den Toten,
Selber aber besteht, ewig, in freiestem Geist.
Aber sie muß uns auch, daß in der zaudernden Weile,
Daß im Finstern für uns einiges Haltbare sei,
Uns die Vergessenheit und das Heiligtrunkene gönnen,
Gönnen das strömende Wort, das, wie die Liebenden, sei,
Schlummerlos, und vollern Pokal und kühneres Leben,
Heilig Gedächtnis auch, wachend zu bleiben bei Nacht.

3.

Auch verbergen umsonst das Herz im Busen, umsonst nur
Halten den Mut noch wir, Meister und Knaben, denn wer
Möcht es hindern und wer möcht uns die Freude verbieten?
Göttliches Feuer auch treibet, bei Tag und bei Nacht,
Aufzubrechen. So komm! daß wir das Offene schauen,
Daß ein Eigenes wir suchen, so weit es auch ist.
Fest bleibt Eins; es sei um Mittag oder es gehe
Bis in die Mitternacht, immer bestehet ein Maß,
Allen gemein, doch jeglichem auch ist eignes beschieden,
Dahin gehet und kommt jeder, wohin er es kann.
Drum! und spotten des Spotts mag gern frohlockender Wahnsinn,
Wenn er in heiliger Nacht plötzlich die Sänger ergreift.
Drum an den Isthmos komm! dorthin, wo das offene Meer rauscht
Am Parnaß und der Schnee delphische Felsen umglänzt,
Dort ins Land des Olymps, dort auf die Höhe Cithärons,
Unter die Fichten dort, unter die Trauben, von wo
Thebe drunten und Ismenos rauscht im Lande des Kadmos,
Dorther kommt und zurück deutet der kommende Gott.

4.

Seliges Griechenland! du Haus der Himmlischen alle,
Also ist wahr, was einst wir in der Jugend gehört?

2.

The kindness of exalted Night is wonderful, and no one
Knows where she comes from, or what will emerge from her.
Thus she moves the world, and the hopeful minds of humans:
Not even a sage knows what she's up to.
The highest god, who loves you very much, wants it so;
Therefore you prefer reasonable day to the night.
But occasionally a clear eye loves the shadows as well,
And tries to sleep just for pleasure, before it's necessary,
Or a brave person likes to gaze directly into the Night:
Surely it's right to dedicate wreaths and songs to her,
Since she is holy to those who are lost or dead, although
She herself exists totally free in spirit, forever.
But she must grant us oblivion and holy drunkenness,
That in the hesitating interval, in the darkness,
There'll be something for us to hold on to.
She must grant us flowing words, sleepless
As lovers are, and a fuller cup, and bolder life, and
Holy remembrance as well, to stay wakeful at night.

3.

We, masters and apprentices both, hide our hearts
In vain, and repress our enthusiasm for no reason.
For who could stop it, or forbid us our pleasure?
The fire of the gods drives us to set forth by day
And by night. So come, let us look at what is apparent,
And seek what is ours, as distant as it may be!
One thing is certain: a standard always exists, at noon
Or at midnight, common to all of us. But also
To each of us something personal is granted;
Everyone goes and comes where he can.
Thus playful madness may mock mockery itself,
Seizing singers suddenly in the holy night.
Then let's be off to the Isthmus! There, where
The open sea roars at Parnassus, and the snow
Shines around the Delphian cliffs,
There in the land of Olympus, on Cithaeron's peak,
Under the pines, amid vineyards, from which
Thebes and Ismenos roar in the land of Cadmus.
The approaching god comes from there, and points back.

4.

Holy Greece! Home of all the gods – so it's true,
What once we heard when we were young?

687

Festlicher Saal! der Boden ist Meer! und Tische die Berge,
Wahrlich zu einzigem Brauche vor alters gebaut!
Aber die Thronen, wo? die Tempel, und wo die Gefäße,
Wo mit Nektar gefüllt, Göttern zu Lust der Gesang?
Wo, wo leuchten sie denn, die fernhintreffenden Sprüche?
Delphi schlummert und wo tönet das große Geschick?
Wo ist das schnelle? wo brichts, allgegenwärtigen Glücks voll,
Donnernd aus heiterer Luft über die Augen herein?
Vater Aether! so riefs und flog von Zunge zu Zunge
Tausendfach, es ertrug keiner das Leben allein;
Ausgeteilet erfreut solch Gut und getauschet, mit Fremden,
Wirds ein Jubel, es wächst schlafend des Wortes Gewalt:
Vater! heiter! und hallt, so weit es gehet, das uralt
Zeichen, von Eltern geerbt, treffend und schaffend hinab.
Denn so kehren die Himmlischen ein, tiefschütternd gelangt so
Aus den Schatten herab unter die Menschen ihr Tag.

5.

Unempfunden kommen sie erst, es streben entgegen
Ihnen die Kinder, zu hell kommet, zu blendend das Glück,
Und es scheut sie der Mensch, kaum weiß zu sagen ein Halbgott,
Wer mit Namen sie sind, die mit den Gaben ihm nahn.
Aber der Mut von ihnen ist groß, es füllen das Herz ihm
Ihre Freuden und kaum weiß er zu brauchen das Gut,
Schafft, verschwendet und fast ward ihm Unheiliges heilig,
Das er mit segnender Hand töricht und gütig berührt.
Möglichst dulden die Himmlischen dies; dann aber in Wahrheit
Kommen sie selbst und gewohnt werden die Menschen des Glücks
Und des Tags und zu schaun die Offenbaren, das Antlitz
Derer, welche, schon längst Eines und Alles genannt,
Tief die verschwiegene Brust mit freier Genüge gefüllet,
Und zuerst und allein alles Verlangen beglückt;
So ist der Mensch; wenn da ist das Gut, und es sorget mit Gaben
Selber ein Gott für ihn, kennet und sieht er es nicht.
Tragen muß er, zuvor; nun aber nennt er sein Liebstes,
Nun, nun müssen dafür Worte, wie Blumen, entstehn.

6.

Und nun denkt er zu ehren in Ernst die seligen Götter,
Wirklich und wahrhaft muß alles verkünden ihr Lob.
Nichts darf schauen das Licht, was nicht den Hohen gefället,
Vor den Aether gebührt Müßigversuchendes nicht.
Drum in der Gegenwart der Himmlischen würdig zu stehen,
Richten in herrlichen Ordnungen Völker sich auf

A festival hall, whose floor is the ocean, whose tables
Are the mountains – anciently built for a single purpose.
But where are the thrones? Where the temples, the songs,
The vases full of nectar for the pleasure of the gods?
Where are the oracles that shine for miles and miles?
Delphi sleeps, and where does great Fate resound?
Where does Fate suddenly break forth, full of omnipresent
Joy, thundering out of clear air over our eyes?
Father Aether! It called and flew from tongue to tongue
A thousand times, and nobody had to endure life alone.
Shared, such fortune is a joy; exchanged with strangers,
It becomes jubilant. Sleeping, the power of the word grows:
Father! Joyful! The ancient sign resounds, as far it reaches,
Inherited from the elders, striking, creating.
Thus the gods enter; thus the season of the gods falls
From the shadows down to men, shaking the depths.

5.

At first the gods come unperceived. Children try to get
Near them. But their glory dazzles and blinds and
Awakens fear. A demi-god scarcely knows the people
By name, who now approach him with gifts. But their
Courage is great. Their joy fills his heart, and he hardly
Knows what to do with the offerings. He busies himself
And becomes wasteful, and unholy things almost become holy,
Which he touches with a blessing hand, foolishly and kindly.
The gods tolerate it as long as they can, and then in truth
They appear themselves. And people become accustomed
To this fortune, to the daytime, and to the sight of the manifest
Ones, the faces of those formerly called the 'One and All,'
Deeply making every silent breast content, and first and alone
Filling every desire. It's the way people are. When something
Good appears, and even when it's a god that provides them
With gifts, they don't see or recognize it. First they have
To get used to it; then they call it their closest possession.
And only then will words of praise arise, like flowers.

6.

And now they prepare in earnest to honor the holy gods.
Everything must really and truly proclaim their praise.
Nothing displeasing to the high ones may come to light.
Idle endeavors aren't proper for the Aether.
Therefore, to stand worthily in the presence of the gods,
Nations rise in splendid order and beautiful

Untereinander und baun die schönen Tempel und Städte
Fest und edel, sie gehn über Gestaden empor –
Aber wo sind sie? wo blühn die Bekannten, die Kronen des Festes?
Thebe welkt und Athen; rauschen die Waffen nicht mehr
In Olympia, nicht die goldnen Wagen des Kampfspiels,
Und bekränzen sich denn nimmer die Schiffe Korinths?
Warum schweigen auch sie, die alten heilgen Theater?
Warum freuet sich denn nicht der geweihete Tanz?
Warum zeichnet, wie sonst, die Stirne des Mannes ein Gott nicht,
Drückt den Stempel, wie sonst, nicht dem Getroffenen auf?
Oder er kam auch selbst und nahm des Menschen Gestalt an
Und vollendet' und schloß tröstend das himmlische Fest.

7.

Aber Freund! wir kommen zu spät. Zwar leben die Götter,
Aber über dem Haupt droben in anderer Welt.
Endlos wirken sie da und scheinens wenig zu achten,
Ob wir leben, so sehr schonen die Himmlischen uns.
Denn nicht immer vermag ein schwaches Gefäß sie zu fassen,
Nur zu Zeiten erträgt göttliche Fülle der Mensch.
Traum von ihnen ist drauf das Leben. Aber das Irrsal
Hilft, wie Schlummer, und stark machet die Not und die Nacht,
Bis daß Helden genug in der ehernen Wiege gewachsen,
Herzen an Kraft, wie sonst, ähnlich den Himmlischen sind.
Donnernd kommen sie drauf. Indessen dünket mir öfters
Besser zu schlafen, wie so ohne Genossen zu sein,
So zu harren, und was zu tun indes und zu sagen,
Weiß ich nicht, und wozu Dichter in dürftiger Zeit?
Aber sie sind, sagst du, wie des Weingotts heilige Priester,
Welche von Lande zu Land zogen in heiliger Nacht.

8.

Nämlich, als vor einiger Zeit, uns dünket sie lange,
Aufwärts stiegen sie all, welche das Leben beglückt,
Als der Vater gewandt sein Angesicht von den Menschen,
Und das Trauern mit Recht über der Erde begann,
Als erschienen zuletzt ein stiller Genius, himmlisch
Tröstend, welcher des Tags Ende verkündet' und schwand,
Ließ zum Zeichen, daß einst er da gewesen und wieder
Käme, der himmlische Chor einige Gaben zurück,
Derer menschlich, wie sonst, wir uns zu freuen vermöchten,
Denn zur Freude, mit Geist, wurde das Größre zu groß
Unter den Menschen und noch, noch fehlen die Starken zu höchsten
Freuden, aber es lebt stille noch einiger Dank.

Temples and cities are built, strong and noble, which rise
Above the banks of the waters –but where are they?
Where are the famous, flourishing cities, crowning the festival?
Thebes and Athens are fading. Don't the weapons clash
At Olympus, or golden chariots at the games? Are there
No longer wreaths to decorate the ships of Corinth?
Why are the ancient holy theaters silent?
What happened to the joyful ceremonial dancing?
Why doesn't a god place his sign on a human forehead,
Leaving his mark on the person he has struck?
Or, as gods used to, come comfortingly, and assume human
Shape, then complete and close the festival of the gods?

7.

But friend, we come too late. It's true that the gods live,
But up over our heads, up in a different world.
They function endlessly up there, and seem to care little
If we live or die, so much do they avoid us.
A weak vessel cannot hold them forever; humans can
Endure the fullness of the gods only at times. Therefore
Life itself becomes a dream about them. But perplexity
And sleep assist us: distress and night-time strengthen,
Until enough heroes have grown in the bronze cradle,
With hearts as strong as the gods', as it used to be.
Thundering they arise. Meanwhile I often think it is
Better to stay asleep, than to exist without companions,
Just waiting it out, not knowing what to do or say
In the meantime. What use are poets in times of need?
But you'll say they're like holy priests of the wine god,
Moving from land to land in the holy night.

8.

Some time ago – to us it seems like a long time –
All those who made our lives happy climbed upwards.
The Father turned his face away from people,
And sorrow came rightly upon the earth.
Finally a quiet genius appeared, comforting in a god-like
Way, who announced the end of the day, and disappeared.
The choir of gods left some gifts behind, as a sign
Of their presence and eventual return, which we
May appreciate in our human fashion, as we used to.
That which is superior had grown too great for pleasure
With spirit among men. And to this day no one's strong enough
For the highest joys, although some gratitude survives quietly.

Brot ist der Erde Frucht, doch ists vom Lichte gesegnet,
Und vom donnernden Gott kommet die Freude des Weins.
Darum denken wir auch dabei der Himmlischen, die sonst
Da gewesen und die kehren in richtiger Zeit,
Darum singen sie auch mit Ernst, die Sänger, den Weingott
Und nicht eitel erdacht tönet dem Alten das Lob.

9

Ja! sie sagen mit Recht, er söhne den Tag mit der Nacht aus,
Führe des Himmels Gestirn ewig hinunter, hinauf,
Allzeit froh, wie das Laub der immergrünenden Fichte,
Das er liebt, und der Kranz, den er von Efeu gewählt,
Weil er bleibet und selbst die Spur der entflohenen Götter
Götterlosen hinab unter das Finstere bringt.
Was der Alten Gesang von Kindern Gottes geweissagt,
Siehe! wir sind es, wir; Frucht von Hesperien ists!
Wunderbar und genau ists als an Menschen erfüllet,
Glaube, wer es geprüft! aber so vieles geschieht,
Keines wirket, denn wir sind herzlos, Schatten, bis unser
Vater Aether erkannt jeden und allen gehört.
Aber indessen kommt als Fackelschwinger des Höchsten
Sohn, der Syrier, unter die Schatten herab.
Selige Weise sehns; ein Lächeln aus der gefangnen
Seele leuchtet, dem Licht tauet ihr Auge noch auf.
Sanfter träumet und schläft in Armen der Erde der Titan,
Selbst der neidische, selbst Cerberus trinket und schläft.

[1800–1801] [*Friedrich Hölderlin, Sämtliche Werke. Kleine Stuttgarter Ausgabe.*
Ed., Friedrich Beißner. Stuttgart: Cotta 1944–1962. II (1953). 94–99]

V.e.2. FRIEDRICH SCHLEIERMACHER, *Über die Religion. Reden an die*
Gebildeten unter ihren Verächtern, aus Rede II: 'Über das Wesen der Religion'

Stellet Euch auf den höchsten Standpunkt der Metaphysik und der Moral, so werdet Ihr finden,
daß beide mit der Religion denselben Gegenstand haben, nämlich das Universum und das
Verhältnis des Menschen zu ihm. Diese Gleichheit ist von lange her ein Grund zu mancherlei
Verirrungen gewesen; daher ist Metaphysik und Moral in Menge in die Religion eingedrungen,
und manches was der Religion angehört, hat sich unter einer unschicklichen Form in die Metaphysik oder die Moral versteckt. Werdet Ihr aber deswegen glauben, daß sie mit einer von
beiden einerlei sei? Ich weiß, daß Euer Instinkt Euch das Gegenteil sagt, und es geht auch aus
Euren Meinungen hervor; denn Ihr gebt nie zu, daß sie mit dem festen Tritte einhergeht, dessen
die Metaphysik fähig ist, und Ihr vergesset nicht fleißig zu bemerken, daß es in ihrer Geschichte
eine Menge garstiger unmoralischer Flecken gibt. Soll sie sich also unterscheiden, so muß sie
ihnen ungeachtet des gleichen Stoffs auf irgendeine Art entgegengesetzt sein; sie muß diesen
Stoff ganz anders behandeln, ein anderes Verhältnis der Menschen zu demselben ausdrücken
oder bearbeiten, eine andere Verfahrungsart oder ein anderes Ziel haben: denn nur dadurch

Bread is the fruit of the earth, yet it's blessed also by light.
The pleasure of wine comes from the thundering god.
We remember the gods thereby, those who were once
With us, and who'll return when the time is right.
Thus poets sing of the wine god in earnest, and their
Ringing praises of the old one aren't devised in vain.

9.

Yes, they say rightly that he reconciles day with night,
And leads the stars of heaven up and down forever –
Joyful always, like the boughs of evergreen pine
That he loves, and the wreath he chose of ivy,
Since it endures, and brings a trace of the fugitive gods
Down to the darkness of those who must live in their absence.
What the sons of the ancients foretold of God's children:
Look, it's us, the fruit of Hesperia!
Through humans it is wonderfully and exactly fulfilled;
Let those believe who've examined the matter. But so much
Goes on, yet nothing succeeds: we are like heartless shadows
Until our Father Aether recognizes us and belongs to us all.
Meanwhile the Son, the Syrian, comes down among
The shadows, as torchbearer of the Highest.
Holy sages observe it; a smile shines out from
The imprisoned soul; their eyes thaw in the light.
Titans dream more softly, asleep in the arms of the earth–
Even jealous Cerberus drinks and falls asleep.

Poems of Friedrich Hölderlin. Selected and translated by James Mitchell.
San Francisco: Ithuriell's Spear 2007. 7–29 [1800–1801]

V.e.2. FRIEDRICH SCHLEIERMACHER, *On Religion: Speeches to its Cultured Despisers,* from Speech 2: 'On the Essence of Religion'

If you put yourselves on the highest standpoint of metaphysics and morals, you will find that both have the same object as religion, namely, the universe and the relationship of humanity to it. This similarity has long since been a basis of manifold aberrations; metaphysics and morals have therefore invaded religion on many occasions, and much that belongs to religion has concealed itself in metaphysics and morals under an unseemly form. But shall you, for this reason, believe that it is identical with one of these? I know that your instinct tells you the contrary, and it also follows from your opinions; for you never admit that religions walks with the firm step of which metaphysics is capable, and you do not forget to observe diligently that there are quite a few ugly immoral blemishes on its history. If religion is thus to be differentiated, then it must be set off from those in some manner, regardless of the common subject matter. Religion must treat this subject matter completely differently, express or work out another relationship of humanity to it, have another mode of procedure or another goal; for only in this way can that which is similar in its subject matter to something else achieve a determinate

kann dasjenige, was dem Stoff nach einem andern gleich ist, eine besondere Natur und ein eigentümliches Dasein bekommen. Ich frage Euch also: was tut Euere Metaphysik oder wenn Ihr von dem veralteten Namen, der Euch zu historisch ist, nichts wissen wollt Euere Transzendentalphilosophie? sie klassifiziert das Universum und teilt es ab in solche Wesen und solche, sie geht den Gründen dessen was da ist nach, und deduziert die Notwendigkeit des Wirklichen, sie entspinnet aus sich selbst die Realität der Welt und ihre Gesetze. In dieses Gebiet darf sich also die Religion nicht versteigen, sie darf nicht die Tendenz haben Wesen zu setzen und Naturen zu bestimmen, sich in ein Unendliches von Gründen und Deduktionen zu verlieren, letzte Ursachen aufzusuchen und ewige Wahrheiten auszusprechen. Und was tut Euere Moral? Sie entwickelt aus der Natur des Menschen und seines Verhältnisses gegen das Universum ein System von Pflichten, sie gebietet und untersagt Handlungen mit unumschränkter Gewalt. Auch das darf also die Religion nicht wagen, sie darf das Universum nicht brauchen um Pflichten abzuleiten, sie darf keinen Kodex von Gesetzen enthalten. »Und doch scheint das, was man Religion nennt, nur aus Bruchstücken dieser verschiedenen Gebiete zu bestehen.« Dies ist freilich der gemeine Begriff. Ich habe Euch letzthin Zweifel gegen ihn beigebracht; es ist jetzt Zeit ihn völlig zu vernichten. Die Theoretiker in der Religion, die aufs Wissen über die Natur des Universums und eines höchsten Wesens, dessen Werk es ist, ausgehen, sind Metaphysiker; aber artig genug, auch etwas Moral nicht zu verschmähen. Die Praktiker, denen der Wille Gottes Hauptsache ist, sind Moralisten; aber ein wenig im Stile der Metaphysik. Die Idee des Guten nehmt Ihr und tragt sie in die Metaphysik als Naturgesetz eines unbeschränkten und unbedürftigen Wesens, und die Idee eines Urwesens nehmt Ihr aus der Metaphysik und tragt sie in die Moral, damit dieses große Werk nicht anonym bleibe, sondern vor einem so herrlichen Kodex das Bild des Gesetzgebers könne gestochen werden. Mengt aber und rührt wie Ihr wollt, dies geht nie zusammen. Ihr treibt ein leeres Spiel mit Materien, die sich einander nicht aneignen. Ihr behaltet immer nur Metaphysik und Moral. Dieses Gemisch von Meinungen über das höchste Wesen oder die Welt, und von Geboten für ein menschliches Leben (oder gar für zwei) nennt Ihr Religion! und den Instinkt der jene Meinungen sucht, nebst den dunklen Ahndungen, welche die eigentliche letzte Sanktion dieser Gebote sind, nennt Ihr Religiosität! Aber wie kommt Ihr denn dazu, eine bloße Kompilation, eine Chrestomathie für Anfänger für ein eignes Werk zu halten, für ein Individuum eignen Ursprunges und eigener Kraft?

[...]

Ihr mögt die Religion nicht, davon sind wir schon neulich ausgegangen; aber indem Ihr einen ehrlichen Krieg gegen sie führt, der doch nicht ganz ohne Anstrengung ist, wollt Ihr doch nicht gegen einen Schatten gefochten haben, wie dieser, mit dem wir uns herumgeschlagen haben; sie muß doch etwas eigenes sein, was in der Menschen Herz hat kommen können, etwas denkbares, wovon sich ein Begriff aufstellen läßt, über den man reden und streiten kann, und ich finde es sehr unrecht, wenn Ihr selbst aus so disparaten Dingen etwas Unhaltbares zusammennäht, das Religion nennt, und dann so viel unnütze Umstände damit macht. Ihr werdet leugnen, daß Ihr hinterlistig zu Werke gegangen seid. Ihr werdet mich auffordern, alle Urkunden der Religion weil ich doch die Systeme, die Kommentare und die Apologien schon verworfen habe, alle aufzurollen von den schönen Dichtungen der Griechen bis zu den heiligen Schriften der Christen, ob ich nicht überall die Natur der Götter finden werde, und ihren Willen, und überall den heilig und selig gepriesen, der die erstere erkennt und den letztern vollbringt. Aber das ist es ja eben, was ich Euch gesagt habe, daß die Religion nie rein erscheint, das alles sind nur die fremden Teile, die ihr anhängen, und es soll ja unser Geschäft sein, sie von diesen zu befreien. Liefert Euch doch die Körperwelt keinen Urstoff als reines Naturprodukt Ihr müßtet dann, wie

nature and a unique existence. I ask you, therefore, What does your metaphysics do – or, if you want to have nothing to do with the outmoded name that is too historical for you, your transcendental philosophy? It classifies the universe and divides it into this being and that, seeks out the reasons for what exists, and deduces the necessity of what is real while spinning the reality of the world and its laws out of itself. Into this realm, therefore, religion must not venture too far. It must not have the tendency to posit essences and to determine natures, to lose itself in an infinity of reasons and deductions, to seek out final causes, and to proclaim eternal truths.

And what does your morality do? It develops a system of duties out of human nature and our relationship to the universe; it commands and forbids actions with unlimited authority. Yet religion must not even presume to do that; it must not use the universe in order to derive duties and is not permitted to contain a code of laws. 'And yet what one calls religion seems to consist only of fragments of these various fields.' This is indeed the common concept. I have just imparted to you doubts about that; now it is time to annihilate it altogether. The theorists in religion, who aim at knowledge of the nature of the universe and a highest being whose work it is, are metaphysicians, but also discreet enough not to disdain some morality. The practical people, to whom the will of God is the primary thing, are moralists, but a little in the style of metaphysics. You take the idea of the good and carry it into metaphysics as the natural law of an unlimited and plenteous being, and you take the idea of a primal being from metaphysics and carry it into morality so that this great work should not remain anonymous, but so that the picture of the lawgiver might be engraved at the front of so splendid a code. But mix and stir as you will, these never go together; you play an empty game with materials that are not suited to each other. You always retain only metaphysics and morals. This mixture of opinions about the highest being or the world and of precepts for a human life (or even for two) you call religion! And the instinct, which seeks those opinions, together with the dim presentiments that are the actual final sanction of these precepts, you call religiousness! But how then do you come to regard a mere compilation, an anthology for beginners, as an integral work, as an individual with its own origin and power?

[. . .]

You do not like religion; we started from that assumption. But in conducting an honest battle against it, which is not completely without effort, you do not want to have fought against a shadow like the one with which we have struggled. Religion must indeed be something integral that could have arisen in the human heart, something thinkable from which a concept can be formulated about which one can speak and argue. I find it very unjust if you yourselves stitch together something untenable out of such disparate things, call it religion, and then make so much needless ado about it. You will deny that you have begun deceitfully. You will call upon me to roll out all of the ancient sources of religion – since I have, after all, already rejected systems, commentaries, and apologies – from the beautiful compositions of the Greeks to the holy writings of the Christians, and to state whether I would not find the nature of the gods and their will everywhere, and everywhere praise persons as holy and blessed, who acknowledge the former and fulfill the latter.

But that is precisely what I have said to you. Religion never appears in a pure state. All these are only the extraneous parts that cling to it, and it should be our business to free it from them. After all, the corporeal world provides you with no primal element as nature's pure product – you would then, as happens to you in the intellectual world, have to regard very rough things as simple – but rather it is only the ceaseless aim of analytic skill to be able to depict such a primal

es Euch hier in der intellektuellen ergangen ist, sehr grobe Dinge für etwas Einfaches halten, sondern es ist nur das unendliche Ziel der analytischen Kunst, einen solchen darstellen zu können; und in geistigen Dingen ist Euch das Ursprüngliche nicht anders zu schaffen, als wenn Ihr es durch eine ursprüngliche Schöpfung in Euch erzeugt, und auch dann nur auf den Moment wo Ihr es erzeugt. Ich bitte Euch, verstehet Euch selbst hierüber, Ihr werdet unaufhörlich daran erinnert werden. Was aber die Urkunden und die Autographa der Religion betrifft, so ist in ihnen diese Einmischung von Metaphysik und Moral nicht bloß ein unvermeidliches Schicksal, sie ist vielmehr künstliche Anlage und hohe Absicht. Was als das erste und letzte gegeben wird, ist nicht immer das wahre und höchste. Wüßtet Ihr doch nur zwischen den Zeilen zu lesen! Alle heilige Schriften sind wie die bescheidenen Bücher, welche vor einiger Zeit in unserem bescheidenen Vaterlande gebräuchlich waren, die unter einem dürftigen Titel wichtige Dinge abhandelten. Sie kündigen freilich nur Metaphysik und Moral an, und gehen gern am Ende in das zurück, was sie angekündigt haben, aber Euch wird zugemutet diese Schale zu spalten. So liegt auch der Diamant in einer schlechten Masse gänzlich verschlossen, aber wahrlich nicht um verborgen zu bleiben, sondern um desto sicherer gefunden zu werden. Proselyten zu machen aus den Ungläubigen, das liegt sehr tief im Charakter der Religion; wer die seinige mitteilt, kann gar keinen andern Zweck haben, und so ist es in der Tat kaum ein frommer Betrug, sondern eine schickliche Methode bei dem anzufangen und um das besorgt zu scheinen, wofür der Sinn schon da ist, damit gelegentlich und unbemerkt sich das einschleiche, wofür er erst aufgeregt werden soll. Es ist, da alle Mitteilung der Religion nicht anders als rhetorisch sein kann, eine schlaue Gewinnung der Hörenden, sie in so guter Gesellschaft einzuführen. Aber dieses Hilfsmittel hat seinen Zweck nicht nur erreicht, sondern überholt, indem selbst Euch unter dieser Hülle ihr eigentliches Wesen verborgen geblieben ist. Darum ist es Zeit die Sache einmal beim andern Ende zu ergreifen, und mit dem schneidenden Gegensatz anzuheben, in welchen sich die Religion gegen Moral und Metaphysik befindet. Das war es was ich wollte. Ihr habt mich mit Euerem gemeinen Begriff gestört; er ist abgetan, hoffe ich, unterbrecht mich nun nicht weiter. Sie entsagt hiermit, um den Besitz ihres Eigentums anzutreten, allen Ansprüchen auf irgend etwas, was jenen angehört, und gibt alles zurück, was man ihr aufgedrungen hat. Sie begehrt nicht das Universum seiner Natur nach zu bestimmen und zu erklären wie die Metaphysik, sie begehrt nicht aus Kraft der Freiheit und der göttlichen Willkür des Menschen es fortzubilden und fertig zu machen wie die Moral. Ihr Wesen ist weder Denken noch Handeln, sondern Anschauung und Gefühl. Anschauen will sie das Universum, in seinen eigenen Darstellungen und Handlungen will sie es andächtig belauschen, von seinen unmittelbaren Einflüssen will sie sich in kindlicher Passivität ergreifen und erfüllen lassen. So ist sie beiden in allem entgegengesetzt was ihr Wesen ausmacht, und in allem was ihre Wirkungen charakterisiert, Jene sehen im ganzen Universum nur den Menschen als Mittelpunkt aller Beziehungen, als Bedingung alles Seins und Ursach alles Werdens; sie will im Menschen nicht weniger als in allen andern Einzelnen und Endlichen das Unendliche sehen, dessen Abdruck, dessen Darstellung. Die Metaphysik geht aus von der endlichen Natur des Menschen, und will aus ihrem einfachsten Begriff, und aus dem Umfang ihrer Kräfte und ihrer Empfänglichkeit mit Bewußtsein bestimmen, was das Universum für ihn sein kann, und wie er es notwendig erblicken muß. Die Religion lebt ihr ganzes Leben auch in der Natur, aber in der unendlichen Natur des Ganzen, des Einen und Allen; was in dieser alles Einzelne und so auch der Mensch gilt, und wo alles und auch er treiben und bleiben mag in dieser ewigen Gärung einzelner Formen und Wesen, das will sie in stiller Ergebenheit im Einzelnen anschauen und ahnden. Die Moral geht vom Bewußtsein der Freiheit aus, deren Reich will sie ins Unendliche erweitern, und ihr alles

element. In spiritual things the original cannot be brought forth for you, except when you beget it through an original creation in yourselves, and even then only in the moment when you beget it. I beg you, understand yourselves on this point, for you shall be ceaselessly reminded of it. But as far as the sources and original documents of religion are concerned, this interference of metaphysics and morals with them is not merely an unavoidable fate; it is rather an artificial plan and a lofty intention. What is presented at the first and last is not always the truest and highest. If you only knew how to read between the lines! All holy writings are like the modest books that were in use some time ago in our modest fatherland, which treated important matters under a sketchy title. To be sure, they only give notice of metaphysics and morals, and in the end are happy to return to that which they have announced, but you are encouraged to crack open this shell. Thus even the diamond lies wholly enclosed in a base substance, yet surely not in order to remain hidden but rather to be found all the more certainly. To make proselytes out of unbelievers is deeply engrained in the character of religion; those who impart their own religion can have no other purpose. Thus it is in fact hardly a pious deception but an appropriate method to begin with and appear concerned about a matter for which the sensibility already exists, so that something may occasionally and unnoticeably slip in for which the sensibility must first be aroused. Since all communication of religion cannot be other than rhetorical, it is a clever engagement of an audience to introduce them into such good company. Yet this device has not only reached but overstepped its goal, since even for you religion's essence has remained hidden under this mask. Therefore is it time to take up the subject from the other end and start with the sharp opposition in which religion is found over against morals and metaphysics. That was what I wanted. You distracted me with your ordinary concept; I hope it is now settled and you will interrupt me no more.

In order to take possession of its own domain, religion renounces herewith all claims to whatever belongs to those others and gives back everything that has been forced upon it. It does not wish to determine and explain the universe according to its nature as does metaphysics; it does not desire to continue the universe's development and perfect it by the power of freedom and the divine free choice of a human being as does morals. Religion's essence is neither thinking nor acting, but intuition and feeling. It wishes to intuit the universe, wishes devoutly to overhear the universe's own manifestations and actions, longs to be grasped and filled by the universe's own immediate influences in childlike passivity. Thus, religion is opposed to these two in everything that makes up its essence and in everything that characterizes its effects. Metaphysics and morals see in the whole universe only humanity as the center of all relatedness, as the condition of all being and the cause of all becoming; religion wishes to see the infinite, its imprint and its manifestation, in humanity no less than in all other individual and finite forms. Metaphysics proceeds from finite human nature and wants to define consciously, from its simplest concept, the extent of its powers, and its receptivity, what the universe can be for us and how we necessarily must view it. Religion also lives its whole life in nature, but in the infinite nature of totality, the one and all; what holds in nature for everything individual also holds for the human; and wherever everything, including man, may press on or tarry within this eternal ferment of individual forms and beings, religion wishes to intuit and to divine this in detail in quiet submissiveness. Morality proceeds from the consciousness of freedom; it wishes to extend freedom's realm to infinity and to make everything subservient to it. Religion breathes there where freedom itself has once more become nature; it apprehends man beyond the play of his particular powers and his personality, and views him from the vantage point where he must be what he is, whether he likes it or not.

unterwürfig machen; die Religion atmet da, wo die Freiheit selbst schon wieder Natur geworden ist, jenseit des Spiels seiner besondern Kräfte und seiner Personalität faßt sie den Menschen, und sieht ihn aus dem Gesichtspunkte, wo er das sein muß was er ist, er wolle oder wolle nicht. So behauptet sie ihr eigenes Gebiet und ihren eigenen Charakter nur dadurch, daß sie aus dem der Spekulation sowohl als aus dem der Praxis gänzlich herausgeht, und indem sie sich neben beide hinstellt, wird erst das gemeinschaftliche Feld vollkommen ausgefüllt, und die menschliche Natur von dieser Seite vollendet. Sie zeigt sich Euch als das notwendige und unentbehrliche Dritte zu jenen beiden, als ihr natürliches Gegenstück, nicht geringer an Würde und Herrlichkeit, als welches von ihnen Ihr wollt. Spekulation und Praxis haben zu wollen ohne Religion, ist verwegener Übermut, es ist freche Feindschaft gegen die Götter, es ist der unheilige Sinn des Prometheus, der feigherzig stahl, was er in ruhiger Sicherheit hätte fordern und erwarten können. Geraubt nur hat der Mensch das Gefühl seiner Unendlichkeit und Gottähnlichkeit, und es kann ihm als unrechtes Gut nicht gedeihen, wenn er nicht auch seiner Beschränktheit sich bewußt wird, der Zufälligkeit seiner ganzen Form, des geräuschlosen Verschwindens seines ganzen Daseins im Unermeßlichen. Auch haben die Götter von je an diesen Frevel gestraft. Praxis ist Kunst, Spekulation ist Wissenschaft, Religion ist Sinn und Geschmack fürs Unendliche. Ohne diese, wie kann sich die erste über den gemeinen Kreis abenteuerlicher und hergebrachter Formen erheben? wie kann die andere etwas besseres werden als ein steifes und mageres Skelett?

[...]

Vom Anschauen muß alles ausgehen, und wem die Begierde fehlt das Unendliche anzuschauen, der hat keinen Prüfstein und braucht freilich auch keinen, um zu wissen, ob er etwas ordentliches darüber gedacht hat.

[...]

Anschauen des Universums, ich bitte befreundet Euch mit diesem Begriff, er ist der Angel meiner ganzen Rede, er ist die allgemeinste und höchste Formel der Religion, woraus Ihr jeden Ort in derselben finden könnt, woraus sich ihr Wesen und ihre Grenzen aufs genaueste bestimmen lassen. Alles Anschauen gehet aus von einem Einfluß des Angeschaueten auf den Anschauenden, von einem ursprünglichen und unabhängigen Handeln des ersteren, welches dann von dem letzteren seiner Natur gemäß aufgenommen, zusammengefaßt und begriffen wird. Wenn die Ausflüsse des Lichtes nicht (was ganz ohne Euere Veranstaltung geschieht) Euer Organ berührten, wenn die kleinsten Teile der Körper die Spitzen Eurer Finger nicht mechanisch oder chemisch affizierten, wenn der Druck der Schwere Euch nicht einen Widerstand und eine Grenze Eurer Kraft offenbarte, so würdet Ihr nichts anschauen und nichts wahrnehmen, und was Ihr also anschaut und wahrnehmt, ist nicht die Natur der Dinge, sondern ihr Handeln auf Euch. Was Ihr über jene wißt oder glaubt, liegt weit jenseits des Gebiets der Anschauung. So die Religion; das Universum ist in einer ununterbrochenen Tätigkeit und offenbart sich uns jeden Augenblick. Jede Form die es hervorbringt, jedes Wesen dem es nach der Fülle des Lebens ein abgesondertes Dasein gibt, jede Begebenheit die es aus seinem reichen immer fruchtbaren Schöße herausschüttet, ist ein Handeln desselben auf Uns; und so alles Einzelne als einen Teil des Ganzen, alles Beschränkte als eine Darstellung des Unendlichen hinnehmen, das ist Religion; was aber darüber hinaus will, und tiefer hineindringen in die Natur und Substanz des Ganzen ist nicht mehr Religion ...

[1799] [*Hamburg: Felix Meiner, 1958. 23–32*]

Thus religion maintains its own sphere and its own character only by completely removing itself from the sphere and character of speculation as well as from that of praxis. Only when it places itself next to both of them is the common ground perfectly filled out and human nature completed from this dimension. Religion shows itself to you as the necessary and indispensable third next to those two, as their natural counterpart, not slighter in worth and splendor than what you wish of them. To want to have speculation and praxis without religion is rash arrogance. It is insolent enmity against the gods; it is the unholy sense of Prometheus, who cowardly stole what in calm certainty he would have been able to ask for and to expect. Man has merely stolen the feeling of his infinity and godlikeness, and as an unjust possession it cannot thrive for him if he is not also conscious of his limitedness, the contingency of his whole form, the silent disappearance of his whole existence in the immeasurable. The gods have also punished this crime from the very beginning. Praxis is an art, speculation is a science, religion is the sensibility and taste for the infinite. Without religion, how can praxis rise above the common circle of adventurous and customary forms? How can speculation become anything better than a stiff and barren skeleton?

[...]

Everything must proceed from intuition, and those who lack the desire to intuit the infinite have no touchstone and indeed need none in order to know whether they have given any respectable thought to the matter.

[...]

I entreat you to become familiar with this concept: intuition of the universe. It is the hinge of my whole speech; it is the highest and most universal formula of religion on the basis of which you should be able to find every place in religion, from which you may determine its essence and its limits. All intuition proceeds from an influence of the intuited on the one who intuits, from an original and independent action of the former, which is then grasped, apprehended, and conceived by the latter according to one's own nature. If the emanations of light – which happen completely without your efforts – did not affect your sense, if the smallest parts of the body, the tips of your fingers, were not mechanically or chemically affected, if the pressure of weight did not reveal to you an opposition and a limit to your power, you would intuit nothing and perceive nothing, and what you thus intuit and perceive is not the nature of things, but their action upon you. What you know or believe about the nature of things lies far beyond the realm of intuition.

The same is true of religion. The universe exists in uninterrupted activity and reveals itself to us every moment. Every form that it brings forth, every being to which it gives separate existence according to the fullness of life, every occurrence that spills forth from its rich, ever-fruitful womb, is an action of the same upon us. Thus to accept everything individual as a part of the whole and everything limited as a representation of the infinite is religion. But whatever would go beyond that and penetrate deeper into the nature and substance of the whole is no longer religion [...]

[1799] [*Edited and translated by Richard Coulter. London: Cambridge UP, 1996. 19–25*]

f. MAGYAR

V.f.1. KÖLCSEY FERENC, *Töredékek a vallásról* (Részlet)

4

Insani sapiens nomen ferat, aequus iniqui,
Ultra quam satis est virtutem si petat ipsam

Azon *communis maxima mensura*,[1] melyhez minden lépéseinket, gondolatainkat, tetteinket mérnünk kell: *az egésznek boldogsága*. Szív és ész ezen tárgynak vagynak alárendeltetve. Minden törekedés a tökéletesség s világosodás felé, minden társasági egybeköttetés, törvényadás, filozófia s több ilyenek, csak azon oszcilláció által hozatnak elő, melyet ezen tárgyhoz egyenes vagy nem egyenes közelgetés vagy közelgetni akarás elejétől fogva okozott. Gazdagság, testi kény, virtus, felvilágosodás látnivaló, hogy nem tehetik az élet végcélját, hanem csak eszközei lehetnek azon végcélnak, s aszerint jók vagy rosszak, amint azt hátráltatják, vagy nem hátráltatják. *Bolondnak mondassék a bölcs*, mond Horatius, *s igazságtalanságnak az igaz, ha magát a virtust mérték felett kívánja.* Azt teszem hozzá: *Részegnek mondassék a józan, ha magát a világosodást mérték felett kívánja.* Ezen mértéknél, ezen ítéletnél fogva óhajtanám, hogy valaki a vallást, s annak tisztogatását, modifikációját s befolyását megvizsgálja.

A vallás első beléptével boldogságra hív, és boldogít is, s ahol ezt emberi környűlmények miatt nem teheti, legalább vigasztal s remélni hágy. Reményt, vigasztalást s boldogságot nem adhat egyéb, hanem amit igaznak, valónak, csalhatatlannak hiszünk, s ennél fogva tiszteletben tartunk, s ezen igaznak, valónak, csalhatatlannak s tiszteltetettnek ideája az, amit *szent* névvel nevezünk. Szent légyen tehát a vallás előttünk, ha benne nyugalmat, boldogságot lelni akarunk. Ez legyen ama befátyolozott kép, melyet felfedni nem szabad, s a filozófia, mely ehhez ér, nem nyert egyebet, hanem vagy megkábulást, vagy megcsalattatást. Nem mondom, hogy egy igazán filozóf, bármily rezultátumokra vitte is okoskodása, nyugodt nem lehetne. De itt az egésznek, azon nagy népnek, mely emberiségnek neveztetik, boldogságáról van szó; s feltévén, hogy a filozófia vihetne bizonyos s értelmesb rezultátumokra, mint a *vallás és hit*: de hanyad része az emberi nemzetnek bír erővel vizsgálódni, magát önmagában megnyugtatni, s a világosodást elbírni? Semmi sincs könnyebb, mint valakitől a hitet elvenni; de semmi sincs nehezebb, mint egy kételkedő valakit megnyugtatni. Mert a hit, mely a szívet vezérlette, nem kívánt vizsgálódást; a kételkedés pedig csak bizonyosság által enyészik el.

Vizsgálódás nélkül nincs tudomány, s tudomány nélkül kultúra. De ti jól tudjátok azt, hogy a való tudomány csak ezerek közül jutott egynek, s jótéteményei milliomokra csak ki- és vissza-sugárzás által hathatnak el. Azon milliomoknak semmire sincs oly múlhatatlan szükségök, mint vallásra, mégpedig oly vallásra, melyhez ragaszkodjanak, mely őket a szívnél fogva szelídségre és moralitásra vezesse, s ezáltal boldogságra.

Jól mondja Montesquieu: *lelki valót kell a vallásnak imádtatni, hogy nagyobb ragaszkodást szerezzen magához híveiben.* A nép, mely az istenség képét márványból, vagy fából, vagy szalmából formáltatva látja maga előtt, ha majd isméretei szélesednek, s a kultúrának lépcsőin elő kezd menni, észre fogja venni, hogy az ő istenségei tehetetlenek, s azt teszi, amit Diogenész: ha könyörgését, hogy tüzet szerezzen, meg nem hallgatja, fabálványát vagdalja fel, s melegszik darabjainál. A lelki valót imádás nagymértékű kultúrának következése, s az abban hívéstől valamint a filozófot csak a feszített okoskodás viheti el, úgy a közembert semmi el nem vonhatja.

[1] legfőbb közös mérték

f. HUNGARIAN

V.f.1. FERENC KÖLCSEY, from *Fragments on Religion*

4

Insani sapiens nomen ferat, aequus iniqui,
Ultra quam satis est virtutem si petat ipsam.[2]

That *communis maxima mensura*[3] against which we have to assess our every step, thought and act is *the happiness of the whole*. Heart and mind are subordinate to this matter. All striving towards perfection and enlightenment, all social unification, lawgiving, philosophy and the like are only the product of that oscillation which is caused from the very outset by the approach – direct or indirect – or the desire to approach that object. Wealth, physical pleasure, virtue and enlightenment clearly cannot constitute the aim of life, but can only be means to that end, and so are good or bad as they do or do not bar the way to it. *Let the wise man be called a fool*, says Horace, *and he that is just unjust if he calls for virtue itself to excess*. To that I will add: *Let the sober be called drunken, if he calls for enlightenment itself to excess*. With that measure, that opinion, in mind, I would wish that one should examine religion, its purification, modification and influence.

Religion primarily calls us to happiness, and makes us happy too, and where human circumstances prevent it from so doing it at least consoles us and gives us hope. Nothing can give hope, consolation and happiness but that which we believe to be just, real and infallible, and therefore hold in honour, and the concept of that just, real, infallible and honoured thing is what we designate by the name of *holy*. Let religion, therefore, be holy in our eyes if in it we wish to find repose and happiness. Let it be that veiled image which may not be revealed, and the philosophy which reaches towards it has attained nothing but either confusion or disappointment. I do not mean that one that is truly a philosopher, whatever outcome his deliberations led him to, could not be content. But here we are speaking of the happiness of the whole, that great people named humanity, and supposing that philosophy could lead to results more certain and intelligible than *religion* and *faith*, what fraction of the human race has the power to think deeply, to reassure itself inwardly and to endure enlightenment? There is nothing easier than to take away a person's faith, but nothing harder than to assure one that doubts. Because faith, which has led the heart, calls for no examination; doubt, however, is only removed by certainty.

Without examination there is no knowledge, and without knowledge there is no culture. You know very well, however, that real knowledge has come to only one among thousands, and its benefits have their effect on millions only by radiation and reflection. Those millions have no so imperative need of anything as of religion, and especially a religion to which they may hold fast, and which may lead them by the heart to gentleness and morality, and thereby to happiness.

Montesquieu is right in saying that *a spiritual being must be worshipped by religion in order that it may obtain greater loyalty in its adherents*. The people, who see before them the image of the divinity carved in marble or wood or shaped in straw, if their awareness broadens and they begin to ascend the ladder of culture, will realise that its divine qualities are powerless, and will do as did Diogenes: if it does not hear their plea for fire they will cut up its wooden idol and warm themselves at its pieces. Worship of a spiritual being is the consequence of a high degree of culture, and just as only rigorous argument can dissuade the philosopher from believing in it, so nothing can dissuade the common man.

[2] See Horace, Epist. I. VI. 15–16.
[3] The greatest common measure

De a teizmus csak filozófus fejéből vehette eredetét, s ennek egyedül az értelmet foglalatoskodtató ideája a közembernek felette van. A néphez közelebb a poéta, mint a filozóf, azaz, az érzés, mint a vizsgálódás. Ezen idea: *Isten; egy nemtesti való; ok,* melyből minden következések kifejtőznek; *szellem,* mely hevít, tenyészt s fenntart, melynek sajátságait a látszó természetnek ezer jelenségeiből ezeren magyarázták, de magát önnön individualitásában senki meg nem határozhatta, senki nem gondolhatta, nem is sejdíthette: mondjátok meg világnak bölcsei, volt-e valaha nép, mely egy ilyen ideát felfoghatott volna, mely az ilyen ideával fejében lépett volna templomainak küszöbeikre, s hajtotta volna meg térdeit? Minden filozófnak, minden teológusnak fejében másképen asszimiláltatik ezen idea, s ti azt kívánjátok-e, hogy a nép azt így vagy amúgy a ti tanításaitok szellemökben tegye magáévá.

Ha ti az emberi szívnek mozdulatit úgy ismeritek, mint ismernetek kell: könnyen általláthatjátok, hogy a legtisztább vallást is a filozófiának együgyűségére redukálni képtelenség. Izraelnek fiai hányszor nem tértenek el a láthatatlan Istent imádástól, mert értelmök gyenge volt azon egyszerű, tiszta ideában megnyugodni? *A frigyláda, a jeruzsálemi fényes templom, a szent rejtekben lakó cherubim, a magasságban épült oltárok* (excelsa), *az áldozatok* arra szolgáltanak, hogy a vallásnak az istenségről való magas s értelmi tanításai a népnek érezhetőkké tétessenek, s a gyenge értelem a képzelet és szív hevülései által segítessék. Jézus a maga egyszerű vallását titkos sejdítésekkel szőtte keresztül, hogy az értelmi vizsgálatok elakasztatván, a szívet tegye foglalatosságba s a szív által a fantáziát. Mert nem mindezen megjegyzés alá tartoznak-e a *váltságot illető titkok; a háromság; az eredeti romlás hathatós éreztetése; a jutalmakról s büntetésekről tétetett ígéretek s fenyegetések;* s maga az a *képekkel gazdag előadás,* melybe Jézus a legtisztább s legegyszerűbb morált öltözteté? Valóban Montesquieu a természetből merítette azon jegyzést: *hogy a vallásnak a lelki valóval oly ideákat is kell öszvekötnie, melyek az értelmi világot az érzékivel neműneműképpen egybekapcsolják.* Az emberi léleknek lépcsőkre volt szüksége, melyeken magát az alacsonyságból a legfelsőbb magasságig felemelhesse. Ezért van, hogy az írásokban angyalok jelennek meg. Ezért van, hogy a kereszténységnek századai az eget szentekkel elnépesítették.

Kettő van még, ami a vallás kötelékeit erősekké teheti: ceremónia és tiszta erkölcsiség. A ceremónia semmi nem egyéb, hanem forma, mely nélkül a vallások filozófi szektákká lennének, s hidegségbe süllyednének el. A ceremónia bizonyos setét-tisztában tünteti fel a vallási tárgyakat; az értelemnek megfoghatatlan dolgokat a szívnek sejdítéseivé varázsolja; s a fantázia előtt azon termékeny régiónak kárpitjait vonja fel, hol csak az nem talál boldogságot, ki elég kegyetlen magát mindig és mindenütt hideg vizsgálatokkal s gáncsolódásokkal gyötreni. Magában következik, hogy a vallást erősítő minden gyámolok közt a ceremóniának gyámolai legerősebbek. Tedd hozzá: és legtartósabbak. Emlékeznünk kell a népre, melynek Mózes adott törvényeket, s ez legyen minden bizonyság helyett bizonyság.

Ha van vallás, melynek fundamentomába erkölcstelenség öntötte magát, azon vallásnak előbb utóbb a világosodó emberiség előtt tekintetét[4] el kell vesztenie. Törvényadó és filozóf, a jónak s rossznak felébredező gondolatja és közbátorság[5] fel fogják a népnek szemeit nyitni. Így tűntek ki a históriából az emberáldozatok, a prostitúciók. Így töröltettek el Romában a bacchanáliák. De a tiszta morállal egybeolvadt vallás felette áll minden megvettetésnek. Hiában gyújtja meg fáklyáját az emberi nyugtalan elme; hiában tűn elő a kételkedés minden gáncsaival: rendületlen áll az épület, mert célját betöltötte; s revolúciók mennek és jőnek, de végtére is törvényadó, filozóf és nép kénytelenek lesznek oda visszaindulni, hol lélek és szív, társasági alkotvány és társasági boldogság *egyedül* találhatnak biztos álláspontot magoknak.

[4] tekintélyét
[5] közbiztonság

Theism, however, can only spring from the head of the philosopher, and the concept of this, which concerns itself with understanding alone, is too high for the common man. This concept is that *God is an incorporeal being; the cause* from which all consequences ensue; *a spirit* which animates, cultivates and sustains, the characteristics of which a thousand expound from a thousand phenomena of visible nature, but which itself in its own individuality no one has been able to define, conceive or even guess at. Say, wise men of the world, was there ever a people that could have accepted such a concept, would have gone to the doors of its temples with such a concept in its head and bent the knee? This concept is differently formulated in the head of every philosopher, every theologian – do you expect the people to imbibe it this way or that in the spirit of your teachings?

If you are as familiar with the motions of the human heart as you must be, you can easily perceive that to reduce even the clearest religion to the simplicity of a philosophy is absurd. How often did the people of Israel not turn from the worship of the invisible God because their understanding was too weak to be satisfied with that simple, clear concept? *The ark of the covenant, the shining temple in Jerusalem, cherubim that dwelt in holy seclusion, altars built in high places* (excelsa), *sacrifices,* all served to make the lofty and intellectual teachings of religion concerning the divinity more palpable to the people, and to assist feeble intellect by fervour of imagination and heart. Jesus wove into his own simple religion mysterious hints so as to suspend enquiry and bring the heart into play, and through the heart the fantasy. For do not *the mysteries of redemption, the Trinity, the powerful imparted sense of original corruption, the promises and threats of rewards and punishments, and the image-rich delivery* with which Jesus clothed the clearest and simplest morals, all belong under this heading? Indeed, Montesquieu was right to draw from nature the observation that *religion must combine with the spiritual being such concepts as will in some way connect the world of the intellect with that of the senses.* The human spirit needed steps by which to raise itself from the depths to the supreme heights. This is why angels appear in scripture. This is why the centuries of Christianity have peopled heaven with saints.

Two more things make the bonds of religion strong: ceremony and clear morality. Ceremony is nothing other than form, without which religions would become philosophical sects and sink into frigidity. Ceremony shows religious matters in a certain dark-clarity; charms things inconceivable to the intellect into surmises of the heart; and raises before the fantasy the curtains of that fertile region in which only he cannot find happiness who, at every trick and turn, torments his quite cruel self with cold examination and censure. It follows of itself that of all the supports that strengthen religion that of ceremony is the strongest. Add to that, and the most enduring. We must remember the people to whom Moses gave laws, and let that be the proof of proofs.

If there is a religion into the foundations of which immorality has seeped, that religion must sooner or later lose the esteem of enlightened men. Lawgiver and philosopher, awaking sense of moral judgement and public safety will open the people's eyes. In this way human sacrifice vanished from history, as did prostitution. Thus at Rome the Bacchanalia were abolished. The religion that blends itself with clear morals stands above all disdain. The restless mind of man will light its torch in vain; in vain will doubt come forth with all its censures; the house stands unshaken, because it has achieved its goal; revolutions will come and go, but finally lawgiver, philosopher and people will be obliged to return thither where *alone* heart and soul, communal constitution and communal happiness can find themselves a secure stance.

A vallás az az isteni folyam, mely az egész pallérozatlan emberi nemzeten keresztülhabzik; az a talizmán, mely sok népeknél és sok esetekben minden tudomány, polgári alkotvány és törvény helyett szolgála; az a talpkő, melyhez minden törvényhozó és statusalkotó a maga princípiumit úgy forrasztotta, hogy csak általa s rajta találjanak maradást; az a menedék, mely a természeti jusnak gyengeségét legelőszer oltalomba vette, s melyből a nemzeteknek jusaik, a magok kicsinységében, legelébb kiszállani merészeltek; az az erő, mely az erőszaknak és bűnnek legfoganatosban vethetett határt, midőn túl az emberi törvény és fenyíték határain a jövendőben mutatott reményt és félelmet.

Mózes a maga vallását a kezdetről szóló tradíciókon fundálta meg. A keresztyénségnek szép épülete a mózesi fundamentumból emelkedett fel. Így minden vallás, egyszerű vagy öszvetett, tiszta vagy homályos, olyan eredetre viszi fel magát, mely túl a históriának emlékein, túl minden tudománynak, vizsgálatnak kezdetén, a legrégibb, legtávolabb s csak alig sejdíthető kornak homályában enyészik el. Önmaga, az arabs próféta is kénytelen vala egyfelől a mózesi, másfelől a nemzeti tradíciókhoz kötni hálóját, hogy szövedékei önkényt széjjel ne bomoljanak.

Jele, hogy a vallások, a magok alkotórészeikben, nem emberi találmányok. Egy oly vászon ez, melyre az emberi kéz időről időre sok különböző színeket mázolt fel: de a vászon ezer évek után is, s ezer különböző színek alatt is, mindig ugyanaz marad, s a figyelmes nézőnek tekintete elől soha nem tűnik el. Az emberiség kezdetében, s ahhoz közel tisztábbak s bizonyosbak voltak azon tradíciók, melyek ezen planéta mostani alakjának kezdetét, az emberiség eredetét, első lakhelyét, állapotát, változásait illeték. Ezen tradíciók keresztülszőve homályos sejdítésekkel az istenség s az istenséghez köttetett ideák felől, melyek annyira természetében fekszenek az emberi léleknek, hogy azokat inkább érzelem, mint reflexió következéseinek kell tartanunk; ezen tradíciók generációról-generációra szállongottak által, s száz meg százféle alakot nyertek, s az időnek folytában száz meg százféle vallásokat szültenek. Mert a vallások a hagyományokon épültek fel, s a hagyományokból vett lételt a filozófia is. S íme, ezen két annyira különböző szellemű testvérek itt találkoznak egy kis korig, hogy innen különböző arányokat vévén fel, ugyanazon tárgyakat ellenkező pontok felé keressék.

Az a bölcs, ki a tétovázó s ezerféleképen megcsonkított, kitoldozott, s önmagával ellenkezésbe jött hagyományokat tisztító és formáló kezek alá vette, vagy felette vagy kívüle volt a filozófi kételkedő vizsgálódásnak. Hit és belső nyugalom voltak az ő céljai. Megfoghatóvá tenni egy felső valóságnak lételét, vagyis inkább az arról való ideákat a tradíció homályitól elválasztani; ugyanazon hagyományokban az emberi nemzetnek eredetét nyomozni; a világbeli jó és rossz miatt emberemlékezetétől fogva fennálló gyanúkat s hánykódásokat elcsendesíteni; a lelki és testi embert, a látszó és nem látszó természetet öszvekötni; s egy elmúlt s egy jövendő életnek belénk ömlött sejdítéseit érezhetőkké képezni: ilyenek voltak az igyekezetek, melyekből a memphisi titkok, a Zoroaster tanításai, az orphicum szisztéma s több ilyenek származtak. S minden vallás (revelációval vagy reveláció nélkül) itt állapodik meg. Azaz, megtanít bennünket arra, amit oly forrón tudni óhajtunk, de amit vizsgálódás által soha bizonyosan nem tudhatunk: felmutat előttünk bizonyos célt, mely bennünk nemesb, mint állati törekedést, s nagyobb, mint végeshez illő szenvedelmeket gerjesszen; kíván hitet, s ígér nyugodalmat; parancsol engedelmességet, s jutalommal biztat vagy rettent büntetéssel. Jehova és Demiurgus, a paradicsomi kígyó és Arimán, mennyország és metempsychosis tagadhatatlanul egyforma forrásokból merített, s egyforma cél felé siettető ideák.

Religion is that divine stream which foams through the race of uncouth men; that talisman which, in many peoples and on numerous occasions, serves in place of all knowledge, civil constitution and law; that foundation-stone to which every law-bringer and state-founder has so based his concepts that only through and on it can stability be found; that sanctuary which first gave protection to the weakness of natural law, and from which the rights of infant nations first ventured to take wing; that power which was able most effectively to curb violence and crime as it revealed hope and fear in the future beyond the reach of human law and punishment.

Moses based his religion on traditions that spoke of the Creation. The fine building of Christianity has risen on the Mosaic foundation. Thus every religion, simple or complex, clear or obscure, harks back to a source that vanishes in the mists of the most ancient, most remote, only barely imaginable age, beyond the monuments of history, beyond the beginning of all knowledge, all enquiry. Even the Arab prophet himself was compelled to secure his web on the one hand on Mosaic, on the other hand on national traditions so that his fabric should not tear apart of itself.

It is the sign that religions, in their constituent parts, are not human inventions. This is a canvas on which human hands have, from time to time, daubed many and various colours; but even after a thousand years, even beneath a thousand different colours, the canvas always remains the same, and never disappears from the sight of the attentive observer. In the beginning of mankind, and near to that, those traditions which concerned the beginning of the present form of this planet, the beginning of mankind, his first abode, condition and vicissitudes were clearer and more certain. These traditions were shot through with obscure surmises about divinity and the concepts associated with divinity, which are so much embedded in the nature of the human soul that we must consider them the consequences rather of feelings than of reflection; these traditions have drifted on from generation to generation, acquiring hundreds upon hundreds of forms, and in the course of time have given rise to hundreds and hundreds of sorts of religion. For religions were built on traditions, and from traditions philosophy too came into being. And see, those two siblings, intellectually so different, come together here for a little space, only to take different courses and seek the same things in opposite directions.

The wise man who submitted to a clarifying or reforming hand traditions which were wavering, mutilated in a thousand ways, deformed and self-contradictory was either above or beyond doubting philosophical examination. Faith and inner repose were his aims. To render conceivable the existence of higher reality or rather disentangle the concepts concerning it from the mists of tradition; to trace the origin of the human race in those traditions; to still the ever-lingering suspicions and uncertainty caused by man's awareness of good and bad in the world; to unite spiritual and physical man, nature seen and unseen, and to portray in more palpable form the surmises that arise within us of a past and a future life – such have been the endeavours from which sprang the mysteries of Memphis, the teachings of Zoroaster, the Orphic system and others like them. This is the point on which all religions (with or without revelations) concur. That is to say, they teach us that which we so ardently wish to know, but which we can never know for certain by means of enquiry; they hold up before us certain aims to stir within us strivings more noble than animal and passions greater than befits the transient; they require faith and promise peace; command obedience, assure of reward and threaten punishment. Jehovah and Demiurge,[6] the serpent of paradise and Ahriman,[7] heaven and metempsychosis[8] are concepts undeniably drawn from similar sources and aiming for similar goals.

[6] A creator deity
[7] The destructive spirit in later Zoroastrianism
[8] The passing of a soul after death into some other body, either human or animal

De eljött az idő, midőn az embernek nem lőn elég a tudomány hit által, hanem akart tudományt vizsgálódás által. Thales emelte fel legelől a fáklyát, s erőkről s princípiumokról kezde szólani. Csakhamar száz meg száz értelmek toldúltak rakásra, s kevés századok alatt nem maradt el semmi lehetséges út, melyet az ember meg nem próbált volna, hogy rajta Isten, világ, s önmaga felől magyarázatokat találjon. Mit nyert a tudomány? Egyfelől szofistákat, másfelől Pyrrhót. Azaz, dévajkodást és kételkedést. S nem maradt az emberiségnek egyéb, hanem vagy örök vetélkedések s ellenmondások közt függőben maradni, vagy visszatérni oda, ahonnan eltévelygett: a *hithez*. Ezen hit készen várta a görög filozófiának küszködő maradványait; s e maradványok, leginkább pedig a Pythagoras titkaiból és Pláton fellengezéseiből öszvealkottatott tudomány, a keresztyén vallás kebelében kerestek nyugalmat.

Nem lehetett, hogy ezen nyugalmat kereset filozófiának messzebb terjedő befolyása ne lett légyen. Jézus tökéletes, de magányos vonásokkal rajzolta előnkbe a vallást, melyre az ő követői egy egész nagy tudományt, egy mesterséges teológiát alkottak. S ezen teológiának sokfelé ágazó szövedékein lehetetlen az elsőbb századoki filozófoknak kezeiket meg nem ismerni.

Feszegetés, különböztetés, egyezgetés, titokszaporítás, titokmagyarázat, megfoghatatlanokat bebizonyítani akarás, hipotézisek, dialektikázás, szofistáskodás stb., amiket vagy a nyughatatlanság szelleme, vagy a vetekedés tüze s kénytelensége tüntettek fel, okozták azt, hogy egyfelől képtelen eretnekségek toldúltak rakásra; másfelől maga az ortodoxia végremehetetlen szubtilitásokra feszült ki, s mint később a kontroverzisták állíták vala, toldásokat s kiegészítéseket szenvedett. Arisztotelésznek bölcsessége is feléledett végre a feledékenységből, s egy mesterséges, félig filozófiai, félig teológiai alkotványt hagyott maga után a revolúciókhoz készülő világnak.

Azonban az emberi szívnek természetes indulati a vallásnak értelmi tárgyait mind inkábbinkább megtestesítették, azaz levonták az érzéki körbe, s a titokból fátyolt szőttek felébe. Így a vallás, mely a teológiában egyedül a feszegető okosságnak tárgya volt, a külső tiszteletben egyedül a sejdítgető érzelemnek sajátjává varázsoltatott. S e kettős állapotban találta azt a revolúciónak százada.

A reformáció a maga szerző okaiban, s közvetetlen rezultátumiban nem lehetett egyéb, mint Rómával való pör. Nem lehetett tehát azt várni, hogy a vallás egy józan nyugalomnak, s egy nyugodtan fellengő léleknek ideálja szerint fog modifikáltatni. Felek állottak egymás ellen, kiknek bíróra volt szükségök. *Az írás a bíró:* mondá a reformáló fél. *Tartassék meg minden, ami azokban van; töröltessék el minden, ami nincs azokban.* De hibázott[9] még egy valaki, aki meghatározza: mi az, ami azokban van? és mi az, ami nincs azokban? Mert a transsubstantiátiót állítók és tagadók; valamint a háromságot, predestinációt, szakramentomokat stb. állítók és tagadók: nem mindnyájan az írásokon építik-e véleményeiket? Mi van egyéb hátra, hanem hogy maga az istenség, mint Jóbnak és az ő barátainak, közvetlen megszólaljon, s előnkbe szabja az ingadozást ismerni nem fogó tudományt?

Vissza, ezt mondjátok, az emberi okosságnak örök törvényeire! De vigyázzatok, nehogy csalóka tüzet vettetek legyen csalóka vezérül. Ki nem tudja, minő romlásokat nem szerzett ezen okosság, valahányszor filozófia küszködött religióval, azaz, hit hittel? Az okosság, lépcsőkről lépcsőkre hág, a vallásnak alsó tartományából nyugtalanul törekszik a felsőbb felé, s jaj nekie, ha a titkokig felbátorkodik!

Az emberi nép időről időre revolúciókon megyen keresztül, s minden revolúció után bizonyos többé vagy kevesebbé megváltozott formák közt marad. Hagyni kell őtet azon formák között nyugodtan. Jaj annak, aki eléggé erős a maga egykorúit saját magasságához felvonni! Felvonhatta

---

[9] hiányzott

The time came, however, when men were not satisfied with knowledge through faith, but wanted knowledge through enquiry. Thales was first to hold aloft the torch and began to speak of forces and principles. Very soon hundreds and hundreds of minds crowded to the task, and in a few centuries there remained no possible way for man to find explanations of God, the world and himself that he had not explored. What had learning achieved? On the one hand the sophists, on the other Pyrrho.[10] That is, hair-splitting and scepticism. And there was nothing left for man but either to remain in suspense among everlasting disputes and contradictions or to return to where he had strayed from – *faith*. This faith was ready and waiting for the struggling posterity of Greek philosophy; and that posterity, or rather the combined knowledge of the Pythagorean mysteries and Plato's lofty disquisitions, found rest in the bosom of Christianity.

This peace-seeking philosophy had to have quite a far-reaching influence. Jesus portrayed religion to us in perfect but isolated lines, on which his followers constructed a whole great science, an artificial theology. And it is impossible not to recognise the hands of the earlier philosophers in the widely-branching framework of this theology.

Enquiry, discrimination, accord, increase of mysteries, exposition of mysteries, desire to prove the inconceivable, hypotheses, dialectics, sophistry etc., which either the spirit of restlessness or the fire and necessity of rivalry brought into being, caused on the one hand foolish heresies to push themselves forward, while on the other hand orthodoxy itself became involved in endless subtleties and, as later protesters maintained, suffered by supplementation and amplification. The philosophy of Aristotle too was eventually resurrected from oblivion, and left behind it a semi-artificial, semi-theological framework for the world that was preparing for revolution.

The natural tendency of the human heart, however, more and more gave bodily form to the abstract things of religion, that is, they lowered them into the sphere of the palpable and wove over them a veil of mystery. In this way religion, which was in theology only the object of inquisitive intelligence, in outward respect was magically changed into being only that of conjectural feeling. And in this dual state the century of revolutions found it.

In its fundamental causes and its immediate results the Reformation could not be anything other than a dispute with Rome. It could not therefore be expected that religion would be modified in accordance with the concepts of sober tranquillity and a calmly soaring spirit. Parties opposed one another and needed a judge. *Scripture is the judge*, said the reforming party; *let all that is in it be kept, all that is not be done away with*. But there was still need of someone to decide what was in it and what was not. Because did not all those that were for and against transubstantiation, the Trinity, predestination, sacraments etc. base their views on the scriptures? What else remained but for the godhead itself, as in the case of Job and his friends, to speak directly and set before us knowledge that would be incontrovertible?

Back, you will say, to the eternal laws of human intelligence! But beware lest you have taken a will-o'-the-wisp as your false leader. Who does not know what ruination this intelligence has not brought about whenever philosophy has fought against religion, that is, faith against faith? Intelligence mounts from step to step, striving restlessly upwards from the lowest reaches of religion towards the topmost, and woe betide if it braves the mysteries!

The human race goes through revolutions from time to time, and after every revolution is left among more or less changed forms. It has to be left undisturbed among those forms. Grief awaits him that is strong enough to draw his contemporaries up to his own height! He can do it,

---

[10] Pyrrho (c.360–c.272 BC), a philosopher of Elis who believed that equal arguments could be offered on both sides of any propositions, and therefore dismissed the search for truth as a vain endeavour.

ugyan őket, de a szédüléstől meg nem óvhatta; s azon dicsőséggel szálland sírjába, hogy a századnak nyugalmát magával temette el.

Azt tanítjátok, hogy az így eltemetkezett nyugalom gazdag aratásra leszen egykor felvirulandó. Azt tanítjátok, hogy a gondviselés nem hagyja el az emberi nemzetet; s hogy ezen szenvedésekkel gazdagon kikészült emberi nemzetnek bizonyos isteni célok felé kell közelgetnie; s hogy ezen célokat szükségesképpen és egyedül megrázó rendületek által fogja elérhetni. Oh tegyétek nekem azon nagy, azon isteni célt csak oly világossá, csak oly látszóvá, mint Herschelnek legtökéletesb csővén a legtávolabb feltűnő csillagzatnak legaprányibb pontja látszatik! Íme, most a babiloni birodalom eldőltétől fogva nagy Sándoron, Rómán, a nemzetek költözéseiken, nagy Károly császáron, s Lutheren keresztül a francia vérontásokig ezredekről ezredekre nyomozom azon rettentő vészeknek következéseiket, s mutassátok meg, hol találhatok bizonyos közönséges céltól távozást, vagy célhoz közelítést? Mi gyengék, mi szédelgő fejűek akarunk e borzasztó rázkódásokban erőt, s szédítő magasságokon s mélységek felett biztos álláspontot találni?

Az emberi nemzet látszik ugyan bizonyos időkben, bizonyos ismeretlen centrum körül most kisebb majd nagyobb tolongásban, most kisebb majd nagyobb gyorsasággal kerengeni. De ezen kerengések megszűnnek, és újra kezdődnek, s mindannyiszor újabb alakú tüneményeket hoznak magokkal anélkül, hogy a centrumtól való távolság észrevehetőképpen kisebbednék. A francia lélek szilajkodása ezer ideákat tett közönségesekké, melyek különben csak kevés embernek sajáti voltanak: mint hajdan a reformáció. S mit nyert mindezzel az emberiség? Mirajtunk keresztülment az orkán, szenvedtünk és jajgattunk; s lesz idő, mikor a nép, melyben a reformatorok születtek, mikor a nép, melyben a királyölők születtek, úgy enyészik el, mint Babilon és Athéna; s egy új generáció ismét ezer évekig fog küzdeni, hogy a mostaninak minden tökéletességeit és tökéletlenségeit, virtusit és hibáit, tudományát és tudatlanságát új meg új színek alatt magának megszerezze, s a maga során ezen planétáról eltűnjön.

Akármint legyenek ezek, annyi való marad: hogy az emberiség bizonyos magvakat rejt kebelében, de amelyek annyi ezredek folytokban sohasem indultak virágzatba; s ha elvégeztetett, hogy valaha kivirágozzanak, annak másutt, nem ezen életben, s máshol, nem ezen planétán kell s lehet történnie. Az emberi nemzet felett és körül úgy, amint ezen bujdosó csillagon él és bolyong, *világosságnak és homálynak* bizonyos jóltevő egyarányúságban kell elterjednie. Bontsd meg az egyarányt, s akár világosság a homályon, akár homály a világosságon vegyen erőt, mindenik esetben elvakítottad az emberi gyenge szemeket, s kit fogsz majd a sötétben tévelygő mellé vezetőül rendelni?

[The whole treatise consists of four parts, the last of which has been republished in this volume. It was written in 1823 and published by the author in an expurgated and fragmented form: Élet és Literatúra, 1827 24–46. After Kölcsey's death it was published according to the original manuscript: Kölcsey, Ferenc, Kölcsey Ferencz' minden munkái, vol. 4, Philosophiai, nyelvészeti és vegyes dolgozatok. Eds Eötvös, József, Szalay, László and Szemere, Pál. Pest: Heckenast, 1842 77–88. The modern edition is based on that of 1842: Kölcsey, Ferenc, Kölcsey Ferenc összes művei, 3 vols. Budapest: Szépirodalmi, 1960, vol. 1 1071–1081]

but cannot protect them against dizziness, and will go to the grave with the reputation of having buried the calm of the century.

You teach that the calm that has thus been buried will one day flourish and yield a rich harvest. You teach that Providence will not desert the human race; and that the human race, well prepared by these sufferings, must be approaching certain divine purposes; and that it will attain these purposes of necessity and only through appalling catastrophes. Oh, make that great, that divine purpose as clear to me, as visible, as the most minute point of the remotest constellation seems in Herschel's most perfect telescope! See, from the fall of the Babylonian empire on, through Alexander the Great, Rome, the great migrations, Charlemagne and Luther to the French bloodbath, I can trace from millennium to millennium the consequences of those terrible disasters – show me where I can find a certain departure from, or approach to, a common goal? Do we weaklings, we witless men expect to find strength in these fearsome disasters, a secure stance on dizzying heights above the abyss?

The human race seems indeed at times to be whirling around a certain unknown centre in greater or lesser density, at greater or lesser speed. But this whirling ceases and begins anew, and on each occasion brings with it new phenomena without the distance from the centre becoming perceptibly less. The turbulence of the French spirit rendered universal a thousand concepts which otherwise were the property of only a few, as did the Reformation in years past. And what did humanity gain thereby? The hurricane passed through us, we suffered and cried out; and the time will come when the people in which the reformers were born, the people in which the regicides were born, will vanish like Babylon and Athens; and a new generation will struggle for another thousand years to acquire for itself in another guise all the perfections and imperfections of the present one, its virtues and faults, its knowledge and ignorance, and this too will, in its turn, vanish from the planet.

However these things may be, so much will remain: humanity conceals in its bosom certain seeds, ones which have never come into flower in the course of all these thousands of years; and if it has been decided that at some time they are to flower – at some other time, not in this life, and somewhere else, not on this planet – it must and can happen. As it lives and moves on this wandering star light and darkness must spread in a certain beneficial balanced proportion over and about the human race. Disturb the balance and either light will gather strength in the darkness, or darkness in the light; in either case you will blind weak human eyes, and who will you appoint as a guide to the wanderer in the dark?

[*Translated by Bernard Adams*]

V.f.2. ARANY JÁNOS, *Dante*

Állottam vizének mélységei felett,
Sima volt a fölszín, de sötét, mint árnyék;
Alig mozzantá meg a rózsalevelet,
Mint rengéskor a föld, csak alig hullámlék.
Acéltiszta tükre visszaverte híven
A külső világot – engem is: az embert;
De örvényeibe nem hatott le a szem,
Melyeket csupán ő – talán ő sem – ismert.

Csodálatos szellem! egy a mérhetetlen
Éggel, amely benne tükrödzik alattam!
Egy csak a fönségben és a terjedetben
És mivel mindenik oly megfoghatatlan.
Az ember ... a *költő* (mily bitang ez a név!)
Hitvány koszorúját, reszketvén, elejti
És, mintha lábait szentegyházba tenné,
Imádva borul le, mert az Istent sejti. –

E mélység fölött az értelem mér-ónja,
Mint könnyű pehelyszál, fönnakad, föllebben:
De a lélek érzi, hogy az örvény vonja,
S a gondolat elvész csodás sejtelemben.
Nem-ismert világnak érezi nyomását,
Rettegő örömnek elragadja kéje,
A leviathánnak hallja hánykodását...
Az *Úr lelke* terült a víznek föléje.

Lehet-é e szellem az istenség része?
Hiszen az istenség egy és oszthatatlan;
Avagy lehet-é, hogy halandó szem nézze
A szellemvilágot, teljes öntudatban?
Évezred hanyatlik, évezred kel újra,
Míg egy földi álom e világba téved,
Hogy a *hitlen* ember imádni tanulja
A köd oszlopában rejlő Istenséget.

[*First published: Budapesti Visszhang. Vol. 1, no. 5, 5 June 1852. Critical edition:*
János Arany, Arany János összes művei. Vol. 1. Kisebb költemények. Ed.
Voinovich, Géza. Budapest: Akadémiai, 1951. 160–161]

V.f.2. JÁNOS ARANY, *Dante*

By his waters deep, I stood there contemplating.
Flat the surface lay, and full of shadows grave;
And atop it, petals, gently undulating,
Like a hardly-noticed earthquake's subtle wave.
Clear as steel, its mirror faithfully reflected
What it found outside – and me: the human world;
He alone – perhaps not even he – detected
Turbulence with which, deep down, the water swirled.

Marvelous his spirit! One with the unending
Heaven that's reflected here before my eyes!
Just as far beyond all grasping, comprehending,
Equal in its grandeur, equal in its size!
And the man . . . the *poet* (wretched rascal's label!)
Trembling, drops his worthless laurels to the sod;
And, as if before a church's altar table,
Prayerful, he kneels earthward, for he senses God.

Such a depth makes reason's plumbline grows unsteady,
Float as if with feather weighted, not with lead.
Consciousness accepts it's caught up in the eddy.
Wondrous divination fills the human head.
It can feel the pull of other-worldly quarters;
Shudders at the dread and pleasures they afford;
Hears Leviathan go thrashing in the waters . . .
Onto which has passed the *presence of the Lord.*

Is it part of the one Godhead, then, this spirit?
After all, the Godhead's one unbroken whole.
And the spirit world, could mortal see or hear it,
When his conscious mind is fully in control?
One millennium sets and one millennium rises,
Till a mortal's dream into that world will stray,
Till the *unbelieving* person recognizes
That mist-hidden Godhead to which he must pray.

[*Translated by David Hill*]

g. ITALIANO

V.g.1. ALESSANDRO MANZONI, da *Lettera al Marchese Cesare Taparelli D'Azeglio sul Romanticismo*

Nella sua gentilissima lettera Ella ha parlato d'una *causa*, per la quale io tengo, d'una parte, che seguo; e questa parte è quel sistema letterario, a cui fu dato il nome di *romantico*. Ma questa parola è applicata a così vari sensi, ch'io provo un vero bisogno d'esporle, o d'accennarle almeno quello ch'io c'intendo, perché troppo m'importa il di Lei giudizio. Oltre la condizione comune a tutti i vocaboli destinati a rappresentare un complesso d'idee e di giudizi, quella, cioè, d'essere intesi più o meno diversamente dalle diverse persone, questo povero romanticismo ha anche de' significati espressamente distinti, in Francia, in Germania, in Inghilterra. Una simile diversità, o una maggior confusione, regna, se non m'ingano, in quelle parti d'Italia dove se n'è parlato, giacché credo che, in alcune, il nome stesso non sia stato proferito, se non qualche volta per caso, come un termine di magia. In Milano, dove se n'è parlato più e più a lungo che altrove, la parola *romanticismo*, è stata, se anche qui non m'ingano, adoperata a rappresentare un complesso d'idee più ragionevole, più ordinato, più generale, che in nessun altro luogo.

[...]

La prima [parte] tende principalmente a escludere – l'uso della mitologia – l'imitazione servile dei classici – le regole fondate su fatti speciali, e non su princìpi generali, sull'autorità de' retori, e non sul ragionamento, e specialmente quella delle così dette unità drammatiche, di tempo e di luogo apposte ad Aristotele.

[...]

Non parlerò dell'idee nove messe in campo da quelli; le opposizioni stesse ne provocarono assai. Ma il nesso delle antiche; ma la relazione scoperta e indicata tra di esse; ma la luce e la forza reciproca, che venivano a tutte dal solo fatto di classificarle sotto ad un principio, il sistema insomma, da chi era stato immaginato, da chi proposto, da chi ragionato mai? Dalle ricchezze intellettuali sparse, dal deposito confuso delle cognizioni umane, raccogliere pensieri staccati e accidentali, verità piuttosto sentite che comprese, accennate piuttosto che dimostrate; subordinarle a una verità più generale, che riveli tra di esse un'associazione non avvertita in prima; cambiare i presentimenti di molti uomini d'ingegno in dimostrazioni, levare a molte idee l'incertezza, e l'esagerazione; sceverare quel misto di vero e di falso, che le faceva rigettare in tutto da molti, e ricevere in tutto da altri con un entusiasmo irragionevole; collocarle con altre, che servono ad esse di limite e di prova a un tempo, non è questa la lode d'un buon sistema? e è forse una lode tanto facile a meritarsi? E chi ha mai desiderato, o immaginato un sistema, che non contenesse, fuorché idee tutte nove?

[...]

Se la disputa fosse continuata, o, per dir meglio, se, invece d'una disputa si fosse fatta una investigazione comune, dall'escludere si sarebbe passati al proporre, anzi in questo si sarebbe fissata la maggiore intenzione degli ingegni. E allora, si potrebbe credere che le opinioni sarebbero state tanto più varie quanto più abbondanti; e che molti ingegni, movendo da un centro comune, si sarebbero però avviati per tanti raggi diversi, allontanandosi anche talvolta l'uno dall'altro a misura che si sarebbero avanzati: tale è la condizione delle ricerche intellettuali intraprese da molti. Ma il sistema romantico non potè arrivare, o piuttosto, non arrivò a questo periodo. E ciò nonostante, un gran rimprovero, che veniva fatto ai suoi sos-

g. ITALIAN

V.g.1. ALESSANDRO MANZONI, from *Letter to Marchese Cesare Taparelli D'Azeglio on Romanticism*

You mentioned in your dear letter a *cause* that I favour and partly follow, and this cause is the literary movement that goes by the name 'Romanticism'. This last word, however, is applied in so many senses that I feel a real need to explain them all, or at least to describe to you my intentions in using the term, because I value your opinion so highly. In addition to the problem inherent in all words designed to represent complex ideas and judgments – such words are generally understood in different ways by different people – this poor Romanticism has different meanings in France, Germany and England. If I am not mistaken, a similar diversity of opinion, or indeed a greater confusion, about this word 'Romantic' reigns in the part of Italy where it has been discussed. I believe that the situation is such that in some parts of Italy the name 'Romanticism' has never been invoked, unless sometimes by accident, as if it were a magical term. If I am again not mistaken, in Milan, where there has been more discussion about the matter than elsewhere, the word 'Romanticism' has come to represent a system of ideas that are more reasonable, ordered and comprehensive than anywhere else.

[...]

The first part of Romanticism tends primarily toward excluding the following: the use of mythology, servile imitation of the classics, rules founded on specific cases and not general principles, and rules founded on the authority of rhetoricians and not on reason, especially with regard to the so-called dramatic unities of time and space attributed to Aristotle.

[...]

I will not speak of the new ideas fielded by the Romantics; the opposition to these ideas in itself already created a great many new ideas. But the cohesion of the old ideas, the relation discovered and indicated between them – and the illumination and reciprocal force that came to all these ideas from the sole fact of classifying them according to a single principle, namely, Romantic theory – who ever imagined, proposed, or reasoned it out? Is it not a praiseworthy theory that gathers disconnected and accidental thoughts, truths felt rather than understood and suggested rather than proved, from the dispersed intellectual riches and confused depositary of human cognition? that subordinates these truths to a general precept that establishes among them a previously unnoticed link? That changes the intuitions of brilliant people into demonstrable knowledge and removes uncertainty and exaggeration from many ideas? that dissolves the mix of truth and falsehood that had previously led many to reject these ideas wholesale and others to accept them with an unreasonable enthusiasm? that links these ideas with others, which serve simultaneously to limit and prove them? Is it easy to achieve such praise? Who ever desired or imagined a theory that contained only new ideas?

[...]

Had the Romantic dispute continued – or, to put it better, if instead of a dispute there had been a united inquiry – one would have passed from exclusion to proposal; indeed, the majority of brilliant intentions would have focused on this. The opinions, presumably, would have been as varied as they were abundant, and many brilliant people, moving outward from a common centre, would have radiated in many directions, even distancing themselves at times from one another as they proceeded. Such is the general rule for intellectual inquiry undertaken by many. But Romantic theory could not, or did not, arrive at this point. This fact notwithstanding, a great

tenitori, era, che non s'intendevano nemmeno fra di loro: cominciassero, si diceva, ad accordarsi perfettamente nelle idee, prima di proporle agli altri come verità. Rimprovero, al quale non posso tuttavia pensare senza maraviglia. In regola generale, quelli, che così parlavano, chiedevano una cosa che l'ingegno non ha data, né può dar mai. Mai questa concordia perfetta di più persone in tutti i punti d'un sistema morale non ha avuto luogo: bisognerebbe, a ottenerla, che per tutti questi punti si adottassero da ciascheduno altrettanti giudizi, altrettante formule uniche e invariabili; anzi che tanti uomini diventassero uno solo, per potere a ogni novo caso fare una identica applicazione di quei giudizi generici. C'è bene un ordine di cose, nel quale esiste una essenziale e immutabile concordia; ma quest'ordine è unico; i suoi caratteri, le sue circostanze sono incomunicabili. Quest'ordine è la religione: essa dà una scienza, che l'intelletto non potrebbe scoprire da sé, una scienza, che l'uomo non può ricevere, che per rivelazione, e per testimonianza; ora una sola rivelazione include una sola dottrina, e quindi produce una sola credenza. E anche in quest'ordine, la concordia delle menti non è comandata, se non dove è sommamente ragionevole; cioè in quei punti, nei quali la verità non si può sapere, che per la testimonianza di chi ne ha ricevuta la rivelazione, cioè della Chiesa; e non è comandata questa concordia, se non dal momento, che l'unico testimonio ha parlato. Ma, nelle cose umane, questo testimonio non esiste, non è stata né fatta, né promessa ad alcuno una comunicazione di scienza, un'assistenza nelle decisioni; quindi i giudizi variano secondo la varietà degl'ingegni, e riescono generalmente così dissimili, che a chiamar uno un sistema, non si ricerca mai il fatto impossibile, che esso riunisca tutti i giudizi in una materia qualunque, ma il fatto difficile e raro, che ne riunisca molti, nei punti principali di essa.

[...]

Dove poi l'opinioni de' Romantici erano unanimi, m'è parso, e mi pare, che fosse in questo: che la poesia deva proporsi per oggetto il vero come l'unica sorgente d'un diletto nobile e durevole; giacché il falso può bensì trastullar la mente, ma non arricchirla, né elevarla; e questo trastullo medesimo è, di sua natura instabile e temporario, potendo essere, come è desiderabile che sia, distrutto, anzi cambiato in fastidio, o da una cognizione sopravvegnente del vero, o da un amore cresciuto del vero medesimo. Come il mezzo più naturale di render più facili e più estesi tali effetti della poesia, volevano che essa deva scegliere de' soggetti che, avendo quanto è necessario per interessare le persone più dotte, siano insieme di quelli per i quali un maggior numero di lettori abbia una disposizione di curiosità e d'interessamento, nata dalle memorie e dalle impressioni giornaliere della vita; e chiedevano, per conseguenza, che si dasse finalmente il riposo a quegli altri soggetti, per i quali la classe sola de' letterati, e non tutta, aveva un'affezione venuta da abitudini scolastiche, e un'altra parte del pubblico, non letterata né illetterata, una reverenza, non sentita, ma cecamente ricevuta.

[...]

il materiale dei fatti, che devono servire agli esperimenti, è così abbondante, che è da credersi, che un tale principio sia per ricevere, di mano in mano, svolgimenti, spiegazioni e conferme, di cui ora non è possibile prevedere in concreto, né il numero, né l'importanza. Tale almeno è l'opinione, che ho fitta nella mente, e che m'arride anche perché in questo sistema, mi par di vedere una tendenza cristiana. Era questa tendenza nelle intenzioni di quelli, che l'hanno proposto, e di quelli, che l'hanno approvato? Sarebbe leggerezza l'affermarlo di tutti, poiché in molti scritti di teorie romantiche, anzi nella maggior parte, le idee letterarie non sono espressamente subordinate al cristianesimo, sarebbe temerità il negarlo, anche d'uno solo, perché in nessuno di

criticism made against its supporters was that they did not even agree with one another. They should begin, it was suggested, by harmonising their ideas before proposing them to others as the truth. I cannot think about this criticism without wonder. Those that reasoned thus asked something that genius, as a general rule, has not ever given and can never give. This perfect concord among people in all points of a moral system has never existed. To attain it, everyone would have to adopt a fixed set of opinions and formulas for judging the points of the moral system. Many men would have to become one, so that they could apply their generic judgments identically to each new case. There is indeed an order of things in which an essential and immutable concord exists, but this order is unique, and its characteristics and circumstances are incommunicable. This order is religion, which imparts a knowledge that the intellect cannot discover on its own, a knowledge that man can only receive by revelation and the testimony of the Church. This single revelation includes a single doctrine, and therefore a single faith. Even within this religious order, the concord is not ordained, except where it is eminently reasonable for it to be so – that is, in those points wherein the truth cannot be known except from the testimony of those who have received its revelation, namely, from the Church. This concord is not commanded except for the moment in which the sole witness to the divine has spoken. In human matters, however, this form of testimony does not exist. No one is given or promised knowledge or assistance with decisions. Judgments, therefore, vary according to the variety of intellects and tend to be generally so dissimilar that when we call a judgment a system, we do not ask of it the impossible – that it harmonize all judgments about an unspecified general topic. Rather, we ask of it the difficult and rare task of harmonizing many judgments made on the principal points of this subject.

[. . .]

The area then, in which the opinions of the Romantics were unanimous, it seemed and seems to me, was this: that poetry should make truth its objective, as the unique source of a noble and enduring delight. Although the false can fascinate the mind, it can neither enrich nor elevate it. This pseudofascination is, by its nature, unstable and temporary, since it is capable, as should be the case, of being destroyed or even changed into something tedious. Such a change may be brought about by a transcendent sense of truth or by an ever-increasing love of truth. As the most natural means of rendering such poetic effects easier to produce and more accessible, Romantics wanted poets to choose subjects that, while sufficiently interesting to the most learned, also appealed to many readers' natural curiosity and interest, born of memories and daily impressions of life. Consequently, Romantics asked poets to give final burial to subjects that interested only the literary class – and not the entire literary class but only the part of it that derived its predilections from scholastic habit – and another part of the public, neither literate nor illiterate, holding a reverence for these subjects that was not heartfelt but was certainly accepted.

[. . .]

The factual material needed for experimentation is so abundant as to make us believe that, in its original form, Romantic theory may actually be transmitting from one person to the next ideas, explanations, and assertions whose quantity and importance may be impossible to foresee concretely at present. In any case, this is the opinion I have created in my mind – an opinion that elates me because in Romantic theory I seem to discern a Christian inclination. Did those who first proposed and approved Romantic theory ever intend this Christian inclination? It would be frivolous to asset that this was everyone's intention, since in many Romantic theoretical writings, indeed in the greater part of them, literary ideas are not subordinated expressly to Christianity. It would be cowardly, however, to deny this Christian component, even in a single writer,

quegli scritti, almeno dei letti da me, il cristianesimo è escluso. Non abbiamo, né i dati, né il diritto, né il bisogno di fare un tal giudizio: quella intenzione, certo desiderabile, certo non indifferente, non è però necessaria per farci dare la preferenza a quel sistema. Basta che quella tendenza ci sia. Ora, il sistema romantico, emancipando la letteratura dalle tradizioni pagane, disobbligandola, per dir così, da una morale voluttuosa, superba, feroce, circoscritta al tempo, e improvida anche in questa sfera; antisociale, dov'è patriotica, e egoista, anche quando non è ostile; tende certamente a render meno difficile l'introdurre nella letteratura le idee, e i sentimenti, che dovrebbero informare ogni discorso. E dall'altra parte, proponendo anche in termini generalissimi il vero, l'utile, il bono, il ragionevole concorre, se non altro, con le parole, allo scopo del cristianesimo; non lo contraddice almeno nei termini.

> (1823) [*D'Azeglio sul Romanticismo Edizioni di riferimento: Alessandro Manzoni, Scritti di teoria letteraria, con note e traduzioni a cura di Adelaide Sozzi Casanova, introduzione di Cesare Segre, Rizzoli, Milano 1981; Alessandro Manzoni, Opere varie, Stabilimento Redaelli dei fratelli Rechiedei, Milano, 1870*]

i. POLSKI

V.i.1. ADAM MICKIEWICZ, *Księgi pielgrzymstwa polskiego* (fragmenty) księgi XIII i XVIII

XIII

Nie spierajcie się o zasługi Wasze i o pierwszeństwo, i o znaki.

Do pewnego miasta szturmowali żołnierze mężni i postawiono na murze drabinę, a wojsko krzyknęło: Kto pierwszy postawi nogi na murze, będzie miał znak wielki wojskowy

Przybiegła pierwsza rota; a iż każdy chciał pierwszy wstąpić na szczeble, zaczęli się odpychać i obalili drabinę, i pobici są z murów.

Postawiono więc drugą drabinę i nadbiegła druga rota; a który najpierwej wskoczył na szczeble, puszczono go, a drudzy postępowali za nim.

Ale pierwszy żołnierz w pół drabiny stracił siłę i zatrzymał się, drugim zawalając drogę. A więc następujący żołnierz targał się z nim i oderwał go, i w dół rzucił, i innych zepchnął; zrobiło się zamieszanie wielkie, i wszyscy pobici są.

Aż postawiono trzecią drabinę i wbiegła trzecia rota; pierwszy żołnierz dostał ranę i iść dalej nie chciał. Ale następujący po nim był mąż silny i ogromny, więc nic nie mówiąc porwał go i niósł przed sobą, i zastawiał się nim jak tarczą i postawił go na murze; za czym wbiegli inni porządkiem i miasto zdobyli.

A wojsko potem weszło w radę i chciało dać znak wielki owemu żołnierzowi silnemu. On zaś tak im mówił:

Bracia żołnierze, okrzyknęliście, iż kto pierwszy na murze nogi postawi, znak weźmie, a oto jest żołnierz ranny, który stanął przede mną; on tedy znak weźmie. Przez niego BÓG miasto zdobył.

Nie ważcie go lekce, mówiąc, iż tylko prędkości nóg winien pierwsze miejsce, bo i prędkość jest przymiot w żołnierzu, jako siła i męstwo.

Nie mówcie, iż on nic nie sprawił, bo gdyby go nie raniono przede mną, tedy ja odniósłbym tę ranę, i może byśmy miasta dziś nie wzięli. A ten, kto zasłania, równy temu, kto walczy, i tarcz ma równą cenę jak miecz. Znaku nie potrzebuję, bo wszyscy wiedzą com zrobił.

for in none of these Romantic writings, at least in those I have read, is Christianity excluded. We have neither the facts, the right, nor the need to make such a judgment. Such a possible Christian intent, while certainly desirable and no small matter to us, is not, however, necessary to make us voice our preference for Romantic theory. It is enough for us that this Christian tendency is present in Romantic thought. Romantic theory, let us remember, freed literature from paganism and liberated writers from, so to speak, a moral voluptuousness that was haughty, fierce, circumscribed by time, and improvident in this sphere; antisocial, even when it was patriotic; and egoistical, even when it was not hostile. In this regard, Romantic theory tends to make it less difficult for one to introduce into literature the ideas and sentiments that should inform any discussion. In another sense, because Romantic theory proposes in general terms the true, useful, good, and reasonable, its words, if nothing else, converge with the goals of Christianity, or, at least, the terms of Romanticism do not contradict those of Christianity.

(1823) [*Translated by Joseph Luzzi. PMLA, March 2004.*]

i. POLISH

V.i.1. ADAM MICKIEWICZ, from *The Books of Polish Pilgrimage, (fragments)* from Books XIII and XVIII

XIII

Do not quarrel over your merits, precedence and decorations.

Once brave soldiers who were storming a city set up a ladder against the wall, and the army cried: He who first sets foot on the wall will have the great military medal.

The first squad rushed forward, and since all wanted to be first on the ladder, they began to struggle among themselves, overturned the ladder and were killed one after the other from the top of the walls.

Therefore they raised a second ladder, and a second squad rushed forward; and he who first reached the rungs of the ladder was allowed to climb, and his comrades followed.

But the first soldier, mid-way in his climb, weakened and halted, blocking the way to the others. Therefore the soldier who followed struggled with him and threw him down to the ground, together with all the rest; there was great confusion, and all were killed.

Finally they raised a third ladder, and the third squad ran forward and climbed; the first soldier was wounded, and did not want to advance. Bu the man following was huge and powerful, and so without a word he clasped him in his arms and carried him upward, protecting himself with his burden as with a shield, and set him on the top of the wall. And the others ran up one after the other, and they took the city.

And later the army held council, and wanted to award the great decoration to the strong soldier. But he said to them:

Comrades, you have proclaimed that the first to set foot on the wall should have the medal. Here is a wounded soldier who arrived before me; the decoration is his. Through him God conquered the city.

Do not think lightly of him, saying that he owes his place in the forefront only to his swiftness of limb, for swiftness too is a soldierly quality, like strength and courage.

BÓG daje zwycięstwo używając prędkości jednego, męstwa drugiego, siły trzeciego; a skoro człowiek zręczny lub silny, zamiast nieść w górę towarzysza słabszego, strąca go, tedy robi zamieszanie i klęskę; a jeśli chwali się z zasługi swej, zasiewa niezgodę.

XVIII

[...]

Wszedł do domu opustoszałego człowiek dziki, z żoną i z dziećmi. A widząc okna rzekł: Przez to okno będzie patrzeć żona moja, a przez drugie ja sam, a przez trzecie mój syn. Patrzyli więc, a kiedy odchodzili od okien, zasłaniali je obyczajem ludzi dzikich, aby światło do nich należące innym nie dostało się. A reszta rodziny okien nie miała.

I rzekł człowiek dziki: Przy tym piecu ja sam tylko grzać się będę, bo jeden tylko piec był. A inni niech sobie zrobią każdy po jednym piecu. I rzekł potem: Wybijmy wdomu drzwi dla każdego oddzielne; przetoż popsuli dom i bili się często o światło, ciepło i granice izby.

Otóż tak robią Narody europejskie, zazdroszczą sobie handlu książek i handlu wina, i bawełny, nie wiedząc, iż nauka i dostatek do jednego domu należą, do wolnych ludów należą.

[*Edited by Czesław Zgorzelski, Dzieła, volume I: Wiersze. Warszawa: Czytelnik, 1993*]

V.i.2.   ADAM MICKIEWICZ, 'Snuć Miłość'

Snuć miłość, jak jedwabnik nić wnętrzem swym snuje,
Lać ją z serca, jak źródło wodę z wnętrza leje,
Rozkładać ją jak złotą blachę, gdy się kuje
Z ziarna złotego; puszczać ją w głąb, jak nurtuje
Źródło pod ziemią. – W górę wiać nią, jak wiatr wieje,
Po ziemi ją rozsypać, jak się zboże sieje.
Ludziom piastować, jako matka swych piastuje.

Stąd będzie naprzód moc twa jak moc przyrodzenia,
A potem będzie moc twa jako moc żywiołów,
A potem będzie moc twa jako moc krzewienia,
Potem jak ludzi, potem jako moc aniołów,
A w końcu będzie jako moc Stwórcy stworzenia

[*From Liryki lozańskie (1839–1840). Ed. Czesław Zgorzelski. Warszawa: Czytelnik, 1993*]

Do not say that he has accomplished nothing, for if he had not been injured before me I would have received that wound, and perhaps the city would not be ours today. He who protects is equal to one who strikes, and the shield has the worth of the sword. I do not need the medal, for all know what I have done.

God grant victory through the swiftness of one, the courage of another, and the strength of a third; and when an able or strong man does not lift his weaker comrade upward but rather throws him down, he creates disorder and brings defeat; and if he boasts of his merit, he sows discord.

XVIII

[. . .]

A savage entered an empty house together with his wife and children. And, upon seeing the windows, he said, 'My wife will look through this window, I through the next, and my son through the third.' They all looked, and when they came away from the windows, they covered them up after the fashion of savages, so that the light belonging to each would not go to another. And the rest of the family had no windows at all.

And the savage said, 'I alone shall warm myself by this stove' – for there was only one stove – 'and, as for the others, let each one make himself a stove.' And then he said, 'Let us knock out a door for each of us in the house.' So doing they tore apart the house, and continually fought over the light, heat, and limits of the rooms.

Thus are the European nations. They begrudge one another's trade in books, or wine, or cotton, not knowing that knowledge and fortune are parts of one house and belong to the peoples who are free.

[*Book 13 translated by Ludwick Krzyzanowski and Book XVIII translated by John F. Leich. Mickiewicz, Adam, From The Books of Polish Pilgrimage. Ed. Clark Mills. Trans. Ludwick Krzyzanowski. New York: The Noonday Press, 1956. Book 13.*]

V.i.2. ADAM MICKIEWICZ, 'Spin Love'

Spin love, spin love out of your heart
    As from the worm the silk is wound,
As from the spring the waters start,
    As flows the river underground.
Unroll love like those glittering sheets,
    Papyrus-thin, and bright with glamour,
Which patiently the goldsmith beats
    Out of an ingot with a hammer.
And blow love as the zephyr blows,
    Upward and outward, far and wide,
And cast it as the farmer sows
    The prodigal grain on every side.
Love men and women everywhere,
    All human creatures brought to birth,
As mothers for their children care.
    Your hands will have more power on earth

V.i.3.   ADAM MICKIEWICZ, 'Nad wodą wielką i czystą'

Nad wodą wielką i czystą
Stały rzędami opoki,
I woda tonią przejrzystą
Odbiła twarze ich czarne;

Nad wodą wielką i czystą
Przebiegły czarne obłoki,
I woda tonią przejrzystą
Odbiła kształty ich marne;

Nad wodą wielką i czystą
Błysnęło wzdłuż i grom ryknął,
I woda tonią przejrzystą
Odbiła światło, głos zniknął.

A woda, jak dawniej czysta,
Stoi wielka i przejrzysta.

Tę wodę widzę dokoła
I wszystko wiernie odbijam,
I dumne opoki czoła,
I błyskawice – pomijam.

Skałom trzeba stać i grozić,
Obłokom deszcze przewozić,
Błyskawicom grzmieć i ginąć,
Mnie płynąć, płynąć i płynąć –

(1839–1840)

[Liryki lozańskie (1839–1840). Ed. Czesław Zgorzelski. Warszawa: Czytelnik, 1993]

Than nature has; and then your strength,
    Indomitable, shall equate
That of the elements, and at, length,
    Shall be the power to propagate,
Then be the power of the people,
    Then power of a heavenly horde
Of angels flying round a steeple –
    At last, the power of the Lord.

        [*Translated by Kimball Flaccius. Ed.Clark Mill. New York: The Noonday Press, 1956.*]

V.i.3.   ADAM MICKIEWICZ, 'Within Their Silent, Perfect Glass'

Within their silent, perfect glass
The mirror waters, vast and clear,
Reflect the silhouette of rocks,
Dark faces brooding on the shore.

Within their silent, perfect glass
The mirror waters show the sky;
Clouds skim across the mirror's face,
And dim its surface as they die.

Within their silent, perfect glass
The mirror waters image storm;
They glow with lightning, but the blasts
Of thunder do not mar their calm.

These mirror waters, as before,
Still lie in silence, vast and clear.

They mirror me, I mirror them,
As true as glass as they I am;
And as I turn away I leave
The images that gave them form.

Dark rocks must menace from the shore,
And thunderheads grow large with rain;
Lightning must flash above the lake,
And I must mirror and pass on,
Onward and onward without end.

        (1839–1840)

[*Translated by Cecil Hemley, published in Adam Mickiewicz, 1798–1855. Selected Poems. Ed.
Clark Mills. New York: The Noonday Press, 1956*]

j. PORTUGUÊS

V.j.1. ALEXANDRE HERCULANO, «*Eu e o Clero* (excertos)»

Ainda algumas palavras sobre o antagonismo, em que de nenhum modo V. SS. me quer ver col-locado, em relação á maioria do clero. Foram apenas alguns que me provocaram do púlpito, e eu chamo á autoria o grande numero, É verdade. Não sei com certeza senão de alguns factos de aggressão, mas a noticia de parte desses factos obtive-a casualmente: alguns constaram-me apenas, porque um jornal a elles alludem de passagem, dizendo que se praticavam por diversos logares de Entre-Douro e Minho. É acaso provável que se não repetissem por outras dioceses? Em Lisboa, onde eu resido; onde os sacerdotes podem ter mais illustração; onde até o fanatismo deve ser mais raro, porque a própria fé é mais tibia; onde, emfim, os pregadores mais devem recear que o seu auditório se ria delles, houve dois exemplos. Não me será licito inferir que, não tendo eu uma policia ás minhas ordens, ignoro muitos successos análogos? Depois, houve á vista desses factos repetidos, não digo punição deste abuso do ministério sagrado, o que não peço, o que até me contristaria, porque me lembro das palavras de Christo «Perdoa-lhes Pae, que não sabem o que fazem»; mas a mínima providencia para impedir a renovação de taes escândalos? Para que servem os vigários da vara, os arcediagos, os representantes ou delegados do poder episcopal? Como informam os respectivos prelados do que se passa entre o clero dioc-esano? Não tenho eu direito a suppôr que elles também entendem que a sanctidade dos papas da idade média ou o apparecirnento de Ourique são partes integrantes da crença catholica, e que se trepassem ao púlpito, e lhes viesse a talho, me chamariam do mesmo modo ímpio ou hereje? Se não estão de accôrdo com os pregadores, como se esquecem de que os padres de Trenio prohibiram aos bispos que consentissem aos oradores sagrados *divulgar ou tractor factos incertos, ou que tenham caracteres, de falsidade*, e de que os do concilio 1.º de Colónia ordenam aos mesmos oradores que *não fallem impudentemente de milagres, limitando-se aos que refere a Bíblia, ou aos que forem narrados por escriptores de peso, estribados em sólidos fundamentos históricos*? Como quer pois V. SS. que eu não increpe o maior numero; que não o supponha alistado contra mim nesta vergonhosa cruzada d'ignorancia?

[...]

(...) Como homem, como príncipe temporal, os seus actos públicos são do domínio da imprensa; se esses actos pelo seus effeitos moraes e politicos poderem trazer graves turbações, dias de amargura á igreja, não é lícito a todo e qualquer christão deplorar essas consequencias, reprehender esses actos? Quando eu digo que Roma *parece* ter jurado o exterminio do catholicismo, accuso o papa, a cúria, alguém de ter a intenção directa de o destruir? Ou eu não sei portuguez, ou empreguei uma phrase trivial, e cujo alcance todos comprehendem. Que se diz do valetudinário que despreza os conselhos dos médicos? Parece que se quer matar! E quando dizemos isto passa-nos acaso pelo espirito a idéa de attrihuir a esse indivíduo a intenção directa do suicídio? Ou será que os expressões simples, as phrases innocentes dos outros homens se convertam em peste e veneno, quando sabem da bocca do feroz hereje que ousou duvidar do testemunho posthumo, e bem posthumo, de S. Bernardo acerca do milagre de Ourique?

j. PORTUGUESE

V.j.1. ALEXANDRE HERCULANO, from *Me and the Clergy*

The following are excerpts from a letter written by Herculano to A Nação, a Portuguese periodical, concerning the religious polemics that arose from the publication of the first volume of his History of Portugal. The letter mentions 'Ourique,' a legendary confrontation between Christians and Moors, which Herculano's work discredits. According to the myth, a divine vision appeared to the Portuguese Christians, establishing Portugal as a nation according to divine will. Most of this excerpt illustrates Herculano's notorious hostility toward nineteenth-century Christianity in Europe, especially toward the doctrine of papal infallibility.

[. . .] Allow me some words concerning what some perceive as my antagonism toward the greater part of the clergy. Doubtless you agree that this is a distorted perception of the truth. It has been said that I attribute to the majority what is only being said by a few. This may be true; I only know of a few cases of the clergy attacking me from their pulpits, but from what I have read in newspapers the attacks are more widespread, especially in several parts of Entre-Douro e Minho.[1] Is it not likely that the harangues I have experienced from the pulpits in Lisbon, where fanaticism should be less because the faith is weaker, are not even more common in dioceses where religion has a stronger hold? Where preachers should most fear ridicule, there have been two cases; is it not legitimate for me to infer, without having the authorities check every parish, that I am ignorant of more such cases? I do not resent the fact that these abuses of the sacred ministry have gone unpunished; punishment would indeed sadden me, for I remember the words of Christ, 'Forgive them Father, for they know not what they do.' I do condemn, however, the lack of effort to prevent further such scandals. What use are the Church leaders, the arch-deacons, the representatives of papal authority, if they do not inform their superiors about what goes on among the lower clergy? Have I not reason to infer that they too, like the lower clergy, uphold the sanctity of Middle Age Popes or the miracle at Ourique as part and parcel of Catholic creeds, or that they too might call me ungodly and heretical from the pulpit if it suited their purposes? How can they forget that the Council of Trent prohibited bishops and other ministers to 'divulge or address uncertain facts or facts associated with falsity,'[2] or that the Council of Cologne ordered leaders to 'prevent ministers from talking recklessly about miracles, mentioning only those in the Bible or those narrated by relevant authorities using sound historical support'?[3] How can you, Sir, imagine that I do not suspect the majority of the clergy to be implicated in this problem? Indeed, how can you imagine that I do not consider even you among the ranks of those attacking me in this shameful crusade of ignorance? [. . .]

[*The following is a discussion about an earlier argument against Herculano's views of the medieval Papacy and early modern Protestants.*]

As a man, as a prince of this world, the Pope's public actions are in the domain of the press. Is it not licit for every Christian to condemn his public actions when they, by force of their moral and political effects, cause distress for the whole Church? When I say that Rome *appears* to have condemned Catholicism to extermination, do I accuse the Pope, the Church, or anyone of having the direct intention of destroying it? Either I do not know Portuguese or I meant exactly what I wrote in a very clear and simple sentence. What is said of the patient who ignores the

---

[1] Northern, very Catholic region of Portugal.
[2] Council of Trent. Session 25, Decree Concerning Purgatory. [Herculano's note].
[3] Council of Cologne. I, tit. 6 c. 25. [Herculano]

Em que tempos estamos nós? Para onde caminha a reacção religiosa? Que!? Eu não poderia appreciar como entendesse o procedimento político de um papa, em relação aos futuros destinos da igreja, e S. Thomaz de Cantuaria poderia sem ser um réprobo lançar em rosto a Alexandre III as gravíssimas accusações de o trahir, e de querer conduzi-lo á morte? Poderia S. Thomaz de Aquino, o mais profundo philosopho do século XIII, ao observar-lhe Innocencio IV que tinha passado o tempo em que S. Pedro dizia «não possuo nem ouro nem prata» – responder-lhe «que tambem era passado o tempo em que S. Pedro dizia ao paralítico – levanta-te e anda» epigramma pungente atirado ás faces de um papa, cuja cubiça não conheceu limites; poderia, digo, S. Thomás ser um doutor da igreja, depois deste attentado? Podia sequer ser papa o successor do mesmo Innocencio, Alexandre IV, que lhe chamava o vendilhão de igrejas? Riscae do catalogo dos bemaventurados S. Antonino de Florença, que não duvidou de pintar com as mais negras cores os vícios hediondos de Clemente. Não chameis o ultimo padre da igreja a Bossuet, porque taxou de velhaco o papa Eugęnio IV. Rejeitae do grémio catholico o erudito e pio Fleury, porque escreveu o 4.º discurso sobre a Historia Ecclesiastica. Para serdes lógicos despovoae a igreja de sanctos, de doutores, de homens illustres, se credes que dentro dela eu, que não sou nenhuma dessas cousas, não tenho direito de aferir pęlos principies eternos da moral, da justiça, e da caridade evangélica as acçőes dos papas sem renegar da igreja.

Não disputarei com V. SS. sobre os successos de Roma nos últimos tempos. Cada qual pôde vę-los á luz que julgar verdadeira. Ao que, porém, eu tenho jus, é a averiguar se é exacta a proposição absoluta de V. SS. de que o futuro da igreja é muito sabido, claro e indisputável para os catholicos. Por este modo V. SS. parece excluir-me do grémio do catholicismo, porque hesito sobre o seu futuro. Advertiu acaso V. SS. em que a proposição, assim absolutamente enunciada, conduziria ao impossível? O que é certo, sabido, e claro para a igreja, e para cada um dos seus membros é que ella será perpetua, indestructivel. Mas por quaes phases tem de passar; se esperam dias serenos, se dias de tribulação; se acres resentimentos, imprudentemente preparados, virão ou não como a procella despir a folhagem, lascar os troncos da arvore eterna do christianismo, eis o que nem a igreja, nem eu, nem V. SS. sabemos. Está acaso V. SS., que eu creio profundamente catholico, habilitado para me dizer de um modo certo e claro, se a idéa revolucionaria da Itália apodreceu para sempre encharcada no sangue que as balas e bayonetas francezas e austríacas derramaram á voz da cúria romana? Se a política das masmorras, dos desterros, da compressão inexorável, preferida â política evangélica da tolerância, do perdão das injurias, da caridade sem limites, poderá varrer para sempre dos ânimos italianos o ódio do dominio estrangeiro (quer directo, quer indirecto) e o amor da liberdade política? Esse ódio e esse amor pôde V. SS. julga-los gloriosos ou deploráveis: não disputarei sobre isso. Mas que elles não existam; que elles não possam triumphar algum dia, eis o que V. SS., por certo, não affirmará com a mão na consciência. E nessa hypothese, quem saberá dizer até onde chegarão os excessos da cólera e da vingança, azedadas pelo padecer, e até certo ponto legitimadas por elle, se legitimidade se pôde dar em taes sentimentos? Parece-me que ao homem catholico é licito imaginar, sem que por isso vacille a sua fé acerca da perpetuidade do catholicismo, que a igreja

medical doctor's advise? That it *seems* he wants to kill himself! When we say this we do not even consider attributing to the patient direct intentions of suicide. The same can be said of the Church. But it seems that innocent sentences written by other men become poisonous when uttered by a ferocious heretic like me who dares to doubt the posthumous testimony of Saint Bernard concerning the miracle of Ourique!

What is this age we are living in? What is the source of this religious intolerance? How can it exist?! I cannot judge, as I would like to, the effects of the Pope's politics on the future of the Church, but Saint Thomas of Canterbury could make charges, without becoming an outcast in the eyes of Alexander III, of betrayal against his Pope grave enough to condemn him to death.[4] So too could Saint Thomas Aquinas, the most profound philosopher of the thirteenth century, respond to Innocent IV's claim that the time in which Peter had said, 'I have no gold nor silver' had come to an end, by saying, 'So too is the time past in which Peter said to the invalid, ìget up and walk,"'[5] a poignant indictment of a Pope whose ambition knew no limits. Could Saint Thomas be a doctor of the Church after such an offence? Could Innocent's successor have been Alexander IV, who had called him the 'Church's salesman'?[6] By the logic of our own day, we should strike from the catalogue of saints Antonine of Florence, who did not hesitate to portray the hideous vices of Clement.[7] And we should not consider Boussuet as the last Church father, for he said that Pope Eugene IV was a scoundrel.[8] We should discard the learned and pious Fleury from the Christian community for writing the 4th discourse on Ecclesiastical History. The Church should be deprived of all of these saints and illustrious men if it believes that I – who am neither saintly nor illustrious – have no right to judge the Pope's actions according the universal principles of morality, justice, and evangelical charity without offending the whole Church.

I will not argue with you about the Church's recent successes, but I do want to examine your statement, your absolute proposition, that Catholics can and must have complete confidence in the future of the Church. This statement excludes me from Catholic community as someone who has doubts about the Church's future. The only thing the Church and each one of its members can know for sure about the Church is that she is perpetual and indestructible. But more specific knowledge about her future, whether she will enjoy peace or face strong opposition, is uncertain. Neither you nor I nor the Church authorities can know if the latent resentment toward the Church will develop into a storm powerful enough to strip the leaves and branches from the tree of Christendom. Are you, who I assume to be profoundly Catholic, in a position to tell me with absolute confidence that the revolutionary spirit in Italy rots irrevocably with the blood spilled by French and Austrian bullets and bayonets under the command of the Roman Church?[9] Are you certain that the politics of oppression and violence which you prefer over the evangelical politics of tolerance and charity can expel the Italian spirit of hatred toward foreign rule and establish love for religious freedom in Portugal? I will not argue with you about the merits and dangers of such hate and such love; however, I do argue that you cannot declare with a clear conscience that the spirit of hate will not one day triumph again in the Church. Who can

[4] Scriptore Ver. Francicar. T. XVII. 553. [Herculano]
[5] Art de Verif. les Dates vol. 1. 299. [Herculano]
[6] Matth. Paris. 607 col. 2. [Herculano]
[7] Chron. Pag. Mihi 287. [Herculano]
[8] Def. de la Declar. I. 6. [Herculano]
[9] Herculano is commenting on the Vatican's nineteenth-century resistance to the unification of Italy.

se entristece, ou deve entristecer, aterrada pelo porvir; é licito suppôr que as lagrimas dos seus futuros martyres vem já de antemão cair-lhe ardentes sobre o seio materno. Se attribuir ao grémio dos fiéis, composto de homens, os affectos de dor e amargura desdiz de alguma cousa, não é, de certo, das tradições evangélicas, nem das tradições dos antigos padres. Já no VI século S. Hilário de Poitiers observava quão frequente era pintar-nos o evangelho como triste e afflicto o Filho de Deus; e S. Gregorio Magno não duvidava de dizer: «*A sancta igreja em quanto vive esta vida de corrupção, não cessa de chorar os damnos das vicissitudes porque passa:*» e noutra parte: «*A dor esmaga a igreja quando vê os perversos prosperarem na própria maldade.*» É dessas vicissitudes a que allude o sancto pontífice, que eu fallo; é a essas vicissitudes, demasiado prováveis, que os erros dos homens, as paixões anti-christãs do sacerdócio triumphante ajuntam, nas minhas previsões, um carácter de terribilidade.

(...)

[1850]

tell how far the latent anger and desire for revenge toward the Church may reach, especially when legitimized to a certain extent (if such feelings can be legitimized at all) by the persistence of suffering? It seems to me that the Catholic man must be allowed to question, without his faith in the perpetuity of the Church being shaken, whether the church should be saddened or even scared by continued suffering under the Church's authority. We must be allowed to believe that the motherly bosom of the Church is ready for the tears of her future martyrs, which have already started to fall. The belief that the bitterness and suffering of the community of the faithful is offensive to the Church as an institution is not orthodox in either the ancient or the evangelical traditions of faith. As soon as the sixth century, Saint Hilaire of Poitiers remarked how frequently the gospels portray the Son of God as sad and worried.[10] And Saint Gregory the Great said without hesitation, 'The Holy Church, while living in the corrupt world, mourns the effects of the suffering the world endures,' and 'pain crushes the Church when it sees the wicked prosper in their wickedness.'[11] It is because of the mistakes of men and the anti Christian passions of the clergy toward men's suffering that I foresee terrible effects. [. . .]

[1850] [*Translated by Carlos Leone and Bethany Smith*]

---

[10] Saint Hilaire. Pictav., in Psalm. 53. [Herculano]
[11] Gregory the Great, *Expositions on the Book of Job* Book 8 section 6; book 13 section 4. [Herculano]

k. ROMÂNĂ

V.k.1. ALECU RUSSO, from 'Cântarea României'

1

Domnul Dumnezeul părinţilor noştri înduratu-sa de lacrămile tale, norod nemângâiet, înduratu-sa de durerea plămânilor tale, ţara mea?... [...]

2

Neamurile auziră ţipetul chinuirei tale, pământul se mişcă. Dumnezeu numai să nu-l fi auzit?... Răzbunătoriul prevestit nu s-a născut oare?

7

Nu eşti frumoasă, nu eşti înavuţită?... N-ai ficiori mulţi care te iubesc? N-ai cartea de vitejie a trecutului, şi a viitorului înaintea ta?... pentru ce curg lacrămile tale?...

8

Pentru ce tresari? Trupul ţi se topeşte de slăbiciune, şi inima ţi se frământă cu iuţeală... cetit-ai oare în cartea ursitei?... Aerul mişcă turburat... vântul dogoreşte... Îngerul peirei arătatu-ţi-s-a? Nopţile tale sunt reci, visurile turburate ca valurile mărei bătută de fortună... ce-ţi prevestesc?

62

Deşteaptă-te, pământ român! Biruie-ţi durerea, e vremea să ieşi din amorţire, seminţie a domnitorilor lumei!... Aştepţi oare, spre a învia, ca strămoşii să se scoale din morminte?... Într-adevăr, într-adevăr ei s-au sculat, şi tu nu i-ai văzut... Ei au grăit, şi tu nu i-ai auzit... Cinge-ţi coapsa ta, caută şi ascultă... Ziua dreptăţii se apropie... toate popoarele s-au mişcat... căci furtuna mântuirei a început!...

[1850]

k. ROMANIAN

V.k.1. ALECU RUSSO, from 'Hymn to Romania'[1]

1

The Lord Almighty, God of our fathers, hath He taken pity on thy tears, uncomforted people, hath He taken pity on thy spirit, my country? ... [...]

2

The peoples have heard the cries of thy suffering, the earth is moving. Can God alone be deaf to it? Can the promised saviour be yet unborn?

7

Art thou not beauteous, art thou not wealthy?... Hast thou not countless sons who love thee? Hast thou not the book of thy heroic past, and thy future extending before thyself?... Wherefore dost thou weep?...

8

Why art thou startled? Thy body melts with weakness, thy heart throbs and pants ... hast thou read in the book of fate? ... The air is thick with dread ... the wind is burning ... hath the angel of Death shown himself to thee? Thy nights are cold, thy dreams are troubled like waves beaten by tempests ... What do they foretell?
Wake up, Romanian land! Vanquish thy suffering, it is time you were free of this drowsiness, thou, home of kings and princes! ... Dost thou expect to be resurrected by thy forefathers rising from their graves? Verily, verily, they have risen, and thou hast not sent them ... They have spoken, and thou hast not heard them ... Gird up thy loins, and try to hear ... The day of justice is approaching ... all the peoples have moved ... for the day of redemption hath begun! ...

[1850] [*Translated by Mihaela Anghelescu Irimia, Adina Ciugureanu and Virginia Jarrell*]

[1] Félicité Robert de Lamennais (1782–1854), author of *Paroles d'un croyant* (1834) and *Le livre du people* (1837), is a minor French writer who caused a mimetic contagion throughout Romanian Romanticism. He was particularly influential in the case of Alecu Russo, who changed his name to make it sound like Jean Jacques Rousseau. Lamennais reads between the lines of Russo's *Hymn to Romania*, composed in the manner of Gospel exhortation at a time of Lamartinian and Youngian poetical fashion on the Continent, in which the social tone overlaps with the apocalyptic vision. Written in French and later translated into Romanian by Nicolae Bălcescu, this biblically phrased text combines archaic language with encomiastic nationalistic accents against a messianic background.

l. РУССКИЙ

V.l.1. НИКОЛАЙ ГОГОЛЬ, «Портрет»

ЧАСТЬ II

Множество карет, дрожек и колясок стояло перед подъездом дома, в котором производилась аукционная продажа вещей одного из тех богатых любителей искусств, которые сладко продремали всю жизнь свою, погруженные в зефиры и амуры, которые невинно прослыли меценатами и простодушно издержали для этого миллионы, накопленные их основательными отцами, а часто даже собственными прежними трудами. Таких меценатов, как известно, теперь уже нет, и наш XIX век давно уже приобрел скучную физиономию банкира, наслаждающегося своими миллионами только в виде цифр, выставляемых на бумаге. Длинная зала была наполнена самою пестрою толпой посетителей, налетевших, как хищные птицы на неприбранное тело. Тут была целая флотилия русских купцов из Гостиного двора и даже толкучего рынка, в синих немецких сюртуках. Вид их и выраженье лиц были здесь как-то тверже, вольнее и не означались той приторной услужливостью, которая так видна в русском купце, когда он у себя в лавке перед покупщиком. Тут они вовсе не чинились, несмотря на то что в этой же зале находилось множество тех аристократов, перед которыми они в другом месте готовы были своими поклонами смести пыль, нанесенную своими же сапогами. Здесь они были совершенно развязны, щупали без церемонии книги и картины, желая узнать доброту товара, и смело перебивали цену, набавляемую графами-знатоками. Здесь были многие необходимые посетители аукционов, постановившие каждый день бывать в нем вместо завтрака; аристократы-знатоки, почитавшие обязанностью не упустить случая умножить свою коллекцию и не находившие другого занятия от 12 до 1 часа; наконец, те благородные господа, которых платья и карманы очень худы, которые являются ежедневно без всякой корыстолюбивой цели, но единственно, чтобы посмотреть, чем что кончится, кто будет давать больше, кто меньше, кто кого перебьет и за кем что останется. Множество картин было разбросано совершенно без всякого толку; с ними были перемешаны и мебели, и книги с вензелями прежнего владетеля, может быть, не имевшего вовсе похвального любопытства в них заглядывать. Китайские вазы, мраморные доски для столов, новые и старые мебели с выгнутыми линиями, с грифами, сфинксами и львиными лапами, вызолоченные и без позолоты, люстры, кенкеты – все было навалено, и вовсе не в таком порядке, как в магазинах. Все представляло какой-то хаос искусств. Вообще ощущаемое нами чувство при виде аукциона страшно: в нем все отзывается чем-то похожим на погребальную процессию. Зал, в котором он производится, всегда как-то мрачен; окна, загроможденные мебелями и картинами, скупо изливают свет, безмолвие, разлитое на лицах, и погребальный голос аукциониста, постукивающего молотком и отпевающего панихиду бедным, так странно встретившимся здесь искусствам. Все это, кажется, усиливает еще более странную неприятность впечатленья.

Аукцион, казалось, был в самом разгаре. Целая толпа порядочных людей, сдвинувшись вместе, хлопотала о чем-то наперерыв. Со всех сторон раздававшиеся слова: «Рубль, рубль, рубль», – не давали времени аукционисту повторять надбавляемую цену, которая уже возросла вчетверо больше объявленной. Обступившая толпа хлопотала из-за портрета, который не мог не остановить всех, имевших сколько-нибудь понятия в живописи. Высокая кисть художника выказывалась в нем очевидно. Портрет, по-видимому, уже несколько раз был ресторирован и поновлен и представлял смуглые

I. RUSSIAN

V.I.1. NIKOLAI GOGOL, *The Portrait, Part II*

Masses of carriages, chaises, and coaches were standing round the entrance of the house in which an auction was taking place. It was a sale of all the belongings of one of those wealthy art connoisseurs who sweetly slumber away their lives plunged in zephyrs and amours, who are naively reputed to be Maecenases,[1] and good-naturedly spend on keeping up that reputation the millions accumulated by their businesslike fathers, and often, indeed, by their own earlier labors. As is well known, there are no longer such Maecenases, for the nineteenth century long ago acquired the aspect of a stingy banker who delights himself only with the figures written in ledgers. The long drawing room was filled with the most motley crowd of visitors who had come swooping down like birds of prey on an abandoned body. Here was a regular flotilla of Russian merchants from the bazaar, and even from the old-clothes market, in dark blue coats of German cut. They had here a harder and more free-and-easy air and appearance, and were not marked by the obsequiousness which is so prominent a feature of the Russian merchant. They did not stand on ceremony, in spite of the fact that there were in the room many distinguished aristocrats, before whom in any other place they would have been ready to bow down to the ground till they swept away the dust brought in by their own boots. Here they were completely at ease and they fingered books and pictures without ceremony, trying to feel the quality of the goods, and boldly outbid aristocratic connoisseurs. Here were many of those persons who are invariably seen at auctions, who make it a rule to attend one every day as regularly as they have their breakfast; distinguished connoisseurs who look upon it as a duty not to miss a chance of increasing their collections, and have nothing else to do between twelve and one o'clock; and finally there were those excellent gentlemen whose coats and pockets are not well lined but who turn up every day at such functions with no mercenary motives, solely to see how things will go: who would give more and who less, who would outbid whom, and to whom the goods would be sold. Many of the pictures had been flung down here and there without any system; they were mixed up with the furniture and books, which all bore the monogram of their owner, though he probably had not had the laudable curiosity to look into them. Chinese vases, marble tabletops, furniture both modern and antique with curved lines adorned with the paws of griffins, sphinxes, and lions, chandeliers gilt and not gilt, and knickknacks of all sorts were heaped together, not arranged in order as in shops. It was a chaos of works of art. Generally the impression made by an auction is strange. There is something in it suggestive of a funeral procession. The room in which it takes place is always rather gloomy, the windows are blocked up with furniture and pictures, the light filters in sparingly; there is silent attention on all the faces, and the effect of a funeral procession is enhanced by the voice of the auctioneer, as he taps with his hammer and recites the requiem over the poor works of art so strangely gathered together. All this further accents the singular unpleasantness of the impression.

The auction was at its height. A throng of respectable people were gathered in a group and were excitedly discussing something. From all sides resounded the words, 'Rubles, rubles,' allowing the auctioneer no opportunity to repeat the last bid which had already mounted to a sum quadruple the original price announced. The surging crowd was bidding for a portrait which could not fail but attract the attention of anyone who had any knowledge of art. The gifted hand of a master was easily discernible in it. Apparently the portrait had been restored and refinished

---

[1] That is, patrons of art. Maecenas was the patron of Horace and Vergil.

черты какого-то азиатца в широком платье, с необыкновенным, странным выраженьем в лице; но более всего обступившие были поражены необыкновенной живостью глаз. Чем более всматривались в них, тем более они, казалось, устремлялись каждому вовнутрь. Эта странность, этот необыкновенный фокус художника заняли вниманье почти всех. Много уже из состязавшихся о нем отступились, потому что цену набили неимоверную. Остались только два известные аристократа, любители живописи, не хотевшие ни за что отказаться от такого приобретенья. Они горячились и набили бы, вероятно, цену до невозможности, если бы вдруг один из тут же рассматривавших не произнес:

– Позвольте мне прекратить на время ваш спор. Я, может быть, более, нежели всякий другой, имею право на этот портрет.

Слова эти вмиг обратили на него внимание всех. Это был стройный человек, лет тридцати пяти, с длинными черными кудрями. Приятное лицо, исполненное какой-то светлой беззаботности, показывало душу, чуждую всех томящих светских потрясений; в наряде его не было никаких притязаний на моду: все показывало в нем артиста. Это был, точно, художник Б., знаемый лично многими из присутствовавших.

– Как ни странны вам покажутся слова мои, – продолжал он, видя устремившееся на себя всеобщее внимание, – но если вы решитесь выслушать небольшую историю, может быть, вы увидите, что я был вправе произнести их. Всё меня уверяют, что портрет есть тот самый, которого я ищу.

Весьма естественное любопытство загорелось почти на лицах всех, и самый аукционист, разинув рот, остановился с поднятым в руке молотком, приготовляясь слушать. В начале рассказа многие обращались невольно глазами к портрету, но потом все вперились в одного рассказчика, по мере того как рассказ его становился занимательней.

– Вам известна та часть города, которую называют Коломною. – Так он начал. – Тут все непохоже на другие части Петербурга; тут не столица и не провинция; кажется, слышишь, перейдя в коломенские улицы, как оставляют тебя всякие молодые желанья и порывы. Сюда не заходит будущее, здесь все тишина и отставка, все, что осело от столичного движенья. Сюда переезжают на житье отставные чиновники, вдовы, небогатые люди, имеющие знакомство с сенатом и потому осудившие себя здесь почти на всю жизнь; выслужившиеся кухарки, толкающиеся целый день на рынках, болтающие вздор с мужиком в мелочной лавочке и забирающие каждый день на пять копеек кофию да на четыре сахару, и, наконец, весь тот разряд людей, который можно назвать одним словом: пепельный, – людей, которые с своим платьем, лицом, волосами, глазами имеют какую-то мутную, пепельную наружность, как день, когда нет на небе ни бури, ни солнца, а бывает просто ни се ни то: сеется туман и отнимает всякую резкость у предметов. Сюда можно причислить отставных театральных капельдинеров, отставных титулярных советников, отставных питомцев Марса с выколотым глазом и раздутою губою. Эти люди вовсе бесстрастны: идут, ни на что не обращая глаз, молчат, ни о чем не думая. В комнате их не много добра; иногда просто штоф чистой русской водки, которую они однообразно сосут весь день без всякого сильного прилива в голове, возбуждаемого сильным приемом, какой обыкновенно любит задавать себе по воскресным дням молодой немецкий ремесленник, этот удалец Мещанской улицы, один владеющий всем тротуаром, когда время перешло за двенадцать часов ночи.

Жизнь в Коломне страх уединенна: редко покажется карета, кроме разве той, в которой ездят актеры, которая громом, звоном и бряканьем своим одна смущает всеобщую тишину. Тут всё пешеходы; извозчик весьма часто без седока плетется, таща сено для бородатой лошаденки своей. Квартиру можно сыскать за пять рублей в месяц, даже с кофием поутру.

several times, and it showed the dark features of an Asiatic in a wide robe who wore a peculiar expression on his face. But it was the remarkable liveliness of the eyes that struck the buyers most of all. The longer the people looked at them, the more did they seem to bore right into every man's heart. This peculiarity, this mysterious illusion created by the artist, forced the attention of almost all upon it. Many of those who had bid for the picture finally withdrew from the bidding when the price rose to an incredible sum. Only two well-known, art-collecting aristocrats remained, both absolutely determined not to forgo such a purchase. In the heat of excitement they would probably have continued out-bidding each other until the price had finally assumed incredible proportions if one of those in attendance had not suddenly said, 'Allow me to interrupt your competition for a while. I, perhaps, have more right to his picture than anyone else.' Immediately these words drew the attention of everyone upon him. He was a tall man of thirty-five, with long black hair. His pleasant face, full of a kind of gay nonchalance, showed a soul devoid of all mundane concerns. His clothes made no pretense to be fashionable. Everything about him indicated the artist. In fact, he was the artist B., well known personally to many of those present.

'Regardless of how strange my words may seem to you,' he continued, noticing that all attention was focused on him, 'you will see, if you agree to listen to a little story, that I was right to speak them. Everything convinces me that this is the portrait for which I have been looking.'

A very natural curiosity took hold of nearly everyone, and even the auctioneer, with an open mouth and a raised hammer, paused and prepared to listen. At the beginning of the story many people involuntarily looked at the portrait, but later all attention was fixed on the narrator as what he said grew more and more interesting.

'You all know that part of the city which is called Kolomna,' he began. 'Everything there is different from any other part of Petersburg. There we have neither capital nor provinces. It seems, indeed, that when you walk through the streets of Kolomna, all the youthful desires and passions are drained from you. There the future never comes; all is still and desolate. Everything suggests withdrawal from the life of the capital. Retired officials move there to live, and widows and poor people who are familiar with the senate and therefore sentence themselves to this district for nearly all of their lives; cooks who have retired and spend the whole day haggling in the market, gossiping with the peasants in the milkshop, buying five kopeks' worth of coffee and four kopeks' worth of sugar every day; and that class of people whom I call ashen, whose clothes and faces and hair all have a dingy appearance like ashes. They are like a gray day when the sun does not dazzle with its brilliance, nor the storm whistle with thunder, rain, and hail, but when the sky is neither one thing nor the other: there is a veil of mist that blurs the outline of every object. And to these must be added retired people who were ushers in the theater, titular councilors, retired disciples of Mars with swollen lips and eyes poked out. These people are quite without passions. Nothing matters to them; they go about without taking the slightest notice of anything, and remain quite silent thinking of nothing at all. In their room they have nothing but a bed and a bottle of pure Russian vodka, which they imbibe with equal regularity every day, without any of the rush of ardor to the head that is provoked by a strong dose, such as the young German artisan, that bully of Meshchansky Street, who has undisputed possession of the pavement after twelve o' clock at night, loves to give himself on Sundays.

'Life in Kolomna is dull: rarely does a carriage rumble through its quiet streets, unless it be one full of actors, which disturbs the general stillness with its bells, its creaking and rattling. Here almost everyone goes on foot. Only at rare intervals a cab crawls along lazily, almost always without a fare, taking a load of hay for its humble nag. An apartment can be rented for five

Вдовы, получающие пенсион, тут самые аристократические фамилии; они ведут себя хорошо, метут часто свою комнату, толкуют с приятельницами о дороговизне говядины и капусты; при них часто бывает молоденькая дочь, молчаливое, безгласное, иногда миловидное существо, гадкая собачонка и стенные часы с печально постукивающим маятником. Потом следуют актеры, которым жалованье не позволяет выехать из Коломны, народ свободный, как все артисты, живущие для наслажденья. Они, сидя в халатах, чинят пистолет, клеют из картона всякие вещицы, полезные для дома, играют с пришедшим приятелем в шашки и карты, и так проводят утро, делая почти то же ввечеру, с присоединеньем кое-когда пунша. После сих тузов и аристократства Коломны следует необыкновенная дробь и мелочь. Их так же трудно поименовать, как исчислить то множество насекомых, которое зарождается в старом уксусе. Тут есть старухи, которые молятся; старухи, которые пьянствуют; старухи, которые и молятся и пьянствуют вместе; старухи, которые перебиваются непостижимыми средствами, как муравьи – таскают с собою старое тряпье и белье от Калинкина мосту до толкучего рынка, с тем чтобы продать его там за пятнадцать копеек; словом, часто самый несчастный осадок человечества, которому бы ни один благодетельный политический эконом не нашел средств улучшить состояние.

Я для того привел их, чтобы показать вам, как часто этот народ находится в необходимости искать одной только внезапной, временной помощи, прибегать к займам; и тогда поселяются между ними особого рода ростовщики, снабжающие небольшими суммами под заклады и за большие проценты. Эти небольшие ростовщики бывают в несколько раз бесчувственней всяких больших, потому что возникают среди бедности и ярко выказываемых нищенских лохмотьев, которых не видит богатый ростовщик, имеющий дело только с приезжающими в каретах. И потому уже слишком рано умирает в душах их всякое чувство человечества. Между такими ростовщиками был один... но не мешает вам сказать, что происшествие, о котором я принялся рассказать, относится к прошедшему веку, именно к царствованию покойной государыни Екатерины Второй. Вы можете сами понять, что самый вид Коломны и жизнь внутри ее должны были значительно измениться. Итак, между ростовщиками был один – существо во всех отношениях необыкновенное, поселившееся уже давно в сей части города. Он ходил в широком азиатском наряде; темная краска лица указывала на южное его происхождение, но какой именно был он нации: индеец, грек, персиянин, об этом никто не мог сказать наверно. Высокий, почти необыкновенный рост, смуглое, тощее, запаленное лицо и какой-то непостижимо страшный цвет его, большие, необыкновенного огня глаза, нависнувшие густые брови отличали его сильно и резко от всех пепельных жителей столицы. Самое жилище его не похоже было на прочие маленькие деревянные домики. Это было каменное строение, вроде тех, которых когда-то настроили вдоволь генуэзские купцы, – с неправильными, неравной величины окнами, с железными ставнями и засовами. Этот ростовщик отличался от других ростовщиков уже тем, что мог снабдить какою угодно суммою всех, начиная от нищей старухи до расточительного придворного вельможи. Пред домом его показывались часто самые блестящие экипажи, из окон которых иногда глядела голова роскошной светской дамы. Молва, по обыкновению, разнесла, что железные сундуки его полны без счету денег, драгоценностей, бриллиантов и всяких залогов, но что, однако же, он вовсе не имел той корысти, какая свойственна другим ростовщикам. Он давал деньги охотно, распределяя, казалось, весьма выгодно сроки платежей; но какими-то арифметическими странными выкладками заставлял их восходить до непомерных процентов. Так, по крайней мере, говорила молва. Но что страннее всего и что не могло не поразить многих – это была странная судьба всех тех, которые получали от него деньги: все они оканчивали жизнь

rubles a month, morning coffee included. The widows of government clerks, in receipt of a pension, are the most substantial inhabitants of the quarter. They behave with great propriety, keep their rooms fairly clean, and talk to their female neighbors and friends of the high price of beef and cabbages. They not infrequently have a young daughter, a silent creature who has nothing to say for herself, though sometimes rather nice-looking; they have also a disgusting little dog and an old-fashioned clock with a dismally ticking pendulum. Next to them in precedence come the actors, whose salaries don't allow of their leaving Kolomna. They are rather a free and easy group, like all artists, and live for their own pleasure. Sitting in their dressing gowns they either clean a pistol or glue pieces of cardboard together to make something of use in the house, or play checkers or cards with a friend, and so they spend their mornings; they follow the same pursuits in the evening, mingling them with punch. Below these swells, these aristocrats of Kolomna, come the smaller fry, and it is as hard for the observer to reckon up all the people occupying the different corners and nooks in one room as it is to enumerate all the creatures that breed in stale vinegar. What people does one not meet there! Old women who say their prayers, old women who get drunk, old women who both get drunk and say their prayers; old women who live from hand to mouth by means that pass all understanding, who like ants drag old rags and linen from Kalinkin Bridge to the flea market, to sell them there for fifteen kopeks – in fact all the pitiful and luckless dregs of humanity whose lot not even a benevolent economist could improve.

'I have listed them so that you will understand how often people like this are driven by need to seek immediate temporary help by borrowing. And among these people a certain kind of moneylender settles, and he lends them small loans on little security and charges exorbitant interest. These petty usurers often are more heartless than the major moneylenders because they live in the midst of poverty among people dressed in rags that the rich usurer who deals only with the carriage trade never sees, and every humane feeling in them is soon extinguished. Among these usurers there was one . . . but I must not forget to mention that the events which I have begun to relate refer to the last century in the reign of our late Empress Catherine II.[2] You will realize that since then the very appearance of Kolomna and its life has altered significantly. Now, among these usurers there was a certain person, a remarkable being in every respect, who had long before settled in that part of the city. He went about in a voluminous Asiatic robe. His dark complexion bespoke his southern origin, but as to his nationality, whether he belonged to India, or Greece, or Persia, no one was certain. He was tall and of enormous height, and had a dark, haggard, scorched face, and in his large eyes there was the blaze of strange fire, and he had heavy protruding eyebrows which made him so different from all the ash-colored inhabitants of the capital. Even his house was different from the other small wooden houses. It was made of stone, of a style which Genoese merchants had once preferred. It had irregular windows of various sizes and iron shutters and bars. This usurer was different from other usurers because he was willing to lend anyone any required amount, from that needed by a penurious beggar-woman to that required by a profligate courtier. And in front of his house there were often to be seen splendid carriages, and sometimes, out of their windows, there would appear the head of an elegant lady of society. It was rumored, as usual, that his iron chests were brimming with gold, treasures, diamonds, and all sorts of pledged articles, but nevertheless, that he was not so enslaved by greed as other usurers were. He lent money avidly and the terms of payment were

---

[2] Catherine the Great (1729–1796) was of German birth, but she became thoroughly Russian and was extremely popular. Greatly influenced by the Enlightenment, she planned vast reforms which were never carried out because of the Pugachev rebellion and the French Revolution. (Translator's note)

несчастным образом. Было ли это просто людское мнение, нелепые суеверные толки или с умыслом распущенные слухи – это осталось неизвестно. Но несколько примеров, случившихся в непродолжительное время пред глазами всех, были живы и разительны.

Из среды тогдашнего аристократства скоро обратил на себя глаза юноша лучшей фамилии, отличившийся уже в молодых летах на государственном поприще, жаркий почитатель всего истинного, возвышенного, ревнитель всего, что породило искусство и ум человека, пророчивший в себе мецената. Скоро он был достойно отличен самой государыней, вверившей ему значительное место, совершенно согласное с собственными его требованиями, место, где он мог много произвести для наук и вообще для добра. Молодой вельможа окружил себя художниками, поэтами, учеными. Ему хотелось всему дать работу, все поощрить. Он предпринял на собственный счет множество полезных изданий, надавал множество заказов, объявил поощрительные призы, издержал на это кучи денег и наконец расстроился. Но, полный великодушного движенья, он не хотел отстать от своего дела, искал везде занять и наконец обратился к известному ростовщику. Сделавши значительный заем у него, этот человек в непродолжительное время изменился совершенно: стал гонителем, преследователем развивающегося ума и таланта. Во всех сочинениях стал видеть дурную сторону, толковал криво всякое слово. Тогда, на беду, случилась французская революция. Это послужило ему вдруг орудием для всех возможных гадостей. Он стал видеть во всем какое-то революционное направление, во всем ему чудились намеки. Он сделался подозрительным до такой степени, что начал наконец подозревать самого себя, стал сочинять ужасные, несправедливые доносы, наделал тьму несчастных. Само собой разумеется, что такие поступки не могли не достигнуть наконец престола. Великодушная государыня ужаснулась и, полная благородства души, украшающего венценосцев, произнесла слова, которые хотя не могли перейти к нам во всей точности, но глубокий смысл их впечатлелся в сердцах многих. Государыня заметила, что не под монархическим правлением угнетаются высокие, благородные движенья души, не там презираются и преследуются творенья ума, поэзии и художеств; что, напротив, одни монархи бывали их покровителями; что Шекспиры, Мольеры процветали под их великодушной защитой, между тем как Дант не мог найти угла в своей республиканской родине; что истинные гении возникают во время блеска и могущества государей и государств, а не во время безобразных политических явлений и терроризмов республиканских, которые доселе не подарили миру ни одного поэта; что нужно отличать поэтов-художников, ибо один только мир и прекрасную тишину низводят они в душу, а не волненье и ропот; что ученые, поэты и все производители искусств суть перлы и бриллианты в императорской короне: ими красуется и получает еще больший блеск эпоха великого государя. Словом, государыня, произнесшая сии слова, была в эту минуту божественно прекрасна. Я помню, что старики не могли об этом говорить без слез. В деле все приняли участие. К чести нашей народной гордости надобно заметить, что в русском сердце всегда обитает прекрасное чувство взять сторону угнетенного. Обманувший доверенность вельможа был наказан примерно и отставлен от места. Но наказание гораздо ужаснейшее читал он на лицах своих соотечественников. Это было решительное и всеобщее презрение. Нельзя рассказать, как страдала тщеславная душа; гордость, обманутое честолюбие, разрушившиеся надежды – все соединилось вместе, и в припадках страшного безумия и бешенства прервалась его жизнь.

Другой разительный пример произошел тоже в виду всех: из красавиц, которыми не бедна была тогда наша северная столица, одна одержала решительное первенство над всеми. Это было какое-то чудное слиянье нашей северной красоты с красотой полудня, бриллиант,

fairly stipulated, but by some devious method of figuring, he made the payments amount to an enormous rate of interest. At least, that's how rumor had it. But what was most striking of all, and that which could not fail to arouse the attention of many, was the strange fate of all those who had borrowed money from him: all came to a miserable end. Whether all this was merely the kind of thing that people said about him or some superstition-born talk or reports spread for the purpose of harming him, is not known, but several things which happened within a short time of each other, and before everybody's eyes, were remarkable and striking.

'Among the aristocracy of that day there was one young man of a fine family who quickly attracted the attention of all. While still young he had distinguished himself in court circles. He was an ardent admirer of all that was true and noble. He was a patron of all which art or the mind of man produced, and a man who gave promise of becoming a Maecenas. Soon, deservedly, he was rewarded by the Empress; she appointed him to an important office which was exactly what he wished for, and in which he could accomplish much for science and the general good. The youthful statesman surrounded himself with artists, poets, and men of learning. He desired to give work to everyone, to encourage everyone and, at his own expense, he undertook very many useful publications, placed many orders, and offered many prizes to encourage the different arts. He spent a great deal of money and finally ruined himself financially. Full of noble impulses, however, he did not want to stop his work, and he looked for a loan wherever he could find it, and finally he came to the well-known moneylender. After obtaining a loan of considerable size from him, the man changed completely in a short time. He became a persecutor and oppressor of young artists and intellectuals. He saw only the bad side in everything published, and every word he spoke perverted the truth. Unfortunately, at this time, the French Revolution took place, and this supplied him with an excuse for every sort of suspicion.[3] He began discovering a revolutionary tendency in everything; everything hinted of subversion, and he finally became so suspicious that he began even to suspect himself. He began to fabricate terrible and unjust accusations and he made scores of people miserable. Obviously, news of this behavior finally reached the throne of the Empress. The kindhearted Empress, full of the noble spirit which adorns crowned heads, was shocked. She uttered words which, despite their failure to have been preserved, have yet had the memory of their meaning impressed upon many hearts. The Empress observed that it was not under a monarchy that the high and noble impulses of souls were persecuted, not under such a government were the finest achievements of the intellect, of poetry, and of the arts condemned and persecuted; that on the contrary, the monarchs alone were their protectors, and that Shakespeare and Molière flourished under their gracious protection,[4] while Dante could not even find a spot for himself in his republican birthplace,[5] that true geniuses arose at the time when emperors and empires were at the zenith of their brilliance and power, and not at the time of monstrous political unrest and republican terror which had, up to that time, never given the world a single poet;[6] that poets must be marked for favour, for they brought peace and divine contentment, and not excitement and discontent; that learned men and poets and all producers and all those who work in the arts were, indeed, the pearls and diamonds in

[3] During the French Revolution the Czarist regime became more reactionary than ever. (Translator's note)

[4] Shakespeare flourished under the reign of the brilliant Elizabeth I. Jean Baptiste Moliere found Louis XIV a generous patron and a protector against his many enemies. (Translator's note)

[5] Dante Alighieri went into exile with the White Guelphs (a political faction) in 1302 and died in exile in Ravenna. (Translator's note)

[6] Gogol's strongly conservative point of view finds clear expression here. (Translator's note)

какой попадается на свете редко. Отец мой признавался, что никогда он не видывал во всю жизнь свою ничего подобного. Все, казалось, в ней соединилось: богатство, ум и душевная прелесть. Искателей была толпа, и в числе их замечательнее всех был князь Р., благороднейший, лучший из всех молодых людей, прекраснейший и лицом, и рыцарскими, великодушными порывами, высокий идеал романов и женщин, Грандисон во всех отношениях. Князь Р. был влюблен страстно и безумно; такая же пламенная любовь была ему ответом. Но родственникам показалась партия неровною. Родовые вотчины князя уже давно ему не принадлежали, фамилия была в опале, и плохое положенье дел его было известно всем. Вдруг князь оставляет на время столицу, будто бы с тем, чтобы поправить свои дела, и спустя непродолжительное время является окруженный пышностью и блеском неимоверным. Блистательные балы и праздники делают его известным двору. Отец красавицы становится благосклонным, и в городе разыгрывается интереснейшая свадьба. Откуда произошла такая перемена и неслыханное богатство жениха, этого не мог наверно изъяснить никто; но поговаривали стороною, что он вошел в какие-то условия с непостижимым ростовщиком и сделал у него заем. Как бы то ни было, но свадьба заняла весь город. и жених и невеста были предметом общей зависти. Всем была известна их жаркая, постоянная любовь, долгие томленья, претерпенные с обеих сторон, высокие достоинства обоих. Пламенные женщины начертывали заранее то райское блаженство, которым будут наслаждаться молодые супруги. Но вышло все иначе. В один год произошла страшная перемена в муже. Ядом подозрительной ревности, нетерпимостью и неистощимыми капризами отравился дотоле благородный и прекрасный характер. Он стал тираном и мучителем жены своей и, чего бы никто не мог предвидеть, прибегнул к самым бесчеловечным поступкам, даже побоям. В один год никто не мог узнать той женщины, которая еще недавно блистала и влекла за собою толпы покорных поклонников. Наконец, не в силах будучи выносить долее тяжелой судьбы своей, она первая заговорила о разводе. Муж пришел в бешенство при одной мысли о том. В первом движенье неистовства ворвался он к ней в комнату с ножом и, без сомнения, заколол бы ее тут же, если бы его не схватили и не удержали. В порыве исступленья и отчаянья он обратил нож на себя – и в ужаснейших муках окончил жизнь.

Кроме сих двух примеров, совершившихся в глазах всего общества, рассказывали множество случившихся в низших классах, которые почти все имели ужасный конец. Там честный, трезвый человек делался пьяницей; там купеческий приказчик обворовал своего хозяина; там извозчик, возивший несколько лет честно, за грош зарезал седока. Нельзя, чтобы такие происшествия, рассказываемые иногда не без прибавлений, не навели род какого-то невольного ужаса на скромных обитателей Коломны. Никто не сомневался о присутствии нечистой силы в этом человеке. Говорили, что он предлагал такие условия, от которых дыбом поднимались волоса и которых никогда потом не посмел несчастный передавать другому; что деньги его имеют прожигающее свойство, раскаляются сами собою и носят какие-то странные знаки... словом, много было всяких нелепых толков. И замечательно то, что все это коломенское население, весь этот мир бедных старух, мелких чиновников, мелких артистов и, словом, всей мелюзги, которую мы только поименовали, соглашались лучше терпеть и выносить последнюю крайность, нежели обратиться к страшному ростовщику; находили даже умерших от голода старух, которые лучше соглашались умертвить свое тело, нежели погубить душу. Встречаясь с ним на улице, невольно чувствовали страх. Пешеход осторожно пятился и долго еще озирался после того назад, следя пропадавшую вдали его непомерную высокую фигуру. В одном уже образе было столько необыкновенного, что всякого заставило бы невольно

the imperial crown, for they glorified and immortalized the epic which the great ruler adorned, and made it more brilliant. In short, the Empress, speaking these words, was divinely beautiful for the moment. I recall old men who could not speak of it without tears. Everyone was interested in that affair. It must be noted, to the honor of our national pride, that in the Russian's heart there is always an impulse to aid the persecuted. The statesman who had betrayed his trust was punished in an exemplary manner and degraded from his post. But a much worse punishment could be read in the faces of his countrymen: sharp and universal scorn. Nothing could describe the sufferings of this vainglorious soul: pride, frustrated ambitions, destroyed aspirations, all joined together, and he died in a horrible attack of raving madness.

'Another striking example also occurred in the sight of all. Among the beauties in which our northern capital is decidedly not poor, one completely surpassed all the others. Her beauty was a blend of our northern charm with the charm of the south, a diamond only rarely seen in the world. My father told me that during his whole life he had never seen any woman like her. Everything seemed combined in her – wealth, intelligence, and spiritual charm. Throngs of admirers surrounded her, and the most distinguished of them all was Prince R., the most noble and best of all young men, the handsomest of face and in chivalrous character, the great ideal of novels and women, a Grandison[7] in every respect. Prince R. was passionately, desperately in love, and his love was returned. But the girl's parents did not approve of the match. The Prince's ancestral estates had long before gone out of his hands and his family was in disfavor. Everyone knew of the sad state of his affairs. The prince suddenly left the capital, leaving the impression that he was bent upon improving his affairs, and he reappeared not long afterward surrounded with luxury and remarkable splendor. Those at court came to know him because of his brilliant balls and parties. The father of the beauty removed his objection, and the town soon witnessed one of the most fashionable weddings. What the real reason was for this change in fortune, and what the source was for this enormous wealth, no one fully knew, but it was whispered that he had made a deal with the mysterious usurer, and that he had borrowed money from him. Be that as it may, the wedding occupied the whole town, and the bride and the bridegroom were the objects of general envy. Everyone knew of their warm and devoted love, how long they had endured persecution from every quarter, the great virtue of both. Romantic women already spoke of the heavenly happiness which the young couple would enjoy. But it turned out very differently. In one year a frightful change took place in the husband. His character, which until that time had been so fine and noble, was poisoned with jealous suspicions, intolerance, and inexorable caprice. He became a tyrant and torturer of his wife, which no one could have foreseen, and he indulged in the most abominable acts, even beating her. In only a year no one recognized the woman who only so recently had been so radiant and who had drawn around her crowds of submissive admirers. Finally, finding it impossible to endure her misery, she suggested a divorce, but at the mere suggestion of such a thing her husband flew into a rage. In the first outpouring of emotion he stormed into her room, and had he not been seized and restrained, he would undoubtedly have murdered her then and there. In a fit of madness and despair he turned the knife against himself, and he ended his life in the most horrible suffering.

'In addition to these two instances which occurred before the eyes of the whole world, there were many stories told of such happenings among the lower classes, nearly all of which ended tragically. An honest, sober man became a drunkard; a shopkeeper's assistant stole from his

---

[7] Hero of Sir Charles Grandison, third novel of Samuel Richardson (1689–1761), who was designed to portray the perfect gentleman. (Translator's note)

приписать ему сверхъестественное существование. Эти сильные черты, врезанные так глубоко, как не случается у человека; этот горячий бронзовый цвет лица; эта непомерная гущина бровей, невыносимые, страшные глаза, даже самые широкие складки его азиатской одежды – все, казалось, как будто говорило, что пред страстями, двигавшимися в этом теле, были бледны все страсти других людей. Отец мой всякий раз останавливался неподвижно, когда встречал его, и всякий раз не мог удержаться, чтобы не произнести: «Дьявол, совершенный дьявол!» Но надобно вас поскорее познакомить с моим отцом, который, между прочим, есть настоящий сюжет этой истории.

Отец мой был человек замечательный во многих отношениях. Это был художник, каких мало, одно из тех чуд, которых извергает из непочатого лона своего только одна Русь, художник-самоучка, отыскавший сам в душе своей, без учителей и школы, правила и законы, увлеченный только одною жаждою усовершенствованья и шедший, по причинам, может быть, неизвестным ему самому, одною только указанною из души дорогою; одно из тех самородных чуд, которых часто современники честят обидным словом «невежи» и которые не охлаждаются от охулений и собственных неудач, получают только новые рвенья и силы, и уже далеко в душе своей уходят от тех произведений, за которые получили титло невежи. Высоким внутренним инстинктом почуял он присутствие мысли в каждом предмете; постигнул сам собой истинное значение слова «историческая живопись»; постигнул, почему простую головку, простой портрет Рафаэля, Леонардо да Винчи, Тициана, Корреджио можно назвать историческою живописью и почему огромная картина исторического содержания все-таки будет tableau de genre, несмотря на все притязанья художника на историческую живопись. И внутреннее чувство, и собственное убеждение обратили кисть его к христианским предметам, высшей и последней ступени высокого. У него не было честолюбия или раздражительности, так неотлучной от характера многих художников. Это был твердый характер, честный, прямой человек, даже грубый, покрытый снаружи несколько черствой корою, не без некоторой гордости в душе, отзывавшийся о людях вместе и снисходительно и резко. «Что на них глядеть, – обыкновенно говорил он, – ведь я не для них работаю. Не в гостиную понесу я мои картины, их поставят в церковь. Кто поймет меня – поблагодарит, не поймет – все-таки помолится Богу. Светского человека нечего винить, что он не смыслит живописи; зато он смыслит в картах, знает толк в хорошем вине, в лошадях, – зачем знать больше барину? Еще, пожалуй, как попробует того да другого да пойдет умничать, тогда и житья от него не будет! Всякому свое, всякий пусть занимается своим. По мне, уж лучше тот человек, который говорит прямо, что он не знает толку, нежели тот, который корчит лицемера, говорит, будто бы знает то, чего не знает, и только гадит да портит». Он работал за небольшую плату, то есть за плату, которая была нужна ему только для поддержанья семейства и для доставленья возможности трудиться. Кроме того, он ни в каком случае не отказывался помочь другому и протянуть руку помощи бедному художнику; веровал простой, благочестивой верою предков, и оттого, может быть, на изображенных им лицах являлось само собою то высокое выраженье, до которого не могли докопаться блестящие таланты. Наконец постоянством своего труда и неуклонностью начертанного себе пути он стал даже приобретать уважение со стороны тех, которые честили его невежей и доморощенным самоучкой. Ему давали беспрестанно заказы в церкви, и работа у него не переводилась. Одна из работ заняла его сильно. Не помню уже, в чем именно состоял сюжет ее, знаю только то – на картине нужно было поместить духа тьмы. Долго думал он над тем, какой дать ему образ; ему хотелось осуществить в лице его все тяжелое, гнетущее человека. При таких размышлениях иногда проносился в голове его

employer; an honest cabby cut the throat of his passenger for a few kopeks. Naturally such incidents, often told with embellishment, inspired horror in the simple hearts of Kolomna's inhabitants. No one at all doubted that the devil resided in this man. They said that he imposed conditions on a man which made the hair rise on one's head and which the poor wretch never dared to repeat to anyone else; that his money had the power to attract, possessed the power of becoming incandescent, and that it bore strange symbols. In short, there were many fantastic tales which circulated about him. It is worth noting that the entire population of Kolomna, the entire world of poor old women, petty officials, petty artists, and all those insignificant people we earlier mentioned, agreed that they would endure anything and suffer any misery rather than go to the terrible usurer. There were even old women who had died of hunger, preferring to starve to death rather than lose their souls. Anyone who met him in the street felt an involuntary fear. Pedestrians were careful to move away from him as he walked, and for a long time they gazed at the receding tall figure. Even in his face there was so much that was strange that they could not help but ascribe to him supernatural powers. The powerful features, so deeply chiseled that they were unlike those in any other man; the glowing bronze of his complexion; the incredible thickness of his eyebrows; those intolerable, terrible eyes; even the wide folds of his Asiatic robe – everything seemed to note that all the passions within other men paled when compared to the passions which raged within him. Whenever my father met him he stopped short, and he could not help but say, 'A devil, a real devil!' But I must, as speedily as possible, introduce you to my father, who is the true hero of this story.

'In many respects my father was a remarkable man. He was an artist of unusual ability, a self-taught artist who without teachers or schools discovered in his own soul the rules and laws of art, and, for reasons he did not understand, motivated only by his passion for perfection, he walked on the path which his spirit pointed out to him. He was one of those natural geniuses whom their contemporaries so often honor with the contemptuous word 'ignorant' and who are not disheartened by sneers or their own lack of success, who gain fresh strength and are, constantly, in their own minds, far beyond those works because of which they had earned the title 'ignorant.' Through some lofty and basic instinct, he perceived the presence of a soul in every object. He grasped, with his untutored mind, the true significance of the words 'historical painting.' He understood why a simple head, a simple portrait by Raphael, Leonardo da Vinci, Titian, or Correggio could be appreciated as an historical painting, while a huge picture of historical subjects remained, nevertheless, nothing more than a genre picture, despite all the artist's pretensions to historical painting. And this inherent instinct and personal conviction turned his brush to Christian subjects, the highest and loftiest degree of the sublime. He was devoid of vanity and irritability, which are so much a part of the character of many artists. His character was strong. He was honorable, frank, even a man with rough manners, covered with a hard shell, but not lacking in pride, and he always expressed himself about people both gently and scornfully. 'What are they looking at?' he usually said. 'I am not working for them. I don't take my pictures to the tavern! He who understands me will thank me. The worldly man cannot be held at fault because he comprehends nothing of painting; he understands cards, and he knows wine and horses – what more need a gentleman know? If he tries one thing and then another, he becomes too much to endure. Let every man concern himself with his own business. So far as I am concerned, I much prefer a man who honestly admits that he does not understand a thing to one who pretends to know something he really does not know and is simply base and intolerable.' He worked for very little pay, that is to say, for just enough with which to keep his family and to buy the tools necessary for his work. Further, under no circumstances did he ever refuse to help

образ таинственного ростовщика, и он думал невольно: «Вот бы с кого мне следовало написать дьявола». Судите же об его изумлении, когда один раз, работая в своей мастерской, услышал он стук в дверь, и вслед за тем прямо вошел к нему ужасный ростовщик. Он не мог не почувствовать какой-то внутренней дрожи, которая пробежала невольно по его телу.

– Ты художник? – сказал он без всяких церемоний моему отцу.

– Художник, – сказал отец в недоуменье, ожидая, что будет далее.

– Хорошо. Нарисуй с меня портрет. Я, может быть, скоро умру, детей у меня нет; но я не хочу умереть совершенно, я хочу жить. Можешь ли ты нарисовать такой портрет, чтобы был совершенно как живой?

Отец мой подумал: «Чего лучше? – он сам просится в дьяволы ко мне на картину». Дал слово. Они уговорились во времени и цене, и на другой же день, схвативши палитру и кисти, отец мой уже был у него. Высокий двор, собаки, железные двери и затворы, дугообразные окна, сундуки, покрытые старинными коврами, и, наконец, сам необыкновенный хозяин, севший неподвижно перед ним, – все это произвело на него странное впечатление. Окна, как нарочно, были заставлены и загромождены снизу так, что давали свет только с одной верхушки. «Черт побери, как теперь хорошо осветилось его лицо!» – сказал он про себя и принялся жадно писать, как бы опасаясь, чтобы как-нибудь не исчезло счастливое освещенье. «Экая сила! – повторил он про себя. – Если я хотя вполовину изображу его так, как он есть теперь, он убьет всех моих святых и ангелов; они побледнеют пред ним. Какая дьявольская сила! он у меня просто выскочит из полотна, если только хоть немного буду верен натуре. Какие необыкновенные черты!» – повторял он беспрестанно, усугубляя рвенье, и уже видел сам, как стали переходить на полотно некоторые черты. Но чем более он приближался к ним, тем более чувствовал какое-то тягостное, тревожное чувство, непонятное себе самому. Однако же, несмотря на то, он положил себе преследовать с буквальною точностью всякую незаметную черту и выраженье. Прежде всего занялся он отделкою глаз. В этих глазах столько было силы, что, казалось, нельзя бы и помыслить передать их точно, как были в натуре. Однако же во что бы то ни стало он решился доискаться в них последней мелкой черты и оттенка, постигнуть их тайну... Но как только начал он входить и углубляться в них кистью, в душе его возродилось такое странное отвращенье, такая непонятная тягость, что он должен был на несколько времени бросить кисть и потом приниматься вновь. Наконец уже не мог он более выносить, он чувствовал, что эти глаза вонзались ему в душу и производили в ней тревогу непостижимую. На другой, на третий день это было еще сильнее. Ему сделалось страшно. Он бросил кисть и сказал наотрез, что не может более писать с него. Надобно было видеть, как изменился при этих словах странный ростовщик. Он бросился к нему в ноги и молил кончить портрет, говоря, что от сего зависит судьба его и существование в мире, что уже он тронул своею кистью его живые черты, что если он передаст их верно, жизнь его сверхъестественною силою удержится в портрете, что он чрез то не умрет совершенно, что ему нужно присутствовать в мире. Отец мой почувствовал ужас от таких слов: они ему показались до того странны и страшны, что он бросил и кисти и палитру и бросился опрометью вон из комнаты.

Мысль о том тревожила его весь день и всю ночь, а поутру он получил от ростовщика портрет, который принесла ему какая-то женщина, единственное существо, бывшее у него в услугах, объявившая тут же, что хозяин не хочет портрета, не дает за него ничего и присылает назад. Ввечеру того же дни узнал он, что ростовщик умер и что собираются уже хоронить его по обрядам его религии. Все это казалось ему неизъяснимо странно. А между тем с этого времени оказалась в характере его ощутительная перемена: он чувствовал

anyone or to offer assistance to a destitute artist. He believed with the simple, reverent faith of his ancestors, and, because of that, a lofty expression appeared in all the faces he painted, an expression which even the most brilliant artists could not reproduce. Finally, by dedicated labor and perseverance in the path he had marked out for himself, he began to win the respect of those who had before derided his amateur status and his self-taught talent. They constantly commissioned him to do churches, and he was never without employment. In particular, one of his paintings interested him very strongly. What its precise subject was I can't recall; I know only that he had to represent the Prince of Darkness in it. For a long time, he pondered over what kind of form to present him in because he wanted to represent in that face all that weighs down and oppresses man. And while involved with these thoughts, there suddenly raced through his mind the image of the mysterious moneylender, and he could not help but say, 'That's who ought to be the model for the devil!' Imagine his surprise when, while at work in his studio one day, he heard a knock at the door and immediately the same terrible usurer entered the room. My father could not repress a cold chill which ran through every limb.

" 'Are you an artist?' he asked my father quickly.

" 'I am,' answered my surprised father, wondering what was to come next.

" 'Good. Paint my portrait. It is possible that I may be dead soon. I have no children, and I don't want to die completely. I wish to live. Can you do a portrait that will look as though it were alive?'

'My father thought, 'What could be better? He offers himself as the devil I'm painting in my picture.' So he agreed. They came to terms about time and price, and on the very next day, my father took his palette and his brushes and went to his house. The high walls encircling the court-yard, dogs, iron doors and locks, arched windows, chests draped with strange rugs, and finally, the singular owner himself who was seated motionless before him: all this produced a strange impression upon him. The lower half of the windows were covered so that only from the top of the windows was the light admitted. 'Damn it. How remarkably well his face is lighted up!' he said to himself, and he began to paint feverishly, as though he were afraid that the favorable light would somehow disappear. 'What power!' he said to himself. 'If I even capture half of how he appears now, all my other works will be surpassed. He'll just leap from the canvas even if I capture only a little of his nature. What remarkable features!' he kept repeating to himself, redoubling his energy, and soon he himself began to see how certain traits were already appearing on the canvas. But the closer he approached them the more he became aware of an oppressive uneasiness which was beyond his explanation. Despite this, he began to reproduce them exactly as they were. But he made up his mind, at any price, to discover their most minute characteristics and shades and to penetrate their secret . . . But as soon as he painted them with redoubled efforts, there arose in him such a terrible revulsion, such a feeling of inexplicable oppression, that he was forced to put aside his brush for a while and then to begin afresh. At last he could endure it no longer. He felt as though those eyes pierced into his very soul and filled it with intolerable alarm. On the second and third days this feeling became stronger. He became frightened. He threw down his brush and bluntly announced that he could paint no longer. You should have seen how the sinister usurer's face changed at these words. He fell at his feet, begged him to finish the portrait, pleading that his fate and his very existence in the world depended on it, that he had already captured his promi-nent features, and if he would accurately reproduce them his life would be preserved in some supernatural manner in the portrait, and then he would not die completely, for it was necessary for him to remain in the world. These words terrified my father; they seemed so strange and so terrible that he discarded his brushes and his palette and dashed out of the room.

неспокойное, тревожное состояние, которому сам не мог понять причины, и скоро произвел он такой поступок, которого бы никто не мог от него ожидать. С некоторого времени труды одного из учеников его начали привлекать внимание небольшого круга знатоков и любителей. Отец мой всегда видел в нем талант и оказывал ему за то свое особенное расположение. Вдруг почувствовал он к нему зависть. Всеобщее участие и толки о нем сделались ему невыносимы. Наконец, к довершенью досады, узнает он, что ученику его предложили написать картину для вновь отстроенной богатой церкви. Это его взорвало. «Нет, не дам же молокососу восторжествовать! – говорил он. – Рано, брат, вздумал стариков сажать в грязь! Еще, слава Богу, есть у меня силы. Вот мы увидим, кто кого скорее посадит в грязь». И прямодушный, честный в душе человек употребил интриги и происки, которыми дотоле всегда гнушался; добился наконец того, что на картину объявлен был конкурс и другие художники могли войти также с своими работами. После чего заперся он в свою комнату и с жаром принялся за кисть. Казалось, все свои силы, всего себя хотел он сюда собрать. И точно, это вышло одно из лучших его произведений. Никто не сомневался, чтобы не за ним осталось первенство. Картины были представлены, и все прочие показались пред нею как ночь пред днем. Как вдруг один из присутствовавших членов, если не ошибаюсь, духовная особа, сделал замечание, поразившее всех. «В картине художника, точно, есть много таланта, – сказал он, – но нет святости в лицах; есть даже, напротив того, что-то демонское в глазах, как будто бы рукою художника водило нечистое чувство». Все взглянули и не могли не убедиться в истине сих слов. Отец мой бросился вперед к своей картине, как бы с тем, чтобы поверить самому такое обидное замечание, и с ужасом увидел, что он всем почти фигурам придал глаза ростовщика. Они так глядели демонски-сокрушительно, что он сам невольно вздрогнул. Картина была отвергнута, и он должен был, к неописанной своей досаде, услышать, что первенство осталось за его учеником. Невозможно было описать того бешенства, с которым он возвратился домой. Он чуть не прибил мать мою, разогнал детей, переломал кисти и мольберт, схватил со стены портрет ростовщика, потребовал ножа и велел разложить огонь в камине, намереваясь изрезать его в куски и сжечь. На этом движенье застал его вошедший в комнату приятель, живописец, как и он, весельчак, всегда довольный собой, не заносившийся никакими отдаленными желаньями, работавший весело все, что попадалось, и еще веселей того принимавшийся за обед и пирушку.

– Что ты делаешь, что собираешься жечь? – сказал он и подошел к портрету. – Помилуй, это одно из самых лучших твоих произведений. Это ростовщик, который недавно умер; да это совершеннейшая вещь. Ты ему просто попал не в бровь, а в самые глаза залез. Так в жизнь никогда не глядели глаза, как они глядят у тебя.

– А вот я посмотрю, как они будут глядеть в огне, – сказал отец, сделавши движенье швырнуть его в камин.

– Остановись, ради Бога! – сказал приятель, удержав его, – отдай его уж лучше мне, если он тебе до такой степени колет глаз.

Отец сначала упорствовал, наконец согласился, и весельчак, чрезвычайно довольный своим приобретением, утащил портрет с собою.

По уходе его отец мой вдруг почувствовал себя спокойнее. Точно как будто бы вместе с портретом свалилась тяжесть с его души. Он сам изумился своему злобному чувству, своей зависти и явной перемене своего характера. Рассмотревши поступок свой, он опечалился душою и не без внутренней скорби произнес:

– Нет, это Бог наказал меня; картина моя поделом понесла посрамленье. Она была замышлена с тем, чтобы погубить брата. Демонское чувство зависти водило моею кистью, демонское чувство должно было и отразиться в ней.

'All day and all night he was vexed by what had happened, but on the next morning he received the portrait from the moneylender. It was brought by a woman who was the only human being the usurer employed, and she declared that her master did not want the portrait, that he would not pay for it, and that he had, therefore, sent it back. He learned that the usurer had died on the evening of the very same day, and that preparations were being made for him to be buried according to the rites of his religion. This seemed inexplicably strange, but from that day on there was a decided change in my father's character. An uneasy and restless feeling which he could not explain possessed him and, soon after, he did something which no one would have expected of him. For some time the paintings of one of his pupils had attracted the attention of a small group of connoisseurs and art lovers. My father appreciated his talent and because of that had always been very helpful. Suddenly, and the conversations which centered about it became unbearable to my father. Finally, to heighten his annoyance, he learned that a rich church which had recently been rebuilt had commissioned him to do a picture. He was enraged. 'No, this youngster must not be permitted to defeat me!' he said. 'It's too soon for you, my friend, to think of relegating the old men to the gutters. Thank God I am not without strength! We will see who will defeat whom!' And this straightforward and honorable man planned intrigues and schemes which he had hitherto detested. Finally, he succeeded in arranging a competition for the commission so that other artists were offered the opportunity of entering their own works. And then he shut himself up in his room and began painting feverishly. It was as if he wanted to use all his strength for this one occasion, and, indeed, it turned out to be one of his best works. No one doubted that he would win. The pictures were exhibited, and all the others were as night to day compared to his. Then suddenly one of the members present (If I am not mistaken, a person in holy orders) said something which surprised everyone: 'Certainly there is much talent in the picture of this artist,' he said, 'but there is nothing holy in the faces; on the contrary, in fact, there is even something demoniacal in the eyes, as though some evil feeling had guided the artist's hand.' And everyone looked at the picture and could not help admitting that these words were true. My father rushed up to his picture to see for himself whether this offensive remark was justified, and with horror he saw that the usurer's eyes were contained in nearly all the figures. They gazed with such a devastatingly diabolical gaze that he could not help but shudder. The picture was rejected and, to his great vexation, he was forced to hear that his pupil had won the competition. It is impossible to describe the degree of fury in him when he returned home. He almost murdered my mother, he drove all the children away, he smashed his brushes and his easels; and he ripped the usurer's portrait from its place on the wall, demanded a knife, and ordered a fire to be built in the fireplace, intending to slash it to pieces and to burn it. An artist friend caught him in the act upon entering the room. He was a jovial fellow, like my father, who was content, aspired to nothing unobtainable, did anything that came to hand happily, and was especially gay at dinner or at parties.

"'What are you doing? What are you going to burn?' he asked, walking up to the portrait. 'Why, this is one of your best works. It's the usurer who recently died. It's a very fine painting. You didn't cease your efforts until you captured his very eyes. Even in life eyes never look like that.'

"'Well, I'll see how they look in the fire!' said my father, seizing the portrait to fling it into the flames.

'For God's sake, stop!' shouted his friend, restraining him. 'If it offends you so much, give it to me.' My father began to insist on his way at first, but at length he gave in, and his jovial friend, pleased with his new acquisition, carried the portrait home with him.

"My father was calmer after he had left; it was as if that which oppressed him was removed with the portrait. He was himself surprised at his previous evil feelings, his jealousy, and the apparent change in his character. Reviewing what he had done, he grew sad and, not without

Он немедленно отправился искать бывшего ученика своего, обнял его крепко, просил у него прощенья и старался сколько мог загладить пред ним вину свою. Работы его вновь потекли по-прежнему безмятежно; но задумчивость стала показываться чаще на его лице. Он больше молился, чаще бывал молчалив и не выражался так резко о людях; самая грубая наружность его характера как-то умягчилась. Скоро одно обстоятельство еще более потрясло его. Он уже давно не видался с товарищем своим, выпросившим у него портрет. Уже собирался было идти его проведать, как вдруг он сам вошел неожиданно в его комнату. После нескольких слов и вопросов с обеих сторон он сказал:

– Ну, брат, недаром ты хотел сжечь портрет. Черт его побери, в нем есть что-то странное... Я ведьмам не верю, но, воля твоя: в нем сидит нечистая сила...

– Как? – сказал отец мой.

– А так, что с тех пор как повесил я к себе его в комнату, почувствовал тоску такую... точно как будто бы хотел кого-то зарезать. В жизнь мою я не знал, что такое бессонница, а теперь испытал не только бессонницу, но сны такие... я и сам не умею сказать, сны ли это или что другое: точно домовой тебя душит, и все мерещится проклятый старик. Одним словом, не могу рассказать тебе моего состояния. Подобного со мной никогда не бывало. Я бродил как шальной все эти дни: чувствовал какую-то боязнь, неприятное ожиданье чего-то. Чувствую, что не могу сказать никому веселого и искреннего слова; точно как будто возле меня сидит шпион какой-нибудь. И только с тех пор, как отдал портрет племяннику, который напросился на него, почувствовал, что с меня вдруг будто какой-то камень свалился с плеч: вдруг почувствовал себя веселым, как видишь. Ну, брат, состряпал ты черта!

Во время этого рассказа отец мой слушал его с неразвлекаемым вниманием и наконец спросил:

– И портрет теперь у твоего племянника?

– Куда у племянника! не выдержал, – сказал весельчак, – знать, душа самого ростовщика переселилась в него: он выскакивает из рам, расхаживает по комнате; и то, что рассказывает племянник, просто уму непонятно. Я бы принял его за сумасшедшего, если бы отчасти не испытал сам. Он его продал какому-то собирателю картин, да и тот не вынес его и тоже кому-то сбыл с рук.

Этот рассказ произвел сильное впечатление на моего отца. Он задумался не в шутку, впал в ипохондрию и наконец совершенно уверился в том, что кисть его послужила дьявольским орудием, что часть жизни ростовщика перешла в самом деле как-нибудь в портрет и тревожит теперь людей, внушая бесовские побуждения, совращая художника с пути, порождая страшные терзанья зависти, и проч., и проч. Три случившиеся вслед за тем несчастия, три внезапные смерти – жены, дочери и малолетнего сына – почел он небесною казнью себе и решился непременно оставить свет. Как только минуло мне девять лет, он поместил меня в Академию художеств и, расплатясь с своими должниками, удалился в одну уединенную обитель, где скоро постригся в монахи. Там строгостью жизни, неусыпным соблюдением всех монастырских правил он изумил всю братью. Настоятель монастыря, узнавши об искусстве его кисти, требовал от него написать главный образ в церковь. Но смиренный брат сказал наотрез, что он недостоин взяться за кисть, что она осквернена, что трудом и великими жертвами он должен прежде очистить свою душу, чтобы удостоиться приступить к такому делу. Его не хотели принуждать. Он сам увеличивал для себя, сколько было возможно, строгость монастырской жизни. Наконец уже и она становилась ему недостаточною и не довольно строгою. Он удалился с благословенья настоятеля в пустынь, чтоб быть совершенно одному. Там из древесных ветвей выстроил он себе келью, питался одними сырыми

inward sorrow, he said, 'It was God who punished me! My picture deserved disgrace. It was intended to ruin a fellow man. A fiendish feeling of envy controlled my brush and the fiendish feeling was reflected in what it produced!' Immediately he went out to find his former pupil, and he embraced him warmly and begged his forgiveness and, as far as possible, he did all he could to assuage the wrongs he had committed. His work continued as undisturbed as it had once been, but his face was more frequently thoughtful. He prayed more often, he became more taciturn, he spoke less negatively about people, and even the coarse exterior of his character was somehow changed. But something soon happened which disturbed him more than ever. For some time he had seen nothing of the friend who had begged him for the portrait. He had been contemplating looking him up when he suddenly appeared in my father's room, and, after the usual words exchanged between friends, he said, 'Well, friend, there was a reason why you wished to burn that portrait. Damn it, there's something strange about it! . . . I don't believe in sorcery, but, and I beg your pardon, there's something evil in it. . .'

" 'What is it?' asked my father.

" 'Well, from the instant I hung it up in my room, I've been so depressed, as if I was thinking of murdering someone. Never before did I know what insomnia was, but now I suffer not only insomnia, but from terrible dreams! . . . I hardly know whether they can be called dreams or something else. It's as if a domovoi was strangling me, and the old man appears to me in my sleep. In short, I simply can't describe my state of mind to you. Nothing of the sort ever happened to me before. I have been wandering about in misery all this time – obsessed with fear, expecting something awful. I felt as if I couldn't say a friendly word, a sincere word, to anyone. It's as if a spy were watching over me. And only after I had given that portrait to my nephew who asked for it did I feel as if a stone had been rolled from my shoulders. Immediately I felt as happy as you see me now. Well, brother, you made the devil!'

"My father listened to this story with absolute attention, and he finally asked, 'Does your nephew now have the portrait?'

" 'My nephew, no! He couldn't stand it!' said the jovial fellow. 'Do you know that the soul of that usurer is in that portrait? He leaps out of the frame and walks about the room, and the story my nephew tells of him is beyond comprehension. I would have thought him a lunatic if I myself had not experienced some of it. He sold it to an art collector who couldn't stand it either and who finally got rid of it by getting someone else to take it.' "The story produced a deep impression on my father, and now he was seriously worried, oppressed with melancholy, and finally he became convinced that his brush had been a tool of the devil and that a part of the usurer's life had somehow or other really passed into the portrait and was now plaguing people, inspiring diabolical ideas, beguiling artists from the righteous path, inflicting the horrible torments of jealousy, and so forth. Three catastrophes which happened afterwards, the sudden deaths of his wife and his daughter and his infant son, he regarded as divine punishment, and he firmly resolved to remove himself from the world. As soon as I reached nine years of age he placed me in an art academy and, paying his debts, he retired to a lonely monastery where he soon took the vows. There he amazed everyone with the austerity of his life and his absolute observance of all the monastic rules. The prior of the monastery ordered him to paint the principal, but he refused, noting that he was unworthy of touching a brush, that it had been contaminated, that he must first purify his spirit with hard work and great sacrifice before he would deem himself worthy of undertaking such a task. They did not want to force the issue. He increased the rigors of monastic life as much as possible until even this life no longer satisfied him because it did not demand sufficient austerity. With the approval of the prior, he retired into the wilderness so that

кореньями, таскал на себе камни с места на место, стоял от восхода до заката солнечного на одном и том же месте с поднятыми к небу руками, читая беспрерывно молитвы. Словом, изыскивал, казалось, все возможные степени терпенья и того непостижимого самоотверженья, которому примеры можно разве найти в одних житиях святых. Таким образом долго, в продолжение нескольких лет, изнурял он свое тело, подкрепляя его в то же время живительною силою молитвы. Наконец в один день пришел он в обитель и сказал твердо настоятелю: «Теперь я готов. Если Богу угодно, я совершу свой труд». Предмет, взятый им, было Рождество Иисуса. Целый год сидел он за ним, не выходя из своей кельи, едва питая себя суровой пищей, молясь беспрестанно. По истечении года картина была готова. Это было, точно, чудо кисти. Надобно знать, что ни братья, ни настоятель не имели больших сведений в живописи, но все были поражены необыкновенной святостью фигур. Чувство божественного смиренья и кротости в лице Пречистой Матери, склонившейся над Младенцем, глубокий разум в очах Божественного Младенца, как будто уже что-то прозревающих вдали, торжественное молчанье пораженных божественным чудом царей, повергнувшихся к ногам Его, и, наконец, святая, невыразимая тишина, обнимающая всю картину, – все это предстало в такой согласной силе и могуществе красоты, что впечатление было магическое. Вся братья повергласть на колена пред новым образом, и умиленный настоятель произнес: «Нет, нельзя человеку с помощью одного человеческого искусства произвести такую картину: святая, высшая сила водила твоею кистью, и благословенье небес почило на труде твоем».

В это время окончил я свое ученье в Академии, получил золотую медаль и вместе с нею радостную надежду на путешествие в Италию – лучшую мечту двадцатилетнего художника. Мне оставалось только проститься с моим отцом, с которым уже двенадцать лет я расстался. Признаюсь, даже самый образ его давно исчезнул из моей памяти. Я уже несколько наслышался о суровой святости его жизни и заранее воображал встретить черствую наружность отшельника, чуждого всему в мире, кроме своей кельи и молитвы, изнуренного, высохшего от вечного поста и бденья. Но как же я изумился, когда предстал предо мною прекрасный, почти божественный старец! И следов измождения не было заметно на его лице: оно сияло светлостью небесного веселия. Белая, как снег, борода и тонкие, почти воздушные волосы такого же серебристого цвета рассыпались картинно по груди и по складкам его черной рясы и падали до самого вервия, которым опоясывалась его убогая монашеская одежда; но более всего изумительно было для меня услышать из уст его такие слова и мысли об искусстве, которое, признаюсь, я долго буду хранить в душе и желал бы искренно, чтобы всякий мой собрат сделал то же.

– Я ждал тебя, сын мой, – сказал он, когда я подошел к его благословенью. – Тебе предстоит путь, по которому отныне потечет жизнь твоя. Путь твой чист, не совратись с него. У тебя есть талант; талант есть драгоценнейший дар Бога – не погуби его. Исследуй, изучай все, что ни видишь, покори всё кисти, но во всем умей находить внутреннюю мысль и пуще всего старайся постигнуть высокую тайну созданья. Блажен избранник, владеющий ею. Нет ему низкого предмета в природе. В ничтожном художник-создатель так же велик, как и в великом; в презренном у него уже нет презренного, ибо сквозит невидимо сквозь него прекрасная душа создавшего, и презренное уже получило высокое выражение, ибо протекло сквозь чистилище его души. Намек о божественном, небесном рае заключен для человека в искусстве, и по тому одному оно уже выше всего. И во сколько раз торжественный покой выше всякого волненья мирского; во сколько раз творенье выше разрушенья; во сколько раз ангел одной только чистой невинностью светлой души своей выше всех несметных сил и гордых страстей сатаны, – во столько раз выше всего,

he could be absolutely alone. And there he built a hut of tree branches, and he ate only uncooked roots, and he dragged a large stone from place to place, and he stood on the same spot with his hands lifted to heaven from the time the sun went up till the time it went down, and, without stop, he recited his prayers. In brief, he experienced, it seems, every possible degree of suffering and pitiless self-abnegation, examples of which can only be found in some Lives of the Saints. In this manner, he long – for several years – exhausted his body and strengthened it at the same time only through fervent prayer. At last, one day he returned to the monastery and firmly said to the prior, 'I am ready now. If God wills, I shall do my task.' And he selected for his subject the birth of Christ. And he worked on it for a whole year without ever leaving his cell, barely sustaining himself with coarse food and praying incessantly. The picture was finished at the end of the year. It was a remarkable achievement. It should be understood that neither the prior nor the monks knew much about painting, but they were all struck by the wonderful holiness of the figures. The expression of divine humility and gentleness on the face of the Holy Mother as she bent over the Child; the profound intelligence in the eyes of the Holy Child, as though they perceived something from afar; the triumphant silence of the Magi, amazed by the Divine Miracle as they prostrated themselves at His feet, and finally, the ineffable tranquillity which pervaded the entire picture – all this was presented with such harmonious strength and great beauty that the impression it created was magical. All of the brethren fell on their knees before the new icon, and the deeply moved prior said, 'No, it is impossible for any artist to produce such a picture solely with the aid of human art alone: your brush was guided by a holy and divine power, and heaven's blessing rested upon your labours!'

"At that time, I had just finished my education at the Academy and had been awarded a gold medal, and with it the joyful hope of going to Italy – the greatest dream of a twenty-year-old artist. I had only to say goodbye to my father whom I had not seen for twelve years. I admit that I had quite forgotten even what he looked like. I had heard some comment about his austerity, and I expected to meet a recluse of rough exterior, a man who had become estranged from everything in the world but his cell and his prayers, a man who was worn out and shriveled from eternal fasting and penance. How great was my surprise when I beheld before me a handsome, almost inspired old man! And on his face there was no trace of exhaustion. It shone with the light of heavenly joy. His beard was white as snow, and his thin, almost transparent hair, of the same silvery hue, fell picturesquely over his breast, and on the folds of his black frock, to the rope which encircled his humble, monastic garb. But still more surprising to me was to hear such words and thoughts about art which, I confess, I will long keep in my mind, and I sincerely wish that all of my friends would do the same.

" 'I awaited you, my son,' he said as I approached him for his blessing. The path in which, henceforth, your life is to flow awaits you. It is clear. Do not desert it. You have talent; do not destroy it, for it is the most priceless of God's gifts. Search, study everything you see, master everything, but in everything try to discover the hidden meaning and, above all else, endeavor to attain comprehension of the great mystery of creation. Blessed is he who masters that! For him there is nothing low in nature. A creative artist is as great in lowly things as he is in great ones; in the despicable there is nothing for him to despise, for the glorious spirit of the Creator imbues it, and what is despicable receives glory because it has passed through the purifying fire of His spirit. An intimation of God's heavenly paradise is found in art, and it is for this reason that art is higher than all else. As life spent in triumphant contemplation of God is nobler than a life involved with earthly turmoil, so is the lofty creation of art higher than anything else on earth. As much as the angel is by the purity and innocence of its bright spirit above all invisible

что ни есть на свете, высокое созданье искусства. Все принеси ему в жертву и возлюби его всею страстью. Не страстью, дышащей земным вожделением, но тихой небесной страстью; без нее не властен человек возвыситься от земли и не может дать чудных звуков успокоения. Ибо для успокоения и примирения всех нисходит в мир высокое созданье искусства. Оно не может поселить ропота в душе, но звучащей молитвой стремится вечно к Богу. Но есть минуты, темные минуты... Он остановился, и я заметил, что вдруг омрачился светлый лик его, как будто бы на него набежало какое-то мгновенное облако.

– Есть одно происшествие в моей жизни, – сказал он. – Доныне я не могу понять, что был тот странный образ, с которого я написал изображение. Это было точно какое-то дьявольское явление. Я знаю, свет отвергает существованье дьявола, и потому не буду говорить о нем. Но скажу только, что я с отвращением писал его, я не чувствовал в то время никакой любви к своей работе. Насильно хотел покорить себя и бездушно, заглушив все, быть верным природе. Это не было созданье искусства, и потому чувства, которые объемлют всех при взгляде на него, суть уже мятежные чувства, тревожные чувства, – не чувства художника, ибо художник и в тревоге дышит покоем. Мне говорили, что портрет этот ходит по рукам и рассевает томительные впечатленья, зарождая в художнике чувство зависти, мрачной ненависти к брату, злобную жажду производить гоненья и угнетенья. Да хранит тебя Всевышний от сих страстей! Нет их страшнее. Лучше вынести всю горечь возможных гонений, нежели нанести кому-либо одну тень гоненья. Спасай чистоту души своей. Кто заключил в себе талант, тот чище всех должен быть душою. Другому простится многое, но ему не простится. Человеку, который вышел из дому в светлой праздничной одежде, стоит только быть обрызнуту одним пятном грязи из-под колеса, и уже весь народ обступил его, и указывает на него пальцем, и толкуют об его неряшестве, тогда как тот же народ не замечает множества пятен на других проходящих, одетых в будничные одежды. Ибо на будничных одеждах не замечаются пятна.

Он благословил меня и обнял. Никогда в жизни не был я так возвышенно подвигнут. Благоговейно, более нежели с чувством сына, прильнул я к груди его и поцеловал в рассыпавшиеся его серебряные волосы. Слеза блеснула в его глазах.

– Исполни, сын мой, одну мою просьбу, – сказал он мне уже при самом расставанье. – Может быть, тебе случится увидеть где-нибудь тот портрет, о котором я говорил тебе. Ты его узнаешь вдруг по необыкновенным глазам и неестественному их выражению, – во что бы то ни было истреби его...

Вы можете судить сами, мог ли я не обещать клятвенно исполнить такую просьбу. В продолжение целых пятнадцати лет не случалось мне встретить ничего такого, что бы хотя сколько-нибудь походило на описание, сделанное моим отцом, как вдруг теперь, на аукционе...

Здесь художник, не договорив еще своей речи, обратил глаза на стену, с тем чтобы взглянуть еще раз на портрет. То же самое движение сделала в один миг вся толпа слушавших, ища глазами необыкновенного портрета. Но, к величайшему изумлению, его уже не было на стене. Невнятный говор и шум пробежал по всей толпе, и вслед за тем послышались явственно слова: «Украден». Кто-то успел уже стащить его, воспользовавшись вниманьем слушателей, увлеченных рассказом. И долго все присутствовавшие оставались в недоумении, не зная, действительно ли они видели эти необыкновенные глаза или это была просто мечта, представшая только на миг глазам их, утружденным долгим рассматриванием старинных картин.

powers and the proud passions of Satan, by exactly that much is the great creation of art higher than anything on earth. Sacrifice everything to it and love it with great passion, not with the passion born of earthly lust, but with a gentle and heavenly passion. Without it a man is power-less to raise himself above the earth, and he cannot produce the wonderful sounds which bespeak contentment. For the great creations of art come into the world in order to soothe and reconcile everything. It cannot sow discord in the soul, but it aspires, like a resounding prayer, to God. But there are moments, dark moments . . .' He paused, and I saw a darkness on his face as though some cloud had for a moment passed before him. 'There is one incident in my life,' he said. 'To this very moment, I cannot grasp what that terrible being was whose portrait I painted. It was surely some manifestation of something diabolical. I am aware that the world denies the existence of the devil, and because of that, I will not speak of him. I will only note that it was with revulsion that I painted him. Even at that time I felt no love for my work. I tried to force myself to be true to nature, and I stifled every emotion in me. It was not a work of art, and, therefore, the feelings which are aroused in everyone who looks at it are feelings of revulsion, disturbing feelings, not the feelings of an artist, for an artist puts peace into turmoil. I have been told that this portrait passes from hand to hand and sows dissatisfaction and creates jealousy and black hatred in artists toward their fellow artists, and evil desires to persecute and oppress. May God keep you from such passions. Nothing is more terrible. Better to endure the anguish of the most horrible persecution than to inflict anyone with even a hint of persecution. Keep your mind pure. He who is talented must be purer than all others. Much must be forgiven him. A man who goes forth from his house dressed in brilliant holiday garments has only to be spat-tered with a single spot of mud from a wheel and people encircle him and point a finger at him and talk of his lack of cleanliness, while the same people do not notice the very many spots on the ordinary garments of other passers-by, for spots on ordinary clothes are never seen.'

"He blessed me and he embraced me. Never in my life was I so deeply moved. I leaned upon his breast reverently rather than with the feeling of a son, and I kissed his flowing silver hair.

"Tears glistened in his eyes. 'Fulfill one request, dear son,' said he at the moment of parting. 'You may one day come across the portrait I have mentioned. You will recognize it at once by its strange eyes and unnatural expression. If you find it, I beg you, destroy it at any cost.'

'You may yourselves judge whether I could refuse to promise to fulfill this request. For fifteen years I have never come across anything which even slightly corresponded to the description of the portrait which my father had given me, until suddenly, at this auction . . .'

The artist did not finish the sentence; he turned his eyes to the wall to look at the portrait once more. And everyone who had listened to him instinctively did the same thing. To their amazement, however, it was no longer on the wall. A soft murmur ran through the crowd, fol-lowed suddenly by the word 'stolen' which was distinctly heard. Someone had succeeded in taking it away, taking advantage of the fact that the attention of the listeners was distracted by the story. And for a long time those who were present were bewildered, wondering whether they had really seen those remarkable eyes or whether it was merely a dream which had flashed before their eyes, strained from long examination of old pictures.

(1835) [*Translated by Constance Garnett*]

V.1.2. АФАНАСИЙ ФЕТ, «Измучен жизнью, коварством надежды…»

Die Gleichmassigkeit des Laufes der Zeit in allen Köpfen beweist mehr, als irgend etwas, das wir Alle in denselben Traum versenkt sind, ja das es ein Wesen ist, welches ihn träumt.

*Schopenhauer**

1

Измучен жизнью, коварством надежды,
Когда им в битве душой уступаю,
И днем и ночью смежаю я вежды
И как-то странно порой прозреваю.

Еще темнее мрак жизни вседневной,
Как после яркой осенней зарницы,
И только в небе, как зов задушевный,
Сверкают звезд золотые ресницы.

И так прозрачна огней бесконечность,
И так доступна вся бездна эфира,
Что прямо смотрю я из времени в вечность
И пламя твое узнаю, солнце мира.

И неподвижно на огненных розах
Живой алтарь мирозданья курится,
В его дыму, как в творческих грезах,
Вся сила дрожит и вся вечность снится.

И всё, что мчится по безднам эфира,
И каждый луч, плотской и бесплотный,-
Твой только отблеск, о солнце мира,
И только сон, только сон мимолетный.

И этих грез в мировом дуновеньи
Как дым несусь я и таю невольно,
И в этом прозреньи, и в этом забвеньи
Легко мне жить и дышать мне не больно.

V.1.2.   AFANSY FET, 'When I am Tired with Life . . .'

Die Gleichmassigkeit des Laufes der Zeit in allen Köpfen beweist mehr, als irgend etwas, das wir Alle in denselben Traum versenkt sind, ja das es ein Wesen ist, welches ihn träumt.

Schopenhauer[8]

1

When I am tired with life, with the treachery of hope,
In my soul, I surrender to the battle of despair;
Day and night, I close my eyes
And at times, so strangely, my sight returns.

The darkness of everyday life is darker yet,
Just as after a bright autumn lightning,
When, in the sky, like a intimate summons,
The golden eyelashes of the stars are sparking.

The infinity of lights is so translucent,
That the entire chasm of the heavens becomes visible,
And I look from time straight into eternity
And recognize your flame, O sun of the world.

And on fiery roses, motionlessly,
Smoke rises from this living altar of the universe,[9],
In its smoke, as in creative dreams,
All force is trembling[10], and all eternity appears in a dream.

Everything which is rushing through the chasm of the heavens,
Every ray, corporeal and incorporeal,
Is only your brightness, O sun of the world,
But only a dream, a fleeting dream.

And with the universal breeze of these dreams
I am rushing like a puff of smoke, and I too fade away,
And in this recovery of sight, in this oblivion
It is easy for me to live and painless for me to breathe.

---

[8] Evenness of the course of time in all minds proves more than anything else that we all have been submerged in one and the same dream; moreover, it proves that all dreaming this dream are one and the same being.' (Schopenhauer)
[9] Lit., 'smoking,' emitting smoke like when incense is burned.
[10] Fet seems to be using 'trembling' in a sense of vibrating, shaking, rather than trembling with fear.

2

В тиши и мраке таинственной ночи
Я вижу блеск приветный и милый,
И в звездном хоре знакомые очи
Горят в степи над забытой могилой.

Трава поблекла, пустыня угрюма,
И сон сиротлив одинокой гробницы,
И только в небе, как вечная дума,
Сверкают звезд золотые ресницы.

И снится мне, что ты встала из гроба,
Такой же, какой ты с земли отлетела,
И снится, снится: мы молоды оба,
И ты взглянула, как прежде глядела

* Равномерность течения времени во всех головах доказывает более, чем что-либо другое, что мы все погружены в один и тот же сон; более того, что все видящие этот сон являются единым существом.

Шопенгауэр (нем.)

m. ESPAÑOL

V.m.1. JOSÉ de ESPRONCEDA, 'Al sol. Himno'

Para y óyeme ¡oh Sol! Yo te saludo
y extático ante ti me atrevo a hablarte:
ardiente como tú mi fantasía,
arrebatada en ansia de admirarte,
intrépidas a ti sus alas guía.
¡Ojalá que mi acento poderoso,
sublime resonando,
del trueno pavoroso
la temerosa voz sobrepujando,
¡oh Sol! a ti llegara,
y en medio de tu curso te parara!
¡Ah! Si la llama que mi mente alumbra
diera también su ardor a mis sentidos,
al rayo vencedor que los deslumbra,
los anhelantes ojos alzaría,
y en tu semblante fúlgido atrevidos
mirando sin cesar los fijaría.

2

In the silence and dark of the mysterious night
I see the brilliance, welcoming and dear,
Amid the chorus of stars, of familiar eyes
Shining in the steppe above a forgotten grave.

The grass has withered, the wilderness is somber,
And the orphaned grave sleeps on alone,
Only in the sky, like an eternal thought,
The golden eyelashes of the stars are sparkling.

And in my dream I see that you have risen[11] from the grave,
Appearing just as you did when you departed from the world,
And in my dream we both are young again,
And you looked at me the way you used to.

[Translated by Yelena Borisova. Edited by
Jamie S. Crouse]

m.   SPANISH

V.m.1.   JOSÉ de ESPRONCEDA, 'To the Sun: A Hymn'

Stop and listen to me, O Sun, I salute you and, ecstatic before you, I dare to address you. My imagination, like you, burns and it is carried away in a fever and in admiration of you, and guides its wings towards you intrepidly. Would that my powerful accents, resounding sublimely, surpassing the frightened voice of the fearful thunderclap, O Sun, reach up to you and that you would pause in the middle of your transit! Ah! If only the flame that lights up my mind were also to give ardour to my senses, and my longing eyes were to rise up to the conquering ray that dazzles them, and were to fix them, gazing ceaselessly and with daring on your brilliant face. How long have I loved you, O refulgent Sun! With what simple desire, as an innocent child, did I long to follow you in the extended heavens and watched you ecstatically and grew fascinated in the contemplation of your light! August sovereign, you stretch out in pomp the fringes of your fiery apparel from the golden limits of the Orient, which the rich Ocean girdles with pearls, to the shadowy limit of the West, and you bathe the world in your pure light. Vivid, you launch the day from your brow and, soul and life of the world, your disc sends, in peace, placid fecund warmth, and you raise yourself up in triumph, the scintillating crown of the orbs. Tranquilly you rise from the golden zenith to the royal throne in the centre of the

---

[11] Feminine singular form, that is, Fet is addresses a woman.

¡Cuánto siempre te amé, sol refulgente!
¡Con qué sencillo anhelo,
siendo niño inocente,
seguirte ansiaba en el tendido cielo,
y extático te vía
y en contemplar tu luz me embebecía!
De los dorados límites de Oriente,
que ciñe el rico en perlas Océano,
al término sombroso de Occidente
las orlas de tu ardiente vestidura
tiendas en pompa, augusto soberano,
y el mundo bañas en tu lumbre pura.
Vívido lanzas de tu frente el día,
y, alma y vida del mundo,
tu disco en paz majestuoso envía
plácido ardor fecundo,
y te elevas triunfante,
corona de los orbes centellante.
Tranquilo subes del Cenit dorado
al regio trono en la mitad del cielo,
de vivas llamas y esplendor ornado,
y reprimes tu vuelo.
Y desde allí tu fúlgida carrera
rápido precipitas,
y tu rica, encendida cabellera
en el seno del mar, trémula agitas,
y tu esplendor se oculta,
y el ya pasado día
con otros mil la eternidad sepulta.
¡Cuántos siglos sin fin, cuántos has visto
en su abismo insondable desplomarse!
¡Cuánta pompa, grandeza y poderío
de imperios populosos disiparse!
¿Qué fueron ante ti? Del bosque umbrío
secas y leves hojas desprendidas,
que en círculos se mecen,
y al furor de Aquilón desaparecen.
Libre tú de la cólera divina,
viste anegarse el universo entero,
cuando las aguas de Jehová lanzadas,
impelidas del brazo justiciero,
y a mares por los vientos despeñadas,
bramó la tempestad; retumbó en torno
el ronco trueno, y con temblor crujieron
los ejes de diamante de la tierra;
montes y campos fueron

heavens, adorned with living flames and splendour, and you curb your flight. And from thence you rapidly descend in your refulgent course and, trembling, you tremulously shake your rich burning tresses in the bosom of the sea and your splendour is hidden and eternity buries the day that has passed with other thousand days. How many centuries without end, how many have you seen slide into the unfathomable abyss! What pomp, grandeur and power and populous empires have vanished! What existed before you? The dry and light leaves snatched from the dark wood which swirl in circles disappear at the fury of the North Wind. You were freed from the divine rage, you were witness to the drowning of the entire universe when the waters, thrust by the righteous arm of Jehovah, were cast down, and the tempest roared and the seas were hurled by the winds; the hoarse thunder boomed all around, and in fear the diamond pivots of the Earth creaked; mountains and meadows became mutinous seas, the tomb of mankind. The deep shuddered and then you, like the Lord of the world, raised up your throne over the tempest, dressed in darkness, and you paraded your face, and you shone on other worlds in peace. And you saw, once more, new centuries, new peoples come, flee, disappear in an eternal whirlwind, just as the waves of the Ocean come, break and flee and come again and again; while you, unchanging, alone and radiant, O Sun!, continuously rise up and triumph over a thousand ages and a thousand traces. And are you to be eternal, inextinguishable, so that your immense fire will never lose its radiance, never tiring, audaciously following your immortal course, contemplating the disappearance of ages and alone, eternal, perennial, sublime, dominating as a powerful monarch? No; for death, even if it stalks you from afar, no less desiring pursues you. Who knows that if, perhaps, you are the pale flash of another sun which from another greater univers than ours once shone with double brilliance? Enjoy your youth and your beauty O Sun!, for when the dread day comes when the orb explodes and slips from the potent hand of the Sovereign Father and, there, too, you will fall into eternity, fragmented into a thousand horrible din of a hundred storms your pure flame will die amid endless darkness. Gloomy night will cover for eternity the heavenly firmament; and not a trace of your light will remain!

(1834) [1840]

[*Possibly in response to* Byron's 'Darkness' *(1816) Espronceda paints a bleak scenario of the end of the world. In this poem, after 85 lines of orchestrated and evocative rhetoric demanding a positive response in the reader, with a single negative, Espronceda calls into question the accepted Christian view of the world by employing the new evolutionist theories which challenged Bishop Usher's dating of the moment of Creation. He not only implies a much longer time span for the history of the world but also that the Creator seems incapable of controlling the mechanisms of a universe he supposedly created omnipotently. In* 'To Jarifa' *(above) the mysterious voice seems also to imply the existence of a cruel and unjust God who punishes man for seeking after knowledge, a radical and blasphemous idea which challenged the Catholic teaching of his day.*]

alborotado mar, tumba el hombre.
Se estremeció el profundo,
y entonces tú, como Se–or del mundo,
sobre la tempestad tu trono alzabas,
vestido de tinieblas,
y tu faz engreías,
y a otros mundos en paz resplandecías.
Y otra vez nuevos siglos, nuevas gentes,
viste llegar, huir, desvanecerse
en remolino eterno, cual las olas
llegan, se agolpan y huyen de Océano
y tornan otra vez a sucederse;
mientras inmutable tú, solo y radiante
¡oh Sol! siempre te elevas
y edades mil y mil huellas triunfante.
¿Y habrás de ser eterno, inextinguible,
sin que nunca jamás tu inmensa hoguera
pierda su resplandor, siempre incansable,
audaz siguiendo tu inmortal carrera,
hundirse las edades contemplando,
y solo, eterno, perenal, sublime,
monarca poderoso dominando?
No; que también la muerte,
si de lejos te sigue,
no menos anhelante te persigue.
¿Quién sabe si tal vez pobre destello
eres tú de otro sol que otro universo
mayor que el nuestro un día
con doble resplandor esclarecía?
Goza tu juventud y tu hermosura,
¡oh Sol! que cuando el pavoroso día
llegue que el orbe estalle y se desprenda
de la potente mano
del Padre Soberano,
y allá a la eternidad también descienda,
deshecho en mil pedazos, destrozado
y en piélagos de fuego
envuelto para siempre y sepultado.
De cien tormentas al horrible estruendo,
en tinieblas sin fin tu llama pura
entonces morirá. Noche sombría
cubrirá eterna la celeste cumbre;
ni aun quedará reliquia de tu lumbre!!!

(1834) [*Published in Poesías 1840*]

V.m.2.   JOSÉ SOMOZA, 'El sepulcro de mi hermano: Oda'

Del tiempo la corriente
los a–os precipita.
¿Mas dónde está su fuente?
¿En qué mar deposita
los a–os y los siglos que nos quita?
Si al hombre fuera dado
hundir su vista en la caverna oscura
que tragó lo pasado,
desde allí por ventura
lograra ver la eternidad futura.
La misteriosa esfera
del saber y virtud abarcaría
y el término midiera
de la encantada vía
que hacia su perfección los seres guía.
¿Por qué este mármol frío
no me muestra la huella silenciosa
del caro hermano mío?
¡Con mano poderosa
la muerte entre los dos echó esta losa!
En ella suspiraba
mientras la noche el manto tenebroso
sobre mí desplegaba
y el viento quejumbroso
dejaba los cipreses en reposo.
La luna que se alzara,
un débil rayo entonces enviando,
el sepulcro alumbrara,
las sombras alargando
y la luz a mis cansados ojos dando.
Vi alzar su incierto vuelo
a una pintada mariposa en tanto,
cual si para consuelo
viniera en mi quebranto
a darme aliento y enjugar mi llanto,
como si me dijera:
"Quien muertes llora, admire mi alegría,
vencí a la Parca fiera
como la noche el día.
Tres vidas cuenta la vida mía.
Era gusano inerte
y hoy vuelo ante la luz como la aurora,
que en la tumba la muerte
mi existencia mejora,

V.m.2.   JOSÉ SOMOZA, 'The Tomb of My Brother: Ode'

The current of time thrusts the years along. But where is its source? In which sea does it deposit the years and the centuries of which we are robbed? If man were given to sink his gaze into the dark cavern which the past has swallowed, perhaps from there he might succeed in seeing a future eternity. It would embrace the mysterious sphere of knowledge and virtue and would measure the final point of the enchanted path which guides human souls to its perfection. Why does the cold marble not show me the silent outline of my dear brother? Death with powerful hand thrust this slab between us! He sighed within it while night enfolded over me its dark mantle and the complaining wind left the cypresses in repose. The moon, which sent a weak ray at that moment, illuminated the tomb, making the shadows lengthen, giving light to my dejected eyes. I saw then a butterfly raise itself up in uncertain flight as if it came as a consolation to my sorrow and give me respite and dry my tears as if to say: 'He who mourns the dead, admire my happiness. I have conquered the fierce Parcae (the three Fates = death) as day does night. My life has summed three lives. I was once an inert grub and today I fly in the light like the dawn, death in its tomb improves my existence, it gives me a life of love, it gilds my wings.' Ah! Beautiful butterfly, guide me by the stair of hope which reaches to the highest star from the earth and raises up humans from one world to another!

[1842]

[*Somoza was a notable liberal in a conservative age and, here, he expresses a revisionist view of the Catholic view of death. He raises the question of man's seeking after the nature of existence beyond that permitted by Catholic teaching and balances a sense of loss and a sense of nothingness with a vain hope, expressed through the butterfly, of a form of rebirth, a metempsychosis. In this he seems to reject a Christian God of redemption and places trust in a form of eternal return.*]

me da vida de amor, mis alas dora."
¡Ay, mariposa bella,
guíame por la escala de esperanza
que a la más alta estrella
desde la tierra alcanza
y los seres de un mundo en otro lanza!

[From Poesías *1842]*

V.m.3.   GABRIEL GARCÍA TASSARA, from 'El desaliento'

"La ignorancia es la fe", me dijo el mundo,
y te huí con desdén cuando volviste,
y ora te llamo en mi dolor profundo
y ya no vienes a alegrar a un triste.
Los himnos se acabaron,
Los cielos se cerraron,
...
Exclamo sin cesar: "¡La fe me falta!"

(Excerpts, c.1840)
[Published in Poesías *1872]*

V.m.4.   GUSTAVO ADOLFO BÉCQUER, 'Rima'

¿De dónde vengo?... El más horrible y áspero
de los sendas busca.
Las huellas de unos pies ensangrentados
sobre la roca dura;
los despojos de un alma hecha jirones
en las zarzas agudas,
te dirán el camino
que conduce a mi cuna.
¿A dónde voy? El más sombrío y triste
de los páramos cruza,
valle de eternas nieves y de eternas
melancólicas brumas.
En donde esté una piedra solitaria
sin inscripción alguna,
donde habite el olvido,
allí estará mi tumba.

[From Libro de los gorriones 1868]

V.m.3. GABRIEL GARCÍA TASSARA, from 'Despair'

'Ignorance is faith', the world told me, and I fled from you with disdain when you returned, and either I call on you in my profound pain or you no longer come to afford a smile to a sad man. Hymns have ceased, the heavens closed down, . . . I exclaimed endlessly, 'I want for faith'.

(1840) [1872]

[*García Tassara's pessimism extends to a complete loss of faith and a rejection of the Catholic view that man must not question Church teaching nor seek answers to ultimate metaphysical issues.*]

V.m.4. GUSTAVO ADOLFO BÉCQUER, *'Rhyme'*

Whence came I . . .? Seek the most horrible and bitter of paths. The prints of bloody feet on the harsh rock; the spoil of a soul torn into shreds on sharp thorns will point the way to my cradle. Whence go I? Cross the most gloomy and sad of wasteland, valley of eternal snows and eternal melancholy mists, where stands a solitary stone without inscription, there will be my tomb.

[1868]

[*One of Bécquer's most pessimistic poems questioning the very nature of man's being, his origins and of his final existence. Here he echoes Byron's celebrated questioning in* Don Juan: *'What are we? Whence came we? What shall be our ultimate existence?' This type of metaphysical questioning is to be reinvigorated in the literature of the early XXth century.*]

VI. Nature

Nature in Romanticism has a different status from nature as seen either in the light of tradi-tional theology or of the scientific conceptions of the Enlightenment. Nature becomes a resource for meaning when traditional theological certainties dissolve. It is also, though, the source of darker thoughts, when the awareness grows of the destructive aspects of human instinct that seem most intimately connected to 'nature'. We try to illustrate conflicting conceptions of nature and humankind's place within it by a selection of literary and philosophical texts that paint both a positive and a negative picture (from Rousseau to Wordsworth to de Sade and Baudelaire), but it will also recall that, from the very first, as in Coleridge's and Wordsworth's co-operative plan for the Lyrical Ballads, the natural and the supernatural could be closely allied. Theological debates over the status of nature and the problem of pantheism mingle with more secular conceptions.

a. BRITISH

VI.a.1.   WILLIAM WORDSWORTH, 'Lines Written a Few Miles above
. Tintern Abbey, On Revisiting the Banks of the Wye During a Tour, July 13, 1798'

Five years have past; five summers, with the length
Of five long winters! and again I hear
These waters, rolling from their mountain-springs
With a soft inland murmur. – Once again
Do I behold these steep and lofty cliffs,
That on a wild secluded scene impress
Thoughts of more deep seclusion; and connect
The landscape with the quiet of the sky.
The day is come when I again repose
Here, under this dark sycamore, and view
These plots of cottage-ground, these orchard-tufts,
Which at this season, with their unripe fruits,
Are clad in one green hue, and lose themselves
'Mid groves and copses. Once again I see
These hedge-rows, hardly hedge-rows, little lines
Of sportive wood run wild: these pastoral farms,
Green to the very door; and wreaths of smoke
Sent up, in silence, from among the trees!
With some uncertain notice, as might seem

Of vagrant dwellers in the houseless woods,
Or of some Hermit's cave, where by his fire
The Hermit sits alone.

              These beauteous forms,
Through a long absence, have not been to me
As is a landscape to a blind man's eye:
But oft, in lonely rooms, and 'mid the din
Of towns and cities, I have owed to them,
In hours of weariness, sensations sweet,
Felt in the blood, and felt along the heart;
And passing even into my purer mind
With tranquil restoration: – feelings too
Of unremembered pleasure: such, perhaps,
As have no slight or trivial influence
On that best portion of a good man's life,
His little, nameless, unremembered, acts
Of kindness and of love. Nor less, I trust,
To them I may have owed another gift,
Of aspect more sublime; that blessed mood,
In which the burthen of the mystery,
In which the heavy and the weary weight
Of all this unintelligible world,
Is lightened: – that serene and blessed mood,
In which the affections gently lead us on, –
Until, the breath of this corporeal frame
And even the motion of our human blood
Almost suspended, we are laid asleep
In body, and become a living soul:
While with an eye made quiet by the power
Of harmony, and the deep power of joy,
We see into the life of things.

                    If this
Be but a vain belief, yet, oh! how oft –
In darkness and amid the many shapes
Of joyless daylight; when the fretful stir
Unprofitable, and the fever of the world,
Have hung upon the beatings of my heart –
How oft, in spirit, have I turned to thee,
O sylvan Wye! thou wanderer thro' the woods,
How often has my spirit turned to thee!

And now, with gleams of half-extinguished thought,
With many recognitions dim and faint,
And somewhat of a sad perplexity,
The picture of the mind revives again:

While here I stand, not only with the sense
Of present pleasure, but with pleasing thoughts
That in this moment there is life and food
For future years. And so I dare to hope,
Though changed, no doubt, from what I was when first
I came among these hills; when like a roe
I bounded o'er the mountains, by the sides
Of the deep rivers, and the lonely streams,
Wherever nature led: more like a man
Flying from something that he dreads, than one
Who sought the thing he loved. For nature then
(The coarser pleasures of my boyish days
And their glad animal movements all gone by)
To me was all in all. – I cannot paint
What then I was. The sounding cataract
Haunted me like a passion: the tall rock,
The mountain, and the deep and gloomy wood,
Their colours and their forms, were then to me
An appetite; a feeling and a love,
That had no need of a remoter charm,
By thought supplied, not any interest
Unborrowed from the eye. – That time is past,
And all its aching joys are now no more,
And all its dizzy raptures. Not for this
Faint I, nor mourn nor murmur; other gifts
Have followed; for such loss, I would believe,
Abundant recompense. For I have learned
To look on nature, not as in the hour
Of thoughtless youth; but hearing oftentimes
The still sad music of humanity,
Nor harsh nor grating, though of ample power
To chasten and subdue. – And I have felt
A presence that disturbs me with the joy
Of elevated thoughts; a sense sublime
Of something far more deeply interfused,
Whose dwelling is the light of setting suns,
And the round ocean and the living air,
And the blue sky, and in the mind of man:
A motion and a spirit, that impels
All thinking things, all objects of all thought,
And rolls through all things. Therefore am I still
A lover of the meadows and the woods
And mountains; and of all that we behold
From this green earth; of all the mighty world
Of eye, and ear, – both what they half create,
And what perceive; well pleased to recognise

In nature and the language of the sense
The anchor of my purest thoughts, the nurse,
The guide, the guardian of my heart, and soul
Of all my moral being.

                      Nor perchance,
If I were not thus taught, should I the more
Suffer my genial spirits to decay:
For thou art with me here upon the banks
Of this fair river; thou my dearest Friend,
My dear, dear Friend; and in thy voice I catch
The language of my former heart, and read
My former pleasures in the shooting lights
Of thy wild eyes. Oh! yet a little while
May I behold in thee what I was once,
My dear, dear Sister! and this prayer I make,
Knowing that Nature never did betray
The heart that loved her; 'tis her privilege,
Through all the years of this our life, to lead
From joy to joy: for she can so inform
The mind that is within us, so impress
With quietness and beauty, and so feed
With lofty thoughts, that neither evil tongues,
Rash judgments, nor the sneers of selfish men,
Nor greetings where no kindness is, nor all
The dreary intercourse of daily life,
Shall e'er prevail against us, or disturb
Our cheerful faith, that all which we behold
Is full of blessings. Therefore let the moon
Shine on thee in thy solitary walk;
And let the misty mountain-winds be free
To blow against thee: and, in after years,
When these wild ecstasies shall be matured
Into a sober pleasure; when thy mind
Shall be a mansion for all lovely forms,
Thy memory be as a dwelling-place
For all sweet sounds and harmonies; oh! then,
If solitude, or fear, or pain, or grief,
Should be thy portion, with what healing thoughts
Of tender joy wilt thou remember me,
And these my exhortations! Nor, perchance –
If I should be where I no more can hear
Thy voice, nor catch from thy wild eyes these gleams
Of past existence – wilt thou then forget
That on the banks of this delightful stream
We stood together; and that I, so long

A worshipper of Nature, hither came
Unwearied in that service: rather say
With warmer love – oh! with far deeper zeal
Of holier love. Nor wilt thou then forget,
That after many wanderings, many years
Of absence, these steep woods and lofty cliffs,
And this green pastoral landscape, were to me
More dear, both for themselves and for thy sake!

(1798)

VI.a.2.   SAMUEL TAYLOR COLERIDGE, 'Frost at Midnight'

The Frost performs its secret ministry,
Unhelped by any wind. The owlet's cry
Came loud – – and hark, again! loud as before.
The inmates of my cottage, all at rest,
Have left me to that solitude, which suits
Abstruser musings: save that at my side
My cradled infant slumbers peacefully.
'Tis calm indeed! so calm, that it disturbs
And vexes meditation with its strange
And extreme silentness. Sea, hill, and wood,
This populous village! Sea, and hill, and wood,
With all the numberless goings-on of life,
Inaudible as dreams! the thin blue flame
Lies on my low-burnt fire, and quivers not;
Only that film, which fluttered on the grate,
Still flutters there, the sole unquiet thing.
Methinks, its motion in this hush of nature
Gives it dim sympathies with me who live,
Making it a companionable form,
Whose puny flaps and freaks the idling Spirit
By its own moods interprets, every where
Echo or mirror seeking of itself,
And makes a toy of Thought.

                        But O! how oft,
How oft, at school, with most believing mind,
Presageful, have I gazed upon the bars,
To watch that fluttering stranger! and as oft
With unclosed lids, already had I dreamt
Of my sweet birth-place, and the old church-tower,
Whose bells, the poor man's only music, rang
From morn to evening, all the hot Fair-day,
So sweetly, that they stirred and haunted me

With a wild pleasure, falling on mine ear
Most like articulate sounds of things to come!
So gazed I, till the soothing things, I dreamt,
Lulled me to sleep, and sleep prolonged my dreams!
And so I brooded all the following morn,
Awed by the stern preceptor's face, mine eye
Fixed with mock study on my swimming book:
Save if the door half opened, and I snatched
A hasty glance, and still my heart leaped up,
For still I hoped to see the stranger's face,
Townsman, or aunt, or sister more beloved,
My play-mate when we both were clothed alike!

Dear Babe, that sleepest cradled by my side,
Whose gentle breathings, heard in this deep calm,
Fill up the interspersed vacancies
And momentary pauses of the thought!
My babe so beautiful! it thrills my heart
With tender gladness, thus to look at thee,
And think that thou shalt learn far other lore,
And in far other scenes! For I was reared
In the great city, pent 'mid cloisters dim,
And saw nought lovely but the sky and stars.
But thou, my babe! shalt wander like a breeze
By lakes and sandy shores, beneath the crags
Of ancient mountain, and beneath the clouds,
Which image in their bulk both lakes and shores
And mountain crags: so shalt thou see and hear
The lovely shapes and sounds intelligible
Of that eternal language, which thy God
Utters, who from eternity doth teach
Himself in all, and all things in himself.
Great universal Teacher! he shall mould
Thy spirit, and by giving make it ask.

Therefore all seasons shall be sweet to thee,
Whether the summer clothe the general earth
With greenness, or the redbreast sit and sing
Betwixt the tufts of snow on the bare branch
Of mossy apple-tree, while the nigh thatch
Smokes in the sun-thaw; whether the eave-drops fall
Heard only in the trances of the blast,
Or if the secret ministry of frost
Shall hang them up in silent icicles,
Quietly shining to the quiet Moon.

[*1798*]

VI.a.3.   SIR WALTER SCOTT, from *Waverley*

Having gained the open air by a postern door, they walked a little way up the wild, bleak, and narrow valley in which the house was situated, following the course of the stream that winded through it. In a spot, about a quarter of a mile from the castle, two brooks, which formed the little river, had their junction. The larger of the two came down the long bare valley, which extended, apparently without any change or elevation of character, as far as the hills which formed its boundary permitted the eye to reach. But the other stream, which had its source among the mountains on the left hand of the strath, seemed to issue from a very narrow and dark opening betwixt two large rocks. These streams were different also in character. The larger was placid, and even sullen in its course, wheeling in deep eddies, or sleeping in dark blue pools; but the motions of the lesser brook were rapid and furious, issuing from between precipices, like a maniac from his confinement, all foam and uproar.

It was up the course of this last stream that Waverley, like a knight of romance, was conducted by the fair Highland damsel, his silent guide. A small path, which had been rendered easy in many places for Flora's accommodation, led him through scenery of a very different description from that which he had just quitted. Around the castle, all was cold, bare, and desolate, yet tame even in desolation; but this narrow glen, at so short a distance, seemed to open into the land of romance. The rocks assumed a thousand peculiar and varied forms. In one place, a crag of huge size presented its gigantic bulk, as if to forbid the passenger's farther progress; and it was not until he approached its very base, that Waverley discerned the sudden and acute turn by which the pathway wheeled its course around this formidable obstacle. In another spot, the projecting rocks from the opposite sides of the chasm had approached so near to each other, that two pine-trees laid across, and covered with turf, formed a rustic bridge at the height of at least one hundred and fifty feet. It had no ledges, and was barely three feet in breadth.

While gazing at this pass of peril, which crossed, like a single black line, the small portion of blue sky not intercepted by the projecting rocks on either side, it was with a sensation of horror that Waverley beheld Flora and her attendant appear, like inhabitants of another region, propped, as it were, in mid air, upon this trembling structure. She stopped upon observing him below, and, with an air of graceful ease, which made him shudder, waved her handkerchief to him by way of signal. He was unable, from the sense of dizziness which her situation conveyed, to return the salute; and was never more relieved than when the fair apparition passed on from the precarious eminence which she seemed to occupy with so much indifference, and disappeared on the other side. Advancing a few yards, and passing under the bridge which he had viewed with so much terror, the path ascended rapidly from the edge of the brook, and the glen widened into a sylvan amphitheatre, waving with birch, young oaks, and hazels, with here and there a scattered yew-tree. The rocks now receded, but still showed their grey and shaggy crests rising among the copse-wood. Still higher, rose eminences and peaks, some bare, some clothed with wood, some round and purple with heath, and others splintered into rocks and crags. At a short turning, the path, which had for some furlongs lost sight of the brook, suddenly placed Waverley in front of a romantic waterfall. It was not so remarkable either for great height or quantity of water, as for the beautiful accompaniments which made the spot interesting. After a broken cataract of about twenty feet, the stream was received in a large natural basin filled to the brim with water, which, where the bubbles of the fall subsided, was so exquisitely clear, that, although it was of great depth, the eye could discern each pebble at the bottom. Eddying round this reservoir, the brook found its way over a broken part of the ledge, and formed a second fall, which

seemed to seek the very abyss; then, wheeling out beneath from among the smooth dark rocks, which it had polished for ages, it wandered murmuring down the glen, forming the stream up which Waverley had just ascended. The borders of this romantic reservoir corresponded in beauty; but it was beauty of a stern and commanding cast, as if in the act of expanding into grandeur. Mossy banks of turf were broken and interrupted by huge fragments of rock, and decorated with trees and shrubs, some of which had been planted under the direction of Flora, but so cautiously, that they added to the grace, without diminishing the romantic wildness of the scene.

Here, like one of those lovely forms which decorate the landscapes of Poussin, Waverley found Flora, gazing on the waterfall. Two paces further back stood Cathleen, holding a small Scottish harp, the use of which had been taught to Flora by Rory Dall, one of the last harpers of the Western Highlands. The sun, now stooping in the west, gave a rich and varied tinge to all the objects which surrounded Waverley, and seemed to add more than human brilliancy to the full expressive darkness of Flora's eye, exalted the richness and purity of her complexion, and enhanced the dignity and grace of her beautiful form. Edward thought he had never, even in his wildest dreams, imagined a figure of such exquisite and interesting loveliness. The wild beauty of the retreat, bursting upon him as if by magic, augmented the mingled feeling of delight and awe with which he approached her, like a fair enchantress of Boiardo or Ariosto, by whose nod the scenery around seemed to have been created, an Eden in the wilderness.

[1814]

VI.a.4. PERCY BYSSHE SHELLEY, 'Mont Blanc: Lines Written in the Vale of Chamouni'

I

The everlasting universe of things
Flows through the mind, and rolls its rapid waves,
Now dark – now glittering – now reflecting gloom –
Now lending splendour, where from secret springs
The source of human thought its tribute brings
Of waters – with a sound but half its own,
Such as a feeble brook will oft assume,
In the wild woods, among the mountains lone,
Where waterfalls around it leap for ever,
Where woods and winds contend, and a vast river
Over its rocks ceaselessly bursts and raves.

II

Thus thou, Ravine of Arve – dark, deep Ravine –
Thou many-coloured, many-voiced vale,
Over whose pines, and crags, and caverns sail
Fast cloud-shadows and sunbeams: awful scene,
Where Power in likeness of the Arve comes down

From the ice-gulfs that gird his secret throne,
Bursting through these dark mountains like the flame
Of lightning through the tempest; – thou dost lie,
Thy giant brood of pines around thee clinging,
Children of elder time, in whose devotion
The chainless winds still come and ever came
To drink their odours, and their mighty swinging
To hear – an old and solemn harmony;
Thine earthly rainbows stretched across the sweep
Of the etherial waterfall, whose veil
Robes some unsculptured image; the strange sleep
Which when the voices of the desert fail
Wraps all in its own deep eternity; –
Thy caverns echoing to the Arve's commotion,
A loud, lone sound no other sound can tame;
Thou art pervaded with that ceaseless motion,
Thou art the path of that unresting sound –
Dizzy Ravine! and when I gaze on thee
I seem as in a trance sublime and strange
To muse on my own separate fantasy,
My own, my human mind, which passively
Now renders and receives fast influencings,
Holding an unremitting interchange
With the clear universe of things around;
One legion of wild thoughts, whose wandering wings
Now float above thy darkness, and now rest
Where that or thou art no unbidden guest,
In the still cave of the witch Poesy,
Seeking among the shadows that pass by
Ghosts of all things that are, some shade of thee,
Some phantom, some faint image; till the breast
From which they fled recalls them, thou art there!

III

Some say that gleams of a remoter world
Visit the soul in sleep, – that death is slumber,
And that its shapes the busy thoughts outnumber
Of those who wake and live. – I look on high;
Has some unknown omnipotence unfurled
The veil of life and death? or do I lie
In dream, and does the mightier world of sleep
Spread far around and inaccessibly
Its circles? For the very spirit fails,
Driven like a homeless cloud from steep to steep
That vanishes among the viewless gales!

Far, far above, piercing the infinite sky,
Mont Blanc appears – still, snowy, and serene;
Its subject mountains their unearthly forms
Pile around it, ice and rock; broad vales between
Of frozen floods, unfathomable deeps,
Blue as the overhanging heaven, that spread
And wind among the accumulated steeps;
A desert peopled by the storms alone,
Save when the eagle brings some hunter's bone,
And the wolf tracks her there – how hideously
Its shapes are heaped around! rude, bare, and high,
Ghastly, and scarred, and riven. – Is this the scene
Where the old Earthquake-daemon taught her young
Ruin? Were these their toys? or did a sea
Of fire envelop once this silent snow?
None can reply – all seems eternal now.
The wilderness has a mysterious tongue
Which teaches awful doubt, or faith so mild,
So solemn, so serene, that man may be,
But for such faith, with Nature reconciled;
Thou hast a voice, great Mountain, to repeal
Large codes of fraud and woe; not understood
By all, but which the wise, and great, and good
Interpret, or make felt, or deeply feel.

IV

The fields, the lakes, the forests, and the streams,
Ocean, and all the living things that dwell
Within the daedal earth; lightning, and rain,
Earthquake, and fiery flood, and hurricane,
The torpor of the year when feeble dreams
Visit the hidden buds, or dreamless sleep
Holds every future leaf and flower; the bound
With which from that detested trance they leap;
The works and ways of man, their death and birth,
And that of him and all that his may be;
All things that move and breathe with toil and sound
Are born and die; revolve, subside, and swell.
Power dwells apart in its tranquillity,
Remote, serene, and inaccessible:
And *this*, the naked countenance of earth,
On which I gaze, even these primaeval mountains
Teach the adverting mind. The glaciers creep
Like snakes that watch their prey, from their far fountains,
Slow rolling on; there, many a precipice

Frost and the Sun in scorn of mortal power
Have piled: dome, pyramid, and pinnacle,
A city of death, distinct with many a tower
And wall impregnable of beaming ice.
Yet not a city, but a flood of ruin
Is there, that from the boundaries of the sky
Rolls its perpetual stream; vast pines are strewing
Its destined path, or in the mangled soil
Branchless and shattered stand; the rocks, drawn down
From yon remotest waste, have overthrown
The limits of the dead and living world,
Never to be reclaimed. The dwelling-place
Of insects, beasts, and birds, becomes its spoil;
Their food and their retreat for ever gone,
So much of life and joy is lost. The race
Of man flies far in dread; his work and dwelling
Vanish, like smoke before the tempest's stream,
And their place is not known. Below, vast caves
Shine in the rushing torrents' restless gleam,
Which from those secret chasms in tumult welling
Meet in the vale, and one majestic River,
The breath and blood of distant lands, for ever
Rolls its loud waters to the ocean-waves,
Breathes its swift vapours to the circling air.

V

Mont Blanc yet gleams on high: – the power is there,
The still and solemn power of many sights,
And many sounds, and much of life and death.
In the calm darkness of the moonless nights,
In the lone glare of day, the snows descend
Upon that Mountain; none beholds them there,
Nor when the flakes burn in the sinking sun,
Or the star-beams dart through them. – Winds contend
Silently there, and heap the snow with breath
Rapid and strong, but silently! Its home
The voiceless lightning in these solitudes
Keeps innocently, and like vapour broods
Over the snow. The secret Strength of things
Which governs thought, and to the infinite dome
Of Heaven is as a law, inhabits thee!
And what were thou, and earth, and stars, and sea,
If to the human mind's imaginings
Silence and solitude were vacancy?

[1817]

VI.a.5. JOHN KEATS, 'To Autumn'

I

Season of mists and mellow fruitfulness,
    Close bosom-friend of the maturing sun;
Conspiring with him how to load and bless
    With fruit the vines that round the thatch-eves run;
To bend with apples the moss'd cottage-trees,
    And fill all fruit with ripeness to the core;
      To swell the gourd, and plump the hazel shells
With a sweet kernel; to set budding more,
    And still more, later flowers for the bees,
    Until they think warm days will never cease,
      For Summer has o'er-brimm'd their clammy cells.

II

Who hath not seen thee oft amid thy store?
    Sometimes whoever seeks abroad may find
Thee sitting careless on a granary floor,
    Thy hair soft-lifted by the winnowing wind;

Or on a half-reap'd furrow sound asleep,
    Drows'd with the fume of poppies, while thy hook
        Spares the next swath and all its twined flowers:
And sometimes like a gleaner thou dost keep
    Steady thy laden head across a brook;
    Or by a cyder-press, with patient look,
        Thou watchest the last oozings hours by hours.

III

Where are the songs of Spring? Ay, where are they?
    Think not of them, thou hast thy music too, –
While barred clouds bloom the soft-dying day,
    And touch the stubble plains with rosy hue;
Then in a wailful choir the small gnats mourn
    Among the river sallows, borne aloft
        Or sinking as the light wind lives or dies;
And full-grown lambs loud bleat from hilly bourn;
    Hedge-crickets sing; and now with treble soft
    The red-breast whistles from a garden-croft;
        And gathering swallows twitter in the skies.

[1820]

b. ČEŠTINA

VI.b.1. KAREL HYNEK MÁCHA, *Máj*

1

Byl pozdní večer – první máj –
večerní máj – byl lásky čas.
Hrdličin zval ku lásce hlas,
kde borový zaváněl háj.
O lásce šeptal tichý mech;
květoucí strom lhal lásky žel,
svou lásku slavík růži pěl,
růžinu jevil vonný vzdech.
Jezero hladké v křovích stinných
zvučelo temně tajný bol,
břeh je objímal kol a kol;
a slunce jasná světů jiných
bloudila blankytnými pásky,
planoucí tam co slzy lásky.

I světy jich v oblohu skvoucí
co ve chrám věčné lásky vzešly;
až se – milostí k sobě vroucí
změnivše se v jiskry hasnoucí –
bloudící co milenci sešly.
Ouplné lůny krásná tvář –
tak bledě jasná, jasně bledá,
jak milence milenka hledá –
ve růžovou vzplanula zář;
na vodách obrazy své zřela
a sama k sobě láskou mřela.
Dál blyštil bledý dvorů stín,
jenž k sobě šly vzdy blíž a blíž,
jak v objetí by níž a níž
se vinuly v soumraku klín,
až posléze šerem v jedno splynou.
S nimi se stromy k stromům vinou. –
Nejzáze stíní šero hor,
tam bříza k boru, k bříze bor
se kloní. Vlna za vlnou
potokem spěchá. Vře plnou –
v čas lásky – láskou každý tvor.

Za růžového večera
pod dubem sličná děva sedí,
se skály v břehu jezera

b. CZECH

VI.b.1.   KAREL HYNEK MÁCHA, *May*

1

Late evening, on the first of May –
The twilit May – the time of love.
Meltingly called the turtle-dove,
Where rich and sweet pinewoods lay.
Whispered of love the mosses frail,
The flowering tree as sweetly lied,
The rose's fragrant sigh replied
To love-songs of the nightingale.
In shadowy woods the burnished lake
Darkly complained a secret pain,
By circling shores embraced again;
And heaven's clear sun leaned down to take
A road astray in azure deeps,
Like burning tears the lover weeps.

A haze of stars in heaven hovers –
That church of endless love's communion –
Each jewel blanches and recovers
As blanch and burn long-parted lovers
In the high rapture of reunion.
How clear, to her full beauty grown,
How pale, how clear, the moon above,
Like maiden seeking for her love,
A rosy halo round her thrown!
Her mirrored image she espied,
And of self-love, beholding, died.
Forth from the farms pale shadows strayed,
Lengthening longing to their kind,
Till they embraced, and close entwined,
Coiled low into the lap of shade,
Grown all one twilight unity.
Tree in the shadows writhes to tree.
In the far mountains' dark confine
Pine leans to birch and birch to pine.
Wave haunting wave the streamlets move.
For love's sake – in the time of love –
Anguished goes every living thing.

A fair girl at the rim of land
Watches the evening's rosy phases;
Under the oak-tree by the strand

daleko přes jezero hledí.
To se jí modro k nohoum vine,
dále zeleně zakvítá,
vždy zeleněji prosvítá,
až v dálce v bledé jasno splyne.
Po šírošíré hladině
umdlelý dívka zrak upírá;
po šírošíré hladině
nic mimo promyk hvězd nezírá;
Dívčina krásná, anjel padlý,
co amarant na jaro svadlý,
v ubledlých lících krásy spějí.
Hodina jenž jí všecko vzala,
ta v usta, zraky, čelo její
půvabný žal i smutek psala. –

Tak zašel dnes dvacátý den,
v krajinu tichou kráčí sen.
Poslední požár kvapně hasne,
i nebe, jenž se růžojasné
nad modrými horami míhá.
"On nejde – již se nevrátí! –
Svedenou žel tu zachvátí!"
Hluboký vzdech jí ňadra zdvíhá,
bolestný srdcem bije cit,
a u tajemné vod stonání
mísí se dívky pláč a lkání.
V slzích se zhlíží hvězdný svit,
jenž po lících co jiskry plynou.
Vřelé ty jiskry tváře chladné
co padající hvězdy hynou;
kam zapadnou, tam květ uvadne.

Viz, mihla se u skály kraje;
daleko přes ní nahnuté
větýrek bílým šatem vlaje.
Oko má v dálku napnuté. –
Teď slzy rychle utírá,
rukou si zraky zastírá
upírajíc je v dálné kraje,
kde jezero se v hory kloní,
po vlnách jiskra jiskru honí,
po vodě hvězda s hvězdou hraje.

Jak holoubátko sněhobílé
pod černým mračnem přelétá,
lílie vodní zakvétá

Far out across the lakes she gazes.
Blue to her feet it coils and glimmers,
And green beyond, and greener, sleeps,
Till in the distances and deeps
In clear, pale light all melts and shimmers.
Over the wide and watery plain
The girl has fixed her weary gaze;
Over the wide and watery plain
Only the glint of starlight plays.
A lovely girl, an angel ravaged,
A bud that April winds have savaged,
In her pale cheeks doomed beauty hastens.
One hour has swallowed up her morrow,
One hour her promise chills and chastens,
Marries her May to grief and sorrow.

Of twenty days the last has died;
Still dreams the quiet countryside.
The last light hastens to its close,
And heaven, like a great, clear rose,
Over the deep blue mountains flushes.
'He comes not! Ah, such anguish takes me!
Another spoiled, and he forsakes me!'
A heavy sigh her sad voice hushes,
Her aching heart burns in her breast,
And with the water's plaint unsleeping
Mingles the note of bitter weeping.
Snared in her tears the stars find rest,
Down her pale cheeks like bright sparks flowing
Till like quenched stars they burn to shades there,
On her cold countenance briefly glowing.
And where they fall, the blossom fades there.

At the rock's rim she glimmers whitely;
A silken standard flies her gown,
In evening zephyrs fluttering lightly.
Her eyes on distance fix and frown –
In haste she dries her blinding tears,
Beneath her shading hand she peers,
And on the distant shore she fastens,
Where in the hills the lake creeps hiding;
Over the waves live sparks go gliding,
Star after watery starlet hastens.

Even as snow-white virgin doves
Against dark wastes of cloud in flight,
On water-lily flowering white

nad temné modro, tak se číle –
kde jezero se v hory níží –
po temných vlnách cosi blíží,
rychle se blíží. Malá chvíle,
a již co čápa vážný let,
ne již holoubě či lílie květ,
bílá se plachta větrem houpá.
Štíhlé se veslo v modru koupá,
a dlouhé pruhy kolem tvoří.
Těm zlaté růže, jenž při doubí
tam na horách po nebi hoří,
růžovým zlatem čela broubí.
"Rychlý to člůnek! blíž a blíže!
To on, to on! Ty péra, kvítí,
klobouk, oko, jenž pod ním svítí,
ten plášť!" Již člun pod skalou víže.

Vzhůru po skále lehký krok
uzounkou stezkou plavce vede.
Dívce se zardí tváře bledé
za dub je skryta. – Vstříc mu běží,
zaplesá – běží – dlouhý skok –
již plavci, již na prsou leží –
"Ha! Běda mi!" Vtom lůny zář
jí známou osvítila tvář;
hrůzou se krev jí v žilách staví.
"Kde Vilém můj?"

"Viz," plavec k ní
    tichými slovy šepce praví:
"Tam při jezeru vížka ční
nad stromů noc; její bílý stín
hlubokoť stopen v jezera klín;
však hlouběji ještě u vodu vryt
je z mala okénka lampy svit;
tam Vilém myšlenkou se baví,
že příští den jej žití zbaví.
On hanu svou, on tvoji vinu
se dozvěděl; on svůdce tvého
vraždě zavraždil otce svého.
Msta v patách kráčí jeho činu. –
Hanebně zemře. – Poklid mu dán,
až tváře, jenž co růže květou,
zbledlé nad kolem obdrží stán,
až štíhlé oudy v kolo vpletou.
Tak skoná strašný lesů pán! –

On deepest blue – so something moves –
Where in the hills the lake creeps hiding –
Over the dark waves nearer gliding,
Nearer in haste. A moment proves
Now as the stork's grave flight it looms,
No dove so flies nor lily blooms,
But a white sail rocked by hasting breezes.
A slender oar the blue wave teases,
With flaming furrows the surface hazing.
The golden rose of heaven's hold,
High in the mountain oakwoods blazing,
Gilds the ripples with rosy gold.
'Swift little boat! Near, nearer bounding!
'Tis he! 'Tis he! Those plumes bright beaming,
The hat, the eyes beneath it gleaming –
His cloak – 'The boat in the beach is grounding.

Over the rocks his light step rings,
By a known path he climbs and closes.
The girl's pale face flowers into roses;
From the tree's shade in wild hope flying
She runs, high-calling, runs and springs,
And on the rower's breast she's lying–
'Alas, my heart!: The moonlight shows
In its full flood a face she knows.
Her pounding blood to terror knells her.
Where is Vilem?'

'See, by the lake,'
In low grim tone the boatman tells her,
'Above the night the forests make
Rises a tower, its image white
Deep in the lake's heart drowned from sight;
But deeper, see, at the water's rim,
From a little window a lantern's gleam;
This night to vigil Vilem is giving:
Tomorrow sets him free from living.
His heavy guilt and yours he carries:
Deep your seducer's blood has stained him,
That stroke a parricide arraigned him.
Still, still revenge the avenger harries!
A felon's death! Peace to him bring,
Lord, when that face, the rose outshining,
In its high place stands withering,
And in the wheel his limbs are twining!
So dies the dreaded Forest King!

Za hanbu jeho, za vinu svou
měj hanu světa, měj kletbu mou!"

Obrátí se. – Utichl hlas –
Po skále slezl za krátký čas,
při skále člun svůj najde.
Ten rychle letí, co čápa let,
menší a menší, až co lílie květ
mezi horami po vodě zajde.

Tiché jsou vlny, temný vod klín,
vše lazurným se pláštěm krylo;
nad vodou se bílých skví šatů stín,
a krajina kolem šepce: "Jarmilo!"
V hlubinách vody: "Jarmilo! Jarmilo!!"

Je pozdní večer – první máj –
večerní máj – je lásky čas.
Zve k lásky hrám hrdliččin hlas:
"Jarmilo! Jarmilo!! Jarmilo!!!"

2

Klesla hvězda s nebes výše,
mrtvá hvězda, siný svit;
padá v neskončené říše
padá věčně v věčný byt.
Její pláč zní z hrobu všeho,
strašný jekot, hrůzný kvíl.
"Kdy dopadne konce svého?"
Nikdy – nikde – žádný cíl.
Kol bílé věže větry hrají,
při níž si vlnky šepotají.
Na bílé zdě stříbrnou zář
rozlila bledá lůny tvář;
však hluboko u věži je temno pouhé;
neb jasna měsíce světlá moc
uzounkým oknem u sklepení dlouhé
proletši se změní v pološerou noc.
Sloup sloupu kolem rameno si podává
temnotou noční. Z venku větru vání
přelétá zvražděných vězňů co lkání,
vlasami vězně pohrává.
Ten na kamenný složen stůl
hlavu o ruce opírá;
polou sedě a kleče půl
v hloub myšlenek se zabírá.

Bear for his guilt, and your own shame,
My bitter curse, and the world's blame!'

He turns. His voice to silence falls;
Down he climbs through the rocky walls,
Outward his boat goes gliding.
Swift as the stork's flight, beating fast,
Dwindling, dwindling, a lily at last,
Over the lake in the mountains hiding.

Hushed are the waters, dark, forlorn,
In deep dusk all things crouch to cover.
A white dress gleams on the waves that mourn
Over her: 'Jarmila!' like a lover,
And the woods sigh: 'Jarmila!' over and over.

Late evening, on the first of May –
The twilit May–the time of love.
To dalliance woos the turtle-dove:
'Jarmila! Jarmila!! Jarmila!!!'

2

Out of heaven a star falls questing,
Dying through the wastes of space,
Endlessly it falls unresting
Through its endless resting-place;
From the unbounded grave wild crying
Beats at heaven with bitter breath.
'Is there then no end of dying?'
Nowhere – never an end of death.
Around the white tower breezes shiver,
Beneath, the whispering wavelets quiver.
On the blanched walls in silver glance
The argent moon sheds radiance.
But deep within the tower is darkness only,
For the clear moon's pale wealth of light
Through narrow window into the cell gropes lonely,
And dims into the assault of night.
Column by column the sombre vault's recesses
Melt into darkness. The entering wind sighing
Circles the cell like murdered felons crying,
And stirs the prisoner's tresses.
Beside a table hewn of stone,
His head upon his hands inclining
Half-sits, half-kneels this wretched one,
To deeps of thought his soul resigning.

Po měsíce tváři jak mračna jdou,
zahalil vězeň v ně duši svou;
myšlenka myšlenkou umírá.

"Hluboká noc! ty rouškou svou
teď přikrýváš dědinu mou,
a ona truchlí pro mě! –
Že truchlí? – pro mě? – pouhý sen!
Ta dávno neví o mně.
Sotvaže zítra jasný den
nad její lesy vstane,
já hanebně jsem odpraven,
a ona – jak v můj první den –
vesele, jasně vzplane."

Umlknul; po sklepení jen,
jenž nad sloupy se zdvíhá,
dál, dál se hlas rozlíhá;
až – jakby hrůzou přimrazen –
na konci síně dlouhé
usne v temnotě pouhé.

Hluboké ticho té temnosti
zpět vábí časy pominulé,
a vězeň ve svých snách dny mladosti
zas žije dávno uplynulé.
To vzpomnění mladistvých let
mladistvé sny vábilo zpět;
a vězně oko slzy lilo,
srdce se v citech potopilo; –
marná to touha v zašlý svět.

Kde za jezerem hora horu
v západní stíhá kraje,
tam – zdá se mu – si v temném boru
posledně dnes co dítko hraje.
Od svého otce v svět vyhnán,
v loupežnickém tam roste sboru.
Později vůdcem spolku zván,
dovede činy neslýchané,
všude jest jméno jeho znané,
každémuť: "Strašný lesů pán!"
Až poslez láska k růži svadlé
nejvejš roznítí pomstu jeho,
a poznav svůdce dívky padlé
zavraždí otce neznaného.
Protož jest u vězení dán;

As clouds the moon's face veil and cover,
He draws their web his spirit over;
Thought into thought flows undesigning.

'Deep night, now in your veiling hold
My native village you enfold,
And friends weep for my end there.
Weep? – and for me? A dream outworn!
Long since I have no friend there.
The first gleam of tomorrow's morn
Over her forest breaking,
Will send me to my death forlorn,
And gild, as when her child was born,
Her merry, mild awaking.'

Silent he falls; but through the night,
About the high vault flying,
Far, far his voice goes sighing,
Till as with horror frozen in flight
At the cell's end it chills there,
And into darkness stills there.

The silence in the darkness grieving
Calls back to heart the days departed;
Again in waking dreams he's living
The long-lost life of a boy light-hearted.
Remembrance of green years and kind
Brings back a young man's dreams to mind;
The prisoner's eyes with tears are flowing,
And in his heart a great pain growing –
A lost world how shall the seeker find?

Mountain on mountain westward presses
Beyond the lake high-piled
And there in the pinewoods' sweet recesses,
He dreams himself once more a child.
Early thrust from his father's care,
Bred up by brigands in strives and stresses,
Last to their leader fallen heir,
Gallant and daring they acclaim him.
Known to all men, thus all men name him,
Lord of the Woods, a name of fear.
Till the love of a broken rose inflames him;
His hand, to bitter vengeance straying,
Seeks the seducer, strikes him, claims him,
His stranger father strangely slaying.
Wherefore a prisoner he lies,

a kolem má být odpraven
již zítra strašný lesů pán,
jak první z hor vyvstane den.

Teď na kamenný složen stůl
hlavu o ruce opírá,
polou sedě a kleče půl
v hloub myšlenek se zabírá;
po měsíce tváři jak mračna jdou,
zahalil vězeň v ně duši svou,
myšlenka myšlenkou umírá.

"Sok – otec můj! Vrah – jeho syn,
on svůdce dívky mojí! –
Neznámý mně. – Strašný můj čin
pronesl pomstu dvojí.
Proč rukou jeho vyvržen
stal jsem se hrůzou lesů?
Čí vinu příští pomstí den?
Čí vinou kletbu nesu?
Ne vinou svou! – V života sen
byl jsem já snad jen vyváben,
bych ztrestal jeho vinu?
A jestliže jsem vůli svou
nejednal tak, proč smrtí zlou
časně i věčně hynu? –
Časně i věčně? – věčně – čas – "
Hrůzou umírá vězně hlas
obražený od temných stěn;
hluboké noci němý stín
daleké kobky zajme klín,
a paměť vězně nový sen.

"Ach – ona, ona! Anjel můj!
Proč klesla dřív, než jsem ji znal?
Proč otec můj? – Proč svůdce tvůj?
Má kletba – " Léč hluboký žal
umoří slova. Kvapně vstal;
nocí řinčí řetězů hřmot
a z mala okna vězně zrak
zalétá ven za hluky vod. –
Ouplný měsíc přikryl mrak,
než nade temný horní stín
vychází hvězdy v noci klín;
i po jezeru hvězdný svit,
co ztracené světlo se míhá.
Zrak vězně tyto jiskry stíhá,

Doomed to the wheel's embrace that kills;
Lord of the Woods, at dawn he dies,
At the first kindling of the hills.

Now at a table hewn of stone,
His head upon his hands reposing,
Half-sits, half-kneels this wretched one,
The abyss of thought his soul enclosing:
As clouds the moon's face veil and cover,
He draws their web his spirit over,
Thought evermore new thought disclosing.

'He, sire and foe!–I, death and seed!
And he my love's betrayer!
I knew him not! My fearful deed
Recoiled and slew the slayer.
Why was I banished from his sight
The lawless woods to harry?
Whose crime does the dawn's death requite?
Whose guilt is this I carry?
Not mine! ah, surely I was bent
A mute, unwitting instrument
God's judgment to deliver.
Not mine the deed! Why, then, ah, why
Out to this hideous death go I
So soon–and, ah, for ever?
Soon, and for ever! Endless – death – '
For horror fails the prisoner's breath,
Echoing from the dungeon wall;
The voiceless shadow of the night
In iron grip shuts sound and sight.
A new dream holds his mind in thrall.

'Ah, she, my saint, my rose embowered!
Why lost ere ever she was found?
Why at my father's hands deflowered?
Accursed I! – ' Deep anguish drowned
The struggling words. With sudden sound
Of clamorous chains he springs upright,
And from the little window strains
Over the waves his tortured sight.
Cloud veils the moon, and shadow reigns
Over the earth, but no shade mars
The zenith glittering with stars;
With points of fire the lake they stain,
That flash and fade in waters hollow.
Their glimmering flight his fixed eyes follow,

a v srdce bolný vodí cit.
"Jak krásnáť noc! Jak krásný svět!
Jak světlo – stín se střídá!
Ach – zítra již můj mrtvý hled
nic více neuhlídá!
A jako venku šedý mrak
dál – dál se rozestírá:
tak –" Sklesl vězeň, sklesl zrak,
řetězů řinčí hřmot, a pak
u tichu vše umírá.

Již od hor k horám mraku stín –
ohromna ptáka peruť dlouhá –
daleké noci přikryl klín,
a šírou dálkou tma je pouhá.
Slyš! za horami sladký hlas
pronikl nocí temnou,
lesní to trouba v noční čas
uvádí hudbu jemnou.
Vše uspal tento sladký zvuk,
i noční dálka dřímá.
Vězeň zapomněl vlastních muk,
tak hudba ucho jímá.
"Jak milý život sladký hlas
v krajinu noční vdechne;
než zítřejší – ach – mine čas,
tu ucho mé ach nikdy zas
těch zvuků nedoslechne!"
Zpět sklesne vězeň – řetěz hluk
kobkou se rozestírá; – –
hluboké ticho. – V hloubi muk
se opět srdce svírá,
a dálné trouby sladký zvuk
co jemný pláč umírá. – – –
"Budoucí čas?! – Zítřejší den?! –
Co přes něj dál, pouhý to sen,
či spaní je bez snění?
Snad spaní je i život ten,
jenž žiji teď; a příští den
jen v jiný sen je změní?
Či po čem tady toužil jsem,
a co neměla šírá zem,
zítřejší den mi zjeví?
Kdo ví? – Ach žádný neví." –

A opět mlčí. Tichá noc
kolkolem vše přikrývá.

And all his heart is wrenched with pain.
'How fair the world! How rich the night!
Silver and shade agreeing!
Ah, tomorrow shuts my dying sight
On all the bliss of seeing!
And as grey cloud across the skies
Far, far and wide goes flying,
So – 'Down he sinks, his hungering eyes
Torn from the scene, his chains' harsh cries
Soon into silence dying.

A monstrous bird's extended wing,
From peak to peak the cloud is driven,
Under one vast pall gathering
In blackest marriage earth and heaven.
Hark! from the high hills lost to sight
A poignant voice is trilling,
A forest piper of the night,
The song of heaven distilling.
To all things which have wakeful lain
It charms down sleep's completeness;
The prisoner in his mortal pain
Finds Lethe in its sweetness.
'How beautiful, dear voice, the song
On the night's breast you're flinging!
But one more night–ah, God, not long!–
And deaf to your enchanted tongue,
No more I'll hear such singing.'
Again he sinks–the clank of chains
Rings through the cell, despairing–
Deep silence. Once again the pains
Of death his heart are tearing,
And fading far the voice complains
An anguish beyond bearing.
'Time yet to come? Tomorrow's day?
Still, still some dream will time repay,
Or sleep too deep for dreaming?
Perhaps this life which here I live
Is but a sleep, and dawn will give
Only another seeming?
Or that best rose, long longed-for here,
That fruit the wide earth did not bear,
Will dawn and death disclose?
Who knows? – Ah, no one knows!'

Silence again. The hush of night
On all the earth is draped there.

Zhasla měsíce světlá moc,
i hvězdný svit, a kol a kol
je pouhé temno, šírý dol
co hrob daleký zívá.
Umlkl vítr, vody hluk,
usnul i líbý trouby zvuk,
a u vězení síni dlouhé
je mrtvé ticho, temno pouhé.
"Hluboká noc – temná je noc! –
Temnější mně nastává – – –
Pryč, myšlenko!!" – A citu moc
myšlenku překonává.

Hluboké ticho. – Z mokrých stěn
kapka za kapkou splyne,
a jejich pádu dutý hlas
dalekou kobkou rozložen,
jako by noční měřil čas,
zní – hyne – zní a hyne –
zní – hyne – zní a hyne zas.

"Jak dlouhá noc – jak dlouhá noc –
však delší mně nastává. – – –
Pryč, myšlenko!" – A hrůzy moc
myšlenku překonává. –
Hluboké ticho. – Kapky hlas
svým pádem opět měří čas.

"Temnější noc! – – – Zde v noční klín
ba lůny zář, ba hvězdný kmit
se vloudí – – tam – jen pustý stín,
tam žádný – žádný – žádný svit,
pouhá jen tma přebývá.
Tam všecko jedno, žádný díl –
vše bez konce – tam není chvíl,
nemine noc, nevstane den,
tam času neubývá. –
Tam žádný – žádný – žádný cíl –
bez konce dál – bez konce jen
se na mne věčnost dívá.
Tam prázdno pouhé – nade mnou
a kolem mne i pode mnou
pouhé tam prázdno zívá. –
Bez konce ticho – žádný hlas –
bez konce místo – noc – i čas – – –
To smrtelný je mysle sen,
toť, co se ‚nic' nazývá.

Quenched is the moon's benignant light,
Quenched are the stars, and all around
Is purest darkness, black, profound,
As if the grave's mouth gaped there.
No winds blow more, nor waves complain,
Nor even the far, sweet pipe of pain,
And in the bosom in the cell
Dead silence, utter darkness dwell.
'How deep the night–how dark the night!
On me a darker closes –
Away, thought!' Panic shuts from sight
The grave his thought discloses.

Deep silence. From the streaming wall
Flows down a small, slow river,
And echoing drops the silence fret;
Through the long cell their hollow fall,
Measuring night's moments of regret,
Chimes – ceases – chimes and ceases ever,
Chimes – ceases – chimes and ceases yet.

'How long the night – how long the night!
On me a longer closes –
Away, thought!' Horror shuts from sight
The grave his thought discloses.
Deep silence. Once again the chime
Of slow drops falling metes out time.

"A darker night! Here in the womb
Of veriest midnight shines some beam
Of moon or star – there – hideous gloom,
There never – never – never a gleam,
Only the dark for ever.
All's one there, without part–they send
No hours, no moments to befriend,
Night fails not, never dawns the day,
For there time passes never.
There never – never – never an end!
From death that passes not away
Who shall my soul deliver?
There utter emptiness, beneath,
Around, above, the void of death,
Quenching all life's endeavour.
Unending silence – never a sound –
Unending space, night, time, surround
The dead mind dreaming on decay –
Mere nothingness – for ever!

A než se příští skončí den,
v to pusté nic jsem uveden. – – – ”
Vězeň i hlas omdlívá.

A lehounce si vlnky hrají
jezerní dálkou pode věží,
s nimi si vlnky šepotají,
vězně uspávati se zdají,
jenž v hlubokých mrákotách leží.

Strážného vzbudil strašný hřmot,
jejž řetězů činí padání;
se světlem vstoupil. – Lehký chod
nevzbudil vězně z strašných zdání.
Od sloupu k sloupu lampy svit
dlouhou zalétá síní,
vzdy bledší – bledší její kmit,
až vzadu zmizí její moc,
a pustopustá temná noc
ostatní díl zastíní.
Leč nepohnutý vězně zrak –
jak by jej ještě halil mrak –
zdá se, že nic nezírá;
ač strážce lampy rudá zář
ubledlou mu polila tvář,
a tma již prchla čírá.
On za kamenný složen stůl
hlavu o ruce opírá,
polou sedě a kleče půl
znovu v mdlobách umírá;
a jeví hlasu šepot mdlý,
že trapnýť jeho sen i zlý.

“Duch můj – duch můj – a duše má!”
Tak slova mu jednotlivá
ze sevřených ust plynou.
Než však dostihne ucho hlas,
tu slova strašná ničím zas –
jakž byla vyšla – hynou.

Přistoupí strážce, a lampy zář
před samou vězně vstoupí tvář.
Obličej vězně – strašný zjev –
oko spočívá nehnuté
jak v neskončenost napnuté,
po tváři slzy – pot a krev;
v ustech spí šepot – tichý zpěv.

And I to nothing – but one more day,
And I to nothing am cast away – '
He faints, he falls aquiver.

Lightly the waves at play come springing
Under the tower, their small spray flying,
Ever a gentle murmur bringing,
A cradle-song for captive singing,
Who in a deep half-death is lying.

The fearful clash of chains awakes
The guard, who with his lamp comes hasting;
So light a step, it scarcely breaks
The prisoner's trance of dread unresting.
Pillar to pillar the lantern bright
Puts forth its little gleaming:
Still paler, paler grows its light,
Till fails at last the exhausted spark,
And absolute and moveless dark
On all beyond lies dreaming.
But still the prisoner's eyes, adaze
As if night shrouded still their gaze,
Strain forward, nothing seeing,
Although the lantern's reddening ray
Lights his wan face, and drives away
The timid shadows fleeing.
Beside the table hewn of stone,
His head upon his hands inclining,
Half-sits, half-kneels the wretched one,
To sick despair his soul resigning;
And the faint whispering of his breath
Tells forth tormenting dreams of death.

'Alas, my soul–Alas, my love–'
Single and slow the sad words move
Out of his shut lips sighing.
Scarcely they reach the straining ear
When, newly born in pain and fear,
Already they are dying.

The gaoler's light before him goes,
And on the prisoner's face it glows.
The prisoner's face – ah, dread and pain! –
His fixed eyes glare in wild distress
After an end of endlessness,
Tears, sweat and blood his pallor stain,
For speech his lips contend in vain.

Tu k ustům vězně ucho své
přiklonil strážce bázlivé;
a jak by lehký větřík vál,
vězeň svou pověst šepce dál.
A strážný vzdy se níž a níž
ku vězni kloní – blíž a blíž,
až ucho s usty vězně spojí.
ten šepce tíše – tíš a tíš,
až zmlkne – jak by pevně spal.

Leč strážný nepohnutě stojí,
po tváři se mu slzy rojí,
ve srdci jeho strašný žal. –
Dlouho tak stojí přimrazen,
až sebrav sílu kvapně vstal,
a rychlým krokem spěchá ven.
On sice – dokud ještě žil –
co slyšel, nikdy nezjevil,
než navzdy bledé jeho líce
neusmály se nikdy více.

Za strážným opět temný stín
zahalil dlouhé síně klín;
hlubokou nocí kapky hlas
svým pádem opět měřil čas.

A vězeň na kamenný stůl
složený – klečí – sedí půl.
Obličej jeho – strašný zjev –
oko spočívá nehnuté,
jak v neskončenost napnuté,
po tváři slzy – pot – a krev.

A ustavičně kapky hlas
svým pádem dále měří čas.
A kapky – vod i větrů zpěv
vězňovi blízký hlásá skon,
jenž myšlenkami omdlívá. –
Z dálky se sova ozývá,
a nad ním půlnoc bije zvon.

Intermezzo I
Půlnoc
(*Krajina*)

V rozlehlých rovinách spí bledé lůny svit,
kolem hor temno je, v jezeru hvězdný kmit,
nad jezerem pahorek stojí.

The frightened gaoler stoops to snare
The thread of utterance from the air,
Lighter than lightest breeze he hears
The prisoner's tale of blood and tears.
Lower he leans, and closer yet
To the wan mouth his ear is set,
Hard on the labouring lips now leaning,
Till fainting, fainting, they forget
Speech, as if sleep came unawares.

Still stands the guard in dreadful dreaming,
Like bees in swarm his tears come teeming,
Sorrow his heart within him sears.
Long he stands frozen there aghast,
Till thrusting off his helpless fears,
Out of the cell he flies in haste.
Long as he lived, he told no word
Of what his ears this night had heard:
Rather his whole life through thereafter
His pale lips said farewell to laughter.

The guard is fled, fast-closed the door.
Deep darkness shrouds the cell once more;
And through the night once more the chime
Of slow drops falling metes out time.

Beside the table hewn of stone
Half-sits, half-kneels Vilem alone;
His face a sight for fear and pain,
With fixed eyes staring in distress
After an end of endlessness –
Tears, sweat and blood his pallor stain.

Incessantly the watery chime
Of slow drops falling metes out time,
And wind and waves as one complain;
To Vilem's ear of death they tell.
He faints beneath the thought appalling.
Far through the night an owl is calling,
And louder beats the midnight bell.

Intermezzo I
Midnight
(*a lonely place in the countryside*)

In the wide plains sleeps sound the pale moon's argent light,
Darkness is on the hills, the lake with stars is bright.
A hillock by the lake-shore rises,

797

Na něm se sloup, s tím kolo zdvíhá,
nad tím se bílá lebka míhá,
kol kola duchů dav se rojí;
hrůzných to postav sbor se stíhá.

Sbor duchů

"V půlnočních ticho je dobách;
světýlka bloudí po hrobách,
a jejich modrá mrtvá zář
svítí v dnes pohřbeného tvář,
jenž na stráži – co druzí spí –
o vlastní křížek opřený
poslední z pohřbených zde dlí.
V zenitu stojí šedý mrak
a na něm měsíc složený
v ztrhaný mrtvý strážce zrak,
i v pootevřené huby
přeskřípené svítí zuby."

Jeden hlas

"Teď pravý čas! – připravte stán –
neb zítra strašný lesů pán
mezi nás bude uveden."

Sbor duchů
(sundávaje lebku)

"Z mrtvého kraje vystup ven,
nabudiž život – přijmi hlas,
buď mezi námi – vítej nám.
Dlouho jsi tady bydlil sám,
jiný tvé místo zajme zas."

Lebka
(mezi nimi kolem se točíc)

"Jaké to oudů toužení,
chtí opět býti jedno jen.
Jaké to strašné hemžení,
můj nový sen. – Můj nový sen! – "

Jeden hlas

"Připraven jestiť jeho stán.
Až zítra půlnoc nastane,
vichr nás opět přivane.
Pak mu buď slavný pohřeb dán."

Sbor duchů

"Připraven jestiť jeho stán.
Až zítra půlnoc nastane,
vichr nás opět přivane.
Pak mu buď slavný pohřeb dán."

A stake thereon, a wheel raised lightly,
Whereon a bleached skull glistens whitely,
While ghostly rout a dance devises,
About the high wheel revelling rightly.

Chorus of Phantoms

'Silent the midnight graveyard lies;
Through the graves the marshlight flies,
Its dead blue radiance lights the head
Of the newly-buried dead,
Who, while his fellows sleep, stands guard,
Last of the sepulchred, dead today,
Beside his own cross keeping ward.
A grey cloud in the zenith stays,
No moon beneath it but the ray
Of the dead man's glassy gaze,
And through half-open lips beneath
The glitter of his gnashing teeth.'

A Voice

'This is the hour! The place prepare!
Lord of the Woods, the lord of fear,
Is one with us at dawn of day.'

Chorus of Phantoms (lifting down the skull)

'From death's dim threshold come away,
Inherit life – a voice receive.
Be one among us, know us well,
No more be doomed alone to dwell.
Another must your place achieve.'

The Skull (joining in their dance)

'How my limbs long to join again
In one whole creature, only one!
What is this rout of terror and pain?
My newest dream – I still dream on!'

Voice

'His place of honour ready see!
When tomorrow's course is o'er
The storm shall bear us here once more.
Glorious may his burial be!'

Chorus of Phantoms

'His place of honour ready see!
When tomorrow's course is o'er
The storm shall bear us here once more.
Glorious may his burial be!'

Jeden hlas

"Rozlehlým polem leť můj hlas;
pohřeb v půlnoční bude čas!
Co k pohřbu dá, každý mi zjev!"

Čekan s kolem

"Mrtvému rakví budu já."

Žáby z bažiny

"My odbudem pohřební zpěv."

Vichr po jezeru

"Pohřební hudbu vichr má."

Měsíc v zenitu

"Já bílý příkrov tomu dám."

Mlha po horách

"Já truchlroušky obstarám."

Noc

"Já černá roucha doručím."

Hory v kolo krajiny

"Roucha i roušky dejte nám."

Padající rosa

"A já vám slzy zapůjčím."

Suchopar

"Pak já rozduji vonný dým."

Zapadající mračno

"Já rakev deštěm pokropím."

Padající květ

"Já k tomu věnce uviji."

Lehké větry

"My na rakev je donesem."

Svatojánské mušky

"My drobné svíce ponesem."

Bouře z hluboka

"Já zvonů dutý vzbudím hlas."

Krtek pod zemí

"Já zatím hrob mu vyryji."

Čas

"Náhrobkem já ho přikryji."

Přes měsíc letící hejno nočního ptactva

"My na pohřební přijdem kvas."

Jeden hlas

"Slavný mu pohřeb připraven.

Voice
'Fly, voice, across the fields with power!
At midnight is the funeral hour.
His votive gift let each make known!'
　The Stake and Wheel
'I'll be the coffin to his repose.'
　Frogs in the Marsh
'The burial anthem we'll intone.'
　Storm over the Lake
'The gale funeral music knows.'
　The Moon in the Zenith
'I'll cover him with snow-white pall.'
　Mist on the Mountains
'With veils I'll drape his funeral.'
　　Night
'I'll give black weeds to mourn the dead.'
　The Hills Standing Round
'Give veils and garments to us all.'
　The Falling Dew
'And I will give you tears to shed.'
　The Barren Soil
'I'll incense with sweet smoke his head.'
　The Sinking Cloud
'With rain will I asperge his bed.'
　The Falling Blossom
'I will weave garlands for his bier.'
　　Light Breezes
'We'll bear them to the coffin lightly.'
　St John's Fireflies
'Our tiny candles shall burn up brightly.'
　Thunder out of the Depths
'I'll wake the great bell's hollow tone.'
　The Mole under the Earth
'I'll dig his grave, I, lowly here.'
　　Time
'Over his bones a tomb I'll rear.'
Flocks of Night-Birds Crossing the Moon
'We'll make the funeral feast our own.'
　　Voice
'All honour to his grave we pay!

Ubledlý měsíc umírá,
Jitřena brány otvírá,
již je den, již je den!"
   Sbor duchů
"Již je den, již je den!"
   (*Zmizí*)

3

Nad temné hory růžný den
vyvstav májový budí dol,
nad lesy ještě kol a kol –
lehká co mlha – bloudí sen.
Modravé páry z lesů temných
v růžové nebe vstoupají,
i nad jezerem barev jemných
modré se mlhy houpají;
a v břehu jeho – v stínu hory –
i šírým dolem – dál a dál –
za lesy – všude bílé dvory
se skvějí; až – co mocný král,
ohromný jako noci stín   ·
v růžový strmě nebes klín –
nejzáz vrchů nejvyšší stál.

Ledvaže však nad modré temeno hor
brunatné slunce rudě zasvitnulo,
tu náhle ze sna všecko procitnulo,
a vesel plesá vešken živý tvor.
V jezeru zeleném bílý je ptáků sbor,
a lehkých člůnků běh i rychlé veslování
modravé stíny vln v rudé pruhy rozhání.
Na břehu jezera borový šumí háj,
z něj drozdů slavný žalm i jiných ptáků zpěv
mísí se u hlasy dolem bloudících děv;
veškeren živý tvor mladistvý slaví máj.
A větru ranního – co zpěvu – líbé vání
tam v dolu zeleném roznáší bílý květ,
tam řídí nad lesy divokých husí let,
tam zase po horách mladistvé stromky sklání. –
Leč výjev jediný tu krásu jitra zkalí.
Kde v šíré jezero uzounký ostrov sahá,
z nějž města malého i bílé věže stín
hlubokoť stopený v zelený vody klín,
náramný křik a hřmot mladým se jitrem vzmahá,
a valný zástup se z bran mala města valí.
Zdaleka spěchá lid – vzdy větší zástup ten –

The moon pales in the heaven's heart,
The gates of morning draw apart –
It is day! It is day!'
   Chorus of Phantoms (as they vanish)
'It is day! It is Day!'

3

Over the dark hills rosy day
Arises, the May valley wakes;
Above the woods, as morning breaks,
Like mist lies long the dream of May.
Out of the forests bluely lifting
Faint vapours climb the rose-flushed sky,
And on the lake more bluely drifting
In delicate colours melt and die;
And on the shore, and in the shadow
Of hills and valleys flowering,
Shine out white courts through wood and meadow,
Waking; till like a mighty king –
Colossal as the shade of night
Against the heaven's rosy light –
The highest peak stands towering.

But now the sun his first red blessing gives
Over the blue, dark hills, and by that token
Suddenly all the spell of dreams is broken,
And joy possesses everything that lives.
Whitely the lake's green glass the flight of birds receives,
And fleets of little craft, and small, swift-rowing shallops,
Pattern the dim blue waves with glancing, fiery scallops.
Murmurous by the shore the pinewoods greet the day,
Sweet with the song of birds, the thrush's shower of pearls,
And mingling with their psalm the mirth of straying girls,
As all that lives draws breath to praise the youthful May.
The morning wind, like song, through the green valley blowing,
Bears on its incensed breath a sweet white foam of flowers,
And wild geese ride its flight above the forest bowers,
And to its touch young trees unfold their eager growing.
One scene, and only one, the fair young morn defaces,
Where to the wide lake's heart a narrow isle goes straying,
Bearing the little town, and the white tower, whose shade
Deep in the waters green in quiveringly laid.
Here wakes a clamorous cry, babel of human baying,
As from the gates of the town the hungry man-pack races.
From far the people haste, a swift stream rushing by,

vzdy větší – větší jest – vzdy roste tento pluk;
nesmírné množství již. – Vzdy větší jeho hluk.
Nešťastný zločinec má býti vyveden.

Teď z mala města bran vojenský pluk vychází,
povolným krokem on zločince doprovází,
jenž v středu jeho jde jak jindy ozdoben.
Utichl množství hluk – leč znovu počne zas,
a mnohý v hluku tom vynikne silný hlas:
"To on, to on! Ty péra, kvítí,
klobouk, oko, jenž pod ním svítí!
Ten jeho plášť, to on, to on! To strašnýť lesů pán!"
Tak lidem ode všech voláno bylo strán;
a větší vzdy byl hluk – zbouřených jako vod –
čím blíže zločince zdlouhavý vedl chod.
Kolem něj zástup jde – co nebem černý mrak,
z něho – co blesku svit – v slunci se leskne zbraň.
Volně jde nešťastný – upřený v zemi zrak.
Z městečka zvonku hlas. Množství se modlí zaň.

Na břehu jezera malý pahorek stojí,
na něm se dlouhý kůl, na kůlu kolo zdvíhá.
Blíž strmí kolmý vrch, na vrchu vrchol dvojí,
na vyšším vrcholi bílá se kaple míhá.
U volném průvodu ku kapli přišel sbor;
všickni teď ustoupí – zločinec stojí sám.
Posledněť vyveden v přírody slavný chrám,
by ještě popatřil do lůna temných hor,
kde druhdy veselý dětinství trávil věk;
by ještě jedenkrát v růžový nebe klín
na horu vyveden, před bílé kaple stín,
nebe i světů všech pánovi svůj vzdal vděk.
Umlknul vešken hluk, nehnutý stojí lid,
a srdce každého zajímá vážný cit.
V soucitu s nešťastným v hlubokém smutku plál
slzící lidu zrak obrácen v hory výš,
kde nyní zločinec, v přírody patře říš,
před Bohem pokořen v modlitbě tiché stál.

Vyšlého slunce rudá zář
zločince bledou barví tvář,
a slzy s oka stírá,
jenž smutně v dálku zírá.
Hluboko pod ním krásný dol,
temné jej hory broubí kol,
lesů věnec objímá.
Jasné jezero dřímá

And ever swells the food, a river strongly rolling,
A mighty multitude, its voice to thunder tolling;
The unhappy felon comes, led forth at dawn to die.

Now from the little town a troop of guards comes swinging,
In slow and sombre march the hapless prisoner bringing,
Whose old, proud habit soon the eager watchers spy.
The clamour stills around – a hush falls on the crowd –
Till babel bursts anew, with many a cry and loud:
"Tis he! The flowers, the plumes he's wearing,
The hat, the eye beneath it glaring –
His very cloak – 'Tis he,' tis he! The dreaded Forest King!'
About him beats the cry, his old name echoing;
And louder still it rings, as thundering waters clear,
As with a heavy step the criminal draws near.
Round him darkens the throng – like heavy clouds in heaven –
A sword flames from the dark – as heaven's lightnings flare;
Slowly the doomed man goes, his gaze to earth is given.
The town bell tolls; the crowd pities and falls to prayer.

There stands a little mound, on the lake-shore leaning lightly,
A long stake raised thereon, a wheel above it rearing,
A steep hill looms above, twin peaks its summit sharing,
And on the higher point a chapel gleaming whitely.
In sombre march thereto company is come;
Now all men move aside – the felon stands alone.
A last time led forth here, still he beholds his own,
The dark, deep-breasted hills which were his early home,
Where the lost coin was spent, the golden childhood days.
Yet once more, only once, in the rosy dawning light,
Let forth to the hills, a shade before the chapel white,
To the lord of heaven and earth his reverence he pays.
Hushed is all sound; transfixed the people stand apart,
And deep compassion folds its hands on every heart.
His grief their grief inflames, they suffer his despair,
Fixing their eyes through tears on the summit where he stands
Adoring the fair earth well-fashioned at God's hands,
A murderer praising God in the humbled hush of prayer.

The rising sun with ruddy grace
Flushes the prisoner's pallid face;
His eyes, through mists of weeping,
A last love-tryst are keeping.
Beneath him deep the lovely vale
Dreams in its rugged mountain pale,
By forests circled greenly.
The lucid lake serenely

u středu květoucího dolu.
Nejblíž se modro k břehu vine,
dále zeleně zakvítá,
vzdy zeleněji prosvítá
až posléz v bledé jasno splyne.
Bílé dvory u velkém kolu
sem tam jezera broubí břeh.
V jezeru bílých ptáků sbor,
a malých člůnků rychlý běh,
až kde jezero v temno hor
v modré se dálce níží.
Loďky i bílé v břehu dvory –
věž – město – bílých ptáků rod –
pahorky vkolo – temné hory –
vše stopeno v lůno vod,
jak v zrcadle se zhlíží.
Tam v modré dálce skály lom
květoucí břeh jezera tíží,
na skále rozlehlý je strom –
starý to dub – tam – onen čas,
kde k lásce zval hrdliččin hlas,
nikdy se nepřiblíží. –
Nejblíže pahorek se zdvíhá,
na něm se kůl a kolo míhá.
Po hoře – na níž stojí – háj
mladistvý hučí – smutný stesk –
nad šírým dolem slunce lesk,
a ranní rosa – jitřní máj.

To vše zločinec ještě jednou zřel,
to vše, jež nyní opustiti měl,
a hluboký srdce mu žel uchvátí;
hluboce vzdechne – slza slzu stíhá –
ještě jednou – posledně – vše probíhá,
pak slzavý v nebe svůj zrak obrátí.
Po modrém blankytu bělavé páry hynou,
lehounký větřík s nimi hraje;
a vysoko – v daleké kraje
bílé obláčky dálným nebem plynou,
a smutný vězeň takto mluví k nim:
"Vy, jenž dalekosáhlým během svým,
co ramenem tajemným zemi objímáte,
vy hvězdy rozplynulé, stíny modra nebe,
vy truchlenci, jenž rozsmutnivše sebe,
v tiché se slzy celí rozplýváte,
vás já jsem posly volil mezi všemi.

Nursed in the flowering valley drowses.
Blue to the shore it coils and glimmers,
And green beyond, and greener, sleeps,
Till in the distances and deeps
In clear, pale light all melts and shimmers.
About the wheel the white farmhouses
Dimpling the sunlit lake-shore lie.
Across the mirroring waters fast
Flocks of white birds and small boats fly,
Till bluely hides the lake at last,
Far in the hills retreating.
And white craft in the scalloped beaches –
The tower – the town – the white birds' flight –
Hillocks and shadowy mountain reaches –
Gaze on that mirror with delight,
Their deep-drowned beauty greeting.
Rocks are piled heavy on that far shore
Where flowering land and lake are meeting,
And there an oak-tree old and hoar
Roots in the rocks–once, once the dove
Called there deliciously to love –
Oh, fair lost hour and fleeting!
Never again! The mound is nearing,
The column and the wheel appearing.
Beyond the hill there slips away
A young wood, murmuring mournfully;
Radiant the sun on vale and lea –
The morning dew – the dawning May.

Beauty once more the felon's eyes receive,
Beauty which now for ever he must leave,
And passionate regret his heart possesses:
Deeply he sighs – tear after tear flows over –
One last long look, lingering as looks the lover,
Then to the sky his tear-dimmed eyes he raises.
In the azure vault of heaven the blanching mists are dancing,
In light dissolving zephyrs tattered,
And on the far horizon scattered
White cloudlets over the placid sky go glancing.
The grieving prisoner greets them as they race:
'You clouds, who in your wandering course embrace
Like secret circling arm the earth her own course keeping,
You dissolutions of stars, shades in the blue of heaven,
You mourners ever to mutual sorrow given,
Who know so well the ways of silent weeping –
Bear you my charge, of all things that have birth.

Kudy plynete u dlouhém dálném běhu,
i tam, kde svého naleznete břehu,
tam na své pouti pozdravujte zemi.
Ach zemi krásnou, zemi milovanou,
kolébku mou i hrob můj, matku mou,
vlasť jedinou i v dědictví mi danou,
šírou tu zemi, zemi jedinou! –
A až běh váš onu skálu uhlídá,
kde v břehu jezera – tam dívku uplakanou – "
Umlkl již, slza s slzou se střídá.
Teď s výše hory s vězněm kráčí pluk
širokou stezkou v středu mlada borku,
doleji – dole – již jsou na pahorku –
a znovu ztichl šíra množství hluk.
Přichystán již popravce s mečem stojí,
jedenkrát ještě vězeň zdvihl zrak,
pohlédl vůkolím – povzdechl – pak
spustiv je zas – k blízké se smrti strojí.
Obnažil vězeň krk, obnažil ňádra bílé,
poklekl k zemi, kat odstoupí, strašné chvíle –
pak blyskne meč, kat rychlý stoupne krok,
v kolo tne meč, zločinci blyskne v týle,
upadla hlava – skok i – ještě jeden skok –
i tělo ostatní ku zemi teď se skloní.
Ach v zemi krásnou, zemi milovanou,
v kolébku svou i hrob svůj, matku svou,
v vlasť jedinou i v dědictví mu danou,
v šírou tu zemi, zemi jedinou,
v matku svou, v matku svou, krev syna teče po ní.

Po oudu lámán oud, až celé vězně tělo
u kolo vpleteno nad kůlem v kole pnělo,
i hlava nad kolem svůj obdržela stán;
tak skončil života dny strašný lesů pán;
na mrtvé tváři mu poslední dřímá sen.
Na něj se dívajíc – po celý dlouhý den
nesmírné množství v kol mala pahorku stálo;
teprv až k západu schýlivši slunce běh
veselo v mrtvý zrak sťaté hlavy se smálo,
utichl jezera šírý – večerní břeh.

Nad dálkou temných hor poslední požár plál;
v hluboké ticho to měsíce vzešla zář,
stříbřící hlavy té ubledlou mrtvou tvář
i tichý pahorek, jenž v břehu vody stál.
Města jsou vzdálená co bílý v modru mrak,

Where you pass from me on your long, wide way
To the distant shore, there for a moment stay,
There, pilgrim clouds, greet reverently the earth.
Ah, well-beloved earth, beautiful earth,
My cradle and grave, the womb that gave me birth,
My sweet, sole land, left to my spirit's keeping,
Ah, vast and single of beauty as of worth!–
Seek there that rock, and when your swift sails gain it –
If you shall see – by the shore – a woman weeping – '
There fails his voice, the strangling tears have slain it.
Down from the height the guards their prisoner lead
By a wide pathway through young pinewoods threading,
Down and still down; now on the mound they're treading;
And now the multitude is hushed indeed.
The executioner with his sword stands ready.
Yet one more time the prisoner lifts his eyes,
Worships the sweet, encircling world–once sighs–
And on the approaching death his soul makes steady.
His breast and throat he bares, kneeling to earth he leaves it;
Back steps the headsman–an age the frozen mind believes it! –
The sword flashes; a rapid forward stride –
The sword circles; the bent white neck receives it –
The head falls – a tremor – and yet a tremor beside –
And falls the body after, one with the grieved earth growing.
Into the earth, so beautiful, so beloved.
His cradle and grave, the womb that gave him birth,
His sweet, sole land, his heritage approved,
In the generous earth, the single, holy earth,
Into the mother's heart the blood of her son is flowing.

The prisoner's shattered shell, limb after long limb broken,
Twined in the wheel's embrace is raised, a terrible token,
And over the wheel his head, a blind, oblivious thing.
So died the lord of the woods, the dreaded Forest King.
On the dead countenance the last dream lingers still.
Gazing upon his face, mute round the little hill
The unquiet multitude awaits the long day's ending,
Till the declining sun draws to the west once more,
Into the head's blind eyes its gay last laughter sending.
Hushed is the broad lake–hushed is the evening shore.

Above the far dark hills the last radiance blazed.
The pale, dead face of the head is softly silvered o'er,
Silvered the silent mound, hushed by the lake-shore,
As in the evening hush the moon's fair face is raised.
Distant are grown the towns, far as a cloud in air,

přes ně v kraj daleký nesl se mrtvý zrak,
v kraj, kde co dítě on – Ó krásný – krásný věk!
Daleko zanesl věk onen časů vztek,
dalekoť jeho sen, umrlý jako stín,
obraz co bílých měst u vody stopen klín,
takť jako zemřelých myšlenka poslední,
tak jako jméno jich, pradávných bojů hluk,
dávná severní zář, vyhaslé světlo s ní,
zbořtěné harfy tón, ztrhané strůny zvuk,
zašlého věku děj, umřelé hvězdy svit,
zašlé bludice pouť, mrtvé milenky cit,
zapomenutý hrob, věčnosti skleslý byt
vyhasla ohně kouř, slitého zvonu hlas,
to jestiť zemřelých krásný dětinský čas.

Je pozdní večer – druhý máj –
večerní máj – je lásky čas,
hrdliččin zve ku lásce hlas:
"Viléme! Viléme!! Viléme!!!"

Intermezzo II

Stojí hory proti sobě,
z jedné k druhé mrak přepnutý
je, co temný strop klenutý,
jednu k druhé pevně víže.
Ouvalem tím v pozdní době
ticho, temno jako v hrobě.
Za horami, kde pod mrakem
ve vzdálí se rozestupují –
v temné dálce, něco blíže
než hory se sestupují,
takže siným pod oblakem
skály ouzkou bránu tvoří.
Za tou v dálce pode mrakem
temnorudý požár hoří,
dlouhý pruh v plamenné záři
západní rozvinut stranou,
po jehožto rudé tváři
noční ptactvo kola vedší,
jako by plamennou branou
nyní v dálku zalétalo.
Hasnul požár – bledší – bledší,
až se šírošíré nebe
noční rosou rozplakalo,
rozesmutnivši zem i sebe.

Beyond to the edge of seeing the dead eyes steadily stare,
To the edge of sight, to his youth–Oh, brief, bright childhood day!
Time in its headlong flight has carried that Spring away.
Far fled is his dream, a shadow no more found,
Like visions of white towns, deep in the waters drowned,
The last indignant thoughts of the defeated dead,
Their unremembered names, the clamour of old fights,
The worn-out northern lights, after their gleam is fled,
The untuned harp, whose strings distil no more delights,
The deeds of time gone by, quenched starlight overhead,
Heresy's pilgrimage, the loving, lovely dead,
The deep forgotten grave, eternal board and bed;
As the smoke of burned-out fires, as the shattered bell's chime,
Are the dead years of the dead, their beautiful childhood time!

Late eve – the second eve of May –
The twilit May – the time of love –
Meltingly calls the turtle-dove:
Vilem! Vilem! Vilem!!

Intermezzo II

Close the hills lean to each other,
Underneath a dark cloud hiding,
Like a vaulted ceiling riding
Taut from one peak to his brother.
Dark this place by evening gloom is,
Dark and silent as the tomb is.
In the portal deeply-shaded,
Where the hills shrink back dividing,
Sharp rocks in the opening spaces
Steeply rear their frowning faces,
Lower, narrower, blackly biding;
Underneath the cloud dark-braided
Shuts this gate of rocks and boulders.
In the valley's heart deep-gladed,
Darkly red a camp-fire smoulders,
Broken from the west bright-beaming,
A long sliver of the sunset;
Round its red nocturnal gleaming
Circle night-birds, wheeling, plaining,
In a red and restless onset,
Till the hue of night they borrow.
Sinks the fire, still waning–waning,
Till the broad and bounteous heaven
Melts in nightly dews of sorrow,
And the earth to grief is given.

V hlubokém ouvalu klínu,
ve stověkých dubů stínu,
sbor u velkém kole sedí.
Zahalení v pláště bílé
jsou to druzi noční chvíle.
Každý před se v zemi hledí
beze slova, bez pohnutí,
jak by kvapnou hrůzou jmutí
v sochy byli proměnění.
Večerních co krajin pění.
tichý šepot – tiché lkání –
nepohnutým kolem plynul,
tichý šepot bez přestání:
"Vůdce zhynul! – vůdce zhynul!" –

V kotouči jak vítr skučí,
nepohnutým kolem zvučí:
"Vůdce zhynul! – vůdce zhynul!" –

Jako listů šepotání
pode skálou při ozvěně,
znělo kolem bez přestání,
jednozvučně, neproměnně:
"Vůdce zhynul! – vůdce zhynul!" –

Zachvěly se lesy dalné,
ozvaly se nářky valné:
"Pán náš zhynul! – zhynul!! – zhynul!!!"

4

Krásný máj uplynul, pohynul jarní květ,
a léto vzplanulo; – pak letní přešel čas,
podzim i zima též – i jaro vzešlo zas;
až mnohá léta již přenesl časů let.

Byl asi sedmý rok, poslední v roce den;
hluboká na něj noc. – S půlnocí nový rok
právě se počínal. V vůkolí pevný sen,
jen blíže jezera slyšeti koně krok.
Mého to koně krok. – K městu jsem nocí jel;
a přišed k pahorku, na němž byl tichý stán
dávno již obdržel přestrašný lesů pán,
po prvé Viléma bledou jsem lebku zřel.
Půlnoční krajinou, kam oko jen dosáhlo,
po dole, po horách, lesy, jezerem, polem,
co příkrov daleký sněhu se bělmo táhlo,

Oaks a hundred years a-growing,
Darkness within darkness throwing,
Hide a company of friends there.
Cloaked in white, as in the bright time,
Sit the comrades of the night-time.
Each before him groundward bends there,
Wordless, motionless, his vision,
As if terror's chill transition
Into stone their flesh had stricken.
Through the valley seems to quicken
Whispered breath of lamentation
Round the moveless men who plain him,
Secretly, without cessation:
'Lost, our leader! – they have slain him!'

And the wind, the smoke-wreaths plying,
To the moveless men is crying:
'Lost, our leader!–they have slain him!'

And the restless leaves aquiver
Underneath the cold cliff-faces,
Trembling, murmuring, utter ever
These insistent, changeless phrases:
'Lost, our leader!–they have slain him!'

All the forests in their station
Sound the great, sad accusation:
'They have slain him – slain him!! – slain him – !!!'

4

Beautiful May is passed, withered the bloom of Spring;
The summer fire burns high, wanes, and as soon is gone,
Autumn, and winter after; another Spring comes on,
As time bears off the years on its unresting wing.

The seventh year it was, the seventh year's last day;
Deep on it lay the night, and with the midnight chime
A new year would be born. The cold earth dreaming lay.
Lone hoof-beats by the lake troubled the silent time.
I was that wayfarer, bound for the town by night,
Led by chance to the mound, where, long ago at rest,
The dreaded Forest King lingered a quiet guest;
There first I saw Vilem– a bare skull glistening white.
There in the midnight land, far as the eye's reach ranging,
Through valleys, over hills, by forest, lake and meadow,
A wide, white pall of snow lay level and unchanging,

co příkrov rozstřený – nad lebkou i nad kolem.
V hlubokých mrákotách bledý se měsíc ploužil,
časem zněl sovy pláč, ba větru smutné chvění,
a větrem na kole kostlivce rachocení,
že strach i ňadra má i mého koně oužil.
A tam, kde města stín, v cvál poletěl jsem s koněm,
i po kostlivci jsem hned druhý den se tázal:
starý mi hospodský ku pahorku ukázal,
a – již jsem dříve psal – smutnou dal zprávu o něm.

Pak opět žití běh v šírý mě vedl svět,
mnohý mě bouřný vír v hluboký smutek zchvátil;
leč smutná zpráva ta vzdy vábila mě zpět,
až s mladým jarem jsem ku pahorku se vrátil.
S západem slunce jsem tam na pahorku seděl,
nade mnou kolo – kůl – kostlivec – lebka bledá;
smutným jsem okem v dál krajiny jarní hleděl,
až tam, kde po horách mlha plynula šedá.

Byl opět večer – první máj –
večerní máj – byl lásky čas;
hrdliččin zval ku lásce hlas,
kde borový zaváněl háj.
O lásce šeptal tichý mech,
květoucí strom lhal lásky žel,
svou lásku slavík růži pěl,
růžinu jevil vonný vzdech.
Jezero hladké v křovích stinných
zvučelo temně tajný bol,
břeh je objímal kol a kol,
co sestru brat ve hrách dětinných.
A kolem lebky pozdní zář
se vložila, co věnec z růží;
kostlivou, bílou barví tvář
i s pod bradu svislou jí kůží.
Vítr si dutou lebkou hrál,
jak by se mrtvý z hloubi smál.
Sem tam polétal dlouhý vlas,
jejž bílé lebce nechal čas,
a rosné kapky zpod se rděly
jako by lebky zraky duté,
večerní krásou máje hnuté,
se v žaluplných slzách skvěly.

Tak seděl jsem, až vzešlá lůny zář
i mou i lebky té bledší činila tvář,
a – jako příkrovu – bělost její rozsáhlá

Over the skull and wheel–all white without a shadow.
Deep clouds hemmed in the moon, which seemed to droop and sicken;
Sometimes the weird owl cried, ever the sad wind's shaking
Plucked at the wheel above, and set the loud bones quaking,
So that my horse and I with panic dread were stricken.
Forward I spurred in fear, there where the safe town hailed me,
And asked what wheel, what bones were these which grimly grew there,
The old innkeeper told the story all men knew there–
The story I have told–and on that wheel impaled me.

Far I went through the world–and the world has enough of pain,
Many a storm of heart blew over me and bled me;
But still this old, worn woe beckoned me back again,
Till in a young Spring season home to the mound it led me.
Under the stake I sat, just as the sun descended,
Under the wheel which bore the skeleton and skull there,
Gazing sad-eyed on Spring, whose cup was fair and full there,
Even to the misty rim where earth and heaven blended.

Evening once more, the first of May–
The twilit May–the time of love.
Meltingly called the turtle-dove,
Where rich and sweet the pinewoods lay.
Whispered of love the mosses frail,
The flowering tree as sweetly lied
The rose's fragrant sigh replied
To love-songs of the nightingale.
The lake within the dark woods straying
Softly complained a secret pain,
By circling shores embraced again
As brother sister in their playing.
About the head the sunset bright
Lay like a wreath of roses growing,
Gilding the bony face with light,
On fretted skin and white jaw glowing.
In the hollow skull the breezes sped
As if grim laughter mocked the dead,
and lifted lightly here and there
What time had left of his long hair;
Beneath his brows the dewdrops borrow
The sunset light, as if, discerning
The evening beauty of May's returning,
His dead eyes brim with tears of sorrow.

There I sat on, until the young moon's light
Blanched both my face and his with rays as pale as bright;
Now like a snowy pall its whiteness spreads before him

815

po dole – po lesích – po horách v dál se táhla.
Časem se z daleka žežhulčino volání
ještě v dol rozléhá, časem již sova stůně;
z vůkolních dvorů zní psů vytí i štěkání.
V kol suchoparem je koření líbá vůně,
pahorkem panny jsou slzičky zkvétající.
Tajemné světlo je v jezera dálném lůně;
a mušky svítivé – co hvězdy létající –
kol kola blysknavé u hře si kola vedou.
Časem si některá zasedši v lebku bledou,
vbrzku zas odletí co slza padající.

I v smutném zraku mém dvě vřelé slzy stály,
co jiskry v jezeru, po mé si tváři hrály;
neb můj též krásný věk, dětinství mého věk
daleko odnesl divoký času vztek.
Dalekoť jeho sen, umrlý jako stín,
obraz co bílých měst u vody stopen klín,
takť jako zemřelých myšlenka poslední,
tak jako jméno jich, pradávných bojů hluk,
dávná severní zář, vyhaslé světlo s ní,
zbortěné harfy tón, ztrhané struny zvuk,
zašlého věku děj, umřelé hvězdy svit,
zašlé bludice pouť, mrtvé milenky cit,
zapomenutý hrob, věčnosti skleslý byt,
vyhasla ohně kouř, slitého zvonu hlas,
mrtvé labutě zpěv, ztracený lidstva ráj,
to dětinský můj věk.
                              Nynější ale čas
jinošství mého – je, co tato báseň, máj.
Večerní jako máj ve lůně pustých skal;
na tváři lehký smích, hluboký v srdci žal.

Vidíš-li poutníka, an dlouhou lučinou
spěchá ku cíli, než červánky pohynou?
Tohoto poutníka již zrak neuzří tvůj,
jak zajde za onou v obzoru skalinou,
nikdy – ach nikdy! To budoucí život můj.
Kdo srdci takému utěchy jaké dá?
Bez konce láska je! – Zklamánať láska má!

Je pozdní večer – první máj –
večerní máj – je lásky čas;
hrdliččin zve ku lásce hlas:
"Hynku! Viléme!! Jarmilo!!!"

(1836)

Over the vales and woods to the distant hills that bore him.
Sometimes from far away the cuckoo's greeting sounds here,
Flung from the flowering vale, sometimes the owl's grave warning;
From many a farmyard near the bark of dogs rebounds here;
Out of the dust arises a sweet incense of mourning,
The little tears of the Virgin upon the hill are flowering,
Deep in the heart of the lake a secret light is burning;
And the fireflies, shooting stars, about the wheel are showering,
Glittering in their play, touching the pale skull brightly,
Lighting to launch again, and launch again as lightly,
Like fiery falling tears, all his spent tears embowering.

And in my grieving eyes two hot tears rise and break,
Glittering down my cheeks as sparks play in the lake;
For my young years, mine too, my childhood golden-gay,
Time in its headlong flight has seized and borne away.
Far is that lost dream now, a shadow no more found,
Like visions of white towns, deep in the waters drowned,
The last indignant thoughts of the defeated dead,
Their unremembered names, the clamour of old fights,
The worn-out northern lights after their gleam is fled,
The untuned harp, whose strings distil no more delights,
The deeds of time gone by, quenched starlight overhead,
Heresy's pilgrimage, the loving, lovely dead,
The deep, forgotten grave, eternal board and bed,
The smoke of burned-out fires, the scattered bell's chime –
Like the song of dead swan, like Eden snatched away,
So is my childhood time –
                              But what of following time?
My youth, alas, my youth! My season and song are May!
An eventide of May on a rocky, desolate shore:
Light laughter on the lips, deep grief in the heart's core.

See you the pilgrim there, hastening on his quest
Through the long, sunset fields, beneath the dimming west?
Strain your eyes as you will, the end you cannot see,
As over the edge of vision he falters and finds no rest.
Never–ah, never! And this is all life offers me!
Comfort? Who comforts me? What charm this heart can move?
Love is without an end! – And bitter is my love!

Late evening, on the first of May –
The twilit May–the time of love –
Meltingly calls the turtle-dove:
'Hynek! Vilem! Ah, Jarmila!!!'

(1836)

[*Translated by Edith Pargeter. Prague: Artia Publishers, 1965*]

d. FRANÇAIS

VI.d.1. FRANÇOIS RENÉ DE CHATEAUBRIAND, de *Le Génie du christianisme*, Part II, Book 4, Chapter 1

Le spectacle de l'univers ne pouvait faire sentir aux Grecs et aux Romains les émotions qu'il porte à notre âme. Au lieu de ce soleil couchant, dont le rayon allongé tantôt illumine une forêt, tantôt forme une tangente d'or sur l'arc roulant des mers; au lieu de ces accidents de lumière qui nous retracent chaque matin le miracle de la création, les anciens ne voyaient partout qu'une uniforme machine d'opéra.

Si le poète s'égarait dans les vallées du Taygète, au bord du Sperchius, sur le Ménale aimé d'Orphée, ou dans les campagnes d'Elore, malgré la douceur de ces dénominations, il ne rencontrait que des faunes, il n'entendait que des dryades; Priape était là sur un tronc d'olivier, et Vertumme avec les zéphyrs menait des danses éternelles. Des sylvains et des naïades peuvent frapper agréablement l'imagination, pourvu qu'ils ne soient pas sans cesse reproduits; nous ne voulons point

– – – – Chasser les tritons de l'empire des eaux,
Oter à Pan sa flûte, aux Parques leurs ciseaux...

Mais, enfin, qu'est-ce que tout cela laisse au fond de l'âme? qu'en résulte-t-il pour le coeur? quel fruit peut en tirer la pensée? Oh! que le poète chrétien est plus favorisé dans la solitude où Dieu se promène avec lui! Libres de ce troupeau de dieux ridicules qui les bornaient de toutes parts, les bois se sont remplis d'une Divinité immense. Le don de prophétie et de sagesse, le mystère et la religion, semblent résider éternellement dans leurs profondeurs sacrées.

Pénétrez dans ces forêts américaines aussi vieilles que le monde: quel profond silence dans ces retraites quand les vents reposent! quelles voix inconnues quand les vents viennent à s'élever! Etes-vous immobile, tout est muet; faites-vous un pas, tout soupire. La nuit s'approche, les ombres s'épaississent: on entend des troupeaux de bêtes sauvages passer dans les ténèbres; la terre murmure sous vos pas; quelques coups de foudre font mugir les déserts; la forêt s'agite, les arbres tombent, un fleuve inconnu coule devant vous. La lune sort enfin de l'Orient; à mesure que vous passez au pied des arbres, elle semble errer devant vous dans leur cime et suivre tristement vos yeux. Le voyageur s'assied sur le tronc d'un chêne pour attendre le jour; il regarde tour à tour l'astre des nuits, les ténèbres, le fleuve; il se sent inquiet, agité, et, dans l'attente de quelque chose d'inconnu, un plaisir inouï, une crainte extraordinaire font palpiter son sein comme s'il allait être admis à quelque secret de la Divinité: il est seul au fond des forêts, mais l'esprit de l'homme remplit aisément les espaces de la nature, et toutes les solitudes de la terre sont moins vastes qu'une seule pensée de son coeur. Oui, quand l'homme renierait la Divinité, l'être pensant, sans cortège et sans spectateur, serait encore plus auguste au milieu des mondes solitaires que s'il y paraissait environné des petites déités de la fable; le désert vide aurait encore quelques convenances avec l'étendue de ses idées, la tristesse de ses passions et le dégoût même d'une vie sans illusion et sans espérance.

Il y a dans l'homme un instinct qui le met en rapport avec les scènes de la nature. Eh! qui n'a passé des heures entières assis, sur le rivage d'un fleuve, à voir s'écouler les ondes! Qui ne s'est plu, au bord de la mer, à regarder blanchir l'écueil éloigné! Il faut plaindre les anciens, qui n'avaient trouvé dans l'Océan que le palais de Neptune et la grotte de Protée; il était dur de ne voir que les aventures des tritons et des néréides dans cette immensité des mers, qui semble nous donner une mesure confuse de la grandeur de notre âme, dans cette immensité qui fait naître en nous un vague désir de quitter la vie pour embrasser la nature et nous confondre avec son auteur.

d. FRENCH

VI.d.1. FRANÇOIS RENÉ DE CHATEAUBRIAND, from *The Genius of Christianity,* Part II, Book 4, Chapter 1

The prospect of the universe could not excite in the bosoms of the Greeks and Romans those emotions which it produces in our souls. Instead of that setting sun, whose lengthened rays sometimes light up the forest, at others form a golden tangent on the rolling arch of the seas, – instead of those beautiful accidents of light which every morning remind us of the miracle of the creation, – the ancients beheld around them naught but a uniform system, which reminds us of the machinery of an opera.

If the poet wandered in the vales of the Taygetus, on the banks of the Sperchius, on the Mćnalus, beloved of Orpheus, or in the plains of the Elorus, whatever may have been the charm of this Grecian geography, he met with nothing but fauns, he heard no sounds but those of the dryads. Apollo and the Muses were there, and Vertumnus with the Zephyrs led eternal dances. Sylvans and Naiads may strike the imagination in an agreeable manner, provided they be not incessantly brought forward. We would not

– – – – Expel the Tritons from the watery waste,
Destroy Pan's pipe, snatch from the Fates their shears.

But then what impression does all this leave on the soul? What results from it for the heart? What moral benefit can the mind thence derive? Oh, how far more highly is the Christian poet favored! Free from that multitude of absurd deities which circumscribed them on all sides, the woods are filled with the immensity of the Divinity; and the gift of prophecy and wisdom, mystery and religion, seem to have fixed their eternal abode in their awful recesses.

Penetrate into those forests of America coeval with the world. What profound silence pervades these retreats when the winds are hushed! What unknown voices when they begin to rise! Stand still, and every thing is mute; take but a step, and all nature sighs. Night approaches: the shades thicken; you hear herds of wild beasts passing in the dark; the ground murmurs under your feet; the pealing thunder roars in the deserts; the forest bows; the trees fall; an unknown river rolls before you. The moon at length bursts forth in the east; as you proceed at the foot of the trees, she seems to move before you at their tops, and solemnly to accompany your steps. The wanderer seats himself on the trunk of an oak to await the return of day; he looks alternately at the nocturnal luminary, the darkness, and the river: he feels restless, agitated, and in expectation of something extraordinary. A pleasure never felt before, an unusual fear, cause his heart to throb, as if he were about to be admitted to some secret of the Divinity; he is alone in the depth of the forests, but the mind of man is equal to the expanse of nature, and all the solitudes of the earth are less vast than one single thought of his heart. Even did he reject the idea of a Deity, the intellectual being, alone and unbeheld, would be more august in the midst of a solitary world than if surrounded by the ridiculous divinities of fabulous times. The barren desert itself would have some congeniality with his discursive thoughts, his melancholy feelings, and even his disgust for a life equally devoid of illusion and of hope.

There is in man an instinctive melancholy, which makes him harmonize with the scenery of nature. Who has not spent whole hours seated on the bank of a river contemplating its passing waves? Who has not found pleasure on the sea-shore in viewing the distant rock whitened by the billows? How much are the ancients to be pitied, who discovered in the ocean naught but the palace of Neptune and the cavern of Proteus! It was hard that they should perceive only the adventures of the Tritons and the Nereids in the immensity of the seas, which seems to give an indistinct measure of the greatness of our souls, and which excites a vague desire to quit this life, that we may embrace all nature and taste the fullness of joy in the presence of its Author.

[*Translated by Charles White, Baltimore, 1856*]

VI.d.2.   VICTOR HUGO, from 'Á Albert Dürer'

Dans les vieilles forêts où la sève à grands flots
Court du fût noir de l'aulne au tronc blanc des bouleaux,
Bien des fois, n'est-ce pas? à travers la clairière,
Pâle, effaré, n'osant regarder en arrière,
Tu t'es hâté, tremblant et d'un pas convulsif,
O mon maître Albert Düre, ô vieux peintre pensif!
On devine, devant tes tableaux qu'on vénère,
Que dans les noirs taillis ton oeil visionnaire
Voyait distinctement, par l'ombre recouverts,
Le faune aux doigts palmés, le sylvain aux yeux verts,
Pan, qui revêt de fleurs l'antre où tu te recueilles,
Et l'antique dryade aux mains pleines de feuilles.
Une forêt pour toi, c'est un monde hideux.
Le songe et le réel s'y mêlent tous les deux.
Là se penchent rêveurs les vieux pins, les grands ormes
Dont les rameaux tordus font cent coudes difformes,
Et dans ce groupe sombre agité par le vent
Rien n'est tout à fait mort ni tout a fait vivant.
Le cresson boit; l'eau court; les frênes sur les pentes,
Sous la broussaille horrible et les ronces grimpantes,
Contractent lentement leurs pieds noueux et noirs;
Les fleurs au cou de cygne ont les lacs pour miroirs;
Et, sur vous qui passez et l'avez réveillée,
Mainte chimère étrange à la gorge écaillée,
D'un arbre entre ses doigts serrant les larges noeuds,
Du fond d'un antre obscur fixe un oeil lumineux.
O végétation! esprit! matière! force!
Couverte de peau rude ou de vivante écorce!
Aux bois, ainsi que toi, je n'ai jamais erré,
Maître, sans qu'en mon coeur l'horreur ait pénétré,
Sans voir tressaillir l'herbe, et, par le vent bercées,
Pendre à tous les rameaux de confuses pensées.
Dieu seul, ce grand témoin des faits mystérieux,
Dieu seul le sait, souvent, en de sauvages lieux,
J'ai senti, moi qu'échauffe une secrète flamme,
Comme moi palpiter et vivre avec une âme,
Et rire, et se parler dans l'ombre à demi-voix,
Les chênes monstrueux qui remplissent les bois.

(20 avril 1837)

VI.d.2.   VICTOR HUGO, from 'To Albert Dürer'

Through ancient forests – where like flowing tide
The rising sap shoots vigour far and wide,
Mounting the column of the alder dark
And silv'ring o'er the birch's shining bark –
Hast thou not often, Albert Dürer, strayed
Pond'ring, awe-stricken – through the half-lit glade,
Pallid and trembling – glancing not behind
From mystic fear that did thy senses bind,
Yet made thee hasten with unsteady pace?
Oh, Master grave! whose musings lone we trace
Throughout thy works we look on reverently.
Amidst the gloomy umbrage thy mind's eye
Saw clearly, 'mong the shadows soft yet deep,
The web-toed faun, and Pan the green-eyed peep,
Who decked with flowers the cave where thou might'st rest.
Leaf-laden dryads, too, in verdure drest.
A strange weird world such forest was to thee,
Where mingled truth and dreams in mystery;
There leaned old ruminating pines, and there
The giant elms, whose boughs deformed and bare
A hundred rough and crooked elbows made;
And in this sombre group the wind had swayed,
Nor life – nor death – but life in death seemed found.
The cresses drink – the water flows – and round
Upon the slopes the mountain rowans meet,
And 'neath the brushwood plant their gnarled feet,
Intwining slowly where the creepers twine.
There, too, the lakes as mirrors brightly shine,
And show the swan-necked flowers, each line by line.
Chimeras roused take stranger shapes for thee,
The glittering scales of mailéd throat we see,
And claws tight pressed on huge old knotted tree;
While from a cavern dim the bright eyes glare.
Oh, vegetation! Spirit! Do we dare
Question of matter, and of forces found
'Neath a rude skin – in living verdure bound.
Oh, Master – I, like thee, have wandered oft
Where mighty trees made arches high aloft,
But ever with a consciousness of strife,
A surging struggle of the inner life.
Ever the trembling of the grass I say,
And the boughs rocking as the breezes play,
Have stirred deep thoughts in a bewild'ring way.
Oh, God! alone Great Witness of all deeds,

e. DEUTSCH

VI.e.1.   JOHANN WOLFGANG von GOETHE, aus *Die Leiden des jungen Werthers*

Am 18. August

Mußte denn das so sein, daß das, was des Menschen Glückseligkeit macht, wieder die Quelle seines Elendes würde?

Das volle, warme Gefühl meines Herzens an der lebendigen Natur, das mich mit so vieler Wonne überströmte, das rings umher die Welt mir zu einem Paradiese schuf, wird mir jetzt zu einem unerträglichen Peiniger, zu einem quälenden Geist, der mich auf allen Wegen verfolgt. Wenn ich sonst vom Felsen über den Fluß bis zu jenen Hügeln das fruchtbare Tal überschaute und alles um mich her keimen und quellen sah; wenn ich jene Berge, vom Fuße bis auf zum Gipfel, mit hohen, dichten Bäumen bekleidet, jene Täler in ihren mannigfaltigen Krümmungen von den lieblichsten Wäldern beschattet sah, und der sanfte Fluß zwischen den lispelnden Rohren dahinglei- tete und die lieben Wolken abspiegelte, die der sanfte Abendwind am Himmel herüberwiegte; wenn ich dann die Vögel um mich den Wald beleben hörte, und die Millionen Mückenschwärme im letzten roten Strahle der Sonne mutig tanzten, und ihr letzter zuckender Blick den summenden Käfer aus seinem Grase befreite, und das Schwirren und Weben um mich her mich auf den Boden aufmerksam machte, und das Moos, das meinem harten Felsen seine Nahrung abzwingt, und das Geniste, das den dürren Sandhügel hinunter wächst, mir das innere, glühende, heilige Leben der Natur eröffnete: wie faßte ich das alles in mein warmes Herz, fuhlte mich in der überfließenden Fülle wie vergöttert, und die herrlichen Gestalten der unendlichen Welt bewegten sich allbelebend in meiner Seele. Ungeheure Berge umgaben mich, Abgründe lagen vor mir, und Wetterbäche stürzten herunter, die Flüsse strömten unter mir, und Wald und Gebirg erklang; und ich sah sie wirken und schaffen ineinander in den Tiefen der Erde, alle die unergründlichen Kräfte; und nun über der Erde und unter dem Himmel wimmeln die Geschlechter der mannigfaltigen Geschöpfe. Alles, alles bevölkert mit tausendfachen Gestalten; und die Menschen dann sich in Häuslein zusammen sichern und sich annisten und herrschen in ihrem Sinne über die weite Welt! Armer Tor! der du alles so gering achtest, weil du so klein bist. — Vom unzugänglichen Gebirge über die Einöde, die kein Fuß betrat, bis ans Ende des unbekannten Ozeans weht der Geist des Ewig- schaffenden und freut sich jedes Staubes, der ihn vernimmt und lebt. — Ach damals, wie oft habe ich mich mit Fittichen eines Kranichs, der über mich hin flog, zu dem Ufer des ungemessenen Meeres gesehnt, aus dem schäumenden Becher des Unendlichen jene schwelende Lebenswonne zu trinken und nur einen Augenblick in der eingeschränkten Kraft meines Busens einen Tropfen der Seligkeit des Wesens zu fühlen, das alles in sich und durch sich hervorbringt.

Of thoughts and acts, and all our human needs,
God only knows how often in such scenes
Of savage beauty under leafy screens,
I've felt the mighty oaks had spirit dower –
Like me knew mirth and sorrow – sentient power,
And whisp'ring each to each in twilight dim,
Had hearts that beat – and owned a soul from Him!

(20 April, 1837) [*Translated by Mrs Newton Crosland, 1812. London:*
George Bell and Sons, 1887]

e. GERMAN

VI.e.1. JOHANN WOLFGANG von GOETHE, from *The Sorrows of Young Werther,*

August 18, a.m.

Must it always be so – that the source of our happiness becomes the fountain of our misery?

The rich and ardent feeling which filled my heart with a love of Nature, overwhelmed me with a torrent of delight, and brought all paradise before me, has now become an insupportable torment – a demon which perpetually pursues me. When I used to gaze from these rocks upon the mountains across the river and upon the green valley before me, and saw everything around budding and bursting; the hills clothed from foot to peak with tall, thick trees; the valleys in all their variety, shaded with the loveliest woods; and the river gently gliding along among the whispering reeds, mirroring the clouds which the soft evening breeze wafted across the sky – when I heard the groves about me melodious with the music of birds, and saw the million swarms of insects dancing in the last golden beams of the sun, whose setting rays awoke the humming beetles from their grassy beds, while the subdued tumult around me drew my attention to the ground, and I there observed the hard rock giving nourishment to the dry moss, while the heather flourished upon the arid sands below me – all this conveyed to me the holy fire which animates all Nature, and filled and glowed within my heart. I felt myself exalted by this overflowing fullness, as if a god myself, and the glorious forms of an infinite universe stirred within my soul! Stupendous mountains encompassed me, abysses yawned at my feet, and cataracts fell headlong down before me; rivers rolled through the plains below, and the rocks and mountains resounded from afar. In the depths of the earth I saw the mysterious powers at work; on its surface, and beneath the heavens there teemed ten thousand living creatures. Everything is alive with an infinite variety of forms; and mankind safeguards itself in little houses and settles and rules in its own way over the wide universe. Poor fool! in whose petty estimation all things are little. From the inaccessible mountains, across the wilderness which no mortal foot has trod, far as the edge of the immeasurable ocean, the spirit of the eternal Creator breathes; and every speck of dust which He has made finds favor in His sight – Ah, how often then did the flight of a crane, soaring above my head, inspire me with the desire to be transported to the shores of the immeasurable ocean, there to drink the pleasures of life from the foaming goblet of the Infinite, and to realize, if but for a moment with the confined powers of my soul, the bliss of that Creator Who accomplishes all things in Himself, and through Himself!

823

Bruder, nur die Erinnerung jener Stunden macht mir wohl. Selbst diese Anstrengung, jene unsäglichen Gefühle zurückzurufen, wieder auszusprechen, hebt meine Seele über sich selbst und läßt mich dann das Bange des Zustandes doppelt empfinden, der mich jetzt umgibt.

Es hat sich vor meiner Seele wie ein Vorhang weggezogen, und der Schauplatz des unendlichen Lebens verwandelt sich vor mir in den Abgrund des ewig offenen Grabes. Kannst du sagen: *Das ist!* da alles vorübergeht? da alles mit der Wetterschnelle vorüberrollt, so selten die ganze Kraft seines Daseins ausdauert, ach, in den Strom fortgerissen, untergetaucht und an Felsen zerschmettert wird? Da ist kein Augenblick, der nicht dich verzehrte und die Deinigen um dich her, kein Augenblick, da du nicht ein Zerstörer bist, sein mußt; der harmloseste Spaziergang kostet tausend armen Würmchen das Leben, es zerrüttet ein Fußtritt die mühseligen Gebäude der Ameisen und stampft eine kleine Welt in ein schmähliches Grab. Ha! nicht die große, seltne Not der Welt, diese Fluten, die eure Dörfer wegspülen, diese Erdbeben, die eure Städte verschlingen, rühren mich; mir untergräbt das Herz die verzehrende Kraft, die in dem All der Natur verborgen liegt; die nichts gebildet hat, das nicht seinen Nachbar, nicht sich selbst zerstörte. Und so taumle ich beängstigt. Himmel und Erde und ihre webenden Kräfte um mich her: ich sehe nichts als ein ewig verschlingendes, ewig wiederkäuendes Ungeheuer.

(1775) [*Johann Wolfgang von Goethe, Werke. Hamburger Ausgabe. Ed. Erich Trunz, 14 vols. Hamburg: Wegner (later Munich: Beck), 1948–60. VI. 51–53*]

VI.e.2.   NOVALIS, 'Wenn nicht mehr Zahlen und Figuren'

Wenn nicht mehr Zahlen und Figuren
Sind Schlüssel aller Kreaturen
Wenn die so singen, oder küssen,
Mehr als die Tiefgelehrten wissen,
Wenn sich die Welt ins freye Leben
Und in die Welt wird zurück begeben,
Wenn dann sich wieder Licht und Schatten
Zu ächter Klarheit wieder gatten,
Und man in Mährchen und Gedichten
Erkennt die wahren Weltgeschichten,
Dann fliegt vor Einem geheimen Wort
Das ganze verkehrte Wesen fort.

[Novalis. Schriften, *Historisch-kritische Ausgabe* by *Paul Kluckhohn, Richard Samuel, Hans-Joachim Mähl, Gerhard Schulz. 7 vols. Stuttgart, Berlin, Cologne, Mainz: Kohlhammer, 1960–. III. 675*]

My dear friend, the mere recollection of those hours consoles me. Even the effort to recall those ineffable emotions, and give them utterance, exalts my soul above itself, and makes me feel doubly the intensity of my present anguish.

It is as if a curtain had been drawn from before my eyes, and, instead of prospects of eternal life, the abyss of an ever-open grave yawned before me. Can we say of anything that it is when all passes away – when time, with the speed of a storm, carries all things onward – and our transitory existence, hurried along by the torrent, is swallowed up by the waves or dashed against the rocks? There is not a moment that doesn't consume you and yours – not a moment in which you don't yourself destroy something. The most innocent walk costs thousands of poor insects their lives; one step destroys the delicate structures of the ant and turns a little world into chaos. No, it is not the great and rare catastrophes of the world, the floods which sweep away villages, the earthquakes that swallow up our towns, that affect me. My heart is wasted by the thought of that destructive power which lies latent in every part of universal Nature. Nature has formed nothing that does not destroy itself, and everything near it. And so, surrounded by earth and air and all the active forces, I stagger on in sheer anxiety. The universe to me is an all-consuming, devouring monster.

(1775) [*Johann Wolfgang von Goethe. Collected Works. Ed. Victor Lange, Eric A. Blackall and Cyrus Hamlin, 12 vols. New York: Suhrkamp, 1983–1989, XI (1988). 36–37.*]

VI.e.2.   NOVALIS, 'When No Longer Numbers and Figures . . .'

When no longer numbers and figures
Are keys to all creatures,
When those who sing or kiss
Know more than all the learned scholars,
When the world returns to itself
In a life of freedom,
When once again the light and shadow wed
And these united give the real clarity,
When man can know the true world story
In myths and in the form of poems,
Then will the whole deformed being
Vanish before one single secret word

(*Heinrich von Ofterdingen, Part II*)

[*From Stein, W. J. The Ninth Century and the Holy Grail.
Sussex: Temple Lodge Publishing, 2001. 90*]

VI.e.3.   NOVALIS, aus *Die Lehrlinge zu Sais*

Vor langen Zeiten lebte weit gegen Abend ein blutjunger Mensch. Er war sehr gut, aber auch über die Maaßen wunderlich. Er grämte sich unaufhörlich um nichts und wieder nichts, ging immer still für sich hin, setzte sich einsam, wenn die Andern spielten und fröhlich waren, und hing seltsamen Dingen nach. Höhlen und Wälder waren sein liebster Aufenthalt, und dann sprach or immer fort mit Thieren und Vögeln, mit Bäumen und Felsen, natürlich kein vernünftiges Wort, lauter närrisches Zeug zum Todtlachen. Er blieb aber immer mürrisch und ernsthaft, ungeachtet sich das Eichhörnchen, die Meerkatze, der Papagay und der Gimpel alle Mühe gaben ihn zu zerstreuen, und ihn auf den richtigen Weg zu weisen. Die Gans erzählte Mährchen, der Bach klimperte eine Ballade dazwischen, ein großer dicker Stein machte lächerliche Bockssprünge, die Rose schlich sich freundlich hinter ihm herum, kroch durch seine Locken, und der Epheu streichelte ihm die sorgenvolle Stirn. Allein der Mißmuth und Ernst waren hartnäckig. Seine Eltern waren sehr betrübt, sie wußten nicht was sie anfangen sollten. Er war gesund und aß, nie hatten sie ihn beleidigt, er war auch bis vor wenig Jahren fröhlich und lustig gewesen, wie keiner; bei allen Spielen voran, von allen Mädchen gern gesehn. Er war recht bildschön, sah aus wie gemahlt, tanzte wie ein Schatz. Unter den Mädchen war Eine, ein köstliches, bildschönes Kind, sah aus wie Wachs, Haare wie goldne Seide, kirschrothe Lippen, wie ein Püppchen gewachsen, brandrabenschwarze Augen. Wer sie sah, hätte mögen vergehn, so lieblich war sie. Damals war Rosenblüthe, so hieß sie, dem bildschönen Hyacinth, so hieß er, von Herzen gut, und er hatte sie lieb zum Sterben. Die andern Kinder wußtens nicht. Ein Veilchen hatte es ihnen zuerst gesagt, die Hauskätzchen hatten es wohl gemerkt, die Häuser ihrer Eltern lagen nahe beisammen. Wenn nun Hyacinth die Nacht an seinem Fenster stand und Rosenblüthe an ihrem, und die Kätzchen auf den Mäusefang da vorbeyliefen, da sahen sie die Beiden stehn, und lachten und kickerten oft so laut, daß sie es hörten und böse wurden. Das Veilchen hatte es der Erdbeere im Vertrauen gesagt, die sagte es ihrer Freundinn der Stachelbeere, die ließ nun das Sticheln nicht, wenn Hyacinth gegangen kam; so erfuhrs denn bald der ganze Garten und der Wald, und wenn Hyacinth ausging, so riefs von allen Seiten: Rosenblüthchen ist mein Schätzchen! Nun ärgerte sich Hyacinth, und mußte doch auch wieder aus Herzensgrunde lachen, wenn das Eidechschen geschlüpft kam, sich auf einen warmen Stein setzte, mit dem Schwänzchen wedelte und sang:

Rosenblüthchen, das gute Kind,
Ist geworden auf einmal blind,
Denkt, die Mutter sey Hyacinth,
Fällt ihm um den Hals geschwind;
Merkt sie aber das fremde Gesicht,
Denkt nur an, da erschrickt sie nicht,
Fährt, als merkte sie kein Wort,
Immer nur mit Küssen fort.

Ach! wie bald war die Herrlichkeit vorbey. Es kam ein Mann aus fremden Landen gegangen, der war erstaunlich weit gereist, hatte einen langen Bart, tiefe Augen, entsetzliche Augenbrauen, ein wunderliches Kleid mit vielen Falten und seltsame Figuren hineingewebt. Er setzte sich vor das Haus, das Hyacinths Eltern gehörte. Nun war Hyacinth sehr neugierig, und setzte sich zu ihm und hohlte ihm Brod und Wein. Da that er seinen weißen Bart von einander und erzählte bis tief

VI.e.3.   NOVALIS, from The Disciples at Sais

There lived once upon a time in the land of the setting sun a young man. He was very good, but above the ordinary extraordinary. He fretted himself incessantly about nothing and yet again nothing, went quietly about on his own account when others played together and were merry, and indulged in strange things. Caves and woods were his favorite haunts; he talked continually with quadrupeds and birds, with trees and rocks; of course in no sensible words, but only such foolish twaddle as would make one die of laughing. But he ever remained morose and solemn notwithstanding that the squirrels and monkeys, the parrots and bullfinches gave themselves all the trouble in the world to distract him and put him in the right path again. The goose told him tales, the stream rippled a roundelay, a great heavy stone made comic leaps and a rose crept round him amicably and twined herself in his locks, while the ivy caressed his thoughtful brow. But his solemnity and depression were stubborn. His parents were very grieved; they knew not what they ought to do. He was healthy and ate well; they had never crossed him. Only a few years back he was cheerful and blithe as anyone, first in all games, and approved by every maiden. He was really beautiful, looked like a picture and danced like an angel. Amongst the maidens there was one, a precious, exquisite child; she seemed to be of wax, her hair was like gold silk, her lips were cherry red like a doll's, her eyes burning black. Who saw her might have thought to perish of it, so lovely was she. At that time Rosenblütchen, for so she was called, was dear to the beautiful Hyacinth, for that was his name, and in fact he loved her to the point of death. The other children knew nothing about it. The violet had whispered it to them first. The house kittens had noticed it, for the houses of their parents lay close together. When at night Hyacinth stood at his window and Rosenblütchen at hers, and the little cats passed by on their mouse-hunt and saw the two there they laughed and giggled so loud that it made the lovers quite cross. The violet had told it in confidence to the strawberry, who told it to her friend the gooseberry, who did not omit to scratch Hyacinth as he came along. So very soon the whole garden and wood knew all about it, and when Hyacinth went out there rang from all sides: 'Little Rosenblütchen is my darling!' Then Hyacinth was annoyed, but he had to laugh with all his heart when a little lizard came gliding past, sat himself on a warm stone, and waving his little tail, sang: –

> Rosenblütchen, little pet,
> Once upon a time went blind,
> So when Hyacinth she met
> She embraced him. Being blind
> She just thought he was her mother,
> When she found it was another
> Did she mind? no not a bit,
> Only kissed him as before.
> Was she frightened? not a whit,
> Merely kissed him more and more.

Alas, how soon this glorious time was over. There came a man from foreign parts who had travelled astonishingly far, who had a long beard, deep eyes, fearsome eyebrows, and who wore a marvellous robe of many folds with strange figures woven into it. He sat himself down before the house belonging to Hyacinth's parents. Hyacinth was filled with curiosity, and went out to him and brought him bread and wine. He parted his white beard, and told his story far on into

in die Nacht, und Hyacinth wich und wankte nicht, und wurde auch nicht müde zuzuhören. So viel man nachher vernahm, so hat er viel von fremden Ländern, unbekannten Gegenden, von erstaunlich wunderbaren Sachen erzählt, und ist drey Tage dageblieben, und mit Hyacinth in tiefe Schachten hinuntergekrochen. Rosenblüthchen hat genug den alten Hexenmeister verwünscht, denn Hyacinth ist ganz versessen auf seine Gespräche gewesen, und hat sich um nichts bekümmert; kaum daß er ein wenig Speise zu sich genommen. Endlich hat jener sich fortgemacht, doch dem Hyacinth ein Büchelchen dagelassen, das kein Mensch lesen konnte. Dieser hat ihm noch Früchte, Brod und Wein mitgegeben, und ihn weit weg begleitet. Und dann ist er tiefsinnig zurückgekommen, und hat einen ganz neuen Lebenswandel begonnen. Rosenblüthchen hat recht zum Erbarmen um ihn gethan, denn von der Zeit an hat er sich wenig aus ihr gemacht und ist immer für sich geblieben. Nun begab sichs, daß er einmal nach Hause kam und war wie neugeboren. Er fiel seinen Eltern um den Hals, und weinte. Ich muß fort in fremde Lande; sagte er, die alte wunderliche Frau im Walde hat mir erzählt, wie ich gesund werden müßte, das Buch hat sie ins Feuer geworfen, und hat mich getrieben, zu euch zu gehn und euch um euren Segen zu bitten. Vielleicht komme ich bald, vielleicht nie wieder. Grüßt Rosenblüthchen. Ich hätte sie gern gesprochen, ich weiß nicht, wie mir ist, es drängt mich fort; wenn ich an die alten Zeiten zurück denken will, so kommen gleich mächtigere Gedanken dazwischen, die Ruhe ist fort, Herz und Liebe mit, ich muß sie suchen gehn. Ich wollt' euch gern sagen, wohin, ich weiß selbst nicht, dahin wo die Mutter der Dinge wohnt, die verschleyerte Jungfrau. Nach der ist mein Gemüth entzündet. Lebt wohl. Er riß sich los und ging fort. Seine Eltern wehklagten und vergossen Thränen, Rosenblüthchen blieb in ihrer Kammer und weinte bitterlich. Hyacinth lief nun was er konnte, durch Thäler und Wildnisse, uber Berge und Ströme, dem geheimnißvollen Lande zu. Er fragte überall nach der heiligen Göttin (Isis) [:] Menschen und Thiere, Felsen und Bäume. Manche lachten [,] manche schwiegen, nirgends erhielt er Bescheid. Im Anfange kam er durch rauhes, wildes Land, Nebel und Wolken warfen sich ihm in den Weg, es stürmte immerfort; dann fand er unabsehliche Sandwüsten, glühenden Staub, und wie er wandelte, so veränderte sich auch sein Gemüth, die Zeit wurde ihm lang und die innre Unruhe legte sich, er wurde sanfter und das gewaltige Treiben in ihm allgemach zu einem leisen, aber starken Zuge, in den sein ganzes Gemüth sich auflöste. Es lag wie viele Jahre hinter ihm. Nun wurde die Gegend auch wieder reicher und mannichfaltiger, die Luft lau und blau, der Weg ebener, grüne Büsche lockten ihn mit anmuthigem Schatten, aber er verstand ihre Sprache nicht, sie schienen auch nicht zu sprechen, und doch erfüllten sie auch sein Herz mit grünen Farben und kühlem, stillem Wesen. Immer höher wuchs jene süße Sehnsucht in ihm, und immer breiter und saftiger wurden die Blätter, immer lauter und lustiger die Vögel und Thiere, balsamischer die Früchte, dunkler der Himmel, wärmer die Luft, und heißer seine Liebe, die Zeit ging immer schneller, als sähe sie sich nahe am Ziele. Eines Tages begegnete er einem krystallnen Quell und einer Menge Blumen, die kamen in ein Thal herunter zwischen schwarzen himmelhohen Säulen. Sie grüßten ihn freundlich mit bekannten Worten. Liebe Landsleute, sagte er, wo find' ich wohl den geheiligten Wohnsitz der Isis? Hier herum muß er seyn, und ihr seid vielleicht hier bekannter, als ich. Wir gehn auch nur hier durch, antworteten die Blumen; eine Geisterfamilie ist auf der Reise und wir bereiten ihr Weg und Quartier, indeß sind wir vor kurzem durch eine Gegend gekommen, da hörten wir ihren Namen nennen. Gehe nur aufwärts, wo wir herkommen, so wirst du schon mehr erfahren. Die Blumen und die Quelle lächelten, wie sie das sagten, boten ihm einen frischen Trunk und gingen weiter. Hyacinth folgte ihrem Rath, frug und frug und kam endlich zu jener längst gesuchten Wohnung, die unter Palmen und andern köstlichen Gewächsen versteckt lag. Sein Herz klopfte in unendlicher Sehnsucht, und

the night. Hyacinth kept awake and did not fidget nor grow tired of listening. From what transpired afterwards he told a great deal about strange lands, of unexplored regions, of amazing extraordinary things. He stayed there three days and descended with Hyacinth into profound depths. Rosenblütchen heartily cursed the old warlock, for Hyacinth became quite possessed by his discourse, and concerned himself with nothing else. He would scarcely take his food. At last the old man went away, but he left with Hyacinth a little book in which no one could read. Hyacinth gave him more fruit, bread, and wine, and accompanied him far upon his way. He returned pensive and from thenceforward began a new way of life. Rosenblütchen certainly had a right to be pitied for from that time he made little enough of her, and was always self-engrossed. Now it happened that one day he came home, and was as though new born. He fell on the necks of his parents and wept. 'I must away into strange lands,' he said; 'the old Sibyl in the forest has told me how I am to become whole; she threw the book into the fire, and bade me come to you and ask your blessing. Perhaps I may return soon, perhaps never. Greet little Rosenblütchen; I would willingly have spoken with her. I know not how it is with me; something urges me away. If I try to think of the old days, mightier thoughts intervene. Peace is fled together with heart and love. I must go seek them. I would like to tell you whither, but I do not know. Thither where the Mother of All Things lives, the Veiled Virgin. My desire is aflame for her. Farewell.' He tore himself away from them and departed. His parents lamented and shed tears. Rosenblütchen stayed in her chamber and wept bitterly. Hyacinth hastened through valleys and deserts, over mountains and streams, towards the Mysterious Land. He questioned men and animals, rocks and trees concerning Isis, the sacred Goddess. Many laughed, many kept silence, from none did he receive the information he sought. At first he passed through a rude wild country; mists and clouds intercepted his passage and never-ceasing storms. Then he passed through interminable deserts of sand and fiery dust, and as he wandered his humour also was changed. The time seemed long to him; the inward tumult was appeased, he grew more gentle and the mighty urgence was gradually reduced to a quiet but intense aspiration in which his whole spirit was melted. It was as though many years had passed over him. The country became at the same time richer and more varied, the air warm and azure, the road more level. Green bushed allured him with pleasant shade. But he did not understand their speech. Besides they did not seem to speak while yet they filled his heart with green colors and a cool still perfume. That sweet longing waxed higher and higher in him, and the leaves expanded with sap; birds and beasts were noisier and more joyous, the fruits more aromatic, the heavens a deeper blue, the air milder, his love warmer, time went faster as if it saw itself nearing the goal. One day he lighted on a crystal brook, and on a cloud of flowers that came tripping down the valley between black mountain peaks as high as heaven. They greeted him kindly, with familiar words. 'Dear country folk,' he said, 'where can I really find the sacred dwelling-place of Isis? It must needs be somewhere near here, and you are perhaps more at home than I.' 'We are only passing through,' answered the flowers; 'a family of spirits is traveling abroad, and we prepare their way and resting-place. Yet we have but just come through a place where we heard your name. Only go upwards whence we came, and you will learn more.' The flowers and the brook laughed as they said this, offered him a refreshing draught, and went on their way. He followed their advice, asked again and again, and finally came to that long-sought dwelling that lay hidden beneath palms and other rare trees. His heart beat with an infinite yearning, and the sweetest shyness overcame him in this habitation of the eternal centuries. He slumbered enveloped by heavenly perfumes, for it was only a dream that could lead him to the Holy of Holies. Mysteriously his dream led him to the sound of loud, delicious music and alternating harmonies through endless halls full of curious

die süßeste Bangigkeit durchdrang ihn in dieser Behausung der ewigen Jahreszeiten. Unter himmlischen Wohlgedüften entschlummerte er, weil ihn nur der Traum in das Allerheiligste führen durfte. Wunderlich führte ihn der Traum durch unendliche Gemächer voll seltsamer Sachen auf lauter reitzenden Klängen und in abwechselnden Accorden. Es dünkte ihm alles so bekannt und doch in niegesehener Herrlichkeit, da schwand auch der letzte irdische Anflug, wie in Luft verzehrt, und er stand vor der himmlischen Jungfrau, da hob er den leichten, glänzenden Schleyer, und Rosenblüthchen sank in seine Arme. Eine ferne Musik umgab die Geheimnisse des liebenden Wiedersehns, die Ergießungen der Sehnsucht, und schloß alles Fremde von diesem entzückenden Orte aus. Hyacinth lebte nachher noch lange mit Rosenblüthchen unter seinen frohen Eltern und Gespielen, und unzählige Enkel dankten der alten wunderlichen Frau für ihren Rath und ihr Feuer; denn damals bekamen die Menschen so viel Kinder, als sie wollten.

(1798–1800)

[Novalis. Schriften, *Historisch-kritische Ausgabe by Paul Kluckhohn, Richard Samuel, Hans-Joachim Mähl, Gerhard Schulz. 7 vols. Stuttgart, Berlin, Cologne, Mainz: Kohlhammer, 1960– I. 91–95*]

VI.e.4. JOSEPH von EICHENDORFF, 'Wünschelrute'

Schläft ein Lied in allen Dingen,
Die da träumen fort und fort,
Und die Welt hebt an zu singen,
Triffst du nur das Zauberwort.

[*Joseph von Eichendorff, Werke. Eds Wolfgang Frühwald, Brigitte Schillbach, Hartwig Schultz. 6 vols. Frankfurt a. M.: Deutscher Klassiker Verlag, 1985–1993. I, 328*]

things. It all seemed to him so familiar, and yet of an hitherto unrecognized splendor. Then the last vestiges of earthliness disappeared as though consumed in air, and he stood before the Celestial Virgin. He raised the diaphanous glistening veil, and Rosenblütchen sank into his arms. A distant music encompassed the secrets of the lovers' meeting, and the effusions of their love, and shut away everything inharmonious from this abode of rapture. Hyacinth lived ever after with Rosenblütchen, among his glad parents and his playfellows, and innumerable grand-children thanked the old Sibyl for her counsel and her fire, for at that time people had as many children as they wished for.

[*Translated by F.V.M.T. and Una Birch. London:*
Methuen, 1903. 112–119]

VI.e.4.   JOSEPH von EICHENDORFF, 'Divining Rod'

Sleeps a song in things abounding
that keep dreaming to be heard:
And the world begins to sing
if you find the magic word.

[*Translated by Walter A. Aue (This translation can be found at http://myweb.*
dal.ca/waue/Trans/Eichendorff-Wuenschelrute.html(modified))]

f. MAGYAR

VI.f.1. PETŐFI SÁNDOR, *A Tisza*

Nyári napnak alkonyúlatánál
Megállék a kanyargó Tiszánál
Ott, hol a kis Túr siet beléje,
Mint a gyermek anyja kebelére.

A folyó oly símán, oly szelíden
Ballagott le parttalan medrében,
Nem akarta, hogy a nap sugára
Megbotoljék habjai fodrába'.

Síma tükrén a piros sugárok
(Mint megannyi tündér) táncot jártak,
Szinte hallott lépteik csengése,
Mint parányi sarkantyúk pengése.

Ahol álltam, sárga föveny-szőnyeg
Volt terítve, s tartott a mezőnek,
Melyen a levágott sarju-rendek,
Mint a könyvben a sorok, hevertek.

Túl a réten néma méltóságban
Magas erdő: benne már homály van,
De az alkony üszköt vet fejére,
S olyan, mintha égne s folyna vére.

Másfelől, a Tisza tulsó partján,
Mogyoró- s rekettye-bokrok tarkán,
Köztök egy csak a nyilás, azon át
Látni távol kis falucska tornyát.

Boldog órák szép emlékeképen
Rózsafelhők usztak át az égen.
Legmesszebbről rám merengve néztek
Ködön át a mármarosi bércek.

Semmi zaj. Az ünnepélyes csendbe
Egy madár csak néha füttyentett be.
Nagy távolban a malom zugása
Csak olyan volt, mint szunyog dongása.

Túlnan, vélem átellenben épen,
Pór menyecske jött. Korsó kezében.
Korsaját mig telemerítette,
Rám nézett át; aztán ment sietve.

f. HUNGARIAN

VI.f.1. SÁNDOR PETŐFI, *The Tisza*

When in the dusk a summer day had died,
I stopped by winding Tisza's river-side,
just where the little Túr flows in to rest,
a weary child that seeks its mother's breast.

Most smooth of surface, with most gentle force,
the river wandered down its bankless course,
lest the faint sunset-rays, so close to home,
should stumble in its lacery of foam.

On its smooth mirror, sunbeams lingered yet,
dancing like fairies in a minuet;
one almost heard the tinkle of their feet,
like tiny spurs in music's ringing beat.

Low flats of yellow shingle spread away,
from where I stood, to meet the meadow hay
where the long shadows in the after-glow
like lines upon a page lay row on row.

Beyond the meadow in mute dignity
the forest towered o'er the darkening lea,
but sunset rested on its leafy spires
like embers red as blood and fierce with fires.

Elsewhere, along the Tisza's farther bank,
the motley broom and hazels, rank on rank,
crowded, but for one cleft, through which was shown
the distant steeple of the tiny town.

Small, rosy clouds lay floating in the sky
in memory-pictures of the hours gone by.
Far in the distance, lost in reverie,
the misty mountain-summits gazed at me.

The air was still. Across the solemn hush
fell but the fitful vespers of a thrush.
Even the murmur of the far-off mill
seemed faint as a mosquito humming shrill.

To the far bank before me, within hail,
a peasant-woman came to fill her pail;
she, as she brimmed it, wondered at my stay,
and with a glance went hastily away.

Ottan némán, mozdulatlan álltam,
Mintha gyökeret vert volna lábam.
Lelkem édes, mély mámorba szédült
A természet örök szépségétül.

Oh természet, oh dicső természet!
Mely nyelv merne versenyezni véled?
Mily nagy vagy te! mentül inkább hallgatsz,
Annál többet, annál szebbet mondasz. –

Késő éjjel értem a tanyára
Fris gyümölcsből készült vacsorára.
Társaimmal hosszan beszélgettünk.
Lobogott a rőzseláng mellettünk.

Többek között szóltam én hozzájok:
„Szegény Tisza, miért is bántjátok?
Annyi rosszat kiabáltok róla,
S ő a föld legjámborabb folyója."

Pár nap mulva fél szendergésemből
Félrevert harang zugása vert föl.
Jön az árvíz! jön az árvíz! hangzék,
S tengert láttam, ahogy kitekinték.

Mint az őrült, ki letépte láncát,
Vágtatott a Tisza a rónán át,
Zúgva, bőgve törte át a gátot,
El akarta nyelni a világot!

[*First published: Honleányok Könyve. Eds Röszler, Ágnes and Oroszhegyi, Jósa.
Pest. Vol. 1. May, 1847. 12–13. Critical edition: Petőfi, Sándor, Petőfi
Sándor összes művei, Petőfi Sándor költeményei. Vol. 3. Ed.
Béla Varjas. Budapest: Akadémiai, 1951. 286–287*]

But I stood there in stillness absolute
as though my very feet had taken root.
My heart was dizzy with the rapturous sight
of Nature's deathless beauty in the night.

O Nature, glorious Nature, who would dare
with reckless tongue to match your wondrous fare?
How great you are! And the more still you grow,
the lovelier are the things you have to show!

Late, very late, I came back to the farm
and supped upon fresh fruit that made me warm,
and talked with comrades far into the night,
while brushwood flames beside us flickered bright.

Then, among other topics, I exclaimed:
'Why is the Tisza here so harshly blamed?
You wrong it greatly and belie its worth:
surely, it's the mildest river on the earth!'

Startled, a few days later in those dells
I heard the frantic pealing of the bells:
'The flood, the flood is coming!' they resound.
And gazing out, I saw a sea around.

There, like a maniac just freed from chains,
the Tisza rushed in rage across the plains;
roaring and howling through the dyke it swirled,
greedy to swallow up the whole wide world.

[*Translated by Watson Kirkconnell and reprinted from* In Quest of the 'Miracle Stag':
The Poetry of Hungary. *Ed. Adam Makkai. Chicago and Budapest,
Atlantis-Centaur, M. Szivárvány and Corvina, 1996. 315–317,
with the kind permission of Adam Makkai*]

g. ITALIANO

VI.g.1.   GIACOMO LEOPARDI, 'La quiete dopo la tempesta'

In Giacomo Leopardi, Canti, a cura di Giuseppe e Domenico De Robertis, Oscar Studio Mondadori, Milano 1978

Passata è la tempesta:
Odo augelli far festa, e la gallina,
Tornata in su la via,
Che ripete il suo verso. Ecco il sereno
Rompe là da ponente, alla montagna;
Sgombrasi la campagna,
E chiaro nella valle il fiume appare.
Ogni cor si rallegra, in ogni lato
Risorge il romorio
Torna il lavoro usato.
L'artigiano a mirar l'umido cielo,
Con l'opra in man, cantando,
Fassi in su l'uscio; a prova
Vien fuor la femminetta a còr dell'acqua
Della novella piova;
E l'erbaiuol rinnova
Di sentiero in sentiero
Il grido giornaliero.
Ecco il Sol che ritorna, ecco sorride
Per li poggi e le ville. Apre i balconi,
Apre terrazzi e logge la famiglia:
E, dalla via corrente, odi lontano
Tintinnio di sonagli; il carro stride
Del passegger che il suo cammin ripiglia.

Si rallegra ogni core.
Sì dolce, sì gradita
Quand'è, com'or, la vita?
Quando con tanto amore
L'uomo a' suoi studi intende?
O torna all'opre? o cosa nova imprende?
Quando de' mali suoi men si ricorda?
Piacer figlio d'affanno;
Gioia vana, ch'è frutto
Del passato timore, onde si scosse
E paventò la morte
Chi la vita abborria;
Onde in lungo tormento,
Fredde, tacite, smorte,
Sudàr le genti e palpitàr, vedendo
Mossi alle nostre offese
Folgori, nembi e vento.

g. ITALIAN

VI.g.1. GIACOMO LEOPARDI, 'The Calm after the Storm'

The storm has passed
I hear the birds singing and the hen
Returning to the street
Repeating her refrain. See the serene sky
Breaks through from the west, at the mountain,
Liberating the countryside
And the river appears clearly in the valley.
Every heart rejoices, from everywhere
Noise rises again and
Usual work resumes.
The artisan looking at the humid sky
With work in hand, singing,
He comes to the door.
The young woman comes out
Looking for water from the fresh rainfall;
And the vegetable seller resumes
From street to street
His daily cry.
Here the Sun returns, here smiling
Amongst the hills and villas.
Families open balconies, terraces
And loggias. And from the main roads the far off
Clinking of bell-harnesses can be heard; The carriage creaks
From the traveler who resumes his journey.

Every heart rejoices
When life, so sweet so enjoyed,
Is like this?
When with much love
Man approaches his studies?
Or resumes his work? Or learns new things?
When not even his ills are remembered?
Pleasure, son of suffering,
Vain joy, fruit
Of previous fear
When death shook and scared
He who abhorred life
When in long torment,
Cold, silent, pale
People sweated and shook, seeing
Moved by our offences
Lightening, clouds and wind.

O natura cortese,
Son questi i doni tuoi,
Questi i diletti sono
Che tu porgi ai mortali. Uscir di pena
È diletto fra noi.
Pene tu spargi a larga mano; il duolo
Spontaneo sorge: e di piacer, quel tanto
Che per mostro e miracolo talvolta
Nasce d'affanno, è gran guadagno. Umana
Prole cara agli eterni! assai felice
Se respirar ti lice
D'alcun dolor: beata
Se te d'ogni dolor morte risana.

[1829]

h. NORSK

VI.h.1. HENRIK WERGELAND, 'Til en Gran'

Bekrandste, høie Ætling af
den Gran, som først de Gother gav
den djærve Kunstmodell
til Kathedral paa Kathedral,
til Notredamens Høiportal,
til Münstren, til Vestminsterhal,
til Pisas Taarn paaheld! –

Her i den skumle Dal forglemt
Du sørgende i Skyen gjemt
din stolte Isse har.
Du speider mørkt derovenhen
mod graneformte Taarn af Steen,
og kjender sukkende igjen
et Billed af din Far.

Dig venter feige Øx ved Rod.
Som Herkules i Drageblod
du døer i seige Ild.
Dog døe du stolt, min Gran! Thi vid:
Europas Kraft ei rækker did
At forme slig en Pyramid,
som være kan dit Bild.

Klag ei; thi mangtet Hjerte, der
Modell for Himmeldomer er,

O gentle nature
These are your gifts
These are the joys
You offer to mortals. To escape from pain
Is a joy for us.
You liberally spread travails, suffering appears
Spontaneously and, that little pleasure, which
Strangely and at times miraculously grows
From toil, is a great gain. Human kind
Dear to the gods! You are happy
If you are allowed breathing space
From pain: blessed are you
If death restores you from all pain.

[1829] [*Translated by Anne O'Connor*]

h.   NORWEGIAN

VI.h.1.   HENRIK WERGELAND, 'To a Pine-Tree'

Crowned, lofty scion of the pine
Whence Gothic architect's design
Derived the grace and power
For churches planned in noblest style,
For Notre Dame's majestic pile,
Westminster Hall, or Münster's aisle,
Or Pisa's leaning tower, –

In this dark valley laid aside,
Thou in thy grief thy crown of pride
Dost in the clouds retire;
And far thy somber glance has flown
To spires like pine-trees shaped in stone,
Perceiving, with a wistful groan,
The portrait of thy sire.

The dastard axe awaits thy wood:
Like Hercules in dragon's blood,
Thou in slow flames must die.
Yet perish proudly, pine, for know
Not all of Europe's skill can show
How such a pyramid may grow,
So stately and so high.

Lament not thou, for many a heart,
Fit model for the loftiest art,

ukjendt, i Pjalter slaaer.
Tungsindig sidder paa sit Fjell,
en ledig Helt, en ubrugt Tell;
en Byron tidt, en Platos Sjel
i Folkets Sværm forgaaer.

Den Tell, i Brist af en Tyran,
kun Spurv og Krage skyder han.
Og Han, hvis Hjerne Slør
for cherubinske Genius var,
mens en Trompeter Krandsen bar,
en Siljuqvist til Pibe skar
for gode Folkes Dør.

– Min Gran! Du ødsler hen som Dem
din Høihed i dit skjulte Hjem
i usel Veddekamp
med lave Kirkespiir i Dal.
– Det Himlens Skuur! Du heller skal
forgaae, Naturens Kathedral,
i herostratisk Damp.

Meer Herlig Tempel staaer du der.
Blyhvide Dome Skyen er.
I pavens Lateran
ei straaler Kjerterad saa reen
og fuld som din bedugg'de Green.
Hvor lød en Messe from som den
en Fugl sang i min Gran?

Hvo mon i Tempelhvælvet fandt
Tropæer, Sejerherre vandt
I mere ærlig Strid,
end disse Fenniker forvist
der perleglimre paa din Qvist,
dem Kinglen i langvarig Tvist
tilkjæmpet sig af Flid?

En vellugtopfyldt Dunkelhed,
et Chor du har, et hellig Sted;
Men intet Billed der.
Uskyldige Natur, som har
dig reist, til Gud umiddelbar
tør tale, mens et Sonaltar
Den Faldnes Midler er.

Unknown in rags has pined;
There, brooding over work denied,
Some hero sits, some Tell Untried;
A Byron, Plato, oft has died
Unnoticed by mankind.

Yon Tell, for lack of tyrant foe,
Wars on the sparrow and the crow,
And he whose brain could soar
To match the master-minstrel's lays –
Some trumpeter usurps his bays,
While on his rustic pipe he plays
For alms from door to door.

Like theirs, my pine, obscurely placed,
Thy nobleness must run to waste,
With lowly village spires –
Unworthy hovels – must contend,
Thou, Nature's temple! Fortune send
Thee first a Herostratic end,
Immortalised in fires.

Thou stand'st a nobler temple there,
Thy dome the leaden clouds of air;
No Lateran tapers fling
A beam so radiant and so fine
As those dew-spangled boughs of thine,
What sacred strains are so divine
As those thy linnets sing?

Beneath what temple arches are
Such trophies of victorious war,
So honourably won,
As are these pennons pearly bright,
Flecking thy darkest twigs with white,
Which spiders, in a hard-fought fight,
Have established where they spun.

Dim spaces filled with incense fine,
A choir thou hast, a holy shrine,
But ne'er an image there;
For sinless Nature, who did base
Thy root, to God speaks face to face,
Nor needs, like man, who fell from grace,
To mediate her prayer.

Af Stormen gjennemorgles Du
med et Tedeums søde Gru –
Tedeum? – Ak min Sjel,
syng Psalmen med som synges der:
"Naturens Tempel Himlens er;
selv vesle Moseblomme skjær
er Himmelens Capel".

[1833]

VI.h.2. AASMUND OLAFSSON VINJE, 'Ved Rundarne'

No seer eg atter slike Fjøll og Dalar,
Som deim eg i min fyrste Ungdom saag,
Og sama Vind den heite Panna svalar;
Og Gullet ligg paa Snjo, som fyrr det laag.
Det er eit Barnemaal, som til meg talar,
Og gjer' meg tankefull, men endaa fjaag.
Med Ungdomsminni er den Tala blandad:
Det strøymer paa meg, so eg knapt kann anda.

Ja, Livet strøymer paa meg, som det strøymde,
Naar under Snjo eg saag det grøne Straa.
Eg drøymer no, som fyrr eg alltid drøymde,
Naar slike Fjøll eg saag i Lufti blaa.
Eg gløymer Dagsens Strid, som fyrr eg gløymde,
Naar eg mot Kveld af Sol eit Glimt fekk sjaa.
Eg finner vel eit Hus, som vil meg hysa,
Naar Soli heim til Notti vil meg lysa.

Alt er som fyrr, men det er meir forklaarat,
So Dagsens Ljos meg synest meire bjart,
Og det, som beit og skar meg, so det saarat,
Det gjerer sjølve Skuggen mindre svart;
Sjølv det, som til at synda tidt meg daarat,
Sjølv det gjer' harde Fjøllet mindre hardt.
Forsonad' koma atter gamle Tankar:
Det sama Hjarta er, som eldre bankar.

Og kver ein Stein eg som ein Kjenning finner,
For slik var den, eg flaug ikring som Gut.
Som det var Kjæmpur spyr eg, kven som vinner
Af den og denne andre haage Nut.

Upon thine organ-pipes the storm
Its wild Te Deum can perform,
So awful, yet so fair:
Join thou, my soul, that anthem's strain; –
'The house of God is Nature's fane;
No moss so small, no weed so plain,
But builds a chapel there.'

[1833] [*Translated by G.M. Gathorne-Hardy. 1960*]

VI.h.2. AASMUND OLAFSSON VINJE, 'Recollections'

These mountains wake in me the self-same feeling
As those where as a boy I used to dwell;
The cool wind as of old is full of healing,
The same light bathes yon snow-crowned citadel.
Like a lost language from my childhood stealing,
It makes me pensive and yet glad as well.
The early memories rise so thick before me
I scarce can breathe as they come flooding o'er me.

Yes, life again through every vein is streaming
As when through snow I saw green grass arise;
I dream now, as I once was always dreaming
When I saw mountains pierce the azure skies.
I can escape from frenzied strife and scheming,
When the rich sunset spreads its glowing dyes.
I find a home where comfort and repose is,
When such a sea of light the world encloses.

But all is lovelier now than I had feigned me,
More limpidly I see the daylight burn;
And that which cut so sharply that it pained me
Softens the shadows now at eve's return.
What tempted to the misdeeds that have stained me
Makes now the very mountain side less stern.
Old thoughts grow ever kinder with repeating;
'Tis the same heart in me more calmly beating.

Each stone I knew. I find a comrade in it,
For there it was, a boy, I used to play.
And if there was a fight, why, who could win it,
Came out more strong for each and every fray.

Alt minner meg; det minner, og det minner,
Til Soli burt i Snjoen sloknar ut.
Og inn i siste Svevn meg eigong huggar
Dei gamle Minni og dei gamle Skuggar.

[*First printed in Ferdaminni fraa Sumaren 1860, a special edition of the poet's journal
Dølen, Kristiania, 1861. He undertook a journey from Oslo to Trondheim
in 1860. Passing the mountains of Rondane he remembers the
mountains of his childhood in Telemark*]

i. POLSKI

VI.l.1.   ADAM MICKIEWICZ, *Pan Tadeusz*, Księga I, 'Gospodarstwo' (fragment)

Litwo! Ojczyzno moja! ty jesteś jak zdrowie;
Ile cię trzeba cenić, ten tylko się dowie,
Kto cię stracił. Dziś piękność twą w całej ozdobie
Widzę i opisuję, bo tęsknię po tobie.

Panno święta, co Jasnej bronisz Częstochowy
I w Ostrej świecisz Bramie! Ty, co gród zamkowy
Nowogródzki ochraniasz z jego wiernym ludem!
Jak mnie dziecko do zdrowia powróciłaś cudem
(Gdy od płaczącej matki pod Twoję opiekę
Ofiarowany, martwą podniosłem powiekę   10
I zaraz mogłem pieszo do Twych świątyń progu
Iść za wrócone życie podziękować Bogu),
Tak nas powrócisz cudem na Ojczyzny łono.
Tymczasem przenoś moję duszę utęsknioną
Do tych pagórków leśnych, do tych łąk zielonych,
Szeroko nad błękitnym Niemnem rozciągnionych;
Do tych pól malowanych zbożem rozmaitem,
Wyzłacanych pszenicą, posrebrzanych żytem;
Gdzie bursztynowy świerzop, gryka jak śnieg biała,
Gdzie panieńskim rumieńcem dzięcielina pała,   20
A wszystko przepasane jakby wstęgę, miedzą
Zieloną, na niej z rzadka ciche grusze siedzą.
    Śród takich pól przed laty, nad brzegiem ruczaju,
Na pagórku niewielkim, we brzozowym gaju,
Stał dwór szlachecki, z drzewa, lecz podmurowany;
Świeciły się z daleka pobielane ściany,
Tym bielsze, że odbite od ciemnej zieleni
Topoli, co go bronią od wiatrów jesieni.
Dóm mieszkalny niewielki, lecz zewsząd chędogi,
I stodołę miał wielką, i przy niej trzy stogi   30

It all comes back, as minute after minute
The sun behind the snow-crest fades away.
And so at last they cradle me in slumber,
Old shadows and old memories without number.

[1860] [*Translated by Charles Wharton Stork, 1942*]

i. POLISH

VI.l.1. ADAM MICKIEWICZ, from *Pan Tadeusz*, 'Gospodarstwo' ('The Farm')

O Lithuania, my country, thou
Art like good health; I never knew till now
How precious, till I lost thee. Now I see
Thy beauty whole, because I yearn for thee.

O Holy Maid, who Częstochowa's shrine   5
Dost guard and on the Pointed Gateway shine
And watchest Nowogródek's pinnacle!
As Thou didst heal me by a miracle
(For when my weeping mother sought Thy power,
I raised my dying eyes, and in that hour   10
My strength returned, and to Thy shrine I trod
For life restored to offer thanks to God),
So by a miracle Thou'lt bring us home.
Meanwhile, bear off my yearning soul to roam
Those little wooded hills, those fields beside   15
The azure Niemen, spreading green and wide,
The vari-painted cornfields like a quilt,
The silver of the rye, the wheatfields' gilt;
Where amber trefoil, buck-wheat white as snow,
And clover with her maiden blushes grow,   20
And all is girdled with a grassy band
Of green, whereon the silent pear trees stand.
Such were the fields where once beside a rill
Among the birch trees on a little hill
There stood a manor house, wood-built on stone;   25
From far away the walls with whitewash shone,
The whiter as relieved by the dark green
Of poplars, that the autumn winds would screen.
It was not large, but neat in every way,
And had a mighty barn; three stacks of hay   30

Użątku, co pod strzechą zmieścić się nie może;
Widać, że okolica obfita we zboże,
I widać z liczby kopic, co wzdłuż i wszerz smugów
Świecą gęsto jak gwiazdy, widać z liczby pługów
Orzących wcześnie łany ogromne ugoru,
Czarnoziemne, zapewne należne do dworu,
Uprawne dobrze na kształt ogrodowych grządek:
Że w tym domu dostatek mieszka i porządek.
Brama na wciąż otwarta przechodniom ogłasza,
Że gościnna i wszystkich w gościnę zaprasza.   40

[*Mickiewicz, Adam, Dzieta*, volume IV: *Pan Tadeusz. Ed. Zbigniew Jerzy Nowak,
Warszawa: Czytelnik, 1995*]

VI.i.2.   ADAM MICKIEWICZ, *Pan Tadeusz,* Księga IV,
         'Dyplomatyka i łowy' (fragment)

Któż zbadał puszcz litewskich przepastne krainy
Aż do samego środka, do jądra gęstwiny?
Rybak ledwie u brzegów nawiedza dno morza;
Myśliwiec krąży koło puszcz litewskich łoża,
Zna je ledwie po wierzchu, ich postać, ich lice,
Lecz obce mu ich wnętrzne serca tajemnice;
Wieść tylko albo bajka wie, co się w nich dzieje.
Bo gdybyś przeszedł bory i podszyte knieje,
Trafisz w głębi na wielki wał pniów, kłod, korzeni,
Obronny trzęsawicą, tysiącem strumieni
I siecią zielsk zarosłych, i kopcami mrowisk,
Gniazdami os, szerszeniów, kłębami wężowisk.
Gdybyś i te zapory zmógł nadludzkim męstwem,
Dalej spotkać się z większym masz niebezpieczeństwem;
Dalej co krok czyhają, niby wilcze doły,
Małe jeziorka, trawą zarosłe na poły,
Tak głębokie, że ludzie dna ich nie dośledzą
(Wielkie jest podobieństwo, że diabły tam siedzą).
Woda tych studni sklni się, plamista rdzą krwawą,
A z wnętrza ciągle dymi, zionąc woń plugawą,
Od której drzewa wkoło tracą liść i korę;
Łyse, skarłowaciałe, robaczliwe, chore,
Pochyliwszy konary mchem kołtunowate
I pnie garbiąc brzydkimi grzybami brodate,
Siedzą wokoło wody, jak czarownic kupa
Grzejąca się nad kotłem, w którym warzą trupa.

Stood near it, that the thatch could not contain;
The neighbourhood was clearly rich in grain;
And from the stooks that every cornfield filled
As thick as stars, and from the ploughs that tilled
The black-earthed fields of fallow, broad and long,   35
Which surely to the manor must belong,
Like well-kept flower beds – everyone could tell
That plenty in that house and order dwell.
The gate wide open to the world declared
A hospitable house to all who feared.   40

[*Translated by Kenneth Mackenzie, New York: Hippocrene, 1992*]

VI.i.2.   ADAM MICKIEWICZ, from *Pan Tadeusz*, Book IV,
       'Diplomacy and Hunting'

Who has explored the innermost recess
Within the Lithuanian wilderness?
The fisherman knows but the ocean shore,
The huntsman skirts the forests and no more,
And only sees their face, the outward part,
Nor knows the secret mysteries of their heart;
What happens there to fable's only known.
For when you pass the thickets undergrown,
You find a wall of stumps and roots and logs,
Defended by a thousand streams and bogs,
And ant-hills and a net of tangled brakes,
And hornets' nests and wasps', and coiling snakes.
All these by superhuman courage passed,
You meet with peril greater yet at last.
At every step like dens of wolves amid
The overgrowing grass small pools lie hid,
So deep that none their bottom ever found.
(It's probable that devils there abound.)
Their water with a rusty bloodstain gleams,
From which a filthy stinking vapour steams;
And round about, the stunted, worm-like trees
Are reft of leaves and bark by foul disease.
With branches tangled up in mossy knots,
And hump-backed trunks and beards of fungus clots
They sit around the waters like a crew
Of witches huddled round a corpse's brew.

Za tymi jeziorkami już nie tylko krokiem,
Ale daremnie nawet zapuszczać się okiem;
Bo tam już wszystko mglistym zakryte obłokiem,
Co się wiecznie ze trzęskich oparzelisk wznosi.
A za tą mgłą na koniec (jak wieść gminna głosi)
Ciągnie się bardzo piękna, żyzna okolica,
Główna królestwa zwierząt i roślin stolica.
W niej są złożone wszystkich drzew i ziół nasiona,
Z których się rozrastają na świat ich plemiona;
W niej, jak w arce Noego, z wszelkich zwierząt rodu
Jedna przynajmniej para chowa się dla płodu.
W samym środku (jak słychać) mają swoje dwory:
Dawny Tur, Żubr i Niedźwiedź, puszcz imperatory.
Około nich na drzewach gnieździ się Ryś bystry
I żarłoczny Rosomak, jak czujne ministry;
Dalej zaś, jak podwładni szlachetni wasale,
Mieszkają Dziki, Wilki i Łosie rogale.
Nad głowami Sokoły i Orłowie dzicy,
Żyjący z pańskich stołów, dworscy zausznicy.
Te pary zwierząt główne i patryjarchalne,
Ukryte w jądrze puszczy, światu niewidzialne,
Dzieci swe ślą dla osad za granicę lasu,
A sami we stolicy używają wczasu;
Nie giną nigdy bronią sieczną ani palną,
Lecz starzy umierają śmiercią naturalną.
Mają też i swój smętarz, kędy, bliscy śmierci,
Ptaki składają pióra, czworonogi sierci.
Niedźwiedź, gdy zjadłszy zęby strawy nie przeżuwa,
Jeleń zgrzybiały, gdy już ledwie nogi suwa,
Zając sędziwy, gdy mu już krew w żyłach krzepnie.
Kruk, gdy, już posiwieje, sokoł, gdy oślepnie,
Orzeł, gdy mu dziób stary tak się w kabłąk skrzywi,
Że zamknięty na wieki już gardła nie żywi –
Idą na smętarz. Nawet mniejszy zwierz, raniony
Lub chory, bieży umrzeć w swe ojczyste strony.
Stąd to w miejscach dostępnych, kędy człowiek gości,
Nie znajdują się nigdy martwych zwierząt kości.
Słychać, że tam w stolicy, między zwierzętami
Dobre są obyczaje, bo rządzą się sami;
Jeszcze cywilizacją ludzką nie popsuci,
Nie znają praw własności, która świat nasz kłóci,
Nie znają pojedynków ni wojennej sztuki.
Jak ojce żyły w raju, tak dziś żyją wnuki,
Dzikie i swojskie razem, w miłości i zgodzie,
Nigdy jeden drugiego nie kąsa ni bodzie.
Nawet gdyby tam człowiek wpadł, chociaż niezbrojny,

Beyond these pools it were in vain to try
To penetrate on foot or e'en with eye.
For from the quaking bog misty pall
Of vapour rises and envelopes all.
Beyond this vapour (fables so declare),
A region stretches fertile and most fair.
The capital of beasts and plants is there.
There seeds of every tree and herb are pent,
And thence their species o'er the world are sent;
And, as in Noah's ark, one pair at least
Is kept for breeding there of every beast.
Midmost the emperors of the forest hold
Their court, the Bison, Bear, and Buffalo old.
And in the trees like ministers on guard
Lie greedy Wolverine and fleet-foot Pard,
While further off like chiefs inferior
Dwell Wolf and long-horned Elk and forest Boar.
The Eagles overhead and soaring Kites
Live off their lords like courtly parasites.
These patriarchs, these archetypal pairs
Of beasts, live in their secret forest lairs,
And send their children to the world outside
As colonists, while they in peace abide.
They perish not by wound of gun or knife,
But meet a natural end to their long life.
They have their graveyard too, where near to death
Birds shed their feathers, beasts their fur bequeath.
The bear with blunted teeth that cannot eat,
The senile stag that scarcely lifts his feet,
The aged hare whose blood more stiffly flows,
The raven grey, the falcon blind that grows,
The eagle whose old beak with age grown bent
No longer serves to give him nourishment,
The sick or wounded, e'en the lesser kind,
Return to their own land a grave to find.
Wherefore it is that on man-trodden ground
The bones of animals are never found.
They say the beasts in this metropolis
Do rule themselves and thence good order is;
No civilising human custom spoils,
No law of property their world embroils;
They know no duels nor in battles strive.
In their ancestral paradise they live,
The wild beast with the tame lives as a brother,
Nor either ever bites or butts the other.
E'en though a man should go there all unarmed,

Toby środkiem bestyi przechodził spokojny;
One by nań patrzyły tym wzrokiem zdziwienia,
Jakim w owym ostatnim, szóstym dniu stworzenia
Ojce ich pierwsze, co się w ogrójcu gnieździły,
Patrzyły na Adama, nim się z nim skłóciły.
Szczęściem, człowiek nie zbłądzi do tego ostępu,
Bo Trud i Trwoga, i Śmierć bronią mu przystępu.
Czasem tylko w pogoni zaciekłe ogary,
Wpadłszy niebacznie między bagna, mchy i jary,
Wnętrznej ich okropności rażone widokiem,
Uciekają skowycząc, z obłąkanym wzrokiem;
I długo potem, ręką pana już głaskane,
Drżą jeszcze u nóg jego strachem opętane.
Te puszcz stołeczne, ludziom nie znane tajniki
W języku swoim strzelcy zowią: mateczniki.

Głupi niedźwiedziu! gdybyś w mateczniku siedział,
Nigdy by się o tobie Wojski nie dowiedział;
Ale czyli pasieki zwabiła cię wonność,
Czy uczułeś do owsa dojrzałego skłonność,
Wyszedłeś na brzeg puszczy, gdzie się las przerzedził,
I tam zaraz leśniczy bytność twą wyśledził,
I zaraz obsaczniki, chytre nasłał szpiegi,
By poznać, gdzie popasasz i gdzie masz noclegi;
Teraz Wojski z obławą, już od matecznika
Postawiwszy szeregi, odwrót ci zamyka.

[*Edited by Jerzy Nowak, Warszawa: Czytelnik, 1995*]

He would pass through the midst of them unharmed,
And they would see him with such admiration
As on the last, the sixth day of creation,
Their fathers that in Eden first did dwell
On Adam looked, ere strife with him befell.
But happily in this domain none strays,
For Toil and Death and Terror bar the ways.
But sometimes in hot chase the furious dogs
Incautious enter these deep mossy bogs,
And horror-stricken when they see their error,
They run off whining and with looks of terror,
And even by their master's hand caressed
They tremble at his feet by fright possessed.
The secret places of this capital
The huntsmen motherlands are wont to call.

O foolish bear! If you had never strayed
Beyond the woods, you had not been betrayed;
But by the fragrance of the honey drawn
Or too great longing for the ripening corn,
You left the forest where the trees grew thin,
And so the woodman traced where you had been.
At once like cunning spies the beaters sped
To find where you had spent the night and fed.
So now the Seneschal and all the beat
Drew out their lines and cut off your retreat.

[*Translated by Kenneth Mackenzie. New York: Hippocrene, 1992. 176–182*]

k. ROMÂNĂ

VI.k.1. MIHAI EMINESCU, from 'Floare albastră'

– Iar te-ai cufundat în stele
Şi în nori şi-n ceruri nalte?
De nu m-ai uita încalte,
Sufletul vieţii mele.

În zadar râuri în soare
Grămădeşti-n a ta gândire
Şi câmpiile asire
Şi întunecata mare;

Piramidele-nvechite
Urcă-n cer vârful lor mare –
Nu căta în depărtare
Fericirea ta, iubite!

Astfel zise mititica,
Dulce netezindu-mi părul.
Ah! ea spuse adevărul;
Eu am râs, n-am zis nimica.

– Hai în codrul cu verdeaţă,
Und-izvoare plâng în vale,
Stânca stă să se prăvale
În prăpastia măreaţă.

Acolo-n ochi de pădure,
Lângă balta cea senină
Şi sub trestia cea lină
Vom şedea în foi de mure.

....

Când prin crengi s-a fi ivit
Luna-n noaptea cea de vară,
Mi-i ţinea de subsuoară,
Te-oi ţinea de după gât.

Pe cărare-n bolţi de frunze,
Apucând spre sat în vale,
Ne-om da sărutări pe cale,
Dulci ca florile ascunse.

k. ROMANIAN

VI.k.1. MIHAI EMINESCU, from 'Sky-Blue Flower'[1]

'Are you rapt in stars again
And in clouds of lofty skies?
Mind you don't forget my eyes,
You, the dearest of all men!'

'Vainly do you cram up notions
Of a sun criss-crossed by rills
Of Assyrian plains and hills
Of the ever darkling oceans;'

'Pyramids of some old day
Raise their tapers to the sky
Oh, my soul's life, never try
To seek bliss so far away!'

So my darling used her craft –
Gently she caressed my hair;
She had told the truth, I swear:
I made no reply, just laughed.

'Let us flee to forests green
Where in valleys springs lament
And a rock is downwards bent
Over each deep-cleft ravine.'

'Where the forest's brow is split
By the pond that's free from weeds,
In the shade of quiet reeds
'Mong the blackberries we'll sit.'

....

'When through boughs we see the moon –
Empress of the summer night –
By the waist you'll hold me tight
And together we shall spoon.'

'While descending under bowers
To our village in the glen
I'll give you a kiss again
Sweet as shyly hiding flowers.'

---

[1] The blue flower is particularly significant in Eminescu. It is the very copy of the skies and the waters and is one with the cosmic infinite, from which we come and into which we are bound to dissolve, as he implies over and over again. The urge to look into the book of nature, by far more potent and richer in learning than the books of erudition, recalls Keats's words to his brother George.

Şi sosind l-al porţii prag,
Vom vorbi-n întunecime:
Grija noastră n-aib-o nime,
Cui ce-i pasă că-mi eşti drag?

Înc-o gură – şi dispare...
Ca un stâlp eu stam în lună!
Ce frumoasă, ce nebună
E albastra-mi, dulce floare!

....

Şi te-ai dus, dulce minune,
Ş-a murit iubirea noastră –
Floare-albastră! floare-albastră!...
Totuşi este trist în lume!

[1873]

VI.k.2. MIHAI EMINESCU, 'Lacul'

Lacul codrilor albastru
Nuferi galbeni îl încarcă;
Tresărind în cercuri albe
El cutremură o barcă.

Şi eu trec de-a lung de maluri,
Parc-ascult şi parc-aştept
Ea din trestii să răsară
Şi să-mi cadă lin pe piept;

Să sărim în luntrea mică,
Îngânaţi de glas de ape,
Şi să scap din mână cârma,
Şi lopeţile să-mi scape;

Să plutim cuprinşi de farmec
Sub lumina blândei lune –
Vântu-n trestii lin foşnească,
Unduioasa apă sune!

Dar nu vine... Singuratic
În zadar suspin şi sufăr
Lângă lacul cel albastru
Încărcat cu flori de nufăr.

[1876]

'And, if reaching mother's gate,
We shall whisper in the dark,
Nobody will mind our lark:
Just who cares my love's so great?'

One more kiss – she vanishes
I stay in the moonlight dazed:
Of, how beautiful, how crazed,
And how sweet my flower is!

....

Wonder sweet, you left your thrall:
Our love lived but an hour.
Sky-blue flower, sky-blue flower! . . .
Sad is this world after all.

[1873] [*Translated by Andrei Bantaș*]

VI.k.2.   MIHAI EMINESCU, 'The Lake'[2]

In the forest, yellow lilies
Carpet the lake-waters blue;
Of a sudden, whitish circles
Do unfasten a canoe.

And I roam along the border
And half list, half wait, most blest
If she comes out of the rushes
And falls gently on my breast.

Into the canoe we'll hurry
Tempted by the waters' chant,
And I shall let slip the rudder,
And the oar I'll put aslant;

We shall, lit by friendly moonbeams,
Float within the magic ring –
May the winds through rushes rustle,
May the rippling waters sing!

But she will not come. O, vainly,
All alone, I sigh and ache
Near the host of yellow lilies,
On the brink of the blue lake.

[1876] [*Translated by Leon Levițchi*]

---

[2] The lake is another favourite topos in Eminescu's nature poetry putting one in mind of Blake's or Coleridge's verse. As the reflection of the skies, the lake conceals in its mysterious depth the secrets of a world full of peerless wonders.

l. РУССКИЙ

VI.l.1. АЛЕКСЕЙ КОЛЬЦОВ, *«Лес»*

Что, дремучий лес,
Призадумался, –
Грустью темною
Затуманился?

Что Бова-силач
Заколдованный,
С непокрытою
Головой в бою, –

Ты стоишь – поник,
И не ратуешь
С мимолетною
Тучей-бурею.

Густолиственный
Твой зеленый шлем
Буйный вихрь сорвал –
И развеял в прах.

Плащ упал к ногам
И рассыпался...
Ты стоишь – поник,
И не ратуешь.

Где ж девалася
Речь высокая,
Сила гордая,
Доблесть царская?

У тебя ль, было,
В ночь безмолвную
Заливная песнь
Соловьиная...

У тебя ль, было,
Дни – роскошество, –
Друг и недруг твой
Прохлаждаются...

У тебя ль, было,
Поздно вечером
Грозно с бурею
Разговор пойдет;

l. RUSSIAN

VI.l.1. ALEXEY KOLTSOV, 'The Forest'

In the memory of A. S. Pushkin

O primeval forest,
Why art thou so pensive,-
Why art thou so clouded
By deep dark sorrow?

Like the valiant knight
Bova, under spell,
Standing bareheaded
On a battlefield,-

Standst thou drooping low
And thou strugglest not
With the swift storm-cloud
That passeth thee by.

Thy thick-leaved helm
That would shine so green
Is torn off by whirlwind,
Dispelled into dust.

At thy feet thy cloak
Fallen, moulded lies . . .
Thou standst drooping low,
Struggling not a bit.

Hast thou lost indeed
All thy glorious speech,
All thy force so proud,
All thy royal might?

Was it thou who sang
That wide warbling song
On a silent night
Like a nightingale?

Was it thou who hadst
Days of lavishing living,-
When thou entertain'dst
Both thy friends and foes?

Was it thou who hadst
In the late of night
Formidable talks
With the thunder-storm;

Распахнет она
Тучу черную,
Обоймет тебя
Ветром-холодом.

И ты молвишь ей
Шумным голосом:
«Вороти назад!
Держи около!»

Закружит она,
Разыграется...
Дрогнет грудь твоя,
Зашатаешься;

Встрепенувшися,
Разбушуешься:
Только свист кругом,
Голоса и гул...

Буря всплачется
Лешим, ведьмою, –
И несет свои
Тучи за море.

Где ж теперь твоя
Мочь зеленая?
Почернел ты весь,
Затуманился...

Одичал, замолк...
Только в непогодь
Воешь жалобу
На безвременье.

Так-то, темный лес,
Богатырь-Бова!
Ты всю жизнь свою
Маял битвами.

Не осилили
Тебя сильные,
Так дорезала
Осень черная.

It would open wide
Its dark feathery cloud
And embrace you all
With its icy wind.

Thou wouldst say to it
In a shrill voice: 'Halt!
'Turn around, I pray,
'Keep away from me!'

It would turn and lurch,
It would blow great guns . . .
And thy breast would stir
And begin to reel;

Thou wouldst shudder then,
Thou wouldst rage and seethe:
Whistling all amidst
Voices, boom and hum . . .

And the storm would weep
Like Puck or a witch,-
And would carry its
Clouds beyond the sea.

Where is now thy power?
Where is thy green strength?
Thou hast all grown dark,
Misty is thy sight . . .
Silent . . . only when
Elements are foul
Thou wilt wail about
Time that runs in vain.

Thus, primeval forest,
Bova, valiant knight,
Hast thou spent thy life
Ever struggling hard.

It was not strong foes
Who did master thee,
It was autumn black
That brought thee an end.

Знать, во время сна
К безоружному
Силы вражие
Понахлынули.

С богатырских плеч
Сняли голову –
Не большой горой,
А соломинкой...

m. ESPAÑOL

VI.m.1. JOSÉ SOMOZA, 'Soneto'

La luna mientras duermes te acompaña,
tiende su luz por tu cabello y frente,
va del semblante al cuello y lentamente
cumbres y valles de tu seno baña.
Yo, Lesbia, que al umbral de tu cabaña
hoy velo, lloro y ruego inútilmente,
el curso de la luna refulgente
dichoso he de seguir o amor me engaña.
He de entrar cual la luna en tu aposento,
cual ella al lienzo en que tu faz resposa
y cual ella a tus labios acercarme;
cual ella el disco de la casta diosa,
puro, trémulo, mudo retirarme.

(1824?) [*Published in Poesías 1842*]

While thou wast asleep,
Unaware, unarmed,
Treacherously foes
Came in throng to thee.

They cut off thine head
From the shoulders strong –
With a thin small straw,
Not a heavy hill . . .

(1837) [*Translated by Dmitry Usenco*]

m.   SPANISH

VI.m.1.   JOSÉ SOMOZA, 'Sonnet'

The moon accompanies you while you sleep, it extends its light over your head and brow, it moves from your face to your throat and slowly bathes the hills and valleys of your breasts. I, Lesbia, who now watch from the portal of your cabin, weep and vainly beg a happy course of the refulgent moon which I must follow or love deceives me. I have to enter like the moon into your room, and, like her, onto the linen on which your face reposes and, like her, come close to your lips; like her breath your sweet breath and, like the disc of the chaste goddess, pure, tremulous, silent, I steal away.

(1824?) [1842]

Somoza began writing in a neoclassical vein reminiscent of English writers like Young and Thomson. Here he takes up the traditional theme of the lover contemplating his sleeping beloved bathed in (romantic) moonlight, both sensual and chaste at the same moment. Nature is used as a complicit agency in the expression of love and desire.

VI.m.2.   ROSALÍA DE CASTRO, 'Los Robles', Section II

Bajo el hacha implacable, ¡cuán presto
en tierra cayeron
encina y robles!
Y a los rayos del alba risueña
¡que calva aparece
la cima del monte!
Los que ayer fueron bosques y selvas
de agreste espesura,
donde envueltas en dulce misterio
al rayar el día,
flotaban las brumas,
y brotaba la fuente serena
entre flores y musgos oculta,
hoy son áridas lomas que ostentan,
deformes y negras,
sus hondas cisuras.
Ya no entornan en ellas los pájaros
sus canciones de amor, ni se juntan
cuando mayo alborea en la fronda
que quedó de sus robles desnuda,
sólo el viento al pasar trae el eco
del cuervo que grazna
del lobo que aúlla.

[From 'Los robles', En las orillas del Sar 1884]

n.   SVENSKA

VI.n.1.   ERIK JOHAN STAGNELIUS, "Suckarnes Mystèr"

Suckar, suckar äro Elementet,
I hvars sköte Demiurgen andas.
Se dig om! Hvad glädde dina sinnen?
Kom ditt hjerta fortare att klappa,
Och med fröjdens milda rosenskimmer
Flyktigt stänkte dina bleka kinder?
Säg, hvad var det? Blott en suck af vemod,
Som, ur andelifvets källa fluten,
Vilsefor i tidens labyrinter.

Tvenne lagar styra menskolifvet
Tvenne krafter hvälfva allt, som födes
Under Månens vanskeliga skifva.
Hör, o menska! Makten att begära
Är den första. Tvånget att försaka
Är den andra. Skilda åt i himlen,

862

VI.m.2.   ROSALÍA DE CASTRO, from 'The Oak Trees', Section II

Under the implacable blades of the axe how swiftly holm oak and oak tree crash to the ground! And under the beams of smiling dawn how bare the crests of the hills appear! That which yesteryear was woods and groves both wild and overgrown, where mists floated wrapped in sweet mystery as dawn appeared, and the serene springs bubbled up hidden between flowers and mosses, today are arid slopes which display their deformed and blackened stumps. Birds no longer fill them with their songs of love, nor gather together when the May dawn breaks through the naked foliage which remain of the oaks, only the passing echo of the croaking raven and the wolf who howls.

[1884]

While Rosalía uses the felling of the Galician oak forests in the mid-XIXth century as a screen onto which she projects her own sense of personal loss – the Romantic contrast of a felicitous past and a bleak present – she also expresses in this group of poems dedicated to the oak trees, a sense of the wounding of the very soul of Galicia and of the natural wonders of the great forests of the province. Galicia, as George Borrow remarks in The Bible in Spain, was famous for the density of its woodlands and their beauty. The Castilian entrepreneurial felling of the oaks seemed to Galician nationalists like Rosalía and her husband Murguía to be an assault on national ideals and symbols. Thus nature is used to evoke both spiritual and political concerns.

n.   SWEDISH

VI.n.1.   ERIK JOHAN STAGNELIUS, 'The Mystery of Sighs'

Sighs constitute the element
In which the Demiurge breathes.
Look back! What did gladden your senses,
Making your heart beat faster,
A mild rose glow of delight
Furtively spattering your pale cheeks?
What was it? Only a sigh of melancholy,
Risen from the source of the life of spirits,
Going astray in the labyrinths of time.

Two laws govern the life of men,
Two forces arch over all that is born
Beneath the awkward disc of the moon.
Listen, human! The power to desire
Is the first one. The compulsion to resign
The second one. Separated in heaven,

En och samma äro dessa lagar
I de land der Achamot befaller,
Och som evig dubbelhet och enhet
Fram i suckarnes mystèr de träda.
Mellan lifvets sorgesuck och dödens
Menskohjertat vacklar här på jorden,
Och hvart enda andedrag förkunnar
Dess bestämmelse i sinneverlden.

Ser du hafvet? Ilande det kommer,
Vill med blåa längtansfulla armar
Under fästets bröllopps-facklor sluta
Till sitt bröst den liljekrönta jorden.
Se, det kommer. Hur dess hjerta svallar
Högt af längtan! Hur dess armar sträfva!
Men förgäfves. Ingen önskan fylles
Under månen. Sjelfva månens fullhet
Är minutlig. Med bedragen väntan
Dignar hafvet och dess stolta böljor
Fly tillbaka suckande från stranden.

Hör du vinden? Susande han sväfvar
Mellan lundens höga poppelkronor.
Hör du? växande hans suckar tala,
Liksom trånsjukt han en kropp begärde
Att med sommarns Flora sig förmäla.
Dock re'n tyna rösterna. På löfvens
Eolsharpa klingar svanesången
Ständigt mattare och dör omsider.

Hvad är våren? Suckar blott från jordens
Dunkla barm, som himlens Konung fråga
Om ej Edens Maj en gång begynner?
Hvad är lärkan, morgonstrålens älskling?
Näktergalen, skuggornas förtrogna?
Suckar blott i växlande gestalter.

Menska! vill du lifvets vishet lära,
O, så hör mig! Tvenne lagar styra
Detta lif. Förmågan att begära
Är den första. Tvånget att försaka
Är den andra. Adla du till frihet
Detta tvång, och, helgad och försonad,
Öfver stoftets kretsande planeter,
Skall du ingå genom ärans portar.

(1820)

These laws are one and the same
In the countries where Achamot rules,
And as eternal unity and duality
They appear in the mystery of sighs.
Between Life's sigh of sorrow and Death's
The human heart falters here on earth,
And each single breath teaches
Its mission in the world of senses.

Do you see the ocean? With haste it comes,
Wanting to clutch with blue longful arms
Beneath the wedding torches of the firmament
To its breast the earth, covered with lilies.
Lo! It comes. How its heart heaves
High with longing! How its arms strive!
But in vain. No wish is fulfilled
Beneath the moon. Even the moon's fullness
Is momentaneous. Deceived by longing
The ocean recedes and its noble billows
Go back sighing from the shore.

Do you hear the wind? Soughing he soars
Amidst the high poplar heads of the grove.
Hark! Crescending his sighs do speak,
As if yearning for a body of his own,
To let him wed the Flora of summer.
But already the voices wane. On the Aeolic
Harp of the leaves the swan song plays
Constantly duller, and finally dies.

What is spring? Nothing but sighs from earth's
Sombre bosom, to ask the King of heaven
Whether the May of Eden shall ever begin?
What is the lark, the darling of the morning beam?
The nightingale, the confident of shadows?
Nothing but sighs, changeling vicissitudes.

Human! If you wish the wisdom of life
Then listen to me! Two laws govern
This life. The capacity to desire
Is the first one. The compulsion to resign
Is the second one. Elevate to freedom
This compulsion, and, hallowed and redeemed,
Above the circling planets of the dust,
Enter you shall through the gates of glory.

(1820)[*Translated by John Swedenmark*]

VI.n.2. ESAIAS TEGNÉR, "Sång till solen"

Dig jag sjunger en sång
du högtstrålande sol!
Kring din konungastol,
djupt i blånande natt,
har du verldarna satt
som vasaller. Du ser
på de bedjande ner; –
men i ljus är din gång.

Se, naturen är död.
Natten, vålnaders vän,
på dess bleknade pragt
har sitt bårtäcke lagt.
Mången nattlampa ser
uti sorghuset ner.
Men du stiger igen
utur östern i glöd.
Som en ros ur sin knopp
växer skapelsen opp.
Den får lif, den får färg,
men du nedblickar glad
på de gnistrande blad,
på de flammande berg.
Lifvets rinnande flod,
som var frusen och stod,
nu framsorlar han mild
med din vaggande bild,
tills du nedblickar sval
mot den vestliga sal,
der för anande hopp,
der för uttröttad dygd
till de saligas bygd
springa portarna opp.

O du himmelens son
hvadan kommer du från?
Var du med, var du med
då den Evige satt
och i ljusnande natt
sådde flammande säd?
Eller stod du kanske
vid hans osedda thron
(öfver verlden står hon)
att som engel tillbe;

VI.n.2.   ESAIAS TEGNER, 'Song to the Sun'

I will sing unto thee,
O thou radiant sun,
High aloft on thy throne
In the deep, azure night,
With the worlds left and right
As thy vassals. Below
In thy glance they may glow;
But their light thou must be.

Behold! Nature is dead.
Now, when ghosts walk about,
On her form night has cast
A black mort-cloth at last.
Many lamps lend relief
To the mansion of grief.
Thou again steppest out
When the east burneth red.
Like a rosebud unfurled
Now awakens the world.
It takes life, it takes hue,
But with joy thou look'st down
On the glittering dew,
And the hills' flaming crown.
And Life's flowing stream,
That was stilled in a dream,
Now goes murmuring on
With thine image, O sun,
Till, more cool, thy rays fall
On the great western hall,
Where fulfilled is each hope
And where virtue may rest
When the portals shall ope
To the realm of the blest.

O celestial one, say
Whence thou camest, I pray.
Wert thou by at the time
The Almighty sublime
Sowed the glittering night
With the seed of the light?
Or perchance was thy place
By the throne of the Lord –
Far aloft above Space –
Where the angels adored;

tills du stolt ej fördrog
hvad från thronen befalls,
och han vredgad dig tog
öfver strålande hals,
och dig hof med förakt
som en boll i det blå,
att förkunna ändå
hans förnekade makt?
Derför ilar du än
så orolig, så snar;
ingen tröstande vän
bjuder vandraren qvar.
Derför ännu ibland
drar du skyarnas dok
öfver kindernas brand.
Ty du sörjer den dag
då dig hämnaren vrok
ur sitt heliga lag,
och du föll från hans knän
uti öcknarna hän.

Säg mig, blir du ej trött
på din ensliga gång?
Blir ej vägen dig lång
som så ofta du nött?
I mångtusende år
har du kommit igen;
och dock gråna ej än
dina gullgula hår?
Som en hjelte går du
på din glänsande stig,
dina härar ännu
hvälfva trygge kring dig.
Men det kommer en stund,
då din gyllene rund
springer sönder: dess knall
manar verlden till fall.
Och som ramlande hus
störta skapelsens hörn
efter dig uti grus;
och den flygande tid,
lik en vingskjuten örn,
faller död derbredvid.

Far en engel då fram
der du fordomdags sam

Till no more thou wouldst brook
The commands from on high,
And He wrathfully took
Thee and flung through the sky
With supernal disdain
Like a ball in the blue
Which might show to full view
That He only doth reign?
Therefore on thou dost roll
With so restless a will
That no friend may console
Thee or bid thee be still.
And anon thou dost seek
With a cloud to enfurl
The hot shame of thy cheek,
For thou ruest the day
The Avenger did hurl
From His presence away,
And thou fell'st from His knees
To the sky's desert seas.

Seems it long thou hast strode
On thy journey alone?
Dost thou tire of the road
Thou so often hast gone?
As in ages untold
Thou hast come the same way,
Have thy tresses of gold
Never softened to gray?
Thou'rt a warrior strong
In the radiant strath,
And thy bold legions throng,
Over-arching the path.
But the hour draws near
When thy great yellow sphere
With a loud noise will break,
And Creation shall quake.
Like a tottering wall
Will the universe fall
Into atoms with thee;
And Time, that on high
Like an eagle sped free,
Shall fall, wounded, and die.

Now an angel doth soar,
Where thou swammest of yore

som en gyllene svan
genom blå ocean,
se, då blickar han stum
kring de ödsliga rum;
men dig finner han ej,
ty din pröfning har slut,
och försonad alltnog
dig den Evige tog
som ett barn på sin arm,
och nu hvilar du ut
invid faderlig barm. –

Väl, så rulla ditt klot
uti ljus och gå gladt
din förklaring emot.
Efter långvarig natt
skall jag se dig en gång
i ett skönare blå;
jag skall helsa dig då
med en skönare sång.

(1817) [1828]

Like a swan gold of hue
On the ocean of blue;
He looks dumbly around
On the empty Profound,
But he sees thee not there.
For, thy long trial o'er,
The Almighty thee bore
On His arm like a child,
And received thee to rest
On His fatherly breast.

Do thou roll on the way
And be glad in the light
Till thou reachest that day!
We shall win through the night,
Be it never so long,
And in fairer blue then
I shall hail thee again
With a lovelier song.

(1817) [1828] [*Translated by Charles Wharton*]

VII. The Exotic

The Romantic preoccupation with the exotic, and, in particular, the Orient, has complex origins – in ideas of nature, voyages of exploration, in a search for origins, in a quest for some 'other' that might define or offer an alternative to European modes of thought, sometimes for satire, sometimes for imperial ambitions, but often for sheer fascination with human differences. China/Japan, Australia, Egypt and America all served this role. Within Europe, the association of freedom, simplicity and the sublime even gave Switzerland a similar role for Wordsworth and the Shelleys.

a. BRITISH

VII.a.1.   WILLIAM BECKFORD, from *Vathek*

Vathek in the midst of this curious harangue, seized the basket, and long before it was finished the fruits had dissolved in his mouth; as he continued to eat his piety increased, and in the same breath which recited his prayers he called for the Koran and sugar.

Such was the state of his mind when the tablets, which were thrown by at the approach of the dwarfs, again attracted his eye; he took them up, but was ready to drop on the ground when he beheld, in large red characters, these words inscribed by Carathis, which were indeed enough to make him tremble: 'Beware of thy old doctors, and their puny messengers of but one cubit high; distrust their pious frauds, and, instead of eating their melons, impale on a spit the bearers of them. Shouldst thou be such a fool as to visit them, the portal of the subterranean palace will be shut in thy face, and with such force as shall shake thee asunder; thy body shall be spit upon, and bats will engender in thy belly.'

To what tends this ominous rhapsody?' cries the Caliph. 'And must then perish in these deserts with thirst, whilst I may refresh myself in the valley of melons and cucumbers! Accursed be the Giaour, with his portal of ebony! he hath made me dance attendance too long already. Besides, who shall prescribe laws to me? I forsooth must not enter any one's habitation! Be it so; but what one can I enter that is not my own?' Bababalouk, who lost not a syllable of this soliloquy, applauded it with all his heart, and the ladies for the first time agreed with him in opinion.

The dwarfs were entertained, caressed, and seated with great ceremony on little cushions of satin. The symmetry of their persons was the subject of criticism; not an inch of them was suffered to pass unexamined; knick-knacks and dainties were offered in profusion, but all were declined with respectful gravity. They clambered up the sides of the Caliph's seat, and, placing themselves each on one of his shoulders, began to whisper prayers in his ears; their tongues quivered like the leaves of a poplar, and the patience of Vathek was almost exhausted, when the acclamations of the troops announced the approach of Fakreddin, who was come with a hundred

old grey-beards and as many Korans and dromedaries; they instantly set about their ablutions, and began to repeat the Bismillah; Vathek, to get rid of these officious monitors, followed their example, for his hands were burning.

The good Emir, who was punctiliously religious, and likewise a great dealer in compliments, made an harangue five times more prolix and insipid than his harbingers had already delivered. The Caliph, unable any longer to refrain, exclaimed – 'For the love of Mahomet, my dear Fakred-din, have done! let us proceed to your valley, and enjoy the fruits that Heaven hath vouchsafed you.' The hint of proceeding put all into motion; the venerable attendants of the Emir set forward somewhat slowly, but Vathek, having ordered his little pages in private to goad on the dromedaries, loud fits of laughter broke forth from the cages, for the unwieldy curvetting of these poor beasts, and the ridiculous distress of their superannuated riders, afforded the ladies no small entertainment. They descended, however, unhurt into the valley, by the large steps which the Emir had cut in the rock; and already the murmuring of streams and the rustling of leaves began to catch their attention. The cavalcade soon entered a path which was skirted by flowering shrubs, and extended to a vast wood of palm-trees, whose branches overspread a building of hewn stone. This edifice was crowned with nine domes, and adorned with as many portals of bronze, on which was engraven the following inscription: 'This is the asylum of pil-grims, the refuge of travellers, and the depository of secrets for all parts of the world.'

Nine pages, beautiful as the day, and clothed in robes of Egyptian linen, very long and very modest, were standing at each door. They received the whole retinue with an easy and inviting air. Four of the most amiable placed the Caliph on a magnificent taktrevan, four others, some-what less graceful, took charge of Bababalouk, who capered for joy at the snug little cabin that fell to his share; the pages that remained waited on the rest of the train.

When everything masculine was gone out of sight the gate of a large enclosure on the right turned on its harmonious hinges and a young female of a slender form came forth; her light brown hair floated in the hazy breeze of the twilight; a troop of young maidens, like the Pleiades, attended her on tip-toe. They hastened to the pavilions that contained the sultanas, and the young lady, gracefully bending, said to them: 'Charming Princesses, everything is ready; we have prepared beds for your repose, and strewed your apartments with jasmine; no insects will keep off slumber from visiting your eyelids, we will dispel them with a thousand plumes; come then, amiable ladies! refresh your delicate feet and your ivory limbs in baths of rosewater; and, by the light of perfumed lamps your servants will amuse you with tales.' The sultanas accepted with pleasure these obliging offers, and followed the young lady to the Emir's harem, where we must for a moment leave them, and return to the Caliph.

Vathek found himself beneath a vast dome, illuminated by a thousand lamps of rock crystal; as many vases of the same material, filled with excellent sherbet, sparkled on a large table, where a profusion of viands were spread; amongst others were sweetbreads stewed in milk of almonds, saffron soups, and lamb a la creme, of all which the Caliph was amazingly fond. He took of each as much as he was able, testified his sense of the Emir's friendship by the gaiety of his heart, and made the dwarfs dance against their will, for these little devotees durst not refuse the Commander of the Faithful; at last he spread himself on the sofa, and slept sounder than he had ever before.

Beneath this dome a general silence prevailed, for there was nothing to disturb it but the jaws of Bababalouk, who had untrussed himself to eat with greater advantage, being anxious to make amends for his fast in the mountains. As his spirits were too high to admit of his sleeping, and not loving to be idle, he proposed with himself to visit the harem, and repair to his charge of the ladies, to examine if they had been properly lubricated with the balm of Mecca, if their eyebrows

and tresses were in order, and, in a word, to perform all the little offices they might need. He sought for a long time together, but without being able to find out the door; he durst not speak aloud, for fear of disturbing the Caliph, and not a soul was stirring in the precincts of the palace; he almost despaired of effecting his purpose, when a low whispering just reached his ear; it came from the dwarfs who were returned to their old occupation, and for the nine hundred and ninety-ninth time in their lives, were reading over the Koran. They very politely invited Bababalouk to be of their party, but his head was full of other concerns. The dwarfs, though scandalised at his dissolute morals, directed him to the apartments he wanted to find; his way thither lay through a hundred dark corridors, along which he groped as he went, and at last began to catch from the extremity of a passage the charming gossiping of the women, which not a little delighted his heart. 'Ah, ha! what, not yet asleep!' cried he; and, taking long strides as he spoke. 'Did you not suspect me of abjuring my charge? I stayed but to finish what my master had left.'

Two of the black eunuchs, on hearing a voice so loud, detached a party in haste, sabre in hand, to discover the cause; but presently was repeated on all sides: "Tis only Bababalouk! no one but Bababalouk!' This circumspect guardian, having gone up to a thin veil of carnation-coloured silk that hung before the doorway, distinguished, by means of the softened splendour that shone through it, an oval bath of dark porphyry, surrounded by curtains festooned in large folds; through the apertures between them, as they were not drawn close, groups of young slaves were visible, amongst whom Bababalouk perceived his pupils, indulgingly expanding their arms, as if to embrace the perfumed water and refresh themselves after their fatigues. The looks of tender languor, their confidential whispers, and the enchanting smiles with which they were imparted, the exquisite fragrance of the roses, all combined to inspire a voluptuousness, which even Bababalouk himself was scarce able to withstand.

He summoned up, however, his usual solemnity, and, in the peremptory tone of authority, commanded the ladies instantly to leave the bath. Whilst he was issuing these mandates the young Nouronihar, daughter of the Emir, who was sprightly as an antelope, and full of wanton gaiety, beckoned one of her slaves to let down the great swing, which was suspended to the ceiling by cords of silk, and whilst this was doing, winked to her companions in the bath, who, chagrined to be forced from so soothing a state of indolence, began to twist it round Bababalouk, and tease him with a thousand vagaries.

When Nouronihar perceived that he was exhausted with fatigue, she accosted him with an arch air of respectful concern, and said: 'My lord, it is not by any means decent that the chief eunuch of the Caliph, our Sovereign, should thus continue standing; deign but to recline your graceful person upon this sofa, which will burst with vexation if it have not the honour to receive you.'

Caught by these flattering accents, Bababalouk gallantly replied: 'Delight of the apple of my eye! I accept the invitation of thy honeyed lips; and, to say truth, my senses are dazzled with the radiance that beams from thy charms.'

'Repose, then, at your ease,' replied the beauty, and placed him on the pretended sofa, which, quicker than lightning, gave way all at once. The rest of the women, having aptly conceived her design, sprang naked from the bath, and plied the swing with such unmerciful jerks, that it swept through the whole compass of a very lofty dome, and took from the poor victim all power of respiration; sometimes his feet rased the surface of the water, and at others the skylight almost flattened his nose; in vain did he pierce the air with the cries of a voice that resembled the ringing of a cracked basin, for their peals of laughter were still more predominant.

(1786)

VII.a.2. SAMUEL TAYLOR COLERIDGE, 'Kubla Khan:
Or a Vision in a Dream. A Fragment'

In Xanadu did Kubla Khan
A stately pleasure-dome decree:
Where Alph, the sacred river, ran
Through caverns measureless to man
   Down to a sunless sea.
So twice five miles of fertile ground
With walls and towers were girdled round:
And there were gardens bright with sinuous rills,
Where blossomed many an incense-bearing tree;
And here were forests ancient as the hills,
Enfolding sunny spots of greenery.

But oh! that deep romantic chasm which slanted
Down the green hill athwart a cedarn cover!
A savage place! as holy and enchanted
As e'er beneath a waning moon was haunted
By woman wailing for her demon-lover!
And from this chasm, with ceaseless turmoil seething,
As if this earth in fast thick pants were breathing,
A mighty fountain momently was forced:
Amid whose swift half-intermitted burst
Huge fragments vaulted like rebounding hail,
Or chaffy grain beneath the thresher's flail:
And 'mid these dancing rocks at once and ever
It flung up momently the sacred river.
Five miles meandering with a mazy motion
Through wood and dale the sacred river ran,
Then reached the caverns measureless to man,
And sank in tumult to a lifeless ocean:
And 'mid this tumult Kubla heard from far
Ancestral voices prophesying war!

   The shadow of the dome of pleasure
   Floated midway on the waves;
   Where was heard the mingled measure
   From the fountain and the caves.
It was a miracle of rare device,
A sunny pleasure-dome with caves of ice!

   A damsel with a dulcimer
   In a vision once I saw:
   It was an Abyssinian maid,
   And on her dulcimer she played,

Singing of Mount Abora.
Could I revive within me
Her symphony and song,
To such a deep delight 'twould win me
That with music loud and long
I would build that dome in air,
That sunny dome! those caves of ice!
And all who heard should see them there,
And all should cry, Beware! Beware!
His flashing eyes, his floating hair!
Weave a circle round him thrice,
And close your eyes with holy dread,
For he on honey-dew hath fed
And drunk the milk of Paradise.

(1816)

VII.a.3. GEORGE GORDON, LORD BYRON, from *Don Juan,* Canto II

188

They were alone, but not alone as they
    Who shut in chambers think it loneliness;
The silent ocean, and the starlight bay,
    The twilight glow which momently grew less,
The voiceless sands and dropping caves, that lay
    Around them, made them to each other press,
As if there were no life beneath the sky
Save theirs, and that their life could never die.

189

They fear'd no eyes nor ears on that lone beach,
    They felt no terrors from the night, they were
All in all to each other: though their speech
    Was broken words, they thought a language there, –
And all the burning tongues the passions teach
    Found in one sigh the best interpreter
Of nature's oracle – first love, – that all
Which Eve has left her daughters since her fall.

190

Haidde spoke not of scruples, ask'd no vows,
    Nor offer'd any; she had never heard
Of plight and promises to be a spouse,
    Or perils by a loving maid incurr'd;

877

She was all which pure ignorance allows,
    And flew to her young mate like a young bird;
And, never having dreamt of falsehood, she
    Had not one word to say of constancy.

191

She loved, and was beloved – she adored,
    And she was worshipp'd; after nature's fashion,
Their intense souls, into each other pour'd,
    If souls could die, had perish'd in that passion, –
But by degrees their senses were restored,
    Again to be o'ercome, again to dash on;
And, beating 'gainst his bosom, Haidee's heart
Felt as if never more to beat apart.

192

Alas! they were so young, so beautiful,
    So lonely, loving, helpless, and the hour
Was that in which the heart is always full,
    And, having o'er itself no further power,
Prompts deeds eternity can not annul,
    But pays off moments in an endless shower
Of hell-fire – all prepared for people giving
Pleasure or pain to one another living.

193

Alas! for Juan and Haidee! they were
    So loving and so lovely – till then never,
Excepting our first parents, such a pair
    Had run the risk of being damn'd for ever;
And Haidee, being devout as well as fair,
    Had, doubtless, heard about the Stygian river,
And hell and purgatory – but forgot
Just in the very crisis she should not.

194

They look upon each other, and their eyes
    Gleam in the moonlight; and her white arm clasps
Round Juan's head, and his around hers lies
    Half buried in the tresses which it grasps;
She sits upon his knee, and drinks his sighs,
    He hers, until they end in broken gasps;

And thus they form a group that's quite antique,
Half naked, loving, natural, and Greek.

195

And when those deep and burning moments pass'd,
    And Juan sunk to sleep within her arms,
She slept not, but all tenderly, though fast,
    Sustain'd his head upon her bosom's charms;
And now and then her eye to heaven is cast,
    And then on the pale cheek her breast now warms,
Pillow'd on her o'erflowing heart, which pants
With all it granted, and with all it grants.

196

An infant when it gazes on a light,
    A child the moment when it drains the breast,
A devotee when soars the Host in sight,
    An Arab with a stranger for a guest,
A sailor when the prize has struck in fight,
    A miser filling his most hoarded chest,
Feel rapture; but not such true joy are reaping
As they who watch o'er what they love while sleeping.

197

For there it lies so tranquil, so beloved,
    All that it hath of life with us is living;
So gentle, stirless, helpless, and unmoved,
    And all unconscious of the joy 't is giving;
All it hath felt, inflicted, pass'd, and proved,
    Hush'd into depths beyond the watcher's diving:
There lies the thing we love with all its errors
And all its charms, like death without its terrors.

198

The lady watch'd her lover – and that hour
    Of Love's, and Night's, and Ocean's solitude,
O'erflow'd her soul with their united power;
    Amidst the barren sand and rocks so rude
She and her wave-worn love had made their bower,
    Where nought upon their passion could intrude,
And all the stars that crowded the blue space
Saw nothing happier than her glowing face. (II, ll. 1497–1584)

(1819)

VII.a.4.   SIR WALTER SCOTT, from *Ivanhoe*

To his great surprise he found himself in a room magnificently furnished, but having cushions instead of chairs to rest upon, and in other respects partaking so much of Oriental costume, that he began to doubt whether he had not, during his sleep, been transported back again to the land of Palestine. The impression was increased, when, the tapestry being drawn aside, a female form, dressed in a rich habit, which partook more of the Eastern taste than that of Europe, glided through the door which it concealed, and was followed by a swarthy domestic.

As the wounded knight was about to address this fair apparition, she imposed silence by placing her slender finger upon her ruby lips, while the attendant, approaching him, proceeded to uncover Ivanhoe's side, and the lovely Jewess satisfied herself that the bandage was in its place, and the wound doing well. She performed her task with a graceful and dignified simplicity and modesty, which might, even in more civilized days, have served to redeem it from whatever might seem repugnant to female delicacy. The idea of so young and beautiful a person engaged in attendance on a sick-bed, or in dressing the wound of one of a different sex, was melted away and lost in that of a beneficent being contributing her effectual aid to relieve pain, and to avert the stroke of death. Rebecca's few and brief directions were given in the Hebrew language to the old domestic; and he, who had been frequently her assistant in similar cases, obeyed them without reply.

The accents of an unknown tongue, however harsh they might have sounded when uttered by another, had, coming from the beautiful Rebecca, the romantic and pleasing effect which fancy ascribes to the charms pronounced by some beneficent fairy, unintelligible, indeed, to the ear, but, from the sweetness of utterance, and benignity of aspect, which accompanied them, touching and affecting to the heart. Without making an attempt at further question, Ivanhoe suffered them in silence to take the measures they thought most proper for his recovery; and it was not until those were completed, and this kind physician about to retire, that his curiosity could no longer be suppressed. – 'Gentle maiden,' be began in the Arabian tongue, with which his Eastern travels had rendered him familiar, and which he thought most likely to be understood by the turban'd and caftan'd damsel who stood before him – 'I pray you, gentle maiden, of your courtesy' – –

'But here he was interrupted by his fair physician, a smile which she could scarce suppress dimpling for an instant a face, whose general expression was that of contemplative melancholy. 'I am of England, Sir Knight, and speak the English tongue, although my dress and my lineage belong to another climate.'

(1819)

VII.a.5.   THOMAS DE QUINCEY, from *Confessions of an English Opium Eater*

And, by the way, now that I speak of giving laudanum away, I remember, about this time, a little incident, which I mention, because, trifling as it was, the reader will soon meet it again in my dreams, which it influenced more fearfully than could be imagined. One day a Malay knocked at my door. What business a Malay could have to transact amongst English mountains I cannot conjecture; but possibly he was on his road to a seaport about forty miles distant.

The servant who opened the door to him was a young girl, born and bred amongst the mountains, who had never seen an Asiatic dress of any sort; his turban therefore confounded her not a little; and as it turned out that his attainments in English were exactly of the same extent as hers in the Malay, there seemed to be an impassable gulf fixed between all communication of ideas, if either party had happened to possess any. In this dilemma, the girl, recollecting the reputed

learning of her master (and doubtless giving me credit for a knowledge of all the languages of the earth besides perhaps a few of the lunar ones), came and gave me to understand that there was a sort of demon below, whom she clearly imagined that my art could exorcise from the house. I did not immediately go down, but when I did, the group which presented itself, arranged as it was by accident, though not very elaborate, took hold of my fancy and my eye in a way that none of the statuesque attitudes exhibited in the ballets at the Opera-house, though so ostentatiously complex, had ever done. In a cottage kitchen, but panelled on the wall with dark wood that from age and rubbing resembled oak, and looking more like a rustic hall of entrance than a kitchen, stood the Malay – his turban and loose trousers of dingy white relieved upon the dark panelling. He had placed himself nearer to the girl than she seemed to relish, though her native spirit of mountain intrepidity contended with the feeling of simple awe which her countenance expressed as she gazed upon the tiger-cat before her. And a more striking picture there could not be imagined than the beautiful English face of the girl, and its exquisite fairness, together with her erect and independent attitude, contrasted with the sallow and bilious skin of the Malay, enamelled or veneered with mahogany by marine air, his small, fierce, restless eyes, thin lips, slavish gestures and adorations. Half-hidden by the ferocious-looking Malay was a little child from a neighbouring cottage who had crept in after him, and was now in the act of reverting its head and gazing upwards at the turban and the fiery eyes beneath it, whilst with one hand he caught at the dress of the young woman for protection. My knowledge of the Oriental tongues is not remarkably extensive, being indeed confined to two words – the Arabic word for barley and the Turkish for opium (madjoon), which I have learned from Anastasius; and as I had neither a Malay dictionary nor even Adelung's Mithridates, which might have helped me to a few words, I addressed him in some lines from the Iliad, considering that, of such languages as I possessed, Greek, in point of longitude, came geographically nearest to an Oriental one. He worshipped me in a most devout manner, and replied in what I suppose was Malay. In this way I saved my reputation with my neighbours, for the Malay had no means of betraying the secret. He lay down upon the floor for about an hour, and then pursued his journey. On his departure I presented him with a piece of opium. To him, as an Orientalist, I concluded that opium must be familiar; and the expression of his face convinced me that it was. Nevertheless, I was struck with some little consternation when I saw him suddenly raise his hand to his mouth, and, to use the schoolboy phrase, bolt the whole, divided into three pieces, at one mouthful. The quantity was enough to kill three dragoons and their horses, and I felt some alarm for the poor creature; but what could be done? I had given him the opium in compassion for his solitary life, on recollecting that if he had travelled on foot from London it must be nearly three weeks since he could have exchanged a thought with any human being. I could not think of violating the laws of hospitality by having him seized and drenched with an emetic, and thus frightening him into a notion that we were going to sacrifice him to some English idol. No: there was clearly no help for it. He took his leave, and for some days I felt anxious, but as I never heard of any Malay being found dead, I became convinced that he was used to opium; and that I must have done him the service I designed by giving him one night of respite from the pains of wandering.

This incident I have digressed to mention, because this Malay (partly from the picturesque exhibition he assisted to frame, partly from the anxiety I connected with his image for some days) fastened afterwards upon my dreams, and brought other Malays with him, worse than himself, that ran 'a-muck' at me, and led me into a world of troubles. But to quit this episode, and to return to my intercalary year of happiness. I have said already, that on a subject so important to us all as happiness, we should listen with pleasure to any man's experience or experiments,

881

even though he were but a plough-boy, who cannot be supposed to have ploughed very deep into such an intractable soil as that of human pains and pleasures, or to have conducted his researches upon any very enlightened principles. But I who have taken happiness both in a solid and liquid shape, both boiled and unboiled, both East India and Turkey – who have conducted my experiments upon this interesting subject with a sort of galvanic battery, and have, for the general benefit of the world, inoculated myself, as it were, with the poison of 8000 drops of laudanum per day (just for the same reason as a French surgeon inoculated himself lately with cancer, an English one twenty years ago with plague, and a third, I know not of what nation, with hydrophobia), I (it will be admitted) must surely know what happiness is, if anybody does. And therefore I will here lay down an analysis of happiness; and as the most interesting mode of communicating it, I will give it, not didactically, but wrapped up and involved in a picture of one evening, as I spent every evening during the intercalary year when laudanum, though taken daily, was to me no more than the elixir of pleasure. This done, I shall quit the subject of happiness altogether, and pass to a very different one – THE PAINS OF OPIUM.

(1821)

d. FRANÇAIS

VII.d.1. FRANÇOIS RENÉ DE CHATEAUBRIAND, de *Atala*

Souvent, dans les grandes chaleurs du jour, nous cherchions un abri sous les mousses des cèdres. Presque tous les arbres de la Floride, en particulier le cèdre et le chêne-vert, sont couverts d'une mousse blanche qui descend de leurs rameaux jusqu'à terre. Quand la nuit, au clair de la lune, vous apercevez sur la nudité d'une savane une yeuse isolée revêtue de cette draperie, vous croiriez voir un fantôme, traînant après lui ses longs voiles. La scène n'est pas moins pittoresque au grand jour; car une foule de papillons, de mouches brillantes, de colibris, de perruches vertes, de geais d'azur, vient s'accrocher à ces mousses, qui produisent alors l'effet d'une tapisserie en laine blanche, où l'ouvrier européen auroit brodé des insectes et des oiseaux éclatants.

C'étoit dans ces riantes hôtelleries, préparées par le Grand-Esprit, que nous nous reposions à l'ombre. Lorsque les vents descendoient du ciel pour balancer ce grand cèdre, que le château aérien bâti sur ses branches alloit flottant avec les oiseaux et les voyageurs endormis sous ses abris, que mille soupirs sortoient des corridors et des voûtes du mobile édifice, jamais les merveilles de l'ancien monde n'ont approché de ce monument du désert.

Chaque soir nous allumions un grand feu, et nous bâtissions la hutte du voyage avec une écorce élevée sur quatre piquets. Si j'avois tué une dinde sauvage, un ramier, un faisan des bois, nous le suspendions devant le chêne embrasé, au bout d'une gaule plantée en terre, et nous abandonnions au vent le soin de tourner la proie du chasseur. Nous mangions des mousses appelées *tripes de roches*, des écorces sucrées de bouleau, et des pommes de mai, qui ont le goût de la pêche et de la framboise. Le noyer noir, l'érable, le sumac fournissoient le vin à notre table. Quelquefois j'allois chercher parmi les roseaux une plante dont la fleur allongée en cornet contenoit un verre de la plus pure rosée. Nous bénissions la Providence, qui sur la foible tige d'une fleur avoit placé cette source limpide au milieu des marais corrompus, comme elle a mis l'espérance au fond des coeurs ulcérés par le chagrin, comme elle a fait jaillir la vertu de sein des misères de la vie.

d. FRENCH

VII.d.1. FRANÇOIS RENÉ DE CHATEAUBRIAND, from *Atala*

During the great heat of the day, we frequently sought shelter beneath the moss of the cedars. Nearly all the Floridan trees, especially the cedar and the oak, are covered with a white moss, which decends from their branches down to the very ground. At night-time, by moonlight, should you happen to see, in the open savanna, an isolated holm dressed in such drapery, you would imagine it to be a phantom dragging after it a number of long veils. The scene is not less picturesque by day, when a crowd of butterflies, brilliant insects, colibris, green paraquets, and blue jackdaws entangle themselves among the moss, and thus produce the effect of a piece of white woolen tapestry embroidered by some clever European workman with beautiful birds and sparkling insects.

It was in the shade of such smiling quarters prepared by the Great Spirit that we stopped to repose ourselves. When the winds come down from heaven to rock the great cedar, when the aerial castles built upon its branches undulate with the birds and travelers sleeping beneath its shelter, when thousands of sighs pass through the corridors of the waving edifice, there is nothing among the wonders of the ancient world to be compared with this moment of the desert.

Every evening we lighted a large fire and built a traveling hut of bark raised upon four stakes. When I had killed a wild turkey, a pigeon, or a wood-pheasant, we attached it to the end of a pole before a pile of burning oak, and left the care of turning the hunter's prey to the caprices of the wind. We used to eat a kind of moss called rock-tripe, sweetened bark, and May-apples that tasted of the peach and raspberry. The black walnut-tree, the maple-tree, and the sumach furnished our table with wine. Sometimes I went and fetched from among the reeds a plant whose flower, in the form of an elongated cup, contained a glass of the purest dew. We blessed heaven for having placed this limpid spring upon the stalk of a flower in the midst of the corrupted marshes, just as it has placed hope at the bottom of hearts ulcerated by grief; just also as it has caused virtue to well up from the bosom of the miseries of life!

[Translated by James Spence Harry. New York: Cassell, 1884]

VII.d.2.   ALFRED DE MUSSET, 'Venise'

Dans Venise la rouge,
Pas un bateau qui bouge
Pas un pêcheur dans l'eau,
Pas un falot.
Seul, assis à la grève,
Le grand lion soulève,
Sur l'horizon serein,
Son pied d'airain.
Autour de lui, par groupes,
Navires et chaloupes,
Pareils à des hérons
Couchés en ronds,
Dorment sur l'eau qui fume,
Et croisent dans la brume,
En légers tourbillons,
Leurs pavillons.
La lune qui s'efface
Couvre son front qui passe
D'un nuage étoile
Demi-voilé.
Ainsi, la dame abbesse
De Sainte-Croix rabaisse
Sa cape aux larges plis
Sur son surplis
Et les palais antiques,
Et les graves portiques,
Et les blancs escaliers
Des chevaliers,
Et les ponts, et les rues,
Et les mornes statues,
Et le golfe mouvant
Qui tremble au vent,
Tout se tait, fors les gardes
Aux longues hallebardes,
Qui veillent aux créneaux
Des arsenaux.
-Ah! maintenant plus d'une
Attend, au clair de lune,
Quelque jeune muguet,
L'oreille au guet.
Pour le bal qu'on prépare,
Plus d'une qui se pare,
Met, devant son miroir
Le masque noir.

VII.d.2. ALFRED DE MUSSET, 'Venice'

In Venice the red,
Never a boat that's sped,
No fisher on the mere,
No lantern near.
Seated alone on shore,
The Lion grand lifts o'er
Horizon without flaw,
His bronzed paw.
Around him, ranged in groups,
Great vessels and shallops,
Like herons all adoze
In silent rows,
On smoking waves reclined;
And o'er the mist entwined,
Their standards, hovering
In airy ring.
The moon that groweth pale,
Her fading brow doth veil,
A cloud all starry lined
Half hidd'n behind.
The lady abbess, so,
Of Sainte Croix folds low
Her cape of vast contour
Her surplice o'er.
Palace of olden time,
And porticoes sublime,
And the broad stairways white
Of ancient knight,
And streets, and bridge of stone,
And statues sad and lone,
And gulf that onward glides
In rippling tides,
The guards in midnight hour
With halberds on the tower,
And arsenal turrets steep,
Their watches keep.
Ah, more than one sweet maid
'Neath light of moon, hath stayed,
Some boyish flow'ret dear,
With listening ear.
More than one hurrying lass,
Ere leaving, at her glass
The mask of jet doth tie,
For the ball's nigh.

Sur sa couche embaumée,
La Vanina pâmée
Presse encor son amant,
En s'endormant;
Et Narcisa, la folle,
Au fond de sa gondole,
S'oublie en un festin
Jusqu'au matin.
Et qui, dans l'Italie,
N'a son grain de folie?
Qui ne garde aux amours
Ses plus beaux jours?
Laissons la vieille horloge,
Au palais du vieux doge,
Lui compter de ses nuits
Les longs ennuis.
Comptons plutôt, ma belle,
Sur ta bouche rebelle
Tant de baisers donnés...
Ou pardonnés.
Comptons plutôt tes charmes,
Comptons les douces larmes,
Qu'à nos yeux a coûté
La volupté!

VII.d.3.   VICTOR HUGO, *Les Orientales,* 'Les Djinns'

Murs, ville,
Et port,
Asile
De mort,
Mer grise
Où brise
La brise,
Tout dort.
Dans la plaine
Naît un bruit.
C'est l'haleine
De la nuit.
Elle brame
Comme une âme
Qu'une flamme
Toujours suit!

On couch of balmy scent,
La Vanina, outspent,
Still fast her lover keeps,
And sweetly sleeps,
And Narcissa, the bold,
In her gondola's hold,
Forgets herself till day,
Feasting away.
And who, o'er Italy,
Breeds not frivolity?
Who keeps not for love's ways
His fairest days?
Leave antique horologe,
On palace of old doge,
Of weary nights to count
The dull amount.
Better to count, ma belle,
On thy lips that rebel,
So many kisses given . . .
Or forgiven.
Better thy charms repeat,
Better, the tear-drops sweet,
That love's voluptuous sighs
Have cost our eyes.

(1828)

[*Translated by Andrew Lang, Charles Conner Hayden and Marie Agathe Clarke. Boston: C. T. Brainard, 1908*]

VII.d.3.   VICTOR HUGO, from *Eastern Lyrics*, 'The Djinns'

Walls, town,
And port,
Asylum
Of death,
Gray sea
Where breaks
The breeze,
All sleeps.
In the plain
Is born a noise.
It's the breath
Of the night
It bawls
Like a soul
That a flame
Always follows!

La voix plus haute
Semble un grelot.
D'un nain qui saute
C'est le galop.
Il fuit, s'élance,
Puis en cadence
Sur un pied danse
Au bout d'un flot.
La rumeur approche.
L'écho la redit.
C'est comme la cloche
D'un couvent maudit;
Comme un bruit de foule,
Qui tonne et qui roule,
Et tantôt s'écroule,
Et tantôt grandit,
Dieu! la voix sépulcrale
Des Djinns!... Quel bruit ils font!
Fuyons sous la spirale
De l'escalier profond.
Déjà s'éteint ma lampe,
Et l'ombre de la rampe,
Qui le long du mur rampe,
Monte jusqu'au plafond.
C'est l'essaim des Djinns qui passe,
Et tourbillonne en sifflant!
Les ifs, que leur vol fracasse,
Craquent comme un pin brûlant.
Leur troupeau, lourd et rapide,
Volant dans l'espace vide,
Semble un nuage livide
Qui porte un éclair au flanc.
Ils sont tout près! – Tenons fermée
Cette salle, où nous les narguons.
Quel bruit dehors! Hideuse armée
De vampires et de dragons!
La poutre du toit descellée
Ploie ainsi qu'une herbe mouillée,
Et la vieille porte rouillée
Tremble, à déraciner ses gonds!
Cris de l'enfer! voix qui hurle et qui pleure!
L'horrible essaim, poussé par l'aquilon,
Sans doute, ô ciel! s'abat sur ma demeure.
Le mur fléchit sous le noir bataillon.
La maison crie et chancelle penchée,
Et l'on dirait que, du sol arrachée,

The highest voice
Seems a sleigh bell.
Of a jumping dwarf
It's the gallop.
It flees, rushes,
Then in cadence
On one foot dances
At the tip of a wave.
The hum approaches.
The echo repeats it.
It is like the bell
Of a cursed convent;
Like a crowd's noise
Booming and rolling,
Now collapsing,
Now growing,
God! the sepulchral voice
Of the Djinns! . . . What a noise!
Let's flee under the spiral
Of the deep staircase.
Already my lamp goes out,
And the shadow of the ramp,
Which slithers across the wall,
Climbs up to the ceiling.
The swarm of Djinns is passing
And swirls around while whistling!
The yews, which their flight smashes,
Crackle like a burning pine.
Their herd, heavy and rapid,
Flying in empty space,
Seems to be a livid cloud
Carrying lightning at its side.
They are so close! – Let us hold closed
This room, in which we scoff at them.
Such noise outside! Hideous army
Of vampires and of dragons!
The roof-beam, pulling free,
Bends just like a damp blade of grass,
And the old and rusty door
Trembles, and uproots its hinges!
Shouts from hell! voice which screams and cries!
The horrible swarm, pushed by the north wind,
Doubtless, oh Heaven! crashes down on my home.
The wall bends under the black battalion.
The house cries out and totters, leaning,
And one would think that, torn out of the ground,

Ainsi qu'il chasse une feuille séchée,
Le vent la roule avec leur tourbillon!
Prophète! si ta main me sauve
De ces impurs démons des soirs,
J'irai prosterner mon front chauve
Devant tes sacrés encensoirs!
Fais que sur ces portes fidèles
Meure leur souffle d'étincelles,
Et qu'en vain l'ongle de leurs ailes
Grince et crie à ces vitraux noirs!
Ils sont passés! – Leur cohorte
S'envole, et fuit, et leurs pieds
Cessent de battre ma porte
De leurs coups multipliés.
L'air est plein d'un bruit de chaînes,
Et dans les forêts prochaines
Frissonnent tous les grands chênes,
Sous leur vol de feu pliés!
De leurs ailes lointaines
Le battement décroît,
Si confus dans les plaines,
Si faible, que l'on croit
Ouïr la sauterelle
Crier d'une voix grêle,
Ou pétiller la grêle
Sur le plomb d'un vieux toit.
D'étranges syllabes
Nous viennent encor; –
Ainsi, des Arabes
Quand sonne le cor,
Un chant sur la grève
Par instants s'élève,
Et l'enfant qui rêve
Fait des rêves d'or.
Les Djinns funèbres,
Fils du trépas,
Dans les ténèbres
Pressent leurs pas;
Leur essaim gronde:
Ainsi, profonde,
Murmure une onde
Qu'on ne voit pas.
Ce bruit vague
Qui s'endort,
C'est la vague
Sur le bord;

Just as it chases a dry leaf,
The wind rolls it with their whirlwind!
Prophet! if your hand saves me,
From these impure nighttime demons,
I will go prostrate my bald forehead
Before your sacred censers!
On these faithful doors, cause
Their breath of sparks to die,
And in vain the nail of their wings
To scrape and wail at these black windows!
They have passed! – Their cohort
Takes wing, and flees, and their feet
Cease beating on my door
With their redoubled blows.
The air is full of a noise of chains,
And in the nearby forests
Shiver all the great oaks,
Bent under their fiery flight!
Of their far-off wings
The beating fades away,
So confused in the plains,
So weak that one believes
That one hears the grasshopper
Shouting in a shrill voice,
Or hail fizzing
On the leads of an old roof.
Strange syllables
Still come to us; –
As of the Arabs
When the horn sounds,
A song on the strand
Rises in snatches
And the dreaming child
Has golden dreams.
The gloomy Djinns,
Sons of demise,
In the shadows
Hurry their step;
Their swarm growls:
As does, deeply,
Murmur a wave
Which goes unseen.
This vague noise
Going to sleep,
Is the wave
On the shore;

C'est la plainte
Presque éteinte
D'une sainte
Pour un mort.
On doute
La nuit...
J'écoute: –
Tout fuit,
Tout passe
L'espace
Efface
Le bruit.

(1829)

e. DEUTSCH

VII.e.1. NOVALIS, aus *Heinrich von Ofterdingen*

Das Gespräch lief über ehmalige Kriegsabentheuer hin. Heinrich hörte mit großer Aufmerksamkeit den neuen Erzählungen zu. Die Ritter sprachen vom heiligen Lande, von den Wundern des heiligen Grabes, von den Abentheuern ihres Zuges, und ihrer Seefahrt, von den Sarazenen, in deren Gewalt einige gerathen gewesen waren, und dem frölichen und wunderbaren Leben im Felde und im Lager. Sie äußerten mit großer Lebhaftigkeit ihren Unwillen jene himmlische Geburtsstätte der Christenheit noch im frevelhaften Besitz der Ungläubigkeit zu wissen. Sie erhoben die großen Helden, die sich eine ewige Krone durch ihr tapfres, unermüdliches Bezeigen gegen dieses ruchlose Volk erworben hätten. Der Schloßherr zeigte das kostbare Schwerdt, was er einem Anführer derselben mit eigner Hand abgenommen, nachdem er sein Castell erobert, ihn getödtet, und seine Frau und Kinder zu Gefangenen gemacht, welches ihm der Kayser in seinem Wappen zu führen vergönnet hatte. Alle besahen das prächtige Schwerdt, auch Heinrich nahm es in seine Hand, und fühlte sich von einer kriegerischen Begeisterung ergriffen. Er küßte es mit inbrünstiger Andacht. Die Ritter freuten sich über seinen Antheil. Der Alte umarmte ihn, und munterte ihn auf, auch seine Hand auf ewig der Befreyung des heiligen Grabes zu widmen, und das wunderthätige Kreuz auf seine Schultern befestigen zu lassen. Er war überrascht, und seine Hand schien sich nicht von dem Schwerdte losmachen zu können. Besinne dich, mein Sohn, rief der alte Ritter. Ein neuer Kreuzzug ist vor der Thür. Der Kayser selbst wird unsere Schaaren in das Morgenland führen. Durch ganz Europa schallt von neuem der Ruf des Kreuzes, und heldenmüthige Andacht regt sich aller Orten. Wer weiß, ob wir nicht übers Jahr in der großen weltherrlichen Stadt Jerusalem als frohe Sieger bey einander sitzen, und uns bey vaterländischem Wein an unsere Heymath erinnern. Du kannst auch bey mir ein morgenländisches Mädgen sehn. Sie dünken uns Abendländern gar anmuthig, und wenn du das Schwerdt gut zu führen verstehst, so kann es dir an schönen Gefangenen nicht fehlen. Die Ritter sangen mit lauter Stimme den Kreuzgesang, der damals in ganz Europa gesungen wurde:

It's the plea
Very faint
Of a saint
For a dead man.
One doubts
The night . . .
I listen: –
All flees,
All passes
The space
Erases
The noise.

(1829) [*Translated by Anne Gwin*]

e. GERMAN

VII.e.1.   NOVALIS, from *Henry of Ofterdingen*

The conversation turned to former adventures in war. Henry listened very attentively to these new stories. The knights talked about the Holy Land, about the marvels of the Holy Sepulcher, about the adventures on their crusade and their journey at sea, about the Saracens into whose hands several of them had fallen, and about the jolly and wonderful life in the field and in camp. With great passion they uttered their indignation that the heavenly birthplace of Christianity was still in the impious possession of infidels. They extolled the great heroes who had earned for themselves an eternal crown by their tireless, courageous behavior towards that villainous people.

The lord of the castle displayed the costly sword which he with his own hand had taken from one of their chiefs after having stormed his castle, killed him, and taken his wife and children prisoner – exploits which the emperor permitted him to add to the heraldic devices on his escutcheon. They all looked at the splendid sword; Henry also took it in his hands and felt gripped by a war-like enthusiasm. He kissed it with fervid admiration. The knights were delighted at his interest. The old lord put his arms around him and encouraged him also to dedicate his hand forever to the liberation of the Holy Sepulcher and to have the wonder-working cross fastened on his shoulders. He was surprised and his hand appeared unable to let go of the sword.

'Think about this, my son,' the old knight said. 'A new crusade is at hand. The emperor himself will lead our hosts to the Holy Land. The call of the cross is resounding anew throughout all Europe, and a heroic devotion is stirring everywhere. Who knows but that in a year we shall be sitting together as joyful victors in the great world-renowned city of Jerusalem and over our native wine calling to mind our homeland. You can also see an oriental girl in my house. They look very attractive to us of the West, and if you know how to handle a sword well, you cannot want for lovely prisoners.' In a loud voice the knights sang the crusade song sung at that time in all Europe:

893

Das Grab steht unter wilden Heyden;
Das Grab, worinn der Heyland lag,
Muß Frevel und Verspottung leiden
Und wird entheiligt jeden Tag.
Es klagt heraus mit dumpfer Stimme:
Wer rettet mich von diesem Grimme!

*

Wo bleiben seine Heldenjünger?
Verschwunden ist die Christenheit!
Wer ist des Glaubens Wiederbringer?
Wer nimmt das Kreuz in dieser Zeit?
Wer bricht die schimpflichsten der Ketten,
Und wird das heil'ge Grab erretten?

*

Gewaltig geht auf Land und Meeren
In tiefer Nacht ein heil'ger Sturm;
Die trägen Schläfen aufzustören,
Umbraust er Lager, Stadt und Thurm,
Ein Klaggeschrey um alle Zinnen:
Auf, träge Christen, zieht von hinnen.

*

Es lassen Engel aller Orten
Mit ernstem Antlitz stumm sich sehn,
Und Pilger sieht man vor den Pforten
Mit kummervollen Wangen stehn;
Sie klagen mit den bängsten Tönen
Die Grausamkeit der Sarazenen.

*

Es bricht ein Morgen, roth und trübe,
Im weiten Land der Christen an.
Der Schmerz der Wehmuth und der Liebe
Verkündet sich bey Jedermann.
Ein jedes greift nach Kreuz und Schwerdte
Und zieht entflammt von seinem Heerde.

*

Ein Feuereifer tobt im Heere,
Das Grab des Heylands zu befreyn.
Sie eilen frölich nach dem Meere,
Um bald auf heil'gem Grund zu seyn.
Auch Kinder kommen noch gelaufen
Und mehren den geweihten Haufen.

*

The grave in pagandom's possession,
The Sepulcher where Jesus lay,
Must suffer mocking and transgression,
Is desecrated day by day.
Hear ye its muffled lamentation:
'O save me from this degradation!'

Where do its loyal heroes linger?
Ah, Europe's Christendom is gone.
And will no warrior raise a finger
Or to the Holy Cross be drawn?
Who comes this bondage to dissever
And save the Sepulcher forever?

In darkest night on land and ocean
A holy tempest rages deep,
In cote and castle makes commotion
To call men from their slothful sleep.
A wailing cry surrounds each tower:
'Ye languid, O how late the hour!'

Allwheres are angels, white immortals,
With voiceless lips and earnest eyes;
And pilgrims wait before their portals,
Grim faces lifted to the skies.
They wail the Saracens's dominion,
That infidel, that slaughters' minion.

A red and gloomy morn is breaking
Over all the lands of Christendom;
And hearts with holy love are shaking
And yearning toward Jerusalem.
Lo, true men hear the call of tabor
And fly from hearth to cross and saber.

The hosts are touched with zeal and burning
The Holy Sepulcher to save,
And toward the East as one are turning
To stand before the Holy Grave.
And even children haste with longing
To swell the consecrated thronging.

Hoch weht das Kreuz im Siegspaniere,
Und alte Helden stehn voran.
Des Paradieses sel'ge Thüre
Wird frommen Kriegern aufgethan;
Ein jeder will das Glück genießen
Sein Blut für Christus zu vergießen.

*

Zum Kampf ihr Christen! Gottes Schaaren
Ziehn mit in das gelobte Land.
Bald wird der Heyden Grimm erfahren
Des Christengottes Schreckenshand.
Wir waschen bald in frohem Muthe
Das heilige Grab mit Heydenblute.

*

Die heil'ge Jungfrau schwebt, getragen
Von Engeln, ob der wilden Schlacht,
Wo jeder, den das Schwerdt geschlagen,
In ihrem Mutterarm erwacht.
Sie neigt sich mit verklärter Wange
Herunter zu dem Waffenklange.

*

Hinüber zu der heilgen Stätte!
Des Grabes dumpfe Stimme tönt!
Bald wird mit Sieg und mit Gebete
Die Schuld der Christenheit versöhnt!
Das Reich der Heyden wird sich enden,
Ist erst das Grab in unsern Händen.

Heinrichs ganze Seele war in Aufruhr, das Grab kam ihm wie eine bleiche, edle, jugendliche Gestalt vor, die auf einem großen Stein mitten unter wildem Pöbel säße, und auf eine entsetzliche Weise gemißhandelt würde, als wenn sie mit kummervollen Gesichte nach einem Kreuze blicke, was im Hintergrunde mit lichten Zügen schimmerte, und sich in den bewegten Wellen eines Meeres unendlich vervielfältigte.

Seine Mutter schickt eben herüber, um ihn zu holen, und der Hausfrau des Ritters vorzustellen. Die Ritter waren in ihr Gelag und ihre Vorstellungen des bevorstehenden Zuges vertieft, und bemerkten nicht, daß Heinrich sich entfernte. Er fand seine Mutter in traulichem Gespräch mit der alten, gutmuthigen Frau des Schlosses, die ihn freundlich bewillkommte. Der Abend war heiter; die Sonne began sich zu neigen, und Heinrich, der sich nach Einsamkeit sehnte, und von der goldenen Ferne gelockt wurde, die durch die engen, tiefen Bogenfenster in das düstre Gemach hineintrat, erhielt leicht die Erlaubniß, sich außerhalb des Schlosses besehen zu dürfen. Er eilte ins Freye, sein ganzes Gemüth war rege, er sah von der Höhe des alten Felsen zunächst in das waldige Thal, durch das ein Bach herunterstürzte und einige Mühlen trieb, deren Geräusch man kaum aus der gewaltigen Tiefe vernehmen konnte, und dann in eine unabsehliche Ferne

The bannered cross on high is waving
To seasoned warriors stout and bold;
The gates of paradise are craving
The blessed heroes to enfold.
All men desire – the young, the hoary –
To shed their blood for Jesus' glory.

Christians, to arms! the hosts of heaven
March with us to the Promised Land;
The heathen might will soon be riven
By great Jehovah's awful hand.
Soon we shall wash in joyful mood
The Holy Grave with pagan blood.

The angels bear the Virgin Mary
On wings above the battle plain,
And to her mother arm they carry
Each warrior whom the sword has slain.
She bends down with transfigured graces
Toward the clang of battle places.

O haste we to the Sanctuary!
The Sepulcher is making moan!
The guilt of Christendom we carry
Our prayers and triumphs shall atone.
If once the Grave is in our power,
Then ends the heathen's reigning hour.

Henry's whole soul was in a tumult; the Sepulcher appeared to him like the form of a pale, noble youth sitting on a large stone amid a wild rabble and being horribly mistreated, as if he were gazing with sorrowful mien towards a cross which shimmered in the background with luminous outlines and was endlessly multiplied by reflections in the rocking waves of a sea.

His mother just then sent for him to present him to the mistress. The knights were so taken up by their drinking and their ideas of the coming crusade that they did not notice Henry's leaving. He found his mother chatting familiarly with the kindly old mistress of the castle, who welcomed him pleasantly. The evening was clear, the sun was beginning to sink, and Henry, yearning for solitude and allured by the golden distance, which came into the gloomy room through the deep, narrow bay windows, easily obtained permission to look around outside the castle.

He hastened out into the open; his whole soul was excited. He looked first from the top of the old cliff down into the wooded valley through which a stream plunged and turned some mill wheels, the sound of which could hardly be heard from the great depth. And then he gazed into

von Bergen, Wäldern und Niederungen, und seine innere Unruhe wurde besänftigt. Das krieg-erische Getümmel verlor sich, und es blieb nur eine klare bilderreiche Sehnsucht zurück. Er fühlte, daß ihm eine Laute mangelte, so wenig er auch wußte, wie sie eigentlich gebaut sey, und welche Wirkung sie hervorbringe. Das heitere Schauspiel des herrlichen Abends wiegte ihn in sanfte Fantasieen: die Blume seines Herzens ließ sich zuweilen, wie ein Wetterleuchten in ihm sehn. — Er schweifte durch das wilde Gebüsch und kletterte über bemooste Felsenstücke, als auf einmal aus einer nahen Tiefe ein zarter eindringender Gesang einer weiblichen Stimme von wunderbaren Tönen begleitet, erwachte. Es war ihm gewiß, daß es eine Laute sey; er blieb ver-wunderungsvoll stehen, und hörte in gebrochner deutscher Aussprache folgendes Lied:

Bricht das matte Herz noch immer
Unter fremdem Himmel nicht?
Kommt der Hoffnung bleicher Schimmer
Immer mir noch zu Gesicht?
Kann ich wohl noch Rückkehr wähnen?
Stromweis stürzen meine Thränen,
Bis mein Herz in Kummer bricht.

*

Könnt ich dir die Myrthen zeigen
Und der Zeder dunkles Haar!
Führen dich zum frohen Reigen
Der geschwisterlichen Schaar!
Sahst du im gestickten Kleide,
Stolz im köstlichen Geschmeide
Deine Freundinn, wie sie war.

*

Edle Jünglinge verneigen
Sich mit heißem Blick vor ihr;
Zärtliche Gesänge steigen
Mit dem Abendstern zu mir.
Dem Geliebten darf man trauen;
Ewge Lieb' und Treu den Frauen,
Ist der Männer Losung hier.

*

Hier, wo um krystallne Quellen
Liebend sich der Himmel legt,
Und mit heißen Balsamwellen
Um den Hayn zusammenschlägt,
Der in seinen Lustgebieten,
Unter Früchten, unter Blüthen
Tausend bunte Sänger hegt,

*

an endless distance of mountains, woods, and valleys, and his inner unrest was allayed. The tumult of war faded away, and there remained only a clear yearning crowded with imagery. He felt the want of a lute, little as he knew how one really looked and what kind of effect it produced. The bright spectacle of the glorious evening lulled him into soothing fancies: from time to time the flower of his heart flashed upon his inward eye like heat lightning. He was rambling through the wild thickets and clambering over mossy boulders when all at once out of a deep vale nearby the tender, affecting singing of a female voice with a wonderful, melodious accompaniment woke to life. He felt certain it was a lute; he stood there filled with amazement and listened to the following song in broken speech:

Ah, my faint heart not yet broken
Underneath this alien sky?
Is there still a sallow token
Breathing of a hope that I
May return across the water?
Tears will flow, O sweet my daughter,
Till for woe my heart must die.

Could I show you but the myrtles
And the cedar's darksome hair!
Lead you where the maids in kirtles
Gaily dance in evening air!
Face you in embroidered dresses
Proud with gems and flowing tresses,
As of old when I was fair.

Noble swains there bow before me
Gaze on me with ardent eyes.
Tender serenadings woo me
While the evening stars arise.
There a maid may trust her lover;
Never will an eye discover
Faithless heart beneath those skies.

Here around the crystal fountains
Heaven bends in eastern mauve
And from balsam-fragrant mountains
Clings around the sacred grove,
Where amid the pleasure bowers
And amid lush fruits and flowers
Minstrels find a soft alcove.

899

Fern sind jene Jugendträume!
Abwärts liegt das Vaterland!
Langst gefällt sind jene Bäume,
Und das alte Schloß verbrannt.
Fürchterlich, wie Meereswogen
Kam ein rauhes Heer gezogen,
Und das Paradies verschwand.

*

Fürchterliche Gluten flossen
In die blaue Luft empor,
Und es drang auf stolzen Rossen
Eine wilde Schaar ins Thor.
Säbel klirrten, unsre Brüder,
Unser Vater kam nicht wieder,
Und man riß uns wild hervor.

*

Meine Augen wurden trübe;
Fernes, mütterliches Land,
Ach! sie bleiben dir voll Liebe
Und voll Sehnsucht zugewandt!
Wäre nicht dies Kind vorhanden,
Langst hätt' ich des Lebens Banden
Aufgelöst mit kühner Hand.

Heinrich hörte das Schluchzen eines Kindes und eine tröstende Stimme. Er stieg tiefer durch das Gebüsch hinab, und fand ein bleiches, abgehärmtes Mädchen unter einer alten Eiche sitzen. Ein schönes Kind hing weinend an ihrem Halse, auch ihre Thränen flossen, und eine Laute lag neben ihr auf dem Rasen. Sie erschrack ein wenig, als sie den fremden Jüngling erblickte, der mit wehmüthigem Gesicht sich ihr näherte.

Ihr habt wohl meinen Gesang gehört, sagte sie freundlich. Euer Gesicht dünkt mir bekannt, laßt mich besinnen — Mein Gedächtniß ist schwach geworden, aber euer Anblick erweckt in mir eine sonderbare Erinnerung aus frohen Zeiten. O! mir ist, als gleicht ihr einem meiner Brüder, der noch vor unserm Unglück von uns schied, und nach Persien zu einem berühmten Dichter zog. Vielleicht lebt er noch, und besingt traurig das Unglück seiner Geschwister. Wüßt ich nur noch einige seiner herrlichen Lieder, die er uns hinterließ! Er war edel und zärtlich, und kannte kein größeres Glück als seine Laute. Das Kind war ein Mädchen von zehn his zwölf Jahren, das den fremden Jüngling aufmerksam betrachtete und sich fest an den Busen der unglücklichen Zulima schmiegte. Heinrichs Herz war von Mitleid durchdrungen; er tröstete die Sängerin mit freundlichen Worten, und bat sie, ihm umständlicher ihre Geschichte zu erzählen. Sie schien es nicht ungern zu thun. Heinrich setzte sich ihr gegenüber und vernahm ihre von häufigen Thränen unterbrochne Erzählung. Vorzüglich hielt sie sich bei dem Lobe ihrer Landsleute und ihres Vaterlandes auf. Sie schilderte den Edelmuth derselben, und ihre reine starke Empfänglichkeit für die Poesie des Lebens und die wunderbare, geheimnißvolle Anmuth der Natur. Sie beschrieb die romantischen Schönheiten der fruchtbaren Arabischen Gegenden, die wie glückliche Inseln in

Dreams of youth are transitory,
Distant lies my fatherland;
And my house – how old my story! –
Victim fell to firebrand.
Frightful as the stormy breakers
Came the wild invading wreckers,
And my paradise was sand.

Blazing embers darted, marging
Far and wide the azure sky.
Knights on horses wildly charging
Stormed our caravanserai.
Brothers fell to sabers' clashing,
Father under rooftree's crashing,
We in harsh captivity.

Then my eyes grew dimmed and troubled –
O my mother's far countree! –
And their love for thee is doubled
As they turn their tears to thee.
Were not this my child beside me,
To the grave I would have hied me,
Boldly sought eternity.

Henry heard the sobbing of a child and a comforting voice. He went down through the thickets and found a pale, careworn girl sitting under an old oak tree. A beautiful child clung around her neck and wept; her tears flowed also, and a lute lay beside her on the grass. She was somewhat startled as she perceived the strange youth, who approached her with troubled face.

'You probably heard my song,' she said amiably. 'Your face seems familiar to me; let me think – my memory is getting weak, but the sight of you calls up strange recollections of happy times. O it seems to me you resemble one of my brothers who, before our misfortune, went to a famous poet in Persia. Perhaps he is still living and lamenting in song the misfortune of his brothers and sisters. If only I could remember some of the splendid songs he left us! He was noble and sensitive and knew no greater happiness than his lute.'

The child was a girl ten or twelve years old, who attentively observed the strange youth and pressed close to the bosom of the unhappy Zulima. Henry's heart was filled with compassion; he confronted the singer with kind words and asked her to tell about her life in more detail. She appeared not unwilling. Henry sat opposite her and listened to her story, which was frequently interrupted by tears. She lingered especially on the praise of her country and her people. She depicted their magnanimity and their pure, great sensitiveness to the poetry of life and to the wonderful, mysterious charm of nature. She described the romantic beauties of the fruitful regions in Arabia, which lie like happy isles amid the pathless sand wastes, like refuges for the weary and oppressed, like colonies of paradise. She described these colonies full of fresh springs that ripple through dense grass and over sparkling stones among venerable old groves. She told

unwegsamen Sandwüsteneien lägen, wie Zufluchtsstätte der Bedrängten und Ruhebedürftigen, wie Kolonien des Paradieses, voll frischer Quellen, die über dichten Rasen und funkelnde Steine durch alte, ehrwürdige Haine rieselten, voll bunter Vögel mit melodischen Kehlen und anziehend durch mannichfaltige Überbleibsel ehemaliger denkwürdiger Zeiten. Ihr würdet mit Verwunderung, sagte sie, die buntfarbigen, hellen, seltsamen Züge und Bilder auf den alten Steinplatten sehn. Sie scheinen so bekannt und nicht ohne Ursach so wohl erhalten zu seyn. Man sinnt und sinnt, einzelne Bedeutungen ahnet man, und wird um so begieriger den tiefsinnigen Zusammenhang dieser uralten Schrift zu errathen. Der unbekannte Geist derselben erregt ein ungewöhnliches Nachdenken, und wenn man auch ohne den gewünschten Fund von dannen geht, so hat man doch tausend merkwürdige Entdeckungen in sich selbst gemacht, die dem Leben einen neuen Glanz und dem Gemüth eine lange, belohnende Beschäftigung geben. Das Leben auf einem längst bewohnten und ehemals schon durch Fleiß, Thätigkeit und Neigung venherrlichten Boden hat einen besondern Reiz. Die Natur scheint dort menschlicher und verständlicher geworden, eine dunkle Erinnerung unter der durchsichtigen Gegenwart wirft die Bilder der Welt mit scharfen Umrissen zurück, und so genießt man eine doppelte Welt, die eben dadurch das Schwere und Gewaltsame verliert und die zauberische Dichtung und Fabel unserer Sinne wird. Wer weiß, ob nicht auch ein unbegreiflicher Einfluß der ehemaligen, jetzt unsichtbaren Bewohner mit ins Spiel kommt, und vielleicht ist es dieser dunkle Zug, der die Menschen aus neuen Gegenden, sobald eine gewisse Zeit ihres Erwachens kömmt, mit so zerstörender Ungeduld nach der alten Heymath ihres Geschlechts treibt, und sie Gut und Blut an den Besitz dieser Länder zu wagen anregt. Nach einer Pause fuhr sie fort: Glaubt ja nicht, was man euch von den Grausamkeiten meiner Landsleute erzählt hat. Nirgends wurden Gefangene großmüthiger behandelt, und auch eure Pilger nach Jerusalem wurden mit Gastfreundschaft aufgenommen, nur daß sie selten derselben werth waren. Die Meisten waren nichtsnutzige, böse Menschen, die ihre Wallfahrten mit Bubenstücken bezeichneten, und dadurch freylich oft gerechter Rache in die Hände fielen. Wie ruhig hätten die Christen das heilige Grab besuchen können, ohne nöthig zu haben, einen fürchterlichen, unnützen Krieg anzufangen, den alles erbittert, unendliches Elend verbreitet, und auf immer das Morgenland von Europa getrennt hat. Was lag an dem Namen des Besitzers? Unsere Fürsten ehrten andachtsvoll das Grab eures Heiligen, den auch wir für einen göttlichen Profeten halten; und wie schön hätte sein heiliges Grab die Wiege eines glücklichen Einvenständnisses, der Anlaß ewiger wohlthätiger Bündnisse werden können!

Der Abend war unten ihren Gesprächen herbeygekommen. Es fing an Nacht zu werden, und der Mond hob sich aus dem feuchten Walde mit beruhigendem Glanze herauf. Sie stiegen langsam nach dem Schlosse; Heinrich war voll Gedanken, die kriegerische Begeisterung war gänzlich verschwunden. Er merkte eine wunderliche Verwirrung in der Welt; der Mond zeigte ihm das Bild eines tröstenden Zuschauers und erhob ihn über die Unebenheiten der Erdoberfläche, die in der Höhe so unbeträchtlich erschienen, so wild und unersteiglich sie auch dem Wanderer vorkamen. Zulima ging still neben ihm her, und führte das Kind. Heinrich trug die Laute. Er suchte die sinkende Hoffnung seiner Begleiterinn, ihr Vaterland dereinst wieder zu sehn, zu beleben, indem er innerlich einen heftigen Beruf fühlte, ihr Retter zu seyn, ohne zu wissen, auf welche Art es geschehen könne. Eine besondere Kraft schien in seinen einfachen Worten zu liegen, denn Zulima empfand eine ungewohnte Beruhigung und dankte ihm für seine Zusprache auf die rührendste Weise. Die Ritter waren noch bey ihren Bechern und die Mutter in häuslichen Gesprächen. Heinrich hatte keine Lust in den lärmenden Saal zurückzugehn. Er fühlte sich müde, und begab sich bald mit seiner Mutter in das angewiesene Schlafgemach. Er erzählte ihr vor dem Schlafengehn, was ihm begegnet sey, und schlief bald zu unterhaltenden

how these groves are vocal with gay-colored birds of melodious throats, and attractive because of many vestiges of memorable bygone ages.

'You would be amazed,' she said, 'to see the strange, bright and many-colored figures and scenes on the old stone slabs there. They look so familiar, it appears to be not without reason that they are preserved so well. You meditate and meditate and guess at a meaning now and then and get all the more eager to unravel the profound connection of these primitive inscriptions. The unknown spirit of these arouses uncommon reflection; and even if one leaves without the wished-for revelation, still one has made a thousand remarkable discoveries within oneself, which give a new splendor to life and provide the mind with a long and rewarding occupation.

'Life has a special charm on land inhabited for ages and glorified by former diligence, activity, and affection. Nature appears to have become more human and intelligible there. An obscure recollection amid the transparent present reflects the images of the world in sharp outlines, and thus one enjoys a double world which in that very way sloughs off its crude and violent nature and turns into the magical poesy and fables of our senses. Who knows whether an incomprehensible influence of former, now invisible inhabitants does not also play a part, and perhaps it is this obscure drive which with such destructive impatience urges people from new homes back to the land of their forefathers as soon as a certain time of their awakening comes and spurs them to risk goods and blood for the possession of these lands.'

After a pause she continued: 'By no means believe the stories they tell you about the cruelty of my countrymen. Nowhere were prisoners treated more magnanimously, and your pilgrims to Jerusalem were hospitably received; only they were seldom worthy of it. Most of them were good-for-nothing wicked men, who disgraced their pilgrimages with knavish deeds and hence, to be sure, often fell into the hands of righteous vengeance. How tranquilly the Christians could have visited the Holy Sepulcher without the need of starting a terrible, useless war which has embittered everything, spread endless wretchedness, and separated the East from Europe forever. What importance did the name of the possessor have? Our sovereigns reverently honored the Sepulcher of your Holy One, whom we also regard as a divine prophet; and how splendidly could his Holy Sepulcher have become the cradle of a happy mutual understanding and the occasion of everlastingly beneficent alliances!'

While they were talking dusk had come. Night began to fall, and the moon rose out of the damp woods with calming radiance. They climbed slowly toward the castle. Henry was full of thoughts; his martial enthusiasm had completely vanished. He observed an odd confusion in the world; the moon presented to him the picture of a comforting guardian and exalted him above the roughnesses of the earth's surface, which from on high appeared as inconsiderable as they seemed wild and insurmountable to the wayfarer. Zulima walked silent at his side, leading her daughter. Henry carried the lute. He was trying to revive Zulima's sinking hopes of seeing her country again, while inwardly feeling a strong call to rescue her without knowing how it could be done. A special power seemed to lie in his simple words, for Zulima was comforted into unusual tranquility and thanked him for his consolation in the most affecting manner.

The knights were still at their cups and his mother deep in domestic discussions. Henry had no desire to return to the noisy hall. He felt tired and soon went with his mother to the bed-chamber assigned to them. Before he went to sleep he told his mother what he had encountered and soon fell asleep and into pleasant dreams. The merchants had also retired betimes and were up again bright and early. As they rode away, the knights were still sound asleep; the mistress however bade them an affectionate farewell.

Träumen ein. Die Kaufleute hatten sich auch zeitig fortbegeben, und waren früh wieder munter. Die Ritter lagen in tiefer Ruhe, als sie abreisten; die Hausfrau aber nahm zärtlichen Abschied. Zulima hatte wenig geschlafen, eine innere Freude hatte sie wach erhalten; sie erschien beym Abschiede, und bediente die Reisenden demüthig und emsig. Als sie Abschied nahmen brachte sie mit vielen Thränen ihre Laute zu Heinrich, und bat mit rührender Stimme, sie zu Zulimas Andenken mitzunehmen. Es war meines Bruders Laute, sagte sie, der sie mir beym Abschied schenkte; es ist das einzige Besitzthum, was ich gerettet habe. Sie schien euch gestern zu gefallen, und ihr laßt mir ein unschätzbares Geschenk zurück, süße Hoffnung. Nehmt dieses geringe Zeichen meiner Dankbarkeit, und laßt es ein Pfand eures Andenkens an die arme Zulima seyn. Wir werden uns gewiß wiedersehn, und dann bin ich vielleicht glücklicher. Heinrich weinte; er weigerte sich, diese ihr so unentbehrliche Laute anzunehmen: gebt mir, sagte er, das goldene Band mit den unbekannten Buchstaben aus euren Haaren, wenn es nicht ein Andenken eurer Eltern oder Geschwister ist, und nehmt dagegen einen Schleyer an, den mir meine Mutter gern abtreten wird. Sie wich endlich seinem Zureden und gab ihm das Band, indem sie sagte, Es ist mein Name in den Buchstaben meiner Muttersprache, den ich in bessern Zeiten selbst in dieses Band gestickt habe. Betrachtet es gern, und denkt, daß es eine lange, kummervolle Zeit meine Haare festgehalten hat, und mit seiner Besitzerin verbleicht ist. Heinrichs Mutter zog den Schleyer heraus, und reichte ihr ihn hin, indem sie sie an sich zog und weinend umarmte.

(1800) [*Novalis. Schriften, Historisch-kritische Ausgabe by Paul Kluckhohn, Richard Samuel, Hans-Joachim Mähl, Gerhard Schulz, 7 vols. Stuttgart, Berlin, Cologne, Mainz: Kohlhammer, 1960–, I. 230–239*]

VII.e.2.   HEINRICH HEINE, 'Jehuda ben Halevy (Fragment.)'

"Lechzend klebe mir die Zunge
An dem Gaumen, und es welke
Meine rechte Hand, vergäß' ich
Jemals dein, Jerusalem –"

Wort und Weise, unaufhörlich
Schwirren sie mir heut' im Kopfe,
Und mir ist als hört' ich Stimmen,
Psalmodirend, Männerstimmen –

Manchmal kommen auch zum Vorschein
Bärte, schattig lange Bärte –
Traumgestalten, wer von euch
Ist Jehuda ben Halevy?

Doch sie huschen rasch vorüber;
Die Gespenster scheuen furchtsam
Der Lebend'gen plumpen Zuspruch –
Aber ihn hab' ich erkannt –

Ich erkannt' ihn an der bleichen
Und gedankenstolzen Stirne,

Zulima had not slept much; an inner joy had kept her awake. She appeared at the departure and waited upon the travelers diligently and humbly. When they bade farewell, Zulima brought her lute to Henry with many tears and asked him in a quivering voice to take it as a remembrance of her. 'It was my brother's lute,' she said; 'he gave it to me when he left. It is the only possession I rescued. It seemed to please you yesterday, and you are leaving me an inestimable gift, sweet hope. Take this small token of my gratitude and let it be a pledge of your remembering poor Zulima. We shall certainly meet again, and then I may be more fortunate.'

Henry wept; he refused to take the lute so indispensable to her. He said, 'Give me the ribbon with the unknown letters you have in your hair, if it is not a keepsake from your parents or brothers and sisters, and receive in exchange a veil my mother will gladly give me.' She finally yielded to his persuasion, gave him the ribbon, and said, 'It is my name in the letters of my mother's tongue, which I myself in happier times embroidered on the ribbon. Look at it with pleasure and remember that it bound my hair for a long, sad time and that it faded along with its possessor.' Henry's mother drew forth the veil and gave it to her, drawing the girl close and embracing her with tears.

> [*Novalis. Henry von Ofterdingen. A Novel. Translated by Palmer Hilty. New York: Ungar, 1964. 54–62*]

VII.e.2.   HEINRICH HEINE, 'Jehuda ben Halevy'; Fragment

'Dry with thirst, oh let my tongue cleave
To my palate – let my right hand
Wither off, if I forget thee ·
Ever, O Jerusalem –'

Words and melody keep buzzing
In my head today, unceasing,
And I seem to make out voices
Singing psalms, I hear men's voices –

Sometimes, too, I catch a glimpse of
Shadowy long beards in darkness –
Phantom figures, which of you
Is Jehuda ben Halevy?

But they scurry by me quickly –
Ghosts will shun with fear the clumsy
Consolations of the living –
Yet I recognized him there –

I could recognize his pallid
Forehead, proudly worn with thinking,

An der Augen süßer Starrheit –
Sahn mich an so schmerzlich forschend –

Doch zumeist erkannt ich ihn
An dem räthselhaften Lächeln
Jener schön gereimten Lippen,
Die man nur bey Dichtern findet.

Jahre kommen und verfließen.
Seit Jehuda ben Halevy
Ward geboren, sind verflossen
Sieben hundert fünfzig Jahre –

Hat zuerst das Licht erblickt
Zu Toledo in Castilien,
Und es hat der goldne Tajo
Ihm sein Wiegenlied gelullet.

Für Entwicklung seines Geistes
Sorgte früh der strenge Vater,
Der den Unterricht begann
Mit dem Gottesbuch, der Thora.

Diese las er mit dem Sohne
In dem Urtext, dessen schöne,
Hieroglyphisch pittoreske,
Altcaldäische Quadratschrift

Herstammt aus dem Kindesalter
Unsrer Welt, und auch deswegen
Jedem kindlichen Gemüthe
So vertraut entgegenlacht.

Diesen echten alten Text
Rezitirte auch der Knabe
In der uralt hergebrachten
Singsang-Weise, Tropp geheißen –

Und er gurgelte gar lieblich
Jene fetten Gutturalen,
Und er schlug dabey den Triller,
Den Schalscheleth, wie ein Vogel.

Auch den Targum Onkelos,
Der geschrieben ist in jenem
Plattjudäischen Idiom,
Das wir aramäisch nennen

And his eyes, so gentle-stubborn –
Pained, inquiring eyes that pierce me –

But I recognized him mostly
By his enigmatic way of
Smiling with those rhyming lips,
Which are found in poets only.

Years come round and years go fleeting.
Since Jehuda ben Halevy
Saw the light, the world has counted
Seven hundred years and fifty;

It was in Castile's Toledo
That he came into the world,
And the golden Tagus crooned him
Lullabies beside the cradle.

His strict father early nurtured
His development and thinking,
And his education started
With the book of God, the Torah.

And the youngster read this volume
In the ancient text, whose lovely
Picturesquely hieroglyphic
Old Chaldean squared-off letters

Are derived out of the childhood
Of the world, and for this reason
Show familiar, smiling features
To all childlike minds and spirits.

This authentic ancient text
Was recited by the youngster
In the old, original singsong
Known as *Tropp* down through the ages –

And with loving care he gurgled
Those fat gutterals right gladly,
And the quaver, the Shalsheleth,
He trilled like feathered warbler.

As for Onkelos's Targum,
Which is written in that special
Low-Judaic idiom
That we call the Aramaic

Und zur Sprache der Propheten
Sich verhalten mag etwa
Wie das Schwäbische zum Deutschen –
Dieses Gelbveiglein-Hebräisch

Lernte gleichfalls früh der Knabe,
Und es kam ihm solche Kenntniß
Bald darauf sehr gut zu Statten
Bey dem Studium des Talmuds.

Ja, frühzeitig hat der Vater
Ihn geleitet zu dem Talmud,
Und da hat er ihm erschlossen
Die Halacha, diese große

Fechterschule, wo die besten
Dialektischen Athleten
Babylons und Pumpedithas
Ihre Kämpferspiele trieben.

Lernen konnte hier der Knabe
Alle Künste der Polemik;
Seine Meisterschaft bezeugte
Späterhin das Buch Cosari.

Doch der Himmel gießt herunter
Zwey verschiedne Sorten Lichtes:
Grelles Tageslicht der Sonne
Und das milde Mondlicht – Also,

Also leuchtet auch der Talmud
Zwiefach, und man theilt ihn ein
In Halacha und Hagada.
Erstre nannt' ich eine Fechtschul' –

Letztre aber, die Hagada,
Will ich einen Garten nennen,
Einen Garten, hochphantastisch
Und vergleichbar jenem andern,

Weicher ebenfalls dem Boden
Babylons entsprossen weiland –
Garten der Semiramis,
Achtes Wunderwerk der Welt.

Königin Semiramis,
Die als Kind erzogen worden

And which bears the same relation
To the language of the prophets
That the Swabian has to German –
In this garlic-sausage Hebrew

Was the boy instructed likewise,
And this knowledge soon provided
Solid service to his efforts
In the study of the Talmud.

Yes, his father early led him
To the pages of the Talmud,
And thereby he laid before him
The Halacha, that prodigious

School of fencing, where the greatest
Of the dialectic athletes
In the Babylonian contests
Used to carry on their war games.

Here the boy could master every
Art and science of polemic;
And his mastery was later
Witnessed by his book *Kuzari*.

But the heavens shed upon us
Two quite different kinds of luster:
There's the sun's harsh-glaring daylight
And the milder moonlight – likewise,

Likewise, shining in the Talmud
Is a double light, divided
In Halacha and Haggada.
Fencing school I called the former,

But the latter, the Haggada,
I would rather call a garden,
A phantasmagoric garden
That is very like another

That once bloomed and sprouted also
From the soil of Babylonia—
Queen Semiramis' great garden,
That eighth wonder of the world.

Queen Semiramis was brought up
As a child by birds, and always

Von den Vögeln, und gar manche
Vögelthümlichkeit bewahrte,

Wollte nicht auf platter Erde
Promeniren wie wir andern
Säugethiere, und sie pflanzte
Einen Garten in der Luft -

Hoch auf kolossalen Säulen
Prangten Palmen und Cypressen,
Goldorangen, Blumenbeete,
Marmorbilder, auch Springbrunnen,

Alles klug und fest verbunden
Durch unzähl'ge Hänge-Brücken,
Die wie Schlingepflanzen aussahn
Und worauf sich Vögel wiegten –

Große, bunte, ernste Vögel,
Tiefe Denker, die nicht singen,
Während sie umflattert kleines
Zeisigvolk, das lustig trillert –

Alle athmen ein, beseligt,
Einen reinen Balsamduft,
Welcher unvermischt mit schnödem
Erdendunst und Mißgeruche.

Die Hagada ist ein Garten
Solcher Luftkindgrillen-Art,
Und der junge Talmudschüler,
Wenn sein Herze war bestäubet

Und betäubet vom Gezänke
Der Halacha, vom Dispute
Ueber das fatale Ey,
Das ein Huhn gelegt am Festtag,

Oder über eine Frage
Gleicher Importanz – der Knabe
Floh alsdann sich zu erfrischen
In die blühende Hagada,

Wo die schönen alten Sagen,
Engelmärchen und Legenden,
Stille Märtyerhistorien,
Festgesänge, Weisheitsprüche,

Later on retained a number
Of their birdlike traits and temper,

And so she refused to walk on
Lowly ground like common mammals
And insisted on the planting
Of a garden in the air: –

Rising high on giant pillars
Cypresses and palm trees flourished,
Orange trees and beds of flowers,
Marble statues, even fountains,

All secured with cunning braces
Formed by countless hanging bridges,
Made to look like vines and creepers,
On which birds would swing and teeter –

Big and bright-hued birds, deep thinkers
Much too solemn-faced to warble,
While around them fluttered bands of
Little finches, gaily trilling.

All of them were blithely breathing
Air distilled of balsam fragrance,
Unpolluted by the reek of
Earth's miasma and malodors.

The Haggada is a garden
Of such childlike airy fancy.
And the young Talmudic scholar –
When his heart felt dry and dusty,

Musty from the noisy squabbling
Over the Halacha, over
Quarrels on the plaguy egg
That a hen laid on a feast day,

Or about some other question
Equally profound – the youngster
Fled for solace of the spirit
To the blossom-filled Haggada,

With its lovely olden fables,
Tales of angels, myths and legends,
Tranquil stories of the martyrs,
Festive songs and wise old sayings,

Auch Hyperbeln, gar possirlich,
Alles aber glaubenskräftig,
Glaubensglühend – O, das glänzte,
Quoll und sproß so überschwenglich –

Und des Knaben edles Herze
Ward ergriffen von der wilden,
Abenteuerlichen Süße,
Von der wundersamen Schmerzlust

Und den fabelhaften Schauern
Jener seligen Geheimwelt,
Jener großen Offenbarung,
Die wir nennen Poesie.

Auch die Kunst der Poesie,
Heitres Wissen, holdes Können,
Welches wir die Dichtkunst heißen,
Tat sich auf dem Sinn des Knaben.

Und Jehuda ben Halevy
Ward nicht bloß ein Schriftgelehrter,
Sondern auch der Dichtkunst Meister,
Sondern auch ein großer Dichter.

Ja, er ward ein großer Dichter,
Stern und Fackel seiner Zeit,
Seines Volkes Licht und Leuchte,
Eine wunderbare, große

Feuersäule des Gesanges,
Die der Schmerzenskarawane
Israels vorangezogen
In der Wüste des Exils.

Rein und wahrhaft, sonder Makel
War sein Lied, wie seine Seele –
Als der Schöpfer sie erschaffen,
Diese Seele, selbstzufrieden

Küßte er die schöne Seele,
Und des Kusses holder Nachklang
Bebt in jedem Lied des Dichters,
Das geweiht durch diese Gnade.

Wie im Leben, so im Dichten
Ist das höchste Gut die Gnade –

Droll exaggerations also,
Yet it all had faith's old power,
Faith's old fire – Oh, how it sparkled,
Bubbling with exuberance –

And the youngster's noble spirit
Was enraptured by the sweetness,
Wild and wonderful adventure,
And the strangely aching gladness,

And the fabled thrills and shivers
Of that blissful secret world,
Of that mighty revelation
Which we title poesy.

And the art of poesy –
Gaia scienza, gracious talent
That we call the poet's art –
Also worked upon his spirit.

Thus Jehuda ben Halevy
Grew to be not just a scholar
But a master of poetics
And a great and mighty poet.

Yes, he was a mighty poet,
Star and beacon for his age,
Light and lamp among his people,
And a wonderful and mighty

Pillar of poetic fire
In the vanguard of all Israel's
Caravan of woe and sorrow
In the desert waste of exile.

Pure and truthful, without blemish,
Was his song – his soul was also.
On the day his Maker fashioned
This great soul, He paused contented,

Kissed the soul whose beauty sparkled;
And those kisses still go thrilling
Through the poet's every measure
Hallowed by this grace and bounty.

Both in poetry and life,
It's the gift of grace that governs –

Wer sie hat, der kann nicht sündgen
Nicht in Versen, noch in Prosa.

Solchen Dichter von der Gnade
Gottes nennen wir Genie:
Unverantwortlicher König
Des Gedankenreiches ist er.

Nur dem Gotte steht er Rede,
Nicht dem Volke – In der Kunst,
Wie im Leben, kann das Volk
Töten uns, doch niemals richten.

(1851) [*Heinrich Heine. Historisch-kritische Gesamtausgabe der Werke.*
Edited by Manfred Windfuhr, 16 vols. Hamburg: Hoffmann & Campe,
1973–1997, III/1. 130–134]

g. ITALIANO

VII.g.1. GIUSEPPE VERDI, da *Nabucco,* 'Coro di schiavi ebrei'
Libretto: Temistocle Solera

Va, pensiero, sull'ali dorate;
va, ti posa sui clivi, sui colli
ove olezzano tepide [libere] e molli
l'aure dolci del suolo natal!
Del Giordano le rive saluta,
di Sionne le torri atterrate.
Oh, mia patria sì bella e perduta!
Oh, membranza sì cara e fatal!
Arpa d'or dei fatidici vati,
perché muta dal salice pendi?
Le memorie nel petto raccendi,
ci favella del tempo che fu!
O simile di Solima ai fati
traggi un suono di crudo lamento,
o t'ispiri il Signore un concento
che ne infonda al patire virtù!

(1842)

He who has this highest good can
Never sin in prose or verse.

Any poet who possesses
This, God's grace, we call a genius:
Monarch in the realm of thought, he
Is responsible to no man.

He accounts to God, God only,
Not the people; both in art
And in life, the people can
Kill us but can never judge us.

(1851) [*The Complete Poems of Heinrich Heine. A Modern English Version.
Translated by Hal Draper. Oxford: OUP, 1982. 655–659*]

g. ITALIAN

VII.g.1. GIUSEPPE VERDI, from *Nabucco*, 'The Chorus of the Hebrew Slaves'
Libretto: Temistocle Solera

Go, thought, on wings of gold,
go alight upon the slopes and the hills
where the sweet breezes of our
native land smell warm [free] and gentle!
Greet the banks of the river Jordan
and Zion's fallen towers.
Oh, my fatherland, so beautiful and lost!
Oh remembrance so dear and unhappy!
Golden harp of the prophetic bards,
why hang so silently from the willows?
Rekindle the memories in our hearts,
tell us about the times gone by!
O like Solomon to the fates
draw us the sound of a sad lament
or may the Lord inspire in you an accord
which infuses our suffering with virtue.

(1842) [*Translated by Anne O'Connor*]

i. POLSKI

VII.i.1. ANTONI MALCZEWSKI, *Maria. Powieść ukraińska* (fragment)

PIEŚŃ I

> Wszystko się dziwnie plecie
> Na tym tu biednym świecie:
> A kto by chciał rozumem wszystkiego dochodzić,
> I zginie, a nie będzie umiał w to ugodzić.
> *– Jan Kochanowski*

I

Ej! ty na szybkim koniu gdzie pędzisz, kozacze?
Czy zaoczył zająca, co na stepie skacze?
Czy rozigrawszy myśli, chcesz użyć swobody
I z wiatrem ukraińskim puścić się w zawody?
Lub może do swej lubej, co czeka wśród niwy,
Nucąc żałosną dumkę lecisz niecierpliwy?
Bo i czapkęś nasunął, i rozpuścił wodze,
A długi tuman kurzu ciągnie się na drodze:
Zapał jakiś rozżarza twojej twarzy śniadość,
I jak światełko w polu błyszczy na niej radość;
Gdy koń, co jak ty, dziki, lecz posłuszny żyje,
Porze szumiący wicher wyciągnąwszy szyję.
Umykaj, Czarnomorcu, z swą mażą skrzypiącą,
Bo ci synowie stepu twoją sól roztrącą.
A ty, czarna ptaszyno, co każdego witasz,
I krążysz, i zaglądasz, i o coś się pytasz,
Spiesz się swą tajemnicę odkryć kozakowi –
Nim skończysz twoje koło, oni ujść gotowi.

II

Pędzą – a wśród promieni zniżonego słońca,
Podobni do jakiego od Niebianów gońca –
I długo, i daleko, słychać kopyt brzmienie:
Bo na obszernych polach rozległe milczenie;
Ani wesołej szlachty, ni rycerstwa głosy,
Tylko wiatr szumi smutnie uginając kłosy;
Tylko z mogił westchnienia i tych jęk spod trawy
Co śpią na zwiędłych wieńcach swojej starej sławy.
Dzika muzyka – dziksze jeszcze do niej słowa,
Które Duch dawnej Polski potomności chowa –
A gdy cały ich zaszczyt krzaczek polnej róży,
Ah! Czyjeż serce, czyje, w żalu się nie nuży?

i. POLISH

VII.i.1.   ANTONI MALCZEWSKI, from *Marya. A Tale of Ukraine*

CANTO I

All is strangely twisted here
Upon this poor old earthly sphere,
And he who would some pattern see
Perishes, nor e'er finds harmony.
                    – *Jan Kochanowski*

I

HEY! thou Cossack, whither on thy fleet-hoofed horse are flying?
Yonder hare that skims the steppe art spying?
Or, heartsick of meditation, dost thou strain
To free thyself, to race the charging winds of the Ukraine?
Perhaps unto thy love who on some distant plain awaiteth thee,
Murmuring thy melancholy air, thou fli'st impatiently.
For thou hast pulled down thy cap and loosed the rein,
And now a cloud of dust hangs thick above the plain.
Thy tawny face is shining with some ardor half-concealed,
And joy, like sudden light from darksome field,
Breaks, when thy charger, wild but curbed like thee,
Stretching his neck, bursts through the winds that lure him free.
Yon Black Sea Cossacks with the squeaking carts, Run! Hide!
The scions of the steppe will thrust your salt aside.
And all you little black birds with your friendly greeting,
Who circle overhead and look about entreating,
Quick! Tell your secret to the Cossack, fly!
Before you circle 'round he will rush by!

II

ON, on they speed, amid the sun's departing glow,
Swift as couriers of the Gods they go,
And still from far away persists that steady beat,
And over all the wilderness broods silence, dark and deep.
No voice is heard of merry squire, nor knight, upon this plain,
Only the rushing wind that sadly stirs the ears of grain,
Only from all the graves the sadly murmured story,
The tale of those who sleep amid the tokens of their glory.
Music, wild and mad . . . madder still the chorus runs;
Words the Soul of Ancient Poland cherishes for future sons.
When here a single rose marks all their ancient glory,
Whose heart, whose, breaks not at man's despairing story?

III

Minął już kozak bezdnię i głębokie jary,
Gdzie się lubią, ukrywać wilki i Tatary;
Przyleciał do figury (co jej wzgorek znany,
Bo pod nią już od dawna upior pochowany),
Uchylił przed nią czapki, żegnał się trzy razy
I jak wiatr świsnął stepem z pilnymi rozkazy.
I koń rzeski, żadnym się urokiem nie miesza,
Tylko parschnął, i wierzgnął, i dalej pośpiesza.
Ciemny Boh po granitach srebrne szarfy snuje,
A śmiały wierny kozak myśl pana zgaduje –
Szumi młyn na odnodze, i wróg w łozie szumi,
A żwawy wierny konik kozaka rozumi –
I przez kwieciste łąki, przez ostre bodiaki
Lżej się nie przesuwają pierszchliwe sumaki;
I jak strzała schylony na wysokiej kuli,
Czai się zwinny kozak, do konia się tuli;
I przez puste bezdroża król pustyni rusza –
A step – koń – kozak – ciemność – jedna dzika dusza.
O! ktoż mu tam przynajmniej pohulać zabroni?
Zginął – w rodzinnym stepie nicht go nie dogoni.

(First Polish edition 1825) [*Edited by Halina Krukowska. Białystok: Trans Humana, 2002*]

VII.i.2. ADAM MICKIEWICZ, *Sonety krymskie* (wybór)

VI. Bakczysaraj

Jeszcze wielka, już pusta Girajów dziedzina!
Zmiatane czołem baszów ganki i przedsienia,
Sofy, trony potęgi, miłości schronienia
Przeskakuje sarańcza, obwija gadzina.

Skróś okien różnofarbnych powoju roślina,
Wdzierając się na głuche ściany i sklepienia,
Zajmuje dzieło ludzi w imię przyrodzenia
I pisze Balsazara głoskami «RUINA».

W środku sali wycięte z marmuru naczynie;
To fontanna haremu, dotąd stoi cało
I perłowe łzy sącząc woła przez pustynie:

«Gdzież jesteś, o miłości, potęgo i chwało!
Wy macie trwać na wieki, źródło szybko płynie,
O hańbo! wyście przeszły, a źródło zostało.»

III

NOW flew the Cossack horseman over gorges dread and deep,
Where wolves are like to hide themselves and Tartars vigil keep.
His racing steed he guided straight past a well-known hill
Where ancient ghosts are lurking and spectres watching still.
His cap he doffed before it, three times his bosom crossed,
Then, like the wind across the steppe, horse and Cossack passed.
No phantom frightened his charger, impatient to go on,
He only snorted, gave a kick, and like a flash was gone.
The dark Boh draws its silver thread across the granite plain,
And now the faithful little steed has sensed his Cossack's game –
The osiers hide dread foemen, the osiers by the mill,
But the nimble little charger knows at once his master's will,
They fly o'er flowery meadows, through thistles sharp and keen,
As swiftly as the mountain goat, as lightly as a dream,
Bent low above his saddle, like arrow poised for flight,
Close lies the nimble Cossack, against his horse pressed tight,
So through the empty, trackless waste the steppe-king seeks his goal,
Steppe and Cossack, horse and night, a wild, unfettered soul.
And who would fain forbid him this hour of revelry?
He's gone! His native steppe-land will enfold him tenderly.

(First edition 1825) [*Translated by Arthur Prudden Coleman and Marion Moore Coleman.*
Schenectady, New York: Electric City Press, Inc., 1935]

VII.i.2. ADAM MICKIEWICZ, from *The Crimean Sonnets*

VI. Bakhchisarai

Still vast, but desolate, the dwelling of the Girey kings!
On stairs, in vestibules once brushed by Pashas' brows
And across sofas that were thrones of power, sanctuaries of love,
Grasshoppers veer and bounce, the serpent winds,

And rank vines crawl through myriad-colored windows
To invade mute vaults and voiceless halls, conquer
Man's labor in the name of nature, and inscribe
There in the letters of Balthazar: DESTRUCTION.

In the center of a hall, a basin hewn in marble:
The fountain of the harem, still intact,
Whispers its tearful pearls alone, as if to ask:

Where are they, grandeur, power and love? Their term
Was to have been forever, and the stream's, ephemeral,
But they have passed and the white fount is here.

[*Translated by Angelica Caro*]

X. Bajdary

Wypuszczam na wiatr konia i nie szczędzę razów;
Lasy, doliny, głazy, w kolei, w natłoku
U nóg mych płyną, giną jak fale potoku;
Chcę odurzyć się, upić tym wirem obrazów.

A gdy śpieniony rumak nie słucha rozkazów,
Gdy świat kolory traci pod całunem mroku,
Jak w rozbitym źwierciedle, tak w mym spiekłym oku
Snują się mary lasów i dolin, i głazów.

Ziemia śpi, mnie snu nie ma; skaczę w morskie łona,
Czarny, wydęty bałwan z hukiem na brzeg dąży,
Schylam ku niemu czoło, wyciągam ramiona,

Pęka nad głową fala, chaos mię okrąży;
Czekam, aż myśl, jak łódka wirami kręcona,
Zbłąka się i na chwilę w niepamięć pogrąży.

XIII. Czatyrdah

Drżąc muślimin całuje stopy twej opoki,
Maszcie krymskiego statku, wielki Czatyrdachu!
O minarecie świata! o gór padyszachu!
Ty, nad skały poziomu uciekłszy w obłoki,

Siedzisz sobie pod bramą niebios, jak wysoki
Gabryjel pilnujący edeńskiego gmachu.
Ciemny las twoim płaszczem, a janczary strachu
Twój turban z chmur haftują błyskawic potoki.

Nam czy słońce dopieka, czyli mgła ocienia,
Czy sarańcza plon zetnie, czy giaur pali domy –
Czatyrdahu, ty zawsze głuchy, nieruchomy,

Między światem i niebem jak drogman stworzenia,
Podesławszy pod nogi ziemie, ludzi, gromy,
Słuchasz tylko, co mówi Bóg do przyrodzenia.

(1826) [*Edited by Czesław Zgorzelski. Warszawa: Czytelnik, 1993*]

X. Baidar

Urging my horse into the wind, I spare
No spur. Woods, valleys, rocks, in surge rush by
And vanish like a torrent's furious foam;
And by the swirl of images I'm stunned.

But when my charger races out of hand,
And all the world's brave colour's dimmed in dusk,
Then, in my burning eyes, as in grey glass,
The ghosts of forest, valley, rock, flash past.

The wave in chaos breaks above my head:
I wait – till all my thoughts be whirled away
And swept into oblivion for a while.

[*Translated by George Reavey*]

XIII. Chatir Dah

Trembling the Muslim comes to kiss the foot of your crags,
Mast on Crimea's raft, towering Chatir Dah!
Minaret of the World! Mightiest Padishah
Of Mountains! From the plain Fugitive into the Clouds!

As great Gabriel once stood over portals of Eden,
You at Heaven's Gate watch, wrapped in your forest cloak,
And, in turban of clouds with lightning flashes bespangled,
On your forehead you wear janissaries of dread.

Hot sun may roast our limbs, mountain mists blind our eyes,
Locusts may eat our grain, infidels burn our homes,
You, Chatir Dah, would still, unmindful of man's fate,

Rise between earth and sky, Dragoman of Creation;
Far spreads the plain at your feet, home of men and of thunder,
But you can only hear what God to nature speaks.

[*Translated by John Saly. Edited by Clark Mills. New York: Noonday, 1956*]

k. ROMÂNĂ

VII.k.1.   ION ELIADE RĂDULESCU, din 'Zburătorul'

"Vezi, mamă, ce mă doare! şi pieptul mi se bate,
Mulţimi de vineţele pe sân mi se ivesc;
Un foc s-aprinde-n mine, răcori mă iau la spate,
Îmi ard buzele, mamă, obrajii-mi se pălesc!

Ah! inima-mi zvâcneşte!... şi zboară de la mine!
Îmi cere... nu-ş' ce-mi cere! şi nu ştiu ce i-aş da;
Şi cald, şi rece, uite, că-mi furnică prin vine,
În braţe n-am nimica şi parcă am ceva;

Că uite, mă vezi, mamă? aşa se-ncrucişează,
Şi nici nu prinz de veste când singură mă strâng,
Şi tremur de nesaţiu, şi ochii-mi văpăiază,
Pornesc dintr-înşii lacrămi, şi plâng, măicuţă, plâng.

Ia pune mâna, mamă, – pe frunte, ce sudoare!
Obrajii... unul arde şi altul mi-a răcit!
Un nod colea m-apucă, ici coasta rău mă doare;
În trup o piroteală de tot m-a stăpânit.

Oar' ce să fie asta? Întreabă pe bunica:
O şti vrun leac ea doară... o fi vrun zburător!
Or aide l-alde baba Comana, or Sorica,
Or du-te la moş popa, or mergi la vrăjitor.

....

Aşa plângea Florica şi, biet, îşi spunea dorul
Pe prispă lângă mă-sa, ş-obida o neca;
Junicea-n bătătură mugea, căta oborul,
Şi mă-sa sta pe gânduri, şi fata suspina.

....

"Dar ce lumină iute ca fulger trecătoare
Din miazănoapte scapă cu urme de schintei?
Vro stea mai cade iară? vrun împărat mai moare?
Or e – să nu mai fie! – vro pacoste de zmei?

k. ROMANIAN

VII.k.1. ION ELIADE RĂDULESCU, from 'The Ballad of the Flying Dragon'[1]

'See, mother, how it hurts me? And how my breast it beats,
How veins on my white bosom turn purple lesion;
A blaze in me is burning, the frost again it meets,
My lips afire, mother, my cheeks are cold anon!

Ah! My heart throbs . . . And flies away from me, you see!
It wants of me . . . Who knows what? And what can I give it?
Now hot, now cold, it flows through all my veins and in me,
I hold nought in my arms, my arms with lead are fit;

For you see, most sweet mother? The way it comes across
My own body, mother, before I can surmise,
And then desire takes me, and then my eyes do gloss
And tears they shed, O mother, and how can I be wise?

Just lay your hand, sweet mother, my forehead is in sweat!
My cheeks . . . the one is burning, the other icy is!
A pain me here possesses, my rib it gnaws, I bet;
My body in mild languor, I feel it all amiss.

What can this be, O mother? Does grannie know, think you?
She could devise some cure . . . It could some dragon be,
Of those that fly up there, the women maybe knew,
Or maybe does the priest, mum, or wizards do maybe.'

....

Thus cried poor Florica[2] and thus she told her sorrow;
Below the porch her mother she everything retold;
Her heifer lower'd softly, the lass felt prone to borrow
The tales the mother murmured from memories of old.

....

'But what quick light like lightning that dazzles in a wink
From up the north escapes now and sparkles far away?
Some shooting star can it be? Maybe some dying king?
Or, God forbid! Some ogre that flies perching astray?

[1] As in Lermontov's *Demon* and Eminescu's *Hyperion*, the male protagonist in Eliade Rădulescu's *Zburătorul* (*The Flying Dragon*) is at once superhuman and earthly. He descends at night to meet his mortal female counterpart and accomplishes a rite of passage: as the virgin awakes to sexual awareness, she projects her baffled physiology onto a mythical image. The flying dragon is equally unhappy in the world down here and the eventual separation of the two is a case in Romantic irony. Byron's *Oriental Poems*, Shelley's *Alastor* and Keats' *La Belle Dame sans Merci* share this otherworldly experience.

[2] A common Christian name in the Romanian countryside, Florica, literally 'little flower', reveals the natural background of this mythical encounter. It also sets in Romantic contrast the ordinary and the extraordinary, by focusing on the ominous intervention of the otherworldly in everyday life.

Tot zmeu a fost, surato. Văzuşi, împeliţatu,
Că ţintă l-alde Floarea în clipă străbătu!
Şi drept pe coş, leicuţă! ce n-ai gândi, spurcatu!
Închină-te, surato! – Văzutu-l-ai şi tu?

Balaur de lumină cu coada-nflăcărată,
Şi pietre nestimate lucea pe el ca foc.
Spun, soro, c-ar fi june cu dragoste curată;
Dar lipsa d-a lui dragosti! departe de ast loc!

Pândeşte, bată-l crucea! şi-n somn colea mi-ţi vine
Ca brad un flăcăiandru, şi tras ca prin inel,
Bălai, cu părul d-aur! dar slabele lui vine
N-au nici un pic de sânge, ş-un nas – ca vai de el!

O! biata fetişoară! mi-e milă de Florica
Cum o fi chinuind-o! vezi, d-aia a slăbit
Şi s-a pălit copila! ce bine-a zis bunica:
Să fugă fata mare de focul de iubit!

Că-ncepe de visează, şi visu-n lipitură
Începe-a se preface, şi lipitura-n zmeu,
Şi ce-i mai faci pe urmă? că nici descântătură,c
Nici rugi nu te mai scapă, ferească Dumnezeu!"

[1844]

l. РУССКИЙ

VII.l.1. АЛЕКСАНДР ПУШКИН, «Цыганы»

It was an ogre, you, lass! Did you not see the dragon?
He straight unto Florica his wings beat up to fan!
And down the chimney, goodness! Who would have pondered on
The ogre, who descended, so everybody ran?

He was of light an ogre, with a big tail of fire
And precious stones ablaze set as truly he did shine,
I say, a young lad he could, with pure love afire,
Be to her, but, o dear, why should she lie supine?

He ambushes the lasses, as in deep sleep they lie,
As slender as the fir tree, the fair-haired lad,
With bloodless tender veins he so gently draws nearby
And in his weird covers the ogre he is clad.

The little lass, o dear! Florica, tender, pure,
How much her he must torture, see how slim has she gone
How pale she is, the poor girl! And right was grannie, sure,
To say that a young virgin with love can be forlorn.

For now she dreams of tales fine which new tales can engender
And the engendered dreams then the dragon do restore,
And, oh, the evil eye, then, or charms or spirits slender,
None can release the lass now from sufferings of yore.

[1844]

[*Translated by Mihaela Anghelescu Irimia, Adina Ciugureanu and Virginia Jarrell*]

l. RUSSIAN

VII.l.1. ALEXANDER PUSHKIN, *The Gypsies*

Introductory Note

The Gypsies (begun in 1823/24 in Odessa, finished in October 1824, at Mikhailovskoe) is an anti-Rousseauian drama built on Rousseauian premises. It is a tragedy of ungovernable human drives – the 'fateful passions' of the rueful closing lines of the epilogue. These urges possess man and destroy him regardless of his own volition, and the central dramatic issue of flaw or guilt becomes almost irrelevant. Aleko, the haunted hero who bears a variant of Pushkin's own name, is twice undone by the elemental passion of possessive jealousy; once (it is barely hinted in the nightmare scene) during his life in urban civilization, another time in the free, simple environment which he has himself sought in a vain attempt to escape personal guilt and 'enlightened corruption' – civilization and sophistication seen as a curse in the manner of Rousseau. Of the triad of principle actors, only artistically subdued central figure, the old gypsy, has conquered, at great cost, the helpless serfdom of the human condition and thus achieving full harmony with frugal nature and a life reduced to the bare essentials, attained the peace and wisdom of resignation. This achievement, however, has no explicit parallel among the other followers of the nomad life, whether 'naturals' or romantic fugitives from the city – for 'ot sudeb zascity net': there is no refuge from the fates.

The Gypsies is the most mature and thoughtful of Pushkin's southern narrative poems. In it he has completely discarded the romantic vagueness of background and the arid habit of narcissistic

ЦЫГАНЫ

Цыганы шумною толпой
По Бессарабии кочуют.
Они сегодня над рекой
В шатрах изодранных ночуют.
Как вольность, весел их ночлег
И мирный сон под небесами;
Между колесами телег,
Полузавешанных коврами,
Горит огонь; семья кругом
Готовит ужин; в чистом поле
Пасутся кони; за шатром
Ручной медведь лежит на воле.
Всё живо посреди степей:
Заботы мирные семей,
Готовых с утром в путь недальний,
И песни жен, и крик детей,
И звон походной наковальни.
Но вот на табор кочевой
Нисходит сонное молчанье,
И слышно в тишине степной
Лишь лай собак да коней ржанье.
Огни везде погашены,
Спокойно всё, луна сияет
Одна с небесной вышины
И тихий табор озаряет.
В шатре одном старик не спит;
Он перед углями сидит,
Согретый их последним жаром,
И в поле дальнее глядит,
Ночным подернутое паром.
Его молоденькая дочь
Пошла гулять в пустынном поле.
Она привыкла к резвой воле,
Она придет; но вот уж ночь,
И скоро месяц уж покинет
Небес далеких облака, –
Земфиры нет как нет; и стынет
Убогий ужин старика.

Но вот она; за нею следом
По степи юноша спешит;

self-projection, which he had come to condemn in the Byronic poem and its thinly disguised author-hero – both powerful influences upon him in the earlier years of his 'southern exile.'

THE GYPSIES

Between Moldavian settlements
In clamorous throng the gypsies wander.
Tonight they spread their tattered tents
Encamped beside the river yonder.
Gay is their camp, like freedom gay,
Their sleep beneath the stars untroubled;
Amid the wheels of van and dray,
Their sides with hanging carpets doubled,
The campfire burns, and over it bent
They cook their meal; at pasture scattered,
The horses graze; behind the tent
A tame bear lies at ease, unfettered.
A lively bustle stirs the scene:
The peaceful cares of clansmen keen
To move at daybreak, women singing
And children's shouts around the wains,
Above the traveling anvil's ringing.
But now the night with slumbrous balm
Descends on the nomadic camping,
And nothing stirs the prairie calm
But barks and horses' neighs and stamping.
Extinct at last the winking lights,
All lies in stillness, moonbeams shimmer
Alone from heaven's distant heights
And set the silent camp aglimmer.
But in one tent an aged man
Still lingers by the charcoal pan,
His limbs at dying embers warming,
And his old eyes alertly scan
The steppe, where mists of night are forming.
His youthful daughter, scarcely grown,
Has gone to roam the prairie yonder.
In willful freedom bred to wander,
She will be back; but day has flown,
And soon the moon will have receded
From heaven's far-beclouded fold
Zemfira's still abroad; unheeded
Her father's poor repast grows cold.

But here she is; with her together –
A stranger to the old man's gaze

Цыгану вовсе он неведом.
«Отец мой, – дева говорит, –
Веду я гостя; за курганом
Его в пустыне я нашла
И в табор на´ ночь зазвала.
Он хочет быть как мы цыганом;
Его преследует закон,
Но я ему подругой буд
Его зовут Алеко – он
Готов идти за мною всюду».

Старик

Я рад. Останься до утра
Под сенью нашего шатра
Или пробудь у нас и доле,
Как ты захочешь. Я готов
С тобой делить и хлеб и кров.
Будь наш – привыкни к нашей доле,
Бродящей бедности и воле –
А завтра с утренней зарей
В одной телеге мы поедем;
Примись за промысел любой:
Железо куй – иль песни пой
И селы обходи с медведем.

Алеко

Я остаюсь.

Земфира

Он будет мой:
Кто ж от меня его отгонит?
Но поздно... месяц молодой
Зашел; поля покрыты мглой,
И сон меня невольно клонит...

———————

Светло. Старик тихонько бродит
Вокруг безмолвного шатра.
«Вставай, Земфира: солнце всходит,
Проснись, мой гость! пора, пора!..
Оставьте, дети, ложе неги!..»
И с шумом высыпал народ;
Шатры разобраны; телеги
Готовы двинуться в поход.
Всё вместе тронулось – и вот
Толпа валит в пустых равнинах.

A lad comes striding through the heather.
'My father,' thus the maiden says,
'I bring a guest, found in the distance
Beyond the barrow as I went;
I bade him slumber in our tent.
He wants to share our own existence,
And I shall be his gypsy love;
For where he dwelt, the law pursues him.
His name – Aleko. He will rove,
He vows, where I rove; and I choose him.'

OLD MAN

My welcome to you; if you meant
To rest till morning in our tent,
Or if indeed you came preparing
A longer sojourn, I am glad
To share my shelter and my bread.
Be ours – and our own lot preferring,
Espouse our humble, wayward faring,
And share my wagon too; and so
At dawn we shall set forth together;
Choose any of the trades we know:
Forge iron, or to market go
With songs and dancing-bear atether.

ALEKO

I choose to stay.

ZEMFIRA

  He will be mine;
And who is there to drive him from me?
But it grows late . . . the new moon's rim
Has sunk from sight; the plains are dim
With mist, and sleep will overcome me . . .

———————

Day breaks. The elder ambles nearer
About the sleep-enveloped tent.
'The sun is up. Arise, Zemfira,
Wake up, my guest; it's time we went!
Come, children, end your blissful slumber . . .'
Out pours the tribe in noisy swarms,
The tents are struck, and wagons lumber
As the accustomed cart train forms.
All moves at once, by wonted norms
Across the barren lowlands swaying,

Ослы в перекидных корзинах
Детей играющих несут;
Мужья и братья, жены, девы,
И стар и млад вослед идут;
Крик, шум, цыганские припевы,
Медведя рев, его цепей
Нетерпеливое бряцанье,
Лохмотьев ярких пестрота,
Детей и старцев нагота,
Собак и лай и завыванье,
Волынки говор, скрып телег,
Всё скудно, дико, всё нестройно,
Но всё так живо-неспокойно,
Так чуждо мертвых наших нег,
Так чуждо этой жизни праздной,
Как песнь рабов однообразной!

––––––––––––

Уныло юноша глядел
На опустелую равнину
И грусти тайную причину
Истолковать себе не смел.
С ним черноокая Земфира,
Теперь он вольный житель мира,
И солнце весело над ним
Полуденной красою блещет;
Что ж сердце юноши трепещет?
Какой заботой он томим?

Птичка божия не знает
Ни заботы, ни труда;
Хлопотливо не свивает
Долговечного гнезда;
В долгу ночь на ветке дремлет;
Солнце красное взойдет,
Птичка гласу бога внемлет,
Встрепенется и поет.
За весной, красой природы,
Лето знойное пройдет –
И туман и непогоды
Осень поздняя несет:
Людям скучно, людям горе;
Птичка в дальные страны,
В теплый край, за сине море
Улетает до весны.

The donkeys carry children playing
In baskets slung behind the reins,
Husbands and brothers, wives and maidens,
All ages line the wagon trains,
Hails, clamor, tunes of gypsy cadence,
The dance-bear's growling and his chain's
Impatient jangle, colors sparkling
From tattered motley rags of dress
On gnarled or tender nakedness,
The dogs' unending howl and barking,
The bagpipe's skirling, axles' creak –
All squalid, savage, all unsettled,
But how vivacious, highly mettled,
How alien to our pastimes bleak,
How foreign to those vapid pleasures,
Stale as a slave song's tuneless measures!

—————————

The youth in gloom of spirit viewed
The even steppelands, now deserted,
His reason fearfully averted
From the deep sources of his mood.
Black-eyed Zemfira's love to treasure,
The wide world his to roam at leisure,
The lofty sun above him gay
In festive noontime glamour shining –
What sets the youthful heart to pining,
What private torment, what dismay?

Little bird, God's winged neighbor,
Knows not toil or heart's unrest,
Nor in unremitting labor
Weaves a long enduring nest;
Seeks a twig-perch when it darkens
And till sunrise folds its wings;
Come the dawn, God's voice it hearkens,
Shakes its feathers down and sings.
Spring, the year's adornment, fading,
In its turn the summer's blaze,
Tardy autumn will be shading,
Shrouding all in rain and haze,
Fretful sloth to humans bringing –
Past blue seas denied to men,
Southward bound the bird is winging
Till the spring returns again.

Подобно птичке беззаботной
И он, изгнанник перелетный,
Гнезда надежного не знал
И ни к чему не привыкал.
Ему везде была дорога,
Везде была ночлега сень;
Проснувшись поутру, свой день
Он отдавал на волю бога,
И жизни не могла тревога
Смутить его сердечну лень.
Его порой волшебной славы
Манила дальная звезда;
Нежданно роскошь и забавы
К нему являлись иногда;
Над одинокой головою
И гром нередко грохотал;
Но он беспечно под грозою
И в вёдро ясное дремал.
И жил, не признавая власти
Судьбы коварной и слепой;
Но боже! как играли страсти
Его послушною душой!
С каким волнением кипели
В его измученной груди!
Давно ль, на долго ль усмирели?
Они проснутся: погоди!

Земфира

Скажи, мой друг: ты не жалеешь
О том, что бросил навсегда?

Алеко

Что ж бросил я?

Земфира

    Ты разумеешь:
Людей отчизны, города.

Алеко

О чем жалеть? Когда б ты знала,
Когда бы ты воображала
Неволю душных городов!
Там люди, в кучах за оградой,
Не дышат утренней прохладой,

He, like that careless feathered singer,
A transient exile, would not linger
In safety by a sturdy nest,
Clove to no custom, sought no rest.
For him no beaten road was needed,
No inn bespoke, no route to chart,
Aroused by each new morn, he ceded
His day to God, life's cares unheeded
Stirred not the torpor of his heart.
At times, like far-off constellations,
He glimpsed renown's alluring ray,
And rare delights and dissipations
All unexpected came his way.
Though crashing thunderbolts not seldom
Above his lonely head would strike,
The same oblivious slumber held him
In storm and quietude alike.
His life ignored blind Fate and yielded
To her malignant guile no toll;
But God! what sway the passions wielded
Within his unresisting soul!
How in his ravaged breast their torment
They used to wreak and rage their fill!
How briefly, how much longer dormant,
Will they flare up once more? They will!

ZEMFIRA

Tell me, my friend: you are not grieving
For what you will not know again?

ALEKO

Know what again?

ZEMFIRA

    I mean your leaving
The cities, your own countrymen.

ALEKO

What should I grieve for? If you knew it,
Could comprehend – why would I rue it,
The bondage of the stifling towns!
There man in throngs, hemmed in by fences,
Tastes not the morning cool, nor senses

933

Ни вешним запахом лугов;
Любви стыдятся, мысли гонят,
Торгуют волею своей,
Главы пред идолами клонят
И просят денег да цепей.
Что бросил я? Измен волненье,
Предрассуждений приговор,
Толпы безумное гоненье
Или блистательный позор.

Земфира

Но там огромные палаты,
Там разноцветные ковры,
Там игры, шумные пиры,
Уборы дев там так богаты!..

Алеко

Что шум веселий городских?
Где нет любви, там нет веселий.
А девы... Как ты лучше их
И без нарядов дорогих,
Без жемчугов, без ожерелий!
Не изменись, мой нежный друг!
А я... одно мое желанье
С тобой делить любовь, досуг
И добровольное изгнанье!

Старик

Ты любишь нас, хоть и рожден
Среди богатого народа.
Но не всегда мила свобода
Тому, кто к неге приучен.
Меж нами есть одно преданье:
Царем когда-то сослан был
Полудня житель к нам в изгнанье.
(Я прежде знал, но позабыл
Его мудреное прозванье.)
Он был уже летами стар,
Но млад и жив душой незлобной –
Имел он песен дивный дар
И голос, шуму вод подобный –
И полюбили все его,
И жил он на брегах Дуная,

The vernal perfume of the downs;
There love is furtive, thought in bridles,
There liberty is bought and sold,
They bow in worship before idols
And beg for shackles and for gold.
What did I leave? Betrayers' babble,
Rank prejudice's smug decree,
The hounding of the mindless rabble
Or else resplendent infamy.

ZEMFIRA

But there they have apartments spacious,
With rugs of many-colored plaid,
And games and festivals vivacious –
The girls there go so richly clad!

ALEKO

What of the city's noisy mirth?
Where love is not, there is no pleasure.
The girls . . . Of how much greater worth
Are you than they, for all your dearth
Of costly garments, pearls, and treasure!
Don't ever change, my lovely fair!
And I . . . have but a single mission,
Your pastimes and your love to share,
An exile by my own volition.

OLD MAN

You like us and the life we lead,
Though nurtured by a wealthy nation.
Not always, though, is liberation
Dear to a man of tender breed.
Here an old tale is still related:
A dweller of the South[1] once came
Amongst us, by the Emperor fated
To live in exile here, the same
As you (the legend stated,
But I forget his curious name).
Though old in body, far from strong,
His guileless soul was younger, firmer
He had the wondrous gift of song,
His voice like to the waters' murmur.
And long, beloved of everyone,

[1] The legend alludes to Ovid, the Roman poet banished by Augustus in AD 8 to Tomi on the Black Sea, not far from Bessarabia, the setting of The Gypsies and Pushkin's own temporary place of exile.

Не обижая никого,
Людей рассказами пленяя;
Не разумел он ничего,
И слаб и робок был, как дети;
Чужие люди за него
Зверей и рыб ловили в сети;
Как мерзла быстрая река
И зимни вихри бушевали,
Пушистой кожей покрывали
Они святаго старика;
Но он к заботам жизни бедной
Привыкнуть никогда не мог;
Скитался он иссохший, бледный,
Он говорил, что гневный бог
Его карал за преступленье...
Он ждал: придет ли избавленье.
И всё несчастный тосковал,
Бродя по берегам Дуная,
Да горьки слезы проливал,
Свой дальный град воспоминая,
И завещал он, умирая,
Чтобы на юг перенесли
Его тоскующие кости,
И смертью – чуждой сей земли
Не успокоенные гости!

           Алеко

Так вот судьба твоих сынов,
О Рим, о громкая держава!..
Певец любви, певец богов,
Скажи мне, что такое слава?
Могильный гул, хвалебный глас,
Из рода в роды звук бегущий?
Или под сенью дымной кущи
Цыгана дикого рассказ?

           ————————

Прошло два лета. Так же бродят
Цыганы мирною толпой;
Везде по-прежнему находят
Гостеприимство и покой.
Презрев оковы просвещенья,
Алеко волен, как они;
Он без забот в сожаленья
Ведет кочующие дни.

Here on the banks of Danube dwelling,
He lived, and gave offense to none
But charmed them with his storytelling.
As shy and feeble as a child,
He knew not how to make his living,
And fed on creatures of the wild,
On fish and fowl of strangers' giving.
When storm winds raged and winter came,
The rapid flow in frost entrapping,
They used to guard with furry wrapping
The saintly stranger's aged frame.
Yet years and habitude could never
Endear our humble, toilsome way,
But, pale and gaunt, he strayed forever
Amongst us and was wont to say
That an immortal's vengeful passion
Pursued him for some old transgression.
Deliverance his only thought,
Throughout his span, with piteous crying
The exile, restless and distraught,
Bestrode the banks of Danube, sighing
For his far city; lastly, dying,
He charged them earnestly to send
To the warm land of his allegiance
His sorrowing bones – this alien region's
Reluctant guests unto the end!

ALEKO

Is such the fate, then, of your sons,
Majestic Rome of song and story!
Thou bard of the immortal ones,
Love's singer, tell me, what is glory?
Sepulchral echoes, honor's hail,
Renown from age to age redawning?
Or, told beneath a smoky awning,
An errant nomad's artless tale?

———————

Two years have passed. The gypsies wander
Upon their wonted peaceful quest,
As ever finding here and yonder
Both hospitality and rest.
Civilization's bonds disdaining,
Aleko wanders free as they;
Exempt from cares and uncomplaining,
He shares their ever-ranging day.

937

Всё тот же он; семья всё та же;
Он, прежних лет не помня даже,
К бытью цыганскому привык.
Он любит их ночлегов сени,
И упоенье вечной лени,
И бедный, звучный их язык.
Медведь, беглец родной берлоги,
Косматый гость его шатра,
В селеньях, вдоль степной дороги,
Близ молдаванского двора
Перед толпою осторожной
И тяжко пляшет, и ревет,
И цепь докучную грызет;
На посох опершись дорожный,
Старик лениво в бубны бьет,
Алеко с пеньем зверя водит,
Земфира поселян обходит
И дань их вольную берет.
Настанет ночь; они все трое
Варят нежатое пшено;
Старик уснул – и всё в покое...
В шатре и тихо и темно.

———————————

Старик на вешнем солнце греет
Уж остывающую кровь;
У люльки дочь поет любовь.
Алеко внемлет и бледнеет.

Земфира

Старый муж, грозный муж,
Режь меня, жги меня:
Я тверда; не боюсь
Ни ножа, ни огня.

Ненавижу тебя,
Презираю тебя;
Я другого люблю,
Умираю любя.

Алеко

Молчи. Мне пенье надоело,
Я диких песен не люблю.

Земфира

Не любишь? мне какое дело!
Я песню для себя пою.

He is the same, so are his dear ones,
Their life is his; to all appearance
He scarce remembers former years.
He loves the dusk of their nocturnal
Bivouacs, sweet indolence eternal,
Their tuneful speech upon his ears.
Fled from the lair where once he bedded,
The shaggy sharer of his tent
In hamlets on the steppe-trail threaded,
Near some Moldavian settlement,
Performed his ponderous dance and snorted
Before a cautious gathering
And gnawed the noxious iron sling;
While, on his traveler's staff supported,
The elder with a lazy swing
Would set the cymbaled hand-drum ringing,
Aleko sang, Zemfira bringing
Their freely given offering.
Night falls; all three prepare their diet
Of unreaped millet gleaned and crushed;
The old man sleeps – and all is quiet . . .
The tent within is dark and hushed.

———————————

The ancient's failing pulses quicken,
New life the vernal sunshine brings;
And by the cot his daughter sings
Of love. Aleko listens, stricken.

ZEMFIRA

Graying man, cruel man,
Spare me not fire or knife,
Stab you can, burn you can,
Firm I am, spurn your strife.

And your love I deny,
And your wrath I defy,
For another I love,
For his love I will die.

ALEKO

Be still. Your singing wearies me,
I do not like those uncouth airs.

ZEMFIRA

Too bad! but it is not for thee
That I am singing them. Who cares?

Режь меня, жги меня;
Не скажу ничего;
Старый муж, грозный муж,
Не узнаешь его.

Он свежее весны,
Жарче летнего дня;
Как он молод и смел!
Как он любит меня!

Как ласкала его
Я в ночной тишине!
Как смеялись тогда
Мы твоей седине!

Алеко

Молчи, Земфира! я доволен...

Земфира

Так понял песню ты мою?

Алеко

Земфира!

Земфира

Ты сердиться волен,
Я песню про тебя пою.

Уходит и поет: Старый муж и проч.

Старик

Так, помню, помню – песня эта
Во время наше сложена,
Уже давно в забаву света
Поется меж людей она.
Кочуя на степях Кагула,
Ее, бывало, в зимню ночь
Моя певала Мариула,
Перед огнем качая дочь.
В уме моем минувши лета
Час от часу темней, темней;
Но заронилась песня эта
Глубоко в памяти моей.

———————

Stab you may, burn you may,
Not a word will I say,
Graying man, cruel man,
You shall not learn his name.

How much fresher than spring,
Hot as summer-day gold,
Is my lad young and bold,
Is his love that I sing.

What caresses we shared
In the still of the night!
How we laughed at the sight
Of the gray in your hair!

ALEKO

Enough, Zemfira! Hush, be quiet . . .

ZEMFIRA

So thou hast read my song's intent?

ALEKO

Zemfira!

ZEMFIRA

Scold, then! Why deny it?
It is for thee my song is meant.

Goes off, singing 'Graying man . . . .'

OLD MAN

Yes, I remember – that old ditty
Was first in my young manhood sung,
And often since in mart and city
It has delighted old and young.
When in the steppelands of Kagula
We wandered, of a winter night –
Dandling her daughter, my Mariula
Would sing it by the firelight.
The years gone by with every hour
Grow dark and darker now, I find
But that refrain some secret power
Has graven deep into my mind.

———————

Всё тихо; ночь. Луной украшен
Лазурный юга небосклон,
Старик Земфирой пробужден:
«О мой отец! Алеко страшен.
Послушай: сквозь тяжелый сон
И стонет, и рыдает он».

　　　Старик

Не тронь его. Храни молчанье.
Слыхал я русское преданье:
Теперь полунощной порой
У спящего теснит дыханье
Домашний дух; перед зарей
Уходит он. Сиди со мной.

　　　Земфира

Отец мой! шепчет он: Земфира!

　　　Старик

Тебя он ищет и во сне:
Ты для него дороже мира.

　　　Земфира

Его любовь постыла мне.
Мне скучно; сердце воли просит –
Уж я... Но тише! слышишь? он
Другое имя произносит...

　　　Старик

Чье имя?

　　　Земфира

　　　Слышишь? хриплый стон
И скрежет ярый!.. Как ужасно!..
Я разбужу его...

　　　Старик

　　　Напрасно,
Ночного духа не гони –
Уйдет и сам...

　　　Земфира

　　　Он повернулся,
Привстал, зовет меня... проснулся –
Иду к нему – прощай, усни.

Night; all is still. The moon has brightened
The southern heaven's azure span;
Zemfira wakens the old man:
'Oh, father, listen! I am frightened.
Such troubled sleep Aleko sleeps!
He groans as if in pain, and weeps.'

OLD MAN

Keep silent, daughter. Do not touch him.
I often heard the Russians tell:
At midnight a domestic elf
May haunt the sleeper's rest and clutch him
To choke his breath; at dawn the spell
Is loosed. Sit by me, calm yourself.

ZEMFIRA

Oh, Father! Now he sobs: Zemfira!

OLD MAN

His very dreams reach out for thee:
Than all the world he holds thee dearer.

ZEMFIRA

His love is wearisome to me.
For freedom pines my soul and mutters –
Already . . . Hush! I hear him moaning . . .
It is another name he utters.

OLD MAN

Whose name?

ZEMFIRA

　　Oh, listen! Hoarsely groaning,
Gnashing his teeth as one insane!
I must awaken him.

OLD MAN

　　In vain;
Break not a nightbound spirit's spell
Before its own time.

ZEMFIRA

　　It is broken.
He's rising, calling . . . he has woken.
I'll go to him – sleep on; farewell.

943

Алеко

Где ты была?

Земфира

С отцом сидела.
Какой-то дух тебя томил;
Во сне душа твоя терпела
Мученья; ты меня страшил:
Ты, сонный, скрежетал зубами
И звал меня.

Алеко

Мне снилась ты.
Я видел, будто между нами...
Я видел страшные мечты!

Земфира

Не верь лукавым сновиденьям.

Алеко

Ах, я не верю ничему:
Ни снам, ни сладким увереньям,
Ни даже сердцу твоему.

––––––––––––

Старик

О чем, безумец молодой,
О чем вздыхаешь ты всечасно?
Здесь люди вольны, небо ясно,
И жены славятся красой.
Не плачь: тоска тебя погубит.

Алеко

Отец, она меня не любит.

Старик

Утешься, друг: она дитя.
Твое унынье безрассудно:
Ты любишь горестно и трудно,
А сердце женское – шутя.
Взгляни: под отдаленным сводом
Гуляет вольная луна;
На всю природу мимоходом
Равно сиянье льет она.
Заглянет в облако любое,

ALEKO

Where have you been?

ZEMFIRA

I have been sitting
With Father; there was plaguing thee
An evil sprite; thy soul unwitting
Knew agonies. It frightened me,
For in thy slumber thou wert gritting
Thy teeth and calling me.

ALEKO

I dreamed
Of you. Between us, so it seemed . . .
I fancied horrors past endurance!

ZEMFIRA

Trust not dream fancies – they depart.

ALEKO

Ah, I trust nothing – not the art
Of dreams, or that of sweet assurance,
I do not even trust your heart.

———————

OLD MAN

Wherefore, unruly youth, confess,
Wherefore forever sighing, pining?
Here men are free, the heavens shining,
And women tamed for comeliness.
Weep not – grief will undo you. Rather . . .

ALEKO

Zemfira does not love me, Father.

OLD MAN

She is a child, friend; be consoled.
Perversely, foolishly you languish.
Your love is drudgery and anguish,
A woman's is all play. Behold!
Across the vaulted darkness soaring,
The heedless moon serenely strays,
On all creation gently pouring
Her undiscriminating rays.
She calls upon a cloudbank yonder,

Его так пышно озарит –
И вот – уж перешла в другое;
И то недолго посетит.
Кто место в небе ей укажет,
Примолвя: там остановись!
Кто сердцу юной девы скажет:
Люби одно, не изменись?
Утешься.

Алеко

Как она любила!
Как нежно преклонясь ко мне,
Она в пустынной тишине
Часы ночные проводила!
Веселья детского полна,
Как часто милым лепетаньем
Иль упоительным лобзаньем
Мою задумчивость она
В минуту разогнать умела!..
И что ж? Земфира неверна!
Моя Земфира охладела!...

Старик

Послушай: расскажу тебе
Я повесть о самом себе.
Давно, давно, когда Дунаю
Не угрожал еще москаль –
(Вот видишь, я припоминаю,
Алеко, старую печаль.)
Тогда боялись мы султана;
А правил Буджаком паша
С высоких башен Аккермана –
Я молод был; моя душа
В то время радостно кипела;
И ни одна в кудрях моих
Еще сединка не белела, –
Между красавиц молодых
Одна была... и долго ею,
Как солнцем, любовался я,
И наконец назвал моею...

Ах, быстро молодость моя
Звездой падучею мелькнула!

Bedews it with a silver haze –
Lo! to another she will wander,
Again for but a fleeting gaze.
How fix on one among the stellar
Redoubts and bid her: Cease to range!
How fix a maiden's heart and tell her:
This you shall love, and never change?
Console yourself, my friend.

ALEKO

How tender
Her love! How willingly she sank
To my embraces as we drank
The wilderness' tranquil splendor!
Forever playful, childish-gay,
How often has she sweetly chattered
Or with her magic kisses scattered
Dark fancies, banished gloom away,
And to the moment's joy restored me!
And now? Zemfira gone astray!
Zemfira grown unkind toward me! . . .

OLD MAN

Attend, my son, and you shall know
What once befell me long ago:
When yet the Danube did not echo
To Moskal[2] arms encroaching here
(An ancient grief, you see, Aleko,
I must recall), we lived in fear
Of the Great Turk; and from the aerie
Of lofty-towered Ak-Kerman
A Turkish pasha ruled the prairie
Of the Budzhak[3] still. I was young,
My fervent spirits sparkled brightly,
And of my curly tresses none
Was yet with silver threaded whitely.
Among our youthful beauties one
There shone . . . and long my eyes upon her
In worship gazed, as on the sun,
And in the end, at last, I won her . . .

Alas, my youthful years were gone
Like fallen stars as soon as kindled!

---

[2] Derogatory Slavic, especially Polish, term for 'Muscovite.'
[3] The Budzhak (Turkish: bucak, 'corner,' probably from the angle between the Prut and the Danube) is the extensive puszta-like prairieland of southern Bessarabia.

Но ты, пора любви, минула
Еще быстрее: только год
Меня любила Мариула.

Однажды близ Кагульских вод
Мы чуждый табор повстречали;
Цыганы те, свои шатры
Разбив близ наших у горы,
Две ночи вместе ночевали.
Они ушли на третью ночь, –
И, бродя маленькую дочь,
Ушла за ними Мариула.
Я мирно спал; заря блеснула;
Проснулся я, подруги нет!
Ищу, зову – пропал и след.
Тоскуя, плакала Земфира,
И я заплакал – с этих пор
Постыли мне все девы мира;
Меж ими никогда мой взор
Не выбирал себе подруги,
И одинокие досуги
Уже ни с кем я не делил.

Алеко

Да как же ты не поспешил
Тотчас вослед неблагодарной
И хищникам и ей коварной
Кинжала в сердце не вонзил?

Старик

К чему? вольнее птицы младость;
Кто в силах удержать любовь?
Чредою всем дается радость;
Что было, то не будет вновь.

Алеко

Я не таков. Нет, я не споря
От прав моих не откажусь!
Или хоть мщеньем наслажусь.
О нет! когда б над бездной моря
Нашел я спящего врага,
Клянусь, и тут моя нога
Не пощадила бы злодея;
Я в волны моря, не бледнея,
И беззащитного б толкнул;
Внезапный ужас пробужденья

But you, fulfillment's season, dwindled
More swiftly still; for not above
One year I held Mariula's love.

Not far from the Kagulan waters
We met a tribe; they staked their ropes
And pitched beside our canvas quarters
Their tents upon the mountain slopes.
Two nights that band spent near us, breaking
Their trek, and on the third decamped;
With them, Mariula left, forsaking
Her baby daughter, while I dreamt
In peaceful sleep. At dawn's first shining
I woke – my love was gone! I flew
To search, I called – no trace. Repining,
Zemfira cried, and I wept too!
That dark hour taught me to abhor
All this earth's maidens; I forbore
Henceforth to let my eyes admire,
Nor my lone idleness desire
The solace of a tender guest.

ALEKO

You gave not chase, then, to arrest
The faithless ingrate and to chasten
Her vile abductors, did not hasten
To plunge a dagger in their breast?

OLD MAN

To what end? Who would vainly try
To hold young love, free as a bird?
On each in turn is bliss conferred
What was, returns not.

ALEKO

    No – not I
Would thus have cravenly resigned
My rights in a usurper's favor;
Or at the meanest I would savor
A sweet revenge. Were I to find
My foe on the deep sea, I swear,
Unarmed, asleep – I would not spare
The knave my foot: straightway, unblanching,
Into the raging waves would launch him;
The sudden terror of his waking

949

Свирепым смехом упрекнул,
И долго мне его паденья
Смешон и сладок был бы гул.

————————

Молодой цыган

Еще одно... одно лобзанье...

Земфира

Пора: мой муж ревнив и зол.

Цыган

Одно... но доле!.. на прощанье.

Земфира

Прощай, покамест не пришел.

Цыган

Скажи – когда ж опять свиданье?

Земфира

Сегодня, как зайдет луна,
Там, за курганом над могилой...

Цыган

Обманет! не придет она!

Земфира

Вот он! беги!.. Приду, мой милый.

————————

Алеко спит. В его уме
Виденье смутное играет;
Он, с криком пробудясь во тьме,
Ревниво руку простирает;
Но обробелая рука
Покровы хладные хватает –
Его подруга далека...
Он с трепетом привстал и внемлет...
Всё тихо – страх его объемлет,
По нем текут и жар и хлад;
Встает он, из шатра выходит,
Вокруг телег, ужасен, бродит;
Спокойно всё; поля молчат;
Темно; луна зашла в туманы,

With savage laughter I would cheer,
And long his thrashings would be breaking
Like gleeful music on my ear.

_____

YOUNG GYPSY

One more . . . one more kiss . . .

ZEMFIRA

Time is fleeting,
My man mean-spirited and cross.

GYPSY

Just one . . . but longer! One last greeting.

ZEMFIRA

Farewell, or he might follow us.

GYPSY

When shall we have another meeting?

ZEMFIRA

Tonight, then, when the moon takes cover,
Upon that tomb, beyond the mound.

GYPSY

She plays me false – will not be found!

ZEMFIRA

Run! Here he is! . . . I'll come, my lover.

_____

Aleko sleeps, but in his mind
A vague and troubling vision lingers,
Till with a cry he wakes – to find
All darkness. His mistrustful fingers
Reach out . . . and shrink as they uncover
Cold blankets – far off is his lover . . .
Half-rearing with a shuddering start,
He listens: silence; sick at heart,
His limbs now chill, now fever-damp,
He rises, leaves the tent, goes walking
Between the wagons, grimly stalking
The slumbering fields about the camp.
Deep gloom; the moon is mist-beclouded,
The faltering starlight barely hints

Чуть брезжит звезд неверный свет,
Чуть по росе приметный след
Ведет за дальные курганы:
Нетерпеливо он идет,
Куда зловещий след ведет.

Могила на краю дороги
Вдали белеет перед ним...
Туда слабеющие ноги
Влачит, предчувствием томим,
Дрожат уста, дрожат колени,
Идет... и вдруг... иль это сон?
Вдруг видит близкие две тени
И близкой шепот слышит он –
Над обесславленной могилой.

   1-й голос

Пора...

   2-й голос

 Постой...

   1-й голос

 Пора, мой милый.

   2-й голос

Нет, нет, постой, дождемся дня.

   1-й голос

Уж поздно.

   2-й голос

 Как ты робко любишь.
Минуту!

   1-й голос

Ты меня погубишь.

   2-й голос

Минуту!

   1-й голос

 Если без меня
Проснется муж?..

The faintest trail of dewy prints
Toward the mounds in distance shrouded.
He follows with impatient haste
The path these ill-starred footprints traced.

White in the hazy dusk before him
There gleamed afar a roadside tomb . . .
And there his dragging footsteps bore him,
Weighed down by prescience of doom,
With quivering lips and shaking knees;
Until – is it a dream he sees? –
Nearby is heard a whispering sound,
And at his feet twin shadows hover
Upon the desecrated mound.

       FIRST VOICE

It's time . . .

       SECOND VOICE

   No, wait . . .

       FIRST VOICE

   It's time, dear lover.

       SECOND VOICE

Don't go – let us await the day.

       FIRST VOICE

It's late.

       SECOND VOICE

   Be bolder, love, be joyous.
One moment more!

       FIRST VOICE

   You will destroy us.

       SECOND VOICE

One moment!

       FIRST VOICE

   While I am away,
My husband may wake up! . . .

Алеко

Проснулся я.
Куда вы! не спешите оба;
Вам хорошо и здесь у гроба.

Земфира

Мой друг, беги, беги...

Алеко

Постой!
Куда, красавец молодой?
Лежи!

Вонзает в него нож.

Земфира

Алеко!

Цыган

Умираю...

Земфира

Алеко, ты убьешь его!
Взгляни: ты весь обрызган кровью!
О, что ты сделал?

Алеко

Ничего.
Теперь дыши его любовью.

Земфира

Нет, полно, не боюсь тебя! –
Твои угрозы презираю,
Твое убийство проклинаю...

Алеко

Умри ж и ты!

Поражает ее.

ALEKO

He may.
No, stay, you two, where are you flitting?
The graveside here is fine, is fitting.

ZEMFIRA

Run, dearest, hurry . . .

ALEKO

Where away?
Oh, no, my bonny lad, you stay!
Lie there!

Thrusts his knife into him.

ZEMFIRA

Aleko!

GYPSY

I am dying!

ZEMFIRA

Aleko, you will be his death!
Look: you are all with blood bespattered!
What have you done?

ALEKO

As if it mattered.
Now go and drink your lover's breath.

ZEMFIRA

Ah, no – I am not frightened of
Your rage! I scorn it, I abhor it,
Your bloody deed, I curse you for it.

ALEKO

Then die you too!

Strikes her.

Земфира

Умру любя...

———————

Восток, денницей озаренный,
Сиял. Алеко за холмом,
С ножом в руках, окровавленный
Сидел на камне гробовом.
Два трупа перед ним лежали;
Убийца страшен был лицом.
Цыганы робко окружали
Его встревоженной толпой.
Могилу в стороне копали.
Шли жены скорбной чередой
И в очи мертвых целовали.
Старик-отец один сидел
И на погибшую глядел
В немом бездействии печали;
Подняли трупы, понесли
И в лоно хладное земли
Чету младую положили.
Алеко издали смотрел
На всё... когда же их закрыли
Последней горстию земной,
Он молча, медленно склонился
И с камня на траву свалился.

Тогда старик, приближась, рек:
«Оставь нас, гордый человек!
Мы дики; нет у нас законов,
Мы не терзаем, не казним –
Не нужно крови нам и стонов –
Но жить с убийцей не хотим...
Ты не рожден для дикой доли,
Ты для себя лишь хочешь воли;
Ужасен нам твой будет глас:
Мы робки и добры душою,
Ты зол и смел – оставь же нас,
Прости, да будет мир с тобою».

Сказал – и шумною толпою
Поднялся табор кочевой
С долины страшного ночлега.
И скоро всё в дали степной
Сокрылось; лишь одна телега,
Убогим крытая ковром,
Стояла в поле роковом.

ZEMFIRA

I die in love . . .

Resplendent Venus, star of morrow,
Across the dawning orient shone.
Upon the tomb beyond the barrow,
Blood-dabbled, knife in hand, alone
Aleko sat. And thus they found him,
Hunched by those dead, his stare insane.
Abashed, the gypsies shrank around him;
Some sidled to inter the twain
Not far away. In mournful train
The women followed one another
To kiss their eyelids. On the slain
In numb bereavement her old father,
Bleak desolation in his heart,
Sat gazing mutely and apart.
They lifted and bore off the supple,
Now lifeless, forms and laid the couple
Into the chilly earthen womb.
Aleko from the farther tomb
Looked on . . . but when the two were covered
With that last offering of earth,
Still mute, he teetered forward, hovered,
And sprawled headlong upon the turf.

Then spoke the ancient by his side:
'Depart from us, oh man of pride!
We are but wild, a lawless nation,
We keep no rack or hempen knot,
Need neither blood nor lamentation –
But live with slayers we will not.
The heathen freedom you have known,
You claim it for yourself alone;
Your voice henceforth would awe and grieve us,
For we are meek and kind of heart,
And you are fierce and wicked – leave us,
And peace be with you as we part.'

He spoke – and with a bustling start
The light encampment rose as bidden
To leave the night's dread vale behind.
And soon the prairie's depth had hidden
The nomad train. A single cart,
Its frame with wretched cover vested,
Stood in the fateful field arrested,

Так иногда перед зимою,
Туманной, утренней порою,
Когда подъемлется с полей
Станица поздних журавлей
И с криком вдаль на юг несется,
Пронзенный гибельным свинцом
Один печально остается,
Повиснув раненым крылом.
Настала ночь: в телеге темной
Огня никто не разложил,
Никто под крышею подъемной
До утра сном не опочил.

Эпилог

Волшебной силой песнопенья
В туманной памяти моей
Так оживляются виденья
То светлых, то печальных дней.

В стране, где долго, долго брани
Ужасный гул не умолкал,
Где повелительные грани
Стамбулу русский указал,
Где старый наш орел двуглавый
Еще шумит минувшей славой,
Встречал я посреди степей
Над рубежами древних станов
Телеги мирные цыганов,
Смиренной вольности детей.
За их ленивыми толпами
В пустынях часто я бродил,
Простую пищу их делил
И засыпал пред их огнями.
В походах медленных любил
Их песен радостные гулы –
И долго милой Мариулы
Я имя нежное твердил.

Но счастья нет и между вами,
Природы бедные сыны!..
И под издранными шатрами
Живут мучительные сны,
И ваши сени кочевые
В пустынях не спаслись от бед,
И всюду страсти роковые,
И от судеб защиты нет.

Thus late in autumn one may find,
On plains where morning mists are clinging,
With cries above their gathering-stead
A tardy crane-flight southward winging;
But one, pierced through by mortal lead,
Forlorn in empty fields is lagging,
Its wounded pinion sadly dragging.
Dusk fell; behind the wagon's awning
That night no flickering fire arose,
And no one till a new day's dawning
Lay down there for a night's repose.

EPILOGUE

Thus song-craft with its potent magic
From memory's beclouded haze
Will conjure visions, now of tragic,
Now of serenely shining days.

Where long, so long, the conflagrations
Of warlike ardor did not cool,
Where once the Russian showed his nation's
Imperious borders to Stambul,
Where our old eagle double-headed
For parted glories still is dreaded,
There in the steppelands would see
On some abandoned rampart's traces
The gypsies' peaceful camping places,
Wild freedom's humble progeny.
And often through those untamed shires
Behind their lazy troops I fared,
Their simple nourishment I shared,
And fell asleep before their fires.
As on those leisured treks I came,
Their cheerful ringing tunes I cherished,
And long with fond recital nourished
Sweet Mariula's tender name.

Yet you, too, Nature's sons undaunted,
Are strange to happiness, it seems!
Your ragged shelters, too, are haunted
By omens and oppressive dreams,
Deep in your wilderness, disaster
For wandering tents in ambush waits;
Grim passion everywhere is master,
And no one can elude the Fates.

[*Translated by Walter Arndt*]

m. ESPAÑOL

VII.m.1. JUAN AROLAS BONET, 'La hermosa Halewa'

El prudente Almanzor, emir glorioso,
el cordobés imperio dirigía;
Hixcén, su rey, en el harén dichoso
los blandos sueños del placer dormía.
Cisnes de oro purísimo, labrados
sobre conchas de pórfido en las fuentes,
en medio de jardines regalados
derramaban las linfas transparentes.
Los limpios baños de marmóreas pilas
do el agua pura mil esencias toma
cercaban lirios y agrupadas lilas
de tintas bellas y profuso aroma.
Damascos y alcatifas tunecinas
del palacio adornadan los salones,
perlas en colgaduras purpurinas,
perlas en recamadas almohadones.
Olores de Arabia respiraban
lechos de blanda pluma en los retretes
y las fuentes de plata reflejaban
del alcázar los altos minaretes.
Del regio templo celebrada diosa,
Halewa fue en su plácida fortuna
ídolo del monarca por hermosa,
tierna como una lágrima en la cuna.
Feliz si de un esclavo que sabía
enamorar con trova cariñosa.
Más amor no aprendiera que armonía
al son del arpa dulce y sonorosa.
Iba del docto mancebo modulando
los ayes del amor en vario tono.
La bella favorita suspirando
hizo el primer desprecio al regio trono.
Un día... Nunca el sol su rayo activo
lanzó con más ardor ni más hermoso
fue el pensil y la sombra del olivo
para gozar del celestial reposo.
Sediento del halago y del cariño,
buscaba Hixcén los suspirados lazos
y, cual sus juegos inocente niño,
apetecía el rey tiernos abrazos.
¡Infeliz!, ¡ah!, repara aquella rosa
que el roedor insecto ha deshojado.
No muevas, no, la planta vagorosa;

960

m. SPANISH

VII.m.1.   JUAN AROLAS BONET, 'The Beautiful Halewa'

Prudent Almansur, glorious emir, ruled the Cordoban empire; Hisham, his king, in the pleasant harem slept the soft dreams of pleasure. In the fountains, swans of the purest gold, worked on shells of porphyry in the midst of richly planted gardens, spilled out transparent water. The limpid baths of marble basins, where the pure water takes a thousand essences are enclosed in irises and clumps of lilacs of beautiful tints and profuse scents. Damascenes and carpets from Tunis adorned the rooms of the palace, pearls in goldthreaded tapestries, pearls on embroidered cushions. The perfumes of Arabia breathed out from beds of soft down in the side chambers and the silver fountains reflected the tall minarets of the royal palace. The renowned goddess of the royal temple, Halewa, was, in her good fortune, the idol of the monarch for her beauty, tender as a tear in a cradle. If she was the joy of a slave who knew how to enamour her with a loving troubador's song, she learned more harmony than love at the sound of his sweet and sonorous harp. The skilled young man came tuning the sighs of love in varied tones. The beautiful favourite, sighing, made the first slight to the royal throne. One day . . . Never had the sun thrust down his active ray with more heat nor was the flowerbed and the shade of the olive tree more beautiful to enjoy the heavenly repose. Thirsty for flattery and endearments, Hisham sought sighing encounters and, like the games of an innocent child, he yearned for tender embraces. Unhappy man, alas!, take heed of that rose which the gnawing insect has deflowered. Move not, no, the unreliable plant: the tomb of pain is at your side. He saw, sleeping in the grotto which, at the end of the walkway was covered with a climbing ivy, with fresh-plucked roses on her brow, the inconstant beauty whose breast he adored. He saw the slave sleeping . . . Fresh flowers crowned his brow . . . His impure lip murmured his love in his dreams, and the slip of the other lip perjured him. The harp forgotten on the grass moved its strings in the wind and seemed to weep the agony of its enamoured and accomplished owner. The lion roars and the serpent hisses through offended love, the woman weeps and the man washes, with his sinful blood which dishonours him, the heavy slab. Hisham groans; an infernal fury rends his heart; he places his hand on the hilt of his curved scimitar and the unhappy Halewa opens her eyes. She opens them to see the wild blow against the slave who loved her beauty, the livid corpse at her side and, rent from its shoulders, the head. She saw blood on her garments and on her veil, and the grotto and path were tinted with blood as the head rolled along the floor in a cold tremor and a horrible convulsion. She is dragged off to a gloomy dungeon by six black slaves . . . Ah! her tears of pure jewels and timid gaze cannot bend the disdainful Moor. The new light of the clouded day glimpsed, on the point of a pole in the gardens, the horrid cold head of the slave and the jasmines spattered with blood.

[1838]

[*Arguably, Arolas was the most erotic poet of his time despite being in religious orders. He was also the most Orientalist, setting his poems in Moorish Spain, Turkey and Arabia. He was a precursor of the European Decadence in his admixture of eroticism, violence and death and an influence on the Spanish Decadence of the late nineteenth century and early twentieth.*]

la tumba del dolor está a tu lado.
Vio en la gruta que al fin de los andenes
se cubre con la hiedra trepadora
dormir con frescas rosas en las sienes
la inconstante beldad que el pecho adora.
Vio dormido el esclavo... Frescas flores
coronaban su sien... Su labio impuro
en sueños murmuraba sus amores
y el desliz de otro labio más perjuro.
El arpa sobre el césped olvidada
con el viento sus fibras conmovía
y de su docto dueño enamorada
parece que lloraba su agonía.
Ruge el león y silba la serpiente
por ofendido amor, la mujer llora
y el hombre con la sangre delincuente
lava el torpe baldón que le desdora.
Suspira Hixcén; su corazón desgarra
una furia infernal; su mano lleva
al puño de la corva cimitarra
y abre los ojos la infeliz Halewa.
Los abre para ver el golpe airado
contra el siervo que amaba su belleza,
el lívido cadáver a su lado
y fuera de los hombros la cabeza.
Sangre vio en su vestido y en su velo,
que en sangre se tiñó la gruta y senda
al rodar la cabeza por el suelo
en temblor frío y convulsión horrenda.
A lóbrega mazmorra es arrastrada
por seis esclavos negros... ¡Ah!, su lloro
de aljófar puro y tímida mirada
no pueden doblegar a esquivo moro.
La nueva luz del nebuloso día
vio en la punta de un palo en los jardines
la cabeza del siervo horrenda y fría
y con gotas de sangre los jazmines.

[*In Diario Mercantil, 1838*]

n. **SVENSKA**

VII.n.1.   C. J. L. ALMQVIST, ur *Parjumouf. Saga ifrån Nya Holland*

Då jag för ungefär halftannat år sedan var i London, inlopp en dag oförmodadt den Rapporten till Ministrarne och Parlamentet ifrån Guvernören öfver Botany Bay, att denne, på andra sidan om Blå Bergen, upptäckt ett herrligt, fruktbärande Land, och att han redan vid en flod hade gjort anstalt till en ny Stads uppbyggande. – Såsom jag just då var i begrepp, att företaga någon lång Resa, men icke kunnat bestämma mig, hvilken Verldsdel jag skulle välja; så beslöt jag nu hastigt, att resa till Port Jackson, för att sjelf få bese, kanske också sjelf göra några upptäckter i en trakt af Verlden, som ännu ingen Europé besett.

Jag begaf mig också genast till Plymouth, hvarest ett Skepp låg segelfärdigt till Söderhafvet. Kaptenen var en städad och skicklig man. Han skulle både besöka Java och Moluckiske Öarne. Han hade dessutom en betydande transport af Trädvaror för Colonierne i Sidney Cove; – han skulle således sjelf till Botany Bay – och min resa var aldeles förenad med hans.

Vädret var ganska vackert; resan geck fort: en besynnerlig rysning öfverföll mig, då jag såg de ödsliga, ofantliga Sandkusterne af det stora Ulimaroa. – Jag blef mycket väl emottagen af Guvernören i Botany Bay. Han biföll med den största glädje min begäran, att i förening med de öfriga engelska Officerarne resa inåt Landet på upptäckter. Derefter tillbringade jag någon tid med inhämtande af de Vildars språk, som redan Engelsmännen kände, och gjorde dessutom några andra tillredelser för mina ernade Resor.

Jag förbigår nu de tre första Resorna vi gjorde. Jag vill blott nämna om den fjerde. – I sällskap med en ung engelsk Officer, vid namn *Sandwich*, företog jag denna förtjusande resa. Vi hade redan ifrån Port Jackson kommit till den ofantliga Bergås, som stänger utsigten af landet innanföre, och som erhållit namn af de Blå Bergen. Då vi öfverstigit höjden af dessa berg, och under nedstigandet på andra sidan vände oss mera åt Norden, än vi vanligen förut gjort, upptäckte vi snart en liten klar Ström, som flöt ned ifrån Bergsryggen och som rigtade sin gång åt Norden. Vi följde strömmens lopp. Snart kommo vi i trakter, som allt mer och mer utmärkte sig genom sin lefvande Grönska: en Grönska, som var så mycket mer uppfriskande för oss, som alla trakterna kring vår Colonie vid Botany Bay äro förfärande ödsliga. – Vi gingo några timmar genom de herrligaste Bokskogar, kommo derefter in i andra Skogar bevuxna med sköna Träd, hvars Namn och Natur vi icke kände; och i hvilka vi visserligen utan compassens tillhjelp skulle hafva förvillat oss. – Slutligen kommo vi fram till en Äng. Intet spår syntes efter Menniskor; men i det höga gräset betade ett slags Djur, som förut aldrig i NaturalHistorien varit kände, men som jag tyckte mycket liknade Antiloper. Vi gingo öfver ängen och fingo åter se en ström, men som var mycket stridare och större än den förra. Den verkligt gudomligen vackra Trakten började nu afväxla med kullar, ängar, lundar och små skogar. Ingen Menniska syntes.

Genom dessa sköna Landskap vandrade vi ännu några timmar, då vi slutligen kommo in i en dyster Lund. Den var beväxt med det tjusande vackra Trädslag jag nyss nämndt, men som ännu för NaturalHistorien var okändt. Detta Träd liknade till en del Palmen, genom sin lummighet och höjd: till en del Cypressen, genom sin dystra svalka och mörka färg. – Vi hvilade oss en liten stund i denna Lund, och såsom vi hörde en källa porla på litet afstånd, så beslöto vi att gå dit, för att släcka vår törst.

Vi gingo dit – men gripne af häpnad stadnade vi tvärt. En underskön Flicka låg på knä framföre källan, och tycktes vara försänkt i betraktande, antingen af vattnet, eller af sin egen bild uti vattnet. – Hon var, efter vårt sätt att se saken, mycket besynnerligt klädd. Håret nedföll från

n.   SWEDISH

VII.n.1.   C. J. L. ALMQVIST, from *Parjumouf: A Tale from New Holland*

When I was in London some six months ago, the unexpected Report to the Ministers and Parliament from the Governor of Botany Bay arrived telling that he had discovered a wonderful and fructiferous Land on the far side of the Blue Mountains, and that he already had made preparations for the founding of a new town by a river. – Since I was about to venture on a long voyage, not having decided which continent to select, I hastily decided to travel to Port Jackson in order to see for myself, and perhaps also make some discoveries in a part of the World, where no European had yet went.

I therefore immediately went to Portsmouth where a Ship lay ready to sail to the South Pacific. The captain was a respectable and able man. He would go to both Java and the Islands of the Moluccas. He also had a significant cargo of timber for the Colonies at Sidney Cove; – he would thus himself go to Botany Bay – and my travels were indeed conjoined to his.

The weather was quite fair; the journey went fast by: a peculiar shudder came over me when I saw the barren, immense Dunes of the great Ulimaroa. – I was very well received by the Governor of Botany Bay. He contentedly granted my request to journey inland for discoveries together with the other British officers. I thereafter spent some time making myself acquainted with the language of the Savages familiar to the British, and also made some other preparations for my planned Travels.

I will now omit the first three journeys we made. I only want to mention the fourth. – I made this delightful journey in the company of a young British Officer by the name of *Sandwich*. Having left Port Jackson, we had already arrived at the massive Ridge that shuts off the view from the inland territory, and that has been named the Blue Mountains. When we had climbed the peaks of these mountains, and turned North during the descent on the other side, we soon discovered a small clear mountain stream that set its course North down the Ridge. We followed the reaches of the stream. We soon arrived at pastures that were characterised by their living Greenery: a Greenery that was all the more refreshing to us, as the regions surrounding our Colony are horribly barren. – We walked for a few hours through the most wonderful Beech woods, came thence into other forests of beautiful trees whose name and nature we did not know; and among which we surely would have been lost had we not had the help of the compass. – We finally arrived in a meadow. There were no traces of Men; but some kind of Beast hitherto unknown to Natural Science, but that I found very similar to the Antelope, was grazing in the tall grass. We crossed the meadow and came upon another stream, but one that was more rapid and wider than the previous. These exceedingly divine and beautiful pastures now began to change into hills, meadows, groves and small forests. No Human being was to be seen.

Through these scenic Landscapes we wandered a few more hours yet, before we finally came into a gloomy grove. It was draped in the enchanting beautiful variety of tree that I just mentioned, but that was still unknown to Natural Science. In its lushness and height, this tree did somewhat look like the Palm Tree: in its gloomy shade and dark colour somewhat like the Cypress. – We rested for a short while in this Grove, and as we heard a rippling spring at some distance, we decided to go there to quench our thirst.

We went there – but seized by astonishment we stopped all at once. A wondrously beautiful Girl lay on her knees by the spring, and she seemed lost in contemplation, either of the water or of her own reflection in the water. – She was, from our way of looking at it, very peculiarly dressed. The

Hufvudet i långa, oflätade lockar, men rundt omkring Hufvudet gick ett band, hvaruti fjädrar af de skönaste färgor voro instuckna, och hvilka utgjorde liksom en krona öfver hennes hufvud. Halsen och brösten voro obetäckte: och, det som vi här minst väntade, hennes hy och skin af en bländande hvithet. Vi kunde alldeles icke begripa af hvad slags tyg hennes kläder voro gjorde: men de syntes vara ganska fina. På fötterna bar hon blott Sandaler.

Slutligen uppsteg hon. Jag nalkades henne vördsamt, och tänkte tilltala henne på samma Språk, som de öfrige Indianerne tala, som vi förut upptäckt på andra sidan om Blå Bergen. – "Sköna Flicka, sade jag, vredgas icke, om vi stört dig i din djupa betraktelse öfver Källans Vatten –"

Hon förstod rätt väl hvad jag sade, och, sedan hon med någon liten häpnad betraktat oss bägge, svarte hon mig småleende, men tillika med ett slags ljuft alfvar, som jag svårligen kan beskrifva: "Sköna Främling, du har visst icke begått något ondt, derigenom att du störde mig; min betraktelse var nu slutad: jag skådade blott i det klara vattnet mitt eget ansigte, för att efterse, om jag deruti skulle finna något fult och afskyvärdt, – ty det skulle ganska mycket förtörna Tiono." – Hon skyndade bort och försvann emellan Löfven. Vi stodo nästan orörlige af förundran, gjorde blott några utrop öfver hennes sköna Växt, och jag tillade, att Tiono var ett Namn, jag förut bland de andra Indianerne hade hört, och hvarmed de beteckna det högsta Väsendet, eller Himmelens Herre.

Efter en liten stund kom Indianskan tillbaka. Nu var all allvarsamhet försvunnen: en ljuf glädtighet strålade öfver hela hennes Väsende. "Bli inte onda öfver, att jag så hastigt lemnade Er, sade hon, men det var nödvändigt: – jag finner nog, att Ni är främlingar här, så väl af ert tal, som klädedrägt; – om det derföre roar Er, så följ mig; jag skall då visa Er hvarest jag nyss var."

Vi biföllo. En lätt rodnad flög öfver hennes kinder. Hon geck framföre: vi följde hennes knappt märkbara spår i gräset, och efter ett ögonblick stodo vi framför ett slags stor Löfsal; – om jag så får kalla det. Dess skönhet vill jag ej försöka att beskrifva. Det var ett stort rum, ungefär i form af en italiensk Rotunda. En mängd af de stora, sköna Träd, jag förut beskrifvit, stodo omkring i en tät rundel. Deras svarta stammar liknade nästan Colonner af svart Marmor. Deras lummiga blad och qvistar hade sammanflätat sig till de ogenomträngligaste skönaste Väggar, och topparne förenat sig i ett enda Hvalf till tak. Utom igenom ingången, inslapp icke något ljus, annars än från öster, der en trekantig öppning var gjord högt upp på väggen i Löfverket. Under det sken, som således inträngde från öster, var af blommor och gräs en liten kulle eller upphöjning bygd, liksom i form af ett altare. Jag gissade straxt, att detta var någon slags Pagod.

"Här, sade vår förtjusande Ledsagarinna, här knäfaller jag alltid inför Tiono, så snart jag upptäcker något fult i mina anletsdrag; ty det är alltid ett säkert tecken, att jag då bär något styggt i mitt Hjerta: och Tiono utplånar det alltid straxt, så snart jag bönfaller derom. Honom älskar jag öfver allting; till och med mer än min Far... mer än *Dujoumon...*"

"*Dujoumon*?" upprepade jag med en frågande mine

Hennes kinder stego i dunkel purpur. "Ja, sade hon, *Dujoumon* är den skönaste Yngling på Jorden. Också du är inte ful, ehuru något besynnerligt klädd. Dock är *Dujoumon* skönare, och hans ädla Växt är icke tvungen genom några trånga, konstiga kläder." – Nu tog hon hastigt min hand, och lade den på vänstra sidan, under sitt svallande obetäckta bröst. "Känner du, huru här slår? sade hon; i de dalar, hvarifrån du kommer, finnas väl också Flickor? – Då förstår du nog, hvarför hela mitt Väsende darrar och klappar, då jag talar om *Dujoumon*." –

Jag log, och darrade nästan lika så mycket som hon. "*Dujoumon* är då din Make," svarade jag något stammande.

hair fell from her Head in long, unbraided curls, but circumfering the Head there was a ribbon wherein feathers of the most beautiful colours were stuck, and that formed what seemed like a crown above her head. The neck and the breasts were uncovered: and, that which we expected the least, her hue and skin were of a blinding whiteness. We could not understand of what fabric her clothes were made: but they seemed quite exquisite. On her feet she wore only Sandals.

Finally, she got up. I approached her respectfully, and thought to address her in the same Language, that the other Indians spoke, whom we had discovered earlier on the other side of the Blue Mountains. – 'Fair Girl,' I said, 'be not angry, if we have disturbed you in your deep contemplation of the Water of the Spring–'

She understood fairly well what I said, and, after having looked upon us with some amazement, she answered with a faint smile, but also with a kind of sweet sincerity, that I scarcely can describe: 'Fair Stranger, you have not committed any evilry, when you disturbed me; my meditation was over: I saw in the clear water only my own face, and looked to see if I would find anything ugly and abominable therein, – for it would greatly anger Tiono.' She hurried away and disappeared between the Leaves. We stood nearly motionless out of wonder, only making a few exclamations on her fair Appearance, and I added, that Tiono was a name, that I had previously heard among the other Indians, and that it was one that used to signify the highest Being, or the Lord of Heaven.

The Indian returned after a short while. Now all earnestness was gone: a lovely cheerfulness radiated from her entire Being. 'Do not be angry because I left You so hastily,' she said, 'but it was necessary: – I do understand that You are strangers here, from your words, as from your dress; – if it pleases You, come with me; and I will show You whence I just was.'

We agreed. A slight blush came over her cheeks. She went in front: we followed her barely discernible tracks in the grass, and after a while we stood before a grand Hall of leaves of sorts, if I may call it thus. Its beauty I will not try to describe. It was a great hall, approximately the shape of an Italian Rotunda. A number of the big, beautiful trees I described previously stood densely around a circular space. Their black trunks looked almost like Columns of black Marble. Their lush leaves and sprigs had intertwined themselves into the most impenetrable and beautiful Walls, and the treetops had joined into one vault for a ceiling. Other than through the entrance, no light entered but from the east, where a triangular opening had been made high up the foliage wall. In the light that thus entered from the east a grassy and flower-covered knoll or elevation had been erected, as in the shape of an altar. Not before long, I soon guessed that this was some kind of Pagoda.

'Here,' our lovely escort said, 'here I always kneel before Tiono, as soon as I discover something ugly in my features; for it is a certain sign, that I carry something nasty in my heart: and Tiono always blots it out as soon as I pray him to. Him, I love above everything; even more than my Father . . . more than *Dujoumon* . . .'

'Dujoumon?' I repeated with an inquiring expression.

Her cheeks rose to a dark purple. 'Yes,' she said, '*Dujoumon* is the most beautiful young man on Earth.' 'You may not be ugly, if somewhat peculiarly dressed, but *Dujoumon* is more beautiful, and his noble Appearance is not forced into tight, strange clothes.' – Here she hastily took my hand, and placed it on her left side, under her heaving uncovered breast. 'Can you feel how it beats here?' she said; 'in the valleys where you come from, there must be Girls too?' – Then you understand why my whole Being trembles and pounds when I speak of *Dujoumon*?' –

I smiled, and trembled nearly as much as she did. 'Then *Dujoumon* must be your Husband,' I answered, somewhat faltering.

"Nej, han är det icke; men blir det snart. Hvar dag, sedan jag slutat fläta mina röda Korgar, springer jag bort till honom, eller kommer han till mig. Också i afton, tillade hon småleende, i afton skola vi äfven träffas. Då komma vi visst att tala länge, länge. Kanske långt inpå natten skola vi sitta tillsammans; ty i morgon...."

"Nå, i morgon?" sade jag med häftighet.

"Ja, bäste Främling, sade hon med någon förlägenhet, jag vet ej, om du rätt skulle kunna fatta, det jag ville säga: derföre afbröt jag. Nog märker jag på dina kläder, att du ej är kommen från närliggande Dalar. – Brukas det också hos Er, såsom hos oss? – När hos oss en Flicka och en Gosse hålla af hvarandra, så mycket, som *Dujoumon* och jag, så komma de alltid bägge öfverens, att lefva tillsammans, så länge de lefva. De underrätta då sina Föräldrar derom, och en viss dag utsättes, som vi kalla Förenings-Högtiden. – På denna dag falla de bägge på knä bredvid den åt Tiono helgade Blomsterkullen. Då ställer sig en af Fäderne midt framför dem, tar bägge deras händer och lägger i sin högra hand. De bägge unga förklara då fritt och högtidligt, att de inför Tionos ansigte önska få lefva tillsammans så länge de lefva. Derpå lägger Fadren sina Händer på deras Hufvuden och frågar: om de nånsin kysst hvarandra? Bägge bedyra de då heligt inför Tiono, att de aldrig nånsin kysst hvarandras mun. Nu tar Fadren den heliga blomman, som vi kalla Imla, och stryker dermed sakta öfver bägges munnar. Så lägger han deras armar om hvarandra, och sluter dem tillsammans i en enda famn. Bägge blunda de nu, och gifva hvarann så den första kyssen. Då säger Ynglingen till henne: *Nu är Du min!* – men Flickan...."

"Nå hvad säger då Flickan? ropade jag, hvad säger Flickan?"

"Hon säger inte också till honom: Nu är Du min! – utan hon säger: *Nu är Jag din!* – och det är just detta, som jag i morgon skall säga åt *Dujoumon.*"

Sandwich och jag sågo på hvarandra med leende nästan tårfulla blickar, liksom frågande, om det var till Ulimaroa vi hade farit, för att med så fina nuancer af känslor få en Beskrifning på, hvad ett Bröllop ville säga.

Den lilla Flickan, som ej förstod orsaken till vår tystnad, men förmodligen märkte rörelsen i mitt ansigte, tillade: "Också Du är visst en god Yngling, det ser jag. – – Men nu har min Far låtit uppbygga ett vackert Tält åt oss. Alldeles på samma sätt, som han och min Mamma bo tillsammans, så skall också *Dujoumon* bo med mig i det Tältet, sedan vi i morgon till tecken af vår förening gifvit hvarandra den första Kyssen...."

"Den första? – Söta Flicka, sade jag, du träffar ju din älskade *Dujoumon* hvarje dag, hvarje afton, huru kan du då i morgon vid Blomsterkullen heligt bedyra, att du aldrig förr kysst honom? Det har du dock visst gjort många gånger?"

Den lilla Flickan skakade bekymrad på hufvudet. "Hvarföre frågar du så? sade hon med ömhet; Tiono har ju befallt, att innan den heliga Föreningsdagen får ingen Gosse och Flicka kyssa hvarandras mun? Det vet du ju? Hvarför frågar du mig då, om jag gjort det, som är omöjligt att göra? – Förlåt, gode Främling; jag är mycket enfaldig, och förstår så litet: jag förstod ej din mening?" –

(1817)

'No, he is not; but will soon become it. Every day since I stopped weaving my red Baskets, I run to him, or he comes to me.' 'Tonight too,' she added with a smile, 'we will meet again tonight. We will speak for a long, long time. Maybe into the night; for tomorrow . . .'

'Well, tomorrow?' I said fiercely.

'Yes, good Stranger,' she said somewhat warily, 'I know not if you could rightly understand what I had to say, and that is why I interrupted you. I can well tell from your dress that you do not come from any Valley close by. – Is it Your custom too, as it is ours? – When a Girl and a Boy among us are fond of each other, as much as *Dujoumon* and I am, then they always agree to live together for as long as they live. They then inform their Parents, and a certain day is set, that we call the Union Feast – On this day they both kneel down before the mound of flowers sanctified to Tiono. Then one of the Fathers will stand before them, take their hands and place them in his right hand. The two young ones then declare openly and solemnly before Tiono's face that they wish to live together for as long as they live. The Father then places his Hands upon their Heads and asks: if they have ever kissed each other? Both then solemnly swear before Tiono, that they have never kissed each other's lips. The Father now takes the holy flower, that we call Imla, and rubs it gently on both their lips. And the Father places their arms on each other, and joins them together in one embrace. Both now shut their eyes, and give each other the first kiss. Then the young man says to her: *Now you are mine!* – but the Girl . . .'

'Well, what says the Girl?' I cried, 'what says the Girl?'

'She does not repeat to him: Now you are mine! – But she says: *Now I am yours!* – and it is this, that I will say to *Dujoumon* tomorrow.'

Sandwich and I looked at each other with smiling almost tearful eyes, as if asking if we had gone to Ulimaroa so that we could be given with so subtle feelings a Description of what a Wedding meant.

But the little Girl who could not understand the reason for our silence, but who probably could trace the emotion in my face, added: 'I can tell that You too are a good Young man. – – But now my Father has had a beautiful Tent raised for us. In the very same way that he and my Mother live together, so shall *Dujoumon* live with me in that Tent, after we have given each other the first Kiss as a sign of our union . . . .'

'The first? – Dear Girl,' I said, 'you meet with your beloved *Dujoumon* every day, every night, how can you then swear at the flower-covered mound tomorrow, that you have never kissed him before? You have surely done it many times?'

The little Girl shook her head in consternation. 'Why do you ask this?' she said tenderly; 'Tiono has commanded that before the holy day of Union no Boy and Girl can kiss each other's lips? You know this? Why do you ask me if I have done this, which is impossible to do? – Forgive me, good Stranger; I am very simple, and understand so little: I did not understand your intention?' –

(1817) [*Translated by Mattias Bolkéus Blom*]

VIII. Science

Romanticism has often been assumed to be somehow 'anti-science'. While there are significant texts that are concerned with the possible negative effects of the way the sciences 'disenchant' nature, there are also many major Romantic writers and thinkers who were themselves scientists or who sought inspiration from scientists. Humphrey Davey and Shelley are closely linked by a common interest in the detailed workings of the physical world. The ambivalent role of science in modernity, which can be the source of human well-being and the source of utter misery, is reflected in Romanticism's divided approaches to the status and role of the natural sciences. Texts by Romantic scientists themselves are juxtaposed with other texts welcoming, satirizing and fearful of the results of the sciences.

a. BRITISH

VIII.a.1. THOMAS ROBERT MALTHUS, from *An Essay on the Principle of Population*

[From Chapter 1]

I think I may fairly make two postulata.

First, That food is necessary to the existence of man.

Secondly, That the passion between the sexes is necessary and will remain nearly in its present state.

These two laws, ever since we have had any knowledge of mankind, appear to have been fixed laws of our nature, and, as we have not hitherto seen any alteration in them, we have no right to conclude that they will ever cease to be what they now are, without an immediate act of power in that Being who first arranged the system of the universe, and for the advantage of his creatures, still executes, according to fixed laws, all its various operations.

I do not know that any writer has supposed that on this earth man will ultimately be able to live without food. But Mr Godwin has conjectured that the passion between the sexes may in time be extinguished. As, however, he calls this part of his work a deviation into the land of conjecture, I will not dwell longer upon it at present than to say that the best arguments for the perfectibility of man are drawn from a contemplation of the great progress that he has already made from the savage state and the difficulty of saying where he is to stop. But towards the extinction of the passion between the sexes, no progress whatever has hitherto been made. It appears to exist in as much force at present as it did two thousand or four thousand years ago. There are individual exceptions now as there always have been. But, as these exceptions do not appear to increase in number, it would surely be a very unphilosophical mode of arguing to infer, merely from the existence of an exception, that the exception would, in time, become the rule, and the rule the exception.

Assuming then my postulata as granted, I say, that the power of population is indefinitely greater than the power in the earth to produce subsistence for man.

Population, when unchecked, increases in a geometrical ratio. Subsistence increases only in an arithmetical ratio. A slight acquaintance with numbers will shew the immensity of the first power in comparison of the second.

By that law of our nature which makes food necessary to the life of man, the effects of these two unequal powers must be kept equal. This implies a strong and constantly operating check on population from the difficulty of subsistence. This difficulty must fall somewhere and must necessarily be severely felt by a large portion of mankind.

Through the animal and vegetable kingdoms, nature has scattered the seeds of life abroad with the most profuse and liberal hand. She has been comparatively sparing in the room and the nourishment necessary to rear them. The germs of existence contained in this spot of earth, with ample food, and ample room to expand in, would fill millions of worlds in the course of a few thousand years. Necessity, that imperious all pervading law of nature, restrains them within the prescribed bounds. The race of plants and the race of animals shrink under this great restrictive law. And the race of man cannot, by any efforts of reason, escape from it. Among plants and animals its effects are waste of seed, sickness, and premature death. Among mankind, misery and vice. The former, misery, is an absolutely necessary consequence of it. Vice is a highly probable consequence, and we therefore see it abundantly prevail, but it ought not, perhaps, to be called an absolutely necessary consequence. The ordeal of virtue is to resist all temptation to evil.

This natural inequality of the two powers of population and of production in the earth, and that great law of our nature which must constantly keep their effects equal, form the great difficulty that to me appears insurmountable in the way to the perfectibility of society. All other arguments are of slight and subordinate consideration in comparison of this. I see no way by which man can escape from the weight of this law which pervades all animated nature. No fancied equality, no agrarian regulations in their utmost extent, could remove the pressure of it even for a single century. And it appears, therefore, to be decisive against the possible existence of a society, all the members of which should live in ease, happiness, and comparative leisure; and feel no anxiety about providing the means of subsistence for themselves and families.

Consequently, if the premises are just, the argument is conclusive against the perfectibility of the mass of mankind.

I have thus sketched the general outline of the argument, but I will examine it more particularly, and I think it will be found that experience, the true source and foundation of all knowledge, invariably confirms its truth.

(1798)

VIII.a.2. JAMES COOK, from *The Journals*

Journal on Board His majesty's Bark Resolution

THURSDAY *17th* [March 1774] PM . . . No Nation will ever contend for the honour of the discovery of Easter Island as there is hardly an Island in this sea which affords less refreshments and conveniences for Shipping than it does; Nature has hardly provided it with any thing fit for man to eat or drink, and as the Natives are but few and may be supposed to plant no more than sufficient for themselves, they cannot have much to spare to new comers.

The Inhabitants of this isle from what we have been able to see of them do not exceed six or seven hundred souls and above two thirds of these are Men, they either have but few Women

among them or else many were not suffer'd to make their appearance, the latter seems most Probable. They are certainly of the same race of People as the New Zealanders and the other islanders, the affinity of the Language, Colour and some of their customs all tend to prove it, I think they bearing more affinity to the Inhabitants of Amsterdam and New Zealand, than those of the more northern isles which makes it probable that there lies a chain of isles in about this Parallel or under, some of which have at different times been seen . . .

Of their Religion, Government &c we can say nothing with certainty. The Stupendous stone statues errected in different places along the Coast are certainly no representation of any Deity or places of worship; but the most probable Burial Places for certain Tribes or Families. I my self saw a human Skeleton lying in the foundation of one just covered with Stones, what I call the foundation is an oblong square about 20 or 30 feet by 10 or 12 built of and faced with hewn stones of a vast size, executed in so masterly a manner as sufficiently shews the ingenuity of the age in which they were built. The Statue is errected in the middle of its foundation, it is about [15 to 30 feet] high and [from 16 to 24] round for this is its shape, all the appearances it has of a human figure is in the head where all the parts are in proportion to its Size; the head is crow[n] ed with a Stone of the shape and full size of a drum, we could not help wondering how they were set up, indeed if the Island was once Inhabited by a race of Giants of 12 feet high as one of the Authors of Roggewein's Voyage tells us, than this wonder ceaseth and gives place to another equally as extraordinary, viz. to know what is become of this race of giants. . . .

(1774) [1955–1967]

VIII.a.3. JOHN KEATS, 'On First Looking into Chapman's Homer'

> Much have I travell'd in the realms of gold,
>   And many goodly states and kingdoms seen;
>   Round many western islands have I been
> Which bards in fealty to Apollo hold.
> Oft of one wide expanse had I been told
>   That deep-brow'd Homer ruled as his demesne;
>   Yet did I never breathe its pure serene
> Till I heard Chapman speak out loud and bold:
> Then felt I like some watcher of the skies
>   When a new planet swims into his ken;
> Or like stout Cortez when with eagle eyes
>   He star'd at the Pacific – and all his men
> Look'd at each other with a wild surmise –
>   Silent, upon a peak in Darien.

(1817)

VIII.a.4. CHARLES LYELL, from *Principles of Geology*

In our first volume we treated of the changes which have taken place in the inorganic world within the historical era, and we must next turn our attention to those now in progress in the animate creation. In examining this class of phenomena, we shall treat first of the vicissitudes to

which *species* are subject, and afterwards consider the influence of the powers of vitality in modifying the surface of the earth and the material constituents of its crust.

The first of these divisions will lead us, among other topics, to inquire, first, whether species have a real and permanent existence in nature; or whether they are capable, as some naturalists pretend, of being indefinitely modified in the course of a long series of generations? Secondly, whether, if species have a real existence, the individuals composing them have been derived originally from many similar stocks, or each from one only, the descendants of which have spread themselves so gradually from a particular point over the habitable lands and waters? Thirdly, how far the duration of each species of animal and plant is limited by its dependence on certain fluctuating and temporary conditions in the state of the animate and inanimate world? Fourthly, whether there be proofs of the successive extermination of species in the ordinary course of nature, and whether there be any reason for conjecturing that new animals and plants are created from time to time, to supply their place?

Before we can advance a step in our proposed inquiry, we must be able to define precisely the meaning we attach to the term species. This is even more necessary in geology than in the ordinary studies of the naturalist; for they who deny that such a thing as species exists, concede nevertheless that a botanist or zoologist may reason as if the specific character were constant, because they confine their observations to a brief period of time.

(1830–1833)

d. FRANÇAIS

VIII.d.1. HONORÉ DE BALZAC, *La recherche de l'absolu*

– Quoi! dit Balthazar en se dressant dans la chambre et jetant un regard perçant à sa femme, tu blâmes ton mari de s'élever au-dessus des autres hommes, afin de pouvoir jeter sous tes pieds la pourpre divine de la gloire, comme une minime offrande auprès des trésors de ton coeur! Mais tu ne sais donc pas ce que j'ai fait, depuis trois ans? des pas de géant! ma Pépita, dit-il en s'animant. Son visage parut alors à sa femme plus étincelant sous le feu du génie qu'il ne l'avait été sous le feu de l'amour, et elle pleura en l'écoutant. – J'ai combiné le chlore et l'azote, j'ai décomposé plusieurs corps jusqu'ici considérés comme simples, j'ai trouvé de nouveaux métaux. Tiens, dit-il en voyant les pleurs de sa femme, j'ai décomposé les larmes. Les larmes contiennent un peu de phosphate de chaux, de chlorure de sodium, du mucus et de l'eau. Il continua de parler sans voir l'horrible convulsion qui travailla la physionomie de Joséphine, il était monté sur la Science qui l'emportait en croupe, ailes déployées, bien loin du monde matériel. – Cette analyse, ma chère, est une des meilleures preuves du système de l'Absolu. Toute vie implique une combustion. Selon le plus ou moins d'activité du foyer, la vie est plus ou moins persistante. Ainsi la destruction du minéral est indéfiniment retardée, parce que la combustion y est virtuelle, latente ou insensible. Ainsi les végétaux qui se rafraîchissent incessamment par la combinaison d'où résulte l'humide, vivent indéfiniment, et il existe plusieurs végétaux contemporains du dernier cataclysme. Mais, toutes les fois que la nature a perfectionné un appareil, que dans un but ignoré elle y a jeté le sentiment, l'instinct ou l'intelligence, trois degrés marqués dans le système organique, ces trois organismes veulent une combustion dont l'activité est en raison directe du résultat obtenu. L'homme, qui représente le plus haut point de l'intelligence et qui nous offre le seul appareil d'où résulte un pouvoir à demi créateur, *la pensée!* est, parmi les créations zoologiques, celle où la combustion se rencontre dans son degré le plus intense et dont les puissants effets

d. FRENCH

VIII.d.1. HONORÉ DE BALZAC, from *The Alkahest or The House of Claës*

'What!' says Balthazar drawing himself up in his bedroom and throwing a piercing look at his wife, 'you blame your husband for raising himself above other men, in order to be able to throw under your feet the divine purple of glory, like a tiny offering next to the treasures of your heart! But then do you not know at all what I have done, for three years? Giant steps! My Pépita,' he said, growing animated. His face then appeared to his wife more gleaming under the fire of genius than it had ever been under the fire of love, and she wept while listening to him. 'I have combined chlorine and nitrogen, I have decomposed several substances until now considered simples, I have discovered new metals. Look,' he says, seeing his wife's tears, 'I have decomposed tears. Tears contain a little phosphate of lime, sodium chloride, mucus, and water.' He continued speaking without seeing the horrible convulsion which tormented the face of Joséphine, he was mounted pillion upon Science, which was carrying him off, wings unfolded, far away from the material world. 'This analysis, my dear, is one of the best proofs of the system of the Absolute. All life involves combustion. According to the greater or lesser amount of activity in the furnace, life is more or less persistent. Thus the destruction of minerals is indefinitely delayed, because the combustion in them is virtual, latent, or imperceptible. Thus plants, which are continually refreshed by the combination from which humidity results, live indefinitely, and there exist some plants contemporary with the last cataclysm. But, every time that nature perfects an apparatus, that, for an unknown purpose, she cast into it sentiment, instinct, or intelligence, three marked degrees in the organic system, these three organisms desire a combustion whose activity is in direct proportion to the result obtained. Man, who represents the highest point of intelligence and who offers us the only apparatus from which there results an ability to be half a creator – thought! – is, among members of the animal kingdom, the one where combustion is found in the most intense

sont en quelque sorte révélés par les phosphates, les sulfates et les carbonates que fournit son corps dans notre analyse. Ces substances ne seraient-elles pas les traces que laisse en lui l'action du fluide électrique, principe de toute fécondation? L'électricité ne se manifesterait-elle pas en lui par des combinaisons plus variées qu'en tout autre animal? N'aurait-il pas des facultés plus grandes que toute autre créature pour absorber de plus fortes portions du principe absolu, et ne se les assimilerait-il pas pour en composer dans une plus parfaite machine, sa force et ses idées! Je le crois. L'homme est un matras. Ainsi selon moi, l'idiot serait celui dont le cerveau contiendrait le moins de phosphore ou tout autre produit de l'électro-magnétisme, le fou celui dont le cerveau en contiendrait trop, l'homme ordinaire celui qui en aurait peu, l'homme de génie celui dont la cervelle en serait saturée à un degré convenable. L'homme constamment amoureux, le porte-faix, le danseur, le grand mangeur, sont ceux qui déplaceraient la force résultante de leur appareil électrique. Ainsi, nos sentiments...

– Assez, Balthazar; tu m'épouvantes, tu commets des sacrilèges. Quoi! mon amour serait...

– De la matière éthérée qui se dégage, dit Claës, et qui sans doute est le mot de l'Absolu. Songe donc que si moi, moi le premier! si je trouve, si je trouve, si je trouve! En disant ces mots sur trois tons différents, son visage monta par degrés à l'expression de l'inspiré. Je fais les métaux, je fais les diamants, je répète la nature, s'écria-t-il.

– En seras-tu plus heureux? cria-t-elle avec désespoir. Maudite Science, maudit démon! tu oublies, Claës, que tu commets le péché d'orgueil dont fut coupable Satan. Tu entreprends sur Dieu.

– Oh! oh! Dieu!

– Il le nie! s'écria-t-elle en se tordant les mains. Claës, Dieu dispose d'une puissance que tu n'auras jamais.

A cet argument qui semblait annuler sa chère Science, il regarda sa femme en tremblant.

– Quoi! dit-il.

– La force unique, le mouvement. Voilà ce que j'ai saisi à travers les livres que tu m'as contrainte à lire. Analyse des fleurs, des fruits, du vin de Malaga; tu découvriras certes leurs principes qui viennent, comme ceux de ton cresson, dans un milieu qui semble leur être étranger; tu peux, à la rigueur, les trouver dans la nature; mais en les rassemblant, feras-tu ces fleurs, ces fruits, le vin de Malaga? auras-tu les incompréhensibles effets du soleil, auras-tu l'atmosphère de l'Espagne? Décomposer n'est pas créer.

– Si je trouve la force coërcitive, je pourrai créer.

(1834)

e. DEUTSCH

VIII.e.1. NOVALIS, *Das allgemeine Brouillon* (1798)

89. Phys[ikalische] Kunstl[ehre]

Wie wenig Menschen haben *Genie* zum Experimentiren. Der ächte Experimentator muß ein *dunkles Gefühl der Natur* in sich haben, das ihn, je vollkomner seine Anlagen sind, um so sicherer auf seinem Gange leitet und mit desto größerer *Genauigkeit* das versteckte entscheidende Phaenomèn finden und bestimmen läßt. Die Natur *inspirirt* gleichsam den

degree and of which the powerful effects are in some way revealed by the phosphates, sulfates, and carbonates which his body furnishes in our analysis. Are these substances not the traces which are left in him by the action of the electric fluid, the principle of all fertility? Would not electricity be made manifest in him by more varied combinations than in any other animal? Would he not have greater faculties than any other creature for absorbing larger amounts of the absolute principle, and would he not assimilate them in order to create from them, in a more perfect machine, his strength and his ideas? I believe it. Man is a laboratory flask. So, in my opinion, the idiot would be the one whose brain contained the least phosphorus or any other product of electromagnetism; the madman, the one whose brain contained too much of it; the ordinary man, the one who had little of it; and the man of genius, the one whose brain was saturated with it to a suitable degree. The constantly amorous, the porter, the dancer, the big eater, would be those who displace the strength resulting from their electric apparatus. Thus, our sentiments . . .'

'Enough, Balthazar; you're scaring me, you're committing sacrilege. What! My love would be . . .'

'Of the ethereal material that is emitted,' said Claës, 'and which without doubt is the word of the Absolute. Think, then, that if I – I, the first! – if I find it, if I find it, if I find it!' In saying these words in three different tones, his face rose by degrees to the expression of one inspired. 'I make metals, I made diamonds, I repeat nature,' he exclaimed.

'Will it make you happier?' she cried with despair. 'Cursed Science, cursed demon! You forget, Claës, that you are committing the sin of pride, of which Satan was guilty. You're infringing on God.'

'Oh! Oh! God!'

'He denies him,' she exclaimed, wringing her hands. 'Claës, God wields a power that you will never have.'

At this argument, which seemed to annul his precious Science, he looked at his wife, trembling. 'What!' he said.

'Unique force, movement. See what I have understood through the books that you compelled me to read. Analysis of flowers, of fruits, of Malaga wine; you will certainly discover their principles which come, like those of your watercress, to an environment that seems strange to their being; you can, if necessary, find them in nature; but, in gathering them together, will you make these flowers, these fruits, this Malaga wine? Will you have the incomprehensible effects of the sun, will you have the atmosphere of Spain? Decomposing is not creating.'

'If I find the coercive force, I will be able to create.'

[*Translated by David J. White. Edited by Anne Gwin*]

e. GERMAN

VIII.e.1. NOVALIS, excerpts from *Notes for a Romantic Encyclopaedia*

89. Physical Theory of Art:

How few people have a *genius* for experimenting. The true experimenter must have a *dim feeling for Nature* within himself, which – depending on the perfection of his faculties – guides him with unfailing surety along his path, allowing him to discover and determine with much greater *precision*, the hidden and decisive phenomenon. Nature *inspires* the true

ächten Liebhaber und offenbart sich um so vollkommner durch ihn — je harmonischer seine *Constitution* mit ihr ist. Der ächte Naturliebhaber zeichnet sich eben durch seine Fertigkeit die Experimente zu vervielfältigen, zu vereinfachen, zu combiniren, und zu analysiren, zu romantisiren und popularisiren, durch seinen Erfindungsgeist neuer Experimente — durch seine Naturgeschmackvolle oder Natursinnreiche Auswahl und Anordnung derselben, durch Schärfe und Deutlichkeit der Beobachtung, und artistische, sowohl zusammengefaßte, als ausführliche Beschreibung, oder Darstellung der Beobachtung aus. Also — Auch Experimentator ist nur das Genie.

911.

Experimentiren mit Bildern und Begriffen im Vorstell[ungs] V[ermögen] ganz auf eine dem phys[ikalischen] Experim[entiren] analoge Weise. Zus[ammen] Setzen. Entstehn lassen — etc.

924.

Plotin war schon in Betreff der meisten Resultate — kritischer Idealist und Realist./ Fichtes und Kants Methode ist noch nicht vollst[ändig] und genau genug dargestellt. Beyde wissen noch nicht mit Leichtigkeit und Mannichfaltigkeit zu experimentiren — uberhaupt nicht *poëtisch* — Alles ist so steif, so ängstlich noch.

Die freye *Generationsmethode* d[er] Wahrheit kann noch sehr erweitert und simplificirt - überhaupt verbessert werden. Da ist nun diese ächte Experimentirkunst - Die *Wissenschaft* des *thätigen Empirismus*. (Aus d[er] *Tradition* ist *Lehre* geworden) (Alle *Lehre* bezieht sich auf Kunst — Praxis.)

Man muß d[ie] Wahrheit überall vergegenwärtigen — überall *repraesentiren* (im thätigen, producirenden Sinn) können.

934.

Schon das Gewissen beweißt unser Verhältniß — Verknüpfung — (Die Übergangsmöglichk[eit]) mit einer andern Welt — eine innre unabhängige Macht und einen Zustand außer der *gemeinen Individualitaet*. Die Vernunft ist nichts anders. Der État de Raison ist *ekstatisch*. (D[urch] d[ie] *Connexion* mit dem *Vater* kann man Wunder thun.) Auf diesem *Beweise* beruht die Möglichkeit des thätigen Empirismus. Wir werden erst Physiker werden, wenn wir *imaginative* — Stoffe und Kr[äfte] zum regulat[iven] Maaßstab der Naturstoffe und Kr[äfte] machen.

1093.

Der *Poët* versteht die Natur besser, wie der wissenschaftliche Kopf.

> [*Novalis. Schriften, Historisch-kritische Ausgabe by Paul Kluckhohn, Richard Samuel, Hans-Joachim Mähl, Gerhard Schulz, 7 vols. Stuttgart, Berlin, Cologne, Mainz: Kohlhammer, 1960–, III. 256, 443, 445, 468*]

lover, as it were, and reveals herself all the more completely through him – the more his *constitution* is in harmony with her. Thus the true lover of Nature distinguishes himself by his skill in multiplying and simplifying, combining and analyzing, romanticizing and popularizing the experiments, by his ability in inventing new experiments – by his tasteful and ingenious selection and arrangement of Nature, his acuteness and clarity of observation, and by his artistic and concise, as well as extensive, descriptions, or presentations of his observations,

Thus –

the genius alone is the experimenter.

911.

Experimenting with images and concepts within the faculty of representation in a manner wholly analogous to physical experimenting. Associating. Allowing to arise – etc.

924.

With respect to the majority of results, Plotinus was already – a critical idealist and realist./ The method of Fichte and Kant is not yet complete or presented precisely enough. Both still do not know how to experiment with facility and diversity – absolutely *unpoetic* – Everything is still so awkward, so tentative.

The *method for the free generation* of truth may yet become greatly broadened and simplified – thoroughly improved. There now exists a true art of experimenting – The *science of active empiricism*. (*Theory* arises from *tradition*) (All *theory* relates to art – praxis).

We must everywhere call to mind the truth – everywhere be capable of *representing* (in the active, productive sense).

934.

Conscience already demonstrates our relationship – connection – (the possibility of a transition) to another world – an inner independent power, and a state apart from the *common* individuality. Reason is no different. The *état de raison* is *ecstatic*. (One can perform wonders through the *connection* with the *Father*).

The possibility of active empiricism is based on this *proof*. We will only become physicists if we make *imaginative* substances and forces – into the regulative standard for natural substances and forces.

1093.

The *poet* understands Nature better than the scientific mind.

[*Notes for a Romantic Encyclopaedia. Das allgemeine Brouillon. Novalis.
Translated, edited, and with an Introduction by David M. Wood.
Albany: SUNY, 2007. 14–15, 162, 164, 166, 182*]

VIII.e.2. Goethe on Polarität und Steigerung Die Natur; Erläuterung

DIE NATUR

Fragment

(Aus dem "Tiefurter Journal" 1783)

Natur! Wir sind von ihr umgeben und umschlungen – unvermögend aus ihr herauszutreten, und unvermögend tiefer in sie hineinzukommen. Ungebeten und ungewarnt nimmt sie uns in den Kreislauf ihres Tanzes auf und treibt sich mit uns fort, bis wir ermüdet sind und ihrem Arme entfallen.

Sie schafft ewig neue Gestalten; was da ist war noch nie, was war kommt nicht wieder – Alles ist neu und doch immer das Alte.

Wir leben mitten in ihr und sind ihr fremde. Sie spricht unaufhörlich mit uns und verrät uns ihr Geheimnis nicht. Wir wirken beständig auf sie und haben doch keine Gewalt über sie.

Sie scheint alles auf Individualität angelegt zu haben und macht sich nichts aus den Individuen. Sie baut immer und zerstört immer und ihre Werkstätte ist unzugänglich.

Sie lebt in lauter Kindern, und die Mutter, wo ist sie? – Sie ist die einzige Künstlerin: aus dem simpelsten Stoffe zu den größten Kontrasten: ohne Schein der Anstrengung zu der größten Vollendung – zur genausten Bestimmtheit immer mit etwas Weichem überzogen. Jedes ihrer Werke hat ein eigenes Wesen, jede ihrer Erscheinungen den isoliertesten Begriff und doch macht alles eins aus.

Sie spielt ein Schauspiel: ob sie es selbst sieht, wissen wir nicht, und doch spielt sies für uns, die wir in der Ecke stehen.

Es ist ein ewiges Leben, Werden und Bewegen in ihr und doch rückt sie nicht weiter. Sie verwandelt sich ewig und ist kein Moment Stillestehen in ihr. Fürs Bleiben hat sie keinen Begriff und ihren Fluch hat sie ans Stillestehen gehängt. Sie ist fest. Ihr Tritt ist gemessen, ihre Ausnahmen selten, ihre Gesetze unwandelbar.

Gedacht hat sie und sinnt beständig; aber nicht als ein Mensch, sondern als Natur. Sie hat sich einen eigenen allumfassenden Sinn vorbehalten, den ihr niemand abmerken kann.

Die Menschen sind all in ihr und sie in allen. Mit allen treibt sie ein freundliches Spiel, und freut sich, je mehr man ihr abgewinnt. Sie treibts mit vielen so im verborgenen, daß sies zu Ende spielt, ehe sies merken.

Auch das Unnatürlichste ist Natur. Wer sie nicht allenthalben sieht, sieht sie nirgendwo recht.

Sie liebet sich selber und haftet ewig mit Augen und Herzen ohne Zahl an sich selbst. Sie hat sich auseinander gesetzt um sich selbst zu genießen. Immer läßt sie neue Genießer erwachsen, unersättlich sich mitzuteilen.

Sie freut sich an der Illusion. Wer diese in sich und andern zerstört, den straft sie als der strengste Tyrann. Wer ihr zutraulich folgt, den drückt sie wie ein Kind an ihr Herz.

Ihre Kinder sind ohne Zahl. Keinem ist sie überall karg, aber sie hat Lieblinge, an die sie viel verschwendet und denen sie viel aufopfert. Ans Große hat sie ihren Schutz geknüpft.

Sie spritzt ihre Geschöpfe aus dem Nichts hervor, und sagt ihnen nicht, woher sie kommen und wohin sie gehen. Sie sollen nur laufen. Die Bahn kennt sie.

Sie hat wenige Triebfedern, aber nie abgenutzte, immer wirksam, immer mannigfaltig.

Ihr Schauspiel ist immer neu, weil sie immer neue Zuschauer schafft. Leben ist ihre schönste Erfindung, und der Tod ist ihr Kunstgriff viel Leben zu haben.

Sie hüllt den Menschen in Dumpfheit ein und spornt ihn ewig zum Lichte. Sie macht ihn abhängig zur Erde, träg und schwer und schüttelt ihn immer wieder auf.

VIII.e.2: Goethe on Polarity and Intensification; 'Nature'; Commentary on 'Nature'

Nature

[A Fragment by Georg Christoph Tobler]

Nature! We are surrounded and embraced by her – powerless to leave her and powerless to enter her more deeply. Unasked and without warning she sweeps us away in the round of her dance and dances on until we fall exhausted from her arms.

She brings forth ever new forms: what is there, never was; what was, never will return. All is new, and yet forever old.

We live within her, and are strangers to her. She speaks perpetually with us, and does not betray her secret. We work on her constantly, and yet have no power over her.

All her effort seems bent toward individuality, and she cares nothing for individuals. She builds always, destroys always, and her workshop is beyond our reach.

She lives in countless children, and the mother – where is she? She is the sole artist, creating extreme contrast out of the simplest material, the greatest perfection seemingly without effort, the most definite clarity always veiled with a touch of softness. Each of her works has its own being, each of her phenomena its separate idea, and yet all create a single whole.

She plays out a drama: we know not whether she herself sees it, and yet she plays it for us, we who stand in the corner.

There is everlasting life, growth, and movement in her and yet she does not stir from her place. She transforms herself constantly and there is never a moment's pause in her. She has no name for respite, and she has set her curse upon inactivity. She is firm. Her tread is measured, her exceptions rare, her laws immutable.

She thought and she thinks still, not as man, but as nature. She keeps to herself her own all-embracing thoughts which none may discover from her.

All men are in her and she in all. With all she plays a friendly game, and is glad as our winnings grow. With many she plays a hidden game which is ended before they know it.

Even what is most unnatural is nature. The one who does not see her everywhere sees her nowhere clearly.

She loves herself, she adores herself eternally with countless eyes and hearts. She has scattered herself to enjoy herself. She brings forth ever new enjoyers, insatiable in her need to share herself.

She delights in illusion. Whoever destroys this in himself and others she punishes as the sternest tyrant. Whoever follows her trustingly she takes to her heart like a child.

Her children are without number. From none does she withhold all gifts, but upon her favorites she lavishes much and for them she sacrifices much. She has lent her protection to greatness.

Her creatures are flung up out of nothingness with no hint of where they come from or where they are going – they are only to run; she knows the course.

She has few mainsprings to drive her, but these never wind down; they are always at work, always varied.

Her drama is ever new because she creates ever new spectators. Life is her most beautiful invention and death her scheme for having much life.

She wraps man in shadow and forever spurs him to find the light. She makes him a creature dependent upon the earth, sluggish and heavy, and then again and again she shakes him awake.

Sie gibt Bedürfnisse, weil sie Bewegung liebt. Wunder, daß sie alle diese Bewegung mit so weni-
gem erreichte. Jedes Bedürfnis ist Wohltat. Schnell befriedigt, schnell wieder erwachsend. Gibt sie
eins mehr, so ist's ein neuer Quell der Lust. Aber sie kommt bald ins Gleichgewicht.

Sie setzt alle Augenblicke zum längesten Lauf an und ist alle Augenblicke am Ziele.

Sie ist die Eitelkeit selbst; aber nicht für uns, denen sie sich zur größten Wichtigkeit gemacht hat.

Sie läßt jedes Kind an sich künsteln, jeden Toren über sie richten, tausend stumpf über sie hinge-
hen und nichts sehen, und hat an allen ihre Freude und findet bei allen ihre Rechnung.

Man gehorcht ihren Gesetzen, auch wenn man ihnen widerstrebt, man wirkt mit ihr, auch wenn
man gegen sie wirken will.

Sie macht alles, was sie gibt, zur Wohltat, denn sie macht es erst unentbehrlich. Sie säumet, daß
man sie verlange, sie eilet, daß man sie nicht satt werde.

Sie hat keine Sprache noch Rede, aber sie schafft Zungen und Herzen durch die sie fühlt und spricht.

Ihre Krone ist die Liebe. Nur durch sie kommt man ihr nahe. Sie macht Klüfte zwischen allen
Wesen und alles will sich verschlingen. Sie hat alles isoliert um alles zusammenzuziehen. Durch
ein paar Züge aus dem Becher der Liebe hält sie für ein Leben voll Mühe schadlos.

Sie ist alles. Sie belohnt sich selbst und bestraft sich selbst, erfreut und quält sich selbst. Sie ist
rauh und gelinde, lieblich und schröklich, kraftlos und allgewaltig. Alles ist immer da in ihr. Ver-
gangenheit und Zukunft kennt sie nicht. Gegenwart ist ihr Ewigkeit. Sie ist gütig. Ich preise sie mit
allen ihren Werken. Sie ist weise und still. Man reißt ihr keine Erklärung vom Leibe, trutzt ihr kein
Geschenk ab, das sie nicht freiwillig gibt. Sie ist listig, aber zu gutem Ziele, und am besten ists, ihre
List nicht zu merken.

Sie ist ganz und doch immer unvollendet. So wie sies treibt, kann sies immer treiben.

Jedem erscheint sie in einer eigenen Gestalt. Sie verbirgt sich in tausend Namen und Termen und
ist immer dieselbe.

Sie hat mich hereingestellt, sie wird mich auch herausführen. Ich vertraue mich ihr. Sie mag mit
mir schalten. Sie wird ihr Werk nicht hassen. Ich sprach nicht von ihr. Nein, was wahr ist und was
falsch ist, alles hat sie gesprochen. Alles ist ihre Schuld, alles ist ihr Verdienst.

ERLÄUTERUNG

ZU DEM APHORISTISCHEN AUFSATZ "DIE NATUR"

Goethe an den Kanzler v. Müller

Jener Aufsatz ist mir vor kurzem aus der brieflichen Verlassenschaft der ewig verehrten Her-
zogin Anna Amalia mitgeteilt worden; er ist von einer wohlbekannten Hand geschrieben, deren
ich mich in den achtziger Jahren in meinen Geschäften zu bedienen pflegte.

Daß ich diese Betrachtungen verfaßt, kann ich mich faktisch zwar nicht erinnern, allein sie
stimmen mit den Vorstellungen wohl überein, zu denen sich mein Geist damals ausgebildet
hatte. Ich möchte die Stufe damaliger Einsicht einen Komparativ nennen, der seine Richtung
gegen einen noch nicht erreichten Superlativ zu äußern gedrängt ist. Man sieht die Neigung zu
einer Art von Pantheismus, indem den Welterscheinungen ein unerforschliches, unbedingtes,
humoristisches, sich selbst widersprechendes Wesen zum Grunde gedacht ist, und mag als Spiel,
dem es bitterer Ernst ist, gar wohl gelten.

Die Erfüllung aber, die ihm fehlt, ist die Anschauung der zwei großen Triebräder aller Natur:
der Begriff von *Polarität* und von *Steigerung*, jene der Materie, insofern wir sie materiell, diese
ihr dagegen, insofern wir sie geistig denken, angehörig; jene ist in immerwährendem Anziehen

She gives us needs because she loves movement. A miracle, how little she uses to achieve all this movement. Every need is a favor. Soon satisfied, soon roused again. When she gives us another it is a source of new pleasure. But soon she comes into balance.

At every moment she prepares for the longest race and at every moment she is done with it. She is vanity itself, but not our vanity. For us she has given herself paramount importance.

She lets every child practice his arts on her, every fool judge her; she allows thousands to pass over her dully, without seeing her. In all this she takes joy and from it she draws her profit.

We obey her laws even in resisting them; we work with her even in working against her.

All she gives she makes a blessing, for she begins by making it a need. She delays so that we long for her; she hurries so that we never have our fill of her.

She has neither language nor speech, but she makes tongues and hearts with which to feel and speak.

Her crown is love. Only through love do we come to her. She opens chasms between all beings, and each seeks to devour the other. She has set all apart to draw all together. With a few draughts from the cup of love she makes good a life full of toil.

She is all. She rewards herself and punishes herself, delights and torments herself. She is rough and gentle, charming and terrifying, impotent and all-powerful. All is eternally present in her. She knows nothing of past and future. The present is eternity for her. She is kind. I praise her with all her works. She is wise and still. We may force no explanation from her, wrest no gift from her, if she does not give it freely. She is full of tricks, but to a good end, and it is best not to take note of her ruses.

She is whole and yet always unfinished. As she does now she may do forever.

To each she appears in a unique form. She hides amid a thousand names and terms, and is always the same.

She has brought me here, she will lead me away. I trust myself to her. She may do as she will with me. She will not hate her work. It is not I who has spoken of her. No, what is true and what is false, all this she has spoken. Hers is the blame, hers the glory.

A Commentary on the Aphoristic Essay

'Nature'

(Goethe to Chancellor von Müller)

This essay recently came to me from the estate of the late, revered Duchess Anna Amalia. It is in a familiar hand, one I often employed in my affairs during the eighties.

I cannot, in fact, remember having composed these remarks, but they reflect accurately the ideas to which my understanding had then attained. I could call the level of my insight at the time a 'comparative' which strove to express its development toward a 'superlative' not yet reached. The tendency toward a form of pantheism is apparent in the thought that what meets us in the world springs from an unfathomable, limitless, humorous, self-contradictory being. It may be considered a game in deadly earnest.

The missing capstone is the perception of the two great driving forces in all nature: the concepts of *polarity* and *intensification,* the former a property of matter insofar as we think of it as material, the latter insofar as we think of it as spiritual. Polarity is a state of constant attraction and repulsion, while intensification is a state of ever-striving ascent. Since, however, matter can

und Abstoßen, diese in immerstrebendem Aufsteigen. Weil aber die Materie nie ohne Geist, der Geist nie ohne Materie existiert und wirksam sein kann, so vermag auch die Materie sich zu steigern, so wie sichs der Geist nicht nehmen läßt, anzuziehen und abzustoßen; wie derjenige nur allein zu denken vermag, der genugsam getrennt hat, um zu verbinden, genugsam verbunden hat, um wieder trennen zu mögen.

In jenen Jahren, wohin gedachter Aufsatz fallen möchte, war ich hauptsächlich mit vergleichender Anatomie beschäftigt und gab mir 1786 unsägliche Mühe, bei anderen an meiner Überzeugung: *dem Menschen dürfe der Zwischenknochen nicht abgesprochen werden*, Teilnahme zu erregen. Die Wichtigkeit dieser Behauptung wollten selbst sehr gute Köpfe nicht einsehen, die Richtigkeit leugneten die besten Beobachter, und ich mußte, wie in so vielen andern Dingen, im stillen meinen Weg für mich fortgehen.

Die Versatilität der Natur im Pflanzenreiche verfolgte ich unablässig und es glückte mir Anno 1787 in Sizilien die Metamorphose der Pflanzen, so im Anschauen wie im Begriff, zu gewinnen. Die Metamorphose des Tierreichs lag nahe dran und im Jahre 1790 offenbarte sich mir in Venedig der Ursprung des Schädels aus Wirbelknochen; ich verfolgte nun eifriger die Konstruktion des Typus, diktierte das Schema im Jahre 1795 an Max Jacobi in Jena und hatte bald die Freude von deutschen Naturforschern mich in diesem Fache abgelöst zu sehen.

Vergegenwärtigt man sich die hohe Ausführung, durch welche die sämtlichen Naturerscheinungen nach und nach vor dem menschlichen Geiste verkettet worden, und liest alsdann obigen Aufsatz, von dem wir ausgingen, nochmals mit Bedacht; so wird man nicht ohne Lächeln jenen Komparativ, wie ich ihn nannte, mit dem Superlativ, mit dem hier abgeschlossen wird, vergleichen und eines funfzigjährigen Fortschreitens sich erfreuen.

Weimar, 24. Mai 1828.

[Johann Wolfgang von Goethe, Werke. Hamburger Ausgabe. Edited by Erich Trunz, 14 vols. Hamburg: Wegner (later Munich: Beck), 1948–1960. XIII, 45–49]

f. MAGYAR

VIII.f.1. VÖRÖSMARTY MIHÁLY, *Gondolatok a könyvtárban*

Hová lépsz most, gondold meg, oh tudós,
Az emberiségnek elhányt rongyain
Komor betűkkel, mint a téli éj,
Leírva áll a rettentő tanulság:
„Hogy míg nyomorra milliók születnek,
Néhány ezernek jutna üdv a földön,
Ha istenésszel, angyal érzelemmel
Használni tudnák éltök napjait."
Miért e lom? hogy mint juh a gyepen
Legeljünk rajta? s léha tudománytól
Zabáltan elhenyéljük a napot?
Az isten napját! nemzet életét!
Miért e lom? szagáról ismerem meg
Az állatember minden bűneit.
Erény van írva e lapon; de egykor

never exist and act without spirit, nor spirit without matter, matter is also capable of undergoing intensification, and spirit cannot be denied its attraction and repulsion. Similarly, the capacity to think is given only to someone who has made sufficient divisions to bring about a union, and who has united sufficiently to seek further divisions.

During the years in which this essay probably falls I was largely occupied with comparative anatomy. In 1786 I was at enormous pains to arouse support for my conviction that *the existence of the intermaxillary bone in man may not be denied.* Even good minds would not admit the importance of this assertion; the best observers denied its validity. As in so many other things, I was forced to go my own way quietly and alone.

I continued to apply myself to the study of nature's versatility in the plant kingdom, and while visiting Sicily in 1787 I succeeded in grasping the metamorphosis of plants both perceptually and conceptually. Metamorphosis in the animal kingdom is closely related, and in 1790 it became clear to me in Venice that the skull originates from the vertebrae. I then pursued the construction of the prototype with more vigor, dictated my schematic outline to Max Jacobi in 1795 in Jena, and soon had the pleasure of seeing other German researchers continue my work in this area.

If we recall the sublime way in which all natural phenomena have been linked bit by bit in human thought, and if we then take a second look at the above essay as our point of departure, we cannot but smile when we contrast that 'comparative' (as I termed it) to the 'superlative' which forms our end point – thus we will find pleasure in fifty years of progress.

Weimar, 24 May 1828.

[Johann Wolfgang von Goethe, Scientific Studies. Edited and translated by Douglas Miller (Goethe, Collected Works. Edited by Victor Lange, Eric A. Blackall and Cyrus Hamlin, 12 vols. New York: Suhrkamp), 1983–1989. XII. 3–5]

f. HUNGARIAN

VIII.f.1. MIHÁLY VÖRÖSMARTY, *Thoughts in the Library*

Consider, scholar, when you enter here,
on cast-off rags,[1] man's stigma freshly marked,
with words as stark as the dark winter night,
there looms, written blood-black, the awesome lesson:
'While into misery millions are born
a few thousand might find in life salvation
could they but make use of the days of their lives,
had they the mind divine, the Seraph's temper.'
Why all this rubbish? So, like sheep on grass
we may graze on it? Sated with fodder
and idle hours synthesized by science amoral
to waste God's day, a nation's energy?
Why this rubbish? From its stench I recall
all the sins of the animal man – they reek!
Virtue is written on this page, which once

[1] Vörösmarty alludes to the fact that good quality paper was made of rags.

Zsivány ruhája volt. S amott?
Az ártatlanság boldog napjai
Egy eltépett szűz gyönge öltönyén,
Vagy egy dühös bujának pongyoláján.
És itt a törvény – véres lázadók,
Hamis birák és zsarnokok mezéből
Fehérre mosdott könyvnek lapjain.
Emitt a gépek s számok titkai!
De akik a ruhát elszaggaták
Hogy majd belőle csínos könyv legyen,
Számon kivül maradtak: Ixion
Bőszült vihartól űzött kerekén
Örvény nyomorban, vég nélkül kerengők.
Az őrült ágyán bölcs fej álmodik;
A csillagászat egy vak koldus asszony
Condráin méri a világokat:
Világ és vakság egy hitvány lapon!
Könyv lett a rabnép s gyávák köntöséből
S most a szabadság és a hősi kor
Beszéli benne nagy történetét.
Hűség, barátság aljas hitszegők
Gunyáiból készült lapon regél.
Irtózatos hazudság mindenütt!
Az írt betűket a sápadt levél
Halotti képe kárhoztatja el.
          Országok rongya! könyvtár a neved,
De hát hol a könyv, mely célhoz vezet?
Hol a nagyobb rész boldogsága? – Ment-e
A könyvek által a világ elébb?
Ment, hogy minél dicsőbbek népei,
Salakjok annál borzasztóbb legyen,
S a rongyos ember bőszült kebele
Dögvészt sohajtson a hír nemzetére.
          De hát ledöntsük, amit ezredek
Ész napvilága mellett dolgozának?
A bölcsek és a költők műveit,
S mit a tapasztalás arany
Bányáiból kifejtett az idő?
Hány fényes lélek tépte el magát,
Virrasztott a sziv égő romja mellett,
Hogy tévedt, sujtott embertársinak
Irányt adjon s erőt, vigasztalást.
Az el nem ismert érdem hősei,
Kiket – midőn már elhunytak s midőn
Ingyen tehette – csúfos háladattal
Kezdett imádni a galád világ,

as rag has garbed an outlaw. This other page?
perhaps – oh happy days of innocence –
the frail dress ripped from a ravished virgin,
perhaps a lust-enraged whore's negligee.
And here on these leaves, the law whitewashed from
remnants of bloody rebels and false judges,
from masks of sanguine tyrants washed white;
the secrets of machines and of numbers laid bare,
but those who tore garments, stripped man naked,
flayed dignity that bindings might be vellum,
these, unaccounted for, must render account –
they spin on Ixion's tempest-driven wheel
within the vortex, misery without end
and, gnashing their teeth, wail in the dark outside.
On the madman's sheets ponders a sage's head;
the astronomer, on eyeless beggar's rags
measures bursting universes piled on end –
light and blindness, all on a flimsy page!
The coward and the captive, both hapless roles
are bound forever in one book that sings
of freedom and heroes hewing history. . .
Stainless sheets, pulped from traitor's rags, now
reward the friend and thus honour the faithful;
yet over all, all-polluting, the Big Lie!
The Word, cursed by the pallid winding sheet
its black image adorns, suffers damnation.

      Rag-lure of countries, your name is library!
Where, then, is the volume that answers all?
The greater part of Man – where is his joy?
Is the world no better for any book?
Yes! The more gloriously man's societies arise
the greater the human refuse at the bottom.
The bursting breast of rags stuffed with man
must breathe contagion into the empire's heart.

      Should we, after all, topple what countless brains
have wrought in the linked sunbursts of their minds?
Void the golden knowledge rare brains have
chopped and torn away from the mines of time?
How many bright souls immolated themselves
in vigil at the burning ruins of the heart
to give purpose, strength and comfort
to erring humans humbled by destiny?
Those heroes of unrecognized merit
whom the contemptible public mocked
were praised after death, when praise cost but words:

Népboldogító eszmék vértanúi,
Ők mind e többi rongykereskedővel,
Ez únt fejek- s e megkorhadt szivekkel,
Rosz szenvedélyek oktatóival
Ők mind együtt – a jók a rosz miatt –
Egy máglya üszkén elhamvadjanak?

      Oh nem, nem! amit mondtam, fájdalom volt,
Hogy annyi elszánt lelkek fáradalma,
Oly fényes elmék a sár fiait
A sűlyedéstől meg nem menthették!
Hogy még alig bír a föld egy zugot,
Egy kis virányt a puszta homokon
Hol legkelendőbb név az emberé,
Hol a teremtés ősi jogai
E névhez „ember!" advák örökűl –
Kivéve aki feketén született,
Mert azt baromnak tartják e dicsők
S az isten képét szíjjal ostorozzák.

      És mégis – mégis fáradozni kell.
Egy újabb szellem kezd felküzdeni,
Egy új irány tör át a lelkeken:
A nyers fajokba tisztább érzeményt
S gyümölcsözőbb eszméket oltani,
Hogy végre egymást szívben átkarolják,
S uralkodjék igazság, szeretet.
Hogy a legalsó pór is kunyhajában
Mondhassa bizton: nem vagyok magam!
Testvérim vannak, számos milliók;
Én védem őket, ők megvédnek engem.
Nem félek tőled, sors, bármit akarsz.

      Ez az, miért csüggedni nem szabad.
Rakjuk le, hangyaszorgalommal, amit
Agyunk az ihlett órákban teremt.
S ha összehordtunk minden kis követ,
Építsük egy újabb kor Bábelét,
Míg oly magas lesz, mint a csillagok.
S ha majd benéztünk a menny ajtaján,
Kihallhatók az angyalok zenéjét,
És földi vérünk minden csepjei
Magas gyönyörnek lángjától hevültek,
Menjünk szét, mint a régi nemzetek,
És kezdjünk újra tűrni és tanulni.

      Ez hát a sors és nincs vég semmiben?
Nincs és nem is lesz, míg a föld ki nem hal
S meg nem kövűlnek élő fiai.
Mi dolgunk a világon? küzdeni,

their thoughts beatified by the martyring mob!
Should the great burn to ashes at the same stake
with rag peddlers, numbskulls, and mildewed hearts?
Glow in embers with dark passion-panders
indiscriminate? Good on account of bad, with them?

    Never! That which I said was pain.
The travail of many a bold spirit,
even those luminous minds could not save
the sons of dust from sinking in the mud.
There is barely a corner of the world,
one little oasis on the barren sand
where the most sought-after name is not that of Man,
where the ancient rites of generation
yield as heritage the name of Man!
Except for those who have been born to blackness,
labelled cattle by the glorious elite
who caress the dark image of God with whips.

    Despite all, despite all, one must travail –
a new spirit is fighting its way up,
through the soul of man bursts a new approach –
to nurture fruitful ideals in races
primitive, to culture finer sentiments
that they may embrace, at last, each other,
and within their hearts reign love and justice.
So the lowest peasant may, in his hut,
say with assurance: 'I am not alone,
my brothers and sisters number millions,
I protect them, and me they defend;
fate, I fear thee not, despite thy dread will!'

    That is why one must not succumb to despair.
Let us, steadfast as ants, set down that which
our brains, in the rare inspired hours, create,
and when we have assembled every stone,
we'll erect the Babel of a newer age,
build it until it towers among the stars,
and when we have looked through the gates of Heaven,
having heard from without the Angels' song,
with every drop of our earthly blood
aglow from elevated flames of delights,
let us then scatter like the ancient peoples
and begin anew, to endure and to learn.

    Is this then our fate, and nothing our goal?
It is not – nor will be while the earth yields life,
and its mortal sons are not turned to stone;
what, in this world, is our task? To struggle,

És tápot adni lelki vágyainknak.
Ember vagyunk, a föld s az ég fia.
Lelkünk a szárny, mely ég felé viszen,
S mi ahelyett, hogy törnénk fölfelé,
Unatkozzunk s hitvány madár gyanánt
Posvány iszapját szopva éldegéljünk?
Mi dolgunk a világon? küzdeni
Erőnk szerint a legnemesbekért.
Előttünk egy nemzetnek sorsa áll.
Ha azt kivíttuk a mély sülyedésből
S a szellemharcok tiszta sugaránál
Olyan magasra tettük, mint lehet,
Mondhatjuk, térvén őseink porához:
Köszönjük élet! áldomásidat,
Ez jó mulatság, férfi munka volt!

[*First published Pesti Divatlap, vol. 1, no. 1, January 1, 1845. 4–5. Critical edition: Vörösmarty, Mihály, Vörösmarty Mihály összes művei, vol. 3, Kisebb költemények 3, (1840–1855). Edited by Tóth, Dezső. Budapest: Akadémiai 1962. 101–104*]

g. ITALIANO

VIII.g.1. PIETRO BORSIERI, da *Avventure letterarie di un giorno*

Non si può chiamar fiorente la coltura di una nazione quando ella vanta soltanto qualche grande Scrittore; ma bensì quando, oltre i rari ottimi, ella ne possiede molti buoni, mediocri moltissimi, cattivi pochi, e v'aggiunge infiniti lettori giudiziosi. Allora si forma, dirò così, un'invisibile catena d'intelligenza e di idee tra il genio che crea e la moltitudine che impara; si sente e s'indaga il bello con più profondità; i falsi giudizi sono più facilmente combattuti; ai veri grand'uomini è concessa la gloria e agli ingegni minori la fama.

Così, per modo d'esempio, quando fiorivano Michelangelo e Raffaello, coprivano essi col raggio della loro gloria il nome pur chiaro d'altri artisti che in epoca di decadenza sarebbero riputati eccellenti, e che ora infatti veneriamo come grandi maestri. Così, quando l'Ariosto ed il Tasso stampavano orme profonde di poesia, avevano intorno a loro una turba d'altri poeti meno insigni, ma pure distinti in quella età. Facile è l'applicazione di questo principio al presente periodo della letteratura italiana, ed ognuno può farla per se stesso.

Ma riguardo a coloro che, a proposito di bella letteratura e di scienze morali ripetono continuamente i nomi di alcuni fisici, o matematici, od artisti, od eruditi, soggiungo che noi esaltiamo i nostri grand'uomini dopo che furono onorati dagli Stranieri; e che allora cominciamo ad incoraggiare l'ingegno, quando ha già compiuto il suo corso senza l'aiuto della stima comune, anzi vincendo la guerra che gli moviamo.

Sì certo, Lagrange è nato in Italia, e noi possediamo il liceo ov'egli spandeva la prima luce di se stesso. Di lui dissero i dotti delle altre nazioni ch'egli stava dappresso a Newton nell'ingegno, e lo sorpassava nel sapere. Ma Newton dorme glorioso i suoi sonni nelle tombe dei Re d'Inghilterra, mentre le ceneri di Lagrange giacciono in terra straniera! Né le ceneri solo; ma

and to nourish the needs of the spirit;
we are Man, son to both the earth and sky,
our soul is the wing beating toward heaven,
but we, instead of striving up to soar,
would rather, dully, like some bird beneath contempt,
eke out existence sucking mud from swamps.
What, in this world, is our task? To struggle,
according to our strength, for noble goals.
Before us stands the fate of a nation –
when we, from the irrevocable fall
have preserved it and restored it to its heights,
fighting under the clear beam of the spirit,
we can say, returning to our ancestors
in the dust: Thank you, life, for thy blessings –
this has been great joy, yea, the Work of Men!

> [*Translated by Hyman H. Hart (& Adam Makkai) and reprinted from In Quest of the
> 'Miracle Stag': The Poetry of Hungary. Edited by Adam Makkai. Chicago and
> Budapest, Atlantis-Centaur, M. Szivárvány and Corvina, 1996.
> 230–233, with the kind permission of Adam Makkai*]

g. ITALIAN

VIII.g.1.   PIETRO BORSIERI, from *A Day of Literary Adventures*

One cannot say that a nation is flourishing when it boasts only a few great writers; but rather when, as well as the rare excellent writers, it has many good ones, very many mediocre ones and few bad ones, and I may add infinite judicious readers. So then I will put it like this, an invisible chain of intelligence and ideas is formed between the genius that creates and the multitude that learns; it feels and examines beauty with more depth, false judgments are more easily fought against; glory is granted to truly great men and fame to minor geniuses.

Thus, for example, when Michelangelo and Raphael were flourishing they covered with the rays of their glory the distinguished names of other artists, who would have been considered excellent in an age of decadence, and who, in fact, we venerate today as great masters. Thus, when Ariosto and Tasso produced profound examples of poetry, they were surrounded by a multitude of poets, who were also distinguished but less illustrious at that time. It is easy to apply this principle to the present period of Italian literature, and everybody can do it for himself.

But with regard to those people who, when talking about great literature and moral sciences, continuously repeat the names of some physicists, or mathematicians, or artists, or scholars, I add that we exalt our great men only after they have been honoured by foreigners; and that we begin to promote genius when it has already completed its course without the help of the common esteem, instead, winning the war that we wage on it.

Yes, certainly, Lagrange was born in Italy and we own the school where he first shone. The learned men of other nations say of him that he was close to Newton in genius, and that he surpassed him in knowledge. But Newton sleeps his glorious sleep in the tombs of the Kings of England, while the ashes of Lagrange lie in foreign soil! Not just his ashes, but he as a person

tutta la miglior vita di lui trascorse lontana dalla patria la quale non seppe onorarlo che troppo tardi; ed egli la rimeritò degnamente non dettando mai veruna opera sua nella lingua nativa.

Volta è il Franklin dell'Europa. Penetrando con acutissime esperienze nel magistero della creazione, egli comandò all'elettricità di trascorrere sotto il freno di una stessa legge gli spazii dell'aria, le superficie de' metalli, e le fibre degli animali, e trovò così un filo segreto con che la materia inanimata si congiunge alla natura vivente.

Ma dimanderò a tutti coloro che ne citano ora il nome con orgoglio, se sappiano infatti venerare questo grand'uomo come gli Americani veneravano il loro sommo fisico e legislatore; dimanderò se la fama di lui era tanto altamente predicata fra noi, prima che l'Istituto di Francia lo chiamasse nel suo seno a presentare alla meditazione di que' dotti, quasi in una festiva solennità della sapienza, le sue mirabili esperienze?

(1816) [*Edizione di riferimento: I manifesti romantici del 1816 e gli scritti principali del «Conciliatore» sul Romanticismo, a cura di Carlo Calcaterra, Unione tipografico-editrice torinese, Torino, ristampa*]

h. NORSK

VIII.h.1.   HENRIK IBSEN, 'Bergmanden'

Bergvæg, brist med drøn og brag
for mit tunge hammerslag!
Nedad må jeg vejen bryde,
til jeg hører malmen lyde.

Dybt i fjeldets øde nat
vinker mig den rige skat, –
diamant og ædelstene
mellem guldets røde grene.

Og i dybet er der fred, –
fred og ørk fra evighed; –
bryd mig vejen, tunge hammer
til det dulgtes hjertekammer!

Engang sad som gut jeg glad
under himlens stjernerad,
trådte vårens blomsterveje,
havde barnefred i eje.

Men jeg glemte dagens pragt
i den midnatsmørke schakt,
glemte liens sus og sange
i min grubes tempelgange.

Den gang først jeg steg herind,
tænkte jeg med skyldfrit sind:
Dybets ånder skal mig råde
livets endeløse gåde. –

spent the best part of his life far from the homeland which did not know how to honour him until it was too late: and he repaid this by never penning any work in his native tongue.

Volta is the Franklin of Europe. Delving with honed experience into the mastery of creation, he commanded electricity to pass through space, the surfaces of metals and the fibres of animals, under the restraints of a common law, and he thus found a secret thread with which inanimate material is linked to living nature.

But I will ask all those people who now cite his name with pride, if they indeed know how to venerate this great man as the Americans venerated their greatest physicist and legislator; I will ask if his fame was so very highly proclaimed here before the French Institute called him to its membership to present his wonderful experiences for the consideration of those learned men almost in a joyful solemnity of knowledge?

(1816) [*Translated by Marayde O'Brien and*
Anne O'Connor]

h. NORWEGIAN

VIII.h.1. HENRIK IBSEN, 'Miner'

Rock-face, burst and boom and ring
to my heavy hammering!
Downwards must I burrow, pounding
till I hear the metals sounding.

Deep in mountain's night obscure
treasures beckon and allure,
diamond and stones past pricing,
veins of gold, red-branched, enticing.

In the depth, too, there is peace, –
peace eternal, wilderness; –
break my way, you hammer, batter
to the secret heart of matter.

Once, a boy, I'd sit and play
under heaven's starred array;
tread the springtime's path of flowers,
tranquil in those childhood hours.

I forgot day's splendid light
in the pit's dense gloom of night,
hill-side too, its sighs and singing,
in my lode's harsh temple – ringing.

When at first I made descent,
all my thought was innocent:
'Earth's deep spirits will unravel
life's great maze that I must travel'.

End har ingen ånd mig lært,
hva mig tykkedes så sært;
end er ingen stråle runden,
som kan lyse op fra grunden.

Har jeg fejlet? Fører ej
frem til klarhed denne vej?
Lyset blinder jo mit øje,
hvis jeg søger i det høje.

Nej, i dybet må jeg ned;
der er fred fra evighed.
Bryd mig vejen, tunge hammer,
til det dulgtes hjertekammer! –

Hammerslag på hammerslag
indtil livets siste dag.
Ingen morgenstråle skinner;
ingen håbets sol oprinder.

[*First published 1851; revised 1863 and 1871; 1851 version rendered here*]

i. **POLSKI**

VIII.i.1.   ADAM MICKIEWICZ, 'Romantyczność'

> *Zdaje me się, że widzę... gdzie? Przed*
> *oczyma duszy mojej.*
> – Shakespeare

Słuchaj, dzieweczko!
– Ona nie słucha –
To dzień biały! To miasteczko!
Przy tobie nie ma żywego ducha.
Co tam wkoło siebie chwytasz?
Kogo wołasz, z kim się witasz?
– Ona nie słucha. –

To jak martwa opoka
Nie zwróci w stronę oka,
To strzela wkoło oczyma,
To się łzami zaleje;
Coś niby chwyta, coś niby trzyma;
Rozpłacze się i zaśmieje.

But no spirit solved for me
puzzle or complexity;
and no sun has risen shining
from this darkened realm of mining.

A mistake then? Can this be
no new path to clarity?
For the brightness blinds my sight
if I seek that in the light.

No, still delve I must, not cease;
here lives my eternal peace.
Break my way, you hammer, batter
to the secret heart of matter.

Hammering and hammering
to the last day life shall bring.
Never beam of brightness dawning,
never sun-of-hope's full morning.

[*Translated by John Northam. Oslo: Norwegian UP, 1986*]

i. POLISH

VIII.i.1. ADAM MICKIEWICZ, 'The Romantic'

> *Methinks, I see. . . where? – In my mind's*
> *eye.*
> – Shakespeare

'Silly girl, listen!'
But she doesn't listen
While the village roofs glisten,
Bright in the sun.
'Silly girl, what do you do there,
As if there were someone to view there,
A live form warmly to meet there,
When there is no one, none, do you hear!'
But she doesn't hear.

Like a dead stone
She stands there alone,
Staring ahead of her, peering around
For something that has to be found
Till, suddenly spying it,
She touches it, clutches it,
Laughing and crying.

«Tyżeś to w nocy? – To ty, Jasieńku!
Ach! I po śmierci kocha!
Tutaj, tutaj, pomaleńku,
Czasem usłyszy macocha!

Niech sobie słyszy, już nie ma ciebie!
Już po twoim pogrzebie!
Ty już umarłeś? Ach! Ja się boję!
Czego się boję mego Jasieńka?
Ach, to on! Lica twoje, oczki twoje!
Twoja biała sukienka!

I sam ty biały jak chusta,
Zimny, jakie zimne dłonie!
Tutaj połóż, tu na łonie,
Przyciśnij mnie, do ust usta!

Ach, jak tam zimno musi być w grobie!
Umarłeś! Tak, dwa lata!
Weź mię, ja umrę przy tobie,
Nie lubię świata.

Źle mnie w złych ludzi tłumie
Płaczę a oni szydzą;
Mówię, nikt nie rozumie;
Widzę, oni nie widzą!

Śród dnia przyjdź kiedy... To może we śnie?
Nie, nie... trzymam ciebie w ręku.
Gdzie znikasz, gdzie, mój Jasieńku?
Jeszcze wcześnie, jeszcze wcześnie!

Mój Boże! kur się odzywa,
Zorza błyska w okienku.
Gdzie znikłeś? Ach! stój, Jasieńku!
Ja nieszczęśliwa.»

Tak się dziewczyna z kochankiem pieści,
Bieży za nim, krzyczy, pada;
Na ten upadek, na głos boleści,
Skupia się ludzi gromada.

«Mówcie pacierze! – krzyczy prostota –
Tu jego dusza być musi.
Jasio być musi przy swej Karusi,
On ją kochał za żywota!»

I ja to słyszę, i ja tak wierzę,
Płaczę i mówię pacierze.

Is it you, my Johnny, my true love, my dear?
I knew you would never forget me,
Even in death! Come with me, let me
Show you the way now! Hold your breath, though,
And tiptoe lest stepmother hear!

What can she hear? They have made him
A grave, two years ago laid him
Away with the dead.
Save me, Mother of God! I'm afraid.
But why? Why should I flee you now?
What do I dread?
Not Johnny! My Johnny won't hurt me.
It is my Johnny! I see you now,
Your eyes, your white shirt.

But it's pale as linen you are,
Cold as winter you are!
Let my lips take the cold from you,
Kiss the chill of the mould from you.

Dearest love, let me die with you,
In the deep earth lie with you,
For this world is dark and dreary,
I am lonely and weary!

Alone among the unkind ones
Who mock at my vision,
My tears their derision,
Seeing nothing, the blind ones!

Dear God! A cock is crowing,
Whitely glimmers the dawn.
Johnny! Where are you going?
Don't leave me! I am forlorn!

So, caressing, talking aloud to her
Lover, she stumbles and falls,
And her cry of anguish calls
A pitying crowd to her.

'Cross yourselves! It is, surely,
Her Johnny come back from the grave:
While he lived, he loved her entirely.
May God his soul now save!'

Hearing what they are saying,
I, too, start praying.

«Słuchaj, dzieweczko!» – krzyknie śród zgiełku
Starzec i na lud zawoła:
«Ufajcie memu oku i szkiełku,
Nic tu nie widzę dokoła.

Duchy karczemnej tworem gawiedzi,
W głupstwa wywarzone kuźni.
Dziewczyna duby smalone bredzi,
A gmin rozumowi bluźni».

«Dziewczyna czuje – odpowiadam skromnie –
A gawiedź wierzy głęboko;
Czucie i wiara silniej mówi do mnie
Niż mędrca szkiełko i oko.

Martwe znasz prawdy, nieznane dla ludu,
Widzisz świat w proszku, w każdej gwiazd iskierce.
Nie znasz prawd żywych, nie obaczysz cudu!
Miej serce i patrzaj w serce!»

(1821) [*Edited by Czesław Zgorzelski. Warszawa: Czytelnik, 1993*]

l. РУССКИЙ

VIII.l.1. ВЛАДИМИР ОДОЕВСКИЙ, Последнее самоубийство, из сборника
«Русские ночи»

Наступило время, предсказанное философами XIX века: род человеческий размножился; потерялась соразмерность между произведениями природы и потребностями человечества. Медленно, но постоянно приближалось оно к сему бедствию. Гонимые нищетою, жители городов бежали в поля, поля обращались в селы, селы в города, а города нечувствительно раздвигали свои границы; тщетно человек употреблял все знания, приобретенные потовыми трудами веков, тщетно к ухищрениям искусства присоединял ту могущественную деятельность, которую порождает роковая необходимость, – давно уже аравийские песчаные степи обратились в плодоносные пажити; давно уже льды севера покрылись туком земли; неимоверными усилиями химии искусственная теплота живила царство вечного хлада... но все тщетно: протекли века, и животная жизнь вытеснила растительную, слились границы городов, и весь земной шар от полюса до полюса обратился в один обширный, заселенный город, в который перенеслись вся роскошь, все болезни, вся утонченность, весь разврат, вся деятельность прежних городов; но над роскошным градом вселенной тяготела страшная нищета и усовершенные способы сообщения разносили во все концы шара лишь вести об ужасных явлениях голода и болезней; еще возвышались здания; еще нивы в несколько ярусов, освещенные искусственным солнцем, орошаемые искусственною водою, приносили обильную жатву, – но она исчезала прежде, нежели успевали собирать ее: на каждом шагу, в каналах, реках, воздухе, везде теснились люди, все кипело жизнию, но жизнь умерщвляла сама себя. Тщетно люди молили друг у друга средства воспротивиться всеобщему бедствию: старики воспоминали о протекшем, обвиняли во всем роскошь и испорченность нравов; юноши призывали в помощь силу ума, воли и воображения; мудрейшие искали средства продолжать существование без пищи, и над ними никто не смеялся.

'The girl is out of her senses!'
Shouts a man with a learned air,
'My eye and my lenses
Know there's nothing there.

Ghosts are a myth
Of ale-wife and blacksmith.
Clodhoppers! This is treason
Against King Reason!'

'Yet the girl loves,' I reply diffidently,
'And the people believe reverently:
Faith and love are more discerning
Than lenses or learning.

You know the dead truths, not the living,
The world of things, not the world of loving.
Where does any miracle start?
Cold eye, look in your heart!'

(1821) [*Translated by W. H. Auden. New York: Noonday Press, 1956*]

l.   RUSSIAN

VIII.l.1.   V. F. ODOEVSKY, 'The Last Suicide' from *Russian Nights*

The time predicted by the philosophers of the nineteenth century arrived: the human race had multiplied; the balance between nature's production and the needs of mankind was lost. Slowly but incessantly it had been approaching this catastrophe. Driven by destitution the city dwellers ran to the fields, the fields turned into villages, villages into towns, and the towns imperceptibly expanded their limits. In vain did man apply all the knowledge he had acquired during centuries in the sweat of his brow, in vain did he add to the contrivances of art the powerful activity stimulated by fateful necessity: The sandy steppes of Arabia had long been turned into fruitful fields; northern ice had been long covered by a layer of soil; by enormous efforts of chemistry artificial heat enlivened the kingdom of eternal cold . . . but all this was to no avail: centuries passed, and the animal world forced out the plant world; cities' limits merged, and the whole earth, from pole to pole, turned into an immense inhabited city with all the luxury, all the diseases, refinements, and depravity, all the activities of former cities. But an awful destitution weighed upon this luxurious universal city, and perfected means of communications carried news of the horrible phenomenon of starvation and diseases into all parts of the globe. Buildings still rose high; more fields, arranged in several tiers, illuminated by an artificial sun and irrigated by artificial water, brought an abundant harvest – but it would disappear before it was gathered: at every step, in canals, in rivers, and in the air, there were crowds of people, everything was bursting with life, but life was killing itself. In vain, people implored each other to find means of opposing the all-enveloping disaster: old men remembered the days gone by, and blamed luxury and depraved morals for everything; young people called the power of intellect, of will and imagination to their assistance; wise men searched for means of continuing existence without food, and no one laughed at them.

Скоро здания показались человеку излишнею роскошью; он зажигал дом свой и с дикою радостию утучнял землю пеплом своего жилища; погибли чудеса искусства, произведения образованной жизни, обширные книгохранилища, больницы, – все, что могло занимать какое-либо пространство, – и вся земля обратилась в одну обширную, плодоносную пажить.

Но не надолго возбудилась надежда; тщетно заразительные болезни летали из края в край и умерщвляли жителей тысячами; сыны Адамовы, пораженные роковыми словами писания, росли и множились.

Давно уже исчезло все, что прежде составляло счастие и гордость человека. Давно уже погас божественный огонь искусства, давно уже и философия, и религия отнесены были к разряду алхимических знаний; с тем вместе разорвались все узы, соединявшие людей между собою, и чем более нужда теснила их друг к другу, тем более чувства их разлучались. Каждый в собрате своем видел врага, готового отнять у него последнее средство для бедственной жизни: отец с рыданием узнавал о рождении сына; дочери прядали при смертном одре матери; но чаще мать удушала дитя свое при его рождении, и отец рукоплескал ей. Самоубийцы внесены были в число героев. Благотворительность сделалась вольнодумством, насмешка над жизнию – обыкновенным приветствием, любовь – преступлением.

Вся утонченность законоискусства была обращена на то, чтобы воспрепятствовать совершению браков; малейшее подозрение в родстве, неравенство в летах, всякое удаление от обряда делало брак ничтожным и бездною разделяло супругов. С рассветом каждого дня люди, голодом подымаемые с постели, тощие, бледные, сходились и обвиняли друг друга в пресыщении или упрекали мать многочисленного семейства в распутстве; каждый думал видеть в собрате общего врага своего, недосягаемую причину жизни, и все словами отчаяния вызывали на брань друг друга: мечи обнажались, кровь лилась, и никто не спрашивал о причине брани, никто не разнимал враждующих, никто не помогал упавшему.

Однажды толпа была раздвинута другою, которая гналась за молодым человеком; его обвиняли в ужасном преступлении: он спас от смерти человека, в отчаянии бросившегося в море; нашлись еще люди, которые хотели вступиться за несчастного. "Что вы защищаете человеконенавистника? – вскричал один из толпы. – Он эгоист, он любит одного себя!" Одно это слово устранило защитников, ибо эгоизм тогда был общим чувством; он производил в людях невольное презрение к самим себе, и они рады были наказать в другом собственное свое чувство. "Он эгоист, – продолжал обвинитель, – он нарушитель общего спокойствия, он в своей землянке скрывает жену, а она сестра его в пятом колене!"

– В пятом колене! – завопила разъяренная толпа.

– Это ли дело друга? – промолвил несчастный.

– Друга? – возразил с жаром обвинитель. – А с кем ты несколько дней тому назад,

– прибавил он шопотом, – не со мною ли ты отказал поделиться своей пищею?

– Но мои дети умирали с голоду, – сказал в отчаянии злополучный.

– Дети! дети! – раздалось со всех сторон. – У него есть дети! – Его беззаконные дети съедают хлеб наш! – и, предводимая обвинителем, толпа ринулась к землянке, где несчастный скрывал от взоров толпы все драгоценное ему в жизни. – Пришли, ворвались, – на голой земле лежали два мертвых ребенка, возле них мать; ее зубы стиснули руку грудного младенца. – Отец вырвался из толпы, бросился к трупам, и толпа с хохотом удалилась, бросая в него грязь и каменья.

– –

Soon man began to think of buildings as a superfluous luxury; he would set his house aflame and, wild with joy, cover the soil with the ashes of his dwelling; marvels of art, the creations of cultured life, huge libraries, hospitals – everything that might occupy some space, everything was destroyed and all the earth turned into a single fruitful field.

But hope didn't last long; it was to no avail that contagious diseases spread from one end to another, killing thousands of inhabitants; Adam's sons, struck by the fateful words of the Scriptures, kept growing and multiplying.

Long ago everything that formerly had meant the happiness and pride of man had disappeared. The divine flame of the arts burned no more, and both philosophy and religion were considered knowledge similar to alchemy. Along with this all bonds uniting people among themselves were torn apart, and the more their destitution forced them together, the more their feelings parted. Everyone saw in his fellowman an enemy ready to deprive him of the last means of his destitute life: a father would cry when learning that a son had been born; daughters would dance around their mother's deathbed; but most frequently a mother would strangle her child at birth, while the father would applaud her. Suicides ranked as heroes. Charity became an act of freethinking, scorn at life became a usual greeting, love became a crime.

All the refinements of legislation were used to prevent marriages from taking place: the slightest suspicion of relationship, age difference, any deviation from the ceremony annulled marriages and created an abyss between husband and wife. At the dawn of each day, wakened by hunger from their sleep, emaciated, pale people would gather and accuse one another of overeating, or reproach the mother of a large family of dissoluteness; everyone thought of seeing his general enemy in his fellowman, an unattainable cause of life, and with words of despair they challenged one another to fight: swords were drawn, blood was shed, and there was no one to part them, no one to help the one who fell.

Once a crowd was parted by another crowd chasing after a young man; he was accused of a horrible crime: he saved the life of a man whose despair made him jump into the sea. There were still some people who wanted to protect the poor fellow. 'Why do you defend the man-hater?' shouted one of the crowd, 'he is an egoist, he loves only himself!' This word alone put off the defenders, because egoism was a common feeling then; it created an unconscious contempt toward themselves in people, and they were glad to punish their own feelings in another person. 'He is an egoist,' continued the accuser; 'he violated the general peace; he hides his wife in his hut but she is his sister in the fifth generation.'

'In the fifth generation!' roared the infuriated crowd.

'Is this my friend speaking in you?' uttered the wretched fellow.

'Your friend?' interjected his fiery accuser, and then went on in a whisper, 'And with whom did you refuse to share your food just a few days ago?'

'But my children were starving' said the ill-fated man in despair.

'Children! children!' resounded from all around. 'He has children! His illegal children eat up our bread!' – and, with the accuser at their head, the crowd rushed toward the hut where the poor wretch was hiding everything dear to him in life from the sight of the crowd. They broke inside – on the bare ground lay two dead children, with their mother next to them; her teeth pressing the hand of her baby. The father tore himself from the crowd, and rushed toward the bodies, while the laughing crowd moved away, throwing dirt and stones at him.

– –

Мрачное, ужасное чувство зародилось в душе людей. Этого чувства не умели бы назвать в прежние веки; тогда об этом чувстве могли дать слабое понятие лишь ненависть отверженной любви, лишь цепенение верной гибели, лишь бессмыслие терзаемого пыткою; но это чувство не имело предмета. Теперь ясно все видели, что жизнь для человека сделалась невозможною, что все средства для ее поддержания были истощены, – но никто не решался сказать, что оставалось предпринять человеку? Вскоре между толпами явились люди, – они, казалось, с давнего времени вели счет страданиям человека – и в итоге выводили все его существование. Обширным, адским взглядом они обхватывали минувшее и преследовали жизнь с самого ее зарождения. Они вспоминали, как она, подобно татю, закралась сперва в темную земляную глыбу и там, посреди гранита и гнейса, мало-помалу, истребляя одно вещество другим, развила новые произведения, более совершенные; потом на смерти одного растения она основала существование тысячи других; истреблением растений она размножила животных; с каким коварством она приковала к страданиям одного рода существ наслаждения, самое бытие другого рода! Они вспоминали, как, наконец, честолюбивая, распространяя ежечасно свое владычество, она все более и более умножала раздражительность чувствования – и беспрестанно, в каждом новом существе, прибавляя к новому совершенству новый способ страдания, достигла наконец до человека, в душе его развернулась со всею своею безумною деятельностию и счастие всех людей восставила против счастия каждого человека. Пророки отчаяния с математическою точностию измеряли страдание каждого нерва в теле человека, каждого ощущения в душе его. "Вспомните, – говорили они, – с каким лицемерием неумолимая жизнь вызывает человека из сладких объятий ничтожества. – Она закрывает все чувства его волшебною пеленою при его рождении, – она боится, чтобы человек, увидев все безобразие жизни, не отпрянул от колыбели в могилу. Нет! коварная жизнь является ему сперва в виде теплой материнской груди, потом порхает перед ним бабочкою и блещет ему в глаза радужными цветами; она печется о его сохранении и совершенном устройстве его души, как некогда мексиканские жрецы пеклись о жертвах своему идолу; дальновидная, она дарит младенца мягкими членами, чтоб случайное падение не сделало человека менее способным к терзанию; несколькими покровами рачительно закрывает его голову и сердце, чтоб вернее сберечь в них орудия для будущей пытки; и несчастный привыкает к жизни, начинает любить ее: она то улыбается ему прекрасным образом женщины, то выглядывает на него из-под длинных ресниц ее, закрывая собою безобразные впадины черепа, то дышит в горячих речах ее; то в звуках поэзии олицетворяет все несуществующее; то жаждущего приводит к пустому кладезю науки, который кажется неисчерпаемым источником наслаждений. Иногда человек, прорывая свою пелену, мельком видит безобразие жизни, но она предвидела это и заранее зародила в нем любопытство увериться в самом ее безобразии, узнать ее; заранее поселила в человеке гордость видом бесконечного царства души его, и человек, завлеченный, упоенный, незаметно достигает той минуты, когда все нервы его тела, все чувства его души, все мысли его ума – во всем блеске своего развития спрашивают: где же место их деятельности, где исполнение надежд, где цель жизни? Жизнь лишь ожидала этого мгновения, – быстро повергает она страдальца на плаху: сдергивает с него благодетельную пелену, которую подарила ему при рождении, и, как искусный анатом, обнажив нервы души его – обливает их жгучим холодом.

Иногда от взоров толпы жизнь скрывает свои избранные жертвы; в тиши, с рачением воскормляет их таинственною пищею мыслей, острит их ощущения; в их скудельную

A dark and horrible feeling was born in men's souls. People of former days wouldn't have known what to call this feeling; in those days only the hatred of denied love, only the fear of sure death, and a senselessly tortured man could give a faint idea of this feeling; but this feeling had no object. Now everybody saw clearly that man's life had become impossible, that all the means of supporting it were exhausted, but no one could make up his mind to say what there was left for man to do. Soon there appeared among them men who seemed to have been keeping count of man's sufferings from ancient times – and as a result they deduced his entire existence. Their boundless insight grasped the past and pursued Life from the moment of its inception. They recalled her, thief-like, creeping first into a dark clod of earth, and there, between granite and gneiss, destroying one matter by another and slowly developing new, more perfect creations; then she made the death of one kind of plant bring about the existence of thousands of others; by destroying plants she multiplied animals. With what cunning she made the enjoyment, the very existence of one kind depend on the sufferings of the other! They recalled, finally, how ambitious Life, extending her authority from hour to hour, kept increasing the irritability of feelings, constantly adding new ways of suffering to a new perfection in each new being until she created a human being, and in his soul she unfolded with all her reckless activity, and placed the happiness of all people against the happiness of each man. The prophets of despair measured the suffering of each nerve in man's body, of each feeling in his soul with mathematical preci- sion. 'Remember,' they said, 'the hypocrisy with which inexorable Life calls man out of the sweet embraces of nothingness. She covers all his feelings with a magic veil at his birth, she is afraid that man, seeing all the ugliness of life, would recoil from his cradle into a grave. No! cunning Life appears to him first in the shape of his mother's warm breast; then she flutters like a butterfly before him and entices his eyes with gay colors; she takes great care to safe- guard him and the state of his soul, as Mexican priests used to take care of the sacrifices for their idol. With foresight she endows a child with soft limbs, so that an accidental fall might not make man less capable of suffering; she carefully covers his head and heart to keep the instruments of future torture within them intact; and poor man becomes accustomed to Life, begins to love her: now she smiles at him in the guise of a beautiful woman; now she glances at him from under her long eyelashes, covering the ugly holes of her skull; now she breathes passionate words; now, in poetic sounds, she personifies all non-existent things; now she takes him to an empty well of science, which seems to him an inexhaustible source of enjoy- ment. Sometimes man tears the shroud enveloping him, and catches sight of Life's ugliness, but she had anticipated that and implanted in him curiosity to assure himself of her ugliness, to learn to know her; she endowed man with the pride of seeing the infinite kingdom of his soul, and man, enticed and intoxicated, unnoticeably reaches the moment when all the nerves of his body, all the feelings of his heart, all the thoughts of his mind, at the high point of their development, begin to ask: What is the point of their activity? Where is the fulfillment of their hopes? Where is the purpose of their life? And Life was only waiting for this moment – she quickly throws him upon an executioner's block, strips off the protective veil which she gave him at the moment of his birth, and, like a skillful anatomist, having bared the nerves of his soul, she pours the burning cold over him.

'Sometimes Life hides her chosen victims from the sight of crowds: in silence and with care she nourishes them with mysterious food of thoughts, sharpens their feelings, pours all her end- less activity into their frail breasts, and, having elevated their spirits to heaven, scornfully throws them into the midst of the crowd. There they are strangers; no one understands their language; they lack their usual food, and, tormented by inner hunger, enclosed in the fetters of social

грудь вмещает всю безграничную свою деятельность – и, возвысив до небес дух их, жизнь с насмешкою бросает их в средину толпы; здесь они чужеземцы, – никто не понимает языка их, – нет их привычной пищи, – терзаемые внутренним гладом, заключенные в оковы общественных условий, они измеряют страдание человека всею возвышенностию своих мыслей, всею раздражительностию чувств своих; в своем медленном томлении перечувствуют томление всего человечества, – тщетно рвутся они к своей мнимой отчизне, – они издыхают, разуверившись в вере целого бытия своего, и жизнь, довольная, но не насыщенная их страданиями, с презрением бросает на их могилу бесплодный фимиам позднего благоговения.

Были люди, которые рано узнавали коварную жизнь, – и, презирая ее обманчивые призраки, с твердостию духа рано обращались они к единственному верному и неизменному союзнику их против ее ухищрений – ничтожеству. В древности слабоумное человечество называло их малодушными; мы, более опытные, менее способные обманываться, назвали их мудрейшими. Лишь они умели найти надежное средство против врага человечества и природы, против неистовой жизни; лишь они постигли, зачем она дала человеку так много средств чувствовать и так мало способов удовлетворять своим чувствам. Лишь они умели положить конец ее злобной деятельности и разрешить давний спор об алхимическом камне.

В самом деле, размыслите хладнокровно, – продолжали несчастные, – что делал человек от сотворения мира?.. он старался избегнуть от жизни, которая угнетала его своею существенностию. Она вогнала человека свободного, уединенного, в свинцовые условия общества, и что же? человек несчастия одиночества заменил страданиями другого рода, может быть ужаснейшими; он продал обществу, как злому духу, блаженство души своей за спасение тела. Чего не выдумывал человек, чтоб украсить жизнь или забыть о ней. Он употребил на это всю природу, и тщетно в языке человеческом забывать о жизни – сделалось однозначительным с выражением: быть счастливым; эта мечта невозможная; жизнь ежеминутно напоминает о себе человеку. Тщетно он заставлял другого в кровавом поте лица отыскивать ему даже тени наслаждений, – жизнь являлась в образе пресыщения, ужаснейшем самого голода. В объятиях любви человек хотел укрыться от жизни, а она являлась ему под именами преступлений, вероломства и болезней. Вне царства жизни человек нашел что-то невыразимое, какое-то облако, которое он назвал поэзиею, философией, – в этих туманах он хотел спастись от глаз своего преследователя, а жизнь обратила этот утешительный призрак в грозное, тлетворное привидение. Куда же еще укрыться от жизни? мы переступили за пределы самого невыразимого! чего ждать еще более? мы исполнили, наконец, все мечты и ожидания мудрецов, нас предшествовавших. Долгим опытом уверились мы, что все различие между людьми есть только различие страданий, – и достигли, наконец, до того равенства, о котором так толковали наши предки. Смотрите, как мы блаженствуем: нет между нами ни властей, ни богачей, ни машин; мы тесно и очень тесно соединены друг с другом, мы члены одного семейства! – О люди! люди! не будем подражать нашим предкам, не дадимся в обман, – есть царство иное, безмятежное, – оно близко, близко!"

Тиха была речь пророков отчаяния – она впивалась в душу людей, как семя в разрыхленную землю, и росла, как мысль, давно уже развившаяся в глубоком уединении сердца. Всем понятна и сладка была она – и всякому хотелось договорить ее. Но, как во всех решительных эпохах человечества, недоставало избранного, который бы вполне выговорил мысль, крывшуюся в душе человека.

conditions, they measure human sufferings with the loftiness of their thinking, with all the irritability of their feelings; in their slow languor they experience the languor of all mankind: their longing after their own imaginary land remains futile, and they die, having lost faith in their entire existence; and Life, satisfied, but not satiated with their sufferings, contemptuously throws the barren incense of a long-delayed veneration upon their graves.

'There were men who learned about Life's nature early enough, and, despising her deceitful phantoms, turned in the firmness of their spirits to their only true and unfailing ally against her contrivances – to nothingness. In ancient times weak-minded mankind called them cowards; we, being more experienced and less liable to deceit, have called them wise. Only they knew how to find sure means against the enemy of mankind and nature, against violent Life. Only they understood why she gave man so many means to feel and so few ways to satisfy their feelings. Only they knew how to end her malicious activity and to solve the age-old argument about the alchemic stone.

'Indeed, consider it in cold blood,' continued the ill-fated men, 'what has man done since the creation of the world? He tried to escape from Life, which burdened him with her reality. She drove a free and solitary man into leaden social conditions, and what happened? Man replaced his pain of loneliness by another pain, perhaps a worse kind: for the sake of his body he sold the bliss of his soul to society, as to an evil spirit. He employed all his ingenuity to adorn his life or to forget about it. He employed all nature but to no avail: to forget Life became synonymous with the expression to be happy. But this is an unattainable dream. Life keeps reminding man about itself at every moment. It didn't help him to set another man in the sweat of his brow to seek out for him even the shadows of enjoyments – Life appeared as superabundance, more horrible than hunger. In the embraces of love man sought to hide from Life, but it came to him again under the name of crimes, perfidy, and diseases. Outside Life's domain man found something inexpressible, some sort of cloud which he called poetry, philosophy. In these clouds he sought salvation from the sight of his persecutor, but Life turned this consoling phantom into a fearful, pernicious ghost. Where else could one hide himself from Life? We had crossed the limits of the most inexpressible. What else could we expect? We have finally fulfilled all the dreams and expectations of the wise men who preceded us. We learned through long experience that the only difference between people lies in a variety of sufferings, and, finally, we reached the state of equality our ancestors dreamed about. See how blissfully happy we are: there is no authority; there are no rich men, no machines among us; we are very tightly united with one another; we are members of one family! Oh, people! people! let us not imitate our ancestors; let us not be deceived – there is another, serene realm, and it is very near!'

The speech of the prophets of despair was quiet; it penetrated men's souls like seed into ready soil, and it grew like an idea that has long been developing in the heart's deep solitude. Everyone understood it; it was sweet to the ear, and everyone wanted to say it to the end. But, as was the case in all decisive moments of mankind, there was no man who could fully express the idea hidden in man's soul.

Then, at last he came, the Messiah of despair! His look was cold, his voice was loud, and his words dispersed the last remnants of ancient beliefs. He was swift in pronouncing the last word of the last thought of mankind – and everything was set in motion. All the efforts of ancient art, all ancient achievements of anger and vengeance, everything that could ever kill man, everything was summoned, and the vaults of the earth crumbled under the light cover of soil; and artificially refined nitrate, sulphur, and carbon filled them from one end of the equator to another. At a fixed, solemn hour, people finally fulfilled the dreams of ancient philosophers

Наконец, явился он, мессия отчаяния! Хладен был взор его, громок голос, и от слов его мгновенно исчезали последние развалины древних поверий. Быстро вымолвил он последнее слово последней мысли человечества – и все пришло в движение, – призваны были все усилия древнего искусства, все древние успехи злобы и мщения, все, что когда-либо могло умерщвлять человека, и своды пресеклись под легким слоем земли, и искусством утонченная селитра, сера и уголь наполнили их от конца экватора до другого. В уреченный, торжественный час люди исполнили, наконец, мечтанья древних философов об общей семье и общем согласии человечества, с дикою радостию взялись за руки; громовой упрек выражался в их взоре. Вдруг из-под глыбы земли явилась юная чета, недавно пощаженная неистовою толпою; бледные, истощенные, как тени мертвецов, они еще сжимали друг друга в объятиях.

"Мы хотим жить и любить посреди страданий", – восклицали они и на коленях умоляли человечество остановить минуту его отмщения; но это мщение было возлелеяно вековыми щедротами жизни; в ответ раздался грозный хохот, то был условленный знак – в одно мгновение блеснул огонь; треск распадавшегося шара потряс солнечную систему; разорванные громады Альпов и Шимборазо взлетели на воздух, раздались несколько стонов... еще ... пепел возвратился на землю... и все утихло... и [вечная] жизнь впервые раскаялась!..

[*В. Ф. Одоевский. Повести и рассказы, Художественная литература, Москва, 1988*]

m.   ESPAÑOL

VIII.m.1.   FELIPE JACINTO SALA, 'El Aeronauta'

Rompe el Aeronauta
las ligaduras fuertes
que el ímpetu fogoso
del mongolfier detienen,
y ciego de locura,
con él en los espacios va a cernerse.
Al verse a cierta altura, más su osadía crece
y arroja temerario todo el lastre
y hasta los cielos escalar pretende.
¡Quimérica ilusión! A poco rato
¿sabéis lo que sucede?
Que el leve gas que daba vida al globo,
fugaz se desvanece,
y con frecuencia el hombre en su caída
halla segura muerte.
¿Verdad que el ambicioso
también al Aeronauta se parece?
Entrambos buscan siempre las alturas,
y entrambos elevándose se pierden.

about a common family and general agreement of mankind. Wild with joy they joined their hands. Thundering reproach was in their eyes. Suddenly a young couple, recently saved by the furious crowd, appeared from under a clod of earth; pale and exhausted, like shadows of corpses, they kept pressing each other in an embrace. 'We want to live and to love amidst sufferings,' they shouted, and falling to their knees they implored mankind to stop the moment of its vengeance; but this vengeance had been nursed by centuries of life's generosity; terrible laughter came as an answer; it was a prearranged signal – the next moment fire flashed high, the roar of the disintegrating earth shook the solar system, torn masses of Alps and Chimborazo flew up into the air, groans were heard . . . then . . . again . . . ashes returned to ashes . . . everything became quiet . . . and eternal Life repented for the first time!

[*Translated by Olga Koshansky-Olienikov and Ralph E. Matlaw*]

m.   SPANISH

VIII.m.1.   FELIPE JACINTO SALA, 'The Aeronaut'

The aeronaut breaks the strong bonds which hold back the spirited impulse of the Montgolfier balloonist and, blinded by insanity, with him he is about to soar into space. Rising to a certain height, his daring grows and the fearless pilot throws over all the ballast and strives to scale the heavens. A fantastical illusion! In a short while, guess what happens? The light gas which gives life to the balloon, fugitive seeps away and, most often, the man finds a certain death in his fall. Is it not true that the ambitious man also seems like the aeronaut? Both always seek the heights and both, rising up, lose all.

[*The Montgolfier brothers (Joseph and Jacques) made the first public balloon ascent in 1783. While Salas is interested in the science of flight he uses the daring experiment as a moral tale. Spain was a latecomer to the Industrial Revolution and literature only tardily reflected its impact. Trains, electricity, gas, etc. all made their appearance in literature and the arts in the mid-nineteenth century as exemplars of the thrill of scientific achievement.*]

n. SVENSKA

VIII.n.1. JONAS BRAG, 'Stjärnhimmelen'

adspice hoc, sublime candens. Ennius.

Kom räck mig handen! du förtryckte Broder
   Du plågans offer, oförrätters mål!
Kom räck mig handen, lämnom denna moder,
   Som blott vår smärta, våra suckar tål!
Kom! följ mig opp på hoppets ljusa vingar
   Med lättat bröst från livets långa sorg,
Att söka opp bland högre världars ringar
   Vårt rätta Manhem och vår Faders borg.

O! säkert var jag en gång i det höga!
   O! säkert kom jag från en bättre sfär!
Och när dess ljus ej vinkar mer mitt öga,
   Så är min ande säkert åter där.
Vem var den Lethe, säg mig, som fördränkte
   De ljuva minnen av Olympens dar?
Nej! vem du var, jag tackar Dig, som skänkte,
   Den enda tröst mitt sorgsna hjärta har.

Djupt låg dock kvar i varje bröst en aning
   Av plågan väckt, av värdets känsla stödd.
Med denna syftning, denna sinnets daning
   Blev mänskan blott till kval och villor född?
Blev ej ett land, en fristad henne ämnad,
   Där inga tårar fukta vänners grav?
Där ingen Cimon fäders bygd ser lämnad
   Och ingen Cato flyr för Caesars glav.

Förgäves såg i väntans långa timma
   Dess våta öga över jordens rund,
Det såg blott sorgens stränder, tvivlets dimma,
   Lik höstens i en regnig morgonstund.
Nu såg det opp i himlens sköna spegel
   Och dimman svann, som lätta hindars tropp.
Var låga brann, en bättre världs insegel,
   En fackla tänd för evighetens hopp.

Se detta klot, som nattens skuggor jagar,
   Som väcker sippan milt ur drivans bädd,
Som ammar rosens knopp i vårens dagar
   Och hösten ter i rika skördar klädd.
Vad! bär det ej sitt ursprungs rätta stämpel?
   Vad! prisar det ej högre himlars Gud,

n. SWEDISH

VIII.n.1. JONAS BRAG, 'The Starry Sky'

adspice hoc, sublime candens. Ennius

Come, let me take your hand! Oppressed Brother,
 Victim of torment, target of injustice!
Come, let me take your hand, this mother let us leave,
 Who only wishes us pain and sighing!
Come! follow me on the bright wings of hope,
 With bosom relieved from life's long sorrow,
To find among the circles of higher worlds
 Our rightly Home of man and our Father's castle.

Oh! surely I was once up high!
 Oh! surely I come from a better sphere!
And when its light waves to my eye no more,
 Then surely will my spirit go back there.
Tell me, who was the Lethe that drowned
 The sweet memories of Olympian days?
No! whoever you were, I do thank You, who gave
 My sad heart its only solace.

Deep in each bosom lay the premonition
 Woken by torment, maintained by value of sense.
With this aim, this formation of mind
 Was Man born just for agony and delusions?
Was there not a land or a sanctuary intended for him
 Where no tears moist the grave of dear friends?
Where no Cimo deserts the land of his ancestors
 And no Cato flees away from Caesar's spear.

In vain, through the long hour of waiting
 His wet eye all over the earth's round,
Saw but the shores of sorrow, the mist of doubt,
 Like rain on an early autumn morning.
It looked up into the beautiful mirror of heaven
 And the mist ran off, like a flock of light deer.
Each flame was burning, the seal of a better world
 A torch lit for the hope of eternity.

Behold this ball, chased by the shadows of night,
 That gently wakes the anemone from the bed of snow,
That feeds the rosebud in days of spring
 And displays autumn covered in rich harvests.
What? Should it not carry the proper imprint of its origin?
 What? Should it not praise a God of heavens higher

Än hämndens bud från fanatismens tempel
  Och kall sofism i vetenskaplig skrud?

Och Luna, du! med dina blyga strålar,
  Med oskuldens och lugnets rena färg;
Hur skön din bild sig för den sorgsne målar,
  Hur längtar ej hans blick till dina berg
Och vilar ljuv på dina silverslätter,
  Där dagens glans ej flyr för molnets vind
Och säkert ej för våldets oförrätter
  En vissnad ros på dina söners kind.

Re'n flyr du bort från Västerns ljusa branter,
  Re'n ler din bild i Skandiens lugna Sund,
Re'n tindra fram de slocknade demanter
  I renad glans på mörknad azurgrund.
Vem räknar er, I himlens legioner!
  Vad skådar Bode där från sin altan?
Vad speglar Herschel över nya zoner?
  En droppa mer i stjärnors ocean!

Hur skön där över Deianiras hjälte
  Orfei lyra stämd till sfärers dans;
Se där Orion med sitt gyllne bälte;
  Se där Caelano i en syskonkrans;
Där vandrar Zeus, glömsk av sin härskarinna,
  Bland fyra tärnors leende behag,
Där Venus, lik en trogen älskarinna,
  Som sist flyr bort för evighetens dag.

Jag ser ej bilder mer bland dessa under,
  Jag ser ett verk utav naturens Far,
Där vart sin form, sin bana, sina stunder,
  Men samma grundkraft, samma syfte har.
Jag ser hur, styrd af Keplers lag, kometen,
  I blodig rustning klädd, i hotat språng
Ej krossar mer den skälvande planeten,
  Ej bådar mer dess rikens undergång!

Från dagens bloss till nattens milda låga
  Allt i systemers trygga kretsar rörs,
Den Drott, kring vilken elva Furstar tåga,
  Själv kring en för oss okänd Konung förs.
Och dennes spira högre makter styra
  Och så igenom Centrers million

Than the decree of revenge from the temples of fanatism
    Or cold sophistry in the guise of science?

And Luna, you! With your shy beams,
    Your pure colour of innocence and calm;
How fair your picture is to the sadful one,
    How his gaze does long for your mountains
And sweetly rest upon your silver plains
    Where day's splendour flees not the wind of the cloud
And surely not the violence of injustice
    A withered rose on the cheeks of your sons.

Already you are fleeing from the bright slopes of the west,
    Already your image smiles over Scandia's calm straits.
Already glimmer anew the burnt-out diamonds
    In purified splendour on the darkened azure.
Who counts you, legions of heaven!
    What does Bode behold there from his terrace?
What new zones are mirrored by Herschel?
    Another drop in the ocean of stars!

How fair up above the hero of Dejanira,
    The lyre of Orpheus tuned to the dance of the spheres;
Look at Orion with his golden belt;
    Look at Caelano in a wreath of siblings;
There walks Zeus, forgetful of his ruleress,
    Amidst the charms of four smiling maidens,
There Venus, like a faithful lover,
    The last to run off from Eternity's day.

I no more see images among these wonders,
    I see the works of the Father of Nature,
Where each one has its own form, its orbit, its moments,
    But the same basic force, the same purpose.
I observe the comet, governed by the law of Kepler
    In blood-stained armour, in a threatened leap.
No more crushing the frightened planet,
    No more foretelling the decline of its nations!

From the flare of day to the gentle flame of night
    All is moved within safe circles of systems,
The Prince around which eleven Nobles march,
    Is himself brought before a King unknown to us.
And that one's sceptre rules higher powers
    And so through a million Centres

Jag nalkas slutligt i min höga yra
   Till alla världars Centrum, Skaparns tron.

Förmätna öga, lyft till Gudazonen!
   Re'n tusen solar blända där din syn!
Mot deras glans, som omger himlatronen,
   En skymning är den dag, som skingrat skyn.
När Moses fick den Helige beskåda,
   Han Honom såg blott klädd i molnets skrud,
Men ingen såg mer Moses utan våda
   Och täckelset beviste, han sett Gud.

Jag har ej Mosis anda, Mosis sinne
   – (Mitt svaga hjärta ofta brottsligt var,
Begären storma mången gång därinne), –
   Jag vågar dock att nalkas Dig, min Far!
Själv bjöd du Hoppets stjärna för mig brinna,
   Själv lyste Du den väg, mitt öga lopp,
Och dit mitt fjärrrglas icke kunde hinna
   Du förde mig på tankens vingar opp.

Ifrån Din tron i världens morgontimma
   Jag hör O Gud! ett 'Varde!' och jag ser
Millioner klot ur österns purpur glimma,
   Millioner liv tillbedja på vår sfär.
Från Dig till alla liv och kraft sig sprida,
   Kring Dig systemer vid harmonisk sång,
Än längre bort i långa kretsar skrida,
   Än närmre fly, som blixten i sitt språng.

Jag skådar genom seklers vikna stunder,
   Jag far från zon till zon, från pol till pol.
Än hylla dig i samma banors runder
   Den minsta jord, de största världars sol,
Bild av dig själv, bild av odödligheten
   Står för din tron i första ungdomsglans
Din Uranie, din bild; och evigheten
   Ser ej en blomma vissnad i dess krans.

Var är Du? Var är jorden? Gode Fader!
   Är hon väl långt ifrån din boning? Säg!
I vilken av systemers många grader
   Beskriver hon sin trygga cirkelväg?
Jag vet det ej! En blick på jordens dårar
   Bortflyttar mig till Firmamentets gräns;

I finally approach in my high frenzy
    The Centre of all worlds, the Creator's throne.

Presumptuous eye, lifted to the zone Divine!
    Where already a thousand suns blind your sight!
Compared to the splendour of those who surround the throne of heaven
    The day that shattered the clouds is a dusk.
When Moses was allowed to behold the Holy one
    He only saw him shrouded in a cloud,
But no one could look at Moses without peril
    And this cover proved that he had seen God.

I do not have the spirit of Moses, the mind of Moses
    (My weak heart was oftentimes criminal,
Many a time desires are rageing in there) –
    And yet I dare approach You my Father!
You ordered the star of Hope to burn for me,
    You lit up the course that my eye ran,
And to where my farglasses could not reach
    You brought me on the wings of thought.

From your throne in the world's hour of dawn
    I hear, Oh God! A 'Let there be!' and I see
Millions of balls gleaming from the purple of East,
    Millions of life in worship on our sphere.
From You to all do life and force spread,
    Around you systems in harmonic singing
Further away in long circles glide,
    Or run nigh, like the leap of lightning.

I look through moments of centuries passed,
    I go from zone to zone, from pole to pole.
Still celebrated you around these trajectories
    The pettiest earth, suns of the biggest worlds,
An image of You, an image of immortality
    Stands before your throne in the first splendour of youth,
Your Urania, your image; and eternity
    Sees not one wilted flower in its wreath.

Where are You? Where is the Earth? Good Father!
    Is she far away from your abode? Pray tell?
In which one of the many grades of the system
    Does she describe her safe circular way?
I do not know! One look at the fools on Earth
    Transport me to the edge of the Firmament;

En blick på snillet, på den Ädles tårar!
   Och vägen flyr och Din närvaro känns.

Och var du är ditt öga mig dock hinner,
   Bland Änglars lovsång hörs min matta röst!
Var morgonsol din godhet mig påminner,
   Var aftonsol din milda fadersröst!
Förgäves stormen sina vingar skakar,
   Förgäves ljungar viggen kring vårt tjäll.
Högt över oss din gode Ande vakar,
   Som Nordens stjärna över Nordens fjäll!

(1811)

One look at the genius, at the tears of a Noble man
    Removes the way and makes your presence felt.

And wherever you are your eye reaches me,
    Among the extolation of Angels my dull voice is heard!
Each morning sun reminds me of your goodness,
    Each evening sun of your mild paternal voice!
In vain the gale shakes its wings,
    In vain the bolt thunders around our abode.
High above us your Good spirit keeps wake,
    Like the Polar star over the mountains of the North!

(1811) [*Translated by John Swedenmark*]

INDEX

Note: Page numbers in **bold** denote detailed discussion.

CPSIA information can be obtained
at www.ICGtesting.com
Printed in the USA
LVHW080719051221
705203LV00021B/22

9 781472 535443